The Cambridge Handbook of the Learning Sciences
Second Edition

The interdisciplinary field of the learning sciences encompasses educational psychology, cognitive science, computer science, and anthropology, among other disciplines. *The Cambridge Handbook of the Learning Sciences*, first published in 2006, is widely acknowledged to be the definitive introduction to this innovative approach to teaching, learning, and educational technology. In this dramatically revised second edition, leading scholars incorporate the latest research to provide practical advice on a wide range of issues. The authors address the best ways to write textbooks, design educational software, prepare effective teachers, organize classrooms, and use the Internet to enhance student learning. They illustrate the importance of creating productive learning environments both inside and outside school, including after school clubs, libraries, and museums. Accessible and engaging, the *Handbook* has proven to be an essential resource for graduate students, researchers, teachers, administrators, consultants, software designers, and policy makers on a global scale.

R. KEITH SAWYER is the Morgan Distinguished Professor in Educational Innovations at the University of North Carolina at Chapel Hill School of Education. He studies creativity, innovation, and learning, with a focus on collaborating groups and teams. He is the author or editor of 13 previous books, including *Group Genius: The Creative Power of Collaboration* (2007); *Explaining Creativity: The Science of Human Innovation* (2012); and *Zig Zag: The Surprising Path to Greater Creativity* (2013).

learning

This word cloud was generated using the complete text of the book, and displays the 100 most frequently used words in the book. The size of each word represents how often it appears in the book. Common words like "the" and "of" were excluded, and plural and singular occurrences were combined. The smallest words occur approximately 150–200 times. The biggest word counts are: Learning – 3,266; students – 1,726; knowledge – 1,029; research – 931; learners – 697; teachers – 687. Generated by R. Keith Sawyer using wordle.net.

The Cambridge Handbook of the Learning Sciences

Second Edition

Edited by

R. Keith Sawyer

CAMBRIDGE
UNIVERSITY PRESS

One Liberty Plaza, 20th Floor, New York, NY 10006, USA

Cambridge University Press is part of the University of Cambridge.

It furthers the University's mission by disseminating knowledge in the pursuit of education, learning, and research at the highest international levels of excellence.

www.cambridge.org
Information on this title: www.cambridge.org/9781107626577

First edition published 2006
First paperback edition 2006
Second edition 2014
8th printing 2019

Printed in the United Kingdom by TJ International Ltd. Padstow Cornwall

A catalog record for this publication is available from the British Library.

Library of Congress Cataloging in Publication data
The Cambridge handbook of the learning sciences / [edited by]
R. Keith Sawyer. – Second edition.
    pages   cm. – (Cambridge handbooks in psychology)
Includes bibliographical references and index.
ISBN 978-1-107-03325-2 (hardback) – ISBN 978-1-107-62657-7 (paperback)
1. Learning, Psychology of.   2. Cognitive learning.   3. Learning – Social aspects.   I. Sawyer, R. Keith (Robert Keith)
LB1060.C35   2014
370.15'23–dc23   2014002493

ISBN 978-1-107-03325-2 Hardback
ISBN 978-1-107-62657-7 Paperback

Contents

Part V. Learning Disciplinary Knowledge

Part VI. Moving Learning Sciences Research into the Classroom

Figures

Tables

Contributors

DOR ABRAHAMSON, University of California, Berkeley

JERRY ANDRIESSEN, Wise & Munro Learning Research

ROGER AZEVEDO, North Carolina State University

MICHAEL BAKER, Centre National de la Recherche Scientifique

RYAN BAKER, Teachers College, Columbia University

SASHA BARAB, Arizona State University

CARL BEREITER, University of Toronto

SUSAN BRIDGES, University of Hong Kong

MARIO CARRETERO, Autonoma University of Madrid

CAROL K. K. CHAN, University of Hong Kong

CLARK A. CHINN, Rutgers University

PAUL COBB, Vanderbilt University

ALLAN COLLINS, Northwestern University

KEVIN CROWLEY, University of Pittsburgh

ELIZABETH A. DAVIS, University of Michigan

CHRIS DEDE, Harvard University

SHARON J. DERRY, University of North Carolina at Chapel Hill

ANDREA A. DISESSA, University of California, Berkeley

MICHAEL EISENBERG, University of Colorado, Boulder

YRJÖ ENGESTRÖM, University of Helsinki

NOEL ENYEDY, University of California, Los Angeles

BARRY J. FISHMAN, University of Michigan

RICKI GOLDMAN, New York University

JAMES G. GREENO, University of Pittsburgh

ERICA ROSENFELD HALVERSON, University of Wisconsin

CINDY E. HMELO-SILVER, Indiana University

MICHAEL J. JACOBSON, University of Sydney

SANNA JÄRVELÄ, University of Oulu

YASMIN B. KAFAI, University of Pennsylvania

YAEL KALI, University of Haifa

MANU KAPUR, National Institute of Education, Nanyang Technological University

PAUL A. KIRSCHNER, Open University of the Netherlands

KAREN KNUTSON, University of Pittsburgh

TIMOTHY KOSCHMANN, Southern Illinois University School of Medicine

JOSEPH S. KRAJCIK, Michigan State University

CAROL D. LEE, Northwestern University

PETER LEE, Institute of Education, London

ROBB LINDGREN, University of Illinois at Urbana-Champaign

JINGYAN LU, University of Hong Kong

RICHARD E. MAYER, University of California, Santa Barbara

NAOMI MIYAKE, University of Tokyo

NA'ILAH SUAD NASIR, University of California, Berkeley

MITCHELL J. NATHAN, University of Wisconsin

NARCIS PARES, Universitat Pompeu Fabra, Barcelona

ROY PEA, Stanford University

JAMES W. PELLEGRINO, University of Illinois, Chicago

WILLIAM R. PENUEL, University of Colorado, Boulder

PALMYRE PIERROUX, University of Oslo

BRIAN J. REISER, Northwestern University

K. ANN RENNINGER, Swarthmore College

ANN S. ROSEBERY, TERC

R. KEITH SAWYER, University of North Carolina at Chapel Hill

MARLENE SCARDAMALIA, University of Toronto

ANNA SFARD, University of Haifa

MIKE SHARPLES, The Open University

KIMBERLY M. SHERIDAN, George Mason University

BRUCE L. SHERIN, Northwestern University

NAMSOO SHIN, Seoul National University

GEORGE SIEMENS, Athabasca University

PETER SMAGORINSKY, University of Georgia, Athens

NANCY BUTLER SONGER, University of Michigan

JAMES P. SPILLANE, Northwestern University

KURT SQUIRE, University of Wisconsin

GERRY STAHL, Drexel University

CONSTANCE STEINKUEHLER, University of Wisconsin

REED STEVENS, Northwestern University

DANIEL SUTHERS, University of Hawai'i at Manoa

IRIS TABAK, Ben Gurion University of the Negev

BETH WARREN, TERC

URI WILENSKY, Northwestern University

PHILIP H. WINNE, Simon Fraser University

CARMEN ZAHN, University of Applied Sciences and the Arts

Preface

R. Keith Sawyer

This book is for everyone who wants to know what scientists have discovered about how people learn – education researchers, teachers, administrators, policy makers, consultants, and software designers. This handbook is your introduction to a powerful approach to reforming education and schools, an approach that builds on the learning sciences to design new learning environments that help people learn more deeply and more effectively.

In 2006, the first edition of *The Cambridge Handbook of the Learning Sciences* (*CHLS*) was published. As the first comprehensive overview of learning sciences research, *CHLS* found a broad audience and was widely adopted as a text in university learning sciences programs. The impact was international, with particularly large numbers of readers in the United States and in Europe, and with translated editions in Chinese and Japanese also selling well. Because of this significant impact, and exciting new advances in the field, the need has increased for a second edition.

This second edition represents developments in the field since the text of the first edition was finished in 2005. This new second edition, *CHLS 2E*, shows how educators can use the learning sciences to design effective and innovative learning environments – including school classrooms and informal settings such as science centers or after school clubs, online learning, and educational software. Each chapter in *CHLS 2E* describes exciting new classroom environments, based on the latest science about how people learn. These classroom environments combine new curricular materials, new collaborative activities, support for teachers, and innovative educational software, often using the unique advantages of the Internet to extend learning beyond the walls of the school. *CHLS 2E* is a true "handbook" in that readers can use it to design the schools of the future – schools that are based on learning sciences research and that draw on the full potential of computer and Internet technology to improve students' experiences. The learning sciences are supporting deep links between formal schooling and the many other learning institutions available to students – libraries, science centers and history museums, after school clubs, online activities that can be accessed from home, and even collaborations between students and working professionals.

In particular, this handbook describes how to use the new sciences of learning to design effective learning environments, in classrooms and outside, often taking advantage of new computer technology. As Chapter 2, "Foundations of the Learning Sciences," points out, learning sciences is a "design science" that incorporates both research and practice. Redesigning schools so that they are based on scientific research is a mammoth undertaking, and it will require the participation of all of the groups that read this book: teachers, parents, school leaders, policy makers, and education researchers.

The Second Edition

This second edition has some overlap with the first edition, but most of it is completely new: of the 36 chapters here, 23 of them are written by authors whose work did not appear in the first edition, and 20 of them discuss topics that did not have dedicated chapters in the first edition. The 13 chapters that are repeated from the first edition have been substantially rewritten.

In this second edition, the chapter topics and their authors were selected by a distributed, collective process that involved the entire learning sciences community, as well as input from readers and users of the first edition. To determine the chapter topics to be included in this second edition, I gathered three sources of information:

- I conducted an online survey, using SurveyMonkey, that was distributed to the membership of the International Society of the Learning Sciences (ISLS), asking which topics from the first edition should remain in the second edition, and which new topics should be added. I received 90 responses to this survey.
- The publisher, Cambridge University Press, distributed the same survey to seven instructors who were using the first edition in their university courses.
- I used Google Scholar to determine the number of citations each of the chapters had received.

These three information sources were largely consistent with each other, and I used this information to identify the 36 chapter topics. Then I distributed a second survey to the ISLS membership, asking them to suggest authors for each of these chapter topics. Because of the increasing international scope of the learning sciences, one of my personal goals was to increase the number of non-U.S. contributors in the second edition. After all, the annual learning sciences conferences have now been held in many different countries, all with active learning sciences research programs. The ISLS hosts two conferences, the International Conference of the Learning Sciences (ICLS) conference (in even years) and the Computer Supported Collaboration Learning (CSCL) conference (in odd years). The ICLS has been held in The Netherlands (2008) and in Australia (2012). The CSCL has been held in Canada (1999),

The Netherlands (2001), Norway (2003), Taiwan (2005), Greece (2009), and Hong Kong (2011).

Because the field has such broad international participation – the ISLS includes members from six continents – in my second survey I asked ISLS members to suggest names of both U.S. and non-U.S. experts on each topic. The contributors to the second edition come from almost every country with active learning sciences research. Of the 72 contributors, 47 are from the United States; 11 are from Europe; 4 are from Canada; 6 are from Asia; 3 are from Israel; and 1 is from Australia. (Contrast this with the first edition: only 5 authors were from outside the United States.)

The 36 chapters of the *CHLS* are organized into six parts.

- **Part I: Foundations**. Each of these chapters focuses on a foundational concept that has been influential in learning sciences research from the origin of the field in the 1980s and 1990s. These foundational concepts are introduced in Chapter 2.
- **Part II: Methodologies**. Learning scientists use a broad range of methodologies, including experimental psychological methods. I chose not to provide a chapter on experimental designs – although they have contributed substantially to learning sciences research – because such introductions are easy to find elsewhere, and also because experimental designs are not typically used in designing real-world learning environments. The chapters here focus on innovative methodologies that have, at least in part, been developed by the learning sciences community – often to bring together research and practice, and to bridge the elemental and systemic levels of analysis (see Chapter 2).
- **Part III: Practices that Foster Effective Learning**. Each of these chapters describes an innovative classroom practice, based in learning sciences research, that has been documented to lead to enhanced learning outcomes.
- **Part IV: Learning Together**. A wide range of educational research has found that collaboration contributes to learning. Unlike an older generation of educational software, where each student worked in isolation at his or her own computer, the advent of the Internet and of wireless handheld devices supports students in learning collaborations, so that computers bring students together instead of pulling them apart. These chapters show how learning environments can be designed to foster more effective learning conversations.
- **Part V: Learning Disciplinary Knowledge**. This section is new in the second edition. These chapters are written primarily for a broad audience of learning scientists, and secondarily for education researchers working in that discipline. The focus of each chapter is: What unique epistemologies, practices, and findings – inspired by this discipline's content – change the

way we think about learning more generally? How does studying learning in this discipline add to what we know from studies of learning more generally?

• **Part VI: Moving Learning Sciences Research into the Classroom**. Globally, many education systems are looking to learning sciences research to help them redesign their schools for a 21st-century knowledge and innovation age. Learning sciences researchers are prepared to offer practical solutions, because the discipline works to bridge research and practice. These chapters summarize the key messages from learning sciences for education policy makers, and explore what might happen when we take learning sciences findings and use them to reform schools, classrooms, and teacher practices.

In my own introduction and conclusion to this handbook, I explain why the learning sciences are important not only to education, but to our entire society. The major advanced nations and the entire global economy are rapidly changing. In these two chapters, I draw on a large body of recent scholarship that describes the mismatch between the schools we have today and the demands of the knowledge age. Because the learning sciences are discovering how to teach the deep knowledge, skills, and attitudes required in the knowledge society, they are positioned to provide the blueprint for the schools of the future.

This six-part structure does not reflect established divisions within the field – far from it. The chapter topics that emerged from the process I described earlier seemed to me to fall naturally into these six groupings, but another editor might have come up with a different organizational structure. Many of the chapters touch on themes common to more than one part, and could have been placed in more than one location in the handbook. There is a lot of cross-referencing between chapters both within and among these six parts, and this coherence and interconnection is one of the strengths of the learning sciences.

A book like *CHLS* is a massive undertaking; 72 authors have contributed to this book, and many other members of the learning sciences community have contributed indirectly, by reading and commenting on chapter drafts. As with any professional community, the knowledge that emerges is collectively created by all of the participants. Many important scholars whose names do not appear as authors nonetheless have contributed to the collective endeavor of the learning sciences. While editing this handbook, I have discovered that the members of this professional community are deeply aware that they are each only one participant in a broad community of practice, and that the knowledge generated cannot be considered to be owned or possessed by any one researcher. By sharing openly and working collaboratively, learning sciences researchers have made great strides in less than two decades. I hope that

CHLS functions as a resource that will allow a significant expansion of this community of practice, allowing everyone involved with education to tap into these new findings and begin the task of designing the schools of the future.

I would like to thank my editors at Cambridge University Press, whose commitment to this project was an inspiration. Over the years, I discussed the structure and timing of a second edition with many different editors who successively served as the psychology editor at Cambridge. Phil Laughlin was the original editor on the 2006 first edition. He was replaced by Eric Schwartz, who was replaced by Simina Calin, who was replaced by Emily Spangler, who was replaced by Adina Berk. Ms. Berk reviewed the second edition proposal and issued a contract in March 2012. Ms. Berk left Cambridge in August 2012. In March 2013, David Repetto took over as my editor, and he expertly took the project into production.

I would like to thank the leadership of the International Society of the Learning Sciences (ISLS). In preparing this second edition, I relied heavily on two surveys, described above, that the ISLS passed on to their membership list. The Board of Directors of the ISLS also provided me with several statistics that demonstrate the increasing impact of the learning sciences, and I drew on these while preparing this Preface.

I am grateful to each of the authors for the hard work they invested. It was a true pleasure to work with such a deeply professional group of scholars, with everyone delivering their chapters "on time and under budget," as they say. I am particularly grateful that the authors were willing to respond to my suggestions – in many cases I offered very detailed comments that required them to invest a significant amount of time to write a second draft. My goal was to read with the mindset of our target reader, a newcomer to the field of learning sciences. I worked to identify passages or terms that might be difficult for a newcomer to understand. A second goal was to ensure that each chapter was as concise and focused as possible; because there are 36 chapters, each one had rather strict length limitations. Having worked so closely with these scholars through their multiple drafts, I have a deeper understanding of why the learning sciences is having such a significant impact on education.

1 Introduction

The New Science of Learning

R. Keith Sawyer

The learning sciences is an interdisciplinary field that studies teaching and learning. Learning scientists study a variety of settings, including not only the formal learning of school classrooms, but also the informal learning that takes place at home, on the job, and among peers. The goal of the learning sciences is to better understand the cognitive and social processes that result in the most effective learning and to use this knowledge to redesign classrooms and other learning environments so that people learn more deeply and more effectively. The sciences of learning include cognitive science, educational psychology, computer science, anthropology, sociology, information sciences, neurosciences, education, design studies, instructional design, and other fields. In the late 1980s, researchers in these fields who were studying learning realized that they needed to develop new scientific approaches that went beyond what their own disciplines could offer and to collaborate with other disciplines. The field of learning sciences was born in 1991, when the first international conference was held and the *Journal of the Learning Sciences* was first published.

By the 20th century, all major industrialized countries offered formal schooling to all of their children. When these schools took shape during the 19th and 20th centuries, scientists didn't know very much about how people learn. Even by the 1920s, when schools began to grow into the large bureaucratic institutions that we know today, there was still no sustained study of how people learn. As a result, the schools we have today were designed around commonsense assumptions that had never been tested scientifically:

- Knowledge is a collection of *facts* about the world and *procedures* for how to solve problems. Facts are statements like "the earth is tilted on its axis by 23.45 degrees" and procedures are step-by-step instructions like instructions on how to do multi-digit addition by carrying to the next column.
- The goal of schooling is to get these facts and procedures into students' heads. People are considered educated when they possess a large collection of these facts and procedures.
- Teachers know these facts and procedures, and their job is to transmit them to students.
- Simpler facts and procedures should be learned first, followed by progressively more complex facts and procedures. The definitions of "simplicity"

and "complexity" and the proper sequencing of material were determined by teachers, by textbook authors, or by expert adults like mathematicians, scientists, or historians – not by studying how children actually learn.

- The way to determine the success of schooling is to test students to see how many of these facts and procedures they have acquired.

This traditional vision of schooling is known as *instructionism* (Papert, 1993). Instructionism prepared students for the industrialized economy of the early 20th century. But the world today is much more technologically complex and economically competitive, and instructionism is increasingly failing to educate our students to participate in this new kind of society. Economists and organizational theorists have reached a consensus that today we are living in a knowledge economy, an economy that is built on knowledge work (Bereiter, 2002; Drucker, 1993). In the knowledge economy, memorization of facts and procedures is not enough for success. Educated graduates need a deep conceptual understanding of complex concepts and the ability to work with them creatively to generate new ideas, new theories, new products, and new knowledge. They need to be able to critically evaluate what they read, to be able to express themselves clearly both verbally and in writing, and to be able to understand scientific and mathematical thinking. They need to learn integrated and usable knowledge, rather than the sets of compartmentalized and decontextualized facts emphasized by instructionism. They need to be able to take responsibility for their own continuing, lifelong learning. These abilities are important to the economy, to the continued success of participatory democracy, and to living a fulfilling, meaningful life. Instructionism is particularly ill suited to the education of creative professionals who can develop new knowledge and continually further their own understanding; instructionism is an anachronism in the modern innovation economy.

In the 1970s, a new science of learning was born – based on research emerging from psychology, computer science, philosophy, sociology, and other scientific disciplines. As they closely studied children's learning, scientists discovered that instructionism was deeply flawed. By the 1990s, after about 20 years of research, learning scientists had reached a consensus on the following basic facts about learning – a consensus that was published by the United States National Research Council (see Bransford, Brown, & Cocking, 2000):

- *The importance of deeper conceptual understanding.* Scientific studies of knowledge workers demonstrate that expert knowledge does include facts and procedures, but simply acquiring those facts and procedures does not prepare a person for performance as a knowledge worker. Factual and procedural knowledge is only useful when a person knows which situations to apply it in and exactly how to modify it for each new situation. Instructionism results in a kind of learning that is very difficult to use outside of the classroom. When students gain a deeper conceptual understanding, they learn facts and procedures in a much more useful and profound way that transfers to real-world settings.

- *Focusing on learning in addition to teaching.* Students cannot learn deeper conceptual understanding simply from better instruction. Students can only learn this by actively participating in their own learning. The new science of learning focuses on student learning processes, as well as instructional techniques.
- *Creating learning environments.* The job of schools is to help students learn the full range of knowledge required for expert adult performance: facts and procedures, of course, but also the deeper conceptual understanding that will allow them to reason about real-world problems. Learning sciences research has identified the key features of those learning environments that help students learn deeper conceptual understanding.
- *The importance of building on a learner's prior knowledge.* Learners are not empty vessels waiting to be filled. They come to the classroom with preconceptions about how the world works; some of them are basically correct, and some of them are misconceptions. The best way for children to learn is in an environment that builds on their existing knowledge; if teaching does not engage their prior knowledge, students often learn information just well enough to pass their tests, and then revert to their misconceptions outside of the classroom.
- *The importance of reflection.* Students learn better when they express their developing knowledge – either through conversation or by creating papers, reports, or other artifacts – and then receive opportunities to reflectively analyze their state of knowledge.

This handbook is an introduction to this new science of learning and to how researchers are using this science to lay the groundwork for the schools of the future. This new science is called *the learning sciences* because it is an interdisciplinary science: it brings together researchers in psychology, education, computer science, and anthropology, among others, and the collaboration among these disciplines has resulted in new ideas, new methodologies, and new ways of thinking about learning. Many people – parents, teachers, policy makers, and even many educational researchers – are not aware of the important discoveries emerging from the learning sciences. Without knowing about the new science of learning, many people continue to assume that schools should be based on instructionism. Parents and policy makers remember being taught that way and are often uncomfortable when their children have different educational experiences. Many teachers have spent entire careers mastering the skills required to manage an instructionist classroom, and they understandably have trouble envisioning a different kind of school. The purpose of this handbook is to build on the new science of learning by showing various stakeholders how to design innovative learning environments and classrooms.

- For *teachers*, reading about the new science of learning can help you be more effective in your classrooms.
- For *parents*, reading about the new science of learning can help you become an informed consumer of schools. The learning sciences explains why and when instructionism fails and which alternative learning environments are based in contemporary science.
- For *administrators*, reading about the new science of learning can help you lead your school into the 21st century.
- For *policy makers*, reading about the new science of learning can help you understand the problems with today's curricula, teacher education programs, and standardized tests, and understand how to form a vision for the future.
- For *education entrepreneurs*, reading about the new science of learning can help you ground your innovations in how people learn and design more effective learning environments.
- For *professionals*, reading about the new science of learning can help you understand why the general public is so poorly informed about science, technology, international relations, economics, and other knowledge-based disciplines.
- And finally, for *education researchers*, reading about the new science of learning can help you learn how your own studies relate to the learning sciences and to see how you can participate in building the schools of the future.

The Goals of Education

The traditional role of educational research has been to tell educators how to achieve their curriculum objectives, but not to help set those objectives. But when learning scientists went into classrooms, they discovered that many schools were not teaching the deep knowledge that underlies intelligent performance. By the 1980s, cognitive scientists had discovered that children retain material better – and are able to generalize and apply it to a broader range of contexts – when they learn deep knowledge rather than surface knowledge, and when they learn how to use that knowledge in real-world social and practical settings (see Table 1.1).

One of the central underlying themes of the learning sciences is that students learn deeper knowledge when they engage in activities that are similar to the everyday activities of professionals who work in a discipline. Authentic practices are the keystone of many recent educational standards documents in the United States. In the subject of history, for example, reforms call for learning history by doing historical inquiry rather than by memorizing dates and sequences of events: working with primary data sources and using the methods of historical analysis and argumentation that historians use (National Center for History in the Schools, 1996). In the subject of science,

Table 1.1. *Deep learning versus traditional classroom practices*

Learning knowledge deeply (findings from cognitive science)	Traditional classroom practices (instructionism)
Deep learning requires that learners relate new ideas and concepts to previous knowledge and experience.	Learners treat course material as unrelated to what they already know.
Deep learning requires that learners integrate their knowledge into interrelated conceptual systems.	Learners treat course material as disconnected bits of knowledge.
Deep learning requires that learners look for patterns and underlying principles.	Learners memorize facts and carry out procedures without understanding how or why.
Deep learning requires that learners evaluate new ideas and relate them to conclusions.	Learners have difficulty making sense of new ideas that are different from what they encountered in the textbook.
Deep learning requires that learners understand the process of dialogue through which knowledge is created, and that they examine the logic of an argument critically.	Learners treat facts and procedures as static knowledge handed down from an all-knowing authority.
Deep learning requires that learners reflect on their own understanding and their own process of learning.	Learners memorize without reflecting on the purpose or on their own learning strategies.

the National Science Education Standards calls for students to engage in the authentic practices of scientific inquiry: constructing explanations and preparing arguments to communicate and justify those explanations (National Research Council, 1996, p. 105).

To better understand how to engage students in authentic practices, many learning sciences reforms are based on studies of professional practice.

• Professionals engage in a process of inquiry, in which they start with a driving question and then use discipline-specific methods to propose hypothetical answers to the question and to gather and evaluate evidence for and against competing hypotheses.
• Professionals use complex representations to communicate with each other during collaboration.
• Scientists and mathematicians work with concrete, visual models, so students should too.

This focus on authentic practice is based on a new conception of the expert knowledge that underlies knowledge work in today's economy. In the 1980s and 1990s, scientists began to study science itself, and they discovered that newcomers become members of a discipline by learning how to participate in all of the practices that are central to professional life in that discipline. And increasingly, cutting-edge work in the sciences is being done at the boundaries of disciplines; for this reason, students need to learn the underlying models, mechanisms, and practices that apply across many scientific disciplines, rather than learning in the disconnected and isolated units that are found in instructionist science classrooms – moving from studying the solar system to studying photosynthesis to studying force and motion, without ever learning about the connections between these topics.

Studies of knowledge workers show that they almost always apply their expertise in complex social settings, using a wide array of technologically advanced tools along with old-fashioned pencil, paper, chalk, and blackboards. These observations have led learning sciences researchers to a *situativity* view of knowledge (Greeno & Engeström, Chapter 7, this volume). Situativity means that knowledge is not just a static mental structure inside the learner's head; instead, knowing is a process that involves the person, the tools and other people in the environment, and the activities in which that knowledge is being applied. The situativity perspective moves us beyond a transmission and acquisition conception of learning; in addition to acquiring content, what happens during learning is that patterns of participation in collaborative activity change over time (Rogoff, 1990, 1998). This combined research has led the learning sciences to focus on how children learn in groups and from collaboration (as discussed in the chapters in Part 4).

Of course, students are not capable of doing exactly the same things as highly trained professionals; when learning scientists talk about engaging students in authentic practices, they are referring to developmentally appropriate versions of the situated and meaningful practices of experts. One of the most important goals of learning sciences research is to identify exactly what practices are appropriate for students to engage in and learn and how to design age-appropriate learning environments without losing the authenticity of professional practice.

The Nature of Expert Knowledge

Should we reduce auto emissions because of global warming? Should we avoid growing and eating genetically modified organisms (GMOs)? Should we allow stem cell research to proceed? Are market-based mechanisms capable of helping to address pressing social problems? Today's public debates about such controversial issues show a glaring lack of knowledge about scientific practice. The U.S. National Science Education Standards observes that "Americans are confronted increasingly with questions in their lives that require scientific information and scientific ways of thinking for informed decision making" (National Research Council, 1996, p. 11).

By the early 1900s, major industrial countries had realized the important role that science and engineering played in their rapid growth, and many scholars began to analyze the nature of scientific knowledge. In the first half of the 20th century, philosophers came to a consensus on the nature of scientific knowledge: scientific knowledge consisted of statements about the world and of logical operations that could be applied to those statements. This consensus was known as *logical empiricism* (McGuire, 1992; Suppe, 1974). Logical empiricism combined with behaviorism and traditional classroom practice to form the instructionist approach to education: disciplinary knowledge consisted of facts and procedures, and teaching was thought of as transmitting the facts and procedures to students.

In the 1960s, sociologists, psychologists, and anthropologists began to study how scientists actually did their work, and they increasingly discovered that scientific knowledge was not simply a body of statements and logical operations. In this new view, scientific knowledge is an understanding about how to go about doing science, combined with deep knowledge of models and explanatory principles connected into an integrated conceptual framework (Songer & Kali, Chapter 28, this volume). Learning scientists often refer to logical empiricism, and to this expanded view of scientific knowledge, as distinct *epistemologies* of science. This newer epistemology holds that the practice of science involves experimentation, trial and error, hypothesis testing, debate, and argumentation. And science is not a solo endeavor; it involves frequent encounters with peers in the scientific community. Scientists frequently talk about evaluating other scientists' claims and think about how best to support and present their claims to others.

In this new view, scientific knowledge is situated, practiced, and collaboratively generated. The traditional science classroom, with its lectures and step-by-step lab exercises, completely leaves out these elements of science. But this kind of knowledge would be extremely useful to members of the general public as they read reports of an experimental drug in the daily paper, as they discuss the potential risks of upcoming surgeries with their doctors, or as they evaluate the health risks of new construction near their neighborhoods.

This new view of expert knowledge has extended beyond science to other forms of knowledge work. For example, literacy scholars have discovered that advanced literacy involves much more than knowing which sounds correspond to which letters; literacy involves knowing how to participate in a complex set of literate practices – like reading a recipe, scanning the classifieds for a specific product, or writing an e-mail to a colleague (Smagorinsky & Mayer, Chapter 30, this volume). Social science educators have discovered that historians are experts because they know how to engage in the complex practices of historical inquiry and argumentation (Carretero & Lee, Chapter 29, this volume).

Processes Involved in Learning

The learning sciences are centrally concerned with exactly what is going on in a learning environment and exactly how it is contributing to improved student performance. The learning environment includes the people in the environment (teachers, learners, and others), the computers in the environment and the roles they play, the architecture and layout of the room and the physical objects in it, and the social and cultural environment. Key questions include: How does learning happen? How do different learning environments contribute to learning, and can we improve the design of learning environments to enhance learning? Some researchers work on specific components of the learning environment – software design, the roles that teachers should play, or the specific activities each student performs. Others examine the entire learning environment as a system and focus on more holistic questions: How much support for the student should come from the teacher, the computer software, or from other students? How can we create a culture where learners feel like a "learning community"? How can we design materials and activities that keep students motivated and sustain their engagement? Chapter 2, "Foundations of the Learning Sciences," further explores this synergistic contrast between *elemental* and *systemic* approaches in the learning sciences.

How Does Learning Happen?: The Transition from Novice to Expert Performance

One of the legacies of early cognitive science research was its close study of knowledge work. Many artificial intelligence researchers interviewed and observed experts, with the goal of replicating that expert knowledge in a computer program. Before it was possible to simulate expertise in a program, these researchers had to describe in elaborate detail the exact nature of the knowledge underlying that expertise. When these researchers turned their attention to education, they had to consider a new twist: How do experts acquire their expertise? What mental stages do learners go through as they move from novice to expert? These questions were the purview of cognitive development research, which combined developmental psychology and cognitive psychology. Cognitive development has been an important foundation for the learning sciences.

Because learning scientists focus on the expert knowledge underlying knowledge work, they study how novices think and what misconceptions they have; then, they design curricula that leverage those misconceptions appropriately so that learners end up at the expert conception in the most efficient way (diSessa, Chapter 5, this volume).

How Does Learning Happen?: Using Prior Knowledge

One of the most important discoveries guiding learning sciences research is that learning always takes place against a backdrop of existing knowledge.

Students don't enter the classroom as empty vessels; they enter the classroom with half-formed ideas and misconceptions about how the world works – sometimes called "naïve" physics, math, or biology. Many cognitive developmentalists have studied children's theories about the world, and how children's understanding of the world develops through the preschool and early school years. The basic knowledge about cognitive development that has resulted from this research is absolutely critical to reforming schooling so that it is based on the basic sciences of learning.

Instructionist curricula were developed under the behaviorist assumption that children enter school with empty minds, and the role of school is to fill up those minds with knowledge. Instructionist curricula were designed before the learning sciences discovered how children think and what knowledge structures they bring to the classroom.

Promoting Better Learning: Scaffolding

The learning sciences are based on a foundation of constructivism. The learning sciences have convincingly demonstrated that when children actively participate in constructing their own knowledge, they gain a deeper understanding, more generalizable knowledge, and greater motivation. Learning sciences research has resulted in very specific findings about what support the learning environment must provide for learners to effectively construct their own knowledge.

To describe the support that promotes deep learning, learning scientists use the term *scaffolding*. *Scaffolding* is the help given to a learner that is tailored to that learner's needs in achieving his or her goals of the moment (see Reiser & Tabak, Chapter 3, this volume). The best scaffolding provides this help in a way that contributes to learning. For example, telling someone how to do something, or doing it for them, may help them accomplish their immediate goal; but it is not good scaffolding because the child does not actively participate in constructing that knowledge. In contrast, effective scaffolding provides prompts and hints that help learners to figure it out on their own. Effective learning environments scaffold students' active construction of knowledge in ways similar to the way that scaffolding supports the construction of a building. When construction workers need to reach higher, additional scaffolding is added, and when the building is complete, the scaffolding can be removed. In effective learning environments, scaffolding is gradually added, modified, and removed according to the needs of the learner, and eventually the scaffolding fades away entirely.

Promoting Better Learning: Externalization and Articulation

The learning sciences have discovered that when learners externalize and articulate their developing knowledge, they learn more effectively (Bransford, Brown, & Cocking, 2000). This is more complex than it might sound, because it's not the case that learners first learn something and then express it. Instead, the best learning takes place when learners articulate their unformed and still developing understanding and continue to articulate it throughout the process of learning. Articulating and learning go hand in hand, in a mutually reinforcing feedback loop. In many cases, learners don't actually learn something until they start to articulate it – in other words, while thinking out loud, they learn more rapidly and deeply than while studying quietly.

This fascinating phenomenon was first studied in the 1920s by Russian psychologist Lev Vygotsky. In the 1970s, when educational psychologists began to notice the same phenomenon, Vygotsky's writings were increasingly translated into English and other languages, and Vygotsky is now considered one of the foundational theorists of the learning sciences (see Nathan & Sawyer, Chapter 2, this volume). Vygotsky's explanation for the educational value of articulation is based on a theory of mental development; he argued that all knowledge began as visible social interaction, and then was gradually internalized by the learner to form thought. Learning scientists have widely debated the exact nature of this internalization process, but, regardless of the specifics of one or another explanation, the learning sciences are unified in their belief that collaboration and conversation among learners is critical because it allows learners to benefit from the power of articulation.

One of the most important topics of learning sciences research is how to support students in this ongoing process of articulation, and which forms of articulation are the most beneficial to learning. The learning sciences have discovered that articulation is more effective if it is scaffolded – channeled so that certain kinds of knowledge are articulated, and in a certain form that is most likely to result in useful reflection. Students need help in articulating their developing understandings; they don't yet know how to think about thinking, and they don't yet know how to talk about thinking. The chapters in Part 4, "Learning Together," describe several examples of learning environments that scaffold effective learning interactions.

Promoting Better Learning: Reflection

One of the reasons that articulation is so helpful to learning is that it makes possible *reflection* or *metacognition* – thinking about the process of learning and thinking about knowledge (see Winne & Azevedo, Chapter 4, this volume). Learning scientists have repeatedly demonstrated the importance of reflection in learning for deeper understanding. Many learning sciences classrooms are designed to foster reflection, and most of them foster reflection by providing students with tools that make it easier for them to articulate their developing understandings. Once students have articulated their developing understandings, learning environments should support them in reflecting on what they have just articulated. One of the most central topics in learning sciences research is how to support students in educationally beneficial reflection.

Promoting Better Learning: Building from Concrete to Abstract Knowledge

One of the most accepted findings of developmental psychologist Jean Piaget is that the natural progression of learning starts with more concrete information and gradually becomes more abstract. Piaget's influence in schools during the 1960s and 1970s led to the widespread use of "manipulatives," blocks and colored bars used in math classrooms. Not every important abstract idea that we teach in schools can be represented using colored blocks, but the sophistication of computer graphics allows very abstract concepts to be represented in a visible form.

The learning sciences have taken Piaget's original insight and have developed computer software to visually represent a wide range of types of knowledge. Even very abstract disciplinary practices have been represented visually in the computer; the structure of scientific argument can be represented (Andriessen & Baker, Chapter 22, this volume), and the step-by-step process of scientific inquiry can be represented.

In the process of making the abstract concrete, these systems also scaffold students in the articulation of rather abstract conceptual knowledge; their articulation can be visual or graphic rather than simply verbal, and in many cases, visual and spatial understandings precede verbal understandings and can be used to build verbal understanding.

Educational Technology

In the 1950s, B. F. Skinner presented his "teaching machines" and claimed that they made the teacher "out of date" (Skinner, 1954/1968, p. 22). The first educational software was designed in the 1960s and was based on Skinner's behaviorist theories; these programs are known as *computer-assisted instruction* or *CAI*, and such programs are still in use. In the 1970s, a few artificial intelligence (AI) researchers started working in education, developing automated tutoring systems and other applications (Bobrow & Collins, 1975; Sleeman & Brown, 1982; Wenger, 1987). In the 1980s, cognitive scientists like Roger Schank and Seymour Papert made widely popularized claims that computers would radically transform schools.

By the 1990s, a strong consensus had formed in many countries, among politicians, parents, and the business community, that it was essential to get computers into schools (Cuban, 2001). There was a major push to install computers in schools and to grant students access to the Internet. In the United States, this push included federal government programs like E-rate that paid for Internet connection in schools. By 2009, in the United States, 97 percent of teachers had one or more computers in their classrooms every day, and 93 percent of these computers were connected to the Internet. On average, there were 5.3 students for each computer; this was a dramatic drop from 12.1 students in 1998, when this statistic was first reported (Gray, Thomas, & Lewis, 2010; Parsad & Jones, 2005).

However, the impact of all of this investment has been disappointing. By 2000, no studies had convincingly shown that computer use was correlated with improved student performance. When researchers began to look more closely at why computers were having so little impact, they discovered that computer use was not based on the learning sciences; instead, teachers were using computers as quick add-ons to the existing instructionist classroom (Cuban, 2001). Learning scientists are well aware that computers have generally failed teachers and students; that they are, in Larry Cuban's (2001) famous words, "oversold and underused."

Computers only benefit learning when they are designed to take into account what we know about how children learn and are closely integrated with teacher and student interactions in the classroom. Learning sciences research explains why the promise of computers in schools has not yet been realized. It's because, to date, educational software has been designed based on instructionist theories, with the computer performing roles that are traditionally performed by the teacher – the software acts as an expert authority, delivering information to the learner. In contrast, learning sciences research suggests that the computer should take on a more facilitating role, helping learners have the kinds of experiences that lead to deep learning – for example, helping them to collaborate or to reflect on their developing knowledge.

Many of the chapters in this handbook describe the next generation of educational software and technology – solidly based on the sciences of learning and designed in close collaboration with teachers and schools. Computers are used only as part of overall classroom reform and only where research shows they will have the most impact. Computer software is an important aspect of learning sciences research and practice because the graphics and the processing power of today's computers support deep learning.

- Computers can represent abstract knowledge in concrete form.
- Computer tools allow learners to articulate their developing knowledge in a visual and verbal way.
- Computers allow learners to manipulate and revise their developing knowledge via the user interface in a complex process of design that supports simultaneous articulation, reflection, and learning.
- Computers support reflection in a combination of visual and verbal modes.

- Internet-based networks of learners can share and combine their developing understandings and benefit from the power of collaborative learning.

But computer software is only one component of this handbook; various chapters also propose new teaching strategies, alternative ways of bringing students together in collaborating groups, and new forms of curriculum that cross traditional grades and disciplines. Some chapters even propose radical new ways of thinking about schooling and learning.

A Design Science

As scientists who are focused on creating effective learning environments, learning scientists ask questions like: How can we measure learning? How can we determine which learning environments work best? How can we analyze a learning environment, identify the innovations that work well, and separate out those features that need additional improvement? In other words, how can we marshal all of our scientific knowledge to design the most effective learning environments? These questions are fundamental to scientific research in education (Shavelson & Towne, 2002).

The gold standard of scientific methodology is the *experimental design*, in which students are randomly assigned to different learning environments. Many education studies are also quasi-experimental – rather than randomly assigning students to environments, they identify two existing classrooms that seem identical in every way, and use one teaching method in one classroom and a different teaching method in the other classroom, and analyze which students learn more and better (Shavelson & Towne, 2002). Experimental and quasi-experimental designs can provide educators and policy makers with important information about the relative merits of different approaches. But they can't tell us very much about why or how a teaching method is working – the minute-by-minute structure of the classroom activity that leads to student learning. If we could study those classroom processes, we would be in a much better position to improve teaching methods by continually revising them. Learning scientists combine a range of methodologies to better understand learning processes, as described in the chapters in Part 2, "Methodologies." The chapters in this book report on experimental comparisons of classrooms, experiments in cognitive psychology laboratories, studies of social interaction using the methodologies of sociology and anthropology, and a new hybrid methodology known as *design-based research* (Barab, Chapter 8, this volume).

Learning scientists have discovered that deep learning is more likely to occur in complex social and technological environments. To study learning in rich social and technological environments, learning scientists have drawn on ethnography (from anthropology), ethnomethodology and conversation analysis (from sociology), and sociocultural psychology (from developmental psychology). Anthropological methods have been influential since the 1980s, when ethnographers like Lucy Suchman, Ed Hutchins, and Jean Lave began to document exactly how learning takes place within the everyday activities of a community (Hutchins, 1995; Lave, 1988; Scribner & Cole, 1973; Suchman, 1987).

Many learning scientists study the moment-to-moment processes of learning, typically by gathering large amounts of videotape data, and they use a range of methodologies to analyze these videotapes back in the laboratory – a set of methodologies known as *interaction analysis* (Enyedy & Stevens, Chapter 10, this volume). Interaction analysis is used to identify the moment-to-moment unfolding of three things simultaneously: (1) the relations among learners, their patterns of interaction, and how they change over time; (2) the practices engaged in by the learners – individual and group procedures for solving problems, and how they change over time; and (3) individual learning. Individual learning can only be understood alongside the first two kinds of change.

However, deep knowledge cannot be learned in one class session. As a result, learning scientists also study longer-term learning, over the entire school year and even from grade to grade. During the course of a research study, learning scientists continually shift their focus closer and then farther back, studying the microgenetics of one classroom (Chinn & Sherin, Chapter 9, this volume) and then analyzing how that class session contributes to the longer-term development of deeper conceptual understanding.

Learning sciences research is complex and difficult. A typical learning sciences research project takes a minimum of a year, as researchers work closely with teachers and schools to modify the learning environment, allow time for the modification to take effect, and observe how learning emerges over time. Some projects follow learners over several years, or follow a particular teacher's classes for several years as that teacher introduces new activities and software tools to each successive class. And after the years of observation are complete, the hard work begins, because the researchers have shelves of videotapes – in some cases hundreds of hours – that need to be closely watched, multiple times, and many of them transcribed for even more detailed analysis, including quantitative coding and statistical analysis.

The Emergence of the Field of Learning Sciences

In the 1970s and 1980s, many cognitive scientists used artificial intelligence technologies to design software that could promote better learning (e.g., Bobrow & Collins, 1975; Sleeman & Brown, 1982). During this period, they initiated the "Artificial Intelligence in Education" (AIED) conferences that are still held today. In 1987, Northwestern University decided to make a major commitment to this emerging field, and hired cognitive scientist Roger Schank from Yale University to lead what became known as the Institute of the Learning Sciences (ILS). Also in 1987, John Seely Brown and James Greeno were cofounders, along with David Kearns, CEO of Xerox, Corp., of the Institute for Research on Learning (IRL) in Palo Alto, California. At about the same time, Vanderbilt University's Center for Learning and Technology was applying cognitive science to develop technology-based curriculum, and Seymour Papert's Logo group at MIT was building constructivist learning environments on the computer.

In the summer of 1989, Roger Schank, Allan Collins, and Andrew Ortony began to discuss founding a new journal that would focus on applying the cognitive sciences to learning. Janet Kolodner was chosen as the editor of the new journal, and the first issue of the *Journal of the Learning Sciences* was published in January 1991. Also in 1991, the AI and Education conference was held at Northwestern at the ILS, and Schank dubbed it the first International Conference of the Learning Sciences. But the newly formed learning sciences community and the AI and Education community found that they had somewhat different interests. AI and Education researchers continued to design tutoring systems and other educational tools based on AI technologies, while the learning sciences community was more interested in studying learning in real-world learning environments, and in designing software that focused on learners' needs, whether or not AI technology was needed. For example, supporting articulation, reflection, and collaboration required different kinds of technologies from those the AI and Education community was considering at that time. After the 1991 conference, the AI community and the learning sciences community parted ways. The second learning sciences conference was held in 1996 and conferences have been held every two years since then, with conferences focusing on computer support for collaborative learning (CSCL) held in the intervening years. In 2002, the International Society of the Learning Sciences (ISLS) was founded, and it is now the organization that plans both the ICSL and the CSCL conferences, provides intellectual support for the *Journal of the Learning Sciences* (*JLS*), and helped to found the *International Journal of Computer Supported Collaborative Learning* (iJCSCL; see www.isls.org).

Conclusion

Since the beginning of the modern institution of schools, there has been debate about whether education is a science or an art. The language of science makes some educators nervous. Everyone can remember the artistry of a great teacher – a teacher who somehow against all odds got every student to perform better than they thought they could. Teachers themselves know how complex their job is – every minute of every hour, a thousand different things are going on, and it can seem so unlikely that the cutting-and-slicing reductionist approach of science could ever help us understand what's happening. The history of scientific approaches to education is not promising; in the past, scientists studied learning in a university laboratory and then delivered pronouncements from the Ivory Tower that teachers were expected to adopt unquestioningly (Cremin, 1961).

Unlike these previous generations of educational research, learning scientists spend a lot of time in schools – many of us were full-time teachers before we became researchers. And learning scientists are committed to improving classroom teaching and learning – many are in schools every week, working directly with teachers and districts. Some even take time off from university duties and return to the classroom, teaching alongside teachers and learning how to make theories work in the real world. This is a new kind of science, with the goal of providing a sound scientific foundation for educational innovations.

References

Baron, J. (1985). *Rationality and intelligence*. New York: Cambridge.

Bereiter, C. (2002). *Education and mind in the knowledge age*. Mahwah, NJ: Erlbaum.

Bobrow, D. G., & Collins, A. (1975). *Representation and understanding: Studies in cognitive science*. New York: Academic Press.

Bransford, J. D., Brown, A. L., & Cocking, R. R. (Eds.). (2000). *How people learn: Brain, mind, experience, and school*. Washington, DC: National Academy Press.

Burtis, P. J., Bereiter, C., Scardamalia, M., & Tetroe, J. (1983). The development of planning in writing. In B. M. Kroll & G. Wells (Eds.), *Explorations in the development of writing: Theory, research, and practice* (pp. 153–174). New York: Wiley.

Cole, M. (1996). *Cultural psychology: A once and future discipline*. Cambridge, MA: Harvard University Press.

Collins, A., & Brown, J. S. (1988). The computer as a tool for learning through reflection. In H. Mandl & A. Lesgold (Eds.), *Learning issues for intelligent tutoring systems* (pp. 1–18). New York: Springer.

Cremin, L. A. (1961). *The transformation of the school: Progressivism in American education, 1876–1957*. New York: Knopf.

Cuban, L. (2001). *Oversold and underused: Computers in the classroom*. Cambridge, MA: Harvard University Press.

Drucker, P. F. (1993). *Post-capitalist society*. New York: HarperBusiness.

Dunbar, K., & Klahr, D. (1989). Developmental differences in scientific discovery strategies. In D. Klahr & K. Kotovsky (Eds.), *Complex information processing: The impact of Herbert A. Simon* (pp. 109–143). Mahwah, NJ: Erlbaum.

Flower, L., & Hayes, J. R. (1980). The cognition of discovery: Defining a rhetorical problem. *College Composition and Communication, 31*, 21–32.

Gray, L., Thomas, N., & Lewis, L. (2010). *Teachers' use of educational technology in U. S. public schools: 2009* (NCES 2010–040). Washington, DC: National Center for Education Statistics, Institute of Education Sciences, U.S. Department of Education.

Heath, C., & Luff, P. (1991). *Collaborative activity and technological design: Task coordination in the London Underground control rooms.* Paper presented at the Proceedings of ECSCW '91.

Hughes, J. A., Shapiro, D. Z., Sharrock, W. W., Anderson, R. J., & Gibbons, S. C. (1988). *The automation of air traffic control* (Final Report SERC/ESRC Grant no. GR/D/86257). Lancaster, UK: Department of Sociology, Lancaster University.

Hutchins, E. (1995). *Cognition in the wild.* Cambridge: MIT Press.

Kahneman, D., Slovic, P., & Tversky, A. (Eds.). (1982). *Judgment under uncertainty: Heuristics and biases.* New York: Cambridge.

Kuhn, D. (1989). Children and adults as intuitive scientists. *Psychological Review, 96*, 674–689.

Kuhn, D. (1990). Introduction. In D. Kuhn (Ed.), *Developmental perspectives on teaching and learning thinking skills* (pp. 1–8). Basel: Karger.

Lave, J. (1988). *Cognition in practice: Mind, mathematics, and culture in everyday life.* New York: Cambridge.

Liebowitz, J. (Ed.). (1998). *The handbook of applied expert systems.* Boca Raton, FL: CRC Press.

McGuire, J. E. (1992). Scientific change: Perspectives and proposals. In M. Salmon, J. Earman, C. Glymour, J. Lennox, P. Machamer, J. McGuire, J. Norton, W. Salmon, & K. Schaffner (Eds.), *Introduction to the philosophy of science* (pp. 132–178). Englewood Cliffs, NJ: Prentice Hall.

National Center for History in the Schools. (1996). *National standards for history.* Los Angeles, CA: National Center for History in the Schools.

National Research Council. (1996). *National science education standards.* Washington, DC: National Academy Press.

Newell, A., & Simon, H. A. (1972). *Human problem solving.* Englewood Cliffs, NJ: Prentice Hall.

Palincsar, A. S., & Brown, A. L. (1984). Reciprocal teaching of comprehension fostering and comprehension monitoring. *Cognition and Instruction, 1*(2), 117–175.

Papert, S. (1980). *Mindstorms: Children, computers, and powerful ideas.* New York: Basic Books.

Papert, S. (1993). *The children's machine: Rethinking school in the age of the computer.* New York: Basic Books.

Parsad, B., & Jones, J. (2005). *Internet access in U.S. public schools and classrooms: 1994–2003* (NCES 2005–015). Washington, DC: National Center for Education Statistics.

Rogoff, B. (1990). *Apprenticeship in thinking: Cognitive development in social context.* New York: Oxford University Press.

Rogoff, B. (1998). Cognition as a collaborative process. In D. Kuhn & R. S. Siegler (Eds.), *Handbook of child psychology, 5th edition, Volume 2: Cognition, perception, and language* (pp. 679–744). New York: Wiley.

Salomon, G. (Ed.). (1993). *Distributed cognitions: Psychological and educational considerations.* New York: Cambridge.

Saxe, G. B. (1991). *Culture and cognitive development: Studies in mathematical understanding.* Hillsdale, NJ: Erlbaum.

Schauble, L. (1990). Belief revision in children: The role of prior knowledge and strategies for generating evidence. *Journal of Experimental Child Psychology,* 49, 31–57.

Scribner, S., & Cole, M. (1973). Cognitive consequences of formal and informal education. *Science,* 182(4112), 553–559.

Shavelson, R. J., & Towne, L. (2002). *Scientific research in education.* Washington, DC: National Academy Press.

Siegler, R. S. (1998). *Children's thinking.* (Third ed.). Upper Saddle River, NJ: Prentice Hall.

Skinner, B. F. (1954/1968). The science of learning and the art of teaching. In B. F. Skinner (Ed.), *The technology of teaching* (pp. 9–28). New York: Appleton-Century-Crofts. (Original work published in 1954 in the *Harvard Educational Review,* 24(2), 86–97).

Sleeman, D., & Brown, J. S. (Eds.). (1982). *Intelligent tutoring systems.* New York: Academic Press.

Suchman, L. A. (1987). *Plans and situated actions: The problem of human-machine communication.* New York: Cambridge University Press.

Suppe, F. (1974). The search for philosophic understanding of scientific theories. In F. Suppe (Ed.), *The structure of scientific theories* (pp. 3–241). Urbana: University of Illinois Press.

Voss, J. F., Perkins, D. N., & Segal, J. W. (Eds.). (1991). *Informal reasoning and education.* Mahwah, NJ: Erlbaum.

Wenger, E. (1987). *Artificial intelligence and tutoring systems: Computational and cognitive approaches to the communication of knowledge.* San Francisco, CA: Morgan Kaufmann.

PART I

Foundations

2 Foundations of the Learning Sciences

Mitchell J. Nathan and R. Keith Sawyer

The learning sciences (LS) studies the design and implementation of effective learning environments, in addition to basic scientific research on learning (Kolodner, 1991). In this sense, LS embraces Stokes's (1997) notion of "use-inspired basic research." In its pursuits, LS research draws on a variety of theoretical perspectives on learning phenomena as they occur across a broad range of physical, social, and technological spaces. In this chapter, we describe the intellectual foundations that have influenced the learning sciences from its beginnings, and we identify the core elements of LS that unify the many chapters of this handbook.

Principles and Themes of the Learning Sciences

Bridging Research and Practice

Learning scientists work on the design and implementation of real-world educational systems – curricula, software, teaching practices, and social and interactional patterns – and also conduct basic scientific investigations. As a result of this joint focus, learning scientists are centrally concerned with bridging research and practice. This approach contrasts with the history of education research, where researchers and practitioners have long viewed each other with extreme skepticism and little trust. This focus on bridging research and practice distinguishes LS from related fields that are "basic sciences" – cognitive psychology, educational psychology, and anthropology – and those that are more "use inspired," such as instructional design and educational technology. An early example of a prototypical learning sciences project was the *Schools for Thought* classrooms implemented with funding from the James S. McDonnell Foundation throughout North America (Lamon et al., 1996). The innovations that were incorporated into *Schools for Thought* classrooms included: *Knowledge Forum* (science and rhetoric; see Scardamalia & Bereiter, Chapter 20, this volume), *The Adventures of Jasper Woodbury* (mathematics; Cognition and Technology Group at Vanderbilt, 1997), *Reciprocal Teaching* (reading; Palincsar & Brown, 1984), and *Fostering Communities of Learners* (classroom culture; Brown & Campione, 1994). *Schools for Thought* advanced our scientific understanding of the nature of classroom learning, teaching, and assessment in an intellectually, socially, and technologically dynamic learning environment. It also contributed substantially to the development and implementation of empirically based principles of learning environment design.

Scaling up: From Research Intervention to Widespread Implementation

The ideal progress of an LS project is to begin by developing an educational innovation, using an iterative design process that involves frequent evaluation in real-world settings; to then document the effectiveness of the innovation in a carefully observed test site – typically one classroom or one school with participating teachers who work closely with the research team; and then to *scale up* the innovation beyond the test site in order to broadly shape pedagogical practices, design principles, and education policies (Spillane, Reiser, & Reimer, 2002). Although scaling up effective interventions is critical for education reform, successful scale-up initiatives are rare (Penuel, Fishman, Cheng, & Sabelli, 2011). Members of the LS community, however, have been responsible for several successful scale-up efforts, including *Schools for Thought* (Lamon et al., 1996); *Cognitive Tutor Algebra* (Koedinger & Corbett, 2006); *Web-based inquiry science environment (WISE)* (Linn & Slotta, 2000); *Quest Atlantis* (Barab, Thomas, Dodge, Carteaux, & Tuzun, 2005); and *SimCalc* (Tatar et al., 2008); among others. These successful projects have provided valuable experience in taking research-based innovations and translating them into real-world practices that enhance student learning outcomes.

Scaling up has traditionally been defined in terms of the breadth of the dissemination and level of fidelity of an innovation (RAND, 2004). In contrast, contemporary evaluations of successful scale-up research tend to highlight the importance of tailoring the measures and practices to the specific implementation context (Dede, 2006; McDonald, Keesler, Kauffman, & Schneider, 2006). Recent evaluations suggest that effective reform must conform to the constraints of the local learning environments, and that practitioners must be recognized for the central role they play in carrying out fundamental change. Education scale-up researchers advocate forming collaborative relationships with teachers, school leaders, and designers in order to customize each implementation. Scale-up researchers strive to improve the implementation with each successive iteration of the design-implement-evaluate-redesign cycle.

Scientific and Engineering Approaches to the Study of Learning

The goal of basic research on the human mind – for example, a cognitive psychology perspective – is to produce reliable models and broad theories that describe, explain, and predict human behavior and development in ways that stand up to scrutiny by a community of scientific peers. Scientific theories advance our understanding of learning and pave the way for the design of new, effective innovations. This scientific ethos has dominated studies of human behavior, learning, education, workplace training, and human factors for more than a century (Cremin, 1961).

However, if the goal is to develop scalable educational innovations that transform schools and classrooms, scientific approaches have serious limitations, as follows. Scientific accounts of complex social phenomena are commonly based on the study of greatly simplified behaviors in methodologically favorable contexts (for example, the isolated individual studied in the psychological laboratory), which compromises their ecological validity and makes it difficult to scale up to a wide variety of authentic settings. Scientific theories are *descriptive* of learning and performance, but are rarely *prescriptive* of the instructional supports needed to foster that learning (Schwartz, Martin, & Nasir, 2005). Thus, scientific theories of learning "under-constrain" instructional design (Nathan, 1998), meaning that designers of learning environments must make many atheoretical decisions during planning and implementation.

LS is a *design science* drawn from an engineering ethos. In an engineering approach, success is seldom defined in terms of theoretical accounts of how the world operates, but by developing *satisficing* solutions for how things ought to be – innovations that *satisfy* existing conditions and *sufficiently* meet the stated goals within prevailing constraints (Simon, 1996). Efforts to design effective learning environments and activities cannot be based solely on scientifically validated theories of learning: theoretical advances are often too slow in coming, too blunt, and too idealistic. Engineering and other design-based approaches use faster methods of testing innovation. Design-based approaches (see Barab, Chapter 8, this volume) are goal directed and contextualized and often employ frequent, formative assessment (see Pellegrino, Chapter 12, this volume) as part of iterative design-implement-evaluate-redesign methods. This allows for highly responsive, evidence-based course corrections so that it is possible to realign solutions to suit local constraints and to resolve on-the-fly decisions that are underspecified by prevailing scientific models.

Influential Theories of Learning

Cognitive Science

Cognitive science is an interdisciplinary field, drawing primarily on cognitive psychology and computer science, which frames cognition as computation (Chalmers, 1993/2011). *Computation* is broadly defined to include the many classes of computational systems that computer scientists have developed and studied, from rule-based or algorithmic systems to connectionist or "massively parallel" systems. The goal of cognitive science is to develop an empirically based and computationally verifiable (i.e., programmable) theory of cognition

(Newell & Simon, 1976). The mental processes and structures that cognitive scientists study most often are attention, perception, semantic and episodic memory, language development and use, concepts and categorization, reasoning and decision making, problem solving, procedural and conceptual learning, and consciousness. Many cognitive scientists hold to the principle of computational equivalence, also known as *multiple realizability*: a cognitive system can achieve the same output (e.g., a behavior) for a specific set of inputs (e.g., words and images on a screen) using vastly different "realizing" lower-level substrates of algorithms, representations, and material substrates (e.g., the silicon chips of computers or the neurons of the human brain).

Situated Cognition

Situated cognition is heavily influenced by phenomenological philosophy and its central insight that we know and make sense of the world through direct perception of the actionable possibilities of our interactions with our environment (Gibson, 1977). Phenomenologists argue that perception and representation exist as grounded interaction *with* the world, rather than as internal mental representations *about* the world (Dreyfus, 2002). Phenomenologists focus on the contextualized activity of complex organizations of people, technology and information resources, and the physical environment (Greeno, 1997). Thus, phenomenology places agency and action in the world, rather than internal mental processing, at its core (Anderson, 2003; Larkin, Eatough, & Osborn, 2011). Situated cognition rejects models of cognition that are based primarily on computational processes and structures composed of symbol systems that are abstract, amodal, and arbitrarily mapped to the world.

The situated cognition perspective holds that cognitive behavior is embodied, embedded, and extended. An *embodied cognition* approach (Abrahamson & Lindgren, Chapter 18, this volume; Nathan, 2014) is valuable when body states and body-based resources are inextricably tied to intellectual behavior (Glenberg, 1997). *Embedded cognition* (closely related to *distributed cognition*) holds that cognition is mediated by the physical and social environment of the individual in cases where the environment is used to off-load task demands that might otherwise be performed mentally. An influential example of distributed cognition was Hutchins's (1995) study of the emergence of navigation as the work of a team interacting with instruments and tools, maps, and the space the team inhabits. Theories of *extended cognition* go further, arguing that in some cases the social and physical environment, along with the individuals in it, jointly *constitute* the cognitive system (Clark & Chalmers, 1998).

Constructivism

Constructivism posits that learning involves the active creation of mental structures, rather than the passive internalization of information acquired from others or from the environment. Jean Piaget, the originator of constructivism, argued that all learning was mediated by the construction of mental objects that he called *schemas*, which were essentially Kantian a priori categories (e.g., space, time, causality). Piaget's original articulation focused on how schemas emerge from the interaction and experimentation of the child with the physical world. For Piaget, schemas first emerge as concrete actions and gradually develop into more abstract and conceptual mental entities.

Constructivism has been broadly influential in education and forms one of the core elements of learning sciences approaches. Some learning scientists have also been influenced by variants of constructivism. For example, *radical constructivists* (e.g., von Glasersfeld, 1989) hold that because we each form our own realities there can be no external truth. *Social constructivists* (e.g., Mead, Vygotsky) posit that the knowledge construction process is inherently mediated by social interaction, including the use of language.

The emergence of the San Francisco Exploratorium and other interactive science centers (see Crowley, Pierroux, & Knutson, Chapter 23, this volume) was directly inspired by the dissemination of Piagetian ideas in America in the 1960s (Flavell, 1963). One of the seminal contributions of constructivism to education was the development of the Logo programming language by Seymour Papert (1980), soon after he returned from studying with Piaget in Geneva. Logo enables children to construct notions of geometry and computation through the exploration of space and the control of actions as mediated through programming of an animated "turtle." Constructivism also figured prominently in the "Great Debate" on reading (whole language versus phonics), and the "Math Wars" (back to basics versus constructivist approaches), and remains influential in educational reform and the emergence of a convergent set of curriculum and instructional standards in primary and secondary education content areas.

Sociocultural Theory

By the 1980s, after the burst of activity associated with 1970s artificial intelligence (AI) and cognitive science, many of these scholars had begun to realize that their goal – to understand and simulate human intelligence in the computer – was still very far off. The 1980s disillusionment with AI was so severe that it was informally known as "the AI winter." Researchers began to step back and think about why the cognitive sciences had not been more successful. The most influential answer was provided by a group of interrelated approaches, including the sociocultural, situative, and distributed cognition approaches (Greeno & Engeström, Chapter 7, this volume; Salomon, 1993). Socioculturalists began with the observation that all intelligent behavior was realized in a complex environment – a human-created environment filled with tools and machines, but also a deeply social environment with collaborators and partners.

Some of the most interesting work along these lines focused on informal learning in non-Western societies without formal schooling (Cole, 1996; Lave, 1988; Rogoff, 1990; Saxe, 1991). Equally influential studies examined the socially distributed nature of knowledge work – including studies of navy ship navigation (Hutchins, 1995), of London Underground control rooms (Heath & Luff, 1991), of office systems (Suchman, 1987), and of air traffic control centers (Hughes, Shapiro, Sharrock, Anderson, & Gibbons, 1988). This research revealed that, outside of formal schooling, almost all learning occurs in a complex social environment and that learning is hard to understand if one thinks of it as a mental process occurring within the head of an isolated learner.

Sociocultural scholars draw on the classic theories of Russian psychologist Lev Vygotsky (1978), who argued that social interaction was the primary driver of intellectual development. He contended that thought emerged during development as social interaction gradually became internalized. Through mechanisms like scaffolding (see Reiser & Tabak, Chapter 3, this volume), children could perform at a higher level than when operating alone, and these opportunities could accelerate intellectual development.

The sociocultural approach has been widely influential in all of the disciplines participating in the learning sciences.

- Artificial intelligence researchers began to emphasize distributed cognition in part because of the rapidly evolving network technologies of the 1980s and 1990s.
- Cognitive psychology researchers began to study teamwork, collaboration, group dynamics, and the role of social context in cognitive development.
- Education researchers began to study classroom collaboration, collaborative discourse in student groups, and project teams.

Learning scientists use these approaches in particular to explain *informal learning* (Crowley et al., Chapter 23, this volume) – learning outside of schools, whether at home with the family, on the playground with peers, or in apprenticeship settings where youth learn a trade or other culturally valued skills (Lave & Wenger, 1991; also see Collins and Kapur, Chapter 6, this volume).

American Pragmatism

Pragmatist John Dewey developed *child centered pedagogy*, where the child's interest and experience drove the learning environment design. Dewey's theories emphasized the importance of *inquiry* – that children learn best when they interact with the world much as a scientist or philosopher does, by posing hypotheses and testing them against reality and reason. There are close parallels with Piaget's theory; Piaget and Dewey were contemporaries and both were widely influential through much of the 20th century.

George Herbert Mead, another pragmatist working during the first half of the 20th century, argued that thought is *emergent* from the organism's interaction with reality, and that communication and language begin as concrete and simple gestures and gradually become more abstract (again, note the close parallels with Piaget). Blumer, a student of Mead's, developed *symbolic interactionism*, which focused on the close analysis of how people exchange symbols – whether verbal symbols (words) or gestures and body language. During the 1960s and 1970s, Blumer's ideas were further developed by Garfinkel's *ethnomethodology*, which holds that the best way to understand social phenomena is to ask participants what they are doing and how they are interpreting it. A variant of ethnomethodology, *conversation analysis*, likewise proposes that the best way to analyze the social context of an encounter is to closely examine how participants talk about that social context and convey its relevance to them. These approaches remain influential in LS, particularly among researchers who use qualitative and ethnographic methods to study videotapes of naturally occurring learning encounters (see Goldman, Zahn, & Derry, Chapter 11, this volume).

The Scope of Learning Behaviors

Time Scales of Learning

LS studies learning across levels of space, time, and scale. Figure 2.1 (adapted from Nathan & Alibali, 2010) reflects one way to visualize the unified nature of learning phenomena as they emerge through variation of only a single parameter: time (Newell, 1990). From an individualist psychological perspective, what unifies all learning phenomena is a set of shared mental *processes*. In contrast, LS holds that what unites learning phenomena is that learning occurs in the context of *designed learning environments* – classrooms, the home, workplaces, museums, even the psychology laboratory. In each case, the learning environment is an artifact designed in a historical context, in

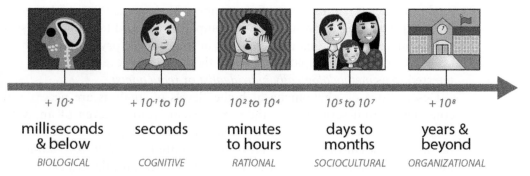

$+10^{-2}$	$+10^{-1}$ to 10	10^2 to 10^4	10^5 to 10^7	$+10^8$
milliseconds & below	seconds	minutes to hours	days to months	years & beyond
BIOLOGICAL	COGNITIVE	RATIONAL	SOCIOCULTURAL	ORGANIZATIONAL

Figure 2.1. *Log_{10} time scale of human learning. Adapted from Nathan and Alibali (2010).*

response to cultural constraints and expectations, which is intended to bring about societally desirable learning outcomes.

Elemental Research

To investigate the range of learning phenomena within LS more fully, in addition to a time scale analysis, Nathan and Alibali (2010) drew a distinction between *systemic* and *elemental* approaches to learning research. *Elemental* approaches are so called because they focus on the component elements of a complex learning environment – and as such, they rely on the *factoring assumption*: they assume that the many components of the system (such as context) can be "factored out" and analyzed independently (Greeno & Engeström, Chapter 7, this volume). *Systemic* approaches reject the factoring assumption. Thus, they analyze learning at the level of the entire complex system.

Elemental approaches include research performed using correlational and experimental methods, structural equation modeling and factor analysis, and computer modeling approaches. While much cognitive psychology research is elemental in nature, some of it – for example, research from a situated cognition perspective – can be systemic. Thus, it would be erroneous to assign all quantitative methods or all methods that lie in the lower time bands of Figure 2.1 to elemental approaches. Methods that draw on learning analytics, such as educational data mining (Baker & Siemens, Chapter 13, this volume) and whole-brain methods in cognitive neuroscience, for example, contradict this pattern. Similarly, though a great deal of qualitative research aligns with systemic approaches, some, such as think aloud reports, are used to factor out elemental processes from task and environmental influences.

Levels of Analysis

Scientists study complex systems at different *levels of analysis*: some phenomena are better studied by analyzing the complete system (the "higher" level of analysis), and other phenomena are better studied by reductively analyzing the system in terms of its component elements ("lower" levels of analysis). Learning environments are complex social and technological systems, and approaches that analyze them in terms of the psychological characteristics of the participating individuals are "lower level" and often are referred to as *methodologically individualist* or *reductionist*.

Descriptions of phenomena at higher levels of analysis are necessarily consistent with descriptions of the same systems at lower levels of analysis. This is because all such systems are characterized by *supervenience*: properties and entities at the higher level of analysis are *realized* or *instantiated* in lower-level component properties and processes. Technically, *supervenience* refers to a system where any change in the higher-level description must

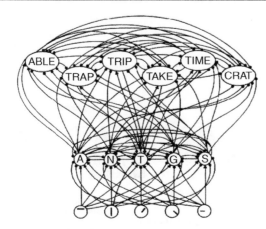

Figure 2.2. *An example of supervenience: Pen strokes combine to form letters; letters combine to form words. Copied from McClelland and Rumelhart (1986).*

necessarily result in a corresponding change in the lower-level description (Sawyer, 2005).

Figure 2.2 provides an illustrative example of a simple system of supervenience, where individual pen strokes (bottom of the figure) are combined in conventional ways to form letters, and letters combine to form words. Words are the "higher level" and they supervene on letters, while letters supervene on strokes.

Systemic Research

In the history of science, elemental reductionist approaches have had great success. This had led some education researchers to suggest that lower-level analysis (for example, psychological studies of individual learners) is the most promising approach for education research. LS research, in contrast, is distinguished by its regard for both elemental and systemic research, with the approach determined by the nature of the phenomenon.

In complex systems, higher levels always supervene on lower levels. And yet, in some complex systems, higher levels can exhibit emergent properties that are difficult to analyze and explain in elemental terms. Systemic approaches assume that context and behavior cannot be "factored out"; these approaches include situated cognition and cultural-historical activity theory (CHAT), social learning theory (Miyake & Kirschner, Chapter 21, this volume), and ethnomethodological methods. These approaches all choose a system-level unit of analysis, maintaining that this better preserves the essential qualities of the learning environment than does analyzing the phenomenon by reducing it to a set of factorable elements (Leont'ev, 1981; Wertsch, 1985).

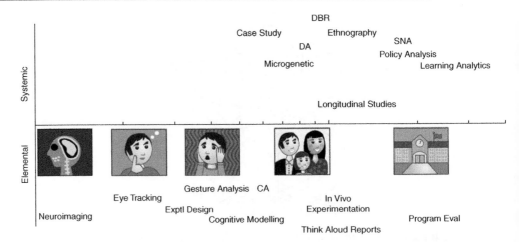

Figure 2.3. *Systemic (above) and elemental (below) research plotted on a logarithmic time scale.*

Learning Sciences as a Design Science

As a field, LS draws on research from both elemental and systemic perspectives when developing, implementing, and evaluating effective learning environment designs for behaviors observed at various time scales (Figure 2.3). In this section, we review some of the key findings from these two research perspectives, and offer guidance for how elemental and systemic perspectives can be productively combined to achieve the broad aims of LS: to advance our basic understanding of learning while applying that understanding to the design of real-world learning environments.

Elemental View: Evidence-Based Principles of Learning and Design

The core findings that have emerged from several decades of elemental learning research have been summarized in several review articles (Dunlosky, Rawson, Marsh, Nathan, & Willingham, 2013; Graesser, Halpern, & Hakel, 2008; Pashler et al., 2007). These reviews converge on a small number of overarching principles for facilitating learning: the importance of repetition and practice; managing the demands on cognitive and attentional resources; engaging the learner in the active construction of meaning and knowledge; and metacognitive awareness. This body of research suggests the following design guidelines for how to develop effective learning environments.

Strategically Regulated Repetition and Practice

Learning benefits immensely from strategically regulated repetition and practice, especially when it is accompanied by reliable and timely feedback.

Performance is generally superior when repetition and practice are spaced apart in time. The feedback practice testing provides is valuable, in part because it emulates the assessment experience that is to come, and the necessary *retrieval practice* – the generation of responses by retrieving information from memory. For certain kinds of test performance, such as rapid and accurate performance of a narrow set of perceptual or motor skills, practice that is *blocked* – continuous repetition of the same behavior, rather than mixing practice of differing behaviors – is most beneficial. In more conceptually oriented testing, it is more beneficial to *interleave* practice by mixing multiple types of tasks. The benefit is thought to result because interleaving provides learners with the opportunity to practice item discrimination as well as strategy selection.

Managing Cognitive Demands while Integrating across Information Sources

Exposure to and integration across varied sources of information is key to many forms of learning. Often, we recall things more reliably and for longer periods of time when they are presented in complementary modalities – such as when people combine verbal associations with mental imagery.

Although people can remember an enormous amount of information over a lifetime, cognition is mediated by a much smaller capacity "working memory" system that attends to and encodes information. These limitations are further restricted when there are substantial, real-time demands – sometimes referred to as *cognitive load* – such as making decisions based on rapidly changing events. Learning environments can reduce cognitive load, and thus enhance learning, by minimizing split attention across sources of information, or reducing the demands to connect and combine conceptual relations across different modalities. Cognitive load can also be reduced with well-structured learning materials, with experiences that are organized and coherent, and by segmenting complex information into manageable parts. Cognitive load can also be reduced by presenting material in the form of stories and case studies, because these genres provide organization by using familiar narrative forms.

Engaging the Learner in the Active Construction of Meaning and Knowledge

Learning is more effective when learners are actively engaged in the construction of meaning and knowledge. If cognitive load is reduced too much – if material is too organized and task demands are too easy – then people will process the information passively and shallowly, with little learning occurring (e.g., McNamara, Kintsch, Songer, & Kintsch, 1996).

Learning is more effective when learners are encouraged to ground new experiences and concepts in perceptual and motor experiences, language, and prior knowledge. Activities that tend to ground meaning, and thus result in more effective knowledge construction, include practice testing, asking and answering deep questions, participating in dialog and argumentation that requires one to articulate one's position and explain one's reasoning (see Andriessen & Baker, Chapter 22, this volume), and participating in project-based collaboration (see Krajcik & Shin, Chapter 14, this volume). It can also be productive to encounter desirable difficulties, and even to engage in failure, because this activates relevant prior knowledge, varies the learning experiences, elicits explanations, distributes practice, and targets knowledge gaps for repair (see Collins & Kapur, Chapter 6, this volume).

Active construction of meaning is particularly important in making sense of abstract formalisms such as formulas and diagrams. Formalisms support analogical mapping, generalization, and the flexible transfer of knowledge to new domains. Yet they are steeped in technical and arbitrary systems of notation, which separate them from the real-world contexts to which they apply. Grounding formalisms in concrete and familiar ideas and experiences through methods such as *progressive formalization* supports meaningful interpretation of these abstract representations and improves learners' abilities to access and apply them when it is relevant and efficient to do so (Nathan, 2012).

Metacognitive Awareness

Metacognition (Winne & Azevedo, Chapter 4, this volume), including the ability to monitor one's level of understanding and reflect on what and how one learns, is a cornerstone of human cognition. Its value is evident whenever learners pause to evaluate their progress and use the outcome of that evaluation to direct their own reasoning process or to restructure their learning environment. Yet most learners need help doing effective monitoring and self-regulation, and they require feedback to verify their self-evaluations. For example, students make many poor choices about study methods and can be wildly inaccurate at predicting their effectiveness (Dunlosky et al., 2013). With proper support, however, students can develop good monitoring and self-regulation skills and can improve their efficiency, retention, and self-monitoring.

Systemic View: Evidence-Based Principles of Learning and Design

Systemic research asserts that it is not possible to analytically separate participants' actions from one another or from the learning environment. From this perspective, context cannot be treated as a container in which isolated elemental "regularities" occur; it is an integral part of the complex causal field that gives rise to the phenomenon under study. Lave powerfully illustrated this point when she stated that everyday cognition is *"stretched over, not divided among* – mind, body, activity and culturally organized settings" (1988, p. 1; emphasis added).

Methods of Systemic Research

Systemic research aims to document the situated learning practices and resources people use in learning environments – including classrooms, but also workplace settings, museums, and their everyday lives as members of their communities – to establish social order and make sense of their world. Systemic research methods include microgenetic analysis (Chinn & Sherin, Chapter 9, this volume), conversation analysis, interaction analysis, and ethnomethodology. Interaction analysis methodology has been particularly influential within the LS community (Enyedy & Stevens, Chapter 10, this volume), and views learning as "a distributed, ongoing social process, in which evidence that learning is occurring or has occurred must be found in understanding the ways in which people collaboratively do learning and do recognize learning as having occurred" (Jordan & Henderson, 1995, p. 42).

Design-based research (DBR; Barab, Chapter 8, this volume) is another systemic methodology that documents learning interactions, mechanisms of change, and the influences that bring about these changes (Brown, 1992; Cobb, Confrey, Lehrer, & Schauble, 2003; Collins, Joseph, & Bielaczyc, 2004; Design-Based Research Collective, 2003; Hawkins, 1997). Consistent with the design sciences, DBR is not primarily concerned with describing existing behaviors, but with designing learning environments to foster maximally effective behaviors (Barab & Squire, 2004; Simon, 1996). A variant of DBR has formed around policy and implementation research (Penuel & Spillane, Chapter 32, this volume). Thus, DBR blurs traditional distinctions between research and development, contributing to both.

Summary Findings from Systemic Research

Systemic approaches analyze learning in holistic terms, as a complex system phenomenon. Learning environment designs that are influenced by systemic research focus on the level of the group, or the sociotechnical learning environment. For example, they might address the nature of interpersonal interactions in the service of meeting social, participatory, and identity-related goals. Many prominent LS-inspired curricular designs are grounded in systemic research, including problem-based learning (Lu, Bridges, & Hmelo-Silver, Chapter 15, this volume), project-based learning (Krajcik & Shin, Chapter 14, this volume), and inquiry-based learning. Findings from systemic research can be organized into three general areas: support for collaboration and argumentation; engaging learners in disciplinary practices; and providing appropriate levels of support for guided inquiry and project-based learning.

Collaborative Discourse and Argumentation

Conversation mediates between group participation and individual learning. Members of cooperative groups exhibit greater learning gains than those in competitive or individualistically structured learning environments (Cohen,

1994). Furthermore, the quality of the collaborative discourse influences subsequent transfer performance by individual students (Barron, 2003). *Computer-supported collaborative learning* (CSCL; Stahl, Koschmann, & Suthers, Chapter 24, this volume) fosters intersubjective meaning making through shared representations and task structure.

There are several potential explanations for how collaboration and argumentation improve individual participants' learning. For example, learning is enhanced when people generate and listen to explanations. Participants must generate precisely formulated statements and questions to argue effectively (Andriessen & Baker, Chapter 22, this volume). Interlocutors must make their knowledge explicit, which fosters new connections. Collaboration can reveal knowledge gaps and misconceptions that may be repaired. Argumentation invites speakers to reflect on their reasoning processes, which can promote conceptual change (diSessa, Chapter 5, this volume). Co-elaboration and co-construction of ideas and representations can influence subsequent, ongoing interaction (Cobb et al., 1997).

Unfortunately, learners do not spontaneously collaborate effectively (Azmitia, 1996). Students often need modeling, guidance, or direct instruction and scripts to develop and apply collaboration skills, such as turn taking, active listening, critical evaluation, and respecting others' opinions (Krajcik, Czerniak, & Berger, 2002).

Engaging in Accessible Forms of Authentic Disciplinary Practices

Research shows that active engagement in authentic disciplinary practices results in enhanced learning outcomes – such as those promoted by programs like *The Adventures of Jasper Woodbury* (Cognition and Technology Group at Vanderbilt, 1997), *Fostering Community of Learners* (Brown & Campione, 1994), and *Kids as Global Scientists* (Songer, 1996). Engaging learners in authentic practices is effective for several reasons (Edelson, 2006). Disciplinary practices provide a meaningful context that *anchors* students' emerging understanding to authentic contexts and legitimate practices. They provide coherence to new practices and information, and orient learners toward future application of their learning. Disciplinary practices can increase student motivation. Authentic disciplinary practices also assist students in understanding the *epistemology* of a discipline – the ways knowledge in a field is structured and produced.

Just as with collaboration and argumentation, learners do not naturally know how to engage in authentic practices. Care must be taken to structure the learning environment and activities in ways that are accessible and that follow a developmental progression. Skillful pedagogical practices are necessary to encourage and support students' development, and then, just as skillfully, foster their autonomy. Technological tools can be designed to present phenomena (e.g., weather system data) that are accessible, engaging, and yet not overwhelming to students (Songer & Kali, Chapter 28, this volume).

Exploiting the distributed nature of cognition in these sociotechnical learning environments helps individuals manage the potentially high cognitive load (Edelson, 2006). Outside experts can help students navigate some of the complexities. Pedagogical approaches, such as cognitive apprenticeship, organize the use of methods such as modeling, coaching, scaffolding, and fading to facilitate development of both conceptual and procedural skills through guided participation. Learning environments need to make explicit the "tacit knowledge" underlying the professional practices of experts – the deeply ingrained expertise that they have automatized and no longer have conscious access to.

Guided Inquiry and Project-Based Learning

Guided inquiry results in more effective learning than unguided discovery learning or than simply hearing the information to be learned (Furtak, Seidel, Iverson, & Briggs, 2012; Hmelo-Silver, Duncan, & Chinn, 2007). Guided inquiry is effective because it elicits many of the most effective learning mechanisms discussed earlier, all in one coherent system. Students repeatedly generate and articulate their knowledge, ask deep questions, self-explain, and justify their reasoning. Inquiry experiences frequently incorporate repeated testing.

Like guided inquiry, project-based learning (PBL; Krajcik & Shin, Chapter 14, this volume) allows students to learn by doing, explaining, and applying ideas to solve meaningful problems. Students in PBL classrooms show better test performance than students in lecture and demonstration classrooms, regardless of gender or ethnicity (Marx et al., 2004). As Graesser and colleagues (2008) noted, students are unlikely to spontaneously take up inquiry, disciplinary, and project-based practices, and they need substantial assistance or "scaffolding" to discover key principles, connect prior knowledge, and employ effective learning and monitoring strategies (Reiser & Tabak, Chapter 3, this volume).

Rethinking Scale-up: Integrating Systemic and Elemental Views

Scale-up is a central aim for LS research. The systemic perspective addresses the important interrelationships between a design innovation and its context and use. However, it is difficult to manage the complexity of systems (Wilensky & Jacobson, Chapter 16, this volume), and attempts to control them can lead to unintended consequences. Elemental approaches bring powerful methods for precision and control that enable the research design team to establish causal relations that inform scale-up efforts. But the reductionism of elemental approaches is insensitive to local constraints and seldom scales up (Dede, 2006). Bridging systemic and elemental perspectives would result in more efficient means of developing effective learning innovations, with designs that bridge research and practice.

As an alternative to traditional scale-up approaches, Nathan and Alibali (2010) proposed the *scale-down method* as one way of integrating systemic and elemental approaches. The scale-down method begins by studying a system from a systemic perspective – by examining the learning environment in the complex settings in which it naturally occurs (e.g., a classroom). Then, analysis of these systemic observations is used to develop hypotheses for how to improve system performance, first by identifying potential subsystems within *nearly decomposable systems* that impact system performance; second, by modifying the design and performance of these subsystems; third, by reintegrating modified subsystems into the system; and finally, by observing behavior of the system as a whole in its natural context.

Fully decomposable systems are relatively simple systems made up of modules that function independently. In contrast, *nearly* decomposable systems are marked by components of a system, where "the short-run behavior of each of the component subsystems is approximately independent of the short-run behavior of the other components," though "in the long run, the behavior of any one of the components depends in only an aggregate way on the behavior of the other components" (Simon, 1962, p. 474). Thus, interactions in nearly decomposable systems are relatively strong within subsystems, while interactions between the subsystem and the rest of the system are relatively weak, although they cannot be ignored. For example, saccades, which direct eye movement, are fully decomposable from many other aspects of visual tasks, while reading comprehension strategies are nearly decomposable, in that they can be measured and improved in relative isolation, but ultimately interact with the environment and task goals (Perfetti, 1989).

The aim of scale-down is to improve systemic performance by improving, when possible, the design of subsystems – whether curricular materials, interaction patterns, or teacher behaviors. Refinement of the design and performance of a subsystem can draw on the precision and control that characterize elemental methods, as well as systemic methods of investigation and design. In this way, refinement of a nearly decomposable system is performed in a recursive manner, alternately using elemental and systemic methods when necessary. The development of measurement instruments used in service of systemic research, for example, relies on near decomposability, in that one needs to develop a means of extracting one aspect of the system's behavior and subjecting it to an analytic framework that supports categorization or quantification.

Engineering efforts use near decomposability when designing, evaluating, and improving complex technological and social systems. One method used historically in engineering is *functional decomposition* (Bradshaw, 1992). Functional decomposition allows designers to optimize performance of a nearly decomposable subsystem, such as a wing design for an airplane, using elemental methods (measurements of lift) as well as systemic methods (observing behavior in the context of a wind tunnel) to improve the overall performance of the system. Functional decomposition is efficient because it is cheaper and easier to test and modify the design of subsystems of a complex system than to redesign the system as a whole.

Because the behaviors and aims of people differ radically from those of designed technological systems, education may not directly lend itself to functional decomposition methods, per se. But learning environment design may nonetheless draw some inspiration from techniques like functional decomposition. Laboratory experimentation offers one set of elemental methods used to support scale-down. Computer-based learning companions, pedagogical agents, and simulated students also offer ways to isolate and improve complex collaboration and pedagogical interactions (Biswas, Leelawong, Schwartz, & Vye, 2005; Dillenbourg & Self, 1992; Ur & VanLehn, 1995). *Standardized students* and *standardized parents* – drawing on *standardized patient* work in medical training and assessment – have live actors in authentic settings who provide personable interactions for teacher training and assessment (Dotger, 2010), which can enhance the overall learning environment design.

The problem with using elemental methods exclusively to analyze complex systems is that the factoring assumption neglects the inherent interactions of the specific participants and local context with the functioning of the component elements once they are reintroduced into the system. The scale-down method emphasizes the important role of the *reintegration process*. Redesigned subsystems must be thoughtfully reintegrated by practitioners familiar with the elemental qualities of interest as well as with the particulars of the larger system, and then studied in real-world learning environments using systemic methods.

New programs of research are emerging that are consistent with the scale-down method, especially in mathematics education. Davenport (2013) reported on the carefully coordinated use of experimental methods, learning analytics, and eye tracking for the redesign of a widely used middle school mathematics curriculum, *Connected Mathematics 2*. The organization and content of the words and images in the printed booklets, the practice schedule for gaining mastery of concepts and skills, the testing practices, the use of worked examples and self-explanation for homework activities, and teacher professional development are treated as nearly decomposable subsystems, which a team of specialists observed, modified, and then reintegrated for classroom implementation as a systemic whole. In a second example, Lehrer, Kim, Ayers, and Wilson (in press) used a series of design experiments to support middle school students' statistical reasoning. Although the emphasis was the formation of a system within which students showed development along a hypothesized learning progression, nearly decomposable components were identified to structure performance measures and staff development. Teachers with experience from prior design work led aspects of the system implementation and integration of components.

Scale-down is one way to productively address tensions between systemic and elemental approaches (Anderson, Reder, & Simon, 2000). Much of LS research and development foregrounds the systemic perspective, with primary attention to the complex interactions and authentic practices as they occur in ecologically valid settings. Elemental approaches then serve a subordinate though complementary role by aiding in the control, analysis, and redesign of subsystems. By strategically combining elemental and systemic approaches, scale-down enhances design, development, and implementation of promising educational innovations, while contributing to the efficient advancement of empirically based theories of learning.

Conclusions

The learning sciences is an interdisciplinary field that emerged from a historical intersection of multiple disciplines focused on learning and learning environment design. Consequently, learning sciences blends research and practice – and views the two approaches as synergistic. For example, observing what happens when a new learning environment is implemented often results in new foundational understandings about mechanisms of learning and new design principles.

The theoretical foundations of LS include a broad range of social scientific theories. Some of these theories – such as cognitivism and constructionism – focus on learning at the level of the individual. These theories are generally associated with elemental research methodologies. Other theories are used to better understand embedded and situated learning – how learning is influenced by, and in some cases inextricably interwoven with, social and cultural context. These theories are generally associated with systemic research methodologies.

The chapters of this handbook share the two core defining features of LS research: they bridge research and practice, and they combine elemental and systemic perspectives on learning across a range of scales. We believe such research has great potential to enhance our scientific understanding of learning, while at the same time resulting in innovative and effective learning environment designs that foster enhanced learning outcomes.

References

Anderson, J. R., Reder, L. M., & Simon, H. A. (1996). Situated learning and education. *Educational Researcher*, 25(4), 5–11.

Anderson, M. L. (2003). Embodied cognition: A field guide. *Artificial Intelligence*, 149, 91–130.

Azmitia, M. (1996). Peer interactive minds: Developmental, theoretical, and methodological issues. In P. B. Baltes & U. M. Staudinger (Eds.), *Interactive minds:*

Life-span perspectives on the social foundation of cognition (pp. 133–162). New York: Cambridge University Press.

Barab, S., & Squire, K. (2004). Design-based research: Putting a stake in the ground. *The Journal of the Learning Sciences*, 13(1), 1–14.

Barab, S., Thomas, M., Dodge, T., Carteaux, R., & Tuzun, H. (2005). Making learning fun: Quest Atlantis, a game without guns. *Educational Technology Research and Development*, 53(1), 86–107.

Barron, B. (2003). When smart groups fail. *The Journal of the Learning Sciences, 12*, 307–359.

Barsalou, L. W. (2008). Grounded cognition. *Annual Review of Psychology*, 59, 617–645.

Biswas, G., Leelawong, K., Schwartz, D., Vye, N., & The Teachable Agents Group at Vanderbilt. (2005). Learning by teaching: A new agent paradigm for educational software. *Applied Artificial Intelligence*, 19(3–4), 363–392.

Bradshaw, G. F. (1992). The airplane and the logic of invention. In R. N. Giere (Ed.), *Cognitive models of science* (pp. 239–250). Minneapolis: University of Minnesota Press.

Brown, A. L. (1992). Design experiments: Theoretical and methodological challenges in creating complex interventions in classroom settings. *The Journal of the Learning Sciences*, 2(2), 141–178.

Brown, A. L., & Campione, J. C. (1994). Guided discovery in a community of learners. In K. McGilly (Ed.), *Classroom lessons: Integrating cognitive theory and classroom practice* (pp. 229–270). Cambridge, MA: MIT Press/Bradford Books.

Chalmers, D. J. (1993/2011). A computational foundation for the study of cognition. *Journal of Cognitive Science*, 12(4), 323–357.

Clark, A., & Chalmers, D. (1998). The extended mind. *Analysis*, 58(1), 7–19.

Cobb, P., Gravemeijer, K., Yackel, E., McClain, K., & Whitenack, J. (1997). Mathematizing and symbolizing: The emergence of chains of signification in one first-grade classroom. In D. Kirshner & J. A. Whitson (Eds.), *Situated cognition: Social, semiotic, and psychological perspectives* (pp. 151–233). Mahwah, NJ: Lawrence Erlbaum Associates.

Cobb, P., Confrey, J., Lehrer, R., & Schauble, L. (2003). Design experiments in educational research. *Educational Researcher*, 32(1), 9–13.

Cognition and Technology Group at Vanderbilt. (1997). *The Jasper Project: Lessons in curriculum, instruction, assessment, and professional development.* Mahwah, NJ: Lawrence Erlbaum Associates.

Cohen, E. G. (1994). Restructuring the classroom: Conditions for productive small groups. *Review of Educational Research*, 64(1), 1–35.

Collins, A., Joseph, D., & Bielaczyc, K. (2004). Design research: Theoretical and methodological issues. *The Journal of the Learning Sciences*, 13(1), 15–42.

Cremin, L. A. (1961). *The transformation of the school: Progressivism in American education, 1876–1957* (vol. 519). New York: Knopf.

Davenport, J. (2013). Reciprocal relations between research and practice: How improving curricular materials led to new research questions. Paper presentation to the Annual Meeting of the American Educational Research Association (San Francisco).

Dede, C. (2006). Evolving innovations beyond ideal settings to challenging contexts of practice. In R. K. Sawyer (Ed.), *The Cambridge handbook of the learning sciences* (pp. 551–566). New York: Cambridge University Press.

Design-Based Research Collective. (2003). Design-based research: An emerging paradigm for educational inquiry. *Educational Researcher*, 32(1), 5–8.

Dillenbourg, P., & Self, J. (1992). People power: A human-computer collaborative learning system. In C. Frasson, G. Gauthier, & G. McCalla (Eds.), The 2nd International Conference of Intelligent Tutoring Systems, Lecture Notes in Computer Science, 608, Springer-Verlag, 651–660.

Dotger, B. H. (2010). "I had no idea": Developing dispositional awareness and sensitivity through a cross-professional pedagogy. *Teaching and Teacher Education*, 26(4), 805–812.

Dreyfus, H. L. (2002). Intelligence without representation – Merleau-Ponty's critique of mental representation: The relevance of phenomenology to scientific explanation. *Phenomenology and the Cognitive Sciences*, 1(4), 367–383.

Dunlosky, J., Rawson, K. A., Marsh, E. J., Nathan, M. J., & Willingham, D. T. (2013). Improving students' learning with effective learning techniques: Promising directions from cognitive and educational psychology. *Psychological Science in the Public Interest*, 14(1), 4–58.

Edelson, D. C., & Reiser, B. J. (2006). Making authentic practices accessible to learners: Design challenges and strategies. In R. K. Sawyer (Ed.), *The Cambridge handbook of the learning sciences* (pp. 335–354). New York: Cambridge University Press.

Flavell, J. H. (1963). *The developmental psychology of Jean Piaget* (vol. 1). Princeton, NJ: Van Nostrand.

Furtak, E. M., Seidel, T., Iverson, H., & Briggs, D. C. (2012). Experimental and quasi-experimental studies of inquiry-based science teaching: A meta-analysis. *Review of Educational Research*, 82(3), 300–329.

Garfinkel, H. (1967). *Studies in ethnomethodology*. Englewood Cliffs, NJ: Prentice Hall.

Gibson, J. J. (1977). The concept of affordances. In R. Shaw & J. Bransford (Eds.), *Perceiving, acting, and knowing: Toward an ecological psychology* (pp. 67–82). Hillsdale, NJ: Lawrence Erlbaum Associates.

Glenberg, A. M. (1997). What memory is for: Creating meaning in the service of action. *Behavioral and brain sciences*, 20(01), 41–50.

Graesser, A. C., Halpern, D. F., & Hakel, M. (2008). 25 principles of learning. Washington, DC: Task Force on Lifelong Learning at Work and at Home. Retrieved December 8, 2008, from http://www.psyc.memphis.edu/learning/whatweknow/index.shtml.

Greeno, J. G. (1997). On claims that answer the wrong questions. *Educational Researcher*, 26(1), 5–17.

Hawkins, J. (1997). *The National Design Experiments Consortium: Final Report.* New York: Center for Children and Technology, Educational Development Center.

Hmelo-Silver, C. E., Duncan, R. G., & Chinn, C. A. (2007). Scaffolding and achievement in problem-based and inquiry learning: A response to Kirschner, Sweller, and Clark (2006). *Educational Psychologist*, 42(2), 99–107.

Hutchins, E. (1995). *Cognition in the wild*. Cambridge, MA: MIT Press.

Jordan, B., & Henderson, A. (1995). Interaction analysis: Foundations and practice. *The Journal of the Learning Sciences*, 4(1), 39–103.

Koedinger, K. R., & Corbett, A. T. (2006). Cognitive tutors: Technology bringing learning science to the classroom. In R. K. Sawyer (Ed.), *The Cambridge handbook of the learning sciences*. New York: Cambridge University Press.

Kolodner, J. L. (1991). The Journal of the Learning Sciences: Effecting changes in education. *Journal of the Learning Sciences*, 1, 1–6.

Krajcik, J., Czerniak, C., & Berger, C. (2002). *Teaching science in elementary and middle school classrooms: A project-based approach* (2nd ed.). Boston, MA: McGraw-Hill.

Lamon, M., Secules, T., Petrosino, A. J., Hackett, R., Bransford, J. D., & Goldman S. R. (1996). Schools for thought: Overview of the project and lessons learned from one of the sites. In L. Schauble & R. Glaser (Eds.), *Innovation in learning: New environments for education* (pp. 243–288). Mahwah, NJ: Lawrence Erlbaum Associates.

Larkin, M., Eatough, V., & Osborn, M. (2011). Interpretative phenomenological analysis and embodied, active, situated cognition. *Theory & Psychology*, 21(3), 318–337.

Lave, J. (1988). *Cognition in practice: Mind, mathematics and culture in everyday life*. New York: Cambridge University Press.

Lave, J., & Wenger, E. (1991). *Situated learning: Legitimate peripheral participation*. New York: Cambridge University Press.

Lehrer, R., Kim, M. J., Ayers, E., & Wilson, M. (in press). Toward establishing a learning progression to support the development of statistical reasoning. To appear in A. P. Mahoney, J. Confrey, & K. H. Nyugen (Eds.), *Learning over time: Learning trajectories in mathematics education*. Charlotte, NC: Information Age Publishers.

Leont'ev, A. N. (1981). The problem of activity in psychology. In J. V. Wertsch (Ed.), *The concept of activity in Soviet psychology* (pp. 37–71). Armonk, NY: Sharpe.

Linn, M. C., & Slotta, J. D. (2000). WISE science. *Educational Leadership*, 58(2), 29–32.

Marx, R. W., Blumenfeld, P. C., Krajcik, J. S., Fishman, B., Soloway, E., Geier, R., & Tal, R. T. (2004). Inquiry-based science in the middle grades: Assessment of learning in urban systemic reform. *Journal of Research in Science Teaching*, 41(10), 1063–1080.

McDonald, S. K., Keesler, V. A., Kauffman, N. J., & Schneider, B. (2006). Scaling-up exemplary interventions. *Educational Researcher*, 35(3), 15–24.

McNamara, D. S., Kintsch, E., Songer, N. B., & Kintsch, W. (1996). Are good texts always better? Interactions of text coherence, background knowledge, and levels of understanding in learning from text. *Cognition and instruction*, 14(1), 1–43.

Nathan, M. J. (1998). The impact of theories of learning on learning environment design. *Interactive Learning Environments*, 5, 135–160.

Nathan, M. J. (2012). Rethinking formalisms in formal education. *Educational Psychologist*, 47(2), 125–148.

Nathan, M. J. (2014). Grounded mathematical reasoning. In L. Shapiro (Ed.), *The Routledge handbook of embodied cognition* (pp. 171–183). Routledge: New York.

Nathan, M. J., & Alibali, M. W. (2010). Learning sciences. *Wiley Interdisciplinary Reviews: Cognitive Science*, 1(3), 329–345.

Newell, A. (1990). *Unified theories of cognition*. Cambridge, MA: Harvard University Press.

Newell, A., & Simon, H. A. (1976). Computer science as empirical inquiry: Symbols and search. *Communications of the ACM*, 19(3), 113–126.

Palinscar, A. S., & Brown, A. L. (1984). Reciprocal teaching of comprehension-fostering and comprehension-monitoring activities. *Cognition and instruction*, 1(2), 117–175.

Papert, S. (1980). *Mindstorms: Children, computers, and powerful ideas*. New York: Basic Books.

Pashler, H., Bain, P. M., Bottge, B. A., Graesser, A., Koedinger, K., McDaniel, M., & Metcalfe, J. (2007). Organizing Instruction and Study to Improve Student Learning. IES Practice Guide. NCER 2007–2004. *National Center for Education Research*.

Penuel, W. R., Fishman, B. J., Cheng, B. H., & Sabelli, N. (2011). Organizing research and development at the intersection of learning, implementation, and design. *Educational Researcher*, 40(7), 331–337.

Perfetti, C. A. (1989). There are generalized abilities and one of them is reading. In L. Resnick (Ed.), *Knowing, learning, and instruction: Essays in honor of Robert Glaser* (pp. 307–335). Hillsdale, NJ: Lawrence Erlbaum Associates.

RAND (2004). *Expanding the Reach of Education Reforms: What Have We Learned about Scaling Up Educational Interventions?*. RAND Health.

Robbins, P., & Aydede, M. (Eds.) (2010). *The Cambridge handbook of situated cognition*. New York: Cambridge University Press.

Rumelhart, D. E., & McClelland, J. L. (1986). *Parallel distributed processing: Explorations in the microstructure of cognition.* (vol. 1). Foundations. Cambridge, MA: MIT Press.

Sawyer, R. K. (2005). *Social emergence: Societies as complex systems*. New York: Cambridge University Press.

Schwartz, D. L., Martin, T., & Nasir, N. (2005). Designs for knowledge evolution: Towards a prescriptive theory for integrating first- and second-hand knowledge. In P. Gardenfors & P. Johansson (Eds.), *Cognition, education, and communication technology* (pp. 21–54). Mahwah, NJ: Lawrence Erlbaum Associates.

Simon, H. A. (1962). The architecture of complexity. *Proceedings of the American Philosophical Society*, 106(6), 467–482.

Simon, H. A. (1996). *The sciences of the artificial*. Cambridge, MA: MIT Press.

Songer, N. B. (1996). Exploring learning opportunities in coordinated network-enhanced classrooms: A case of kids as global scientists. *The Journal of the Learning Sciences*, 5(4), 297–327.

Spillane, J. P., Reiser, B. J., & Reimer, T. (2002). Policy implementation and cognition: Reframing and refocusing implementation research. *Review of Educational Research*, 72(3), 387–431.

Stevens, R., & Hall, R. (1998). Disciplined perception: Learning to see in technoscience. In M. Lampert & M. L. Blunk (Eds.), *Talking Mathematics in School: Studies of Teaching and Learning*, (pp. 107–149). Cambridge: Cambridge University Press.

Stokes, D. E. (1997). *Pasteur's quadrant: Basic science and technological innovation.* Washington, DC: Brookings Institution Press.

Tatar, D., Roschelle, J., Knudsen, J., Shechtman, N., Kaput, J., & Hopkins, B. (2008). Scaling up innovative technology-based mathematics. *The Journal of the Learning Sciences*, 17(2), 248–286.

Ur, S., & VanLehn, K. (1995). Steps: A simulated, tutorable physics student!. *Journal of Artificial Intelligence in Education*, 6, 405–437.

Von Glasersfeld, E. (1989). Cognition, construction of knowledge, and teaching. *Synthese*, 80(1), 121–140.

Vygotsky, L. S. (1978). *Mind in society: The development of higher mental process.*

Wertsch, J. V. (1985). *Vygotsky and the social formation of mind.* Cambridge, MA: Harvard University Press.

3 Scaffolding

Brian J. Reiser and Iris Tabak

A classroom of 7th grade students is developing a scientific model of the factors influencing water quality in their local stream. They run a dynamic simulation of the model to test it, yet they are able to do so without having to produce sophisticated mathematical representations for these relationships. In another classroom, 11th graders are reading primary historical texts and engaging in argumentation to develop a coherent explanation of events, despite lacking the extensive disciplinary knowledge and experience historians use to analyze primary documents. How can these learners participate in activities that share elements of expert practices, but that call on knowledge and skills that they do not yet possess? These feats are possible in the same way that young children can ride two-wheelers using training wheels before they have mastered balancing, or that construction workers can use scaffolding to work on the penthouse before the lower floors have been fully constructed.

The Historical Roots of Scaffolding

Drawing on the metaphor of scaffolding in building construction, Wood, Bruner, and Ross (1976) proposed the concept of *scaffolding* to describe how children, with the help of someone more knowledgeable to share and support their problem solving, can perform more complex tasks than they would otherwise be capable of performing on their own[1] (Palincsar, 1998; Rogoff, 1990). Scaffolding may be provided by a variety of different

[1] The term *scaffolding* also appears in Ausubel's work to refer to the ways advance organizers facilitate learning from texts (Ausubel, 1963). The advance organizers, short expository texts or concept maps, introduce novel terms and concepts, as well as their meaning and the relationships between the terms and concepts. These advance organizers enable learners to form an initial mental structure Ausubel called an "ideational scaffold" that can help process subsequent text by providing an organization for integrating new knowledge. In this way, the advance organizer forms conceptual scaffolding for subsequent knowledge, similar to the way a building is built with the aid of scaffolding. This use of the term *scaffolding* is not typically referenced in the research on scaffolding within the learning sciences, which is mostly associated with sociocultural approaches to learning. However, it points to the alignment between how scaffolding is conceived of within the learning sciences and the broad perspective of constructivism, in which learners are seen as active agents who construct their own knowledge based on their prior knowledge and their interaction with new experiences.

mechanisms. In the example cited earlier, in the history classroom, scaffolding is provided by interaction with guidance from the teacher and curriculum materials (Reisman, 2012), while in the water quality model, part of the assistance is provided by a supportive software environment (Fretz et al., 2002).

A central idea in scaffolding is that the work is shared between the learner and some more knowledgeable other or agent. Scaffolding enables not only the performance of a task more complex than the learner could handle alone, but also enables learning from that experience. In the example of modeling water quality, experts would use fairly complex mathematical models to explore conjectured relationships between factors, such as amount of leaves and levels of oxygen, but they would also test whether their conjectures are consistent with empirical evidence, and examine, through argumentation over competing models, which model best explains the world around them. Middle school learners may be able to reason about the interaction of factors relevant to water quality long before they are able to represent and test those relationships in mathematical terms. If the students are unaided, these mathematical challenges might stand in the way of exploring the causal relationships between these factors. The scaffolded environment enables students to explore models by specifying relationships between factors verbally (e.g., when the amount of leaves increases, the amount of dissolved oxygen increases), while offloading the underlying mathematics (Fretz et al., 2002). This provides a context in which students can explore and contrast competing models to debate and reach consensus on the underlying causal mechanisms (Schwarz et al., 2009), without overloading the task with mathematical calculations.

In the example of reading historical texts, historians have a set of conceptual questions that they ask of texts and that shape their reading and interpretation, such as questions about the author and about how writing the document in this way may have served the author's interests, or about how events occurring at the time might explain what information is included or omitted (Reisman, 2012). While the learners might be able to make progress in reasoning about these issues, they likely would not have brought these questions to bear in their investigation by themselves. The teacher's verbal and written prompts introduce these considerations and make learners continually aware of these questions as they read primary period sources. The teacher can present these conceptual guiding questions, taking over the monitoring and regulation aspects of the task, so that learners can focus on building their proficiency in answering the questions. In this way, the prompts the teacher or curriculum materials provide scaffold the learners' work, enabling them to pursue investigations and analyses they would not have been able to plan, monitor, and execute themselves.

The concept of scaffolding and its use in the learning sciences draws on multiple research traditions. The idea arises from Vygotskian-based study of adult-child and peer interactions, primarily in the context of language development (e.g., Cazden, 1979, 1997; Ratner & Bruner, 1978; Rogoff, 1990; Wertsch, 1979; Wood et al., 1976). It draws on Vygotsky's notion of development and learning as occurring in a *zone of proximal development (ZPD)* (Rogoff, 1990). The ZPD refers to a range of tasks that are outside of the learners' current independent ability but are achievable with appropriate help, thereby extending their range of independent activity (Rogoff, 1990; Stone, 1998; Wood et al., 1976). By actively participating in working through these more complex tasks, children learn from the experience and go beyond what they can accomplish alone. Another influence is the study of classical apprenticeship in which learning occurs as people with varying degrees of expertise engage in context in authentic tasks (Collins & Kapur, Chapter 6, this volume; Greenfield, 1984; Hutchins, 1996; Jordan, 1989; Lave, 1997).

How Does Scaffolding Help Learning?

The collaboration with a "more knowledgeable other" (typically called a *tutor* in early work on scaffolding) can help learners bridge from their current knowledge to more sophisticated practices. Several aspects of knowledge and skills may need to be bridged. Learners may have an incomplete definition of the problem, not able to fully determine the goal of the task, the expected products, or the resources involved. Their relevant skill set may be incomplete. Regulating the problem solving process, determining which actions to take, and when and how, often pose serious challenges for learners. Thus, what learners need to acquire through the scaffolded activity is an inventory of relevant actions and proficiency in the orchestration of these actions (Wertsch, 1979).

The more knowledgeable other providing scaffolding proceeds as though the learner already does possess this knowledge and skill. Thus, learners may encounter directives that they do not understand and are pushed to construct an understanding of the directive and to associate it with their emerging definition of the task (Wertsch, 1979; Wertsch & Stone, 1985). This understanding is built by having the tutor perform the required action for the learner (modeling) or animate the actions of the learners (Goffman, 1974) by helping to implement their actions, such as in manipulating their hands in a loom (Greenfield, 1984) or rephrasing their words to better align with the task (Cazden, 1979; O'Connor & Michaels, 1993). This process is also true for nonverbal actions and directives (Reid & Stone, 1991). Over repeated interactions, the learner imitates the modeled actions and associates them with the directive and the definition of the task. This is one of the mechanisms that explains how learning occurs through scaffolding, and is referred to as *prolepsis* (Wertsch & Stone, 1985).

Similarly, the joint activity of scaffolding tends to begin with other-regulated behavior, in which the tutor directs, hints, or offers prompts that help regulate the sequence of relevant actions. Over time, learners appropriate this guidance and begin to regulate their own actions as the tutor gradually reduces guidance, resulting in *fading* of scaffolding. Eventually, the learners regulate their activity without overt speech, as the "other speech" becomes internalized and eternal guidance is no longer needed (Wertsch, 1979).

Scaffolding is fundamentally different from instructional approaches based on the decomposition of complex skills and tasks into minimal constituent components. The instructional design approach of breaking skills and tasks into component parts has its roots in behaviorist approaches to learning and education (Greeno, Collins, & Resnick, 1996). Based on behaviorist theory, learners acquire more complex behaviors from simpler learned behaviors, for example, adding a new step to a known sequence. Analyzing tasks into constituent components, teaching these first, and then building up to more complex behaviors has become a common approach in traditional instructional design (Gagné, 1965). In these approaches, learning requires small-scale tasks created specifically for developing a particular subskill. Such tasks may not reflect actual tasks outside the learning environment.

In contrast, scaffolding is an element of contextualized approaches that situate the learning of new skills in more complex tasks such as apprenticeship and project-based learning (Collins & Kapur, Chapter 6, this volume; Krajcik & Shin, Chapter 14, this volume). In these contextualized approaches, learners work on real-world or expert complex tasks, which motivate developing subskills and requisite knowledge, in context, as needed, applying the knowledge and skills as they are constructed (Edelson, 2001). Embedding guidance in context as learners perform a full contextualized expert-like task is the essence of the pedagogical logic of scaffolding.

Because scaffolding is a contextualized holistic approach, it facilitates transfer, and it cultivates an understanding of the objectives of a discipline and of the relationship between objectives and procedures. Understanding the ultimate aim and application context of component skills is often absent from instruction that is organized around the decomposition of requisite skills. In traditional instruction, learners see the particular skill, such as solving linear equations or learning the formula for photosynthesis, as an aim in and of itself, and they do not learn the potential relevance and applicability of this knowledge. This results in inert knowledge (Bransford, Brown, & Cocking, 2000), in which learners cannot apply what they learn. In contrast, when learners work on component skills in the context of the full target application task, they learn how the component skills should work in concert (Collins et al., 1989; Edelson, 2001) and when and how they should be applied, which facilitates their independent and appropriate use in the future.

How Can Scaffolding Transform Learning Tasks?

The primary focus of research in the learning sciences has been designing effective learning environments for disciplinary learning, such as learning to read, learning to engage in scientific inquiry, or learning mathematics. A major emphasis has been involving learners in building, using, and refining knowledge, rather than taking in the ideas as fixed or "final-form" knowledge (see Scardamalia & Bereiter, Chapter 20, this volume). As a result, considerable research has explored how scaffolding can be purposefully designed, and the concept broadened to an analysis of the rich interactions between a learner and other learners, teachers, and the tools they are using to do the work (Lajoie, 2005; Puntambekar & Hubscher, 2005). We consider what functions scaffolding serves in these settings and how design elements accomplish these functions.

To analyze the functions scaffolding can play in learning (Wood et al., 1976), we need to consider how scaffolding transforms the task to make it both more achievable and more productive for learning (Sherin, Reiser, & Edelson, 2004). Challenges in disciplinary learning may arise when learners are unaware of relevant disciplinary strategies, are not able to perform or orchestrate these strategies well, or do not have a strong conception of the aims of the discipline and how they drive disciplinary practices. For example, mathematics learners may not be familiar with particular procedures, they may have difficulty applying procedures, and they may not understand that the goal is to develop elegant solutions, not only simply correct solutions (Lampert, 1990; McClain & Cobb, 2001).

Quintana and colleagues (2004) identified *sensemaking, articulation and reflection*, and *managing investigation and problem-solving processes* as three aspects of work for which scaffolding can transform tasks to make them more productive for learning (see also Guzdial, 1994). Scaffolding sensemaking entails helping learners make sense of problems or data. Scaffolding the process refers to helping learners with strategic choices and executing processes to achieve solutions. This type of scaffolding goes beyond helping learners make sense of individual elements of a solution and addresses the strategic knowledge that can guide their work (Many, 2002; van de Pol, Volman, & Beishuizen, 2010). Scaffolding articulation and reflection refers to helping learners articulate their thinking as they progress on problems, and reflect on their solutions in ways productive for learning (see Winne & Azevedo, Chapter 4, this volume). The means by which scaffolding can be effective can be considered in light of these three aspects of disciplinary work.

Scaffolding simplifies elements of tasks so they are within reach of learners. This is one of the essential functions Wood and colleagues (1976) described. Scaffolding can transform tasks so that learners can succeed by engaging in simpler tasks that are still valuable for learning. For example, a tutor working with a student on an algebra problem might handle some of the more difficult calculations in the problem, enabling learners to focus on algebraic manipulations without the cognitive load of simultaneously handling strategy and arithmetic calculations. Scaffolding might also catch errors that would be disruptive, while allowing errors more productive for learning to occur (Merrill, Reiser, Merrill, & Landes, 1995).

Scaffolding can manage the process so that learners can engage in elements of the disciplinary work in real problem contexts. Strategic help has emerged as central to scaffolding approaches. Learners often make poor strategic choices that can easily disrupt problem solving. Strategic guidance at opportune points can help problem solving stay on track, enabling learners to continue performing much of the work, and thereby learn from the problem-solving experiences (Hmelo-Silver, Duncan, & Chinn, 2007; Merrill et al., 1995).

Scaffolding can offset frustration and risk and maintain interest. From the earliest use of the scaffolding metaphor, the motivational side of scaffolding has been considered alongside its cognitive benefits (Wood et al., 1976). The aim of scaffolding is to balance learners' participation in active problem solving, building both expertise and confidence, while minimizing the motivational and cognitive cost of floundering and failure (Hmelo-Silver et al., 2007; Lepper, Woolverton, Mumme, & Gurtner, 1993).

Scaffolding can focus learners' attention on aspects of the problem they may take for granted. While scaffolding is often summarized as "helping" learners or making their work "easier," in fact an important role for scaffolding is to help learners in the long term by encouraging them to engage in difficult aspects of the work they may be inclined to overlook. Wood and colleagues (1976) pointed out how scaffolding can help by "marking critical features" that point the learner to "discrepancies" between the learner's work so far and desired outcomes. Scaffolding can help by problematizing aspects of the work learners might otherwise take for granted and avoid (Reiser, 2004) and by encouraging learners to engage in complexities that are productive for learning (Kapur & Bielaczyc, 2012).

Scaffolding can prompt learners to explain and reflect. A focus of scaffolding design research has been prompting learners to explain and reflect. While learning by doing has been a strong emphasis in recent approaches to disciplinary learning, reaching successful solutions to a problem or challenge does not ensure learning from that experience (Barron et al., 1998). Scaffolding needs to go beyond helping learners reach successful answers and help them construct explanations for why a particular mathematical approach was successful or identify the scientific mechanism responsible for some natural phenomenon. Scaffolding can prompt learners to articulate and explain their ideas as they work on problems in a way that is more productive for learning (Linn, Bell, & Davis, 2004; Quintana et al., 2004; Scardamalia & Bereiter, Chapter 20, this volume; Winne & Azevedo, Chapter 4, this volume).

Scaffolding can enable learning by doing in context. These advantages combine to make it more feasible and productive for learners to learn in the context of more expert-like tasks and connect what they are learning to authentic contexts (Collins et al., 1989; Edelson, 2001). In addition to learning component skills, they learn how to coordinate and orchestrate these actions to accomplish complex disciplinary goals. Moreover, this contextualized approach can help develop the values and epistemological understandings of the discipline (Smith, Maclin, Houghton, & Hennessey, 2000). In addition, this larger purpose can be more motivating than engaging in activities without understanding their aim or utility (Blumenfeld et al., 1991).

How Can Scaffolding Be Embedded in Learning Environments?

In designed learning environments, these scaffolding strategies and functions can be accomplished by embedding scaffolding in various designed elements. Scaffolding may be embedded in teacher strategies supported in an intervention, designed activity structures, verbal prompts built in the written or software materials students use to do their work, or the structure of the tools students use to represent their ideas. We consider examples of these different scaffolding designs.

Embedding Scaffolding in Teaching and Learning Interactions

Teachers (whether interacting one on one, in small groups, or with the whole class) can model actions, make suggestions, and ask questions that bridge gaps between learners' current abilities and the demands of expert-like disciplinary performance (van de Pol et al., 2010). Teachers can help learners attend to aspects of the situation that are salient to the discipline, but that learners consider ancillary (i.e., problematize) (Engle & Conant, 2002). They can model discipline-specific strategies and elicit articulation (C. D. Lee, 2001). In classroom settings, there are multiple zones of proximal development (Palincsar, 1998) where different learners have different levels of knowledge and skill. In such a setting, the learners can provide scaffolding along with the teacher. For example, as two learners work together on a problem, one student might model and justify a strategy to the other. The teacher can then present this strategy to the class, sanctioning the learner's spontaneous strategy and making it public and available to the whole class (C. D. Lee, 2001).

Teacher scaffolding through classroom talk can also foster a disciplinary cultural climate. Assuming the role of a critical audience for student work, teachers can cultivate the norms and values that provide purpose to disciplinary practices, encouraging learners to go beyond a possible correct solution to develop more culturally valued solutions, such as a more elegant mathematical solution or a more detailed chain of scientific causality (Herrenkohl, Tasker, & White, 2011; McClain & Cobb, 2001; Tabak, 1999). This is a critical element of scaffolding – unlike traditional apprenticeship, the learning setting is disconnected from real-world communities of practice. The cultural climate that typically engulfs apprenticeship-based learning that drives participants' actions and reflects the community's values and norms must be created in the classroom (Berland & Reiser, 2011; Herrenkohl, Palincsar, DeWater, & Kawasaki, 1999; Michaels, O'Connor, & Resnick, 2008).

Embedding Scaffolding in the Structure of Activities and Artifacts

The disconnect between a learning community cultivated in the classroom and the target community of practice, with its consequential absence of an encompassing target culture, imposes challenges that are not present in classical scaffolding. The many-to-one student-teacher ratio can make this even more difficult. Designed activity structures (configurations of roles and actions) that reflect disciplinary practices address these challenges. For example, cognitive strategies derived from disciplinary practice can be used to structure activity so that different phases of the activity are identified to make strategies explicit. The strategy or practice represented in each labeled phase of the activity can be modeled by the teacher followed by gradual transfer of responsibility to students. One of the pioneering designs using this approach is *reciprocal teaching* (Palincsar & Brown, 1984), in which the labeled phases of the activity are the strategies that proficient readers use to comprehend texts: questioning, clarifying, summarizing, and predicting. Similarly designed activity structures are used to mark strategies and process models in other disciplines, such as engineering design (Hmelo, Holton, & Kolodner, 2000), scientific inquiry (Metz, 2011), argumentation in social studies (Nussbaum & Edwards, 2011), and scientific argumentation (Berland, 2011; McNeill & Krajcik, 2009).

These strategies may also be supported by assigning learners explicitly labeled intellectual roles (Herrenkohl et al., 1999). Explicit roles to organize and support disciplinary activity can be introduced through classroom talk and embedded in artifacts. An example of artifact-embedded activity structures are *collaboration scripts* (Kollar, Fischer, & Hesse, 2006), written materials that structure collaboration by prompting productive ways to participate in disciplinary reasoning.

Embedding Scaffolding in Computational Tools

Guzdial (1994) coined the term *software-realized scaffolding* to describe scaffolding embedded within software tools. Software-realized scaffolding can offload work not productive for learning, provide strategic guidance, make the structure of the domain more transparent, and support articulation and reflection (de Jong, 2006; Quintana et al., 2004). For example, computational tools can offload unhelpful complexity, enabling learners to create and test scientific models without complex mathematics (Fretz et al., 2002) and to work with scientific visualizations of complex datasets without being overwhelmed by the complexity (Edelson & Reiser, 2006). Software tools can help students articulate their contributions to the knowledge-building discourse such as new questions, ideas, or disagreements (Scardamalia & Bereiter, Chapter 20, this volume). Such tools can support discipline-specific practices such as structure-function reasoning (Vattam et al., 2011) or theory-driven queries of data (Tabak & Reiser, 2008), and can support both general and discipline-specific aspects of argumentation, helping learners articulate and reflect on an argument's structure (Andriessen & Baker, Chapter 22, this volume; de Vries, Lund, & Baker, 2002; Suthers, Vatrapu, Medina, Joseph, & Dwyer, 2008). Software tools can also make problem-solving steps selectively available to guide students in complex investigations (Guzdial, 1994; Vattam et al., 2011).

Another prevalent use of computational tools for scaffolding is the use of prompts. Scaffolding prompts are sentence stems or questions – embedded in simulations, data analysis, or explanation construction tools – that guide learners by asking specific questions about process or suggesting particular actions. Prompts can serve the function of a more knowledgeable other providing disciplinary or process knowledge that the learner may not possess, and presenting it at relevant junctures (Davis, 2003; Demetriadis, Papadopoulos, Stamelos, & Fischer, 2008; C.-Y. Lee & Chen, 2009; McNeill & Krajcik, 2009). Just like scaffolding in caregiver-child interactions, students can take up these questions as inner speech that guides their subsequent independent activity. Artificial intelligence techniques can also be used to provide advice on next steps or feedback on errors (Koedinger & Corbett, 2006; Wu & Looi, 2012).

The mechanism of prolepsis that underlies the effectiveness of scaffolding in human interaction can also be supported in software interfaces. Labels and prompts can reflect the underlying expert model of the domain. Learners engage in tasks with these representations, trying to create meaning and connections between their actions and the representations. Over time, through successful, supported performance of the task, the learners come to understand the meaning of the interface labels and their role as conceptual entities in the discipline (Greeno, 1983).

Distributed Scaffolding

Distributed scaffolding (Puntambekar & Kolodner, 2005) is a concept that describes those cases in which scaffolding is embedded productively in multiple aspects of a learning environment – in teaching, peer interactions, activity structures and material, and computational artifacts (Dillenbourg & Jermann, 2010). With distributed scaffolding, a variety of material and social tools with different affordances and constraints can be employed strategically to provide the large assortment of support learners need to develop disciplinary ways of knowing, doing, and communicating. There are three types of distributed scaffolding: *differentiated*, *redundant*, and *synergistic* (Tabak, 2004).

Differentiated Scaffolding

The design strategy in differentiated scaffolding is to *use different means to support different aspects of performance*. Ambitious learning goals create many support needs that cannot be adequately addressed through a single method of support. Moreover, different tools may be more or less suited for different needs, and differentiated scaffolding aims to provide the best support for each need. For example, software scaffolding may be better for supporting fine-grained analysis and sensemaking, because it is continually present at every relevant step of student work, while teachers may be better for supporting metacognitive and regulation strategies, because this requires complex evaluation of the learners' progress and an articulation of rationale (e.g., Raes, Schellens, De Wever, & Vanderhoven, 2012).

Redundant Scaffolding

Scaffolding is designed to support learning while learners engage in the performance of real-time consequential tasks. Consequently, there is a risk that some learners may take a path through the task that causes them to miss a scaffolding opportunity (Greenfield, 1984). This is especially true for classrooms, where there are multiple learners with different support needs. Redundant scaffolding, in which *the same aspect of performance is supported through different means*, aims to minimize this risk. Redundant scaffolding provides different supports through different modalities, thus enabling learners who did not benefit from one scaffolding to benefit later, or learners who require greater assistance to receive more help. For example, students learning science through design projects might be prompted to describe the considerations they raised in deciding between alternative design options. Prompts might appear as sentence starters in a design diary. Some learners may not understand the intent of the prompt, or might be immersed in the execution of the design, and thereby fail to consider the reasoning behind their design choices. Yet considering the reasoning behind design alternatives is key to gaining competence. Thus, redundant scaffolding in the form of subsequent teacher verbal prompts in whole-class discussion can help more learners benefit from this support (Puntambekar & Kolodner, 2005).

Synergistic Scaffolding

Unlike classical apprenticeship, in which there is little division between educable and daily professional contexts, schooling takes place in isolated settings that are very different from professional disciplinary contexts. It can be challenging for learners to connect their own developing proficiencies with the goals and values of professionals in the discipline. Scaffolding in these settings may require an additional strategy of *providing different concurrent means of support for the same performance that are synergistic in scaffolding learners*. In this design strategy, some of the supports help the learners make use of the other concurrent supports.

For example, earlier we described how the mechanism of prolepsis can operate in software-realized scaffolding, in which menu selections represent conceptual entities of the discipline, helping learners move from interactions that are absent task meaning to interactions that associate task meaning with menu selections (Tabak & Reiser, 2008). In classical scaffolding, if a directive does not hold meaning for the child initially, the caregiver can explicitly manipulate the child's actions until the directive becomes associated with meaning. Additional support, that helps learners to ascribe meaning to the menu representations, may be needed to augment software-realized scaffolding. For instance, the teacher can manipulate the software as the learner's partner, while verbalizing her thoughts and rationale (Tabak & Baumgartner, 2004). Essentially, she is providing the modeling and articulation functions of scaffolding in concert with the "assumed knowledge" directives of the software (Tabak, 2004). Classroom studies suggest that teacher guidance and embedded scaffolding prompts can operate synergistically to support learning (McNeill & Krajcik, 2009).

Challenges in Using Scaffolding in the Learning Sciences

Designed learning environments, like classrooms, are very different cultural contexts than the real-world settings where the learned knowledge will eventually be applied (Squire, MaKinster, Barnett, Luehmann, & Barab, 2003). In classrooms, the equivocal nature of the scaffolded learning process can be an impediment to learning, potentially resulting in an emphasis on the product rather than the process. Consider history classrooms where learners are asked to compare different, potentially conflicting, historical sources (Reisman, 2012). Such activities to build knowledge may conflict with existing school culture, which values receiving answers from authority (Jimenez-Aleixandre, Rodriguez, & Duschl, 2000; Scardamalia & Bereiter, Chapter 20, this volume).

Design researchers attempt to imbue representations and activities with the norms and values of the target community of practice (Berland & Hammer, 2012; Enyedy & Goldberg, 2004; Lehrer & Schauble, 2006), so that learners are more likely to recognize the steps that they take as salient rather than ancillary to the task. In the history classroom example, this would mean that the creation of defensible accounts would drive activity in the classroom.

Consequently, learners would see analyzing differences between sources as a way of reading documents carefully to develop evidence-based accounts, and see this as what it means to do history.

Another central challenge for implementing scaffolding in classroom settings is the difficulty in providing just the right degree of support and fading that support at just the right rate. These elements are essential features of scaffolding that not only ensure that learners perform in their zones of proximal development, but that they have the opportunity to extend their abilities as supports fade. However, until recently, much of the research on scaffolding in the learning sciences has made more progress in understanding how to support learners in performing complex disciplinary practices–such as scientific modeling, evidence-based reasoning, or historical sourcing–and less so in how to customize supports for individual learners and to fade supports over time as learners gain competence. Incorporating more individualized support and fading has been difficult in software-realized scaffolds, because until recently, it has been difficult to design tools that could effectively align with the learners' current abilities and dynamically tailor the software representations to the learners' real-time changing competencies. Teachers' redundant or synergistic scaffolds that complement software supports appear to provide more of this dynamic support, but a clear model for teachers' fading has not been developed. Fading has also been explored through curricular structure–by moving from simpler and highly supported activities to more complex and less supported activities (Linn, Clark, & Slotta, 2003), so that the scaffolding faded over time, even if within each activity the supports were fairly constant.

There is always a tension between having learners engage with meaningful complex tasks that maximize potential for growth and transfer to out-of-school contexts, and providing sufficient support so that learners are neither overwhelmed nor under-challenged (Sawyer, 2011). This tension introduces the risk of hypermediation (Gutiérrez & Stone, 2002) or over-scripting (Dillenbourg, 2002), which could occur in any form of scaffolding – spontaneous caregiver interactions, classical apprenticeship, classrooms, or other learning settings. There is the risk of inaccurately assessing the learners' capacity for independent performance and providing more support than the learners currently need, stifling their ability to extend their range of competencies. This challenge might be heightened in classroom settings where it is difficult to enact customized support and fading. If supports are not well calibrated to an individual or group's ability or do not fade as learners gain competence, then even if they are aligned with learners' abilities at the beginning, they may eventually provide too much support as learners gain competence.

In scaffolding research, it is difficult to tease apart evidence of scaffolding's effectiveness from other aspects of design. Scaffolding is inherent to complex multifaceted learning environments, so it is difficult to "control" for scaffolding versus other supports. However, a corpus of research on learning environments that include scaffolding shows promising outcomes in helping young learners overcome challenges and engage successfully in tasks that seemed inconceivable for learners to accomplish in the past (de Jong, 2006; Hmelo-Silver et al., 2007; Kali, Linn, & Roseman, 2008; van de Pol et al., 2010).

Scaffolding in the Learning Sciences: Future Outlook

Most learning scientists think of scaffolding as a designed element in a learning environment. The means that have been developed to address the support needs and unique challenges of these settings, such as the use of computational agents and activity structures, have broadened previous views of scaffolding. Yet despite the contribution to advancing complex learning in classroom settings (Puntambekar & Hubscher, 2005), this dominant interpretation of "scaffolding" has raised some debate over the use of the term and whether it has been stripped of its meaning (Palincsar, 1998; Pea, 2004; Puntambekar & Hubscher, 2005; Stone, 1998).

Using too rigid a definition would not be productive, because it might exclude innovations such as recent explorations of scaffolding in gaming (Wong, Boticki, Sun, & Looi, 2011) or gesture and scaffolding (Alibali & Nathan, 2007). At the same time, if we begin to think of scaffolding as synonymous with "instructional support," we will lose sight of key design goals that may not be implied by other theories of instruction. Our conception of scaffolding is valuable because it focuses analyses on how tasks can be transformed to be more achievable and more productive for learning (Sherin et al., 2004). Scaffolding analyses must identify obstacles for learning and restructure tasks using talk, activity structures, or technology to be more productive for learning by doing (Quintana et al., 2004), without losing useful complexity and the cultural relevance of the tasks. In our conception of scaffolding, mediated action and cultural relevance are central. If the conception becomes so broad as to lose these elements, it runs the risk of stripping the resulting pedagogical design of its potential to produce robust rather than inert learning.

As we look forward to future research on scaffolding, it is important to address some of the challenges of enacting scaffolding in designed learning environments. Two central questions are how to cultivate a disciplinary culture in these settings so that learners can recognize and take up the aims and purposes of the activities, and how to better achieve the appropriate levels of support and fading. The field of the learning sciences is in a good position to make headway in addressing these issues, through recent advances in the study of learning as it crosses physical and social boundaries of communities and learning settings (Looi et al., 2011; Luckin, 2010; Moje, 2004), and in machine learning, learning analytics, and artificial intelligence (Mu,

Stegmann, Mayfield, Rosé, & Fischer, 2012; Shen, 2010; Slotta, Tissenbaum, & Lui, 2013; Suthers & Verbert, 2013; Wu & Looi, 2012).

References

Alibali, M. W., & Nathan, M. J. (2007). Teachers' gestures as a means of scaffolding students' understanding: Evidence from an early algebra lesson. In R. Goldman, R. D. Pea, & S. J. Derry (Eds.), *Video research in the learning sciences* (pp. 349–365). Mahwah, NJ: Erlbaum.

Ausubel, D. P. (1963). *The psychology of meaningful verbal learning: An introduction to school learning.* New York: Grune and Stratton.

Barron, B., Schwartz, D. L., Vye, N. J., Moore, A., Petrosino, A., Zech, L., & Bransford, J. D. (1998). Doing with understanding: Lessons from research on problem- and project-based learning. *Journal of the Learning Sciences,* 7(3–4), 271–311.

Berland, L. K. (2011). Explaining variation in how classroom communities adapt the practice of scientific argumentation. *Journal of the Learning Sciences,* 20(4), 625–664.

Berland, L. K., & Hammer, D. (2012). Students' framings and their participation in scientific argumentation. In M. S. Khine (Ed.), *Perspectives on scientific argumentation* (pp. 73–93). New York: Springer.

Berland, L. K., & Reiser, B. J. (2011). Classroom communities' adaptations of the practice of scientific argumentation. *Science Education,* 95(2), 191–216.

Blumenfeld, P., Soloway, E., Marx, R., Krajcik, J., Guzdial, M., & Palincsar, A. S. (1991). Motivating project-based learning: Sustaining the doing, supporting the learning. *Educational Psychologist,* 26, 369–398.

Bransford, J. D., Brown, A., & Cocking, R. R. (Eds.). (2000). *How people learn: Brain, mind, experience and schools.* Washington, DC: National Academy Press.

Cazden, C. B. (1979). *Peekaboo as an instructional model: Discourse development at home and at school.* Stanford, CA: Department of Linguistics, Stanford University.

Cazden, C. B. (1997). Performance before competence: Assistance to child discourse in the zone of proximal development. In M. Cole, Y. Engeström, & O. Vasquez (Eds.), *Mind, culture, and activity: Seminal papers from the laboratory of comparative human cognition* (pp. 303–310). New York: Cambridge University Press.

Collins, A., Brown, J. S., & Newman, S. E. (1989). Cognitive apprenticeship: Teaching the crafts of reading, writing, and mathematics. In L. B. Resnick (Ed.), *Knowing, learning, and instruction: Essays in honor of Robert Glaser* (pp. 453–494). Hillsdale, NJ: Erlbaum.

Davis, E. A. (2003). Prompting middle school science students for productive reflection: Generic and directed prompts. *Journal of the Learning Sciences,* 12(1), 91–142.

de Jong, T. (2006). Scaffolds for scientific discovery learning. In J. Elen & R. E. Clark (Eds.), *Handling complexity in learning environments: Theory and research* (pp. 107–128). Amsterdam: Elsevier.

de Vries, E., Lund, K., & Baker, M. (2002). Computer-mediated epistemic dialogue: Explanation and argumentation as vehicles for understanding scientific notions. *Journal of the Learning Sciences*, 11, 63–103.

Demetriadis, S. N., Papadopoulos, P. M., Stamelos, I. G., & Fischer, F. (2008). The effect of scaffolding students' context-generating cognitive activity in technology-enhanced case-based learning. *Computers & Education*, 51(2), 939–954.

Dillenbourg, P. (2002). Over-scripting CSCL: The risks of blending collaborative learning with instructional design. In P. A. Kirschner (Ed.), *Three worlds of CSCL: Can we support CSCL?* (pp. 61–91). Heerlen: Open Universiteit Nederland.

Dillenbourg, P., & Jermann, P. (2010). Technology for classroom orchestration. In M. S. Khine and I. M. Saleh (Eds.), *New science of learning* (pp. 525–552). New York: Springer.

Edelson, D. C. (2001). Learning-for-use: A framework for integrating content and process learning in the design of inquiry activities. *Journal of Research in Science Teaching*, 38(3), 355–385.

Edelson, D. C., & Reiser, B. J. (2006). Making authentic practices accessible to learners: Design challenges and strategies. In R. K. Sawyer (Ed.), *The Cambridge handbook of the learning sciences* (pp. 335–354). New York: Cambridge University Press.

Engle, R. A., & Conant, F. R. (2002). Guiding principles for fostering productive disciplinary engagement: Explaining an emergent argument in a community of learners classroom. *Cognition and Instruction*, 20(4), 399–483.

Enyedy, N., & Goldberg, J. (2004). Inquiry in interaction: How local adaptations of curricula shape classroom communities. *Journal of Research in Science Teaching*, 41(9), 905–935.

Fretz, E. B., Wu, H. -K., Zhang, B., Davis, E. A., Krajcik, J. S., & Soloway, E. (2002). An investigation of software scaffolds supporting modeling practices. *Research in Science Education*, 32(4), 567–589.

Gagné, R. M. (1965). *The conditions of learning*. New York: Holt, Rinehart, and Winston.

Goffman, E. (1974). *Frame analysis: An essay on the organization of experience*. New York: Harper & Row.

Greenfield, P. M. (1984). A theory of teacher in the learning activities of everyday life. In B. Rogoff & J. Lave (Eds.), *Everyday cognition: Its development in social context* (pp. 117–138). Cambridge, MA: Harvard University Press.

Greeno, J. G. (1983). Conceptual entities. In D. Gentner & A. L. Stevens (Eds.), *Mental models*. Hillsdale, NJ: Erlbaum.

Greeno, J. G., Collins, A. M., & Resnick, L. B. (1996). Cognition and learning. In D. C. Berliner & R. C. Calfee (Eds.), *Handbook of educational psychology* (pp. 15–46). New York; London: MacMillian Library Reference USA; Prentice Hall International.

Gutiérrez, K., & Stone, L. (2002). Hypermediating literacy activity: How learning contexts get reorganized. In O. Saracho & B. Spodek (Eds.), *Contemporary perspectives in literacy in early childhood education* (pp. 25–51). Greenwich, CT: Information Age Publishing.

Guzdial, M. (1994). Software-realized scaffolding to facilitate programming for science learning. *Interactive Learning Environments, 4*, 1–44.

Herrenkohl, L. R., Palincsar, A. S., DeWater, L. S., & Kawasaki, K. (1999). Developing scientific communities in classrooms: A sociocognitive approach. *Journal of the Learning Sciences*, 8(3–4), 451–493.

Herrenkohl, L. R., Tasker, T., & White, B. (2011). Pedagogical practices to support classroom cultures of scientific inquiry. *Cognition and Instruction*, 29(1), 1–44.

Hmelo, C. E., Holton, D. L., & Kolodner, J. L. (2000). Designing to learn about complex systems. *The Journal of the Learning Sciences*, 9(3), 247–298.

Hmelo-Silver, C. E., Duncan, R. G., & Chinn, C. A. (2007). Scaffolding and achievement in problem-based and inquiry learning: A response to Kirschner, Sweller, and Clark (2006). *Educational Psychologist*, 42(2), 99–107.

Hutchins, E. (1996). Learning to navigate. In S. Chaiklin & J. Lave (Eds.), *Understanding practice: Perspectives on activity and context* (pp. 35–63). New York: Cambridge University Press.

Jimenez-Aleixandre, M. P., Rodriguez, A. B., & Duschl, R. A. (2000). "Doing the lesson" or "doing science": Argument in high school genetics. *Science Education*, 84, 757–792.

Jordan, B. (1989). Cosmopolitical obstetrics: Some insights from the training of traditional midwives. *Social Science & Medicine*, 28(9), 925–937.

Kali, Y., Linn, M. C., & Roseman, J. E. (2008). *Designing coherent science education: Implications for curriculum, instruction, and policy*: Teachers College, Columbia University.

Kapur, M., & Bielaczyc, K. (2012). Designing for productive failure. *Journal of the Learning Sciences*, 21(1), 45–83.

Koedinger, K., & Corbett, A. T. (2006). Cognitive tutors: Technology bringing learning sciences to the classroom. In R. K. Sawyer (Ed.), *The Cambridge handbook of the learning sciences* (pp. 61–96). West Nyack, NY: Cambridge University Press.

Kollar, I., Fischer, F., & Hesse, F. W. (2006). Collaboration scripts – a conceptual analysis. *Educational Psychology Review*, 18(2), 159–185.

Lajoie, S. P. (2005). Extending the scaffolding metaphor. *Instructional Science*, 33(5–6), 541–557.

Lampert, M. (1990). When the problem is not the question and the solution is not the answer: Mathematical knowing and teaching. *American Educational Research Journal*, 27, 29–63.

Lave, J. (1997). The culture of acquisition and the practice of understanding. In D. Kirshner & J. A. Whitson (Eds.), *Situated cognition: Social, semiotic, and psychological perspectives* (pp. 63–82). Mahwah, NJ: Erlbaum.

Lee, C.-Y., & Chen, M.-P. (2009). A computer game as a context for non-routine mathematical problem solving: The effects of type of question prompt and level of prior knowledge. *Computers & Education*, 52(3), 530–542.

Lee, C. D. (2001). Is October Brown Chinese? A cultural modeling activity system for underachieving students. *American Educational Research Journal*, 38(1), 97–141.

Lehrer, R., & Schauble, L. (2006). Scientific thinking and science literacy: Supporting development in learning in contexts. In W. Damon, R. M. Lerner, K. A. Renninger, & I. E. Sigel (Eds.), *Handbook of child psychology, 6th ed.* (vol. 4). Hoboken, NJ: John Wiley and Sons.

Lepper, M. R., Woolverton, M., Mumme, D. L., & Gurtner, J. (1993). Motivational techniques of expert human tutors: Lessons for the design of computer-based tutors. In S. P. Lajoie & S. J. Derry (Eds.), *Computers as cognitive tools* (pp. 75–105). Hillsdale, NJ: Erlbaum.

Linn, M. C., Bell, P., & Davis, E. A. (2004). Specific design principles: Elaborating the scaffolded knowledge integration framework. In M. C. Linn, E. A. Davis, & P. Bell (Eds.), *Internet environments for science education.* Mahwah, NJ: Erlbaum.

Linn, M. C., Clark, D., & Slotta, J. D. (2003). WISE design for knowledge integration. *Science Education,* 87(4), 517–538.

Looi, C. K., Zhang, B., Chen, W., Seow, P., Chia, G., Norris, C., & Soloway, E. (2011). 1:1 mobile inquiry learning experience for primary science students: A study of learning effectiveness. *Journal of Computer Assisted Learning,* 27(3), 269–287.

Luckin, R. (2010). *Re-designing learning contexts: Technology rich, learner centred ecologies.* New York: Routledge.

Many, J. E. (2002). An exhibition and analysis of verbal tapestries: Understanding how scaffolding is woven into the fabric of instructional conversations. *Reading Research Quarterly,* 37(4), 376–407.

McClain, K., & Cobb, P. (2001). An analysis of development of sociomathematical norms in one first-grade classroom. *Journal for Research in Mathematics Education,* 32(3), 236–266.

McNeill, K. L., & Krajcik, J. (2009). Synergy between teacher practices and curricular scaffolds to support students in using domain-specific and domain-general knowledge in writing arguments to explain phenomena. *Journal of the Learning Sciences,* 18, 416–460.

Merrill, D. C., Reiser, B. J., Merrill, S. K., & Landes, S. (1995). Tutoring: Guided learning by doing. *Cognition and Instruction,* 13(3), 315–372.

Metz, K. E. (2011). Disentangling robust developmental constraints from the instructionally mutable: Young children's epistemic reasoning about a study of their own design. *Journal of the Learning Sciences,* 20, 50–110.

Michaels, S., O'Connor, C., & Resnick, L. B. (2008). Deliberative discourse idealized and realized: Accountable talk in the classroom and in civic life. *Studies in Philosophy and Education,* 27, 283–297.

Moje, E. B. (2004). Powerful spaces: Tracing the out-of-school literacy spaces of Latino/a youth. In K. Leander & M. Sheehy (Eds.), *Spatializing literacy research and practice* (pp. 15–38). New York: Peter Lang.

Mu, J., Stegmann, K., Mayfield, E., Rosé, C., & Fischer, F. (2012). The ACODEA framework: Developing segmentation and classification schemes for fully automatic analysis of online discussions. *International Journal of Computer-Supported Collaborative Learning,* 7(2), 285–305.

Nussbaum, E. M., & Edwards, O. V. (2011). Critical questions and argument stratagems: A framework for enhancing and analyzing students' reasoning practices. *Journal of the Learning Sciences,* 20, 443–488.

O'Connor, M. C., & Michaels, S. (1993). Aligning academic task and participation status through revoicing: Analysis of a classroom discourse strategy. *Anthropology and Education Quarterly,* 24(4), 318–335.

Palincsar, A. S. (1998). Keeping the metaphor of scaffolding fresh – a response to C. Addison Stone's "the metaphor of scaffolding: Its utility for the field of learning disabilities." *Journal of Learning Disabilities,* 31(4), 370–373.

Palincsar, A. S., & Brown, A. L. (1984). Reciprocal teaching of comprehension-fostering and comprehension-monitoring activities. *Cognition and Instruction*, 1, 117–175.

Pea, R. D. (2004). The social and technological dimensions of scaffolding and related theoretical concepts for learning, education, and human activity. *Journal of the Learning Sciences*, 13(3), 423–451.

Puntambekar, S., & Hubscher, R. (2005). Tools for scaffolding students in a complex learning environment: What have we gained and what have we missed? *Educational Psychologist*, 40(1), 1–12.

Puntambekar, S., & Kolodner, J. L. (2005). Distributed scaffolding: Helping students learn science from design. *Journal of Research in Science Teaching*, 42(2), 185–217.

Quintana, C., Reiser, B. J., Davis, E. A., Krajcik, J., Fretz, E., Duncan, R. G., ... Soloway, E. (2004). A scaffolding design framework for software to support science inquiry. *The Journal of the Learning Sciences*, 13(3), 337–386.

Raes, A., Schellens, T., De Wever, B., & Vanderhoven, E. (2012). Scaffolding information problem solving in Web-based collaborative inquiry learning. *Computers & Education*, 59(1), 82–94.

Ratner, N., & Bruner, J. (1978). Games, social exchange and the acquisition of language. *Journal of Child Language*, 5(3), 391–401.

Reid, D. K., & Stone, C. A. (1991). Why is cognitive instruction effective? Underlying learning mechanisms. *Remedial and Special Education*, 12(3), 8–19.

Reiser, B. J. (2004). Scaffolding complex learning: The mechanisms of structuring and problematizing student work. *The Journal of the Learning Sciences*, 13(3), 273–304.

Reisman, A. (2012). Reading like a historian: A document-based history curriculum intervention in urban high schools. *Cognition and Instruction*, 30(1), 86–112.

Rogoff, B. (1990). *Apprenticeship in thinking: Cognitive development in social context.* New York: Oxford University Press.

Sawyer, R. K. (2011). What makes good teachers great? The artful balance of structure and improvisation. In R. K. Sawyer (Ed.), *Structure and improvisation in creative teaching*, 1–24. New York: Cambridge University Press.

Schwarz, C. V., Reiser, B. J., Davis, E. A., Kenyon, L., Acher, A., Fortus, D., ... Krajcik, J. (2009). Developing a learning progression for scientific modeling: Making scientific modeling accessible and meaningful for learners. *Journal of Research in Science Teaching*, 46(6), 632–654.

Shen, J. (2010). Nurturing students' critical knowledge using technology-enhanced scaffolding strategies in science education. *Journal of Science Education and Technology*, 19(1), 1–12.

Sherin, B. L., Reiser, B. J., & Edelson, D. C. (2004). Scaffolding analysis: Extending the scaffolding metaphor to learning artifacts. *The Journal of the Learning Sciences*, 13(3), 387–421.

Slotta, J. D., Tissenbaum, M., & Lui, M. (2013). Orchestrating of complex inquiry: Three roles for learning analytics in a smart classroom infrastructure. Paper presented at the Proceedings of the Third International Conference on Learning Analytics and Knowledge.

Smith, C., Maclin, D., Houghton, C., & Hennessey, M. G. (2000). Sixth-grade students' epistemologies of science: The impact of school science experiences on epistemological development. *Cognition and Instruction,* 18(3), 349–422.

Squire, K. D., MaKinster, J. G., Barnett, M., Luehmann, A. L., & Barab, S. L. (2003). Designed curriculum and local culture: Acknowledging the primacy of classroom culture. *Science Education,* 87(4), 468–489.

Stone, C. A. (1998). The metaphor of scaffolding: Its utility for the field of learning disabilities. *Journal of Learning Disabilities,* 31(4), 344–364.

Suthers, D. D., Vatrapu, R., Medina, R., Joseph, S., & Dwyer, N. (2008). Beyond threaded discussion: Representational guidance in asynchronous collaborative learning environments. *Computers and Education,* 50, 1103–1127.

Suthers, D. D., & Verbert, K. (2013). Learning analytics as a middle space. Paper presented at the Proceedings of the Third International Conference on Learning Analytics and Knowledge.

Tabak, I. (1999). Unraveling the development of scientific literacy: Domain-specific inquiry support in a system of cognitive and social interactions. *Dissertation Abstracts International* (vol. A 60, p. 4323). Evanston, IL: Northwestern University.

Tabak, I. (2004). Synergy: A complement to emerging patterns of distributed scaffolding. *Journal of the Learning Sciences,* 13(3), 305–335.

Tabak, I., & Baumgartner, E. (2004). The teacher as partner: Exploring participant structures, symmetry and identity work in scaffolding. *Cognition and Instruction,* 22(4), 393–429.

Tabak, I., & Reiser, B. J. (2008). Software-realized inquiry support for cultivating a disciplinary stance. *Pragmatics & Cognition,* 16(2), 307–355.

van de Pol, J., Volman, M., & Beishuizen, J. (2010). Scaffolding in teacher-student interaction: A decade of research. *Educational Psychology Review,* 22(3), 271–296.

Vattam, S., Goel, A. K., Rugaber, S., Hmelo-Silver, C. E., Jordan, R., Gray, S., & Sinha, S. (2011). Understanding complex natural systems by articulating structure-behavior-function models. *Educational Technology & Society,* 14(1), 66–81.

Wertsch, J. V. (1979). From social-interaction to higher psychological processes – clarification and application of Vygotsky theory. *Human Development,* 22(1), 1–22.

Wertsch, J. V., & Stone, C. A. (1985). The concept of internalization in Vygotsky's account of the genesis of higher mental functions. In J. V. Wertsch (Ed.), *Culture, communication, and cognition: Vygotskian perspectives* (pp. 162–179). Cambridge: Cambridge University Press.

Wong, L.-H., Boticki, I., Sun, J., & Looi, C.-K. (2011). Improving the scaffolds of a mobile-assisted Chinese character forming game via a design-based research cycle. *Computers in Human Behavior,* 27(5), 1783–1793.

Wood, D., Bruner, J. S., & Ross, G. (1976). The role of tutoring in problem solving. *Journal of Child Psychology and Psychiatry,* 17, 89–100.

Wu, L., & Looi, C.-K. (2012). Agent prompts: Scaffolding for productive reflection in an intelligent learning environment. *Educational Technology & Society,* 15(1), 339–353.

4 Metacognition

Philip H. Winne and Roger Azevedo

At the simplest level, metacognition is thinking about the contents and processes of one's mind. A large body of research in cognitive psychology, extending back to the mid-1960s, has demonstrated that metacognition plays an important role in essentially all cognitive tasks, from everyday behaviors and problem solving to expert performance in the disciplines. Building on this groundbreaking research, more recent studies have demonstrated how metacognition plays an important role in learning. We review this research and identify findings that help illuminate how people learn and guide better designs for learning environments.

We begin by tackling a crucial question: "What is meta?" Then we break down metacognition in terms of two typologies, one about forms of knowledge and a second about how knowledge is used. With these distinctions as our foundation, we review empirical work on metacognition. We conclude by discussing several future directions for research in metacognition and learning.

What Is Meta?

Metacognition is cognition where the information on which a learner operates describes features of cognition. Metacognition can occur before the cognitive event when a learner forecasts whether knowledge and skills are available to successfully engage in a cognitive task. It can occur simultaneous with the event, when a learner monitors progress and considers whether cognitive tactics and strategies currently being applied might be adapted or replaced to improve progress. And, metacognition can occur after the event when a learner retrospectively considers a learning event, evaluates how effective it was, and engages in *forward-reaching transfer* by making decisions about how to approach similar tasks in the future (Salomon & Perkins, 1989).

Uses of the prefix "meta" in learning science are many, including "meta-comprehension, metaattention, metalearning, metacommunication, meta-components, and metamemory to name a few" (Tarricone, 2011, p. 1). An important misconception is afoot in this landscape. It is that metacognitive processing is 'higher order" or more abstract than "regular" cognitive processing. Our view is that what differentiates metacognition from cognition per se is only the topics a learner thinks about, not the processes a learner applies. Two important corollaries arise from this view. First, research on metacognition and on cognition share the same general paradigm. Methods that reveal how cognition unfolds also can reveal how metacognition unfolds. Second, theories and principles developed about metacognition should mirror or at least strongly parallel theories and principles that describe cognition. The benefit of this overlap is that the vast literature on cognition should be mined to advance understanding about metacognition.

The First Typology: Metacognition about Different Forms of Knowledge

Cognitive psychologists have traditionally studied three distinct forms of knowledge:

- *Declarative knowledge* refers to propositions of the form "This is the case." Declarative forms of metacognitive knowledge include beliefs about: self-efficacy, knowledge (epistemological beliefs, Muis & Duffy, 2012), and tasks (task understanding; Greene, Hutchison, Costa, & Crompton, 2012). This class also includes beliefs about the applicability of particular strategies (Jacobs & Paris, 1987) and the probability they will be successful (outcome expectations; Bandura, 2001).
- *Procedural knowledge* is knowledge of how to carry out cognitive work that accomplishes tasks. For example, a learner may know how to construct a first-letter mnemonic or a method for narrowing a search on the Internet by forming literal strings as phrases in quotes. Procedures can be domain specific or general if they span multiple domains. They can be algorithmic in the sense of (within statistical limits) guaranteeing a sought-for product or heuristic in the sense of likely but not certain to achieve a particular product.
- *Conditional knowledge* identifies circumstances under which a proposition is the case or a procedure is appropriate for approaching a goal. A common representation for conditional knowledge has the form IF-THEN. For example, if a word is styled with bold font, then it's probably important to test (monitor) whether it is understood.

Metacognition about Declarative Knowledge

Metacognition about declarative knowledge is, simply, being aware that one possesses that knowledge. This is usually straightforward: if you know that Paris is the capital of France, then you almost always know that you know that Paris is the capital of France. A core characteristic of metacognitive declarative knowledge is that declarative knowledge can be verbalized.

Declarative knowledge is any knowledge that takes the form of a factual or declarative statement. Thus, in addition to school subjects, declarative knowledge also includes statements or beliefs about a task and its context, judgments about the applicability of particular strategies (Jacobs & Paris, 1987), estimates of what one needs to know, and knowledge of what will meet task demands. Of course, learners may hold false beliefs; for example, a learner may think that he is not proficient in using conceptually demanding learning strategies (e.g., hypothesizing and making inferences – strategy characteristic) to collaborate on solving science problems using a software simulation (task characteristic) and, therefore, he should not invest much effort to complete the task. This learner may miscategorize as well as underestimate or overestimate the status of these factors, their relevance, and influence.

Possessing metacognitive declarative knowledge does not guarantee that a learner will engage in appropriate (learning) strategies. The learner may lack motivation or capability to enact appropriate strategies because of obstacles in the environment (see Järvelä & Renninger, Chapter 33, this volume). Consequently, metacognitive declarative knowledge about a learner's own learning often poorly predicts learning outcomes (Veenman, 2007).

Metacognition about Procedural Knowledge

Procedural knowledge is knowledge of processes and actions for addressing a task, often called *know-how* (Chi, 1987; Jacobs & Paris, 1987; Kluwe, 1982; Kuhn, 2000; Paris, Lipson, & Wixson, 1983; Schraw, 1998, 2001; Schraw & Moshman, 1995). Developed through application and experience, procedural knowledge can become automatic in familiar problem-solving situations (Garner, 1987; Hartman, 2001; Paris, 1988; Schraw & Moshman, 1995; Slusarz & Sun, 2001).

As long ago as the 1970s, cognitive psychologists documented a learning trajectory of procedural knowledge. At first, the learner is highly metacognitively aware, in part because the procedure needed to accomplish a task is so challenging. Gradually, as elements of the procedure are mastered, they become *automatized* – sequences of behavior are internalized and can be executed without requiring conscious attention or control. Highly automatized routines are often largely or entirely implicit. As a result, metacognitive awareness is very low, in contrast to metacognition about declarative knowledge about which a person almost always is aware.

The implications for learning are that learning designs should require learners early in learning a complex procedure to make explicit and externalize that procedural knowledge. This is particularly important when learners arrive with preexisting automatized behaviors, because they are likely to be unaware of how this automatized procedural knowledge is influencing their behavior. Particularly if the desired learning outcome is a change in procedural knowledge, it is correspondingly more important to guide learners in metacognitive awareness of their procedural knowledge.

Metacognition about Conditional Knowledge

Conditional knowledge is knowing when and why declarative and procedural knowledge are relevant to tasks (Schraw, 1998), particularly knowledge and awareness of factors that affect learning, such as "why strategies are effective, when they should be applied and when they are appropriate" (Jacobs & Paris, 1987, p. 259). Conditional knowledge involves sensitivity to the task or context, as well as sensitivity to strategy selection that is influenced by the task context.

Without conditional knowledge, declarative and procedural knowledge would not be useful (Jacobs & Paris, 1987; Paris et al., 1983; Pintrich, 2002; Schneider & Lockl, 2002; Schraw, 2001). Conditional knowledge plays a key role in adapting and transferring strategies in unfamiliar, complex problems and contexts (Desoete, 2008). But adaptation and transfer can be inhibited by inadequate domain knowledge, weak or inaccurate cognitive monitoring, ineffective strategies, and lack of awareness of task demands and goals (Garner, 1990; Hartman, 2001). Context influences strategy use, transfer, and regulation of cognition. Strategies are driven by task goals and affected by task complexity and demands, and they are also strongly influenced by context and changes in context (Pintrich, 2002). Additionally, novel, complex problems require the identification of applicable, effective strategies (Pintrich, 2002; Zimmerman, 2011), and these task demands require not only monitoring and regulation of strategic processes, but also knowledge about contextual conditions or conditional knowledge and self-efficacy when dealing with complexity, uncertainty, and limited or vague feedback.

The Second Typology: Metacognitive Forms of Thinking

Metacognition also can be modeled in terms of the form of thinking involved. Again, three distinctions can be made:

- *Metacognitive monitoring* generates awareness about the match between a particular instance of metacognitive knowledge to standards for that knowledge.
- *Metacognitive control* takes the results of metacognitive monitoring as input and generates an intention to direct thinking and action toward a goal.
- *Self-regulated learning* spans multiple instances of metacognitive monitoring and metacognitive control to shape and adapt thinking over the time span of engaging in an extended complex task.

Metacognitive Monitoring

Hart (e.g., 1965, 1967) studied the *tip-of-the-tongue* (TOT) phenomenon, a feeling that one knows information that cannot be recalled at the moment. This is a form of metacognition because it is an awareness about one's own cognitive processes. Hart's studies (and many others afterward) investigated *metacognitive monitoring*; they addressed whether and how accurately people gauge acts of cognition, and factors that affect whether and how accurately people metacognitively monitor cognitive activities.

Metacognitive Control

A landmark in learning science – Miller, Galanter, and Pribram's *Plans and the Structure of Behavior* (1960) – described successful cognitive systems as capable of changing future responses to the environment based on feedback generated by prior responses. Such "forward transfer" is an important form of learning in which people take action in response to their metacognitive monitoring. These responsive actions constitute *metacognitive control*.

Young children are typically not yet effective at metacognitive control, but it has been demonstrated to develop with increasing age. Flavell, Friedrichs, and Hoyt (1970) studied children ranging from nursery school through grade four. They first worked to memorize a list of items for recall in serial order without error. They studied the list by pressing one of several buttons in an array to reveal a picture of an object. Children's behavior was coded into four categories as they prepared for recall: naming the object pictured after pressing a button, naming an object they anticipated would be shown when a finger pointed at but had not yet pressed the button, rehearsing the name of the object pictured after pressing the button, and gesturing across the array of buttons to mentally review the sequence of objects. Older children but not younger children shifted their pattern of study across time – they monitored their progress toward the goal of perfect serial recall – and metacognitive control: they adapted their study methods in response to how well they had memorized the list.

Self-Regulating Learning

To engage metacognition productively, learners must realize there are alternative paths forward – they need multiple forms of procedural knowledge, that is, various tactics and strategies to use for learning. Also, they need knowledge of which tactics and strategies work under which conditions – conditional knowledge – as well as knowledge of what is the case in a particular task – declarative knowledge. But just having such knowledge is not enough. Productive learners need to match what they know to results that unfold as they work through tasks. Productive learners engage in self-regulating learning (SRL). They bring together, over the course of engaging with a learning task, the three forms of knowledge and the three forms of thinking to approach goals in a particular task and to adapt how they learn to improve their capacity to reach goals (Winne, 2011).

Topics learners address as they carry out metacognitively powered SRL range widely. They include: conditions that affect learning (conditional knowledge), setting goals and designing plans predicted to reach them, tracking how plans unfold as a task is engaged and diagnosing faults, and making adjustments as a task unfolds and for future engagements in similar learning tasks (see Azevedo, Johnson, Chauncey, & Graesser, 2011; Baumeister & Vohs, 2004; Boekaerts, 1999; Corno, 1986; Paris & Paris, 2001; Pintrich, 2000; Winne, 1995, 2011; Zimmerman, 1986, 1989, 2008; Zimmerman & Schunk, 2001, 2011).

A useful representation for SRL extends the model for conditional knowledge to open a door to options: IF-THEN-ELSE. IF a particular form of cognition is predicted to be successful, THEN choose to apply it. But, if that isn't productive, select something ELSE that is predicted to have a stronger chance of succeeding. For example, a learner may start out using Google to develop knowledge about how gene sequencing helped to discover how humans spread over the globe. If the material is too perplexing (monitored as requiring too much effort to understand), the learner likely will turn to another approach, such as chatting with a knowledgeable friend.

Empirical Studies of the Role of Metacognition in Learning

We review empirical studies of metacognition in six categories:

1. Studies of calibration: the fit between metacognition and performance.
2. Studies of motivation and metacognition.
3. Self-reports about metacognition: Studies of reported confidence or ease of learning after a learning task is completed.
4. Studies of metacognition and self-regulated learning.
5. Studies of domain-general metacognitive abilities.
6. Embedded online measures that study metacognitive processing during learning.

1. Calibration: The Fit between Metacognition and Performance

Calibration is the degree to which a person's judgment about his or her performance corresponds to his or her actual performance. Thus, calibration measures an important attribute of effective metacognitive monitoring

(Nelson, 1996). The accuracy of calibration is proportional to the potential for productive self-regulation (Zimmerman & Moylan, 2009). For example, students studying for a test need to accurately monitor their comprehension of information and their retention of knowledge to successfully guide further studying; for example, depending on their level of comprehension, they might restudy using the same method, or switch to a different method, or move forward to new information.

Calibration is not easily achieved. Learners quite often develop a false sense of their mastery of studied material and overestimate how well they will perform. This can lead them to prematurely terminate studying and fail to transform information into knowledge (Hacker, Bol, & Bahbahani, 2008). In contrast, learners may underestimate how well they will perform. This negative bias in calibration can undermine academic performance because students unnecessarily allocate study time to what they already know well, rather than investing that time studying what they don't yet know well. Calibration processes are important in text comprehension, multimedia learning, exam preparation, learning with computerized learning environments, and collaborative learning in a classroom setting.

Studies of calibration have explored six key questions.

(a) How does calibration vary with a learner's level of knowledge and with the task difficulty?

Many studies show that calibration accuracy is linked to levels or qualities of one's knowledge (e.g., Bol, Hacker, O'Shea, & Allen, 2005; Hacker, Bol, Horgan, & Rakow, 2000; Nietfeld, Cao, & Osborne, 2005). In general, higher-achieving learners tend to be more accurately calibrated. However, they are under-confident in judging their performance relative to lower-achieving peers. Another consistent finding is that postdictions – estimates of how well one performed after completing a task – are typically more accurate than predictions (Maki & Serra, 1992; Pressley & Ghatala, 1990).

Task difficulty also influences calibration accuracy. For example, Juslin, Winman, and Olsson (2000) identified the *hard-easy effect* by which learners tend to be more accurate but under-confident on easy items, and less accurate but overconfident on difficult items.

(b) How does calibration accuracy differ as a function of incentives and task authenticity?

Several studies of calibration examined the role of incentives and task authenticity. For example, an incentive might be course credit, such as is often given to undergraduates for participating in a pool of participants. An example of task authenticity would be learning something that aligns with students' personal goals, such as learning how to search the Internet more efficiently. In contrast, many tasks used in calibration research are inauthentic – they ask participants, for example, to learn word pairs in a remote tribal language (to control for prior learning; that is, to ensure that participants do not already know the word pairs).

In an ecologically valid study manipulating an external condition potentially affecting metacognition, Hacker and colleagues (2008) varied incentives in a quasi-experiment conducted in a college course. Students in an extrinsic reward condition could gain one to four additional points on each of three exams, depending on their calibration accuracy for test items, with more points given for greater accuracy. In this study, incentives improved calibration accuracy but only among lower-achieving students, perhaps because of greater motivation on their part to earn additional points. In a similar study by Schraw and colleagues (1993), students received extra credit either for improving performance on a test or increasing their calibration accuracy. Although performance improved in both incentive conditions, extra credit for accurate calibration was more effective than extra credit for improved test performance.

In these studies it was not possible to isolate the independent effects of incentives and task authenticity (Bol & Hacker, 2012). Future research should attempt to isolate the effects of incentives and task authenticity in the same study. For example, in a within-subjects design, calibration accuracy might be examined when students complete more authentic tasks versus contrived tasks, crossed with conditions where incentives are or are not present.

(c) What do students themselves report to be the basis of their calibration judgments?

The research indicates that learners predict how much they have learned from how much effort (time) they spent studying or methods they used to study (e.g., Bol, Riggs, Hacker, & Nunnery, 2010). Similar results are found in studies of test-taking ability, where expectations of test ease, effort exerted in studying, and learners' global sense of self confidence increase judgments of learning (e.g., Hacker et al., 2008).

(d) How do group interactions and social comparisons affect calibration accuracy?

Recent studies were able to improve calibration accuracy by experimentally manipulating various conditions of learning, such as providing guidelines for solo learning or in a group context (e.g., Bol et al., 2010; Kramarski & Dudai, 2009). Other studies demonstrated that combining group learning with guiding questions resulted in increased metacognitive monitoring and achievement (e.g., Kramarski & Dudai, 2009). One reason is that group work can elicit explicit social comparison; some experimental designs present learners with information about the average performance of fictitious peers. The results indicated that social comparisons increased the learner's confidence; greater confidence was associated with higher performance. Other results suggested that participants with little confidence in their judgments may be particularly susceptible to social influences.

(e) What is the relation between absolute and relative accuracy?

Calibration research studies two forms of accuracy. *Absolute accuracy* refers to the level of retrieval of knowledge from memory (Nietfeld, Enders, & Schraw, 2006), for example, what percent of test items can be accurately answered. For instance, a learner may judge he or she will correctly answer 80 percent of test items and, in fact, score at that level. This is perfect absolute accuracy. In contrast, *relative accuracy* (also called *discrimination*) measures the extent to which a learner can accurately differentiate which items of knowledge are more likely to be retrieved from memory and which are less likely (Nelson, 1996). While both types of accuracy are important for students to effectively self-regulate learning (Maki, Shields, Wheeler, & Zacchilli, 2005) and make gains in academic achievement, there is little to no relation between absolute and relative accuracy (Maki et al., 2005).

(f) To what extent does calibration accuracy predict achievement?

Despite the intuition that accurate metacognitive monitoring is essential to effective self-regulated learning, researchers have paid limited attention to the empirical question of whether achievement is enhanced by accurate monitoring. Correlational and experimental studies have established that good metacognitive monitoring can beneficially impact decisions about what to study (e.g., Metcalfe & Finn, 2008), but whether that studying leads to gains in achievement is unclear (Dunlosky & Rawson, 2011). Some calibration studies have shown a positive relation between calibration accuracy and achievement level (e.g., Hacker et al., 2000): greater accuracy is related to greater retention, and learners who are overconfident stopped studying too early. Nietfeld and colleagues (2006) and Bol and colleagues (2012) demonstrated that learners who participated in interventions designed to improve calibration accuracy obtained higher gains in achievement than students who did not participate in those interventions.

In conclusion, studies on calibration have demonstrated that: (1) Internal conditions that anchor metacognitive monitoring and external conditions that provide incentives and task authenticity affect calibration judgments. (2) External conditions in the form of social influences can bias learners' calibration accuracy and positively affect the relationship between absolute and relative accuracy. And (3) feedback on performance and self-reflection influences subsequent, cyclical phases of self-regulated learning.

2. Motivation and Metacognition

Several studies have explored links between learners' self-reports of motivation – reasons learners give for choices they make and for temperamental features of their behavior – and their metacognitive abilities. Some of these studies have used the Motivated Strategies for Learning Questionnaire (Pintrich, Smith, Garcia, & McKeachie, 1993) and the Motivational Strategies of Learning Scales (Suárez & Fernández, 2011) as a measure of several motivational dispositions, including metacognitive strategies as well as rehearsal, organization, and elaboration strategies. Using these two questionnaires, Suárez and Fernández (2011) found that generating positive expectations and defensive pessimism related positively to self-reported metacognitive self-regulation, and self-handicapping related negatively.

Pierce and Lange (2000) explored relations among self-reported knowledge of strategies (internal conditions), strategy use (metacognitive control), and attributions for success or failure, to effort, ability, task difficulty, luck, or outside help. Grade two and three students in a Midwestern U.S. city studied information represented by pictures, and then sorted and recalled the information. A day later, students responded to self-report measures of attributions for success or failure and of knowledge about learning tactics. A path analysis showed that attributing their success or failure to the amount of effort they invested positively related to self-reported knowledge of tactics for studying, and both of these positively related to self-reported strategy use (metacognitive control) while they were studying. These results contradicted an earlier study by Schneider, Korkel, and Weinert (1987) in which effort attributions in a German sample were not related to metacognitive control while studying.

Theories of *achievement goal orientation* are designed to explain the various motives for why one wants to learn. Typically, these theories contrast a *mastery goal orientation* (desire to truly learn and understand new material) with a *performance goal orientation* (desire to be able to demonstrate one's ability to others; Meece, Anderman, & Anderman, 2006). This view on motivation was adopted in a study by Ford, Smith, Weissbein, Gully, and Salas (1998) where undergraduates practiced identifying ambiguous targets in a computer simulation of radar tracking. Participants could select the degree of complexity of successive practice tasks under penalty conditions for making errors. Self-reported mastery goal orientation, but not performance goal orientation, was associated with self-reported level of metacognitive monitoring; higher levels of mastery goal orientation predicted greater metacognitive engagement.

Using the same radar tracking computer simulation, Bell and Kozlowski (2008) contrasted an *exploratory approach* to learning (where learners actively inquired and explored the material) with a *proceduralized approach* (where learners executed a predetermined sequence to learn, instead of open-ended exploration). The learning environment that fostered an exploratory approach led to increased metacognition (monitoring learning, planning, et cetera). A mastery goal orientation also led to increased metacognition. In turn, increased metacognition led to increased processing of feedback (metacognitive control).

Miele, Molden, and Gardner (2009) investigated how learners exercised metacognitive control in reading by examining the degree to which learners were motivated by a desire to avoid mistakes while they attempted to comprehend a text. Rereading paragraphs was considered evidence of exercising metacognitive control to avoid errors of comprehension. Making forward progress in reading the texts was taken to be evidence of metacognitive control to promote achievement. In experiment 1, undergraduates studied conceptually challenging texts after priming instructions designed to induce either a prevention (performance avoidance) orientation or a promotion (mastery) orientation. In experiment 2, undergraduates were classified according to self-report surveys according to their dispositional orientation toward prevention versus promotion. When participants reported that their comprehension was weak, their motivational orientation moderated choices about how to exercise metacognitive control. Participants with either a situational (primed) or dispositional orientation to avoid errors reread more often and longer than those with an orientation to pursue meaning. These motivational orientations led learners to metacognitively forecast (or monitor) which study tactic would be more effective.

In a study in which undergraduates took one test that counted for grades and another that did not, Sungur (2007a) administered a battery of self-report measures including: mastery goal orientation, performance goal orientation, knowledge of factors affecting cognition (metacognitive knowledge), and approaches to regulating cognition (planning, managing information, monitoring, debugging, and evaluating; Schraw & Dennison, 1994). Moderately positive correlations were observed between each measure of goal orientation (internal conditions) and both measures of self-reported metacognitive knowledge (another internal condition).

High school science students participating in a study by Sungur (2007b) responded to the self-report Motivated Strategies for Learning Questionnaire (Pintrich et al., 1993) to generate scale scores relating to motivation: intrinsic (mastery) goal orientation, task value, control of learning beliefs, and self-efficacy; and two scales relating to metacognition: regulation of metacognition and regulation of effort. Both metacognitive scales showed moderate to moderately strong correlations with all motivation variables. In a path analysis, all four motivation variables (internal conditions) positively influenced students' self-reported use of metacognition (metacognitive control). Self-reported use of metacognition and self-efficacy positively influenced self-reported regulation of effort, another expression of metacognitive control.

Stavrianopoulos (2007) administered undergraduates a self-report instrument gauging goal orientation scores on three scales: mastery, performance approach, and performance avoidance. Participants in this study also predicted their knowledge of vocabulary items, which was later compared to scores on multiple-choice items testing knowledge of those definitions. This provided an objective against which to calibrate self-reported metacognitive monitoring. After the multiple-choice test, participants could choose to review up to 25 percent of the items. Calibration of metacognitive monitoring accuracy correlated moderately positively with all three measures of goal orientation and accounted for a statistically nonzero amount of variance in review of items (metacognitive control).

Vrugt and Oort researched relations of self-reported mastery and performance goal orientations to several variables related to metacognition. Metacognitive knowledge was tapped by self-report items regarding knowledge about one's self, learning strategies, and tasks. Views about regulating cognition were operationalized by self-reports about planning, monitoring and evaluating study, and alertness to cognitive states. Perceptions about studying were elicited using self-report items describing the use of deep cognitive strategies, elaboration, organization, and critical thinking to learn. Self-reports items also reflected students' regulation of effort. A large undergraduate sample in The Netherlands participated in the study. Vrugt and Oort divided their sample into two groups who invested relatively more and relatively less effort toward learning. A structural equation model using data from more effortful learners identified that mastery orientation was strongly related to self-reported metacognitive knowledge and modestly related to self-reported use of deep cognitive strategies and metacognitive strategies. Orientation toward avoiding settings where incompetence might be publically revealed was modestly negatively related to metacognitive knowledge. Self-reported orientations toward proving competence (performance approach orientation) were modestly positively related to self-reports of learning by applying deep cognitive strategies, elaboration, organization, or critical thinking. In the group that reported applying relatively less effort to learning, essentially the same model was observed. The only difference was that orientation toward avoiding situations where incompetence might be demonstrated had a slight negative relation to reports of using deep cognitive strategies while learning.

Overall, these studies demonstrate that motives, particularly learners' orientations toward goals for learning – mastery, performance and approach, avoidance – influence learners' metacognitive monitoring and how they exercise metacognitive control. However, the variety of motives so far researched is narrow; and measures of metacognition are almost solely limited to learners' self-reports, a methodology that has well-known shortcomings (Winne, 2011; Winne & Perry, 2000; Winne, Zhou, & Egan, 2011). Furthermore, effect sizes in these studies are slight to modest. Because metacognitive behavior requires deliberate effort, motivation almost surely plays a role in metacognitive monitoring. But, on the basis of available research, too little is known about the interplay of motives and metacognition.

3. Self-Reports about Metacognition

Measures of metacognition predominantly have been off-line measures gathered before or after a learning episode. Common formats include self-reports about beliefs, ability, and expectations about kinds or levels of performance (see Dunlosky & Bjork, 2008; Dunlosky & Metcalfe, 2009; Schraw, 2010; Winne, 2010). For example, metacomprehension research conventionally emphasizes judgments about one's learning expressed as a judgment about *ease of learning (EOL)*, *judgment of learning (JOL)*, or *retrospective confidence judgments (RCJ)*. According to Nelson and Naren's (1990) framework, EOLs typically are obtained prior to learning and evaluate how easy or difficult information will be to learn. EOLs are interpreted as a prediction of task difficulty and are associated with the planning phase of self-regulated learning (e.g., determining how much time to allocate to studying) (Winne, 2010). RCJs are solicited after a learner has responded to a learning measure, usually a test, by asking participants to rate confidence in their response. RCJs are likely to influence subsequent EOLs as well as future choices of learning strategies (Dunlosky & Bjork, 2008; Dunlosky & Metcalfe, 2009). JOLs can occur at any point during learning, but are often elicited by researchers at strategic points, for example, after studying specific sections of material or at the end of a learning session. Participants are asked to rate the likelihood that they can recall recently studied information or, less commonly, how well material they have just studied is understood. JOLs are associated with the acquisition phase of learning and are perhaps the most frequently studied metacognitive judgments in current literature (see Dunlosky & Ariel, 2010).

4. Metacognition and Self-Regulated Learning (SRL)

Learners find it difficult to productively self-regulate learning for several reasons. First, learners often monitor features of cognition that mislead their exercise of metacognitive control, such as whether to review or how much attention to pay to a task. In these cases, they use inappropriate standards to metacognitively monitor cognition (Koriat, 1997). For example, learners often are overconfident about what they can recall because they mistake a feeling of knowing for actual knowledge (Koriat & Bjork, 2006). Or, learners judge they know something, not because they can actually retrieve it, but because they recognize it (Dunlosky & Rawson, 2012). As well, learners sometimes suffer the hard-easy effect wherein the more difficult they judge a task is, the greater their overconfidence (Koriat, Ma'ayan, & Nussinson, 2006). Also, when learners engage in complex tasks, cognitive load intrinsic to the task can occupy cognitive resources to an extent that metacognition suffers (Pieschl, Stahl, Murray, & Bromme, 2013).

As important as metacognition is to productive SRL, SRL depends on other critical factors. Self-regulating learners are also motivationally committed, goal-oriented, persistent, and attentive to their knowledge, beliefs, and volition (see Järvelä & Renninger, Chapter 33, this volume). Productive SRL depends on a strong sense of self, including self-control, self-efficacy, self-esteem, self-attainment, and self-actualization (McCombs, 1986; Zimmerman, 1995, 2000). As well, effective self-regulating learners have learning strategies to attain desired learning goals and monitor the effectiveness of these strategies (Corno, 1986; Purdie, Hattie, & Douglas, 1996; Wolters, 1998, 2005; Zimmerman, 1989).

Personal expectations for achievement and needs for attainment facilitate the development of self-regulatory skills (see Järvelä & Renninger, Chapter 33, this volume). Learners' perceptions of their self-regulatory learning abilities also are influenced by a combination of internal and external comparisons, which can directly affect self-regulatory processes (Butler & Winne, 1995; Miller, 2000). For example, volitional control is important in managing motivation, emotion, and environmental factors (Boekaerts, 2011; Corno, 1986; Pintrich, 2000). Also, self-talk can address personal beliefs and learning strategies for goal attainment that influence the development of self-regulation (Schunk, 1986; Vygotsky, 1978). Other key factors that impact self-regulation include self-awareness, self-judgments, self-concept, and self-efficacy (Bandura, 2001; McCombs, 1986; Zimmerman, 1989, 1995). Although these factors are often separated from metacognition, they are intrinsically entwined with metacognitive processes (Bandura, 2001; Boekaerts, 1995).

5. Studies of Domain-General Metacognitive Abilities

Almost all studies of metacognition are domain specific. This makes sense; metacognition is by definition cognition about knowledge, and knowledge is commonly domain specific. However, some researchers have posited that metacognitive abilities may be based on domain-general mental abilities. Several self-report instruments have been developed to assess domain-general metacognition (Schraw & Dennison, 1994) and self-regulation (Pintrich, 2000) in terms of how learners perceive themselves, as reflected in the common response scale where learners indicate "how true of me is this description." However, perceptions may not match reality (Winne, 2010; Winne & Perry, 2000). The debate in this area of research is the extent to which learning and metacognition in the moment – as learners are working on an unfolding task – can be accurately reflected by learners' responses to questions posed about more general contexts outside the bounds of working on a specific task (Cromley & Azevedo, 2011; McNamara, 2011; Schellings & Hout-Wolters, 2011; Veenman, 2011; Winne, 2010; Winne & Muis, 2011).

6. Embedded Tracking of Metacognitive Processing

In contrast to measures of metacognition and SRL that are not temporally co-occurring as learners engage in tasks, embedded tracking measures gather data during learning (see Azevedo & Aleven, 2013; Winne, 2010). These approaches can be grouped into *unobtrusive* and *obtrusive* performance measures (see Schraw, 2010). Measures are considered *obtrusive* to the extent that the learner is aware of them and, therefore, the act of gathering data may affect task engagement and performance (Kirk & Ashcraft, 2001). A prevalent example of an obtrusive online measure is a concurrent think aloud protocol in which a learner is asked to talk about cognitive and metacognitive processes while engaged in a learning task (e.g., Azevedo et al., 2011, 2013). It is not clear whether such measures impede, have no effect on, or enhance performance.

A recent technological development is using *computer-based learning environments* (CBLEs) to unobtrusively collect trace data about learners' cognitive and metacognitive processes during learning, problem solving, and reasoning (e.g., Aleven et al., 2010; Azevedo et al., 2013; Biswas, Kinnebrew, & Segedy, 2013; Greene et al., 2013; Hadwin, Oshige, Gress, & Winne, 2010; Lester, Mott, Robison, Rowe, & Shores, 2013; Moos & Stewart, 2013; Veenman, 2013; Winne & Hadwin, in press; Winne, Hadwin, & Gress, 2010). This allows researchers to capture temporally unfolding cognitive and metacognitive processes during a learning episode (also see Pellegrino, Chapter 12, this volume, on embedded assessment). Traces can be gathered using eye-tracking technologies, log files of learners' keystrokes, video and audio time-stamped data, screen recordings, and dialogues between the CBLE and the learner. For example, Azevedo and colleagues (2011, 2013) used *MetaTutor*, an intelligent multi-agent hypermedia system, to collect traces of cognitive and metacognitive processes during learning about complex human biology.

Interpretations of trace data as reliable reflections of metacognition and SRL rest on several key assumptions. First, there must be a strong mapping of a trace to its hypothesized theoretical construct (Azevedo et al., 2011; Winne & Perry, 2000). For example, when a learner highlights a specific segment of a sentence, were particular standards used to metacognitively monitor meaning and did the learner actually apply metacognitive control to mark the text corresponding to those standards? Second, it must be assumed that different features of metacognition and SRL correspond to differentiable expressions – different traces. When a learner tags one paragraph "important" and another paragraph "review this," does the learner actually intend to use those judgments to impact future metacognitive control? Third, because self-regulated learning is adaptive, can patterns of traces be compared to detect changes over time as learners make decisions about the success of their history in reaching goals? (Azevedo & Witherspoon, 2009; Schunk, 2001; Winne, 2001; Winne & Perry, 2000; Zimmerman, 2008).

Traces can be generated in multiple ways. For example, a trace of goal-directed planning might be a learner's utterance, "I want to learn about the valves in the heart, their function, and how they support the healthy function of the circulatory system," captured during a concurrent think aloud while studying with MetaTutor. Alternatively, the learner might click through a table of contents and tag entries referring to those topics as "my focus." Or the learner might enter expressions into a search field to locate content relating to these topics.

Other trace data can be gathered in MetaTutor in the form of text a learner enters in a dialog with one of the system's pedagogical agents. For example, a trace of help seeking is recorded when the learner "texts" a pedagogical agent asking it to model how to make an inference based on a complex diagram of the human heart. Supplemental sensors also can yield informing traces, for example, tracking the learner's eye gaze to trace choices among learning strategies such as skimming, reading a caption, or coordinating informational sources, for example, between text and a diagram. Log-file data in systems like MetaTutor are time-stamped, which allows scanning for patterns of interaction that indicate routine approaches to learning and how learners use conditional knowledge to switch among learning strategies.

Trace data are analyzed quantitatively using various methods, ranging over traditional inferential statistics, recent methods such as educational data mining (see Baker & Siemens, Chapter 13, this volume; Baker & Winne, 2013), and graph theoretical methods (Winne, Gupta, & Nesbit, 1994). Qualitative analyses of think aloud traces can expose motives and other factors affecting decisions learners make to change metacognitive processes.

Embedded studies of learning that gather trace data demonstrate that learners' SRL can be supported when the learning environment provides scaffolding that fosters metacognitive monitoring. Such scaffolding should be designed to encourage learners to externalize their developing understanding, which enhances their metacognitive knowledge (Azevedo, in press).

Future Directions

We have reviewed a substantial amount of research on metacognition. However, there is not very much study of the targets monitored in metacognition; that is, what do people notice about their cognition? In the area of self-regulated learning, we need more research to discover which strategies learners use (or misuse) in metacognitive monitoring. For example, various studies have shown that experiences of *fluency* or ease of retrieval shape metacognitive judgments of learning (e.g., Metcalfe, 2009). But what other strategies are applied? For example, might strategies include judgments of completeness or organization? Do strategies differ when a learner is monitoring learning an organized collection of knowledge (e.g., an argument) versus learning a single cognitive event (e.g., a learning strategy)?

We suggest three other topics that need study. First, what triggers a metacognitive event in a real-world learning environment rather than in a research setting when a researcher intervenes in the natural flow of engagement to ask the learner to report about metacognition? Think aloud protocols are one method to investigate this question (e.g., Azevedo et al., 2011; Greene et al., 2011). Traces offer a promising alternative (e.g., Aleven et al., 2010; Azevedo et al., 2013; Biswas et al., 2010; Winne et al., 2011). We recommend research that investigates using traces to predict think aloud data. That is, can patterns in trace data accurately predict when a learner will engage in metacognitive monitoring and what they will describe?

A second area we recommend for further research is whether individual differences, such as various indicators of ability, knowledge, motivation, and the like, correlate with metacognition. At present, too little is known about why people differ in the frequency and forms of metacognition. As well, does an individual's metacognition change as other individual difference variables change? For example, is there a trajectory of change in metacognition as a learner moves along a track from novice to expert and develops a growing sense of self-efficacy?

Third, too little is known about how people make the decisions that lead to exercising particular forms of metacognitive control. Is the nature of decision making in metacognitive monitoring that underlies metacognitive control like other forms of decision making? For example, do factors identified in classical studies of decision making (Weber & Johnson, 2009) and heuristic decision making (Gigerenzer & Gaissmaier, 2011) affect metacognitive control similarly? Can methods from these related areas of research be adapted to illuminate how options are chosen in exercising metacognitive control? As noted previously, what standards do learners use in choosing the form of metacognitive control they exercise?

Conclusion

Studies of metacognition have many significant implications for our understanding of how people learn and how to design learning environments that support learning. To sum up the key findings from our review of research in this chapter:

1. Learning is intrinsically shaped by features of metacognitive monitoring, metacognitive control, and metacognitive knowledge.
2. Metacognition operates differently, and impacts learning in different ways, depending on whether the object of the metacognition is declarative knowledge, procedural knowledge, or conditional knowledge.
3. To foster effective metacognition, learning environments should offer appropriate scaffolding (Reiser & Tabak, Chapter 3, this volume) that is aligned with the nature of the task, the nature of the knowledge being studied, and characteristics of each learner.

4. How learners self-regulate learning is shaped by metacognition. To help learners engage in productive SRL, learning environments should be designed to foster effective use of metacognitive strategies.
5. Motivation and metacognition are closely intertwined in complex ways. Understanding this relationship is essential to designing effective learning environments.

In summary, metacognition is a fundamental feature in learning, problem solving, and performance. Consequently, research on metacognition has many implications for the learning sciences. Empirical studies of metacognition that draw on a spectrum of methods for gathering and analyzing data about metacognition offer strong potential for discovering principles that can improve designs for learning environments.

References

Aleven, V., Roll, I., McLaren, B., & Koedinger, K. (2010). Automated, unobtrusive, action-by-action assessment of self-regulation during learning with an intelligent tutoring system. *Educational Psychologist,* 45, 224–233.

Azevedo, R. (in press). Metacognition and multimedia learning. In R. E. Mayer (Ed.), *The Cambridge handbook of multimedia learning.* (2nd ed.). Cambridge, MA: Cambridge University Press.

Azevedo, R., & Aleven, V. (Eds.) (2013a). *International handbook of metacognition and learning technologies.* Amsterdam, the Netherlands: Springer.

Azevedo, R., Feyzi-Behnagh, R., Duffy, M., Harley, J., & Trevors, G. (2012). Metacognition and self-regulated learning in student-centered leaning environments. D. Jonassen & S. Land (Eds.), *Theoretical foundations of learning environments* (2nd ed., pp. 171–197). New York: Routledge.

Azevedo, R., & Hadwin, A. F. (2005). Scaffolding self-regulated learning and metacognition: Implications for the design of computer-based scaffolds. *Instructional Science,* 33, 367–379.

Azevedo, R., Harley, J., Trevors, G., Feyzi-Behnagh, R., Duffy, M., Bouchet, F., & Landis, R. S. (2013). Using trace data to examine the complex roles of cognitive, metacognitive, and emotional self-regulatory processes during learning with multi-agent systems. In R. Azevedo & V. Aleven (Eds.), *International handbook of metacognition and learning technologies* (pp. 427–449). Amsterdam, the Netherlands: Springer.

Azevedo, R., Johnson, A., Chauncey, A., & Graesser, A. (2011). Use of hypermedia to convey and assess self-regulated learning. In B. Zimmerman & D. Schunk (Eds.), *Handbook of self-regulation of learning and performance* (pp. 102–121). New York: Routledge.

Azevedo, R., & Witherspoon, A. M. (2009). Self-regulated learning with hypermedia. In D. J. Hacker, J. Dunlosky, & A. C. Graesser (Eds.), *Handbook of metacognition in education* (pp. 319–339). Mahwah, NJ: Routledge.

Baker, R. S. J. D., & Winne, P. H. (Eds.) (2013). Special issue on motivation, metacognition, and self-regulated learning. *Journal of Educational Data Mining,* 5(1).

Bandura, A. (2001). Social cognitive theory: An agentic perspective. *Annual Review of Psychology,* 52, 1–26.

Baumeister, R. F., & Vohs, K. D. (Eds.) (2004). *Handbook of self-regulation: Research, theory, and applications.* New York: Guilford.

Bell, B. S., & Kozlowski, S. W. J. (2008). Active learning: Effects of core training design elements on self-regulatory processes, learning, and adaptability. *Journal of Applied Psychology,* 93(2), 296–316.

Biswas, G., Jeong, H., Kinnebrew, J., Sulcer, B., & Roscoe, R. (2010). Measuring self-regulated learning skills through social interactions in a teachable agent environment. *Research and Practice in Technology-Enhanced Learning,* 5(2), 123–152.

Biswas, G., Kinnebrew, J. S., & Segedy, J. R. (2013). Analyzing students' metacognitive strategies in open-ended learning environments. *Proceedings of the 35th annual meeting of the Cognitive Science Society.* Berlin, Germany.

Boekaerts, M. (1995). Self-regulated learning: Bridging the gap between meta-cognitive and metamotivation theories. *Educational Psychologist,* 30(4), 195–200.

Boekaerts, M. (Ed.) (1999). Self-regulated learning. *International Journal of Educational, Research,* 31(6), 445–457.

Boekaerts, M. (2011). Emotions, emotion regulation, and self-regulation of learning. In B. Zimmerman & D. Schunk (Eds.), *Handbook of self-regulation of learning and performance* (pp. 408–425). New York: Routledge.

Bol, L., & Hacker, D. J. (2012). Calibration research: Where do we go from here? *Frontiers in Psychology,* 3, 299.

Bol, L., Hacker, D. J., O'Shea, P., & Allen, D. (2005). The influence of overt practice, achievement level, and explanatory style on calibration accuracy and performance. *Journal of Experimental Education,* 73, 269–290.

Bol, L., Hacker, D. J., Walck, C. C., & Nunnery, J. (2012). The effects of individual or group guidelines on the calibration accuracy and achievement of high school biology students. *Contemporary Educational Psychology,* 37, 280–287.

Bol L., Riggs R., Hacker D. J., & Nunnery J. (2010). The calibration accuracy of middle school students in math classes. *Journal of Research in Education,* 21, 81–96.

Butler, D., & Winne, P. (1995). Feedback and self-regulated learning: A theoretical synthesis. *Review of Educational Research,* 65(3), 245–281.

Chi, M. T. (Ed.) (1983). *Trends in memory development research.* (vol. 9). Hillsdale, NJ: Erlbaum.

Corno, L. (1986). The metacognitive control components of self-regulated learning. *Contemporary Educational Psychology,* 11, 333–346.

Cromley, J., & Azevedo, R. (2011). Measuring strategy use in context with multiple-choice items. *Metacognition and Learning,* 6(2), 155–177.

Desoete, A. (2008). Multi-method assessment of metacognitive skills in elementary school children: How you test is what you get. *Metacognition and Learning,* 3, 189–306.

Dunlosky, J., & Ariel, R. (2011). Self-regulated learning and the allocation of study time. In B. Ross (Ed.), *Psychology of learning and motivation, Vol 54* (pp. 103–140). San Diego, CA: Elsevier Academic Press.

Dunlosky, J., & Bjork, R. (Eds.) (2008). *Handbook of metamemory and memory.* New York: Taylor & Francis.

Dunlosky, J., & Metcalfe, J. (2009). *Metacognition.* Thousand Oaks, CA: Sage.

Dunlosky, J., & Rawson, K.A. (2012). Overconfidence produces underachievement: Inaccurate self-evaluations undermine students' learning and retention. *Learning and Instruction, 22,* 271–280.

Flavell, J. H., Friedrichs, A. G., & Hoyt, J. D. (1970). Developmental changes in memorization processes. *Cognitive Psychology,* 1(4), 324–340.

Ford, J. K., Smith, E. M., Weissbein, D. A., Gully, S. M., & Salas, E. (1998). Relationships of goal orientation, metacognitive activity, and practice strategies with learning outcomes and transfer. *Journal of Applied Psychology,* 83, 218–233.

Garner, R. (1987). Strategies for reading and studying expository text. *Educational Psychologist,* 22(3), 299–312.

Garner, R. (1990). When children and adults do not use learning strategies: Toward a theory of settings. *Review of Educational Research,* 60, 517–529.

Gigerenzer, G., & Gaissmaier, W. (2011). Heuristic decision making. *Annual Review of Psychology,* 62, 451–482.

Greene, J. A., Costa, L-J., & Dellinger, K. (2011). Analysis of self-regulated learning processing using statistical models for count data. *Metacognition and Learning,* 6, 275–301.

Greene, J. A., Dellinger, K., Binbasaran Tuysuzoglu, B., & Costa, L. (2013). A two-tiered approach to analyzing self-regulated learning process data to inform the design of hypermedia learning environments. In R. Azevedo & V. Aleven (Eds.), *International Handbook of Metacognition and Learning Technologies* (pp. 117–128). New York: Springer.

Greene, J. A., Hutchison, L. A., Costa, L., & Crompton, H. (2012). Investigating how college students' task definitions and plans relate to self-regulated learning processing and understanding of a complex science topic. *Contemporary Educational Psychology, 37,* 307–320.

Hacker, D. J., Bol, L., & Bahbahani, K. (2008). Explaining calibration in classroom contexts: The effects of incentives, reflection, and attributional style. *Metacognition and Learning,* 3, 101–121.

Hacker, D. J., Bol, L., Horgan, D., & Rakow, E. A. (2000). Test prediction and performance in a classroom context. *Journal of Educational Psychology,* 92, 160–170.

Hacker, D. J., Dunlosky, J., & Graesser, A. (Eds.) (2009). *Handbook of metacognition in education.* New York: Routledge.

Hacker, D. J., Keener, M. C., & Kircher, J. C. (2009). Writing is applied metacognition. In A. Graesser, J. Dunlosky, & D. Hacker (Eds.), *Handbook of metacognition in education.* (pp. 154–172). Mahwah, NJ: Erlbaum.

Hadwin, A. F., Oshige, M., Gress, C. L. Z., & Winne, P. H. (2010). Innovative ways for using study to orchestrate and research social aspects of self-regulated learning. *Computers in Human Behavior,* 26, 794–805.

Hart, J. T. (1965). Memory and the feeling-of-knowing experience. *Journal of Educational Psychology,* 56(4), 208–216.

Hart, J. T. (1967). Memory and the memory-monitoring process. *Journal of Verbal Learning and Verbal Behavior,* 6, 685–691.

Hartman, H. J. (2001). *Metacognition in learning and instruction: Theory, research and practice.* Amsterdam, the Netherlands: Springer.

Jacobs, J. E., & Paris, S. G. (1987). Children's metacognition about reading: Issues in definition, measurement, and instruction. *Educational Psychologist, 22,* 255–278.

Juslin, P., Winman, A., & Olsson, H. (2000). Naïve empiricism and dogmaticism in confidence research: A critical examination of the hard-easy effect. *Psychological Review,* 107, 384–396.

Kirk, E. P., & Ashcraft, M. H. (2001). Telling stories: The perils and promise of using verbal reports to study math strategies. *Journal of Experimental Psychology: Learning, Memory, and Cognition,* 27(1), 157–175.

Kluwe, R. H. (1982). Cognitive knowledge and executive control: Metacognition. In D. R. Griffin (Ed.), *Animal mind – Human mind* (pp. 201–224). Springer-Verlag.

Koriat, A. (1997). Monitoring one's own knowledge during study: A cue-utilization approach to judgments of learning. *Journal of Experimental Psychology: General,* 126, 349–370.

Koriat, A., & Bjork, R. A. (2006). Illusions of competence during study can be remedied by manipulations that enhance learners' sensitivity to retrieval conditions at test. *Memory & Cognition,* 34(5), 959–972.

Koriat, A., Ma'ayan, H., & Nussinson, R. (2006). The intricate relationship between monitoring and control in metacognition: Lessons for the cause-and effect relation between subjective experience and behavior. *Journal of Experimental Psychology: General,* 135, 36–69.

Kramarski, B., & Dudai, V. (2009). Group-metacognitive support for online inquiry in mathematics with differential self-questioning. *Journal of Educational Computing Research,* 40(4), 377–404.

Kuhn, D. (2000). Metacognitive development. *Current Directions in Psychological Science,* 5, 178–181.

Lester, J. C., Mott, B. W., Robison, J., Rowe, J., & Shores, L. (2013). Supporting self-regulated science learning in narrative-centered learning environments. In R. Azevedo & V. Aleven (Eds.), *International handbook on metacognition and learning technologies* (pp. 471–483). Amsterdam, the Netherlands: Springer.

Maki, R. H., & Serra, M. (1992). The basis of test predictions for text material. *Journal of Experimental Psychology: Learning, Memory, and Cognition,* 18(1), 116–126.

Maki, R. H., Shields, M., Wheeler, A. E., & Zacchilli, T. L. (2005). Individual differences in absolute and relative metacomprehension accuracy. *Journal of Educational Psychology,* 97, 723–731.

McCombs, B. L. (1986). The role of the self-system in self-regulated learning. *Contemporary Educational Psychology,* 11, 314–332.

McNamara, D. (2011). Measuring deep, reflective comprehension and learning strategies: Challenges and successes. *Metacognition and Learning,* 6, 195–203.

Meece, J. L., Anderman, E. M., & Anderman, L. H. (2006). Classroom goal structure, student motivation, and academic achievement. *Annual Review of Psychology,* 57, 487–503.

Metcalfe, J. (2009). Metacognitive judgments and control of study. *Current Directions in Psychological Science,* 18(3), 159–163.

Metcalfe, J., & Finn, B. (2008). Evidence that judgments of learning are causally related to study choice. *Psychonomic Bulletin & Review,* 15, 174–179.

Miele, D. B., Molden, D. C., & Gardner, W. L. (2009). Motivated comprehension regulation: Vigilant versus eager metacognitive control. *Memory & Cognition, 37*(6), 779–795.

Miller, G. A., Galanter, E., & Pribram, K. H. (1960). *Plans and the structure of behavior.* New York: Holt, Rinehart & Winston.

Moos, D. C. & Stewart, C. (2013). Self-regulated learning with hypermedia: Bringing motivation into the conversation. In R. Azevedo and V. Aleven (Eds), *International handbook of metacognition and learning technologies* (pp. 683–697). New York: Springer.

Muis, K., & Duffy, M. (2013). Epistemic climate and epistemic change: Instruction designed to change students' epistemic beliefs and learning strategies and improve achievement. *Journal of Educational Psychology, 105,* 213–222.

Nelson, T. O. (1996). Gamma is a measure of the accuracy of predicting performance on one item relative to another item, not of the absolute performance on an individual item. *Applied Cognitive Psychology, 10,* 257–260.

Nelson, T. O., & Narens, L. (1990). Metamemory: A theoretical framework and some new findings. In G. H. Bower (Ed.), *The psychology of learning and motivation* (pp. 125–173). New York: Academic Press.

Nietfeld, J. L., Cao, L., & Osborne, J. W. (2005). Metacognitive monitoring accuracy and student performance in the classroom. *Journal of Experimental Education, 74*(1), 7–28.

Nietfeld, J. L., Enders, C. K., & Schraw, G. (2006). A Monte Carlo comparison of two measures of monitoring accuracy. *Educational and Psychological Measurement, 66,* 258–271.

Paris, S. G., Lipson, M. Y., & Wixson, K. K. (1983). Becoming a strategic reader. *Contemporary Educational Psychology, 8,* 293–316.

Paris, S. G., & Paris, A. H. (2001). Classroom applications of research on self-regulated learning. *Educational Psychologist, 36*(2), 89–101.

Pierce, S. H., & Lange, G. (2000). Relationships among metamemory, motivation and memory performance in young school-age children. *British Journal of Developmental Psychology, 18,* 121–135.

Pieschl, S., Stahl, E., & Bromme, R. (2013). Is adaptation to task complexity really beneficial for performance? *Learning and Instruction, 22,* 281–289.

Pintrich, P. R. (2000). The role of goal orientation in self-regulated learning. In M. Boekaerts, P. Pintrich, & M. Zeidner (Eds.), *Handbook of self-regulation* (pp. 451–502). San Diego, CA: Academic Press.

Pintrich, P. R. (2003). A motivational science perspective on the role of student motivation in learning and teaching contexts. *Journal of Educational Psychology, 95*(4), 667–686.

Pintrich, P. R., Smith, D., Garcia, T., & McKeachie, W. (1993). Predictive validity and reliability of the Motivated Strategies for Learning Questionnaire (MSLQ). *Educational and Psychological Measurement, 53,* 801–813.

Pressley, M., & Ghatala, E. S. (1990). Self-regulated learning: Monitoring learning from text. *Educational Psychologist, 25*(1), 19–33.

Purdie, N., Hattie, J., & Douglas, G. (1996). Students' conceptions of learning and their use of self-regulated learning strategies: A cross-cultural comparison. *Journal of Educational Psychology, 88,* 87–100.

Salomon, G., & Perkins, D. N. (1989). Rocky roads to transfer: Rethinking mechanisms of a neglected phenomenon. *Educational Psychologist,* 24, 113–142.

Schellings, G., & Hout-Wolters, B. (2011). Measuring strategy use with self-report instruments: theoretical and empirical considerations. *Metacognition and Learning,* 6(2), 83–90.

Schneider, W., Korkel, J., & Weinert, F. R. (1987). The effects of intelligence, self-concept, and attributional style on metamemory and memory behaviour. *International Journal of Behavioral Development, 10,* 281–299.

Schneider, W., & Lockl, K. (2002). The development of metacognitive knowledge in children and adolescents. In T. J. Perfect & B. L. Schwartz (Eds.), *Applied metacognition* (pp. 224–258). Cambridge University Press.

Schraw, G. (1998). Promoting general metacognitive awareness. *Instructional Science,* 26, 113–125.

Schraw, G. (2001). Current themes and future directions in epistemological research: A commentary. *Educational Psychology Review, 14,* 451–464.

Schraw, G. (2009). Measuring metacognitive judgements. In D. J. Hacker, J. Dunlosky, & A. C. Graesser (Eds.), *Handbook of metacognition in education.* New York: Routledge.

Schraw, G., & Dennison, R. S. (1994). Assessing metacognitive awareness. *Contemporary Educational Psychology, 19,* 460–475.

Schraw, G., & Moshman, D. (1995). Metacognitive theories. *Educational Psychology Review, 7,* 351–371.

Schraw, G., Potenza, M. T., & Nebelsick-Gullet, L. (1993). Constraints on the calibration of performance. *Contemporary Educational Psychology, 18,* 455–463.

Schunk, D. (1986). Verbalization and children's self-regulated learning. *Contemporary Educational Psychology,* 11, 347–369.

Schunk, D. (2001). Social cognitive theory of self-regulated learning. In B. Zimmerman & D. Schunk (Eds.), *Self-regulated learning and academic achievement: Theoretical perspectives* (pp. 125–152). Mahwah, NJ: Erlbaum.

Slusarz, R., & Sun, R. (2001). The interaction of explicit and implicit learning: An integrated model. In J.D. Moore & K. Stenning (Eds.), *Proceedings of the 23rd annual conference of the Cognitive Science Society* (pp. 952–957). Edinburgh: Erlbaum.

Stavrianopoulos, K. (2007). Adolescents' metacognitive knowledge monitoring and academic help seeking: The role of motivation orientation. *College Student Journal,* 41I, 444–453.

Suárez, J. M. & Fernández, A. P. (2011). Evaluación de las estrategias de autorregulación afectivo-motivacional de los estudiantes: Las EEMA-VS. *Anales de Psicología,* 27(2), 369–380.

Sungur, S. (2007a). Contribution of motivational beliefs and metacognition to students' performance under consequential and nonconsequential test conditions. *Educational Research and Evaluation, 13(2),* 127–142.

Sungur, S. (2007b). Modeling the relationships among students' motivational beliefs, metacognitive strategy use, and effort regulation. *Scandinavian Journal of Educational Research,* 51(3), 315–326.

Tarricone, P. (2011). *The taxonomy of metacognition.* New York: Psychology Press.

Veenman, M. J. (2007). The assessment and instruction of self-regulation in computer-based environments: A discussion. *Metacognition and Learning, 2,* 177–183.

Veenman, M. (2011). Alternative assessment of strategy use with self-report instruments: a discussion. *Metacognition and Learning, 6,* 205–211.

Veenman, M. (2013). Assessing metacognitive skills in computer-based learning environments. In R. Azevedo & V. Aleven (Eds.), *International handbook of metacognition and learning technologies* (pp. 157–168). Amsterdam, the Netherlands: Springer.

Vrugt, A., & Oort, F. J. (2008). Metacognition, achievement goals, study strategies and academic achievement: pathways to achievement. *Metacognition and Learning,* 3(2), 123–146.

Vygotsky. L. (1978). *Mind in society: The development of higher psychological processes.* Cambridge, MA: Harvard University Press.

Weber, E. U., & Johnson, E. J. (2009). Mindful judgment and decision making. *Annual Review of Psychology,* 60(1), 53–85.

Winne, P. H. (1995). Inherent details of self-regulated learning. *Educational Psychologist, 30,* 173–187.

Winne, P. H. (2001). Self-regulated learning viewed from models of information processing. In B. Zimmerman & D. Schunk (Eds.), *Self-regulated learning and academic achievement: Theoretical perspectives* (pp. 153–189). Mahwah, NJ: Erlbaum.

Winne, P. H. (2010). Improving measurements of self-regulated learning. *Educational Psychologist, 45,* 267–276.

Winne, P. H. (2011). A cognitive and metacognitive analysis of self-regulated learning. In B. J. Zimmerman and D. H. Schunk (Eds.), *Handbook of self-regulation of learning and performance* (pp. 15–32). New York: Routledge.

Winne, P., Gupta, L., & Nesbit, J. (1994). Exploring individual differences in studying strategies using graph theoretic statistics. *Alberta Journal of Educational Research, 40,* 177–193.

Winne, P. H., & Hadwin, A. F. (2013). Study: Tracing and supporting self-regulated learning in the Internet. In R. Azevedo & V. Aleven (Eds.), *International handbook of metacognition and learning technologies* (pp. 293–308). New York: Springer.

Winne, P. H., Hadwin, A. F., & Gress, C. L. Z. (2010). The Learning Kit Project: Software tools for supporting and researching regulation of collaborative learning. *Computers in Human Behavior,* 26, 787–793.

Winne, P. H., & Muis, K. R. (2011). Statistical estimates of learners' judgments about knowledge in calibration of achievement. *Metacognition and Learning, 6,* 179–193.

Winne, P. H., & Perry, N. E. (2000). Measuring self-regulated learning. In M. Boekaerts, P. Pintrich, & M. Zeidner (Eds.), *Handbook of self-regulation* (pp. 531–566). Orlando, FL: Academic Press.

Winne, P. H., Zhou, M., & Egan, R. (2011). Designing assessments of self-regulated learning. In G. Schraw & D. H. Robinson (Eds.), *Assessment of higher-order thinking skills* (pp. 89–118). Charlotte, NC: Information Age Publishing.

Wolters, C. (1998). Self-regulated learning and college students' regulation of motivation. *Journal of Educational Psychology,* 90, 224–235.

Wolters, C. (2005). Regulation of motivation: Evaluating an underemphasized aspect of self-regulated learning. *Educational Psychologist, 38,* 189–205.

Zimmerman, B. (1986). Becoming a self-regulated learner: Which are the key processes? *Contemporary Educational Psychology, 11,* 307–313.

Zimmerman, B. (1989). A social cognitive view of self-regulated learning and academic learning. *Journal of Educational Psychology, 81,* 329–339.

Zimmerman, B. (1995). Self-regulation involves more than metacognition. A social cognitive perspective. *Educational Psychologist, 30,* 217–221.

Zimmerman, B. (2000). Attaining self-regulation: A social cognitive perspective. In M. Boekaerts, P. Pintrich, & M. Zeidner (Eds.), *Handbook of self-regulation* (pp. 13–39). San Diego, CA: Academic Press.

Zimmerman, B. (2001). Theories of self-regulated learning and academic achievement: An overview and analysis. In B. Zimmerman & D. Schunk (Eds.), *Self-regulated learning and academic achievement: Theoretical perspectives* (pp. 1–37). Mahwah, NJ: Erlbaum.

Zimmerman, B. (2008). Investigating self-regulation and motivation: Historical background, methodological developments, and future prospects. *American Educational Research Journal, 45*(1), 166–183.

Zimmerman, B. (2011). Motivational sources and outcomes of self-regulated learning and performance. In B. J. Zimmerman & D. H. Schunk (Eds.), *Handbook of self-regulation of learning and performance* (pp. 49–64). New York: Routledge.

Zimmerman, B. J., & Moylan, A. R. (2009). Self-regulation: Where metacognition and motivation intersect. In D. Hacker, J. Dunlosky, & A. Graesser (Eds.), *Handbook of metacognition in education* (pp. 299–315). New York: Routledge.

Zimmerman, B. J., & Schunk, D. H. (Eds.) (2001). *Self-regulated learning and academic achievement: Theoretical perspectives.* Mahwah, NJ: Erlbaum.

Zimmerman, B. J., & Schunk, D. H. (Eds.) (2011). *Handbook of self-regulation of learning and performance.* New York: Routledge.

5 A History of Conceptual Change Research: Threads and Fault Lines

Andrea A. diSessa

Some topics seem systematically extremely difficult for students, and conventional methods of teaching usually fail. Topics like this are found at all age levels, including, in physics; matter and density, Newtonian mechanics, electricity, and relativity; in biology: evolution and genetics.[1] These topics are difficult to learn, because learning them requires students to undergo a conceptual change. Conceptual change contrasts with less problematic learning, such as skill acquisition (learning a physical skill or an algorithm for long division) and acquisition of facts (such as "basic number facts" for addition or multiplication). If there are difficulties in these areas, they are for more apparent reasons such as sheer mass of learning or the necessity of practice to produce quick, error-free performance.

The name "conceptual change" embodies a first approximation of the primary difficulty: students must build new ideas in the context of old ones, hence the emphasis on "change" rather than on simple accumulation or (*tabula rasa*, or "blank slate") acquisition. Evidence strongly suggests that prior ideas constrain learning in many areas. The "conceptual" part of the conceptual change label must be treated less literally. Various theories locate the difficulty in such entities as "beliefs," "theories," or "ontologies," in addition to "concepts."

Conceptual change is among the most central areas in the learning sciences for several reasons. First, many critically important ideas in science cannot be successfully learned unless learners undergo conceptual change. Second, understanding conceptual change requires us to engage with some of the deepest theoretical issues concerning learning. What is knowledge? When and why is it difficult to acquire? What is deep understanding? How can it be fostered? Conceptual change is important not only to education, but also to developmental psychology, epistemology, and the history and philosophy of science. For example, how did Newton, Copernicus, and Darwin accomplish their dramatic scientific revolutions?

---

[1] The conceptual change paradigm is less often applied to other areas of science, and much less in mathematics.

Conceptual change research is difficult to review. Problems (what changes; why is change difficult; how does it happen?) have led only slowly to solutions, and solutions have been tentative and partial. Many academic disciplines have examined conceptual change, resulting in a wide range of perspectives that can be hard to reconcile. There are no widely accepted, well-articulated, and tested theories of conceptual change. Instead, the field consists of multiple perspectives that combine many commonsense and theoretical ideas in kaleidoscopic fashion. In this chapter I highlight critical *threads* and *fault lines* – the former through a historical orientation and the latter by noting a few important changes in perspective and differences of opinion.

Preview

The concept of force provides an excellent example of conceptual change. Figure 5.1 shows an expert's conceptualization of a simple event, tossing a ball into the air. Physicists maintain that only one force, gravity (thick arrow in the figure), acts on the ball after it has left the hand. Gravity acts on the speed of the ball (thin arrow), diminishing it until the object reaches zero speed at the peak of the toss. Then, gravity continues to "pull" the speed of the ball downward, accelerating the ball downward.

Before conceptual change research began, instructors would have attributed student difficulties with the toss to the abstractness of physics or to its complexity. Instructional interventions might include reorganizing or simplifying exposition. "Say it better" is a "blank slate" reaction to student difficulties; it assumes a simple acquisition model of learning. In contrast, listening closely to student explanations yields a stunning discovery. Students do not just lack knowledge; they think differently than experts. Figure 5.2 illustrates a typical novice explanation involving two forces. Your hand imparts a force that overcomes gravity and drives the ball upward. The upward force gradually dies away until it balances gravity at the peak. Then, gravity takes over and pulls the ball downward.

The two-force explanation illustrates that students have a prior concept of force and what forces do that is different from experts' perception. Instruction must deal with prior ideas and change them: enter conceptual change.

How should one deal with students' "misconceptions," such as this one? Early on, most people assumed that students' ideas were coherent, like physicists'. If that is the case, one has little choice but to argue students out of their prior ideas, convincing them to accept the scientifically correct conceptualization. But a very different view has gradually developed. Rather than a coherent whole, students' ideas consist of many quasi-independent elements. Instead of rejecting students' conceptions altogether, one can pick and choose the most productive ideas and refine them to create normative concepts. For example, students see balancing at the peak of the toss. But

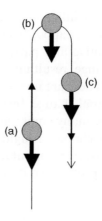

Figure 5.1. *The expert explanation of a toss: (a) There is only one force, gravity (thick arrow), that drives the ball's velocity (thin arrow) downward, (b) bringing it to zero at the peak, (c) then gravity extends velocity downward in the fall.*

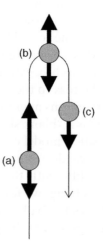

Figure 5.2. *A novice explanation of a toss that involves two forces: (a) An upward force, imparted by the hand, overcomes gravity and drives the ball upward, (b) but the imparted force gradually dies away and comes into balance with gravity; (c) finally, the imparted force is overcome by gravity.*

balancing is a rough version of an incredibly important principle in physics, conservation of energy. Similarly, the upward "force" in the incorrect explanation is not absent, but it is what physicists call *momentum*.

The opposing views of students' naïve ideas as either coherent and strongly integrated or fragmented constitute a watershed fault line in the history of conceptual change. That fault line will permeate this chapter, as it has permeated the history of conceptual change research.

I turn to a chronology of conceptual change research.

Premonitions in the Work of Piaget

Jean Piaget contributed an immense body of work on children's understanding (Gruber & Voneche, 1977). He found that children think quite differently than adults. This discovery had a strong influence on the foundations of conceptual change. Piaget introduced the idea of *genetic epistemology* – the study of the slow growth of knowledge and intelligence – which contrasted with philosophers' (e.g., Plato, Descartes, Kant) prior emphasis on timelessness and certainty. His empirical work touched many domains, including biology (the concept of "alive"), physics ("force"), space and time (perspective and simultaneity), representation (drawing), categorization, and logic. His biological work has been particularly influential on conceptual change research.

Piaget established the core idea of *constructivism*: new ideas always emerge from old ones. Indeed, this orientation seeded conceptual change itself. Constructivism and the astounding revelation that children systematically think quite differently than adults constitute the most important threads from Piagetian studies into conceptual change.

Some of Piaget's other methodologies and theories have also influenced conceptual change research. For example, Piaget introduced the idea of clinical interviews as a way of investigating children's thinking. His grand epistemological program sought to find similarities, if not identical principles of development, between children's developing ideas and the history of science. Other elements of his thinking – the idea of disequilibration and re-equilibration as a mechanism of change, assimilation versus accommodation, reflective abstraction, and others – were important mainly at early stages of conceptual change research.

There is one important way that modern conceptual change research contrasts with Piaget: Piaget developed a domain-independent "stage theory" of intelligence, where concepts in every domain reflect the same global changes in thinking. In contrast, contemporary conceptual change research takes a domain-specific approach; each domain follows its own sequence of conceptions.

The Influence of the Philosophy and History of Science

Thomas Kuhn was an influential historian of science whose work has had substantial impact on conceptual change research. Kuhn, however, had strong opposition within the history of science, and the contrasting ideas of his critics have more recently begun to influence conceptual change research. In particular, Stephen Toulmin anticipated important opposition to Kuhn's ideas. The enduring fault line between coherence and fragmentation, which I introduced in the Preview section, can be traced back to Kuhn (coherence) versus Toulmin (fragmentation).

Kuhn's Scientific Revolutions

In his landmark work, *The Structure of Scientific Revolutions* (1970), Kuhn broke from his predecessors in his view of progress in science. Kuhn rejected the idea that science progresses incrementally. Instead, he claimed that ordinary "puzzle-solving" periods of science, called *Normal Science*, are punctuated by revolutions, periods of radical change that work completely differently than Normal Science. In particular, the entire *disciplinary matrix* (referred to ambiguously but famously as a "paradigm" in the earliest edition) gets shifted in a revolution. What counts as a sensible problem, how proposed solutions are judged, what methods are reliable, and so on, all change at once in a revolution. Kuhn famously compared scientific revolutions to gestalt switches (consider Jastrow's duck-rabbit, Necker cubes, etc.), where practitioners of the "old paradigm" and those of the "new paradigm" simply do not see the same things in the world. Gestalt switches happen when the coherence of ideas forces many things to change at once.

Kuhn articulated his belief in scientific revolutions in terms of *incommensurability*. Incommensurability means that claims of the new theory cannot be stated in the terms of the old theory, and vice versa. Incommensurability constitutes both a definitional property of conceptual revolutions and an explanation for their problematic nature. As such, Kuhn's argument for incommensurability established an enduring thread in conceptual change work. In contrast, sociological aspects of Kuhn's views were not imported into conceptual change work:

> Scientific knowledge, like language, is intrinsically the common property of a group, or else nothing at all. To understand it we shall need to know the special characteristics of the groups that create and use it. (Kuhn, 1970, p. 208)

Toulmin's Rejection of Strong Coherence

The main thrust of early conceptual change research followed Kuhn, and it ignored competing perspectives. Stephen Toulmin's *Human Understanding* (1972) appeared only a few years after *The Structure of Scientific Revolutions*, and this work perspicuously introduces the other side of the coherence versus fragmentation fault line.

Human Understanding begins with an extensive review and rejection of assumptions about the level and kind of coherence (Toulmin used the term *systematicity*) that philosophers assumed in scientific thought. Toulmin traces the "cult of systematicity" back to the model of logico-mathematical coherence taken from certain mathematical forms, such as an axiomatic view of Euclidean geometry.[2]

---

[2] Toulmin does not restrict his critique to strictly logical forms of systematicity. For example, he also rejects Collingwood's model of "systematicity in hierarchical presumptions," which will be relevant in later discussion.

Presumptions of coherence were, for Toulmin, pernicious. Not only is there no global framework for all science (as the philosopher Kant claimed), but the assumption that particular theories are strongly coherent fails also. Toulmin directly criticizes Kuhn's argument for incommensurability; Toulmin countered that incommensurability appears only when one makes the mistake of assuming strong coherence. Furthermore, if one mistakenly perceives incommensurability, that also guarantees that change will always appear mysterious – everything changes at once (Kuhn's "gestalt switch").

> Rather than treating the content of a natural science as a tight and coherent logical system, we shall therefore have to consider it as a conceptual aggregate, or "population," with which there are – at most – localized pockets of logical systematicity. (Toulmin, 1972, p. 128)

In the context of his attack on coherence, Toulmin made an important methodological observation. He maintained that the dominant "before and after" (revolutionary) view of conceptual change had to be abandoned.

> This change of approach [away from strong coherence] obliges us to abandon all those static, "snapshot" analyses.... Instead, we must give a more historical, "moving picture" account. (Toulmin, 1972, p. 85)

This parallels a gradual shift from before-and-after studies of conceptual change to process-based accounts.

Misconceptions

> Even the brightest students in the class have false ideas based on enduring misconceptions that traditional instructional methods cannot overcome. (Promo materials for *A Private Universe*: Harvard-Smithsonian Center for Astrophysics (1987), http://www.learner.org/resources/series28.html)

Starting in the mid-1970s, a huge social movement, which we dub "misconceptions," began modern conceptual change studies in education and in developmental and experimental psychology. The movement exploded to prominence in the early 1980s, spawned a huge literature, and tailed off somewhat in the early 1990s, although its influence is still strong. The strength of the movement can be gauged by the fact that an early bibliography collected hundreds of studies (Pfundt & Duit, 1988). Confrey (1990) provided an excellent review of misconceptions in physics, biology, and mathematics.

Three European scholars were important contributors. R. Driver, L. Viennot, and A. Tiberghien did foundational studies, often involving instructional interventions, of topics like elementary school students' conceptions of matter, middle school heat and temperature, and high school force and motion (Driver, 1989; Tiberghien, 1980; Viennot, 1979). These and other researchers discovered, documented, and theoretically considered "false beliefs" such as: "tiny specks of matter don't weigh anything," "an object's speed is proportional to the force on it" (Newton found that force controls *acceleration*, not velocity), and "heat and cold are different things."

In the United States, important early misconceptions researchers included D. Hawkins (1978), J. Clement (1982), J. Minstrell (1982), and M. McCloskey (1983a, 1983b). Hawkins described the presence of false ideas that systematically block science learning as "critical barriers." Others used different terms for the same idea, such as *alternative conceptions*, *alternative frameworks*, *intuitive* or *naïve theories*, and *naïve beliefs*. The term *misconceptions* was most used.

A positive influence of misconceptions studies was bringing the importance of educational research into practical instructional circles. Teachers saw vivid examples of students responding to apparently simple conceptual questions in incorrect ways. Poor performance in response to basic questions, often years into instruction, could not be dismissed. Apparently, students had entrenched, "deeply held," but false prior ideas. The obvious solution was usually phrased in terms of "overcoming" misconceptions, convincing students to abandon prior ideas.

This simple story – entrenched but false prior beliefs interfere with learning and need to be overcome – was compelling to educators and resulted in significant funding and publicity. Many leading researchers would go on to develop more refined views, some elements of which are reviewed later in this chapter. However, public impact and most research remained largely at the primitive level of documenting misconceptions, rather than approaching deeper questions, such as: What is a concept? Can we decompose concepts into pieces, or are they unitary? Do multiple concepts fit into coherent wholes? If so, how coherent is the whole? Most important for the learning sciences, how do genuine scientific concepts develop out of naïve ones?

Three Early Threads

The Analogy with the History of Science

Three important and related threads in conceptual change research came to prominence simultaneously early in the misconceptions movement. Arguably the most influential was the analogy of the development of students' ideas with the history of science, which was first explored by Piaget. Susan Carey (1991, 1999) was one of the most consistent in drawing on Kuhn's ideas about scientific change in the context of children's conceptual change. She has systematically used the idea of incommensurability as a primary earmark of conceptual change. Incommensurability distinguishes conceptual change from "enrichment" (adding new ideas or beliefs) or even mere change of beliefs. Carey's main work was in biology, where she argued that children undergo a spontaneous and important conceptual revolution (Carey, 1985). For example, the concepts "alive," "real," and "intentional" (meaning having psychological wishes and desires) are confused in children's minds before they sort out a true biology, wherein "alive" means precisely that the bodily machine continues to work, sustaining life. Carey was influenced by Piaget but argued that domain-independent theories of intelligence cannot explain changes in childhood biology. Carey's extensive empirical and theoretical argumentation constituted an influential landmark, especially among developmental psychologists.

Carey worked with Marianne Wiser in the domain of heat and temperature, where a prominent sub-thread of the analogy with the history of science appeared. Not only are the *forms* (structures and processes, such as concepts, theories, incommensurability, and radical restructuring) similar in children's conceptual change and in the history of science, but *content* itself shows remarkable commonalities as well. Wiser and Carey (1983) built the case that naïve conceptions of heat and temperature parallel the ideas of an early group of scientists.

Researchers have used the analogy with history of science in multiple ways. Karmiloff-Smith (1988) denied or downplayed content parallelism between child development and the history of science, but she highlighted process-of-change parallelisms. Nercessian advocated the use of "cognitive-historical analysis" empirically to determine the processes scientists use in changing theories. Those processes include using analogical and imagistic models to bootstrap from simpler to more advanced theories, thought experiments, and extreme cases. Nercessian suggested that educators should encourage use of the same processes to help foster students' conceptual change in school (Nercessian, 1992, p. 40).

The Theory Theory

The theory theory is the claim that children or beginning students have theories in very much the same sense that scientists do. Carey has consistently advocated a version of the theory theory. With respect to "theories of mind," Allison Gopnik advocates very strong parallels between children and scientists (Gopnik & Wellman, 1994). Others are more conservative in supporting weaker parallels (Vosniadou, 2002). Theory theorists generally align themselves with the coherence side of the coherence/fragmentation fault line.

Michael McCloskey (1983a, 1983b) performed a series of studies that became perhaps the most famous of all misconceptions studies. He claimed that students entered physics with a remarkably coherent and articulate theory (suggested in Figure 5.2) that competed directly with Newtonian physics in instruction. McCloskey's theory theory included a strong parallel in content to medieval scientists' ideas, such as those of John Buridan and Galileo. In contrast to others, however, he did not say much about process-of-change similarities and, for example, did not refer in any depth to Kuhn or the philosophy of science. He took content parallels to ideas in the history of science as empirical facts, unrelated to theories of change.

McCloskey's work was incredibly influential. Despite empirical and theoretical claims by others, McCloskey has often been cited authoritatively as showing that naïve ideas in physics are strongly coherent, and, indeed, theoretical in the same way that scientific theories are (e.g., Wellman & Gelman, 1992, p. 347).

A Rational View of Conceptual Change

Introducing rational models of conceptual change marked another early landmark. Rational models hold that students, like scientists, maintain current ideas unless there are good reasons to abandon them. Posner, Strike, Hewson, and Gertzog (1982) established the first and best-known rational model. They argued that students and scientists change their conceptual systems only when several conditions are met: (1) they become *dissatisfied* with their prior conceptions (experience a "sea of anomalies" in Kuhn's terms); (2) the new conception is *intelligible*; (3) beyond intelligible, the new conception is *plausible*; (4) the new conception appears *fruitful* for future pursuits (in Lakatos's, 1970, terms: should offer a *progressing paradigm*).

Posner and colleagues' framework was eclectic. It drew from both Kuhn and Lakatos, despite Lakatos's criticism of Kuhn as viewing science as "mob rule." The framework drew equally from Kuhn's opponent, Toulmin, appropriating the idea of "conceptual ecology." A later version of this framework retreated from a purely rational framework, admitting such factors as motivation and nonverbal forms of knowledge (Strike & Posner, 1990).

Posner and colleagues maintained that their framework was epistemological and did not reflect psychological reality or provide a model for instruction. Still, many science educators organized instruction around the framework (e.g., Smith, Maclin, Grosslight, & Davis, 1997). Some even introduced students explicitly to the framework (Hewson & Hennessey, 1992).

Assessing the Misconceptions Movement

Positive Contributions:
1. Misconceptions highlighted qualitative understanding and explanation against a historical background that emphasized only quantitative problem solving.
2. Misconceptions established visibility for constructivist thinking, in contrast to "blank slate" models of learning.
3. Misconceptions provided foci for instructional problems and new measures of learning. It diminished attention to domain-general difficulties (e.g., Piagetian stages) and emphasized domain-specific issues.

Negative Contributions:
1. Most misconceptions studies were relatively devoid of theory. The "depth" of misconceptions was often uncalibrated, and the meaning of "concept" or "theory" remained unexamined.

2. Misconceptions work exclusively emphasized negative contributions of prior knowledge.
3. How learning is actually possible was minimally discussed.
4. Misconceptions led to a preemptive dominance for theory theory points of view and "conflict" models of instruction (Posner et al.'s framework; Hewson & Hewson, 1983; McCloskey, 1983a).

See Smith, diSessa, and Roschelle (1993) for a more extended analysis of the misconceptions movement.

Beyond Misconceptions

Conceptual Change in Particular Domains

What, in detail, do students or children know about any particular domain at any particular age? Since Piaget, this has been an important question. However, modern conceptual change research is asking this question with greater precision and empirical support, in more instructionally relevant domains, than previously.

In the domain of biology,[3] a substantial community of researchers (Carey, Keil, Hatano, Inagaki, Atran, and others) shared innovative methods, critiqued, and built on each other's ideas. Carey argued that a domain-specific conceptual change – which involves "radical restructuring" rather than a mere "accretion of ideas" – occurs in childhood (1985, 1988). She maintained that the early concept of "animal" was embedded in a naïve theory of psychology; animals are distinct from inanimate objects in their goal-directed (psychological) activities. In contrast, biologists attend to animals' structure and internal processes, the "bodily machine" of which young children are nearly completely ignorant. She claimed that a true biology appears only by about age 10.

The burgeoning field of children's biology revised and refined Cey's ideas, leading to a wonderfully enriched view of the emergence of biological knowledge. Two prime innovators were Frank Keil and Giyoo Hatano (with his collaborator, Kayoko Inagaki). These researchers pushed the emergence of distinctively biological thinking back about six years. Keil developed an extensive program that isolated children's sensitivity to biological phenomena in multiple strands, including the biological essence of animals, inheritance, biological contagion, and the distinctive properties of the "insides" of living things. In the latter category, Keil (1994) showed that children age four or younger expect the insides of rocks to be random while plants and animals have more organized insides. Keil showed that very young children

---

[3] Naïve psychology and naïve physics were other notable domains of study. Coverage was most spotty in physics. Studies of baby cognition revealed stunning early physics competence (Baillargeon, 1986; Spelke, Philips, & Woodword, 1995). But middle years received less attention. Late development was left to misconceptionists.

believe it is easy to paint or in other ways physically change a skunk into a raccoon, while older children, still before the age of six, feel such operations cannot essentially change the creature. He showed that children come early to the idea that inheritance ("nature") is more important than environment ("nurture") in establishing the essential characteristics of animals.

Inagaki and Hatano (2002) brought a new order to early biology by describing a core naïve theory, a *vitalist* biology. In this theory, the ingestion and use of a "vital force" accounts for animals' activity, health, and growth. Experiments showed that vitalist biology emerged by age six. Hatano, Inagaki, and Keil argued and empirically disputed Carey's claim that biology emerged from psychology. However, Inagaki and Hatano agreed with Carey that the shift from childhood to mechanistic biology (age 10–12) constituted true conceptual change.

Knowledge in Pieces

The theory theory thread dominated studies of naïve biology, psychology, and physics. It represents the "coherence" (Kuhnian) side of the coherence/fragmentation fault line. A contrasting approach, "knowledge in pieces," takes the "fragmented" side. Minstrell and diSessa were early advocates of knowledge in pieces. Their critique of the theory theory approach was analogous to Toulmin's critique of strong coherence.

Minstrell (1982, 1989) viewed naïve ideas as resources for instruction much more than blocks to conceptual change in physics. This directly challenged the misconceptions view that naïve ideas are simply wrong, and it also challenged the theory theory notion that naïve ideas must be taken or rejected as a whole. Minstrell described intuitive ideas as *facets*, "threads" that, rather than rejecting, need to be "rewoven" into a different, stronger, and more scientific conceptual fabric. Facet work has charted hundreds of ideas that students have on entering instruction in many topics (Hunt & Minstrell, 1994). Coherent naïve theories are nowhere to be seen.

diSessa (1983) introduced the idea that naïve physics consisted largely of hundreds or thousands of elements called p-prims, similar to Minstrell's facets. P-prims provide people with their sense of which events are natural (when a p-prim applies), which are surprising, and why. P-prims are many, loosely organized, and sometimes highly contextual, categorically unlike "theories." With good instructional design, p-prims can be enlisted – rather than rejected – into excellent learning trajectories. For example, "Ohm's p-prim" prescribes that more effort begets more result, and a greater resistance begets less result. Ohm's p-prim accounts for the easy learnability of Ohm's law in electrical circuit theory, and it can be invoked to help students understand other physics, such as thermal equilibration (diSessa, in press).

Knowledge in pieces was, at best, a minority opinion in early educational studies of conceptual change (Driver, 1989; Smith et al., 1997). It remains largely ignored in developmental psychology. See diSessa, Gillespie, and Esterly (2004) for a historical review. However, the viewpoint has gained visibility and adherents in educational circles. Marcia Linn (2006), for example, elaborated "scaffolded knowledge integration" as an instructional framework. In this view, the multiplicity of intuitive ideas is explicitly recognized, and integration (increasing coherence) is virtually the definition of conceptual advancement.

Fragments of Theory

I referred earlier to conceptual change research as kaleidoscopic; many threads are combined in diverse ways into many different theoretical perspectives. This section sketches the theoretical landscape of conceptual change in terms of some of those threads.

I discuss two groups of theoretical issues. First, what are the mental entities involved in conceptual change, and how are they organized? Second, why is conceptual change difficult, and how does it happen when it does? The various answers to these questions radically shift how we think about the design of good instruction.

Components and Systems in Conceptual Change

What changes in conceptual change? The obvious answer is "concepts." Shockingly, there is very little agreement in the field on the meaning of the term *concept* and concepts' role in conceptual change.

Carey (1988) distinguished beliefs from concepts. Beliefs are relational entities. For example, "people are animals" relates two concepts, people and animals; Newton's laws ($F = ma$) relate the concepts of force, mass, and acceleration. Carey believed that belief change is relatively easy, and that the difficulty is change in the very concepts in which beliefs are expressed. When children finally believe that people are animals, a very different concept of animal is implicated compared to their earlier conceptions.

In Carey's theory theory perspective, concepts are components of larger-scaled systems, intuitive theories, which strongly constrain concepts. Most theories of conceptual change are *nested* in this way. At least two levels exist (concepts are *components* in a theoretical *system*), and the relational constraints involved at the system level are critical. Systemic relations constrain individual concepts, and therefore incremental change is difficult. This brings us directly to the core of the coherence versus fragmentation fault line. If systemic constraints are too strong (that is, if coherence is high), then change is unimaginable, as Toulmin advised. So a great deal rests precisely on understanding relations at the system level, which is the naïve theory in Carey's case.

Vosniadou has proposed two versions of how knowledge might involve nesting components within systems. First, concerning children's models of the earth's shape (sphere, pancake, etc.), she implicated *framework theories* at the system level. When children are asked questions about the shape of the earth, their framework theories constrain generation of specific models (at the component level) to a few possibilities. In this case, *models* are nested in and constrained by framework theories. Models change relatively easily, but framework theories take a long time. In more recent work, Vosniadou extended her ideas to force and motion, and developed a second version of nesting. For example, in Ioannides and Vosniadou (2002), framework theories constrain *meanings* (not models) such as "force," and the higher, relational level (theories) is still the real locus of difficulty in change.[4]

Another nested view of conceptual change involves concepts as components, but the higher level is not theories, but ontologies (fundamental categories, like matter, processes, or ideas). Micheline Chi (1992) posited that concepts are strongly constrained by their presumed ontology. In early work, Chi maintained that concepts of intuitive physics were nested in the matter ontology, but Newtonian concepts lie in an ontology very different from matter, "constraint-based processes." Shifting ontologies, like shifting theories, is very difficult. Instructionally, Chi suggested teaching the new ontology first, and then revised concepts can grow naturally within that ontology.

Adherents of the knowledge-in-pieces view feel that classical knowledge terms (*concepts, theories, ontologies*) are not up to the scientific job of explaining conceptual change; we need new terms. Minstrell introduced *facets*. I introduced a series of constructs, each with its own definition: for example, *p-prims*, *mental models*, and *coordination classes* (diSessa, 1996; diSessa & Wagner, 2005). A coordination class is a model of a certain kind of concept. Coordination classes are complex systems that include many coordinated parts, including p-prims. There is recursive nesting here: p-prims are nested in coordination classes (concepts), and coordination classes – along with mental models and other entities – constitute the "conceptual ecology" of students, which is parallel to but different from "theory."

The fact that concepts (coordination classes) are explicitly modeled is virtually unique to this view of conceptual change[5] and has important consequences for instructional design. Knowing the internal pieces of concepts is much like having an ingredient list for baking a cake. Knowing how those internal pieces are configured is almost like having a recipe.

Models of Constraint and Change

Following Kuhn, if successive stages in conceptual development are indeed characterized by incommensurability, this would certainly account for the

---

[4] Vosniadou often emphasizes the nature of framework theories as "background assumptions," similar to Collingwood's view, which Toulmin criticized for lack of rendering such assumptions explicit and testable.

[5] Neither Carey, Vosniadou, nor Chi describe the internal structure of concepts.

difficulty of conceptual change. But critics of incommensurability raise a serious challenge: How is conceptual change at all possible? Inspired by the history of science, various researchers proposed mechanisms like analogy and developing imagistic models. A common assumption is that differentiation of diffuse initial concepts (heat and temperature become distinct), and coalescence of old categories (plants and animals become joined in the category of living things) are important processes that take place in overcoming incommensurability (Carey, 1988, 1999; Smith et al., 1997).

A generic difficulty in the knowledge-in-pieces view is: How do learners collect a large set of elements (say, p-prims) into a system (say, a scientific concept)? Unlike baking a cake, one cannot collect conceptual ingredients all from a store. Instead, students need to have diverse experiences while they are developing a concept. In addition, the conceptual ingredients must be coordinated into a smoothly operating system. Coordination class theory specifies a kind of coherence, called *alignment*, that poses systematic and empirically tractable difficulties for students. The theory also delineates some standard paths to overcoming them.

In cases where there might be no intuitive theory (chemistry?; mathematics?), incommensurability cannot be an accurate description of learning. In these domains of knowledge, coherence theories of conceptual change cannot explain learning difficulties. Knowledge in pieces approaches are more appropriate in such cases, because even without an intuitive theory, learners still collect and coordinate pieces of knowledge.

Rational models remain surprisingly well regarded, despite sparse evidence for their adequacy in dealing with conceptual change. Gopnik and Wellman (1994) mention most of the same elements as Posner and colleagues. They also mention quasi-rational processes resonant with professional science, such as denial of the need for change and the formation of auxiliary hypotheses to fend off deep change.

Although Piaget's argument that development is driven by the drive toward equilibration has diminished in popularity, new versions have appeared. Inagaki and Hatano provide two models of conceptual change where new ideas disturb the coherence of prior ideas and reestablishing coherence drives conceptual change (Inagaki and Hatano, 2002, pp. 173–175). See also Ioannides and Vosniadou (2002, p. 58).

Instruction

Working out the implications of conceptual change research for instruction is as complex as surveying the field of conceptual change itself. However, here is a series of observations about the knowledge-in-pieces (KiP) perspective and its implications for instruction.

1. *KiP allows "watching" conceptual change*: Teachers or tutors organize students' attention over short periods of time. KiP has a small enough grain size of analysis to allow real-time tracking of learning (diSessa, in press). This means, in particular, that instructional design can use, not just before/after studies, but also process data for formative feedback.

2. *KiP explains why conceptual change takes time.* Every view of conceptual change assumes that it takes a long time. However, KiP proposes its own distinctive reasons, which allows one to monitor and remediate difficulties. One such problem is that creating a coherent concept requires aligning (in the technical sense discussed earlier) multiple distinct ways of using that concept.

3. *KiP requires learning in many contexts.* Complex contextuality is a fact of the matter in a KiP perspective. There is no alternative to exposing students to multiple contexts during learning, so that they may learn in each.

4. *Students have rich conceptual resources on which to draw.* A nearly unique property of KiP in the field of conceptual change is that it sees "naïve" students as full of ideas, many of which can or even must be reused in developing scientific understanding (diSessa, in press).

5. *Confront and replace is an implausible instructional strategy.* With hundreds of relevant ideas in their conceptual ecology, the idea of separately eliminating all the wrong ones is implausible, even if it were desirable.

6. *Coaching students meta-conceptually is very different from a KiP perspective.* Most contemporary researchers feel that students should learn about their own learning and about the nature of scientific concepts (see Winne & Azevedo, Chapter 4, this volume). As Kuhn differed from Toulmin, KiP differs from theory theory views with respect to the nature of both students' and scientists' ideas.

7. *KiP is flexible and fine-grained enough to track individual differences in learning.* "One theory fits all" does not work. The grain size of KiP analyses allows one to characterize student differences and to see how they influence learning (Kapon & diSessa, 2012).

In contrast to KiP approaches, a coherence or theory theory view might lead to different instructional designs. To date, we do not have solid empirical evidence that instructional designs based on any one of the aforementioned theoretical approaches is superior to any other. There are several potential reasons for this:

1. Instruction is a complex mixture of design and theory. Good intuitive design can override the power of current theory to prescribe successful methods. Almost all reported conceptual change-inspired interventions work; none of them leads to unquestionably superior results.

2. Researchers of different theoretical persuasions advocate similar instructional strategies. Both adherents of knowledge in pieces and of theory

theories advocate student discussion, whether to draw out and reweave elements of naïve knowledge, or to make students aware of the faults in their prior theories. The use of instructional analogies, metaphors, and visual models is widespread and not theory distinctive.

3. Many or most evaluations of interventions, at present, rely primarily on pre/post evaluations, which do little to discern specific processes of conceptual change.

Mapping the Frontier

Coherence: A Central Fault Line

Thomas Kuhn had a huge influence in the early days of conceptual change research, with the idea that scientific theories change drastically and holistically. His ideas influenced the theory theory, that conceptual change replaces one coherent theory with another, and the sticking point is precisely the coherence of the prior theory. Coherence is a byword for theory theorists, and it is taken to be the defining attribute that makes the term *theory* applicable to naïve ideas (Wellman & Gelman, 1992). More recently, Toulmin's critique of Kuhn – that scientific understanding is not strongly coherent – has been expanded by contemporary conceptual change researchers in the learning sciences. These "fragmentation" theorists note that almost no models of coherence exist,[6] and data for coherence has been ambiguous and contested. There is increasing evidence that the knowledge-in-pieces perspective provides a more apt framework for instructional difficulties and possibilities concerning conceptual change, even though some influential researchers ignore the issue of coherence and others dismiss it as unimportant (Chi, 1992, p. 161).

Recent studies have explicitly provided empirical and theoretical argument and counterargument concerning coherence in naïve ideas (Ioannides & Vosniadou, 2002; diSessa et al., 2004; Hammer & Elby, 2002). Today, fragmentation views seem ascendant. For example, Minstrell's facet analysis has been extensively developed and brought to widespread instructional practice; I am unaware of instruction based on the theory theory that has passed beyond research prototypes.

Biology also offers coherence/fragmentation lessons. The modern view of naïve biology, despite many researchers' commitment to the idea of naïve theories, contains trends that undermine strong coherence. The multiple lines in biological knowledge developed by Keil and others beg the question of how much they cohere with each other. Vitalism, as described by Inagaki

---

[6] Thagard (2000) is a notable exception.

and Hatano, is only a part of naïve biology, not a full, pervasive theory. And the "theory" that defines the mechanistic phase of intuitive biology is not succinctly characterized, nor is its coherence empirically measured. Inagaki and Hatano show that more primitive ways of reasoning about biology than naïve theories (based, for example, on similarity rather than biological categories) persist into adulthood. Adults also use vitalism long past the "transition to mechanistic biology." These observations are not consistent with strongly coherent "theories" and gestalt switch transitions.

Settling the coherence/fragmentation dispute requires further theory development and additional empirical work. We need better cognitive models and more precise empirical support. The metaphor of "theory" drawn from the history of science ambiguously covers both strongly and weakly systematic knowledge systems, as exemplified by Kuhn and Toulmin's debate. Specifications such as "theories embody causal notions, license distinct types of explanations, support distinct predictions, and reflect basic ontological commitments" (Gopnik & Meltzoff, 1997) are similarly ambiguous. The field must do better.

Debate over coherence versus fragmentation is subtle. No one thinks children are completely unsystematic in their thinking about physics or biology. Furthermore, all existing views of scientific competence, when actually achieved, entail substantial systematicity.[7] The central issue, rather, is specification of the *nature* and *extent* of systematicity.[8]

Foci for Near-Future Work

Here is a list of specific suggestions for future research.

1. *Pursue detailed specification of the content development of conceptual domains.* For example, the rich empirical studies of naïve biology provide important resources for developing and testing theories of conceptual change. Furthermore, educational application will likely depend as much on domain-specific content as on general theories of conceptual change.

2. *Make contextuality a central concern.* Research on intuitive physics reveals sensitive dependence on problem context, on framing of questions, on modality (viewing, drawing, enacting), and so on (diSessa et al., 2004). In naïve biology, subjects reveal early vitalist sensitivities only when explicitly prompted. But, in contrast, no students of physics would

---

[7] See diSessa (1993) for a knowledge-in-pieces point of view on the development of systematicity.

[8] Few if any researchers believe that intuitive ideas are deductively coherent. Yet explicit alternative forms of coherence are both rare and vague. Wellman and Gelman (1992) mention two meanings for coherence: lack of contradiction (which, as they point out, applies to a set of beliefs that have nothing to do with one another), and the idea that concepts "refer to each other" (where "reference" is undefined).

be said to understand Newton's laws if they only thought of them when prompted. Understanding physics includes consciously knowing what concepts you are using and thoughtfully applying them. Surely this must be consequential. More generally, developmental studies consistently report "intrusion" of one way of thinking into others (e.g., psychology intrudes on biology; or weight intrudes on density). But one must ask about the relevant contextuality. When are there intrusions? Why?

3. *Assume variation across domains, and empirically validate commonalities (or differences).* Almost all conceptual change research assumes common difficulties and common psychological mechanisms across domains. But there is increasing evidence that conceptual change proceeds differently in different domains.

4. *Develop explicit models of constructs like "concept" and "theory," and test them against data; models need to highlight relational structure (coherence).* Researchers need to commit themselves to particular constructs with specified meanings. What, after all, is an "entrenched belief"? I have also systematically highlighted the critical importance of understanding the nature and level of coherence in naïve and instructed competences.

5. *Accept the challenge of process validation of models of entities and change.* Toulmin argued for abandoning both snapshot models of conceptual change and snapshot validation of theories of change. Everyone agrees change is slow; but few theories exist to track the slow progress. Shockingly, almost no research on conceptual change tracks students' moment-by-moment thinking while learning (although see Chinn & Sherin, Chapter 9, this volume). Filling in the big "before-and-after" views of change with the details of exactly what changes when may be the gold ring of conceptual change research.

References

Baillargeon, R. (1986). Representing the existence and the location of hidden objects: Object permanence in 6- and 8-month infants. *Cognition, 23,* 21–41.

Carey, S. (1985). *Conceptual change in childhood.* Cambridge, MA: MIT Press/Bradford Books.

Carey, S. (1988). Reorganization of knowledge in the course of acquisition. In S. Strauss (Ed.), *Ontogeny, phylogeny, and historical development* (pp. 1–27). Norwood, NJ: Ablex.

Carey, S. (1991). Knowledge acquisition: Enrichment or conceptual change? In S. Carey & R. Gelman (Eds.), *The epigenesis of mind* (pp. 257–291). Mahwah, NJ: Lawrence Erlbaum Associates.

Carey, S. (1999). Sources of conceptual change. In E. Scholnick, K. Nelson, S. Gelman, & P. Miller (Eds.), *Conceptual development: Piaget's legacy* (pp. 293–326). Mahwah, NJ: Lawrence Erlbaum Associates.

Chi, M. T. H. (1992). Conceptual change across ontological categories: Examples from learning and discovery in science. In F. Giere (Ed.), *Cognitive models of science: Minnesota studies in the philosophy of science* (pp. 129–160). Minneapolis: University of Minnesota Press.

Clement, J. (1982). Students' preconceptions in introductory mechanics. *American Journal of Physics*, 50(1), 66–71.

Confrey, J. (1990). A review of the research on student conceptions in mathematics, science, and programming. In C. Cazden (Ed.), *Review of Research in Education*, *16* (pp. 3–56). Washington, DC: American Educational Research Association.

diSessa, A. A. (1983). Phenomenology and the evolution of intuition. In D. Gentner & A. Stevens (Eds.), *Mental models* (pp. 15–33). Hillsdale, NJ: Lawrence Erlbaum Associates.

diSessa, A. A. (1993). Toward an epistemology of physics. *Cognition and Instruction*, 10(2–3), 105–225; Responses to commentary, 261–280. (*Cognition and Instruction* Monograph No. 1).

diSessa, A. A. (1996). What do "just plain folk" know about physics? In D. R. Olson & N. Torrance (Eds.), *The Handbook of Education and Human Development: New Models of Learning, Teaching, and Schooling* (pp. 709–730). Oxford: Blackwell Publishers, Ltd.

diSessa, A. A. (2002). Why "conceptual ecology" is a good idea. In M. Limón & L. Mason (Eds.), *Reconsidering conceptual change: Issues in theory and practice* (pp. 29–60). Dortrecht: Kluwer.

diSessa, A. A. (in press). The construction of causal schemes: Learning mechanisms at the knowledge level. *Cognitive Science*.

diSessa, A. A., Gillespie, N., & Esterly, J. (2004). Coherence vs. fragmentation in the development of the concept of force. *Cognitive Science*, 28, 843–900.

diSessa, A. A., & Wagner, J. F. (2005). What coordination has to say about transfer. In J. Mestre (Ed.), *Transfer of learning from a modern multidisciplinary perspective* (pp. 121–154). Greenwich, CT: Information Age Publishing.

Driver, R. (1989). Students' conceptions and the learning of science. *International Journal of Science Education*, 11, 481–490.

Gopnik, A., & Meltzoff, A. (1997). *Words, thoughts, and theories*. Cambridge, MA: MIT Press.

Gopnik, A., & Wellman, H. (1994). The theory theory. In L. A. Hirschfeld & S. A. Gelman (Eds.), *Mapping the mind: Domain specificity in cognition and culture* (pp. 257–293). New York: Cambridge University Press.

Gruber, H., & Voneche, J. (1977). *The essential Piaget*. New York: Basic Books.

Hammer, D., & Elby, A. (2002). On the form of a personal epistemology. In B. Hofer & P. Pintrich (Eds.), *Personal epistemology* (pp. 169–190). Mahwah, NJ: Lawrence Erlbaum Associates.

Harvard-Smithsonian Center for Astrophysics (1987). *A private universe*. Video. Annenberg/CPB: www.learner.org.

Hawkins, D. (1978). Critical barriers to science learning. *Outlook*, 29, 3–23.

Hewson, P., & Hennesy, M. G. (1992). Making status explicit: A case study of conceptual change. In R. Duit, F. Goldberb, & H. Niedderer (Eds.), *Research in physics learning: Theoretical and empirical studies* (pp. 176–187). Kiel, Germany: IPN.

Hewson, W. H., & Hewson, M. G. A. (1983). The role of conceptual conflict in conceptual change and the design of science instruction. *Instructional Science*, 13, 1–13.

Hunt, E., & Minstrell, J. (1994). A cognitive approach to the teaching of physics. In K. McGilly (Ed.), *Classroom lessons: Integrating cognitive theory and classroom practice* (pp. 51–74). Cambridge, MA: MIT Press.

Inagaki, K., & Hatano, G. (2002). *Young children's naive thinking about the biological world*. New York: Psychology Press.

Ioannides, C., & Vosniadou, C. (2002). The changing meanings of force. *Cognitive Science Quarterly*, 2, 5–61.

Kapon, S., & diSessa, A. A. (2012). Reasoning through instructional analogies. *Cognition and Instruction*, 30(3), 261–310.

Karmiloff-Smith, A. (1988). The child as a theoretician, not an inductivist. *Mind and Language* 3(3), 183–195.

Keil, F. (1994). The birth and nurturance of concepts by domains: The origins of concepts of living things. In L. Hirschfield & S. Gelman (Eds.), *Mapping the mind: Domain specificity in cognition and culture* (pp. 234–254). Cambridge: Cambridge University Press.

Kuhn, T. S. (1970). *The structure of scientific revolutions*. Second Edition. Chicago: University of Chicago Press.

Lakatos, I. (1970). Falsification and the methodology of scientific research programmes. In I. Lakatos & A. Musgrave (Eds.), *Criticism and the growth of knowledge* (pp. 91–196). London; NY: Cambridge University Press.

Linn, M. C. (2006). The knowledge integration perspective on learning and instruction. In R. K. Sawyer (Ed.), *The Cambridge handbook of the learning sciences* (pp. 243–264). New York: Cambridge University Press.

McCloskey, M. (1983a). Naive theories of motion. In D. Gentner & A. Stevens (Eds.), *Mental models* (pp. 299–323). Hillsdale, NJ: Lawrence Erlbaum Associates.

McCloskey, M. (1983b, April). Intuitive physics. *Scientific American*, 122–130.

Minstrell, J. (1982). Explaining the "at rest" condition of an object. *The Physics Teacher*, 20, 10–14.

Minstrell, J. (1989). Teaching science for understanding. In L. Resnick & L. Klopfer (Eds.), *Toward the thinking curriculum* (pp. 129–149). Alexandria, VA: Association for Supervision and Curriculum Development.

Nercessian, N. (1992). How do scientists think? In F. Giere (Ed.), *Cognitive models of science: Minnesota studies in the philosophy of science* (pp. 3–44). Minneapolis: University of Minnesota Press.

Pfundt, H, & Duit, R. (1988). *Bibliography: Students' alternative frameworks and science education*. Second Edition. Kiel, Germany: IPN.

Posner, G. J., Strike, K. A., Hewson, P. W., & Gertzog, W. A. (1982). Accommodation of a scientific conception: Toward a theory of conceptual change. *Science Education*, 66(2), 211–227.

Smith, C., Maclin, D., Grosslight, L., & Davis, H. (1997). Teaching for understanding: A study of students' preinstruction theories of matter and a comparison of the effectiveness of two approaches to teaching about matter and density. *Cognition and Instruction*, 15, 317–393.

Smith, J. P., diSessa, A. A., & Roschelle, J. (1993). Misconceptions reconceived: A constructivist analysis of knowledge in transition. *Journal of the Learning Sciences*, 3(2), 115–163.

Spelke, E. S., Phillips, A., & Woodword, A. (1995). Infants' knowledge of object motion and human action. In D. Sperber, D. Premack, & A Premack (Eds.), *Causal cognition: A multidisciplinary debate* (pp. 44–78). Oxford: Clarendon Press.

Strike, K. A., & Posner, G. J. (1990). A revisionist theory of conceptual change. In R. Duschl & R. Hamilton (Eds.), *Philosophy of science, cognitive science, and educational theory and practice* (pp. 147–176). Albany, NY: SUNY Press.

Thagard, P. (2000). *Coherence in thought and action.* Cambridge, MA: MIT Press.

Tiberghien, A. (1980). Modes and conditions of learning: The learning of some aspects of the concept of heat. In W. Archenhold, R. Driver, A. Orton, & C. Wood-Robinson (Eds.), *Cognitive development research in science and mathematics: Proceedings of an international symposium* (pp. 288–309). Leeds, UK: University of Leeds.

Toulmin, S. (1972). *Human understanding.* Vol. 1. Oxford: Clarendon Press.

Viennot, L. (1979). Spontaneous reasoning in elementary dynamics. *European Journal of Science Education, 1,* 205–221.

Vosniadou, S. (2002). On the nature of naïve physics. In M. Limón & L. Mason (Eds.), *Reconsidering conceptual change: Issues in theory and practice* (pp. 61–76). Dordrecht: Kluwer Academic Publishers.

Wellman, H., & Gelman, S. (1992). Cognitive development: Foundational theories of core domains. *Annual Review of Psychology, 43,* 337–375.

Wiser, M., & Carey, S. (1983). When heat and temperature were one. In D. Gentner & A. Stevens (Eds.), *Mental models* (pp. 267–298). Mahwah, NJ: Lawrence Erlbaum Associates.

6 Cognitive Apprenticeship

Allan Collins and Manu Kapur

Throughout most of history, teaching and learning have been based on apprenticeship. Children learned how to speak, grow crops, construct furniture, and make clothes. But they didn't go to school to learn these things; instead, adults in their families and in their communities showed them how, and helped them do it. Even in modern societies, we learn some important things through apprenticeship: we learn our first language from our families, employees learn critical skills on the job, and scientists learn how to conduct research by working side by side with senior scientists as part of their doctoral training. But for most other kinds of knowledge, schooling has replaced apprenticeship. The number of students pursuing an education has dramatically increased in the past two centuries, and it gradually became impossible to use apprenticeship on the large scale of modern schools. Apprenticeship requires a very small teacher-to-learner ratio that is not realistic in the large educational systems of modern economies.

Even in modern societies, when someone has the resources and a strong desire to learn, they often hire a coach or tutor to teach them by apprenticeship – demonstrating that apprenticeship continues to be more effective even in modern societies. If there were some way to tap into the power of apprenticeship without incurring the costs of hiring a teacher for every two or three students, it could be a powerful way to improve schools. In the 1970s and 1980s, researchers in computers and education were studying how technology could help to transform schooling. In a series of articles (e.g., Collins & Brown, 1988; Collins, Brown, & Newman, 1989), we explored how to provide students with apprenticeship-like experiences, providing the type of close attention and immediate response associated with apprenticeship.

From Traditional to Cognitive Apprenticeship

In her study of a tailor shop in Africa, Lave (1988) identified the central features of traditional apprenticeship. First, traditional apprenticeship focuses on specific methods for carrying out tasks. Second, skills are instrumental to the accomplishment of meaningful real-world tasks, and learning is embedded in a social and functional context, unlike schooling where skills and knowledge are usually abstracted from their use in the world. Apprentices learn domain-specific methods through a combination of what Lave called observation, coaching, and practice. In this sequence of activities, the apprentice repeatedly observes the master modeling the target process, which usually involves a number of different but interrelated subskills. The apprentice then attempts to execute the process with guidance and coaching from the master. A key aspect of coaching is guided participation: the close support, which the master provides, to help the novice complete an entire task, even before the novice has acquired every skill required. As the learner develops the needed skills, the master reduces his or her participation, providing fewer hints and less feedback to the learner. Eventually, the master fades away completely, when the apprentice has learned to smoothly execute the whole task.

Of course, most people think of traditional trades when they hear the term *apprenticeship* – like shoemaking or farming. We realized that the concept of apprenticeship must be updated to make it relevant to modern subjects like reading, writing, and mathematics. We called this updated concept "cognitive apprenticeship" to emphasize two issues (Brown, Collins, & Duguid, 1989; Collins, Brown, & Newman, 1989).

First, the term *apprenticeship* emphasizes that cognitive apprenticeship was aimed primarily at teaching the processes that experts use to handle complex tasks. Like traditional apprenticeship, cognitive apprenticeship emphasizes that knowledge must be used in solving real-world problems. Conceptual knowledge is learned in a variety of contexts, encouraging both a deeper understanding of the meaning of the concepts themselves, and a rich web of memorable associations between them and the problem-solving contexts. This dual focus on expert processes and learning in context are shared by both traditional apprenticeship and cognitive apprenticeship.

Second, the term *cognitive* emphasizes that the focus is on cognitive skills, rather than physical ones. Traditional apprenticeship evolved to teach domains in which the target skills are externally visible, and thus readily available to both student and teacher for observation, refinement, and correction, and bear a transparent relationship to concrete products. But given the way that most subjects are taught in school, teachers cannot make fine adjustments in students' application of skill and knowledge to tasks, because they can't see the cognitive processes in students' heads. By the same token, students do not usually have access to the problem-solving processes of instructors as a basis for learning through observation. Before apprenticeship methods can be applied to learn cognitive skills, the learning environment has to be changed to make these thought processes visible. Cognitive apprenticeship is designed to bring these cognitive processes into the open, where students can observe and practice them.

There are two major differences between cognitive apprenticeship and traditional apprenticeship. First, because traditional apprenticeship is set in the workplace, the problems and tasks given to learners arise not from pedagogical concerns, but from the demands of the workplace. Because the job selects the tasks for students to practice, traditional apprenticeship is limited in what it can teach. Cognitive apprenticeship differs from traditional apprenticeship in that tasks and problems are chosen to illustrate the power of certain techniques, to give students practice in applying these methods in diverse settings, and to increase the complexity of tasks slowly, so that component skills can be integrated. In short, tasks are sequenced to reflect the changing demands of learning.

Second, whereas traditional apprenticeship emphasizes teaching skills in the context of their use, cognitive apprenticeship emphasizes generalizing knowledge so that it can be used in many different settings. Cognitive apprenticeship extends practice to diverse settings and articulates the common principles, so that students learn how to apply their skills in varied contexts.

A Framework for Cognitive Apprenticeship

Cognitive apprenticeship focuses on four dimensions that constitute any learning environment: content, method, sequence, and sociology (see Table 6.1).

Content

Recent cognitive research has begun to differentiate the types of knowledge required for expertise. Of course, experts have to master the explicit concepts, facts, and procedures associated with a specialized area – what researchers call *domain knowledge*. This is the type of knowledge that is generally found in school textbooks, lectures, and demonstrations. Examples of domain knowledge in reading are vocabulary, syntax, and phonics rules.

Domain knowledge is necessary but not sufficient for expert performance. In addition, experts know how use their domain knowledge to solve real-world problems. We call this second kind of knowledge *strategic knowledge*. Research has identified three kinds of strategic knowledge:

1. *Heuristic strategies* are generally effective techniques and approaches for accomplishing tasks that might be regarded as "tricks of the trade"; they don't always work, but when they do, they are quite helpful. Most heuristics are tacitly acquired by experts through the practice of solving problems. However, there have been noteworthy attempts to address heuristic learning explicitly (Schoenfeld, 1985). In mathematics, a heuristic for solving problems is to try to find a solution for simple cases and see if the solution generalizes.
2. *Control strategies*, or *metacognitive strategies*, control the process of carrying out a task. Control strategies have monitoring, diagnostic, and remedial components; decisions about how to proceed in a task depend

Table 6.1. *Principles for designing cognitive apprenticeship environments*

Content	*types of knowledge required for expertise*
Domain knowledge	subject matter specific concepts, facts, and procedures
Heuristic strategies	generally applicable techniques for accomplishing tasks
Control strategies	general approaches for directing one's solution process
Learning strategies	knowledge about how to learn new concepts, facts, and procedures
Methods	*ways to promote the development of expertise*
Modeling	teacher performs a task so students can observe
Coaching	teacher observes and facilitates while students perform a task
Scaffolding	teacher provides supports to help students perform a task
Articulation	teacher encourages students to verbalize their knowledge and thinking
Reflection	teacher enables students to compare their performance with others
Exploration	teacher invites students to pose and solve their own problems
Sequencing	*keys to ordering learning activities*
Increasing complexity	meaningful tasks gradually increasing in difficulty
Increasing diversity	practice in a variety of situations to emphasize broad application
Global to local skills	focus on conceptualizing the whole task before executing the parts
Sociology	*social characteristics of learning environments*
Situated learning	students learn in the context of working on realistic tasks
Community of practice	communication about different ways to accomplish meaningful tasks
Intrinsic motivation	students set personal goals to seek skills and solutions
Cooperation	students work together to accomplish their goals

on an assessment of one's current state relative to one's goals, on an analysis of current difficulties, and on the strategies available for dealing with difficulties. For example, a comprehension monitoring strategy might be to try to state the main point of a section one has just read; if one cannot do so, it might be best to reread parts of the text.

3. *Learning strategies* are strategies for learning domain knowledge, heuristic strategies, and control strategies. Knowledge about how to learn ranges from general strategies for exploring a new domain to more specific strategies for extending or reconfiguring knowledge in solving problems or carrying out complex tasks. For example, if students want to learn to solve problems better, they need to learn how to relate each step in the example problems worked in textbooks to the principles discussed in the text (Chi, Bassok, Lewis, Reimann, & Glaser, 1989). If students want to write better, they need to learn to analyze others' texts for strengths and weaknesses.

Method

Strategic knowledge is often *tacit knowledge*: experts apply strategies without being consciously aware of exactly what they are doing. Domain knowledge alone provides insufficient clues for many students about how to solve problems and accomplish tasks in a domain. Teaching methods that emphasize apprenticeship are designed to give students the opportunity to observe, engage in, and discover expert strategic knowledge in context.

The six teaching methods associated with cognitive apprenticeship fall roughly into three groups. The first three methods (modeling, coaching, and scaffolding) are the core of traditional apprenticeship. They are designed to help students acquire an integrated set of skills through processes of observation and guided practice. The next two methods (articulation and reflection) are designed to help students focus their observations and gain conscious access and control of their own problem-solving strategies. The final method (exploration) is aimed at encouraging learner autonomy, not only in carrying out expert problem-solving processes, but also in formulating the problems to be solved.

1. *Modeling* involves an expert performing a task so that the students can observe and build a conceptual model of the processes that are required to accomplish it. In cognitive domains, this requires the externalization of usually internal processes and activities. For example, a teacher might model the reading process by reading aloud in one voice, while verbalizing her thought processes in another voice (Collins & Smith, 1982). In mathematics, Schoenfeld (1985) models the process of solving problems by thinking aloud while trying to solve novel problems students bring to class. Recent research suggests that delaying expert modeling of a task until students have tried to generate their own ideas and strategies for performing the task is particularly effective (Kapur, 2008; Schwartz & Martin, 2004).

2. *Coaching* consists of observing students while they carry out tasks and offering hints, challenges, scaffolding, feedback, modeling, reminders, and new tasks aimed at bringing their performance closer to expert performance. Coaching relates to specific problems that arise as the student attempts to accomplish a task. In Palincsar and Brown's (1984) reciprocal teaching of reading, the teacher coaches students while they formulate questions on the text, clarify their difficulties, generate summaries, and make predictions about what will come next.

3. *Scaffolding* refers to the supports the teacher provides to help the student carry out a task (Wood, Bruner, & Ross, 1976). Coaching refers broadly to all the different ways that coaches foster learning, whereas scaffolding refers more narrowly to the supports provided to the learner. These supports can take the form of either suggestions or help, as in Palincsar and Brown's (1984) reciprocal teaching, or they can take the form of

physical supports, as with the cue cards used by Scardamalia, Bereiter, and Steinbach (1984) to facilitate writing, or the short skis used to teach downhill skiing (Burton, Brown, & Fisher, 1984). The timing of the supports is critical. One approach is to provide support at the beginning, and then *fade* the support by gradually removing it until students are on their own. Another approach is to provide the support only after the learner is at an impasse or has failed to perform a task. Research suggests that withholding support up front and providing it only after learners have failed to perform a task is very effective (Kapur, 2012; Schwartz & Martin, 2004; VanLehn, Siler, Murray, Yamauchi, & Baggett, 2003).

4. *Articulation* includes any method of getting students to explicitly state their knowledge, reasoning, or problem-solving processes in a domain. Inquiry teaching (Collins & Stevens, 1983) is a strategy of questioning students to lead them to articulate and refine their understanding. Also, teachers can encourage students to articulate their thoughts as they carry out their problem solving, or have students assume the critic or monitor role in cooperative activities in order to articulate their ideas to other students. For example, an inquiry teacher in reading might question students about why one summary of the text is good but another is poor, in order to get them to formulate an explicit model of a good summary. In mathematics, a teacher may ask for a comparison of incorrect, suboptimal, and correct solutions in order to get students to attend to the critical features of the targeted concept (Kapur & Bielaczyc, 2012).

5. *Reflection* involves enabling students to compare their own problem-solving processes with those of an expert, another student, and ultimately, an internal cognitive model of expertise. Reflection is enhanced by the use of various techniques for "replaying" the performances of both expert and novice for comparison. Some form of "abstracted replay," in which the critical features of expert and student performance are highlighted, is desirable (Collins & Brown, 1988). For reading, writing, or problem solving, methods to encourage reflection might consist of recording students as they think out loud and then replaying the tape for comparison with the thinking of experts and other students.

6. *Exploration* involves guiding students to problem solving on their own. Enabling them to do exploration is critical, if they are to learn how to frame questions or problems that are interesting and that they can solve. Exploration as a method of teaching involves setting general goals for students and then encouraging them to focus on particular subgoals of interest to them, or even to revise the general goals as they come upon something more interesting to pursue. For example, the teacher might send the students to the library to investigate and write about theories as to why the dinosaurs disappeared. In mathematics, a teacher might ask students to design solutions to complex problems that target concepts they have not learned yet. Even though exploration of the problem and

solution spaces might initially lead to incorrect solutions, the teacher can consolidate and build on such an exploration to teach the targeted concepts (Kapur & Rummel, 2012).

Sequencing

Cognitive apprenticeship provides some principles to guide the sequencing of learning activities.

1. *Increasing complexity* refers to sequencing of tasks, such that more of the skills and concepts necessary for expert performance are required (Burton, Brown, & Fisher, 1984; White, 1984). For example, in reading, increasing task complexity might consist of progressing from relatively short texts – with simple syntax and concrete description – to texts in which complexly interrelated ideas and the use of abstractions make interpretation difficult.
2. *Increasing diversity* refers to sequencing of tasks so that a wider variety of strategies or skills is required. As a skill becomes well learned, it becomes increasingly important that tasks requiring a diversity of skills and strategies be introduced, so that the student learns to distinguish the conditions under which they apply. Moreover, as students learn to apply skills to more diverse problems, their strategies acquire a richer net of contextual associations and thus are more readily available for use with unfamiliar or novel problems. For mathematics, task diversity might be attained by intermixing very different types of problems, such as asking students to solve problems that require them to use a combination of algebraic and geometric techniques.
3. *Global before local skills*. In tailoring, apprentices learn to put together a garment from precut pieces before learning to cut out the pieces themselves (Lave, 1988). The chief effect of this sequencing principle is to allow students to build a conceptual map of the task before attending to the details of the terrain (Norman, 1973). Having a clear conceptual model of the overall activity helps learners make sense of the part they are carrying out, thus improving their ability to monitor their progress and develop self-correction skills. In algebra, for example, computers might carry out low-level computations – the local skills – so that students can concentrate on the global structure of the task, and the higher-order reasoning and strategies required to solve a complex, authentic problem.

Sociology

Tailoring apprentices learn their craft not in a special, segregated learning environment, but in a busy tailoring shop. They are surrounded by both masters and other apprentices, all engaged in the target skills at varying levels of expertise. And they are expected to engage in activities that contribute directly to the production of garments, advancing toward independent skilled production. As a result, apprentices learn skills in the context of their application to real-world problems, within a culture focused on expert practice. Furthermore, aspects of the social organization of apprenticeship encourage productive beliefs about the nature of learning and expertise that are significant to learners' motivation, confidence, and most importantly, their orientation toward problems they encounter as they learn. These considerations suggest several characteristics affecting the sociology of learning.

1. *Situated learning.* A critical element in fostering learning is having students carry out tasks and solve problems in an environment that reflects the nature of such tasks in the world (Brown, Collins, & Duguid, 1989; Lave & Wenger, 1991). For example, reading and writing instruction might be situated in the context of students creating a Web site about their town. Dewey created a situated learning environment in his experimental school by having the students design and build a clubhouse (Cuban, 1984), a task that emphasizes arithmetic and planning skills.

2. *Community of practice* refers to the creation of a learning environment in which the participants actively communicate about and engage in the skills involved in expertise (Lave & Wenger, 1991; Wenger, 1998). Such a community leads to a sense of ownership characterized by personal investment and mutual dependency. It cannot be forced, but it can be fostered by common projects and shared experiences. Activities designed to engender a community of practice for reading might engage students in discussing how they interpret difficult texts.

3. *Intrinsic motivation.* Related to the issue of situated learning and the creation of a community of practice is the need to promote intrinsic motivation for learning. Lepper and Greene (1979) discuss the importance of creating learning environments in which students perform tasks because the tasks are intrinsically related to a goal of interest to the students, rather than for some extrinsic reason, like getting a good grade or pleasing the teacher. In reading and writing, for example, intrinsic motivation might be achieved by students communicating with students in another part of the world using electronic mail.

4. *Exploiting cooperation* refers to having students work together in a way that fosters cooperative problem solving. Learning through cooperative problem solving is both a powerful motivator and a powerful mechanism for extending learning resources. In reading, activities to exploit cooperation might involve having students break up into pairs, where one student articulates their thinking process while reading, and the other student questions the first student about different inferences.

Themes in Research on Cognitive Apprenticeship

In the years since cognitive apprenticeship was first introduced, scholars have conducted extensive research toward developing learning environments that embody many of these principles. Several of these principles have been developed further, in particular situated learning, communities of practice, communities of learners, scaffolding, articulation, and reflection.

Situated Learning

Goal-based scenarios (Nowakowski et al., 1994; Schank, Fano, Bell, & Jona, 1994) embody many of the principles of cognitive apprenticeship. They can be set either in computer-based environments or naturalistic environments. Learners are given real-world tasks and the scaffolding they need to carry out such tasks. For example, in one goal-based scenario, learners are asked to advise married couples as to whether their children are likely to have sickle-cell anemia, a genetically linked disease. To advise the couples, learners must find out how different genetic combinations lead to the disease and run tests to determine the parents' genetic makeup. There are scaffolds in the system to support learners, such as various recorded experts who offer advice. Other goal-based scenarios support learners in a wide variety of challenging tasks, such as putting together a news broadcast, solving an environmental problem, or developing a computer reservation system for a hotel. Goal-based scenarios make it possible to embed cognitive skills and knowledge in the kinds of contexts where they are to be used. So people learn not only basic competencies, but also when and how to apply the competencies.

Video and computer technology has enhanced the ability to create simulation environments where students are learning skills in context. A novel use of video technology is the Jasper series developed by the Cognition and Technology Group (1997) at Vanderbilt University to teach middle school mathematics. In a series of 15–20-minute videos, students are put into various problem-solving contexts, such as developing a business plan for a school fair or a rescue plan for a wounded eagle. The problems are quite difficult to solve and reflect the complex problem solving and planning that occurs in real life. Middle school students work in groups for several days to solve each problem. Solving the problems develops a much richer understanding of the underlying mathematical concepts than traditional school mathematics problems.

These kinds of situated learning tasks are different from most school tasks, because school tasks are decontextualized. Imagine learning tennis by being told the rules and practicing the forehand, backhand, and serve without ever playing or seeing a tennis match. If tennis were taught that way, it would be hard to see the point of what you were learning. But in school, students are taught algebra and history without being given any idea of how they might be useful in their lives. That is not how a coach would teach you to play tennis. A coach might first show you how to grip and swing the racket, but very soon you would be hitting the ball and playing games. A good coach would have you go back and forth between playing games and working on particular skills – combining global and situated learning with focused local knowledge. The essential idea in situated learning is to tightly couple a focus on accomplishing tasks with a focus on the underlying competencies needed to carry out the tasks.

Communities of Practice

Lave and Wenger (1991; Wenger, 1998) have written extensively about communities of practice and how learning takes place in these contexts. They introduced the notion of *legitimate peripheral participation* to describe the way that apprentices participate in a community of practice. They described four cases of apprenticeship and emphasized how apprentices' identities derive from becoming part of the community of workers, as they become more central members in the community. They also noted that an apprenticeship relationship can be unproductive for learning, as in the case of the meat cutters they studied, where the apprentices worked in a separate room and were isolated from the working community. Productive apprenticeship depends on opportunities for apprentices to participate legitimately in the community practices that they are learning.

The degree to which people play a central role and are respected by other members of a community determines their sense of identity (Lave & Wenger, 1991). The central roles are those that most directly contribute to the collective activities and knowledge of the community. The motivation to become a more central participant in a community of practice can provide a powerful incentive for learning. Frank Smith (1988) argues that children will learn to read and write if the people they admire read and write. That is, they will want to join the community of literate people and will work hard to become members. Learning to read is part of becoming the kind of person they want to become. Identity is central to deep learning.

Wenger argues that people participate in a variety of communities of practice – at home, at work, at school, and in hobbies. In his view, a community of practice is a group of people participating together to carry out different activities, such as garage bands, ham radio operators, recovering alcoholics, and research scientists. "For individuals, it means that learning is an issue of engaging in and contributing to the practices of their communities. For communities, it means that learning is an issue of refining their practice and ensuring new generations of members. For organizations, it means that learning is an issue of sustaining the interconnected communities of practice through which an organization knows what it knows and thus becomes effective and valuable as an organization" (Wenger, 1998, pp. 7–8).

Communities of Learners

In recent years there has developed a "learning communities" approach to education that builds on Lave and Wenger's (1991) notion of a community of practice. In a learning community, the goal is to advance the collective knowledge of the community, with the belief that this will ultimately support the growth of individual knowledge (Scardamalia & Bereiter, 1994). The defining quality of a learning community is that there is a culture of learning, in which everyone is involved in a collective effort of understanding (Brown & Campione, 1996).

A learning community should ideally have these four characteristics (Bielaczyc & Collins, 1999): (1) diversity of expertise among its members, who are valued for their contributions and given support to develop, (2) a shared objective of continually advancing the collective knowledge and skills, (3) an emphasis on learning how to learn, and (4) mechanisms for sharing what is learned. It is not necessary that each member assimilate everything that the community knows, but each should know who within the community has relevant expertise to address any problem. This marks a departure from the traditional view of schooling, with its emphasis on individual knowledge and performance, and the expectation that students will acquire the same body of knowledge at the same time.

Brown and Campione (1996) have developed a model they call Fostering a Community of Learners (FCL) for grades one through eight. The FCL approach promotes a diversity of interests and talents in order to enrich the knowledge of the classroom community as a whole. The focus of FCL classrooms is on the subject areas of biology and ecology, with central topics such as endangered species and food chains. There is an overall structure of students (1) carrying out research on the central topics in small groups where each student specializes in a particular subtopic area, (2) sharing what they learn with other students in their research group and in other groups, and (3) preparing for and participating in some "consequential task" that requires students to combine their individual learning so that all members in the group come to a deeper understanding of the main topic and subtopics. Teachers orchestrate students' work and support students when they need help.

In the FCL model there are usually three research cycles per year. A cycle begins with a set of shared materials meant to build a common knowledge base. Students then break into research groups that focus on a specific research topic related to the central topic. For example, if the class is studying food chains, then the class may break into five or six research groups that each focus on a specific aspect of food chains, such as photosynthesis, consumers, energy exchange, and so forth. Students research their subtopic as a group and individually, with individuals "majoring" by following their own research agendas within the limits of the subtopic. Students also engage in regular "crosstalk" sessions, where the different groups explain their work to the other groups, ask and answer questions, and refine their understanding. The research activities include reciprocal teaching (Palincsar & Brown, 1984), guided writing and composing, consultation with subject matter experts outside the classroom, and cross-age tutoring. In the final part of the cycle, students from each of the subtopic groups come together to form a "jigsaw" group (Aronson, 1978) in order to share learning on the various subtopics and to work together on some consequential task. Thus, in the jigsaw, all pieces of the puzzle come together to form a complete understanding. The consequential tasks "bring the research cycle to an end, force students to share knowledge across groups, and act as occasions for exhibition and reflection" (Brown & Campione, 1996, p. 303).

A key idea in the learning communities approach is to advance the collective knowledge of the community, and in that way to help individual students learn. The culture of schools often discourages sharing of knowledge by preventing students from working on problems or projects together and from sharing or discussing their ideas. Testing and grading are administered individually, and when taking tests, students are prevented from relying on other resources, such as other students, books, or computers. This traditional approach, often referred to as *instructionism* (see Sawyer, Chapter 1, this volume), is aimed at ensuring that individual students have all the knowledge in their heads that is included in the curriculum. Thus the learning community approach is a radical departure from the instructionist approach that dominates in many schools.

Scaffolding

Scaffolding is a form of support that enables students to tackle complex, difficult tasks that are beyond their ability to engage with independently (Reiser & Tabak, Chapter 3, this volume). Scaffolding can take the form of structured or highly constrained tasks; help systems that give advice when the learner does not know what to do or is confused; guided tours on how to do things; or hints when needed. One common form of scaffolding is to provide an overall structure of a complex task, such that students are guided to individual components of the task at the appropriate moment. The overall structure shows them how each component fits into the overall task. Quintana and colleagues (2004) suggest twenty specific strategies for designing scaffolds to support sense making, inquiry, articulation, and reflection in computer-based learning environments. In most situations, scaffolding naturally *fades* as learners are able to accomplish tasks on their own.

Reiser (2004; Reiser & Tabak, Chapter 3, this volume) points out that most of the work on scaffolding has focused on *structuring* the task for students, in order to make it easier for learners to accomplish the task. But he emphasizes that scaffolding plays another important role – *problematizing* students' performance, or explicitly questioning the key content and strategies used during the task, so that students reflect more on their learning. While this may make the task more difficult, it can facilitate their learning.

The term *scaffolding* was first applied to teaching and learning by Wood, Bruner, and Ross (1976). The term later became associated with Vygotsky's (1978) notion of the *zone of proximal development*, which described how adults can support learners to accomplish tasks that they cannot accomplish on their own. This requires a dynamic determination of what and how learners fail to accomplish a task, and using this information to adapt subsequent instruction and teaching. Hence, the focus of research on scaffolding (see, for example, Davis & Miyake, 2004; Reiser & Tabak, Chapter 3, this volume) has been on supporting individuals in their learning. But Kolodner and colleagues (2003) point out that it is important to scaffold groups as well as individuals. So for example, in their work teaching science, they first provide students with focused collaboration activities to solve simple problems, which they call "launcher units." Engaging in these activities and reflecting on them helps students to collaborate more effectively and to understand the value of collaboration.

In schools, needing to ask for extra help often implies that the student is inferior. Hence, students are reluctant to ask for help for fear of being stigmatized. When scaffolding is provided by computers, it comes without criticism and without others knowing that the student needed help. Computers offer the kind of scaffolding that avoids stigmatization and provides individualized instructional support.

Articulation

In order to abstract learning from particular contexts so that it will transfer to new contexts, it is important to articulate one's thinking and knowledge in terms that are not specific to a particular context (Bransford, Brown, & Cocking, 2000). There have been several very successful examples of how effective group discussions can be as learning environments in classrooms. For example, Lampert (Lampert, Rittenhouse, & Crumbaugh, 1996) showed how fifth grade children can form a community of learners about important mathematical concepts. She engaged students in discussion of their conjectures and interpretations of each other's reasoning. Techniques of this kind have been very successful with even younger children (Cobb & Bauersfeld, 1995) and may partly underlie the success of Japanese mathematical education (Stigler & Hiebert, 1999).

A notable method for fostering articulation in science is the Itakura method developed in Japan (Hatano & Inagaki, 1991). First, students make different predictions about what will happen in a simple experiment, where they are likely to have different expectations. For example, one experiment involves lowering a clay ball on a string into water and predicting what will happen. After students make their initial predictions, they discuss and defend among themselves why they think their predictions are correct. After any revisions in their predictions, the experiment is performed and discussion ensues as to why the result came out the way it did.

Sandoval and Reiser (2004) have developed a computer system called the Biology Guided Inquiry Learning Environment (BGuILE) that supports students in making scientific arguments in the context of population genetics. The system presents the students with a mystery: Why did some of the finches in the Galapagos Islands die during a period of drought while others survived? To solve the mystery, students have to analyze extensive data that were collected by scientists and come up with a reasoned conclusion as to why some finches died while others survived. The Explanation Constructor tool in the system prompts the students to put in all the pieces of a sound genetics-based argument, after they have decided what caused some of the finches to die. Hence, the system scaffolds students to articulate their argument in a much more explicit form than they would normally do.

The Knowledge Forum environment developed by Scardamalia and Bereiter (Chapter 20, this volume; 1994) is an environment where students articulate their ideas in writing and exchange their ideas through a computer network. The model involves students investigating problems in different subject areas over a period of weeks or months. As students work, they enter their ideas and research findings as notes in a knowledge base that is accessible to all computers in the network. The software scaffolds students in constructing their notes through features such as theory-building scaffolds (e.g., "My Theory," "I Need to Understand") or debate scaffolds (e.g., "Evidence For"). Students can read through the knowledge base, adding text, graphics, questions, links to other notes, and comments on each other's work. When someone has commented on another student's work, the system automatically notifies them about it.

The central activity of the community is contributing to the communal knowledge base. Contributions can take the form of (a) *individual notes*, in which students state problems, advance initial theories, summarize what needs to be understood in order to progress on a problem or to improve their theories, provide a drawing or diagram, and so forth, (b) *views*, in which students or teachers create graphical organizations of related notes, (c) *build-ons*, which allow students to connect new notes to existing notes, and (d) *"Rise Above It" notes*, which synthesize notes in the knowledge base. Any of these kinds of contributions can be jointly authored. The goal is to engage students in progressive knowledge building, where they continually develop their understanding through problem identification, research, and community discourse. The emphasis is on progress toward collective goals of understanding, rather than individual learning and performance.

Learning designs that foster *productive failure* (Kapur, 2008) give students opportunities to articulate and externalize their domain knowledge to generate representations and solutions to a novel problem. In the first phase of such a learning design, students struggle to come up with a solution to a problem that is just beyond what they have learned previously – such as writing a formula to characterize the variance of a mathematical distribution or solving an ill-structured problem in kinematics. This *generation phase* provides opportunities for students to explore the benefits and weaknesses of multiple representations and solutions, as well as reason with and refine them in a flexible and adaptive manner. The generation phase is followed by a *consolidation phase* where students are provided with an explanation and solution to the problem (e.g., Kapur, 2012), or an opportunity to discern the deep structure of the problem (e.g., Kapur, 2008). In the consolidation phase, students learn the targeted concept by organizing their student-generated representations and solutions into canonical ones (for a fuller description, see Kapur & Bielaczyc, 2012). Over a series of studies, Kapur and colleagues have demonstrated that productive-failure learning designs give students a level of procedural fluency similar to direct instruction, but result in significantly better conceptual and transfer gains.

Reflection

Reflection encourages learners to look back on their performance in a situation and compare their performance to other performances, such as their own previous performances and those of experts. Reflection has received much attention as a vital aspect of the learning process for both children and adults. Schon (1983) describes how systematic reflection on practice is critical for many professionals engaged in complex activities. Designers of learning environments often build supports for reflection into tasks by asking students to discuss and reflect on the strategies used to guide their actions. Reflection can highlight the critical aspects of a performance and encourage learners to think about what makes for a good performance and how they might improve in the future.

There are two forms that reflection can take, both of which are enhanced by technology: 1) comparison of your performance to that of others, and 2) comparison of your performance to a set of criteria for evaluating performances:

- *Comparison of your performance to that of others:* Because technology makes it possible to record performances, people can look back at how they did a task. One useful form of reflection is an "abstracted replay," where the critical decisions made are replayed (Collins & Brown, 1988). One system that teaches complex problem solving allows learners to compare their decisions in solving a complex problem to those of an expert, so that they can see how they might have done better. This is called *perceptual learning* (Bransford, Franks, Vye, & Sherwood, 1989) because it helps learners perceive what factors are associated with successful problem solving.

- *Comparison of your performance to a set of criteria for evaluating performances:* One of the most effective ways to improve performance is to evaluate how you did with respect to a set of explicitly articulated criteria that are associated with good performance. For example, White and Frederiksen (1998) showed that students who evaluated their performance on projects using a set of eight diverse criteria improved much more than students who carried out the same tasks but did not reflect on their performance in the same way. Furthermore, self-evaluation on the eight criteria helped the weaker students much more than the stronger students.

Effective cognitive apprenticeship asks learners to think about what they are going to do beforehand, try to do what they have planned, and reflect back on how well what they did came out (Gardner, 1991). If learners are presented with criteria to evaluate what they did, this will help them as they plan what they do on the next cycle.

The wide availability of computers and other recording technologies makes performances easier to produce and to reflect on. For example, students can now produce their own news broadcasts, musical performances, or plays, either on audiotape, videotape, or cable television, that go out to other schools or to parents. Furthermore, they can play these back, reflect on them, and edit them until they are polished. One of the best examples of the use of technology for recording performances has been in Arts Propel (Gardner, 1991) with its cycle of performing, reflecting on the performance in terms of a set of criteria, and then performing again.

Conclusion

As these examples illustrate, extensive research over the past 25 years has incorporated the principles of cognitive apprenticeship in the design of learning environments. As computer-based learning environments become more pervasive, there is likely to be continued development of new ways to embody these principles in their design.

References

Aronson, E. (1978). *The jigsaw classroom.* Beverly Hills, CA: Sage Publications.

Bielaczyc, K., & Collins, A. (1999). Learning communities in classrooms: A reconceptualization of educational practice. In C. M. Reigeluth (Ed.), *Instructional-design theories and models: A new paradigm of instructional theory* (pp. 269–292). Mahwah, NJ: Lawrence Erlbaum Associates.

Bransford, J. D., Brown, A. L., & Cocking, R. (2000). *How people learn: Brain, mind, experience and school.* Expanded Edition. Washington, DC: National Academies Press.

Bransford, J. D., Franks, J. J., Vye, N. J., & Sherwood, R. D. (1989). New approaches to instruction: Because wisdom can't be told. In S. Vosniadou & A. Ortony (Eds.), *Similarity and analogical reasoning* (pp. 470–497). New York: Cambridge University Press.

Brown, A., & Campione, J. (1996). Psychological theory and the design of innovative learning environments: On procedures, principles, and systems. In L. Schauble & R. Glaser (Eds.), *Innovations in learning: New environments for education* (pp. 289–325). Mahwah, NJ: Lawrence Erlbaum Associates.

Brown, J. S., Collins, A., & Duguid, P. (1989). Situated cognition and the culture of learning. *Educational Researcher*, 18(1), 32–42.

Burton, R., Brown, J. S., & Fischer, G. (1984). Skiing as a model of instruction. In B. Rogoff & J. Lave (Eds.), *Everyday cognition: Its developmental and social context* (pp. 139–150). Cambridge, MA: Harvard University Press.

Chi, M. T. H., Bassok, M., Lewis, M. W., Reimann, P., & Glaser, R. (1989). Self-Explanations: How students study and use examples in learning to solve problems. *Cognitive Science*, 13, 145–182.

Cobb, P., & Bauersfeld, H. (Eds.) (1995). *The emergence of mathematical meaning: Interaction in classroom cultures*. Mahwah, NJ: Lawrence Erlbaum Associates.

Cognition and Technology Group at Vanderbilt. (1997). *The Jasper Project: Lessons in curriculum, instruction, assessment, and professional development*. Mahwah, NJ: Lawrence Erlbaum Associates.

Collins, A., & Brown, J. S. (1988). The computer as a tool for learning through reflection. In H. Mandl & A. Lesgold (Eds.), *Learning issues for intelligent tutoring systems* (pp. 1–18). New York: Springer.

Collins, A., Brown, J. S., & Newman, S. E. (1989). Cognitive apprenticeship: Teaching the craft of reading, writing, and mathematics. In L. B. Resnick (Ed.), *Knowing, learning, and instruction: Essays in honor of Robert Glaser* (pp. 453–494). Hillsdale, NJ: Lawrence Erlbaum Associates.

Collins, A., & Smith, E. E. (1982). Teaching the process of reading comprehension. In D. K. Detterman & R. J. Sternberg (Eds.), *How much and how can intelligence be increased?* (pp. 173–185). Norwood, NJ: Ablex.

Collins, A., & Stevens, A. L. (1983). A cognitive theory of interactive teaching. In C. M. Reigeluth (Ed.), *Instructional design theories and models: An overview* (pp. 247–278). Hillsdale, NJ: Lawrence Erlbaum Associates.

Cuban, L. (1984). *How teachers taught*. New York: Longman.

Davis, E. A., & Miyake, N. (Eds.) (2004). Special issue: Scaffolding. *Journal of the Learning Sciences*, 13(3), 265–451.

Gardner, H. (1991). Assessment in context: The alternative to standardized testing. In B. Gifford & C. O'Connor (Eds.), *Future assessments: Changing views of aptitude, achievement, and instruction* (pp.77–120). Boston: Kluwer.

Hatano, G., & Inagaki, K. (1991). Sharing cognition through collective comprehension activity. In L. Resnick, J. Levin, & S. D. Teasley (Eds.), *Perspectives on socially shared cognition* (pp. 331–348). Washington, DC: American Psychological Association.

Kapur, M. (2008). Productive failure. *Cognition and Instruction*, 26(3), 379–424.

Kapur, M. (2012). Productive failure in learning the concept of variance. *Instructional Science*, 40(4), 651–672.

Kapur, M., & Bielaczyc, K. (2012). Designing for productive failure. *Journal of the Learning Sciences*, 21(1), 45–83.

Kapur, M., & Rummel, N. (2012). Productive failure in learning and problem solving. *Instructional Science*, 40(4), 645–650.

Kolodner, J. L., Camp, P. J., Crismond, D., Fasse, B., Gray, J., Holbrook, J., Puntambekar, S., & Ryan, M. (2003). Problem-based learning meets case-based reasoning in the middle-school science classroom: Putting learning-by-design into practice. *Journal of the Learning Sciences,* 12(4), 495–547.

Lampert, M., Rittenhouse, P., & Crumbaugh, C. (1996). Agreeing to disagree: Developing sociable mathematical discourse. In D. Olson & N. Torrance (Eds.), *Handbook of Education and Human Development* (pp. 731–764). Oxford: Blackwell's Press.

Lave, J. (1988). *The culture of acquisition and the practice of understanding* (Report No. IRL88–0007). Palo Alto, CA: Institute for Research on Learning.

Lave, J., & Wenger, E. (1991). *Situated learning: Legitimate peripheral participation.* New York: Cambridge University Press.

Lepper, M. R., & Greene, D. (1979). *The hidden costs of reward.* Hillsdale, NJ: Lawrence Erlbaum Associates.

Norman, D. A. (1973). Memory, knowledge, and the answering of questions. In R. L. Solso (Ed.), *Contemporary issues in cognitive psychology: The Loyola symposium* (pp. 135–165). Washington, DC: Winston.

Nowakowski, A., Campbell, R., Monson, D., Montgomery, J., Moffett, C., Acovelli, M., Schank, R., & Collins, A. (1994). Goal-based scenarios: A new approach to professional education. *Educational Technology*, 34(9), 3–32.

Palincsar, A. S., & Brown, A. L. (1984). Reciprocal teaching of comprehension-fostering and monitoring activities. *Cognition and Instruction*, 1(2), 117–175.

Quintana, C., Reiser, B. J., Davis, E. A., Krajcik, J., Fretz, E., Duncan, R. G., Kyza, E., Edelson, D., & Soloway, E. (2004). A scaffolding design framework for software to support science inquiry. *Journal of the Learning Sciences*, 13(3), 337–386.

Reiser, B. J. (2004). Scaffolding complex learning: The mechanisms of structuring and problematizing student work. *Journal of the Learning Sciences*, 13(3), 273–304.

Sandoval, W. A., & Reiser, B. J. (2004). Explanation-driven inquiry: Integrating conceptual and epistemic scaffolds for scientific inquiry. *Science Education*, 88, 345–372.

Scardamalia, M., & Bereiter, C. (1994). Computer support for knowledge-building communities. *Journal of the Learning Sciences*, 3(3), 265–283.

Scardamalia, M., Bereiter, C., & Steinbach, R. (1984). Teachability of reflective processes in written composition. *Cognitive Science*, 8, 173–190.

Schank, R. C., Fano, A., Bell, B., & Jona, M. (1994). The design of goal-based scenarios. *Journal of the Learning Sciences*, 3(4), 305–346.

Schoenfeld, A. H. (1985). *Mathematical problem solving.* Orlando, FL: Academic Press.

Schon, D. A. (1983). *The reflective practitioner: How professionals think in action.* New York: Basic Books.

Schwartz, D. L., & Martin, T. (2004). Inventing to prepare for future learning: The hidden efficiency of encouraging original student production in statistics instruction. *Cognition and Instruction, 22*(2), 129–184.

Smith, F. (1988). *Joining the literacy club.* Portsmouth, NH: Heinemann.

Stigler, J., & Hiebert, J. (1999). *The teaching gap: Best ideas from the world's teachers for improving education in the classroom.* New York: Free Press.

VanLehn, K., Siler, S., Murray, C., Yamauchi, T., & Baggett, W. B. (2003). Why do only some events cause learning during human tutoring? *Cognition and Instruction, 21*(3), 209–249.

Vygotsky, L. S. (1978). *Mind in society: The development of higher mental processes.* (M. Cole, V. John-Steiner, S. Scribner, & E. Souberman, Eds.) Cambridge, MA: Harvard University Press.

Wenger, E. (1998). *Communities of practice: Learning, meaning, and identity.* New York: Cambridge University Press.

White, B. Y. (1984). Designing computer games to help physics students understand Newton's laws of motion. *Cognition and Instruction, 1*(1), 69–108.

White, B. Y., & Frederiksen, J. R. (1998). Inquiry, modeling, and metacognition: Making science accessible to all students. *Cognition and Instruction, 16*(1), 3–118.

Wood, D., Bruner, J. S., & Ross, G. (1976). The role of tutoring in problem solving. *Journal of Child Psychology and Psychiatry and Allied Disciplines, 17,* 89–100.

7 Learning in Activity

James G. Greeno and Yrjö Engeström

In traditional psychology, learning is studied at the level of the individual. This is true of behaviorism, which studies behaviors of individual organisms, and also of cognitivism, which studies mental processes and structures within individuals' minds. This chapter presents an approach to the study of learning in which the unit of analysis is larger than an individual person – either two or more people, such as a dyad, a group, a classroom, a community, or an individual person working with objects and technological systems. Many learning scientists conduct research at these levels of analysis, and this is part of what distinguishes the field from experimental cognitive psychology, where the usual level of analysis is the individual. We refer to these higher-level learning systems as *activity systems* because the focus of learning sciences research is often on how people learn by engaging in activities in these systems, such as solving a problem or making or designing something. An activity system can be as large as a classroom of students with a teacher, or as small as a single individual interacting with some text or a computer program. Research on activity systems focuses on the ways the individual components act and interact with each other, and also focuses on larger contextualizing systems that provide resources and constraints for those actions and interactions. This definition of activity system is designed to be broad enough to incorporate a range of perspectives that theorize activity systems; these include cultural-historical activity theory (e.g., Engeström, 1987), situated learning (Lave & Wenger, 1991), situated action (Suchman, 1987), distributed cognition (Hutchins & Klauson, 1998), and cultural psychology (Cole, 1996; Rogoff, 2003). We use the term *situative* in this chapter, intending it to refer to the general approach of all these research programs.

In an activity system, regular and recurring patterns of activity are called its *practices*. People who know how to participate in the same shared practices are called a *community of practice*. When individuals want to join a community of practice, they do not know how to participate in these shared practices. Consequently, at first they are *peripheral* members of the community, and their learning trajectory gradually leads them toward participating more fully in the community's practices (Lave & Wenger, 1991).

To illustrate the concept of practices, consider patterns of discourse that occur in school classrooms. Schools are organizations with distinctive practices, and for students to learn in the way that educators value, they need to adapt to the practices associated with the activity systems of schools, including participating in classrooms, study groups, and homework.

A type of episode that occurs frequently in school classrooms is labeled IRE or IRF (Initiation, Response, Evaluation or Feedback). The teacher takes the first turn, I, usually asking a question. Then the teacher calls on a student who takes the second turn, R, giving an answer. The teacher takes the third turn, evaluating the student's answer, E, sometimes adding feedback or providing clarification or elaboration, F (Wells, 1993).

Conversation analysts, especially Schegloff (2007), have intensively studied patterns of turn taking in brief episodes. Schegloff's analyses focus on adjacency pairs, in which two turns complete a functional unit of conversation. We hypothesize that IRE and IRF units are extensions of a common adjacency pair, QA, a question followed by an answer. In much ordinary discourse, QA functions to provide the questioner with information he or she did not have. In IRE or IRF, the teacher who asks a question knows the answer, and information generated in the exchange is whether one or more of the students know the answer. IRE and IRF units are common in much school practice (Bellack, Kliebard, Hyman, & Smith, 1966; Mehan, 1979; Sinclair & Coulthard, 1975).

In IRE and IRF units, the student participant is positioned as a passive participant: someone whose knowledge is being assessed, not as someone who is expected to actively contribute an idea or information toward progress in understanding an issue in the subject matter domain. (See Harré & Van Langenhove, 1999, and Holland, Lachicotte, Skinner, & Cain, 1998, for discussions of positioning and positional identities.) In contrast, learning scientists are working actively with teachers to develop discourse practices in which students are actively participating. Examples include Mercer (1995), who referred to exploratory talk; Resnick, Michaels, and O'Connor (2010), who referred to Accountable Talk;[1] and Chapin, O'Connor, and Anderson (2009), who referred to academically productive talk. For example, Engle and Conant (2002) studied interaction of fifth grade students and their teachers in classroom activities developed in the Fostering Communities of Learners project (Brown & Campione, 1994) as the students worked in groups to

---

[1] Accountable Talk is a registered trademark of the Institute for Learning, University of Pittsburgh. "In the accountable talk form of classroom interaction, the teacher poses a question that calls for a relatively elaborated response. As initial responses come forth, the teacher then presses a group of students to develop explanations, challenges, counterexamples, and questions. The process includes extended exchanges between teacher and student and among students and includes a variety of "talk moves," such as asking other students to explain what the first responder has said, challenging students – sometimes via 'revoicing' a student's contribution ('So let me see if I've got your idea right. Are you saying …?') which makes the students' idea, reformulated by the teacher, available to the entire group" (Resnick et al., 2010, p. 179).

write reports about some endangered species. The analysis focused on the occurrence of an extended debate among the students about how orcas (often called "killer whales") should be classified, as whales or as dolphins.[2] Engle and Conant hypothesized that students would be more deeply engaged and motivated to learn science if they were positioned with authority and accountability. Consequently they attempted to foster a new discourse practice that encouraged problematizing substantive issues in science and that provided resources that supported the students' taking, challenging, and supporting positions on these substantive issues. (We discuss another analysis of the data obtained in this classroom setting, by Engle (2006), later in this chapter.)

In many societies and throughout history, individuals have primarily interacted in activity systems that contained only other members of the same community of practice. In complex modern societies, and specifically in schools, activity systems often include participants who are members of different communities of practice – this can make their participation problematic (see Eckert, 1990), or the resulting diversity can be a source of creative productivity (e.g., Engeström, 2001).

In the remainder of this chapter, we discuss three issues. In Section 2, we present a framework for analyzing the behavior of activity systems and we hypothesize that changes in one of the systems' components – specifically, the desired learning outcome as understood by the students – can be a key component of significant learning by the system. In Section 3, we discuss relations between theories at different levels, specifically between theories that focus on learning by individual participants and theories that focus on learning considered as changes in practices of activity systems (also see Miyake & Kirschner, Chapter 21, this volume, for another way of addressing these distinct levels of analysis). In Section 4, we discuss research on understanding and learning concepts, using the situative perspective that focuses on understanding and learning at the level of activity systems.

A Framework for Analyzing System-Level Activity and Learning

Engeström (1987), building on Vygotsky's (1987) theorizing, developed a framework for analyzing activity systems. In Engeström's framework (see Figure 7.1), the three major components of an activity system are a subject or agent (which can be an individual but also could be a group of people),

---

[2] Both are correct, but the students' sources were inconsistent. Orcas are classified as being in the same phylogenetic family with dolphins, different from whales, but orcas, dolphins, and whales are all included in the phylogenetic order Cetaceans, often referred to as the whales. The "big ol' argument," as the students referred to it, that extended over twelve weeks of their activity, was sparked when they were on a field trip to Sea World, where a staff person told them that many people think that orcas are whales, but they're not – they're dolphins.

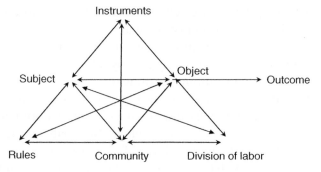

Figure 7.1. *General model of an activity system (from Engeström, 1987, p. 78).*

an object (what the subject works on), and resources, which the subject uses in its effort to transform the object according to a goal. This framework assumes that an activity system has the goal of transforming the object toward a desired outcome. For example, the activity systems found in learning environments have the goal of leading learners toward a desired learning outcome.

To illustrate use of this analytical scheme, consider a task analyzed by Hutchins (1995a). The object of the activity was to determine the location of a U.S. Navy ship, and to represent that position on a chart and in the ship's log. This task, called "fixing a position," was performed by a team of ten seamen and officers at least once per hour. To take a position fix near land, members of the crew sighted known landmarks using instruments called *alidades*, which provide numerical measures of the directions between the ship and the landmarks. These were communicated via a telephone line to the room on the ship's bridge where an officer drew lines, called *Lines of Position*, on a chart from each of the landmarks in the directions reported from the deck. Three Lines of Position were drawn, and they intersected on the chart at the location of the ship. Finally, the officer drew a line from this location in the direction corresponding to the ship's current bearing, and of a length corresponding to the ship's current speed, to indicate the projected path of the ship up to the next position fix.

Using Engeström's framework, the subject (or agent) of this activity was the set of ten naval personnel, and the object was the ship's position at the time of the fix and its representation. The resources used included the alidades, the telephones, and the chart itself.

In this example, no learning necessarily takes place. An analysis of learning by an activity system involves identifying a change in the practices of the system and giving an account of how that change was accomplished. Several recent studies have concluded that an important mechanism leading to change in practices is *an expansion of the subject's understanding of the object*. For example, Engeström (2001) found that a group of children's caregivers expanded the object of their activity from discrete single consultations to long-term care relationships involving more cooperation and communication across administrative units.

In the situative perspective, this *expansivity* is an important quality of learning in activity. Expansivity suggests hypotheses about a distinction made by theorists of organizational learning (e.g., Argyris and Schön, 1978): the distinction between "single-loop learning" and "double-loop learning." In single-loop learning, activities and practices change without changing the underlying understanding of the participants, the goals of the activity, or the uses of resources that can be relevant for achieving the system's goals. Double-loop learning involves a change in the participants' understanding of some fundamental aspect of the activity. Double-loop learning can bring about a radical expansion of the scope and impact of activity in a system, and this expansivity is often observed in learning in activity.

The notion of expansion was theoretically elaborated by Engeström (1987), and the theory of expansive learning has generated a line of studies reviewed by Engeström and Sannino (2010). An example would be the expansion of the object of a health care activity from a discrete single consultation to a long-term care relationship involving various caregivers (Engeström, 2001). This example demonstrates that expansion minimally includes a temporal and a socio-spatial dimension (Engeström, Puonti, & Seppänen, 2003). The learning challenge for the participants is to acquire mastery of work on the expanded object while designing and implementing the necessary changes in the activity system.

A limited version of the object of classroom instruction is for students to acquire routine knowledge and procedural skill, so they can perform well on tests in which they need to recite accurately or apply procedures correctly. A more expansive understanding of the object of instruction is for students to understand concepts and principles of a domain and develop productive habits of mind that support productive and generative use of concepts and principles. Learning scientists are engaged in research and development that investigates conditions in which this more expansive object of learning takes place.

Another aspect of activity that can be involved in double-loop learning is the role of the subject (or, alternatively, the agency of the participants). An example is provided by Ginnett's (1993) early study of airline crews at work. Ginnett had the opportunity to observe and compare the performance of two kinds of captains: those assessed by check airmen as being exceedingly good at creating highly efficient teams (HI-E captains) and those who received low ratings on this same ability (LO-E captains). The performance Ginnett observed was a formal crew briefing before the first leg of a new crew complement, conducted in the terminal one hour before departure. The most interesting finding had to do with how the captains talked about the crew boundaries. The HI-E captains worked to expand the team boundaries. They included in "we" the total flight crew, as opposed to some of the LO-E captains, who only included the cockpit crew and referred to flight attendants as "you." The HI-E captains also tried to include gate personnel, maintenance workers, air traffic controllers, and in some cases even the passengers as part of the group – not as outsiders (Ginnett, 1993, p. 87).

Ginnett also found that the best captains kept "elaborating and expanding" the routines of the crew (Ginnett, 1993, pp. 96–97). In Ginnett's data, such expansive moves were initiated by skilled captains who had the courage to deviate from the routine by "disavowing perfection": "They make a statement suggesting they don't know something about a particular issue even though the information is often quite readily available.... They are open about dealing with their own vulnerabilities" (Ginnett, 1993, p. 90).

In another example, Engle (2006) hypothesized that *expansive framing of interactions* (as opposed to restrictive framing) that occur during learning results in more productive learning and greater transfer. Expansive framing includes an expansive understanding of the object of learning, and an expanded understanding of learner agency that includes learners actively participating in the construction of their knowing and understanding of the subject matter. The idea of expansive framing was empirically studied by Engle, Nguyen, and Mendelson, who stated that "contexts are framed expansively as opportunities for students to actively contribute to larger conversations that extend across times, places, people, and activities" (Engle et al., 2011, p. 605). The boundaries of expansive learning contexts are framed as wide-ranging and permeable, increasing the number of contexts that can become linked with them.

Learning new skills and concepts is radically enhanced when those skills and concepts are not handled as isolated actions of answering "what?" and "how?" questions but are instead embedded in envisioning and constructing the structure and future of the entire activity system, that is, answering "why?" and "where to?" questions. This aspect of expansion has been characterized as *contextualizing* or *anchoring upward* (Engeström, 1990, p. 194).

In recent studies of learning, the notion of "learning object" has been systematically used by Marton and his colleagues (e.g., Marton & Tsui, 2004; Marton & Pang, 2006). Marton distinguishes among three aspects of the learning object, namely the (a) instructor's intended object of learning, (b) the enacted object of learning that "defines what it is possible to learn in the actual setting" (Marton & Tsui, 2004, p. 4), and (c) the eventual outcome as the student's lived object of learning (Figure 7.2). In Marton's conceptualization there may be serious discrepancies among the three perspectives on the object of learning.

Especially for studies of learning in activity systems, Marton's conceptualization is problematic. The intended object is depicted as a monopoly of the instructor. However, learners also have intentions. Their life interests and work concerns may become intended learning objects that may more or less openly clash with the intended object of the instructor. This issue of learners' agency has been emphasized in several studies of expansive learning

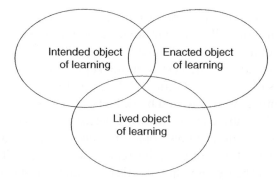

Figure 7.2. *Three aspects of the learning object according to Marton and Tsui (2004, pp. 4–5).*

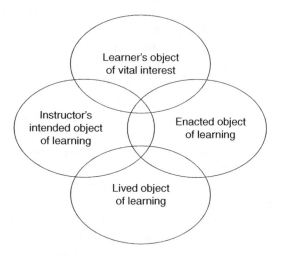

Figure 7.3. *Extended view of the learning object.*

(e.g., Engeström, 2011; Sannino, 2008). It calls for an extended version of Marton's conceptualization (Figure 7.3).

Expansive learning understood as expansion of the object or the subject (agent), or both, of an activity is typically a lengthy process that calls for longitudinal research designs. To facilitate and compress processes of expansive learning in activity systems, formative intervention methods such as the Change Laboratory (Engeström, 2011; Virkkunen & Newnham, 2013) have been developed. A Change Laboratory typically consists of ten weekly sessions in which practitioners of an activity system (or multiple collaborating activity systems) analyze developmental contradictions in their activity, design a new object and a corresponding new pattern for their activity, and take steps toward implementation of the new design. The relatively compact format of the Change Laboratory allows for effective data collection and detailed analysis of steps and interactions in an expansive learning process. Recent analyses have focused on discursive manifestations of contradictions

(Engeström & Sannino, 2011) and cycles of learning actions (Engeström, Rantavuori, & Kerosuo, 2013) in Change Laboratory interventions.

Expansive learning often involves negotiation between different perspectives on the learning object. In Change Laboratory interventions, this is typically manifested in the form of deviations from the initial plans and intentions of the interventionists, as the participants take over and redirect the course of learning by articulating novel versions of the object (Engeström et al., 2013; Engeström & Sannino, 2012).

These sequences resemble the processes Gutiérrez and her coauthors described (Gutiérrez, 2008; Gutiérrez, Baguedano-López, & Tejeda, 1999; Gutiérrez, Rymes, & Larson, 1995). Gutiérrez and her colleagues analyzed how the gap between the instructor's object or authoritative "script" and the learners' object or "counter-script" led to collisions and conflicts. Occasionally the parties found common ground on which they could build an expanded hybrid object for meaningful negotiated learning. Gutiérrez and her colleagues characterize these events as emergence of "third spaces" in the teaching-learning process.

The expanded hybrid object may emerge by means of fairly straightforward mapping of the learner's object of vital interest onto the instructor's intended object. An example is shown in the Brazilian film *City of Men* (2007). A teacher in the primary school of a *favela* tries to teach the students the history of the Napoleonic wars but faces mainly indifference, resistance, and disturbance. As the conflict is aggravated and a field trip promised to the students is about to be canceled, a boy suddenly comes up with his own account of the unfolding of the Napoleonic wars, explaining them in some detail in terms of the gang wars in the *favelas*. This depiction of recruiting a perspective of a learner illustrates an important general idea that Luis Moll and his colleagues refer to as *Funds of Knowledge* (González, Moll, & Amanti, 2005), in which perspectives and knowledge that is held in a community are recruited to diversify and authenticate the contents of school instruction.

In Change Laboratory interventions, an expanded object of learning is more commonly worked out by means of inventing a novel idea or model that deviates from the intended object of the interventionist and from the initial interests of the practitioner-learners. Such a novel idea is often suggested by one or a few learners in opposition to both the interventionist and some of the other learners and it may take repeated efforts to gain reception and support from them (Engeström, Pasanen, Toiviainen, & Haavisto, 2005; Engeström et al., 2013; Sannino, 2008).

Patterns of Explanation Involving Activity System-Level Phenomena and Concepts

Traditional cognitive psychology studies knowledge and learning of individuals. With the experimental designs cognitive psychologists use, the individual learner is intentionally removed from the usual contexts of learning. If other people, materials, and practices are considered or theorized by cognitive psychologists, they are considered to be a context for what that individual does and learns. This is in contrast to the situative perspective we present in this chapter. However, the cognitive perspective and the situative perspective are not incompatible; rather, we argue that analyses of learning and cognition that focus on individuals and analyses that focus on activity systems are complementary (also see Enyedy & Stevens, Chapter 10, this volume): they pursue explanations of the same phenomena at different levels of analysis.

A focus on activity systems can provide three different forms of explanation of how learning happens, two of which involve integrative links between individual and activity-system levels of theorizing:

1. An individual learns by participating in an activity system, and that individual's learning is explained by properties and processes within the activity system. One might call this a "top-down" explanation, because learning of one component of the activity system – one participant – is explained by the higher-level activity system.
2. The activity system as a whole learns when practices evolve or interactional routines change over time, and that learning is explained in terms of mental representations and behaviors of the participating individuals. This would be a "bottom-up" explanation, sometimes referred to as a *reductionist, individualist,* or *mechanist* explanation.
3. The activity system as a whole learns, and this learning is explained in terms of properties and processes of the activity system. This would be a horizontal form of explanation, because the cause and the effect are both at the same level of analysis.

(Traditional cognitive psychology focuses on a fourth form of explanation: explaining how an individual learns in terms of properties, processes, and behaviors of that individual. This form of explanation is horizontal and generally neglects the role of activity systems, shared social practices, and context in learning.)

Pattern 1: Individual Learning Explained by System-Level Hypotheses

The phenomenon to be explained is learning by one or more individuals, and the explanatory concepts and variables are properties of activity systems (Figure 7.4).

One example is a study of teaching and learning a concept of place value by Bowers, Cobb, and McClain (1999). The teacher led her third grade class in activities of representing, calculating, and reasoning about quantities that included diagrams that distinguished single objects, groups of 10, and groups of 100. Individual students were interviewed before and after

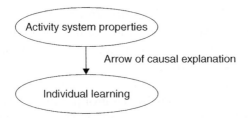

Figure 7.4. *Individual learning phenomena explained by system-level hypotheses.*

this instruction, and they increased their conceptual understanding of the quantitative meanings of numerical symbols and operations. This learning outcome was causally explained in terms of properties of the activity system – the activities and practices associated with the teacher's lesson plan.

In another example, by Moss and Case (1999), fourth grade students participated in classroom activities – collective practices – designed to advance their understanding of concepts and representations of rational numbers. Moss and Case found that the activities they had designed were effective; the individual students in the classroom attained the desired individual learning goals, and the learning was again explained as a causal outcome of participation in the collective practices.

In these classroom examples, the independent variables – the phenomena to be explained – were learning outcomes at the individual level of analysis: changes in the answers given by individual students to questions posed by interviewers, or performances on tests. The activities included using and discussing representations of objects with quantitative properties; these objects were interpreted as referents of numerical symbols that were used to pose problems involving arithmetic operations. As a result of participating in these practices, individual students came to interpret numerical symbols as referring to quantities and their reasoning was more successful.

In another example, Bowers and colleagues (1999) discussed norms of interaction, including general social norms (e.g., attending to others' solutions and explanations) and socio-mathematical norms (e.g., using quantitative terms in explanations), and reported that the teacher and students attended to the establishment of these norms. In Figure 7.1, these norms function as rules of practice that constrain the classroom's discourse activity. (These rules also function as resources, which facilitate participation by shaping ways members of the system interact with each other as they collaborate in activity.) The norms also relate to the way responsibility for different aspects of activity is distributed among the participants (the division of labor), by expecting students to develop meaningful explanations of their work, not just procedures that result in correct answers.

Engle (2006) also documented conceptual learning by individual students that resulted from their participation in an activity system. Engle studied fifth grade students who worked in groups to write reports about endangered species. The students' explanations and evaluations of habitats were more advanced after they participated in an activity in which they were asked to discuss habitats for species different from those they studied in their projects. This enhanced learning was demonstrated in interviews with individual students, and also in evaluations by the group. Engle (2006) also examined records of students' interactions with their teacher during the students' work on their report, and found that the teacher frequently framed students' contributions in ways that attributed *authorship* to a student rather than to the source; the teacher attributed *generality* to the source and to the information that the student contributed. Engle referred to this pattern of interaction as *expansive framing*, and subsequently conducted another empirical study and found that when a tutor used expansive framing, students were able to transfer their learning to new contexts more successfully than students in a control condition (Engle, Nguyen, & Mendelson, 2011). Like the classroom examples by Bowers and colleagues (1999) and by Moss and Case (1999), we propose that the instructional activities in Engle's studies involve expansive changes in the object of activity. In other words, the content of the knowledge to be learned was not presented as static facts to be memorized; rather, it was transformed into a different category – one of active engagement with material and knowledge building. The students' activity could have been presented as constructing text only to satisfy the requirements of an assignment; instead, the teacher framed students' contributions as having significance for broader audiences and for events on a broad time scale. And this resulted in deeper conceptual learning and greater transfer.

Pattern 2. Explaining Changes in Activity Systems in Terms of the Individual Participants in the System

In this explanatory pattern, *learning* refers to a change over time in the activity system as a whole; for example, patterns of participation in joint activity may change (Rogoff, 1990), or the sequences of an interactional routine may evolve. In Pattern 2, changes in activity systems are explained in terms of the actions and interactions of components of the system – a reductionist or "bottom-up" form of explanation.

In an example of Pattern 2, Hutchins and Klausen (1998) used the concept of *distributed cognition* to explain the process whereby an airplane crew successfully made a case that supported their request to be cleared to change the altitude of their flight. The crew's explanation of the need to change altitude depended on knowledge that no single member of the crew possessed, so their success depended on coordinating and combining their individual knowledge into a coherent argument. Distributed cognition has also been documented by Hutchins (1995b), who analyzed how the crew members of an airplane cockpit, supported by material resources, remembered to change the settings

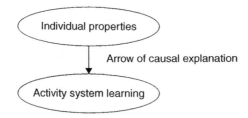

Figure 7.5. *Explaining changes in activity systems in terms of the individual participants in the system.*

of flaps and slats during the plane's descent toward landing. Hutchins (1993, 1995a) also analyzed conditions of participation by members of the navigation team of a naval ship, focusing on the opportunities that participation afforded for junior members to learn the capabilities they would need as they advanced in rank and to master the responsibilities for performing more complex tasks in the team's activity. Hutchins documented that the success of the learning environment that activity system provided resulted from an aspect of their working arrangement in which the more junior members had access to the information that was communicated and what was done with that information by more advanced members of the team.

When changes in an activity system are explained in terms of individual components, these lower-level explanations are sometimes referred to as the underlying *mechanisms* of phenomena at the activity system (see Machamer, Darden, & Craver, 2000).

An example of this sort of mechanistic explanation is the analysis by Van de Sande and Greeno (2012) of cases in which participants in problem-solving discourse succeeded in reaching mutual understanding after there was a lack of understanding by at least one of them. Van de Sande and Greeno accounted for these cases by hypothesizing a mechanism in which the participants (and in one case, an interactive computer program used by the participants) developed a common ground (Clark & Schaefer, 1989) that enabled them to align their framings, thus supporting their continued joint work on the problem.

Pattern 3: Activity System-Level Phenomena Explained by Hypotheses of Activity System Properties

Nersessian, Kurz-Milke, Newstetter, and Davies (2003) took this third approach in their analysis of a biomedical engineering lab, where the goal was to discover a way to synthesize artificial blood vessels that could function in human bodies. Like Hutchins, they referred to the lab as a *distributed cognitive system*. They defined learning at the level of the activity system as a change in the capabilities of the entire lab to conduct research and develop artificial systems. They documented a learning trajectory that involved

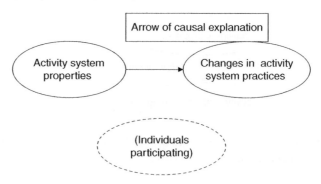

Figure 7.6. *Activity system-level phenomena explained by hypotheses of activity-system properties.*

modifications in the material devices that the researchers developed and used, as well as changes in individual researchers' understandings of the functioning and history of these synthetic devices. They considered problem solving to be *distributed model-based reasoning*, in which researchers and devices combine in a complex socio-technical system that collectively increases its capabilities. They explicitly contrasted their explanatory approach with individualist and reductionist cognitive psychological notions.

These studies demonstrate the value of explanations at the activity-system level of analysis, particularly when the phenomenon to be explained is transformation, change, and learning that occurs in the activity system as a whole, rather than the learning of any one participant only.

Learning Concepts in Activity

Much learning sciences research has emphasized the importance of deeper conceptual understanding, as opposed to a form of learning that results only in memorization of disconnected facts (Sawyer, Chapter 1, this volume). Experimental cognitive psychologists have mainly limited their studies of learning concepts to studies of individuals in laboratories, engaged in the task of learning rules for classifying stimuli. In this section we instead argue that "concepts and their meanings develop and evolve in settings of practice and are maintained in practices because they are useful in conducting the community's activities" (Hall and Greeno, 2008, p. 213). In particular, with "functional concepts" (Greeno, 2012) – those that are shaped and used as integral resources in the daily practices of collectives as individuals – a situative approach may provide better explanations than an individualist analysis of cognitive processes.

To illustrate the distinction between formal and functional concepts, consider the example of instruction of the concept of place value in addition and subtraction by Bowers and colleagues (1999), which we discussed in Section 2. In most math instruction, place value is defined as a formal concept, with values of digits in different places equal to multiples of powers of 10; rules for carrying or borrowing can be applied without reference to the quantities that the numerals refer to. In the Candy Factory microworld that Bowers developed and McClain used in her teaching, the learning environment was designed to provide students with functional concepts for place as well as formal concept. Toward this end, the students were shown three types of objects: pieces, rolls (containing 10 pieces), and boxes (square displays containing 100 pieces or 10 rolls), and students were presented with two operations: packing (pieces to rolls or rolls to boxes) and unpacking (boxes to rolls or rolls to pieces). The learning environment supported activities in which students reasoned functionally about manufacturing or taking away quantities of candy. In parallel, they reasoned formally about adding or subtracting numbers, represented by numerals. McClain's teaching emphasized coordination of these two uses of the concept of place value, with apparent success for the students' understanding.

This functional reasoning about place value provides groups of learners with *common ground* (Clark & Schaefer, 1989) or *anchors* (Hutchins, 2005) that help them communicate more smoothly and efficiently. Because they are embedded in shared situated activity, functional concepts are often distributed across people as well as tools and artifacts that are used in the activity. In working on understanding and solving a problem, these shared functional concepts function as resources. In Engeström's framework (Figure 7.1) concepts are among the tools that the subject can draw on in the activity of working to transform the object according to the system's goal.

It can be productive to consider a conceptual domain metaphorically as a space, and learning its concepts as becoming able to move around in the space, recognizing conceptual resources that can be used productively in activity. Considering a domain of concepts as analogous to a search space supports the general situative idea that reasoning and problem solving are carried out by systems, which comprise an individual person or persons interacting with other systems that provide resources for the person's or persons' activity.

This idea also fits with Davydov's (1990) version of becoming adept at ascending to the concrete, where the conceptual field may have numerous conceptual germ cells that are interrelated, and someone, or a group, is adept at recognizing the potential utility of these conceptual resources. Greeno (1991) and Schoenfeld (1998) proposed that a conceptual domain, such as mathematics, may be thought of metaphorically as a physical environment. Schoenfeld (1998) proposed that knowing and understanding mathematics is analogous to an expert cook's knowing and understanding the properties of ingredients that can be used to contribute to the flavor and texture of a dish that he or she is deciding to prepare, along with the cook's knowledge of procedures that are performed in its preparation.

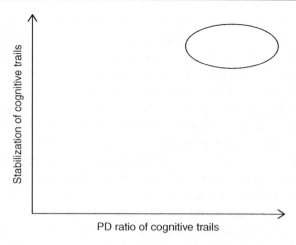

Figure 7.7. *Generality as high PD ratio and high stabilization (Cussins, 1992, p. 683).*

Cussins (1992, 1993) proposed a philosophical theory of embodied cognition where the basic metaphor is that of a *cognitive trail* – a person moving through a territory. Cussins's key concepts are *perspective dependence (PD)* and *stabilization*. To demonstrate these concepts, imagine a person standing somewhere in the middle of a city. If that person can find his or her way to any desired location regardless of his or her initial position, they have a maximum "perspective independence" ratio of one. The PD ratio is close to zero when that person is completely unable to find his or her way to any desired location in the territory. People learn to move around in a territory by moving around in the territory. In so doing, they make cognitive trails. According to Cussins, trails are "in" the environment, but they are also cognitive objects; they are experiential but also relatively durable environmental markings (Cussins, 1992, pp. 673–674). As multiple cognitive trails are marked, some trails intersect, and these intersections are *landmarks*. A territory is structured by means of a network of landmarks. As the structure becomes more elaborated, the PD ratio increases.

The second dimension that characterizes the development of cognitive trails is *stabilization*. Stabilization involves drawing a demarcation line around a phenomenon that is in flux (Cussins, 1992, p. 677). Stabilization is often achieved by *naming*, that is, imposing a linguistic structure on experience (Cussins, 1992, pp. 679–680). Figure 7.7 demonstrates that concepts emerge when the PD ratio is high and stabilization is high.

In communities and workplaces, cognitive trails are typically made in group activity. The trails become explicitly and visibly manifest when there are attempts to articulate ideas or concepts, typically in the form of proposals or definitions.

In a variation of this journey metaphor, anthropologist Tim Ingold (2007) made a distinction between two modes of movement: *wayfaring* and *transport*.

Wayfaring is the fundamental mode by which humans inhabit the earth. The lines of wayfaring are typically winding and irregular, yet comprehensively entangled. They have no ultimate destination. The lines of transport, on the other hand, are typically straight and regular, and intersect only at nodal points of power (Ingold, 2007, p. 81).

In the accounts of Cussins and Ingold, the maker of the cognitive trails, or the wayfarer, is implicitly considered to be an individual moving in relatively pristine space. What is missing in these theories is interaction between wayfarers' trails and already existing paths. The Cussins-Ingold line of analysis needs to be complemented with the notion of encounters between the old and the new – between known information and learners' own knowledge construction.

Wagner provided further evidence that conceptual learning is primarily a process of expansive learning. Wagner interviewed a college student who was taking a statistics course, repeatedly assessing her understanding of the conceptual relation between the size of a sample and properties of the probability distribution of sample means. Wagner found that over time, the student applied the concept of a distribution of sample means in more situations. Wagner interpreted this finding as an example of the idea that learners increasingly learn to respond to features of situations that support the use of a concept. This is consistent with the general idea of expansive learning, as the range of situations in which a concept can be applied expands as the individual learns.

Wagner argued that abstractness is not the key to understanding transfer, but rather that knowledge supporting transfer must somehow account for contextual differences across activities. According to Wagner, transfer was not supported primarily by the subject's ability to state her rule in general terms; "rather it was by an expansive set of underlying, context-dependent knowledge resources and coordination knowledge that permitted her to understand how her rule could be recognized as useful and sensibly applied in varying circumstances" (Wagner, 2006, p. 10). Wagner's findings are consistent with our claim that learning in a conceptual domain is a process of coming to know where to find and how to use resources in a metaphorically spatial environment.

Conclusions

The situative perspective on learning in activity is facing new challenges and possibilities that require continuous theoretical and methodological development. We have provided several examples of studies that analyze learning in and by activity systems, demonstrating how the approach can significantly enrich our understanding of individual and group learning. Our approach to learning is different from the rather global notion of "organization" used in studies of organizational learning, because it offers a way to examine learning beyond the individual without losing sight of the learners as individual subjects.

Our focus on activity systems allowed us to identify three patterns of explanation, two of which involved both individual-level and activity system-level understandings. Each of these three patterns is an important extension to the perspective of traditional cognitive psychology, which represents a fourth "horizontal" form of explanation that remains at the individual level. Studies of learning in activity should be explicit about which pattern of explanation they are using. The most demanding task will be to conduct studies that bring together the three patterns and provide complementary lenses on multilevel learning processes.

We have argued that focusing on expansion of the object of the activity can offer a powerful way to conceptualize learning. We pointed out two aspects of expansivity, one focused on the object and the other focused on the context of learning and the ways members of the activity system, especially students, participate in the learning process. Exploration of the relationship between these two is a promising avenue for future research.

Situative perspectives on learning have sometimes been understood as rejection of the importance of conceptual learning. In contrast, we argue that concepts are foundational for in-depth learning of any domain. But concepts are not merely verbal or symbolic labels or definitions. In particular, functional concepts, embedded in the practices of an activity system, are distributed among material artifacts and embodied enactments of the participants.

References

Argyris, C., & Schön, D. A. (1978). *Organizational learning: A theory of action perspective*. Reading, MA: Addison-Wesley.

Bateson, G. (1972). *Steps to an ecology of mind*. New York: Ballantine Books.

Bellack, A. A., Kliebard, H. M., Hyman, R. T., & Smith, F. L., Jr. (1966). *The language of the classroom*. New York: Teachers College Press.

Bowers, J., Cobb, P., & McClain, K (1999). The evolution of mathematical practices: A case study. *Cognition and Instruction*, 17, 25–64.

Brown, A. L., & Campione, J. C. (1994). Guided discovery in a community of learners. In K. McGilly (Ed.), *Classroom lessons: Integrating cognitive theory and classroom practice* (pp. 229–270). Cambridge, MA: MIT Press.

Chapin, S. H., O'Connor, C., & Anderson, N. C. (2009). *Classroom discussions: Using math talk to help students learn*. Sausalito, CA: Scholastic/Math Solutions.

Clark, H. H., & Schaefer, E. (1989). Contributions to discourse. *Cognitive Science*, 13, 19–41.

Cole, M. (1996). *Cultural psychology: A once and future discipline*. Cambridge, MA: Harvard University Press/Belknap.

Cussins, A. (1992). Content, embodiment and objectivity: The theory of cognitive trails. *Mind*, 101, 651–688.

Cussins, A. (1993). Nonconceptual content and the elimination of misconceived composites! *Mind & Language*, 8, 234–252.

Davydov, V. V. (1990). *Types of generalization in instruction: Logical and psychological problems in the structuring of school curricula*. Reston: National Council of Teachers of Mathematics.

diSessa, A. A. (1993). Toward an epistemology of physics. *Cognition and Instruction*, 10, 105–225.

Eckert, P. (1990). Adolescent social categories: Information and science learning. In M. Gardner, J. G Greeno, F. Reif, A. H. Schoenfeld, A. diSessa, & E. Stage (Eds.), *Toward a scientific practice of science education* (pp. 203–218). Hillsdale, NJ: Lawrence Erlbaum Associates.

Engeström, Y. (1987). *Learning by expanding: An activity-theoretical approach to developmental research*. Helsinki: Orienta-Konsultit.

Engeström, Y. (1990). *Learning, working and imagining: Twelve studies in activity theory*. Helsinki: Orienta-Konsultit.

Engeström, Y. (2001). Expansive learning at work: Toward an activity theoretical reconceptualization. *Journal of Education and Work*, 14, 133–156.

Engeström, Y. (2011). From design experiments to formative interventions. *Theory & Psychology*, 21(4), 598–628.

Engeström, Y., Pasanen, A., Toiviainen, H., & Haavisto, V. (2005). Expansive learning as collaborative concept formation at work. In K. Yamazumi, Y. Engeström, & H. Daniels (Eds.), *New learning challenges: Going beyond the industrial age system of school and work* (pp. 47–77). Kansai: Kansai University Press.

Engeström, Y., Puonti, A., & Seppänen, L. (2003). Spatial and temporal expansion of the object as a challenge for reorganizing work. In D. Nicolini, S. Gherardi, & D. Yanow (Eds.), *Knowing in organizations: A practice-based approach* (pp. 151–186). Armonk: Sharpe.

Engeström, Y., Rantavuori, J., & Kerosuo, H. (2013). Expansive learning in a library: Actions, cycles and deviations from instructional intentions. *Vocations and Learning*, 6, pp. 81–106.

Engeström, Y., & Sannino, A. (2010). Studies of expansive learning: Foundations, findings and future challenges. *Educational Research Review*, 5(1), 1–24.

Engeström, Y., & Sannino, A. (2011). Discursive manifestations of contradictions in organizational change efforts: A methodological framework. *Journal of Organizational Change Management*, 24(3), 368–387.

Engeström, Y., & Sannino, A. (2012). Whatever happened to process theories of learning? *Learning, Culture and Social Interaction*, 1(1), 45–56.

Engle, R. A. (2006). Framing interactions to foster generative learning: A situative account of transfer in a community of learners classroom. *Journal of the Learning Sciences*, 15, 451–498.

Engle, R. A., & Conant, F. (2002). Guiding principles for fostering productive disciplinary engagement: Explaining an emergent argument in a community of learners classroom. *Cognition and Instruction*, 20, 399–484.

Engle, R. A., Nguyen, P. D., & Mendelson, A. (2011). The influence of training on transfer: Initial evidence from a tutoring experiment. *Instructional Science*, 39, 603–628.

Ginnett, R. C. (1993). Crews as groups: Their formation and their leadership. In E. L. Wiener, G. L. Kanki, & R. L. Helmreich (Eds.), *Cockpit resource management*. San Diego, CA: Academic Press.

González, N., Moll, L., & Amanti, C. (Eds.) (2005). *Funds of knowledge: Theorizing practices in households, communities, and classrooms*. Mahwah, NJ: Lawrence Erlbaum Associates.

Greeno, J. G. (1991). Number sense as situated knowing in a conceptual domain. *Journal for Research in Mathematics Education*, 22, 170–218.

Greeno, J. G. (2012). Concepts in activities and discourses. *Mind, Culture, and Activity*, 19, 310–313.

Gutiérrez, K. D. (2008). Developing a sociocritical literacy in the third space. *Reading Research Quarterly*, 43(2), 148–164.

Gutiérrez, K., Baguedano-López, P., & Tejeda, C. (1999). Rethinking diversity: Hybridity and hybrid language practices in the third space. *Mind, Culture, and Activity*, 6(4), 286–303.

Gutiérrez, K. D., Rymes, B., & Larson, J. (1995). Script, counterscript, and underlife in the classroom – Brown, James versus Brown v. Board of Education. *Harvard Educational Review*, 65, 445–471.

Hall, R., & Greeno, J. G. (2008). Conceptual learning. In T. Good (Ed.), *21st Century Education: A Reference Handbook* (pp. 212–221). London: Sage Publications.

Harré, R., & Van Langenhove, L. (1999). *Positioning theory: Moral contexts of intentional action*. Malden: Blackwell.

Heath, S. B. (1983) *Ways with words: Language, life, and work in communities and classrooms*. Cambridge: Cambridge University Press.

Holland, D., Lachicotte, W., Skinner, D., & Cain, C. (1998). *Identity and agency in cultural worlds*. Cambridge, MA: Harvard University Press.

Hutchins, E. (1993). Learning to navigate. In S. Chaiklin & J. Lave (Eds.), *Understanding practice: Perspectives on activity and context* (pp. 35–63). Cambridge: Cambridge University Press.

Hutchins, E. (1995a). *Cognition in the wild*. Cambridge, MA: MIT Press.

Hutchins, E. (1995b). How a cockpit remembers its speeds. *Cognitive Science*, 19, 265–288.

Hutchins, E. (2005). Material anchors for conceptual blends. *Journal of Pragmatics*, 37, 1555–1577.

Hutchins, E., & Klausen, T. (1998). Distributed cognition in an airline cockpit. In Y. Engeström & D. Middleton (Eds.), *Cognition and communication at work* (pp. 15–34.) Cambridge: Cambridge University Press.

Ingold, T. (2007). *Lines: A brief history*. London: Routledge.

Johnson-Laird, P. N. (1983). *Mental models*. Cambridge: Cambridge University Press.

Lave, J., & Wenger, E. (1991). *Situated learning: Legitimate peripheral participation*. Cambridge: Cambridge University Press.

Machamer, P., Darden, L., & Craver, C. F. (2000). Thinking about mechanisms. *Philosophy of Science*, 67, 1–25.

Marton, F., & Pang, M. F. (2006). On some necessary conditions of learning. *The Journal of the Learning Sciences*, 15(2), 193–220.

Marton, F., & Tsui, A. B. M. (2004). *Classroom discourse and the space of learning*. Mahwah, NJ: Lawrence Erlbaum Associates.

Mehan, H. (1979). *Learning lessons: Social organization in the classroom.* Cambridge, MA: Harvard University Press.

Mercer, N. (1995). *The guided construction of knowledge: Talk amongst teachers and learners.* Clevedon: Multilingual Matters.

Mitchell, S. D. (2003). *Biological complexity and integrative pluralism.* Cambridge: Cambridge University Press.

Moss, J., & Case, R. (1999). Developing children's understanding of the rational numbers: A new model and an experimental curriculum. *Journal for Research in Mathematics Education, 30,* 122–147.

Nersessian, N. J., Kurz-Milke, E., Newstetter, W. C., & Davies, J. (2003). Research laboratories as evolving distributed cognitive systems. In R. Alterman & D. Kirsh (Eds.), *Proceedings of the twenty-fifth annual conference of the Cognitive Science Society* (pp. 857–862).

Newell, A., & Simon, H. A. (1972). *Human problem solving.* Englewood Cliffs, NJ: Prentice-Hall.

Resnick, L. R., Michaels, S., & O'Connor, M. C. (2010). How (well-structured) talk builds the mind. In D. D. Preiss & R. J. Sternberg (Eds.), *Innovations in educational psychology: Perspectives on learning, teaching, and human development* (pp. 163–194). New York: Springer.

Rogoff, B. (1990). *Apprenticeship in thinking: Cognitive development in social context.* New York: Oxford University Press.

Rogoff, B. (2003). *The cultural nature of human development.* New York: Oxford University Press.

Sannino, A. (2008). From talk to action: Experiencing interlocution in developmental interventions. *Mind, Culture, and Activity, 15,* 234–257.

Schegloff, E. A. (2007). *Sequence organization in interaction: A primer in conversation analysis, Volume 1.* Cambridge: Cambridge University Press.

Schoenfeld, A. H. (1998). Making mathematics and making pasta: From cookbook procedures to really cooking. In J. G. Greeno & S. V. Goldman (Eds.), *Thinking practices in mathematics and science education* (pp. 299–312). Lawrence Erlbaum Associates.

Schoenfeld, A. H. (2006). Design experiments. In J. L. Green, G. Camilli, & P. B. Elmore (Eds.), *Handbook of complementary methods in education research.* (pp. 193–206). Washington, DC: American Educational Research Association.

Sinclair, J. McH., & Coulthard, R. M. (1975). *Towards an analysis of discourse: The English used by teachers and pupils.* London: Oxford University Press.

Suchman, L. (1987). *Plans and situated action: The problem of human-machine communication.* Cambridge: Cambridge University Press.

Van de Sande, C. C. & Greeno, J. G. (2012). Achieving alignment of perspectival framings in problem-solving discourse. *Journal of the Learning Sciences, 21*(1), 1–44.

Virkkunen, J., & Newnham, D. S. (2013). *The Change Laboratory: A tool for collaborative development of work activities.* Rotterdam: Sense Publishers.

Vygotsky, L. S. (1987). R. W. Rieber & A. S. Carton (Eds.), *The collected works of L. S. Vygotsky, volume 1: Problems of general psychology.* New York: Plenum.

Wagner, J. F. (2006). Transfer in pieces. *Cognition and Instruction, 24*(1), 1–71.

Wells, G. (1993). Reevaluating the IRF sequence: A proposal for the articulation of theories of activity and discourse for the analysis of teaching and learning in the classroom. *Linguists and Education, 5,* 1–37.

PART II

Methodologies

8 Design-Based Research: A Methodological Toolkit for Engineering Change

Sasha Barab

Design-based research (DBR) is used to study learning in environments that are designed and systematically changed by the researcher. DBR is not a fixed "cookbook" method; it is a collection of approaches that involve a commitment to studying activity in naturalistic settings, with the goal of advancing theory while at the same time directly impacting practice. The goal of DBR (sometimes also referred to as *design experiments*) is to use the close study of learning as it unfolds within a naturalistic context that contains theoretically inspired innovations, usually that have passed through multiple iterations, to then develop new theories, artifacts, and practices that can be generalized to other schools and classrooms. In describing design-based research, Cobb, Confrey, diSessa, Lehrer, and Schauble stated:

> Prototypically, design experiments entail both "engineering" particular forms of learning and systematically studying those forms of learning within the context defined by the means of supporting them. This designed context is subject to test and revision, and the successive iterations that result play a role similar to that of systematic variation in experiment. (Cobb et al., 2003, p. 9)

This iterative design process allows the researcher to move beyond simply understanding the world as it is, and involves working to change it in useful ways with the broader goal of examining how these systematic changes influence learning and practice (Barab & Squire, 2004). This innovative aspect of design-based research makes it a useful methodology for advancing new theory and practice.

One way of understanding the focus of design-based research is in terms of Pasteur's Quadrant (Stokes, 1997; see Figure 8.1). In this quadrant model for characterizing scientific research, the upper left-hand cell consists of basic research for the sole purpose of understanding without an eye toward practical use. The lower right-hand cell consists of research that focuses solely on applied goals without seeking a more general understanding of the

This research was supported in part by a grant from the Bill and Melinda Gates Foundation. Also, special thanks to Alan Amory for his valuable feedback, especially because he brought an international perspective to the manuscript. Special thanks also to Alan Gershenfeld, whose valuable feedback is evolving my thinking around what it means to carry out design-based research such that it is likely to bring about scaled and sustained impact.

	Consideration of Use	
	No	Yes
Yes	Pure basic research (Bohr)	Use-inspired basic-research (Pasteur)
No		Pure applied research (Edison)

Figure 8.1. *Quadrant model of scientific research.*

phenomena. While Stokes intentionally left blank the empty bottom left cell, Reeves and Hedberg posited that much of educational research belongs in this sterile quadrant that addresses neither theory nor practice (2003, p. 265). This chapter is primarily concerned with the upper right-hand cell, where DBR is located, in which the focus is on advancing "the frontiers of understanding but is also inspired by considerations of use" (Stokes, 1997, p. 74). Barab and Squire argued that "such a system of inquiry might draw less from traditional positivist science or ethnographic traditions of inquiry, and more from pragmatic lines of inquiry where theories are judged not by their claims to truth, but by their ability to do work in the world (Dewey, 1938)" (Barab & Squire, 2004, p. 6). The design-based researcher must demonstrate local impact while at the same time making a case that this local impact can be explained using the particular theory being advanced.

Design-based research involves more than simply reporting outcomes: DBR moves beyond descriptive accounts to offer what Gee (2013) refers to as "storied truths" from which others can gain process insights that usefully inform their work. Storied truths, while bound to a particular context, are based on a level of reflexive thinking in relation to grounded warrants (Toulmin, 1958; also see Andriessen & Baker, Chapter 22, this volume) that shift the underlying claim from personal sentiment or informed opinion to a warranted argument that is meaningfully tied to the world. Such sharing involves methodological precision and rich accounts so that others can judge the value of the contribution, as well as make connections to their own contexts of innovation. Critics of DBR tend to be advocates of controlled experimental methodologies. These critics argue that DBR does not provide empirical evidence to ground claims; at best, it can provide formative insights that must then be tested through more controlled experimentation. In addition, many academic demands encourage researchers to make use of the "proven" methodologies associated with positivist science, including controlled experiments (Engeström, 2011, p. 598). In this chapter, I argue that design-based research is not simply a precursor to more rigorous, experimental research, but is a form of research that can provide rigorous empirical grounding to theoretical claims and explanations and that can be more illuminative and useful to others because of its emphasis on exposing mechanisms and its articulation of the conditions through which these mechanisms were realized. A well-presented and carefully conducted design narrative has the potential to support what Stake (1995) referred to as "petite generalizations"; that is, work that provides others insights into the challenges and opportunities that might emerge in their own work, as well as strategies for navigating these effectively.

According to educational researchers who use DBR – and contrary to the arguments of those pushing for experimental designs as the gold standard – the messiness of real-world practice must be recognized, understood, and integrated as part of theoretical claims if the claims are to have real-world explanatory value. From this perspective, experimental designs, those that examine teaching and learning as isolated variables within laboratory or other artificial contexts, will necessarily lead to understandings and theories that are incomplete. A key argument in favor of DBR is that demonstrating value in context should be a key component of the theory validation process empirical researchers undertake. Experimental studies can certainly validate theories, but simply demonstrating a variable is significant, while useful as part of the validating story, may be less effective than are rich examples and case narratives for informing how to implement a particular variable or theory within the context of real-world practice. Within learning environments, so called confounding variables necessarily occur and must be taken into account (not controlled) if the findings are to be relevant to practitioners (also see Greeno & Engeström, Chapter 7, this volume). Context is not simply a container within which the disembodied "regularities" under study occur, but is an integral part of the complex causal mechanisms that give rise to the phenomenon under study (Maxwell, 2004).

If researchers only study that which takes place in controlled conditions, they run the risk of developing artificial meanings and interactive dynamics that are so free of contextual realities that any interpretations are suspect with respect to informing real-world practice. Because learning scientists are committed to producing change in real-world learning environments, learning sciences research often occurs in naturalistic contexts and involves confounding variables, political agendas, and multiple alternative hypotheses, and includes rich descriptions of the conditions through which the research was conducted. Given the pragmatic focus of DBR, demonstrating the potential of the intervention to have productive impact at a particular site is key to the methodological process, as well as to justifying the work more generally. However, and while showing local gains is an important element of DBR, the focus is simultaneously on developing a design and generating new theory, with local impact being an important component of the validation process. Barab and Squire stated:

> Although providing credible evidence for local gains as a result of a particular design may be *necessary*, it is not *sufficient*. Design-based research requires more than simply showing a particular design works but demands that the researcher [move beyond a particular design

exemplar to] generate evidence-based claims about learning that address contemporary theoretical issues and further the theoretical knowledge of the field. (Barab & Squire, 2004, pp. 5–6)

To be clear, an essential element of learning sciences research is that it moves beyond observing the world as it is, and actually involves systematically engineering the contexts of study in ways that allow for the generation and advancement of new theory (Barab & Squire, 2004). However, the task of crediting the underlying theory as being responsible for the observed findings is especially challenging given the commitment to researching the designs in naturalistic contexts – so much easier to hold most variables constant when it comes to making causal claims. To further complicate the process, the learning environments DBR studies are often developed by the researchers who are studying it and advancing theoretical claims based on it. The methodology of design-based research emerged specifically in relation to these complex issues, but with the commitment that such complications are necessary when doing research on underlying mechanisms. This is because of the core assumption that the implementation situation will necessarily interact with and co-determine the realization of an intervention, thereby making claims based on more constrained situations such as the laboratory only minimally useful for understanding implications of the underlying theory and for scaling impact to naturalistic contexts.

Setting the Stage

Design-based research is frequently traced back to 1992 when Ann Brown (1992) and Allan Collins (1992) introduced a new methodological approach for conducting research and design work in the context of real-life settings. In complex learning environments, it is difficult to test the causal impact of specific independent variables on specific dependent variables using experimental designs. DBR deals with complexity by iteratively changing the learning environment over time – collecting evidence of the effect of these variations and feeding it recursively into future designs (Brown, 1992; Collins, 1992). DBR is especially useful for understanding the underlying reasons why something is happening (Shavelson & Towne, 2002) or under which conditions a particular interaction or occurrence could happen. Because DBR takes place in naturalistic contexts, it also allows for the identification and examination of multiple interacting variables, thereby providing systems-level understandings.

A second motivation for DBR is the belief that the "factoring assumption" of experimental psychology is not valid in learning environments (Greeno & Engeström, Chapter 7, this volume). The factoring assumption is the assumption that we can analyze individual cognitive processes apart from any particular context. Instead, a core assumption of learning scientists is that the individual and the learning environment are inseparable, with the meaning of any content to be learned being mutually determined through local contextual particulars (Brown, Collins, & Duguid, 1989; Kirshner & Whitson, 1997; Salomon, 1993). Lave argued:

> There is a reason to suspect that what we call cognition is in fact a complex social phenomenon. The point is not so much that arrangements of knowledge in the head correspond in a complicated way to the social world outside the head, but that they are socially organized in such a fashion as to be indivisible. "Cognition" observed in everyday practice is distributed – stretched over, not divided among – mind, body, activity and culturally organized settings which include other actors. (Lave, 1988, p. 1)

Cognition, rather than being a disembodied process occurring in the confines of the mind, is a distributed process spread out across the knower, the environment, and even the meaning of the activity in context (Salomon, 1993). Similarly, knowledge is not abstract and universal, but rather is bound up in numerous contexts and should always be considered "storied" – *storied* being an empirical constraint with respect to the "truthness" of knowledge; an epistemological constraint with respect to how the knowledge should be framed in terms of learning; and a pragmatic constraint in terms of whether the knowledge functions in an impactful manner with respect to its lived impact in the world (Gee, personal communication, 2013). From a situative perspective, studying a phenomenon such as motivation, metacognition, or even learning in a laboratory context might result in scientifically reliable but consequentially limited understandings that have little generalizable value in real-world contexts (Greeno & Engeström, Chapter 7, this volume).

In addition to understanding learning in complex environments and engineering new learning environments, DBR accomplishes a third goal: it improves learning for those participants in the study. This is valuable to learning scientists, because a core commitment of learning sciences research is that the work will have local impact. A challenge then becomes that of generalizing the local findings, or *scaling up*; and this requires understanding the contextual dynamics that surround the implementation of a complex learning environment in such a way that the findings can inform implementation in other contexts. The goal is to advance theory-in-context: the conviction that the theory is always situated in terms of local particulars. Accounts of DBR should describe both the theory and the particulars in a way that allows others to understand how to recontextualize the theory-in-context with respect to their local particulars.

One way of understanding the relations among theory, design, and implementation is in terms of Dewey's (1915) notion of *praxis*; the act of translating theory into action. For Dewey, praxis was not a unidirectional process, but a transactive one involving inquiry and through which theory and practice mutually inform each other. Confrey, commenting on the process of praxis, stated that Dewey "recognizes that in the beginning, there is only the indeterminate, which undergoes a transformation through a problematic to a hypothesis which by means of the activity of inquiry is transformed to a determinate situation producing a set of knowledge claims" (Confrey, 2006, p. 139). In this way, theory can come from action just as action can come from theory. DBR can be thought of as a form of praxis, with design/implementation being the practice. Dewey's notion of praxis as transactive further implies that in practice the theory (and design) will flex according to local particulars, possibly resulting in lethal design mutations even in the context of reasonable theory. Confrey, along similar lines, suggests that DBR results in explanatory frameworks that "cannot predict the outcomes precisely, for each realization is in effect unique, but does yield tendencies that can guide decision-making and the settings of parameters" (Confrey, 2006, p. 139). As such, an essential part of advancing theory-in-context is to communicate the theory as well as the contextual particulars through which it is realized in practice – a process that DBR is particularly effective in illuminating.

Defining Design-Based Research

Conducting DBR requires posing significant questions that can be investigated empirically, linking research to theory, providing a coherent and explicit chain of reasoning, demonstrating impact, disclosing research data and methods to enable and encourage professional scrutiny and critique, and employing methodological practices that are deemed credible and trustworthy and that result in useful claims (Shavelson, Phillips, Towne, & Feuer, 2003). Because this work takes place in naturalistic contexts and involves the systematic tweaking of theoretically inspired aspects of the learning environment, this research can offer insights into *why* and *how* a particular intervention works. Such theoretical and methodological rigor is necessary if DBR is to evolve into an accepted methodology advancing theoretical constructs and designs that are of use to others. Collins and colleagues (1992; Collins, Joseph, & Bielaczyc, 2004) posit seven major differences between traditional experimental psychological methods and DBR, to which I add an eighth difference, the goal of research (see Table 8.1).

Figure 8.2 characterizes the core elements (design, theory, problem, naturalistic context) of DBR, and visually represents how each of these components transact with the others such that the design is predicated on theory and the strength of the theory is bound up with how the design addresses the problem. It is not simply that DBR happens *in* naturalistic settings but, rather, such research *transacts* with these settings such that the design, the problem, and even the theory are fused with these settings in ways that are not easy to disentangle. Finally, DBR usually involves multiple iterations or what Collins (1992) refers to as *progressive refinement*, with each iteration providing a further refinement of the design in order to test the value of the innovation and, hopefully, stimulating the evolution of theory.

Table 8.1. *Contrasting DBR with laboratory experimentation in terms of elements that illuminate key differences*

	DBR	Psychology experiment
Location of research	Real-world learning environment	Laboratory
Complexity of variables	Multiple types of dependent variables	A few dependent variables
Treatment of variables	Not all variables of interest are known in advance; some emerge during the study	A few variables are selected in advance and remain constant during the study
Unfolding of procedures	Research procedures are flexible and evolve during the study	Fixed procedures are used
Social interaction	Complex social interactions with collaboration and sharing	Isolation of individuals
Reporting the findings	Describing design in practice	Report on whether hypotheses were supported
Role of participants	Experimenter and participants are active and influence the design of the research	Experimenter should not influence the subject and subjects do not influence the design
Goal of research	Produce impact and explain mechanism	Validate theory

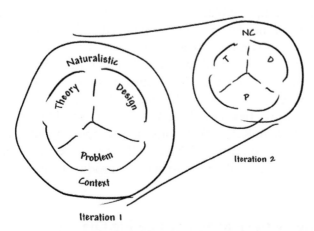

Figure 8.2. *General characterization of design-based research.*

It requires rigorous methods to demonstrate the linkages between theory and design, between design and problem, between theory and problem, and between successive iterations of the design; rigorous methods that make convincing arguments (although they rarely totally rule out alternative explanations). Confrey (2006) suggested that in research, evidence of methodological rigor comes from three sources:

1) the experimentation/investigation has itself been adequately conducted and analyzed;
2) the claims are justified, robust, significant relative to the data and the theory, and subjected to alternative interpretations; and
3) the relevance of the claims to the practices of education is explicit and feasible.

The rigor comes from principled accounts that provide logical chains of reasoning and prove useful to others. Design-based researchers must employ rigorous methods if they wish others to believe (and benefit from) the theoretical claims they wish to advance.

A challenge is to describe the findings in a way that allows others to understand how to recontextualize them with respect to their local particulars. A second challenge is that unlike experimental design, it becomes difficult to rule out alternative explanations. Given these complications, how can the design-based researcher convince others of the credibility of the claims? More often than not, this requires a balance of qualitative and quantitative data, although always taking place in rich naturalistic contexts. Even when conducting experimental comparisons among groups, the researcher is interested in unpacking mechanism and process and not simply reporting that differences did or did not occur. Opening up the black box of theories-in-context reveals complex interactions that cannot be usefully disentangled and reductively analyzed in terms of component variables. Instead, it is necessary to communicate these theories in their full contextual splendor, illuminating process insights while at the same time demonstrating local outcomes. Making convincing arguments from DBR research is challenging and involves complex narratives (Abbott, 1992; Mink, Fay, Golob, & Vann, 1987) and building rich models of interaction (Lesh & Kelly, 2000) – not simply reporting outcomes. Later in this chapter, I expand on some of these challenges, especially when the goal is to shift from theoretical validation to actually producing impact.

Changing Designs to Engineering Change

From Inputs to Outputs to Meaningful Outcomes

McKinsey and Company (2004) distinguished *outputs* – or the direct and tangible products from the activity – from the more significant *outcomes*,

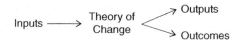

Figure 8.3. *Theory of impact articulation.*

referring to the more lasting changes that occur over time following an intervention. More generally, paying careful consideration to what business refers to as the "return on investment" might prove useful in ensuring learning scientists do not overly focus on theory building research at the expense of scalable and sustainable impact. If we are careful to consider what are the necessary inputs to enact the underlying theory of change,[1] in relation to the production of outputs and outcomes (see Figure 8.3), it would help us to avoid "boutique" research endeavors – that is, research that results in warranted claims and theoretical arguments that cannot be generalized to other classrooms and schools. A theory of change is an articulation of the underlying mechanisms and processes through which a complex organizational change is expected to occur. A core task of DBR involves the instantiation of the theory of change within a particular designed intervention, informed by previous research and consistent with an underlying set of theoretical assumptions.

Another potential problem of DBR, highlighted by Figure 8.3's mapping of inputs to theory of change to outputs to outcomes, is the potential for undesirable local outcomes or consequences – and this would be an even worse outcome than non-scalable theory. Outputs are the direct results of program activities, and can be considered closely connected with respect to causal connections to the program activities. They are often immediately measurable. More complex are outcomes, which are not usually direct and are considered to be longer-term effects expressed in the future. They require more complex causal connections, and are expected to reveal themselves in situations independent of the intervention itself. So, for example, adding fertilizers to soil can directly increase crop production, but do not necessarily guarantee and can even be at odds with self-reliance outcomes. Or, as another example, behavior modification might have the immediate output of increasing or decreasing performance, but runs the risk of negatively affecting such change with respect to longer-term outcomes. Barrett, referring to unintended consequences of food dependency, discusses "the undesirable aspect, 'negative dependency,' [that] arises when meeting current needs comes at the cost of reducing recipients' capacity to meet their own basic needs in the future without external assistance" (Barrett, 2006). I argue that design-based researchers must be responsible for the outcomes of their

[1] According to Connell and Klem (2000), a theory of change should be plausible (the logic makes sense), doable (implementable with available resources), testable (outcomes can be assessed and mechanism can be analyzed), and meaningful (the outcomes are worth the inputs).

work, including such unintended outcomes; considering the unintended consequences of advancing theoretical claims or of particular pedagogical approaches should become a key tenet of such research.

Traditionally, much of the educational psychology and cognitive sciences research from which learning sciences emerged (Brown, 1992) framed outputs in terms of immediate and what might be referred to as sequestered learning and assessment; that is, learning that can be demonstrated without the aid of others or tools. This focus on more immediate and sequestered learning outputs, in fact, has dominated how we evaluate learning. The problem is that when one optimizes system performance for maximizing outputs it often occurs at the expense of outcomes. So, for example, one might argue that schools have been optimized for standardized test performance (an output), and this potentially comes with a cost in that teachers and textbooks end up stripping so much context out to be more efficient with respect to test preparation, that they end up alienating real-world application (an outcome). Schools are often criticized for such output optimization with the more problematic concern that increasing performance on standardized test scores has come at the detriment of achieving more general outcomes such as passion for knowledge, use-inspired understanding, and critical thinking.

Critical theorist Peter McLaren specified "the ability to read and write in no way ensures that literate persons will achieve an accurate or 'deep' political understanding of the world and their place within it" (McLaren, 1988, p. 319). It is time to consider these broader outcomes, using DBR to help uncover at what cost our learning gains come and how our work might be even more influential if we were to consider the immediate outputs and how they were helping achieve the longer-term and more impactful outcomes. Outcomes could be at the level of the individual, differentiating between learning gains and inciting within the learner a passion for knowledge, or a commitment to use the content learned especially when not required to do so (Barab, Thomas, Dodge, Squire, & Newell, 2004). Beyond individual change, learning sciences research also takes place within a broader ecosystem, and it is essential that we consider the implications of our research with respect to the implementation contexts in which our work must scale – especially the changes required to have an infrastructure for successfully implementing the work. The importance of understanding the relations among our designs and the ecosystems in which they are implemented is elaborated in the next section.

From Designs to Services to Optimized Systems

A key component of design-based research is that the research takes place in relation to a theoretically inspired design – whether of a lesson, a product, a policy, a system, or even a program – as long as some theoretical inspiration exists that informed the design decisions and that, if the implementation succeeds, will strengthen the underlying meaningful assumption, theory, or principle. Problematically, it has been quite common to treat the designed lesson, policy, or program as a fixed object. In contrast, I have come to consider the design itself less of an object and more of a *service* whose fidelity is bound up within an ecosystem that does (or does not) have the capacity to usefully support the design in situ. We must consider our *designs as services* (not products) whose effectiveness is always integrated with how well the design engenders the ecosystem to optimize its success.[2] Similar to how situativity theorists have challenged the notion of knowledge as separate from those contexts in which it functions, I have begun to see the "design" of design-based research as a fundamentally situated "service" that requires ongoing optimization and support.

If design is a situated service, it is difficult (if not theoretically naïve) to discuss contexts as somehow separate from the design. This is, in part, what motivated Penuel, Fishman, Cheng, and Sabelli's discussion of design-based implementation research (see Penuel and Spillane, Chapter 32, this volume), which they argue has four key elements: "(a) a focus on persistent problems of practice from multiple stakeholders' perspectives; (b) a commitment to iterative, collaborative design; (c) a concern with developing theory related to both classroom learning and implementation through systematic inquiry; and (d) a concern with developing capacity for sustaining change in systems" (Penuel et al., 2011, p. 331). From this perspective, DBR does not take place *in* naturalistic contexts, but rather the design and the context *together* should be considered as part of a distributed ecosystem – with some contexts being better able to realize the effectiveness of a particular design. This is an even greater challenge if the motivation underlying a design is to introduce an innovation that is paradigm changing, in that one needs an implementation site that is not only "tolerant" of disruptive innovations (Christensen, 2006, 2011), but positioned to maximize their potential.

Learning scientists often distribute their designs to organizations (classrooms, schools, or districts) that may include a facilitator who takes responsibility for the ongoing optimization of the design-in-context. To support these facilitators, many new educational software products include teacher dashboards, where teachers can monitor student learning, and through this interface, can adjust the system parameters to better support learning. We should not study our designs independent of the ecosystems in which they will be integrated; instead, we should engage stakeholders and implementation facilitators as collaborators whose potential actions can become part of the design in situ. In this type of research, a necessary step is for the researcher to spend time with facilitators nested within potential ecosystems – not as

---

[2] In the commercial gaming industry, designers often build the game such that it can be continually optimized in relation to data from "community managers" who employ various methodologies to better understand player/community needs and ensure that designers can optimize player experience.

subjects to be analyzed, but as partners whose insights and functioning are an essential system component. Over time, through design-based implementation research, these insights can result in the development of implementation tools; and these implementation tools should allow the facilitator to remain a dynamic system element able to continually optimize the effectiveness of the intervention. Theoretically and practically, the design, the system, the culture, the stakeholders, and the participants collectively represent the implemented experience with the design and underlying theory each needing to account for these elements in any description.

From Stories to Truths to Storied Truths

Design-based research is a powerful methodological framework for producing usable theory that can be implemented to generate enhanced outputs and outcomes. Although demonstrating such value is an important validation of the success of the intervention, the research will not be completely successful unless the demonstrated value can be explained through some theoretical conjecture about what caused this change. Therefore, a key part of DBR involves unpacking the mechanism underlying the change, in an effort to reveal what Gee (2013) referred to as *storied truths*. It is in this unpacking of the underlying cause, the realizing mechanism, where one transforms the local story into an argument that has generalizable value to others who care about the underlying lessons even if not the particular case. DBR methodology is uniquely well suited to this goal, because it is especially effective at uncovering and illuminating realizing mechanisms. Experimental methodologies are able to identify that something meaningful happened; but they are not able to articulate what about the intervention caused that story to unfold. DBR can articulate the underlying mechanism as a storied truth that has both what Geertz (1976) referred to as *experience-near* meanings to the local story, and at the same time, *experience-distance* significance to others interested in leveraging the core mechanics or assumptions in their own work.

A theory or truth is powerful if it has the ability to transcend the particular, if it is based on general principles independent of any specific instance. To be powerful in this way, the outcome of DBR must transcend the specific case, regardless of how seductive one may find a particular story. Otherwise, such stories would accumulate as disconnected anecdotes rather than building toward a growing understanding of learning and of learning environment design. One risk is that a story's meaning and use remains forever tied to the instances in which it does work; an opposed risk is that to treat it as otherwise is to leave the theory formless and, therefore, unable to impact the world in which its utility is realized. This creates a paradox, one that I believe is in part solved by always discussing theory in relation to the world. I am arguing that a theory is not a truth independent of the world, but rather a storied truth bound up in the world. Such a position supports the idea that "people not only constantly transform and create their environment; they also create and constantly transform their very lives, consequently changing themselves in fundamental ways and, in the process, gaining self-knowledge. Therefore, human activity – material, practical, and always, by necessity, social collaborative processes aimed at transforming the world and human beings themselves with the help of collectively created tools – is the basic form of life for people" (Stetsenko, 2005, p. 72).

Storied truths are built through a process of reflective action, an "interactive conversation with the world" (Gee, 2013, p. 72). In this sense, a storied truth is grounded in actual happenings and not born simply of conjecture. It is through this grounding that any storied truth has value, and if all theories are storied truths, then it is necessary to contextualize any theoretical claim as part of advancing theory. This contextualization is both *illuminative*, in that such a grounded account helps to further articulate the theory, and also *necessary* in that it more clearly specifies the necessary conditions through which the storied truth potentially operates. In a very real way, a storied truth lives in and is bound in the story itself; at the same time, if properly outlined, it can be made relevant to other stories. Here is where our notion of a storied truth has methodological resonance with Stake's (1995) notion that a well-presented and carefully conducted design narrative has the potential to ground "petite generalizations." This grounding occurs because of the design-based researcher's ability, if not insistence, to continually connect the particulars to the general and versa.

A storied truth that is generated from a particular study is powerful, especially to the extent that others see value for their own work. But it is still a particular case. Bringing about change involves stringing together multiple storied truths, some of which are observed, some of which are engineered, and some of which might have been simply aspirational. For Latour (1987), a sociologist of science, truths are not found but made, and the making of truth is a complex process that involves good research but also the assembling of allies and an enabling context through which the claims are seen to be of value. Central to Latour's assertions was the notion that the origin of a truth is actually distributed across time and involves certain moves by the scientist and certain moves by the community with the "cause" of the truth being a dialectic among multiple nodes and links that collectively constitute a truth-making network. Each of the moves, operationalized as nodes and links, are assembled as allies and contextualized in relation to the broader network. This process of making a truth is both intentional and emergent, with the important point being that any one particular and contextualized finding does not constitute a general claim – even, I argue, a storied one – it is here where Glaser and Strauss (1967) discussed the need to "saturate" the theory by building multiple grounded accounts with overlapping claims.

Conclusions and Discussion

Educational researchers have been using design-based methods to develop powerful technological tools, curricular interventions, and especially theory that can be used to improve the teaching and learning process (Bransford, Brown, & Cocking, 2000; Design-based Research Collective, 2003). Further, in contrast to controlled experimental methodologies, these "design experiments" have lent rich insight into the complex dynamics through which theories become contextualized. At the core of this design-based work is the conviction that because these innovations are informed by a particular theoretical perspective, the continual testing and refinement of what works can inform theory that has close resonance to its practical utility. However, and somewhat ironically, while Brown (1992) and Collins (1992) introduced design experiments as a method for understanding learning and developing theory within naturalistic contexts, when learning scientists manipulate learning environments while conducting their research, it may actually undermine the credibility of the claims being made (because they are not objective observers of existing learning contexts). Therefore, in addition to the challenge of working in complex situations, learning scientists face the challenge of justifying that their claims apply generally to other contexts of learning, even though at some level they are responsible for producing the very claims on which they are reporting.

Critics of such research further argue that any interpretation not generated using an experimental methodology can at best provide formative insights that must be then tested through more controlled experimentation. If this is true, then even if learning scientists present rich accounts of learning as it unfolds in complex contexts, they will have a difficult time convincing policy makers, teachers, and other researchers of the theoretical and practical value of our work (Levin & O'Donnell, 1999). It is our responsibility as researchers in this field to address, not dismiss, the concerns of these various parties. If we are going to close the credibility gap between learning scientists and policy makers (as well as colleagues arguing for the primacy of "scientifically based research," by which they mean controlled experimental designs), we need to invest ourselves in changing public opinion with respect to what counts as evidence and in becoming more sophisticated in our methodological prowess. We have the Herculean task of grounding our theory, supporting the development of an innovation, implementing this in a naturalistic context, collecting and analyzing data in rigorous ways, and reporting all of this in a way that will convince others of the local impact of our work while at the same time showing its experience-distant value.

In this chapter, I began by restating key learning sciences assumptions. I augmented these with key challenges that emerged as the work has evolved from small "r" research focused on one study to building a large "R" research framework with the idea of designing for change. This began with a discussion of the differences between outputs and outcomes, highlighting the importance of considering the larger implications of the work beyond the more traditional outputs of learning gains as documented on standardized tests. Along these same lines, Torres emphatically argued that we must "debunk two educational myths of liberalism that have become more suspect at the end of the century than ever before: First, the notion that education is a neutral activity, and second, that education is an apolitical activity" (Torres, 1998, pp. 7–8). An acknowledgment of unintended consequences of even well-motivated work points to the need for broader consideration, a reflective process that occurs when one begins to consider enhancing outcomes and not simply maximizing outputs.

Situating the work in the broader implementation context (Penuel & Spillane, Chapter 32, this volume), I argued that the implementation context needs to be considered a core part of design-based research, not simply a place where it occurs. This involves the reconceptualization of designs not as products, but as services whose success is partly bound up in the way they support ongoing optimization by local stakeholders during the implementation process. Thus the implementation context is not simply a space in which one "tests" the design, but is a fundamental design component – one that in traditional research would be an independent variable or a moderating variable. This is consistent with Engeström's (2011) critique of DBR in which he suggests that the unit of analysis is vague; that such research is linear and excludes practitioners, students, and users; and remains unaware of open-ended social innovation. As one broadens the unit of analysis to be the design in situ, so must the resultant theoretical claims shift from abstracted theory to storied truths. Storied truths are resonant with and warranted within the way they are realized in the natural world, with the responsibility of the researcher being to provide a rich enough accounting such that the reader can make what Stake (1995) referred to as "petite generalizations."

There are multiple avenues for conducting DBR, and it would be impossible to delineate a list of prescriptive steps that all researchers should use regardless of design, theory, or context. However, based on the general principles presented in this chapter, practical steps include:

1) *Make explicit the assumptions and theoretical bases that underlie the work.* At times, this has meant defining assumptions and theory before the design work; at other times, these have evolved out of the work. However, as theoretical claims become apparent, research teams should discuss them as a group and write them down on paper – even if they are only naïve conjectures.

2) *Collect multiple types of theoretically relevant data.* This typically involves field observations, log file data, interviews, questionnaires, and document analysis. An important component of this data should be that it is theoretically relevant, helping to inform evolving theories.

3) *Conduct ongoing data analyses in relation to theory.* I suggest weekly meetings among team members, again positioning the data to support or refute theoretical conjectures, and also determining how to systematically change the design in theoretically informative ways. Here is where the team engages in the process of building storied truths.

4) *Acknowledge the inseparability of the design and implementation.* It is quite common to treat a design as a fixed object, and in contrast I have argued that we need to consider that our designs are services to be optimized within and in response to the ecosystems within which they are expected to work. Treating ecosystem integration as a part of the design process results in more powerful outcomes.

5) *Distinguish between outcomes and outputs.* Many designs focus on optimizing the design and implementation process to achieve desired outputs (generally, student scores on standardized tests), as opposed to longer-term outcomes. It can be beneficial to consider the unintended consequences of various optimizations, and whether outputs are being obtained at the expense of outcomes.

6) *Illuminate the hidden curriculum and accompanying agendas.* All too often we consider education and our designed curriculum to be apolitical. In contrast, I argue that we should deconstruct the hidden assumptions that are bound up in the design decisions, underlying theories, and research interpretations. Taking the time to reflect on one's assumptions can often illuminate biases we had not realized were affecting our work.

7) *Invite multiple voices to critique theory and design.* In many projects, this involves inviting teachers, students, and even external consultants to critique the design and resultant theoretical conjectures. These diverse groups provide different and much needed feedback.

8) *Have multiple accountability structures.* These structures include informal moments like when a student or teacher suggests they do not like a particular design aspect. At other times this might involve more formal meetings with local stakeholders to critique the project, or involve presenting the work at conferences or submitting articles and receiving feedback.

9) *Engage in dialectic among theory, design, and extant literature.* Participate in conferences and attend related talks, as well as talk with colleagues and stay current on both the academic literature as well as other related developments in commercial ventures.

The learning sciences studies learning within its full contextual splendor. This is why our work has the potential to truly change practice; but at the same time, it potentially undermines the generalizability of our claims. It is our responsibility as an emerging community to ensure that we conduct our research, and that we prepare the upcoming generation of learning scientists to conduct their research, in a manner that is methodologically rigorous and that results in theoretically useful claims that others consider informative, convincing, and useful – storied truths. Storied truths emerge over time, growing through a set of smaller research studies and societal happenings. However, over time, they can grow into a big theory, one that gathers momentum because of the work it does in the world and work the world does on reinforcing the theory. Importantly, we should acknowledge that each further node in the network that constitutes the emerging storied truth serves as an important translation, refining the theory and at the same time growing its value, even if what is learned are features of situations in which the theory has no application. The finicky nature of human beings and the contextualized nature of knowing and participation mean that each story has its own details, some of which change the underlying message and some of which serve to reinforce the core message. It is for this reason that a storied truth representing one population might look very different for another and even pass through meaningful translations and require additional frame factors to be relevant to a novel setting.

The best learning sciences research will advance storied truths that withstand translations, persisting even in the context of new actors, new authors, and new settings. The storied truths that can be retold and reapplied in a range of settings are more likely to be paradigm changing, and they are necessary to engineer change. Change will not occur simply through offering richer qualitative accounts, nor simply through employing quantitative methodologies. We need to convince policy makers and our colleagues that conducting good science involves more than employing experimental methods, but also involves demonstrating and evolving theory-in-context. Conducting good science involves using theory to inform real-world practice (through design) at the same time that this practice comes to inform theory – the essence of design-based research. Context, rather than something to be stripped away so as to produce some decontextualized yet ostensibly more generalizable theory, becomes interwoven with the theory in ways that allow others to see the relevance of the theory-in-context with respect to their local situation. Doing this in a manner that convinces others of the value of our work is a core challenge that design-based researchers must engage, especially if we want learning sciences to be a consequential form of social science.

References

Abbott, A. (1992). What do cases do? Some notes on activity in sociological analysis. In C. C. Ragin & H. S. Becker (Eds.), *What is a case? Exploring the foundation of social inquiry* (pp. 53–82). Cambridge, MA: Cambridge University Press.

Barab, S. A., MaKinster, J., & Scheckler, R. (2003). Designing system dualities: Characterizing a web-supported teacher professional development community. *Information Society*, 19(3), 237–256.

Barab, S. A., & Squire, K. (2004). Design-based research: Putting a stake in the ground. *The Journal of the Learning Sciences*, 13(1), 1–14.

Barab, S. A., Thomas, M., Dodge, T., Squire, K., & Newell, M. (2004). Critical design ethnography: Designing for change. *Anthropology & Education Quarterly*, 35(2), 254–268.

Barrett, C. B. (2006). *Food Aid's Intended and Unintended Consequences. FAO. Agriculture and Economics Division.* ESA Working paper No. 06-05

Beane, J. (1996). On the shoulders of giants! The case for curriculum integration. *The Middle School Journal*, 28, 6–11.

Bransford, J. D., Brown, A. L., & Cocking, R. R. (2000). *How people learn: Brain, mind, experience, and school.* Washington, DC: National Academy Press.

Brown, A. L. (1992). Design experiments: Theoretical and methodological challenges in creating complex interventions in classroom settings. *The Journal of the Learning Sciences*, 2(2), 141–178.

Brown, J. S., Collins, A., & Duguid, P. (1989). Situated cognition and the culture of learning. *Educational Researcher,* 18(1), 32–42.

Campbell, D. T., & Stanley, J. C. (1972). *Experimental and quasi-experimental designs for research.* Chicago: Rand McNally & Company.

Christensen, C. M. (2011). *The innovator's dilemma: The revolutionary book that will change the way you do business.* New York: Harper Business.

Christensen, C. M., Baumann, H., Ruggles, R., & Sadtler, T. M. (2006). Disruptive innovation for social change. *Harvard Business Review*, 84(12), 1–11.

Cobb, P., Confrey, J., diSessa, A., Lehrer, R., & Schauble, L. (2003). Design experiments in educational research. *Educational Researcher*, 32(1), 9–13.

Collins, A. (1992). Toward a design science of education. In E. Scanlon & T. O'Shea (Eds.), *New directions in educational technology* (pp. 15–22). New York: Springer-Verlag.

Collins, A., Joseph, D., & Bielaczyc, K. (2004). Design research: Theoretical and methodological issues. *The Journal of the Learning Sciences*, 13(1), 15–42.

Connell, J. P. & Klem, A., M. (2000). You can't get there from here: Using a theory of change approach to plan urban education reform. *Journal of Educational Psychological Consulting,* 11, 93–110.

Confrey, J. (2006). The evolution of design studies as a methodology. In R. K. Sawyer (Ed.), *Cambridge handbook of the learning sciences* (pp. 135–151). New York: Cambridge University Press.

Design-based Research Collective. (2003). Design-based research: An emerging paradigm for educational inquiry. *Educational Researcher*, 32(1), 5–8.

Dewey, J. (1915). *The school and society.* Chicago: University of Chicago Press.

Dewey, J. (1938). *Logic, the theory of inquiry.* New York: H. Holt and Co.

Engeström, Y. (2011). From design experiments to formative interventions. *Theory & Psychology*, 21(5), 598–628.

Gee, J. (2013). *The anti-education era: Creating smarter students through digital learning.* New York: Palgrave Macmillan.

Geertz, C. (1976). From the native's point of view: On the nature of anthropological understanding. In K. Basso & H. A. Selby (Eds.), *Meaning in anthropology.* Albuquerque: University of New Mexico Press.

Glaser, B. G., & Strauss, A. L. (1967). *A discovery of grounded theory: Strategies for qualitative research.* Chicago: Aldine.

Gomez, L. (2005, April). The Learning Sciences: A consequential form of social science. Presented at the American Educational Research Association, Montreal, CA.

Kirshner, D., & Whitson, J. A. (Eds.). (1997). *Situated cognition: Social, semiotic, and psychological perspectives*. Mahwah, NJ: Lawrence Erlbaum Associates.

Lagemann, E. C., & Shulman, L. S. (1999). *Issues in education research: Problems and possibilities*. San Francisco: Jossey-Bass Publishers.

Latour, B. (1987). *Science in action*. Cambridge, MA: Harvard University Press.

Lave, J. (1988). *Cognition in practice: Mind, mathematics, and culture in everyday life*. New York: Cambridge University Press.

Lesh, R. A., & Kelly, A. E. (2000). Multitiered teaching experiments. In A. E. Kelly & R. A. Lesh (Eds.), *Handbook of research design in mathematics and science education* (pp. 197–230). Mahwah, NJ: Lawrence Erlbaum Associates.

Levin, J. R., & O'Donnell, A. M. (1999). What to do about educational research's credibility gaps? *Issues in Education: Contributions from Educational Psychology, 5*, 177–229.

MaKinster, J. G., Barab, S. A., Harwood, W., & Andersen, H. O. (2006). The effect of social context on the reflective practice of pre-service science teachers: Incorporating a web-supported community of teachers. *Journal of Technology and Teacher Education, 14*(3), 543–579.

Maxwell, J. (2004). Causal explanation, qualitative research, and scientific inquiry in education. *Educational Researcher, 33*(2), 3–11.

McKinsey & Co. (2004). *Using Logic models to bring together planning, evaluation, and action: Logic model development guide*. Battle Creek, MI: W. K. Kellogg Foundation.

McLaren, P. L. (1988). On ideology and education: Critical pedagogy and the politics of empowerment. *Social Text, 19/20*, pp. 153–185.

Messick, S. (1992). The interplay of evidence and consequences in the validation of performance assessments. *Educational Researcher, 23*(2), 13–23.

Mink, L. O., Fay, B., Golob, E. O., & Vann, R. T. (1987). *Historical understanding*. Ithaca, NY: Cornell University Press.

Penuel, W., Fishman, B., Cheng, B. H., & Sabelli, N. (2011). Organizing research and development at the intersection of learning, implementation, and design. *Educational Researcher, 40*, 331–337.

Reeves, T. C., & Hedberg, J. G. (2003). *Interactive learning systems evaluation*. Englewood Cliffs, NJ: Educational Technology Publications.

Salomon, G. (Ed.) (1993). *Distributed cognitions: Psychological and educational considerations*. New York: Cambridge University Press.

Shavelson, R. J., Phillips, D. C., Towne, L., & Feuer, M. J. (2003). On the science of education design studies. *Educational Researcher, 32*(1), 25–28.

Shavelson, R. J., & Towne, L. (2002). *Scientific research in education*. Washington, DC: National Academy Press.

Stake, R. (1995). *The art of case study research*. Thousand Oaks, CA: Sage Publications.

Stetsenko, A. (2005). Activity as object-related: Resolving the dichotomy of individual and collective planes of activity. *Mind, Culture, and Activity, 12*(1), 70–88.

Stokes, D. E. (1997). *Pasteur's quadrant: Basic science and technological innovation*. Washington, DC: Brookings Institution Press.

Torres, C. A. (1998). *Education, power, and personal biography: Dialogues with critical educators*. New York: Routledge.

Toulmin, S. (1958). *The uses of argument. New York:* Cambridge University Press.

Wenger, E. (1998). *Communities of practice: Learning, meaning, and identity.* Cambridge: Cambridge University Press.

9 Microgenetic Methods

Clark A. Chinn and Bruce L. Sherin

Microgenetic methods involve the detailed analysis of processes of learning, reasoning, and problem solving. The goal is not merely to identify factors that influence learning, but to understand how these factors mediate learning, step by step, as learning occurs. In this chapter, we discuss a cluster of methods designed to provide an in-depth, detailed understanding of learning processes. Such analyses require reliable methods. Fortunately, it has not been necessary for learning scientists to invent entirely new methods. Prior to the emergence of the learning sciences as a separate field, learning and development were a focus of study in multiple disciplines. Learning scientists have thus been able to borrow methods from these existing disciplines.

However, the learning sciences emerged as a separate field in part because of a set of beliefs about learning that set it off from existing disciplines. These beliefs have, in turn, shaped the methods that we employ. They have dictated which methods we borrow, and they required that we adapt existing methods so that they are better suited for our particular aims. We thus begin this chapter by stating the shared beliefs that are of particular importance for the selection of research methods.

First, in the learning sciences, learning is not typically understood to be a rare and dramatic event, one that happens only in moments of insight. Instead, it occurs continuously, and in small steps, with every moment of thought. Further, mastery of significant knowledge often requires a very long period of time. Second, learning does not occur in a straight line, from lesser to greater understanding; it occurs in parallel on multiple fronts. For this reason, learning can sometimes lead, in the short term, to worse performance. Third, learning and learning events are heterogeneous. "Learning" is not a single, unitary phenomenon about which we can draw general conclusions. Instead, there are multiple kinds of learning, each requiring its own study. Finally, and perhaps most important, learning scientists see learning as fundamentally *mediated*. In general, learning is not driven primarily by the independent cogitations of the individual. We learn from our environment, which includes, most critically, the cultural tools other individuals provide to us.

These beliefs about learning have dramatic implications for the methods that we employ. They imply, for example, that we cannot expect to find a small number of encapsulated moments during which important learning occurs. They also imply that, if we want to foster many important types of learning, we will need to provide a learning environment that contains cultural tools and other individuals that can mediate learning.

In this chapter, we discuss a method that is designed to analyze learning that has these characteristics: the microgenetic method. We discuss its origins, as well as how it has been taken up and extended by researchers in the learning sciences. In the sections that follow, we begin with a general overview of microgenetic methods. We then discuss in some detail a prominent starting point in developmental psychology, the work of Robert Siegler. Then we address a prototypical example of the use of microgenetic methods in the learning sciences, from the work of Schoenfeld, Smith, and Arcavi (1993). Next we discuss some of the variations that exist among applications of microgenetic methods, and the particular ways the learning sciences has adapted them.

Overview of Microgenetic Methods

The goal of microgenetic methods is to illuminate in detail the processes of learning as they occur. This goal cannot be achieved by many other widely used methods to investigate learning. For example, consider the following three methodologies and why they fall short of examining processes of learning as they occur:

- *Cross-sectional developmental studies* investigate the performance of learners at different ages, such as a study that investigates students' performance at simple experimentation tasks at the ages of 6, 8, and 10. These studies may document improvement in performance over time, but they do not show when or how the improved performance occurs. Indeed, each individual child is studied only one time, so change in individuals is not even detected.
- *Longitudinal studies* differ from cross-sectional studies in that they study the same learners at different times. Researchers might examine the same children's performance at simple experimentation tasks at the age of 6, then two years later at age 8, and then again at age 10. If results show improvement, this method indicates that individual children have learned, but the critical learning processes are likely to have occurred sometime during the two-year intervals between observations. Investigators are not present when the learning events occur, and hence the detailed processes of learning cannot be investigated using this method.
- *Instructional experiments* investigate learning by comparing learning under two or more different instructional conditions. For instance,

students learning how to design and interpret experiments might learn either through giving reasons for their design decisions or through stating the rules they used, with pretests and posttests designed to detect learning gains (e.g., Lin & Lehman, 1999). Researchers can draw some inferences about specific learning processes from such a study (e.g., when students explain why inferences are made, this facilitates robust understanding of the logic of experimentation). But, given that no data are collected or analyzed between pretest and posttest, nothing is known of the details of the learning processes in the interim.

In contrast to these methods, microgenetic studies aim to observe learning processes as they occur, and do so in such a way as to permit strong inferences about learning processes. For example, children could be observed conducting experiments in a computer-simulated environment over an extended period of time, with each child conducting many dozens of experiments (Kuhn, Schauble, & Garcia-Mila, 1992). In addition to observing the students as they conduct experiments, the experimenters might have the students think aloud to explain what they are doing in each trial and why they are doing it, what conclusions they draw from each experiment, and why they draw these conclusions (see Enyedy & Stevens, Chapter 10, this volume). Over dozens of trials, students improve both in the design of experiments and in the interpretations they draw. By examining, in detail, what students do and say over dozens of trials, the researchers can draw conclusions about what triggers change, how change occurs, and other questions about the actual processes of knowledge change (also see diSessa, Chapter 5, this volume, on conceptual change). For example, the researchers might discover that more careful controlling of variables in experimental trials is often preceded by several instances of drawing conclusions that focus on what varies across experimental conditions. This might suggest that students first appreciate that controlled experiments afford clear conclusions and only then realize that they should design such experiments.

In a brief historical survey of the microgenetic method, Catán (1986) attributed the invention of the microgenetic method to Werner and other Gestalt psychologists. Microgenetic methods for investigating moment-to-moment processes of learning were developed further by Soviet sociohistorical psychologists including Vygotsky and Luria, as well as by Piaget and scholars influenced by Piaget. In recent years, one prominent approach to microgenetic work has been formulated by developmental psychologists, notably by Robert Siegler and his colleagues (Siegler & Chen, 1998; Siegler & Crowley, 1991; Siegler & Stern, 1998) and by Deanna Kuhn and her colleagues (Kuhn, 1995; Kuhn & Phelps, 1979, 1982). Learning scientists have also adapted this method for use especially in case studies or comparative case studies of learning. Work along these lines within the learning sciences includes Alan Schoenfeld and Andrea diSessa (diSessa, Chapter 5, this volume; Schoenfeld, Smith, & Arcavi, 1993).

The Microgenetic Method in Contemporary Developmental Psychology

A Prototypical Example

According to Siegler (Siegler, 2006; Siegler & Crowley, 1991), the microgenetic method has three essential features:

1. "Observations span the period of rapidly changing competence" (Siegler, 2006, p. 469). Drawing on our earlier example of learning to design and interpret experiments, this has two implications. First, it means that the researchers must begin to observe experimentation skill at a point before students have gained proficiency, and that they continue to observe experimentation trials until many or most of the students have gained mastery. In this way, the observations encompass those moments of change that occur. Second, it means that the researchers create an intensive enough learning environment that the changes occur in a relatively short time – short enough to capture in several hours of investigation. Developmental research suggests that, without intensive learning experiences, complex skills such as experimentation develop slowly. The hope is that the change processes can be accelerated in an intensive learning environment so that there is an opportunity to observe the changes in a study spanning hours rather than months or years.
2. "Within this period, the density of observations is high, relative to the rate of change" (Siegler, 2006, p. 469). In the experimentation example, each and every experimental design that the students make, along with each and every inference they make, is observed. Because change occurs over multiple trials of designing and interpreting experiments – and perhaps over many dozens of trials – the observations are frequent enough to detect changes as they occur.
3. "Observations are analyzed intensively, with the goal of inferring the representations and processes that gave rise to them" (Siegler, 2006, p. 469). In microgenetic studies, the researchers are not merely trying to identify contingencies between behaviors (e.g., determining that the behavior of controlling experiments tends to become more frequent after the behavior of referring to controlled variables when making an inference). The researchers seek to go beyond the behaviors to make claims about the cognitive structures and processes involved. For cognitive developmental psychologists, this may mean postulating cognitive representations. For other scholars, this may mean making inferences, for instance, about patterns of participation in cultural activities.

Siegler and Jenkin's (1989) investigation of the emergence of addition strategies by young children exemplifies the microgenetic method as it has been employed in contemporary developmental psychology. Siegler and Jenkins focused particularly on the emergence of an addition strategy called the *min* strategy; children who use the min strategy will add the two numbers seven and two by saying the larger number ("seven" in this example) and then simply counting upward two times ("eight, nine") in this example. This contrasts with other strategies such as counting from one or guessing. The min strategy is faster and more efficient than strategies such as counting out all the numbers from one to nine. In the study, Siegler and Jenkins gave four- and five-year-olds who did not initially use the min strategy many addition problems to solve over 33 sessions across 11 weeks. No instruction was provided, and all the sessions were video recorded. Siegler and Jenkins inferred the strategy the children used on each problem on the basis of their observed video-recorded behaviors and of the children's explanation of how they had solved each problem.

Using this microgenetic approach, one significant finding was that there was great, ongoing variability in children's use of strategies: children used many different strategies across problems, and, after a new strategy emerged, they also continued to regularly use older strategies. Another finding was that no children used the min strategy until they had used another strategy called the *shortcut sum* strategy; this strategy involves solving a problem such as seven plus two by saying "one, two, three, four, five, six, seven," and then pausing before adding on "eight, nine." Further, students took twice as long to solve the problem *before* they first used the min strategy, despite the fact that these problems were, on average, no harder than other problems the children had solved. Together, these findings led Siegler and Jenkins to conclude that students discover the min strategy through realizing how to make simplifications to the shortcut sum strategy (see also Crowley, Shrager, & Siegler, 1997). This conclusion could be developed only by having detailed, fine-grained, microgenetic information about how children had proceeded one by one through the many problems they had solved.

Because the microgenetic method involves extended observations of learners engaged in similar or the same tasks (e.g., solving many mathematics problems), there is a risk that learners may get tired of working on the same problems. One solution to this is to break up the task into multiple sessions so as to avoid fatigue in any one session. Another is to use problems that children find interesting; at a time when they are still discovering how to add numbers, addition problems may be engaging for young children.

Adapting Microgenetic Methods for the Learning Sciences

Microgenetic studies are diverse in many respects. Although all share the goal of illuminating in detail the processes of learning, there is in practice quite a bit of variability. Furthermore, learning scientists have adapted the method to suit their own characteristic aims. In this section, we discuss some of these dimensions of diversity, and we highlight how researchers in the learning sciences have tended to use these methods.

Variations in Microgenetic Studies

Microgenetic studies are diverse in many respects. We discuss some of the dimensions of this diversity in this section.

Diversity of Topics and Ages

The microgenetic method has proven to be versatile across many different topics of study and ages (see Siegler, 2006, for a detailed account). Studies have addressed learners ranging in age from infants to college students and older adults (Chinn, 2006). Learning domains that have been studied are diverse, including memory strategies, scientific reasoning, spoken and written language use, perception, force and motion, and mathematics problem solving (Chinn, 2006; Siegler, 2006). The microgenetic method is compatible with a range of diverse theoretical perspectives, including Piagetian, dynamic systems, sociocultural, and information-processing perspectives (Siegler, 2006) – basically any theory of learning that focuses on detailed learning processes.

Strategy Use and Conceptual Understanding

Many microgenetic studies have investigated strategy development, as when students are learning strategies for conducting experiments, solving problems, or writing. Strategy development is amenable to microgenetic research because researchers can give participants a long series of problems that invoke the strategies of interest and then examine, problem by problem, what strategies are used and how new strategies emerge. This was the approach used in the Siegler research on the min strategy discussed earlier.

Many studies in the learning sciences have used the microgenetic method to investigate conceptual change (see diSessa, Chapter 5, this volume). Our understanding of conceptual change can benefit from a detailed, moment-by-moment analysis of how students evolve more normative understandings. This focus on conceptual understanding has implications for the way that observations are structured and the type of tasks given to participants. When the focus is on strategy use, participants can be given repeated problem-solving tasks of a similar form. In contrast, when the focus is on conceptual knowledge, studies may take the form of tutorial interactions or clinical interviews, in which an interviewer poses varied questions.

In addition, some studies have examined both conceptual and strategic knowledge. For example, Schauble (1996) had children and adults work on a task in which they investigated learning about the forces on immersed objects through experimentation. She examined growth both in participants' development of experimentation strategies and in their evolving understanding of forces acting on immersed objects

Individuals and Collaborative Groups

Most microgenetic studies have examined individual learning, typically in interview settings. But it is also possible to examine learning in collaborative groups, as Taylor and Cox (1997) did in a study of students learning to solve multiple-step word problems in mathematics. It is further possible to examine learning microgenetically at the classroom level, examining student work through individual writing, through talk in collaborative groups, and through talk in class discussions (Chinn, 2006). For example, Buckland, Chinn, and Duncan (2010) investigated growth in 12 students' scientific modeling and justification over the course of a year's model-based inquiry curriculum. Each model generated by students and each justification were analyzed for changes on each occasion. Because of the focus in the learning sciences on the study of learning "in the wild," where it is mediated by other people and environmental supports, studying group learning has a particular appeal (see Enyedy & Stevens, Chapter 10, this volume).

However, the larger the group, the more likely it is that observations will miss critical learning events. For example, when a group of four students is discussing mathematical problems, one student may seldom speak; no amount of analysis will be able to provide a window into this student's thinking, or into the thinking of any student who was silent at the time she or he made critical insights. Thus, there are analytic trade-offs involved when the microgenetic researchers move away from interviews (or other techniques that focus on a single learner) into more naturalistic group settings.

The Provision of Instructional Support and Experimental Microgenetic Studies

To this point, we have focused on one common form of microgenetic studies – studies that place learners in a common setting and analyze how individual learners progress and how they differ from each other. Many of these studies place students in pure discovery environments and compare and contrast the ways different students progress in these environments. No experimental conditions and no instructions are provided. However, as we stated earlier, researchers in the learning sciences share the belief that most learning is dependent on the provision of mediation in the form of cultural artifacts and situated social practices (often called "scaffolds"). Indeed, ample research has shown that discovery environments without other instructional supports are suboptimal for learning in comparison to guided forms of discovery (Hmelo-Silver, Duncan, & Chinn, 2007; Mayer, 2004).

Such issues are addressed by microgenetic studies that provide instructional guidance to learners. Some of these studies combine microgenetic methods with experimental designs. For example, Rittle-Johnson and Alibali (1999) employed an experimental microgenetic design to teach fourth and fifth graders how to solve equivalence problems such as $3 + 4 + 5 = 3 + \underline{}$. They contrasted conceptual instruction focused on promoting understanding the meaning of the equivalence with procedural instruction focused on the steps needed to carry out the procedure successfully. The trajectory of growth shown by children with conceptual instruction was to demonstrate and maintain gains following instruction. In contrast, the trajectory followed by children with procedural instruction was typically to show improvement shortly after instruction on similar problems, but then on later transfer problems, these students usually reverted to the incorrect problem-solving procedures used prior to instruction. By observing children solve a series of problems in a microgenetic study with an experimental manipulation, the researchers were able to examine and contrast detailed trajectories of change under differing instructional regimens.

Variation in Sample Size and Duration

Microgenetic studies are laborious to conduct and analyze. It is therefore not practical to conduct very long-lasting studies with very dense observations and large sample sizes. If researchers desire to increase the sample size (which they might want to do when conducting a microgenetic experiment, to allow enough statistical power to find differences between conditions), they must necessarily cut back on either the density of observations or the number of problems. Thus, whereas Siegler had nine children solve numerous addition problems over 33 sessions, Rittle-Johnson and Alibali (1999) had 48 students solve about 30 problems over two 15–25-minute sessions. With the larger number of students, Rittle-Johnson and Alibali (1999) gained power to make comparisons across conditions, but they lost the capacity to trace learning over longer periods of time with larger numbers of problems.

Other researchers who increase the sample size may retain a long observation period but reduce the density of observations. For example, if a team of researchers wanted to examine 100 children learning experimentation skills over five weeks under two different instructional conditions, they might make it feasible to do the study by examining performance once a week instead of daily over those five weeks. However, the chance that they miss critical learning events is obviously increased, as critical moments of learning are likely to occur when the researchers are not recording learning events. And as such, these studies would no longer be considered microgenetic.

Thus, variations in sample size, density of observations, and duration of the study arise from the practical need to resolve these trade-offs. When microgenetic methods are employed in the learning sciences, they tend to occupy one region in this space of trade-offs. Rather than consisting of a larger number of short observations, the use of microgenetic methods in the learning sciences frequently consists of a smaller number of longer and sustained observations. For example, a period of continuous observation with individual students may span multiple hours. As the length of observations becomes longer, both the sample size and number of observations may need to be reduced.

A promising new technology, educational data mining (EDM: see Baker & Siemens, Chapter 13, this volume), potentially provides a solution to this problem. When learners are interacting with educational software, their moment-by-moment interactions can be logged, creating a record of the microgenesis of their learning. EDM methods can allow detailed processual analyses of large numbers of learners, but only when learning is mediated by computer software. This is a promising area for future development.

A Prototypical Example from the Learning Sciences

We now present an example of the use of microgenetic methods from the learning sciences. The work we report on is reported on most extensively in a book chapter entitled "Learning: The microgenetic analysis of one student's understanding of a complex subject matter domain" (Schoenfeld, Smith, & Arcavi, 1993). Like the prominent monograph by Siegler and Jenkins we discussed earlier, this chapter has the word "microgenetic" in the title. However, although both deserve to be described as microgenetic, the methods employed are in many respects quite different.

This entire 80+ page book chapter focuses on the work of one student, who the authors refer to as "IN." IN was a 16-year-old volunteer who participated in seven hours of interviews spread over about seven weeks. Each of the sessions was relatively long; the first session was an hour, and this was succeeded by three two-hour sessions. Throughout all of the sessions, IN was guided by a 35-year-old graduate student, JS.

The interviews were originally conducted for the purpose of testing software called Grapher. At the time, Grapher was quite novel. When students typed in parameters, Grapher produced a line based on these parameters. In the part of the software used by IN, the user was given the task of drawing lines so as to pass through targets that appeared on the display.

In some respects, this learning environment was discovery-like. Much of the interviews consisted of IN trying things out – varying parameters and seeing the effect on the lines drawn. Nonetheless, in many important respects, IN was guided by the environment in her learning. The software itself provided significant support. It forced her to adhere to the standard algebraic forms in her descriptions of lines. Furthermore, JS did more than simply observe and ask questions; he sometimes interacted with IN in a more tutorial manner.

What emerged over the 80+ pages of this chapter is a rich description of IN's learning over the seven hours studied. Although the methods Schoenfeld and colleagues employed were very different from those of Siegler, in many respects the features of learning uncovered are similar.

The learning challenge IN faced was essentially to understand the relationship between lines described in the form $y=mx+b$ and the lines drawn by Grapher on the computer display. One could imagine that IN might proceed via the development and modification of relatively straightforward strategies and procedures. But the story of learning Schoenfeld and colleagues describe turns out to be richly conceptual. For example, Schoenfeld and colleagues described one key component of IN's learning as involving movement from what they call a *three-slot schema* to a *two-slot schema*. When a line is described with an expression of the form $y=mx+b$, we can think of the line as determined by the values of m and b, the slope and y-intercept. That is the two-slot schema. In contrast, IN began with a three-slot schema, in which she understood a line as dictated by the slope, the y-intercept, *and* the x-intercept. As described by Schoenfeld and colleagues, the move from the three-slot to a two-slot schema took time; the three-slot schema faded over time, rather than disappearing in a single moment. The authors also discussed the gradual development in IN's understanding of the notions of slope and x-intercept.

Although Schoenfeld and colleagues saw evidence of learning, they saw very few learning *events*. This posed difficulties, as the team attempted to locate and understand the drivers of IN's learning. As an analytic solution to these difficulties, they developed a method of competitive argumentation: the team watched videos together and debated alternative interpretations, while holding themselves to relatively concrete standards of evidence.

The methods Schoenfeld, Smith, and Arcavi employed are very different in many respects from those Siegler and Jenkins used. Nonetheless, the aims and results are very similar. In both cases, the aim is to see learning as it happens, and to understand the factors that engender it. And, at a high level, the conclusions are much the same. Both argue, for example, that learning events can be invisible and that learning can appear to involve steps forward and backward.

Research Questions Suitable for Microgenetic Methods

In this section, we discuss which research questions are particularly suited to the microgenetic method. We also comment on why other common education research methodologies cannot answer these questions. We discuss five classes of research questions that are particularly well suited to microgenetic designs: questions about the variability and stability of strategies, events that precipitate or initiate change, co-occurring events and processes, trajectories or paths of change, and the rate of change.

1. Variability and Stability

Microgenetic studies are particularly strong in analyzing the variability or stability across time in how learners use strategies or express particular ideas. In fact, one of the most strikingly robust findings of microgenetic studies is that strategy use is highly variable at nearly all times. For example, in the Siegler and Jenkins (1989) study of the emergence of the min strategy, the researchers found that children frequently used different strategies on the same problem types, even when those problems were presented just a few trials apart. Rather than using only a single strategy at a time, students seem to sample, more or less randomly, from a pool of available strategies. Over time the frequency of different strategies waxes and wanes, but it is almost never the case that students are found to use only one strategy exclusively.

This finding is general and robust, and it could only have been detected with microgenetic methods that closely examine students' strategy use over many different trials. In contrast, many published educational studies are incapable of determining whether strategy use (or any other kind of knowledge) is stable or variable across problems or contexts. In these studies, students are typically given one or two problems of any given kind, and if students' answers differ across these problems, it is impossible to say whether this reflects fundamental variability or simply that the student consistently prefers one strategy for one kind of problem and a different strategy for the other. One needs the very large number of problems or contexts employed in microgenetic studies to provide trustworthy information about the extent to which cognition is variable. Indeed, the variability of cognition has probably been seriously underestimated because of the prevalence of non-microgenetic studies.

2. Precipitating Events

Microgenetic studies allow researchers to answer the question of whether there are critical events that precipitate learning and, if so, what these events are. For example, it might prove to be the case that a study of children learning the physical concept of "density" in an inquiry environment shows that the development of that concept is precipitated by anomalous data that cannot be explained by a student's current conceptual framework. That is, children who think that density is equivalent to weight may make no move away from this idea until presented with data showing that two objects with the same weight differ in whether they float in water (cf. Chinn & Brewer, 1993;

Smith, Snir, & Grosslight, 1992). Similarly, it might prove to be the case that use of a particular strategy must precede the discovery of another strategy. For example, as we noted earlier in discussing the min strategy study, the use of the shortcut sum strategy always preceded first use of the min strategy (Siegler & Jenkins, 1989). Understanding what precipitates or initiates change can be very useful for designers of learning environments, who can incorporate critical initiating events or promote use of particular facilitative strategies in their designs. Traditional methods of evaluating learning outcomes may miss critical precipitating events, as the density of observation is too small to catch these events. Microgenetic studies are ideally suited to address questions of what precipitates conceptual change.

3. Co-Occurring Processes or Events

Closely related to the issue of precipitating events is the issue of events and processes that co-occur with change. For instance, research on gestures has provided evidence that critical moments of strategy change while children are learning topics such as mathematics are first manifested in gesture rather than in speech – children make gestures that are indicators of a new strategy, even while their vocalizations refer to the older strategy (Broaders, Cook, Mitchell, & Goldin-Meadow, 2007; Goldin-Meadow, Alibali, & Church, 1993). Similarly, in the min strategy study, Siegler and Jenkins (1989) found that students tended to take a long time and were silent on the trial just before using the min strategy for the first time, suggesting that silent reflection contributed to this change. These findings suggest that scaffolds supporting these processes could be incorporated into effective learning environments. For example, if reflection co-occurs with learning gains, designers of learning environments could build in prompts that encourage reflection on problems. This design recommendation could not have been derived from studies that fail to observe learning processes densely enough to catch learning as it occurs.

4. Learning Trajectories

Research questions about learning trajectories are particularly suited to microgenetic methods, such as questions about trajectories by which conceptual change occurs (see diSessa, Chapter 5, this volume). Consider a study in which students' understanding of matter and molecules is investigated microgenetically over an extended period of time. One might find that students change abruptly from a stable pre-instructional theory to a stable correct theory. For example, students might change from an incorrect theory that matter consists of tiny particles of stuff (tiny drops of water, tiny bits of steel, etc.) to the correct theory that matter is composed of molecules that have different properties from the substances they make up (e.g., water molecules are not wet). Alternatively, one might find that students pass through multiple unstable "incorrect" perspectives, and even that some of these perspectives are necessary as way stations toward the accepted scientific theory. For example, students might pass through a belief that water molecules are hard but have water inside a hard shell, and even though incorrect, this belief ultimately leads them to start seeing how a hard molecule could, in the aggregate, have properties like being pourable as water is. Thus, the intermediate step could help set the stage to move toward a more correct molecular theory. Microgenetic studies provide observations dense enough to detect these kinds of changes, whereas traditional studies that only examine students' conceptions at pretest and posttest fail to detect critical intermediate steps that may occur during instruction. Knowledge of these trajectories can again provide critical information to guide the design of learning environments; it may even be desirable to encourage certain nonnormative incorrect models on the path to mastering the accepted scientific models.

5. Rate of Learning

Finally, microgenetic studies allow researchers to examine the rate of change in strategies or concepts. A traditional study with instruction that lasts several weeks, bookended by a pretest and a posttest, can indicate whether change occurs, but it will say little about how rapidly it occurred. Did change occur within a few minutes on one day, or did it occur gradually across the three weeks? Microgenetic studies provide a dense array of observations that allow researchers to identify the rate of learning with greater precision.

Summary

The five issues discussed in the previous section do not exhaust the range of questions that can be asked of data collected in a microgenetic study. For example, as we discussed earlier, microgenetic studies can be combined with other designs such as experiments, thus allowing microgenetic designs to contribute to answering questions that are well addressed by experiments. But the questions discussed in this section are questions that are particularly well addressed by microgenetic designs and that are difficult or impossible to answer with other designs.

Challenges to Using the Microgenetic Method

In this section, we discuss several of the challenges that arise when designing, implementing, and analyzing studies using the microgenetic method.

Cost of Gathering and Analyzing Verbal and Nonverbal Data

In real-world learning environments, whether schools or science centers or wherever, language plays a central role in learning (Mercer, 2000, 2013). Thus, capturing authentic forms of learning requires us to observe learners in environments where they are talking. Furthermore, a growing body of evidence implicates gestures as having an important role in learning (Goldin-Meadow et al., 1993). Hence, to study naturalistic learning environments, it is desirable to capture the verbal and nonverbal activity that mediates learning. This typically requires video recordings of extended periods of learning by learners working, talking, and gesturing in interactions with an interviewer or peers (see Goldman, Zahn, & Derry, Chapter 11, this volume). Large investments of time are needed to implement and analyze the results of such studies. It is typically necessary to transcribe talk and study transcriptions as well as direct study of video and audio records (see Enyedy & Stevens, Chapter 10, this volume). Developing and executing methods of analyzing rich open-ended data are also time consuming.

Although it would be possible to conduct what looks like a microgenetic study by giving students tasks and asking them very frequent written questions, such a study would not capture the verbal and nonverbal events that occur between these written assessments, nor would they show what students are thinking while completing these assessments. If oral interactions are normally a part of learning, written measures alone will not provide access to critical learning processes. In many cases, there will be no substitute for the cost of engaging in extensive analyses of oral data. (Again, a promising possibility is the use of EDM with computer-based learning environments.)

Distortions Introduced by the Method

Some researchers have argued that it is problematic to rely on verbal reports through methods such as encouraging thinking aloud or querying learners about their strategy use (see Enyedy & Stevens, Chapter 10, this volume). Such methods engage students in activities that they may not naturally engage in, and verbal reports may facilitate or impede learning, depending on the task. Essentially, this issue raises questions of verbal protocols that have been extensively addressed in work on the veridicality of verbal reports (Chi, 1997; Ericsson & Simon, 1993; Siegler, 2006). Ericsson and Simon (1993) concluded that verbal reports are accurate when they are directed at reporting traces that are still in working memory, were in working memory for at least one second, and are sufficiently simple to describe (see Siegler, 2006, for a brief overview of this work). Further, verbal articulation of thinking is a method frequently encouraged for effective learning, in encouragements to make students' thinking public and to engage in self-explanation (e.g., Chi, de Leeuw, Chiu, & LaVancher, 1994; Collins, Brown, & Newman, 1989); hence, these behaviors are not unnatural to learning in well-designed educational settings.

Inferring Strategies or Knowledge

Microgenetic methods must deal with a challenge faced by all cognitive psychological research: How can the researcher make inferences about cognitive structures and processes (in this case, knowledge or strategy use) from verbal and nonverbal behavior? In many cases, a particular behavior could have resulted from more than one candidate cognitive process. For instance, a student who inaccurately identifies the x-y coordinates of a point on a graph by referring to point (1, 3) as point (3, 1) may be confused about how to label points or may simply have misspoken (Schoenfeld et al., 1993). Similarly, a student asked to describe a strategy she has used may inaccurately report her strategy use, or may not have the words to accurately describe the strategy she actually used. Or, imagine a microgenetic study investigating students learning the particulate nature of matter, in which a student communicates for the first time that water is composed of small particles. This may represent a large conceptual change in the understanding of matter, or a more modest change limited only to water, or a purely superficial change in wording or expression that is not accompanied by conceptual change at all.

One common solution to this problem is to use multiple sources of behavioral and observational information that converge on a single underlying learning mechanism. For instance, in order to infer which strategies the children had used on each addition problem trial, Siegler and Jenkins (1989) examined children's overt behavior when solving addition problems, and also examined their verbal description of the strategy they had used. Another possible solution to the problem is to have research team members discuss and argue over potential explanations, with subgroups that favor each explanation seeking additional layers of data until the subgroups come to share a single explanation (e.g., Schoenfeld et al., 1993).

Inferring Contingencies in Learning Sequences

In most microgenetic studies, researchers seek to answer questions about learning sequences (also known as *learning progressions* or *learning trajectories*). For example, a research project might examine whether the development of Strategy Y is more likely to occur (or can only occur) once Strategy X has been used regularly. Or to use a more concrete example, from a biology lesson on evolution, a research project might examine the claim that a robust understanding that variation exists among individuals of a species is a cognitive prerequisite for understanding natural selection.

To design microgenetic studies that allow the researcher to identify such contingencies, the researcher must design the study to control for a full range of confounding factors that might influence learning trajectories. Consider a study in which students are given gradually more difficult algebra problems over a period of 10 one-hour sessions. The researchers' goal is to evaluate whether these 10 sessions are sequenced in a way that aligns best with the students' natural learning progression. But now imagine that an instructor interacting with the students provides feedback when students make mistakes, and imagine that the instructor has provided feedback, during the fifth lesson, to reflect on the connection between two different problems. If the student appears to make a major discovery after this feedback, it may be the case that the feedback was responsible for the discovery. However, there are alternative explanations: the student was also working on a new type of problem for the first time; perhaps it is this new task that triggered the change. Or perhaps the student has just then crossed a threshold of sustained engagement with the material; perhaps any student who works intensively on these problems for four or five sessions will make a similar discovery, with or without the interviewer's feedback. Although microgenetic studies allow researchers to draw conclusions that are impossible with other studies that do not detect learning events as they occur, there are inevitable interpretive challenges. These can be addressed by gathering the richest possible information about the learning events so as to narrow down plausible interpretations, but researchers should also acknowledge other possible explanations in their accounts of their data.

Formal Analytic Methods

Microgenetic studies have small samples and repeated measures – often dozens or even hundreds – per participant. As a result, the statistical methods most commonly used in the social sciences cannot be used with microgenetic data. However, there are several formal analytic methods that can be appropriately used (Siegler (2006), Chinn (2006), and Lavelli, Pantoja, Hsu, Messinger, & Fogel (2005)).

(1) Examining conditional probabilities that one event occurs before or after another event. As discussed earlier, Siegler and Jenkins used conditional probabilities in the min studies by examining what preceded the first use of the min strategy, finding that students paused significantly more on the problem before using the min strategy than on problems that did not precede the min strategy. Siegler and Jenkins also found that, prior to children's first use of the min strategy, they usually had encountered an addition problem in which one addend was very large (such as 27 + 3). This kind of analysis is useful for asking what events trigger other events. For example, a microgenetic study of learning evolution might reveal

that students must understand variation within species before they can grasp natural selection processes, as evidenced by students not giving natural selection explanations until *after* they are consistently making note of variation in traits among individuals of the same species.

(2) Lag analysis (Bakeman, Adamson, & Strisik, 1989) is a statistical analytic method that can be used to detect contingencies in a long serious of events. The input to the analysis is a string of coded data – such as a string indicating what kinds of strategies children are using as they work on mathematics problems together. Lag analysis might indicate, for example, that when children ask each other for reasons for their ideas, the children do tend to give reasons, but that their reasons tend to be delayed until two or three turns after the question was posed (Jadallah et al., 2011).

(3) Graphical analyses of trends and trajectories. Many microgenetic researchers have used graphs to show trends and trajectories. This kind of analysis has provided evidence for the variability in strategy use. For example, in graphical analyses of children using strategies while adding, Siegler (1996) graphically demonstrated that at any one time, children were using multiple strategies across problems. These graphs also show that strategies used earlier gradually decrease in frequency, whereas others (such as the min strategy and shortcut sum strategy) become more frequent. The graphs can show how different strategies wax and wane during extended learning periods.

(4) Intensive qualitative case studies analyzing progressions in students' thinking. Microgenetic research demands that we employ methods that are as attentive as possible to the richness of learning phenomena. For this reason, intensive qualitative case studies are a natural fit. For example, Parnafes (2012) presented a case study of one pair of students working to explain the phases of the moon. These students began with a nonnormative explanation and then, over the course of about an hour, worked to construct a sophisticated and largely correct explanation. She argued that the change occurred as the pair successively transitioned from one temporary coherent structure to the next. Parnafes's argument for her account takes the form of a narrative presentation, including excerpts from transcripts, along with an interpretation in terms of her theory. Similarly, Sherin, Krakowski, and Lee (2012), presented narrative cases in which individual students construct explanations of the seasons.

As in the research of Schoenfeld and colleagues, these narrative-based accounts were arrived at through iterative analysis by a research team, as they worked to develop a theoretical framework and to produce an analysis of the data in terms of that framework. Intensive case studies have a number of drawbacks; they are hard to apply to a large number of cases, and the analytic methods applied to the data can be difficult to codify and to communicate when work is written up for publication. The approach also has important strengths. It allows for substantial attention to the richness of learning phenomena. It is also particularly useful for the development of theory and for the discovery of new learning phenomena that can be studied further using other means.

Craft of Design, Implementation, and Analysis

As with other learning sciences methodologies, such as design-based research, researchers conducting microgenetic studies must use a great deal of *craft knowledge*, by which we mean knowledge of practice that is often partly tacit. For example, interviewers cannot simply follow a script when interviewing learners; interviewers must have an ability to engage learners for prolonged periods in tasks that may sometimes seem repetitive. Similarly, there is a great deal of tacit, practical knowledge that goes into setting up tasks that will sustain student engagement through these repetitive tasks. Expertise is also needed to fashion usable transcriptions that include both verbal and nonverbal behaviors of interest; expertise is required to make sense of the oceans of data that are produced.

Conclusions

In this chapter, we have discussed the advantages of the microgenetic method for investigating learning. Most types of learning of interest to learning sciences involve learners gradually learning challenging concepts and strategies over an extended period of time. The microgenetic method is designed to follow these learning events very closely so that learning changes can be detected when they occur, and so that researchers can understand the detailed trajectories by which learning occurs, as well as the critical events that nurture growth, moment by moment. For these reasons, the microgenetic method is an indispensable tool for learning scientists.

References

Bakeman, R., Adamson, L. B., & Strisik, P. (1989). Lags and logs: Statistical approaches to interaction. In Marc H. Bornstein & Jerome S. Bruner (Eds.), *Interaction in human development: Crosscurrents in contemporary psychology* (pp. 241–260). Hillsdale, NJ: Lawrence Erlbaum Associates.

Broaders, S. C., Cook, S. W., Mitchell, Z., & Goldin-Meadow, S. (2007). Making children gesture brings out implicit knowledge and leads to learning. *Journal of Experimental Psychology: General*, 136, 539–550.

Buckland, L. A., Chinn, C. A., & Duncan, R. G. (2010, May). *Epistemic growth in model-based argumentation.* Paper presented at the annual meeting of the American Educational Research Association, Denver, CO.

Catán, L. (1986). The dynamic display of process: Historical development and contemporary uses of the microgenetic method. *Human Development*, 29, 252–263.

Chi, M. T. H. (1997). Quantifying qualitative analyses of verbal data: A practical guide. *The Journal of the Learning Sciences*, 6, 271–315.

Chi, M. T. H., de Leeuw, N., Chiu, M., & LaVancher, C. (1994). Eliciting self-explanations improves understanding. *Cognitive Science*, 18, 439–477.

Chinn, C. A. (2006). The microgenetic method: Current work and extensions to classroom research. In J. L. Green, G. Camilli, & P. Elmore (Eds.), *Handbook of complementary methods in education research* (pp. 439–456). Washington, DC: American Educational Research Association.

Chinn, C. A., & Brewer, W. F. (1993). The role of anomalous data in knowledge acquisition: A theoretical framework and implications for science instruction. *Review of Educational Research*, 63, 1–49.

Collins, A., Brown, J. S., & Newman, S. E. (1989). Cognitive apprenticeship: Teaching the crafts of reading, writing, and mathematics. In L. B. Resnick (Ed.), *Knowing, learning, and instruction: Essays in honor of Robert Glaser* (pp. 453–494). Hillsdale, NJ: Lawrence Erlbaum Associates.

Crowley, K., Shrager, J., & Siegler, R. S. (1997). Strategy discovery as a competitive negotiation between metacognitive and associative mechanisms. *Developmental Review*, 17, 462–489.

Ericsson, K. A., & Simon, H. A. (1993). *Protocol analysis: Verbal reports as data*. Revised Edition. Cambridge, MA: MIT Press.

Goldin-Meadow, S., Alibali, M. W., & Church, R. B. (1993). Transitions in concept acquisition: Using the hand to read the mind. *Psychological Review*, 100, 279–297.

Hmelo-Silver, C. E., Duncan, R. G., & Chinn, C. A. (2007). Scaffolding and achievement in problem-based and inquiry learning: A response to Kirschner, Sweller, and Clark (2006). *Educational Psychologist*, 42, 99–107.

Jadallah, M., Anderson, R. C., Nguyen-Jahiel, K., Miller, B. W., Kim, I.-H., Kuo, L.-J., & Wu, X. (2011). Influence of a teacher's scaffolding moves during child-led small-group discussions. *American Educational Research Journal*, 48, 194–230.

Kuhn, D. (1995). Microgenetic study of change: What has it told us? *Psychological Science*, 6, 133–139.

Kuhn, D., & Phelps, E. (1979). A methodology for observing development of a formal reasoning strategy. *New Directions for Child Development*, 5, 45–57.

Kuhn, D., & Phelps, E. (1982). The development of problem-solving strategies. *Advances in Child Development and Behavior*, 17, 1–44.

Kuhn, D., Schauble, L., & Garcia-Mila, M. (1992). Cross-domain development of scientific reasoning. *Cognition and Instruction*, 9, 285–327.

Lavelli, M., Pantoja, A. P. F., Hsu, H.-C., Messinger, D. S., & Fogel, A. (2005). Using microgenetic designs to study change processes. In D. M. Teti (Ed.), *Handbook of research methods in developmental science* (pp. 40–65). Malden, MA: Blackwell.

Lin, X., & Lehman, J. D. (1999). Supporting learning of variable control in a computer-based biology environment: Effects of prompting college students to reflect on their own thinking. *Journal of Research in Science Teaching,* 36, 837–858.

Mayer, R. E. (2004). Should there be a three-strikes rule against pure discovery learning? The case for guided methods of instruction. *American Psychologist*, 59, 14–19.

Mercer, N. (2000). *Words and minds: How we use language to think together*. London: Routledge.

Mercer, N. (2013). The social brain, language and goal-directed collective thinking: A social conception of cognition and its implications for understanding how we think, teach, and learn. *Educational Psychologist,* 48(3), 148–168.

Parnafes, O. (2012). Developing explanations and developing understanding: Students explain the phases of the moon using visual representations. *Cognition and Instruction*, 30, 359–403.

Rittle-Johnson, B., & Alibali, M. W. (1999). Conceptual and procedural knowledge of mathematics: Does one lead to the other? *Journal of Educational Psychology*, 91, 175–189.

Schauble, L. (1996). The development of scientific reasoning in knowledge-rich contexts. *Developmental Psychology*, 32, 102–119.

Schoenfeld, A. H., Smith, J. P., & Arcavi, A. (1993). Learning: The microgenetic analysis of one student's evolving understanding of a complex subject matter domain. In R. Glaser (Ed.), *Advances in instructional psychology* (vol. 4, pp. 55–175). Hillsdale, NJ: Lawrence Erlbaum Associates.

Sherin, B. L., Krakowski, M., & Lee, V. R. (2012). Some assembly required: How scientific explanations are constructed during clinical interviews. *Journal of Research in Science Teaching*, 49, 166–198.

Siegler, R. S. (1996). *Emerging minds: The process of change in children's thinking*. New York: Oxford University Press.

Siegler, R. S. (2006). Microgenetic analyses of learning. In D. Kuhn & R. Siegler (Eds.), *Handbook of child psychology* (pp. 464–510). Hoboken, NJ: John Wiley & Sons.

Siegler, R. S., & Chen, Z. (1998). Developmental differences in rule learning: A microgenetic analysis. *Cognitive Psychology*, 36, 273–310.

Siegler, R. S., & Crowley, K. (1991). The microgenetic method: A direct means for studying cognitive development. *American Psychologist*, 46, 606–620.

Siegler, R. S., & Jenkins, E. (1989). *How children discover new strategies*. Hillsdale, NJ: Lawrence Erlbaum Associates.

Siegler, R. S., & Stern, E. (1998). Conscious and unconscious strategy discoveries: A microgenetic analysis. *Journal of Experimental Psychology*, 4, 377–397.

Smith, C., Snir, J., & Grosslight, L. (1992). Using conceptual models to facilitate conceptual change: The case of weight-density differentiation. *Cognition and Instruction*, 9, 221–283.

Taylor, J., & Cox, B. D. (1997). Microgenetic analysis of group-based solution of complex two-step mathematical word problems by fourth graders. *The Journal of the Learning Sciences*, 6, 183–226.

10 Analyzing Collaboration

Noel Enyedy and Reed Stevens

The study of collaboration has been part of the learning sciences from its inception. However, articles have appeared that use different definitions of collaboration, that give different reasons for studying it, and that use different methods. This variability has continued to the present. To help make sense of this variety, we propose that the spectrum of methodologies used in collaboration research can be usefully divided into four groups, associated with four different reasons to study collaboration (see Table 10.1): Collaboration-as-a-window, collaboration-for-distal-outcomes, collaboration-for-proximal-outcomes, and collaboration-as-learning.

It is tempting to try to place these four approaches along a single continuum. For example, Howley, Mayfield, and Rose (2013) provide a well-organized discussion of approaches to studying collaboration that range from a focus on the individual as the unit of analysis to a focus on collaborative processes for enculturation as the unit of analysis (also see the "elemental" and "systemic" distinction in Nathan & Sawyer, Chapter 2, this volume). However, we find that a single dimension unnecessarily flattens the research topology on collaboration and learning. Instead, we propose that these four approaches can be distinguished along four dimensions, as shown in Table 10.1: the unit of analysis for describing processes of collaboration and cognition; the unit of analysis for documenting learning outcomes; the degree to which these outcomes are operationalized as proximal (within the collaboration) or distal (outside the collaboration); and the degree to which a normative stance is taken on collaboration. We argue that these four dimensions, and the assumptions that accompany them, provide insight into the methodological choices that researchers have made and may make in the future.

These four dimensions allow us to better characterize the four methodological approaches to studying collaborative discourse, by capturing how they differ along one or more of these dimensions. Our first category – collaboration-as-a-window – uses contexts of collaboration to better understand individual cognition. Our second category – collaboration-for-distal-outcomes – seeks to document how particular patterns of collaboration promote or constrain productive learning activities leading to positive or negative individual outcomes that are operationalized apart from the interaction itself (e.g., performance on a later written test). Our third category – collaboration-for-proximal-outcomes – attempts to link collaborative

Table 10.1. *Four reasons to study collaboration and learning*

Objective for investigating collaboration	Unit for Processes	Unit for Outcomes	Proximal/Distal outcomes	Normative/ Endogenous	Typical methods
Collaboration-as-a-window	Individual	Individual	Proximal (and Distal)	Normative	Code single isolated turns based on the content of what was said
Collaboration-for-distal-outcomes	Collective	Individual	Distal	Normative	Correlate a sequence (IRE), class of talk, or participation framework with distal, individual outcomes
Collaboration-for-proximal-outcomes	Collective	Collective (to explain individual)	Proximal (to explain distal)	Normative	Identify conversational moves that lead to a new, consequential state in the collaboration and explain distal learning outcomes in terms of these processes and proximal outcomes. Use transcript conventions that go beyond the content of talk and document multiparty, multimodal nature of discourse
Collaboration-as-Learning	Collective	Collective	Proximal	Endogenous	Focus on uncovering the organization of collaboration as a members' phenomenon

processes with outcomes within the interaction itself (e.g., intersubjectivity), and (sometimes) uses those outcomes to explain distal learning outcomes. Our fourth category, collaboration-as-learning, treats collaboration as more than a means to proximal or distal outcomes, but as the focal process and outcome itself. Forms of collaboration are themselves outcomes. This view brings with it a commitment to understanding the "endogenous" organization and understandings of collaboration among research participants.

Our goal in this chapter is to frame the choice of methods for studying collaboration and interaction by reviewing the work in each of the four categories described in Table 10.1. In reviewing this work we hope to show that there is more at stake here than merely a choice of methods; these four positions each stake out a theoretical commitment to how collaboration is defined and what counts as learning. It is conscious reflection on these theoretical commitments – the reason one is studying collaboration in the first place – that should drive the choice of methods. This is much preferred to the alternative: that the choice of methods unconsciously drives and constrains one's theory of collaborative learning.

Four Reasons to Study Collaboration and Learning

One simple way to understand our four categories is that they answer the question, "Why study collaboration?" In the following sections, we describe four objectives that drive different paradigms of learning sciences research on collaborative discourse and four corresponding methodological approaches.

1. Collaboration-as-a-Window-onto-Thinking

One reason to study collaboration is to learn more about how individuals think. In such a study, the focus is not on collaborative processes per se, and the methods typically used in these studies reflect this. For example, the learning sciences has strong genealogical roots in cognitive science, and one of the early methods for studying learning and problem solving within cognitive science was the use of verbal protocols. In a verbal protocol study, a person is asked to think aloud, in the presence of a researcher, while carrying out some task (Ericsson & Simon, 1993).

For example, Schoenfeld's (1992) scheme for analyzing mathematical problem solving coded individuals' "thought units" in collaborative talk among group members in terms of the phases of problem solving (reading the problem, analysis, planning, and execution). Although these cognitive actions happened during a social interaction, the interaction itself was treated as epiphenomenal – meaning that it had no causal impact on learning outcomes. Rather, the social interaction was only a convenient way to verbalize the thinking process of the individuals, to allow it to be coded. Other studies of classroom interaction take this same approach. For example, in a recent study by Ellis (2007), whole class discourse, as well as semi-structured interviews, were coded to create a taxonomy of the types of generalizations that students made. The taxonomy included two broad categories – generalizing actions and generalizing statements. Specific codes classified what was said (e.g., relating, searching, and extending). What is telling about Ellis's (2007) methods was that she merged collaborative discourse and the semi-structured interviews, coding and aggregating both using the same coding scheme, thus ignoring the interactional differences between a one-on-one interview and a multiparty conversation. Further, the analysis relied exclusively on the content of what was said, not the interactional context of the conversation. If one accepts the premise that collaboration is just a window into the mind, and that the interactions themselves are epiphenomenal and therefore incidental to the research, then coding individual turns of talk in terms of what they reveal about knowledge states and cognitive processes has the appearance of a warranted simplification. However, we argue that an approach that treats collaboration as epiphenomenal misses the core assumption of collaborative learning – that the ways learners respond to each other matters to both the processes and outcomes of learning.

Methods for Representing and Analyzing Collaboration-as-a-Window onto Thinking

A focus of this chapter is on methods for studying how collaborative discourse impacts learning, and because the collaboration-as-a-window approach treats discourse as epiphenomenal, we will keep our discussion of methods in this category brief. Researchers who conceptualize collaborative discourse as a window onto thinking focus primarily on the content of talk, rather than the interactional processes of talk, which is then coded at the level of single turns, aggregated, quantified, and submitted to statistical analysis (Chi, 1997). Quite often they seek to minimize social influences by using contrived situations such as clinical interviews or problem solving in laboratory conditions. These situations are contrived in the sense that they are not naturally occurring contexts for talk and action, but have the advantage of being well-controlled situations designed to focus the talk on the issues the researchers care most about and to minimize other factors that might complicate access to topics and behavioral displays that are of interest to the researchers. Researchers who ask this kind of research question generally do not analyze variations in interlocutors, the order in which ideas are produced, or the interactions between people that shaped how ideas were expressed.

2. Collaboration as a Context that Promotes (or Constrains) Distal Learning Outcomes

For a second group of researchers, collaboration is treated as a context that promotes and constrains different types of observable actions and forms of thinking. Different types of collaboration can be identified and associated with varying levels of individual learning outcomes, which are identified outside the immediate context of the interaction, such as performance on a later cognitive task or a measure of motivation. This second approach has a long history and has been used in many research studies. Studies have identified many relationships between discourse patterns and any number of measures of distal student outcomes, such as the artifacts produced as a result of collaboration (Mercer, 2008), student achievement (e.g., Nichols, 1996; Webb, 1991; Webb & Mastergeorge, 2003), developmental growth (Sun, Zhang, & Scardamalia, 2010), and motivation (e.g., Jones & Issroff, 2005). Because the foci of these studies are learning outcomes that are correlated with sequences of interaction (i.e., forms of collaborative discourse), these studies have sometimes also been referred to as *effect-oriented research* – studies that aim to document the effect of a particular type of discourse on learning outcomes (Dillenbourg, Baker, Blaye, & O'Malley, 1996; Janssen, Erkens, & Kirschner, 2011; cf. Erickson's critique of "process-product" research, 1986).

One of the earliest and most well-known examples used in this category of studying collaborative discourse is the identification of the common (in school) three-turn dialog sequence known as IRE (Cazden, 1986; Mehan, 1979). IRE typically involves the teacher asking a question to which the answer is known (Initiate) and the student responding with a short response (Respond), which the teacher evaluates as right or wrong (Evaluate). Criticisms of this discourse pattern as a means of promoting learning outcomes valued by the learning sciences are wide and deep. Among these criticisms is that the IRE leads students to view learning as involving quick recall of known facts rather than conceptual learning or critical thinking (e.g., Wood, 1992). Note that the researchers who first identified the pattern of IRE were more interested in it as a common pattern of institutionalized schooling and how it functioned in classrooms, rather than its effectiveness, per se. For the most part they agreed that, "in itself, triadic dialogue is neither good nor bad; rather, its merits – or demerits – depend upon the purposes it is used to serve on particular occasions, and upon the larger goals by which those purposes are informed" (Wells, 1993, p. 3).

However, the now pervasive critique of IRE *based on its effectiveness* is an example of our second category, because it links an identifiable pattern of collaborative discourse with particular learning outcomes, which in this case are largely viewed as deleterious. Unlike the first approach, conversational sequence and processes are the direct foci of the analysis, along with the individual outcomes.

A more positive example of this category of research comes from the seminal study of O'Connor and Michaels (1996), who identified a pattern of discourse that promoted a deep level of conceptual engagement on the part of the students, which they called *revoicing*. Unlike in IRE-patterned discourse, an instance of revoicing begins with a student's turn of talk; the teacher then responds by restating part of what the student said, elaborating or positioning it (e.g., in contrast with another student's idea); which in turn provides an opening for the student to agree or disagree with how the teacher transformed what they said. Revoicing has most often been linked to increased engagement and positive identification with subject matter (Forman, Larreamendy-Joerns, Stein, & Brown, 1998; Strom, Kemeny, Lehrer, & Forman, 2001).

While we characterize this paradigm of research as effect oriented (i.e., driven by finding patterns of collaborative discourse that promote positive learning outcomes), it often involves rich, theoretical descriptions of the collaborative process and why the process leads to effective learning. For example, O'Connor and Michaels theorize the mechanism that connects this pattern of discourse with positive learning outcomes in terms of the productive participation framework it creates. Participation frameworks describe the rights, roles, and responsibilities of participants and how they create the conditions for different ways of learning (Erickson, 1982; O'Connor & Michaels, 1996). Their findings suggest that revoicing increases the degree to which students explicate and expand their reasoning, and it motivates a purposeful search for evidence to support their ideas (see Enyedy, Rubel, Castellon, Mukhopadhyay, & Esmond, 2008, for an expanded list of the functions of revoicing).

This category of research, however, is not limited to identifying short sequences of talk. Researchers have also identified broad classes of talk that correlate with distal, individual learning outcomes. These broad classes of talk do not necessarily map onto a single sequence of turns like the examples given earlier. For example, Mercer identified multiple types of productive talk in classrooms such as "exploratory talk" – marked by broad participation, listening to other people's ideas, and presenting alternatives – and "accountable talk" – characterized by challenging ideas and providing rationale for challenges. Mercer and Hodgkinson (2008) demonstrated empirically how classrooms that routinely display these styles of classroom discourse have better individual student outcomes (e.g., test scores), lead to better individual problem-solving skills, and produce better group products. Likewise, Scardamalia and Bereiter (1994) argued that "knowledge building discourse," characterized by a culture of individual contributions to a shared knowledge base, leads to increased content understanding, higher reading scores, and vocabulary growth (Sun et al., 2010).

Finally, some researchers that are motivated by distal, individual learning describe collaborative discourse in even broader terms, often in terms of the social norms that guide and constrain productive interactions. *Norms* refers to the expectations for what counts as appropriate activity and interaction held by the teachers and students (Cobb, 2002). Cobb (2002) demonstrated how a set of norms can lead students to participate within a classroom so that they end up engaging deeply with the mathematical concepts and as a result have a better facility with the mathematical practices. Similarly, Cornelius and Herrenkohl (2004) investigated how changing the power relations between students and teachers in science classrooms can create democratic participation structures that encourage students to engage deeply with science concepts. Like Cobb (2002), they directly manipulated the classroom's participation framework (the rights, roles, and responsibilities), which in turn led to changes in how students participated and engaged with the science content.

Methods for Correlating Sequences of and Norms for Talk with Distal Learning Outcomes

This second methodological approach requires identifying a collaborative pattern (i.e., either a specific process such as revoicing or a broad class of talk such as accountable talk) within discourse and correlating or relating it to a distal outcome typically reified as a product (Erickson, 1986).

This style of research greatly depends on the researcher's ability to operationalize and define the collaborative phenomena of interest and the outcomes in order to make both observable and measurable. On the process side of the equation, the researcher must choose the scale at which the phenomena of interest becomes visible – in terms of a fixed sequence of turns (e.g., IRE), classes of talk (e.g., accountable talk), or classroom-level structures (e.g., norms). As one moves across these timescales or grain sizes – from particular sequences to classroom-level structures – one increases the number of mappings between specific patterns in discourse to their proposed function. That is, identifying a case of IRE or revoicing is fairly straightforward, whereas there are multiple ways to challenge or justify an idea, all of which would be coded as "accountable talk."

A methodological caution is appropriate here. The process-product method of the collaboration-for-distal-outcomes approach can quickly be reduced to the collaboration-as-a-window approach. Researchers who are ultimately interested in individual outcomes may be tempted to simply treat interaction as a series of successive contributions by individuals that are coded and analyzed independently. We argue that to treat interaction like a back-and-forth exchange – coding and analyzing individual, isolated turns of talk as inputs to individual cognitive processes – is based on the tenuous assumption that the effect of collaboration can be factored out, what Greeno and Engeström (Chapter 7, this volume) refer to as the *factoring assumption*.

The type of research that we are categorizing in our second category fundamentally disagrees with the premise of the collaboration-as-a-window

Matthew   Okay. And how did you think of that?

Sharon   I don't know. Guess. (inaudible). It's like in the middle.

Matthew   In the middle. **That's what I want them to hear. Because if you had totally guessed you might have said a hundred.**

Sharon   Yeah.

Matthew   *So you didn't guess, you thought about it.* Okay.

Figure 10.1. *A standard playscript of a revoicing episode (Enyedy et al., 2008) that uses bolded and italicized text to highlight theoretical constructs such as revoicing but erases interactional details.*

approach, succinctly summarized by Simon, who wrote, "the foundation stone of the entire enterprise is that learning takes place inside the learner and only inside the learner … the murmuring of classroom discussion and study groups – all of these are wholly irrelevant except insofar as they affect what knowledge and skills are stored inside learners' heads" (Simon, 2001, p. 210). Instead, those who take the collaboration-for-distal-outcomes approach typically analyze multi-turn exchanges that they then correlate to distal outcomes/products.

Once the interactional constructs are operationalized, the researcher's task becomes producing a data corpus from the primary audio and video recordings that are amenable to these constructs. This means constructing an intermediate representation (Barron, Pea, & Engle, 2013) of the interaction that can be coded. Most often this is a transcript of the talk in the form similar to a simple theatrical playscript, which identifies who is speaking and what they say, but little in the way of information about timing, intonation, and body position (see Figure 10.1).

On the products/outcomes side of the equation, operationalizing learning outcomes can range from quite simple measures such as time on task or the score on a test (Klein & Pridemore, 1992), to more complex outcomes such as engagement (Engle & Connant, 2002; Forman et al., 1998).

There is a great deal of variation within this basic structure. Studies can be inductive, based on developing codes from the data corpus, or deductive, based on a set of a priori codes (see Erickson, 2006, for in-depth discussion of the implications and histories of these approaches). Studies can be based on a systematic review of all the records in the corpus or based on case studies. Further, studies can be purely qualitative (e.g., O'Connor & Michaels, 1996), can involve mixed methods (e.g., Puntambekar, 2013), or can rely on the aggregation, quantification, and statistical analysis of coded transcripts (e.g., Cress & Hesse, 2013).

3. Collaboration Coordinated with Proximal, Collective Outcomes within the Interaction Itself

A third body of research tightens the focus of collaboration on proximal outcomes, such as intersubjectivity, that are identified within a focal interaction itself and that are believed to mediate the relationship between patterns of discourse and the distal outcomes like those described in the previous section. This is currently one of the most active areas of research in the learning sciences, because its goal is to explain how collaborative processes contribute directly to learning (Chin & Osbourne, 2010; Enyedy, 2003; Hmelo-Silver, 2000).

A paradigmatic example of this approach is Wertsch and Stone's (1999) account of how interaction contributes to learning problem solving. In their study a mother is completing a jigsaw puzzle with her child. The mother begins by verbally directing the child to look at the model first, find a corresponding piece, and then place it in the appropriate part of the puzzle. A bit later on in the same interaction, they show the child having a conversation with herself, using the same questions her mother used to guide her, now used to guide her own activity. Wertsch and Stone argue that interactions were *appropriated* by the child and transformed into mental tools for thought. Their analysis identified a series of semiotic challenges, and other specific interactional moves, that lead to what they call a shared definition of the situation (i.e., what the mother and daughter understand the activity to be about) that allows the child to successfully imitate the mother and appropriate her strategies. What is important here is to note that the analysis centers on the *mutual process* of achieving intersubjectivity, and a proximal outcome that can be identified within the interaction and that is *by definition* a relational property of the pair's activity, rather than a property of either or both individuals.

Taking this perspective does not preclude looking at distal learning outcomes that are assumed to be the property of individual minds. One of the very first papers on collaboration in the *Journal of the Learning Sciences* (Roschelle, 1992) is a good example of an analysis that studied collective processes of sense making that were tied to both collective, proximal outcomes in the conversations (i.e., intersubjectivity) and to individual, distal outcomes (i.e., better individual understanding of the physics concepts). Roschelle's analysis explicitly set out to integrate a collective unit of analysis for collaborative processes with an individual as the unit of analysis for conceptual change. The study detailed how two collaborative processes – iterative cycles of turn taking and progressively higher standards of evidence – contributed to each individual's conceptual change. The analysis of cycles of turn taking demonstrated how contributions of frames, elaborations, and clarifications were provided in response to requests, challenges, and assessments. The construction of shared referents to deep structures of the problem, so critical to conceptual change, was argued to be a joint accomplishment that could not be adequately understood as two independent individual processes.

Methods for Representing and Analyzing Collaborative Discourse with the Evidence for Learning Operationalized Proximally in the Interaction Itself

This close attention to the process of collaboration as a jointly produced activity has been accompanied by a major methodological change in how interactions are represented and studied. Nowhere is this more evident than in the way interactions are represented through transcription conventions. When one brings a collective unit of analysis to the study of collaboration, one needs techniques that allow analysts to track how interactions unfold across participants, for the purposes of identifying units of activity that span different turns, and thereby, different participants in an interaction. This in turn involves capturing all manner of interaction detail that other approaches we have discussed typically "clean up" and leave out of transcripts. These interactional details have been most thoroughly documented by three decades of conversation analysis research (Garfinkel, 1996; Schegloff, 2006); salient details include, among others, the boundaries of when turns at talk start and stop, the prosody of speech, and the pitch contours of particular words. These matter for analysts because they demonstrably matter for the meanings that people in collaboration attribute to each other and act on in interaction. Similarly, people in interaction rely on multiple modalities (e.g., speech, gesture, pointing) and semiotic resources (e.g., texts, pictures, and the affordances of material structures). Finally, groups develop shared meanings, shorthand conventions, and common routines as they work together over time.

This need to make the micro-analytic details of collaborative discourse visible and amenable to analysis has led the field of the learning sciences to develop and borrow transcript conventions from conversation analysis that provide methods for closely looking at the multiparty, multimodal, and temporally unfolding qualities of interaction. For example, many learning sciences studies have borrowed the Jeffersonian transcription conventions of conversation analysis (Atkinson & Heritage, 1984) that represent the timing and order of turns as well as the pauses and prosody within turns (Figure 10.2 and Table 10.2). These elements of interaction problematize simple notions of the "propositional content" of talk (e.g., in protocol analysis), because what people produce in interaction is demonstrably understood by participants in terms of *how* they produce it.

Other transcript conventions have been developed (Erickson, 1996; Goodwin & Goodwin 1987) that display different aspects of collaboratively achieved interaction, such as interaction's music-like rhythms or the relations of talk to representational action (see Figure 10.3). Increasingly, learning scientists have also attended to how material and embodied aspects of interaction (Enyedy, 2005; Stevens & Hall, 1998) – proximity to others, gesture, physical features of the environment, drawings and other representational

Derek: We think the game is unfair. [We think that the game== team A
will win more often because]

Will: [We think that team A...will win
more often because]== (points to team A's outcomes as he counts along
the bottom row)

Derek: ==It, I mean they==

Will: ==have more....have more ==

Derek: ==have..more==

Will: ==more slots.

Derek: Opportunity.

Figure 10.2. *Transcript using Jeffersonian conventions showing, timing, overlap, and latching in an interaction (Enyedy, 2003).*

Table 10.2. *A selection of Jeffersonian transcription conventions (Atkinson & Heritage, 1984)*

Convention	Name	Use
[talk]	Brackets	Indicates the start and end points of overlapping speech.
=	Equal Sign	Indicates latching where there is no pause between turns.
(# of seconds)	Timed Pause	Indicates the time, in seconds, of a pause during speech.
(.)	Micropause	A brief pause, usually less than 0.2 seconds.
. or ↓	Period or Down Arrow	Indicates falling pitch.
? or ↑	Question Mark or Up Arrow	Indicates rising pitch.
,	Comma	Indicates a short rise or fall in intonation.
-	Hyphen	Indicates an abrupt interruption of the utterance.

media – structure collaboration (see Figures 10.4 and 10.5). Taken together these various elements of transcription allow the analyst to produce analyses of how people collaboratively realize an activity. These interactional details are not elective, because it is through these very details that participants orient each other to how a collaborative activity is proceeding and where it might go next.

The point we are making is that no single transcript convention is better than others for all purposes; all select for and highlight different aspects of interaction (Duranti, 2006; Ochs, 1979). What is also critical to keep in mind is that transcripts are to be understood as ongoing relations with

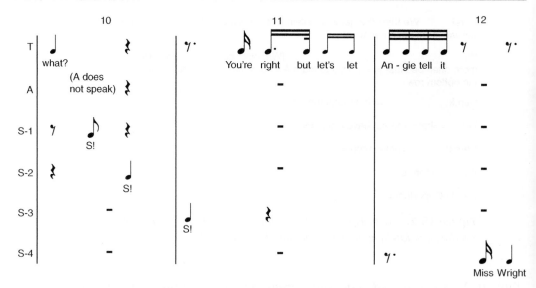

Figure 10.3. *Transcription conventions that attend to the synchronic rhythms of multiparty talk (Erickson, 1996).*

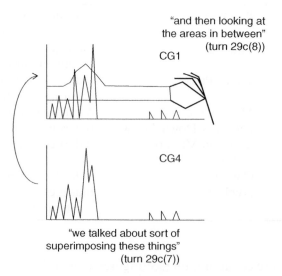

Figure 10.4. *Transcription conventions that display the relations of embodied action to representational media (Hall, Stevens, & Torralba, 2002).*

whatever recording they have been made from (Duranti, 2006; Pomerantz & Fehr, 2011). To reify a transcript as a complete representation of an interaction is a danger to which too many succumb. As an exercise, imagine that you had to reenact an interaction based on one of the transcripts cited earlier. Now imagine that another person also had to reenact the same

Speaker	Dialog
1 Sarah	It will be really hard to show it because uh it is really small to see (.)

How[1] (.) they drew it because it's really-it's like kinda smaller than my finger that I can do it.

*Holds fingers in a "C" shape and shrinks the space as she squints with one eye closed

So it is really small to see how to put the detail inside[2]

[2] puts one hand inside the cupped other hand

and put the blocks together[3]

[3] puts the heels of her hands together

| 2   Teacher | Okay, so absolutely the scale, we call that the scale of the map, right Sarah? |

That it is <u>drawn</u>[4] so small that it might make it difficult. Do people agree with Sarah about that?

[4] motions hand toward the map held in her other hand

Figure 10.5. *Transcription conventions that display the timing of gesture within a turn of talk (Enyedy, 2005).*

interaction based on the same transcript. Like two different stagings of a play, the reenactments would likely differ in significant ways, because the transcript only provided partial information. More significant, both reenactments would likely differ from what was seen on the original video recording.

We suggest that, in early stages of analysis, researchers move back and forth between multiple transcript conventions as well as engage in multiple viewing practices such as watching in groups, watching with the research subjects, or watching at different speeds (Barron et al., 2013). We see this as akin to the basic premises of mixed methods where one uses multiple complementary sources that each shed a different light on the phenomena. Because each rendering of the interaction through the lens of a particular transcript convention is partial and incomplete, multiple transcript conventions of the same interaction are one way for the analyst to study the mutual elaborations that occur in interaction.

Although we have focused on qualitative data analysis here, statistical techniques that preserve the sequence and interdependencies of interaction are still sometimes appropriate for this approach to the study of collaborative discourse. For example, Strom and colleagues (2001) traced the sequences of argument progression with a distributed unit of analysis. Likewise, new techniques such as lag-sequential analysis (Anderson et al., 2001; Jeong, 2005) and social network analysis (Cress & Hesse, 2013) focus on how contributions to collaborative discourse are dependent on one another, as well as other patterns that span multiple turns of collaborative discourse. Regardless of whether the methods are qualitative or quantitative, the critical aspect is that they attend to interaction as collective process and link that process to collective outcomes that occur within the conversation itself.

4. Collaboration-as-Learning: Committing to a Distributed, Endogenous Unit of Analysis

A fourth category within the learning sciences holds that collective units of activity are an important unit of analysis in their own right. Learning is operationalized as relational changes to a system with multiple parts, human and nonhuman – "adaptive reorganization in a complex system" (Hutchins, 1995a, p. 289). To clarify this perspective and how it differs from the other three we have already discussed, let us recall what Hutchins and others mean by "distributed cognition." In using this term, Hutchins is directing attention to units of analysis that stretch across multiple people and tools, interacting in coordination in a "socio-cultural system." Hutchins's "How a Cockpit Remembers Its Speed" (1995b) displays this orientation in its very title. In this article, Hutchins argues that the relevant unit of analysis for the cognitive tasks that matter for landing a large commercial aircraft span a pilot, his or her copilot, and a host of instruments and physical resources. Reducing the analysis of cognition – or by implication, measuring the cognitive processes of the individual pilot or copilot – obscures a lot of what matters to the successful realization of that cognitive task, which is landing the aircraft. As Hutchins says, "the outcomes of interest are not determined entirely by the information processing properties of individuals" (Hutchins, 1999b, p. 265).

In some cases, learning scientists have borrowed from these anthropologically oriented traditions to expand a focus beyond individuals, for both the processes and the outcomes of collaboration. One example of such a study is Stevens's (2000) comparative analysis of a division of labor that emerged among a group of middle school students doing a project-based mathematics architecture unit and the division of labor among professional architects. Here Stevens took *teams* as his primary unit of analysis and examined individual participation and contributions within evolving divisions of labor. In so doing, Stevens showed that the divisions of labor changed and that changes to this distributed unit of analysis could be tied to the performance and outcome of the group's projects in both cases. Parallel to Hutchins's approach, Stevens does not banish the contributions and dispositions of individual participants, but shows that without the distributed, irreducible unit of team division of labor, the individual contributions and learning opportunities cannot be properly understood.

In another important study, Barron's "When Smart Groups Fail" looked at activity within student groups and found that "between-triad differences in problem solving outcomes" (2003, p. 307) could not be reduced to prior measures of individual group members' capacities. Instead, Barron argued that qualities of the interaction among team members – such as how well they recognized, listened to, and made use of contributions by other members of their group – were correlated with these problem solving outcome differences. In both Stevens's and Barron's studies, there was analytic attention to how groups themselves perform as collectives and to qualities of how they "coordinate" their activities – rather than an exclusive focus on the consequences of these interactions for individual outcomes. These joint capacities and achievements are effectively lost when groups or teams, or other sized and shaped collectives, are reduced to the contributions, capacities, and performance outcomes of individuals alone.

Though a handful of learning sciences studies have foregrounded collective units of analysis, the clearly dominant approach has remained one that examines collaboration as a means to understand and promote individual, distal learning outcomes. This imbalance is perhaps puzzling given the clear influence, as evidenced by citations in JLS, to socioculturally oriented authors (e.g., Lave, Cole, Hutchins, Goodwin, and Rogoff) who stress constructs like participation and joint action. One possible explanation for this imbalance is that historically the learning sciences has been closely tied to the values, goals, and institutional practices of schooling. And schooling really only "counts" (i.e., assesses and records) the performances of individuals, paying little more than lip service to the products and processes of joint activity. In short, the learning sciences adopted the units of analysis of schooling and its kindred academic cousin, institutionalized psychology (McDermott & Hood, 1982).

In the past decade, however, learning in contexts other than schools has finally become a real focus for learning sciences research (Bell, Lewenstein, Shouse, & Feder, 2009; Ito et al., 2010; Stevens, Wineburg, Herrenkohl, & Bell, 2005). This shift away from schools as the exclusive site for learning research should, in turn, lead us to expect more studies in the future that take distributed units of cognition and learning as their focus. We expect this because the participants in these nonschool contexts do "count" the performances of its collectives (e.g., teams, groups, families, or firms) alongside and often with more weight than the contributions of individual members.

These insights can be pushed further to suggest that shifts toward distributed units of collaboration, along with a widening focus on learning in nonschool contexts, invite a more distinctly *endogenous* approach to collaboration and learning (Stevens, 2010; cf. Garfinkel, 1996). An endogenous approach tilts away from normative or prescriptive considerations (at least initially) and emphasizes basic descriptive-analytic goals concerning how research participants themselves understand and enact collaboration. What counts as collaboration to the people we are studying? An endogenous approach argues that for every socially organized phenomenon about which outside analysts have a stance, so too do the participants themselves.

We offer two reasons to take an endogenous approach to collaboration. First, as we know from many language use studies, a normative approach often smuggles in cultural values of dominant or majority groups (e.g., Michaels, 2005; Phillips, 1983; Tharp & Gallimore, 1988). What is true of language practice studies in general is equally true of collaboration studies.

An endogenous perspective on collaboration can help inoculate learning sciences researchers against deficit theorizing and imposing culturally specific, normative standards on the collaborative practices of others.

A second reason for taking an endogenous approach to collaboration involves the basic constructivist premise of much learning sciences research. In its original Piagetian formulation, the idea was that children build new ideas out of existing ones. Contemporary learning sciences researchers have expanded the idea of building on prior knowledge – usually thought of as knowledge about the physical world – to include cultural knowledge, arguing that understanding the existing cultural knowledge and practices of youth provides pathways toward new learning. Examples include argumentation in science (Warren & Rosebury, 1995), culturally familiar language practices as a bridge to literary interpretation (Lee, 2001), and culturally relevant mathematics instruction (Enyedy, Danish, & Fields, 2011). In other words, assuming the core theoretical perspective of constructivism, an endogenous approach to collaboration can be seen as a valuable initial step toward achieving normative goals of better collaboration.

The Methods of a Distributed, Endogenous Approach

Methods aligned with either a distributed or endogenous approach to collaboration receive relatively clear guidance from the related approaches to studying social life and interaction known as conversation analysis (CA) and ethnomethodology (EM) (e.g., Goodwin, 2000; Goodwin & Heritage, 1990; Lynch, 1993; Schegloff, 2006). We discussed many of these methods of studying multimodal, multiparty social interaction earlier in this chapter. However, while some of the techniques and transcriptions conventions of CA have been adopted by researchers who study collaboration in other ways (e.g., what we have called collaboration-for-distal-outcomes and collaboration-for-proximal-outcomes), these approaches to collaboration rarely adopt CA/EM's central endogenous heuristic. This heuristic insists that a successful analysis of a socially organized activity like collaboration must render it as a "members' phenomenon" rather than as "one of those things which, as social scientists, we construct and manage" (Sacks, quoted in Stevens, 2010). Therefore, successful endogenous analyses of collaboration will show how members themselves are jointly managing and emergently maintaining collaboration of some particular kind to which they are jointly accountable, regardless of whether outside, normative considerations would regard that collaboration as good or bad, productive or unproductive. Endogenous analyses of collaboration, like those of learning itself (Stevens, 2010), represent a new direction for learning sciences research, one we hope finds expression in future work.

The collaboration as learning approach, with its heuristic of *starting and ending* with collective, distributed units of activity, also exposes an interesting methodological challenge for learning research. As noted earlier, from a typical individualistic ontology (cf. Greeno & Engeström, Chapter 7, this volume on the factoring hypothesis), collaborative forms are simply compositions of multiple individuals, temporarily held together. The collaboration as learning perspective turns this familiar logic upside down (cf. Goodwin, 2003; McDermott, 1993), arguing that in many cases, the distributed unit is historically durable and recognized by the group's members; it is this unit of joint activity and meaning that individual people join. For example, a work group in a professional setting evolves with newcomers coming and old timers going, but it is a rarity for a work group to begin anew, with an entirely new cohort of people who are asked to develop new goals and work practices. This suggests one way to conceive of a distal collective outcome; we need to understand how individuals become integrated to and integrate themselves as members into existing collective units, and use this frame to contextualize what and how individuals learn as they move into these collectives (Lave & Wenger, 1991).

The contrast between the informal sites for collaborative learning and how collaboration is organized in formal schooling is striking. In schools, we isolate individuals via tests and other forms of individual record keeping. But in the many other contexts in which people collaborate and learn together, these forms of isolating individuals are less common or nonexistent. How in these other settings, amidst distributed units of teams, groups, families, and firms are the contributions of individuals recognized and isolated as distinct? This is one of the important and interesting questions that an endogenous and distributed perspective on collaboration brings into view.

Conclusion

The variability we see in the methods adopted in the learning sciences for studying collaboration reflects the breadth of research questions being asked and the range of assumptions within the field about what counts as learning. Many learning scientists study collaboration to better understand how it can reveal or produce knowledge about individual learning, and they adopt a normative perspective on what counts as good learning. However, some of the traditions we borrow methods from (e.g., protocol analysis, clinical interviews) carry with them assumptions and theoretical entailments that were developed within an individual psychological perspective and later expanded to include collaboration. Other traditions the learning sciences borrows methods from (e.g., ethnography and conversational analysis) are committed to a distributed, endogenous unit of analysis. As the field moves forward and expands its horizons outside of the classroom, discussion and debate about the consequences of the approach one takes toward the study of collaboration, about the unit of analysis, and about adopting a commitment to the normative or endogenous stance are critical to unifying or at least understanding important differences in our field's effort to study collaboration and learning in a wide range of contexts.

References

Anderson, R. C., Nguyen-Jahiel, K., McNurlen, B., Archodidou, A., Kim, S., Reznitskaya, A., et al. (2001). The snowball phenomenon: Spread of ways of talking and ways of thinking across groups of children. *Cognition and Instruction*, 19, 1–46.

Atkinson, J. M., & Heritage, J. (1984). Transcription notation. In J. Atkinson & J. Heritage (Eds.), *Structures of social interaction* (pp. ix–xvi). New York: Cambridge University Press.

Barron, B. (2003). When smart groups fail. *The Journal of the Learning Sciences*, 12(3), 307–359.

Barron, B., Pea, R., & Engle, R. (2013). Advancing understanding of collaborative learning with data derived from video records. In C. Hmelo-Silver, C. Chinn, C. Chan, & A. O'Donnell (Eds.), *The International Handbook of Collaborative Learning* (pp. 203–219). New York: Routledge.

Bell, P., Lewenstein, B., Shouse, A. W., & Feder, M. A. (Eds.). National Research Council. (2009). Learning science in informal environments: People, places, and pursuits. Committee on Learning Science in Informal Environments, Board on Science Education, Center for Education, Division of Behavioral and Social Sciences and Education, National Academy of Sciences. Washington, DC: The National Academies Press.

Cazden, C. (1986). Classroom discourse. In M. C. Wittrock (Ed.), *Handbook on teaching*. Third Edition. (pp. 432–460). New York: Macmillan.

Chi, M. T. H. (1997). Quantifying qualitative analyses of verbal data: A practical guide. *The Journal of the Learning Sciences*, 6, 271–315.

Cobb, P. (2002). Reasoning with tools and inscriptions. *The Journal of the Learning Sciences*, 11, 187–216.

Cobb, P., Stephan, M., McClain, K., & Gravemeijer, K. (2001). Participating in classroom mathematical practices. *The Journal of the Learning Sciences*, 10, 113–163.

Cobb, P., Yackel, E., & McClain, K. (Eds.) (2000). *Symbolizing and communicating in mathematics classrooms: Perspectives on discourse, tools, and instructional design*. Mahwah, NJ: Lawrence Erlbaum Associates.

Cornelius, L. L., & Herrenkohl, L. R. (2004). Power in the classroom: How the classroom environment shapes students' relationship with each other and with concepts. *Cognition & Instruction*, 22(4), 467–498.

Cress, U., & Hesse, F. (2013). Quantitative methods for studying small groups. In C. Hmelo-Silver, C. Chinn, C. Chan, & A. O'Donnell (Eds.), *The International Handbook of Collaborative Learning* (pp. 93–111). New York: Routledge.

Dillenbourg, P., Baker, M., Blaye, A., & O'Malley, C. (1996). The evolution of research on collaborative learning. In E. Spada & P. Reiman (Eds.),

Learning in humans and machine: Towards an interdisciplinary learning science (pp. 189–211). Oxford: Elsevier.

Duranti, A. (2006). Transcripts, like shadows on a wall. *Mind, Culture and Activity*, 13(4), 301–310.

Ellis, A. (2007). A taxonomy for categorizing generalizations: Generalizing actions and reflection generalizations. *Journal of the Learning Sciences*, 16(2), 221–262.

Engle, R. A., & Conant, F. R. (2002). Guiding principles for fostering productive disciplinary engagement: Explaining an emergent argument in a community of learners classroom. *Cognition and Instruction*, 20(34), 399–483.

Enyedy, N. (2003). Knowledge construction and collective practice: At the intersection of learning, talk, and social configurations in a computer-mediated mathematics classroom. *The Journal of the Learning Sciences*, 12(3), 361–408.

Enyedy, N. (2005). Inventing mapping: Creating cultural forms to solve collective problems. *Cognition and Instruction*, 23(4), 427–466.

Enyedy, N., Danish, J. A., & Fields, D. (2011). Negotiating the "relevant" in culturally relevant mathematics. *Canadian Journal for Science, Mathematics, and Technology Education*, 11(3), 273–291.

Enyedy, N., Rubel, L., Castellon, V., Mukhopadhyay, S., & Esmond, I. (2008). Revoicing in a multilingual classroom: Learning implications of discourse. *Mathematical Thinking and Learning*, 10(2), 134–162.

Erickson, F. (1982). Classroom discourse as improvisation: Relationships between academic task structure and social participation structure in lessons. In L. C. Wilkinson (Ed.), *Communicating in the classroom* (pp. 153–182). New York: Academic.

Erickson, F. (1986). Qualitative methods in research on teaching. In M. C. Wittrock (Ed.), *Handbook of research on teaching*. Third Edition. (pp. 119–161). New York: Macmillan.

Erickson, F. (1996). Going for the zone: The social and cognitive ecology of teacher-student interaction in classroom conversations. In D. Hicks (Ed.), *Discourse, learning, and schooling* (pp. 29–62). New York: Cambridge University Press.

Erickson, F. (2006). Definition and analysis of data from videotape: Some research procedures and their rationales. In J. Green, G. Camilli, & P. Elmore (Eds.), *Handbook of complementary methods in educational research*. Third Edition. (pp. 177–191). Washington, DC: American Educational Research Association.

Ericsson, K. A., & Simon, H. A. (1993). *Protocol analysis: Verbal reports as data*. Second Edition. Cambridge, MA: MIT Press.

Forman, E., Larreamendy-Joerns, J., Stein, M., & Brown, C. (1998). "You're going to want to find out which and prove it": Collective argumentation in a mathematics classroom. *Learning and Instruction*, 8, 527–548.

Garfinkel, H. (1996). Ethnomethodology's program. *Social Psychology Quarterly*, 59(1), 5–21.

Goodwin, C. (2000). Practices of seeing, visual analysis: An ethnomethodological approach. In T. van Leeuwen & C. Jewitt (Eds.), *Handbook of visual analysis* (pp. 157–187). London: Sage.

Goodwin, C. (2003). Conversational frameworks for the accomplishment of meaning in aphasia. In C. Goodwin (Ed.), *Conversation and brain damage* (pp. 90–116). Oxford: Oxford University Press.

Goodwin, C., & Goodwin, M. (1987). Children's arguing. In S. Philips, S. Steele, & C. Tanz (Eds.), *Language, gender, and sex in comparative perspective* (pp. 200–248). Cambridge, MA: Cambridge University Press.

Goodwin, C., & Heritage, J. (1990). Conversation analysis. *Annual Review of Anthropology*, 19, 283–307.

Hall, R., Stevens, R., & Torralba, A. (2002). Disrupting representational infrastructure in conversations across disciplines. *Mind, Culture, and Activity*, 9, 179–210.

Hmelo-Silver, C. E. (2000). Knowledge recycling: Crisscrossing the landscape of educational psychology in a problem-based learning course for preservice teachers. *Journal on Excellence in College Teaching*, 11, 41–56.

Howley, I., Mayfield, E., & Rose, C. (2013). Linguistic analysis methods for studying small groups. In C. Hmelo-Silver, C. Chinn, C. Chan, & A. O'Donnell (Eds.), *The International Handbook of Collaborative Learning* (pp. 184–202). New York: Routledge.

Hutchins, E. (1995a). *Cognition in the wild*. Cambridge, MA: MIT Press.

Hutchins, E. (1995b). How a cockpit remembers its speeds. *Cognitive Science*, 19, 265–288.

Ito, M., Horst, H. J., Finn, M., Law, L., Manion, A., Mitnick, S., Schlossberg, D., & Yardi, S. (2010). *Hanging out, messing around and geeking out*. Cambridge, MA: MIT Press.

Janssen, J., Erkens, G., & Kirschner, P. A. (2011). Group awareness tools: It's what you do with it that matters. *Computers in Human Behavior*, 27, 1046–1058.

Jeong, A. (2005). A guide to analyzing message-response sequences and group interaction patterns in computer mediated communication. *Distance Education*, 26(3), 367–383.

Jones, A., & Issroff, K. (2005). Learning technologies: Affective and social issues in computer-supported collaborative learning. *Computers & Education*, 44, 395–408.

Klein, J. D., & Pridemore, D. R. (1992). Effects of cooperative learning and need for affiliation on performance, time on task, and satisfaction. *Educational Technology, Research and Development*, 40(4), 39–47.

Lave, J., & Wenger, E. (1991). *Situated learning: Legitimate peripheral participation*. Cambridge: Cambridge University Press.

Lee, C. D. (2001). Signifying in the Zone of Proximal Development. In C. Lee & P. Smagorinsky (Eds.), *Vygotskian perspectives on literacy research: Constructing meaning through collaborative inquiry* (pp. 191–225). Cambridge, MA: Cambridge University Press.

Lynch, M. (1993). *Scientific practice and ordinary action: Ethnomethodology and social studies of science*. Cambridge: Cambridge University Press.

McDermott, R. (1993). The acquisition of a child by a learning disability. In S. Chaiklin & J. Lave (Eds.), *Understanding practice* (pp.269–305). London: Cambridge University Press.

McDermott, R. P., & Hood (Holzman), L. (1982). Institutional psychology and the ethnography of schooling. In P. Gilmore & A. Glatthorn (Eds.), *Children in and out of school: Ethnography and education* (pp. 232–249). Washington, DC: Center for Applied Linguistics.

Mehan, H. (1979). *Learning lessons: Social organization in the classroom*. Cambridge, MA: Harvard University Press.

Mercer, N. (2008). The seeds of time: Why classroom dialogue needs a temporal analysis. *Journal of the Learning Sciences*, 17, 33–59.

Mercer, N., & Hodgkinson, S. (Eds.) (2008). *Exploring classroom talk*. London: Sage.

Michaels, S. (2005).Can the intellectual affordances of working-class storytelling be leveraged in school? *Human Development*, 48, 136–145.

Nichols, J. D. (1996). The effects of cooperative learning on student achievement and motivation in a high school geometry class. *Contemporary Educational Psychology*, 21(4), 467–476.

Ochs, E. (1979). Transcription as theory. In E. Ochs & B. B. Schieffelin (Eds.), *Developmental pragmatics* (pp. 43–72). New York: Academic Press.

O'Connor, M. C., & Michaels, S. (1996). Shifting participant frameworks: Orchestrating thinking practices in group discussion. In D. Hicks (Ed.), *Discourse, learning, and schooling* (pp. 63–103). New York: Cambridge University Press.

Osborne, J. (2010). Arguing to learn in science: The role of collaborative, critical discourse. *Science*, 328, 463–466.

Philips, S. (1983). *The invisible culture: Communication in classroom and community on the Warm Springs Indian Reservation*. Prospect Heights, IL: Waveland Press, Inc.

Pomerantz, A., & Fehr, B. J. (2011). Conversation analysis: An approach to the analysis of social interaction. In T. A. van Dijk (Ed.), *Discourse studies: A multidisciplinary introduction* (pp. 165–190). London: Sage.

Puntambekar, S. (2013). Mixed methods for analyzing collaborative learning. In C. Hmelo-Silver, C. Chinn, C. Chan, & A. O'Donnell (Eds.), *The International Handbook of Collaborative Learning* (pp. 220–230). New York: Routledge.

Roschelle, J. (1992). Learning by collaborating: Convergent conceptual change. *Journal of the Learning Sciences*, 2(3), 235–276.

Scardamalia, M., & Bereiter, C. (1994). Computer support for knowledge-building communities. *Journal of the Learning Sciences*, 3, 265–283.

Schegloff, E. A. (2006). Interaction: The infrastructure for social institutions, the natural ecological niche for language, and the arena in which culture is enacted. In N. J. Enfield and S. C. Levinson (Eds.), *Roots of human sociality: Culture, cognition and interaction* (pp. 70–96). London: Berg.

Schoenfeld, A. H. (Ed.) (1992). Research methods in and for the learning sciences, a special issue of *The Journal of the Learning Sciences*, Volume 2, No. 2.

Simon, H. A. (2001). Learning to research about learning. In S. M. Carver & D. Klahr (Eds.), *Cognition and instruction: Twenty-five years of progress* (pp. 205–226). Mahwah, NJ: Lawrence Erlbaum Associates.

Stevens, R. (2000). Divisions of labor in school and in the workplace: Comparing computer and paper-supported activities across settings. *Journal of the Learning Sciences*, 9(4), 373–401.

Stevens, R. (2010). Learning as a members' phenomenon: Toward an ethnographically adequate science of learning. *NSSE 2010 Yearbook: A Human Sciences Approach to Research on Learning*, 109(1), 82–97.

Stevens, R., & Hall, R. (1998). Disciplined perception: Learning to see in technoscience. In M. Lampert & M. L. Blunk (Eds.), *Talking mathematics in school: Studies of teaching and learning* (pp. 107–149). Cambridge: Cambridge University Press.

Stevens, R., Wineburg, S., Herrenkohl, L., & Bell, P. (2005). The comparative understanding of school subjects: Past, present and future. *Review of Educational Research*, 75(2), 125–157.

Strom, D., Kemeny, V., Lehrer, R., & Forman, E. (2001). Visualizing the emergent structure of children's mathematical argument. *Cognitive Science*, 25, 733–773.

Sun, Y., Zhang, J., & Scardamalia, M. (2010). Knowledge building and vocabulary growth over two years, Grades 3 and 4. *Instructional Science*, 38(2), 247–271.

Tharp, R. G., & Gallimore, R. (1988). *Rousing minds to life: Teaching, learning, and schooling in social context*. Cambridge: Cambridge University Press.

Warren, B., & Rosebery, A. (1995). Equity in the future tense: Redefining relationships among teachers, students and science in linguistic minority classrooms. In W. Secada, E. Fennema, & L. Adajian (Eds.), *New directions for equity in mathematics education* (pp. 298–328). New York: Cambridge University Press.

Webb, N. M. (1991). Task-related verbal interaction and mathematics learning in small groups. *Journal for Research in Mathematics Education*, 22, 366–389.

Webb, N. M., & Mastergeorge, A. M. (2003). The development of students' learning in peer-directed small groups. *Cognition and Instruction*, 21, 361–428.

Wells, G. (1993). Articulation of theories of activity and discourse for the analysis of teaching and learning in the classroom. *Linguistics and Education*, 5, 1–37.

Wertsch, J. V., & Stone, C. A. (1999). *The concept of internalization in Vygotsky's account of the genesis of higher mental functions, Lev Vygotsky: Critical assessments: Vygotsky's theory* (Vol. I, pp. 363–380). Florence, KY: Taylor & Francis /Routledge.

Wood, D. (1992). Teaching talk. In K. Norman (Ed.), *Thinking voices: The work of the National Oracy Project* (pp. 203–214). London: Hodder & Stoughton (for the National Curriculum Council).

11 Frontiers of Digital Video Research in the Learning Sciences: Mapping the Terrain

Ricki Goldman, Carmen Zahn, and Sharon J. Derry

In the highly acclaimed 1975 volume *Principles of Visual Anthropology* edited by Paul Hockings, anthropologist Margaret Mead wrote about the future of video recordings and new tools for conducting research. In 1975, Mead was ahead of her time in observing that continually emerging video-based technologies would enable researchers to record, replay, and learn from the "visual and sound materials" they collected while conducting research. As Mead so aptly noted:

> Many of the situations with which we deal, situations provided by thousands of years of human history, can never be replicated in laboratory settings. But with properly collected, annotated, and preserved visual and sound materials, we can replicate over and over again and can painstakingly analyze the same materials. As finer instruments have taught us about the cosmos, so finer recordings of these precious materials can illuminate our growing knowledge and appreciation of mankind. (Hockings, 1975, p. 10)

This chapter describes various ways learning sciences researchers are using digital video to document, study, and enhance scholarly understanding of complex learning environments. It discusses historical, theoretical, methodological, and technical issues related to collecting and using digital video. This chapter also provides examples of research illustrating specific advances learning scientists have made in applying video research methods over the past 20 years. Our goal is to provide a bird's eye view of the scholarly landscape of video research in the learning sciences. As Margaret Mead reminded us, with the invention of new, refined tools, we may "illuminate our growing knowledge" of how we study learning and, yes, how we learn about humankind.

We start by introducing foundational resources in digital video research in which each of the authors has played a central role. Then we discuss historical and more recent methodological contributions made by innovators and early adopters from visual anthropology, educational ethnography, cognitive ethnography, semiotics, sociology, mathematics and science education, and cognitive studies of *learning with video*. In the third section of this chapter we address a range of methods and tools used with video data. Then, we offer representative cases of current video research in formal and informal learning settings, including the use of digital video in controlled classroom experiments and case studies in naturalistic settings such as museums. We conclude by offering our speculations about the future of using digital video in learning science research.

Foundational Resources for Digital Video Research

This chapter is grounded in four seminal works using digital video research in the learning sciences.

First, we draw on the first pioneering digital video ethnography (1990) using a specifically designed multimedia analysis tool, Learning Constellations™ (circa 1988), for documenting, analyzing, and interpreting the learning approaches of children in a computer-rich elementary school mathematics culture. This study is documented in a dissertation, "Learning Constellations: A Multimedia Ethnographic Research Environment Using Video Technology to Explore Children's Thinking Styles" (Goldman-Segall, 1990a). The more finely tuned book with an accompanying online video Web site, *Points of Viewing Children's Thinking: A Digital Ethnographer's Journey* (Goldman-Segall, 1997), maps a possible future for digital video ethnographic research in education. The book opens with a preface that invites researchers to consider how to rethink the nature of ethnography and learning in a world of multiple representations for capturing, sharing, and analyzing digital data. It also describes two longitudinal studies and the use of pioneering software tools for video data analysis – Constellations™ and Web Constellations™. Innovations to the learning sciences include: software for numerically rating descriptive tags on video segments using a significance measure (Goldman-Segall, 1993); participation of middle school students who shoot, digitize, and edit video; and inclusion of readers of the online video and book as members of the research culture (to comment on video, go to http://www.pointsofviewing.com).

Second, we rely strongly on another resource, *Video Research in the Learning Sciences* (Goldman, Pea, Barron, & Derry, 2007). This handbook-length volume with 67 authors is organized around four cornerstone themes: theoretical and methodological frameworks from ethnography, semiotics, conversational analysis, aesthetics, pleasure, and phenomenology, to conduct and present learning sciences research; video research in peer, family, and informal learning to capture learning processes that arise in settings such as museums, learning centers, and after school clubs; video research in classroom and teacher learning to illuminate how teachers and students learn through study of complex, real-world practices that are captured and represented through digital video media; and video collaboratories and technical futures to explore the value of digital video tools for representation, reflection, interaction, and collaboration to support research.

Third, we draw from a recent report commissioned by the National Science Foundation (NSF) to guide funding agencies and researchers regarding what constitutes quality in video research: *Guidelines for Video Research in Education: Recommendations from an Expert Panel* (Derry, 2007). Representing consensus findings from an NSF-sponsored invitational conference and follow-up by a working panel, the report makes recommendations in five categories: data collection (recording) strategies; selection and sampling guidelines; analytical approaches; models for sharing and reporting video data; how to promote learning with and from video; and ethical issues in conducting video research. Portions of this report, addressing the intersecting problems of selection, analysis, technological support, and ethics, were further refined and peer reviewed for publication in the *Journal of the Learning Sciences* (Derry et al., 2010). Aspects of the report dealing with learning from video, especially teacher learning from classroom video, were refined and published in *The Cambridge Handbook of Multimedia Learning* (Derry, Sherin & Sherin, 2014).

Fourth, we rely on works based on experimental field research on digital learning environments in the classroom published in relevant international books and journals, such as the *Journal of the Learning Sciences* and the *International Journal of Computer Supported Learning* (e.g., Zahn, Krauskopf, Hesse, & Pea, 2010, 2012; Zahn, Pea, Hesse, & Rosen, 2010). This research investigated the paradigm shift in video usage associated with advanced Web-based video and Hypervideo tools (e.g., Chambel, Zahn & Finke, 2005; Pea, Mills, Rosen, Dauber, & Effelsberg, 2004; Zahn & Finke, 2003) as opposed to more traditional forms of video usage in educational settings. Digital video technologies were studied as cognitive and collaborative tools in experimental and field studies that demonstrate how usage patterns of video create new potentials for constructivist learning, for instance in history (Zahn et al., 2010, 2012) and psychology (Stahl, Zahn, & Finke, 2006).

Innovators of Visual and Video Research

Historical Roots

The first film ever shot for research purposes, rather than for illusion or entertainment, was the result of a wager that a Californian racehorse owner, Leland Stanford, made on his claim that all four legs of a horse would be off the ground when trotting. He hired photographer and inventor Eadward Muybridge to prove this claim. Muybridge, in 1878, placed a lineup of cameras on a track, attached wires to camera shutters, and waited for the horse to trip the wires while passing by. By placing the shots from different cameras together, Muybridge created a moving image and proved the Californian correct. Unlike with any previous technology, images placed side by side and played in succession could enable the viewer to perceive what the naked eye could not when watching the actual events.

Early anthropologists who traveled to foreign lands with cameras set the stage for using film as a medium to capture the images of natural life, or so it seemed. In retrospect, there is much ambivalence about their process of representing "others" and about the fruits of their labor – exotic images seen by the most often white and Western "gaze" (Trinh, 1993). They were convinced that collecting specimens, cultural artifacts, and written and visual records of what they experienced was an important contribution of their field, and that they were documenting "native" customs that would die out when Western civilizations intruded (Peck, 1981).

Anthropologists and visual ethnographers agree with Jean Rouch (1975) that anthropologist Margaret Mead and cybernetician Gregory Batson, using analog film, are the earliest and most influential researchers to use the moving image in ethnographic research. Longitudinal filmmaking research was employed when Bateson, working with Mead in Bali, Indonesia from 1936 to 1939, used a wind-up movie camera to study trance dancing (Rony, 2006). Earlier pioneers include Felix-Louis Regnault, who filmed a Wolof (ethnic group from Senegal) woman making pottery without a wheel at the Exposition Ethnographique de l'Afrique Occidentale in 1895; and Robert Flaherty, who realistically staged the life of the Inuit in his silent documentary film, *Nanook of the North* (1922).

The main benefit of this early usage of film was that a researcher could record how people in foreign lands behaved and, months later, share those moving images with colleagues, far away from where they were shot. The films told stories of men, women, and children who shared a different set of customs, signs, symbols, dances, and ways of rearing children.

Contributions from Sociology and Ethnography

As far back as 1888 with the compelling photograph, *Brandt's Roost*, by Jacob Riis, exposing the poverty of Manhattan's Lower East Side, sociologists and ethnographers noted the affordances of the camera as a tool for commenting on the lives of people at home, school, work, or play. The purpose was to affect positive changes in society.

According to Tochon (2007), the aim of semiotics is to address the connection among video research, signs, social effect, and social engagement. He proposes that video becomes a mirror for those who are videotaped to reconsider their actions and transform society. Lemke (2007) describes "the semiotic uses of video in terms of the ways we meaningfully (and feelingfully) move across and through immediate and mediated attentional spaces." Lemke explores this idea in a recent work that addresses the importance of feelingfulness, of videographers and the middle school children who partook in a study about emotion and playing with games in a San Diego after school program (Lemke, 2013).

Koschmann, Stahl, and Zemel (2007) use ethnomethodology of small chunks of video data to closely examine how learners form and act in collaborative communities. They claim that Harold Garfinkel's notion of indexicality underscores the importance of the utterance within a context enabling the analyst to get a handle on what that utterance means. Situating the case within the content and context, McDermott and Goldman (2007) also claim that the case study is embedded in what they call a behavioral and social interactionist theoretical framework. In short, the experienced researcher needs to be cognizant of the context from which video segments are selected.

Scholars have described Clifford Geertz's papers discussing local knowledge (1983) and thick description (1973) as the quintessential ethnographic works because they untangle the common dichotomy between locality and generalization. As Geertz says, "The [ethnographic] effort is to preserve the individuality of things and unfold them in larger worlds of sense at the same time" (Geertz, 1983, p. xi). Following in Geertz's footsteps, Goldman (2007b, 2004) recommends using the perspectivity framework wherein the "individuality" of video data is "unfolded in larger worlds of sense" by enabling all the stakeholders to capture video and analyze the dataset to create what she calls *thick interpretation*.

A related research approach known as *cognitive ethnography* (Williams, 2006) employs traditional ethnographic methods to build knowledge of a community of practice, and then uses this knowledge to situate micro-level analyses of specific episodes or events of activity. The aim of cognitive ethnography is to reveal how cognitive activities are accomplished in real-world settings. Pioneers of this style of research include Goodwin (1996), Hall (e.g., Hall, Stevens, & Torralba, 2002), and Hutchins (2005). These researchers provide models for video collection, analysis, and representation of results, as well as direct advice on the practicalities of doing cognitive ethnographic research with video.

Contributions from Mathematics and Science Education

Researchers studying mathematics and science learning and teaching have made influential methodological contributions to video research. For example, working from a cognitive perspective, Roschelle and colleagues (e.g., Roschelle, 1992) pioneered the use of video to study science learning. A historically significant project was the Third International Mathematics and Science Study (TIMSS; Stigler, Gonzales, Kawanaka, Knoll, & Serrano), the first to videotape a comparative sample of classrooms for the purpose of making international comparisons of mathematics teaching. This study set a standard for international sampling.

Mathematics education researcher Paul Cobb and colleagues (e.g., Cobb & Whitenack, 1996) developed methods for using video to study children's mathematical development in social context. Using data from a classroom study in which two cameras captured pairs of children collaborating on mathematics problem solving over a course of 27 lessons (the children were also recorded in interviews and whole-class interactions), they articulated a three-stage method that begins with interpretive episode-by-episode analyses, which in turn become data for meta-analyses that ultimately produce integrated chronologies of children's social and mathematical development. They characterized their approach as a zigzagging between making conjectures and seeking confirmation or refutation. At all stages the researchers' interpretations were influenced by specific research questions and theoretical assumptions.

Powell, Francisco, and Maher (2003) describe an analytical approach developed in the context of a longitudinal study of children's mathematical development within constructivist learning environments. Their seven-step method begins with attentively viewing video and proceeds through stages of identifying critical events, transcribing, coding, and composing analytic narratives. Like Cobb and Whitenack (1996), they emphasize the importance of interpretive frameworks and research questions while also remaining open to emergent discoveries.

Contributions from Cognitive Studies of Learning with Video

Researchers working in the cognitive tradition have also pioneered a different type of research that develops and uses video cases as cognitive tools to engage learners in complex analyses and problem solving. The goal of these types of research programs is to support and study learners in making various mental connections between real-world problems (depicted in video episodes or "cases") and more abstract, theoretical knowledge. This is illustrated, for example, by research with the "Jasper Woodbury Series," a set of interactive video stories developed by the Cognition and Technology Group (1997) at Vanderbilt University in the late 1980s and 1990s. Students watch the stories of protagonist Jasper Woodbury and his adventures and work collaboratively with the interactive videos in class to solve abstract math problems.

Additional examples include work by Spiro, Collins, and Ramchandran (2007), who explain how systems that provide random access to video can support development of cognitive flexibility, especially in advanced learners. An implementation is described by Derry, Hmelo-Silver, Nagarajan, Chernobilsky, and Beitzel (2006), who demonstrated the effectiveness of teacher education courses offered in STELLAR (sociotechnical environment for learning and learning activity research), a system supporting problem-based learning (PBL) that also facilitated study of video cases integrated with conceptual knowledge, in accordance with cognitive flexibility theory. Similarly, Goeze, Zottmann, Fischer, and Schrader (2010) showed in experiments how the competence to analyze and assess complex classroom situations could be improved substantially and sustainably among novice teachers using an online learning environment (www.videofallarbeit.de) designed in line with cognitive flexibility theory principles where digital video cases were enriched by hyperlinks to conceptual knowledge and multiple perspectives.

While the goals of these types of video research programs (to support learning) can be contrasted with the goals of programs that use video primarily as a tool for collecting data to examine and study learners and learning environments in depth, there are often some overlapping purposes. For example, video cases to support learning are often selectively developed from video datasets collected for basic research on learning (Derry et al., 2010).

Methods and Tools for Digital Video Research

Video researchers have evolved methods and tools to address the problems of capturing, sharing, and analyzing that are inherent in working with video. The concrete video tools at hand and how they are deployed have fundamental impacts on the data, the analyses, and on how data and analyses can be shared with others. Imagine a video showing a classroom situation recorded by a single camera with a perspective from the teacher's front desk into the room. Or imagine a video showing the same classroom situation recorded with multiple cameras capturing different perspectives and edited as a "video case." One also might want to think about how this same classroom situation would be captured by a 360° panoramic camera or by the roving and documentary-style camera observing and *interacting with* learners as they are in the midst of learning. How will the video data differ? How will analyses differ?

Researchers should make informed choices from among available tools to collect, analyze, and archive video data. To make such decisions, researchers need to be aware of available video functions and tools, their different purposes, and their effects on the data collection and analysis. In this section we will describe possible approaches related to capturing, analysis, and sharing video records.

Video Data Collection

Good video research starts with gaining clarity about what research questions will be asked and/or topics will be addressed. It also begins with asking what frameworks and analytic methodologies will be applied. Because video data may be archived, reused, and repurposed to serve goals beyond those conceived at the beginning of a particular study, researchers need to consider that research questions may emerge during and after data collection. Thus, experienced video researchers working in field settings usually find a balance between focusing data collection to ensure its adequacy for addressing initial research topics and questions and planning for flexible adaptability during data collection. The degree of flexibility possible during data capture will depend on what tools and human resources are available.

Before deciding on the technical equipment and data collection procedures, it is important that researchers envision in detail the situation they want to observe in relation to their research goals. In a laboratory setting, one might easily simulate the situation in advance for this purpose. For naturalistic field observations, it is strongly recommended that researchers visit the site beforehand, discuss the endeavor in detail with the relevant people to get a clear picture, and consider where and how to use the cameras.

Ideally, the following questions are asked and answered before data collection begins: What is the focus of my study? If I use a quantitative framework, which research goals and questions will guide my study? What are my hypotheses? What information do I need to collect to answer these questions or test my hypotheses? If using a qualitative framework, the questions are: Which events does the researcher record that provide insights into the nature of the research topic? How is a trusting relationship established within the community of inquiry? Whether qualitative or quantitative, researchers always need to ask: What information do I need to collect? How much of this information is best captured by video versus some other method, such as field notes and surveys? What types of cameras and microphones are needed and available? Given available equipment, what personnel will be needed and available for data collection? What lighting conditions are present? Researchers also have to consider how many people and how much equipment needs to be allocated within the environment to capture as much of the needed information as possible and be willing to adjust the study accordingly.

Video Recording/Capturing

Video capturing starts long before pushing the "on/off" button of a camera with choosing the type of equipment for adequate audio and video capture and determining the number and location of personnel and equipment in relation to the event to be recorded. It includes a careful selection of stand-alone camera position on site, its angle, distance, and perspective, as well as awareness of possible recording strategies (e.g., panning and zooming) and their effects on the data. It also considers the use of handheld documentary-style videography (Goldman-Segall, 1990b, 1991). Detailed guidance on these and other topics can be found in the following published methodological guidelines: Derry (2007) and appendix A of Derry and colleagues (2010).

Available video cameras range from consumer-grade camcorders, mobiles or computer webcams to professional-grade camera kits. Excellent research has been conducted with a single standard consumer-grade video camcorder, a common setup for studies of workplaces and classroom settings. When the recordings are to serve as data for focused analyses or interviews or of small group interactions, the use of a single standard consumer-grade video camcorder is more than adequate given recent improvements in consumer video technologies. Webcams may be more suitable for capturing social interactions at or around a computer screen and when video recordings need to be combined with screen videos capturing the students' computer-based learning activities (e.g., Zahn et al., 2010). A disadvantage of webcams is that they may constrain image and audio quality and therefore can limit the value of the video or audio data, leading to a loss of some data even after careful and repeated viewing or listening. Another alternative is to use multiple cameras, professional-grade cameras, or camera kits with 360° panoramic lenses and high-quality audio devices.

Multiple cameras allow researchers to record events from different distances and perspectives and with different angles. The position of each camera may be defined by the researcher before capturing. For example, in their classroom research on physics education, Seidel, Dalehefte, and Mayer (2005) used an "overview camera" capturing the whole classroom and a separate "teacher camera" capturing teacher-student interactions from an "ideal student perspective." Data from both perspectives were then integrated. And finally, advanced 360° cameras allow researchers to continuously capture whole situations.

Video Analysis: Individual and Social/Collaborative Technologies

There are many choices, and learning scientists are developing new specialized and increasingly complex analytic technologies as part of their ongoing video research efforts. These tools help researchers create and organize video collections, search video data banks, create transcripts, edit, chunk, and annotate video clips, develop coding systems, work collaboratively on analyses, and store processed records and results of analyses in a multimedia information structure.

Proprietary software for qualitative social science research, such as NVivo™ and ATLAS.ti™, possess capabilities for supporting video analyses, especially if based on written transcripts of video. It is also worth mentioning that improvements in easily accessible, inexpensive consumer video tools such as iMovie have increased researchers' options. Although these commercial tools are not oriented to coding or reflection, they can sometimes be successfully adapted and configured with other tools to serve a researcher's toolkit. Researchers must consider what analysis functions are important for their research and what tools that serve those needs are available, supported, and have a user community within the researchers' own environment. The selective overview presented later in this chapter is intended to supply a sense of what kinds of tool capabilities researchers may configure to support video analysis.

A detailed description of digital video analysis tools for working individually or collaboratively with video is provided in Derry and colleagues (2010) and in cornerstone four of *Video Research in the Learning Sciences*. In this chapter, we highlight the following environments:

Based on four generations of experimental software going back to the 1980s, Orion™ is an online prototype for both individual and collaborative video analysis using the constellation metaphor. Using Orion, each researcher has a homepage with collaborative tools to upload, numerically tag, annotate, search, and cluster, as well as collaborative tools either to enable invitees to upload video to that constellation or to create a new constellation (Goldman, 2007a). Several levels of privacy settings are in place for different categories of users.

Transana™ (2005) is an inexpensive open source stand-alone tool with a large user community that has been adapted for varied individual uses, including serving as a platform for videogames and simulations. Transana is appropriate for individual researchers who are building video collections, need to create clips and organize them into annotated categories, apply searchable analytic keywords to clips, and share analytic markup with distant colleagues. It provides support for transcription and offers a number of reporting formats as well as data mining and hypothesis testing capabilities.

The online collaborative HyperVideo™ system (Zahn & Finke, 2003; Zahn et al., 2005) is based on the idea of "annotating movies," that is, selecting video segments from a source video and adding spatiotemporal hyperlinks. Users of the HyperVideo system can create dynamic sensitive regions within video materials and add multiple links to these sensitive regions. The links can consist of data files uploaded from a local computer, as well as URLs. Users can then discuss the links by means of an integrated e-communication tool. Thus, users can include their own annotations and knowledge in a video and share them with others in a group or community.

The DIVER/WebDIVER™ system introduced advanced virtual zooming into a video (Pea & Hoffert, 2007; Pea et al., 2004). Researchers can create a variety of digital video clips from any video record. DIVER provides a virtual camera that can "dive into" or zoom or pan within an overview window of the source video. The virtual camera can take a snapshot of a still image clip, or dynamically record a video path to create a collection of re-orderable "panels," each of which contains a small key video frame that represents a clip, and a text field that can contain an annotation, code, or other interpretation. The user may select visual information by virtually pointing to it in the much larger spatiotemporal data structure of the video.

Given the current focus on social processes in the learning sciences, we want to highlight additional methods and tools for shared video analysis. They also provide researchers with the ability to collect and archive large video datasets, making them widely available for the community of researchers to search through video cases, to tag, to annotate them, and to share transcripts and reorganize selected videos according to a particular research approach. One such environment is used for preservice teacher education (e.g., Derry et al., 2006) and another is used in in-service teachers' professional development.

The Measures of Effective Teaching Project (Bill & Melinda Gates Foundation, 2010) is concerned with systematically developing and testing multiple measures of teaching practice and teaching effectiveness – as well as online video tools that can be used both for reflection and for lesson observations to comparatively evaluate teaching practice at a large scale (e.g., Kane, Wooten, Taylor, & Tyler, 2011).

An additional example of a tool for collaborative video analysis offered by a university library service is Rutgers University's RUAnalytic. Rutgers Library enables selected users to upload and store their video collections in a searchable, annotated streaming database as part of its library services. RUAnalytic allows users to search collections to which they have access, create and annotate clips from the collections, and connect clips to form narrative "analytics" that can be played as movies and, after vetting by the collection's owner, may become part of the video collection. RUAnalytic also supports collaborative development and sharing of analytics. An example of the RUAnalytic is VMCAnalytic (http://videomosaic.org/VMCanalytic), which is the tool associated with the Video Mosaic Collaborative and based on the Robert B. Davis Institute for Learning (RBDIL) video collection on children's mathematical reasoning.

We close this section by mentioning that some configurations for social/collaborative analysis can also be accomplished *without* specialized software. For example, one might imagine sitting at a computer projecting video onto a screen to be viewed by collaborators who are teleconferencing from different sites. The research group might want to quickly find and play video episodes of interest without first having to review and process the entire collection of field materials. Such efficiencies can be easily accomplished if data collection procedures include coordinating cameras and taking time-indexed field notes. Notes collected in a standard searchable database can be linked in various ways to time codes on corresponding video segments.

Findings from Video Research on Classroom and Teacher Learning

Classroom and teacher learning is another large application field of video research in the learning sciences. All the more so since video technology has become widely available for schools, researchers, and teachers to record the physical contexts of classroom situations. Typical goals of applying video research in this area include quantitative and qualitative scientific studies, evaluation, as well as teacher education and teacher professional development (e.g., Tochon, 2007).

In the TIMSS study, Stigler and colleagues (1999) compared 231 eighth grade mathematics classrooms in Germany, Japan, and the United States – a subsample from the large video data sample randomly selected in each country. The TIMSS sample consisted of math and science lessons videotaped in each school that agreed to participate. The capturing of the videos was distributed throughout the school year so that the lessons represented the full range in each country. The researchers generally followed a two-camera strategy, one following the perspective of an "ideal" student and the other following the teacher. Further data, such as teacher and student questionnaires and worksheets and textbook pages used in the lessons, were collected as well. In the Stigler and colleagues (1999) study, math lessons were transcribed and then analyzed on a number of dimensions by teams of coders who were native speakers of the three languages. The analyses focused on cross-cultural comparisons of the content and organization of the lessons (teachers' lesson scripts), as well as on the instructional practices used by teachers visible in the video data. Findings suggest cross-cultural differences among the countries in terms of lesson goals and structuring, as well as the type of mathematical thinking encouraged in the students.

Another more recent approach to classroom research investigates the quality of small group collaboration patterns of students in computer-supported history lessons (e.g., Zahn et al., 2010, 2012; Zahn et al., 2010). Here, student dyads working on a creative design task at a computer were captured by a webcam (the students designed a Web site for a virtual history museum by using an original historical newsreel and a video tool). A screen capturing tool also recorded all activities and interactions of the students with the computer and software. The webcam videos of student-student interactions and screen recordings of student-computer interactions were integrated and transcribed. The videos were previewed by trained observers to develop emergent important behavior categories for a coding scheme that specified task-related activities and dialogue. Then, independent raters coded the videos according to the coding scheme. Several studies using this method revealed how student pairs working at a computer use digital video technology for understanding scientific and history perspectives and how they acquire important analysis skills.

A specific hybrid approach for using video research data in teacher education and professional development is provided by Derry and colleagues (2006). They study the use of prepared video cases showing episodes from teaching situations for preservice teachers. The goal is that the preservice teacher students acquire both perceptual and conceptual knowledge about events they may encounter in a classroom as future teachers. Each video case includes video episodes and transcript of its contents. The video information is additionally connected to theory concepts. Also, several mini-cases relate to (and may illustrate) variations of a concept. The concepts in each video case connect with other resources. In the courses taught on the basis of this research students are required to analyze videos after watching them individually and cooperatively using other resources (e.g., discussion tools) in the learning environment. Results from a recent study indicate that students who participated in such a course using the online environment learned more about the targeted concepts than students in a traditional comparison course (Hmelo-Silver, Derry, Bitterman, & Hattrak, 2009).

Similarly, Goeze, Zottmann, Fischer, and Schrader (2010) showed how the competence to analyze and assess complex classroom situations could be improved substantially and sustainably among novice teachers using an online learning environment designed in line with cognitive flexibility theory (Spiro et al., 1992): digital video cases were enriched by hyperlinks to conceptual knowledge and multiple perspectives. This group is currently exploring how to implement this approach in teacher training programs.

Findings from Video Research in Controlled and Naturalistic Settings

Family, peer, and informal learning are main areas of current video research with long-standing traditions (for review, see Barron, 2007; Derry et al., 2010). Concerning family learning, video-based studies are deeply rooted in developmental psychology, for example, in studies investigating mother and child bonding or intercultural differences of family interactions. In her review, Barron (2007) describes studies of intercultural differences in mothers helping their children to solve complex problems. For instance, Chavajay and Rogoff (2002) captured video data from family groups by recording mothers and three children working together on a totem pole jigsaw puzzle, in order to observe the mothers' problem-solving behavior in relation to the children. One-minute coding intervals were analyzed for the *most prevalent form of coordination* in the task. Diagrams were used to compare different forms of family collaboration patterns – a procedure they called *diagrammatic coding* (Angelillo, Rogoff, & Chavajay, 2007).

Concerning informal learning of families and peers, studies of museum visits are a current issue of growing importance in the learning sciences, because these studies provide important insights into informal science learning mechanisms (e.g., Knipfer, Mayer, Zahn, & Hesse, 2009). Such museum research includes the study of visitor behavior, visitor conversations, visitor interactions, and visitor conduct in museums.

The long ethnographic tradition in working with video recordings for qualitatively studying visitor behavior prefers video recording over note taking, because cameras seem less intrusive in the museum situation than they do in schools. Video is used for studies of individual interactions with exhibits or social interactions among visitors at or around an exhibit (Vom Lehn, Heath, & Hindmarsh, 2002). Some studies analyze video data to evaluate the attractiveness and learning potentials of exhibition designs on the basis of visitor behavior, navigation paths, and patterns of visitors' conduct. Stevens and Hall (1997) report on a video study they conducted that allowed visitors to reflect with an interviewer on video records of their own visits to an exhibit called "Tornado" at the Exploratorium science center in San Francisco, California. Other studies focus on social interactions and learning in museums, investigating in-depth conversation and bodily conduct during visitor interactions (e.g., Vom Lehn, Heath, & Hindmarsh, 2002).

Vom Lehn and Heath (2007) describe how they captured interactions between visitors (talk, gesture, visual and material-related behavior) at exhibits in science centers such as the *Explore* at Bristol (UK). After placing their cameras and microphones at an exhibit, they left the scene. They captured everything the visitors did and said. Video recording was also embedded in beforehand discussions with museum staff, as was taking field notes during recording and conducting interviews with the participants. After recording, researchers examined the data for a first impression that might be important for further data collections and for the analysis. In further steps of analysis of each case the researchers transcribed visitor dialogues and actions in "horizontal" transcripts (Vom Lehn & Heath, 2007, p. 291ff) and analyzed particular actions and activities in depth using conversation analysis techniques. This way, they could evaluate the exhibit in relation to its attractiveness and its effects on visitors' interactions.

Ash (2003) used video data to understand how families make sense of science (e.g., biological themes) in science museums. In one study, she recorded families' 40–60 minute visits at the Monterey Aquarium and then analyzed the video data according to a three-level method (Ash, 2003). On the first level, a flowchart was generated as a rough overview of the entire visit. On the second level, segments of the flowchart were analyzed in depth for significant events on the basis of transcripts. On the third level, a fine-grained dialogue analysis of segments was performed. Based on the analyses the researchers describe scientific meaning making within and across segments that constitute the families' visits.

A new variant of video research in museums is the use of mobile eye tracking (Mayr, Knipfer, & Wessel, 2009; Wessel, Mayr, & Knipfer, 2007). Visitors are provided with a mobile eye-tracking device that captures their eye movements and, thus, records in which direction visitors look and for how long. The eye-tracking data is available as video afterward, and based on the video, researchers can reflect on the visit with the visitors. Based on these combined data, researchers can gain valuable insights into the motivational factors or perception and information processing, and also on the possible cognitive effects of exhibits/exhibitions.

Future of Digital Video in the Learning Sciences

There is no doubt that online digital video has become a welcome member of the investigative toolkit in the learning sciences. In this chapter, we presented a sample of the first 25 years of educational digital video research. Often, using computers and servers to upload their video, pioneering researchers archived datasets to conduct data analysis. In the future we predict the design of even more advanced tools to data mine video repositories. New methods of storing, retrieving, and analyzing data will be developed. High-end digital video cameras and computational devices may meld into one device (such as the iPad is now) using 5-D (and more) surround audio and video technology. These kinds of technologies may enable holographic moving images for people to explore virtually. Imagine being able to virtually move inside an actual classroom you are studying – *same time, different place* (STDP)!

We also predict that every learning sciences program nationally or internationally will offer video research methods courses. University institutional review boards (IRBs) will value the importance of video research and help promote the evolution of institutionally based technological supports that are needed for researchers to collect and archive video data while protecting the privacy and confidentiality of human subjects who are recorded. Most important, we predict that research in the learning sciences will become deeper and broader yet more nuanced and contextual because of the use of sharable and easy-to-use digital video.

The seamlessness of working within the context of international video research communities will become common practice and be encouraged. That said, working in video teams on video-based *Big Data* with tools for massive image crunching and automatic voice recognition should not overshadow the important role of the individual researchers (or small group) using video to build *local knowledge* (Geertz, 1983). As mentioned earlier, Geertz noted, "The effort is to preserve the individuality of things and unfold them in larger worlds of sense at the same time" (Geertz, 1983, p. xi).

Let us build a future where our research conclusions are gleaned from on-the-ground contextual knowledge that is seen, experienced, and interpreted from researchers' perspectives as well as from using a range of data-mining tools of larger video libraries. And may these two paradigms become connected in ways that provide us with valuable insights and conclusions to keep advancing research in the learning sciences.

References

Angelillo, C., Rogoff, B., & Chavajay, P. (2007). Examining shared endeavors by abstracting video coding schemes. In R. Goldman, R. Pea, B. Barron, & S. J. Derry (Eds.), *Video research in the learning sciences* (pp. 189–207). Mahwah, NJ: Lawrence Erlbaum Associates.

Ash, D. (2003). Dialogic inquiry and biological themes and principles: Implications for exhibit design. *Journal of Museum Education*, 28(1), 8–13.

Barron, B. (2007). Video as a tool to advance understanding of learning and development in peer, family and other informal learning contexts. In R. Goldman, R. Pea, B. Barron, & S. Derry (Eds) *Video research in the learning sciences* (159–187). Mahwah, NJ: Lawrence Erlbaum Associates.

Bill & Melinda Gates Foundation. (2010). *Measures of effective teaching (MET) project – Working with teachers to develop fair and reliable measures of effective teaching*. Retrieved on December, 7, 2012 from http://metproject.org/downloads/met-framing-paper.pdf.

Chambel, T., Zahn, C., & Finke, M. (2005). Hypervideo and cognition: Designing video-based hypermedia for individual learning and collaborative knowledge building. In E. M. Alkhalifa (Ed.), *Cognitively informed systems: Utilizing practical approaches to enrich information presentation and transfer* Hershey, PA: Idea Group, Inc.

Chavajay, P., & Rogoff, B. (2002). Schooling and traditional collaborative social organization of problem solving by Mayan mothers and children. *Developmental Psychology*, 38, 55–66.

Cobb, P., & Whitenack, J. W. (1996). A method for conducting longitudinal analyses of classroom videorecordings and transcripts. *Educational Studies in Mathematics*, 30, 213–228.

Cognition and Technology Group at Vanderbilt. (1997). *The Jasper Project: Lessons in curriculum, instruction, assessment, and professional development*. Mahwah, NJ: Lawrence Erlbaum Associates.

Derry, S. (Ed.) (2007). Guidelines for video research in education: Recommendations from an expert panel. Retrieved October 13, 2012 from http://drdc.uchicago.edu/what/video-research.html.

Derry, S., Hmelo-Silver, C., Nagarajan, A., Chernobilsky, E., & Beitzel, B. D. (2006). Cognitive transfer revisited: Can we exploit new media to solve old problems on a large scale? *Journal of Educational Computing Research*, 35(2), 145–162.

Derry, S., Pea, R., Barron, B., Engle, R., Erickson, F., Goldman, R., Hall, R., Koschmann, T., Lemke, J., Sherin, M., & Sherin, B. (2010). Conducting video research in the learning sciences: Guidance on selection, analysis, technology, and ethics. *Journal of the Learning Sciences*, 19, 1–51.

Derry, S., Sherin, M., & Sherin, B. (2014). Multimedia learning with video. In R. Mayer (Ed.), *Cambridge handbook of multimedia learning* (pp. 785–812). New York: Cambridge University Press.

Geertz, C. (1973). *The interpretation of cultures*. New York: Basic Books.

Geertz, C. (1983). *Local knowledge: Further essays in interpretive anthropology*. New York: Basic Books.

Goeze, A., Zottmann, J., Schrader, J., & Fischer, F. (2010). Instructional support for case-based learning with digital videos: Fostering pre-service teachers' acquisition of the competency to diagnose pedagogical situations. In D. Gibson & B. Dodge (Eds.), *Proceedings of the Society for Information Technology and Teacher Education* International Conference, San Diego, CA (pp. 1098–1104). Chesapeake, VA: AACE.

Goldman, R. (2004). A design ethnography: Video perspectivity meets wild and crazy teens. *Cambridge Journal of Education*, 34(2), 147–178.

Goldman, R. (2007a). Orion™, an online digital video analysis tool: Changing our perspectives as an interpretive community. In R. Goldman, R. Pea, B. Barron, & S. Derry (Eds.), *Video research in the learning sciences* (pp. 507–520). Mahwah, NJ: Lawrence Erlbaum Associates.

Goldman, R. (2007b). Video representations and the perspectivity framework: epistemology, ethnography, evaluation, and ethics. In R. Goldman, R. Pea, B. Barron, & S. Derry (Eds.), *Video research in the learning sciences* (pp. 507–520). Mahwah, NJ: Lawrence Erlbaum Associates.

Goldman, R., Pea, R., Barron, B., & Derry, S. J. (Eds.) (2007). *Video Research in the Learning Sciences*. Mahwah, NJ: Lawrence Erlbaum Associates.

Goldman-Segall, R. (1990a). Learning Constellations: A multimedia ethnographic research environment using video technology to explore children's thinking. Unpublished doctoral dissertation. Massachusetts Institute of Technology. Retrieved December 9, 2012 from http://mf.media.mit.edu/pubs/thesis/goldmanPHD.pdf.

Goldman-Segall, R. (1990b). Learning constellations: A multimedia research environment for exploring children's theory-making. In I. Harel (Ed.), *Constructionist learning* (pp. 295–318). Cambridge, MA: MIT Media Lab.

Goldman-Segall, R. (1991). A multimedia research tool for ethnographic investigation. In I. Harel & S. Papert (Eds.), *Constructionism* (pp. 467–496). Norwood, NJ: Ablex Publishers.

Goldman-Segall, R. (1993). Interpreting video data: The importance of a significance measure. *Journal for Educational Multimedia and Hypermedia*, 2(3), 261–282.

Goldman-Segall, R. (1997). *Points of viewing children's thinking: A digital ethnographer's journey*. Mahwah, NJ: LEA. http://pointsofviewing.com.

Goodwin, Charles. (1994). Professional vision. *American Anthropologist*, 96(3), 606–633.

Goodwin, C. (1996). Transparent vision. In E. Ochs, E. A. Schegloff, & S. A. Thompson (Eds.), *Interaction and grammar* (pp. 370–404). New York: Cambridge University Press.

Hall, R., Stevens, R., & Torralba, A. (2002). Disrupting representational infrastructure in conversations across disciplines. *Mind, Culture, and Activity*, 9(3), 179–210.

Hmelo-Silver, C., Derry, S., Bitterman, A., & Hattrak, N. (2009). Targeting transfer in a STELLAR PBL course for preservice teachers. *The Interdisciplinary Journal of Problem-based Learning*, 3(2), 24–42.

Hockings, P. (Ed.) (1975). *Principles of visual anthropology*. Den Hague/Paris: Mouton Publishers, 79–98.

Hutchins, E. (2005). Material anchors for conceptual blends. *Journal of Pragmatics*, 37(10), 1555–1577.

Jacknis, I. (1988). Margaret Mead and Gregory Bateson in Bali: Their use of photography and film. *Cultural Anthropology*, 3(2), 160–177.

Kane, T. J., Wooten, A. L., Taylor, E. S., & Tyler, J. H. (2011). Evaluating teacher effectiveness in Cincinnati public schools. *EducationNext*, 11(3).

Knipfer, K., Mayr, E., Zahn, C., & Hesse, F. W. (2009). Computer support for knowl-edge communication in science exhibitions: Novel perspectives from research on collaborative learning. *Educational Research Review*, 4, 196–209.

Koschmann, T., Stahl, G., & Zemel, A. (2007). The video analyst's manifesto. In R. Goldman, R. Pea, B. Barron, & S. Derry (Eds.), *Video research in the learning sciences*. Mahwah, NJ: Lawrence Erlbaum Associates.

Lemke, J. (2007). Video epistemology in-and-outside the box: Traversing atten-tional spaces. In R. Goldman, R. Pea, B. Barron, & S. J. Derry (Eds.), *Video research in the learning sciences* (pp. 39–52). Mahwah, NJ: Lawrence Erlbaum Associates.

Lemke, J. (2013). Feeling and meaning in the social ecology of learning: Lessons from play and games. In M. Baker, J. Andriessen, & S. Järvelä (Eds.), *Affective learning together: The socio-emotional turn in collaborative learn-ing* (pp. 71–94). New York: Routledge.

Lesh, R., & Lehrer, R. (2000). Iterative refinement cycles for videotape analyses of conceptual change. In: R. Lesh (Ed.), *Handbook of research data design in mathematics and science education* (pp. 665–708). Mahwah, NJ: Lawrence Erlbaum Associates.

Mayr, E., Knipfer, K., & Wessel, D. (2009). In-sights into mobile learning: An explo-ration of mobile eye tracking methodology for learning in museums. In G. Vavoula, N. Pachler, & A. Kukulska-Hulme (Eds.), *Researching mobile learning: Frameworks, tools and research designs* (pp. 189–204). Oxford: Peter Lang.

McDermott, R., & Goldman, S. (2007). Staying the course with video analysis. In R. Goldman, R. Pea, B. Barron, & S. Derry (Eds.), *Video research in the learn-ing sciences* (pp. 101–113). Mahwah, NJ: Lawrence Erlbaum Associates.

Pea, R., & Hoffert, E. (2007). Video workflow in the learning sciences: Prospects of emerging technologies for augmenting work practices. In R. Goldman, R. Pea, B. Baron, & S. Derry (Eds.), *Video research in the learning sciences* (pp. 427–460). Mahwah, NJ: Lawrence Erlbaum Associates.

Pea, R., Mills, M., Rosen, J., Dauber, K., Effelsberg, W., & Hoffert. E. (2004). The DIVER project: Interactive digital video repurposing. *IEEE Multimedia*, 11(1), 54–61.

Peck, A. (Director). (1981). *Margaret Mead: Taking Note*. [Film] In Odessey Series (Series Editor, M. Ambrosino). Boston, MA: Boston Public Broadcasting.

Powell, A. B., Francisco, J. M., & Mager, C. A. (2003). An analytical model for study-ing the development of learners' mathematical ideas and reasoning using videotape data. *Journal of Mathematical Behavior*, 22, 405–435.

Rony, F. T. (2006). Photogenic cannot be tamed: Margaret Mead and Gregory Bateson's Trance and Dance in Bali. *Discourse*, 28(1), 5–27.

Roschelle, J. (1992). Learning by collaborating: Convergent conceptual change. *The Journal of the Learning Sciences*, 2(3), 235–276.

Rouch, J. (1975). The camera and the man. In P. Hockings (Ed.), *Principles of visual anthropology*. Den Hague/Paris: Mouton Publishers, 79–98.

Seidel, T., Dalehefte, I. M., & Meyer, L. (2005). Standardized guidelines – How to collect videotapes. In T. Seidel, M. Prenzel, & M. Kobarg (Eds.), *How to run a video study: Technical report of the IPN video study* (pp. 29–53). Münster, Germany: Waxmann.

Seidel, T., Kobarg, M., & Rimmele, R. (2005). Video data processing procedures. In T. Seidel, M. Prenzel, & M. Kobarg (Eds.), *How to run a video study: Technical report of the IPN video study* (pp. 54–69) Münster, Germany: Waxmann.

Seidel, T., Prenzel, M., Schwindt, K., Stürmer, K. Blomberg, G., & Kobarg, M. (2009). LUV and Observe: Two projects using video to diagnose teacher competence. In T. Janik & T. Seidel (Eds.), *The power of video studies in investigating teaching and learning in the classroom* (pp. 243–259). Münster: Waxmann.

Spiro, R. J., Collins, B. P., & Ramchandran, A. R. (2007). Reflections on a post-Gutenberg epistemology for video use in ill-structured domains: Fostering complex learning and cognitive flexibility. In R. Goldman, R. Pea, B. Barron, & S. Derry (Eds.), *Video research in the learning sciences* (pp. 93–100). Mahwah, NJ: Lawrence Erlbaum Associates.

Spiro, R. J., Feltovich, P. J., Jacobson, M. J., & Coulson, R. L. (1992). Cognitive flexibility, constructivism and hypertext: Random access instruction for advanced knowledge acquisition in ill-structured domains. In T. M. Duffy & D. H. Jonassen (Eds.), *Constructivism and the technology of instruction: A conversation* (pp. 57–75). Hillsdale, NJ: Lawrence Erlbaum Associates.

Stahl, E., Zahn, C., & Finke, M. (2006). Knowledge acquisition by hypervideo design: An instructional program for university courses. *Journal of Educational Multimedia and Hypermedia,* 15(3), 285–302.

Stevens, R., & Hall, R. (1997). Seeing *Tornado*: How video traces mediate visitor understandings of (natural?) phenomena in a science museum. *Science Education,* 81(6), 735–747.

Stigler, J. W., Gonzalez, P., Kawanako, T., Knoll, S., & Serrano, A. (1999). *The TIMSS Video Classroom Study. Methods and Findings from an Exploratory Research Project on Eights Grade Mathematics Instruction in Germany, Japan and the United States.* Washington, DC: National Center for Education Statistics, U.S. Department of Education.

Stigler, J. W., & Hiebest, J. (1999). *The teaching gap.* New York: Free Press.

Tochon, F. (2007). From video cases to video pedagogy: Video feedback in an educational culture sharing differences. In R. Goldman, R. Pea, B. Barron, & S. Derry (Eds.), *Video research in the learning sciences.* Mahwah, NJ: Lawrence Erlbaum Associates.

Trinh, T. Minh-Ha (1993). The totalizing quest of meaning. In M. Reno (Ed.), *Theorizing documentary.* New York: Routledge.

Tochon, F. V. (2007). From video cases to video pedagogy: A framework for video feedback and reflection in pedagogical research practice. In R. Goldman, R. Pea, B. Barron, & S. Derry (Eds.), *Video research in the learning sciences* (pp. 53–66). Mahwah, NJ: Lawrence Erlbaum Associates.

Van Haneghan, J. P., Barron, L., Young, M. F., Williams, S. M., Vye, N. J., & Bransford, J. D. (1992). The Jasper series: An experiment with new ways to enhance mathematical thinking. In D. F. Halpern (Ed.), *Enhancing thinking skills in the sciences and mathematics* (pp. 15–38). Hillsdale, NJ: Lawrence Erlbaum Associates.

Video Mosaic Collaborative (2009). Retrieved December 19, 2011 from videomosaic.org.

Vom Lehn, D., & Heath, C. (2007). Social interaction in museums and galleries: A note on video-based field studies. In R. Goldman, R. Pea, B. Barron, & S. Derry (Eds.), *Video research in the learning sciences.* (pp. 287–301). Mahwah, NJ: Lawrence Erlbaum Associates.

Vom Lehn, D., Heath, C., & Hindmarsh, J. (2002). Video-based field studies in museums and galleries. *Visitor Studies Today, 5(3)*, 15–23.

Wessel, D., Mayr, E., & Knipfer, K. (2007). Re-viewing the museum visitors view. In G. N. Vavoula, A. Kukulska-Hulme, & N. Pachler (Eds.), *Research methods in informal and mobile learning* (pp. 17–23). London: WLE Centre.

Williams, R. F. (2006). Using cognitive ethnography to study instruction. *Proceedings of the 7th International Conference of the Learning Sciences.* Mahwah, NJ: Lawrence Erlbaum Associates.

Zahn, C., & Finke, M. (2003). Collaborative knowledge building based on hyper-linked video. In B. Wasson, R. Baggetun, U. Hoppe, & S. Ludvigsen (Eds.), *Proceedings of the International Conference on Computer Support for Collaborative Learning – CSCL 2003, COMMUNITY EVENTS – Communication and Interaction* (pp. 173–175). Bergen, NO: InterMedia.

Zahn, C., Krauskopf, K., Hesse, F. W., & Pea, R. (2010). Digital video tools in the classroom: How to support meaningful collaboration and advanced thinking of students? In M. S. Chine & I. M. Sale (Eds.), *New science of learning: Cognition, computers and collaboration in education* (pp. 503–523). New York: Springer.

Zahn, C., Krauskopf, K., Hesse, F. W., & Pea, R. (2012). How to improve collaborative learning with video tools in the classroom? Social vs. cognitive guidance for student teams. *International Journal of Computer-Supported Collaborative Learning*, 7(2), 259–284.

Zahn, C., Pea, R., Hesse, F. W., Mills, M., Finke, M., & Rosen, J. (2005). Advanced digital video technologies to support collaborative learning in school education and beyond. In T. Koschmann, D. Suthers,& T.-W. Chan (Eds.), *Computer Supported Collaborative Learning 2005: The Next 10 Years* (pp. 737–742). Mahwah, NJ: Lawrence Erlbaum Associates.

Zahn, C., Pea, R., Hesse, F. W., & Rosen, J. (2010). Comparing simple and advanced video tools as supports for collaborative design processes. *Journal of the Learning Sciences*, 19(3), 403–440.

12 A Learning Sciences Perspective on the Design and Use of Assessment in Education

James W. Pellegrino

From teachers' classroom quizzes and mid-term or final exams, to nationally and internationally administered standardized tests, assessments of students' knowledge and skills have become a ubiquitous part of the educational landscape. Assessments of school learning provide information to help educators, administrators, policy makers, students, parents, and researchers judge the state of student learning and make decisions about implications and actions. The specific purposes for which an assessment will be used are important considerations in all phases of its design. For example, assessments that instructors use in classrooms to assist or monitor learning typically need to provide more detailed information than assessments whose results will be used by policy makers or accrediting agencies.

Assessment to assist learning. In the classroom context, instructors use various forms of assessment to inform day-to-day and month-to-month decisions about next steps for instruction, to give students feedback about their progress, and to motivate students (e.g., Black & Wiliam, 1998; Wiliam, 2007). One familiar type of classroom assessment is a teacher-made quiz, but assessment also includes more informal methods for determining how students are progressing in their learning, such as classroom projects, feedback from computer-assisted instruction, classroom observation, written work, homework, and conversations with and among students – all interpreted by the teacher in light of additional information about the students, the schooling context, and the content being studied.

These situations are referred to as *assessments to assist learning* or the *formative use of assessment*. These assessments provide specific information about students' strengths and difficulties with learning. For example, statistics teachers need to know more than the fact that a student does not understand probability; they need to know the details of this misunderstanding, such as the student's tendency to confuse conditional and compound probability. Teachers can use information from these types of assessment to adapt their instruction to meet students' needs, which may be difficult to

Preparation of this chapter was supported by the following grants to James W. Pellegrino from the U.S. National Science Foundation: 0732090, 0918552, 0920242; and from the U.S. Institute for Education Sciences: R305A090111, R305A100475.

anticipate and are likely to vary from one student to another. Students can use this information to determine which skills and knowledge they need to study further and what adjustments in their thinking they need to make (also see Chinn & Sherin, Chapter 9, this volume).

Assessment of individual achievement. Many assessments are used to help determine whether a student has attained a certain level of competency after completing a particular phase of education, whether it be a two-week curricular unit, a semester-long course, or 12 years of schooling. This is referred to as *assessment of individual achievement* or the *summative use of assessment*. Some of the most familiar forms of summative assessment are those used by classroom instructors, such as end-of-unit or end-of-course tests, which often are used to assign letter grades when a course is finished. Large-scale assessments – which are administered at the direction of people external to the classroom, such as school districts or state boards of education – also provide information about the attainment of individual students, as well as comparative information about how one student performs relative to others. Because large-scale assessments are typically given only once a year and involve a time lag between testing and availability of results, the results seldom provide information that can be used to help teachers or students make day-to-day or month-to-month decisions about teaching and learning.

Assessment to evaluate programs and institutions. Another common purpose of assessment is to help administrators, policy makers, or researchers judge the quality and effectiveness of educational programs and institutions (e.g., Pellegrino, Jones, & Mitchell, 1999). Evaluations can be formative or summative; for example, instructional evaluation is formative when it is used to improve the effectiveness of instruction. School leaders and policy makers increasingly use summative evaluations to make decisions about individuals, programs, and institutions. For instance, public reporting of state assessment results by school and district are designed to provide information to parents and taxpayers about the quality and efficacy of their schools; these evaluations sometimes influence decisions about resource allocations.

No single type of assessment can serve all of these purposes and contexts. Unfortunately, policy makers often attempt to use a single assessment for multiple purposes – either in the desire to save money, or to administer the assessment in less time, or to provide information to teachers to guide instructional improvement. The problem is that when a single assessment is used to serve multiple purposes, it ends up being suboptimal for each specific purpose. The drive to identify a single, one-size-fits-all assessment often results in inappropriate choices of assessments for instructional or research purposes, and this can in turn lead to invalid conclusions regarding persons, programs, and/or institutions.

The ultimate purpose of all assessments is to promote student learning (e.g., Wiggins, 1998). But in some cases, assessments are developed for evaluation purposes that are somewhat distant from this ultimate goal of promoting student learning. Ruiz-Primo, Shavelson, Hamilton, and Klein (2002) proposed a five-point continuum that reflects the proximity of an assessment to classroom instruction and learning: *immediate* (e.g., observations or artifacts from the enactment of a specific instructional activity), *close* (e.g., embedded assessments and semiformal quizzes of learning from one or more activities), *proximal* (e.g., formal classroom exams of learning from a specific curriculum), *distal* (e.g., criterion-referenced achievement tests such as required by the federal No Child Left Behind legislation), and *remote* (broader outcomes measured over time, including norm-referenced achievement tests and national and international achievement measures). The proximity of the assessment to moments of teaching and learning has implications for how and how well it can fulfill the different purposes of assessment (formative, summative, or program evaluation: Hickey & Pellegrino, 2005; NRC, 2003; Pellegrino & Hickey, 2006). For example, an assessment designed to aid teachers in diagnosing the state of student learning to modify instruction has to be contextualized relative to the curriculum and instructional materials that have been in use and it needs to be at a relatively fine grain size regarding specific aspects of knowledge and skill to be instructionally informative. Thus, it cannot cover large amounts of content superficially and it needs to use language and problem contexts familiar to the students. The capacity of such an assessment to function as a good and "fair" summative assessment for all students learning the same content is therefore limited. In contrast, a large-scale state achievement test needs to cover large amounts of content at a relatively coarse grain size and it cannot be curriculum or context dependent to be "fair" to all students tested. Thus, it must use problem formats that are general and curriculum neutral. The capacity of such an assessment to provide instructionally useful information is therefore highly limited. Furthermore, it is typically far removed in time from when instruction and learning have transpired and thus its feedback capacity is similarly limited.

Conceptual Frameworks

Although assessments used in various contexts and for differing purposes and at different timescales often look quite different, they share certain common principles. One such principle is that assessment is always a process of reasoning from evidence. By its very nature, moreover, assessment is imprecise to some degree. I elaborate on these issues in this section.

Assessment as a Process of Evidentiary Reasoning: The *Assessment Triangle*

Assessing educational outcomes is not as straightforward as measuring height or weight; the attributes to be measured are mental representations

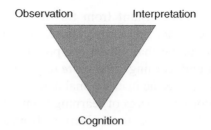

Figure 12.1. *The Assessment Triangle.*

and processes that are not outwardly visible. This is a foundational issue in all cognitive psychology: How can the researcher infer internal mental states and processes from observable behavior? As a result, cognitive psychologists have developed a substantial body of practice and theory to address this issue. An assessment is a tool designed to observe students' behavior and produce data that can be used to draw reasonable inferences about what students know.

It is helpful to portray the process of reasoning from evidence using the *assessment triangle* (Figure 12.1; also see Pellegrino, Chudowsky, & Glaser, 2001). The vertices represent the three key elements underlying any assessment: a model of student *cognition* and learning in the domain of the assessment; a set of assumptions and principles about the kinds of *observations* that will provide evidence of students' competencies; and an *interpretation* process for making sense of the evidence in light of the assessment purpose and student understanding. No assessment can be designed, implemented, or evaluated without incorporating all three (although in many cases, one or more may remain implicit in the design rather than explicitly and consciously chosen).

The *cognition* corner of the triangle refers to theory, data, and a set of assumptions about how students represent knowledge and develop competence in a subject matter domain (e.g., fractions, Newton's laws, thermodynamics). In any particular assessment application, a theory of learning in the domain is needed to identify the set of knowledge and skills that is important to measure for the intended context of use, whether that be to characterize the competencies students have acquired at some point in time to make a summative judgment, or to make formative judgments to guide subsequent instruction so as to maximize learning. Cognitive theories should be consistent with the latest scientific understanding of how learners represent knowledge and develop expertise in a domain (as captured in the various chapters of this handbook).

The *observation* vertex of the assessment triangle represents a description or set of specifications for assessment *tasks* that will elicit illuminating responses from students. Every assessment is based on a set of assumptions and principles about the kinds of tasks or situations that will prompt students to say, do, or create something that demonstrates important knowledge and skills. Assessment tasks (whether answering a multiple choice test, composing a one-paragraph essay, or responding to an oral question from the teacher) must be carefully designed to provide evidence that is linked to the cognitive model of learning and to support the kinds of inferences and decisions that will be made on the basis of the assessment results.

Every assessment is based on assumptions and models for interpreting the evidence collected from observations. The *interpretation* vertex of the triangle encompasses all the methods and tools used to reason from observations. It expresses how the observations derived from a set of assessment tasks constitute evidence about the knowledge and skills being assessed. In the context of large-scale assessment, the interpretation method is usually a statistical model, which is a characterization or summarization of patterns one would expect to see in the data given varying levels of student competency. For example, on a state or country's end-of-year achievement test, the performance of a student is typically reported on a measurement scale that permits various comparisons, for example between students who have taken different forms of the test in a given year, or between the performance of students this year and the performance of students in prior years. In some cases, scores are also classified in terms of achievement levels such as basic, proficient, or advanced. Familiar examples of the use of a statistical model to derive a scale score are the GRE and SAT in the United States and PISA internationally. In the context of classroom assessment, whether the activity is a conversation, a quiz, or a "formal" test, the interpretation is often made informally by the teacher, and is often based on an intuitive or a qualitative model, or on a simple quantitative model such as percent correct, rather than a formal statistical one. Even so, teachers make coordinated judgments about what aspects of students' understanding and learning are relevant, how students have performed on one or more tasks, and what the performances mean about the students' knowledge and understanding. This occurs whether or not they may have used some quantitative metric like total points or percent correct.

The critical final point to note is that each of the three elements of the assessment triangle not only must make sense on its own, but also must align with the other two in a meaningful way to lead to an effective assessment and sound inferences.

Domain-Specific Learning: The Concept of Learning Progressions

As argued earlier, the targets of inference for any given assessment should be largely determined by models of cognition and learning that describe how people represent knowledge and how they develop competence in the domain of interest (the *cognition* element of the assessment triangle) and what are the important elements of such competence, such as how knowledge is organized.

Starting with a model of learning is one of the main features that distinguishes the proposed approach to assessment design from other current approaches. The model suggests the most important aspects of student achievement about which one would want to draw inferences and provides clues about the types of assessment tasks that will elicit evidence to support those inferences (see also Pellegrino, Baxter, & Glaser, 1999; Pellegrino et al., 2001).

Consistent with these ideas, there has been a recent spurt of interest in the topic of "learning progressions" (see Duschl, Schweingruber, & Shouse, 2007; National Research Council, 2012; Wilson & Bertenthal, 2005). A variety of definitions of learning progressions (also called *learning trajectories*) now exist in the literature, with substantial differences in focus and intent (see, e.g., Alonzo & Gotwals, 2012; Corcoran, Mosher, & Rogat, 2009; Daro, Mosher, Corcoran, Barrett, & Consortium for Policy Research in Education, 2011; Duncan & Hmelo-Silver, 2009). Learning progressions are empirically grounded and testable hypotheses about how students' understanding of and ability to use core concepts and explanations and related disciplinary practices grow and become more sophisticated over time, with appropriate instruction (Duschl et al., 2007). These hypotheses describe the pathways students are likely to follow as they master core concepts. The hypothesized learning trajectories are tested empirically to ensure their construct validity (Does the hypothesized sequence describe a path most students actually experience given appropriate instruction?) and ultimately to assess their consequential validity (Does instruction based on the learning progression produce better results for most students?) (see Chinn & Sherin, Chapter 9, this volume, on microgenetic methods). The reliance on empirical evidence differentiates learning trajectories from traditional topical scope and sequence specification. Topical scope and sequence descriptions are typically based only on logical analysis of current disciplinary knowledge and on personal experiences in teaching.

Any hypothesized learning progression has implications for assessment, because effective assessments should be aligned with an empirically grounded cognitive model. A model of a learning progression should contain at least the following elements:

(1) *Target performances or learning goals* that are the end points of a learning progression and are defined by societal expectations, analysis of the discipline, and/or requirements for entry into the next level of education;
(2) *Progress variables* that are the dimensions of understanding, application, and practice that are being developed and tracked over time. These may be core concepts in the discipline or practices central to literary, scientific, or mathematical work;
(3) *Levels of achievement* that are intermediate steps in the developmental pathway(s) traced by a learning progression. These levels may reflect levels of integration or common stages that characterize the development of

student thinking. There may be intermediate steps that are noncanonical but are stepping stones to canonical ideas;

(4) *Learning performances* that are the kinds of tasks students at a particular level of achievement would be capable of performing. They provide specifications for the development of assessments by which students would demonstrate their knowledge and understanding; and

(5) *Assessments*, which are the specific measures used to track student development along the hypothesized progression. Learning progressions include an approach to assessment, as assessments are integral to their development, validation, and use.

Research on cognition and learning has produced a rich set of descriptions of domain-specific learning and performance that can serve to guide assessment design, particularly for certain areas of reading, mathematics, and science (e.g., AAAS, 2001; Bransford et al., 2000; Duschl et al., 2007; Kilpatrick, Swafford, & Findell, 2001; Snow, Burns, & Griffin, 1998; Wilson & Bertenthal, 2005). That said, there is much left to do in mapping out learning progressions for multiple areas of the curriculum in ways that can effectively guide the design of instruction and assessment. Nevertheless, there is a good bit known about student cognition and learning that we can make use of right now to guide how we design systems of assessments, especially those that attempt to cover the progress of learning within and across grades.

Assessment Development: Evidence-Centered Design

The design of educational assessment should be guided by its purpose (e.g., to assist learning, to measure individual attainment, or to evaluate a program), the context in which it will be used (classroom or large scale), and practical constraints (e.g., resources and time). The tendency in assessment design is to work from a somewhat loose description of what students are supposed to know and what they should be able to do (e.g., standards or a curriculum framework) to the development of tasks or problems for them to answer. Given the complexities of the assessment design process, it is unlikely that such a loose process can lead to generation of a quality assessment without a great deal of artistry, luck, and trial and error. As a consequence, many assessments are insufficient on a number of dimensions including representation of the cognitive constructs and content to be covered and uncertainty about the scope of the inferences that can be drawn from task performance.

The solution to this all too common problem is to design assessments grounded in empirical evidence of cognition and learning. This approach is referred to as *evidence-centered design* (e.g., Mislevy & Haertel, 2006; Mislevy & Riconscente, 2006; see Figure 12.2). As shown in Figure 12.2, the process starts by defining as precisely as possible the *claims* that one wants to be able to make about student knowledge and the ways students are supposed to

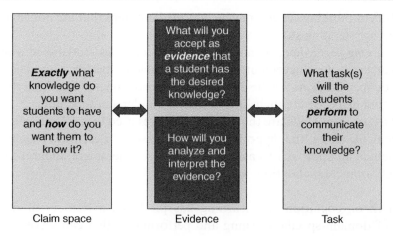

Figure 12.2. *Simplified representation of three critical components of the evidence-centered design process and their reciprocal relationships.*

know and understand some particular aspect of a content domain. Examples might include aspects of algebraic thinking, ratio and proportion, force and motion, heat and temperature, and so forth. One should be as precise as possible about the cognitive elements being studied, and express these in the form of precise verbs of cognition, such as *compare, describe, analyze, compute, elaborate, explain, predict,* or *justify.*

The next step is to specify the forms of *evidence* that would provide support for those claims – for example, features of work products or performances. This includes which features need to be present and how they are weighted in any evidentiary scheme – that is, what matters most and what matters least or not at all. For example, if the claim about a student's knowledge of the laws of motion is that the student can *analyze* a physical situation in terms of the forces acting on all the bodies, then the evidence might be that the student has drawn a free body diagram with all the forces labeled, including their magnitudes and directions.

The third and final step is to design *tasks* that are capable of providing the necessary evidence. When one is precise in stating the claims and the evidence, it becomes much easier to design tasks that can provide the requisite evidence. The tasks should allow students to "show what they know" in a way that is as unambiguous as possible with respect to what the task performance implies about student knowledge and skill – that is, the inferences about student cognition that are permissible and sustainable from a given set of assessment tasks or items.

Assessment Validity: Argumentation and Evidence

The ultimate goal of applying a theory-driven and evidence-based approach to the process of assessment design and use is to create tasks and situations that give us valid and reliable information about student learning. Thus, validity is central in all work on assessment. The joint AERA/APA/NCME Standards frame validity largely in terms of "the concept or characteristic that a test is designed to measure" (AERA/APA/NCME, 1999, p. 5). A contemporary perspective on validity frames it in terms of an argument that "specifies the proposed interpretations and uses of test results by laying out the network of inferences and assumptions leading from the observed performances to the conclusions and decisions based on the performances" (Kane, 2006, p. 23).

Kane (2006) and others (Haertel & Lorie, 2004; Mislevy et al., 2003) distinguish between the interpretive argument, that is, the propositions that underpin test score interpretation, and the evidence and arguments that provide the necessary warrants for the propositions or claims of the interpretive argument. Mislevy and colleagues (2003) have elaborated on this view by asserting that validity evidence can be represented more formally in terms of a structured argument, an approach initially introduced and outlined in the context of legal reasoning by Stephen Toulmin (2003). In Toulmin's view a good argument provides strong evidentiary support for a claim that, in turn, permits it to withstand criticism (also see Andriessen & Baker, Chapter 22, this volume). Toulmin's practical approach begins by explicating the various "claims of interest" and then provides justification for those claims by identifying the evidence (data and/or expert opinion) to support those claims. The approach also calls for supplying a "warrant" that interprets the data and explicates how the data support the claims of interest. Toulmin's work, historically, focused on the formal role of argumentation and was used to evaluate the rational basis of arguments presented typically in the courtroom. Appropriating this approach, contemporary educational measurement theorists have framed test validity as a reasoned argument backed by evidence (e.g., Kane, 2006, 2013). The particular forms of evidence are thus associated with the claims that one wishes to make about what a given assessment is and does and how its scores are to be interpreted. Some of those critical claims are related to the theoretical base underlying the design of a given assessment, and those interpretive claims must be backed up by empirical evidence of various types that the observed performance does in fact reflect the underlying cognitive constructs.

Implications for Assessment Design and Measurement

The Design and Use of Classroom Assessment

Learning scientists generally argue that classroom assessment practices need to change to better support learning (also see Shepard, 2000). The content and character of assessments need to be significantly improved to reflect the latest empirical research on learning; and, given what we now know about learning progressions, the gathering and use of assessment information and insights should become a part of the ongoing learning process. This latter point further suggests that teacher education programs should provide teachers with a deep understanding of how to use assessment in their instruction. Many educational assessment experts believe that if assessment, curriculum, and instruction were more integrally connected, student learning would improve (e.g., Pellegrino et al., 1999; Stiggins, 1997).

According to Sadler (1989), three elements are required if teachers are to successfully use assessment to promote learning:

1. A clear view of the learning goals (derived from the curriculum).
2. Information about the present state of the learner (derived from assessment).
3. Action to close the gap (taken through instruction).

Each of these three elements informs the others. For instance, formulating assessment procedures for classroom use can spur a teacher to think more specifically about learning goals, thus leading to modification of curriculum and instruction. These modifications can, in turn, lead to refined assessment procedures, and so on. The mere existence of classroom assessment along the lines discussed here will not ensure effective learning. The clarity and appropriateness of the curriculum goals, the validity of the assessments in relationship to these goals, the interpretation of the assessment evidence, and the relevance and quality of the instruction that ensues are all critical determinants of the outcome.

Effective teaching must start with a model of cognition and learning in the domain. For most teachers, the ultimate goals for learning are established by the curriculum, which is usually mandated externally (e.g., by state curriculum standards). But the externally mandated curriculum does not specify the empirically based cognition and learning outcomes that are necessary for assessment to be effective. As a result, teachers (and others responsible for designing curriculum, instruction, and assessment) must fashion intermediate goals that can serve as an effective route to achieving the externally mandated goals, and to do so effectively, they must have an understanding of how students represent knowledge and develop competence in the domain (e.g., see the chapters in Part 5 of this handbook). Formative assessment should be based in cognitive theories about how people learn particular subject matter to ensure that instruction centers on what is most important for the next stage of learning, given a learner's current state of understanding.

Preservice teacher education and continuing professional development are needed to help teachers formulate models of learning progressions so they can identify students' naïve or initial sense-making strategies and build on those to move students toward more sophisticated understandings (also see diSessa, Chapter 5, this volume). This will increase teachers' diagnostic expertise so they can make informed decisions about next steps for student learning. Several cognitively based approaches to instruction and assessment, including the Cognitively Guided Instruction program (Carpenter, Fennema, & Franke, 1996) and others (Cobb et al., 1991; Griffin & Case, 1997), have been shown to have a positive impact on student learning.

The Design and Use of Large-Scale Assessment

Large-scale assessments are further removed from instruction but can still benefit learning if well designed and properly used. If the principles of design identified earlier in this chapter were applied, substantially more valid, useful, and fair information would be gained from large-scale assessments. However, before schools and districts can fully capitalize on contemporary theory and research, they will need to substantially change how they approach large-scale assessment. Specifically, they must relax some of the constraints that currently drive large-scale assessment practices, as follows.

Large-scale summative assessments should focus on the most critical and central aspects of learning in a domain – as identified by curriculum standards and informed by cognitive research and theory. Large-scale assessments typically are based on models of learning that are less detailed than classroom assessments. For summative purposes, one might need to know whether a student has mastered the more complex aspects of multicolumn subtraction, including borrowing from and across zero, whereas a teacher needs to know exactly which procedural errors lead to mistakes. Although policy makers and parents may not need all the diagnostic detail that would be useful to a teacher and student during the course of instruction, large-scale summative assessments should be based on a model of learning that is compatible with and derived from the same set of knowledge and assumptions about learning as classroom assessment.

Research on cognition and learning suggests a broad range of competencies that should be assessed when measuring student achievement, many of which are essentially untapped by current assessments. Examples are knowledge organization, problem representation, strategy use, metacognition, and participatory activities (e.g., formulating questions, constructing and evaluating arguments, contributing to group problem solving). These are important elements of contemporary theory and research on the acquisition of competence and expertise and are discussed and illustrated in detail in the various references mentioned earlier in the section on domain-specific learning. Large-scale assessments should not ignore these aspects of competency and should provide information about these aspects of the nature of student understanding, rather than simply ranking students according to general proficiency estimates. If tests are based on a research-grounded theory of cognition and learning, those tests can provide positive direction for instruction, making "teaching to the test" productive for learning rather than destructive (this point is discussed further later in this chapter).

Unfortunately, given current constraints of standardized test administration, only limited improvements in large-scale assessments are possible. These constraints include the need to provide reliable and comparable scores for individuals as well as groups; the need to sample a broad set of curriculum standards within a limited testing time per student; and the need to offer cost efficiency in terms of development, scoring, and administration. To meet these kinds of demands, designers typically create assessments that are given at a specified time, with all students taking the same (or parallel) tests under strictly standardized conditions (often referred to as *on-demand* assessment). Tasks are generally of the kind that can be presented in paper-and-pencil format, that students can respond to quickly, and that can be scored reliably and efficiently. As a result, learning outcomes that lend themselves to being assessed in these ways are assessed, but aspects of learning that cannot be observed under such constrained conditions are not. Designing new assessments that capture the complexity of cognition and learning will require examining the assumptions and values that currently drive assessment design choices and breaking out of the current paradigm to explore alternative approaches to large-scale assessment, including innovative uses of technology (see, e.g., Quellmalz & Pellegrino, 2009).

Models of Measurement

The field of psychometrics focuses on how best to gather, synthesize, and communicate evidence of student understanding in an explicit and formal way. Psychometric models are based on a probabilistic approach to reasoning: a statistical model is developed to characterize the patterns believed most likely to emerge in the data for students at varying levels of cognitive competence. These psychometric models allow one to draw meaning from vast quantities of data and to express the degree of uncertainty associated with one's conclusions.

Various psychometric models are widely used for large-scale summative assessment; they typically have limited usefulness in formative assessment: using assessments to track and guide student learning. Fortunately, we now have alternative measurement models available that can support the kinds of inferences necessary to support teachers and to guide student learning. In particular, it is now possible to characterize student achievement in terms of multiple aspects of proficiency, rather than a single score; chart students' progress over time, instead of simply measuring performance at a particular point in time; deal with multiple paths or alternative methods of valued performance; model, monitor, and improve judgments based on informed evaluations; and model performance not only at the level of students, but also at the levels of groups, classes, schools, and states.

There have been a number of major developments in methods of measurement and the assessment challenges they help address. For example, work on measurement models has progressed from (a) developing models that are intended to measure general proficiency and/or to rank students to (b) adding enhancements to a standard psychometric model to make it more consistent with changing conceptions of learning, cognition, and curricular emphasis to (c) incorporating cognitive elements, including a model of learning and curriculum, directly into psychometric models as parameters to (d) creating a family of models that are adaptable to a broad range of contexts. Each model and adaptation has its particular uses, strengths, and limitations (see Pellegrino et al., 2001).

However, many of the newer models and methods are not widely used because they are not easily understood or because they are not accessible to those without a strong technical background. Technology offers the possibility of addressing this shortcoming. For instance, by building statistical models into technology-based learning environments for use in classrooms, teachers can employ more complex tasks, capture and replay students' performances, share exemplars of competent performance, and in the process gain critical information about student competence (also see Baker & Siemens, Chapter 13, this volume, on learning analytics).

Much hard work remains to focus psychometric model building on the critical features of models of cognition and learning and on observations that reveal meaningful cognitive variation in a particular domain. If anything, the task has become more difficult because an additional step is now required – determining the inferences that must be drawn, the observations needed, the tasks that will provide them, and the statistical models that will express the necessary patterns most efficiently. The long-standing tradition of leaving scientists, educators, task designers, and psychometricians each to their own realms represents another serious barrier to progress (for further discussion, see Pellegrino, DiBello, & Brophy, 2013).

Balanced Assessment Systems

Many different assessments are used in schools, with each serving varying needs and different audiences. Perhaps the biggest divide is between external, large-scale assessments, for purposes of summative evaluation and comparison by policy makers, and classroom assessments designed to assist teachers in their instructional work. One result of this variety is that users can become frustrated when different assessments have conflicting achievement goals and results. Sometimes such discrepancies can be meaningful and useful, such as when assessments are explicitly aimed at measuring different school outcomes. More often, however, conflicting assessment goals and feedback cause much confusion for educators, students, and parents. In this section I describe a vision for coordinated systems of multiple assessments that work together, along with curriculum and instruction, to promote learning.

In many education systems worldwide, assessment is focused on classroom activities designed to provide information about the progress of learning, and external, large-scale standardized assessments play a relatively minor or secondary role in the educational system (see NRC, 2003). In the United States, however, the resources invested in producing and using large-scale tests – in terms of money, instructional time, research, and development – far outweigh the investment in the design and use of effective classroom assessment. And unfortunately, there is ample evidence that the large-scale assessments in use today in the United States and elsewhere negatively impact classroom instruction and assessment. For instance, as discussed earlier, teachers feel pressure to teach to the test, which (given the focus of today's assessments on disconnected facts and skills: see Sawyer, Chapter 1, this volume) results in a narrowing of instruction. This would not necessarily be a problem if the assessments found on such tests were of higher quality and represented the full range of levels of thinking and reasoning that we desire for students to attain. Then we would have tests worth teaching toward and the tasks would be much closer to those that are useful in the context of classroom instruction to promote student learning and engagement. They would be tasks and performances that merit the time and attention of teachers and students. If that was true then we would not have the problem that exists now because teachers model their own classroom tests after the highly limiting and less-than-ideal tasks found on typical standardized tests (Linn, 2000; Shepard, 2000). Given that they will engage in such a modeling exercise when the external tests matter for purposes such as accountability, it would be far better if what they were modeling constituted high-quality and valid assessments of student achievement. So in addition to striking a better balance between classroom and large-scale assessment, we need to coordinate systems of assessments that collectively support a common set of learning and teaching goals, rather than work at cross-purposes. To this end, an assessment system should exhibit three properties: comprehensiveness, coherence, and continuity.

By *comprehensiveness*, I mean that a range of measurement approaches should be used to provide a variety of evidence to support educational decision making. No single test score can be considered a definitive measure of a student's competence. Multiple measures enhance the validity and fairness of the inferences drawn by giving students various ways and opportunities to demonstrate their competence. Multiple measures can also be used to provide evidence that improvements in test scores represent real gains in learning, as opposed to score inflation due to teaching narrowly to one particular test (Heubert & Hauser, 1999).

By *coherence*, I mean that the models of student learning underlying the various external and classroom assessments within a system should be compatible. While a large-scale assessment might be based on a model of learning that is coarser than that underlying the assessments used in classrooms, the conceptual base for the large-scale assessment should be a broader version of one that makes sense at the finer-grained level (Mislevy, 1996). In this way, the external assessment results will be consistent with the more detailed understanding of learning underlying classroom instruction and assessment. As one moves up and down the levels of the system, from the classroom through the school, district, and state, assessments along this vertical dimension should align. As long as the underlying models of learning are consistent, the assessments will complement each other rather than present conflicting goals for learning.

Finally, an ideal assessment system would be designed to be *continuous*. That is, assessments should measure student progress over time, akin more to a videotape record than to the snapshots most current tests provide (also see Chinn & Sherin, Chapter 9, this volume, on microgenetic methods). To provide such pictures of progress, multiple sets of observations over time must be linked conceptually so that change can be observed and interpreted. Models of student progress in learning should underlie the assessment system, and tests should be designed to provide information that maps back to the progression.

Figure 12.3 provides a graphical illustration of how an assessment system might look and some of the factors that would serve to achieve balance and to support these three principles. Figure 12.3 demonstrates that such a system would be (a) coordinated across levels, (b) unified by common learning goals, and (c) synchronized by unifying progress variables. No existing system of assessments has these design features and meets all three criteria of comprehensiveness, coherence, and continuity, but there are examples of assessments that represent steps toward these goals. For instance, Australia's Developmental Assessment program (Forster & Masters, 2001; Masters & Forster, 1996) and the BEAR assessment system (Wilson, Draney, & Kennedy, 2001; Wilson & Sloane, 2000) show how progress maps can be used to achieve coherence between formative and summative assessment, as well as among curriculum, instruction, and assessments. Progress maps also enable the measurement of growth (thus meeting the continuity criterion). The Australian Council for Educational Research has produced an excellent set of resource materials for teachers to support their use of a wide range of assessment strategies – from written tests to portfolios to projects at the classroom level – that can all be designed to link back to the progress maps (thus meeting the criterion of comprehensiveness).

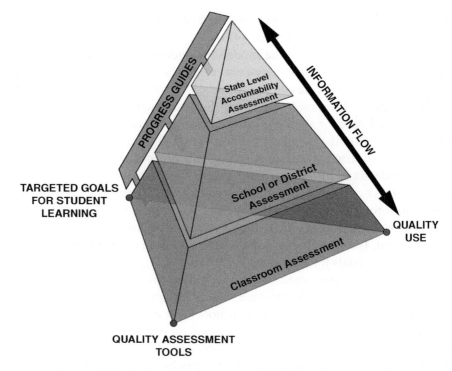

TARGETED GOALS
FOR STUDENT
LEARNING

QUALITY ASSESSMENT
TOOLS

Figure 12.3. *Center for Assessment and Evaluation of Student Learning (CAESL) representation of a coordinated, multilevel assessment system (from Herman, Wilson, Shavelson, Timms, & Schneider, 2005, reprinted with permission of the authors).*

Final Thoughts: The Role of Assessment in Learning Sciences Research

Learning sciences researchers need high-quality evidence that allows us to ask and answer critical questions about the outcomes of learning and instruction – what students know and are able to do. The first requirement for developing quality assessments is that the concepts and skills that signal progress toward mastery of a domain be understood and specified. These activities constitute fundamental components of a prospective learning sciences agenda as applied to multiple courses and content domains. Assessment of the overall outcomes of instruction is important to the learning sciences because it allows us to test program effectiveness. But it is more broadly important because the content of such assessments can drive instructional practice for better or for worse. Assessment of the impact of learning sciences-based curricula is also important. Using assessment for program evaluation requires measures that are sensitive to learning and the impact of quality teaching. Researchers, educators, and administrators must therefore concern themselves with supporting research and development on effective and appropriate assessment procedures that can serve multiple purposes and function as part of a coordinated system of assessments.

So it is important to reemphasize a major theme of this chapter about the nature of what constitutes high-quality and valid assessment from a learning sciences perspective. Such assessments are based on three critical components that work together: (1) they are derived from theories and data about content-based cognition that indicate the knowledge and skills that should be assessed; (2) they include tasks and observations that can provide evidence and information about whether students have mastered the knowledge and skills of interest; and (3) they make use of qualitative and quantitative techniques for interpreting student performance that capture differences in knowledge and skill among students being assessed. Thus, assessment design and use should be seen as a major form of conceptual research *within* the learning sciences. It should not be left to others with limited conceptions of what it means to know and to learn, and it requires multidisciplinary collaborations that integrate across disciplines including researchers in academic disciplines and measurement experts.

From a practical perspective regarding the use of assessment to guide instruction and learning, future research should also explore (a) how new forms of assessment can be made accessible for instructors and practical for use in classrooms, (b) how they can be made efficient for use in K-16+ teaching contexts, (c) how various new forms of assessment affect student learning, instructor practice, and educational decision making, (d) how instructors can be assisted in integrating new forms of assessment into their instructional practices and how they can best make use of information from such assessments, and (e) how structural features of instructional delivery in education (e.g., length of class time, class size, and organization, and opportunities for students and/or instructors to work together) impact the feasibility of implementing new types of assessments and their effectiveness.

As a field, learning sciences continues to make progress on critical issues related to learning and instruction with an increasing awareness of the importance of assessment in that enterprise. I hope this chapter's discussion of ways to think about the design and uses of assessment provides a useful set of ideas and approaches that can further advance the field of learning sciences research. There is a great deal at stake for the field of learning sciences by embracing the challenge of designing assessments that are aligned to our evolving conceptions of what it means to know and to learn. For one, assessment design forces us to be much more explicit about the nature of our constructs and how they are manifest in various aspects of student performance. This also provides the benefit of designing ways to gather evidence that can be used to test and demonstrate the efficacy of the learning environments and tools and technologies for learning that we design. Much of what we can do goes well beyond traditional ways student achievement is assessed, and thus we have the opportunity to also shape the future of educational assessment. It is important that learning scientists engage the educational assessment and policy communities when it comes to the design and use of tasks and situations that provide evidence of student accomplishments – whether that be for purposes of improving educational materials and tools in an era of new standards in mathematics, language arts, and science, or for designing and interpreting assessments that have national and international impact. A good example of the latter context is the participation of the learning sciences community in helping OECD develop a framework for the design of collaborative problem solving for the PISA 2015 international assessment. Not only was engagement in development of the framework useful for guiding the design of a valid assessment of this important 21st-century competency, it was also extremely useful in synthesizing bodies of research related to collaborative learning and problem solving to help learning scientists gauge what we know and don't know and where further theory development and research are needed.

References

Alonzo, A. C., & Gotwals, A. W. (2012). *Learning progression in science: Current challenges and future directions.* Rotterdam, Netherlands: Sense Publishers.

American Association for the Advancement of Science (AAAS). (2001). *Atlas of science literacy.* Washington, DC: Author.

American Educational Research Association, American Psychological Association, and National Council of Measurement in Education (AERA, APA, NCME). (1999). *Standards for educational and psychological testing.* Washington, DC: American Educational Research Association.

Black, P., & Wiliam, D. (1998). Assessment and classroom learning. *Assessment in Education,* 5(1), 7–73.

Bransford, J. D., Brown, A. L., Cocking, R. R., Donovan, M. S., & Pellegrino, J. W. (Eds.) (2000). *How people learn: Brain, mind, experience, and school.* Expanded Edition. Washington, DC: National Academies Press.

Carpenter, T., Fennema, E., & Franke, M. (1996). Cognitively guided instruction: A knowledge base for reform in primary mathematics instruction. *Elementary School Journal,* 97(1), 3–20.

Cobb, P., Wood, T., Yackel, E., Nicholls, J., Wheatley, G., Trigatti, B., & Perlwitz, M. (1991). Assessment of a problem-centered second-grade mathematics project. *Journal for Research in Mathematics Education,* 22(1), 3–29.

Corcoran, T. B., Mosher, F. A., & Rogat, A. (2009). *Learning progressions in science: An evidence-based approach to reform.* New York: Columbia University, Teachers College, Consortium for Policy Research in Education, Center on Continuous Instructional Improvement.

Daro, P., Mosher, F. A., Corcoran, T., Barrett, J., & Consortium for Policy Research in Education. (2011). *Learning trajectories in mathematics: A foundation for standards, curriculum, assessment, and instruction.* Philadelphia, PA: Consortium for Policy Research in Education.

Duncan, R. G., & Hmelo-Silver, C. (2009). Learning progressions: Aligning curriculum, instruction, and assessment. *Journal for Research in Science Teaching*, 46(6), 606–609.

Duschl, R. A., Schweingruber, H. A., & Shouse, A. W. (Eds.) (2007). *Taking science to school: Learning and teaching science in grade K-8*. Washington, DC: The National Academies Press.

Forster, M., & Masters, G. (2001). *Progress maps*. Victoria, Australia: Australian Council for Educational Research.

Griffin, S., & Case, R. (1997). Re-thinking the primary school math curriculum: An approach based on cognitive science. *Issues in Education*, 3(1), 1–49.

Haertel, E. H., & Lorie, W. A. (2004). Validating standards-based test score interpretations. *Measurement: Interdisciplinary Research and Perspectives*, 2(2), 61–103.

Herman, J. L., Wilson, M. R., Shavelson, R., Timms, M., & Schneider, S. (2005, April). *The CAESL assessment model*. Paper presented at American Educational Research Association annual conference, Montreal, Canada.

Heubert, J. P., & Hauser, R. M. (Eds.) (1999). *High stakes: Testing for tracking, promotion, and graduation*. Washington, DC: National Academies Press.

Hickey, D., & Pellegrino, J. W. (2005). Theory, level, and function: Three dimensions for understanding transfer and student assessment. In J. P. Mestre (Ed.), *Transfer of learning from a modern multidisciplinary perspective* (pp. 251–293). Greenwich, CO: Information Age Publishing.

Kane, M. T. (2006). Validation. In R. L. Brennan (Ed.), *Educational measurement*. Fourth Edition. (pp. 17–64). Westport, CT: Praeger.

Kane, M. T. (2013). Validating the interpretations and uses of test scores. *Journal of Educational Measurement*, 50(1), 1–73.

Kilpatrick, J., Swafford, J., & Findell, B. (Eds.) (2001). *Adding it up: Helping children learn mathematics*. Washington, DC: National Academies Press.

Linn, R. (2000). Assessments and accountability. *Educational Researcher*, 29(2), 4–16.

Masters, G., & Forster, M. (1996). *Progress maps. Assessment resource kit*. Victoria, Australia: Commonwealth of Australia.

Mislevy, R. J. (1996). Test theory reconceived. *Journal of Educational Measurement*, 33(4), 379–416.

Mislevy, R. J., & Haertel, G. (2006). Implications of evidence-centered design for educational assessment. *Educational Measurement: Issues and Practice*, 25, 6–20.

Mislevy, R. J., & Riconscente, M. M. (2006). Evidence-centered assessment design: Layers, concepts, and terminology. In S. Downing & T. Haladyna (Eds.), *Handbook of test development* (pp. 61–90). Mahwah, NJ: Lawrence Erlbaum Associates.

Mislevy, R. J., Steinberg, L., & Almond, R. (2003). On the structure of educational assessments. *Measurement: Interdisciplinary Research and Perspectives*, 1, 3–67.

National Research Council. (2003). *Assessment in support of learning and instruction: Bridging the gap between large-scale and classroom assessment*. Washington, DC: National Academies Press.

National Research Council. (2012). *A framework for K–12 science education: Practices, crosscutting concepts, core ideas*. Washington, DC: National Academies Press.

Pellegrino, J. W., Baxter, G. P., & Glaser, R. (1999). Addressing the "two disciplines" problem: Linking theories of cognition and learning with assessment and instructional practice. In A. Iran-Nejad & P. D. Pearson (Eds.), *Review of research in education* (vol. 24, pp. 307–353). Washington, DC: American Educational Research Association.

Pellegrino, J. W., Chudowsky, N., & Glaser, R. (Eds.) (2001). *Knowing what students know: The science and design of educational assessment.* Washington, DC: National Academies Press.

Pellegrino, J. W., DiBello, L., & Brophy, S. (2013). The science and design of assessment in engineering education. In A. Johri & B. Olds (Eds.), *Cambridge handbook of engineering education research.* Cambridge: Cambridge University Press.

Pellegrino, J. W., & Hickey, D. (2006). Educational assessment: Towards better alignment between theory and practice. In L. Verschaffel, F. Dochy, M. Boekaerts, & S. Vosniadou (Eds.), *Instructional psychology: Past, present and future trends. Sixteen essays in honour of Erik De Corte* (pp. 169–189). Oxford: Elsevier.

Pellegrino, J. W., Jones, L. R., & Mitchell, K. J. (Eds.) (1999). *Grading the nation's report card: Evaluating NAEP and transforming the assessment of educational progress.* Washington, DC: National Academies Press.

Quellmalz, E., & Pellegrino, J. W. (2009). Technology and testing. *Science*, 323, 75–79.

Ruiz-Primo, M. A., Shavelson, R. J., Hamilton, L., & Klein, S. (2002). On the evaluation of systemic science education reform: Searching for instructional sensitivity. *Journal of Research in Science Teaching*, 39, 369–393.

Sadler, R. (1989). Formative assessment and the design of instructional systems. *Instructional Science*, 18, 119–144.

Shepard, L. A. (2000). The role of assessment in a learning culture. *Educational Researcher*, 29(7), 4–14.

Snow, C. E., Burns, M., & Griffin, M. (Eds.) (1998). *Preventing reading difficulties in young children.* Washington, DC: National Academies Press.

Stiggins, R. J. (1997). *Student-centered classroom assessment.* Upper Saddle River, NJ: Prentice-Hall.

Toulmin, S. E. (2003). *The uses of argument.* Cambridge: Cambridge University Press.

Wiggins, G. (1998). *Educative assessment: Designing assessments to inform and improve student performance.* San Francisco, CA: Jossey-Bass.

Wiliam, D. (2007). Keeping learning on track: formative assessment and the regulation of learning. In F. K. Lester Jr. (Ed.), *Second handbook of mathematics teaching and learning* (pp. 1053–1098). Greenwich, CT: Information Age Publishing.

Wilson, M., & Sloane, K. (2000). From principles to practice: An embedded assessment system. *Applied Measurement in Education*, 13(2), 181–208.

Wilson, M. R., & Bertenthal, M. W. (Eds.) (2005). *Systems for state science assessments.* Washington, DC: National Academies Press.

13 Educational Data Mining and Learning Analytics

Ryan Baker and George Siemens

During the past decades, the potential of *analytics* and *data mining* – methodologies that extract useful and actionable information from large datasets – has transformed one field of scientific inquiry after another (cf. Collins, Morgan, & Patrinos, 2004; Summers et al., 1992). Analytics has become a trend over the past several years, reflected in large numbers of graduate programs promising to make someone a master of analytics, proclamations that analytics skills offer lucrative employment opportunities (Manyika et al., 2011), and airport waiting lounges filled with advertisements from different consultancies promising to significantly increase profits through analytics. When applied to education, these methodologies are referred to as *learning analytics* (LA) and *educational data mining* (EDM). In this chapter, we will focus on the shared similarities as we review both parallel areas while also noting important differences.

Using the methodologies we describe in this chapter, one can scan through large datasets to discover patterns that occur in only small numbers of students or only sporadically (cf. Baker, Corbett, & Koedinger, 2004; Sabourin, Rowe, Mott, & Lester, 2011); one can investigate how different students choose to use different learning resources and obtain different outcomes (cf. Beck, Chang, Mostow, & Corbett, 2008); one can conduct fine-grained analysis of phenomena that occur over long periods of time (such as the move toward disengagement over the years of schooling – cf. Bowers, 2010); and one can analyze how the design of learning environments may impact variables of interest through the study of large numbers of exemplars (cf. Baker et al., 2009). In the sections that follow, we argue that learning analytics has the potential to substantially increase the sophistication of how the field of learning sciences understands learning, contributing both to theory and practice.

The Emergence of Analytics

Compared to sciences such as physics, biology, and climate science, the learning sciences is relatively late in using analytics. For example, the first journal devoted primarily to analytics in the biological sciences, *Computers in Biology and Medicine*, began publication in 1970. By contrast, the first journal targeted toward analytics in the learning sciences, the *Journal of Educational Data Mining*, began publication in 2009, although it was preceded by a conference series (commencing in 2008), a workshop series (commencing in 2005), and earlier workshops in 2000 and 2004. There are now several venues that promote and publish research in this area – currently including the *Journal of Educational Data Mining*, the *Journal of Learning Analytics*, the *International Conference on Educational Data Mining*, the *Conference on Learning Analytics and Knowledge* (LAK), as well as a growing emphasis on research in this area at conferences such as the *International Conference on Artificial Intelligence in Education*, *ACM Knowledge Discovery in Databases*, the *International Conference of the Learning Sciences*, and the annual meeting of the *American Educational Research Association*.

The use of analytics in education has grown in recent years for four primary reasons: a substantial increase in data quantity, improved data formats, advances in computing, and increased sophistication of tools available for analytics.

Quantity of Data

One of the factors leading to the recent emergence of learning analytics is the increasing quantity of analyzable educational data. Considerable quantities of data are now available to scientific researchers through public archives like the Pittsburgh Science of Learning Center DataShop (Koedinger et al., 2010). Mobile, digital, and online technologies are increasingly utilized in many educational contexts. When learners interact with a digital device, data about that interaction can be easily captured or "logged" and made available for subsequent analysis. Papers have recently been published with data from tens of thousands of students. With the continued growth of online learning (Allen & Seamen, 2013) and the use of new technologies for data capture (Choudhury & Pentland, 2003), even greater scope of data capture during learning activities can be expected in the future, particularly as large companies such as Pearson and McGraw-Hill become interested in EDM, and Massive Online Open Courses (MOOCs) and providers such as Coursera, edX, and Udacity generate additional datasets for research (Lin, 2012).

Data Formats

Baker recalls his first analysis of educational log data; it took almost two months to transform logged data into a usable form. Today, there are standardized formats for logging specific types of educational data (cf. Koedinger et al., 2010), as well as considerable knowledge about how to effectively log educational data, crystallized both in scientific publications and in more informal knowledge that is disseminated at conferences and in researcher training programs like the Pittsburgh Science of Learning Center Summer School and the Society for Learning Analytics Research open online courses.[1]

---

[1] https://learn.canvas.net/courses/33.

Increased Processing/Computation Power

The increase in attention to analytics is also driven by advances in computation (Mayer, 2009). Smartphones today exceed the computational power of desktop computers from less than a decade ago, and powerful mainframe computers today can accomplish tasks that were impossible only a few years ago. Increases in computational power support researchers in analyzing large quantities of data and also help to produce that data in fields such as health care, geology, environmental studies, and sociology.

Development of Analytics Tools

Some of the most significant advances have been in supporting the management of large datasets, making it possible to store, organize, and sift through data in ways that make them substantially easier to analyze. Google developed MapReduce to address the substantial challenges of managing data at the scale of the Internet (Dean & Ghemawat, 2008), including distributing data and data-related applications across networks of computers; previous database models were not capable of managing Web-scale data. MapReduce led to the development of Apache Hadoop, now commonly used for data management.

In addition to tools for managing data, an increasing number of tools have emerged that support analyzing it. In recent years, the sophistication and ease of use of tools for analyzing data make it possible for an increasing range of researchers to apply data mining methodology without needing extensive experience in computer programming. Many of these tools are adapted from the business intelligence field, as reflected in the prominence of SAS and IBM tools in education, tools that were first used in the corporate sector for predictive analytics and improving organizational decision making by analyzing large quantities of data and presenting it in a visual or interactive format (particularly valuable for scenario evaluation). In the early 2000s, many analytics tools were technically complex and required users to have advanced programming and statistical knowledge. Now, even previously complex tools such as SAS, RapidMiner, and SPSS are easier to use and allow individuals to conduct analytics with relatively less technical knowledge. Common desktop software, such as Microsoft Excel, has also incorporated significantly improved visualization and analytics features in recent years. Other tools such as Tableau Software are designed to allow use even if the user does not have advanced technical knowledge of analytics. As easier-to-use tools emerge, they will make EDM and LA accessible to a larger number of learning sciences researchers.

Developing Research Communities

The two research communities we review in this chapter, educational data mining and learning analytics, have adopted complementary perspectives on the analysis of educational data. Siemens and Baker (2012) noted that the two communities have considerable overlap (in terms of both research and researchers), and that the two communities strongly believe in conducting research that has applications that benefit learners as well as informing and enhancing the learning sciences. They also described some of the differences:

1) Researchers in EDM are more interested in automated methods for discovery within educational data; researchers in LA are more interested in human-led methods for exploring educational data. This difference approximately tracks the relationship between data mining and exploratory data analysis, in the wider scientific literature. Automated methods for discovery can help to achieve the best possible prediction; human-led methods of discovery can result in more interpretable and more understandable models of phenomena.

2) Researchers in EDM emphasize modeling specific constructs and the relationships between them; researchers in LA emphasize a more holistic, systems understanding of constructs. This difference parallels long-standing differences in approaches among learning sciences researchers. EDM research in this fashion more closely ties to theoretical approaches such as Anderson's ACT-R Theory (Anderson & Lebiere, 1998) or the PSLC Theoretical Framework (Koedinger, Corbett, & Perfetti, 2012); LA research more closely ties to theory that attempts to understand systems as wholes or that takes a situationalist approach (Greeno, 1998; also see Nathan & Sawyer, Chapter 2, this volume, on elemental and systemic approaches in learning sciences). That said, we believe that researchers from each of these traditions may find methods emerging from each community useful.

3) Researchers in EDM look to applications in automated adaptation, such as supporting learners through having educational software identify a need and automatically change to personalize learners' experience (cf. Arroyo et al., 2007; Baker et al., 2006; Corbett & Anderson, 1995); researchers in LA look for ways to inform and empower instructors and learners, such as informing instructors about ways that specific students are struggling so that the instructor can contact the learner (cf. Arnold, 2010). In this case, EDM and LA methods are each suited to both types of use, and the differences in focus are primarily due to the applications that were historically of interest to researchers in each community.

Both EDM and LA have a strong emphasis on connection to theory in the learning sciences and education philosophy. Most researchers that publish at the EDM and LA conferences use theory from the learning sciences and education to guide their choice of analyses and aim to contribute back to theory with the results of their analyses. The theory-oriented perspective marks a departure of EDM and LA from technical approaches that use data as their sole guiding point (see, for example, Anderson's argument in 2008 that big data will render the scientific method obsolete: "But faced with massive data, this approach to science – hypothesize, model, test – is becoming obsolete.").

Key Methods and Tools

The methodologies used in EDM and LA have come from a number of sources, but the largest two sources of inspiration for the area have been methods from data mining and analytics in general, and from psychometrics and educational measurement. In many cases, the specific characteristics of educational data have resulted in different methods playing a more prominent role in EDM/LA than in data mining in general, or have resulted in adaptations to existing psychometric methods. In this section, we survey some of the key methodologies in the field and discuss a few examples of how these methodologies have been applied. This review draws on past reviews (cf. Baker & Yacef, 2009; Ferguson, 2012; Romero & Ventura, 2010; Siemens & Baker, 2012), but extends them to incorporate recent developments.

Prediction Methods

One of the most prominent categories of EDM methods in the review by Baker and Yacef (2009), and continuing to this day, is *prediction*. In prediction, the goal is to develop a model that can infer a single aspect of the data (the *predicted variable*, similar to dependent variables in traditional statistical analysis) from some combination of other aspects of the data (*predictor variables*, similar to independent variables in traditional statistical analysis). Developing a prediction model depends on knowing what the predicted variable is for a small set of data; a model is then created for this small set of data and statistically validated so that it can be applied at greater scale. For instance, one may collect data on whether 1,000 students dropped out of college, develop a prediction model to infer whether a student will drop out of college, validate it on subsets of the 1,000 students that were not included when creating the prediction model, and then use the model to make predictions about new students. As such, prediction models are commonly used either to predict future events (cf. Dekker, Pechenizkiy, & Vleeshouwers, 2009; Feng, Heffernan, & Koedinger, 2009; Ming & Ming, 2012) or to predict variables that are not feasible to directly collect in real time – for example, collecting data on affect or engagement in real time often requires expensive observations or disruptive self-report measures, whereas a prediction model based on student log data can be completely nonintrusive (cf. Baker et al., 2004; D'Mello, Craig, Witherspoon, McDaniel, & Graesser, 2008; Sabourin et al., 2011).

These methods have successfully supported interventions to improve student outcomes. For example, the Purdue Signals project used prediction models to identify students who were at risk for dropout in courses and university programs. The use of Purdue Signals resulted in more help seeking, better course outcomes, and significantly improved retention rates (Arnold, 2010).

Three types of prediction models are common in EDM/LA: *classifiers*, *regressors*, and *latent knowledge estimation*. In classifiers, the predicted variable can be either a binary (e.g., 0 or 1) or a categorical variable. Popular classification methods in educational domains include decision trees, random forest, decision rules, step regression, and logistic regression. In regressors, the predicted variable is a continuous variable, for example a number. The most popular regressor in EDM is linear regression (note that linear regression is not used the same way in EDM/LA as in traditional statistics, despite the identical name).

A third type of prediction model that is important in EDM/LA (which is actually just a special type of classifier) is latent knowledge estimation. In latent knowledge estimation, a student's knowledge of specific skills and concepts is assessed by their patterns of correctness on those skills (and occasionally other information as well). The models used in online learning typically differ from the psychometric models used in paper tests or in computer-adaptive testing, because with an interactive learning application, the student's knowledge is continually changing. A wide range of algorithms exist for latent knowledge estimation; the two most popular are currently Bayesian Knowledge Tracing (BKT – Corbett & Anderson, 1995) and Performance Factors Analysis (PFA – Pavlik, Cen, & Koedinger, 2009), which have been found to have comparable performance in a number of analyses (see review in Pardos, Baker, Gowda, & Heffernan, 2011). Knowledge estimation algorithms increasingly underpin intelligent tutoring systems, such as the cognitive tutors currently used for algebra in 6 percent of U.S. high school classrooms (cf. Koedinger & Corbett, 2006).

Structure Discovery

Structure discovery algorithms attempt to find structure in the data without an a priori idea of what should be found, a very different goal than in prediction. In prediction, the EDM/LA researcher attempts to model a specific variable; by contrast, structure discovery has no specific variable of interest. Instead, the researcher attempts to determine what structure emerges naturally from the data. Common approaches to structure discovery in EDM/LA include *clustering*, *factor analysis*, *social network analysis*, and *domain structure discovery*.

In clustering, the goal is to find data points that naturally group together, splitting the full dataset into a set of clusters. Clustering is particularly useful in cases where the most common categories within the dataset are not known in advance. If a set of clusters is well selected, each data point in a cluster will generally be more similar to the other data points in that cluster than to data points in other clusters. Clusters have been used to group students (cf. Beal, Qu, & Lee, 2006) and student actions (cf. Amershi & Conati, 2009). For example, Amershi and Conati (2009) found characteristic patterns in how students use exploratory learning environments and used this information to identify more and less effective student strategies.

In factor analysis, a closely related method, the goal is to find variables that naturally group together, splitting the set of variables (as opposed to the data points) into a set of latent (not directly observable) factors. Factor analysis is frequently used in psychometrics for validating or determining scales. In EDM/LA, factor analysis is used for dimensionality reduction (e.g., reducing the number of variables) for a wide variety of applications. For instance, Baker and colleagues (2009) used factor analysis to determine which design choices are made in common by the designers of intelligent tutoring systems (for instance, tutor designers tend to use principle-based hints rather than concrete hints in tutor problems that have brief problem scenarios).

In social network analysis (SNA), models are developed of the relationships and interactions between individual actors, as well as the patterns that emerge from those relationships and interactions. A simple example of its use is in understanding the differences between effective and ineffective project groups, through visual analysis of the strength of group connections (cf. Kay, Maisonneuve, Yacef, & Reimann, 2006). SNA is also used to study how students' communication behaviors change over time (cf. Haythornthwaite, 2001) and to study how students' positions in a social network relate to their perception of being part of a learning community (cf. Dawson, 2008). This is valuable information because patterns of interaction and connectivity can indicate prospect of academic success as well as learner sense of engagement in a course (Macfadyen & Dawson, 2010; Suthers & Rosen, 2011).

SNA reveals the structure of interactions, but does not detail the nature of exchanges or the impact of connectedness. Increasingly, network analysis is paired with additional analytics approaches to better understand the patterns observed through network analytics; for example, SNA might be coupled with discourse analysis (see Enyedy & Stevens, Chapter 10, this volume; Buckingham, Shum, & Ferguson, 2012).

Domain structure discovery consists of finding the structure of knowledge in an educational domain (e.g., how specific content maps to specific knowledge components or skills across students). This could consist of mapping problems in educational software to specific knowledge components in order to group the problems effectively for latent knowledge estimation and problem selection (cf. Cen, Koedinger, & Junker, 2006) or of mapping test items to skills (cf. Tatsuoka, 1995). Considerable work has recently been applied to this problem in EDM for both test data (cf. Barnes, Bitzer, & Vouk, 2005; Desmarais, 2011) and for tracking learning during use of an intelligent tutoring system (Cen et al., 2006).

Relationship Mining

In relationship mining, the goal is to discover relationships between variables in a dataset with a large number of variables. Relationship mining has historically been the most common category of EDM research (Baker & Yacef, 2009), and remains extremely prominent to this day. It may take the form of attempting to find out which variables are most strongly associated with a single variable of particular interest, or may take the form of attempting to discover which relationships between any two variables are strongest. Broadly, there are four types of relationship mining: *association rule mining*, *correlation mining*, *sequential pattern mining*, and *causal data mining*.

In association rule mining, the goal is to find if-then rules of the form that if some set of variable values is found, another variable will generally have a specific value. For instance, Ben-Naim and colleagues (2009) used association rule mining to find patterns of successful student performance in an engineering simulation in order to make better suggestions to students having difficulty. In correlation mining, the goal is to find positive or negative linear correlations between variables (using post hoc corrections or dimensionality reduction methods when appropriate to avoid finding spurious relationships). An example can be found in Baker and colleagues (2009), where correlations were computed between a range of features of the design of intelligent tutoring system lessons and students' prevalence of gaming the system (intentionally misusing educational software to proceed without learning the material), finding that brief problem scenarios lead to a greater proportion of gaming behavior than either rich scenarios or having no scenario at all (just equations to manipulate). In sequential pattern mining, the goal is to find temporal associations between events. One successful use of this approach was work that Perera, Kay, Koprinska, Yacef, and Zaiane (2009) carried out to determine what path of student collaboration behaviors leads to a more successful eventual group project. In causal data mining, the goal is to find whether one event (or observed construct) was the cause of another event (or observed construct), for example to predict which factors will lead a student to do poorly in a class (Fancsali, 2012). All of these methodologies share the potential to find unexpected but meaningful relationships between variables; as such, they can be used for a wide range of applications, generating new hypotheses for further investigation or identifying contexts for potential intervention by automated systems.

Distillation of Data for Human Judgment

For data to be useful to educators, these data have to be timely. When educators have immediate access to visualizations of learner interactions or misconceptions that are reflected in students' writing and interaction, they can incorporate those data quickly into pedagogical activity. For this reason, one methodology that is common in LA is the *distillation of data for human judgment*. There has been a rich history of data visualization methods, which can be leveraged to support both basic research and practitioners (teachers, school leaders, and others) in their decision making. For example, visualizations of student trajectories through the school years can be used to identify common patterns among successful and unsuccessful students or to infer which students are at risk sufficiently early to drive intervention (Bowers, 2010). Visualization methods used in education include *heat maps* (which incorporate much of the same information as scatterplots, but are more scalable – cf. Bowers, 2010), *learning curves* (which show performance over time – cf. Koedinger et al., 2010), and *learnograms* (which show student alternation between activities over time – cf. Hershkovitz & Nachmias, 2008).

Discovery with Models

In *discovery with models* (Baker & Yacef, 2009; Hershkovitz, Baker, Gobert, Wixon, & Sao Pedro, in press), the results of one data mining analysis are utilized within another data mining analysis. Most commonly, a model of some construct is obtained, generally through prediction methods. This model is then applied to data in order to assess the construct the model identifies. The predictions of the model are then used as input to another data mining method. There are several ways that discovery with models can be conducted.

Perhaps the most common way that discovery with models is conducted is when a prediction model is used within another prediction model. In this situation, the initial model's predictions (which represent predicted variables in the original model) become predictor variables in the new prediction model. In this way, models can be composed of other models or based on other models, sometimes at multiple levels. For instance, prediction models of student robust learning (cf. Baker, Gowda, & Corbett, 2011) have generally depended on models of student metacognitive behaviors (cf. Aleven, McLaren, Roll, & Koedinger, 2006), which have in turn depended on assessments of latent student knowledge (cf. Corbett & Anderson, 1995), which have in turn depended on models of domain structure (cf. Koedinger, McLaughlin, & Stamper, 2012).

A second common way that discovery with models is conducted is when a prediction model is used within a relationship mining analysis. In this type of research, the relationships between the initial model's predictions and additional variables are studied. This enables a researcher to study the relationship between a complex latent construct (represented by the prediction model) and a wide variety of other variables. One example of this is seen in work by Beal, Qu, and Lee (2008), who developed a prediction model of gaming the system and correlated it to student individual differences in order to understand which students are most likely to engage in gaming behavior.

It is worth noting that the models used in discovery with models do not have to be obtained through prediction methods. These models can also be obtained through other approaches such as cluster analysis or *knowledge engineering* (Feigenbaum & McCorduck, 1983; Studer, Benjamins, & Fensel, 1998), where a human being rationally develops a model rather than using data mining to produce a model. The merits of knowledge engineering versus data mining for this type of analysis are out of scope for this chapter; greater discussion of this issue can be found in Hershkovitz and colleagues (in press).

Tools for Conducting EDM/LA Methods

In recent years, dozens of tools have emerged for data mining and analytics, from both the commercial and academic sectors. The majority of papers published in the proceedings of the EDM and LAK conferences, or published in the *Journal of Educational Data Mining* and by allied communities (such as Artificial Intelligence in Education, Intelligent Tutoring Systems, and User Modeling and Adaptive Personalization), use publicly available tools including RapidMiner, R, Weka, KEEL, and SNAPP. These tools include algorithms that implement the methods discussed previously and provide support for readying data for use within these methods. They also provide support for conducting statistical validation of model appropriateness for a range of uses (RapidMiner is particularly flexible for conducting sophisticated validation, leading to its increasing popularity among EDM researchers) and for visualizing data.

In addition to these general purpose tools, other tools are available for special purposes. For example, two competing packages are available for estimating student knowledge with Bayesian Knowledge Tracing (e.g., Baker et al., 2010; Chang, Beck, Mostow, & Corbett, 2006). Tools for supporting the development of prediction models, by obtaining data on the predicted variable through hand annotating log files, have also recently become available (Rodrigo, Baker, McLaren, Jayme, & Dy, 2012). Tools for displaying student learning over time and the pattern of student performance for different problems or items have been embedded into the Pittsburgh Science of Learning Center's DataShop, a very large public database on student use of educational software (Koedinger et al., 2010).

Some analytics tools are open source, allowing any researcher to develop add-ons that increase the core functionality of the tool. For example, R (http://www.r-project.org) is an open source statistical computing environment and a very popular tool for statistical and advanced analytics (Muenchen, 2012). A valuable feature for R users is the ability to create specific R packages to address research needs in specific fields. Weka (Witten & Frank, 2005; http://www.cs.waikato.ac.nz/ml/weka) is also open source, and a number of its tools for data mining have been incorporated into other tools, such as

RapidMiner. Open platforms like R and Weka allow researchers to scrutinize the methods and algorithms that other researchers use.

Commercial tools are driving the administrative use of analytics in many schools and districts. Enterprise tools such as IBM Cognos, SAS, and analytics offerings by learning management system providers such as Blackboard, and student systems such as Ellucian, enable an integrated research/application approach. The questions administrators and educators ask can sometimes differ in focus from those EDM researchers ask. For example, a researcher may look for patterns in data and test algorithms or develop analytics models to understand what contributed to learning success. In contrast, institutional analytics activities are likely to focus on improving learner success and providing support programs.

Impacts on Learning Sciences

Educational data mining and learning analytics have had several recent impacts on the learning sciences.

One area where these methods have been particularly useful is in research on *disengagement* within educational software. Prior to the development of analytics, disengagement was difficult to measure (Corno & Mandinach, 1983), but EDM and LA methods have produced models that can infer disengaged behaviors in a fine-grained fashion. Automated detectors of a range of disengaged behaviors have been developed using prediction methods or knowledge engineering methods, including detectors of gaming the system (Baker, Corbett, & Koedinger, 2004; Beal et al., 2008; Muldner, Burleson, Van de Sande, & Van Lehn, 2011; Walonoski & Heffernan, 2006), off-task behavior (Baker, 2007; Cetintas, Si, Xin, & Hord, 2010), carelessness (San Pedro, Baker, & Rodrigo, 2011a), and inexplicable behaviors (Sabourin et al., 2011; Wixon, Baker, Gobert, Ocumpaugh, & Bachmann, 2012).

Researchers have used these detectors to study the relationship between these behaviors and learning (Baker, 2007; Baker et al., 2004; Baker, Gowda, & Corbett, 2011; Cocea, Hershkovitz, & Baker, 2009; Walonoski & Heffernan, 2006), including study of how behaviors lead to differences in learning (e.g., Cocea et al., 2009) and how seemingly disengaged behaviors might, in some cases, paradoxically reflect deep engagement (Shih, Koedinger, & Scheines, 2008). They have also been used to understand what affect is associated with these behaviors (Sabourin et al., 2011; San Pedro, Rodrigo, & Baker, 2011b) and which learner individual differences are associated with these behaviors (Beal et al., 2008; Walonoski & Heffernan, 2006).

Detectors have also been embedded into intelligent tutors that adapt based on student disengagement. For instance, Baker and colleagues (2006) built an automated detector of gaming the system into a software agent that provides alternative exercises to students who game, both giving students an alternate way to learn material bypassed by gaming and making gaming behavior more time consuming. Arroyo and colleagues (2007) used an automated detector of gaming to provide students with information on their recent gaming and to provide an opportunity to give metacognitive messages on how to use the software more effectively. Each of these approaches resulted in less gaming and better learning.

EDM and LA methods have similarly been useful in understanding student learning in various collaborative settings. Collaborative learning behaviors have been analyzed in multiple contexts to determine which behaviors are characteristic of more successful groups and more successful learners, including computer-mediated discussions (McLaren et al., 2007; McLaren, Scheuer, & Mikšátko, 2010), online collaboration using software development tools (Kay et al., 2006), and interactive tabletop collaboration (Martinez, Yacef, Kay, Kharrufa, & AlQaraghuli, 2011). For instance, Prata, Letouze, Costa, Prata, and Brito (2012) found that students who were contradicted by their partners when they were incorrect tended to learn more than students whose partners chose not to correct them. Dyke and colleagues (2012) found that off-topic discussions during collaborative learning are more harmful to learning during some parts of the learning process than during other parts – specifically, off-topic discussion is more harmful when learning basic facts than during discussion of problem-solving alternatives.

Models based on student contributions to online discussion forums have even been able to predict those students' final course grades (Ming & Ming, 2012). This work has been embedded into automated agents that scaffold more effective collaboration (Dyke et al., 2012; McLaren et al., 2010) and into tools to support instructors in scaffolding their students' collaboration (Martinez, Yacef, Kay, & Schwendimann, 2012).

Impacts on Practice

We have often observed a positive feedback loop between research and practice in EDM and LA – with research discoveries leading to changes in practice, which in turn lead to the possibility of studying new issues. One example of this can be seen in research over the years on student knowledge in cognitive tutors (cf. Koedinger & Corbett, 2006). In the mid-1990s, mastery learning (where a student keeps receiving problems of a certain type until he or she successfully demonstrates mastery) was introduced, based on assessments of student mastery from the EDM Bayesian Knowledge Tracing algorithm (Corbett & Anderson, 1995). A prerequisite structure – for example, an ordering of which content must be learned prior to other content because it is needed to understand the later content – was developed for the content in cognitive tutors and applied in the design of tutor lessons. However, instructors were free to deviate from the planned prerequisite structure in line with their pedagogical goals – in other words, if an instructor thought that a prerequisite topic was not actually needed for a later topic, they could skip the prerequisite topic. This enabled later analyses of the pedagogical value of the prerequisite structure (Vuong, Nixon, & Towle, 2011). These results found that it is disadvantageous to students when instructors ignore prerequisite structure.

The development of analytics around social learning and discourse have been important in increasing awareness of the impact of social dimensions of learning and the impact of learning environment design on subsequent learning success. Several open online courses, such as etmooc (http://etmooc.org) and edfuture (http://edfuture.mooc.ca), have incorporated principles from social network theory (and related analytics) in the design of distributed, networked learning systems, in contrast with more centralized platforms such as learning management systems. For example, the analytics options available to researchers in a platform where data collection is centralized (as in an LMS) differ from the analytics approaches possible when data is distributed and fragmented across numerous technical and social spaces. A predictive learner success tool such as Purdue Signals draws data from LMS interactions and from the student information system. In contrast, learning in distributed social networks produces data that reflects learner interest and engagement across multiple spaces that are under the control of individuals. As analytics of learning move into a broader range of settings – such as informal interactions through peer networks in universities, workplace learning, or lifeline learning – EDM and LA can help to evaluate how learning happens across various settings and how patterns of engagement or predictors of success differ in distributed versus centralized learning systems.

EDM/LA and the Learning Sciences: To the Future

Educational data mining and learning analytics, despite being new research areas, have already made contributions to the learning sciences and to practice. The current trend suggests that this contribution will continue and even increase in the years to come.

One key trend is that these methods have been applied to an ever-widening range of data sources. Much of the early work in EDM was conducted within intelligent tutoring systems (as described in Koedinger & Corbett, 2006) and much of the work in LA began in Web-based e-learning and social learning environments. In recent years, this has extended to a wider variety of educational situations, including data from student collaboration around learning resources (Martinez et al., 2012), science simulations (Sao Pedro, Baker, Gobert, Montalvo, & Nakama, 2013), teacher newsgroups (Xu & Recker, 2011), and school district grade data systems (Bowers, 2010).

A second key trend, which can be seen in the examples cited earlier, is the use of EDM methods to answer an expanding range of research questions, in an expanding range of areas represented in this handbook: computer games (Steinkuehler & Squire, Chapter 19, this volume; cf. Hernández, Sucar, & Conati, 2009; Kerr & Chung, 2012), argumentation (Andriessen & Baker, Chapter 22, this volume; cf. Lynch, Pinkwart, Ashley, & Aleven, 2008; McLaren, Scheuer, & Miksatko, 2010), computer-supported collaborative learning (cf. Dyke et al., 2012; Kay et al., 2006; Stahl, Koschmann, & Suthers, Chapter 24, this volume), learning in virtual worlds (Kafai & Dede, Chapter 26, this volume; cf. Sil, Shelton, Ketelhut, & Yates, 2012), and teacher learning (Fishman, Davis, & Chan, Chapter 35, this volume; cf. Xu & Recker, 2011).

As EDM and LA become used in a wider variety of domains, by researchers from a wider variety of disciplines, and within learning systems of a wider variety of types, we will see the potential of these approaches for enhancing both practice and theory in the learning sciences. As this occurs, there will be opportunities to conduct finer-grained, broader-scale research in the learning sciences, benefiting the field and the learners impacted by developments in the field.

Acknowledgments

We would like to thank Lisa Rossi and Keith Sawyer for helpful comments and suggestions.

References

Aleven, V., McLaren, B., Roll, I., & Koedinger, K. (2006). Toward meta-cognitive tutoring: A model of help seeking with a cognitive tutor. *International Journal of Artificial Intelligence and Education*, 16, 101–128.

Allen, I. E., & Seaman, J. (2013). *Changing course: Ten years of tracking online education in the United States*. Sloan Consortium. Available from: http://sloanconsortium.org/publications/survey/changing_course_2012.

Amershi, S., & Conati, C. (2009). Combining unsupervised and supervised machine learning to build user models for exploratory learning environments. *Journal of Educational Data Mining*, 1(1), 71–81.

Anderson, C. (2008). The end of theory: The data deluge makes the scientific method obsolete. *Wired*.

Anderson, J. R., & Lebiere, C. (1998). *Atomic components of thought*. Mahwah, NJ: Lawrence Erlbaum Associates.

Arnold, K. E. (2010). Signals: Applying academic analytics. *Educause Quarterly*, 33, 1–10.

Arroyo, I., Ferguson, K., Johns, J., Dragon, T., Meheranian, H., Fisher, D., Barto, A., Mahadevan, S., & Woolf. B. P. (2007). Repairing disengagement with non-invasive interventions. *Proceedings of the 13th International Conference on Artificial Intelligence in Education,* 195–202.

Baker, R. S., Corbett, A. T., & Koedinger, K. R. (2004). Detecting student misuse of intelligent tutoring systems. *Proceedings of the 7th International Conference on Intelligent Tutoring Systems,* 531–540.

Baker, R. S. J. d. (2007). Modeling and understanding students' off-task behavior in intelligent tutoring systems. *Proceedings of ACM CHI 2007: Computer-Human Interaction,* 1059–1068.

Baker, R. S. J. d., Corbett, A. T., Gowda, S. M., Wagner, A. Z., MacLaren, B. M., Kauffman, L. R., Mitchell, A. P., & Giguere, S. (2010). Contextual slip and prediction of student performance after use of an intelligent tutor. *Proceedings of the 18th Annual Conference on User Modeling, Adaptation, and Personalization,* 52–63.

Baker, R. S. J. d., Corbett, A. T., Koedinger, K. R., Evenson, S. E., Roll, I., Wagner, A. Z., Naim, M., Raspat, J., Baker, D. J., & Beck, J. (2006). Adapting to when students game an intelligent tutoring system. *Proceedings of the 8th International Conference on Intelligent Tutoring Systems,* 392–401.

Baker, R. S. J. d., de Carvalho, A. M. J. A., Raspat, J., Aleven, V., Corbett, A. T., & Koedinger, K. R. (2009). Educational software features that encourage and discourage "gaming the system." *Proceedings of the 14th International Conference on Artificial Intelligence in Education,* 475–482.

Baker, R. S. J. d., Gowda, S. M., & Corbett, A. T. (2011). Automatically detecting a student's preparation for future learning: Help use is key. *Proceedings of the 4th International Conference on Educational Data Mining,* 179–188.

Baker, R. S. J. d., & Yacef, K. (2009). The state of educational data mining in 2009: A review and future visions. *Journal of Educational Data Mining,* 1(1), 3–17.

Barnes, T., Bitzer, D., & Vouk, M. (2005). Experimental analysis of the q-matrix method in knowledge discovery. *Proceedings of the 15th International Symposium on Methodologies for Intelligent Systems,* May 25–28, 2005, Saratoga Springs, NY.

Beal, C. R., Qu, L., & Lee, H. (2006). Classifying learner engagement through integration of multiple data sources. Paper presented at the 21st National Conference on Artificial Intelligence (AAAI-2006), Boston, MA.

Beal, C. R., Qu, L., & Lee, H. (2008). Mathematics motivation and achievement as predictors of high school students' guessing and help-seeking with instructional software. *Journal of Computer Assisted Learning,* 24, 507–514.

Beck, J. E., Chang, K. -M., Mostow, J., & Corbett, A. T. (2008). Does help help? Introducing the Bayesian evaluation and assessment methodology. *Proceedings of Intelligent Tutoring Systems, ITS 2008,* 383–394.

Ben-Naim, D., Bain, M., & Marcus, N. (2009). User-driven and data-driven approach for supporting teachers in reflection and adaptation of adaptive tutorials. *Proceedings of the 2nd International Conference on Educational Data Mining,* 21–30.

Bowers, A. J. (2010). Analyzing the longitudinal K-12 grading histories of entire cohorts of students: Grades, data driven decision making, dropping out and hierarchical cluster analysis. *Practical Assessment, Research & Evaluation (PARE),* 15(7), 1–18.

Buckingham Shum, S., & Ferguson, R. (2012). Social learning analytics. *Educational Technology and Society*, 15(3), 3–26.

Cen, H., Koedinger, K., & Junker, B. (2006). Learning factors analysis – A general method for cognitive model evaluation and improvement. *Proceedings of the 8th International Conference on Intelligent Tutoring Systems*, 164–175.

Cetintas, S., Si, L., Xin, Y., & Hord, C. (2010). Automatic detection of off-task behaviors in intelligent tutoring systems with machine learning techniques. *IEEE Transactions on Learning Technologies*, 3(3), 228–236.

Chang, K.-M., Beck, J., Mostow, J., & Corbett, A. (2006). A Bayes net toolkit for student modeling in intelligent tutoring systems. *Proceedings of the 8th International Conference on Intelligent Tutoring Systems*, 104–113, Jhongli, Taiwan.

Choudhury, T., & Pentland, A. (2003). Sensing and modeling human networks using sociometer. *Proceedings of the Seventh IEEE International Symposium on Wearable Computers (ISWC'03)*.

Cocea, M., Hershkovitz, A., & Baker, R. S. J. d. (2009). The impact of off-task and gaming behaviors on learning: Immediate or aggregate? *Proceedings of the 14th International Conference on Artificial Intelligence in Education*, 507–514.

Collins, F. S., Morgan, M., & Patrinos, A. (2004). The Human Genome Project: Lessons from large-scale biology. *Science*, 300(5617), 286–290.

Corbett, A. T., & Anderson, J. R. (1995). Knowledge tracing: Modeling the acquisition of procedural knowledge. *User Modeling and User-Adapted Interaction*, 4, 253–278.

Corno, L., & Mandinach, E. B. (1983). The role of cognitive engagement in classroom learning and motivation. *Educational Psychologist*, 18(2), 88–108.

D'Mello, S. K., Craig, S. D., Witherspoon, A., McDaniel, B., & Graesser, A. (2008). Automatic detection of learner's affect from conversational cues. *User Modeling and User-Adapted Interaction*, 18, 45–80.

Dawson, S. (2008). A study of the relationship between student social networks and sense of community. *Educational Technology & Society*, 11(3), 224–238.

Dean, J., & Ghemawat, S. (2008). MapReduce: Simplified data processing on large clusters. *Communications of the ACM*, 51(1).

Dekker, G., Pechenizkiy, M., & Vleeshouwers, J. (2009). Predicting students drop out: A case study. *Proceedings of the 2nd International Conference on Educational Data Mining, EDM'09*, 41–50.

Desmarais, M. C. (2011). Conditions for effectively deriving a q-matrix from data with non-negative matrix factorization. In C. Conati, S. Ventura, T. Calders, & M. Pechenizkiy (Eds.), *4th International Conference on Educational Data Mining, EDM 2011* (pp. 41–50). Eindhoven, Netherlands.

Dyke, G., Adamson, D., Howley, I., & Rosé, C. P. (2012). Towards academically productive talk supported by conversational agents. *Intelligent Tutoring Systems*, 531–540.

Fancsali, S. (2012). Variable construction and causal discovery for cognitive tutor log data: Initial results. *Proceedings of the 5th International Conference on Educational Data Mining*, 238–239.

Feigenbaum, E. A., & McCorduck, P. (1983). *The fifth generation: Artificial intelligence and Japan's computer challenge to the world*. Reading, MA: Addison-Wesley.

Feng, M., Heffernan, N., & Koedinger, K. (2009). Addressing the assessment challenge in an intelligent tutoring system that tutors as it assesses. *User Modeling and User-Adapted Interaction*, 19, 243–266.

Ferguson, R. (2012). The state of learning analytics in 2012: A review and future challenges. *Technical Report KMI-12-01*, Knowledge Media Institute, The Open University, UK. http://kmi.open.ac.uk/publications/techreport/kmi-12-01.

Greeno, J. G. (1998). The situativity of knowing, learning, and research. *American Psychologist, 53*(1), 5–26.

Halevy, A. Y., Norvig, P., & Pereira, F. (2009). The unreasonable effectiveness of data. *IEEE Intelligent Systems*, 24(2), 8–12.

Haythornthwaite, C. (2001). Exploring multiplexity: Social network structures in a computer-supported distance learning class. *The Information Society: An International Journal*, 17(3), 211–226.

Hernández, Y., Sucar, E., & Conati, C. (2009). Incorporating an affective behaviour model into an educational game. *Proceedings of FLAIR 2009, 22nd International Conference of the Florida Artificial Intelligence Society*, ACM Press.

Hershkovitz, A., Baker, R. S. J. d., Gobert, J., Wixon, M., & Sao Pedro, M. (in press). Discovery with models: A case study on carelessness in computer-based science inquiry. To appear in *American Behavioral Scientist*.

Hershkovitz, A., & Nachmias, R. (2008). Developing a log-based motivation measuring tool. *Proceedings of the 1st International Conference on Educational Data Mining*, 226–233.

Kay, J., Maisonneuve, N., Yacef, K., & Reimann, P. (2006). The big five and visualisations of team work activity. *Proceedings of the International Conference on Intelligent Tutoring Systems*, 197–206.

Kerr, D., & Chung, G. K. W. K. (2012). Identifying key features of student performance in educational video games and simulations through cluster analysis. *Journal of Educational Data Mining*, 4(1), 144–182.

Koedinger, K. R., Baker, R. S. J. d., Cunningham, K., Skogsholm, A., Leber, B., & Stamper, J. (2010). A data repository for the EDM community: The PSLC DataShop. In C. Romero, S. Ventura, M. Pechenizkiy, & R. S. J. d. Baker (Eds.), *Handbook of educational data mining* (pp. 43–56). Boca Raton, FL: CRC Press.

Koedinger, K. R., & Corbett, A. T. (2006). Cognitive tutors: Technology bringing learning science to the classroom. In K. Sawyer (Ed.), *The Cambridge handbook of the learning sciences* (pp. 61–78). New York: Cambridge University Press.

Koedinger, K. R., Corbett, A. T., & Perfetti, C. The Knowledge-Learning-Instruction (KLI) framework: Bridging the science-practice chasm to enhance robust student learning. *Cognitive Science*, 36(5), 757–798.

Koedinger, K. R., McLaughlin, E. A., & Stamper, J. C. (2012). Automated student model improvement. *Proceedings of the 5th International Conference on Educational Data Mining*, 17–24.

Lin, L. (2012). edX platform integrates into classes. http://tech.mit.edu/V132/N48/801edx.html.

Lynch, C., Ashley, K., Pinkwart, N., & Aleven, V. (2008). Argument graph classification with genetic programming and C4.5. In R. S. J. d. Baker, T.

Barnes, & J. E. Beck (Eds.), *Educational data mining 2008: Proceedings of the 1st International Conference on Educational Data Mining* (pp. 137–146). Montréal, Québec, Canada, June 20–21.

Macfadyen, L. P., & Dawson, S. (2010). Mining LMS data to develop an "early warning system" for educators: A proof of concept. *Computers & Education*, 588–599.

Manyika, J., Chui, M., Brown, B., Bughin, J., Dobbs, R., Roxburgh, C., & Byers, A. H. (2011). *Big data: The next frontier for innovation, competition, and productivity*. McKinsey Global Institute.

Martinez, R., Yacef, K., Kay, J., Kharrufa, A., & AlQaraghuli, A. (2011) Analysing frequent sequential patterns of collaborative learning activity around an interactive tabletop. *Proceedings of the 4th International Conference on Educational Data Mining*, 111–120.

Martinez, R., Yacef, K., Kay, J., & Schwendimann, B. (2012). An interactive teacher's dashboard for monitoring multiple groups in a multi-tabletop learning environment. *Proceedings of Intelligent Tutoring Systems*, 482–492. Springer.

Mayer, M. (2009). The physics of big data. http://www.parc.com/event/936/innovation-at-google.html.

McLaren, B. M., Scheuer, O., DeLaat, M., Hever, R., DeGroot, R., & Rosé, C. P. (2007). Using machine learning techniques to analyze and support mediation of student e-discussions. *Proceedings of the 13th International Conference on Artificial Intelligence in Education (AIED 2007)*.

McLaren, B. M., Scheuer, O., & Mikšátko, J. (2010). Supporting collaborative learning and e-discussions using artificial intelligence techniques. *International Journal of Artificial Intelligence in Education (IJAIED)*, 20(1), 1–46.

Ming, N. C., & Ming, V. L. (2012). Predicting student outcomes from unstructured data. *Proceedings of the 2nd International Workshop on Personalization Approaches in Learning Environments*, 11–16.

Muenchen, R. A. (2012). The popularity of data analysis software. http://r4stats.com/articles/popularity/.

Muldner, K., Burleson, W., Van de Sande, B., & VanLehn, K. (2011). An analysis of students' gaming behaviors in an intelligent tutoring system: Predictors and impacts. *User Modeling and User-Adapted Interaction*, 21(1–2), 99–135.

Pardos, Z. A., Baker, R. S. J. d., Gowda, S. M., & Heffernan, N. T. (2011). The sum is greater than the parts: Ensembling models of student knowledge in educational software. *SIGKDD Explorations*, 13(2), 37–44.

Pavlik, P. I., Cen, H., & Koedinger, K. R. (2009). Performance factors analysis – A new alternative to knowledge tracing. *Proceedings of AIED2009*.

Perera, D., Kay, J., Koprinska, I., Yacef, K., & Zaiane, O. R. (2009). Clustering and sequential pattern mining of online collaborative learning data. *IEEE Transactions on Knowledge and Data Engineering*, 21(6), 759–772.

Prata, D., Letouze, P., Costa, E., Prata, M., & Brito, G. (2012). Dialogue analysis in collaborative learning. *International Journal of e-Education, e-Business, e-Management, and e-Learning*, 2(5), 365–372.

Reimann, P., Yacef, K., & Kay, J. (2011). Analyzing collaborative interactions with data mining methods for the benefit of learning. *Computer-Supported Collaborative Learning Series*, 12, 161–185.

Rodrigo, M. M. T., Baker, R. S. J. d., McLaren, B., Jayme, A., & Dy, T. (2012). Development of a workbench to address the educational data mining bottleneck. *Proceedings of the 5th International Conference on Educational Data Mining*, 152–155.

Romero, C., & Ventura, S. (2010). Educational data mining: A review of the state-of-the-art. *IEEE Transaction on Systems, Man and Cybernetics, part C: Applications and Reviews*, 40(6), 610–618.

Sabourin, J., Rowe, J., Mott, B., & Lester, J. (2011). When off-task is on-task: The affective role of off-task behavior in narrative-centered learning environments. *Proceedings of the 15th International Conference on Artificial Intelligence in Education*, 534–536.

San Pedro, M. O. C., Baker, R., & Rodrigo, M. M. (2011). Detecting carelessness through contextual estimation of slip probabilities among students using an intelligent tutor for mathematics. *Proceedings of 15th International Conference on Artificial Intelligence in Education*, 304–311.

San Pedro, M. O. C., Rodrigo, M. M., and Baker, R. S. J. D. (2011). The relationship between carelessness and affect in a cognitive tutor. *Proceedings of the 4th bi-annual International Conference on Affective Computing and Intelligent Interaction*.

Sao Pedro, M. A., Baker, R. S. J. d., Gobert, J., Montalvo, O., & Nakama, A. (2013). Leveraging machine-learned detectors of systematic inquiry behavior to estimate and predict transfer of inquiry skill. *User Modeling and User-Adapted Interaction*, 23(1), 1–39.

Shih, B., Koedinger, K., & Scheines, R. (2008). A response time model for bottom-out hints as worked examples. *Proceedings of the 1st International Conference on Educational Data Mining*, 117–126.

Siemens, G., & Baker, R. S. J. d. (2012). Learning analytics and educational data mining: Towards communication and collaboration. *Proceedings of the 2nd International Conference on Learning Analytics and Knowledge*.

Sil, A., Shelton, A., Ketelhut, D. J., & Yates, A. (2012). Automatic grading of scientific inquiry. *The 7th Workshop on the Innovative Use of NLP for Building Educational Applications*, 22–32.

Studer, R., Benjamins, V. R., & Fensel, D. (1998). Knowledge engineering: Principles and methods. *Data and Knowledge Engineering (DKE)*, 25(1–2), 161–197.

Summers, D. J., et al. (1992). Charm physics at Fermilab E791. *Proceedings of the XXVIIth Recontre de Moriond, Electroweak Interactions and Unified Theories*, Les Arcs, France, 417–422.

Suthers, D., & Rosen, D. (2011). A unified framework for multi-level analysis of distributed learning. *Proceedings of the 1st International Conference on Learning Analytics and Knowledge*, 64–74.

Tatsuoka, K. K. (1995). Architecture of knowledge structures and cognitive diagnosis: A statistical pattern recognition and classification approach. In P. D. Nichols, S. F. Chipman, & R. L. Brennan (Eds.), *Cognitively diagnostic assessment* (pp. 327–359). Hillsdale, NJ: Lawrence Erlbaum Associates.

Vuong, A., Nixon, T., & Towle, B. (2011). A method for finding prerequisites within a curriculum. *Proceedings of the 4th International Conference on Educational Data Mining*, 211–216.

Walonoski, J. A., & Heffernan, N. T. (2006). Detection and analysis of off-task gaming behavior in intelligent tutoring systems. In M. Ikeda, K. Ashlay, & T.-W. Chan (Eds.), *Proceedings of the 8th International Conference on Intelligent Tutoring Systems* (pp. 382–391). Jhongli, Taiwan; Berlin: Springer-Verlag.

Witten, I. H., & Frank, E. (2005). *Data mining: Practical machine learning tools and techniques*. San Francisco, CA: Morgan Kaufmann.

Wixon, M., Baker, R. S. J. d., Gobert, J., Ocumpaugh, J., & Bachmann, M. (2012). WTF? Detecting students who are conducting inquiry without thinking fastidiously. *Proceedings of the 20th International Conference on User Modeling, Adaptation and Personalization (UMAP 2012)*, 286–298.

Xu, B., & Recker, M. (2011). Understanding teacher users of a digital library service: A clustering approach. *Journal of Educational Data Mining*, 3(1), 1–28.

PART III

Practices that Foster Effective Learning

14 Project-Based Learning

Joseph S. Krajcik and Namsoo Shin

Students living in today's 21st-century society will experience dramatic scientific and technological breakthroughs. These students will also face social and global problems that can only be solved with widespread scientific and technological literacy. The science education community has long argued that society needs scientifically literate citizens, and yet research shows that many educational systems throughout the world are failing to graduate such students (OECD, 2007). To prepare children to live in a global 21st-century society, we need to dramatically change how we educate students.

Learning sciences research can show us how to educate students for these 21st-century developments. Drawing on the cognitive sciences and other disciplines, learning scientists are uncovering the cognitive structure of deeper conceptual understanding and discovering principles that govern learning. This research has found that too many schools teach superficial knowledge rather than integrated knowledge that will allow students to draw on their understanding to solve problems, make decisions, and learn new ideas. Drawing on this research, many learning scientists are developing new types of curricula with the goal of increasing students' engagement and helping them develop deeper understanding of important ideas. One such curricular effort is *project-based learning* (Blumenfeld, Fishman, Krajcik, Marx, & Soloway, 2000; Blumenfeld et al., 1991; Krajcik, Blumenfeld, Marx, & Soloway, 1994). Project-based learning allows students to learn by doing, to apply ideas, and to solve problems. In so doing, students engage in real-world activities similar to those of professional scientists.

Project-based learning is a form of situated learning (Greeno & Engeström, Chapter 7, this volume; Lave & Wenger, 1991) and it is based on the constructivist finding that students gain a deeper understanding of material when they actively construct their understandings by working with and using ideas in real-world contexts. Learning sciences research has shown that students can't learn disciplinary content without engaging in disciplinary practices, and they can't learn these practices without learning the content, and this is the basic underlying premise of situated learning. Unfortunately, all too many classrooms separate disciplinary content from practice (Brown, Collins, & Duguid, 1989). To form useable understanding, knowing and doing cannot be separated, but rather must be learned in a combined fashion that allows for problem solving, decision making, explaining real-world phenomena, and connecting new ideas.

In project-based learning, students engage in real, meaningful problems that are important to them and that are similar to what scientists, mathematicians, writers, and historians do. Within the field of science education, this "doing" aligns with scientific and engineering practices (NRC, 2012). A project-based classroom allows students to investigate questions, propose hypotheses and explanations, argue for their ideas, challenge the ideas of others, and try out new ideas. Research has demonstrated that students in project-based learning classrooms attain better learning outcomes than students in traditional classrooms (Geier et al., 2008; Marx et al., 2004; Rivet & Krajcik, 2004; Williams & Linn, 2003).

Project-based learning environments have six key features (Blumenfeld et al., 1991; Krajcik et al., 1994; Krajcik & Czerniak, 2013):

1. They start with a *driving question*, a problem to be solved.
2. They focus on learning goals that students are required to demonstrate mastery on key science standards and assessments.
3. Students explore the driving question *by participating in scientific practices* – processes of problem solving that are central to expert performance in the discipline. As students explore the driving question, they learn and apply important ideas in the discipline.
4. Students, teachers, and community members *engage in collaborative activities* to find solutions to the driving question. This mirrors the complex social situation of expert problem solving.
5. While engaged in the practices of science, *students are scaffolded with learning technologies* that help them participate in activities normally beyond their ability.
6. Students *create a set of tangible products* that address the driving question. These are shared artifacts, publicly accessible external representations of the class's learning.

In the next section, we summarize the learning sciences theory and research that supports project-based learning. Our own efforts have emphasized applying project-based methods to science classrooms, so in the section after that, we show how our work builds on project-based learning principles. During more than 10 years working in science classrooms, we have learned several important lessons about how to apply project-based learning in schools, and in the bulk of this chapter, we group our lessons around the five key features of project-based learning. We close by discussing issues that we encountered in scaling up our curriculum.

Research Foundations of Project-Based Learning

The roots of project-based learning extend back more than 100 years, to the work of educator and philosopher John Dewey (1959). Dewey argued that the students will develop personal investment in the material if they engage in real, meaningful tasks and problems that emulate what experts do in real-world situations. During the past two decades, learning sciences researchers have refined and elaborated Dewey's original insight that active inquiry results in deeper understanding. New discoveries in the learning sciences have led to new ways of understanding how to promote learning in children (Bransford, Brown, & Cocking, 1999; NRC, 2007). Project-based learning is grounded in four major ideas that emerged from the learning sciences: (1) active construction, (2) situated learning, (3) social interactions, and (4) cognitive tools.

Active Construction

Learning sciences research has found that deep understanding occurs when learners actively construct meaning based on their experiences and interactions in the world, and that only superficial learning occurs when learners passively take in information transmitted from a teacher, a computer, or a book (Sawyer, Chapter 1, this volume). The development of understanding is a continuous, developmental process that requires students to construct and reconstruct what they know from new experiences and ideas and from prior knowledge and experiences (NRC, 2007; Smith, Wiser, Anderson, & Krajcik, 2006). Teachers and materials do not reveal the knowledge to learners; rather, learners actively build knowledge as they explore the surrounding world, observe and interact with phenomena, take in new ideas, make connections between new and old ideas, and discuss and interact with others.

Learning deep understanding takes time and often happens when students work on a meaningful task that forces them to synthesize. By focusing on ideas in depth, students learn the connections between key ideas and principles so that they can apply their understanding to as yet unencountered situations, forming what is known as *integrated understanding* (Fortus & Krajcik, 2011).

Situated Learning

Learning sciences research (Nathan & Sawyer, Chapter 2, this volume; NRC, 2007) has shown that the most effective learning occurs when the learning is situated in an authentic, real-world context. In some scientific disciplines, scientists conduct experiments in laboratories; in others, they systematically observe the natural world and draw conclusions from their observations. Situated learning in science would involve students in experiencing phenomena as they take part in various scientific practices such as designing investigations, making explanations, constructing modeling, and presenting their ideas to others. One of the benefits of situated learning is that students can more easily see the value and meaning of the tasks and activities they perform. When students do a science activity by following detailed steps in the textbook, that's hardly any better than passively listening to a lecture. Either way, it's hard for them to see the meaning in what they're doing. But when they create their own investigation designed to answer a question that they helped to frame and is important to them and their community, they can see how science can be applied to solve important problems. In such environments students develop integrated understanding in which ideas are richly connected to each other (Fortus & Krajcik, 2011).

Compared to traditional classrooms, situated learning generalizes better to a wider range of situations (Kolodner, 2006). When learners acquire information through memorization of discrete facts that are not connected to important and meaningful situations, the superficial understanding that results is difficult for students to generalize to new situations. When students participate in step-by-step science experiments from the textbook, they don't learn how and where to apply these same procedures outside of the classroom. However, when students acquire information in a meaningful context (Blumenfeld et al., 1991; Krajcik & Czerniak, 2013) and relate it to their prior knowledge and experiences, they can form connections between the new information and the prior knowledge to develop better, larger, and more linked conceptual understanding.

Social Interaction

One of the most solid findings to emerge from learning sciences research is the important role of social interaction in learning (Collins & Kapur, Chapter 6, this volume; Greeno & Engeström, Chapter 7, this volume; Scardamalia & Bereiter, Chapter 20, this volume). The best learning results from a particular kind of social interaction: when teachers, students, and community members work together in a situated activity to construct shared understanding. Learners develop understandings of principles and ideas through sharing, using, and debating ideas with others (Blumenfeld, Marx, Krajcik, & Soloway, 1996). This back-and-forth sharing, using, and debating of ideas helps to create a community of learners that supports students making connection between ideas.

Cognitive Tools

Learning sciences research has demonstrated the importance of *cognitive tools* in learning (Salomon, Perkins, & Globerson, 1991). A graph is an example of a cognitive tool that helps learners see patterns in data. Various forms of computer software can be considered cognitive tools because they allow learners to carry out tasks not possible without the software's assistance and support. For instance, new forms of computer software allow learners to visualize complex data sets (Edelson & Reiser, 2006).

These learning technologies can support students (1) by accessing and collecting a range of scientific data and information; (2) by providing visualization and data analysis tools similar to those scientists use; (3) by allowing for collaboration and sharing of information across sites; (4) by planning, building, and testing models; (5) by developing multimedia documents that illustrate student understanding (Novak & Krajcik, 2004); and (6) by providing opportunities to interact, share, and critique the ideas of others. These features expand the range of questions that students can investigate and the multitude and type of phenomena students can experience.

Project-Based Science

In the early 1990s, educators increasingly realized that most students were not motivated to learn science, and that even the best students acquired only a superficial understanding of science. Researchers discovered that these superficial understandings were caused by a combination of ineffective textbook design and instructional style. Science textbooks covered many topics at a superficial level; they focused on technical vocabulary; they failed to consider students' prior knowledge; they lacked coherent explanations of real-world phenomena; and they didn't give students an opportunity to develop their own explanations of phenomena (Kesidou & Roseman, 2002). And although most science teachers have their classes do experiments, most classrooms use materials that specify the exact sequence of steps that students are supposed to perform – often referred to as *cookbook* procedures. Following a cookbook recipe doesn't require a deeper understanding of the material, and at best it results in only superficial learning.

In response to these findings, several researchers began to work collaboratively with middle school and high school science teachers to develop project-based instructions in science (Blumenfeld et al., 2000; Krajcik et al., 1998; Krajcik, McNeill, & Reiser, 2008; Polman, 1999; Tinker, 1997; Williams & Linn, 2003). In project-based science (PBS), students engage in real, meaningful problems that are important to them and that mirror what scientists do. A project-based science classroom allows students to explore phenomena, investigate questions, discuss their ideas, engage in scientific practices, challenge the ideas of others, try out new ideas, and construct and revise models. Research shows that PBL has the potential to help all students – regardless of culture, race, or gender – engage in and learn science (Haberman, 1991; Lee & Buxton, 2010; Moje, Collazo, Carrillo, & Marx, 2001).

PBS responds to science education recommendations made by national organizations. The *Framework for K-12 Science Education* (NRC, 2012) highlights the importance of students using various scientific practices, blended with the core ideas of science, to promote personal decision making, participation in societal and cultural affairs, and economic productivity. By engaging in scientific and engineering practices, learners construct meaning by doing science rather than passively taking in information. Learning scientists have demonstrated that children develop deeper understanding by cognitively engaging in the exploration of phenomena (NRC, 2012). Although some individuals can learn about ecosystems by reading about them, most learners need to grow plants, observe animals in ecosystems, and explore how various animals depend on plants and other animals to construct integrated understandings of ecosystems.

Designing project-based learning environments can be a challenge. During the 1990s and 2000s, several scholars developed strategies for fostering learning in a PBS environment and designed and developed curricular materials using the principles of PBS (Blumenfeld et al., 1991; Krajcik et al., 1998; Krajcik et al., 2008; Krajcik, Reiser, Sutherland, & Fortus, 2011; Marx et al., 2004). These researchers worked with high school teachers to develop PBS environments so that different science disciplines (biology, chemistry, and earth science) were integrated into a three-year program (Schneider, Krajcik, Marx, & Soloway, 2001). They also worked with middle school teachers to transform their teaching (Fishman & Davis, 2006; Novak & Gleason, 2001). More recently, these researchers have developed middle school curriculum materials as one approach to bring about widespread change in the teaching and learning of science (Blumenfeld et al., 2000; Krajcik et al., 2008; Marx et al., 2004).

Features of Project-Based Learning Environments

Through our involvement in the Center for Learning Technologies in Urban Schools (LeTUS) (Blumenfeld et al., 2000; Geier et al., 2008; Marx et al., 2004) and the design, development, and testing of Investigating and Questioning our World through Science and Technology (IQWST) materials (Krajcik et al., 2011), we worked closely with teachers to design, develop, and test PBS curriculum materials. LeTUS was a collaborative effort among Detroit Public Schools, Chicago Public Schools, Northwestern University, and the University of Michigan to improve middle school science teaching and learning. The collaborative work in LeTUS took as its core challenge the use of scientific inquiry and the infusion of learning technologies to support learning in urban classrooms. IQWST was a joint venture among the University of Michigan, Northwestern University, and the Weizmann Institute of Science to develop the next generation of middle school curriculum materials. While engaged in this work, we expanded our understanding of how to design project-based learning environments that foster integrated understanding and we learned many lessons that are relevant to all project-based learning (Krajcik et al., 1998; Krajcik et al., 2008; Krajcik, Slotta, McNeill, & Reiser, 2008; Tinker & Krajcik, 2001). Based on this research, we have identified six key features of effective project-based learning: driving questions, learning goals, engaging in scientific practices, collaboration, learning technologies, and artifacts.

Feature 1: Driving Questions

The hallmark of project-based learning is a *driving question* that guides instruction. Driving questions should be anchored in a real-world situation that learners find meaningful and important (Blumenfeld et al., 1991; Krajcik & Czerniak, 2013; Krajcik & Mamlok-Naaman, 2006). The driving question serves to organize and drive activities of the project, provides a context in which students can use and explore learning goals and scientific practices, and provides continuity and coherence to the full range of project activities. As students pursue solutions to the driving question, they develop integrated understandings of core scientific ideas (NRC, 2012). A good driving question elicits a desire to learn in students (Edelson, 2001), and it makes students realize that there is an important problem that genuinely needs to be solved (Reiser, 2004). Throughout the project, the teacher continually refers back to the driving question to link together the various ideas students explore during the project.

Good driving questions have several features. Driving questions should be (1) *feasible* in that students can design and perform investigations to answer the questions; (2) *worthwhile* in that they contain rich science content that meets important learning goals and relates to what scientists really do; (3) *contextualized* in that they are real world, nontrivial, and important; (4) *meaningful* in that they are interesting and exciting to learners; (5) *ethical* in that they do no harm to individuals, organisms, or the environment (Krajcik & Czerniak, 2013).

In PBL, the teacher or curriculum designer selects the driving question, or sometimes the students work with the teacher to select the question (Krajcik & Czerniak, 2013; Scardamalia & Bereiter, Chapter 20, this volume). Some project-based methods start the process by having students develop their own driving question. This has the advantage that it results in a question that is meaningful to students. However, it is extremely difficult for students to develop driving questions that have all the properties of a good driving question – particularly meeting worthwhile learning goals. Our approach has been to design curriculum around a driving question that we select in collaboration with teachers but that allows students either to explore solutions to their own related questions or to engage in a design project to ask related questions in the unit. In IQWST (Krajcik et al., 2011), we begin with a driving question but then provide opportunities for students to ask their own question related to the driving question of the project. For instance, in the seventh grade energy unit that focuses on the transfer and transformation of energy, students are introduced to the driving question of the unit,

Why do some things stop while others keep going? (Fortus, Abdel-Kareem, Jin, Nordine, & Weizman, 2012), through four *anchoring events* in which students experience phenomena related to the transfer and transformation of energy. Anchoring events help students relate to the new ideas explored in the project (Rivet & Krajcik, 2002; Sherwood, Kinzer, Bransford, & Franks, 1987). Anchoring events also present meaningful contexts for the science ideas explored in the project. During the four anchoring events in the energy unit, students observe, describe, and compare and contrast the motion of four objects. One of the objects is a pendulum and another is a spinner top that appears to keep spinning (because the spinning motion results from a battery-driven device). Students use their observations and descriptions of the anchoring events to generate questions. The anchoring events were carefully chosen so that students would be most likely to ask certain questions. For instance: Why does the top keep spinning, but the motion of the pendulum decreases over time? These questions then get posted on the class's Driving Question Board that serves as a road map for teachers and students to check which questions were answered and to add to the explanations of the driving question and student-generated questions as they proceed with the unit. Often these questions become answered as students work through various project tasks.

In *How can you prevent your good friends from getting sick?* (Hug & Krajcik, 2002; Kolodner, Krajcik, Reiser, Edelson, & Starr, 2009–2013) – an eight-week unit that addresses learning goals related to cells, systems, microbiology, and disease – teachers introduce students to the driving question by reading and discussing a story about a young South African boy who contracted AIDS and became an AIDS activist. This story is an anchoring event that provides a context for discussing how disease relates to them and other middle school children. In a second anchoring event, students participate in an activity that simulates how an infectious disease might spread through a community. First, they each mix a solution in a test tube. Then, students walk around the class and, when they meet another student, they mix the contents of their test tubes. Some test tubes contain an indicator that reacts with a substance in other test tubes, and as this indicator spreads around, more test tubes change color – simulating the transfer of communicable disease. This activity provides a common experience to discuss and relate back to throughout the project (Hug & Krajcik, 2002) as well as allowing learners to generate meaningful questions related to the driving question and the anchoring event.

Feature 2: Focus on Learning Goals

In most schools, students are required to demonstrate mastery on key science standards and assessments. To ensure PBS curriculum aligns with these standards, we use a three-step process. We start by selecting the important ideas aligned with national or state standards (Krajcik et al., 2008). Project-based environments require considerable curriculum time to enable students to focus on ideas, revisit those ideas, collaborate with peers, explore phenomena, and develop integrated understanding. As such, teachers must feel confident that the investment of time is warranted in terms of meeting these districts' and states' mandated learning goals.

In developing the "Investigating and Questioning Our World through Science and Technology" (IQWST) middle school curriculum, we used a learning goals-driven process to ensure that materials would meet key learning goals. The process consisted of three major steps: (a) select core ideas, (b) unpack the ideas, and (c) develop learning performances that express the desired cognitive tasks (Krajcik et al., 2008). To select core ideas, we used two main criteria. First, the core idea must have explanatory power in that it is necessary for understanding a variety of phenomena. Second, the core idea must be necessary for future learning in the sense that it is generative or is needed to understand related topics. The particle nature of matter is one such core idea. The particle nature of matter can be used to explain a host of phenomena from how water evaporates to why mass is conserved during chemical reactions. The *Framework for K-12 Science Education* also identified the particle nature of matter as a Core Idea of Science (2012). The particle nature of matter is also a core idea because it is necessary for understanding many advanced topics, like photosynthesis and respiration.

Once a core idea is selected, it is important for curriculum developers to unpack the idea. The process of unpacking involves decomposing the core idea into its component parts and concepts, and then expanding and identifying those concepts. Unpacking allows designers to develop a much deeper understanding of the core idea and of the essential aspects of that idea that need to be considered in curriculum design (Krajcik et al., 2008). (See Krajcik et al., 2008, for an example of unpacking.) And of course, these component concepts must be suitable for the age and grade level of the students.

To specify what reasoning we expect students to be able to do with core ideas, we write learning goals in terms of *learning performances* (Perkins, Crismond, Simmons, & Unger, 1995). Learning performances blend core ideas with scientific practices (Krajcik et al., 2008). Learning performances reflect the professional disciplinary practices of working scientists: describe phenomena, use models to explain patterns in data, construct scientific explanations, and test hypotheses (Krajcik et al., 2008). Table 14.1 shows an example of forming a learning performance.

Learning performances can then be used as guides for designing the driving question, tasks, and assessments. The focus on learning performances is consistent with our perspective on situated learning: learning performances blend the knowing and the doing.

The goal of this process is to ensure that PBS materials meet important institutionally mandated standards while also supporting students in

Table 14.1. *Developing learning performances*

Core Idea Blended with a Practice to Develop a Learning Performance		
All substances are made from some 100 different types of atoms, which combine with one another in various ways. Atoms form molecules that range in size from two to thousands of atoms. Pure substances are made from a single type of atom or molecule; each pure substance has characteristic physical and chemical properties ... that can be used to identify it. Gases and liquids are made of molecules or inert atoms that are moving about relative to each other. In a liquid, the molecules are constantly in contact with others; in a gas, they are widely spaced except when they happen to collide. In a solid, atoms are closely spaced and may vibrate in position but do not change relative locations (NRC, 2012).	Developing and using models	Constructing and communicating models to predict and explain the motion of molecules in various phases and during phase change.

achieving deeper and more integrated understanding. However, one risk is that when one begins with the standards rather than the driving question, it may be hard to find questions that the students find meaningful and interesting. In the development of one of the first IQWST units, we started with learning goals related to understanding the nature of chemical reactions and the conservations of mass (Krajcik, McNeill, & Reiser, 2008). We had several meetings with teachers to discuss possible driving questions. Some seemed too trivial and did not lead to opportunities for students to explore phenomena. We finally settled on "How do I make new stuff from old stuff?" and we created an anchoring event of making soap as an example of making new stuff from old stuff.

Feature 3: Engaging in Scientific Practices

Beginning with the U.S. science education reforms of the 1960s, policy makers and prominent scientists have argued that science instruction should mirror what scientists do (Hurd, 1970; NRC, 1996, 2007, 2012; Rutherford, 1964). The goal of science is to explain and predict various phenomena – events such as erosion, diseases, rusting, plant growth, and objects falling to the ground. To answer their questions, scientists take part in various

Table 14.2. *Scientific and engineering practices (NRC, 2012)*

• Asking questions (for science) and defining problems (for engineering)
• Developing and using models
• Planning and carrying out investigations
• Analyzing and interpreting data
• Using mathematical and computational thinking
• Constructing explanations (for science) and designing solutions (for engineering)
• Engaging in argument from evidence
• Obtaining, evaluating, and communicating information

scientific practices (see Table 14.2) – asking questions, designing and performing investigations, constructing models, using evidence, and developing explanations (NRC, 2012). Although scientists do not follow a fixed set of steps that leads them to new scientific understandings, all scientists rely on the use of evidence, models, and theories to explain and predict phenomena that occur in the world. Science is truly a nonlinear endeavor. For instance, each component provides feedback that may lead to a different practice. For example, finding information about a topic might lead students to refine their questions or to redesign their investigation, and data analysis might result in revising the experimental design.

In PBS classrooms, students explore the driving questions using new ideas that they're learning, and they investigate the driving question over a sustained period of time. This is different from traditional science classrooms, which are characterized by short-term activities and cookbook procedures. For example, in the project "What is the quality of water in our river?" (Singer, Marx, Krajcik, & Chambers, 2000), students conduct different water quality tests, such as pH, turbidity, temperature, and dissolved oxygen to infer water quality. In the project "How can I smell things from a distance?" (Merritt, Sutherland, Shwartz, Van de Kerkhof, & Krajcik, 2011), students design and conduct investigations to explore various questions about how odors can travel across a room. By exploring these questions, learners take part in a range of scientific practices, including designing and performing investigation, refining questions, constructing and revising models, and developing explanations.

Middle school students find it difficult to engage in various scientific practices, particularly if they've had no previous experiences in science (Edelson & Reiser, 2006; Krajcik et al., 1998). To support teachers, the IQWST materials present very thorough detailed commentary on how to support students in various scientific practices – particularly modeling (Krajcik & Merritt, 2012) and scientific explanation (McNeill & Krajcik, 2012). Unfortunately, many studies have found that students have a hard time developing scientific explanations (McNeill & Krajcik, 2008). Prior research suggests that it is hard for students to use their explanations to articulate and defend their claims (Sadler, 2004), to understand what counts as evidence, to use appropriate evidence (Sandoval & Reiser, 2004), and to not rely on their personal views (Hogan & Maglienti, 2001). Drawing and justifying conclusions using primary evidence requires sophisticated thinking and much experience, and this type of reasoning has not been required of most students in science classes. Because many middle school teachers have experienced working with data from highly structured cookbook experiments, they are less likely to have experience using and inferring from real data. As a result, teachers need support in helping students to create explanations and conclusions (Krajcik et al., 1998).

To overcome this challenge, we have become very explicit in the process and reasons behind how to scaffold students as they write explanations (McNeill & Krajcik, 2008; Moje et al., 2004). Our scaffolding strategies include making the rationale behind explanations explicit, modeling how to construct explanations, providing students with opportunities to engage in explanation construction, and writing scaffolding comments on students' investigation sheets. We have students use an explanation framework that includes three components: a claim, evidence, and reasoning (also see Andriessen & Baker, Chapter 22, this volume). The *claim* makes an assertion that addresses the phenomena students are exploring. The *evidence* supports the claim using scientific data that can come from several sources – observations, reading material, archived data, or an investigation that students complete. The *reasoning* provides a justification that links the claim and evidence together, showing why the data count as evidence to support the claim by using the appropriate scientific ideas (McNeill & Krajcik, 2012). This framework provides a structure to support both students and teachers in constructing explanations in science classrooms.

Feature 4: Collaborations

Project-based learning provides opportunities for students, teachers, and members of society to collaborate with one another to investigate questions and ideas. The classroom becomes a community of learners (Brown & Campione, 1994) as students ask questions, write explanations, form conclusions, make sense of information, discuss data, and present findings. For example, we ask students to critique and provide feedback on each others' explanations. Collaborations helps students build shared understandings of scientific ideas and of the nature of the discipline as they engage in discourse with their classmates and with adults outside the classroom.

Students do not naturally collaborate with other students in the classroom (Azmitia, 1996). Teachers need to help students develop skills in collaborating, including turn taking, listening, and respect for others' opinions. Because students lack skills in collaborating and have had little experience in collaborating, teachers need to build collaborations over the entire school year. Teachers can use a technique in which they first ask students to write down their ideas and then work with a partner to compare their ideas. Written prompts like "My ideas are similar to my partners' ideas in these ways" and "My ideas are different from my partners' ideas in these ways" help students learn to listen to others and compare their ideas to those of others (Krajcik & Czerniak, 2013; Scardamalia & Bereiter, Chapter 20, this volume).

Feature 5: Using Technology Tools to Support Learning

Technology tools can serve as learning tools to help transform the classroom into an environment in which learners actively construct knowledge (Linn, 1997; Tinker, 1997). Edelson (2001) gives three reasons to use technology tools in schools: (1) they align with the practice of science, (2) they can present information in dynamic and interactive formats, and (3) they provide unprecedented opportunities to move teaching away from a transmission-and-acquisition model of instruction.

Students can use learning technologies to access real data on the World Wide Web, to collaborate with others via networks (Novak & Krajcik, 2004; Scardamalia & Bereiter, Chapter 20, this volume; Stahl, Koschmann, & Suthers, Chapter 24, this volume), to gather data, to graph and analyze data (Edelson & Reiser, 2006), to create models (Lehrer & Schauble, 2006), to share and find information, and to produce multimedia artifacts. Learning technologies allow students to extend what they can do in the classroom and serve as powerful cognitive tools that help teachers foster inquiry and student learning (Linn, 1997; Metcalf-Jackson, Krajcik, & Soloway, 2000).

In the water quality project, students use various sensors to gather data about the pH, temperature, and turbidity of the river. The students take handheld computers with them to the river and the data are displayed immediately in a graph. Other sensor devices allow students to collect the data and then view them on computer graphs back in the classrooms. These activities assist students in analyzing and interpreting data and computation reasoning practices. Students use the new ideas they have learned to develop a computer-based model that shows how various factors influence water quality. These technologies help students build connections among the science ideas, forming a deeper and richer understanding.

Mobile technologies have changed lifestyles, and the potential and demand for using them in classroom settings have increased greatly over the past few years (Sharples & Pea, Chapter 25, this volume). Tinker and Krajcik (2001), more than a decade ago, underlined that mobile technologies would become inexpensive so that schools could afford one for each student; today this claim is supported by the work of Norris and Soloway (2009), who encourage the use of mobile devices for every student. Researchers at the University of Michigan (Cahill, Kuhn, Schmoll, Pompe, & Quintana, 2010) have designed

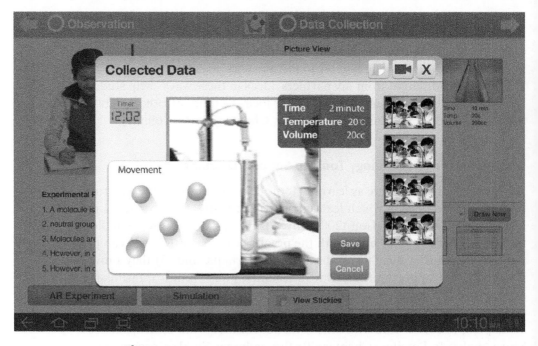

Figure 14.1. *An augmented reality learning environment.*

a mobile tool, Zydeco, that supports students in three important scientific practices: specifying and refining the questions; collecting, sharing, and organizing data; and constructing scientific explanations.

Technologies also hold other advantages for students. Shin and her colleagues have designed augmented reality (AR) to support student understanding of core science ideas in chemistry by linking micro and macro worlds in a mobile learning environment. In this investigation, while students observe macro-world phenomena, the learning tool using AR presents a virtual molecular-level representation showing the movements of molecules to support students' conceptual understanding in a meaningful way. This learning tool has integrated handheld devices (e.g., iPad with camera), and various technologies (e.g., simulation, video, augmented reality) for students to develop understanding of underlying models while they conduct lab experiment in a real classroom. Figure 14.1 shows an example of an augmented reality environment that demonstrates the relationship between gas and volume.

Recently, researchers have designed technology-enhanced materials to create individualized, customized learning environments that provide equal learning opportunities for all students by accommodating the range of ways that diverse students develop their understanding (Choi & Shin, 2009; Rose, Meyer, & Hitchcock, 2005, Shin, Sutherland, & McCall, 2011). The key principle is that given the same learning goals, different students learn in different ways for perceiving and comprehending new information and representing their understanding in a learning environment (Bransford et al., 1999).

Given this perspective, educational materials with multiple representations (e.g., text, picture, video, animation/simulation, audio, augmented reality), various difficulty levels of learning tasks, and different levels of support are necessary to appeal to the interests and meet the needs of individual learners (Rose et al., 2005). For example, Krajcik and Shin, working with information and technology developers in Korea (VisangESL inc.), have designed individualized learning environments using Universal Design for Learning (UDL) principles and Learning Progressions (LP) based on the "How can I smell things from a distance?" unit (Merritt et al., 2011). The materials were adapted from development work initially designed using UDL principles (http://udl-toolkit.cast.org/home). Learning progression (LP) supports the organization and alignment of the science content, instruction, and assessment strategies to provide students with the opportunity to develop better understanding. A learning progression (LP) describes the "successively more sophisticated ways of thinking about a topic that can follow one another as children learn about and investigate a topic over a broad span of time" (Duschl, Schweingruber, & Shouse, 2007, p. 219). We embedded assessment items associated with various levels of the LP into learning tasks to diagnose the level of individual performances before instruction (Shin & Stevens, 2012). An individualized environment is presented to guide each student based on his or her test scores by providing level-appropriate instruction. Figure 14.2 shows an individual path that a student might take in using the materials. The black "flags" that appear in the upper right corners of four of the images indicate a suggested learning path based on a student's test score. We believe that such instructional materials can maximize individualized, independent learning, which can lead to more meaningful learning.

Feature 6: Creation of Artifacts

Learning sciences research shows that students learn more effectively when they develop *artifacts* – external representations of their constructed knowledge. In PBS, these artifacts result from students' investigations into the driving question (Blumenfeld et al., 1991). Students develop physical models and computer models, reports, videos that document their investigations, games, plays, Web sites, and computer programs. To be effective, artifacts need to address the driving question, support students in developing understanding associated with the learning goals of the project, and demonstrate student understanding of the learning goals of the project.

PBS focuses on artifact development for several reasons. First, through the development of artifacts, students construct and reconstruct their understanding. As students build and reflect on their artifacts, they actively manipulate science ideas. Second, because learning does not occur in linear, discrete steps, assessments should not be constructed around small, discrete bits of information (Pellegrino, Chudowsky, & Glaser, 2001). Teachers can use

Figure 14.2. *Individualized learning environment (ILE): Touch pad device. The black "flags" in the upper right corners of four of the images in the bottom half of Figure 14.2 illustrate an individual learning path that a student can follow.*

artifacts to see how student understandings develop throughout and across various projects. Artifact development allows teachers to assess for higher-level cognitive outcomes such as asking questions, designing investigations, gathering and interpreting data, and creating scientific explanations (Atkin & Coffey, 2003; Carver, 2006). Third, when students publish or make publically available what they create, it enhances their motivation to create a product that others will understand. Because artifacts are concrete and explicit, they allow students to share and have their artifacts reviewed by others – teachers, students, parents, and members of the community (Scardamalia & Bereiter, Chapter 20, this volume). Critiquing supports the development of student understanding by providing feedback about what the student knows and doesn't know, permitting learners to reflect on and revise their work.

Learning sciences research shows that providing feedback is critical to the learning process (McNeill & Krajcik, 2009; Pellegrino, Chudowsky, & Glaser, 2001). But unfortunately, teachers rarely give extensive feedback to students. Teachers with large classes and numerous sections do not have enough time in a day or week to give high-quality and individual feedback to students. In addition, many middle school science teachers lack knowledge of how to give quality feedback to students. To help teachers give valuable feedback to students, McNeill and Krajcik (2011) provided them with written descriptions of different levels of quality for student performance to be used for scoring and giving feedback. By providing a common and consistent set of rubrics for PBS tasks such as developing driving questions and providing explanations, teachers learn how to give feedback and students learn how to further their understanding.

Conclusion

Research over the past two decades has shown us how to better design project-based environments. In this chapter, we have emphasized the importance of selecting driving questions that can help students meet important learning goals, help students see the value of the driving questions, and engage students in scientific practices. We have emphasized the importance of developing learning goals that focus on learning performance by blending core ideas and scientific practices. We have described some of the challenges of using technology and explored various techniques to integrate technology throughout the curriculum. We have emphasized the need to support teachers in complex instruction by providing them with explicit strategies.

The research with PBL shows the importance of helping teachers by developing highly developed and highly specified materials that focus instruction on driving questions that students find meaningful and important, and around which students can develop an understanding of central learning goals. Using these materials, teachers can engage students in scientific investigations, make use of cognitive tools, promote collaboration, and teach them the deeper conceptual understating that traditional methods of instruction cannot.

Although the bulk of this chapter has focused on project-based science, the lessons apply to any subject area. Projects are widely used in social studies, arts, and English classes. In these subjects, project ideas tend to be passed down by word of mouth or are developed from scratch by teachers themselves. For the most part these projects are not based in learning sciences research, and researchers have not examined the most effective ways to design these projects. The findings that we summarize in this chapter can improve the educational effectiveness of projects in all subjects, because this research is based on core learning sciences principles and these designs have become progressively better through a process of iterative design experiments. As such, they can provide a model for applying project-based methods to classrooms across the curriculum.

Acknowledgments

We are grateful for the thorough and thoughtful feedback provided by Professor Keith Sawyer.

References

Atkin, J. M., & Coffey, J. E. (2003). *Everyday assessment in the science classroom (science educators' essay collection)*. Arlington, VA: National Science Teachers Associations.

Azmitia, M. (1996). Peer interactive minds: Developmental, theoretical, and methodological issues. In P. B. Baltes & U. M. Staudinger (Eds.), *Interactive minds: Life-span perspectives on the social foundation of cognition* (pp. 133–162). New York: Cambridge University Press.

Blumenfeld, P. C, Fishman, B. J., Krajcik, J., Marx, R. W., & Soloway, E. (2000). Creating usable technology – embedded project-based science in urban schools. *Educational Psychologist*, 35, 149–164.

Blumenfeld, P. C., Marx, R. W., Krajcik, J. S., & Soloway, E. (1996). Learning with peers: From small group cooperation to collaborative communities. *Educational Researcher*, 24(8), 37–40.

Blumenfeld, P. C, Soloway, E., Marx, R. W., Krajcik, J. S., Guzdial, M., & Palincsar, A. (1991). Motivating project-based learning: Sustaining the doing, supporting the learning. *Educational Psychologist*, 26, 369–398.

Bransford, J., Brown, A. L., & Cocking, R. R. (1999). *How people learn: Brain, mind experience, and school*. Washington, DC: National Academy Press.

Brown, A. L., & Campione, J. C. (1994). Guided discovery in a community of learners. In K. McGilly (Ed.), *Classroom lessons: Integrating cognitive theory and classroom practice* (pp. 229–270). Cambridge, MA: MIT Press.

Brown, J. S., Collins, A., & Duguid, P. (1989). Situated cognition of learning. *Educational Researcher*, 18, 32–42.

Cahill, C., Kuhn, A., Schmoll, S., Pompe, A., & Quintana, C. (2010). Zydeco: Using mobile and web technologies to support seamless inquiry between museum and school contexts. In Proceedings of the 9th international Conference on interaction Design and Children (Barcelona, Spain, June 09–12, 2010). IDC '10. ACM, New York, 174–177.

Carver, S. M. (2006). Assessing for deep understanding. In R. K. Sawyer (Ed.), *The Cambridge handbook of the learning sciences* (pp. 205–221). New York: Cambridge University Press.

Choi, J. I., & Shin, N. (2009). Digital textbook design principles Adapting the universal design for learning. *Journal of Educational Technology*, 25(1), 29–59.

Collins, A., Joseph, D., & Bielaczyc, K. (2004). Design research: Theoretical and methodological issues. *Journal of the Learning Sciences*, 13(1), 15–42.

Dewey, J. (1959). *Dewey on education*. New York: Teachers College Press.

Duschl, R., Schweingruber, H., & Shouse, A. (Eds.) (2007). *Taking science to school: Learning and teaching science in grades K-8*. Washington, DC: The National Academies Press.

Edelson, D. C. (2001). Learning-for-use: A framework for integrating content and process learning in the design of inquiry activities. *Journal of Research in Science Teaching*, 38, 355–385.

Edelson, D. C., & Reiser, B. J. (2006). Making authentic practices accessible to learners: Design challenges and strategies. In R. K. Sawyer (Ed.), *Cambridge handbook of the learning sciences* (pp. 335–354). New York: Cambridge University Press.

Fishman, B. J., & Davis, E. A. (2006). Teacher learning research and the learning sciences. In R. K. Sawyer (Ed.), *The Cambridge handbook of the learning sciences* (pp. 535–550). New York: Cambridge University Press.

Fortus, D., Abdel-Kareem, H., Jin, H., Nordine, J. C., & Weizman, A. (2012). Why do some things stop while others continue going? In J. S. Krajcik, B. J. Reiser, L. M. Sutherland, & D. Fortus (Eds.), *Investigating and questioning our world through science and technology (IQWST)*. New York: Sangari Science.

Fortus, D., & Krajcik, J. S. (2011). Curriculum coherence and learning progressions. In B. J. Fraser, K. G. Tobin, & C. J. McRobbie (Eds.), *The international handbook of research in science education*. Second Edition (pp. 783–798). Dordrecht: Springer.

Geier, R., Blumenfeld, P., Marx, R., Krajcik, J., Fishman, B., & Soloway, E. (2008). Standardized test outcomes of urban students participating in standards and project based science curricula. *Journal of Research in Science Teaching,* 45(8), 922–939.

Haberman, M. (1991). The pedagogy of poverty versus good teaching. *Phi Delta Kappan*, 73(4), 290–294.

Hoffman, J., Wu, H-K, Krajcik, J. S., & Soloway, E. (2003). The nature of middle school learners' science content understandings with the use of on-line resources. *Journal of Research in Science Teaching*, 40(3), 323–346.

Hogan, K., & Maglienti, M. (2001). Comparing the epistemological underpinnings of students' and scientists' reasoning about conclusions. *Journal of Research in Science Teaching*, 38(6), 663–687.

Hug, B., & Krajcik, J. (2002). Students, scientific practices using a scaffolded inquiry sequence. In P. Bell, R. Stevens, & T. Satwicz (Eds.), *Keeping learning complex: The proceedings of the Fifth International Conference for the Learning Sciences (ICLS)*. Mahwah, NJ: Lawrence Erlbaum Associates.

Hurd, P. D. (1970). *New directions in teaching secondary school science*. Chicago: Rand McNally.

Kesidou, S., & Roseman, J. E. (2002). How well do middle school science programs measure up? Findings from Project 2061's curriculum review. *Journal Research in Science Teaching*, 39(6), 522–549.

Kolodner, J. L. (2006). Case-based reasoning. In R. K. Sawyer (Ed.), *The Cambridge handbook of the learning sciences* (pp. 225–242). New York: Cambridge University Press.

Kolodner, J., Krajcik, J., Reiser, B., Edelson, D., & Starr, M. (2009–2013). *Project-Based Inquiry Science. It's About Time, Publisher*. (Middle School Science Curriculum Materials). Mt. Kisco, NY.

Krajcik, J. S., Blumenfeld, P. C., Marx, R. W., Bass, K. M., Fredricks, J., & Soloway, E. (1998). Inquiry in project-based science classrooms: Initial attempts by middle school students. *Journal of Learning Sciences*, 7, 313–350.

Krajcik, J. S., Blumenfeld, P. C., Marx, R. W., & Soloway, E. (1994). A collaborative model for helping middle grade teachers learn project-based instruction. *The Elementary Schools Journal*, 94(5), 483–497.

Krajcik, J. S., & Czerniak, C. M. (2013). *Teaching science in elementary and middle school classrooms: A project-based approach*. Fourth Edition. Taylor and Francis: London.

Krajcik, J. S., & Mamlok-Naaman, R. (2006). Using driving questions to motivate and sustain student interest in learning science. In K. Tobin (Ed.), *Teaching and learning science: An encyclopedia*. Westport, CT: Greenwood Publishing Group.

Krajcik, J. S., McNeill, K. L., & Reiser, B., (2008). Learning-goals-driven design model: Developing curriculum materials that align with national standards and incorporate project-based pedagogy. *Science Education*, 92(1), 1–32.

Krajcik, J. S. & Merritt, J. (2012). Engaging students in scientific practices: What does constructing and revising models look like in the science classroom? *Science and Children,* 49(7), 10–13.

Krajcik, J. S., Reiser, B. J., Sutherland, L. M., & Fortus, D. (2011). *IQWST: Investigating and questioning our world through science and technology, (Middle School Science Curriculum Materials)*. Sangari Global Education/ Active Science, USA.

Krajcik, J. S., Slotta, J., McNeill, K. L., & Reiser, B. (2008). Designing learning environments to support students constructing coherent understandings. In Y. Kali, M. C. Linn, & J. E. Roseman (Eds.), *Designing coherent science education*. New York: Teachers College Press.

Lave, J., & Wenger, E. (1991). *Situated learning: legitimate peripheral participation*. New York: Cambridge University Press.

Lee, O., & Buxton, C. A. (2010). *Diversity and equity in science education: Theory, research, and practice*. New York: Teachers College Press.

Lehrer, R., & Schauble, L. (2006). Cultivating model-based reasoning in science education. In R. K. Sawyer (Ed.), *Cambridge handbook of the learning sciences* (pp. 371–387). New York: Cambridge University Press.

Linn, M. C. (1997). Learning and instruction in science education: Taking advantage of technology. In D. Tobin & B. J. Fraser (Eds.), *International handbook of science education* (pp. 265–294). The Netherlands: Kluwer Publishers.

Marx, R. W., Blumenfeld, P. C., Krajcik, J. S., Fishman, B., Soloway, E., Geier, R., & Revital, T. T. (2004). Inquiry-based science in the middle grades: Assessment of learning in urban systemic reform. *Journal of Research in Science Teaching*, 41(10), 1063–1080.

McNeill, K. L. (2009). Teachers' use of curriculum to support students in writing scientific arguments to explain phenomena. *Science Education*, 93(2), 233–268.

McNeill, K. L., & Krajcik, J. S. (2008). Middle school students' use of appropriate and inappropriate evidence in writing scientific explanations. In M. Lovet & P. Shah (Eds.), *Thinking with data* (pp. 233–265). New York: Taylor and Francis.

McNeill, K. L., & Krajcik, J. S. (2012). *Supporting grade 5–8 students in constructing explanations in science: The claim, evidence and reasoning framework for talk and writing*. New York: Pearson Allyn & Bacon.

Merritt, J., Sutherland, L., Shwartz, Y., van de Kerkhof, M. H., & Krajcik, J. (2011). How can I smell things from a distance? In J. Krajcik, B. Reiser, L. Sutherland, & D. Fortus (Eds.), *IQWST: Investigating and questioning our world through science and technology, (Middle School Science Curriculum Materials)*. Sangari Global Education/Active Science, USA.

Metcalf-Jackson, S., Krajcik, J. S., & Soloway, E. (2000). Model-It: A design retrospective. In M. Jacobson & R. B. Kozma (Eds.), *Innovations in science and mathematics education: Advanced designs for technologies and learning* (pp. 77–116). Mahwah, NJ: Lawrence Erlbaum Associates.

Moje, E. B., Collazo, T., Carrillo, R., & Marx, R. W. (2001). "Maestro, what is 'quality'?": Language, literacy, and discourse in project-based science. *Journal of Research in Science Teaching*, 38(4), 469–498.

Moje, E. B., Peek-Brown, D., Sutherland, L. M., Marx, R. W., Blumenfeld, P., & Krajcik, J. S. (2004). Explaining explanations: Developing scientific literacy in middle-school project-based science reforms. In D. Strickland & D. E. Alverman (Eds.), *Bridging the gap: Improving literacy learning for preadolescent and adolescent learners in grades 4–12* (pp. 227–251). New York: Teachers College Press.

National Research Council (NRC). (1996). *National science education standards*. Washington, DC: National Research Council.

National Research Council (NRC). (2007). *Taking science to school: Learning and teaching science in grades K-8*. Washington, DC: National Academies Press.

National Research Council (NRC). (2012). *A framework for K-12 science education: Practices, crosscutting concepts, and core ideas*. Washington, DC: National Academies Press.

Norris, C., & Soloway, E. (2009). A disruption is coming: A primer for educators on the mobile technology revolution. In A. Druin (Ed.), *Mobile technology for children: Designing for interaction and learning* (pp. 125–139). Amsterdam, the Netherlands: Elsevier, Inc.

Novak, A., & Gleason, C. (2001). Incorporating portable technology to enhance an inquiry, project-based middle school science classroom. In R. Tinker & J. S. Krajcik (Eds.), *Portable technologies: Science learning in context* (pp. 29–62). The Netherlands: Kluwer Publishers.

Novak, A., & Krajcik, J. S. (2004). Using learning technologies to support inquiry in middle school science. In L. Flick & N. Lederman (Eds.), *Scientific inquiry and nature of science: Implications for teaching, learning, and teacher education* (pp. 75–102). The Netherlands: Kluwer Publishers.

Organization for Economic Cooperation and Development (OECD). (2007). *PISA 2006 Science Competencies for Tomorrow's World*. Paris: OECD.

Pellegrino, J. W., Chudowsky, N., & Glaser, R. (2001). *Knowing what students know: The science and design of educational assessment*. Washington, DC: National Academy Press.

Perkins, D., Crismond, D., Simmons, R., & Unger, C. (1995). Inside understanding. In D. Perkins, J. Schwartz, M. West, & M. Wiske (Eds.), *Software goes to school: Teaching for understanding with new technologies* (pp. 70–88). New York: Oxford University Press.

Polman, J. (1999). *Designing project-based science: Connecting learners through guided inquiry*. New York: Teachers College Press.

Reiser, B. J. (2004). Scaffolding complex learning: The mechanisms of structuring and problematizing students work. *Journal of the Learning Sciences*, 13(3), 273–304.

Rivet, A., & Krajcik, J. (2002). Contextualizing instruction: Leveraging students' prior knowledge and experiences to foster understanding of middle school science. In P. Bell, R. Stevens, & T. Satwicz (Eds.), *Keeping learning complex: The proceedings of the fifth international conference for the learning sciences (ICLS)*. Mahwah, NJ: Lawrence Erlbaum Associates.

Rivet, A., & Krajcik, J. (2004). Achieving standards in urban systemic reform: An example of a sixth grade project-based science curriculum. *Journal of Research in Science Teaching*, 41(7), 669–692.

Rose, D. H., Meyer, A., & Hitchcock, C. (2005). *The universally designed classroom: Accessible curriculum and digital technologies*. Cambridge, MA: Harvard Education Press.

Rutherford, J. F. (1964). The role of inquiry in science teaching. *Journal of Research in Science Teaching*, 2(2), 80–84.

Sadler, T. D. (2004). Informal reasoning regarding socioscientific issues: A critical review of the research. *Journal of Research in Science Teaching,* 41(5), 513–536.

Salomon, G., Perkins, D. N., & Globerson, T. (1991). Partners in cognition: Extending human intelligence with intelligent technologies. *Educational Researcher*, 20, 2–9.

Sandoval, W. A., & Reiser, B. J. (2004). Explanation-driven inquiry: Integrating conceptual and epistemic scaffolds for scientific inquiry. *Science Education*, 88(3), 345–372.

Schneider, R. M., Krajcik, J., Marx, R., & Soloway, E. (2001). Performance of student in project-based science classrooms on a national measure of science achievement. *Journal of Research in Science Teaching*, 38(7), 821–842.

Sherwood, R., Kinzer, C. K., Bransford, J. D., & Franks, J. J. (1987). Some benefits of creating macro-contexts for science instruction: Initial findings. *Journal of Research in Science Teaching*, 24(5), 417–435.

Shin, N., & Stevens, S. Y. (June 2012). Development and validation of a scale to place students along a learning progression. Paper presented at the International Conferences of the Learning Sciences, Sydney, Australia.

Shin, N., Sutherland, L. M., & McCall, K. (April 2011). Design research of features in inquiry-based science materials. Paper presented at American Educational Research Association, New Orleans, LA.

Singer, J., Marx, R. W., Krajcik, J., & Chambers, J. C. (2000). Constructing extended inquiry projects: Curriculum materials for science education reform. *Educational Psychologist*, 35, 165–178.

Smith, C. L., Wiser, M., Anderson, C. W., & Krajcik, J. (2006). Implications of research on children's learning for standards and assessment: A proposed learning progression for matter and the atomic molecular theory. *Measurement: Interdisciplinary Research and Perspectives* 14(1 and 2), 1–98.

Spitulnik, M. W., Stratford, S., Krajcik, J., & Soloway, E. (1997). Using technology to support student's artifact construction in science. In B. J. Fraser & K. Tobin (Eds.), *International handbook of science education* (pp. 363–382). The Netherlands: Kluwer Publishers.

Stevens, S. Y., & Shin, N. (April 2012). Developing and validating a "ruler" to locate and follow students along a learning progression. Poster presented at American Educational Research Association, Vancouver, Canada.

Tinker, R. (1997). Thinking about science. http://www.concord.org/library/papers.html. Cambridge, MA: Concord Consortium.

Tinker, R., & Krajcik, J. S. (Eds.) (2001). *Portable technologies: Science learning in context. Innovations in science education and technology*. New York, Kluwer Academic/Plenum Publishers.

Weizman A., Shwartz, Y., & Fortus, D. (2008). The driving question board: A visual organizer in project-based learning. *Science Teacher Journal*, 75, 8.

Williams, M., & Linn, M. (2003). WISE inquiry in fifth grade biology. *Research in Science Education*, 32(4), 145–436.

15 Problem-Based Learning

Jingyan Lu, Susan Bridges, and Cindy E. Hmelo-Silver

Problem-based learning (PBL) is an active approach to learning in which learners collaborate in understanding and solving complex, ill-structured problems (Barrows, 2000; Savery, 2006). Because of their complex and ill-structured nature, these problems require learners to share their current knowledge, negotiate among alternative ideas, search for information, and construct principled arguments to support their proposed solutions. The goals of PBL address a large range of cognitive and affective dimensions, with studies indicating that PBL students productively engage in deep approaches to learning and problem solving (Walker & Leary, 2009). As students engage with ill-structured problems, they develop skills in reasoning and self-directed learning and construct flexible knowledge (Hmelo-Silver, 2004). Compared to traditional forms of instruction, PBL enhances students' ability to transfer knowledge to new problems and to achieve more coherent understandings (e.g., Hmelo, 1998).

To provide readers with an idea of how PBL looks, we present two examples from clinical disciplines. The first is an example of how a typical diagnostic PBL problem works in a medical context.[1]

Example 1

A group of second-year medical students attended a PBL tutorial that usually consisted of two two-hour sessions. At the start of the first session, they were presented with a *problem scenario* (also known as a "case") written on a piece of paper. The problem scenario occurred in a curriculum unit organized around the musculoskeletal system and was presented as follows:

> Mr. Ho was a 60 year old machine operator in a garment factory who had enjoyed good health previously. He has married and had a son and a 4 year old grandson. The family had lived for 15 years on the 4th floor of a public housing estate with no elevators. Mr. Ho visited his family physician and complained of discomfort in both knees, worse on the right side. Each morning, he had to walk to the bus stop to get to work. In

---

[1] Case excerpted from the PBL curriculum of the Medical School of The University of Hong Kong.

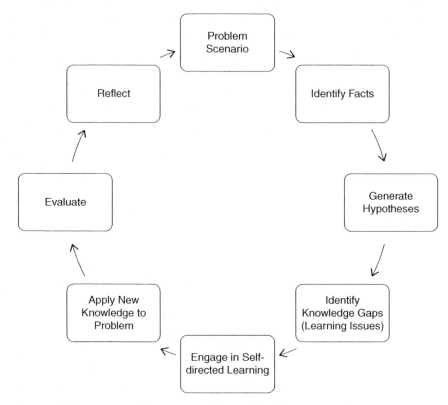

Figure 15.1. *PBL tutorial cycle (adapted from Hmelo-Silver, 2004).*

the past few months, he had found this increasingly difficult, particularly when he was walking down the stairs. Additionally, he was not spending as much time playing with his grandson as he used to.

We show the PBL cycle for how this problem would be enacted in Figure 15.1. After reading the problem scenario, students were asked to *identify important facts*, such as the patient, Mr. Ho, was 60 years old, he was experiencing discomfort in both knees, and was having escalating difficulty walking.

The students then used their background knowledge and the facts they had just identified to *generate initial hypotheses* about Mr. Ho. Students were then given more information about Mr. Ho's medical history and physical examination, which they used to *generate learning issues* and *identify knowledge gaps*, which in turn led them to engage in *self-directed learning* aimed at confirming their diagnosis and at formulating plans for managing the treatment of Mr. Ho. During the second two-hour session, students used what they had learned during the self-directed learning of the first session and applied it to solving problems arising from the presentation of additional information such as the results of laboratory orders and information on clinical and socioeconomic management. They *evaluated* the information and made final decisions on the diagnosis and management of Mr. Ho's medical problems. Finally, the students revisited the learning issues and *reflected on* what they had learned in the PBL unit. During both two-hour sessions, the tutor asked many questions to *scaffold* students' problem solving (see Reiser & Tabak, Chapter 3, this volume), including the causes of symptoms, diagnosis and differential diagnoses, indicators from the physical exam and laboratory tests, treatment plans, side effects of the surgery, and so forth. The whiteboard is an important tool for representing key case information (often listed in a column labeled "Facts" and hypotheses), sometimes labeled "Ideas," and for recording the "learning issues" that will drive self-directed learning, discussion, evaluation, and reflection.

Example 2

Another style of problem in first-year undergraduate dentistry (also at The University of Hong Kong) follows a similar cycle but illustrates the role of educational technologies in PBL. Using the timed release function of the Learning Management System (Moodle, in this case) in the first tutorial (T1), all six groups simultaneously access a video-based problem accompanied with inquiry materials in the form of 3-D anatomical images. The group process of *problem exploration* (facts and ideas) is stimulated and mediated by large-screen visualization and digital object manipulation using an interactive whiteboard (IWB). Moodle resources such as recordings of thematically linked presentations (in-house and open access) and supporting materials for practical workshops (e.g., anatomy) posted after T1 and online discussion forum postings for self-directed learning provide further *scaffolding of learning*. Second tutorial (T2) discussions *share new information and apply this to the problem*, in some groups through generating a collaborative document. Additional use of tools such as concept mapping software (Bridges, Dyson, & Corbett, 2008) *consolidates learning* as a post-problem assignment posted on Moodle after the final tutorial.

In these examples, PBL was a curriculum-level pedagogical strategy. Full, curriculum-level implementation means that PBL is the pedagogical base of a curriculum, not simply one component of a curriculum that is otherwise didactic and instructionist. As such, the careful mapping of content and organization of problems aligned to learning outcomes across the years of the curriculum becomes both the driver and link across disciplines. Characteristics of successful PBL environments include: content integration across a range of disciplines; collaboration and teamwork; application and synthesis of new knowledge toward greater understanding of the dimensions of the problem at hand; reflection on the learning process with self and peer assessment; engagement with real-world problems and issues; and examination processes measuring progress toward the goals of PBL (Savery, 2006). These goals can be achieved at a macro level-- through full implementation of an overarching, integrated curriculum design-- and at a micro level in the complex interactions that occur in small group, student-led, and educator-facilitated discussions.

History of PBL

PBL had its beginnings in medical education at the Health Sciences Centre at McMaster University in the 1960s. The driving rationale was the observation, on the part of the faculty, that medical students were not learning how to apply their basic science knowledge to clinical care (Barrows & Tamblyn, 1980). After its beginnings in medicine, PBL in higher education blossomed – initially in other health sciences curricula, then in professional programs such as engineering, architecture, and education, and finally in gifted education and other primary and secondary school contexts (Walker & Leary, 2009). This swift spread across disciplines was also evident geographically, with PBL first moving across most Western higher education contexts, then extending to medical programs in the Asia-Pacific region in the late 1990s, mainly in Australia and Hong Kong, with recent expansion in Southeast Asia and Mainland China (e.g., Hmelo-Silver, 2012).

Indeed, globally, we are witnessing a rapid change in the way education perceives itself and how it is perceived by society, in an era characterized by uncertainty, continuous risk, and shifting loyalties and trust. As our views of time and knowledge have shifted with current expectations for instant access to information on demand, the impact of these social changes on higher education reflects fundamental shifts in the way we perceive knowledge and learning. These shifts can be described in terms of movement from inert and fragmented knowledge to a notion of knowledge as a tool for thinking and acting; from an individualistic model of the learner to one of learning communities; and from a teaching dynamic to a learning dynamic (Bridges, Whitehill, & McGrath, 2012). This has seen a drive away from learning experiences that focus on content and presentation to those that focus on student activity through the design of learning tasks and environments and the provision of tools for individual and collaborative work.

Theory of PBL

PBL is grounded in the constructivist and sociocultural theories that underlie much learning sciences research (see Nathan & Sawyer, Chapter 2, this volume). For example, PBL problems are designed to situate learning in real-world contexts (Greeno & Engeström, Chapter 7, this volume). In a PBL group, identification of the problem, integration of knowledge, and internalization of knowledge occur as a socially negotiated and constructed process (Downing, 2009; Hmelo-Silver & Barrows, 2006). PBL adopts a process-based approach to knowledge construction, seeking to provide students with ways of knowing – not only in developing the skills to access information and gain knowledge, but also in analyzing and synthesizing the multiple and often conflicting sources so as to manage information. PBL is also grounded in adult learning principles of self-directed learning, with the goal of promoting student-centered education (Barrows & Tamblyn, 1980) in an environment of partnership, honesty, openness, respect, and trust.

In PBL groups, students activate prior knowledge in initial discussions, which helps prepare them to integrate new understanding (Schmidt, Dauphinee, & Patel, 1987). Dolmans and Schmidt's synthesis of studies on cognitive and motivational effects of small group learning in PBL found that engagement in the following aspects of the PBL process was consequential to stimulating students' "intrinsic interest in the subject matter":

- activation of prior knowledge;
- recall of information;
- cumulative reasoning;
- theory building;
- cognitive conflicts leading to conceptual change; and
- collaborative learning construction (Dolmans & Schmidt, 2006, p. 333).

Drawing on constructivist theory, Schmidt, Rotgans, and Yew have recently proposed two related explanations for why PBL is effective. The first is an "activation-elaboration hypothesis" to describe the PBL process whereby students activate prior knowledge to initiate and then refine mental models as they discuss the problem and identify knowledge gaps with peers (Schmidt et al., 2011, p. 792). This is supported by studies into understanding knowledge building across the problem cycle whereby learning in one phase of the PBL process is seen as academically consequential to the next phase (Bridges, McGrath, & Whitehill, 2012). In other words, later parts of the tutorial process build on the earlier tutorial discussions and self-directed learning. The second is a "situational interest hypothesis" that explains how the real-world and applied nature of the presented problem arouses students' interest. This interest then leads to an ongoing engagement and a desire to seek out new information until "hunger for new information related to the problem is satisfied" (Schmidt et al., 2011, p. 793).

Because PBL asks learners to work in teams, PBL results in the social construction of knowledge, as learners engage in collaborative inquiry to solve complex real-world problems. For example, medical students learn by solving real patient problems using the inquiry skills of medical practice. From a cognitive perspective, organized learning experiences foster students' understanding of concepts through problem-solving activities, but from a situative perspective, social interactions are part and parcel of knowledge construction. A situative perspective argues that social practices support the development of students as capable learners, competent in both disciplinary knowledge and problem solving (Greeno & Engeström, Chapter 7, this volume).

These perspectives are integrated in the notion of cognitive apprenticeship (Collins & Kapur, Chapter 6, this volume). A cognitive apprenticeship makes key aspects of expertise visible through modeling and coaching as learners engage in meaningful tasks (Hmelo-Silver, 2004). Facilitators make their expertise visible through questions that scaffold student learning through modeling, coaching, and eventually fading back some of their support. In PBL, the facilitator models learning strategies rather than teaching content knowledge (Hmelo-Silver & Barrows, 2006, 2008). In PBL, the facilitator must continually monitor the discussion, selecting and implementing appropriate strategies as needed. In many cases, these strategies involve posing questions to guide the student team's inquiry process. In other cases, the facilitator may push students to justify their thinking or explain their ideas. This may help group members to realize the limits of their understanding and identify learning issues. As students become more experienced with PBL, facilitators can fade their scaffolding as the learners gradually adopt much of the facilitator's questioning role. A sociocultural perspective provides further theoretical grounds if one is to take the view of PBL as a social system embedded in larger cultural contexts. Additionally, for small group learning, sociocultural perspectives reflect the influence of the Vygotskian notion that the act of speaking transforms thought (John-Steiner & Mahn, 1996). Bridges, McGrath, and Whitehill (2012) traced how semiotic mediation and intervisual links between real and virtual inquiry materials are consequential for learning in a PBL. As, such, the building of academic discourse through negotiation in the PBL process can be seen as highly contingent to learning.

Others have proposed that the knowledge building perspective (Scardamalia & Bereiter, Chapter 20, this volume) can explain learning in PBL. Hmelo-Silver and Barrows (2008) documented the interaction of social and cognitive activity that supported collaborative knowledge building as the PBL groups engaged in joint activity to support the collective improvement of ideas. This aligns with a Vygotskian perspective that knowledge begins in the external world (e.g., the group knowledge building) and is later internalized by the individual.

PBL Pedagogical Design

The heart of PBL is the PBL tutorial process (Figure 15.1) during which students are first presented with information about a problem and then engage in collaborative inquiry to better understand the problem and identify learning issues. Thus, the quality of the problem is the basis for the success of PBL.

The Role of Problems in PBL

PBL presents students in different subject domains with various kinds of problems to solve, such as diagnostic problems, design problems, strategic performance problems, and decision-making problems.

- *Diagnostic problems* are those in which learners have to determine the cause of a problem. The classic example is the medical patient diagnosis problem in which learners need to construct a pathophysiological explanation (e.g., Hmelo-Silver & Barrows, 2008).
- *Design problems* involve creating an artifact, generally based on a set of functional specifications.
- *Strategic performance problems* ask for "applying tactics to meet strategy in real-time complex performance maintaining situational awareness" (Jonassen, 2000, p. 75). Examples include managing an investment portfolio or playing an interactive computer game.
- *Decision-making problems* means a choice/decision needs to be made from a number of competing alternatives. This type of problem is often used in business administration (Stinson & Milter, 1996), leadership education (Bridges & Hallinger, 1996, 1997), or emergency medical care scenarios where personnel are asked to make high-stake decisions in high-risk settings (Lu & Lajoie, 2008).

Although they have important differences, these problems have a number of features in common that are key to the design and success of PBL activities. For instance, problems are often categorized as well structured and ill structured (Newell & Simon, 1972). However, structuredness is a continuum along which problems vary from highly structured problems such as algorithmic problems, to very ill-structured problems such as design problems and dilemmas (Jonassen, 2000). A well-structured problem is a problem for which the goal, problem space, path to solution, and information needed to solve it can be clearly and explicitly specified. An ill-structured problem is a problem for which the goal, problem space, path to solution, and information needed to solve it cannot be clearly and explicitly specified. In PBL, problems are often moderately ill structured, with the degree of structure tailored to the age and expertise of the learners and their learning goals.

PBL problems can also be characterized in terms of their complexity, which refers to the breadth of knowledge needed to solve them, the level of difficulty involved in understanding and applying the relevant concepts, the level of skill and knowledge needed to explore the problem, and the degree of linearity involved in relations among the variables in the problem space (Jonassen & Hung, 2008). Structure and complexity determine how difficult a PBL problem will be for students to solve and how willing they will be to try to solve it. However, in problem design, theory-driven considerations of structure and complexity fail to target student perspectives such as promoting self-directed and significant learning, stimulating critical thinking, and triggering interest. Given that the quality of problems is a major factor in determining learning outcomes (Van Berkel & Schmidt, 2000), features that are valued by researchers and by students should be taken into consideration in the problem design though they might be different. Classically ill-structured problems are multidimensional and may not afford a direct or easy solution. By engaging in a structured reasoning process, however, students gain understanding of the problem complexities and apply appropriate reasoning processes and disciplinary discourse practices.

In a recent meta-analysis, Walker and Leary (2009) found that certain kinds of problems may more effectively promote learning than others. Although in studies of PBL diagnostic problems were most commonly used, other types of problems have been successfully employed in PBL. The meta-analysis showed the greatest achievement effects were for design problems and strategic performance problems. The ill-structured problems used in PBL can serve as the basis for high levels of problem-relevant collaborative interaction; however, groups may need higher-quality facilitation as the problems become less structured to make this interaction productive (Van Berkel & Schmidt, 2000).

Scaffolding

Students would not be successful in PBL without scaffolding for their problem solving and inquiry (Hmelo-Silver & Barrows, 2006). Scaffolding in PBL helps learners manage the complexity of the ill-structured problem space and group dynamics while gently guiding learners toward achieving content and reasoning goals. Scaffolding is temporary support that allows learners to accomplish their goal. It is support that (a) enables a student to accomplish tasks they could not otherwise do and (b) facilitates learning to succeed even without the support. Well-designed scaffolds help ensure that learners succeed at new tasks and can extend their competencies (Reiser & Tabak, Chapter 3, this volume). In general, scaffolding is meant to fade, disappearing over time so that the learner can succeed without the support. In PBL, scaffolding tends to take three forms.

1. *Communicating process* involves presenting the process involved in solving the problem to students, structuring and sometimes simplifying the process. Presenting the process to students can occur through modeling or demonstration. This structure constrains and guides student inquiry. The PBL tutorial process is a good example of this. The whiteboard also helps communicate the process by reminding learners what they need to attend to.

2. *Coaching* refers to providing guidance to learners while they are per-forming a task. This can be accomplished by highlighting critical steps of the process as the student is working on a problem. Coaching can include statements that help frame the problem and articulate inquiry goals. In PBL, the facilitator helps accomplish this through questions that model the kinds of thinking that students should be learning. For example, asking them why they need particular pieces of information helps students focus asking questions on particular goals rather than just trying to gather all possible information.

3. *Eliciting articulation* is asking the student to explain (to themselves or others). This can enhance constructive processing and make thinking vis-ible and therefore an object for discussion and revision. Questions that ask learners to articulate their thinking can lead to significant reflection and subsequent learning. Encouraging reflection helps prepare learn-ers to transfer the knowledge and skills they are learning (Salomon & Perkins, 1989).

Teacher as Scaffold

In PBL, the facilitator's role is to guide active learning on the part of the student team, rather than to provide information through lecture or instruc-tion. PBL facilitators accomplish most of their scaffolding through open-ended questioning and by deploying an array of strategies (Hmelo-Silver & Barrows, 2006, 2008). Hmelo-Silver and Barrows (2006) identified these strategies through an interaction analysis of video of an expert facilitator (see Table 15.1).

Representations as Scaffolds

In PBL, students externalize their developing ideas by inscribing them on a whiteboard for display and discussion. Externalized representations con-tribute to collective knowledge construction in several ways (Roth, 1998). First, representations serve as shared referential objects for group members and provide common ground for discussion. Second, the structure of the representation can guide the students' discussion (Suthers & Hundhausen, 2003). In PBL, several representational artifacts are constructed by student teams under the guidance of a facilitator. One representation is a formally structured PBL whiteboard with facts, ideas or hypotheses, learning issues, and an action plan (Lu, Lajoie, & Wiseman, 2010). This helps guide the students to consider certain issues that the facilitator believes will lead to a more effective learning discussion. The whiteboard serves as an external memory for the students – it reminds them of their ideas, both solidified and tentative, as well as hypotheses that students need to test. One ritual-ized aspect of the PBL tutorial is "cleaning up the boards" (Hmelo-Silver & Barrows, 2006). The whiteboard provides a constant reference point within the learning space, allowing the facilitator (or the students themselves) to

Table 15.1. *Facilitation strategies (adapted from Hmelo-Silver & Barrows, 2006)*

Strategy	How accomplished
Use of open-ended and metacognitive questioning	General strategy to encourage explanations and recognition of knowledge limitations
Pushing for explanation	Construct causal models Students realize limits of their knowledge
Revoicing	Clarify ideas Legitimate ideas of low-status students Mark ideas as important and subtly influence direction of discussion
Summarizing	Ensure joint representation of problem Involve less vocal students Help students synthesize data Move group along in process Reveal facts that students think are important
Generate/evaluate hypotheses	Help students focus their inquiry Examine fit between hypotheses and accumulating evidence
Map between symptoms and hypotheses	Elaborate causal mechanism
Check consensus that whiteboard reflects discussion	Ensure all ideas get recorded and important ideas are not lost
Cleaning up the board	Evaluate ideas Maintain focus Keep process moving
Creating learning issues	Knowledge gaps as opportunities to learn
Encourage construction of visual representation	Construct integrated knowledge structure that ties mechanisms to observable effects

take advantage of this external representation of the students' unfolding ideas about the problem. This occurs at several times but, in particular, after students have discussed the resources they used for their self-directed learning. This is important because it provides an occasion for students to evaluate each of their hypotheses, look at the fit to data, and reflect on what they have gleaned from their self-directed learning. Discussions of which hypotheses are more or less likely often center around what needs to be filled in on the whiteboard (see examples in Figure 15.2).

Students often discuss how hypotheses should be ranked or when they should be added or deleted. These structured whiteboards serve as a focus for students to negotiate their ideas and identify those that can be postponed for later consideration. When students mark something for entry on the whiteboard, it also signifies agreement by the group that the item is worth attending to. The use of the whiteboard supports reasoning, knowledge

Facts	Ideas	Learning Issues

Ann George
 	
72 y/o F
 	
CC: Numbness on Bottoms of Feet
 	
HPI
Numbness in feet 4-5 weeks
 	
Weak tingling in fingers
 	
EXAM
HR 72
T 98.6
RESP 16
Broad-based gait
 	
ROS
0 HA,
Migraines
	Diabetic neuropathy
	
	Multiple sclerosis
	
	~~Alcoholic neuropathy~~
	~~Malnutrition~~
	
	Afferent Neuropathy
	Peripheral neuritis
	
	~~Guillain Barré syndrome~~
	Spinal cord lesion
	
	Herniated Disc
	~~Hypothyroidism~~
	Toxicity
	  Arsenic
	  Lead
	~~Anemia~~
	  ~~Pernicious~~
	~~Scleroderma~~
	Electrolyte
		Guidelines for hypertension
		
		Diabetic neuropathy
		
		Multiple Sclerosis
		
		Peripheral neuritis
		
		Innervations of foot and Blood supply
		
		Pathophysiology of numbness
		
		Guillain Barré Paresthesia
		
		Paralysis
		
		Afferent Tracts

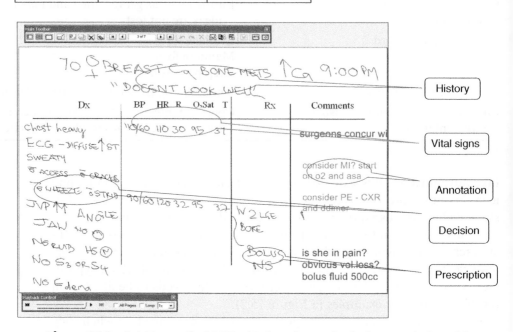

Figure 15.2. *(a) Transcribed PBL whiteboard in medical education (adapted from Hmelo-Silver & Barrows, 2008), (b) Example of PBL electronic whiteboard used in solving medical emergency problems (adapted from Lu et al., 2010).*

construction, and self-directed learning, as students use it to remind them of what they are considering, what they know, and what they still need to learn. Other representational tools students may construct are less formal representations such as flow charts, concept maps (Bridges et al., 2009), and diagrams. Hmelo-Silver and Barrows (2008) provided an example of how the activity of drawing one of these representations led to rich discussion.

Self-Directed Learning

A key feature of PBL is the self-directed learning (SDL) that is initiated through the identification and discussion of learning issues. Students discuss problems initially based on their prior knowledge. The learning issues are concepts that students have identified that are important for the PBL task and that they cannot address with their existing knowledge (Hmelo-Silver, 2004). The student-centered nature of PBL supports SDL as students have to identify knowledge gaps, plan their research to address the learning issues, critically evaluate the information sources they unearth, and engage in self-assessment to see if what they have learned matches their learning goals (Hmelo & Lin, 2000). This involves the use of self-regulated learning strategies as students are required to be metacognitively aware of their knowledge, to plan their research, to allocate time and effort appropriately, and to be intrinsically motivated.

Collaboration

Collaboration requires students to make their thinking visible, as they discuss their developing understandings and hypotheses, thus making their ideas open for negotiation and revisions. One obstacle to implementing PBL is that many medical schools consider small group learning less cost-effective; the financial pressures are toward larger student groups. Conventional practice in PBL has been for groups to be medium-sized, ranging from five to eight students for optimal engagement in the process and academic outcomes (Barrows, 2000; Dolmans & Schmidt, 2006). Lohman and Finkelstein's (2000) design study of the effect of group size in PBL on selected outcome measures found that students' levels of self-directedness increased in small (3 students) and medium (6 students) groups, but decreased in large (9 students) groups. Additionally, they posited that, to promote the development of students' problem-solving skills, PBL needs to be used recurrently over a fairly long period of time, thereby supporting other research findings suggesting that PBL should be the core foundation of the curriculum, rather than one added element to an otherwise instructionist curriculum, such as a single-semester class. Research in the learning sciences suggests that this is because of the time it takes to develop new cultural norms associated with PBL practices (Kolodner et al., 2003).

Reflection for Learning and Transfer

In PBL, learners are encouraged to constantly reflect on their developing understandings in order to support the construction of extensive, flexible, and usable knowledge (Salomon & Perkins, 1989). Reflection helps students: (1) relate their new knowledge to their prior understanding, (2) mindfully abstract knowledge, and (3) understand how the strategies might be reapplied. PBL incorporates reflection throughout the tutorial process, and also when completing a problem. Students take opportunities to reflect on their hypothesis list and their own knowledge relative to the problem. After a problem, students reflect on what they have learned, how well they collaborated with the group, and how effective they were as self-directed learners. As students make inferences that tie general concepts and skills to the specifics of the problem that they are working on, they construct more coherent knowledge. This "mindful abstraction" that occurs during reflection is a critical aspect of the PBL process. The reflection process in PBL helps learners make inferences, identify knowledge gaps, and prepare to transfer problem-solving strategies, self-directed learning strategies, and knowledge to new situations.

Assessment

Given the aspirations of PBL (and other learning sciences-based approaches to 21st-century skill learning) to promote deeper conceptual understanding, integrated and situated knowledge, and adaptive expertise and transfer, we need a better understanding of how to develop appropriate formative and summative assessments. Assessment of PBL may focus on the mastery of knowledge and skills or on the mastery of problem-solving processes. After all, in many practice-oriented professions, knowledge is neither inert nor limited to classroom settings; rather it has the goal of enhancing professional practice. For example, in medicine, students learn basic medical science such as physiology and biochemistry to prepare them for clinical practice. Because the purpose of PBL is to help students apply basic medical knowledge, it would be more meaningful to assess students with respect to their ability to integrate their physiological or biochemistry knowledge into clinical practice rather than ask them to write down the facts about their knowledge. Thus, PBL assessment seeks to emphasize elements involved in clinical practice.

Effects of PBL

A number of meta-analyses have focused on the effectiveness of PBL (Albanese & Mitchell, 1993; Dochy, Segers, Van den Bossche, & Gijbels, 2003; Gijbels, Dochy, Van den Bossche, & Segers, 2005; Strobel & Van Barneveld, 2009; Vernon & Blake, 1993). For instance, its effectiveness has been assessed with respect to academic achievement, cognition, metacognition, attitude, and behavior under different teaching methods. Most assessment has focused on knowledge structure and metacognitive skills (Gijbels et al., 2005). For instance, compared to students receiving lecture-based instruction (Albanese & Mitchell, 1993; Vernon & Blake, 1993), PBL students had stronger procedural knowledge and were better at linking and applying declarative and procedural knowledge to situations, but non-PBL students had more solid basic science knowledge (Gijbels et al., 2005). PBL is predicted to promote metacognitive skills, particularly planning and monitoring skills (see Winne & Azevedo, Chapter 4, this volume). Several studies have confirmed this prediction; for instance, the metacognitive skills of first-year undergraduates in a year-long PBL program were significantly higher than those of students in a non-PBL program on all dimensions (Downing, 2009).

Students tend to have positive attitudes toward PBL. For instance, medical students find PBL programs more engaging and useful, but also more difficult than non-PBL programs (Albanese & Mitchell, 1993). PBL students are more confident in coping with uncertainty and in recognizing the importance of social and emotional factors in illness (Silverstone, 1998). Students find PBL environments more interesting and relevant (de Vries et al., 1989; Schmidt et al., 1987), more conducive to teamwork, and more supportive of doctor-patient relationships (Bernstein, Tipping, Bercovitz, & Skinner, 1995).

PBL is also found to facilitate self-directed learning. Comparing PBL and non-PBL trained medical students, Hmelo and Lin (2000) found that the former were more likely to use hypothesis-driven strategies in planning learning and to integrate new information into revised explanations. PBL students tended to use self-chosen learning resources and non-PBL students tended to use lecture notes (Blumberg & Michael, 1992), and PBL students tended to use more diverse and meaningful study techniques than non-PBL students (Coles, 1985).

With PBL's roots in medical education, outcome assessment tends to focus on the effectiveness of PBL in this field. However, more research is focusing on other fields (Abrandt Dahlgren & Dahlgren, 2002) and on learners at different levels. Further research should examine why, how, and in what contexts PBL might lead to attitude changes, and to what degree.

Most assessment research has focused on measuring types of knowledge and knowledge applications, whereas PBL also supports the development of reasoning (Wood, Cunnington, & Norman, 2000), problem solving (Hmelo, Gotterer, & Bransford, 1997), and decision making (Lu & Lajoie, 2008), all of which should be emphasized in future research on PBL.

PBL in Transition/and Transforming PBL

PBL: Future Practice

Almost four decades have passed since PBL was first introduced, and it has undergone a number of transformations or revisions. For instance, the original McMaster undergraduate MD program has gone through two major curriculum revisions since adopting PBL in 1969 (Neville & Norman, 2007). While the first PBL curriculum emphasized small group tutorials, self-directed learning, and tutorial performance-based assessment, the second curriculum focused on building a foundation based on common medical problems so as to equip students with the knowledge and skills they needed to understand and manage common medical conditions. The third curriculum focused on structuring and arranging concepts and body systems into logical sequences. These revisions reflect changes in the requirements and demands of medical education as well as possible tensions regarding curriculum coherence at the program level.

One of the greatest challenges to curriculum development for any PBL program, especially those adopting PBL at the curriculum design level, is faculty commitment. The silo, course-based approach gives much greater autonomy to individual academics and does not require the level of coordination and faculty collaboration that PBL curricula demand, because careful curriculum mapping is required for content knowledge to be systematically integrated horizontally and vertically in spiral curriculum structures. A single problem, for example, usually integrates knowledge from two to three disciplinary domains. Because no single facilitator can be a content expert for all dimensions of the problem, detailed facilitator guides are devised and shared at regular briefings and debriefings. Some programs have avoided this challenge by introducing PBL at the discipline-specific course level (e.g., Anatomy 101). This requires less cross-disciplinary cooperation and supporting infrastructure, and as such is seen by many as more feasible; however, this changes only classroom method and does not address larger issues of curriculum design and integration that PBL researchers have found consequential to learning (Mok, Dodd, & Whitehill, 2009).

Although PBL emphasizes the role of teachers as facilitators in scaffolding problem-solving processes, little is known about the knowledge and skills teachers bring to such processes and the kinds of knowledge and skills that should be promoted in professional development programs and how to foster them. Ongoing development and quality assurance of PBL facilitators remains a challenge for curriculum managers. While much is done to focus on induction programs for the new facilitator/tutor, there is a pressing need to provide advanced academic development for PBL facilitators. Walker and colleagues (2011) have shown that the training that teachers receive with respect to technology skills and PBL pedagogy leads to differences in how they perceive knowledge and experience and in their confidence in technology integration in PBL, as well as the actual quality of PBL design after the training. The results imply that the ways teachers are trained has an impact on how they design PBL activities, particularly while using technology. With regard to professional development for PBL facilitators and curriculum designers, there is potential for further research to investigate both innovations in the delivery of professional development programs and studies exploring facilitator effectiveness, including in situ judgments regarding tutorial performance. In terms of ongoing quality assurance, the issues of reliability of facilitator feedback and consistency in standards are as increasingly relevant for PBL as for any other education program.

PBL and Technology

The most recent wave of undergraduate PBL students are more increasingly engaged in Web 2.0 technologies that are generally synchronous and interactive. The rise of new educational technologies is seeing Net Generation or tech savvy learners and their facilitators moving into the next generation of blended learning in PBL. Modern PBL curriculum designers in clinical education are building on the initial principles of the traditional PBL tutorial process to adapt to changing programs, students, and technologies (Howe & Schnabel, 2012). As the visual becomes more predominant for digitally engaged learners, intervisual relations between texts can be seen to support and enhance collective and individual cognition whereby in "the social learning process that is PBL, the accessing of visual tools and learning objects in the final tutorial becomes socially and academically relevant" (Bridges, Botelho, & Green, 2012, p. 117).

Other roles for technology in PBL include providing rich contexts, communication spaces, and scaffolds. Hmelo-Silver and colleagues (2013) used video cases as PBL triggers to help medical students learn about communicating bad news. In the STELLAR system (Hmelo-Silver, Derry, Bitterman, & Hatrak, 2009), interactive whiteboards were used to guide students in instructional planning as students engaged in a hybrid PBL model. The whiteboard was adapted from the general PBL whiteboard described earlier to be more specific to these instructional planning tasks with tabs for *Enduring Understanding*, *Evidence of Understanding*, and *Activities*. It served as a communication space for students and the facilitator to comment on and question other students' entries. In another example of a PBL tutorial dealing with medical emergencies, an interactive whiteboard was used as a collaborative argumentation tool where participant students could annotate patient information, comment on, and suggest alternatives for decisions (Lu et al., 2010). Thus, technology was used to scaffold collaborative decision making by promoting the discussion of various proposed actions and plans. These are just a few examples of how technology can support PBL.

Future Directions for PBL Research

Recent work has suggested new directions for research in PBL. Bridges, Whitehill, and McGrath (2012) noted potential research in the areas of student learning outcomes, new research methodologies, and professional development. New studies (particularly comparative and longitudinal studies) are needed to understand the long-term effects of PBL in terms of graduate competences (Shuler, 2012) and effects on professional practice (Toulouse, Spaziani, & Rangachari, 2012).

In particular, we see three general areas that we anticipate would be fruitful for learning scientists investigating PBL:

1. Research in other Disciplines and Grades

PBL research needs to extend to disciplines beyond medical education and to learners in K-12 environments, not only with university students. Most research has focused on medical education, and this has resulted in a lack of research on the development, implementation, and evaluation of PBL in other disciplines – such as history and engineering – and with learners at other levels. This research would be important for the learning sciences to understand under what circumstances PBL might result in enhanced learning outcomes. Part of this research should focus on the adaptations and kinds of scaffolding that might be needed as PBL is used in settings that have larger numbers of groups, differing disciplines (and disciplinary norms), and students of younger ages and with more variable prior knowledge.

2. Research on Evaluation and Assessment of PBL

The effectiveness of PBL with respect to other curricula should be assessed by measuring the components of PBL settings rather than by focusing on PBL programs as a whole. For instance, some PBL programs emphasize the structure of blocks and some focus on integrating technology into the PBL program. Thus, when evaluating or assessing PBL, these components should be highlighted. Further, systematic assessment should go beyond associated knowledge structures or its effectiveness in promoting specifically recognized PBL skills, such as reasoning, problem solving, and decision making, as well as the "soft skills" of self-directed learning and collaboration. The greater tension for PBL may be in the assessment of "process" such as the quality of contributions to the group rather than the standard measurement of student "products" such as written assignments or exams. There is also a tension in creating the kind of embedded formative and summative assessments that are consistent with the values of PBL but that are also psychometrically valid measures of student learning.

3. Research on Supporting PBL on Larger Scales

One question that is important for using PBL on a large scale is figuring out how to distribute scaffolding among facilitators, technology, and other contextual features (Hmelo-Silver et al., 2009). Further, research can focus on designing technology for distributing expertise to facilitators; for sharing and distributing PBL cases to large audiences via online technology; for digitizing PBL tutorials by expert teachers and distributing them to schools; and for digitalized PBL tutorials as teacher development tools.

Implications for the Learning Sciences

Addressing these research areas has the potential to inform learning sciences more broadly. Many of the characteristics of PBL are relevant to other learning sciences-informed instructional approaches:

- Facilitation in PBL is related to the broader issues in supporting student agency in student-centered learning environments.
- Understanding how different scaffolds and representations mediate student learning in PBL as well as other approaches to inquiry.
- Roles for technology in creating contexts, scaffolding, and discursive spaces in PBL would also apply to supporting other forms of inquiry and guided discovery.
- Understanding the nature of generative problems in PBL is part of a broader discussion of design principles.

Exploring the synergies and creating conversations about both common ground and important differences should contribute to our goals of better understanding learning and designing more effective learning environments.

References

Abrandt Dahlgren, M., & Dahlgren, L. O. (2002). Portraits of PBL: Students' experiences of the characteristics of problem-based learning in physiotherapy, computer engineering and psychology. *Instructional Science*, 30, 111–127.

Albanese, M. A., & Mitchell, S. (1993). Problem-based learning: A review of the literature on its outcomes and implementation issues. *Academic Medicine*, 68(1), 52–81.

Barrows, H. S. (2000). *Problem-based learning applied to medical education*. Springfield: Southern Illinois University School of Medicine.

Barrows, H. S., & Tamblyn, R. (1980). *Problem-based learning: An approach to medical education*. New York: Springer.

Bernstein, P., Tipping, J., Bercovitz, K., & Skinner, H. A. (1995). Shifting students and faculty to a PBL curriculum: Attitudes changed and lessons learned. *Academic Medicine*, 70, 245–247.

Blumberg, P., & Michael, J. A. (1992). Development of self directed learning behaviors in a partially teacher directed problem based learning curriculum. *Teaching and Learning in Medicine*, 4, 3–8.

Bridges, S. M., Dyson, J. E., & Corbet, E. F. (2008). Tools for knowledge co-construction: Online concept mapping to support self-directed learning. Paper presented at the 5th International PBL conference, Newport, RI, April 20–24.

Bridges, E. M., & Hallinger, P. (1996). Problem-based learning in leadership education. *New Directions for Teaching and Learning, 1996*(68), 53–61.

Bridges, E. M., & Hallinger, P. (1997). Using problem-based learning to prepare educational leaders. *Peabody Journal of Education*, 72(2), 131–146.

Bridges, S. M., Botelho, M. G., & Green, J. (2012). Multimodality in PBL: An interactional ethnography. In S. Bridges, C. McGrath, & T. Whitehill (Eds.), *Researching problem-based learning in clinical education: The next generation* (pp. 99–120). Netherlands: Springer.

Bridges, S. M., McGrath. C., & Whitehill, T. (2012). *Researching problem-based learning in clinical education: The next generation* Netherlands: Springer.

Bridges, S. M., Whitehill, T., & McGrath, C. (2012). The next generation: Research directions in PBL. In S. Bridges, C. McGrath, & T. Whitehill (Eds.), *Researching problem-based learning in clinical education: The next generation* (pp. 225–232). Netherlands: Springer.

Coles, C. R. (1985). Differences between conventional and problem based curricula in their students' approaches to studying. *Medical Education*, 19, 308–309.

De Vries, M., Schmidt, M., & DeGraaff, E. (1989). Dutch comparisons: Cognitive and motivational effects of problem-based learning on medical students. In H. G. Schmidt, M. Lipkin, M. W. de Vries, & J. M. Greep (Eds.), *New directions for medical education* (pp. 230–240). New York: Springer-Verlag.

Dochy, F., Segers, M., Van den Bossche, P., & Gijbels, D. (2003). Effects of problem-based learning: S meta-analysis. *Learning and Instruction*, 13, 533–568.

Dolmans, D. H. J. M., & Schmidt, H. G. (2006). What do we know about cognitive and motivational effects of small group tutorials in problem-based learning? *Advances in Health Sciences Education*, 11, 321–336.

Downing, K. (2009). Problem-based learning and the development of metacognition. *Higher Education*, 57(5), 609–621.

Gijbels, D., Dochy, F., Van den Bossche, P., & Segers, M. (2005). Effects of problem-based learning: A meta-analysis from the angle of assessment. *Review of Educational Research*, 75, 27–61.

Hmelo, C. E. (1998). Problem-based learning: Effects on the early acquisition of cognitive skill in medicine. *Journal of the Learning Sciences*, 7, 173–208.

Hmelo, C. E., Gotterer, G. S., & Bransford, J. D. (1997). A theory-driven approach to assessing the cognitive effects of PBL. *Instructional Science*, 25, 387–408.

Hmelo, C. E., & Lin, X. (2000). The development of self-directed learning strategies in problem-based learning. In D. Evensen & C. E. Hmelo (Eds.), *Problem-based learning: Research perspectives on learning interactions* (pp. 227–250). Mahwah, NJ: Lawrence Erlbaum Associates.

Hmelo-Silver, C. E. (2004). Problem-based learning: What and how do students learn? *Educational Psychology Review*, 16, 235–266.

Hmelo-Silver, C. E. (2012). International perspectives on problem-based learning: Contexts, cultures, challenges, and adaptations. *Interdisciplinary Journal of Problem-based Learning*, 6, 10–15.

Hmelo-Silver, C. E., & Barrows, H. S. (2006). Goals and strategies of a problem-based learning facilitator. *Interdisciplinary Journal of Problem-based Learning*, 1, 21–39.

Hmelo-Silver, C. E., & Barrows, H. S. (2008). Facilitating collaborative knowledge building. *Cognition and Instruction*, 26, 48–94.

Hmelo-Silver, C. E., Derry, S. J., Bitterman, A., & Hatrak, N. (2009). Targeting transfer in a STELLAR PBL course for pre-service teachers. *Interdisciplinary Journal of Problem-based Learning*, 3(2), 24–42.

Hmelo-Silver, C., Khurna, C. A., Lajoie, S. P., Lu, J., Wiseman, J., Chan, L. K., & Cruz-Panesso, I. (2013). Using online digital tools and video to support international problem-based learning. The 46th Hawaii International Conference on System Sciences (HICSS). January 7–10. Hawaii.

Howe, E. L. C., & Schnabel, M. A. (2012). The changing face of problem-based learning: Social networking and interprofessional collaboration. In S. Bridges, C. McGrath, & T. L. Whitehill (Eds.), *Problem-based learning in clinical education* (pp. 121–137). Dordrecht: Springer.

John-Steiner, V., & Mahn, H. (1996). Sociocultural approaches to learning and development: A Vygotskian framework. *Educational Psychologist*, 31, 191–206.

Jonassen, D. (2000). Toward a design theory of problem solving. *Educational Technology Research and Development*, 48, 63–85.

Jonassen, D. H., & Hung, W. (2008). All problems are not equal: Implications for problem-based learning. *Interdisciplinary Journal of Problem-based Learning*, 2(2), 6–28.

Kolodner, J. L., Camp, P. J., Crismond, D., Fasse, B., Gray, J., Holbrook, J., & Ryan, M. Problem-based learning meets case-based reasoning in the middle-school science classroom: Putting Learning by Design™ into practice. *Journal of the Learning Sciences,* 12, 495–547.

Lohman, M., & Finkelstein, M. (2000). Designing groups in problem-based learning to promote problem-solving skill and self-directedness. *Instructional Science*, 28, 291–307.

Lu, J., & Lajoie, S. P. (2008). Supporting medical decision making with argumentation tools. *Contemporary Educational Psychology*, 33, 425–442.

Lu, J., Lajoie, S. P., & Wiseman, J. (2010). Scaffolding problem based learning with CSCL tools. *International Journal of Computer Supported Collaborative Learning*, 5, 283–298.

Mok, C. K. F., Dodd B., & Whitehill T. L. (2009). Speech-language pathology students' approaches to learning in a problem-based learning curriculum. *International Journal of Speech-Language Pathology*, 11, 472–481.

Neville, A. J., & Norman, G. R. (2007). PBL in the undergraduate MD program at McMaster University: Three iterations in three decades. *Academic Medicine*, 82, 370–374.

Newell, A., & Simon, H. A. (1972). *Human problem solving*. Englewood Cliffs, NJ: Prentice-Hall.

Reiser, B. J. (2004). Scaffolding complex learning: The mechanisms of structuring and problematizing student work. *Journal of the Learning Sciences*, 13, 273–304.

Roth, W.-M. (1998). Inscriptions: Toward a theory of representing as social practice. *Review of educational research*, 68, 35–60.

Salomon, G., & Perkins, D. N. (1989). Rocky roads to transfer: Rethinking mechanisms of a neglected phenomenon. *Educational Psychologist*, 24, 113–142.

Savery, J. (2006). Overview of problem-based learning: Definitions and distinctions. *The Interdisciplinary Journal of Problem-based Learning*, 1(1), 9–20.

Schmidt, H. G., Dauphinee, W. D., & Patel, V. L. (1987). Comparing the effects of problem-based and conventional curricula in an international sample. *Journal of Medical Education*, 62, 305–315.

Schmidt, H. G., Rotgans, J. I., & Yew, E. H. (2011). The process of problem-based learning: What works and why. *Medical Education*, 45, 792–806.

Shuler, C. F. (2012). Comparisons in basic science learning outcomes between students in PBL and traditional dental curricula at the same dental school. In S. Bridges, C. McGrath, & T. L. Whitehill (Eds.), *Problem-based learning in clinical education*. Netherlands: Springer.

Silverstone, Z. (1998). Tomorrow's doctors – tomorrow's attitudes? *Medical Education*, 32(2), 219.

Sockalingam, N., & Schmidt, H. G. (2011). Characteristics of problems for problem-based learning: The students' perspective. *Interdisciplinary Journal of Problem-based Learning*, 5(1), 6–33.

Stinson, J. E., & Milter, R. G. (1996). Problem-based learning in business education: Curriculum design and implementation issues. *New Directions for Teaching and Learning*, 1996(68), 33–42.

Strobel, J., & Van Barneveld, A. (2009). When is PBL more effective? A meta-synthesis of meta-analyses comparing PBL to conventional classrooms. *Interdisciplinary Journal of Problem-based Learning*, 3(1), 44–58.

Suthers, D. D., & Hundhausen, C. D. (2003). An experimental study of the effects of representational guidance on collaborative learning processes. *Journal of the Learning Sciences*, 12, 183–218.

Toulouse, K., Spaziani, R., & Rangachari, P. K. (2012). In S. Bridges, C. McGrath, & T. L. Whitehill (Eds.), *Problem-based learning in clinical education*. Netherlands: Springer.

Van Berkel, H. J. M., & Schmidt, H. G. (2000). Motivation to commit oneself as a determinant of achievement in problem-based learning. *Higher Education*, 40, 231–242.

Vernon, D. T. A., & Blake, R. L. (1993). Does problem-based learning work? A metaanalysis of evaluative research. *Academic Medicine*, 68, 550–563.

Walker, A., Recker, M., Robertshaw, M. B., Osen, J., Leary, H., Ye, L., et al. (2011). Integrating technology and problem-based learning: A mixed methods study of two teacher professional development designs. *Interdisciplinary Journal of Problem-based Learning*, 5(2), 70–94.

Walker, A. E., & Leary, H. (2009). A problem based learning meta analysis: Differences across problem types, implementation types, disciplines, and assessment levels. *Interdisciplinary Journal of Problem-based Learning*, 3, 12–43.

Wood, T. J., Cunnington, J. P. W., & Norman, G. R. (2000). Assessing the measurement properties of a clinical reasoning exercise. *Teaching & Learning in Medicine*, 12, 196–200.

16 Complex Systems and the Learning Sciences

Uri Wilensky and Michael J. Jacobson

A complex system is a system composed of many elements that interact with each other and their environment. For example, an economy is composed of many individual buyers and sellers; an ecological system of many animals and plants; a weather system of fronts, precipitation, and air; and so on. A key feature of complex systems is that it is often difficult to predict or make sense of the behavior of the systems as a whole, even when all the components are known. We use the term *emergence* to describe how large-scale patterns arise from the multiple interactions of individuals; and the resultant patterns are called *emergent phenomena*. Even when we are very familiar with the elements of a system, its emergent pattern is often surprising. Similarly, even when we are very familiar with the overall pattern, it is usually surprising to find out how that pattern arises from underlying elements.

Over the past three decades, a science of complex systems has itself emerged from the recognition of similar patterns of complexity and emergence across many different content domains (Bar-Yam, 1997, 2003; Epstein, 2006; Holland, 1995; Kaput et al., 2001; Kauffman, 1995; Mitchell, 2009; Sawyer, 2005; Waldrop, 1992; Watts & Strogatz, 1998; Wolfram, 2002). Complexity researchers study events and actions that have multiple causes and consequences as well as studying systems that have structures at many different scales of time, space, and organization.

The field of complex systems has grown up alongside advances in computation. Historically, the invention of the telescope enabled advances in astronomy, and in similar fashion more recently, as computers have become faster and more powerful, they enable us to build models of large-scale emergent phenomena and advance the field of complex systems. Complex systems scientists use computer simulations to study emergent phenomena across a very wide range of domains. For example, in animal biology, they have studied the emergence of a bird flock from the movement of individual birds, or the distributed food gathering of ants in an ant colony. In the human world, computer simulations have revealed such dynamics as the emergence of fashion trends, the formation of a traffic jam, and the spread of a disease. All of these complex phenomena are composed of individual elements that follow their own rules of behavior – for example, birds flying with no intention to create a flock, or people driving with no intention to create a traffic jam – but the resultant patterns self-organize and emerge nonetheless.

In this chapter, we argue that students should study complex systems in school (at all educational levels) because virtually all natural and social phenomena are emergent phenomena arising from the interactions of distributed elements – including snowflakes and hurricanes, urban sprawl and cow paths, viral capsids and the Milky Way galaxy. Indeed, the study of complex systems is not the study of some *particular* phenomena, but rather, a perspective on *all* phenomena. All phenomena can be described as complex systems with many simpler components – each with characteristic behaviors – that interact to result in emergent patterns. Even our very selves – our sense of conscious awareness, which we experience as vividly real and unitary – can only be explained scientifically as arising from the interactions of millions of neurons organized into a complex system. The history of science can be seen as a progressive uncovering of the components of observed patterns and how their emergence arises from the interactions of these components.

Complex systems theory has considerably impacted the pure sciences, and insights gained there have also been integrated into the working conceptual frameworks of more applied professions such as engineering, business, and law. This perspective has also informed corporate managers' thinking about their employees and about their relationships with other corporations (e.g., synergistic alliances versus competitive advantages) (Axelrod & Cohen, 1999; Brown & Eisenhardt, 1998; Senge, 1990). Additionally, considerable work has made use of complex systems network-based perspectives on organizational behavior (Gulati, 1998; Reagans & Zuckerman, 2001; Uzzi, 1997; Watts & Strogatz, 1998).

The complex systems perspective provides a framework that integrates many different scientific domains. This is potentially quite valuable to learning scientists, because decades of study have documented that the lack of cross-disciplinary integration in the K–12 curriculum is a source of great confusion for students, resulting in "inert knowledge" that students can repeat back on a test but cannot connect to other knowledge or to real-world experiences. Because it is a broad overarching framework, a complex systems perspective can enable students to connect across domains and to make that knowledge useful outside of the narrow school contexts.

Last, we live in an increasingly connected world. As technology advances, more parts of the world make contact and interact. People can now travel to every conceivable corner of the world. Diseases from remote tropical rain forests find their ways to big cities continents away. Industrial gas emissions affect the polar icecaps, which in turn affect the weather at the equator. Economic downturns in a small European country can cause banks in the United States to fail. In short, the world cannot be understood in terms of isolated systems. To address the many societal and natural challenges we face, it is important for students and an informed citizenry to understand the world as composed of complex systems with many interacting components.

Complex Systems in Education

Complex systems thinking is a dramatic change in perspective that opens up new intellectual horizons, explanatory frameworks, and methodologies that are increasingly important in scientific and professional environments. While some complex systems concepts – such as evolution by natural selection – are found in school curricula in the physical and social sciences, the cross-domain nature of these concepts is not currently identified or exploited. Several concepts and methodologies are becoming key conceptual tools for qualitative reasoning and quantitative modeling and for simulation of real complex systems as well as synthetic or artificial systems. These include interdependence, emergent patterning, cellular automata, agent-based modeling, dynamical attractors, deterministic chaos, scale-free and small-world network topologies, system-environment interaction, fitness landscapes, and self-organization (Bar-Yam, 1997; Pagels, 1988; Simon, 1999).

Unfortunately, little of the conceptual power embodied in the rapidly developing perspectives and tools of complex systems has informed most people's educational experience at almost any level. While some courses in agent-based modeling and network theory have reached the undergraduate curriculum, there is generally little educational exposure to complex systems in university education, and none at all in primary or secondary education. This absence from mainstream education creates many missed opportunities for building links between disparate curricular elements and providing unifying, coherent conceptual frameworks. However, before complex systems perspectives are systematically introduced into precollege and undergraduate curricula, it is important to consider "learnability issues" related to these ideas. We next provide a brief review of literature that explores how learning sciences-based pedagogy can help students understand the important dimensions of complex systems, and then consider ways that concepts and methodologies of studying complex systems raise important theoretical and methodological issues central to the field of learning sciences itself.

Complex Systems and Learning: A Review of the Literature

Contemporary research on learning complex systems ideas and perspectives falls into two main categories: *cognitive* challenges associated with understanding complex systems concepts and *pedagogical* research into learning complex systems perspectives. This section provides a review of the research in these two areas.

Complex Systems Concepts and Cognitive Challenges

Many of the core ideas associated with thinking about complex systems may be challenging for students to learn. Considerable research has documented a variety of difficulties students experience in learning concepts relevant to understanding complex systems that are currently taught in existing science courses. For example, many students – even at the college level – hold to misconceptions such as that chemical reactions stop at equilibrium (Kozma, Russell, Johnston, & Dershimer, 1990; Stieff & Wilensky, 2003) or that evolution is the result of trait use or disuse and that acquired traits are passed down from one generation to the next (Bishop & Anderson, 1990; Samarapungavan & Wiers, 1997). Further, important concepts related to complex systems may be counterintuitive (Casti, 1994; Wilensky & Resnick, 1999). For example, many people believe there is a linear relationship between the size of an action and its corresponding effect: a small action has a small effect; a large action, a correspondingly large effect (Casti, 1994). However, it is now commonly understood that in complex systems, a small action may have system interactions and amplifications that result in large influence (Gleick, 1987; Lorenz, 1963), which some researchers refer to as "tipping points" (Gladwell, 2000) or the "butterfly effect" (Lorenz, 1963).

Other researchers have proposed that people tend to favor explanations that assume centralized control and deterministic causality (Resnick & Wilensky, 1993; Wilensky & Resnick, 1995, 1999), that people harbor deep-seated resistance to ideas that describe phenomena in terms of emergence and self-organization, stochastic and decentralized processes (Feltovich, Spiro, & Coulson, 1989; Resnick, 1994, 1996; Wilensky, 1997; Wilensky & Resnick, 1995). Research suggests that individuals with complex systems expertise have specialized conceptual understandings that novices do not have (beyond their additional formal education) and that complex systems novices and experts use different ontologies when constructing solutions to complex systems problems (Jacobson, 2001). Undergraduate students who were novices with respect to their understanding of complex systems were found to solve complex systems problems using a set of mechanistic ontological statements and centralized sources of control and predictable action paradigms. By contrast, complex systems experts solved these problems using a set of "complex systems" ontologies in which system control emerged as part of decentralized interactions of elements.

Other researchers, for example Hmelo-Silver and Pfeffer (2004), have documented that when children describe a complex aquatic system, they focus on the structures but provide little in the way of functional or mechanistic descriptions. In contrast, experts focus on the structural elements of the system, the elements' behaviors or mechanisms, and the system's functional aspects.

These findings are consistent with other research on expert and novice differences (Bransford, Brown, & Cocking, 2000; Chi, Glaser, & Farr, 1988; Larkin, McDermott, Simon, & Simon, 1980) and with recent theories of conceptual change that propose that cognitive structures – such as individuals' epistemological and ontological beliefs – can strongly affect a learner's ability to understand particular types of higher-order concepts (Chi, 1992, 2005; diSessa, 1993; Vosniadou & Brewer, 1992, 1994). Chi, Roscoe, Slotta, Roy, and Chase have argued (2012) that for students to learn to reason about complex systems, they may need to go through a process of "strong" or "radical" conceptual change, because the standard direct-causal schema used to explain simple systems is inadequate to explain complex systems. To make sense of emergent phenomena such as diffusion, osmosis, and natural selection, they contend that an emergent-causal schema is needed, and that this schema is incommensurate with the direct-causal schema that children bring to the classroom. Others have countered that students do not need to replace their causal schemas, but rather can utilize resources from those schemas to reason about complex systems (Levy & Wilensky, 2008; Sengupta & Wilensky, 2009). There is evidence that students increase their understanding of electricity and natural selection even when they are not directly taught the emergent-causal schema, but rather by using agent-based models to leverage student resources for connecting micro-level direct-causal actions with their emergent outcomes. In a set of 31 interviews about emergent phenomena with 8–16 grade students, Barth-Cohen (2012) found that students' emergent thinking is not a unified entity; rather, it is diverse in nature and varies across problem contexts and the kinds of prior knowledge that students evoke. She concluded that instruction should emphasize the generative process of explaining based on students' prior knowledge, rather than any a priori taxonomy of forms of explanations to be learned. This debate is not yet resolved, and to some extent parallels the debate in conceptual change research as described in diSessa (Chapter 5, this volume).

Pedagogical Research into Learning Complex Systems Ideas

Some of the earliest research projects that investigated students' complex systems learning were conducted by Resnick and Wilensky (Resnick & Wilensky, 1993; Wilensky & Resnick, 1995, 1999). These qualitative studies explored students' use of the StarLogo agent-based modeling program in thinking and learning about common examples of complex systems such as traffic jams and ants foraging for food. This work demonstrated that students were able to use an agent-based modeling tool to support their reasoning and thinking about different types of complex systems. However, students' new knowledge was often fragile and students reverted to noncomplex systems ways of thinking when asked about novel situations.

As noted earlier, a centrally important concept in complex systems research is *emergence*; that is, how local interactions of complex system elements at the micro level contribute to higher-order, macro-level patterns that may have qualitatively different characteristics. However, research by Penner (2000, 2001) has documented that the concept of emergent patterning in complex systems is very difficult for students to learn from classroom activities. Even when micro- and macro-level relationships are appreciated, students were found to ascribe causal primacy to the system's macro level, which is contrary to the complex systems perspective, wherein higher-order properties emerge from the local interactions and not the reverse.

Wilensky and his colleagues at Northwestern's Center for Connected Learning and Computer-Based Modeling have conducted extensive research on student learning about complex systems while using the NetLogo (Wilensky, 1999b) agent-based modeling (ABM) environment. To model a phenomenon with an ABM, the modeler decomposes the phenomenon into its micro-level components, or *agents*, and finds the *rules* for agent action and interaction that generate the macro-level emergent phenomenon (see Sawyer, 2003). Wilensky and colleagues have used NetLogo with a wide variety of contexts and age levels (with a particular focus on middle and high school students in urban schools), exploring, modifying, and constructing ABMs. Case studies of ordinary students doing extraordinary projects in such environments have been conducted, such as middle and high school students deriving the ideal gas law from the micro-level interactions of gas particles in a box (Levy & Wilensky, 2009; Wilensky, 1999a, 2003; Wilensky, Hazzard, & Froemke, 1999), exploring and modeling evolutionary processes (Centola, Wilensky, & McKenzie, 2000; Wagh & Wilensky, 2012; Wilensky & Novak, 2010), exploring core phenomena of materials science (Blikstein & Wilensky, 2009, 2010), and modeling the synchronized flashing of fireflies (Wilensky & Reisman, 2006).

These researchers have also documented difficulties students have in taking on an agent-based perspective and constructing emergent explanations of macro-level phenomena. They have described these difficulties collectively as a "deterministic-centralized mindset" (Resnick & Wilensky, 1993; Wilensky et al., 1999). One way to help students move beyond this mindset is to situate the discussion of complex phenomena in everyday contexts in which students are not merely observers, but also actual participants (Levy & Wilensky, 2004). For example, "participatory simulations" may be used in which students in a classroom act out the roles of micro-level system components and then contrast and compare the results of the classroom system with the behavior of a complex everyday system (Abrahamson & Wilensky, 2004; Abrahamson, Blikstein, & Wilensky, 2007; Colella, Borovoy, & Resnick, 1998; Resnick & Wilensky, 1998; Wilensky & Stroup, 1999). To facilitate innovative participatory simulation, Wilensky and Stroup (1999) have developed the simulation architecture HubNet. HubNet-based participatory simulations have been used to help students learn about a variety of complex systems, from molecular interactions to the spread of epidemics (Wilensky & Stroup, 2000). Analyses of students' reasoning while engaged in participatory simulations and making sense of these different types of complex systems indicated that students need two basic and complementary forms of reasoning: the "agent-based" form, in which students reason from the properties and behavior of individual system elements; and the "aggregate" form, in which students reason about the properties and rates of change of populations and other macro-level structures (Berland & Wilensky, 2005; Levy & Wilensky, 2004; Wilensky & Stroup, 2000; Wilkerson-Jerde & Wilensky, in press).

Students' interactions with simulations of complex phenomena can make them aware of their misconceptions and potentially foster opportunities for the students to articulate and modify these conceptions (Goldstone & Wilensky, 2008). Studying classroom discussions of students engaged in participatory simulations, Wilensky and Abrahamson (2005a) characterized dimensions of complex phenomena that trigger incorrect micro-to-macro inferences. These dimensions include spatial-dynamic cues inherent in the simulations, such as the agents' *velocity* and *density*, and more conceptual or mental-simulation reasoning that interacts with spatial-dynamic cues, such as (a) failing to anticipate *emergence* inherent in agents' rule-based interactions; (b) *proportional/linear* reasoning when it doesn't apply; (c) *randomness versus determinism* confusion; and (d) ignoring the effect of *feedback loops*. Wilensky and Abrahamson concluded that "complex system heuristics" are difficult for learners to develop because they often run counter to "linear system heuristics" that seem more grounded in students' everyday experiences. They recommended that students work with complex systems simulations so as to develop a repertory of cases that may then serve as analogs for reasoning about complex phenomena (see also Goldstone & Wilensky, 2008). They observed students working with such simulations beginning to develop a complex systems mindset enabling them to complexify their models of systemic phenomena to build and defend their assertions.

Wilensky and Stroup (2000) conjectured that "agent-based" (micro-level) and "aggregate" (macro-level) perspectives are complementary – both are needed for a robust understanding of complex systems. Students participating in HubNet simulations were observed to rapidly alternate between bottom-up (micro-level, agent-based) and top-down (macro-level, aggregate) perspectives, which in turn gave them greater explanatory power in discussing different types of complex systems. Wilensky, Hazzard, and Longenecker (2000) achieved promising results by explicitly teaching students this alternation strategy, using what they called "emergent exercises."

In further research on students' understanding of agent and aggregate levels of complex systems, Levy and Wilensky (2008) interviewed sixth grade students about everyday events for which both micro- and macro-level explanations were possible. They found a pervasive strategy among the students that involved constructing a "mid-level" – a new level between the micro and macro levels. A mid-level, typically made up of small groups of individual components in the system, appeared to reduce the amount of information needed to reason about the system. The cognitive construction of a mid-level thus helped students form mental models that students used in two main ways in their more general understanding of complex systems principles. One way was *bottom-up*, in which small groups were formed as a result of local interactions. The bottom-up mid-level way of thinking was associated with a greater understanding of complex systems principles such as equilibration and stochasm. The second way that students formed mid-levels was *top-down*, in which the whole system was dissolved into smaller groups that were treated as single entities. The top-down mid-level approach was associated with a less robust understanding of complex systems.

Research by Yoon (2008) has employed a complexity perspective to help students more deeply understand a challenging scientific area, genetic engineering, as well as to study the dynamics of the classroom interactions as a complex system. Another program of research investigates conceptual change in learning complex systems ideas (Charles, 2003; Charles & d'Appollonia, 2004). Charles (2003) conducted an experimental design that involved a three-day workshop in which students (ages 16–18) in the experimental group heard class lectures on complex systems concepts, ran StarLogoT (Wilensky, 1997) models of different types of complex systems, and had class discussions. Using a revised version of the complex systems analytical framework proposed by Jacobson (2001), students in the experimental group were found to employ an "emergent" explanatory framework to solve near and moderate transfer questions about complex systems phenomena, and to use significantly fewer "clockwork" explanations on near transfer questions than students in the control condition. Charles and Appollonia (2004) conducted a qualitative case study with nine students from the Charles (2003) study who received cognitive coaching while working with a set of StarLogoT complex systems models. The process-oriented data collected in the second study indicated that although students showed learning gains related to four of the six concepts they were taught about emergent causal processes, they had difficulty understanding the concepts of "random actions" and "nonlinear effects" of complex system agents. Recent research also suggests that nonlinearity is a particularly difficult complex systems construct for learners to understand (Jacobson, Kapur, So, & Lee, 2011).

Horn and Wilensky (2012) developed a version of NetLogo, called NetTango, that runs on a tabletop surface. The agents are controlled by placing blocks on the table that are read by a camera and interpreted as commands to the agents. They found that this new interface enabled much younger learners (ages 6–10) to have rich discussions of complex systems concepts (Olson & Horn, 2011; Olson, Horn, & Wilensky, 2010). There is also recent work on developing curriculum materials in which complex systems ideas are integrated with high school biology topics with the goal of enhancing the depth of student understanding of centrally important scientific knowledge in the standard science curriculum (Goh, Yoon, Wang, Yang, & Klopfer, 2012; Wagh & Wilensky, 2012a, 2012b, 2013; Wilensky & Novak, 2010).

While we are still at an early stage of research into learning about complex systems, overall, the studies discussed earlier suggest that K-12 students can learn and benefit from important concepts and perspectives about complex systems. Whereas some may think that complex systems thinking is so difficult that it should only be taught at the graduate level, these studies provide substantial evidence that younger students can understand complex systems ideas. Some of these ideas, such as nonlinearity, emergent properties, and stochastic processes, have been found to be challenging for students to learn. However, the application of diverse theory and research perspectives from the learning sciences is starting to shed light on factors that contribute to learning even difficult ideas such as these. Researchers are developing innovative pedagogies and technologies that may help students develop a richer set of cognitive resources that scaffold their learning about complex systems ideas and methods.

Complex Systems and Curriculum

Current science curricula are often criticized for superficially covering too many subjects, resulting in students failing to gain a solid understanding of any one single domain (Bransford, Brown, & Cocking, 2000; National Research Council, 1996). Consequently, it is vital that educational materials for complex systems not be developed as "add-ons" to an already bloated STEM curriculum.

There are many ways complex systems concepts could be infused into school curricula to form the basis of a new type of scientific literacy (Jacobson, 2001). Concepts derived from the complex systems perspective could provide organization to bewildering properties of diverse phenomena in the physical and social sciences. Complex systems concepts like *self-organization* and *positive feedback* can be applied to biological systems such as insect colonies (Dorigo & Stuetzle, 2004; Resnick, 1994) and to social science systems such as national and global economies (Anderson, Arrow, & Pines, 1988; Epstein & Axtell, 1996; Sawyer, 2005). Research is needed to explore how pedagogies and curricular materials, organized around a complex systems perspective, could help students make conceptual links between traditionally separate subject areas in the natural and social sciences such as chemistry, biology, psychology, and economics. Furthermore, cognitively powerful cross-domain links may be fostered by designing models and simulation tools that help students identify structural and functional similarities across these very different systems. Most students have little reason to believe that a simulation capturing a cell's genetic network and one capturing the topology of the World Wide Web share much in common. Yet many physical and social networks are similar, such as *scale-free networks* (Barabasi & Albert, 1999), that look the same no matter at what level of magnification you view them and that develop over time using simple mechanisms of growth and preferential attachment.[1] Future research could explore whether complex systems-infused curricula allow for additional depth of coverage of traditional physical and social science subjects, or for cross-disciplinary conceptual and cognitive "hooks" that may support far transfer of knowledge to dramatically new situations and problems.

Over the past decade, learning scientists and computer scientists have called for students to learn computational thinking (Bundy, 2007) and to gain computational literacy (diSessa, 2000). While there is still some debate as to the exact meaning of these terms, there is broad agreement that 21st-century students must learn to partner with computers to obtain, manipulate, and analyze large datasets and to work with computational models. As described in the introduction, complex systems grew up alongside and is deeply reliant on computation. As such, it provides both a framework and a context for the practice of computational thinking.

In addition, complex systems phenomena are well suited to problem- and inquiry-centered learning that implements constructivist models of teaching. Research could investigate whether learner-centered curricula that integrate complex systems perspectives ameliorate some students' view of science as rote memorization irrelevant to everyday life. Research could also explore if such a curricular approach helps make cross-disciplinary connections cognitively easier for students to learn.

Implications of Complex Systems for the Learning Sciences

The conceptual frameworks and principles of complex systems raise many important theoretical and methodological issues for the learning sciences. The multidisciplinary fields that study various types of complex systems use a set of conceptual perspectives and scientific methodologies that function as a shared framework for the discourse and representations used in scientific inquiry. The potential scientific value of complex systems is best

[1] See http://ccl.northwestern.edu/netlogo/models/preferentialattachment for a NetLogo model of this mechanism.

reflected by Kauffman's (1995) observation that we may be at a historic juncture at which the relentless reductionism (i.e., increased fragmentation into narrow subspecialties) that has occurred over the past three centuries of scientific work may be coming to an end. For learning sciences researchers, an important question may be asked: What do complex systems perspectives provide that is not already represented in the conceptual and methodological toolkits of the field? Complex systems perspectives can enhance learning sciences theory through the computational modeling of systems of learning and education. Jacobson and Kapur (2012) contend that the traditional qualitative and quantitative methods of the learning sciences do not suffice to explain learning, because learning itself is a complex phenomenon. They argue that existing methods fail to adequately address the issues of nonlinearity, temporality, spatiality, and phase space that are central to understanding emergent phenomena. They propose that these issues can be addressed by integrating computational agent-based methods with existing quantitative and qualitative methods.

In recent years, there has been a major shift in our understanding of what constitutes a legitimate source of scientific information (Jackson, 1996). The origins of modern science are often credited to Aristotle and his use of careful observations to obtain information on which to make informed decisions rather than the logical argumentation of philosophical beliefs. The next phase in the conduct of the inquiry now regarded as science came via the intellectual contributions of Brahe, Galileo, Newton, Kepler, Liebniz, and Euler, who not only advanced the field of mathematics, but also demonstrated how new scientific discoveries could be made through mathematical manipulations of observational data. The remarkable scientific achievements of the ensuing 300 years were predicated on these two approaches; observational and mathematically derived information have been the norm for almost all published research in the learning and cognitive sciences and in education to date.

However, Jackson (1996) has proposed that we are in the midst of a second historical metamorphosis in scientific inquiry, one involving the use of computational tools to generate a third legitimate source of scientific information. Others, such as Pagels (1988), have observed how the use of computational tools in science has dramatically enhanced capabilities to investigate complex and dynamical systems that could not otherwise be systematically investigated. These computational modeling approaches include cellular automata, agent-based modeling, and genetic algorithms, generally used in conjunction with scientific visualization techniques. Examples of complex systems that have been investigated with advanced computational modeling techniques include climate change (West & Dowlatabadi, 1999), urban transportation models (Balmer, Nagel, & Raney, 2004; Helbing & Nagel, 2004; Noth, Borning, & Waddell, 2000), and economics (Anderson et al., 1988; Arthur, Durlauf, & Lane, 1997; Axelrod, 1997; Epstein & Axtell, 1996). New communities of scientific practice have also emerged in which computational modeling techniques, especially agent-based models and genetic algorithms, are being used to create synthetic worlds such as artificial life (Langton, 1989, 1995) and artificial societies (Epstein & Axtell, 1996; Sawyer, 2003) that allow tremendous flexibility to explore theoretical and research questions in the physical and social sciences that would be difficult to impossible in "real," nonsynthetic settings.

Given the development of sophisticated computational modeling tools and their increased acceptance in a wide range of physical and social sciences fields, there is great potential in the application of computational methods to research in the learning sciences on complex learning within educational systems. Use of these methods would have four broad ramifications. First, the articulation of models, particularly "bottom-up" ones such as agent-based models, often help researchers distill their qualitative intuitions about critical factors most responsible for the behavior of the system of interest. Second, complex systems models become scientifically inspectable artifacts that may be compared to real-world data and iteratively revised to improve the fit of the model. Third, models validated with one or more datasets may be used to explore the behavior of the system by varying model parameters (via multiple runs on all parameter combinations to examine the system's stochastic properties). Fourth, such models may assist in generalizing findings from the observed and modeled system(s) to similar system types with different specific local features. The use of models and computation in these four ways can ultimately lead to a reformulation of the content of a knowledge domain in terms of computational representations, what Wilensky and Papert (2010) call "restructurations." The field of learning sciences will need to grapple with creating and choosing such discipline restructurations and evaluating their utility for researchers as well as students.

There are numerous examples of computational modeling of learning systems and learning environments. Lemke and Sabelli (2008) have proposed building "SimSchool" or "SimDistrict" simulation programs that would not just model existing school (or district) systems, but could also be used to create synthetic schools and district systems to study their evolution over time in terms of needs, problems, and probable outcomes. Some actual systems have been developed along these lines, such as agent-based simulations for areas of educational policy like school choice where parents and school officials are agents within the simulation (Lauen, 2007; Maroulis et al., in press; Maroulis et al., 2010; Maroulis & Wilensky, 2005) or modeling factors associated with successful versus nonsuccessful educational policy reforms (Levin & Datnow, 2012). Researchers are also utilizing agent-based modeling methods to articulate and test social science theory, arguing that modeling can support the development of richer theoretical models that integrate contrasting theories. Abrahamson and colleagues (Abrahamson & Wilensky, 2005b; Abrahamson, Wilensky, & Levin, 2007; Blikstein, Abrahamson, &

Wilensky, 2006) have used ABM to embody theories of learning and to contrast Piagetian and Vygotskian theories. Researchers are also using network analysis methods to study topics ranging from how social structure impacts technology's adoption in schools (Frank, Zhao, & Borman, 2004) to the role of social structure on student achievement (Maroulis & Gomez, 2008). Jacobson and Kapur (2012) have also applied network-theoretic methods to bridge between alternative theories of conceptual change. Related, Brown and Hammer (2008) have proposed that the processes of conceptual change may be understood from a complex systems theoretical perspective as being emergent, dynamic, and embedded. In other work, several researchers (e.g., Frey & Goldstone, 2013; Goldstone & Wilensky, 2008) have used participatory simulation environments as data collection tools whereby distributed subjects can be placed in an environment with programmed agents where their behavior and interactions can become data sources. Overall, there appears to be great potential for computational modeling to enhance learning sciences research at other micro and macro levels of cognitive and educational systems, from the evolution of cognitive representational networks and design experiments of technology interventions in classrooms to social network analysis of collaborative interactions patterns and educational policy initiatives.

Conclusion

This chapter has provided an overview of issues, research, and reflections on the potential need for primary and secondary students to learn about complex systems in the physical and social sciences. We expect the learning sciences to continue to generate research on learning that can contribute to our understanding of learning complex systems – research on topics such as conceptual change, knowledge transfer, and sociocultural dynamics of learning that are discussed in many of this handbook's chapters.

During the past few years, new science standards have been created in the United States that foreground the study of systems, modeling, and complexity. The Next Generation Science Standards (NGSS) use seven cross-cutting concepts to structure K-12 science learning: patterns, similarity, and diversity; cause and effect; scale, proportion, and quantity; systems and system models; energy and matter; structure and function; and stability and change. Arguably all of these concepts relate to complex systems and two of them mention complex systems explicitly. This presents an opportunity to infuse scientific understandings about complex systems into primary and secondary curricula. Research that explores student learning of complex systems ideas may expand our views of what kinds of advanced knowledge students are capable of learning, including understandings that are conceptually challenging. Moreover, conceptual perspectives and methodologies from complex systems have the potential to impact important theory and research issues within the field of learning sciences itself.

It has been just more than a decade since researchers began exploring the vast number of cognitive and learning issues associated with complex systems principles, as well as the theory and research implications such perspectives might hold for the learning sciences more generally. How the study of complex systems might impact the field of the learning sciences and the education system at large remains to be determined. In the next phases of research in these areas, we would do well to heed Proust's observation that "the real voyage of discovery lies not in finding new landscapes, but in having new eyes."

References

Abrahamson, D., Blikstein, P., & Wilensky, U. (2007). *Classroom model, model classroom: Computer-supported methodology for investigating collaborative-learning pedagogy*. Proceedings of the Computer Supported Collaborative Learning (CSCL) Conference. New Brunswick, NJ.

Abrahamson, D., & Wilensky, U. (2004). ProbLab: A computer-supported unit in probability and statistics. In M. J. Hoines & A. B. Fuglestad (Eds.), *Proceedings of the 28th Annual Meeting of the International Group for the Psychology of Mathematics Education* (Vol. 1, p. 369). Bergen University College, Norway.

Abrahamson, D., & Wilensky, U. (2005a). Is a disease like a lottery? Classroom networked technology that enables student reasoning about complexity. Paper presented at the annual meeting of the American Educational Research Association, San Francisco, CA.

Abrahamson, D., & Wilensky, U. (2005b). *Piaget? Vygotsky? I'm game: Agent-based modeling for psychology research*. Proceedings of the annual meeting of the Jean Piaget Society, Vancouver, B.C.

Abrahamson, D., Wilensky, U., & Levin, J. (2007). Agent-based modeling as a bridge between cognitive and social perspectives on learning. Paper presented at the annual meeting of the American Educational Research Association. Chicago, IL.

Anderson, P. W., Arrow, K. J., & Pines, D. (Eds.) (1988). *The economy as an evolving complex system* (Vol. 5). Redwood City, CA: Addison-Wesley.

Arthur, B., Durlauf, S., & Lane, D. (Eds.) (1997). *The economy as an evolving complex system* (Vol. II). Reading, MA: Addison-Wesley.

Axelrod, R. (1997). *The complexity of cooperation: Agent-based models of competition and collaboration*. Princeton, NJ: Princeton University Press.

Axelrod, R., & Cohen, M. D. (1999). *Harnessing complexity: Organizational implications of a scientific frontier*. New York: The Free Press.

Balmer, M., Nagel, K., & Raney, B. (2004). Large-scale multi-agent simulations for transportation applications. *Intelligent Transportation Systems*, 8, 1–17.

Bar-Yam, Y. (1997). *Dynamics of complex systems*. Reading, MA: Addison-Wesley.

Bar-Yam, Y. (2003). *Dynamics of complex systems*. New York: Perseus Publishing.

Barabasi, A. L., & Albert, R. (1999). Emergence of scaling in random networks. *Science*, 286(5439), 509–512.

Barthes-Cohen, L. (2012). Theoretical issues: Indicators of decentralized and centralized causality as a gauge for students' understanding of complex systems. In P. Freebody, T. de Jong, E. Kyza, & P. Reimann (Eds.), *Proceedings of the International Conference of the Learning Sciences: Future of Learning (ICLS 2012)*. Sydney: University of Sydney/ICLS.

Berland, M., & Wilensky, U. (2005). Complex play systems: Results from a classroom implementation of VBot. Paper presented at the annual meeting of the American Educational Research Association, Montreal, Canada.

Bishop, B. A., & Anderson, C. W. (1990). Student conceptions of natural selection and its role in evolution. *Journal of Research in Science Teaching*, 27(5), 415–427.

Blikstein, P., Abrahamson, D., & Wilensky, U. (2006). *Minsky, mind, and models: Juxtaposing agent-based computer simulations and clinical-interview data as a methodology for investigating cognitive-developmental theory*. Proceedings of the annual meeting of the Jean Piaget Society, Baltimore, MD.

Blikstein, P., & Wilensky, U. (2009). An atom is known by the company it keeps: A constructionist learning environment for materials science using multi-agent simulation. *International Journal of Computers for Mathematical Learning*, 14(2), 81–119.

Blikstein, P., & Wilensky, U. (2010). MaterialSim: A constructionist agent-based modeling approach to engineering education. In M. J. Jacobson & P. Reimann (Eds.), *Designs for learning environments of the future: International perspectives from the learning sciences* (pp. 17–60). New York: Springer.

Bransford, J. D., Brown, A. L., & Cocking, R. R. (Eds.). (2000). *How people learn: Brain, mind, experience, and school*. Washington, DC: National Academies Press.

Brown, D. E., & Hammer, D. (2008). Conceptual change in physics. In S. Vosniadou (Ed.), *Handbook of research on conceptual change* (pp. 127–154). Hillsdale, NJ: Lawrence Erlbaum Associates.

Brown, S. L., & Eisenhardt, K. M. (1998). *Competing on the edge: Strategy as structured chaos*. Boston, MA: Harvard Business School Press.

Bundy, A. (2007). Computational thinking is pervasive. *J. Scient. Pract. Comput.*, **1**, 67–69.

Casti, J. L. (1994). *Complexificantion: Explaining a paradoxical world through the science of surprise*. New York: HarperCollins.

Centola, D., Wilensky, U., & McKenzie, E. (2000, May). Survival of the groupiest: Facilitating students' understanding of the multiple levels of fitness through multi-agent modeling – The EACH Project. Paper presented at the *International Conference on Complex Systems*. May 21–26, Nashua, NH.

Charles, E. S. (2003). An ontological approach to conceptual change: The role that complex systems thinking may play in providing the explanatory framework needed for studying contemporary sciences. PhD Dissertation at Concordia University, Montreal, Quebec, Canada, April 2003.

Charles, E. S., & d'Apollonia, S. (2004, August). Developing a conceptual framework to explain emergent causality: Overcoming ontological beliefs to achieve conceptual change. In K. Forbus, D. Gentner, & T. Reiger (Eds.),

Proceedings of the 26th Annual Cognitive Science Society (pp. 210–215). Mahwah, N.J.: Lawrence Erlbaum Associates.

Chi, M. T. H. (1992). Conceptual change within and across ontological categories: Implications for learning and discovery in science. In R. Giere (Ed.), *Minnesota studies in the philosophy of science: Cognitive models of science* (vol. XV, pp. 129–186). Minneapolis: University of Minnesota Press.

Chi, M. T. H. (2005). Commonsense conceptions of emergent processes: Why some misconceptions are robust. *The Journal of the Learning Sciences*, 14(2), 161–199.

Chi, M. T. H., Glaser, R., & Farr, M. J. (Eds.) (1988). *The nature of expertise.* Hillsdale, NJ: Lawrence Erlbaum Associates.

Chi, M. T. H., Roscoe, R., Slotta, J., Roy, M., & Chase, M. (2012). Misconceived causal explanations for "emergent" processes. *Cognitive Science,* 36, 1–61.

Colella, V., Borovoy, R., & Resnick, M. (1998). Participatory simulations: Using computational objects to learn about dynamic systems. Paper presented at the Computer Human Interface (CHI) '98 Conference, Los Angeles, CA.

diSessa, A. A. (1993). Towards an epistemology of physics. *Cognition and Instruction,* 10(2), 105–225.

diSessa, A. A. (2000). *Changing minds: Computers, learning, and literacy.* Cambridge, MA: MIT Press.

Dorigo, M., & Stuetzle, T. (2004). *Ant colony optimization.* Cambridge, MA: MIT Press.

Epstein, J. M. (2006). *Generative social science: Studies in agent-based computational modeling.* Princeton, NJ: Princeton University Press.

Epstein, J. M., & Axtell, R. (1996). *Growing artificial societies: Social science from the bottom up.* Washington, DC: Brookings Institution Press/MIT Press.

Feltovich, P. J., Spiro, R. J., & Coulson, R. L. (1989). The nature of conceptual understanding in biomedicine: The deep structure of complex ideas and the development of misconceptions. In D. Evans & V. Patel (Eds.), *The cognitive sciences in medicine* (pp. 113–172). Cambridge, MA: MIT Press.

Frank, K. A., Zhao, Y., & Borman, K. (2004). Social capital and the diffusion of innovations within organizations: Application to the implementation of computer technology in schools. *Sociology of Education*, 77, 148–171.

Frey, S., & Goldstone, R. L. (2013). Cyclic game dynamics driven by iterated reasoning. *PLoS ONE*, 8(2): e56416.

Gell-Mann, M. (1994). *The quark and the jaguar: Adventures in the simple and the complex.* New York: Freeman and Company.

Gladwell, M. (2000). *The tipping point.* New York: Little, Brown.

Gleick, J. (1987). *Chaos: Making a new science.* New York: Viking Penguin.

Goh, S.-E., Yoon, S., Wang, J., Yang, Z., & Klopfer, E. (2012). Investigating the relative difficulty of various complex systems ideas in biology. In J. van Aalst, K. Thompson, M. J. Jacobson & P. Reimann (Eds.), *The future of learning: Proceedings of the 10th international conference of the learning sciences (ICLS 2012) – Volume 1, Full Papers* (pp. 72–79). Sydney, Australia: ISLS.

Goldstone, R. L., & Wilensky, U. (2008). Promoting transfer through grounding complex systems principles. *Journal of the Learning Sciences*, 26(1), 465–516.

Gulati, R. (1998). Alliances and networks. *Strategic Management Journal*, 19(4), 293–317.

Helbing, D., & Nagel, K. (2004). The physics of traffic and regional development. *Contemporary Physics*, 45(5), 405–426.

Hmelo-Silver, C. E., & Pfeffer, M. G. (2004). Comparing expert and novice understanding of a complex system from the perspective of structures, behaviors, and functions. *Cognitive Science*, 1, 127–138.

Holland, J. H. (1995). *Hidden order: How adaptation builds complexity*. Reading, MA: Addison-Wesley.

Horn, M. S., & Wilensky, U. (2012). NetTango: A mash-up of NetLogo and Tern. In Moher, T. (chair) and Pinkard, N. (discussant), *When systems collide: Challenges and opportunities in learning technology mash-ups*. Symposium presented at the annual meeting of the American Education Research Association, Vancouver, British Columbia.

Jackson, E. A. (1996). *The second metamorphosis of science: A second view*. Santa Fe, NM: Santa Fe Institute.

Jacobson, M. J. (2001). Problem solving, cognition, and complex systems: Differences between experts and novices. *Complexity*, 6(3), 41–49.

Jacobson, M. J., & Kapur, M. (2012). Learning environments as emergent phenomena: Theoretical and methodological implications of complexity. In D. Jonassen & S. Land (Eds.), *Theoretical foundations of learning environments*. Second Edition. (pp. 303–334). New York: Springer.

Jacobson, M. J., Kapur, M., So, H. -J., & Lee, J. (2011). The ontologies of complexity and learning about complex systems. *Instructional Science*, 39, 763–783.

Kaput, J., Bar-Yam, Y., Jacobson, M. J., Jakobsson, E., Lemke, J., & Wilensky, U. (2001). Planning documents for a national initiative on complex systems in K–16 education: Two roles for complex systems in education: Mainstream content and means for understanding the education system itself. Final report to the National Science Foundation on Project #REC-9980241. Cambridge, MA: New England Complex Systems Institute.

Kauffman, S. (1993). *The origins of order: Self-organization and selection in evolution*. New York: Oxford University Press.

Kauffman, S. (1995). *At home in the universe: The search for laws of self-organization and complexity*. New York: Oxford University Press.

Kauffman, S. (2000). *Investigations*. New York: Oxford University Press.

Kozma, R., Russell, J., Johnston, J., & Dershimer, C. (1990). College students' conceptions and misconceptions of chemical equilibrium. Paper presented at the meeting of the American Educational Research Association, Boston, MA.

Langton, C. (Ed.) (1989). *Artificial life*. Redwood City, CA: Addison-Wesley.

Langton, C. (Ed.) (1995). *Artificial life: An overview*. Cambridge, MA: MIT Press.

Larkin, J. H., McDermott, J., Simon, D. P., & Simon, H. A. (1980). Expert and novice performance in solving physics problems. *Science*, 208, 1335–1342.

Lauen, L. L. (2007). Contextual explanations of school choice. *Education and Educational Research*, 80(3), 179–209.

Lemke, J., & Sabelli, N. (2008). Complex systems and educational change: Towards a new research agenda. *Educational Philosophy and Theory*, 40(1), 118–129.

Levin, J. A., & Datnow, A. (2012). The principal role in data driven decision making: Using case study data to develop multi-mediator models of educational reform. *School Effectiveness and School Improvement*, 23(2), 179–201.

Levy, S. T., & Wilensky, U. (2004). Making sense of complexity: Patterns in forming causal connections between individual agent behaviors and aggregate group behaviors. Paper presented at the annual meeting of the American Educational Research Association, San Diego, CA.

Levy, S. T., & Wilensky, U. (2008). Inventing a "mid level" to make ends meet: Reasoning between the levels of complexity. *Cognition and Instruction*, 26(1), 1–47.

Levy, S. T., & Wilensky, U. (2009). Students' learning with the connected chemistry (cc1) curriculum: Navigating the complexities of the particulate world. *Journal of Science Education and Technology*, 18(3), 243–254.

Lorenz, E. N. (1963). Deterministic nonperiodic flow. *Journal of Atmospheric Science*, 20, 130–141.

Maroulis, S., Bakshy, E., Gomez, L., & Wilensky, U. (in press). Modeling the transition to public school choice. *Journal of Artificial Societies and Social Simulation*.

Maroulis, S., & Gomez, L. (2008). Does "connectedness" matter? Evidence from a social network analysis of a small school reform. *Teachers College Record*, 110(9), 1901–1929.

Maroulis, S., Guimera, R., Petry, H., Stringer, M., Gomez, L., Amaral, L., & Wilensky, U. (2010). A complex systems approach to educational policy research. *Science*, 330(6000), 38.

Maroulis, S., & Wilensky, U. (2005). Leave no turtle behind: An agent-based simulation of school choice dynamics. Paper presented at the annual meeting of the American Educational Research Association, Montreal, Canada.

Mitchell, M. (2009). *Complexity: A guided tour*. New York: Oxford University Press.

National Research Council. (1996). *National science education standards*. Washington, DC: National Academies Press.

Noth, M., Borning, A., & Waddell, P. (2000). *An extensible, modular architecture for simulating urban development, transportation, and environmental impacts*. Department of Computer Science and Engineering, University of Washington.

Olson, I. C., & Horn, M. (2011). Modeling on the table: Agent-based modeling in elementary school with NetTango. In *Proc. Interaction Design and Children IDC'11*, ACM Press, 189–192.

Olson, I. C., Horn. M. S., & Wilensky, U. (2010). NetLogo Tango: Scaffolding student programming with tangible objects and multi-touch tabletop displays. Workshop paper presented at the 9th International Conference of the Learning Sciences, June 29th, Chicago IL.

Pagels, H. R. (1988). *The dreams of reason: The computer and the rise of the sciences of complexity*. New York: Simon & Schuster.

Penner, D. E. (2000). Explaining systems: Investigating middle school students' understanding of emergent phenomena. *Journal of Research in Science Teaching*, 37, 784–806.

Penner, D. E. (2001). Complexity, emergence, and synthetic models in science education. In K. Crowley, C. D. Schunn, & T. Okada (Eds.), *Designing for science* (pp. 177–208). Mahwah, NJ: Lawrence Erlbaum Associates.

Reagans, R., & Zuckerman, E. W. (2001). Networks, diversity, and productivity: The social capital of corporate R&D teams. *Organization Science*, 12(4), 502–517.

Resnick, M. (1994). *Turtles, termites, and traffic jams: Explorations in massively parallel microworlds*. Cambridge, MA: MIT Press.

Resnick, M. (1996). Beyond the centralized mindset. *The Journal of the Learning Sciences*, 5(1), 1–22.

Resnick, M., & Wilensky, U. (1993). Beyond the deterministic, centralized mindsets: A new thinking for new science. Paper presented at the annual meeting of the American Educational Research Association, Atlanta, GA.

Resnick, M., & Wilensky, U. (1998). Diving into complexity: Developing probabilistic decentralized thinking through role-playing activities. *Journal of Learning Science*, 7(2), 153–172.

Samarapungavan, A., & Wiers, R. W. (1997). Children's thoughts on the origin of species: A study of explanatory coherence. *Cognitive Science*, 21(2), 147–177.

Sawyer, R. K. (2003). Artificial societies: Multi agent systems and the micro-macro link in sociological theory. *Sociological Methods and Research*, 31(3), 37–75.

Sawyer, R. K. (2005). *Social emergence: Societies as complex systems*. New York: Cambridge.

Senge, P. M. (1990). *The fifth discipline: The art and practice of the learning organization*. New York: Doubleday.

Sengupta, P., & Wilensky, U. (2009). Learning electricity with niels: Thinking with electrons and thinking in levels. *International Journal of Computers for Mathematical Learning*, 14(1), 21–50.

Simon, H. A. (1999). Can there be a science of complex systems? In Y. Bar-Yam (Ed.), *Unifying themes in complex systems* (pp. 3–14). Cambridge, MA: Perseus Books.

Stieff, M., & Wilensky, U. (2003). Connected chemistry: Incorporating interactive simulations into the chemistry classroom. *Journal of Science Education and Technology*, 12(3), 285–302.

Uzzi, B. (1997). Social structure and competition in interfirm networks: The paradox of embeddedness. *Administrative Science Quarterly*, 42(1), 35–67.

Vosniadou, S., & Brewer, W. F. (1992). Mental models of the earth: A study of conceptual change in childhood. *Cognitive Psychology*, 24, 535–585.

Vosniadou, S., & Brewer, W. F. (1994). Mental models of the day/night cycle. *Cognitive Science*, 18(1), 123–183.

Wagh, A., & Wilensky, U. (2012a). *Breeding birds to learn about artificial selection: Two birds with one stone?* Proceedings of ICLS, Sydney, Australia, July 2–6.

Wagh, A., & Wilensky, U. (2012b). *Evolution in blocks: Building models of evolution using blocks*. Proceedings of Constructionism, Athens, Greece, August 21–25.

Wagh, A., & Wilensky, U. (2013). *Leveling the playing field: Making multi-level evolutionary processes accessible through participatory simulations*. Proceedings of CSCL, Madison, Wisconsin, June 15–19.

Waldrop, M. M. (1992). *Complexity: The emerging science at the edge of order and chaos*. New York: Simon & Schuster.

Watts, D. J., & Strogatz, S. (1998). Collective dynamics of "small world" networks. *Nature*, (393), 440–442.

West, J. J., & Dowlatabadi, H. (1999). On assessing the economic impacts of sea-level rise on developed coasts. In T. E. Downing, A. A. Olsthoorn, & R. S. J. Tol (Eds.), *Climate change and risk* (pp. 205–220). New York: Routledge.

Wilensky, U. (1997). What is normal anyway? Therapy for epistemological anxiety. *Educational Studies in Mathematics*, 33(2), 171–202.

Wilensky, U. (1999a). GasLab: An extensible modeling toolkit for exploring micro- and macro- views of gases. In N. Roberts, W. Feurzeig, & B. Hunter (Eds.), *Computer modeling and simulation in science education*. Berlin: Springer Verlag.

Wilensky, U. (1999b). *NetLogo*. Evanston, IL: Center for Connected Learning and Computer-Based Modeling. Northwestern University (http://ccl.north-western.edu/netlogo).

Wilensky, U. (2003). Statistical mechanics for secondary school: The GasLab Modeling Toolkit. *International Journal of Computers for Mathematical Learning*, 8(1), 1–41.

Wilensky, U., Hazzard, E., & Froemke, R. (1999). An extensible modeling toolkit for exploring statistical mechanics. Proceedings of the Seventh European Logo Conference – EUROLOGO '99, Sofia, Bulgaria.

Wilensky, U., Hazzard, E., & Froemke, R. (2000). *A bale of turtles: A case study of a middle school science class studying complexity using StarLogoT.* New York: Spencer Foundation. October 11–13.

Wilensky, U., & Novak, M. (2010). Understanding evolution as an emergent process: Learning with agent-based models of evolutionary dynamics. In R. S. Taylor & M. Ferrari (Eds.), *Epistemology and science education: Understanding the evolution vs. intelligent design controversy.* New York: Routledge.

Wilensky, U., & Papert, S. (2010). Restructurations: Reformulations of Knowledge Disciplines through new representational forms. In J. Clayson & I. Kalas (Eds.), *Proceedings of the Constructionism 2010 Conference. Paris, France, Aug 10-14.* p. 97.

Wilensky, U., & Reisman, K. (2006). Thinking like a wolf, a sheep, or a firefly: Learning biology through constructing and testing computational theories. *Cognition and Instruction*, 24(2), 171–209.

Wilensky, U., & Resnick, M. (1995). New thinking for new sciences: Constructionist approaches for exploring complexity. Paper presented at the annual meeting of the American Educational Research Association, San Francisco, CA.

Wilensky, U., & Resnick, M. (1999). Thinking in levels: A dynamic systems perspective to making sense of the world. *Journal of Science Education and Technology*, 8(1), 3–19.

Wilensky, U., & Resnick, M. (1999). Learning through participatory simulations: Network-based design for systems learning in classrooms. Proceedings of the Computer Supported Collaborative Learning Conference (CSCL '99), Palo Alto, CA.

Wilensky, U., & Resnick, M. (2000). Networked gridlock: Students enacting complex dynamic phenomena with the HubNet architecture. In B. Fishman & S. O'Connor-Divelbiss (Eds.), *Fourth international conference of the learning sciences* (pp. 282–289). Mahwah, NJ: Lawrence Erlbaum Associates.

Wilkerson-Jerde, M., & Wilensky, U. (in press). Designed and emergent pedagogical supports for coordinating quantitative and agent-based descriptions of complex dynamic systems. Accepted for presentation at PME-NA 2011.

Wolfram, S. (2002). *A new kind of science*. Champaign, IL: Wolfram Media.

Yoon, S. A. (2008). An evolutionary approach to harnessing complex systems thinking in the science and technology classroom. *International Journal of Science Education*, 30(1), 1–32.

17 Tangible and Full-Body Interfaces in Learning

Michael Eisenberg and Narcis Pares

In the past half century, educational technology has generally been closely associated with computers – so much so that other forms of educational technology are rarely considered. No doubt, over these past 50 years, what we think of as a computer has evolved quite a bit – from the classroom-wide instructional systems pioneered by researchers such as Patrick Suppes in the 1960s, to personal desktop computers in the 1980s, and (more recently) to portable and handheld devices. Nonetheless, all of these educational technologies share the core features of the computer: a central processing unit, a screen (if a smartphone, it might be a tiny touch-sensitive screen), a keyboard (if a tablet, perhaps displayed on the screen itself), and memory (perhaps vastly augmented by the resources of the Web).

The larger field of technological innovation involves much more than computing, however – it includes mechanical, industrial, material, and electrical design, just to name a few major areas. Those elements of technological innovation today contribute to a much broader, more provocative view of the field of educational technology. By expanding our technological lens beyond the computer – by seeing technology as a dynamic ecosystem of techniques, materials, and research – we can likewise view education and learning through a more productive lens. This chapter focuses on the related areas of "tangible" and "full-body" interfaces in learning – essentially, blending computational ideas and devices with the wider landscape of other technologies (e.g., materials science, architectural engineering, mechanical design), such that the user interacts with the technology in a more embodied, more natural way – not through a keyboard and a screen, but through touch and manipulation (in the case of tangible interfaces) and large-scale gesture and bodily movement (for full-body interfaces). Until relatively recently,[1] tangible and full-body computing have rarely been considered in discussions of educational technology.[2]

---

[1] Several key recent references on the subject include Antle (2009, 2013); Buechley and Perner-Wilson (2012); and Zaman and colleagues (2012).

[2] For instance, a 2004 magisterial educational technology reference work (Jonassen, 2004) includes among its 41 chapters discussions of Internet-based learning, virtual reality, and distance education – but nothing on tangible computing. A more recent reference work on mathematics education (Clements et al., 2013) includes eight chapters on "Technology in the Mathematics Curriculum" with no mention of tangibles.

The first section of this chapter provides an overview of recent technological developments that have sparked interest in educational tangible/full-body interfaces. These technologies in turn enable creative new approaches to educational design – for example, for children's crafts, tools, and playgrounds – and we discuss several of the major approaches in the second section, "Learning by combining physical and computational elements." The third section explores the ways tangible interfaces connect with important ideas in the learning sciences – for example, with the affective and kinesthetic (as well as cognitive) dimensions of learning. Finally, in the fourth section, we adopt a societal perspective, discussing the limitations (and perhaps perils) of tangible/full-body interfaces as an approach to learning, and speculating on the role of tangibles in the future development of a broader "do-it-yourself" technological outlook.

Major Technological Themes in Tangible/Full-Body Interfaces for Learning

In this section, we describe several of the most important technological developments that, in concert, form the foundation for design in tangible and full-body educational design. The purpose here is not to focus on detailed technical implementations of these technologies (in any event, a moving target), but rather to give an overview of how "educational computing" is currently evolving into a variety of new forms.

Fabrication and Construction Technologies

Perhaps the most visible and exciting technological developments of the early 21st century are taking place in the realm of accessible, personalized fabrication. Several of the representative devices in this area are:

- 3-D printers (devices that take a specification of a solid object from a computer and output a model of the object in physical form, typically in plastic);
- Laser cutters (devices that use a computer-controlled laser to cut or etch items in wood, acrylic, paper, or textile);
- Milling machines (devices that use a computer-controlled drill to shape materials such as wood, wax, and light metals); and
- Computer-controlled sewing machines (devices that use computational control for embroidering patterns).

Devices of this kind are now increasingly affordable and available for use by hobbyists, amateur engineers, and (most important for our purposes) students and younger children. Briefly, the advent of these technologies enables children to use computers as centerpieces of a vastly empowered "shop" environment in which ideas and models can be translated into physical form in a wide variety of materials. Engineering students can use fabrication tools to make working mechanical models; mathematics students can fashion their own customized handheld puzzles; chemistry students can fashion their own models of complex molecules; physics students can build their own custom-designed tops and balancing toys; history students can create their own models of historical artifacts, battle scenes, or cityscapes.

Gershenfeld (2005) provided an early manifesto for the use of accessible fabrication in educational settings, and his optimism has been progressively vindicated by the steady development of increasingly affordable devices for home and school use. As of this writing there are commercially available desktop 3-D printers, desktop milling machines, and laser cutters, all selling for approximately the same cost as a high-end desktop computer (i.e., less than $5,000). For the purposes of this discussion, the key point is that "tangible computing for the learning sciences" is profoundly influenced by the ability of students to print out a vastly increased range of physical artifacts.

Embedded Computing

A second major technological development of the past decade has been the rapid expansion, in variety and quality, of small computing devices that can be embedded within physical artifacts. Currently, the most popular of these devices is the Arduino microprocessor (www.arduino.cc), which can be programmed via a desktop computer and connected to numerous compatible sensors and actuators. Typical sensors for these purposes include devices that respond to light (in the visible spectrum), sound (within a specified frequency range), touch, or acceleration; typical actuators include LED lights, sound speakers, or small motors. In effect, then, the presence of the Arduino – along with variants and similar devices such as the LilyPad, Flora, Raspberry Pi, Handy Board, Schemer,[3] and many others – allows students and designers to endow a variety of physical objects with programmable behaviors.

The implications of this work for the learning sciences – as with the fabrication devices of the previous discussion – center on the ways embedded devices can empower students to create their own programmable toys, scientific instruments, robots, clothing, jewelry, artwork, and so forth. In other words, the power of tangible computing for learning lies with the youngsters themselves as much as with adult designers. Children can create Lego constructions that respond to light or sound; they can design their own LED-festooned hats and necklaces; they can make plush toys that respond to a squeeze by playing music; they can create self-powered kinetic sculptures.

---

[3] LilyPad: www.sparkfun.com; Flora: www.adafruit.com; Raspberry Pi: www.raspberrypi.org; Handy Board: handyboard.com; Schemer: www.aniomagic.com.

Novel Materials

One of the key areas of technological development for tangible computing – often overlooked in the excitement surrounding fabrication and embedded devices – is in the creation of powerful, innovative materials that collectively open up new realms for design. Among the representative examples here are conductive threads, paints, tape, and ceramics, which permit connections to be sewn or drawn between computational and electronic elements; for example, it is through the use of conductive threads that computational devices such as the LilyPad Arduino are sewn directly onto textile backing and connected to sensors and actuators. Still other materials can be used in combination with computational elements to provide actuation of various sorts: shape memory alloys, for example, can be used to convert current into a mechanical force, while electroluminescent wire and film can be used to produce lighting effects.

Many, though not all, of the most expressive new materials for children derive their utility from direct combination with digital electronics – from their ability to conduct electricity between elements or to change shape (color, viscosity, etc.) in response to an applied voltage. In some cases, the interest of a new material is in its use in some other context – for example, the development of special wax materials for use in milling machines, pigments that change color in the presence of ultraviolet light, or low-melting-point plastics for mold making.

Optics and Tracking: Cameras, Projectors, and GPS

Yet another broad area of enabling technology – perhaps a bit more suited to full-body than (generally smaller-scale) tangible interfaces – involves the use of high-performance optics, projection, and positional sensing. For example, the sensing technology that has become familiar through home entertainment devices such as the Microsoft Kinect™ and Nintendo Wii™ interfaces can also be used to create settings and artifacts that sense the position, gestures, or proximity of users and can respond accordingly. Often, these technologies can be profitably incorporated within large-scale or architectural designs: an exhibit within a science museum, for instance, might respond to specific gestures from viewers or might behave in unexpected ways whenever a large number of viewers happen to be present. Radio frequency identification sensors (RFID) can be used to detect the proximity of particular tagged items; this could, for instance, enable a computational artifact to respond differentially to a wide variety of physical cues. Nor is sensing limited to the short-range technologies of RFID tags or gestural recognition. The use of global positioning system (GPS) technologies can condition the response of some tangible device or structure whenever it (or its user) are in a designated geographical location.

In combination with the use of techniques for positional sensing, there are also a growing number of techniques and devices for customized projection.

A handheld "nano projector," for instance, might allow a user to superimpose projected information onto a physical artifact; or, conversely, the artifact itself might be equipped with a projector and thus employ any nearby flat surface as an informal "screen" for display.

The previous paragraphs have summarized a variety of technological developments that collectively enable innovative educational design beyond the standard computer screen. A crucial point is that these technologies do not operate in isolation, but rather in combination. These technologies (along with others) constitute part of a larger ecosystem. The power of (say) 3-D printers is augmented by the presence of Web sites such as thingiverse.com, through which users can share their 3-D designs; the power of shape memory alloys derives in part from the way they can exert a force in response to Arduino-controlled signals; the utility of RFID tags is increased by the ability to place these tags on (or within) items designed with the use of a laser cutter or milling machine. In other words, "tangible and full-body interfaces" cannot be associated with any one technology, but rather should be seen as an emergent field that arises from widespread and mutually supportive developments.

Learning by Combining Physical and Computational Elements

The technological developments described in the previous section enable designers to create innovative tools and activities for learning. In this section, we outline several of the major directions in "tangible educational design"; in the following section, we discuss the implications of these designs for the learning sciences more generally.

Computational Crafts

There is a long tradition of learning through craftwork in the literature of education; children might (e.g.) learn geometry through origami folding, or ideas of engineering through the design of paper pop-ups, or biology through the construction and decoration of animal models. In some sense, the "curriculum" of traditional children's crafts extends beyond the bald identification of subject matter (geometry, engineering, etc.); one might also argue that the activity of patient, expressive construction is beneficial for affective or motivational reasons, teaching (e.g.) the value of practice or tolerance for failure.

The advent of new technologies has a profound impact on children's activities of this sort. For example, using the LilyPad Arduino, children can not only sew a design into a garment, but now can "program" that design as well (perhaps by having the sewn design respond to being touched by making a sound). Using 3-D printing, children can create their own high-quality dollhouse furnishings, model railroad settings, or diorama elements. Using computer-controlled paper cutters, children can create precise paper cutouts.

Many of the technologies described earlier could be interpreted, then, as natural extensions of the sorts of materials that children have always used in construction. Laser cutters (when used to cut wood) are extensions of hand-held saws and drills; milling machines (when used on wax) are extensions of sculpting tools; conductive threads and paints are extensions of their older, nonconductive cousins. In pursuing these ideas it is important to reflect on what may be gained or lost by the use of particular technologies. Is it (in some sense) *better* for children – more cognitively or motivationally effective – to cut paper with scissors for certain projects than to use a computer-controlled device? There are no easy or immediate answers to such questions; and anyone tempted to reject the use of computational techniques within children's crafts should keep in mind that craft activities have *always* been "high-tech" when viewed in the long term. Human beings did not evolve with scissors, or adhesive tape, or affordable construction paper, or brightly colored yarns; these are relatively recent innovations that have become viewed as traditional for children's work. The point here is not to argue that children's technology is an unmitigated blessing, but rather that its value – for craft activities, say – must be analyzed in terms of educational purpose. What do we want children to accomplish through crafts (and what do *they* want as well), and how do new technologies facilitate or hinder those ends? We return to this question later in this chapter.

Playgrounds, Settings, and Full-Body Interaction

A major genre of full-body interface research involves the creation of "computationally enriched spaces" of various sorts in which children can move about. The roots of this work are by now at least 30 years old: indeed, some current proposals and ideas have been waiting in the files of researchers until the available technology matured to the point at which the ideas could be made affordable for end users. The technological advances described in Section 2 have collectively made it feasible for many of these proposals to jump out of the archives of the labs and to enter homes, schools, and other educational spaces.

Virtual reality (VR) was one of the earliest fields in which researchers began to combine technology that made use of spatial detection of user activity to foster learning. This idea was hardly uncontroversial: even at the outset, there were strong feelings against the potential of VR as a useful educational tool. Surprisingly, some of these came from technologists themselves. Roussos and colleagues (1999) describe this controversy in their work on one of the first immersive learning environments for children, which allowed them to construct simple virtual ecosystems, collaborate with other remotely located children, and create stories from their interactions. They posed serious and reasonable doubts as to whether VR could possibly bring any added value to learning, whether its cost would ever become nonprohibitive, and whether its development, use, and maintenance would require technical knowledge beyond that of most end users and educators.

At that time few people could imagine that technology and interactive media would so quickly evolve to their current levels of miniaturization, availability, and accessibility. Nonetheless, some early researchers believed the potential of these technologies and media had to be explored to see whether the repertoire of educational strategies could be broadened with interesting new possibilities. This led to the subfield called virtual learning environments (VLEs). Whether it was in virtual or physical space or in any mix of both, VR research has experimented with a range of ideas from story rooms to curricular learning environments. This has been done in head-mounted display configurations, in VR surrounding displays like the CAVE, or in desktop versions.

The startling drop in the price of small cameras (and related technologies) has provided widespread access to those interested in creating and exploring similar applications: for example, the Nintendo Wii™ system and wireless positioning and pointing wand-like interface is based on low-cost infrared cameras and sensors. The evolution of such interfaces took another step forward with the arrival of the Microsoft Kinect™ system. This system is also based on a camera-like sensor – the Kinect system detects the depth of the scene, providing what some people call a 2.5-D representation of the scene. This technology has also become accessible within open source tools and languages, and is currently being used to develop many educational, leisure, and creative experiences.

Applications have also evolved in this process, from relatively "instructional" applications – with rigid educational structure – to more experiential and informal learning experiences. Increasingly we even see unorthodox approaches to the notion of education in space-based or full-body interaction: for example, applications for learning social skills through multi-user configurations, or applications to foster children's development through knowledge of their own body (e.g., via kinesthetics or proprioception).

In this sense, technology has penetrated spaces and fields in ways that few could have imagined just one or two decades ago. For example, we now find several commercial enterprises creating urban playgrounds that are technologically furnished to provide interactive experiences. In this manner the traditional benefits of playgrounds (Barbour, 1999) are updated with types of technology that are already familiar and natural to current generations of children and teens.

Classroom-centric educational applications have also evolved into experiences that incorporate embedded technologies. These have changed the way technology and computers are conceived within classrooms, moving away from the desktop toward systems that become part of the classroom, transforming its space into a holistic interactive educational environment for experimenting (Moher et al., 2010).

Nor are homes, classrooms, and playgrounds the only environments in which full-body movement is combined with technology. Science museums, for instance, have been transformed by new approaches that use these space detection systems, providing playground-like environments in which physical properties and laws may be not only experimented with, but also analyzed and even transgressed. Works like those found in the Exploratorium in San Francisco or the Polymechanon in Athens show how learning can become a radically different experience when these technologies are incorporated.

Body Augmentation

For the most part, when researchers use the term *tangible computing*, they are referring to physical artifacts augmented with computational capabilities or (as in the case of fabrication devices) using computers to create or construct physical artifacts. The "tangible" side of the equation – the nature of human touch and the concept of physicality – is interpreted as a constant, or a known quantity, in this description. At the same time, however, it should be noted that the notion of tangibility is (like that of "computing") undergoing steady evolution. Just as simple instruments such as eyeglasses subtly alter the concept of "visibility" over time, we may see a steady change in the assumptions regarding what people themselves bring to their interactions with the physical world.

In a typical instance of augmented reality, human vision of the physical world is complemented through the use of (e.g.) specialized glasses that present computationally derived information superimposed on the physical landscape. Vision is not the only sense that can be augmented in this fashion. One might likewise imagine specialized gloves or handheld tools that act as "augmented touch" for physical objects. The area of wearable computing is especially rich in possibilities for combining the design styles of "computational crafting" (as described earlier) and sensory augmentation. Children might, for example, design programmable garments that are responsive to (among other possibilities) polarized light, high-frequency pitch, or potential allergens in the air.[4]

In short, then, tangible/full-body educational design can be viewed as a combination of various genres. Children can employ tangible technology as an extension of traditional crafts; tangibles and full-body interfaces can be incorporated into children's environments and play spaces in the styles of work associated with "ubiquitous computing" or "pervasive computing";

---

[4] The article by Kirsh (2013), though not directly focused on children or education per se, presents an exciting prospect for this sort of design.

and children can interact with environments and objects through extensions of sensory apparatus.

What Tangible and Full-Body Interfaces Offer to the Learning Sciences

Thus far, we have focused on the design side of tangible/full-body design. In particular, Section 2 explored a variety of recent technological developments that enable this type of work, while Section 3 discussed several genres of design that link tangible and full-body interfaces to education. In this section we focus more on theoretical issues in the learning sciences – and on how tangible and full-body design contribute to investigating those theoretical issues.

Connections to Embodied Cognition

Perhaps the most natural application of tangible computing to the learning sciences is in the study of embodied cognition (or, with mild differences in emphasis, topics such as "grounded cognition" or "extended cognition" as well; cf. Abrahamson & Lindgren, Chapter 18, this volume). Broadly speaking, a growing body of research supports the idea that learning abstract subject matter (e.g., ideas of infinite sets in mathematics (Lakoff & Nuñez, 2000) or conservation of mass in physics (Goldin-Meadow, 2003)) is informed by bodily activity (cf. also Clark, 1997). Just to take a few natural examples: the traditional pedagogical use of mathematical manipulatives such as number rods, balancing beams, and clocks might be seen as a physical, "embodied" way of introducing early mathematical concepts such as number, addition, commutativity, multiplication, and modular arithmetic. Nor is embodied understanding limited to elementary material: for example, one might argue that a puzzle such as Rubik's Cube acts as a "manipulative" in its own right – an embodied introduction to concepts of group theory.

Activity with physical materials can be seen as an embodied foundation for understanding concepts in a wide variety of subject matter: paper acts as an approximation to a two-dimensional surface, a metal rod as a rigid conduit of force, a string as a means for exerting a "pull" (but not a "push") force, billiard balls as approximations to molecules of an ideal gas, and so forth. In all these instances, and many more, experience with physical materials and objects informs intuition and provides a source of metaphorical insights and images. One must keep in mind that such physical experience comes at a certain cost as well: thinking of molecules as billiard balls is reasonable in some contexts (early statistical mechanics) and counterproductive in others (understanding hydrogen bonding). Nonetheless, when thoughtfully employed, physical materials can act as "objects to think with," in the phrase coined by Papert (1980).

Tangible/full-body interface design meshes well with this theoretical interest in embodied cognition for learning. Indeed, there are numerous ways to support research in this area:

- Designers can use novel technologies, including sensors for gesture and movement, to create "manipulatives" that are responsive to bodily actions (e.g., the work of Abrahamson and colleagues (2011) on designing manipulatives that sense the movement of the student's hands to support a kinesthetic understanding of ratio).
- Designers can create tangible artifacts that illustrate advanced or underexplored content such as dynamical systems (e.g., the work of Resnick et al. (1998) on "digital beads" for exploring concepts in dynamical systems).
- Designers can take advantage of accessible fabrication tools to create systems that will enable children to construct or customize their own manipulatives. For example, children could (conceivably) create their own personalized mathematical puzzles, polyhedral models (Eisenberg & Nishioka, 1997), beads, construction kit pieces, and so forth.
- Designers might create novel computationally enriched garments, wearables, or accessories that extend the sensory intuition of students: one might (e.g.) imagine glasses that recognize and signal the presence of "mathematically interesting" objects in the environment, or gloves that respond in interesting ways to certain types of "content-appropriate" hand movements (e.g., counting motions), or handheld musical instruments equipped with sensors that respond to complex rhythmic patterns.

The intent of these examples – some hypothetical, some derived from actual projects – is to suggest the myriad ways a broader view of mathematical and scientific cognition dovetails with an interest in tangible and full-body design. Conversely, it suggests that, for designers of such artifacts, a familiarity with the literature of embodied cognition will help them to create worthwhile educational activities. The two fields – technology and cognitive science – complement each other: to the extent that mathematical or scientific understanding is linked to physical experience and bodily intuition, that experience and intuition can be enriched through the use of tastefully designed technology.

Design beyond the Screen: Design of Children's Places for Learning

Current cognitive theories tell us that we can understand the world because our brain has a body that allows it to act on this world (Dourish, 2001). The field of human-computer interaction (HCI) has incorporated this insight in a very natural way from the moment technology started to allow for full-body or embodied interaction with virtual, physical, or mixed environments. In fact, as Grudin (1990) notes, the history of computer interfaces has been one of reaching out to the physical world; and more recent research on blending physical activity within learning experiences seems to show that it promotes involvement and activeness, increases awareness of one's own actions, enhances creativity, and encourages reflection (Price & Rogers, 2004; Rogers, Scaife, Gabrielli, Harris, & Smith, 2002).

Evolving from an earlier focus on ergonomics – for example, minimizing physical activity and exertion within interfaces – research on space-based or full-body interaction has started to yield many interesting results. Despite the fact that physical activity is often not seen as educational, applications that foster such activity in children and teens have pedagogical relevance. On the one hand, *play* is increasingly acknowledged as an important aspect of human beings and their development (Salen & Zimmerman, 2003). On the other, these applications not only foster physical activity in children who might not otherwise practice sports, but they also teach all children the values behind physical activity: they teach them about health issues, about knowing their bodies, about relating to other children, about negotiating and collaborating in pursuit of common goals.

The games of the Nintendo™ Wii™ console, for instance, are not merely successful because of their element of physical play. They have likewise been successful because of the socialization aspect behind the games developed for them – the fact that users can share a space and interact with the game and with each other. Researchers have studied this effect of playing while doing physical activities. For example Mueller, Agamanolis, and Pickard (2003) coined the term *exertion interfaces* to describe these types of technologies while researching their social effects; they found a greater engagement and binding among users playing a game with an interface that demands some physical effort, in contrast to those who play the same game with an interface that does not ask them to do any physical activity. Berthouze has proposed that a high level of motion in interactive game-like experiences modifies the way users get engaged. She describes this change as a displacement of the experience from what she calls "hard fun" to "easy fun" (Berthouze et al., 2007). This can have an interesting impact in learning and creative processes.

Castañer, Camerino, Pares, and Landry (2011) have used a physical activity platform called the Interactive Slide (Soler-Adillon, Ferrer, & Pares, 2009) to explore the educational aspects of physical activity. Companies such as Kompan in Denmark, Playdale in the United Kingdom, or Lappset in Finland are exploring how the usual benefits of traditional playgrounds can take advantage of space-based interaction and bring these playgrounds closer to current preferences of children and teens (Hodgkins, Caine,

Rothberg, Spencer, & Mallison, 2008). In the same vein, the Playware center was created in Denmark to explore the potential of interactive technologies in play experiences and pay special attention to full-body interaction (Lund, Klitbo, & Jessen, 2005).

If we move toward the goal of understanding the world around us, full-body interaction research has adopted several points of view. For example, the proposal of *embodied metaphors* as defined by Antle and colleagues (2009) takes the work done by Lakoff and Johnson (1980) on how our language – as a reflex of culture and the way we have come to understand our world as human beings – incorporates metaphors that use physical properties of our world. This is a very interesting approach, not only to make interaction more accessible to its users, but also to develop experiences that can help users better understand the mechanics and logic of our world.

Museums have started to experiment with these properties of space-based interaction. The Polymechanon in Athens is completely based on full-body interactive technologies to help children learn about physical laws and properties of our world (Kynigos, 2010). It includes a number of experiences involving physical activity in which users can collaborate or compete in achieving goals. To mention but one more example, the CosmoCaixa science museum in Barcelona has experimented with how the body of the user can become the constant referent while becoming miniaturized in a virtual voyage from human to nano scale (Mora, Pares, & Rodriguez, 2012) or on how collaboration among teens in a mixed reality environment can teach them the need for collaboration in science (Carreras & Pares, 2009).

Technologies such as the Kinect™ are providing new opportunities to make traditional pedagogic strategies evolve into the culture of contemporary children. Two recent examples are the Kinect Nat Geo TV™ and the Kinect Sesame Street TV™. In the first, the classic high-quality documentary format is enhanced by introducing simple games in which children enact the behaviors of animals to better understand their lives and environments. Very interesting disguise strategies are used, for example, in a game in which children see themselves on the screen wearing the head and the wings of an owl. They must gesticulate to catch grasshoppers with their newly acquired beaks and feed the chicks in a nearby nest. Children not only love to wear disguises, but they are also freed from their constraints and are allowed to act spontaneously in very open ways. The second game uses the classical Sesame Street pedagogical scenes and strategies guided by the characters. This time, however, at specific points the characters allow the children to act on the elements or situations depicted. For example, children can be invited to throw coconuts into a box and as they do so the character exhorts them to count how many they have collected. These strategies not only motivate children but also transport them inside the environment in a natural way where the full-body activity provides them with the capacity to understand specific concepts and situations.

The social aspects of full-body interaction design draw on a theoretical tradition in development pioneered by Vygotsky (1978). Vygotsky's theories are part of the foundations for educational constructivism – a body of research that has in turn influenced many interaction designers such as Papert (1980) and Resnick (2005). Specifically in tangible and space-based interaction, Vygotsky's theory of how children start to use tools, not only to manipulate elements in the environment, but also to convert them into symbols that allow them to understand their world, code it, and obtain an internal representation, are affecting the way interactive experiences are being designed. One of the key Vygotskian ideas is that children first develop a new capacity through socialization to later incorporate it in their internalized repertoire. This is consistent with a design philosophy of space-based interaction that allows for multiuser interaction and socializing situations mediated by interactive systems.

Space-based interaction is also helping children with disabilities such as autistic spectrum disorder (ASD). There is a strong potential of full-body interaction with a predictable system and in collaboration with other children, educators, or parents. These provide a powerful support, for example, in ASD children who need to learn to know their body, as in the Pictogram Room project (Casas, Herrera, Coma, & Fernández, 2012). Here children are taught through imitative strategies to become aware of their extremities, of the notions of right and left, and so forth.

The "Tangible Style" of Learning Science Research

As we noted at the outset of this chapter, tangible and full-body interfaces exemplify a relatively recent – and, to many researchers, a relatively unorthodox – way of thinking about educational technology. The field is associated with images that are, for the time being at least, unfamiliar: instead of sitting on desktops, computers now become things that can be strategically placed around a play environment, or things that can be attached to paper surfaces, or things that can be sewn into programmable plush toys, or things that children wear on their clothing. Moreover, because this work gives rise to a novel style of technological design, it lends itself as well to a potentially unorthodox style of thinking about educational design.

Consider how seamlessly the traditional style of educational technology, based on desktop (or laptop) computers, fits with venerable images of education itself: rows of quietly seated children focused on textual or diagrammatic material presented via primarily symbolic (textual or diagrammatic) means. While the means of presentation in this portrait may be new – a high-resolution screen as opposed to a paper surface – and while the technique of presentation may make use of vast underlying computational resources, the larger structure of education itself is familiar: it is something that occurs in designated places and times, and is associated with relatively constrained physical activity.

Tangible/full-body design tends to challenge these images. First, tangible researchers often design artifacts for use in informal (rather than classroom) settings: playgrounds, parks, museums, theme parks, and so forth. This is a natural result of the emphasis on physical activity and movement: after all, classrooms are not generally places where children are encouraged to run around, so the type of educational artifacts designed for such places will be relatively static. Tangible/full-body researchers, however, are naturally drawn to settings in which children learn through movement. The researcher might see an opportunity in a child's walk to school: perhaps the neighborhood could respond to a child's location along the walk (as measured by GPS). Or the researcher might focus her attention on outdoor settings: perhaps the experience of a botanical garden could be enhanced through judiciously employed augmented reality or a playground game could be conducted with infrared signaling instead of physical tagging.

Second, tangible learning researchers tend to think in terms of designing enriching or challenging things for children to do – rather than developing curricular material aimed at traditional academic subject matter. Craft technology, for example, generally imagines novel ways children can spend their creative hours – sewing computers into garments, or building complex pop-up cards, or painting electric circuits onto paper. This approach focuses less on the structure of subject matter, and instead works with less historically "cognitive" notions, such as attitudes, dispositions, perseverance, and aesthetics. A craft technology researcher is more likely to focus on the design of long-term, open-ended, patient opportunities for building; in such settings, the designer has relatively little control over the moment-to-moment presentation of information to the child. Thus, the tangible researcher will focus less on traditional cognitive concerns such as ordering of material, or scheduling of practice, or the design of testing materials. The metric of success, for a craft technologist, tends to be more in whether children are concentrating on content-rich material (circuit design, Arduino programming, paper engineering) over long periods of time, and whether they are experiencing what it is like to be deeply interested in a challenging activity; the particular content learned may well vary from child to child. The affective dimensions of learning – the obsessive desire to create, the pleasure taken in settings associated with one's work, the pride experienced in completion of a project, the likelihood of forming an attachment to intellectual challenge – take on greater importance in the educational literature and research surrounding tangible design.

Third, because tangible and full-body interfaces lend themselves to long-term activities and a wide variety of settings, they likewise suggest a broader view of subject matter itself. Rather than exclusively focusing on classroom staples such as English and mathematics, tangible designers might find themselves creating artifacts for (e.g.) pottery, or gardening, or ballet – the types of subjects associated with (sometimes messy) physical materials or bodily movement. The most natural uses of tangible and full-body design are often precisely those subjects that fit comfortably into studios, or workshops, or playgrounds, as opposed to traditional classrooms.

It should be noted that in all these respects, this philosophy of design may very well represent the cutting edge of educational technology in a plausible near future era when traditional classrooms lose their primacy. The recent explosive growth of formats such as massive open online courses (MOOCs) and online educational enterprises (Khan, 2012) may in fact, over time, give rise to the growth of alternative structures and settings for learning. In future decades, a child whose education is less tied to the classroom altogether may spend portions of her day in a "hackerspace," or local craft center, or nature preserve. (There are far more dystopian future scenarios, of course, but one can at least hope for developments of this kind.) In such alternative settings, the design of novel educational artifacts, geared toward long-term constructive or physical activities, may be seen as a necessary and forceful complement to (e.g.) online lectures, simulations, and quizzes.

Developing Issues in Tangible and Full-Body Design for Learning

This chapter has primarily focused on the opportunities tangible technologies in education present – new affordances of recent technology, new styles of educational design, and new areas of prominent research in the learning sciences. In this final section, we discuss some of the central debates regarding the role of tangible technologies in the learning sciences.

Cognitive Limitations of the Tangible Approach

As noted in the previous section, the tangible/full-body design approach to education dovetails with those cognitive theories that emphasize the roles of physical movement and the body in understanding. In this sense, tangible design and embodied cognition stand in tandem as something of a contrast to more "abstract" types of educational presentations (e.g., via text and other symbolic communication) and more "abstract" types of understanding (e.g., of mathematical notions such as number, function, group, and so forth).

The contrast – perhaps "tension" is a better word – between embodied and abstract understanding is reflected in historical educational debates, particularly in mathematics and the natural sciences. Among mathematicians especially, there has long been a sense that the body is not necessarily a reliable guide to true understanding (a theme associated early on with the writings of Plato and debated by numerous scholars and researchers ever since). We have never actually *seen* or *experienced*, after all, a straight line or a circle: these are abstractions. We have never *touched* a number, or function, or algebraic field. Indeed, our bodies seem to tell us that parallel lines never meet (the subject of Euclid's famous "fifth postulate"), but more abstract 19th-century reasoning tells us that our worldly intuitions on this point are anything but inevitable (Trudeau, 1987).

Mathematics is not the only field in which bodily intuition is suspect. Consider the ideas of modern physics: our bodies are not especially reliable guides to the particulate nature of air, or frictionless movement, or the Heisenberg uncertainty principle, just to name a few troubling concepts. Or biology: our natural, intuitive scales of time make it difficult to conceive of evolutionary change taking place over thousands or millions of years.

In short, mathematics and the natural sciences are shot through with abstract notions and conceptual hurdles that are not especially friendly to bodily understanding. For these reasons, one might argue for caution in focusing too heavily on tangible computing as a basis for educational design: after all, if the crucial challenges of education involve getting *beyond* bodily understanding, then perhaps educational design should focus on exercising precisely the most abstract, nongrounded forms of reasoning.

We argue against this conclusion, taking two lines of argument: first, that tangible experience is itself a "moving target," affected by one's technological or material environment. The tangible experience of (e.g.) working with conductive paints, or shape memory alloys, or electronics kits (to name a few) can form the foundation of a different sort of "grounded cognition" than was available to children a generation ago. Second, even the most abstract concepts in mathematics and science are often informed by some area of tangible experience, even if they run counter to other areas: an air-hockey table can lead to intuitions about (relatively) frictionless motion, even if most day-to-day situations run counter to those intuitions. In summary, then, we would argue that tangible computing can be used to provoke new and unexpected physical intuitions, in many cases precisely aimed at otherwise overly abstract or inaccessible content.

Tangible Computing and the DIY Community

The history of the learning sciences has been deeply interwoven with the parallel history of computing. Cognitive science itself, as an interdisciplinary field, sprang from interest in computational models of mental activity (cf. Gardner, 1987), and learning sciences research has often been characterized by the creative use of computer simulations, cognitive models, and human-computer interfaces.

An interest in tangible and full-body design reflects a natural continuation of the ideas on which the learning sciences were founded. The crucial point is that our ideas about technology, about technological metaphors of mind, and about appropriate technology for children's education continue to change. Computing is not simply a matter of placing a processor on a desk (even if that processor is connected to the Web); the mind is not merely a static, information-processing device; and a fuller portrait of education and learning is one in which technology of various forms is integrated with all sorts of activities and settings.

Tangible/full-body design for the learning sciences plays into a different sort of zeitgeist than that which characterized the growth of the home computer industry in the 1970s and 1980s. Increasingly, there are communities centered on "makers" of various sorts (cf. Anderson, 2012): do-it-yourself (DIY) builders, amateur scientists and engineers, home crafters, and so forth. These communities are supported by sites and commercial enterprises that provide "how-to" information (e.g., instructables.com, makezine.com), or fabrication services (e.g., shapeways.com, ponoko.com), or novel crafting materials (e.g., inventables.com). The "maker movement," as it is sometimes referred to, is a phenomenon that dovetails with an interest in tangible and full-body technology for learning. We see children's work with newly designed physical artifacts and settings as an entree into a world – we hope, a fulfilling and creative world – in which computational and material technologies are expressively intermingled, widely available, and rich in intellectual challenge.

References

Abrahamson, D. et al. (2011). From tacit sensorimotor coupling to articulated mathematical reasoning in an embodied design for proportional reasoning. Presented at AERA 2011. At: edrl.berkeley.edu/sites/default/files/Abrahamson-et-al.AERA2011-EmbLearnSymp.pdf.

Anderson, C. (2012). *Makers*. New York: Crown.

Antle, A. (2009). Embodied child-computer interaction: Why embodiment matters. *ACM Interactions*, (March/April), 27–30.

Antle, A. (2013). Research opportunities: Embodied child-computer interaction. *International Journal of Child-Computer Interaction*, 1(1), 30–36.

Antle, A. N., Corness, G., & Droumeva, M. (2009). What the body knows: Exploring the benefits of embodied metaphors in hybrid physical digital environments. *Interact. Comput.*, 21(1–2) (January), 66–75.

Barbour, A. (1999). The impact of playground design on the play behaviors of children with differing levels of physical competence. *Early Childhood Res. Q.*, 14(1), 75–98.

Berthouze, N. et al. (2007). Does body movement engage you more in digital game play? and why? In *Affective computing and intelligent interaction* (pp. 102–113). Berlin/Heidelberg: Springer.

Buechley, L., & Perner-Wilson, H. (2012). Crafting technology: Reimagining the processes, materials, and cultures of electronics. *ACM Transactions on Computer-Human Interaction*, 19(3), Article 21.

Carreras, A., & Parés, N. (2009). Designing an interactive installation for children to experience abstract concepts. In *New trends on human-computer interaction* (pp. 1–10). New York: Springer.

Casas, X., Herrera, G., Coma, I., & Fernández, M. (2012). A kinect-based augmented reality system for individuals with autism spectrum disorders. *GRAPP/IVAPP*, 440–446.

Castañer, M., Camerino, O., Pares, N., & Landry, P. (2011). Fostering body movement in children through an exertion interface as an educational tool. *Procedia-Social and Behavioral Sciences*, 28, 236–240.

Clark, A. (1997). *Being there*. Cambridge, MA: MIT Press.

Clements, M. A. et al. (Eds.) (2013). *Third international handbook of mathematics education*. New York: Springer.

Dourish, P. (2001). *Where the action is*. Cambridge, MA: MIT Press.

Eisenberg, M., & Nishioka, A. (1997). Orihedra: Mathematical sculptures in paper. *International Journal of Computers for Mathematical Learning*, 1, 225–261.

Feiner, S. et al. (1993). Knowledge-based augmented reality. *Communications of the ACM*, 36(7), 53–62.

Gardner, H. (1987). *The mind's new science*. New York: Basic Books.

Gershenfeld, N. (2005). *Fab*. New York: Basic Books.

Gibson, J. J. (1979). *The ecological approach to visual perception*. Boston: Houghton Mifflin.

Goldin-Meadow, S. (2003). *Hearing gesture*. Cambridge, MA: Harvard University Press.

Grudin, J. (1990). The computer reaches out: The historical continuity of interface design. In *Proceedings of CHI '90*, 261–268.

Hodgkins, P., Caine, M., Rothberg, S., Spencer, M., & Mallison, P. (2008). Design and testing of a novel interactive playground device. *Proceedings of the Institution of Mechanical Engineers, Part B: Journal of Engineering Manufacture*, 222(4), 559–564.

Jonassen, D. (Ed.) (2004). *Handbook of research on educational communications and technology*. Mahwah, NJ: Lawrence Erlbaum Associates.

Khan, S. (2012). *The one world schoolhouse*. New York: Twelve.

Kirsh, D. (2013). Embodied cognition and the magical future of interaction design. *ACM Transactions on Computer-Human Interaction*, 20(1), Article 3.

Kynigos, C., Smyrnaiou, Z., & Roussou, M. (2010). Exploring rules and underlying concepts while engaged with collaborative full-body games. *Proceedings of IDC 2010*, 222–225.

Lakoff, G., & Johnson, M. (1980). *Metaphors we live by*. Chicago: Chicago Press.

Lakoff, G., & Nuñez, R. (2000). *Where mathematics comes from*. New York: Basic Books.

Lund, H. H., Klitbo, T., & Jessen, C. (2005). Playware technology for physically activating play. *Artificial Life and Robotics Journal*, 9.

Moher, T. et al. (2010). Spatial and temporal embedding for science inquiry: An empirical study of student learning. *Proceedings International Conference of the Learning Sciences*. June, Chicago, 1, 826–833.

Mora, J., Pares, N., & Rodriguez, N. (2012). Analysis of an embodied interaction installation for museum to enhance learning of the nanoscale. In *Workshop Designing Interactive Technology for Teens*, NordiCHI 2012, Copenhagen.

Mueller, F., Agamanolis, S., & Picard, R. (2003). Exertion interfaces: Sports over a distance for social bonding and fun. In *Proceedings of CHI '03*, 561–568.

Myron, W., Krueger, Thomas Gionfriddo, & Hinrichsen, Katrin. (1985). VIDEOPLACE – an artificial reality. *Proceedings of CHI '85*, 35–40.

Norman, D. A. (2002). *The design of everyday things*. New York: Basic Books.

Papert, S. (1980). *Mindstorms*. New York: Basic Books.

Price, S., & Rogers, Y. (2004). Let's get physical: The learning benefits of interacting in digitally augmented physical spaces. *Journal of Computers and Education*, 15(2), 169–185.

Resnick, M. et al. (1998). Digital manipulatives: New toys to think with. *Proceedings of CHI '98*, 281–287.

Resnick, M., & Silverman, B. (2005). Some reflections on designing construction kits for kids. *Proceedings of IDC 2005*, 117–122.

Rogers, Y., Scaife, M., Gabrielli, S., Harris, E., & Smith, H. (2002). A conceptual framework for mixed reality environments: Designing novel learning activities for young children. *Presence*, December.

Roussos, M., Johnson, A., Moher, T., Leigh, J., Vasilakis, C., & Barnes, C. (1999). Learning and building together in an immersive virtual world. *Presence: Teleoper. Virtual Environ*, 8(3) (June), 247–263.

Salen, K., & Zimmerman, E. (2003). *Rules of play: Game design fundamentals*. Cambridge, MA: MIT Press.

Soler-Adillon, J., Ferrer, J., & Pares, N. (2009). A novel approach to interactive playgrounds: The interactive slide project. *Proceedings of IDC 2009*, 131–139.

Trudeau, R. (1987). *The non-Euclidean revolution*. Boston: Birkhäuser.

Vygotsky, L. S. (1978). *Mind in society*. Fourteenth Edition. Cambridge, MA: Harvard University Press.

Zaman, B. et al. (2012). Editorial: The evolving field of tangible interaction for children: The challenge of empirical validation. *Personal and Ubiquitous Computing*, 16(4), 367–378.

18 Embodiment and Embodied Design

Dor Abrahamson and Robb Lindgren

Picture this. A preverbal infant straddles the center of a seesaw. She gently tilts her weight back and forth from one side to the other, sensing as each side tips downward and then back up again. This child cannot articulate her observations in simple words, let alone in scientific jargon. Can she learn anything from this experience? If so, what is she learning, and what role might such learning play in her future interactions in the world? Of course, this is a nonverbal bodily experience, and any learning that occurs must be bodily, physical learning. But does this nonverbal bodily experience have anything to do with the sort of learning that takes place in schools – learning verbal and abstract concepts? In this chapter, we argue that the body has everything to do with learning, even learning of abstract concepts.

Take mathematics, for example. Mathematical practice is thought to be about producing and manipulating arbitrary symbolic inscriptions that bear abstract, universal truisms untainted by human corporeality. Mathematics is thought to epitomize our species' collective historical achievement of transcending and, perhaps, escaping the mundane, material condition of having a body governed by haphazard terrestrial circumstance. Surely mathematics is disembodied!

We reject this commonly held view and argue instead that all school subjects, even mathematics, are embodied. An embodied perspective rejects the Platonic notion of mathematical objects as ideal entities whose mere shadows we mortals might hope to apprehend. Furthermore, this perspective promotes an epistemological conceptualization of mathematics, and in fact all STEM content, as grounded not in its sign systems and inscriptional forms (which clearly are pivotal to its practice) but in the situated, spatial-dynamical, and somatic phenomenology of the person who is engaging in activity society marks as "mathematical." We argue even more strongly that fundamental STEM knowledge is itself shaped by the embodied nature of the human mind.

The objective of this chapter is to outline the embodiment approach, explain how it contributes to our understanding of learning, and propose and exemplify how this understanding informs the design of STEM learning environments.

Principles of Embodiment

When we engage in professional practice, we apply particular ways of looking at and discussing situations (Goodwin, 1994). In many fields, particularly science, technology, engineering, and math (STEM), these professional habits can be difficult to acquire, because they introduce analytic perspectives that depart from naturalistic ways of being in the world (Bamberger & diSessa, 2003). And furthermore, in the STEM disciplines, to participate in professional practice one must develop fluency with dedicated semiotic systems that use unfamiliar symbolic notations (Harnad, 1990).

We believe that the embodiment approach can help educators to create learning environments that lead learners toward these disciplinary perspectives. Drawing on a broad range of learning sciences resources, this section spells out three principles that we have found helpful in making sense of and responding to students' persistent difficulty with STEM content. First, we discuss two epistemic systems, the primitive and the formal, and we argue that deep understanding of formal analysis is grounded in meanings from unmediated interactions with the physical world. Second, we claim that even beyond initial learning phases in the disciplines, all ongoing processes of sense making, problem solving, and even manipulating symbolic notation continue to be embodied – they all activate naturalistic perceptuomotor schemes that come from being corporeal agents operating in spatial-dynamical realities. Third, we argue for the pervasive role of equipment – biological, material, epistemic – in supporting and shaping cognitive activity.

Each of these three subsections culminates with a summary and a challenge for the design of STEM learning environments.

Rhyme and Reason: Learning as Coordinating Two Cognitive Systems

When we are immersed in any perceptuomotor activity, we engage a cognitive and motor system that is highly sophisticated yet demands little if any reflection. However, when we stop to think and talk *about* perception and action, we engage a different type of cognitive system, whose activity differs from the bodily experiences it refers to. Understanding the differences between these two epistemic modes – the immediate "doing" and mediated "thinking" – is important for the theory and practice of embodied learning, because educators seek to guide learners from immersive action to structured reflection.

Through structured reflection, the flow of absorbed experience is better understood. As Dewey put it, "Events turn into objects, things with a meaning ... [that can] be infinitely combined and re-arranged in imagination ... [and therefore] infinitely more amenable to management, more permanent and more accommodating" (Dewey, 1958, p. 167). When we make our unconscious, tacit knowledge explicit, it is as though we cast a conceptual screen between ourselves and experience (Polanyi, 1958, p. 197). This *dual-system thesis* has parallels in the foundational literature of the learning sciences; for example, cognitive developmental psychologist Jean Piaget famously differentiated between perceptual and conceptual knowledge (Piaget & Inhelder, 1969, p. 46) and cultural-historical psychologist Lev Vygotsky juxtaposed spontaneous and scientific concepts (Vygotsky, 1962, chapter 6).

Kahneman (2003) distinguished between effortless intuition and deliberate reasoning, the former being rapid, heuristic, and relatively resistant to modification, the latter being slower yet more accurate and amenable to change. Notably, the two systems are permeable, so that deliberate reasoning over time can become more effortless and rapid (Dreyfus & Dreyfus, 1999; Fischbein, 1987). Even working with symbolic notation can become intuitive; recent studies suggest that simple verbal and arithmetic operations can be performed unconsciously (Sklar et al., 2012).

Cognitive psychologists suggest that new knowledge is first acquired in the conscious, deliberate mode and then becomes intuitive. But embodied activities fall into the intuitive, unreflected mode. We argue that meanings experienced in the intuitive holistic mode can lead to quantitative analyses and symbolic articulation typical of disciplinary practice.

Summary: In much of everyday activity, meanings are tacit, contextual, schematized orientations toward obtaining goals under given circumstances – the intuitive mode. STEM disciplines, however, concretize, parse, analyze, and quantify these naturalistic interactions – the analytic mode. To understand STEM content, students must reconcile their unmediated perceptions and actions with the mediated structures of disciplinary practice.

Challenge: Can learning environments be designed to foster grounded learning, in which students sustain a tacit sense of meaning from corporeal activity even as they are guided to rethink this activity formally? And would this result in more significant learning outcomes?

Abstraction as Simulated Action: Learning Is Moving in New Ways

In this section, we argue that manipulating symbolic notation is cognitively quite similar to physically moving objects in space. David Landy contrived an elegant experimental design that demonstrated that the colloquial notion of "manipulating symbols," such as "moving +2 across the equal sign so it becomes -2," is not just a metaphorical form of speech – in our "mind's eye" we literally move those symbols across the equal sign, so that we arrive later at our destination if the moving symbol must brave a counter current (Goldstone, Landy, & Son, 2009).

Many people believe that thinking is a type of psychological activity that is essentially detached from sensory input or action output. Many cognitive science studies have found, in contrast, that "Abstract concepts are perceptual, being grounded in temporally extended simulations of external and internal events" (Barsalou, 1999, p. 603). And if so, thinking is always the evocation and dynamical manipulation of perceptions of the physical world. Melser (2004) argued that thinking is a form of covert, truncated action – "truncated" in that the mental faculties related to planning and executing external physical actions are engaged, but the musculature is not. Empirical evidence from neuroimaging supports these claims, finding that "rational thought … directly uses sensory-motor bodily mechanisms.… [It] is an exploitation of the normal operations of our bodies" (Gallese & Lakoff, 2005, p. 473). For example, when we imagine, we activate by and large the same parts of the brain as in actual seeing (Kosslyn, 2005). And when we hear the verbs *lick*, *pick*, and *kick*, we covertly activate the motor system that controls the mouth, the hands, and the legs, respectively (Hauk, Johnsrude, & Pulvermüller, 2004). These findings have led some scholars to go so far as to abolish traditional conceptualizations of mental represen-tation and rearticulate cognition in terms of agent-environment dynamics (Chemero, 2009; Clark, 2013; Hutto & Myin, 2013; Thelen & Smith, 1994; Varela, Thompson, & Rosch, 1991).

Developmental psychologists broadly agree that bodily action plays a cen-tral role in conceptual development. Famously, Vygotsky stated that, "The word was not the beginning – action was there first" (Vygotsky, 1962). Piaget argued that the same action-oriented mental processes at play in coping with concrete situations are also involved when people learn mathematical or sci-entific ideas, such as the notions of "square" or "gravity." He asserted that "the roots of logical thought are not to be found in language alone.… But … more generally in the coordination of actions, which are the basis of reflec-tive abstraction" (Piaget, 1968, p. 18).

Like Piaget, many contemporary cognitive scientists have proposed models to explain how abstract concepts emerge from concrete sensorimotor experi-ences. Notably, the cognitive semantics theory of conceptual metaphor pos-its that all human reasoning is grounded in *image schemas*, "patterns of our bodily orientations, movements, and interaction … [that] are imaginatively developed to structure our abstract inferences" (Lakoff & Johnson, 1980, p. 90). For example, we can make sense of the mathematical construct of a *set* only because we know what it means for physical objects to be gathered together in a container (Núñez, Edwards, & Matos, 1999).

Several psychologists have studied how people gesture while they speak and solve problems, and these studies have provided further evidence that thinking is embodied. For example, examining how people move their hands as they speak about artifacts they have just learned to manipulate helps us understand how actual interactions develop into simulated actions that impact future physical and cognitive performance (Goldin-Meadow & Beilock, 2010; Kirsh, 2013). Hatano, Miyake, and Binks, who studied abacus experts' mental arithmetic, concluded that "abacus operation tends to interiorize into mental operation through a transition stage wherein the mental operation is not completely independent from the motor system and abacus-simulating finger movement gives important support" (Hatano, Miyake, & Binks, 1977, p. 53). Gestures mediate new ways of looking and thinking.

Summary: Conceptual reasoning originates in physical interaction and becomes internalized as simulated actions.

Challenge: How do we select, create, and facilitate physical interactions that give rise to conceptual reasoning and thinking that is aligned with desired educational learning outcomes?

Equipment and Breakdowns: Learning as Gearing Up with Biological, Material, and Epistemic Tools

The relation between human cognition and technological artifacts has long fascinated scholars. How are these two entities, the mental and the material, the animate and the inanimate, somehow synthesized in human neurobiology? What might it mean to experience conceptual change by manipulating an artifact that is external to the brain (Sfard & McClain, 2002)? After engaging in such an activity, do we retain any useful residual knowledge that we can then apply even in the *absence* of the artifacts (Salomon, Perkins, & Globerson, 1991)?

There is evidence that learners do so; Polanyi offers the following example. Imagine a blind person using a stick to negotiate through a physical space. When the person holds the stick for the first time, the person feels simple sensations – its texture and touch against his fingers and palm. But as one learns to use the stick for feeling one's way, the simple sensation is transformed – gradually, one feels the point of the stick touching the objects being explored (Polanyi, 1958, pp. 13–14).

This example demonstrates that artifacts affect cognition via the incremental adaptation we experience as we develop the skill of operating through these artifacts. As we "instrumentalize" the artifact, we necessarily "instrument" ourselves (Vérillon & Rabardel, 1995). That is, as we figure out how to apply the artifact to the world according to our needs, we develop the skill of controlling and interpreting the world through the mediating artifact. And whenever an artifact fails us, its latent structure and implicit function become transparent (Koschmann, Kuuti, & Hickman, 1998).

There is substantial evidence that thought and action persist in the absence of the artifacts that shaped them. This residual effect of artifact-mediated activity is perhaps most strikingly demonstrated in cases where prosaic structural elements of semiotic media surreptitiously colonize the meanings of signs. For example, Jasmin and Casasanto (2012) have shown that the historical QWERTY configuration of keyboards implicitly paints our affective perception of words in accord with their composition of right-hand side (positive) and left-hand side (negative) characters.

Summary: We use artifacts to extend our perceptuomotor and epistemic capacity. In so doing, we internalize physical and mental habits of interacting with the world via the artifacts' mediating structure. When these somatic, manipulatable, or cognitive artifacts fail to deliver desired effects, we consciously reflect on, recalibrate, or modify our modes of engaging the world. That is, we learn.

Challenge: How do we take learners through an optimal process of engaging with biological, material, and epistemic equipment to accomplish learning?

The embodied perspective, exemplified by the studies reviewed in this section, appears to be gaining a foothold in learning sciences discourse; leading journals and conferences have dedicated special issues and symposia to this perspective (Abrahamson, 2012; Hall & Nemirovsky, 2012; Kiverstein & Clark, 2009; Marshall, Antle, Hoven, & Rogers, 2013; Nemirovsky & Borba, 2004). We have articulated three challenges for educational design emerging from this perspective. Broadly, we have asked how educational designers might help learners ground classroom content knowledge, particularly in STEM disciplines, in their tacit knowledge, and what role action and equipment may play in this process. The next section offers some current responses to these challenges in the form of heuristic guidelines for educational design as well as two examples of their implementation in studies of STEM content learning.

Embodied Design: From Theory to Practice

When we apply an embodiment theory of cognition in the creation of learning environments, we are engaging in embodied design. The phrase *embodied design* was first coined by Thomas van Rompay, then a cognitive-psychologist-turned-industrial-designer, who used conceptual metaphor theory to tune the emotional experience evoked by public structures, such as bus stop shelters (Van Rompay, Hekkert, & Muller, 2005). Abrahamson (2009) imported the phrase into the learning sciences to describe the craft of engineering pedagogical artifacts and activities attuned to how humans naturally perceive the world, yet conducive to disciplinary reanalysis and signification. In an environment based on embodied design principles, learners could approach a problem in chemistry, biology, physics, material science, or mathematics using their natural bodily instincts and movements. This section offers design principles for fostering embodied learning and then describes a couple of designs for STEM content that exemplify these principles, drawing on a range of learning sciences research (Abrahamson, 2013; Antle, Wise, & Nielsen, 2011; Birchfield & Johnson-Glenberg, 2010; Diénès, 1971; Edwards, 1995; Howison, Trninic, Reinholz, & Abrahamson, 2011; Kamii & DeClark, 1985; Levy, 2012; Lindgren, 2012; Montessori, 1967; Papert, 1980; Pratt & Noss, 2010).

Principles for Embodied Design: Physical Experience, Guided Signification

In the previous section, we identified three challenges for pedagogical design:

- Can learning environments be designed to foster grounded learning in which students sustain a tacit sense of meaning from corporeal activity even as they are guided to rethink this activity formally? This is a question about *activities*.
- How do we select, create, and facilitate physical interactions that give rise to conceptual reasoning and thinking that is aligned with desired class-room learning outcomes? This is a question about *materials*.
- How do we take learners through an optimal process of engaging with biological, material, and epistemic equipment to accomplish learning? This is a question about *facilitation*.

We respond to these three challenges with three roughly mapped sets of proposed guidelines for embodied design.

The First Challenge: Activities

The activities most effective for learning draw on students' preexisting capacity to orient and mobilize in real or virtual three-dimensional space. Activities should require that students use their perceptual senses and kinesthetic coordination to judge properties of stimuli and perform new actions.

Initial tasks should include little to no symbolic stimuli, with a preference instead for figurative, iconic, diagrammatic, and graphical representations.

Activities should begin by engaging students in ostensibly simple tasks (making a screen green, hitting a target, etc.). The means of execution should initially be straightforward, but the overall objective may initially be opaque, with more complex objectives emerging over time.

The Second Challenge: Materials

Learning activities should be situated in an orchestrated environment that includes technological artifacts and facilitating agents (e.g., tutors, museum docents, or teachers). Students should have opportunities to find purpose and meaning in these environments, much as they do when navigating the complex material structures of the unmediated world.

The learning environment should be designed so that somatic actions – ranging from the movement of a single finger to the leaping of one's entire body – become coupled with the environment via action-feedback loops.

In the case of computer-based environments, such as augmented reality, virtual worlds, and simulations, students should experience firsthand the manipulation of virtual objects on a screen, tabletop, floor, and so forth.

Breakdowns of the action-environment couplings should be gradually introduced by presenting objectives that cannot be met using solutions and configurations that the learner has already mastered. Tasks might suddenly require that tools be used in new ways or that new tools or frames of reference be used; or the materials themselves might shift to demand novel motor configurations. Students should gradually develop new perceptuomotor schemas that enable them to effectively control objects in service of the more sophisticated task objective.

The Third Challenge: Facilitation

Patterns of movement and body engagement that optimally facilitate conceptual development will not always occur naturally. Students will often need scaffolding (see Reiser & Tabak, Chapter 3, this volume) to take actions and move their bodies in ways that simulate the core mechanisms and spatial relations – to enact *functional metaphors* for the target knowledge domain. Physical cueing and situated real-time feedback should be implemented to reinforce these metaphors and elicit the kinds of movement that lead to desired conceptual insights.

Instructors and other agents in the environment should work to help students' perceptuomotor schemas develop toward those of experts. This typically involves seeing a situation in new ways, becoming attuned to hidden aspects of the environment. Effective pedagogical practices include physical demonstration, co-production, and hands-on coaching, as well as using media technologies to present audiovisual and even haptic (i.e., touch-based) experiences that convey expert perspectives.

Embodied designs will more effectively lead to conceptual development if students are asked to articulate their strategies for interacting with materials in the environment. For example, students may be asked to describe regularities in feedback based on their actions, to elaborate on these regularities relative to the content knowledge evoked by the activity, to develop strategies for utilizing these insights so as to accomplish the task more effectively, and to make requests for particular settings of the variable conditions as well as additional tools.

Having outlined a set of guiding design principles, we now describe several studies of embodied design in mathematics and science.

The Mathematical Imagery Trainer: Concepts as Signified Operatory Schemes

As an example of creating embodied design for mathematics education, we discuss a research project centered on an activity to help students learn the concept of proportion. The concept of proportion is an essential component of early curriculum, because it is key to STEM reasoning in high school, college, and the professions as well as everyday numeracy. However, many students in middle school and beyond experience difficulty in reasoning proportionately, often engaging "additive" rather than "multiplicative" visualizations of problems. For example, students might assert that 1:2 = 2:3, because they attend only to absolute intervals among the numerical values (i.e., 1). A premise of this project was that students would learn proportionality effectively by conceptualizing new multiplicative procedures in terms of familiar additive operations, and that they could achieve this by coordinating among complementary multiplicative and additive visualizations of a proportions situation (Fuson & Abrahamson, 2005; Harel & Confrey, 1994).

The instruction of proportion often begins with a situation that gives rise to some proportional progression. A proportional progression, such as 1:2 = 2:4 = 3:6 = *etc.*, unfolds as a repeating linked adding on the left and right sides of the ":" symbol, that is, 1:2 = (1+1):(2+2) = (1+1+1):(2+2+2) = *etc.* Students learn to produce such successions of number pairs by iterating from each ratio to the next in the form of a ratio table and using multiplication shortcuts. However, what students do not experience when they enact this procedure is the meaning of proportional *equivalence* that the "=" symbol signifies. That is, students never have a structured opportunity to enact, visualize, conceptualize, and calculate exactly what is conserved during additive expansion or multiplicative scaling. Namely, in what sense is 1:2 the same as 2:4 or 3:6? By way of contrast, the equation 2+3 = 4+1 is fairly easily understood because each of the two expressions adds up to the same total – they each denote a set of five things. In contrast, it is harder for learners to understand in what sense 1:2 and 2:4 are the same.

Some curricula attempt to ground the idea of proportional equivalence by using text and pictures to invoke familiar experiences in which two ratios, such as 1:2 and 2:4, are associated with the same perceptual sensation. For example, equivalent ratios are modeled as the identical flavor resulting from mixing two ingredients measured respectively as either 1-and-2 units or 2-and-4 of the same units, or, analogously, the identical color resulting from mixing quantities of blue and yellow paint. However, these sensations are not experienced directly in the classroom but rather are left to children's imaginations. Moreover, the numerical cases are dictated rather than determined. Consequently, a proportion is not directly experienced, and procedures for manipulating proportions are not explored, discovered, calculated, explained, challenged, shared, or elaborated.

A design solution proposed by the Embodied Design Research Laboratory (Abrahamson, Director) is the Mathematical Imagery Trainer for Proportion (MIT-P; see Figure 18.1). The device measures the heights of the user's hands above a designated datum line, calculates the ratio of these two measures, and compares it to a particular ratio on the teacher's console. If the ratio is correct, the screen is green, and otherwise it is red. The goal presented to the student is to move their two hands up and down keeping the screen green rather than red. Note that the student is thus to enact proportional progression qualitatively (without measurement or enumeration), moving their hands simultaneously in continuous space. This design principle is called *dynamical conservation* because the learner needs to discover an action pattern (law of

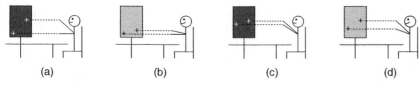

Figure 18.1. *The Mathematical Imagery Trainer for Proportion (MIT-P) set at a 1:2 ratio, so that the right hand needs to be twice as high along the monitor as the left hand in order to achieve a "success." The four-panel figure shows a paradigmatic interaction sequence – while exploring, the student: (a) positions her hands "incorrectly"; (b) stumbles on a "correct" position; (c) raises her hands maintaining a constant interval between them; and (d) corrects position. Compare 1b and 1d and note the different intervals between the cursors.*

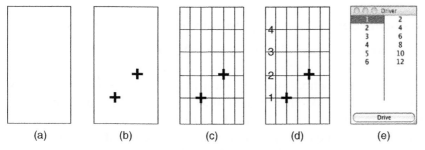

Figure 18.2. *The Mathematical Imagery Trainer for Proportion (MIT-P): schematic representation of the display configuration sequence used in the activity, beginning with (a) a blank screen, and then featuring a set of symbolical objects incrementally overlaid onto the display: (b) a pair of cursors that "mirror" the location of the user's left and right hands, respectively; (c) a grid; (d) numerals along the y-axis of the grid; and (e) a "driver" for controlling the cursors numerically rather than manually.*

progression) that keeps constant a property of the system. Once the student has developed and articulated the new skill, we overlay frames of reference onto the interaction space (see Figure 18.2).

We implemented the MIT-P design in the form of tutorial task-based clinical interviews, wherein 23 grade 4–6 students (ages 9 to 11) participated either individually or in pairs. When students first figured out how to maintain a green screen, they did so by manipulating the interval between their hands, in relation to their hands' elevation above the desk, articulated verbally as, "The higher I go, the bigger the distance." When we introduced mathematical artifacts into their working space (as in Figure 18.2), students tended to adopt these to enhance their performance. And in so doing, students began to talk more mathematically. For example, students utilized the grid (Figure 18.2c) to enact the "higher-bigger" strategy, and doing so led them to reconfigure their strategy into the iteration law of proportional progression, such as "For every 1 I go on the left, I go 2 on the right." Later, when the corresponding numerals were introduced (Figure 18.2d), students suddenly realized the multiplicative relation between the left- and right-hand values and stated, "On the right its double what's on the left" (Abrahamson, Trninic, Gutiérrez, Huth, & Lee, 2011). When we asked students to reason about relations among their various strategies, they were able to explain connections between their non-multiplicative and multiplicative conceptualizations of proportion (Abrahamson, Lee, Negrete, & Gutiérrez, in press).

In a controlled experiment run with 128 students, participants who directly or vicariously engaged activities with the MIT-P outperformed a control group on conceptual items (Petrick & Martin, 2011). Several tablet variations on this design are now available (e.g., Abrahamson, 2012; Rick, 2012).

MEteor: Cueing Body Actions Aligned with Scientific Principles

A second example of embodied design, in the area of science education, comes from a research project on immersive simulation technology for strengthening middle school students' intuitions about kinematics. Students frequently struggle to acquire a formal understanding of the principles that govern how things move, and often fall back on weakly organized systems of knowledge based on their everyday interactions in the world when reasoning about physical phenomena (diSessa, 1993). One way to connect everyday experience to formal concepts is to engage students in analogical thinking and have them reflect critically on their own preconceptions (Clement, 1993). Fully immersive interactive virtual reality environments can support exploration of kinetics concepts by grounding them in the familiar domain of one's own body movements and connecting these experiences to formal representations. Several projects have sought to cultivate physics knowledge with immersive virtual worlds (Kafai & Dede, Chapter 26, this volume; also see Dede et al., 1996; Enyedy, Danish, Delacruz, & Kumar, 2012; Johnson-Glenberg, Birchfield, Megowan-Romanowicz, Tolentino, & Martinez, 2009), but these environments stop short of explicitly prompting learners to enact the movements of an idealized physical system, consistent with the first of our embodied design principles related to facilitation.

The MEteor project is designed to support movement cueing and to combine correctly performed actions with a formal framework for interpreting those actions. MEteor is a room-sized (30' x 10') mixed reality simulation game that attempts to strengthen and structure intuitions about Newton's laws and Kepler's laws by having them enact the movement of an asteroid traveling through space. Students use their whole bodies to make predictions about where the asteroid will move as it encounters planets and other objects with gravitational forces; audio and visual cues guide their movements, allowing them to adjust their predictions in real time. MEteor is a relatively short-term intervention, designed to disrupt preexisting misconceptions and

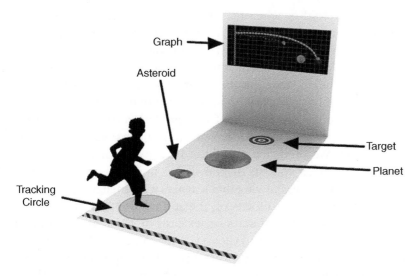

Figure 18.3. *The MEteor simulation game for whole-body metaphor-based interaction. A student launches an asteroid and must predict its motion as it interacts with other objects (e.g., planets) in space. In the scenario above the student has fallen behind the asteroid, causing her tracking circle to change color. A graph on the wall display allows the participant to review the previous trial.*

give rise to new perspectives that have the potential to be built on with formal instruction.

A MEteor user begins by walking onto a platform and linking his or her body movements to the floor-projected image of an asteroid (pronounced visual and audio effects reinforce this connection). The learner now controls the movement of the asteroid up until the point that it enters an area of space where a planet's gravity and other forces influence the asteroid's trajectory. The objective of the learner, through a series of increasingly difficult game levels, is to accurately predict the movement of the asteroid; scoring in the game is dependent on how closely the learner adheres to the correct path, and visual indicators (i.e., a color gradient surrounding the learner's feet) are in place to guide their real-time movement. Level 3 of the game, for example, requires the learner to pass their asteroid through an area of space directly behind a planet placed in the middle of the floor display. To successfully hit the target area, a learner must discover that an asteroid passing near to a planet will curve around it, and accelerate in the process. After completing a trial launch, a learner reviews their attempt via a diagrammatic representation of their movement on a wall display (see Figure 18.3). They are prompted to explain why the asteroid moved the way it did, and the instructor helps them reframe their description, typically first-person models conveyed in everyday language, in terms of gravitation force and orbit. Breakdowns occur when the learner's movement fails to align with that of the launched asteroid or when the objective of a level is not achieved. The data visualizations on the wall display give learners the opportunity to reflect on these actions and recalibrate for the next trial.

In MEteor, a learner is aided in their adoption of functional metaphors through salient cueing mechanisms. If, for example, a learner begins to deviate from the correct trajectory of an object moving through space, all the available dynamic visual elements of the simulation (the color of the tracking circle, the actual position of asteroid, etc.) will change to steer the learner back on course. We predicted that the MEteor experience would result in more highly organized systems of knowledge, and data collected so far suggests that this is the case, showing that learners who engage with the full-body simulation are less likely to focus on the surface features of the simulation experience (e.g., background stars or textures of the planets) compared to participants who used a desktop version of the same simulation (Lindgren & Moshell, 2011). Participants who are given the opportunity to enact the physics concepts with their bodies seem to be more attuned to the important dynamic relationships the simulation conveys, as evidenced by their use of arrows and other representations of movement in their post-simulation diagrams. Additionally, participants using the full-body simulation appear to have a more robust understanding of the simulation space as evidenced by their superior ability to identify the conditions that would lead to a successful versus an unsuccessful launch (Lindgren & Bolling, 2013).

Conclusion and Future Directions

We have argued that all cognition is grounded in bodily experience, and our examples demonstrate specifically that math and science conceptual understandings are grounded in bodily experience. And if so, learning environments for math and science can be made more effective if they are designed to tap into bodily know-how that originates both from existing life experience and new learning experiences.

The studies reviewed in this chapter show that math and science concepts are not abstract, conceptual mental entities, removed from the physical world. Rather they are deeply somatic, kinesthetic, and imagistic. Interactive tasks typical of embodied design thus steer learners to discover, refine, and practice physical action schemes that solve local problems but can then be generalized to math or science conceptual understanding (Trninic & Abrahamson, 2012). Embodied designers design schemes that underlie reasoning in the disciplines.

The embodied turn in the theory and practice of STEM education implies that studying physical skill development (Bernstein, 1996) should bear directly on studying conceptual development (Thelen & Smith, 1994), for example by interfacing neurophysiological and clinical studies with formal models, such as dynamic field theory (Spencer, Austin, & Schutte, 2012, p. 415). Furthermore, the essential role of teachers in guiding students' physical engagement with embodied design suggests the relevance of the fields of cognitive and social anthropology, such as studies of vocational apprenticeship or distributed cognition in the workplace (see Collins & Kapur, Chapter 6, this volume), as bearing theoretical and analytic means for researchers to make sense of how learners come to think through and with their bodies in ways that begin to approximate professional practice (e.g., Becvar Weddle & Hollan, 2010; Ingold, 2011). This marriage of motor-developmental psychology and sociocognitive anthropology bodes well for the learning sciences, as it offers powerful means of realizing the call for dialectical research at the intersection of cognition and sociocultural theory (diSessa, 2008; Greeno & Engeström, Chapter 7, this volume).

A child balancing on a seesaw, it turns out, is developing more than physical coordination – she is building an embodied sense of equivalence that may one day inform her moral reasoning about social justice (Antle, Corness, & Bevans, in press). Even as students develop new physical action schemes as cognitive and social entry into the activity structures of the disciplines, so are scholars developing new conceptualizations of education to explain how embodied knowledge transforms into a body of knowledge. In more than one sense, learning is moving in new ways.

Acknowledgments

For their superb commentary on an earlier draft, we heartily thank Shaun Gallagher, Geoff Saxe, and Katharine G. Young. For inspiring conversations and suggestions, we thank Jeanne Bamberger, Raúl Sanchez Garcia, and Cliff Smyth. We are grateful to Keith Sawyer for constructive critiques and very useful suggestions. Funding for the *Mathematical Imagery Trainer* was provided by a UC Berkeley Committee on Research Faculty Research Grant. Funding for the MEteor project was provided by the National Science Foundation (DRL-1114621). Any opinions, findings, and conclusions or recommendations expressed in this material are those of the authors and do not necessarily reflect the views of UC Berkeley, UI Urbana-Champaign, or NSF.

References

Abrahamson, D. (2009). Embodied design: Constructing means for constructing meaning. *Educational Studies in Mathematics*, 70(1), 27–47. (Electronic supplementary material at http://edrl.berkeley.edu/publications/journals/ESM/Abrahamson-ESM/).

Abrahamson, D. (2012). Mathematical Imagery Trainer – Proportion (MIT-P) IPhone/iPad application (Terasoft): iTunes. Retrieved from https://itunes.apple.com/au/app/mathematical-imagery-trainer/id563185943.

Abrahamson, D. (Chair & Organizer). (2012). You're it! Body, action, and object in STEM learning. In J. v. Aalst, K. Thompson, M. J. Jacobson, & P. Reimann (Eds.), *Proceedings of the International Conference of the Learning Sciences: Future of Learning (ICLS 2012)* (Vol. 1: Full papers, pp. 283–290). Sydney: University of Sydney / ISLS.

Abrahamson, D. (2013). Toward a taxonomy of design genres: Fostering mathematical insight via perception-based and action-based experiences. In J. P. Hourcade, E. A. Miller, & A. Egeland (Eds.), *Proceedings of the 12th Annual Interaction Design and Children Conference (IDC 2013)* (pp. 218–227). New York: The New School and Sesame Workshop.

Abrahamson, D., Lee, R. G., Negrete, A. G., & Gutiérrez, J. F. (in press). Coordinating visualizations of polysemous action: Values added for grounding proportion. In F. Rivera, H. Steinbring, & A. Arcavi (Eds.), Visualization as an epistemological learning tool (Special issue). *ZDM: The International Journal on Mathematics Education.*

Abrahamson, D., Trninic, D., Gutiérrez, J. F., Huth, J., & Lee, R. G. (2011). Hooks and shifts: A dialectical study of mediated discovery. *Technology, Knowledge, and Learning*, 16(1), 55–85.

Antle, A. N., Corness, G., & Bevans, A. (in press). Balancing justice: Exploring embodied metaphor and whole body interaction for an abstract domain. To appear in *International Journal of Arts and Technology, Special Issue on Whole Body Interaction.*

Antle, A. N., Wise, A. F., & Nielsen, K. (2011). Towards utopia: Designing tangibles for learning. In P. Blikstein & P. Marshall (Eds.), *Proceedings of the 10th Annual Interaction Design and Children Conference (IDC 2011)* (Vol. "Full Papers," pp. 11–20). Ann Arbor, MI: IDC.

Artigue, M., Cerulli, M., Haspekian, M., & Maracci, M. (2009). Connecting and integrating theoretical frames: The TELMA contribution. In M. Artigue (Ed.), Connecting approaches to technology enhanced learning in mathematics: The TELMA experience (Special issue). *International Journal of Computers for Mathematical Learning*, 14, 217–240.

Bamberger, J., & diSessa, A. A. (2003). Music as embodied mathematics: A study of a mutually informing affinity. *International Journal of Computers for Mathematical Learning*, 8(2), 123–160.

Barsalou, L. W. (1999). Perceptual symbol systems. *Behavioral and Brain Sciences,* **22**, 577–660.

Becvar Weddle, L. A., & Hollan, J. D. (2010). Scaffolding embodied practices in professional education. *Mind, Culture & Activity*, 17(2), 119–148.

Bernstein, N. A. (1996). On dexterity and its development. In M. L. Latash & M. T. Turvey (Eds.), *Dexterity and its development* (pp. 3–244). Mahwah, NJ: Lawrence Erlbaum Associates.

Birchfield, D., & Johnson-Glenberg, M. C. (2010). A next gen interface for embodied learning: SMALLab and the geological layer cake. *International Journal of Gaming and Computer-Mediated Simulation*, 2(1), 49–58.

Chemero, A. (2009). *Radical embodied cognitive science.* Cambridge, MA: MIT Press.

Clark, A. (2013). Whatever next? Predictive brains, situated agents, and the future of cognitive science. *Behavioral and Brain Sciences,* 36, 181–253.

Clement, J. (1993). Using bridging analogies and anchoring intuitions to deal with students' preconceptions in physics. *Journal of Research in Science Teaching,* 30(10), 1241–1257.

Dede, C., Salzman, M. C., Loftin, R. B., Brusilovsky, P., Kommers, P., & Streitz, N. (1996). *The development of a virtual world for learning Newtonian mechanics: Multimedia, hypermedia, and virtual reality B2 – multimedia, hypermedia, and virtual reality.* Berlin: Springer/Verlag.

Dewey, J. (1958). *Experience and nature.* New York: Dover Publications. (Original work published 1927).

Diénès, Z. P. (1971). An example of the passage from the concrete to the manipulation of formal systems. *Educational Studies in Mathematics,* 3(3/4), 337–352.

diSessa, A. A. (1993). Toward an epistemology of physics. *Cognition and Instruction,* 10(2–3), 105–225.

diSessa, A. A. (2008). A note from the editor. *Cognition and Instruction,* 26(4), 427–429.

Dreyfus, H. L., & Dreyfus, S. E. (1999). The challenge of Merleau-Ponty's phenomenology of embodiment for cognitive science. In G. Weiss & H. F. Haber (Eds.), *Perspectives on embodiment: The intersections of nature and culture* (pp. 103–120). New York: Routledge.

Edwards, L. (1995). Microworlds as representations. In A. A. diSessa, C. Hoyles, & R. Noss (Eds.), *Computers and exploratory learning* (pp. 127–154). New York: Springer.

Enyedy, N., Danish, J. A., Delacruz, G., & Kumar, M. (2012). Learning physics through play in an augmented reality environment. *International Journal of Computer-Supported Collaborative Learning,* 7(3), 347–378.

Even, R., & Ball, D. L. (Eds.) (2003). Connecting research, practice, and theory in the development and study of mathematics education (Special issue). *Educational Studies in Mathematics,* 54(2–3), 139–146.

Fischbein, E. (1987). *Intuition in science and mathematics.* Dordrecht, Holland: D. Reidel.

Fuson, K. C., & Abrahamson, D. (2005). Understanding ratio and proportion as an example of the apprehending zone and conceptual-phase problem-solving models. In J. Campbell (Ed.), *Handbook of mathematical cognition* (pp. 213–234). New York: Psychology Press.

Gallese, V., & Lakoff, G. (2005). The brain's concepts: The role of the sensory-motor system in conceptual knowledge. *Cognitive Neuropsychology,* 22(3–4), 455–479.

Goldin-Meadow, S., & Beilock, S. L. (2010). Action's influence on thought: The case of gesture. *Perspectives on Psychological Science,* 5(6), 664–674.

Goldstone, R. L., Landy, D. H., & Son, J. Y. (2009). The education of perception. *Topics in Cognitive Science,* 2(2), 265–284.

Goodwin, C. (1994). Professional vision. *American Anthropologist,* 96(3), 603–633.

Hall, R., & Nemirovsky, R. (Eds.) (2012). Modalities of body engagement in mathematical activity and learning (Special issue). *Journal of the Learning Sciences,* 21(2).

Harel, G., & Confrey, J. (Eds.) (1994). *The development of multiplicative reasoning in the learning of mathematics*. New York: State University of New York.

Harnad, S. (1990). The symbol grounding problem. *Physica D*, 42, 335–346.

Hatano, G., Miyake, Y., & Binks, M. (1977). Performance of expert abacus operators. *Cognition*, 5, 57–71.

Hauk, O., Johnsrude, I., & Pulvermüller, F. (2004). Somatotopic representation of action words in human motor and premotor cortex. *Neuron*, 41(2), 301–307.

Howison, M., Trninic, D., Reinholz, D., & Abrahamson, D. (2011). The Mathematical Imagery Trainer: From embodied interaction to conceptual learning. In G. Fitzpatrick, C. Gutwin, B. Begole, W. A. Kellogg, & D. Tan (Eds.), *Proceedings of the annual meeting of The Association for Computer Machinery Special Interest Group on Computer Human Interaction: "Human Factors in Computing Systems" (CHI 2011), Vancouver, May 7–12, 2011* (Vol. "Full Papers", pp. 1989–1998). New York: ACM Press.

Hutto, D. D., & Myin, E. (2013). *Radicalizing enactivism: Basic minds without content*. Cambridge, MA: MIT Press.

Ingold, T. (2011). *The perception of the environment: Essays on livelihood, dwelling, and skill*. Second Edition. New York: Routledge.

Jasmin, K., & Casasanto, D. (2012). The QWERTY effect: How typing shapes the meanings of words. *Psychonomic Bulletin & Review*, 19(3), 499–504.

Johnson-Glenberg, M. C., Birchfield, D., Megowan- Romanowicz, C., Tolentino, L., & Martinez, C. (2009). Embodied games, next gen interfaces, and assessment of high school physics. *International Journal of Learning and Media*, 1(2).

Kahneman, D. (2003). A perspective on judgement and choice. *American Psychologist*, 58(9), 697–720.

Kamii, C. K., & DeClark, G. (1985). *Young children reinvent arithmetic: Implications of Piaget's theory*. New York: Teachers College Press.

Kirsh, D. (2013). Embodied cognition and the magical future of interaction design. In P. Marshall, A. N. Antle, E. v.d. Hoven, & Y. Rogers (Eds.), The theory and practice of embodied interaction in HCI and interaction design (Special issue). *ACM Transactions on Human-Computer Interaction*, 20(1), 3:1–30.

Kiverstein, J., & Clark, A. (Eds.) (2009). Introduction: Mind embodied, embedded, enacted: One church or many? *Topoi*, 28(1), 1–7.

Koschmann, T., Kuuti, K., & Hickman, L. (1998). The concept of breakdown in Heidegger, Leont'ev, and Dewey and its implications for education. *Mind, Culture, and Activity*, 5(1), 25–41.

Kosslyn, S. M. (2005). Mental images and the brain. *Cognitive Neuropsychology*, 22(3/4),333–347.

Lakoff, G., & Johnson, M. L. (1980). *Metaphors we live by*. Chicago: University of Chicago Press.

Levy, S. T. (2012). Young children's learning of water physics by constructing working systems. *International Journal of Technology Design Education*.

Lindgren, R. (2012). Generating a learning stance through perspective-taking in a virtual environment. *Computers in Human Behavior*, 28(4), 1130–1139.

Lindgren, R., & Bolling, A. (2013). Assessing the learning effects of interactive body metaphors in a mixed reality science simulation. Paper presented at the

Annual Meeting of the American Educational Research Association, San Francisco, CA.

Lindgren, R., & Moshell, J. M. (2011). Supporting children's learning with body-based metaphors in a mixed reality environment. Paper presented at the Interaction Design and Children, Ann Arbor, MI.

Marshall, P., Antle, A. N., Hoven, E. v.d., & Rogers, Y. (Eds.) (2013). The theory and practice of embodied interaction in HCI and interaction design (Special issue). *ACM Transactions on Human-Computer Interaction*, 20(1).

Melser, D. (2004). *The act of thinking*. Cambridge, MA: MIT Press.

Montessori, M. (1967). *The absorbent mind*. (E. M. 1, Trans.). New York: Holt, Rinehart, and Winston. (Orignal work published 1949).

Nemirovsky, R., & Borba, M. C. (2004). PME Special Issue: Bodily activity and imagination in mathematics learning. *Educational Studies in Mathematics*, 57, 303–321.

Núñez, R. E., Edwards, L. D., & Matos, J. F. (1999). Embodied cognition as grounding for situatedness and context in mathematics education. *Educational Studies in Mathematics*, 39, 45–65.

Overton, W. F. (2012, May). Relationism and relational developmental systems: A paradigm for the emergent, epigenetic, embodied, enacted, extended, embedded, encultured, mind. Paper presented at the "Rethinking Cognitive Development" – the 42nd annual meeting of the Jean Piaget Society, Vancouver.

Papert, S. (1980). *Mindstorms: Children, computers, and powerful ideas*. New York: Basic Books.

Petrick, C. J., & Martin, T. (2011). *Hands up, know body move: learning mathematics through embodied actions*. Manuscript in progress (copy on file with author).

Piaget, J. (1956). *The child's conception of physical causality*. Totowa, NJ: Littlefield, Adams and Company.

Piaget, J. (1968). *Genetic epistemology* (E. Duckworth, Trans.). New York: Columbia University Press.

Piaget, J., & Inhelder, B. (1969). *The psychology of the child* (H. Weaver, Trans.). New York: Basic Books (Original work published 1966).

Polanyi, M. (1958). *Personal knowledge: Towards a post-critical philosophy*. Chicago: University of Chicago Press.

Pratt, D., & Noss, R. (2010). Designing for mathematical abstraction. *International Journal of Computers for Mathematical Learning*, 15(2), 81–97.

Rick, J. (2012). Proportion: A tablet app for collaborative learning. In H. Schelhowe (Ed.), *Proceedings of the 11th Annual Interaction Design and Children Conference (IDC 2012)* (Vol. "Demo Papers," pp. 316–319). Bremen, Germany: ACM-IDC.

Salomon, G., Perkins, D. N., & Globerson, T. (1991). Partners in cognition: Extending human intelligences with intelligent technologies. *Educational Researcher*, 20(3), 2–9.

Sfard, A., & McClain, K. (Eds.) (2002). Analyzing tools: Perspectives on the role of designed artifacts in mathematics learning (Special Issue). *Journal of the Learning Sciences*, 11(2 & 3).

Sklar, A. Y., Levy, N., Goldstein, A., Mandel, R., Maril, A., & Hassin, R. R. (2012). Reading and doing arithmetic nonconsciously. *Proceedings of the National Academy of Sciences*, 109(48), 19614–19619.

Spencer, John P., Austin, Andrew, & Schutte, Anne R. (2012). Contributions of dynamic systems theory to cognitive development. *Cognitive Development*, 27(4), 401–418.

Thelen, E., & Smith, L. B. (1994). *A dynamic systems approach to the development of cognition and action*. Cambridge, MA: MIT Press.

Trninic, D., & Abrahamson, D. (2012). Embodied artifacts and conceptual performances. In J. v. Aalst, K. Thompson, M. J. Jacobson, & P. Reimann (Eds.), *Proceedings of the International Conference of the Learning Sciences: Future of Learning (ICLS 2012)* (Vol. 1: Full papers, pp. 283–290). Sydney: University of Sydney / ISLS.

Van Rompay, T., Hekkert, P., & Muller, W. (2005). The bodily basis of product experience. *Design Studies*, 26(4), 359–377.

Varela, F. J., Thompson, E., & Rosch, E. (1991). *The embodied mind: Cognitive science and human experience*. Cambridge, MA: MIT Press.

Vérillon, P., & Rabardel, P. (1995). Cognition and artifacts: A contribution to the study of thought in relation to instrumented activity. *European Journal of Psychology of Education*, 10(1), 77–101.

Vygotsky, L. S. (1962). *Thought and language*. Cambridge, MA: MIT Press. (Original work published 1934).

19 Videogames and Learning

Constance Steinkuehler and Kurt Squire

The videogames industry has been flourishing. In 2010 in America alone, total consumer spending on the games industry totaled $25.1 billion (Siwek, 2010), surpassing both the music industry ($15.0 billion) and box office movies ($10.5 billion). It is also one of the fastest growing industries in the U.S. economy. From 2005 to 2010, for example, the videogames industry more than doubled while the entire U.S. GDP grew by about 16 percent. The amount of time young people spend with entertainment media in general is staggering. Youth aged 8 to 18 years old consume about 10.45 hours per day of media (compressed into 7.38 hours per day thanks to multitasking; Rideout, Foehr, & Roberts, 2010). Console and handheld videogames alone account for roughly one hour and 13 minutes of that screen time, not including computer games. And the majority of unit sales come from games targeted at children, with ESRB ratings of E for everyone (56% of unit sales), E10+ for ages 10 and up (18%), or T for ages 13 and up (21%) (Entertainment Software Association, 2011). These statistics show that videogames capture a great deal of time and interest from school-aged youth.

But the sheer popularity of videogames with young people is not the primary reason that learning scientists have taken an interest; rather, it is because they have great potential to facilitate learning. Empirical findings on the impact of games come from a broad range of academic disciplines, including neuroscience, social studies education, literacy studies, health, and psychology. Action games have been found to improve visual acuity and attention (Green, Pouget, & Bavelier, 2010). Historical simulations aid systems understanding in world history and geography (Squire & Barab, 2004). Exergames like *Dance Dance Revolution* or Nintendo's *Wii Sports* are shown to increase calorie expenditure and decrease sedentary lifestyles for children (Graf, Pratt, Hester, & Short, 2009). Casual games like *Bejeweled II* have been shown to increase mood and decrease stress (Russoniello, O'Brien, & Parks, 2009). Videogame-related texts for titles like *World of Warcraft* enable struggling readers to perform on par with their more successful counterparts despite the fact that game-related texts typically are written at a high school level (11.8 grade level text) (Steinkuehler, 2012). Online game community discussion boards evidence scientific reasoning (Steinkuehler & Duncan, 2008). The 3-D puzzle platform *FoldIt* has leveraged crowd sourcing against particularly knotty problems in research on protein structures to make genuine scientific discoveries – the findings of which have been published in *Nature* and other leading science journals with the players listed as authors (Eiben et al., 2012).

Across these studies, several themes emerge. First, videogames are remarkably engaging. Few media have been charged with addiction to the extent that games have, and their interactivity and design principles are at the core of their appeal. Second, commercial games often exemplify good pedagogical principles (Gee, 2010). Built into the beginning levels of all successful commercial games are principles for learning that enable players to successfully master not just the game system and interface, but game goals and rules. The fandom communities associated with successful titles show similar learning principles at work, the activities of which complement not just the game content, but the in-game learning mechanics as well. Third, games provide opportunities for learning assessment that are quite rich, ranging from learning analytics applied to a given game title's data exhaust (telemetry or clickstream data; see Baker & Siemens, Chapter 13, this volume) to connected ethnographies that trace student trajectories of learning from within the game to the online game fandom community to participation structures in the home or classroom and back again (see Kafai and Dede's chapter on virtual worlds, Chapter 26, this volume). Fourth and finally, their widespread popularity and existing online distribution channels demonstrate that they can easily scale up to entire schools and school districts.

These themes raise considerable interest in using videogames in learning, both within formal classrooms and beyond them, in after school programs and at home. In this chapter, we review studies of videogames and learning. In the first section, we discuss four functional roles for videogames in learning. In the second section, we summarize the recent debate on evidence of effectiveness of videogames and learning. In the third and final section, we discuss the current and future challenges in the area.

The Roles that Videogames Play

Videogames have played various roles in learning depending on factors such as context, goal, participant structure, nature of the videogame used, topically relevant theme, and demographics of the targeted players. Compare, for example, the use of the historical simulation game *Civilization IV* to teach global material geography to high school students in an AP history course (McCall, 2011) versus the use of the massively multiplayer online game *World of Warcraft* as a context for driving interest in reading in an after school program for struggling readers. In the former, the role of the game is as a content provider and the measure of its effectiveness is contingent on appropriate use in terms of accuracy of the model and structured pedagogical activities linking it to additional resources and AP history content standards. In the latter, the role of the game is as an organizing participation structure and the measure of its effectiveness is the degree to which it effectively motivates its players to tackle texts with the right features (complexity, vocabulary, etc). One measure of the effectiveness for the former might be whether players can critique the simulation underlying the game. For the latter, a better measure might be whether the game is motivating enough to get struggling readers to keep reading even when it is hard. This section details these key roles.

Games as Content

Perhaps the most common conception of the role of videogames in learning is as the content to be learned – most typically as content knowledge and skills, but at times including dispositions as well. Games have been used in nearly all domains for learning, from mathematics (*DragonBox*, *DimensionM*) to health (exergaming titles such as *Dance Dance Revolution*). In this chapter, we focus on three disciplines: history, science, and language learning.

The commercial market success of historical simulation games like the *Civilization* series, *Assassin's Creed*, and *Rome: Total War* has inspired learning scientists to test the mettle of games for learning since the turn of the century. Engaging simulations of world history or specific historical periods allow students to "replay history" (Squire & Barab, 2004), whether on the global material scale (where game play mechanics include development of stable cities, allocation of resources, or negotiations with competing civilizations) or the local scale (where game play mechanics include role play as a historical figure, navigation of historical villages and terrain, and reenactment of key battles or negotiations with other historical figures). In a study by Moshirnia and Israel (2010), modified in-game maps in *Civilization IV* were used to deliver history content related to the American Revolution; customized information displays and pop-ups were also used. The authors found that such treatments were effective at developing students' content knowledge and retention. Additional studies of the impact of history games confirm these findings and demonstrate that these games can engage students more than traditional teaching methods (Devlin-Scherer & Sardone, 2010; Squire & Barab, 2004; Watson, Mong, & Harris, 2011), particularly when they are used in combination with skilled teaching (Lee & Probert, 2010; Squire, 2005; Squire, DeVane, & Durga, 2008). Asking students to reflect on their game play, and to compare the game and actual historical accounts, shows great promise at helping students develop a more nuanced understanding of history (Charsky & Mims, 2008); for example, students realize the limitations of any specific historical account and the potential for misconstruals and inaccuracies.

Perhaps the most well-known use of games to deliver content knowledge is in the sciences, in part because of the national attention brought to the subject through the 2011 National Research Council (NRC) report. Commercial science games like *World of Goo* and noncommercial titles like *FoldIt* or *Citizen Science* have captured both public and research attention, with debates on both sides as to the proper role of games in science learning. According to the NRC, "Simulations and games have great potential to advance multiple science learning goals, including motivation to learn science, conceptual understanding, science process skills, understanding of the nature of science, scientific discourse and argumentation, and identification with science and science learning" (NRC, 2011, p. 25). The key word here, however, is "potential." After examining the evidence, the committee concluded that the evidence for the effect of games on conceptual understanding was intriguing yet still inconclusive, and for science process skills and discourse was inconclusive. Although the report was published in 2011, the committee review of the literature was completed in 2009. Much research and development has happened since that time; our discussion in the second section, "Debate on Evidence of Effectiveness," summarizes this newer research.

The third content area we discuss is language learning, perhaps the most powerful means to which games have been leveraged to date. Example titles include larger game worlds like *XENOS* as well as smaller treatments such as *Peekaboo Barn*. Evidence for dramatic gains is consistent across multiple meta-analyses and reviews, including Peterson (2010), Young and colleagues (2012), and Wouters, Van Nimwegen, Van Oostendorp, and Van der Spek (2013). The rich multimodal environments that games provide ground language learning in the situated context of its meaning and use, thereby enabling meaningful language acquisition to take place. They allow the use of language in a rich context, both virtually and, in many cases, socially. Young and colleagues (2012) add that the current paradigm for language learning instruction, with its focus on immersive experiences and social interaction, is a very good match for the affordances that games provide.

Games as Bait

While videogames can indeed successfully serve as interactive content within the right domains (like science), this is certainly not their only contribution to learning. Recent studies show that engagement in commercial, off-the-shelf titles that are not intended to teach, and with no direct representation of the target domain within them, can – under the right conditions – promote forms of thinking and learning that are valued in school settings. We refer to this function as "games as bait" because players are attracted to the game for noneducational reasons, and the content of the game may have no obvious relation to school learning, and yet as a side effect of playing the game players learn skills and competencies that contribute to success in school subjects. Such results have surfaced across a range of disciplines and research areas, including perception and attention (Green & Bavelier, 2003), collaborative problem solving (Squire, Giovanetto, DeVane, & Durga, 2005; Steinkuehler, 2005), digital and print literacy (Leander & Lovvorn, 2006; Steinkuehler, 2006, 2007, 2008, 2012), computer and information technology fluency (Hayes, 2008), history (Squire, DeVane, & Durga, 2008), systemic thinking (Squire, 2005), ethical reasoning (Simkins & Steinkuehler, 2008), and science reasoning (Steinkuehler & Duncan, 2008). Videogames are, by definition, interactive and involve some form of problem solving: the player is given a goal that does not match their current state and must overcome obstacles to accomplish the goal. In a game, nothing at all happens until the player makes a move (a choice). Thus, even games whose content is not overtly educational can, and frequently do, require intellectual practices that result in educational outcomes as a by-product of the basic problem solving that is required within any title. The question, of course, is whether the player learns content that is, in some way and by some measure, valuable. Moreover, as Young and colleagues point out, "Much of the 'learning' of video game play may come from affinity groups that emerge from game play, consisting of metagame sources such as blogs, wikis, and discussion pages that support hints, cheats, and modding" (Young et al., 2012, pp. 82–83). Such "metagame" community and sources themselves can prove efficacious for learning even when the game title on which they focus is purely for entertainment.

In well-designed games, players have to engage in sophisticated intellectual work in the service of beating the game, including forms of knowledge and skills valued outside of the game, in classrooms and beyond. Classic examples include the ways fantasy baseball requires statistical reasoning (Halverson, 2008), how *The Sims* game franchise leads players to engage in media production and storytelling (Gee & Hayes, 2010), or how online games often lead players to display important forms of leadership (Brown & Thomas, 2006). In many cases, a game's online fan community functions as an intellectual community, promoting valued forms of knowledge and skills among the players. For example, in one study (Steinkuehler & Duncan, 2008), analysis of a representative sample of discussion board forum posts for the commercial games *World of Warcraft* found that 86 percent of the forum discussions engaged in "social knowledge construction" rather than social banter. More than half of the posts evidenced systems-based reasoning, one in ten evidenced model-based reasoning, and 65 percent displayed an *evaluative epistemology* in which knowledge is treated as an open-ended process of evaluation and argument (the very attitude toward knowledge that one needs if one is to truly understand scientific practice; see Songer & Kali, Chapter 28, this volume). In other cases, the texts and other artifacts that players generate while puzzling through a given videogame function as accidental instructional material of sorts. In Steinkuehler (2012), texts regularly involved in videogame play were found to be primarily expository in nature, with an 11.8-grade reading level and 4 percent academic vocabulary.

When reading performance on game-related versus school-related texts was compared using level-appropriate texts on assigned topics, no performance differences were found. However, when participants were allowed to choose topics, so-called struggling readers performed 6.2 grade levels above their diagnosed competency because of doubled self-correction rates (the number of times the reader corrects his or her own error while reading). Thus, game-related reading may be particularly helpful for readers who are struggling in school – not because such reading is game related, but because it is interest driven: fostering persistence in the face of textual challenges among students who might otherwise disengage.

A second notable use of games as a kind of bait is the use of games as *preparation for future learning* (Belenky & Nokes-Malch, 2012; Bransford & Schwartz, 1999). Here, learners engage with a game prior to classroom learning in the target domain, with the goal of providing learners with vicarious, hand-on experience with the phenomenon or domain under study – similar to the ways that field trips to science centers are used (Crowley, Pierroux, & Knutson, Chapter 23, this volume). In this case, game play serves to prime students to subsequently tackle instructional materials in school classroom instruction (Hammer & Black, 2009; Reese, 2007). The work of Arena (2012) is a case in point: In this study, community college students were randomly assigned to receive and play one of two commercial games (*Call of Duty 2*, a first-person shooter, or *Civilization IV*, a historical simulation game) over a period of five weeks as preparation for learning from a lecture about World War II. Participants in the control condition did not play a game in advance. Comparison of pre- and post-lecture tests indicated no differences in performance on the pre-lecture test, but a significant positive effect of game play on the post-lecture test. As hypothesized, playing videogames had prepared students to learn more from the lecture. Additional analysis showed that the two game titles had differentially influenced participants' attention, with the first-person shooter players paying more attention to local tactical elements, and historical simulation players attending more to global strategic elements. Thus, recreational game play, under the appropriate conditions, can help students learn from more traditional materials.

Games as Assessment

Games have the potential to transform assessment, because playing the game successfully and advancing through levels is itself a form of assessment. Gee (2005) observed that we would never think of applying a "test" to assess learning in a game like *Halo*; the game itself assesses your understanding as you play. The potential is that with the shift from a print-based educational media market to a digital one, educational researchers and assessment experts can capture the "data exhaust" of students' choices in online environments and better deliver content and assess learning

(Pellegrino, Chapter 12, this volume; Schoettler, 2012). Tracking and modeling student performance, it is hypothesized, will better enable both the design and delivery of instruction and assessment (Shute & Becker, 2010). The general idea (perhaps best realized by Levy and Mislevy, 2004) is that simulation games could be closely aligned to content standards, could give just-in-time feedback on performance, and could present data on problem solving in situ that would be far superior to those data gathered through traditional measurement instruments such as tests. Research can demonstrate learning gains for students (Barab, Gresalfi, & Ingram-Noble, 2010), and can even correlate in-game success to learning gains, but the idealized vision of an educational game that compels learners to achieve demonstrable excellence through their own volition remains elusive (Klopfer, Osterweil, & Salen, 2009).

Thus far, such techniques have been applied primarily to *discovery games* – games in which players, through their collective activity, make actual contributions to scientific discovery within a given domain – such as *Fold.it*, or games with relatively constrained paths, such as Cisco Systems Aspire (which was designed through Evidence Centered Design; Behrens, Mislevy, Bauer, Williamson, & Levy, 2004; Honey & Hilton, 2011). Recent developments in machine learning offer compelling techniques for measuring learning in game-based learning environments (Dangauthier, Herbrich, Minka, & Graepel, 2008; Gee, 2004). Machine learning techniques, including supervised and unsupervised techniques (such as reinforcement learning and semi-supervised regression) have dramatic potential for reshaping the design of learning systems. As educational systems move toward digital content delivery through mobile systems (see Sharples & Pea, Chapter 25, this volume), it appears certain that such machine learning techniques will be applied to studying learning; bigger questions surround what these learning experiences will look like, how learning will be assessed, and what role different stakeholder groups (learning scientists, academics, teachers, parents, students) will play in shaping it.

An area currently being explored is how to apply such techniques to open-ended games that feature problems that can be solved multiple ways; construction or design tasks; and social mechanics in which learners interact online. Halverson, Owen, Wills, and Shapiro (2012) investigated students playing *ProgenitorX*, a stem cell construction game, and found that efficient game play on the final levels was a predictor of learning gains more broadly. Owen and Halverson are currently applying this framework to other games, and posit that it may be a generalizable model toward using "in game data" (called *telemetry data*) for assessment. They are developing common data structures that can be used in a wide range of games so that researchers can identify play patterns *across* games. With these common data structures, researchers could study (for example) if success in one game predicts success in another.

Games as Architectures for Engagement

Digital games have long been studied as sites of engaged learning (Gee, 2007; Malone & Lepper, 1987). Malone (1981) studied Atari games to develop a theory of intrinsic motivation, and concluded that games use fantasy, control, challenge, and curiosity to motivate players. Later, Malone and Lepper (1987) explored the social context of game play and added collaboration and competition as other intrinsic rewards. Cordova and Lepper (1996) designed games leveraging these principles for mathematics learning and found that more highly motivated students performed better than their peers on similar mathematics tasks.

In the 2000s, socially situated learning theorists studied games as architectures for engagement, using primarily phenomenological, ethnographic, and discursive methods (Davidson, 2011; Gee, 2007). Consistent with a sociocultural approach, this work has examined how and why people play games and how games are designed as systems to be learned (Steinkuehler, Squire, & Barab, 2012). As games grew larger and more complex, good design principles – such as providing just-in-time instruction – emerged (Gee, 2005, 2007). Starting perhaps with *Half Life* (1998), games began jettisoning their lengthy tutorials and manuals. (The manual for *Civilization III*, one of the last such games built this way, is 236 pages; Squire, 2006.) In the hypercompetitive marketplace of entertainment games, these techniques evolve rapidly so that features such as embedded tutorials, just-in-time instruction, or adaptive artificial intelligence (AI) become expected in the marketplace (Sawyer, 2003). Tracking these design innovations across multiple games and platforms is challenging, and Davidson (2011) developed the *Well Played* journal as a venue to publish these innovations. In *Well Played* pieces (which is analogous to being "well read"), authors unpack game design features through deep analysis of select titles. Davidson (2011) and Davidson and LaMarchand (2012) developed a model of engagement in games that describes a player process of *involvement, immersion*, and *investment*. Analyzing *World of Goo*, and later *Uncharted 2*, Davidson demonstrated how specific narrative features contribute to player immersion.

A second branch of research uses character theory to investigate player types (Bartle, 2003). Originally developed through a grounded analysis of user forum interactions, Bartle's (1996) theory emphasizes multiple, discrete motivations for game play (exploration, achievement, competition, and socialization), which one might in engage in at any time. Yee (2006) conducted a factor analysis of game players and proposed an alternative model based on three core motivations (with sub-factors): *achievement, social*, and *immersion*. Yee's model describes these as *components*, as opposed to *types*, suggesting that they fit along a normal distribution, complement one another (as opposed to supplanting one another), and cluster so that a player is a configuration of a cluster of these components. This work reminds learning scientists, particularly those designing games for learning, that different players come to games with different motivations and that designing games to capture broad segments of the population is a challenge.

Gamification is a relatively recent term that describes using game thinking and game mechanics in nongame contexts to engage users (Deterding, 2013). These techniques include narrative structures, quests and challenges, point systems, and achievements. *5th Dimension* is one of the longest-running and most well-researched gamification-type learning systems (Cole, 2006). *5th Dimension* was created in the 1990s as a mechanism for exploring Cole's (1996) theory of cultural psychology. In *5th Dimension*, "clubs" – groups of 5–14 youth – work through a maze of quests, which are assigned to them by a fictional wizard. These quests are presented on task cards, and frequently are based on games such as *Carmen San Diego*, *The Incredible Machine*, or *Oregon Trail*. All learning is situated within a narrative experience of helping the wizard, rather than earning grades or points. Adults (usually college students) play wizards' assistants, who work as mentors. More than 100 research studies and evaluations have been conducted on *5th Dimension*, which has been enacted in sites across the world (Cole, 2006; Mayer, Blanton, Duran, & Schustack, 1999; Simmons, Blanton, & Greene, 1999). Through participation in *5th Dimension*, students develop academic skills that can be used across a variety of contexts (Blanton, Moorman, Hayes, & Warner, 1997; Mayer et al., 1997).

Subsequent learning games, such as *Quest Atlantis*, have created a similarly immersive world, but built around social commitments such as respect for diversity or creative expression (Barab, Thomas, Dodge, Carteaux, & Tuzun, 2005). *Quest Atlantis* targets late elementary school students across a broad swath of the curriculum. *Quest Atlantis* is rendered in real-time 3-D; through completing quests, students seek to improve life for citizens. The quests range from online to offline behaviors, and are usually certified by a teacher through an online dashboard. Students' online profiles include features such as an item inventory, reputation systems, various currencies, and so on. Most *Quest Atlantis* quests are traditionally valued academic practices, but are given meaning through a narrative of the Atlantians. The questing structure also serves as a *motivational* element that repositions learning even traditional academic tasks as a new *activity* (Barab, Zuicker, & Warren, 2007). Students participating in *Quest Atlantis* were motivated by identity, play, immersion, and social relationships, which – for some students – transformed academic activity from reward-based activity to activity driven by a desire to become new kinds of people, to play, or to engage in legitimate social activity. Through its many iterations, the designers Barab, Arici, and Jackson (2005) find that the *Quest Atlantis* narrative was its most engaging feature. Studies of *Quest Atlantis* use in classrooms show that it can improve students' scientific inquiry, reasoning, and argumentation skills – along both traditional and performance measures (cf. Hickey, Ingram-Noble, & Jameson, 2009). Barab and colleagues described this process as "narratizing the curriculum," which suggests one useful way for designers to think about gamifying formal curricular structures.

Debate on Evidence of Effectiveness

Despite nearly a decade of interest in videogames as learning technologies in the field of learning sciences, scholars continue to debate their effectiveness, and the results emerging from different studies are inconsistent. Vogel and colleagues (2006) found that games outperformed more traditional methods in terms of both cognitive and attitudinal effects, but their results were mitigated by variables such as gender and whether navigation through the content was self-driven or teacher or computer driven. Ke's (2009) review of 89 research studies found that games indeed appear efficacious for learning, but the evidence is contradictory in places, with treatments largely underspecified with few if any of the actual game mechanics specified. Clark, Yates, Early, and Moulton (2010), however, found that serious games are not more effective than traditional classroom instruction methods. In contrast, Sitzmann's (2011) meta-analysis found that games – compared to traditional classroom controls – resulted in 20 percent higher self-efficacy, 11 percent higher declarative knowledge, 14 percent higher procedural knowledge, and 9 percent better retention – but only when the comparison treatment was passive and not active learning.

Two recent meta-analyses warrant a bit more discussion and help to tease out these contradictory conclusions in useful ways. Young and colleagues (2012) conducted a meta-analysis of the relationship between playing learning videogames and academic achievement; this study incorporated game implementations in K-12 classrooms. Of the 363 articles found, however, only 10 percent were included (3 in history, 8 in math, 7 in physical education, 11 in science, and 10 in language learning) because of the under-specification of both the treatment variable (i.e., no clear gaming mechanisms were described) and the school-related dependent or outcome variable. The authors concluded that there is evidence for positive effects of videogames on language learning, history, and physical education (specifically exergames), but little support for the academic value of videogames in science and math. This insufficient evidence in the domain of science is corroborated in the National Research Council's (2011) report.

In a second meta-analysis by Wouters and colleagues (2013), the authors analyzed the results from 39 studies that compared games to more conventional instruction methods (lectures, reading, drill and practice, and hypertext environments), the majority of which were conducted in the preceding five years, and found that games were more effective than conventional methods; students learned more knowledge and cognitive skills, and these enhanced gains persisted over time. Games were more effective when supplemented with other instructional methods and when played in groups rather than in isolation. Surprisingly, their results showed that games are *not* more motivating than more conventional methods. The authors posit that the capacity of games to engage may well be mitigated in contexts where game play is mandatory or where the game mechanics are not well aligned with content, and player choice is limited.

Four complications make any reasonable summary of the empirical literature difficult. First and foremost, what technologies fall under the rubric of "games" itself is inconsistent. For Vogel and colleagues (2006), games include "interactive simulations." For Ke (2009), games were defined as computer-based instructional games, but simulations were not included because they do not involve competition. For Clark and colleagues (2010), the focus was on "serious games"; yet there, games were reviewed as one special case of discovery-based instruction more generally (and found wanting). In Sitzmann's (2011), the focus was on computer simulation games. In the NRC (2011) report, computer simulations and games were separate categories but both were included in the review. Only Young and colleagues (2012) and Wouters and colleagues (2013) gave a principled, categorical definition of what exactly was being reviewed and assessed – and even then there is reason to believe that, within those explicit definitions, there is enough variation to raise serious questions about whether videogames enhance learning.

A second reason it is difficult to summarize the research on evidence of effectiveness is that there is not enough specification of the details of game mechanics used and the learning outcomes targeted (National Research Council, 2011; Young et al., 2012). Without drilling down to which specific game mechanics are purported to result in which specific outcomes, substantive conclusions for how to design games for specific curricular goals remain elusive.

Third, because videogames are interactive, individual players often have idiosyncratic goals and play patterns, and as a result each learners' experience is somewhat different (Harris, Yuill, & Luckin, 2008), making generalization within and across conditions difficult. As Young and colleagues wrote:

> [C]urrent methodologies must extend beyond their current parameters to account for the individualized nature of game play, acknowledging the impossibility of the same game being played exactly the same way twice and establishing that game play may need to be investigated as situated learning. (Young et al., 2012, p. 62)

Fourth, the effects of videogames, like any other instructional technique, vary tremendously based on context of use. This context includes not only the ways players tailor game play experiences to reflect their own preferences, but also the social context, the ancillary online or offline texts, and other game-related artifacts accompanying game play, the presence or absence of a more knowledgeable teacher or peer, and the degree of reflection or "metagaming" elicited. Without taking context into consideration, it is difficult to interpret studies of the effectiveness of videogames for learning.

Current and Future Challenges

There are several challenges that should be addressed in future research. First, researchers should develop a working definition of *videogame*, then specify various game play mechanics, and finally, assess each play mechanic's impact on learning. Many definitions of *videogame* have been used; perhaps the most straightforward definition in the literature is the definition provided by Klopfer, Osterweil, and Salen (2009) and used as the basis of the 2011 Science, Technology, Engineering, and Math (STEM) Video Game Challenge conducted by the U.S. Department of Education and the meta-analyses and reports by Thai, Lowenstein, Ching, and Rejeski (2009) and Young and colleagues. Here, learning games are defined as:

> a voluntary activity structured by rules, with a defined outcome (e.g., winning/ losing) or other quantifiable feedback (e.g., points) that facilitates reliable comparisons of in-player performances ... [that] target the acquisition of knowledge as its own end and foster habits of mind and understanding that are generally useful or useful within an academic context. Learning Games may be associated with formal educational environments (schools and universities, online or off), places of informal learning (e.g., museums), or self-learners interested in acquiring new knowledge or understanding. (Young et al., 2012, pp. 11, 21)

Thus, videogames for learning would be defined as digital learning games. Such a definition allows us to exclude other types of simulations and digital visualization tools while including other important forms of contemporary games such as alternate reality games (ARGs) played on mobile devices. This definition is also consistent with the work of Juul (2005) and others in the field of games studies more generally.

Even with this broad working definition in place, "videogames" may very well be too broad a category for drawing useful generalizations. In Young and colleagues' (2012) meta-analysis, for example, this definition of videogames is found to be too broad to meaningfully draw conclusions regarding their effects. With this definition in place, however, we hope to get to the harder business of developing a taxonomy of game mechanics and characteristics and then to study each of their impacts on learning.

Another set of challenges to the field of videogames for learning is how to account for the situational and contextual factors that bear on game-based learning outcomes. Videogames need to be implemented with good teachers who are able to scaffold performance, engage students in reflection, and draw connections between game play and other curricular materials (Baek,

Kim, & Park, 2009; Young et al., 2012). Game-related learning takes place not only within the videogame technology itself, but also and perhaps more crucially through the activities and materials (paratexts, artifacts, interactions, and activities) engaged in outside but in relation to the videogame. Debriefing and reflection practices in particular, as well as individual reflection and peer review (Ke, 2008), play an important role here. An overly narrow focus on the videogame itself may be a poor way to conceptualize how learning is enhanced.

For example, the formal instructional context seems to moderate the effectiveness of any videogame treatment (Sitzmann, 2011) and, in many cases, may work against the unique advantages of videogames for learning. As Young and colleagues noted:

> [T]here appears to be a disconnect between the possible instructional affordances of games and how they are integrated into classrooms. Games are often multiplayer and cooperative and competitive; they engage players in several hours of extended play, allow rich "hint and cheat" websites to develop around player affinity groups, and are played from weeks to years. However, most schools trade off extended immersion for curriculum coverage, individual play, and short exposures, goals that are not well aligned with engaging video game play. (Young et al., 2012, p. 80)

As the interest in videogames and learning grows in the learning sciences, and as we increasingly implement innovative learning environments that incorporate videogames into classrooms, we should be careful not to unintentionally undermine the very features that make videogames provocative and uniquely powerful tools for learning.

References

Arena, D. A. (2012). Commercial video games as preparation for future learning. Dissertation, Stanford University. School of Education.

Baek, Y., Kim, B., & Park, H. (2009). Not just fun, but serious strategies: Using metacognitive strategies in game-based learning. *Computers & Education*, 52, 800–810.

Barab, S., Arica, A., & Jackson, C. (2005). Eat your vegetables and do your homework: A design-based investigation of enjoyment and meaning in learning. *Educational Technology*, 45(1), 15–21.

Barab, S. A., Gresalfi, M. S., & Ingram-Goble, A. (2010). Transformational play: Using games to position person, content, and context. *Educational Researcher*, 39(7), 525–536.

Barab, S., Thomas, M., Dodge, T., Carteaux, R., & Tuzun, H. (2005). Making learning fun: Quest Atlantis, a game without guns. *Educational Technology Research and Development*, 53(1), 86–107.

Barab, S., Zuiker, S., Warren, S., et al. (2007). Situationally embodied curriculum: Relating formalisms and contexts. *Science Education*, 91(5), 750–782.

Bartle, R. (1996). Hearts, clubs, diamonds, spades: Players who suit MUDs. *Journal of MUD Research*, 1(1). Available: http://www.mud.co.uk/richard/hcds.htm (May 19).

Bartle, R. (2003). *Designing virtual worlds.* Indianapolis, IN: New Riders.

Behrens, J. T., Mislevy, R. J., Bauer, M., Williamson, D. M., & Levy, R. (2004). Introduction to evidence centered design and lessons learned from its application in a global e-learning program. *The International Journal of Testing*, 4(4), 295–301.

Belenky, D. M., & Nokes-Malach, T. J. (2012). Motivation and transfer: The role of mastery-approach goals in preparation for future learning. *The Journal of the Learning Sciences*, 21(3), 399–432.

Blanton, W. E., Moorman, G. B., Hayes, B. A., & Warner, M. W. (1997). Effects of participation in the Fifth Dimension on far transfer. *Journal of Educational Computing Research*, 16, 371–396.

Bransford, J., & Schwartz, D. (1999). Rethinking transfer: A simple proposal with multiple implications. In A. Iran-Nejad & P. Pearson (Eds.), *Review of Research in Education*, 24, 61–101.

Brown, J. S., & Thomas, D. (2006). You play World of Warcraft? You're hired! *Wired*, 14(4).

Charsky, D., & Mims, C. (2008). Integrating commercial off-the-shelf video games into school curriculums. *Tech Trends*, 52, 38–44.

Clark, R. E., Yates, K., Early, S., & Moulton, K. (2010). An analysis of the failure of electronic media and discovery-based learning: Evidence for the performance benefits of guided training methods. In K. H. Silber & R. Foshay (Eds.), *Handbook of training and improving workplace performance: Vol. I. Instructional design and training delivery* (pp. 263–297). Somerset, NJ: Wiley.

Cole, M. (1996). *Cultural psychology: A once and future discipline.* Cambridge, MA: Harvard University Press.

Cole, M. (2006). *The Fifth Dimension: An after school program built on diversity.* New York: Sage.

Cordova, D. I., & Lepper, M. R. (1996). Intrinsic motivation and the process of learning: Beneficial effects of contextualization, personalization, and choice. *Journal of Educational Psychology*, 88(4), 715–730.

Dangauthier, P., Herbrich, R., Minka, T., & Graepel, T. (2008). TrueSkill through time: Revisiting the history of chess. *Advances in Neural Information Processing Systems*, 20, 931–938.

Davidson, D. (Ed.) (2011). *Well played.* Pittsburgh, PA: Entertainment Technology Press.

Davidson, D., & Lamarchand, R. (2012). Uncharted 2: Among thieves – How to become a hero. In C. Steinkuehler, K. Squire, & S. Barab (Eds.), *Games+Learning+Society* (pp 75–107). Cambridge: Cambridge University Press.

Devlin-Scherer, R., & Sardone, N. B. (2010). Digital simulation games for social studies classrooms. *Clearing House*, 83, 138–144.

Deterding, S. (2013). Designing gamification: Creating gameful and playful experiences. SIG-CHI Workshop. Proceedings of the Association for Computing Machinery (ACM).

Eiben, C. B., Siegel, J. B., Bale, J. B., Cooper, S., Khatib, F., Shen, B. W., Foldit Players, Stoddard, B. L., Popovic, Z., & Baker, D. (2012). Increased Diels-Alderase activity through backbone remodeling guided by Foldit players. *Nature Biotechnology*, January 22.

Entertainment Software Association. (2011). Industry Facts. Retrieved March 12, 2013 from http://www.theesa.com/facts.

Gee, J. (2004). *Situated language and learning: A critique of traditional schooling*. London: Routledge.

Gee, J. (2005). Learning by design: Good video games as learning machines. *E-Learning*, 2(1), 5–16.

Gee, J. P. (2007). *What video games have to teach us about learning and literacy*. Second Edition. New York: Palgrave Macmillan.

Gee, J. P., & Hayes, E. R. (2010). *Women and gaming: The Sims and 21st century learning*. New York: Palgrave Macmillan.

Graf, D. L., Pratt, L. V., Hester, C. N., & Short, K. R. (2009). Playing active video games increases energy expenditure in children. *Pediatrics*, 124(2), 534–540.

Green, C., & Bavelier, D. (2003). Action videogame modifies visual attention. *Nature*, 423, 534–537.

Green, C. S., Pouget, A., & Bavelier, D. (2010). Improved probabilistic inference as a general mechanism for learning with action video games. *Current Biology*, 23, 1573–1579.

Halverson, E. R. (2008). Fantasy baseball: The case for competitive fandom. *Games and Culture*, 3(3–4), 286–308.

Halverson, R., Owen, E., Wills, N., Shapiro, R. B. (2012, July). *Game-based assessment: An integrating model for capturing learning in play*. ERIA Working Paper.

Hammer, J., & Black, J. (2009). Games and (preparation for future) learning. *Educational Technology*, 49(2), 29–34.

Harris, A., Yuill, N., & Luckin, R. (2008). The influence of context-specific and dispositional achievement goals on children's paired collaborative interaction. *British Journal of Educational Psychology*, 78, 355–374.

Harris, D. N. (2011). *Value-added measures in education: What every educator needs to know*. Cambridge, MA: Harvard University Press.

Hayes, E. (2008). Game content creation & IT proficiency. *Computers & Education*, 51(1), 97–108.

Hickey, D., Ingram-Goble, A., & Jameson, E. (2009). Designing assessments and assessing designs in virtual educational environments. *Journal of Science Education and Technology*, 18, 187–208.

Honey, M. A., & Hilton, M. L. (Eds.) (2011). *Learning science through computer games and simulations*. Washington, DC: National Academies Press.

Juul, J. (2005). *Half-real: Video games between real rules and fictional worlds*. Cambridge, MA: MIT Press.

Ke, F. (2008). A case study of computer gaming for math: Engaged learning from gameplay? *Computers & Education*, 51, 1609–1620.

Ke, F. (2009). A qualitative meta-analysis of computer games as learning tools. In R. E. Ferdig (Ed.), *Handbook of research on effective electronic gaming in education* (Vol. 1, pp. 1–32). Hershey, PA: Information Science Reference.

Klopfer, E., Osterweil, S., & Salen, K. (2009). *Moving learning games forward.* Cambridge, MA: Education Arcade.

Leander, K., & Lovvorn, J. (2006). Literacy networks. *Curriculum & Instruction,* 24(3), 291–340.

Lee, J. K., & Probert, J. (2010). Civilization III and whole-class play in high school social studies. *Journal of Social Studies Research,* 34, 1–28.

Levy, R., & Mislevy, R. J. (2004). Specifying and refining a measurement model for a simulation-based assessment. *International Journal of Testing,* 4, 333–369.

Malone, T. W. (1981). Toward a theory of intrinsically motivating instruction. *Cognitive Science,* (4), 333–369.

Malone, T. W., & Lepper, M. R. (1987). Making learning fun: A taxonomic model of intrinsic motivations for learning. In R. E. Snow & M. J. Farr (Eds.), *Aptitude, learning, and instruction: III. Cognitive and affective process analyses* (pp. 223–253). Hillsdale, NJ: Lawrence Erlbaum Associates.

Mayer, R. E., Blanton, W., Duran, R., & Schustack, M. (1999). *Using new information technologies in the creation of sustainable afterschool literacy activities: Evaluation of cognitive outcomes.* Final Report to the Andrew W. Mellon Foundation.

Mayer, R. E., Quilici, J. H., Moreno, R., Duran, R., Woodbridge, S., & Simon, R. (1997). Cognitive consequences of participation in a Fifth Dimension afterschool computer club. *Journal of Educational Computing Research,* 16, 353–370.

McCall, J. (2011). *Gaming the past: Using video games to teach secondary history.* New York: Routledge.

Moshirnia, A., & Israel, M. (2010). The educational efficacy of distinct information delivery systems in modified video games. *Journal of Interactive Learning Research,* 21, 383–405.

National Research Council (NRC). (2011). *Learning science through computer games and simulations* (Committee on Science Learning: Computer Games, Simulations, and Education, M. A. Honey & M. L. Hilton, Eds.). Washington, DC: National Academies Press, Board on Science Education, Division of Behavioral and Social Sciences and Education.

Peterson, M. (2010). Computerized games and simulations in computer-assisted language learning: A meta-analysis of research. *Simulation & Gaming,* 41, 72–93.

Reese, D. D. (2007). First steps and beyond: Serious games as preparation for future learning. *Journal of Educational Multimedia and Hypermedia,* 16(3), 283–300.

Rideout, V. J., Foehr, U. G., & Roberts, D. F. (2010). *Generation M2: Media in the lives of 8- to 18-year-olds.* Menlo Park, CA: Henry J. Kaiser Family Foundation.

Russoniello, C. V., O'Brien, K., & Parks, J. M. (2009). EEG, HRV and psychological correlates while playing Bejeweled II: A randomized controlled study. *Annual Review of Cybertherapy and Telemedicine,* 7, 189–192.

Sawyer, B. (2003). *Monster gaming.* Phoenix, AZ: Paraglyph.

Schoettler, S. (2012). Learning analytics: What could you do with five orders of magnitude more data about learning? Keynote address at the 2012 Strata Conference, February 29, Santa Clara, CA.

Shute, V. J., & Becker, B. J. (2010). *Innovative assessment for the 21st century*. New York: Springer.

Simkins, D., & Steinkuehler, C. (2008). Critical ethical reasoning & role-play. *Games & Culture*, 3(3–4), 333–355.

Simmons, E. C., Blanton, W. E., & Greene, M. W. (1999). The fifth dimension clearinghouse: One strategy for diffusing, implementing and sustaining core principles. In J. Price et al. (Eds.), *Proceedings of Society for Information Technology & Teacher Education International Conference* (pp. 1135–1140). Chesapeake, VA: AACE.

Sitzmann, T. (2011). A meta-analytic examination of the instructional effectiveness of computer-based simulation games. *Personnel Psychology*, 64, 489–528.

Siwek, S. E. (2010). *Video games in the 21st century: The 2010 report*. Entertainment Software Association.

Squire, K. D. (2005a). Changing the game: What happens when video games enter the classroom? *Innovate: Journal of Online Education*, 1(6). Retrieved from http://www.innovateonline.info/index.php?view=article&id=82.

Squire, K. D. (2005b). Educating the fighter. *On the Horizon*, 13(2), 75–88.

Squire, K. D. (2006). From content to context: Videogames as designed experience. *Educational Researcher*, 35(8), 19–29.

Squire, K., & Barab, S. A. (2004). Replaying history. *Proceedings of the 2004 International Conference of the Learning Sciences*. Los Angeles: UCLA Press.

Squire, K. D., DeVane, B., & Durga, S. (2008). Designing centers of expertise for academic learning through video games. *Theory into Practice*, 47(3).

Squire, K. D., Giovanetto, L., Devane, B., & Durga, S. (2005). From users to designers: Building a self-organizing game-based learning environment. *Technology Trends*, 49(5), 34–42.

Steinkuehler, C. A. (2005). Cognition and learning in massively multiplayer online games: A critical approach. Unpublished dissertation. University of Wisconsin-Madison.

Steinkuehler, C. A. (2006). Massively multiplayer online videogaming as participation in a discourse. *Mind, Culture, & Activity*, 13(1), 38–52.

Steinkuehler, C. A. (2007). Massively multiplayer online gaming as a constellation of literacy practices. *eLearning*, 4(3) 297–318.

Steinkuehler, C. A. (2008). Cognition and literacy in massively multiplayer online games. In J. Coiro, M. Knobel, C. Lankshear, & D. Leu (Eds.), *Handbook of research on new literacies* (pp. 611–634). Mahwah, NJ: Lawrence Erlbaum Associates.

Steinkuehler, C. A. (2012). The mismeasure of boys: Reading and online videogames. In W. Kaminski & M. Lorber (Eds.), *Proceedings of Game-based Learning: Clash of Realities Conference* (pp. 33–50). Munich: Kopaed Publishers.

Steinkuehler, C., & Duncan, S. (2008). Scientific habits of mind in virtual worlds. *Journal of Science Education & Technology*, 17(6), 530–543.

Steinkuehler, C., Squire, K., & Barab, S. (Eds.) (2012). *Games, learning, and society: Learning and meaning in the digital age*. New York: Cambridge University Press.

Thai, A., Lowenstein, D., Ching, D., & Rejeski, D. (2009). *Game changer: Investing in digital play to advance children's learning and health.* New York: Joan Ganz Cooney Center at Sesame Workshop.

Vogel, J. J., Vogel, D. S., Cannon- Bowers, J., Bowers, C. A., Muse, K., & Wright, M. (2006). Computer gaming and interactive simulations for learning: A meta-analysis. *Journal of Educational Computing Research,* 34, 229–243.

Watson, W. R., Mong, C. J., & Harris, C. A. (2011). A case study of in-class use of a video game for teaching high school history. *Computers & Education,* 56, 466–474.

Wouters, P., Van Nimwegen, C., Van Oostendorp, H., & Van der Spek, E. D. (2013, February 4). A meta-analysis of the cognitive and motivational effects of serious games. *Journal of Educational Psychology.*

Yee, N. (2006). Motivations for play in online games. *CyberPsychology and Behavior,* 9, 772–775.

Young, M. F., Slota, S., Cutter, A. B., Jalette, G., Mullin, G., Lai, B., Simeoni, Z., Tran, M., & Yukhymenko, M. (2012). Our princess is in another castle: A review of trends in serious gaming for education. *Review of Educational Research,* 82(1), 61–89.

PART IV

Learning Together

20 Knowledge Building and Knowledge Creation: Theory, Pedagogy, and Technology

Marlene Scardamalia and Carl Bereiter

The terms *knowledge building* and *knowledge creation* entered the applied behavioral science literature at about the same time (Nonaka, 1991; Nonaka & Takeuchi, 1995; Scardamalia & Bereiter, 1991; Scardamalia, Bereiter, & Lamon, 1994), but in different domains: knowledge building in the learning sciences, knowledge creation in organizational science. Because they derive from different epistemologies, it was not immediately apparent that the two terms are essentially synonymous. *Knowledge building* derives from a Popperian epistemology that treats ideas as entities in their own right that can have properties, connections, and potentialities independent of the mental states of the individuals who hold the ideas (Bereiter, 2002; Popper, 1972; Scardamalia et al., 1994). Nonaka and his associates have treated knowledge creation as a sociocognitive process in which the tacit knowledge of individuals figures centrally both as source and as outcome. The two are alike, however, in regarding new knowledge as literally *created* rather than, as older epistemologies viewed it, *discovered*.

In both cases it was necessary to carve out a place for the creation of ideas in a conceptual space dominated by "learning" – as in "inquiry learning" and "learning organization." To demarcate this space in education we have distinguished between learning, conceived of as a change in mental state, and knowledge building, conceived of as the out-in-the-world production of designs, theories, problem solutions, hypotheses, proofs, and the like. The two may go on in parallel, and are expected to do so in education, but from a design standpoint they represent different problem spaces. "Group cognition" (Stahl, 2006), a new kid on the epistemological block, does not obviate the distinction. Groups can learn – that is, acquire skills and understandings best described at the group level. At the same time, but from an importantly different viewpoint, knowledge creation frequently has its origin in group processes. To emphasize the distinction, we have adopted the convention of capitalizing Knowledge Building to refer to the approach elaborated in this chapter, which aims to bring into education both the goals and the processes of knowledge-creating organizations – as represented, for instance, in scientific research groups and industrial design teams.

In successful knowledge-creating organizations, invention and design are "part-and-parcel of the ordinary, if not routine" (Drucker, 1985) and people are recognized for contributions they make to the organization's or community's knowledge, not for what is in their minds. In education, the opposite is normally the case. Although students may be rewarded for doing good work, the "good work" (written assignments and so forth) is usually valued as evidence of what is in the students' minds – hence as evidence of learning. However, in Knowledge Building theory, pedagogy, and technology, students' work is primarily valued for what it contributes to the community and secondarily for what it reveals about individual students' knowledge.

In judging whether students are actually capable of authentic knowledge creation, we have argued that students should not be held to a higher standard than university researchers who publish and earn tenure on the basis of original contributions to knowledge, but who are not the Einsteins or Piagets of their fields (Bereiter & Scardamalia, 2010). Insightful interpretations or explanations of the work of others qualify as knowledge creation, as do identification and clarification of problems, providing supportive or disconfirming findings, offering a different perspective on an issue, and even popularizing knowledge advances – putting them within reach of the less sophisticated. All of these are within the capacity of students working collaboratively (Van Aalst, 2009; Van Aalst & Truong, 2011). The community to which knowledge contributions are made is normally the community of their peers, but this does not exclude occasionally making contributions to world knowledge writ large. The same is true, of course, in the corporate and research worlds.

Despite the recognizable value of group knowledge-creating activity, the fact remains that schools are held responsible for individual students' learning. Educational activities, which may range from taking notes in a lecture to creating a theory or a computer simulation, are ultimately judged according to what individual students learn from them. Such judgments fuel long-running debates about educational policy and no educational approach can stand aloof from them. As far as conventional measures of learning are concerned, evidence indicates that Knowledge Building enhances individual learning in relevant areas and does not diminish it in others (Chuy et al., 2010; Scardamalia et al., 1992), and that as promotion of collaborative knowledge building advances, individual learning of subject matter advances with it (Zhang, Scardamalia, Reeve, & Messina, 2009). Advances in literacy have been documented in the absence of reading instruction, apparently due to students' sustained engagement in knowledge building activities that provide authentic motivation for reading and writing (Sun, Zhang, & Scardamalia, 2010).

Over and above traditional learning objectives, however, is the objective of equipping students for the emerging conditions of life and work in an innovation-driven knowledge society. Many contemporary approaches pursue this objective – some through testing and promoting what are popularly called "21st-century skills," others through engaging students in activities that have some of the characteristics of work in knowledge-creating organizations. Knowledge Building, however, takes a more direct approach, making knowledge creation itself the constitutive basis of subject matter education – in brief, acquiring competence in knowledge creation by actually doing it. In broad terms, this means enabling all students to find respected and positive roles as collaborators in knowledge creation.

Although Knowledge Building and knowledge creation refer to the same process, in practice Knowledge Building encompasses a much greater range of concerns, due in large part to its involvement in issues of learning and human development. These issues are not entirely absent from organizational knowledge management, but they do not have nearly the prominence there that they have in educational Knowledge Building. Thus the term *Knowledge Building* identifies a distinctive design space, even though conceptually it is synonymous with knowledge creation. In the following sections we elaborate five themes that represent special challenges that must be faced when knowledge creation is brought into education.

Community Knowledge Advancement

Creative knowledge work may be defined as work that advances the state of community knowledge, however broadly or narrowly the community may be defined (Scardamalia & Bereiter, 2006). In every scholarly discipline one finds periodic reviews of the state of knowledge (or the "state of the art") in the field. Different scholars might offer different descriptions of the discipline's state of knowledge; however, these disagreements may themselves contribute to advancing the state of knowledge. The state of knowledge is not what everyone in the field or the average person in the field knows, but neither is it what the most knowledgeable people in the field know. Rather, it is an emergent collective phenomenon, a distributed characteristic of the entire discipline. And in this sense, the state of knowledge cannot be found in any one person's mind. If we look back at prehistoric times, using archaeological evidence, we can make statements about the state of knowledge in a certain civilization at a certain time, without knowing anything about any individuals and what they thought or knew.

Knowledge Building pedagogy is based on the premise that authentic creative knowledge work can take place in school classrooms – knowledge work that does not merely emulate the work of mature scholars or designers but that substantively advances the state of knowledge in the classroom community and situates it within the larger societal knowledge building effort. As in the scholarly disciplines, the state of knowledge in the classroom is an emergent distributed phenomenon that cannot be found in any one student's mind. Correspondingly, the state of community knowledge only indirectly reflects the knowledge of individual members of the community.

Some individuals may lag behind, some may be in advance, and some off in another direction from the progress of community knowledge. It is, however, reasonable to expect (as evidence from a variety of sources indicates) that gains in individual achievement will accompany advances in community knowledge. In the previously cited study by Zhang and colleagues (2009), year-by-year changes in a teacher's practice aimed at getting fuller participation in collaborative Knowledge Building resulted in both sociometric changes in the desired direction and in progressive improvements in learning results over successive years.

Idea Improvement

Engineers and designers do not think in terms of a final state of perfection (Petroski, 1998). Advances in a technology open up new problems to be solved and new possibilities for further advancement; there is no end in sight. But many people still think of scholarly knowledge as advancing toward (though perhaps never reaching) final truths: how the universe actually began, the true history of the invasion of Iraq, and so on. But advances in theoretical and historical knowledge raise new problems and open new possibilities, just as do advances in technology. In Knowledge Building, idea improvement is an explicit principle, even at elementary school levels (Scardamalia, 2002). More than a pedagogical principle, idea improvement is promoted as a sociocognitive norm intended to inform the whole way of life in a knowledge-building community. Every idea is to be treated as potentially improvable. In such a sociocultural environment, "critical thinking" is manifested not so much by skepticism or argumentativeness as by the pervasive application of "design thinking" (Martin, 2009) – continual application of a "make it better" heuristic rather than an "arguments for/ arguments against" heuristic (Bereiter & Scardamalia, 2003).

In any educational program, students are expected to leave with better ideas than they held initially. Educational programs vary not only in their methods of promoting idea improvement, but in the allocation of responsibility for bringing such improvement about. In conceptual change teaching, for instance (see diSessa, Chapter 5, this volume), it is generally accepted that idea improvement must come from the students' own reconciliation of conflicting conceptions, but the teacher is responsible for recognizing conceptual inadequacies, arranging activities that will induce cognitive conflict, and assessing results. In Knowledge Building, however, students are expected to take on these responsibilities themselves, with help from teacher, technology, and peers. Whereas idea generation comes naturally to young people, working to improve one's ideas does not. Considerable support is usually required to maintain student engagement in idea improvement, and even more to establish idea improvement as a classroom norm. But once it is established the students themselves become a sustaining force. As later sections of this chapter show, supporting sustained creative efforts at idea improvement is the principal challenge in designing more powerful knowledge-building technology.

Knowledge Building Discourse

In a view of science that was common among philosophers of science 50 years ago, the essential value of discourse among scientists comes from sharing knowledge and subjecting ideas to criticism, as in formal publications and oral presentations, question-and-answer sessions after these presentations, and occasionally debates. Essentially, discourse was viewed as a filter, determining what was accepted into the canon of justified beliefs (Latour & Woolgar, 1979). Lakatos (1976) was perhaps the first to argue that real science does not work this way; instead, discourse often plays a creative role – actively improving on ideas, rather than only acting as a critical filter. Empirical studies of scientific discourse have supported this view. For example, Dunbar (1997) showed that the discourse that goes on inside research laboratories is fundamentally different from the discourse that goes on in presentations and papers; it is more cooperative, more concerned with shared goals of advancing understanding beyond what is currently understood. The creative role of discourse is also widely recognized in the organizational knowledge creation literature; for example, it is the centerpiece of Tsoukas's (2009) theory of knowledge creation. Public discourse and collaborative discourse serve complementary functions, and practitioners of a discipline need to be proficient in both (Woodruff & Meyer, 1997). In Knowledge Building, adversarial argumentation has a role, but collaborative discourse is the driver of creative knowledge work.

Constructive Use of Authoritative Information

The use of authoritative information has presented problems for educators ever since the advent of student-centered and constructivist education. On the one hand, we do not want students to meekly accept authoritative pronouncements. On the other hand, it is impossible to function in society without taking large amounts of information on authority. Even when it comes to challenging authoritative pronouncements, doing so effectively depends on bringing in other authoritative information as evidence. A focus on knowledge building helps to resolve these problems. Information of all kinds, whether derived from firsthand experience or from secondary sources, has value insofar as it contributes to knowledge-building discourse.

The explosive growth of Web-based information has raised the bar on what constitutes adequate literacy. According to Alan Liu (2012), "long forms of shared attention" (of which the scholarly textbook is a salient example) are giving way to short forms (of which the "Tweet" is an extreme example). As a consequence, the job of producing coherence, a responsibility traditionally borne by the author or lecturer, has now devolved on the reader or viewer. Beyond the ability to use a variety of informational and expressive media (multiliteracy), the new "open world" of information requires the ability to construct coherent knowledge out of fragmentary information, which Liu has termed *transliteracy*. Use of multiple documents in learning has become an active research area in the learning sciences (Britt & Rouet, 2012; Goldman & Scardamalia, 2013). Coherence building is a legitimate type of knowledge creation, an essential part of making constructive use of available information rather than a preliminary or an adjunct to it. Students doing Knowledge Building are thus of necessity practicing transliteracy and can profit from technology and pedagogy that supports it.

Understanding through Collaborative Explanation Building

In the kinds of knowledge-creating organizations that organization scientists study, knowledge creation is usually directed toward practical goals such as product innovation and solution of operational problems. In the pure sciences and scholarly disciplines, however, the top-level goals of knowledge creation are typically understanding and explanation. These are also top-level goals of school subjects, increasingly so as standards and achievement tests shift away from emphasis on recall to emphasis on evidence of understanding. In education for a knowledge society, it is important that students have experience in building knowledge serving practical purposes – such as product design and solution of socially significant problems. Although active in promoting innovativeness along practical lines, the Organization for Economic Co-operation and Development (OECD) has emphasized the importance of conceptual understanding as a basis for creative knowledge work of all kinds: "Educated workers need a conceptual understanding of complex concepts, and the ability to work with them creatively to generate new ideas, new theories, new products, and new knowledge" (OECD, 2008, p. 1).

Besides basic theoretical concepts, innovation also depends on a supply of "principled practical knowledge," defined informally as "know-how combined with know-why" and more formally as "explanatorily coherent practical knowledge" (Bereiter, 2014). This is knowledge created in the process of solving problems but requiring additional investment of effort in producing knowledge useful beyond the immediate problem – knowledge sufficient to enable a field of practice to advance. In schools that make use of work-study arrangements, field trips, service learning, and the like, it is common practice to accompany these with discussions aimed at connecting the students' concrete experiences to more generalizable knowledge. In this context, Knowledge Building represents what may be called a principled way of producing principled practical knowledge.

Knowledge Building Pedagogy

Knowledge Building pedagogy puts the emphasis on guiding principles rather than prescribed procedures (Scardamalia, 2002; Zhang, Hong, Scardamalia, Teo, & Morley, 2011). While many innovative educational approaches enunciate guiding principles, most accompany these with explicit procedures to help teachers translate the principles into practice – for instance, the "activity structures" of Brown and Campione's (1996) "communities of learners." "Orchestration scripts" (Dillenbourg & Jermann, 2006) have made headway in instructional science by offering explicit proceduralization (sometimes to foster knowledge creation; Sandoval & Reiser, 2004; Weinberger, Ertl, Fischer, & Mandl, 2005).

Teaching, of course, is carried out through procedures of some kind. A significant drawback of prescribed procedures, however, is that they can easily degenerate into what Brown and Campione (1996) called "lethal mutations" – procedures that take on a life of their own and evolve in ways that undermine the purposes for which they were originally designed. Procedures should evolve. The problem is getting them to evolve in favorable ways, given that the evolution of practices, like biological evolution, is essentially uncontrollable and unpredictable as to specifics. Principles such as "authentic problems, real ideas," "epistemic agency," and "improvable ideas" (Scardamalia, 2002) can serve an important regulative function for both teachers and students, helping to keep higher-level goals in mind and to prevent "lethal mutations" or reversion to older practices. Students themselves can come to use knowledge building principles in conceptualizing their own work. Caswell and Bielaczyk (2001) reported students' productive use of the principle of "improvable ideas." In another class, elementary school students in an inner city school – identified as one of the neediest in Toronto – studied and began to apply such principles as epistemic agency, pervasive knowledge building, and community knowledge, and to describe their work at an international conference. We would not categorically reject procedural prescription; local conditions may sometimes necessitate it. But, as we have emphasized, education for knowledge creation and innovation poses many unsolved problems. Effective solutions require not only design research from the learning sciences community, but also invention by teachers, administrators, engineers, and students themselves. Later in this chapter we indicate technology designs and institutional arrangements for "hubs of knowledge building innovation" intended to support such invention. The point we want to emphasize here, however, is the importance of having regulative principles and generative procedures that stimulate and guide rather than impede pedagogical invention.

Knowledge Building Technology

The Computer Supported Intentional Learning Environment (CSILE), implemented in 1983, represented our first effort to develop networked computer applications to provide these kinds of support for knowledge building. Knowledge Forum®, launched in 1995, based on what we learned from our CSILE research, provided stronger support for community knowledge (Scardamalia, 2004) at all educational levels and in noneducational settings. And now an international open source community is designing extensions to better support the goals identified earlier and to ensure interoperability with other platforms, social media, and mobile technologies.

Knowledge Forum is a multimedia knowledge building environment, with its content and organization created by users. The community knowledge spaces (views) that users create and the ideas they contribute (notes) are themselves collectively emergent phenomena, representing the advancing knowledge of the community. The *view* provides the organizing contexts – possibly a diagram, a scene, a model, a concept map, and so forth – to give structure and meaning to the *notes* whose titles appear in it. The view background can be created before, during, or after work on the view begins, and can be edited at any time. Notes are contributed to the view, with titles on the view providing an overview of issues being addressed. Notes are similarly editable and movable; the same note may appear in multiple views.

Figure 20.1 illustrates a student-generated graphical background, with notes contributed by students as work proceeds. Each learner contributes notes that can then be read by any other student, with notes built on or responded to by others. Lines between notes show note linkages resulting from students building on and referencing each other. In this way, the community builds knowledge, with its collective contribution displayed on the view, and each view represents the emergent collective knowledge.

Figure 20.2 shows one note by one student contributor to the community space. Directly to the left of the note is a pull-down menu of easy-to-use theory-building scaffolds (My Theory, I Need to Understand, New Information, etc.). As the note text indicates, the student has elected the My Theory scaffold. At the bottom of the note are options for actions on notes including "build on," "annotate," and "reference." To the right is a list of notes corresponding to a search (e.g., notes in the view sharing the same scaffold type as the open note, notes sharing keywords, near semantic neighbors).

Wherever one is in a Knowledge Forum database, it is always possible to move downward, producing a lower-level note, comment, or subview;

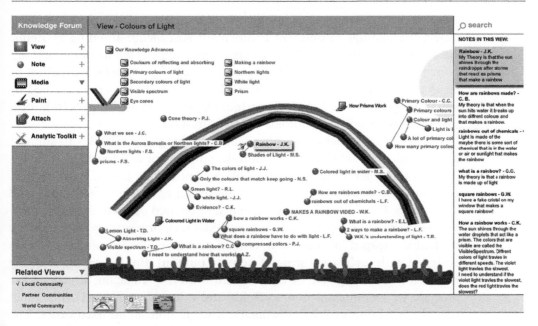

Figure 20.1. *A Knowledge Forum view supporting user-generated graphical representations of notes and note linkages.*

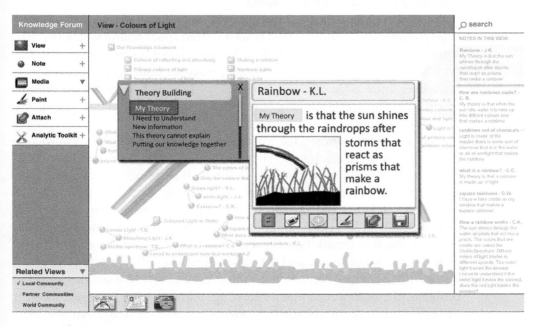

Figure 20.2. *A Knowledge Forum note supporting user-generated graphical representations and text, with a theory-building scaffold.*

upward, producing a more inclusive note or a view of views; and sideways, linking views to views or linking notes in different views. Notes themselves may contain graphics, animations, movies, audio, links to other applications and applets, and so on. Knowledge Forum lends itself to a high level of what we call "epistemic agency" (Scardamalia, 2002). Although the term has different meanings in different contexts, in Knowledge Building epistemic agency refers to the control participants have over the whole range of components of knowledge building – goals, strategies, resources, evaluation of results. Toward this end, views – as well as their contents – are designed by users, or by authorized visitors, partner classes, or invited others from outside the class. Similarly, scaffolds are customizable.

We have seen students actively engaged in designing scaffolds to support more productive thinking. For example, students in one fourth grade class decided that they were doing too much "knowledge telling" and so they introduced new scaffolds to focus attention on advancing their ideas. And Knowledge Forum scaffolds are designed to be used opportunistically, without a set order. Of course, nothing prevents scripting activity so that every student is engaged in a common, phased process (some learning software is designed with such structuring of activity built in). But in keeping with the Knowledge Building goal of learning innovation by engaging directly in the process, we recommend that scaffolds and other Knowledge Forum functions be used opportunistically, as users see fit, and in no fixed order. The results have been impressive and have suggested that students can take on even more demanding roles, as we elaborate in the section titled "Supporting Sustained Creative Work with Ideas."

We designed Knowledge Forum not simply as a tool, but as a knowledge building *environment* – that is, as a virtual space within which the main work of the group takes place (Scardamalia, 2003). Giving pragmatic support to the idea that the same process underlies both school learning and high-level knowledge creation, Knowledge Forum has been used without modification at levels ranging from kindergarten to graduate school and professional work.

Students using Knowledge Forum do not spend all their knowledge-building time at the computer. They read books and magazines, have small-group and whole-class discussions, design and carry out experiments, build things, go on field trips, and do all the other things that make up a rich educational experience. But instead of the online discourse being an adjunct, as it typically is in instructional management systems, Knowledge Forum is where the main work takes place. It is where the "state of knowledge" materializes, takes shape, and advances. It is where the results of the various off-line activities contribute to the overall effort. If students run into a problem, they often recommend starting a space in Knowledge Forum to preserve and work out the ideas. Students come to see it as a valuable place for idea improvement. At the end of grade 1, a child moving to a class without Knowledge Forum asked, "Where will my ideas go? Who will help me improve them?" The grade 2 teacher decided to use Knowledge Forum; the child's grade 1 ideas lived on, to be improved along with new ideas generated in grade 2.

Supporting Sustained Creative Work with Ideas

Supporting the engagement of all students in sustained creative work with ideas (emphasis on *all* and *sustained*) has proved to be the most challenging problem in designing knowledge-building/knowledge-creating technology. It is a design challenge that carries with it the other challenges discussed earlier in the five themes. In this section we discuss design solutions that are currently at an experimental stage prior to being incorporated into the new open source version of Knowledge Forum.

Two planned enhancements to the existing knowledge building environment are intended to support idea work and move it to higher levels. One is supports for *metadiscourse* – student discourse about an ongoing knowledge building discourse, concerned with evaluating progress, recognizing and dealing with obstacles, and so on. The other is stronger visual support for the idea of *rising above* – forming higher-level syntheses of ideas. Figure 20.3 shows one simple tool to aid metadiscourse: a graph of frequency of use of various scaffolds.

In a trial of the "Scaffold Meter" illustrated in Figure 20.3, grade 2 students were working in a view titled "How do birds fly?" On viewing the graph, which was superimposed on their view of the same name, the students quickly focused on the fact that they had generated many theories about how birds fly but not much in the way of authoritative source information (e.g., the "important information + source" scaffold shows low levels of use). They also noted that there was very little effort to explain why source information is important (the scaffold "this information helps explain" was almost never used). The discussion these results stimulated conveyed an awareness of issues not evident to teacher or students previously. And students immediately took responsibility for remedying problems. For example, they decided to read books to find information relevant to their theories. As a result, a discourse that had seemingly come to an end prior to this intervention took a new and productive direction (Resendes, Chen, Acosta, & Scardamalia, 2013; Resendes, Chen, Chuy, & Scardamalia, 2012).

Knowledge Forum supports movement toward higher-level synthesis of ideas through rise-above notes and views. The view shown in Figure 20.1 contains rise-above notes, marked by lines under the note icon (notes titled "Coloured Light in Water" and "How Prisms Work"). Hierarchies of views are represented by the arrangement of view links at the top of the view in Figure 20.1. However, these hierarchical relationships are difficult to see in this view; greater visual impact is needed to convey a sense of ideas existing at different levels of inclusiveness and explanatory power.

Figure 20.4 suggests a possible multilevel design that would make these hierarchical relationships more visible. At the bottom level, students' notes appear as they do now. In relation to a general problem defining the view, individual notes may contain questions, problems of understanding ("I need to

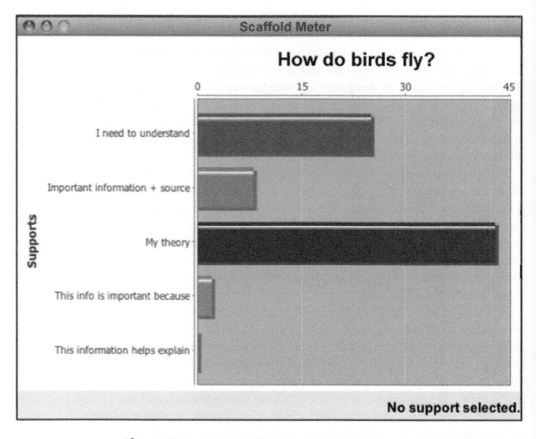

Figure 20.3. *Metadiscourse "Scaffold Meter" showing frequency of use of Knowledge Forum scaffolds by grade 2 students at a midpoint in their work on explaining how birds fly.*

understand"), relevant information drawn from various sources, explanatory ideas, and so on. Ideas selected as promising and warranting further work are represented at the next higher level, with links back to their parent notes. Work on developing and improving these ideas takes place at this higher level. Based on this work, complex idea structures (e.g., theories or theory-like constructions, models, identification of new problems, and action plans) are represented at the next higher level, and so on. Thus progress in knowledge creation is registered not so much by successive approximation to authoritative information (which in essence is what knowledge tests, including essay examinations, generally measure) but by vertical progress toward greater explanatory coherence. Research to date shows that a good predictor of work on exams is level of collaborative engagement and depth of understanding evidenced in work in Knowledge Forum (Chan, Lam, & Leung, 2012).

In addition to a visual metaphor, supports are needed to aid students in reconstructing ideas at progressively higher levels. The most elementary

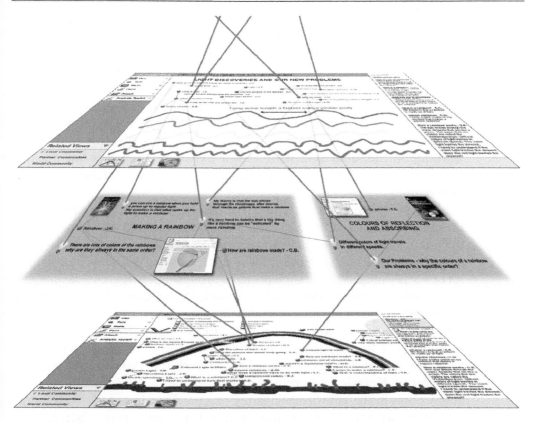

Figure 20.4. *Rise-above graphical user interface for next-generation knowledge building technology. Students' ideas that provide greater explanatory coherence are shown as rising to a higher plane.*

requirement is a way of marking promising ideas at one level and assembling them at the next higher level for further work. The "promisingness" tool (Chen et al., 2012) allows users to clip promising ideas from their own or from peer notes. Selected ideas can then be ordered from most to least promising, based on number of selections of the same idea. The selected ideas can then be made the basis for group discussion of next steps. Or, selected ideas can be exported to new views. A link is preserved to the full note from which an idea was clipped. In keeping with the concept of Knowledge Building discourse discussed earlier, use of the promisingness tool requires that ideas found elsewhere be brought into the collective discourse. Thus, for example, we see, in the middle section of Figure 20.4, promising ideas – marked by light bulb icons – linked to resource material and new student notes. Efforts to synthesize information in an intermediary workspace help students advance their thinking to the next highest level.

In pilot research in a grade 3 class (Chen, Scardamalia, Resendes, Chuy, & Bereiter, 2012), a simple procedure was used: students clipped promising ideas and in a whole-class discussion reviewed ideas selected, ordered from most to least hits, and selected three ideas to be moved to a new view, knowing – as they made selections – that the new view would be their new community workspace. This led to an important discussion regarding ideas worth working on further. The process was repeated. These two iterations of selecting promising ideas and refocusing work on them led to significant knowledge gains, as compared to the rated quality of note contents from the previous year's class of students at the same grade level, working on the same unit, with a more experienced teacher but without access to the tool. The teacher felt the result was clearly attributable to use of the tool.

Learning scientists are exploring whether students can consistently select the most promising ideas from those they have generated, resulting in year-by-year advances in what they can accomplish. Overall, pilot research to date indicates that selecting promising ideas and refocusing discourse on a smaller set of ideas – judged by the students to be promising – helps rekindle interest, reduce information overload, direct knowledge-building effort along more productive routes, and achieve higher levels of individual learning (Chen, Scardamalia, Acosta, Resendes, & Kici, 2013).

To support the actual production of higher-level ideas, more powerful tools are needed. We envision a palette of such tools constituting an integral part of Knowledge Forum, available for use by teachers and students at any point in the knowledge-creating process. Social network analysis has already proved valuable in research on knowledge-building processes (Philip, 2010; Zhang et al., 2009). The Idea Thread Mapper (Zhang, Chen, Chen, & Mico, 2013) re-represents Knowledge Forum notes in time-ordered progressions based on notes referring to preceding notes. Semantic analysis of note content holds the promise of aiding knowledge building efforts, provided it goes beyond identifying note topics and makes connections based on what is being said about the topics. KB-Dex is a highly versatile knowledge building discourse tool that combines social and semantic analysis for rendering social-semantic relations visible and has already been used effectively with students working in Knowledge Forum (Oshima, Oshima, & Matsuzawa, 2012).

The intent in next-generation technology is to support customization, including the analytic tool palette, and to design the tools so that they empower both students and teachers. Making tools accessible for student use poses both usability problems and ethical issues to be addressed by designs that ensure anonymity as appropriate and that provide useful information while avoiding invidious comparisons of students and efforts by them to game the system. Past experience has suggested that students can work with ideas at surprisingly high levels of sophistication, and that they are impressive design partners able to help advance designs for knowledge practices and technologies for sustained work with ideas.

Current Directions

Designing education to meet the emerging needs of a knowledge society is a priority of education systems worldwide. At this writing, it appears that these efforts are dominated by test-driven "21st-century skills" approaches, often sponsored by major corporations. In recent months, however, we have found education officials in widely separated jurisdictions resonating to the idea of "*beyond* 21st-century skills." Although no one is likely to question the value of creativity, problem solving, collaborativeness, and other items that are central 21st-century skills, "21st-century skills" enthusiasts tend to gloss over serious questions of teachability, transfer of learning, and test validity. Experienced educators recognize that tacking the word "skill" onto a desirable human trait does not make it teachable, and so they are likely to find expressions like "empathy skills" ludicrous. Furthermore, to educators who have been in the business for enough years, the skills movement evokes a "been there, done that" reaction. It is not much different from "higher-order thinking skills" and related movements that have come and gone over the past six decades. With the Knowledge Building approach we aim to provide a relatively clear-cut way of going beyond programs focused on assessing and teaching 21st-century skills. By engaging students and teachers as active participants, along with researchers, engineers, and policy makers, we aim to establish pedagogical models and technologies that provide an alternative with potential to exceed existing curriculum standards and expectations.

Researchers and innovators involved in Knowledge Building have launched two initiatives to advance it as an approach to education for a knowledge society. One is a membership association, Knowledge Building International – http://ikit.org/kbi/. The other is an international project called "Building Cultural Capacity for Innovation" (BCCI). It has wide-ranging objectives, including: research to solve problems such as those discussed in this chapter, creation of hubs of innovation to support pedagogical invention and its dissemination, and open source development of Knowledge Building environments, assessment tools, and resources." BCCI has both a knowledge advancement side and a promotional side. As this chapter has suggested, there are major design challenges yet to be satisfactorily met; finding ways to achieve full engagement of all students in sustained efforts at idea improvement is a salient example, but there are others. At the same time, securing a place for Knowledge Building in school programs that are already fully committed to worthwhile educational activities requires more than evidence of good results. It requires putting across a new vision of what is possible. For that reason, one of the important functions of BCCI will be collecting and publicizing examples of schoolchildren producing and elaborating ideas that parents and journalists will recognize as authentic knowledge creation.

We have advocated that all ideas are improvable, and so of course we realize that Knowledge Building itself is grounded in improvable ideas. Some of these are being improved through other research programs. For instance, *explanatory coherence*, which has long been a key idea in Knowledge Building, has undergone extraordinary development by Thagard and his collaborators. What was once a schema mainly relevant to scientific explanation has since been elaborated so that it incorporates not only logical but also social, emotional, and neurologically constrained determinants of explanatory coherence (Thagard, 2000, 2006). This makes it directly applicable to case-based theories in history, social studies, and humanities, where motives are an essential element; and this, in turn, brings theorizing in these areas into the mainstream of educational Knowledge Building (Bereiter & Scardamalia, 2012). Other idea improvements may come about by efforts to synthesize Knowledge Building with other approaches or other cultural forms (Chan, 2011). A number of investigators have explored linking Knowledge Building with related learning sciences research: for example, problem-based learning (Hmelo-Silver & Barrows, 2008; Lu, Bridges, & Hmelo-Silver, Chapter 15, this volume), epistemic games (Bielaczyc & Kapur, 2010), group cognition (Stahl, 2006), and open source communities (Hemetsberger & Reinhardt, 2006). However, the most direct forms of improvement in Knowledge Building are likely to come about through building principled practical knowledge (Bereiter, 2014) in the course of producing pedagogical and technological inventions to solve actual problems of implementing Knowledge Building in diverse settings. That is what the hubs of innovation are expected to produce in the BCCI project.

Conclusion

A case study by Zhang and colleagues (2011) concluded that principle-based knowledge building, if it is to prevail, requires a continuing process of knowledge building by teachers themselves, resulting in educational designs that achieve continually closer approximations to ideal principles. Perhaps more than anything else, however, a principled knowledge building approach must contend with a contrary set of widely held beliefs: namely, (a) basics must be mastered before students can undertake higher-order work with ideas, and (b) instructional planning must start with a clear specification of the skills and concepts to be learned. These *instructionist* notions (see Sawyer, Chapter 1, this volume) date back to an era before the emergent, self-organizing character of learning and cognition was well recognized. They are not based so much on evidence as on what was perceived as common sense in those simpler times.

Although instructionist approaches may have value for the routine conduct of instruction, they are barriers to the more open-ended approach that education for a knowledge society requires. Even such a basic goal as literacy is changing, and will probably continue to change, as a result of new technologies that affect the forms and flow of information. An instructionist approach might be capable of incorporating new informational media as they arrive, and might develop new objectives having to do with skills in the use of the new media.

But deeper things are happening, as noted in our brief discussion of transliteracy. The emerging literacy challenge is to build coherent knowledge out of fragmentary information coming from multiple sources. Although this challenge is beginning to be researched, the requisite skills and strategies are not yet well understood, much less how to foster them. Trying to nail down specific objectives and to order them into a developmental sequence is obviously premature, and yet schools should be trying to do something to help today's students contend with transliteracy challenges (of which they may be quite unaware). More generally, there is a need to go beyond simplistic objectives to deeper and more consequential ones. Getting stakeholders together to formulate objectives (as in the drafting of 21st-century skill goals) is not going to suffice. We need to learn from our students what the next iteration of goals needs to be, and that means putting students into an educational environment where new competencies and new problems have a chance to emerge (Scardamalia, Bransford, Kozma, & Quellmalz, 2012). Knowledge Building aims to provide such an environment. While it may seem a radically optimistic approach, it is actually quite cautious in making assumptions about what is teachable and what the goals of 21st-century education should be. As for the question of what students are actually capable of, the Knowledge Building answer is, "Let's find out."

Acknowledgments

The authors are indebted to the students, teachers, and administrators of the Jackman Institute of Child Study, the Institute for Knowledge Innovation and Technology team (www.ikit.org), and research sponsored by the Social Sciences and Humanities Research Council of Canada. We are also indebted to Keith Sawyer for thoughtful input and help beyond the call of editorial duty.

References

Bereiter, C. (2002). *Education and mind in the knowledge age*. Mahwah, NJ: Lawrence Erlbaum Associates.

Bereiter, C. (2014). Principled practical knowledge: Not a bridge but a ladder. *Journal of the Learning Sciences, 23*(1), 4–17.

Bereiter, C., & Scardamalia, M. (2003). Learning to work creatively with knowledge. In E. D. Corte, L. Verschaffel, N. Entwistle, & J. V. Merriënboer

(Eds.), *Powerful learning environments: Unravelling basic components and dimensions* (pp. 73–78). Oxford: Elsevier Science.

Bereiter, C., & Scardamalia, M. (2010). Can children really create knowledge? *Canadian Journal of Learning and Technology*, 36(1). Published online at http://www.cjlt.ca/index.php/cjlt/article/view/585.

Bereiter, C., & Scardamalia, M. (2012). Theory building and the pursuit of understanding in history, social studies, and literature. In J. R. Kirby & M. J. Lawson (Eds.), *Enhancing the quality of learning: Dispositions, instruction, and learning processes* (pp. 160–177). New York: Cambridge University Press.

Bielaczyz, K., & Kapur, M. (2010). Playing epistemic games in science and mathematics classrooms. *Educational Technology*, 50(5), 19–25.

Britt, M. A., & Rouet, J.-F. (2012). Learning with multiple documents: Component skills and their acquisition. In J. R. Kirby & M. J. Lawson (Eds.), *Enhancing the quality of learning: Dispositions, instruction, and learning processes* (pp. 276–314). New York: Cambridge University Press.

Brown, A. L., & Campione, J. C. (1996). Psychological theory and design of innovative learning environments: On procedures, principles, and systems. In L. Schauble & R. Glaser (Eds.), *Innovations in learning: New environments for education* (pp. 289–325). Mahwah, NJ: Lawrence Erlbaum Associates.

Caswell, B., & Bielaczyc, K. (2001). Knowledge Forum: Altering the relationship between students and scientific knowledge. *Education, Communication & Information*, 1, 281–305.

Chan, C. K. K. (2011). Bridging research and practice: Implementing and sustaining knowledge building in Honk Kong classrooms. *International Journal of Computer-Supported Collaborative Learning*, 6, 147–186.

Chan, C. K. K., Lam, I. C. K., & Leung, R. W. H. (2012). Can collaborative knowledge building promote both scientific processes and science achievement? *International Journal of Educational Psychology*, 1(3), 199–227.

Chen, B., Scardamalia, M., Acosta, A., Resendes, M., & Kici, D. (2013). Promisingness judgments as facilitators of knowledge building. In N. Rummel, M. Kapur, M. Nathan, & S. Puntambekar (Eds.), *To see the world and a grain of sand: Learning across levels of space, time, and scale: CSCL 2013 Conference Proceedings Volume 2 – Short papers, panels, posters, demos & community events* (pp. 231–232). International Society of the Learning Sciences.

Chen, B., Scardamalia, M., Resendes, M., Chuy, M., & Bereiter, C. (2012). Students' intuitive understanding of promisingness and promisingness judgments to facilitate knowledge advancement. In J. van Aalst, K. Thompson, M. J. Jacobson, & P. Reimann (Eds.), *The future of learning: Proceedings of the 10th international conference of the learning sciences (ICLS 2012) – Volume 1, Full Papers* (pp. 111–118). Sydney, Australia: ISLS.

Chuy, M., Scardamalia, M., Bereiter, C., Prinsen, F., Resendes, M., Messina, R., Hunsburger, W., Teplovs, C., & Chow, A. (2010). Understanding the nature of science and scientific progress: A theory-building approach. *Canadian Journal of Learning and Technology*, 36(1). Published online at http://www.cjlt.ca/index.php/cjlt/article/view/580.

Dillenbourg, P., & Jermann, P. (2006). Designing integrative scripts. In F. Fischer, I. Kollar, H. Mandl, & J. Haake (Eds.), *Scripting computer-supported communication of knowledge: Cognitive, computational, and educational perspectives* (pp. 259–288). New York: Springer.

Drucker, P. (1985). *Innovation and entrepreneurship: Practice and principles.* New York: Harper and Row.

Dunbar, K. (1997). How scientists think: Online creativity and conceptual change in science. In T. B. Ward, S. M. Smith, & S. Vaid (Eds.), *Conceptual structures and processes: Emergence, discovery and change* (pp. 461–493). Washington, DC: American Psychological Association.

Goldman, S. R., & Scardamalia, M. (Eds.) (2013). Multiple document comprehension (Special issue). *Cognition and Instruction, 31*(2).

Hemetsberger, A., & Reinhardt, C. (2006). Learning and knowledge-building in open-source communities: A social-experimental approach. *Management Learning, 37*(2), 187–214.

Hmelo-Silver, C. E., & Barrows, H. S. (2008). Facilitating collaborative knowledge building. *Cognition and Instruction, 26*(1), 48–94.

Lakatos, I. (1976). *Proofs and refutations: The logic of mathematical discovery.* New York: Cambridge University Press.

Latour, B., & Woolgar, S. (1979). *Laboratory life: The social construction of scientific facts.* Beverly Hills, CA: Sage Publications.

Liu, A. (2012). This is not a book: Transliteracies and long forms of digital attention. Paper presented at the Translittératies Conference, ENS Cachan, Paris, 7 November 2012. Web: www.stef.ens-cachan.fr/manifs/translit/Alan_Liu_this-is-not-a-book-slides_2012_11_07.pdf.

Martin, R. (2009). *The design of business: Why design thinking is the next competitive advantage.* Cambridge, MA: Harvard Business Press. powerpress http://gsbm-med.pepperdine.edu/gbr/audio/spring2010/designofbiz.mp3.

Nonaka, I. (1991). The knowledge-creating company. *Harvard Business Review, 69*(6), 96–104.

Nonaka, I., & Takeuchi, H. (1995). *The knowledge creating company.* New York: Oxford University Press.

Organization for Economic Co-operation and Development (OECD). (2008). *21st century learning: Research, innovation and policy.* Paris: OECD.

Oshima, J., Oshima, R., & Matsuzawa, Y. (2012). Knowledge Building Discourse Explorer: A social network analysis application for knowledge building discourse. *Educational Technology Research and Development, 60*, 903–921.

Petroski, H. (1998). *Invention by design: How engineers get from thought to thing.* Cambridge, MA: Harvard University Press.

Philip, D. N. (2010). Social network analysis to examine interaction patterns in knowledge building communities. *Canadian Journal of Learning and Technology, 36*(1). Published online at http://cjlt.csj.ualberta.ca/index.php/cjlt/article/view/577.

Popper, K. R. (1972). *Objective knowledge: An evolutionary approach.* Oxford: Clarendon Press.

Resendes, M., Chen, B., Acosta, A., & Scardamalia, M. (2013). The effect of formative feedback on vocabulary use and distribution of vocabulary knowledge in a grade two knowledge building class. In N. Rummel, M. Kapur, M. Nathan, & S. Puntambekar (Eds.), *To see the world and a grain of sand: Learning across levels of space, time, and scale: CSCL 2013 Conference*

Proceedings Volume 1 – Full Papers & Symposia (pp. 391–398). International Society of the Learning Sciences.

Resendes, M., Chen, B., Chuy, M., & Scardamalia, M. (2012, August). The effect of meta-discourse on ways of contributing to an explanation-seeking dialogue in grade 2. Paper presented at the 16th Knowledge Building Summer Institute (KBSI2012), Toronto, Canada. Web: ikit.org/SummerInstitute2012/Papers/3024-Resendes.pdf.

Sandoval, W. A., & Reiser, B. J. (2004). Explanation-driven inquiry: Integrating conceptual and epistemic scaffolds for scientific inquiry. *Science Education*, 8, 345–373.

Scardamalia, M. (2002). Collective cognitive responsibility for the advancement of knowledge. In B. Smith (Ed.), *Liberal education in a knowledge society* (pp. 76–98). Chicago: Open Court.

Scardamalia, M. (2003). Knowledge building environments: Extending the limits of the possible in education and knowledge work. In A. DiStefano, K. E. Rudestam, & R. Silverman (Eds.), *Encyclopedia of distributed learning* (pp. 269–272). Thousand Oaks, CA: Sage Publications.

Scardamalia, M. (2004). CSILE/Knowledge Forum®. In A. Kovalchick & K. Dawson (Eds.), *Education and technology: An encyclopedia* (pp. 183–192). Santa Barbara, CA: ABC-CLIO.

Scardamalia, M., & Bereiter, C. (1991). Higher levels of agency for children in knowledge building: A challenge for the design of new knowledge media. *The Journal of the Learning Sciences*, 1(1), 37–68.

Scardamalia, M., & Bereiter, C. (2006). Knowledge building: Theory, pedagogy, and technology. In K. Sawyer (Ed.), *Cambridge handbook of the learning sciences* (pp. 97–118). New York: Cambridge University Press.

Scardamalia, M., Bereiter, C., Brett, C., Burtis, P. J., Calhoun, C., & Smith Lea, N. (1992). Educational applications of a networked communal database. *Interactive Learning Environments*, 2(1), 45–71.

Scardamalia, M., Bereiter, C., & Lamon, M. (1994). The CSILE project: Trying to bring the classroom into World 3. In K. McGilley (Ed.), *Classroom lessons: Integrating cognitive theory and classroom practice* (pp. 201–228). Cambridge, MA: MIT Press.

Scardamalia, M., Bransford, J., Kozma, R., & Quellmalz, E. (2012). New assessments and environments for knowledge building. In P. Griffin, B. McGaw, & E. Care (Eds.), *Assessment and teaching of 21st century skills* (pp. 231–300). New York: Springer Science+Business Media B.V.

Stahl, G. (2006). *Group cognition: Computer support for building collaborative knowledge*. Cambridge, MA: MIT Press. Web: http://GerryStahl.net/mit.

Sun, Y., Zhang. J., & Scardamalia, M. (2010). Developing deep understanding and literacy while addressing a gender-based literacy gap. *Canadian Journal of Learning and Technology*, 35(1). Web: http://www.cjlt.ca/index.php/cjlt/article/view/576.

Thagard, P. (2000). *Coherence in thought and action*. Cambridge, MA: MIT Press.

Thagard, P. (2006). *Hot thought: Mechanisms and applications of emotional cognition*. Cambridge, MA: MIT Press.

Tsoukas, H. (2009). A dialogical approach to the creation of new knowledge in organizations. *Organization Science*, 20, 941–957.

Van Aalst, J. (2009). Distinguishing knowledge-sharing, knowledge-construction, and knowledge-creation discourses. *International Journal of Computer-Supported Collaborative Learning*, 4(3), 259–287.

Van Aalst, J., & Truong, M. S. (2011). Promoting knowledge creation discourse in an Asian primary five classroom: Results from an inquiry into life cycles. *International Journal of Science Education*, 33(4), 487–515.

Weinberger, A., Ertl, B., Fischer, F., & Mandl, H. (2005). Epistemic and social scripts in computer-supported collaborative learning. *Instructional Science*, 33(1), 1–30.

Woodruff, E., & Meyer, K. (1997). Explanations from intra- and intergroup discourse: Students building knowledge in the science classroom. *Research in Science Education*, 27(1), 25–39.

Zhang, J., Chen, M.-H., Chen, J., & Mico, T. F. (2013). Computer-supported meta-discourse to foster collective progress in knowledge-building communities. *Proceedings of the International Conference of Computer-supported Collaborative Learning* (CSCL). Madison, Wisconsin.

Zhang, J., Hong, H.-Y., Scardamalia, M., Teo, C., & Morley, E. (2011). Sustaining knowledge building as a principle-based innovation at an elementary school. *Journal of the Learning Sciences*, 20(2), 262–307.

Zhang, J., Scardamalia, M., Reeve, R., & Messina, R. (2009). Designs for collective cognitive responsibility in knowledge building communities. *Journal of the Learning Sciences*, 18(1), 7–44.

21 The Social and Interactive Dimensions of Collaborative Learning

Naomi Miyake and Paul A. Kirschner

A broad range of learning sciences research has found that social interaction taking place in collaborative learning contributes to classroom knowledge construction (Sawyer, 2006; see also the other chapters in Part 4 of this book). Yet its exact mechanisms and effective dissemination into classrooms are still uncertain (Rozenblit & Keil, 2002). Computer-mediated worldwide networks have enabled a shift from co-located learning groups to asynchronous distributed learning groups utilizing computer-supported collaborative learning environments (CSCL; see Stahl, Koschmann, & Suthers, Chapter 24, this volume). Although both classroom and CSCL environments can potentially support communication and collaboration, research and field observations reveal that this is not always the case (Kreijns, Kirschner, & Jochems, 2003). The major problem appears to be that while much work has been done to improve the technological and pedagogical aspects of collaborative learning, their social aspects are still slow to develop. Part of this, Kreijns and colleagues (2003) argue, is due to the fact that the social aspects of collaboration are often taken for granted. It is as though the social aspects of learning in general and collaborative learning in particular are so natural or matter of course that educators and researchers assume that they do not need to be addressed specifically – either in practice, in the learning situation, or in theory, in the research situation.

Why is this so? The learning sciences focuses primarily on human learning, especially on research that has implications for formal and informal learning and for helping individuals to achieve their fullest potential and to attain socially desired learning outcomes (Bransford, Brown, & Cocking, 2000) such as 21st-century skills (Collins & Halverson, 2009). One of the core findings of the learning sciences is that effective learning is more likely to occur when learning environments are designed to align with how people learn in everyday and informal settings. Thus many learning scientists have drawn on studies of cognitive development, family interactions, and a range of apprenticeship settings around the world (see Collins & Kapur, Chapter 6, this volume). In many of these naturally occurring learning environments, people learn through social interaction. This is a powerful message, yet what happens naturally tends to take a long time and is hard to study. This could be why the social aspects of learning are taken for granted.

Consequently, the mechanisms of social interaction and learning are still not fully understood, particularly how to implement effective learning collaborations in classrooms. In this chapter, we try to capture some elusive mechanisms of interactive, social, and collaborative learning, with examples of successful implementation, so that we can start activating them in both formal and informal settings (also see Enyedy & Stevens, Chapter 10, this volume).

Some studies emphasize that the situational, social aspects of collaboration are the mechanism that leads to learning, while others emphasize that the mechanism is the natural interaction among individuals. The former features social epistemology – like beliefs about interpersonal context and social cohesion – while the latter regards these as emergent outcomes of collaboration. In the two major sections of this chapter, we present each of these two approaches with the goal of helping readers understand the different strengths of these two approaches.

Studies of the Situational and Social Aspects of Collaboration

Groups of people are increasingly acknowledged as a major source of knowledge construction, particularly when they collectively solve problems or carry out tasks. When solving problems or completing tasks, teams of people with different experiences, values, and knowledge are often more effective than are individuals. However, to be able to adequately solve problems or carry out tasks, they face the challenge of integrating their different perspectives and developing a shared understanding of the problem at hand. This can be established through rich interaction, interactive discussion, and negotiation (Daft & Weick, 1984; Roschelle, 1992). The continuing implementation of group work at schools and of using teamwork in organizations are instances of attempts to build on the potential of solving problems or carrying out tasks in a team.[1] However, research and practice show that this potential effectiveness is not always reached (e.g., Barron, 2003). These studies indicate that fruitful collaboration is not merely a case of putting people with relevant knowledge together. We must understand the factors that make up successful collaboration.

This section examines a team learning model, specifying when and how teams in collaborative learning environments engage in building and maintaining mutually shared cognition, leading to increased performance. This model presents an integrative perspective, building on the strengths of different research strands. It includes both discourse practices that manage the co-construction of mutually shared cognition and conditions in the inter-

---

[1] To facilitate reading, the rest of this chapter will speak of problems, though the meaning is broader than this and also includes the carrying out of working and/or learning tasks.

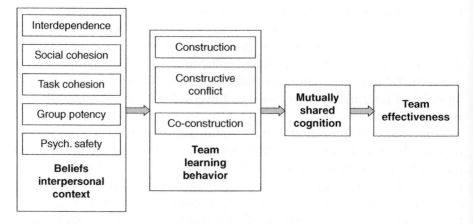

Figure 21.1. *A model of team learning beliefs and behaviors.*

personal context that contribute to engagement in these knowledge-building practices.

We first present our team learning model and identify six hypotheses derived from the model. This is followed by the presentation of a field study that has tested this model.

Team Learning: A Model

The model presented in Figure 21.1 captures how beliefs about the interpersonal context shape a team's willingness to engage in learning behavior. Learning behavior is defined as processes of construction and co-construction of meaning, with constructive conflict as a vehicle to enhance (co-)-construction giving rise to mutually shared cognition, leading to higher team effectiveness.

Two complementary perspectives contributed to this model. First, collaborative learning is analyzed as a fundamentally social process of knowledge building. We present our view on collaborative learning and the characteristics of the discourse in which collaborative knowledge building is taking place. Second, this perspective will be complemented by a description of crucial aspects of the social environment in which this learning takes place and by which this learning discourse is potentially influenced.

Collaborative Learning as Promoting Conceptual Understanding through Mutually Shared Cognition

In a collaborative learning environment, participants are brought together to simultaneously work on a task. The goal is that they learn from this task work and teamwork. Learning through collaboration is primarily a group-level phenomenon (Dillenbourg, Baker, Blaye, & O'Malley, 1996). Collaboration is defined as the process of building and maintaining a shared conception of a problem or task, distributing responsibility across members of the group, sharing expertise, and mutually constructing and negotiating cognition (Roschelle, 1992).

From this viewpoint, the interaction among members of the group and the characteristics of their discourse is considered to be the process through which mutual understanding and shared cognition is reached. In this process, *negotiation* is key to determining which kind of interactions – which patterns in discourse – can be considered to be forms of team learning behavior leading to mutually shared cognition (e.g., Baker, 1995; Dillenbourg et al., 1996). Negotiation is the process of achieving agreement among participants. Baker (1995) points out that achieving "real" agreement presupposes joint understanding, and this joint understanding has two elements. First, interpreting the problem, giving it meaning, and solving it require co-construction; this cannot be done through simple accumulation of the contributions of individuals because each contribution is presumed to build on previous ones. Second, agreement needs to be established on the co-constructed meanings and solutions (Baker, 1995).

Construction and Co-Construction of Meaning

The process of building a shared conception of a problem starts when one of the team members inserts meaning by describing the problem situation and how to deal with it, thereby tuning in to the fellow team members. These fellow team members are actively listening and trying to grasp the given explanation by using this understanding to give meaning to the situation at hand. The outcome of this process is that new meanings emerge that were not previously available to the group.

Toward Agreement: Constructive Conflict

Mutually shared cognition is developed when agreement is reached around the co-constructed understandings. If accepted, the offered meaning can become part of the agreed-on interpretation of the situation, what we call the *mutually shared cognition*.

We propose two hypotheses about the development of mutually shared cognition:

> *Hypothesis 1 (H1)*: Increasing co-construction and constructive conflict in the interaction of the team will positively influence the development of mutually shared cognition.

Mutually shared cognition creates a context for efficient group decision making. First, group members engage in a context that offers possibilities to learn from others' preferences and viewpoints by knowing that there are different viewpoints, by accepting the existence of alternative viewpoints as legitimate, and by considering how they relate to their own viewpoints (Engeström, Engeström, & Kärkkäinen, 1995). Second, the development of shared cognition facilitates coordinated action because it ensures that all participants are solving the same problem and helps exploit the cognitive capabilities of the entire team. Third, the active use of different views in working on and solving problems may entail a consideration of more alternatives and a richer argumentation, and thereby the nature of communication itself and problem solutions may become more creative. This leads to our second hypothesis:

> *Hypothesis 2 (H2):* More developed mutually shared cognition in a team will result in higher team effectiveness.

Groups as Social Systems: Beliefs about the Interpersonal Context

The identification of the social conditions under which teams make this effort to reach mutually shared cognition is an essential prerequisite for developing enhanced understanding of successful collaboration. This section focuses on emerging team-level beliefs about the relations among the team members – in other words, beliefs about the interpersonal context. The main question to be dealt with is: How do team members perceive the interpersonal context formed by their team? Subsequently, these beliefs will influence the behavior of the team (Cohen & Bailey, 1997) and, more specifically, the learning behavior of the team. These beliefs form a context that stimulates or inhibits learning behavior. Which such beliefs about the interpersonal context are most likely to result in learning and cognitive development in teams?

Ample research in social and organizational psychology focuses on the role of beliefs about the interpersonal context in group functioning and performance in out-of-school settings (e.g., Cohen & Bailey, 1997). Group-level beliefs that potentially affect learning behavior in teams include psychological safety, cohesion, potency, and interdependence.

Psychological Safety

Learning in groups can be threatening and stressful (Homan, 2001): team members do not know each other, power games are played, people are left out, people blame each other for making mistakes, and so on. Learning is often facilitated by psychological safety, because participants are then more likely to take risks and think freely. In her work on organizational learning and teamwork, Edmondson (1996, 1999) pointed to the importance of team psychological safety as a facilitating interpersonal context for team learning behavior. Team psychological safety is defined as a shared belief that the team is safe for interpersonal risk taking (Edmondson, 1999). While psychological safety does not play a direct role in the team's performance, it facilitates appropriate behavior leading to better performance (Edmondson, 1999).

> *Hypothesis 3 (H3):* Psychological safety is positively associated with team learning behavior.

Cohesion

Cohesion has been widely studied as an important aspect of group functioning. Festinger defined cohesion as "the resultant of all the forces acting on all the members to remain in the group" (Festinger, 1950, p. 274). Cohesion is a multidimensional construct (Mullen & Copper, 1994). One dimension, *task cohesion*, refers to shared commitment among members to achieve a goal that requires the collective efforts of the group. Another, *social cohesion*, refers to the nature and quality of the emotional bonds of friendship such as liking, caring, and closeness among group members. If the cohesiveness-performance effect is primarily because of interpersonal attraction, group members will exert efforts toward performance for the sake of their well-liked group members. If the effect is primarily because of commitment to the task, group members will exert efforts toward performance for the pleasure of completing that task.

This and related studies lead us to hypothesize that task cohesion will be positively associated with learning behavior because high task motivation shows the existence of shared goals and the motivation to strive for them.

> *Hypothesis 4a (H4a):* Task cohesion is positively related to team learning behavior. *Hypothesis 4b (H4b):* Social cohesion is not related to team learning behavior.

Interdependence

A classic distinction is made between *task interdependence* and *outcome interdependence*. Task interdependence refers to the interconnections among sub-tasks such that the performance of one sub-task depends on the completion of other sub-tasks (Van der Vegt, Emans, & Van de Vliert, 1998). Task interdependence leads to more communication, helping, and information sharing than individualistic tasks (Crawford & Gordon, 1972; Johnson, 1973). Outcome interdependence is defined as the extent to which team members' personal benefits and costs depend on successful goal attainment by other team members (Van der Vegt et al., 1998). Research indicates that team members working under circumstances of positive outcome interdependence are more open minded regarding others' arguments and desires, more concerned about each other's outcomes, and more inclined to search for solutions and compromises (e.g., Deutsch, 1980; Johnson & Johnson, 1989).

> *Hypothesis 5 (H5):* Task and outcome interdependence will be positively related with learning behavior.

Group Potency

Based on the idea of the role of self-efficacy in individual performance (Bandura, 1982), researchers have conceptualized group potency (Shea & Guzzo, 1987) or group efficacy (Jansen, Kirschner, Kirschner, & Paas, 2010) as a key determinant of team performance outcomes. Group potency has been defined as "the collective belief of group members that the group can be effective" (Shea & Guzzo, 1987a, p. 26). In recent studies, Gully, Incalcaterra, Johi, and Beaubien (2002) showed that the sense of confidence generated by high levels of potency helps teams persevere in the face of adversity. This will influence the ability of a team to effectively regulate team processes and share and process information.

> *Hypothesis 6 (H6):* Group potency is positively related to team learning behavior.

Until now, most research has studied these four factors in isolation. So the question remains how these factors influence each other. We hypothesize that the four shared beliefs are complementary – that each of the four shared beliefs has additive positive effects on the occurrence of team learning behaviors: a shared commitment toward the task at hand (task cohesion), the belief that team members need each other for dealing with this task (interdependence), the belief that team members will not be rejected for bringing in new meanings (team psychological safety), and the belief that the team is capable of using this new information to generate useful results (team potency).

Evaluating the Model: Setting and Procedure

One of us (Kirschner) conducted a study to evaluate the model in Figure 21.1. The study took place in two first-year bachelor courses (logistics and international economics) of an international business degree program in the Netherlands. The students had prior experience in working in groups. As a course requirement, students formed groups to work on an assignment during a seven-week period in a face-to-face setting. In one of the courses, the groups were created by the teachers; in the other course, the groups were self-selected. The assignment consisted of advising a company or institution on its strategy, resulting in a paper and a presentation. This assignment was similar in both courses; only the context of the problems was different.

Participants

Data were collected from 99 teams. Data were analyzed from only those teams that had a response of at least two-thirds of the team members (this was possible because group-level constructs were measured; the different individuals in the team can be seen as "repeated measures"). A total of 75 teams was selected for analysis. These teams had an average of 3.45 members ($SD = 0.68$, range $= 3–5$), and on average 0.49 data of team members were missing ($SD = 0.43$). On average, 36 percent of the team members were female.

Instrumentation

A questionnaire (Team Learning Beliefs & Behaviors Questionnaire) was administered in the last week of the course. The following instructions were given to team members before they completed the questionnaire: "Please indicate to what extent you agree with the following statements concerning the team in which you are working and the task with which you are dealing." Assessment of the psychometric properties was carried out through principal component analyses of the scales connected to the same level of the model to confirm the uniqueness of the scales with respect to each other (see Van den Bossche, Gijselaers, Segers, & Kirschner, 2006, for details). The scales and subscales used were:

Team Learning Behaviors. Our conception of collaborative learning leads to a focus on conversational actions enabling team members to become partners in the construction of shared knowledge (Roschelle, 1992). Items operationalizing team learning behaviors (i.e., construction, co-construction, constructive conflict) include: "Team members are listening carefully to each other" (construction), "Information from team members is complemented with information from other team members" (co-construction), and "This team tends to handle differences of opinions by addressing them directly" (constructive conflict).

Beliefs about the Interpersonal Context. To evaluate our hypotheses, the following subscales were used:

- Psychological safety
- Interdependence – both perceived task interdependence and outcome interdependence
- Cohesion – both social cohesion and task cohesion
- Group potency

Factor analysis confirmed the scales as measured, except for one of the items of the task cohesion scale, which also loaded highly onto two other factors, showing the lack of discriminative power; the remaining items loaded onto two factors, both conceptually related to the essence of the construct as defined. The analyses of the internal consistency of the scales confirmed this picture.

Mutually Shared Cognition. This portion of the questionnaire was derived from a questionnaire by Mulder and colleagues (Mulder, 1999; Mulder, Swaak, & Kessels, 2002) that measures shared understanding of the task and of the requirements of the task.

Team Effectiveness. Team effectiveness was measured using four self-report items. Two questioned team performance: one for process and one for product. Two more items were used to grasp team viability and team learning.

Aggregation at the Team Level

The constructs are conceptually meaningful at the team level. Therefore, data gathered from individual team members to assess team-level variables were aggregated to the team level. Within-group agreement was assessed using the

Table 21.1. *Regression models of outcomes*

	Mutually Shared Cognition			Team Effectiveness					
	β	t	p	β	t	P	β	t	p
Team learning behavior	.67	7.644	.000				.41	3.799	.000
Mutually shared cognition				.66	7.514	.000	.39	3.560	.001
Adjusted R^2	.44			.43			.52		

multiple-item estimator r_{wg} (James, Demaree, & Wolf, 1984). This resulted in a mean value of .81 for interdependence, .89 for social cohesion, .76 for task cohesion, .81 for psychological safety, .85 for group potency, .88 for learning behavior, .83 for mutually shared cognition, and .78 for team effectiveness. These results justify creating a group-level dataset.

Methods of Analysis

We present our analysis in three parts. Analogous to the theoretical framework, we first tested whether collaborative learning builds mutually shared cognition. Next, we analyzed whether beliefs about interpersonal context influence team learning behavior. Finally, we analyzed whether the proposed model is a good fit with the data.

The first two parts of the analysis were primarily based on (multiple) regression analyses. The last part of the analysis was informed through the path analyses. Only statistically significant paths are included in the presented diagrams.

The Cognitive Side of Collaborative Learning

To test the hypothesis that team learning behaviors lead to mutually shared cognition and that this is subsequently related to higher team effectiveness, three regression analyses were performed. The results of these computations are presented in Table 21.1, which shows that mutually shared cognition is significantly predicted by team learning behavior (β = .67, p = .000, adj. R^2 = .44), providing support for H1. Mutually shared cognition significantly predicts team effectiveness (β = .66, p = .000, adj. R^2 = .43), supporting H2. The third regression analysis shows that the relation between team learning behavior and team effectiveness is partially mediated by mutually shared cognition.

The Social Side of Collaborative Learning

A multiple regression analysis was conducted to analyze if the four team beliefs of the interpersonal context predict the occurrence of team learning behavior. The results are summarized in Table 21.2. These results provide support for H3, H4a, H4b, H5, and H6 and also support the hypothesis that these beliefs are complementary.

Table 21.2. *Regression model of team learning behavior*

	B	t	p	Adj. R^2
Interdependence	.254	3.317	.001	
Social cohesion	.083	0.866	.390	
Task cohesion	.247	2.550	.013	
Psychological safety	.299	3.243	.002	
Group potency	.202	2.376	.020	
				.70

Note: Standerdized βs are reported.

This second part of the analysis focused on the relation between beliefs about the interpersonal context and team learning behavior. This analysis shows that teams engage in the described sociocognitive processes of team learning behavior under certain conditions. All the identified beliefs about the interpersonal context set the stage for the occurrence of the team learning behavior. Interdependence, task cohesion, psychological safety, and group potency form the context in which teams are motivated to display the crucial learning behavior. Social cohesion is the only measured belief that does not seem to play a role in this context.

Testing the Model

The full team learning model was tested in two steps. A first model explains the development of mutually shared cognition and does not include team effectiveness. The second adds team effectiveness.

Toward a Model of Mutually Shared Cognition

The originally hypothesized model is composed of paths leading from the four constructs measuring beliefs toward team learning behavior and a path from learning behavior toward mutually shared cognition. Though the fit of this model is acceptable for some of the indicators, this can be improved ($\chi^2 = 21.71$, $df = 4$, $p < .05$, CFI = 0.94, NNFI = 0.76, SRMR = 0.065).

Inspection of the modification indices (Sörbom, 1989) suggests one additional path between task cohesion and mutually shared cognition. This model, pictured in Figure 21.2, fits the data better ($\chi^2 = 3.08$, $df = 3$, $p = .38$, CFI = 1.00, NNFI = 1.00, SRMR = 0.022).

The model as confirmed by the data shows that the beliefs about the interpersonal context support team learning behavior, which in turn gives rise to mutually shared cognition. It is important to see that the influence of the beliefs on shared cognition is through the learning behaviors espoused by the team. The only exception is task cohesion, which has also, next to an indirect relation, a direct relation with the rise of mutually

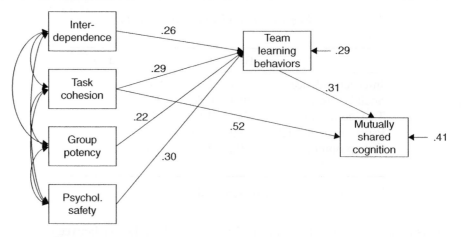

Figure 21.2. *Model toward mutually shared cognition.*

shared cognition. The shared commitment toward the task seems to have effects on mutually shared cognition that are not grasped by the learning behaviors alone.

Toward a Model of Team Effectiveness

First, the model presented in Figure 21.2 was extended with the variable team effectiveness, including a path from mutually shared cognition to team effectiveness. However, the fit indices show that this model is not probable (χ^2 = 43.29, df = 8, p < .05, CFI = 0.91, NNFI = 0.77, SRMR = 0.096). Inspection of the modification indices (Sörbom, 1989) showed that two additional paths are necessary: one path from task cohesion toward team effectiveness and one path from group potency to team effectiveness.

Figure 21.3 contains this adapted model. The values of the fit indices indicate an acceptable fit of the path model applied to the data. The chi-square becomes significant (χ^2 = 13.18, df = 6, p = .04), but all the other fit measures show that this model is acceptable (CFI = 0.98, NNFI = 0.94, SRMR = 0.031). These findings argue for the appropriateness of the model structure as shown in Figure 21.3.

The effectiveness of the team is influenced by the mutually shared cognition that is a result of the team learning behaviors of the team. This means that the data collected through the Team Learning Beliefs & Behaviors Questionnaire confirm the hypotheses associated with our team learning model. The only modifications that needed to be made were (a) an extra path from task cohesion to team effectiveness and (b) an extra path from group potency to team effectiveness. This is probably because a high shared commitment to the task and a high group potency of the team are likely to manifest in other team behavior, leading to effectiveness that is not fully grasped by the identified team learning behaviors.

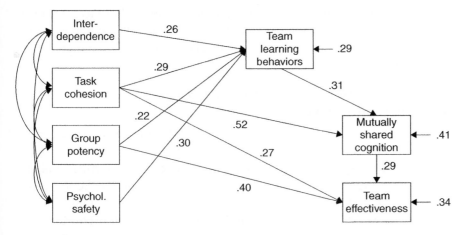

Figure 21.3. *Model toward team effectiveness.*

These analyses show that the relation between team learning behaviors and team effectiveness is fully mediated by mutually shared cognition (see Figure 21.3).

Studies of How Interaction Leads to Collaborative Learning

To better understand how participating individuals learn while collaborating, in this section we shift our focus to interactive, cognitive levels. The study of learning through collaborative discourse could proceed at two different levels of analysis: either the group level or the individual level (see Nathan & Sawyer, Chapter 2, this volume, comparing systemic and elemental approaches). In this section, we focus on the individual level: How does collaboration contribute to individual learning?

The Constructive Interaction Framework

Miyake and her colleagues (Miyake, 1986; Shirouzu, Miyake, & Masukawa, 2002) used pairs of participants to explore "constructive interaction" and how this pattern of collaboration contributes to individual learning. While observing two-person, joint problem-solving situations, participants were observed to work on their own problems in their own way. In this situation, because each participant works from a different starting schema, what is obvious to one may not be to the other. When the listener does not agree, it was the speaker who started to reflect on her/his own solution, shifting the points of view to find yet deeper comprehension, changing their initial ideas into more abstract scientific forms. While they exchange roles of speaking and listening and monitoring, there is ample chance for both to comprehend deeper. Miyake and colleagues concluded that the socially interactive or joint problem solving has a high potential to elicit conceptual change for each participant in different ways.

Mechanisms for Deeper Comprehension through Constructive Interaction

When group participants believe that they understand each other, even if their understandings are incomplete, it can nonetheless enhance social interaction. When a speaker receives some indication from partners that they aren't being understood, they tend to stop talking and to silently explore their own understandings, allowing the listener to begin talking. This role exchange, as well as the incomplete understandings, are almost always potentially constructive in nature.

To examine this iterative process, Miyake (1986) developed two frameworks: the function-mechanism hierarchy to identify the levels of understanding of mechanisms, and another to capture the nature of the cycling of understanding and non-understanding.

Understanding and Non-Understanding on the Function-Mechanism Hierarchy

The process of understanding, for example of a physical device, follows a function-mechanism hierarchy: the function at one level is explained by the mechanism at the next lower level.

When a function in a level n mechanism is identified and questioned (i.e., one puzzles over how that function gets done), this opens up the search for a level n+1 mechanism. A mechanism is then proposed as a tentative solution. This proposal can be criticized, and if it passes this criticism, it is stated as confirmed. Thus, at each level, understanding proceeds through steps of identifying and questioning a function at level n, followed by searching, proposing, criticizing, and confirming the corresponding mechanism at level n+1. The mechanism at level n+1 can then be decomposed into its functions, and those one-level lower functions, when questioned, could then lead to search of a level n+2 mechanism.

When people are engaged in the steps of "identify," "propose," and "confirm," they think they understand the phenomenon at hand. When they "search," "criticize," and "question," they feel they do not understand. Roughly, when one finds an explanation in a level n+1 mechanism for a level n function, it is felt to be understood; when a function of level n is questioned and one starts searching for its mechanisms, this gives a sense of non-understanding. Thus, going through the steps and going down the levels produces an alternation of feelings of understanding and non-understanding.

Results of the Protocol Analysis

Miyake analyzed the interactions of three pairs of participants trying to understand a sewing machine.[2] All participants reached a level 5 mechanism. In terms of the understanding process, analyses confirmed the aforementioned framework: their senses of understanding and non-understanding alternated. Their language revealed that their conceptual viewpoints tended to be stable while they understood and tended to shift often when they did not understand. In addition, analyses of individual protocols in terms of how each descended the levels revealed some fundamental mechanisms of both individualistic as well as socially supported constructive interaction.

All pairs were able to solve the task, but each took a different course. They were often on different levels of the hierarchy while exchanging proposals: for Pair A, out of 91 turn takings, A1 and A2 were on different levels 31 times (36.3%). This discrepancy was greater at the beginning. In the first one-third, when they were talking just with paper and pen, they were out of synchrony 57.7 percent of the time. When interviewed after the experiment, they were unaware of this discrepancy.

Their final models were also different. When asked to explain how a sewing machine works at the end of the experiment, they took different points of view in their explanations. This difference again showed up six months later, when they were asked to do this same task.

Criticisms Provide Validation Checking Mechanisms. Because each participant works from a different starting schema, what is obvious to one may not be so to the other. This leads to "criticisms," defined as utterances expressing insufficiency in another's explanation. Self-criticizing accounted for only 12 percent of the incidents (5 of the total of 41), implying that validation checking is hard for a solitary individual. Interesting, most of the criticisms were "downward," where the person who is criticizing has less understanding than the other (22 times). This seems to mean that the criticizer could not understand the proposed mechanism. These criticisms, although originated in a lesser understanding, nonetheless forced the other person, the one with more understanding, to keep searching for better mechanisms, or better explanations of what s/he wants to propose. Out of 22 observed downward criticisms, 10 pushed the partner to search deeper for their answers.

Motions – The role of the monitors. Motions were suggestions that "moved" the pair forward by proposing a new way to approach the problem. Examples include suggesting taking off the bottom panel of the machine or using cords to simulate the movement of the threads.

There were two different types of motions, either closely related to the topic under discussion or divergent from it. *Topic-related motions* were generated

---

[2] Pairs A, B, and C (each member of a pair is denoted with a number; A1 and A2 formed Pair A).

more by the "task doers" or the people who were leading the problem solving at the moment. Monitors tended to give more *topic-divergent motions*, which showed higher rate of changing the course of problem solving, leading the pair to find broader perspectives. Topic-divergent motions might have their origins in a more global focus that was not easily available to the task doers. In constructive interaction, the observing monitor can contribute by criticizing and giving topic-divergent motions, which are not the primary roles of the task doer.

This set of hypothesized mechanisms of making interactions constructive was independently tested in cognitive, joint problem-solving research and in learning sciences. Yet most of these studies focused on the group level of analyses, tending to neglect how individuals gain more abstract, adaptable perspectives by deepening their own comprehension.

Implementations

The constructive interaction framework suggests a set of design principles that guide its implementation in classroom activities. Constructive interaction requires a shared goal, a problem that all the members want to understand and solve (see Lu, Bridges, & Hmelo-Silver, Chapter 15, this volume, on problem-based learning). It also requires social interaction among members, each of whom is expected to carry ideas, opinions, perspectives, and knowledge different from the others. This difference creates an atmosphere that encourages the exchange of ideas, knowledge, and so forth.

We find these characteristics in many of the best-known collaborative learning environments. Knowledge Forum (Scardamalia & Bereiter, Chapter 20, this volume) makes the differences among ideas clearly visible and enables them to be connected and integrated. Some tools like the Sensemaker of the WISE project make argumentation (Linn, Davis, & Bell, 2008; see Andriessen & Baker, Chapter 22, this volume) highly visible to encourage productive debate between competing scientific ideas. Learning by Design (Kolodner, 2006) encourages learners to carefully check which "physical facts" other groups use when they design a balloon car, all made visibly different from others in the form of white-boarding. They design a car based on the given "evidence," experimented and reported by other groups, to win the race.

In hypothesis-experiment instruction (HEI; Itakura, 1963), a lesson consists of a set of strategic procedures for discussion and a "problem," an experiment whose answer is predicted and discussed by the students. An HEI unit consists of multiple such problems, carefully ordered to guide the development of scientific concepts underlying the problem set. Each student in an HEI class is expected to integrate the results of the experiments in her/his own way to formulate a hypothesis. These differing hypotheses then are used to facilitate whole classroom discussion (Hatano & Inagaki, 1986).

This is similar to the "predict-observe-explain" method used to overcome scientific misconceptions, widely taught in U.S. teacher education programs (Kearney, 2004; Liew & Treagust, 1995; White & Gunstone,1992; see diSessa, Chapter 5, this volume), which encourages students to predict what they think will happen, observe what actually happens, and then try to explain why it happened. But in HEI, the sequence of experiments is designed so that learners create a "hypothesis" that is relevant to, and often surpasses, the materials covered in regular textbooks.

The Knowledge-Constructive Jigsaw

"Making thinking visible" has been a widely used design principle for successful knowledge integration (cf. Linn et al., 2008; Linn & Hsi, 2000). When thinking is made visible, it is more likely to foster constructive interaction. The jigsaw method, first developed by social psychologists for "teaching cooperativeness as a skill" (Aronson and Patnoe, 1997, p. 14), helps increase the diversity of perspectives on a shared task (e.g., Brown, 1997), because it makes it clear to the class that members in different expert groups are tackling different materials, preparing to give different perspectives to solve a shared problem. It is highly flexible, modifiable to facilitate many different types of collaboration (cf. Brown & Campione, 1994; Johnson & Johnson, 1989).

The constructive interaction framework has been used to guide a Japanese school education reform project called Consortium for Renovating Education of the Future (CoREF), to change school practices from teacher-centric, didactic pedagogy to learner-centered, collaborative co-creation of knowledge. CoREF is based on three design principles: (1) Outcomes of constructive interaction are individualistic, not sharable by other members of the same group (or class), thus each learner should be allowed to hold her/his own expression of the solution, to claim ownership of her/his own understanding; (2) a learner who mostly listens and monitors can still learn as much as more active learners, thus the class activity does not have to assume or enforce equal amounts of speaking; and (3) for a constructive interaction to lead to productive learning, there is no need to decide who plays the leader role, but it is essential for the members to share the desire to solve and understand a shared problem.

The exact form of a typical class is provided to the teachers as a starting framework to directly experience the Knowledge Constructive Jigsaw classrooms. This is a strongly scripted, yet dynamically modifiable, collaborative learning situation. Knowledge Constructive Jigsaw emphasizes that each individual student is responsible for integrating their own understanding with perspectives given by the learning materials and from other students. The class design involves a shared question to be answered and relevant learning materials from different perspectives distributed among the different groups – first in expert groups, to be later exchanged and integrated to answer the question in the jigsaw groups that consist of one member from each expert group (Miyake, 2011). The design requires each student to become a task doer in the jigsaw group. It also provides each student with chances to be a monitor who infers what the other students say and why, and to integrate others' ideas with their own. Although how often and how long each participant plays the role of the doer can differ, the proportion itself does not affect the quality of outcome.

Supporting Learning through Collaboration

With the transition to a 21st-century world, the very concept of learning is about to change dramatically (Collins & Halverson, 2009). Technology now enables customized learning – where learners can start learning whenever appropriate for each one of them, whatever content they wish to learn. Yet currently most of these new technologies are designed around one-way information flow, based on a dated "instructionist" model of passive learning (see Sawyer, Chapter 1, this volume). But learning sciences research is pointing toward social and collaborative learning. How can we reconcile the benefits of collaborative learning with the benefits of individualized and customized learning?

We believe that these two trends are not opposed, but are complementary and can be integrated. Learning environments should be designed to foster co-construction of knowledge and meaning and mutually shared sense making. At the same time, the learning environment should foster each individual's self-regulated, sustainable learning. There is no single universal way to do this; it requires learning environment designs that are customized to fit the situation at hand.

In the future, research on collaboration and learning should document learning for each individual participant, to understand the individual unit of learning; and research should also analyze the group level of analysis to understand social and interactional factors.

References

Aronson, E., & Patnoe, S. (1997). *The jigsaw classroom: Building cooperation in the classroom*. New York: Longman.

Baker, M. J. (1995). Negotiation in collaborative problem-solving dialogues. In R.-J. Beun, M. J. Baker, & M. Reiner (Eds.), *Dialogue and instruction* (pp. 39–55). Berlin: Springer-Verlag.

Bandura, A. (1982). Self-efficacy mechanism in human agency. *American Psychologist*, 37, 122–147.

Barron, B. (2003). When smart groups fail. *The Journal of the Learning Sciences*, 12, 307–359.

Bereiter, C. (2002). *Education and mind in the knowledge age.* Mahwah, NJ: Lawrence Erlbaum Associates.

Bereiter, C., & Scardamalia, M. (1993). *Surpassing ourselves: An inquiry into the nature and implications of expertise Knowledge Forum.* Open Court.

Bransford, J. D., Brown, A. L., & Cocking, R. R. (Eds.) (2000). *How people learn: Brain, mind, experience, and school.* Washington, DC: National Academy Press.

Brown, A. (1997). Transforming schools into communities of thinking and learning about serious matters. *American Psychologist*, 52, 399–413.

Brown, A., & Campione, J. (1994). Guided discovery in a community of learners. In K. McGilly (Ed.), *Classroom lessons: Integrating cognitive theory and classroom practice* (pp. 229–270). Cambridge, MA: Bradford Books, MIT Press.

Chang, A., & Bordia, P. (2001). A multidimensional approach to the group cohesion-group performance relationship. *Small Group Research*, 32, 379–405.

Cohen, S. G., & Bailey, D. E. (1997). What makes teams work: Group effectiveness research from the shop floor to the executive suite. *Journal of Management*, 23, 239–290.

Collins, A., & Halverson, R. (2009). *Rethinking education in the age of technology.* New York: Teachers College Press.

Crawford, J. L., & Gordon, A. H. (1972). Predecisional information-seeking and subsequent conformity in the social influence process. *Journal of Personality and Social Psychology*, **23**, 112–119.

Daft, R. L., & Weick, K. E. (1984). Toward a model of organizations as interpretation systems. *Academy of Management Review*, 9, 284–295.

Deutsch, M. (1980). Fifty years of conflict. In L. Festinger (Ed.), *Retrospections on social psychology* (pp. 46–77). New York: Oxford University Press.

Dillenbourg, P., Baker, M., Blaye, A., & O'Malley, C. (1996). The evolution of research on collaborative learning. In E. Spada & P. Reiman (Eds.), *Learning in humans and machine: Towards an interdisciplinary learning science* (pp. 189–211). Oxford: Elsevier.

Edmondson, A. C. (1996). Learning from mistakes is easier said than done: Group and organizational influences on the detection and correction of human error. *Journal of Applied Behavioral Science*, 32(1), 5–28.

Edmondson, A. C. (1999). Psychological safety and learning behavior in work teams. *Administrative Science Quarterly*, 44, 350–383.

Engeström, Y., Engeström, R., & Karkkainen, M., (1995). Polycontextuality and boundary crossing in expert cognition. *Learning and Instruction*, 5, 319–336.

Ericsson, K. A., & Smith, J. (1991). Prospects and limits in the empirical study of expertise: An introduction. In K. A. Ericsson & J. Smith (Eds.), *Toward a general theory of expertise: Prospects and limits* (pp. 1–38). Cambridge: Cambridge University Press.

Festinger, L. (1950). Informal social communication. *Psychological Review*, 57, 271–282.

Greeno, J. G., & Van de Sante, C. (2007). Perspectival understanding of conceptions and conceptual growth in interaction. *Educational Psychologist*, 42(1), 9–23.

Gully, S. M., Incalaterra, K. A., Johi, A., & Beaubien, J. M. (2002). A meta-analysis of team efficacy, potency and performance: Interdependence and level of analysis as moderators of observed relationships. *Journal of Applied Psychology*, 87, 819–832.

Hatano, G., & Inagaki, K. (1986). Two courses of expertise. In H. A. H. Stevenson & K. Hakuta (Eds.), *Child development and education in Japan* (pp. 262–272). New York: Freeman.

Hatano, G., & Inagaki, K. (1991). Sharing cognition through collective comprehension activity. In B. Resnick, J. M. Levine, & S. D. Teasley (Eds.), *Perspectives on socially shared cognition* (pp. 331–348). Washington, DC: American Psychological Association.

Homan, T. (2001). *Teamleren: Theorie en facilitatie.* [Team learning: Theory and facilitation.] Schoonhoven, Nederland: Academic.

Itakura, K. (1963). Kasetsu-Jikken-Jugyo no Teisho [The proposition of hypothesis-experiment-instruction]. *Riko Kyoshitsu [The Journal of Science Education]*, November issue.

Itakura, K. (1997). *Kasetsu-Jikken-Jugyo no ABC, Dai 4 han. (The ABC of the Hypothesis-Experiment-Instruction: Invitation to enjoyable classes, Ver. 4.)*, Kasetsu-Sha. [in Japanese].

James, L. R., Demaree, R. G., & Wolf, G. (1984). Estimating within-group interrater reliability with and without response bias. *Journal of Applied Psychology*, 69(1), 85–98.

Janssen, J., Kirschner, F., Kirschner, P. A., & Paas, F. (2010). Making the black box of collaborative learning transparent: Combining process-oriented and cognitive load approaches. *Educational Psychology Review*, 22, 139–154.

Johnson, D. W. (1973). Communication in conflict situations: A critical review of the research. *International Journal of Group Tensions*, 3, 46–67.

Johnson, D. W., & Johnson, R. T. (1989). *Cooperation and competition: Theory and research*. Edina, MN: Interaction.

Kearney, M. (2004). Classroom use of multimedia-supported predict-observe-explain tasks in a social constructivist learning environment. *Research in Science Education*, 34, 427–453.

Kolodner, J. L. (2006). Case-based reasoning. In R. K. Sawyer (Ed.), *The Cambridge handbook of the learning sciences* (pp. 225–242). New York: Cambridge University Press.

Kolodner, J. L., Camp, P. L., Crismond, D., Fasse, B., Gray, J., Holbrook, J., Puntambekar, S., & Ryan, M. (2003). Problem-based learning meets case-based reasoning in the middle-school science classroom: Putting learning by design into practice. *The Journal of the Learning Sciences*, 12, 495–547.

Kreijns, K., Kirschner, P. A., & Jochems, W. (2003). Identifying the pitfalls for social interaction in computer-supported collaborative learning environments: A review of the research. *Computers in Human Behavior*, 19, 335–353.

Lave, J., & Wenger, E. (1991). *Situated learning: Legitimate peripheral participation*. Cambridge, MA: Cambridge University Press.

Liew, C., & Treagust, D. F. (1995). A predict-observe-explain teaching sequence for learning about students' understanding of heat and expansion of liquids. *Australian Science Teachers' Journal*, 41, 68–71.

Linn, M. C., Davis, E. A., & Bell, P. (Eds.) (2008). *Internet environments for science education* (pp. 29–46). Mahwah, NJ: Lawrence Erlbaum Associates.

Linn, M. C., & Hsi, S. (2000). *Computers, teachers, peers: Science learning partners.* Mahwah, NJ: Lawrence Erlbaum Associates.

Mesch, D., Marvin, L., Johnson, D. W., & Johnson, R. T. (1988). Impact of positive interdependence and academic group contingencies on achievement. *Journal of Social Psychology*, 128, 345–352.

Miyake, N. (1986). Constructive interaction and the iterative process of understanding. *Cognitive Science*, 10, 151–177.

Miyake, N. (2011). Fostering conceptual change through collaboration: Its cognitive mechanism, socio-cultural factors, and the promises of technological support. *Proceedings of the 9th International Conference on Computer-Supported Collaborative Learning (CSCL2011)*, Hong Kong.

Mulder, I. (1999). *Understanding technology mediated interaction processes. A theoretical context*. Enschede, Netherlands: Telematica Instituut.

Mulder, I., Swaak, J., & Kessels, J. (2002). Assessing group learning and shared understanding in technology-mediated interaction. *Educational Technology & Society*, 5(1), 35–47.

Mullen, B., & Copper, C. (1994). The relation between group cohesiveness and performance: An integration. *Psychological Bulletin*, 115(2), 210–227.

Nunally, J. C., & Bernstein, I. H. (1994). *Psychometric theory*. Third Edition. New York: McGraw-Hill.

Roschelle, J. (1992). Learning by collaborating: Convergent conceptual change. *Journal of the Learning Sciences*, 2, 235–276.

Rozenblit, L., & Keil, F. (2002). The misunderstood limits of folk science: An illusion of explanatory depth. *Cognitive Science*, 26, 521–562.

Saito, M., & Miyake, N. (2011) Socially constructive interaction for fostering conceptual change. *Proceedings of the 9th International Conference on Computer-Supported Collaborative Learning (CSCL2011)* (pp. 96–103). Hong Kong.

Sawyer, K. R. (Ed.) (2006). *The Cambridge handbook of the learning sciences*. New York: Cambridge University Press.

Scardamalia, M., & Bereiter, C. (1994). Computer support for knowledge-building communities. *Journal of the Learning Sciences*, 3, 265–283.

Shea, G. P., & Guzzo, R. A. (1987). Group effectiveness: What really matters? *Sloan Management Review*, 28, 25–31.

Shirouzu, H., Miyake, N., & Masukawa, H. (2002). Cognitively active externalization for situated reflection. *Cognitive Science*, 26, 469–501.

Sörbom, D. (1989). Model modification. *Psychometrika*, 54, 371–384.

Stahl, G. A. (2000, June). A model of collaborative knowledge building. Paper presented at the 4th International Conference of the Learning Sciences, Ann Arbor, MI.

Van den Bossche, P., Gijselaers, W., Segers, M., & Kirschner, P. A. (2006). Social and cognitive factors driving teamwork in collaborative learning environments: Team learning beliefs and behaviors. *Small Group Research*, 37, 490–521.

Van der Vegt, G. S., Emans, B. J. M., & Van de Vliert, E. (1998). Motivating effects of task and outcome interdependence in work teams. *Group & Organization Management*, 23(2), 124–143.

Wageman, R. (1995). Interdependence and group effectiveness. *Administrative Science Quarterly*, 40, 145–180.

Webb, N. M., & Palincsar, A. S. (1996). Group processes in the classroom. In D. C. Berliner & R. C. Calfee (Eds.), *Handbook of educational psychology* (pp. 841–873). New York: Macmillan.

White, R. T., & Gunstone, R. F. (1992). *Probing understanding*. Great Britain: Falmer Press.

22 Arguing to Learn

Jerry Andriessen and Michael Baker

Many people think that arguing interferes with learning, and that's true for a certain type of oppositional argument that is increasingly prevalent in our media culture. Tannen (1998) analyzed the aggressive types of argument that are frequently seen on talk shows and in the political sphere, where representatives of two opposed viewpoints spout talking points at each other. In these forms of argument, the goal is not to work together toward a common position, but simply to score points. All teachers and parents have seen children engaged in this type of argumentation, and most would probably agree that it has little to contribute to education.

The learning sciences is studying a different kind of argumentation, which we call *collaborative* argumentation. For example, collaborative argumentation plays a central role in science; science advances not by the accumulation of facts, but by debate and argumentation (Osborne, 2010). Even when two scientists disagree, they still share the common values of science and both of them are interested in achieving the same goals (determining what claim should be upheld). Argumentation in science should not be primarily oppositional and aggressive; it is a form of collaborative discussion in which both parties are working together to resolve an issue, and in which both scientists aim to reach agreement. Engagement in collaborative argumentation can help students learn to think critically and independently about important issues and contested values. Before students can successfully engage in collaborative argumentation, they must overcome the traditional and deep-seated opposition between reason and emotion (Baker, Andriessen, & Järvelä, 2013; Picard et al., 2004), stop being aggressively opposed to others, and instead orient their positive motivations and emotions toward the question being discussed and others' views on it.

When students collaborate in argumentation in the classroom, they are *arguing to learn*. When viewed as a collaborative practice, argumentation can help learners to accomplish a wide variety of important learning goals. There are many ways that argumentation can contribute to learning. First, argumentation involves knowledge elaboration, reasoning, and reflection. These activities have been shown to contribute to deeper conceptual learning (Bransford, Brown, & Cocking, 1999). Second, participating in argumentation helps students learn about argumentative structures (Kuhn, 2001).

Third, because productive argumentation is a form of collaboration, it can help develop social awareness and collaborative ability more generally (Wertsch, 1985). Fourth, groups of people, at work, at home, in social contexts, often share a common tradition of argumentation (Billig, 1987), and effective participation in these groups can enable learning how to argue competently within them (Koschmann, 2003). This is particularly true of the knowledge-based communities that are so central to the knowledge society – groups of highly trained professionals such as scientists, doctors, lawyers, and executives.

Argumentation has been studied for millennia, from many perspectives, notably in philosophy, logic, literature, and public speaking. In recent years, learning scientists have been studying the educational use of argumentation, and this chapter summarizes this research. Studies of arguing to learn have the potential to help learners, teachers, and researchers design learning environments that facilitate collaborative argumentation. First, we discuss argumentation theory for its vocabulary and different viewpoints on argumentation. Then, we discuss the relation between argumentation and learning. Finally, we summarize learning in learning environments, such as chat rooms and Internet newsgroups, where argumentation is mediated by computer networks.

Argumentation Theory

Argumentation theory (Van Eemeren, Grootendorst, & Snoeck Henkemans, 1996) studies the production, analysis, and evaluation of argumentation. The goal is to develop criteria for judging the soundness of an argument. Describing and evaluating arguments are some of the oldest topics of scholarship; Aristotle distinguished several kinds of argumentation: including didactic, dialectical, rhetorical, examination, and eristic. For most of the 20th century, the study of argumentation has been dominated by scholars who focused on the logical, sequential structure of argument. In this tradition, a good argument was thought to have a certain type of structure, and scholars attempted to specify the underlying "grammar" of argument by analogy with the syntax of a well-formed sentence. For example, Toulmin (1958) identified the following elements of sound argumentation in everyday discourse.

> A *claim* states the standpoint or conclusion: "The Kyoto Protocol to reduce global warming is necessary."
>
> The *data* are the facts or opinions that the claim is based on: "Over the past century, the earth's temperature has been rising as a result of greenhouse gas emissions."
>
> The *warrant* provides the justification for using the data as support for the claim: "Scientists agree that there is no other explanation for this rise in temperature."

Optionally, the *backing* provides specific information supporting the warrant. "Scientists have identified the atmospheric mechanisms whereby greenhouse gases cause a warming of the earth's surface."

A *qualifier*, such as "probably," indicates the degree of certainty that the arguers attribute to a claim.

Exceptions to the claim are expressed by a *rebuttal*: "Unless it can be shown that the earth's rise in temperature is entirely due to fluctuations in temperature that have occurred over geological time, independently of human activity."

This type of approach has been very influential, especially in the analysis of spoken and written argumentation (e.g., Voss, 2005). It is a concise description of what appears to be a sound line of reasoning, or even a productive line of inquiry. However, in recent years, the study of argumentation has become a more empirical and scientific study, and empirical analysis has shown that the grammatical approach does not correspond very well to the ways that arguments unfold in collaborative discourse. Van Eemeren and Grootendorst (1999) note that the model fails to consider both sides involved in (real-world) argumentation; it covers only the proponent, not the opponent. A related problem is that it fails to consider argumentation as a discourse phenomenon, which is always embedded in a specific contextual and social environment. For the learning sciences, another serious problem is that the grammatical view doesn't provide any insight into how argument structures might change during development (Leitão, 2001).

In contrast to this grammatical and monological concept of argument, more recent argumentation theory views argumentation as a type of dialog. For example, *formal dialectics* (Barth & Krabbe, 1982) describes argumentation as a dialog between a proponent and an opponent around a certain thesis. *Pragma-dialectics* (Van Eemeren & Grootendorst, 1999) explains the interaction between proponent and opponent in terms of the necessary conditions for critical discussion rather than on rules of logic for generating a debate. Van Eemeren and Grootendorst (1999) show how pragma-dialectics can be applied to the analysis of argumentative discourse. In *dialog theory* (Walton, 2000), an argument is seen as a series of *moves*. Walton described six types of dialog moves – persuasion, inquiry, negotiation, information seeking, deliberation, and eristic (personal conflict).

These newer theories are more useful for learning scientists, because they provide guidance for how to analyze and evaluate students' collaborative argumentation – for example, in terms of whether acceptable moves have been made, and whether the dialog converges toward a constructive outcome. In educational research, similar proposals have been made for analyzing students' dialogs as "types of talk" (e.g., "disputational," "exploratory"), each of which has associated "ground rules." It has been shown that explicitly teaching such ground rules to students improves their collaboration and learning (Mercer, Wegerif, & Dawes, 1999). Several computer-based learning environments have been designed to foster argumentation dialog games (see further on in this chapter).

Argumentation and Learning

In arguing to learn, students are not primarily attempting to convince each other; instead, they are engaged in cooperative explorations of a "dialogical space" of solutions to problems and fundamental concepts underlying them (cf. Nonnon, 1996). Baker (2009) identified five learning mechanisms that are potentially associated with effective arguing to learn. These mechanisms are based on general learning sciences findings that seem to apply broadly to a wide range of content knowledge (Nathan & Sawyer, Chapter 2, this volume):

> **Change in view:** As a result of argumentation, learners may be led to transform their basic beliefs about the problem domain or their overall viewpoints (Harman, 1986). As well as simply changing their minds about beliefs, more subtle changes may occur as students elaborate more reasoned and nuanced views that take alternative views into account.

> **Making knowledge explicit:** Learners who provide explanations, or make explicit the reasoning underlying their problem-solving behavior, show the most learning benefits (Chi & Van Lehn, 1991). Argumentation provides many opportunities for explanation, and preparing a justification or argumentative defense fosters reflection that often leads to deeper learning.

> **Conceptual change:** Debating a question may raise doubt about one's initial conceptions of the problem. Conceptual transformation is supported by argumentation when students make new distinctions between concepts or elaborate new definitions of them (also see diSessa, Chapter 5, this volume).

> **Co-elaboration of new knowledge:** Learners work together to elaborate new meanings. The interactive interpersonal nature of verbal interaction helps to scaffold individual learning.

> **Increasing articulation:** Argumentation obliges learners to precisely formulate question and statements.

The Development of Argumentative Skill

The ability to participate in and comprehend argumentation emerges early in development. By the age of three, children generate and understand the principal components of an argument (Stein & Albro, 2001). The ability to construct detailed, coherent rationales in defense of a favored position improves with age. This development, however, does not guarantee a deeper understanding of one's opponents; in fact, argumentative knowledge develops asymmetrically (Stein & Bernas, 1999). Individuals have more knowledge about the positive benefits of their own position than of those of their opponent's position. Also, they know more about the weaknesses of their opponents than of their own weaknesses. We can train people to understand the opposing position in a more accurate and complex fashion; but only when they are forced to change their stance do learners start generating reasons that favor the opponent's position.

Understanding arguments is related to one's developing knowledge of social conflict and goal-directed action. For example, a conflict may exist between displaying good argument skills and participating in morally and socially responsible negotiations. Sometimes, good arguers have less knowledge about and poorer relationships with their opponents than do poor arguers. We should teach argumentation in a way that leads to interpersonal success rather than personal success at the expense of the other (Stein & Albro, 2001).

Arguing to Learn Contributes to Reasoning Skills

During reasoning, individuals make inferences from given knowledge to reach a conclusion. The inferences that support sound reasoning have a similar structure to an effective argument. Informal reasoning skills develop through argumentation, because argumentation facilitates storage of and access to knowledge in memory, and the development of elaborate mental models, which helps inference generation (Voss & Means, 1991).

Kuhn (1991) studied argumentation skills by asking people to prepare arguments and counterarguments about issues of societal importance such as: What causes prisoners to return to crime after they are released? What causes children to fail in school? Kuhn interviewed 160 individuals in four age groups (teens, 20s, 40s, and 60s) to determine their causal theories, the evidence they used to support their theories, their ability to generate an alternative theory on their own, and their ability to generate counterarguments to their theory and to rebut the counterarguments.

Most of these people provided poorly structured arguments and provided theories along with a list of unrelated causes. Only 16 percent of the participants could generate genuine evidence for their theories. Most of the evidence they presented was of a type that Kuhn called *pseudoevidence* (for example, when asked the question "what causes prisoners to return to crime after being released?" subjects might give a pseudo-reason such as "some of them can have a normal life, you know"). More of the participants (33%), although still a minority, were able to conceive of an alternative theory. An important argumentation skill is the ability to produce counterarguments, and only 34 percent were consistently able to generate a counterargument to their theory. Finally, the percentage of subjects that generated valid rebuttals to their own theories was between 21 percent to 32 percent across topics.

Kuhn argued that argumentative skills are based on a person's epistemological theories, that is, the view they hold about the nature of knowledge and knowing. She proposed that a person's epistemological theory falls on a spectrum between two very different extremes: an *absolutist epistemology* and an *evaluative epistemology*. In the absolutist epistemology, knowing prevails in complete ignorance of alternative possibilities. In the evaluative epistemology, knowing is an ongoing, effortful process of evaluating possibilities, one that is never completed. The evaluative epistemology is associated with argumentative skill and understanding. A minority of the people she studied (between 9% and 22%, depending on the topic) held to the evaluative epistemology. For such learners to progress to a more advanced understanding of argumentation, they first would have to change their epistemology.

Learning to Argue in Small Groups

The learning sciences has shown that collaborative classroom interaction can often contribute to individual learning (Greeno & Engeström, Chapter 7, this volume; Enyedy & Stevens, Chapter 10, this volume; Miyake & Kirschner, Chapter 21, this volume). This is particularly true of collaborative argumentation. For example, Kuhn, Shaw, and Felton (1997) asked participants (students and adults) to write an essay about capital punishment, and then engaged these students in argumentation over this topic for a period of several weeks, following which an essay justifying their positions was elicited again. Arguments took place in pairs, with multiple successive partners, with each argument lasting 10–15 minutes. As a result, students and adults provided significantly more two-sided (as opposed to one-sided) and functional (as opposed to nonfunctional) arguments.

Reznitskaya and colleagues (2001) used a method called *collaborative reasoning*, an approach to discussion that aims to provide elementary schoolchildren with the opportunity to become skilled in argumentation. Collaborative reasoning helps students develop *argument schema* – abstract knowledge structures that represent extended stretches of argumentative discourse. Argument schema enable the organization and retrieval of argument-relevant information, facilitate argument construction and repair, and provide a basis for anticipating objections and for finding flaws in one's arguments and the arguments of others (Reznitskaya et al., 2001). Fifth graders in the experimental group participated in small groups twice a week, during a period of five weeks, in discussions about controversial issues. Students were asked to take positions on an issue (on the basis of story information) and provide supporting reasons and evidence for their opinions. With coaching from their teacher, students challenged each other's viewpoints, offered counterarguments and rebuttals, and asked for clarifications. In addition, the teacher led students in activities that exposed them to formal argument schema. At the end of the five-week period, learning was assessed by analyzing a student's argumentative essay on a realistic story dilemma. The essay was scored on relevant arguments, counterarguments, and rebuttals. Students who participated in collaborative reasoning wrote essays that contained a significantly greater number of arguments, counterarguments, rebuttals, and references to text information than the essays of students who did not experience collaborative reasoning (Reznitskaya et al., 2001).

Learning through Collaborative Argumentation

Argumentation is one of the features of collaborative learning that make student groups so effective at promoting individual learning. Keefer, Zeitz, and Resnick (2000) studied argumentation during oral classroom peer discourse in a fourth grade class. Their point of departure was the idea that statements, assertions, and arguments can be understood as (tacitly agreed) *commitments* that a participant in the dialog is obliged to defend if challenged (Walton & Krabbe, 1995). An important contribution of this study is that it attempts to identify empirically different types of dialog (Walton & Krabbe, 1995). Each type of dialog has an initial starting point, an assigned goal, the participants' goals, and a characteristic means of reaching the goal. Participants' goals may shift during discussion, possibly changing dialog type.

The type of dialog that was most effective in fostering learning of literary content was *critical discussion*. The characteristics of critical discussion are: (1) starting with a difference of opinion; (2) having a goal of accommodation and understanding of different viewpoints; (3) a balance-of-considerations style, in which the most persuasive arguments prevail; (4) the participant goal of persuading others and sharing understanding.

A second type of dialog that was effective for learning is called *explanatory inquiry*, characterized by (1) a lack of knowledge as a starting point; (2) the goal is correct knowledge; (3) achieved by cumulative steps; (4) the participants' goal is convergence on a solution or conclusion.

At the beginning of the school year, and again at the end, students were assessed by asking them to participate in four minutes of conversational reasoning in different peer discussions (six at the beginning and six at the end of the year). The researchers identified a number of features of argumentation, documented in class during the year, that were associated with the largest increase in conversational reasoning. The strongest increase was the degree to which the student held a sustained commitment to the pursuit of an issue. A sustained commitment in a dialog involved a student to grant concessions (to agree potentially to being convinced) accommodating the differences in opinion that existed at the start of the dialog. Sometimes this involved altering a commitment by either attacking arguments that supported conclusions previously presented or by building on arguments that attacked those previously presented conclusions. Dialogs with too many challenges (critical questions or attacks) did not lead to improved outcomes at the end of the year, perhaps because no single challenge was followed by a sustained consideration of its impact on some viewpoint. Dialogs where participants conceded their positions too easily also did not lead to improved outcomes, perhaps because this led to an avoidance of any argumentation at all.

Arguing to Learn in Context

There is some evidence that argumentation proceeds differently in different cultural and social contexts (see the review in Muller Mirza, Perret-Clermont, Tartas, & Iannaccone, 2009). For example, the sort of argumentation that is considered appropriate in school may be a culturally specific school-based form of discourse (Wertsch, 1991). These school-based forms of argumentation are those most likely to align with the idealized forms proposed by argumentation theory. Outside of school, different cultures possess differing norms that influence argumentation; for example, there are cultural differences in the extent to which social conflict is avoided and consensus is preferred. According to Peng and Nisbett (1999), people from Asian countries (notably China and Japan) have a tendency to avoid contradiction and to search for a consensual "middle way." Cultures, such as in Israel, have developed a specific form of discourse – called "dugri speech" ("straight talk") – that is explicitly based on confrontation of views, but with a view to harmonious acknowledgment of differences (Matusov, 2009). In some nations, such as France, certain arguments (for example, those propounding racism) cannot legally be made in public spheres, which include schools (Golder, 1996).

Even within a single culture, one typically finds that a broad range of pedagogical approaches is used in schools. Andriessen and Sandberg (1999) described three basic educational scenarios – "transmission," "studio," and "negotiation" – that differ in terms of how knowledge is supposed to be acquired (from the teacher, by exploratory activities, by discussion). Collaborative argumentation aligns with the negotiation scenario. But even if individual teachers try to introduce negotiation scenarios, encouraging students to discuss and argue, this may be at odds with students' previous school experience, which is more likely to be in instructionist classrooms (Sawyer, Chapter 1, this volume) that implicitly encourage the idea that authoritative texts are simply to be summarized (Andriessen, 2009).

Researchers have identified important differences in argumentation among children in different classes, even within the same school. This has been explained in terms of how the teacher frames the activity, as either a collaborative opportunity to learn about one another's ideas, or as a kind of competition (Berland & Reiser, 2011). Teachers have a complex task to perform in framing activities, involving providing relevant information at the right time, resolving issues, and scaffolding the debate toward a clear and understandable outcome (Simonneaux, 2007).

> The most effective form of collaborative argumentation is likely to vary depending on the school subject. In math and science, students may occasionally engage in heated argument when their proposed solutions are criticized, but this will not challenge their identity and self-esteem nearly as much as when the topic under discussion involves deeply entrenched value systems and personal or group identities, as in history, psychology, sociology, or anthropology (Goldberg, Schwarz, & Porat, 2011).

Summary: Argumentation and Learning

Many people have trouble arguing productively. They are not good at distinguishing evidence from theory and rarely consider alternative positions. And because the social cost of threatening a good relationship is rather high, people avoid arguing when they do not feel at ease. There may be important cultural differences here, but in the Western European and U.S. context, students must be explicitly socialized into collaborative argumentation in school.

The evidence shows that students can benefit from collaborative argumentation, but learning outcomes will be most effective when argumentation is framed as a collaborative activity that benefits all learners. Arguing to learn is most effective when it is embedded in collaborative activity and driven by a desire for understanding and sharing with others (see Scardamalia & Bereiter, Chapter 20, this volume).

Collaborative Argumentation in Electronic Environments

The learning sciences is discovering that much knowledge is learned more effectively in collaboration (see the chapters in Part IV of this handbook). Nevertheless, we have just reviewed a large body of research showing that most people have difficulty arguing collaboratively. Computer technology offers a potential solution. For example, computer-supported collaborative learning systems (CSCL; see Stahl, Koschmann, & Suthers, Chapter 24, this volume) can support and guide productive argumentation, leading to deeper understanding. In this section, we describe several software systems in which students input their contributions to an argument on a computer.

Inform	Question	Challenge
I think...	Why do you think that...?	I disagree because...
Let me explain...	Why is it...?	I'm not so sure...
Let me elaborate...	Can you elaborate...?	How is that relevant...?
Because...	Can you give an example...?	A counter-argument is...
An example...	Is it the case that...?	Is there evidence...?
My evidence...	Don't we need more evidence...?	How reliable is that evidence...?

Reason	Support	Maintain
Therefore...	I agree because...	Yes
What I think you are saying...	I see your point of view...	No
Is your assumption that...?	Also...	Ok
Both are right in that...	That's right	Thank you
To summarize...	Good point	Sorry...
Let's consult...		Is this ok...?
		Would you please...
		Ok. Let's move on.
		Can we...?
		Goodbye...

Figure 22.1. *Sentence openers in AcademicTalk (McAlister et al., 2004).*

These systems aim to *scaffold* student argumentation in some way – by providing structure for the roles of each student and the relationships between them in a dialog, by offering new and multiple ways of *representation* in argument maps, and by allowing students to manipulate the structure and content of the argument.

The topics that we address in this section are: (1) scaffolding argumentation with dialog games; (2) scaffolding text-based argumentative discussions; (3) scaffolding arguments with diagrams; (4) scaffolding scientific argumentation in learning environments.

Scaffolding Argumentation as a Dialog Game

Inspired by dialog theory (Walton, 2000), *dialog game theory* (Levin & Moore, 1980) suggests that we should structure participants' behavior by specifying roles and constraints. Participants are only allowed to make argumentative moves that appear on a list of moves that are appropriate at each point in the argument. Building on dialog game theory, Mackenzie (1979) developed an argumentation computer game called *DC* that allowed the user to select a move and type in its content. The moves provided included "Question," "Statement," "Challenge," "Resolution," and "Withdraw." The system then evaluated the contribution according to a preset list of rules. Rules defined when a move could or must be made and what happened as a result. The rules prevented each player from evading a question, arguing in a circle, or failing to support a claim.

McAlister, Ravenscroft, and Scanlon (2004) developed a tool called AcademicTalk, also based on dialog game theory, that supports synchronous debate between peers. The system requires a learner to choose a sentence opener for each new message (see Figure 22.1), and then to complete the message (note similarities with the scaffolds in Knowledge Forum; Scardamalia & Bereiter, Chapter 20, this volume). The openers were designed to support argumentation, and at each point in the argument certain openers are highlighted as suggestions to be considered. Students prepare for a debate by reading source materials, then engage in the debate, and finally there is a consolidation phase in which a summary of key arguments is presented to the group.

AcademicTalk was compared with a similar tool that allowed online discussion, but with no scaffolding. Results from a group of 34 students indicated that students using AcademicTalk engaged more directly with each other's positions and ideas (claims, challenges, and rebuttals) and produced more extended argumentation. In contrast, students in normal chat did not engage in as much argumentation and instead simply exchanged information.

Scaffolding Argumentation through Computer-Mediated Communication Forums

In a postgraduate university course on computer-mediated communication, Pilkington and Walker (2003) asked their students to adopt one of three *argumentation roles*, based on research showing that when students are forced to adopt these roles, this leads to improved argumentative reasoning (Mercer, Wegerif, & Dawes, 1999). In Role 1, students challenge others to provide evidence and point out alternatives or contradictions (e.g., "No because …," or "Yes, but…"). In Role 2, students ask for explanations and clarifications, and in Role 3, students provide information, either spontaneously or in answer to an inquiry. The teacher and the students had regular electronic discussions throughout the course. At the beginning of the course, the teacher was responsible for a substantial number of argumentative contributions (between 27% and 42% of the challenges). Part way through the semester, the students participated in a role-playing exercise in which they were asked to assume one of the three roles; after this one role-playing session, there was no mention of roles anymore. Even so, after the role-playing session, the teacher's contributions declined to between 21 percent and 25 percent; students increasingly took over responsibility for sustaining the debate. The level of information providing (Role 3) declined, while behaviors associated with the other roles increased. The authors argued that the decline in information providing is evidence for greater student autonomy (possibly relating to learning) because it led to fewer but deeper parallel discussion threads. The exercise showed that students engage in more productive argumentation after they are made aware of the full range of potential roles in discussions via a role-playing activity.

In the 1990s, these text-based discussion forums were thought to be a good way for students to share ideas and also to engage in deep argumentation. Learning scientists were interested in the potential of *asynchronous* forums, because users do not have to be logged in at the same time and can post their responses hours or even days later. Asynchronous forums provide users with unlimited time to formulate well-elaborated contributions (Tiberghien & de Vries, 1997). Unfortunately, the results from using these text-based discussion forums have been disappointing, especially with respect to the frequency and quality of arguments. Andriessen (2005) provides an extensive overview of projects that used forums to engage students in knowledge co-construction discourse, including argumentation, but also forums that aimed to strengthen sense of community and participation. For example, in so-called *theoretical forums*, students were invited to investigate lines of reasoning that authors of scientific papers engaged in. The goal was to engage students in academic argumentation – to introduce students to the discourse of a scientific community, to help them find their own voice, and potentially to form a self-identity as a scientist and a member of that community (Matusov, 2009). An example of such an issue was: *Discuss your ideas about the following statement: For the study of learning processes, phenomenography offers a more promising approach than instructional design, intelligent tutoring systems, or instructional psychology* (see Andriessen, 2005). Questions such as these, although authentic in that they are very similar to what cutting-edge researchers are working on, are now considered too abstract and not engaging for regular students. According to current thinking, there is lack of intersubjectivity in many electronic discussions: although participants may have a sense of others reacting to their contributions, what in fact often happens is co-alienation – the juxtaposition of incompatible representations (arguments) (Schwarz, Kolikant, & Mishenkina, 2012).

Scaffolding Argumentation with Argument Maps

Many systems use the graphical power of today's personal computers to visually display the relations between moves in an argument. Early systems that use visual argument maps to scaffold argumentation include Belvedere, CHENE, and Connect. CHENE (Chaines ENErgetiques; Tiberghien & de Vries, 1997) was designed to be used by two students collaborating to build an electronic circuit; C-CHENE (Baker & Lund, 1997) provided dialog buttons for each of about 10 different dialog moves, as well as dialog buttons for agreeing, disagreeing, and managing the ongoing argument; and CONNECT (de Vries, Lund, & Baker, 2002) displayed every statement made by two students, and provided buttons for both students to agree or disagree with each statement.

Figure 22.2 shows a screen display of the argument map system Belvedere 3.0. Belvedere is intended to support secondary schoolchildren's learning

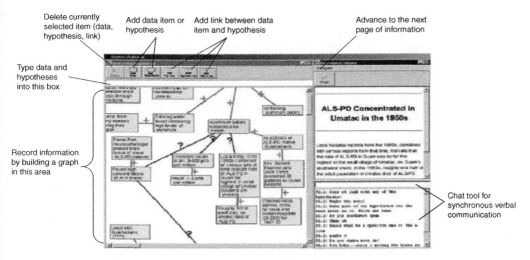

Delete currently selected item (data, hypothesis, link)

Add data item or hypothesis

Add link between data item and hypothesis

Advance to the next page of information

Type data and hypotheses into this box

Record information by building a graph in this area

Chat tool for synchronous verbal communication

Figure 22.2. *Belvedere 3.0. graph interface in the online condition of Suthers and Hundhausen (2003).*

of critical scientific inquiry skills (Suthers & Weiner, 1995). The diagrams were designed to engage students in complex scientific reasoning. The boxes represent hypotheses and data, and the lines show relations of support and disagreement. An earlier version had many more visual primitives than Figure 22.2, allowing propositions to be categorized as *Principal, Theory, Hypothesis, Claim,* or *Report.* Research with this early version showed that the most interesting argumentation was not computer mediated, but instead was the oral discussion between students working together at a single computer. As a result, the diagrams were later simplified, focusing on evidential relations between data and hypotheses, and this is the version depicted in Figure 22.2. Rather than being a medium of communication or a formal record of the argumentation process, the representations served the students as resources for oral conversation and reasoning (Suthers & Hundhausen, 2003).

Learning systems that use argument diagrams have been extensively reviewed (see Andriessen & Baker, 2013, for an overview). Overall, the results show some promise (e.g., Van Amelsvoort, Andriessen, & Kanselaar, 2007). However, students working in small groups with technology and engaging in argumentation presents significant challenges to most students' abilities, both socially and cognitively.

Future systems that use argument diagrams should be clear about the learning goals and the role of the teacher and should make sure that the technology is compatible with the overall classroom context: how students are normally assessed, what experience they have had with collaboration, what their motivation is for the assignment (Andriessen & Baker, 2013). As part of a long-term goal in promoting collaborative reasoning practices (Clark

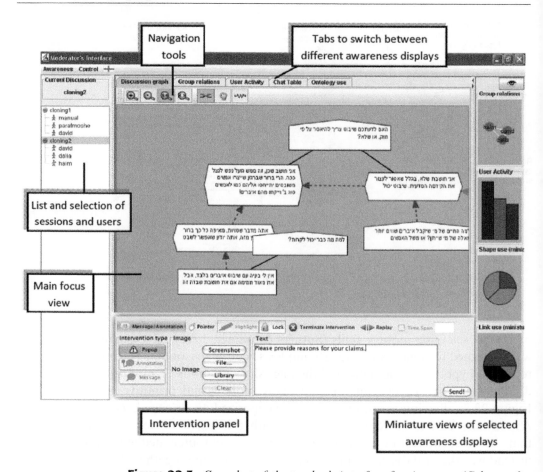

Figure 22.3. *Snapshot of the teacher's interface for Argunaut (Schwarz & Asterhan, 2011).*

et al., 2003) in secondary school classrooms, Schwarz and Asterhan (2011) report a study of the Argunaut system, which uses argument diagrams that meet these requirements. Argunaut allows discourse moves, represented with different geometrical shapes, to be organized in a shared space as (argument) diagrams. Argunaut includes awareness tools that engage in monitoring participation (user activities), argumentation tools, and references to the other actors (group relations) in the discussion. Such tools are meant for teachers to be able to quickly review how collaboration is proceeding for several groups at the same time, as well as to be able to remotely intervene in discussions (by sending pop-up messages or attaching notes) without disrupting the flow (Figure 22.3).

The teacher could detect deficiencies in argumentation through the link use pie chart (bottom right), which could reveal (for example) that only agreement links were used by some groups. The discussion graph and the listed contributions could reveal a lack of depth in the discussion, which was

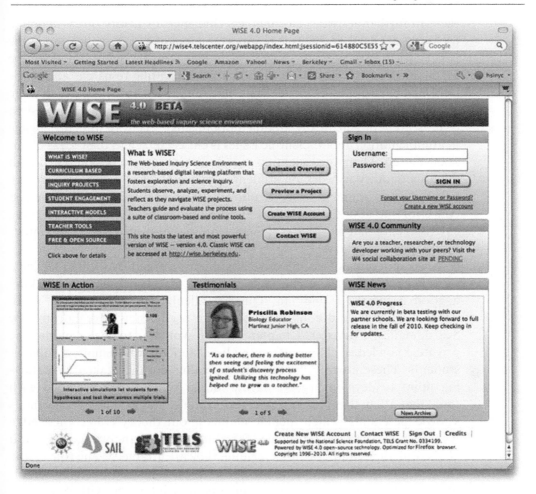

Figure 22.4. *Copy of the WISE interface.*

handled by the teacher with generic prompts early in the discussion and by content-specific hints later on. The teacher also drew the discussants' attention to specific contributions to make a challenging point. What makes the work on Argunaut relevant for arguing to learn is that it offers promising possibilities for teacher support of ongoing argumentation in small groups.

Scaffolding Scientific Argumentation in Learning Environments

In everyday conversation, most of us commonly engage in challenging, counterchallenging, justifying, or agreeing, but according to analytical criteria, our everyday arguments are generally mediocre (Pontecorvo, 1993). However, when it comes to science, very few of us feel qualified to challenge, counterchallenge, or engage with scientific claims at all. Rather, we simply accept expert arguments, and we generally do not use them in further activities to convince, challenge, or justify our viewpoints (Schwarz & Glassner, 2003). An important goal of science education in the 21st century is to prepare students to understand the nature of scientific argumentation, to be critical consumers of scientific research, and to be informed participants in critical national and international debates that are closely tied to scientific argumentation (whether global climate change, stem cell research, or genetically modified organisms). The way students engage in argumentation about scientific issues is closely linked to their ideas about science itself. Therefore, scientific argumentation should be combined with scientific inquiry to work on students' epistemological beliefs rather than on producing arguments only (Sandoval, 2003). In this final section we discuss efforts to develop scientific understanding by using electronic learning environments that scaffold argumentation, but also provide opportunities for interactive inquiry.

You cannot make an effective argument without knowing the facts of a field, but knowing the facts does not necessarily lead to making a good argument (Goldman, Duschl, Ellenbogen, Williams, & Tzou, 2003). Goldman and colleagues' program used Knowledge Forum (see Scardamalia & Bereiter, Chapter 20, this volume) to make public the private knowledge claims of individual students and small groups of students. These now-public knowledge claims are then taken as a starting point to develop argumentation skills. Students are provided with tools that allow them to construct, coordinate, and evaluate each other's knowledge claims, which include claims about theory (what knowledge is important), method (strategies for obtaining and analyzing data), and goals (outcomes and how to determine they are attained). The role of the teacher in whole-class and small-group discussions is to actively monitor the interactions among the students, and intervene with questions, comments, and prompts for additional student input – always oriented toward evidence-based consensus building. Researchers are still exploring the optimal role for the teacher.

Scientists use argumentation to resolve theoretical controversies, and they explicitly use evidence to support competing theories. Linn and her team designed the Web-based Integrated Science Environment (WISE) to scaffold students in these activities (Linn, 2006). Knowledge integration is a dynamic process through which students connect their conceptual ideas to explain phenomena, add experiences from the world to their mix of ideas, and restructure ideas within increasingly more coherent views (Bell & Linn, 2000).

The research team discovered that students focused on one or two pieces of evidence they believed would strongly support their perspective, and ignored counterevidence. In addition, the arguments they produced were not very elaborated. This led Linn's colleague Philip Bell to develop a tool called SenseMaker (Bell, 1997), which allowed students to coordinate claims and evidence with visual argument maps.

When students debated in class without the argument maps, they presented their strongest pieces of evidence to make their points. When the argument maps were incorporated into the debates, the discourse patterns shifted. Students still presented their strongest pieces of evidence, but questions from students in the audience focused on evidence that was not presented. The argument maps became collectively shared scaffolds that allowed students to compare competing interpretations of the same evidence. Audience members used the maps to hold presenters more accountable to the total corpus of evidence involved with the project.

Final evaluations showed that during this debate activity, students developed greater understanding of the evidentiary basis of scientific argumentation, the general connection between argumentation and learning, and the social refinement of their own integrated understanding (Bell & Linn, 2000; also see Clark & Sampson, 2012).

Conclusion

In a sense, all teaching is a form of argument, because the task the teacher faces is to persuade learners to accept a novel point of view (Laurillard, 1993). The research presented in this handbook mostly views learning as a process of active construction and of collaborative knowledge building. And in this sense, all learning can be thought of as an outcome of argumentative processes.

Based on the research summarized in this chapter, we draw seven conclusions.

(1) Arguing to learn is a collaborative process of collective knowledge building. This approach is at odds with the traditional view of argumentation as oppositional. Arguing to learn requires a collaborative attitude and sufficient interest in what others have to say.

(2) Students cannot simply be told to learn by arguing; arguing to learn requires significant scaffolding. Software developed for this purpose has given promising results, but not the final answers.

(3) Argumentation has often been described using abstract schemas or grammars. However, real-world classroom interactions rarely reveal exactly these schemas. This is because such schemas are exclusively epistemic, concerning relations between pieces of knowledge, and do not take account of personal goals and socio-relational and emotional aspects of group work.

(4) The role and nature of argumentation differs across different learning activities in the classroom, such as collaborative writing or a project-based science class. Further research is required to better help students to make the appropriate links between different activities involving individual or collaborative argumentation.

(5) The role of argumentation in learning is deeply intertwined with the commonly held beliefs about knowledge in a community, its *epistemology*. A view of knowledge as relative and always subject to change fits well with arguing to learn. However, this may be taken as a danger to established values and structures by those who uphold other views of knowledge (as certain, unchanging, or essential to national identity; see Carretero & Lee, Chapter 29, this volume). The classroom use of argumentation is always constrained by the epistemology and values of a community.

(6) The type of medium has a major impact on arguing to learn. We have seen some examples of tool use that lead to results similar to argumentation in oral communication contexts, but also, we find possibilities for computer-based scaffolding that would be an improvement over a purely oral situation. The real determinant of the effects of argumentation is not the medium, but the overall design of the learning environment, including learning goals, authentic assignments, and the appropriate role of argumentation in the learning activities.

(7) The educational quality of argumentation decreases if students have to spend a lot of time mastering a software tool. The challenge for developers is to make the user interface as learner centered as possible.

Currently, many learners feel that engaging in arguments with their peers is frustrating, because it takes time and effort; they simply want their teachers to give them the answers. Teachers also experience difficulties in fostering and assessing collaborative argumentation (Baker, 2009). But the research shows that if these difficulties can be overcome, collaborative argumentation is a powerful technique for fostering deeper learning, a productive classroom culture, and an identity as an empowered inquirer and learner. If argumentation in learning situations can be detached in some way from competition, losing or damaging face, and hollow rhetoric – and adequate support for argumentation is designed so that focusing on understanding, explanation, and reasoning is the rule rather than the exception – the virtual promises of arguing to learn and of computer support for learning may become a reality. If this were to happen, students would not want to be presented with answers anymore; they would want to argue toward them. Then they would experience autonomy and powerful learning.

References

Andriessen, J. (2005). Collaboration in computer conferencing. In A. O'Donnell, C. Hmelo, & G. Erkens (Eds.), *Collaboration, reasoning, and technology* (pp. 277–321). Mahwah, NJ: Lawrence Erlbaum Associates.

Andriessen, J. (2009). Argumentation in higher education: Examples of actual practices with argumentation tools. In N. Muller Mirza & A.-N. Perret-Clermont

(Eds.), *Argumentation and education: Theoretical foundations and practices* (pp. 195–213). New York: Springer.

Andriessen, J., & Baker, M. (2013). Argument diagrams and learning: Cognitive and educational perspectives. In G. Schraw, M. McCrudden, & D. Robinson (Eds.), *Learning through visual displays*. Charlotte, NC: Information Age Publishing.

Andriessen, J., & Sandberg, J. (1999). Where is education heading and how about AI? *International Journal of Artificial Intelligence in Education*, 10(2), 130–150.

Baker, M. (2009). Argumentative interactions and the social construction of knowledge. In N. Muller Mirza & A.-N. Perret-Clermont (Eds.), *Argumentation and education: Theoretical foundations and practices* (pp. 127–144). New York: Springer.

Baker, M., Andriessen, J., & Järvelä, S. (Eds.) (2013). *Affective learning together: Social and emotional dimensions of collaborative learning*. London: Routledge.

Baker, M., & Lund, K. (1997). Promoting reflective interactions in a computer-supported collaborative learning environment. *Journal of Computer Assisted Learning*, 13, 175–193.

Barth, E. M., & Krabbe, E. C. W. (1982). *From axiom to dialogue: A philosophical study of logics and argumentation*. Berlin: Walter de Gruyter.

Bell, P. (1997). Using argument representations to make thinking visible for individuals and groups. In R. Hall, N. Miyake, & N. Enyedy (Eds.), *Proceedings of CSCL '97* (pp. 10–19). Toronto: University of Toronto Press.

Bell, P., & Linn, M. C. (2000). Scientific arguments as learning artifacts: Designing for learning from the web with KIE. *International Journal of Science Education*, 22(8), 797–817.

Berland, L. K., & Reiser, B. J. (2009). Making sense of argumentation and explanation. *Science Education*, 93(1), 26–55.

Berland, L. K., & Reiser, B. J. (2011). Classroom communities' adaptations of the practice of scientific argumentation. *Science Education*, 95(2), 191–216.

Billig, M. (1987). *Arguing and thinking: A rhetorical approach to social psychology*. Cambridge: Cambridge University Press.

Bransford, J. D., Brown, A. L., & Cocking, R. (1999). *How people learn: Brain, mind, experience and school*. Washington, DC: National Academies Press.

Chi, M. T. H., & Van Lehn, K. A. (1991). The content of physics self-explanations. *Journal of the Learning Sciences*, 1(1), 69–105.

Clark, A. M., Anderson, R. C., Archodidou, A., Nguyen-Jahiel, K., Kuo, L.-J., & Kim, I. (2003). Collaborative reasoning: Expanding ways for children to talk and think in the classroom. *Educational Psychology Review*, 15, 181–198.

Clark, D. B., Sampson, V., Chang, H.-Y., Zhang, E., & Tate, E. D. (2012). Research on critique and argumentation from the Technology Enhanced Learning in Science Center. In M. S. Khine (Ed.), *Perspectives on scientific argumentation: Theory, practice and research* (pp. 157–199). Heidelberg: Springer.

De Vries, E., Lund, K., & Baker, M. J. (2002). Computer-mediated epistemic dialogue: Explanation and argumentation as vehicles for understanding scientific notions. *The Journal of the Learning Sciences*, 11(1), 63–103.

Goldberg, T., Schwarz, B. B., & Porat, D. (2011). Changes in narrative and argumentative writing by students discussing "hot" historical issues. *Cognition and Instruction*, 29, 185–217.

Golder, C. (1996). *Le développement des discours argumentatifs* (*The development of argumentative discourses*). Lausanne: Delachaux & Niestlé.

Goldman, S. R., Duschl, R. A., Ellenbogen, K., Williams, S., & Tzou, C. T. (2003). Science inquiry in a digital age: Possibilities for making thinking visible. In H. van Oostendorp (Ed.), *Cognition in a digital age* (pp. 253–283). Mahwah, NJ: Lawrence Erlbaum Associates.

Harman, G. (1986). *Change in view: Principles of reasoning*. Cambridge, MA: MIT Press/Bradford Books.

Keefer, M. W., Seitz, C. L., & Resnick, L. B. (2000). Judging the quality of peer-led student dialogues. *Cognition and Instruction*, 18(1), 53–81.

Koschmann, T. (2003). CSCL, argumentation, and Deweyan inquiry: Argumentation is learning. In J. Andriessen, M. Baker, & D. Suthers (Eds.), *Arguing to learn: Confronting cognitions in computer-supported collaborative learning environments* (pp. 259–265). Dordrecht: Kluwer.

Kuhn, D. (1991). *The skills of argument*. Cambridge, MA: Cambridge University Press.

Kuhn, D. (2001). How do people know? *Psychological Science*, 12, 1–8.

Kuhn, D., Shaw, V., & Felton, M. (1997). Effects of dyadic interaction on argumentative reasoning. *Cognition and Instruction*, 15(3), 287–315.

Laurillard, D. (1993) *Rethinking university teaching: A framework for the effective use of educational technology*. London: Routledge.

Leitão, S. (2001). Analyzing changes in view during argumentation: A quest for method. *Forum Qualitative Social Research*, 2, 2.

Levin, J., & Moore, J. (1980). Dialogue-games: Meta-communication structure for natural language interaction. *Cognitive science*, 1(4), 395–420.

Linn, M. C. (2006). The knowledge integration perspective on learning and instruction. In R. K. Sawyer (Ed.), *The Cambridge handbook of the learning sciences* (pp. 243–264). New York: Cambridge University Press.

Mackenzie, J. D. (1979). Question-begging in noncumulative systems. *Journal of Philosophical Logic*, 8, 117–133.

Matusov, E. (2009). *Journey into dialogic pedagogy*. New York: Nova Science Publishers.

McAlister, S., Ravenscroft, A., & Scanlon, E. (2004). Combining interaction and context design to support collaborative argumentation using a tool for synchronous CMC. *Journal of Computer Assisted Learning*, 20(3), 194–204.

Mercer, N., Wegerif, R., & Dawes, L. (1999). Children's talk and the development of reasoning in the classroom. *British Educational Research Journal*, 25(1), 95–111.

Muller Mirza, N., Perret-Clermont, A.-N., Tartas, V., & Iannaccone, A. (2009). Psychosocial processes in argumentation. In N. Muller Mirza & A.-N. Perret-Clermont (Eds.), *Argumentation and education: Theoretical foundations and practices* (pp. 67–90). New York: Springer.

Nonnon, E. (1996). Activités argumentatives et élaboration de connaissances nouvelles: Le dialogue comme espace d'exploration (Argumentative activities and elaboration of new knowledge). *Langue Francaise*, 112, 67–87.

Osborne, J. (2010). Arguing to learn in science: The role of collaborative, critical discourse. *Science*, 328, 463–466.

Peng, K., & Nisbett, E. (1999). Culture, dialectics, and reasoning about contradiction. *American Psychologist*, 54(9), 741–754.

Picard, R. W., Papert, S., Bender, W., Blumberg, B., Breazel, C., Cavallo, D., Machover, T., Resnick, M., Roy, D., & Strohecker, C. (2004). Affective learning – a manifesto. *BT Technology Journal*, 22(4), 253–269.

Pilkington, R., & Walker, A. (2003). Facilitating debate in networked learning: Reflecting on online synchronous discussion in higher education. *Instructional Science*, 31, 41–63.

Pontecorvo, C. (Ed.) (1993). *Cognition and Instruction*, 11 (3 & 4). Special issue: Discourse and Shared Reasoning.

Ravenscroft, A., & McAlister, S. (2008). Investigating and promoting educational argumentation: Towards new digital practices. *International Journal of Research & Method in Education*, 31(3), 317–335.

Reznitskaya, A., Anderson, R. C., McNurlen, B., Nguyen- Jahiel, K., Archodidou, A., & Kim, S. (2001). Influence of oral discussion on written argument. *Discourse Processes*, 32(2–3), 155–175.

Sandoval, W. A. (2003). Conceptual and epistemic aspects of students' scientific explanations. *The Journal of the Learning Sciences*, 12(1), 5–51.

Schwarz, B., & Asterhan, C. S. (2011). E-moderation of synchronous discussions in educational settings: A nascent practice. *The Journal of the Learning Sciences*, 20, 1–48.

Schwarz, B., & Glassner, A. (2003). The blind and the paralytic: Supporting argumentation in everyday and scientific issues. In J. Andriessen, M. Baker, & D. Suthers (Eds.), *Arguing to learn: Confronting cognitions in computer-supported collaborative learning environments* (pp. 227–260). Dordrecht: Kluwer.

Schwarz, B. B., Kolikant, Y. B. D., & Mishenkina, M. (2012). "Co-alienation" mediated by common representations in synchronous e-discussions. *Learning, Culture and Social Interaction,* 1(3–4), 216–231.

Simonneaux, L. (2007). Argumentation in socio-scientific contexts. In S. Erduran & M. P. Jiménez-Aleixandre (Eds.), *Argumentation in science education* (pp. 179–199). New York: Springer.

Stein, N. L., & Albro, E. R. (2001). The origins and nature of arguments: Studies in conflict understanding, emotion, and negotiation. *Discourse Processes*, 32(2–3), 113–133.

Stein, N. L., & Bernas, R. (1999). The early emergence of argumentative knowledge and skill. In J. Andriessen & P. Coirier (Eds.), *Foundations of argumentative text processing* (pp. 97–116). Amsterdam: Amsterdam University Press.

Suthers, D., & Hundhausen, C. D. (2003). An experimental study of the effects of representational guidance on collaborative learning processes. *The Journal of the Learning Sciences*, 12(2), 183–218.

Suthers, D., & Weiner, A. (1995). Groupware for developing critical discussion skills. In J. L. Schnase & E. L. Cunnius (Eds.), *Proceedings of CSCL '95* (pp. 341–348). Mahwah, NJ: Lawrence Erlbaum Associates.

Tannen, D. (1998). *The argument culture: Moving from debate to dialogue*. New York: Random House Trade.

Tiberghien, A., & De Vries, E. (1997). Relating characteristics of learning situations to learner activities. *Journal of Computer Assisted Learning*, 13, 163–174.

Toulmin, S. E. (1958). *The uses of argument*. Cambridge: Cambridge University Press.

Van Amelsvoort, M., Andriessen, J., & Kanselaar, G. (2007). Representational tools in computer-supported collaborative argumentation-based learning: How dyads work with constructed and inspected argumentative diagrams. *Journal of the Learning Sciences*, 16(4), 485–522.

Van Eemeren, F., & Grootendorst, R. (1999). Developments in argumentation theory. In J. Andriessen & P. Coirier (Eds.), *Foundations of argumentative text processing* (pp. 43–57). Amsterdam: Amsterdam University Press.

Van Eemeren, F. H., Grootendorst, R., & Snoeck Henkemans, F. (1996). *Fundamentals of argumentation theory: A handbook of historical backgrounds and contemporary developments*. Hillsdale, NJ: Lawrence Erlbaum Associates.

Voss, J. F. (2005). Toulmin's model and the solving of ill-structured problems. *Argumentation*, 19, 321–329.

Voss, J., & Means, M. (1991). Learning to reason via instruction in argumentation. *Learning and Instruction*, 1, 337–350.

Walton, D. (2000). The place of dialogue theory in logic, computer science and communication studies. *Synthese*, 123, 327–346.

Walton, D. N., & Krabbe, E. C. W. (1995). *Commitment in dialogue*. Albany: State University of New York Press.

Wertsch, J. V. (1985). *Vygotsky and the social formation of mind*. Cambridge, MA: Harvard University Press.

Wertsch, J. V. (1991). *Voices of the mind: A sociocultural approach to mediated action*. Harvard, MA: Harvard University Press.

23 Informal Learning in Museums

Kevin Crowley, Palmyre Pierroux, and Karen Knutson

During the 19th century, educators began to see museums as environments where people might learn. Curators made collections available for public viewing to enlighten the public and to instill the values of the state (Bennett, 1995; Hooper-Greenhill, 1992). During the 20th and 21st centuries, there has been a dramatic increase in the number and types of museums, and a steady movement to identify museums as educational as well as cultural institutions. During the 19th century, museums primarily focused on collections – preserving and curating were their primary functions (think of zoos and art or history museums). Today, many museums, such as interactive science centers and children's museums, have no collections at all. The exhibits in these institutions focus on providing experiences that are often designed explicitly to meet educational goals. The success of this newer interactive form of museum has encouraged many more traditional forms of museum to reposition themselves as educational institutions, especially with respect to school-aged children who visit either with families or in school groups. This new focus on learning is also motivated by increasing pressure on museums to demonstrate that they serve a broader public, and not only an educated and cultured elite.

As museums have become comfortable embracing a learning mission, they have also become more common locations for learning research. In this chapter, we explore new research findings and note what they suggest about how to design museum experiences to support more powerful learning. We also hope this chapter might inspire a new generation of learning scientists to use museums as laboratories for their work. Museums are filled with complex, rich, and fascinating learning problems. They are sometimes referred to as *free choice learning settings* because people are guided by their own interests, goals, or knowledge. As they learn, visitors engage with objects, signs, tools, discourse, and new technologies. And the topics that people learn about are diverse, including all aspects of art, science, history, geography, culture, and more. Museums are public and social places of learning, where it is easy to find learning happening with families or peer groups who need to collectively negotiate how to move through the museum, decide what to do at each exhibit, and figure out how to make sense of what they encounter. Museums also provide a wide range of diverse examples of designs to support learning for audiences ranging from the youngest children to the oldest adults. Because of these features, museums are learning environments that expand our existing definitions of learning; they require learning scientists to account for phenomena that are very different from formal, in-school learning.

The history of learning research might be described as evolution through behavioral, constructivist, and sociocultural paradigms (Greeno, 2006; Nathan & Sawyer, Chapter 2, this volume). The history of learning research in museums in some ways echoes this trajectory. A first wave of research focused on tracking behavior in museums, producing findings about the kinds of exhibits that tend to attract and hold visitors as they move through a museum (Allwood & Montgomery, 1989; Beer, 1987; Bitgood, 1988; Cone & Kendall, 1978). A second wave of constructivist-inspired work explored how individuals make meaning of museum experiences, focusing on the ways that prior knowledge, visitor goals, and different levels of engagement impact understanding and construction of the message of the museum (Falk & Dierking, 1992; Falk, Koran, Dierking, & Dreblow, 1985; Screven, 1986).

The third wave of work, and the focus of this chapter, uses sociocultural theory and notions of participation to understand learning in museums. This work often focuses on the ways that groups of visitors talk and interact with one another, and how these conversations contribute to learning. This approach is perhaps typified by Leinhardt and Knutson (2004), who examined conversations of 207 groups visiting seven exhibitions at a variety of museums. Group visitor conversations were audiotaped and tracked, and after the visit, groups self-conducted a joint interview about the visit. Learning was measured by analyzing the amount of *conversational elaboration* during the interview – the extent to which groups went beyond listing details of exhibitions to synthesizing and explaining exhibitions in ways that connected to disciplinary content. A path analysis found that greater learning was associated with visitor identity, the design of the learning environment, and the extent to which learners engaged in explanatory sense making during the museum visit. This landmark study formed an important bridge between sociocultural perspectives and methods in the learning sciences and studies of informal learning in museums.

By analyzing how group interactions contribute to learning, sociocultural perspectives go beyond constructivist approaches, which often attempt to "factor out" individual learning from the group in a way that ends up neglecting the role of the group (see Greeno & Engeström, Chapter 7, this volume). In the sociocultural approach, the group is the unit of analysis and the focus is on how conversation and interaction contribute to learning (Vygotsky, 1986; Wertsch, 1991). Because conversation and interaction are the focus of the sociocultural approach, video or tracked audio recordings of visitors' interactions are commonly used. Transcripts of talk and interaction may be coded to analyze interactional patterns, participation structures, or group practices, or talk may be analyzed sequentially, adapting methods and conventions from conversation analysis, among other traditions (Derry et al., 2010; see Enyedy & Stevens, Chapter 10, this volume).

We study museums because they foreground aspects of learning that are sometimes overlooked or underemphasized when we study learning in other settings. Through a comparative logic, we thus gain different perspectives on learning that can offer unique and valuable windows into basic questions of how people learn. However, as we study museums, we also uncover knowledge of how to design museum experiences to broaden, deepen, and extend learning impacts. Our review focuses on two areas where strong progress has been made during the past decade in terms of advancing both our understanding of learning and our understanding of how to support it in museums: family learning in museums, and learning during school trips to museums.

Family Learning in Museums: The Role of Parents

Children spend the majority of their waking hours in out-of-school settings and much of what they learn about science, art, technology, and other domains comes not from school, but from informal settings such as museums (e.g., Falk & Dierking, 2010). Yet we still know relatively little about exactly how this informal learning actually occurs. From the perspective of the learning sciences, families are interesting examples of distributed systems for learning. From the perspective of museums, families are an important audience to be served – an audience (and a future audience) who comes to the museum to spend some pleasant time together and perhaps to learn something while they visit. One of the major contributions of museum learning research during the past decade has been to explore systems of family learning and the role of parents as facilitators of children's learning in out-of-school settings.

When visiting museums with their children, parents adopt different roles in the interaction – even enacting multiple roles within the course of a single visit (e.g., Ash, 2004; Melber, 2007). Sometimes parents treat museums more like playgrounds – places for children to explore independently while parents stand back at the edge of the action. But more commonly, parents expect to be involved. After all, most families come to museums to spend time together, and often what parents expect to do together is to learn about science, art, history, or culture (Falk, Mousouri, & Coulson, 1998; Knutson & Crowley, 2010). Thus, adults are often observed enacting the role of coach, guide, or explainer – following the lead of the child, reading signs, suggesting ways to engage, responding to impasses and difficulties, and helping the child to explore the space of possibilities at an exhibit more broadly and more deeply (Gleason & Schauble, 1999).

Parents frequently offer explanations within the child's zone of proximal development (Vygotsky, 1986), thereby scaffolding children's learning. Knutson and Crowley (2010) observed parents in an art museum engaging in the major categories of disciplinary art talk (e.g., criticism, creation, context) as well as making personal connections between art and the family's shared experience outside of the museum context. Parents will sometimes point out causal connections, analogies, and conclusions as they use interactive science exhibits with children (Crowley et al., 2001). In natural history museums, parents often take the lead in asking questions and identifying biological themes and disciplinary big ideas as they view dioramas, fossilized dinosaurs, or live plants and animals (Ash, 2004; Kisiel, Rowe, Vartabedian, & Kopczak, 2012; Palmquist & Crowley, 2007). When children hear these spontaneous adult explanations while using science exhibits, they are more likely to understand exhibits at a deeper, conceptual level, as opposed to a surface and more procedural level (Fender & Crowley, 2007).

What supports parent engagement in productive scaffolding during museum visits? There is undoubtedly some influence of general parent education or specific parent expertise in the content of the museum (e.g., Siegle, Easterly, Callanan, Wright, & Navarro, 2007). But regardless of how knowledgeable they are, it can be a complex task for parents to navigate the museum, interpret exhibits, read, understand, and translate signage for a child, and make connections between the museum and other contexts that the family knows about (Allen, 2004).

Principles of discovery and inquiry-based approaches increasingly inform the design of resources, games, and other technologies that aim to support "learning through play" on family visits to museums (Beale, 2011; Katz, LaBar, & Lynch, 2011). Gutwill and Allen (2010) explored the use of inquiry games to enhance learning through inquiry while families interacted with science museum exhibits. One game was designed to increase collaborative activity and involved groups deciding ahead of time on a shared guiding question. The other game, designed to give individual control to people within the group at the moment when they were learning something valuable, involved normal engagement with the exhibit with the rule that anyone in the group was able to call "hands off" at any time. When this happened, everyone in the group stopped what they were doing to listen to and discuss what the individual had to say. These two strategies were explored in a study in which families were randomly assigned to four conditions: the shared goal game; the individual control game; a condition where the family was guided through the exhibit by an experienced museum educator; or a control condition where the family used the exhibit without any scaffolding or guidance. The study found that groups in the two supported inquiry conditions improved their inquiry more than groups in the educator-led or control conditions.

Signage can also influence interactions in museums. In one study, families were randomly assigned to use an exhibit where they tested the flying properties of paper helicopters in one of two conditions: signage that encouraged them to adopt the scientific goal of discovering how different features changed flying times or signage that encouraged them to adopt the engineering goal of finding the combination of features that had the longest flying time (Kim & Crowley, 2010). Families in the science goal condition talked more, were more collaborative, and were more likely to design informative tests. Families who were encouraged to adopt engineering goals were more likely to have parents who pulled back and allowed children to do more of the design and interpretation without adult scaffolding. As a result, children in the science goal condition learned more about the task than children whose families adopted engineering goals.

Learning technologies have now been designed for museums using inquiry principles so that individualized paths, facilitator roles, and skill levels are adapted to different family members. Family activities modeled on treasure hunts, mysteries, and puzzles are common in museums, as is the use of mobile devices to guide and facilitate the collecting of exhibition information to collaboratively solve tasks. A familiar approach is seen in the design of *Mystery at the Museum* at the Boston Museum of Science (Klopfer, Perry, Squire, Jan, & Steinkuehler, 2005). Family members used handheld PCs to collect information using infrared tags in a collaborative problem-solving activity. In a study of 20 parents and children playing the game, researchers found that the interdependence of roles structured group collaboration and that many participants felt their role had made a unique and essential contribution.

Hatala and colleagues (2009) explored the potential of an adaptive system in *Kurio*, a game that was responsive to both personal and group needs and levels when guiding families through different learning "challenges" at a local history museum. Eighteen family groups comprising 58 individuals participated in studies to identify factors that affected learning when using the system, which was loosely modeled on treasure hunts and involved the use of different kinds of tangibles to collect and share information. Based on analysis of questionnaires, semi-structured interviews, and data logs, the study found that when the pace, level, and number of family challenges were balanced, there was increased learning and the visit as a whole was valued more highly. The study also identified tensions between what individual members experienced as positive and effective for their own learning when solving the shared challenge, and the need for them to help other family members, which was boring and less valued. Further, although family members enjoyed interacting more closely, there was the potential for overload when learning activities dominated the visit. The latter finding is supported in the museum research reviewed earlier, which stresses that families visit museums for a variety of reasons, and motivations related to learning vary among family members. Accordingly, family activities are primarily designed as games, and research on effective learning is secondary to studies that focus on how to support collaboration and interaction among family members.

Across the Formal/Informal Boundary: School Trips to Museums

Formal learning environments, such as schools, are compulsory, include standard curricula, have a limited range of classroom structures, and emphasize accountability through individual testing. Informal learning environments, such as museums, are often defined by being the opposite of schools – they are free choice, include a diverse and nonstandardized range of topics, and have flexible structures, socially rich interaction, and no externally imposed assessments (Callanan, Cervantes, & Loomis, 2011). What happens when these two very different institutional types are brought together – for example on school trips to museums?

Museums have always been popular sites for school excursions, and driven by increasing accountability demands from schools, museum education departments now provide a broad range of activities and resources for teachers that are specifically designed to link museum visits with school curricula. Field trips are planned in advance by teachers to incorporate exhibitions and thematic tours into their study plans, and some measure of cognitive outcome may be required to justify how the museum visit will help them meet required standards (Mortensen & Smart, 2007). School field trips aim to comply with curricular demands, but are also viewed as an essential part of enculturation, empowering young people to use museums independently and purposely, cultivating certain skills and competencies as a kind of "museum literacy" (Stapp, 1984).

Reviews of research on museum field trips suggest modest but positive and lasting impacts on learning concepts and facts (DeWitt & Storksdieck, 2008; Kisiel, 2006), with memories of both subject matter and the social context surrounding a visit particularly strong (Anderson, Storksdieck, & Spock, 2007; Dierking & Falk, 1994). Research on field trips also finds that organizing sequences of pre-visit preparation work in the classroom, guided instruction during the museum visit, and post-visit follow-up work back in school maximizes the potential for learning (DeWitt & Storksdieck, 2008; Kisiel, 2006). However, teachers do not often make time for recommended pre-post visit activities and, in practice, students, chaperones, and many teachers tend to view field trips as "free day" excursions (Kisiel, 2005; Mortensen & Smart, 2007). Generally, museum educators meet classes with mixed expectations regarding learning aims and outcomes and face the challenge of engaging students in activities that are fun, educational, and that will hopefully inspire young people to become lifelong museum visitors.

The use of worksheets (sheets of paper with tasks and problems the students are expected to complete while visiting an exhibition) to meet formal curricular goals also has a long history and is still common today. There is evidence that well-designed worksheets may increase curriculum-related conversations during the museum visit (McManus, 1985; Mortensen & Smart, 2007). However, the design and implementation of worksheets can also make the museum visit too "school-like," with students focused more on procedural aspects of completing a task, such as gathering information from labels, than on conceptually oriented talk based on observations of exhibits and objects (Griffin, 1998). Analyses of field trips using museum worksheets have identified key design characteristics that have implications for student learning (DeWitt & Storksdieck, 2008; Kisiel, 2003; Mortensen & Smart, 2007), including the complexity of the task, the types and location of information sources, and balancing guidance and structure with levels of choice and opportunities to explore the unique qualities of the museum setting.

Students on school trips are often led on guided tours by museum educators. With their field termed the "uncertain profession" during the late 1980s (Dobbs & Eisner, 1987), front-line museum educators often do not have specific training in museum education and the training, skills, and experience of volunteers and staff who lead tours varies, sometimes greatly. Museum educators often fall back on epistemologies and pedagogies that spring from their own personal learning experiences in formal settings (Allen & Crowley, 2014; Bevan & Xanthoudaki, 2008; Cox-Petersen, Marsh, Kisiel, & Melber, 2003). Thus, many guided tours have been based on an IRE (initiation-response-evaluation) whole-class lecture model that constrains a group's movements to objects and displays preselected by the expert. Studies have illustrated tensions between instructional approaches that aim to produce learning outcomes that meet formal education requirements valued in schools and those that foster informal learning and social skills valued in museum environments, such as inquiry, discovery, observing, and conversational elaboration on artworks, historical narratives, or topical issues in science (Griffin & Symington, 1997; Kisiel, 2003; Pierroux, 2005).

Recently, dialogic approaches are increasingly informing guided tour research and practice (Pierroux, 2005, 2010), drawing on sociocultural perspectives on learning conversations in museums (Leinhardt, Crowley, & Knutson, 2002), best practice guidelines (Grinder & McCoy, 1985), and classrom discourse research (Reznitskaya & Glina, 2012; Wells, 1999). This dialogical turn has directed analytic attention to guided tour discourse and instructional approaches to formulating questions, fostering rich descriptions, introducing concepts and disciplinary knowledge, and developing a repertoire of dialogical moves. In a study of different instructional approaches on guided tours in art museums, Pierroux (2010) compared a dialogic method designed to support students' skills in observing and describing artworks with other dialogical methods aimed primarily at teaching art history (see Rice & Yenawine, 2002). The study found that while the first approach effectively engaged students with the artworks and empowered groups of young adults as "meaning makers" through a rich dialogical process, there was no evidence of conceptual development in the discipline of art history, which was the curricular goal of the field trip. Students' difficulties developing disciplinary concepts based solely on interactions with exhibits and one another are a common finding in science museums as well (Achiam, 2012). Analysis of the other approaches in the study suggested that introducing advanced art historical concepts or "leading" information may guide the interpretative process too strongly, similarly stifling learning through students' rejection of interpretations that they did not dialogically develop as their own or were outside their zone of proximal development.

Beyond the educator-led tour, perspectives on creativity and learning motivate a broad range of hands-on educational activities for field trip students that involve games, role play, making, and experimentation. Hands-on activities are often integrated thematically with the guided tour and worksheet activities on field trips in art, history, and science museums. But there is surprisingly little research on learning through such hands-on activities, and much of the literature is anecdotal (Ramey-Gassert, Walberg, & Walberg, 1994). Instructional approaches that involve students in game playing, generating content, making art, and constructing experiments have nonetheless become central in the design of digital technologies for learning on field trips (Hauser, Noschka-Roos, Reussner, & Zahn, 2009; Pierroux, 2013).

Mobile social media, smartphone technologies, and ubiquitous Internet access are pivotal developments in research on how to effectively support inquiry and dialogue within and across school and museum contexts (Naismith, Lonsdale, Vavoula, & Sharples, 2006; Pierroux, 2011; Tallon & Walker, 2008; Wishart and Triggs, 2010). Challenges related to the use of mobile devices as learning tools in museums were identified early on, including problems of "heads-down" behavior, isolation from other group members, and an overall decrease in talk and interaction (Grinter et al., 2002; Heath & Vom Lehn, 2001; Hsi, 2002). There is a history of failed interactive devices and design experiments in museums, and problems are perhaps compounded when applications for mobile devices are designed for field trip use. In a recent study of augmented reality games on mobile devices for zoo field trips, students using the game focused largely on staying on task, spent less time looking at animals than a control group, and talked more about the game than the exhibits (Perry & Nellis, 2012). At the same time, the formal instruction approach in the game design increased the students' conceptual understanding, attitudes, and beliefs in science. Such findings are common and illustrate the need to clarify learning perspectives and aims in the instructional design and to account for users' needs and expectations regarding technology use in museum spaces.

In an early study exploring the potential of mobile phones to support learning on field trips, a class of 23 students used a Web site and phones to access, record, collect, and produce content before, during, and after a museum visit (Vavoula et al., 2009). A three-stage evaluation process based mainly on interviews, observations, and questionnaires found that the mobile application was more motivating for student learning in the museum than traditional worksheets, supported productive on-task interactions during the visit, and effectively prompted students to engage with both their collected material and museum online resources during post-visit activities back in the classroom. Apart from technological issues, the study also identified challenges in designing tasks that aided students in producing their own interpretations rather than merely collecting information provided by the museum. There were also problems for students and teachers to shift from collaborative learning activities in the museum setting to individual work and assessment in the classroom.

Similar studies have since explored how tasks combining mobile phones with social media may be designed to support learning on field trips (Pierroux, Krange, & Sem, 2011). The design approach in the Gidder project emphasized the significance of interactions with authentic objects and other resources in the museum setting for developing art historical interpretations (see Wishart & Triggs, 2010), and explored the potential of student-generated content from the museum to motivate and support critical reflection and analysis back in the classroom. In two design iterations, six classes and more than 150 students were observed over seven nonsequential weeks, with video recordings, blog texts, and data logs as the main empirical material. Working first in small groups in the museum, students collaboratively formulated interpretations of artworks, using their mobile phones to take pictures and make films, record conversations with museum docents, and write text messages (SMS). These were sent to a blog and became chronological entries accessible to everyone in the class. Each group had its own workspace in the blog, which included tasks and resources provided by the museum educator. The classroom task required each group to use the blog entries to create a multimodal summative interpretation, with peers, teachers, and the museum curator an implied audience of "receivers" and "commenters." Assessment was based on the quality of the interpretations in the blog entries. Findings suggested that the direct and abbreviated format of initial text messages motivated students to collaboratively edit, expand on, and clarify their interpretations from the museum, and that blog entries were treated as utterances in dialogues that were open to others (Pierroux et al., 2011).

Field trip research emphasizes the importance of taking advantage of the unique experiences and interactions of the museum learning environment, and also the need for interventions and resources by teachers and museum educators to scaffold the visitor experience so that it contributes to the development of disciplinary knowledge (Pierroux, 2005, 2010). As new technology and social media are increasingly integrated into museum education activities, studies suggest that the most effective designs for learning on field trips have a moderate level of structure and guidance from curators and teachers, with tasks that allow time for inquiry, dialog, and collaboration. These findings are similar to what learning scientists have discovered when studying how to best integrate learning technologies into classroom settings; these studies also show that even the most advanced digital learning environments need to be supplemented with contextual resources and teacher support (Furberg & Arnseth, 2009). The most effective designs for learning on museum field trips will take into account the unique resources provided by museums, will integrate the complementary roles of the teacher and museum educator, and will provide tasks that support collaboration and social interaction.

Looking Forward: 21st-Century Museums and the Learning Sciences

In the coming decade, we expect to see dramatic progress in our ability to conceptualize and assess learning in ways that are rigorous, scalable, and appropriate for museums. Immediate learning impacts are relatively easy to create, observe, and measure in museums. But we suspect that the real value of museum learning revolves around distal outcomes such as fostering a passion for learning, promoting the growth of inquiry skills, learning how to observe, or learning how to talk about science, art, or history – outcomes that are not possible to achieve in a single museum visit. These are habits of mind that need to be cultivated through sustained engagement over time and place. Yet the typical museum learning experience is just a few hours long. The true impact of museum visits might not be fully apparent until visitors have left the museum and had a chance to talk about, wonder about, or use whatever knowledge and practices they learned in the museum.

This is an instance of a general problem facing learning sciences researchers: to explain how a series of relatively short experiences might develop into something much more significant – whether single class sessions or single museum visits. How does a museum visit contribute to longer-term learning trajectories? In retrospective accounts of learning trajectories, we often see adults reporting that their earliest interest in disciplines such as science began in out-of-school settings, including museums (Crowley, Barron, Knutson, & Martin, in press). For many children, early expertise rooted in informal learning experiences will be the first time they encounter the power of discipline-specific knowledge and the first time that they (and their parents) recognize that they might have an interest in pursuing a specific discipline such as science, engineering, or art. Museums, with their rich resources and highly designed learning environments, can be places for engaging deeply with a discipline in ways that are not available in schools or at home. Museums function as learning environments similar to the ways that digital games function as learning environments (Steinkuehler & Squire, Chapter 19, this volume) – both are self-reinforcing and motivating, support deep investigation and learning, encourage the growth of out-of-school learning identities, provide communities of practice for learning and advancement, and can result in considerable engagement throughout a learner's life. As we write this chapter, we see new longitudinal studies of informal learning being launched that focus squarely on transfer between museum experiences and other parts of a child's learning ecology, formal and informal. New pathways are being designed that help connect museums to other learning environments and bring new groups of children into contact with museums.

Although our chapter has focused on how museums can help children learn school subjects, museums are also working to better engage adult audiences. Many museums in the 21st century are struggling to remain relevant and financially viable as adults and children alike turn increasingly to digital resources for out-of-school learning. Recognizing that their 19th- and 20th-century practices are increasingly out of step with audiences who expect to participate and shape their learning experiences, museums are experimenting with ways to reinvent their collections, exhibits, and buildings to act more like town squares, cultural hubs, and more personalized environments for adult learning (Watson & Werb, 2013). One area of active experimentation is in the innovative use of social media (Kelly 2010; Russo et al., 2007) to motivate visitors to share their knowledge and views on museum collections, exhibitions, and events and to engage the museum as discursive partner (Giacardi, 2012; Marty, Sayre, & Fantoni, 2011). Other efforts involve positioning museums as boundary-spanning spaces where disciplinary experts and publics can meet in joint dialogs about data, progress, and civic and social concerns (Irwin, Pegram, & Gay, 2013; Louw & Crowley, 2013; Selvakumar & Storksdieck, 2013). Adults are an important part of museum audiences, but comparatively little learning sciences research has focused on the adult experience in museums.

Museums are generally open to experimentation, are interested in issues of learning, and are becoming familiar with the field of learning sciences. There are still many unanswered questions to be addressed, and we look forward to another decade of rapid progress.

References

Achiam, M. F. (2012). A content-oriented model for science exhibit engineering. *International Journal of Science Education, Part B*, 1–19.

Allen, L., & Crowley, K. (in press). How museum educators change: Changing notions of learning through changing practice. *Science Education*.

Allen, L. B., & Crowley, K. (2014). Challenging beliefs, practices, and content: How museum educators change. *Science Education,* 98(1), 84–105.

Allen, S. (1997). Using scientific inquiry activities in exhibit explanations. *Science Education,* 81, 715–734.

Allen, S. (2004). Designs for learning: Studying science museum exhibits that do more than entertain. *Science Education,* 88 Supplement 1 (July), S17–S33.

Allen, S., & Gutwill, J. P. (2009). Creating a program to deepen family inquiry at interactive science exhibits. *Curator,* 52(3), 289–306.

Allwood, J., & Montgomery, B. (1989). *Exhibition planning and design: A guide for exhibitors, designers and contractors.* London: Batsford.

Anderson, D., Kisiel, J., & Storksdieck, M. (2006). School field trip visits: Understanding the teacher's world through the lens of three international studies. *Curator,* 49(3), 365–386.

Ash, D. (2004). How families use questions at dioramas: Ideas for exhibit design. *Curator,* 47(1), 84–99.

Bamberger, Y., & Tal, T. (2007). Learning in a personal context: Levels of choice in a free choice learning environment in science and natural history museums. *Science Education,* 91, 75–95.

Barab, S. A., & Squire, K. D. (2004). Design-based research: Putting a stake in the ground. *Journal of the Learning Sciences,* 13(1), 1–14.

Beale, K. (Ed.) (2011). *Museums at play – Games, interaction and learning.* Edinburgh: MuseumsEtc.

Beer, V. (1987). Great expectations: Do museums know what visitors are doing? *Curator,* 30(3), 206–215.

Bennett, T. (1995). *The birth of the museum.* London: Routledge.

Bevan, B., & Xanthoudaki, M. (2008). Professional development for museum educators: Underpinning the underpinnings. *The Journal of Museum Education,* 33(2), 107–119.

Bitgood, S. (1988). *A comparison of formal and informal learning.* Technical Report No. 88-10, Jacksonville, AL: Center for Social Design.

Borun, M. J., & Dritsas, J. (1997). Developing family-friendly exhibits. *Curator,* 40(3), 178–196.

Borun, M. J., Dritsas, J. I., Johnson, N. E., Peter, K. F., Fadigan, K., Jangaard, A., ... Wenger, A. (1998). *Family learning in museums: The PISEC perspective.* Philadelphia, PA: The Franklin Institute.

Bruner, J. (1990). *Acts of meaning.* Cambridge, MA: Harvard University Press.

Callanan, M., Cervantes, C., & Loomis, M. (2011). Informal learning. *WIREs Cognitive Science,* 2, 646–655.

Cameron, F., & Kenderdine, S. (Eds.) (2007). *Theorizing digital cultural heritage: A critical discourse.* Cambridge, MA: MIT Press.

Castle, M. C. (2006). Blending pedagogy and content: A new curriculum for museum teachers. *The Journal of Museum Education,* 31(2), 123–132.

Cone, C. A., & Kendall, K. (1978). Space, time, and family interaction: Visitor behavior at the Science Museum of Minnesota. *Curator: The Museum Journal,* 21(3), 245–258.

Cox-Petersen, A. M., Marsh, D. D., Kisiel, J., & Melber, L. M. (2003). Investigation of guided school tours, student learning, and science reform recommendations at a museum of natural history. *Journal of Research in Science Teaching*, 40, 200–218.

Crowley, K., Barron, B. J., Knutson, K., & Martin, C. (in press). Interest and the development of pathways to science. To appear in K. A. Renninger, M. Nieswandt, & S. Hidi (Eds.), *Interest in mathematics and science learning and related activity*. Washington, DC: AERA.

Crowley, K., Callanan, M. A., Jipson, J., Galco, J., Topping, K., & Shrager, J. (2001). Shared scientific thinking in everyday parent-child activity. *Science Education*, 85(6), 712–732.

Crowley, K., & Jacobs, M. (2002). Islands of expertise and the development of family scientific literacy. In G. Leinhardt, K. Crowley, & K. Knutson (Eds.), *Learning conversations in museums*. Mahwah, NJ: Lawrence Erlbaum Associates.

Davis, J., Gurian, E. H., & Koster, E. (2003), Timeliness: A discussion for museums. *Curator: The Museum Journal*, 46, 353–361

Dawson, E., & Jensen, E. (2011). Towards a contextual turn in visitor studies: Evaluating visitor segmentation and identity-related motivations. *Visitor Studies*, 14(2), 127–140.

Derry, S. J., Pea, R. D. et al. (2010). Conducting video research in the learning sciences: Guidance on selection, analysis, technology, and ethics. *Journal of the Learning Sciences*, 19(1), 3–53.

DeSantis, K., & Housen, A. (2001). A brief guide to developmental theory and aesthetic development. *Visual Understanding in Education*, 17.

DeWitt, J., & Storksdieck, M. (2008). A short review of school field trips: Key findings from the past and implications for the future. *Visitor Studies*, 11(2), 181–197.

Dierking, L. H., & Falk, J. H. (1994). Family behavior and learning in informal science settings: A review of the research. *Science Education,* 78(1), 57–72.

Dobbs, S., & Eisner, E. W. (1987). The uncertain profession: Educators in American art museums. *Journal of Aesthetic Education,* 21(4), 77–86.

Eberbach, C. E., & Crowley, K. (2009). From everyday to scientific observation: How children learn to observe the biologist's world. *Review of Educational Research*, 79(1), 39–69.

Falk, J. H. (1997). Testing a museum exhibition design assumption: Effect of explicit labelling of exhibit clusters on visitor concept development. *Science Education*, 6(81), 679–687.

Falk, J. H., & Dierking, L. D. (1992). *The museum experience*. Washington, DC: Whalesback Books.

Falk, J. H., & Dierking, L. D. (2000). *Learning from museums: Visitor experiences and the making of meaning*. New York: AltaMira Press.

Falk, J. H., & Dierking, L. D. (2010). The 95% solution: School is not where most Americans learn most of their science. *American Scientist*, 98, 486–493.

Falk, J. H., Koran, J., Dierking, L. H., & Dreblow, L. (1985). Predicting visitor behavior. *Curator*, 28(4), 249–257.

Falk, J., Mousouri, T., & Coulson, D. (1998). The effects of visitors' agendas on museum learning. *Curator*, 41(2), 107–120.

Fender, J. G., & Crowley, K. (2007). How parent explanation changes what children learn from everyday scientific thinking. *Journal of Applied Developmental Psychology, 28*, 189–210.

Furberg, A., & Arnseth, H. C. (2009). Reconsidering conceptual change from a socio-cultural perspective: Analyzing students' meaning making in genetics in collaborative learning activities. *Cultural Studies of Science Education, 4*, 157–191.

Gates, J. (2010). *Clearing the path for Sisyphus: How social media is changing our jobs and our working relationships.* Museums and the Web 2010: Proceedings, Denver, Colorado, Toronto: Archives & Museum Informatics.

Giaccardi, E. (2012). *Heritage and social media: Understanding heritage in a participatory culture.* New York: Routledge.

Gleason, M. E., & Schauble, L. (1999). Parents' assistance of their children's scientific reasoning. *Cognition and Instruction, 17*(4), 343–378.

Grand, A. (2009). Engaging through dialogue: International experiences of café scientifique. In A. Grand, R. Holliman, J. Thomas, S. Smidt, & E. Scanlon (Eds.), *Practising science communication in the information age: Theorising professional practices* (pp. 209–226). London: Oxford University Press.

Greeno, J. G. (2006a). Learning in activity. In K. Sawyer (Ed.), *The Cambridge handbook of the learning sciences* (pp. 79–96). New York: Cambridge University Press.

Greeno, J. G. (2006b). Theoretical and practical advances through research on learning. In J. L. Green, G. Camilli, & P. B. Elmore (Eds.), *Handbook of complementary methods in education research.* Routledge.

Griffin, J. (1998). Learning science through practical experiences in museums. *International Journal of Science Education, 20*, 655–663.

Griffin, J., & Symington, D. (1997). Moving from task-oriented to learning-oriented strategies on school excursions to museums. *Science Education, 81*, 763–779.

Grinder, A. L., & McCoy, E. S. (1985). *The good guide: A sourcebook for interpreters, docents, and tour guides.* Scottsdale, AZ: Ironwood Press.

Grinter, R. E., Aoki, P. M., Hurst, A., Syzmanski, M. H., Thornton, J. D., & Woodruff, A. (2002). Revisiting the visit: Understanding how technology can shape the museum visit *CSCW'02.* New Orleans: ACM.

Gutwill, J. P., & Allen, S. (2010). Facilitating family group inquiry at science museum exhibits. *Science Education, 94*, 710–742.

Hatala, M., Tanenbaum, K., Wakkary, R., Muise, K., Mohabbati, B., Corness, G., Budd, J., & Loughin, T. (2009). Experience structuring factors affecting learning in family visits to museums. In U. Cress, V. Dimitrova, & M. Specht (Eds.), *Learning in the synergy of multiple disciplines* (Vol. 4th European Conference on Technology Enhanced Learning, EC-TEL 2009 Proceedings. Nice, France, September 29–October 2, pp. 37–52). Berlin: Springer-Verlag.

Hauser, W., Noschka-Roos, A., Reussner, E., & Zahn, C. (2009). Design-based research on digital media in a museum environment. *Visitor Studies, 12*(2), 182–198.

Heath, C., & Vom Lehn, D. (2002). Misconstruing interaction. In Hinton, M. (Ed.), *The proceedings of interactive learning in museums of art and design.* London: Victoria and Albert Museum.

Hein, G. E. (1998). *Learning in the museum.* New York: Routledge.

Hooper-Greenhill, E. (1992). *Museums and the shaping of knowledge.* New York: Routledge.

Horst, H. A., Herr-Stephenson, B. et al. (2008). Media ecologies. Digital Youth Project.

Housen, A. (1999). *Eye of the beholder: Research, theory and practice: Aesthetic and art education: A transdisciplinary approach.* Lisbon, Portugal: Visual Understanding in Education.

Housen, A. (2001–2002). Aesthetic thought, critical thinking and transfer. *Arts and Learning Research Journal,* 18(1), 99–131.

Housen, A. (2001). Voices of viewers: Iterative research, theory, and practice. *Arts and Learning Research Journal,* 17.1, 2–12.

Hsi, S. (2002). The electronic guidebook: A study of user experiences using mobile web content in a museum setting. *IEEE International Workshop on Wireless and Mobile Technologies in Education (WMTE'02).* Växjö, Sweden: IEEE.

Irwin, B., Pegram, E., & Gay, H. (2013). New directions, new relationships: The Smithsonian's Twenty-first Century Learning in Natural History Settings Conference and the Natural History Museum, London. *Curator: The Museum Journal,* 56(2), 273–278.

Katz, J. E., LaBar, W., & Lynch, E. (Eds.) (2011). *Creativity and technology: Social media, mobiles and museums.* Edinburgh: MuseumsEtc.

Kelly, L. (2010). How Web 2.0 is changing the nature of museum work. *Curator: The Museum Journal,* 53(4), 405–410.

Kim, K. Y., & Crowley, K. (2010). Negotiating the goal of museum inquiry: How families engineer and experiment. In M. K. Stein & L. Kucan (Eds.), *Instructional explanations in the disciplines.* New York: Springer.

Kisiel, J. (2003). Teachers, museums and worksheets: A closer look at the learning experience. *Journal of Science Teacher Education,* 14, 3–21.

Kisiel, J. (2006). Making field trips work. *The Science Teacher,* 73(1), 46–48.

Kisiel, J., Rowe, S., Vartabedian, M. A., & Kopczak, C. (2012). Evidence for family engagement in scientific reasoning at interactive animal exhibits. *Sci. Ed.,* 96, 1047–1070.

Klopfer, E., Perry, J., Squire, K., Jan, M.-F., & Steinkuehler, C. (2005). *Mystery at the Museum*: A collaborative game for museum education. Paper presented at the Proceedings of the 2005 Conference on Computer Support for Collaborative Learning: Learning 2005: The Next 10 Years! Taipei, Taiwan.

Knutson, K., & Crowley, K. (2010). Connecting with art: How families talk about art in a museum setting. In M. K. Stein & L. Kucan (Eds.), *Instructional explanations in the disciplines.* New York: Springer.

Knutson, K., Crowley, K., Russell, J., & Steiner, M. A. (2011). Approaching art education as an ecology: Exploring the role of museums. *Studies in Art Education,* 52(4), 310–322.

Leinhardt, G., Crowley, K., & Knutson, K. (Eds.) (2002). *Learning conversations in museums.* Mahwah, NJ: Lawrence Erlbaum Associates.

Leinhardt, G., & Knutson, K. (2004). *Listening in on museum conversations.* Walnut Creek, CA: Altamira Press.

Louw, M. & Crowley, K. (2013). New ways of looking and learning in natural history museums: The use of gigapixel imaging to bring science and publics together. *Curator: The Museum Journal*, 52(1), 87–104.

Marty, P. F., Sayre, S., & Fillipini Fantoni, S. (2011). Personal digital collections: Involving users in the co-creation of digital cultural heritage. In G. Styliaras, D. Koukopoulos, & F. Lazarinis (Eds). *Handbook of research on technologies and cultural heritage: Applications and environments* (pp. 285–304). Hershey, PA: IGI Global.

Matusov, E., & Rogoff, B. (1995). Evidence of development from people's participation in communities of learners. In J. H. Falk & L. D. Dierking (Eds.), *Public institutions for personal learning: Establishing a research agenda* (pp. 97–104). Washington, DC: American Association of Museums.

McManus, P. (1985). Worksheet induced behavior in the British museum (natural history). *Journal of Biological Education,* 19(3), 237–242.

Melber, L. M. (2007). Maternal scaffolding in two museum exhibition halls. *Curator*, 50(3), 341–354.

Miles, R. S. (1993). *Grasping the greased pig: Evaluation of educational exhibits, museum visitor studies in the 90s.* London: Science Museum.

Mortensen, M. F., & Smart, K. (2007). Free-choice worksheets increase students' exposure to curriculum during museum visits. *Journal of Research in Science Teaching,* 44(9), 1389–1414.

Naismith, L., Lonsdale, P., Vavoula, G., & Sharples, M. (2006). Report 11: Literature review in mobile technologies and learning. In FutureLab (Ed.), *FutureLab Series.* Bristol.

National Research Council (NRC). (2009). *Learning science in informal environments: People, places, and pursuits.* Washington, DC: National Academies Press.

Palmquist, S. D., & Crowley, K. (2007). From teachers to testers: Parents' role in child expertise development in informal settings. *Science Education,* 91(5), 712–732.

Perry, J., & Nellis, R. (2012). Augmented learning: Evaluating mobile location-based games at the zoo. Paper presented at the ISTE 2012, San Diego.

Pierroux, P. (2001). Information and communication technology in art museums. In G. Liestøl & T. Rasmussen (Eds.), *Internett i endring (Internet and change)* (pp. 87–103). Oslo: Novus.

Pierroux, P. (2005). Dispensing with formalities in art education research. *Nordisk Museologi,* 2, 76–88.

Pierroux, P. (2010). Guiding meaning on guided tours: Narratives of art and learning in museums. In A. Morrison (Ed.), *Inside multimodal composition* (pp. 417–450). Cresskill, NJ: Hampton Press.

Pierroux, P. (2011). Real life meaning in second life art. In S. Østerud, B. Gentikow, & E. G. Skogseth (Eds.), *Literacy practices in late modernity: Mastering technological and cultural convergences* (pp. 177–198). Cresskill, NJ: Hampton Press.

Pierroux, P., Bannon L., et al. (2007). MUSTEL: Framing the design of technology-enhanced learning activities for museum visitors. International Cultural Heritage Informatics Meeting (ICHIM). Toronto: Archives & Museum Informatics.

Pierroux, P., Krange, I., & Sem, I. (2011). Bridging contexts and interpretations: Mobile blogging on art museum field trips. *Mediekultur. Journal of Media and Communication Research*, 50, 25–44.

Pierroux, P., & Ludvigsen, S. (2013). Communication interrupted: Textual practices and digital interactives in art museums. In K. Schrøder & K. Drotner (Eds.), *The connected museum: Social media and museum communication* (pp. 153–176). London: Routledge.

Ramey-Gassert, L., Walberg, H. J. III, & Walberg, H. J. (1994). Reexamining connections: Museums as science learning environments. *Science Education*, 78(4), 345–363.

Ravelli, L. (1996). Making language accessible: Successful text writing for museum visitors. *Linguistics and Education*, 8, 367–387.

Reisman, M. (2008). Using design-based research in informal environments. *The Journal of Museum Education*, 33(2), 175–185.

Rennie, L. J., & Johnston, D. J. (2004). The nature of learning and its implications for research on learning from museums. *Sci. Ed.*, 88, S4–S16.

Rice, D., & Yenawine, P. (2002). A conversation on object-centered learning in art museums. *Curator: The Museum Journal*, 45(4), 289–301.

Roberts, L. C. (1997). *From knowledge to narrative: Educators and the changing museum*. Washington, DC: Smithsonian Institution Press.

Roth, W.-M. (2001). Situating cognition. *The Journal of the Learning Sciences*, 10(1 & 2), 27–61.

Russo, A., Watkins, J. J. et al. (2007). Social media and cultural interactive experiences in museums. *Nordic Journal of Digital Literacy*, 1, 19–29.

Screven, C. G. (1986). Exhibitions and information centers: Some principles and approaches. *Curator*, 29(2), 109–137.

Selvakumar, M., & Storksdieck, M. (2013). Portal to the public: Museum educators collaborating with scientists to engage museum visitors with current science. *Curator: The Museum Journal*, 56(1), 69–78.

Siegel, D., Esterly, J., Callanan, M., Wright, R., & Navarro. R. (2007). Conversations about science across activities in Mexican-descent families. *International Journal of Science Education*, 29(12), 1447–1466.

Silverman, L. H. (1995). Visitor meaning-making in museums for a new age. *Curator*, 38, 161–170.

Stapp, C. B. (1984). Defining museum literacy. *Roundtable Reports*, 9(1), 3–4.

Steier, R., & Pierroux, P. (2011). "'What is 'the concept'?' Sites of conceptual understanding in a touring architecture workshop. *Nordic Journal of Digital Literacy*, 6(3), 138–156.

Tallon, L., & Walker, K. (Eds.) (2008). *Digital technologies and the museum experience: Handheld guides and other media*. Lanham, MD: AltaMira Press.

Trant, J. (2006). Exploring the potential for social tagging and folksonomy in art museums: Proof of concept. *New Review of Hypermedia and Multimedia*, 12(1), 83–105.

Vavoula, G., Sharples, M., Rudman, P., Meek, J., & Lonsdale, P. (2009). Myartspace: Design and evaluation of support for learning with multimedia phones between classrooms and museums. *Computers & Education*, 53(2), 286–299.

Vom Lehn, D., & Heath, C. (2005). Accounting for new technology in museum exhibitions. *Marketing Management*, 7(3), 11–21.

Vom Lehn, D., Heath, C. et al. (2001). Exhibiting interaction: Conduct and collaboration in museums and galleries. *Symbolic Interaction*, 24(2), 189–216.

Vygotsky, L. S. (1986). *Thought and language*. Cambridge, MIT Press.

Watson, B., & Werb, S. R. (2013). One hundred strong: A colloquium on transforming natural history museums in the twenty-first century. *Curator: The Museum Journal*, 56(2), 255–265.

Wertsch, J. (1991). *Voices of the mind. A sociocultural approach to mediated action*. Cambridge, MA: Harvard University Press.

Wertsch, J. (2002). *Voices of collective remembering*. Cambridge, Cambridge University Press.

Wishart, J., & Triggs, P. (2010). MuseumScouts: Exploring how schools, museums and interactive technologies can work together to support learning. *Computers & Education*, 54(3), 669–678.

Yenawine, P., & Rice, D. (2002). A conversation on object-centered learning in art museums. *Curator* 45.4, 289–299.

24 Computer-Supported Collaborative Learning

Gerry Stahl, Timothy Koschmann, and Daniel Suthers

Computer-supported collaborative learning (CSCL) refers to collaborative learning that is facilitated or mediated by computers and networked devices. CSCL can occur *synchronously*, with learners interacting with each other in real time (e.g., a chat room), or *asynchronously*, with individual contributions stretched out over time (e.g., an e-mail exchange). CSCL can be completely mediated by computers and networks, with individual learners in different buildings or even different countries; or CSCL can involve learners together in the same physical space using computational devices (such as handhelds or tablets) to facilitate their face-to-face communication. CSCL researchers study all of these ways that people learn together with the help of computers.

CSCL researchers have discovered that the interplay of collaborative learning with technology is quite intricate. Bringing the study of collaboration, computer mediation, and distance education into the learning sciences has problematized the very notion of learning and called into question prevailing assumptions about how to study it. In particular, CSCL research demonstrates the power of analytic approaches that focus on situated group practices and interactional processes, and demonstrates the limits and weaknesses of traditional cognitivist approaches that focus on the individual learner.

CSCL within Education

CSCL researchers study all levels of formal education from kindergarten through graduate study as well as informal education, such as museums. Computers have become important at all levels of education, with school districts and politicians around the world setting goals of increasing student access to computers and the Internet. The idea of encouraging students to learn together in small groups has also become increasingly emphasized in the learning sciences (as represented in the other chapters in Part 4 of this handbook). However, the ability to combine these two ideas (computer support and collaborative learning, or technology and education) to effectively enhance learning remains a challenge – a challenge that CSCL research is designed to address.

Computers and Education

Computers in the classroom are often viewed with skepticism. Critics see them as boring and antisocial, a haven for geeks, and a mechanical, inhumane form of training. CSCL is based on precisely the opposite vision: a vision of software and applications that bring learners together and that can offer creative activities of intellectual exploration and social interaction.

CSCL arose in the 1990s in reaction to software that forced students to learn as isolated individuals. The exciting potential of the Internet to connect people in innovative ways provided a stimulus for CSCL research. As CSCL developed, unforeseen barriers to designing, disseminating, and effectively taking advantage of innovative educational software became increasingly apparent. A transformation of the whole concept of learning was required, including significant changes in schooling, teaching, and being a student. These changes are largely consistent with the foundational learning sciences concepts presented in Part 1 of this volume, for instance scaffolding, cognitive apprenticeship, and learning in activity.

E-learning at a Distance

CSCL is often conflated with e-learning, the organization of instruction across computer networks. E-learning is too often motivated by a naïve belief that classroom content can be digitized and disseminated to large numbers of students with little continuing involvement of teachers or other costs, such as buildings and transportation. There are a number of problems with this view.

First, it is simply not true that the posting of content, such as slides, texts, or videos, makes for compelling instruction. Such content may provide important resources for students, just as textbooks always have, but they can only be effective within a larger motivational and interactive social context.

Second, online teaching requires at least as much effort by human teachers as classroom teaching. Not only must the teacher prepare materials and make them available by computer, the teacher must motivate and guide each student through ongoing interaction and a sense of social presence. While online teaching allows students from around the world to participate and allows teachers to work from any place with Internet connectivity, it generally significantly increases the teacher effort per student.

Third, CSCL stresses collaboration among the students, so that they are not simply reacting in isolation to posted materials. The learning takes place largely through interactions among students. Students learn by expressing their questions, pursuing lines of inquiry together, teaching each other, and seeing how others are learning. Computer support for such collaboration is central to a CSCL approach to e-learning. Stimulating and sustaining productive student interaction is difficult to achieve; it requires skillful planning, coordination, and implementation of curriculum, pedagogy, and technology.

Fourth, CSCL is also concerned with face-to-face (F2F) collaboration. Computer support of learning does not always take the form of an online communication medium; the computer support may involve, for instance, a computer simulation of a scientific model or a shared interactive representation. In this case, the collaboration focuses on the construction and exploration of the simulation or representation. Alternatively, a group of students might use a computer to browse through information on the Internet and to discuss, debate, gather, and present what they found collaboratively. CSCL can take the form of distant or F2F interaction, either synchronously or asynchronously.

Cooperative Learning in Groups

The study of group learning began long before CSCL. Since at least the 1960s – before the advent of networked personal computers – education researchers carried out considerable investigation of cooperative learning. Research on small groups has an even longer history within social psychology.

To distinguish CSCL from this earlier investigation of group learning, it is useful to draw a distinction between *cooperative* and *collaborative* learning. In a detailed discussion of this distinction, Dillenbourg defined the distinction roughly as follows:

> In cooperation, partners split the work, solve sub-tasks individually and then assemble the partial results into the final output. In collaboration, partners do the work "together." (Dillenbourg, 1999, p. 8)

He later elaborated that collaboration is "a process by which individuals *negotiate and share meanings* relevant to the problem-solving task at hand ... Collaboration is a coordinated, synchronous activity that is the result of a continued attempt to construct and maintain a shared conception of a problem" (Dillenbourg, 1999, p. 70, emphasis added)

In cooperation, the learning is done by individuals, who then contribute their individual results and present the collection of individual results as their group product. Learning in cooperative groups is viewed as something that takes place individually – and can therefore be studied with the traditional conceptualizations and methods of educational and psychological research.

By contrast, in collaboration, learning occurs socially as the collaborative construction of knowledge. Of course, individuals are involved in this as members of the group, but the activities that they engage in are not individual-learning activities, but group interactions like negotiation and sharing. The participants do not go off to do things individually, but remain engaged with a shared task that is constructed and maintained by and for the group as such. The collaborative negotiation and social sharing of *group meanings* – phenomena central to collaboration – cannot be studied with traditional psychological methods (see Nathan & Sawyer, Chapter 2, this volume).

Collaborative learning involves individual learning, but is not reducible to it. The relationship between viewing collaborative learning as a group process versus as an aggregation of individual change is a tension at the heart of CSCL. Earlier studies of learning in groups treated learning as a fundamentally individual process. The fact that the individuals worked in groups was treated as a contextual variable that influenced the individual learning. In contemporary CSCL research, learning is also analyzed as a group process; analyses of learning at both the individual and the group levels of analysis are necessary.

To some extent, CSCL designs, and CSCL research, have emerged in reaction to previous attempts to use technology within education and to previous approaches to understand collaborative phenomena with the traditional methods of the learning sciences. The learning sciences as a whole has shifted from a narrow focus on individual learning to an incorporation of both individual and group learning, and the evolution of CSCL has paralleled this movement.

The Historical Evolution of CSCL

The Beginnings

Three early projects – the ENFI Project at Gallaudet University, the Computer Supported Intentional Learning Environment (CSILE) Project at the University of Toronto, and the Fifth Dimension (5thD) Project at the University of California San Diego – were forerunners for what was later to emerge as the field of CSCL. All three involved explorations of the use of technology to improve learning related to literacy.

The ENFI Project produced some of the earliest examples of programs for computer-aided composition or "CSCWriting" (Gruber, Peyton, & Bruce, 1995; Nussbaum, 1993). Students who attend Gallaudet are deaf or hearing impaired; many such students enter college with deficiencies in their written communication skills. The goal of the ENFI Project was to engage students in writing in new ways: to introduce them to the idea of writing with a "voice" and writing with an audience in mind. The technologies developed, though advanced for the time, might seem rudimentary by today's standards. Special classrooms were constructed in which desks with computers were arranged in a circle. Software resembling today's chat programs was developed to enable the students and their instructor to conduct textually mediated discussions. The technology in the ENFI Project was designed to support a new form of meaning making by providing a new medium for textual communication.

Another early, influential project was undertaken by Bereiter and Scardamalia at the University of Toronto (see Scardamalia & Bereiter, Chapter 20, this volume). They were concerned that learning in schools is often shallow and poorly motivated. They contrasted the learning that takes place in classrooms with the learning that occurs in "knowledge-building communities" (Bereiter, 2002; Scardamalia & Bereiter, 1996), like the communities of scholars that grow up around a research problem. In the CSILE Project, later known as Knowledge Forum, they developed technologies and pedagogies to restructure classrooms as knowledge-building communities. Like the ENFI Project, CSILE sought to make writing more meaningful by engaging students in joint text production. The texts produced in each case were quite different, however. The ENFI texts were conversational; they were produced spontaneously and were generally not preserved beyond the completion of a class. CSILE texts, however, were archival, like conventional scholarly literatures.

As was the case for CSILE, the Fifth Dimension Project began with an interest in improving reading skills (Cole, 1996). It started with an after school program organized by Cole and colleagues at Rockefeller University. When the Laboratory of Comparative Human Cognition (LCHC) moved to the University of California at San Diego, the 5thD was elaborated into an integrated system of mostly computer-based activities selected to enhance students' skills for reading and problem solving. The "Maze," a board-game type layout with different rooms representing specific activities, was introduced as a mechanism for marking student progress and coordinating participation with the 5thD. Student work was supported by more-skilled peers and by undergraduate volunteers from the School of Education. The program was originally implemented at four sites in San Diego, but was eventually expanded to multiple sites around the world (Nicolopoulou & Cole, 1993).

All of these projects – ENFI, CSILE, and 5thD – shared a goal of supporting learners in a process of making meaning. All three turned to computer and information technologies as resources for achieving this goal, and all three introduced novel forms of organized social activity within instruction. In this way, they laid the groundwork for the subsequent emergence of CSCL.

From Conferences to a Global Community

In 1983, a workshop on the topic of "joint problem solving and microcomputers" was held in San Diego. Six years later, a NATO-sponsored workshop was held in Maratea, Italy. The 1989 Maratea workshop is considered by many to mark the birth of the field, as it was the first public and international gathering to use the term *computer-supported collaborative learning* in its title.

The first full-fledged CSCL conference was organized at Indiana University in the fall of 1995. Subsequent international meetings have taken place biennially, with CSCL conferences in Toronto, Canada in 1997, Palo Alto, California in 1999, Maastricht, The Netherlands in 2001, Boulder, Colorado in 2002, Bergen, Norway in 2003, Taiwan in 2005, New Brunswick, New Jersey in 2007, Rhodes, Greece in 2009, Hong Kong in 2011, and Madison, Wisconsin in 2013.

A specialized literature documenting theory and research in CSCL has developed since the NATO-sponsored workshop in Maratea, Italy. Four of the most influential early monographs are Newman, Griffin, and Cole (1989), Bruffee (1993), Crook (1994), and Bereiter (2002). Additionally, scholars have published a number of edited collections specifically focusing on CSCL research, including O'Malley (1995), Koschmann (1996a), Dillenbourg (1999a), and Koschmann, Hall, and Miyake (2002). A book series on CSCL published by Kluwer (now Springer) includes several volumes to date. The CSCL conference proceedings have been the primary vehicle for publications in the field. A number of journals have also played a role, including the *Journal of the Learning Sciences (JLS)*. The *International Journal of Computer-Supported Collaborative Learning (iJCSCL)* started publishing in 2006. Although the community was centered in Western Europe and Northern America in its early years, it has evolved into a rather well-balanced international presence (Cox, Harrison, & Hoadley, 2009; Kienle & Wessner, 2005). With the 2005 conference in Taiwan, the 2011 conference in Hong Kong, and an international journal, the CSCL research community is truly global.

From Artificial Intelligence to Collaboration Support

The field of CSCL can be contrasted with earlier approaches to using computers in education. Koschmann (1996) identified the following historical sequence of approaches: (a) computer-assisted instruction, (b) intelligent tutoring systems, (c) Logo as Latin, (d) CSCL.

The first use of computers in education was computer-assisted instruction. This behaviorist approach dominated the early years of educational computer applications beginning in the 1960s. It conceived of learning as the memorization of facts. Domains of knowledge were broken down into elemental facts that were presented to students in a logical sequence through computerized drill and practice. Many commercial educational software products still take this approach.

The second use of computers in education was the intelligent tutoring system. These systems – based on a cognitivist philosophy – analyzed student learning in terms of mental models and potentially faulty mental representations. They rejected the behaviorist view that learning could be supported without concern for how students represented and processed knowledge.

Considered particularly promising in the 1970s, this approach created computer models of student understanding and then responded to student actions based on occurrences of typical errors identified in student mental models.

The third use of computers in education began in the 1980s, and was epitomized by the teaching of the Logo programming language. Logo took a constructivist approach, arguing that students must build their knowledge themselves. It provided stimulating environments for students to explore and to discover the power of reasoning, as illustrated in software programming constructs: functions, subroutines, loops, variables, recursion, and so forth.

CSCL represents the fourth and most recent use of computers in education. CSCL approaches explore how computers could bring students together to learn collaboratively in small groups and in learning communities. Motivated by social constructivist and dialogical theories, these efforts seek to provide and support opportunities for students to learn together by directed discourse that would construct shared knowledge.

During the 1970s and 1980s, at a time when mainframe computers were becoming available for school usage and microcomputers started to appear, artificial intelligence (AI) was near the height of its popularity. It was natural that computer scientists interested in educational applications of computer technology would be attracted by the exciting promises of AI. AI is computer software that closely mimics behaviors that might be considered intelligent if done by a human (e.g., to play chess by considering the pros and cons of alternative sequences of legal moves). Intelligent tutoring systems are a prime example of AI, because they replicate the actions of a human tutor – providing responses to student input (e.g., detailed steps in solving a math problem) by analyzing the student problem-solving strategy and offering advice by comparing student actions to programmed models of correct and erroneous understanding. This is still an active research area within the learning sciences (Koedinger, 2006), but is limited to domains of knowledge where mental models can be algorithmically defined. In its most ambitious form, the AI approach sought to have the computer handle certain teaching or guiding functions that would otherwise require a human teacher's time and intervention.

Within CSCL, the focus is on learning through collaboration with other students rather than directly from the teacher. Therefore, the role of the computer shifts from providing instruction – either in the form of facts in computer-aided instruction or in the form of feedback from intelligent tutoring systems – to supporting collaboration by providing media of communication and scaffolding for productive student interaction (see Reiser & Tabak, Chapter 3, this volume, on scaffolding).

The primary form of collaboration support is for a network of computers (typically connected over the Internet) to provide a medium of communication. This may take the form of e-mail, chat, discussion forums, videoconferencing, instant messaging, and so forth. CSCL systems typically provide a combination of several media and add special functionality to them.

In addition, CSCL software environments provide various forms of scaffolding for collaborative learning. These may be implemented with rather complex computational mechanisms, including AI techniques. They can offer alternative views on the ongoing student discussion and emerging shared information. They can provide feedback, possibly based on a model of group inquiry. They can support sociability by monitoring interaction patterns and providing feedback to the students. In most cases, the role of the computer is secondary to the interpersonal collaboration process among the students (and, often, the teacher, tutor, or mentor). The software is designed to support, not replace, these group processes.

The shift from mental models of individual cognition to support for collaborating groups had enormous implications for both the focus and the method of research on learning. The gradual acceptance and unfolding of these implications has defined the evolution of the field of CSCL.

From Individuals to Interacting Groups

At about the time of the first biannual CSCL conference in 1995, Dillenbourg, Baker, Blaye, and O'Malley analyzed the state of evolution of research on collaborative learning as follows.

> For many years, theories of collaborative learning tended to focus on how *individuals* function in a group. This reflected a position that was dominant both in cognitive psychology and in artificial intelligence in the 1970s and early 1980s, where cognition was seen as a product of individual information processors, and where the context of social interaction was seen more as a background for individual activity than as a focus of research. More recently, *the group itself has become the unit of analysis* and the focus has shifted to more emergent, socially constructed, *properties of the interaction.*
>
> In terms of empirical research, the initial goal was to establish whether and under what circumstances collaborative learning was more effective than learning alone. Researchers controlled several independent variables (size of the group, composition of the group, nature of the task, communication media, and so on). However, these variables interacted with one another in a way that made it almost impossible to establish causal links between the conditions and the effects of collaboration. Hence, empirical studies have more recently started to focus less on *establishing parameters for effective collaboration* and more on trying to *understand the role that such variables play in mediating interaction.* This shift to a more process-oriented account requires *new tools for analyzing and modeling interactions.* (Dillenbourg et al., 1996, p. 189, emphasis added)

The research Dillenbourg and colleagues reviewed – which studied the effects of manipulating collaboration variables on the measures of individual learning – did not produce clear results. Effects of gender or group composition (i.e., heterogeneous or homogeneous competence levels) might be completely different at different ages, in different domains, with different teachers, and so on. This not only violated methodological assumptions of variable independence, but raised questions about how to understand what was behind the effects. To get behind the effects meant to understand in some detail what was going on in the group interactions that might cause the effects. This, in turn, required the development of methodologies for analyzing and interpreting group interactions as such. The focus was no longer on what might be taking place "in the heads" of individual learners, but what was taking place between them in their interactions.

From Mental Representations to Interactional Meaning Making

The shift to the group unit of analysis coincided with a focus on the community as the agent of situated learning (Lave & Wenger, 1991) or collaborative knowledge building (Scardamalia & Bereiter, 1991). But it also called for the elaboration of a social theory of mind, such as Vygotsky (1930/1978) had begun to outline, which could clarify the relation of individual learners to collaborative learning in groups or communities.

According to Vygotsky, individual learners have different developmental capabilities in collaborative situations than when they are working alone. His concept of the "zone of proximal development" is defined as a measure of the difference between these two capabilities. This means that one cannot measure the learning – even the individual learning – that takes place in collaborative situations with the use of pre- and post-tests that measure capabilities of the individuals when they are working alone. To get at what takes place during collaborative learning, it does not help to theorize about mental models in the heads of individuals, because that does not capture the shared meaning making that is going on during collaborative interactions.

Collaboration is primarily conceptualized as a process of shared meaning construction. The meaning making is not treated as an expression of mental representations of the individual participants, but as an interactional achievement. Meaning making can be analyzed as taking place across sequences of utterances or messages from multiple participants. The meaning is not attributable to individual utterances of individual students because the meaning typically depends on indexical references to the shared situation, elliptical references to previous utterances, and projective preferences for future utterances.

From Quantitative Comparisons to Micro Case Studies

To observe learning in collaborative situations is different from observing it for isolated learners. First, in situations of collaboration, participants necessarily visibly display their learning as part of the process of collaboration. Second, the observations take place across relatively short periods of group interaction, rather than across long periods between pre- and post-tests.

Ironically, perhaps, it is in principle easier to study learning in groups than in individuals. That is because a necessary feature of collaboration is that the participants display for each other their understanding of the meaning that is being constructed in the interaction (see Enyedy & Stevens, Chapter 10, this volume). Utterances, texts, and diagrams that are produced during collaboration are designed by the participants to display their understanding. That is the basis for successful collaboration. Researchers can take advantage of these displays (assuming that they share the participants' interpretive competencies and can capture an adequate record of the displays, for example, on digital video). Researchers can then reconstruct the collaborative process through which group participants constructed shared meaning, which was learned as a group.

Methodologies like conversation analysis (Have, 1999; Sacks, 1992) or video analysis (Koschmann, Stahl, & Zemel, 2005) based on ethnomethodology (Garfinkel, 1967) produce detailed case studies of collaborative meaning making (Enyedy & Stevens, Chapter 10, this volume). These case studies are not merely anecdotal. They can be based on rigorous scientific procedures with intersubjective validity even though they are interpretive in nature and are not quantitative. They can also represent generally applicable results, in that the methods that people use to interact are widely shared (at least within appropriately defined communities or cultures).

How can the analysis of interactional methods help to guide the design of CSCL technologies and pedagogies? This question points to the complex interplay between education and computers in CSCL.

The Interplay of Learning and Technology in CSCL

The Traditional Conception of Learning

Edwin Thorndike, a founder of the traditional educational approach, once wrote:

> If, by a miracle of mechanical ingenuity, a book could be so arranged
> that only to him who had done what was directed on page one would two
> become visible, and so on, much that now requires personal instruction
> could be managed by print.... Children [could] be taught, moreover to use
> materials in a manner that will be most useful in the long run. (Thorndike,
> 1912, p. 165)

This quotation is notable in two respects. For one, it suggests that the central idea of computer-aided instruction long preceded the actual development of computers; but, more important, it also shows how the goal of research in educational technology is closely tied, indeed indistinguishable from, the conventional goal of educational research, namely to enhance learning as it is operationally defined. Thorndike envisioned an educational science in which all learning is measurable and, on this basis, by which all educational innovations could be experimentally evaluated. Historically, research on educational technology has been tied to this tradition and represents a specialization within it (cf. Cuban, 1986).

In the past, educational researchers have treated learning as a purely individual phenomenon. Learning has been taken to have three essential features. First, it represents a response to and recording of experience. Second, learning is always treated as a change that occurs over time. Finally, learning is generally seen as something that happens to individuals, whether a change in behavior (as in behaviorism) or a change in unobservable mental entities (as in cognitivism) (Koschmann, 2002b). This formulation is so culturally entrenched that it is difficult to conceive of learning in any other way. It rests on established traditions in epistemology and philosophy of mind.

Contemporary philosophy has called these traditions into question, however. The so-called edifying philosophers (Rorty, 1974) – James, Dewey, Wittgenstein, and Heidegger – rebelled against the view of learning as an inaccessible event during which knowledge is inscribed in an individual mind. They aspired to construct a new view of learning and knowing, one that properly located it in the world of everyday affairs. CSCL embraces this more situated view of learning, thereby rejecting the foundations of conventional educational psychology and cognitive psychology. CSCL locates learning in meaning negotiation carried out in the social world rather than in individuals' heads. Of the various socially oriented theories of learning, social practice theory (Lave & Wenger, 1991) and dialogical theories of learning (e.g., Hicks, 1996) speak most directly to a view of learning as socially organized meaning construction. Social practice theory focuses on one aspect of meaning negotiation: the negotiation of social identity within a community. Dialogical theories locate learning in the emergent development of meaning within social interaction. Taken together, they comprise a basis for a new way of thinking about and studying learning.

Designing Technology to Support Learner Meaning Making

The goal for design in CSCL is to create artifacts, activities, and environments that enhance the practices of group meaning making. Rapid advances during recent decades in computer and communication technologies, like the Internet, have dramatically changed the ways we work, play, and learn. No form of technology, however, no matter how cleverly designed or sophisticated, has the capacity, in and of itself, to change practice. To create the possibility of an enhanced form of practice requires more multifaceted forms of design (bringing in expertise, theories, and practices from various disciplines): design that addresses curriculum (pedagogical and didactic design), resources (information sciences, communication sciences), participation structures (interaction design), tools (design studies), and surrounding space (architecture).

As the title of a commentary by LeBaron (2002) suggests, "Technology does not exist independent of its use." Substitute "activities, artifacts, and environments" for "technology" and the message remains the same – these elements themselves cannot define new forms of practice, but are instead constituted within practice. An environment for a desired form of practice becomes such through the organized actions of its inhabitants. Tools and artifacts are only tools and artifacts in the ways they are oriented to and made relevant by participants in directed practice. Even activities are only rendered recognizable as such in the ways that participants orient to them as ordered forms of joint action.

CSCL designs, therefore, must be coupled with analysis of the meanings constructed within emergent practice. Meanings reflect past experience and are open to endless negotiation and reevaluation. Furthermore, neither analysts nor participants have privileged access to others' subjective interpretations. Despite these issues, participants routinely engage in coordinated activity and operate as if shared understanding was both possible and being achieved. A fundamental question, therefore, is: How is this done? In order to design technology to support collaborative learning and knowledge building, we must understand in more detail how small groups of learners construct shared meaning using various artifacts and media.

The question of how *intersubjectivity* is accomplished has been taken up in a variety of specialized disciplines such as pragmatics (Levinson, 2000; Sperber & Wilson, 1986), social psychology (Rommetveit, 1974), linguistic anthropology (Hanks, 1996), and sociology (cf. Goffman, 1974), especially sociological research in the ethnomethodological tradition (Garfinkel, 1967; Heritage, 1984). The problem of intersubjectivity is of particular relevance for those who wish to understand how learning is produced within interaction. Learning can be construed as the act of bringing divergent meanings into contact (Hicks, 1996), and instruction as the social and material arrangements that foster such negotiation. The analysis of meaning making calls for the appropriation of the methods and concerns of psychology (especially the discursive and cultural varieties), sociology (especially the micro-sociological and ethnomethodologically informed traditions), anthropology (including linguistic anthropology and anthropologies of the built environment), pragmatics, communication studies, organizational science, and others.

CSCL research has both analytic and design components. Analysis of meaning making is inductive and indifferent to reform goals. It seeks only to discover what people are doing in moment-to-moment interaction, without prescription or assessment. Design, by contrast, is inherently prescriptive – any effort toward reform begins from the presumption that there are better and worse ways of doing things. To design for improved meaning making, however, requires some means of rigorously studying practices of meaning making. In this way, the relationship between analysis and design is a symbiotic one – design must be informed by analysis, but analysis also depends on design in its orientation to the analytic object (Koschmann et al., 2005).

CSCL must continue with its work of self-invention. New sources of theory are introduced, analyses of learner practice are presented, and artifacts are produced accompanied by theories of how they might enhance meaning making. The design of CSCL technology, which opens new possibilities for collaborative learning, must be founded on an analysis of the nature of collaborative learning.

The Analysis of Collaborative Learning

Koschmann presented a programmatic description of CSCL in his keynote at the 2002 CSCL conference:

> CSCL is a field of study centrally concerned with meaning and the practices of meaning making in the context of joint activity, and the ways in which these practices are mediated through designed artifacts. (Koschmann, 2002a, p. 18)

The definition of CSCL as being concerned with the "practices of meaning making in the context of joint activity" can be understood in multiple ways.

The aspect of collaborative learning that is perhaps hardest to understand in detail is what may be called *intersubjective learning* (Suthers & Hundhausen, 2002) or *group cognition* (Stahl, 2006). This is learning that is not merely accomplished interactionally, but is actually *constituted* of the interactions between participants. Following Garfinkel, Koschmann and colleagues (2005) argue for the study of "member's methods" of meaning making: "how participants in such [instructional] settings actually go about *doing* learning" (emphasis in original). In addition to understanding how the cognitive processes of participants are influenced by social interaction, we need to understand how learning events themselves take place in the interactions between participants.

The study of joint meaning making is not yet prominent within CSCL practice. Even where interaction processes (rather than individual learning outcomes) are examined in detail, the analysis is typically undertaken by assigning coding categories and counting predefined features. The codes, in effect, substitute preconceived categories of behavior for the phenomenon of interest rather than seeking to discover those phenomena in their unique situations (Stahl, 2006).

A few studies published in the CSCL literature have directly addressed this problem of describing the constituting of intersubjectivity in interaction (for example, Koschmann et al., 2005; Koschmann et al., 2003; Roschelle, 1992; Stahl, 2006). Roschelle's early study designed software especially to support meaning making related to physics, defined student activities to engage learners in joint problem solving, and analyzed their collaborative practices in micro detail. Koschmann's work has generally focused on participants' methods of *problematization*: how groups of students collectively characterize a situation as problematic and as requiring further specific analysis.

Stahl (2006) argued that small groups are the most fruitful unit of study, for several reasons. Most simply, small groups are where members' methods for intersubjective learning can be observed. Groups of several members allow the full range of social interactions to play out, but are not so large that participants and researchers alike necessarily lose track of what is going on. The shared construction of meaning is most visible and available for research at the small-group unit of analysis, where it appears as *group cognition*. Moreover, small groups lie at the boundary of and mediate between individuals and a community. The knowledge building that takes place within small groups becomes "internalized by their members as individual learning and externalized in their communities as certifiable knowledge" (Stahl, 2006). However, small groups should not be the only social granularity studied. Analysis of large-scale changes in communities and organizations may lead to an understanding of emergent social-learning phenomena as well as elucidate the role of embedded groups in driving these changes.

The study of the interactional accomplishment of intersubjective learning or group cognition gives rise to interesting questions that are among the most challenging facing any social behavioral science, and even touch on our nature as conscious beings: Do cognitive phenomena take place transpersonally in group discourse? How is it possible for learning, usually conceived of as an individual process, to be distributed across people and artifacts? How can we understand knowledge as accomplished practice rather than as a mental entity?

The Analysis of Computer Support

In CSCL contexts, interactions among individuals are mediated by computer environments. The second half of Koschmann's programmatic definition of the domain of CSCL is "the ways in which these practices [meaning making in the context of joint activity] are mediated through designed artifacts" (Koschmann, 2002b, p. 18). Computer support for intersubjective meaning making is what makes the field unique.

The technology side of the CSCL agenda focuses on the design and study of fundamentally social technologies. To be fundamentally social means that the technology is designed specifically to mediate and encourage social acts that constitute group learning and lead to individual learning. Design should leverage the unique opportunities the technology provides rather than replicate support for learning that could be done through other means, or (worse) try to force the technology to be something for which it is not well suited. What is unique to information technology that can potentially fill this role?

- Computational media are reconfigurable. Representations are dynamic: it is easy to move things around and undo actions. It is easy to replicate those actions elsewhere: one can bridge time and space. These features make information technology attractive as a communication channel, but we should exploit technology for its potential to make new interactions possible, not try to force it to replicate face-to-face interaction.
- Computer-mediated communication environments "turn communication into substance" (Dillenbourg, 2005). A record of activity as well as product can be kept, replayed, and even modified. We should explore the potential of the persistent record of interaction and collaboration as a resource for intersubjective learning.
- Computational media can analyze workspace state and interaction sequences, and reconfigure themselves or generate prompts according to features of either. We should explore the potential of adaptive media as an influence on the course of intersubjective processes, and take advantage of their ability to prompt, analyze, and selectively respond.

Human communication, and the use of representational resources for this communication, are highly flexible: we cannot "fix" meanings or even specify communicative functions (Dwyer & Suthers, 2005). Informed by this fact, CSCL research should identify the unique advantages of computational media and explore how collaborators use these and how they influence the course of their meaning making. This would enable the design of technologies that offer collections of features through which participants can interactionally engage in learning with flexible forms of guidance.

The Multidisciplinarity of CSCL

CSCL consists of three methodological traditions: experimental, descriptive, and iterative design.

Many empirical studies follow the traditional *experimental* paradigm that compares an intervention to a control condition in terms of one or more variables (e.g., Baker-Sennett & Matusov, 1997; Horwitz & Weinberger, 2005; Rummel & Spada, 2005; Suthers & Hundhausen, 2002; Van der Pol, Admiraal, & Simons, 2003). Data analysis in most of these studies is undertaken by "coding and counting": interactions are categorized and/ or learning outcomes measured, and group means are compared through statistical methods to draw general conclusions about the effects of the manipulated variables on aggregate (average) group behavior. These studies do not directly analyze the accomplishment of intersubjective learning. Such an analysis must examine the structure and intention of unique cases of interaction rather than count and aggregate behavioral categories.

The ethnomethodological tradition (exemplified in CSCL by Koschmann et al., 2005; Koschmann et al., 2003; Roschelle, 1992; Stahl, 2006) is more suited for *descriptive* case analyses. Video or transcripts of learners or other members of the community are studied to uncover the methods by which groups of participants accomplish learning. The grounded approach is data driven, seeking to discover patterns in the data rather than imposing theoretical categories. The analysis is often micro-analytic, examining brief episodes in detail. Descriptive methodologies are well suited to existentially quantified claims (e.g., that a community sometimes engages in a given practice). Yet as scientists and designers we would like to make causal generalizations about the effects of design choices. Descriptive methodologies are less suited for claiming that a specific intervention causes an observed outcome; causal claims are the province of experimental methodology.

The traditional analytic methods of experimental psychology are not appropriate to the study of intersubjective meaning making. Nevertheless, this does not imply that all CSCL research should be ethnomethodological. Rather, the foregoing considerations suggest that we explore hybrid research methodologies (Johnson & Onwuegbuzie, 2004). Experimental designs can continue to compare interventions, but the comparisons would be made in terms of microanalyses of how the features of information technology influence and are appropriated for members' methods of joint meaning making. Conceptually, the process analysis changes from "coding and counting" to "exploring and understanding" ways design variables influence support for meaning making. Such analyses are time intensive: we should explore, as research aids, the development of instrumentation for learning environments and automated visualization and querying of interaction logs (as in Cakir, Xhafa, Zhou, & Stahl, 2005; Donmez, Rose, Stegmann, Weinberger, & Fischer, 2005). Traditional analyses, especially measures of learning outcomes but also "coding and counting," might also be retained to obtain quick indicators of where more detailed analyses are merited, thereby focusing the detail work (as in Zemel, Xhafa, & Stahl, 2005).

The *iterative design* tradition is exemplified by Fischer and Ostwald (2005), Lingnau, Hoppe, and Mannhaupt (2003), and Guzdial and colleagues (1997) (also see Barab, Chapter 8, this volume). Driven by the dialectic between theory and informal observations and engaging stakeholders in the process, design-oriented researchers continuously improve artifacts intended to mediate learning and collaboration. Their research is not necessarily either qualitative or quantitative, but may also be "quisitive" (Goldman, 2004). It is not enough to just observe people's behaviors when they use new software.

We need to explore the space of possible designs, pushing into new areas and identifying promising features that should receive further study under the other methodological traditions. Designers also need to conduct micro-analyses of collaborative learning with and through technology in order to identify the features of designed artifacts that seem to be correlated with effective learning. When a new technical intervention is tested, experimental methods can be used to document significant differences while descriptive methods can document how the interventions mediated collaborative inter-actions differently. A conversation between the theoretical assumptions of ethnomethodology and those of design can lead to a "technomethodology" that changes the very objectives of design (Button & Dourish, 1996).

A potential limitation of descriptive methodologies should be noted. If we focus on finding examples of how members accomplish effective learning, we may miss abundant examples of how they also fail to do so. Yet, to find that something is not there, we need to have an idea of what we are looking for. A purely data-driven approach that derives theory but never applies it will not be adequate. Descriptive methods can be modified to address this need. Common patterns found in successful learning episodes subsequently become the theoretical categories we look for elsewhere with analytic methods and perhaps do not find in instances of unsuccessful collaboration. Having identified where the successful methods were *not* applied, we can then exam-ine the situation to determine what contingency was missing or responsible. Unique and un-reproducible instances where collaboration using technology breaks down in interesting ways can often provide the deepest insights into what is happening, and into what is normally taken for granted and invisi-ble. Care should be taken, however, to make sure that in finding examples where the interactional accomplishment of learning is absent, we do not fail to notice where something else of value to the participants *is* being accom-plished! For example, establishment and maintenance of individual and group identity are worthwhile accomplishments as far as the participants are concerned (Whitworth, Gallupe, & McQueen, 2000), and indeed are a form of situated learning, even though researchers may initially identify it as "off topic" social chatting.

CSCL Research in the Future

The CSCL research community includes people from a variety of professional and disciplinary backgrounds and trainings. They bring with them different research paradigms, contrasting views of data, analysis methods, presentation formats, concepts of rigor, and technical vocabu-laries. They come from around the world with various cultures and native languages. Community participants at any given time are operating within diverse conceptions of what CSCL is all about. For instance, Sfard (1998) defined two broad and irreconcilable metaphors of learning that are necessarily relevant to CSCL: the *acquisition* metaphor, in which learning consists of individuals acquiring knowledge stored in their minds, and the *participation* metaphor, in which learning consists of increasing participation in communities of practice (also see Sfard & Cobb, Chapter 27, this volume). Lipponen, Hakkarainen, and Paavola (2004) added a third metaphor based on Bereiter (2002) and Engeström (1987): the *knowledge creation* metaphor, in which new knowledge objects or social practices are created in the world through collaboration. Consequently, it is hard to present a well-defined, consistent, and comprehensive definition of CSCL theory, methodology, findings, or best practices. We suggest that more integrated, hybrid approaches may be possible in the future.

Research methodology in CSCL is largely trichotomized between experimental, descriptive, and iterative design approaches. Although sometimes combined within a single research project, the methodologies are even then typically kept separate in companion studies or separate analyses of a single study. Different researchers sometimes wear different hats on the same project, representing different research interests and methodologies. This situation may still be productive: the experimentalists continue to identify variables that affect general parameters of collaborative behavior, the ethnomethodologists identify patterns of joint activity that are essential to the meaning making, and designers innovate to creatively adapt new technological possibilities. Soon, however, experimentalists within CSCL may start to focus on the dependent variables that directly reflect the phenomenon of interest to the descriptive researchers (Fischer & Granoo, 1995), ethnomethodologists may look for predictive regularities in technology-mediated meaning making that can inform design, and designers may generate and assess promising new technology affordances in terms of the meaning-making activities they enable. Mutual assistance and closer collaboration may be possible through hybrid methodologies, for example by applying richer descriptive analytic methods to the problem of understanding the implications of experimental manipulations and new designs, or through computer support for our own meaning-making activities as researchers.

CSCL researchers form a community of inquiry that is actively constructing new ways to collaborate in the design, analysis, and implementation of computer support for collaborative learning. Having appropriated ideas, methods, and functionality from cognate fields, CSCL may in its next phase collaboratively construct new theories, methodologies, and technologies specific to the task of analyzing the social practices of intersubjective meaning making in order to support collaborative learning. Perhaps the strongest contribution of CSCL research to the learning sciences is that it demonstrates the analytic power of an approach that focuses on the meaning-making practices of collaborating groups and on the design of technological artifacts to mediate interaction, relative to approaches that focus on individual learning.

References

Baker-Sennett, J., & Matusov, E. (1997). School "performance": Improvisational processes in development and education. In R. K. Sawyer (Ed.), *Creativity in performance* (pp. 197–212). Norwood, NJ: Ablex.

Bereiter, C. (2002). *Education and mind in the knowledge age*. Mahwah, NJ: Lawrence Erlbaum Associates.

Bruffee, K. (1993). *Collaborative learning*. Baltimore, MD: Johns Hopkins University Press.

Button, G. Y., & Dourish, P. (1996). Technomethodology: Paradoxes and possibilities. Paper presented at the ACM Conference on Human Factors in Computing Systems (CHI '96), Vancouver, Canada.

Cakir, M., Xhafa, F., Zhou, N., & Stahl, G. (2005). Thread-based analysis of patterns of collaborative interaction in chat. Paper presented at the international conference on AI in Education (AI-Ed 2005), Amsterdam, Netherlands.

Cole, M. (1996). *Cultural psychology: A once and future discipline*. Cambridge, MA: Harvard University Press.

Cox, C., Harrison, S., & Hoadley, C. (2009). Applying the "studio model" to learning technology design. In C. DiGiano, S. Goldman, & M. Chorost (Eds.), *Educating learning technology designers* (pp. 145–164). New York: Routledge.

Crook, C. (1994). *Computers and the collaborative experience of learning*. London: Routledge.

Cuban, L. (1986). *Teachers and machines: The classroom use of technology since 1920*. New York: Teachers College Press.

Dillenbourg, P. (Ed.) (1999a). *Collaborative learning: Cognitive and computational approaches*. Amsterdam: Pergamon, Elsevier Science.

Dillenbourg, P. (1999b). What do you mean by "collaborative learning"? In P. Dillenbourg (Ed.), *Collaborative learning: Cognitive and computational approaches* (pp. 1–16). Amsterdam: Pergamon, Elsevier Science.

Dillenbourg, P. (2005). Designing biases that augment socio-cognitive interactions. In R. Bromme, F. Hesse, & H. Spada (Eds.), *Barriers and biases in computer-mediated knowledge communication – and how they may be overcome*. Dordrecht, Netherlands: Kluwer Academic Publisher.

Dillenbourg, P., Baker, M., Blaye, A., & O'Malley, C. (1996). The evolution of research on collaborative learning. In P. Reimann & H. Spada (Eds.), *Learning in humans and machines: Towards an interdisciplinary learning science* (pp. 189–211). Oxford: Elsevier.

Donmez, P., Rose, C., Stegmann, K., Weinberger, A., & Fischer, F. (2005). Supporting CSCL with automatic corpus analysis technology. Paper presented at the International Conference of Computer Support for Collaborative Learning (CSCL 2005), Taipei, Taiwan.

Dwyer, N., & Suthers, D. (2005). A study of the foundations of artifact-mediated collaboration. Paper presented at the international conference of Computer-Supported Collaborative Learning (CSCL 2005), Taipei, Taiwan.

Engeström, Y. (1987). *Learning by expanding: An activity-theoretical approach to developmental research*. Helsinki, Finland: Orienta-Kosultit Oy.

Fischer, G., & Ostwald, J. (2005). Knowledge communication in design communities. In R. Bromme, F. Hesse, & H. Spada (Eds.), *Barriers and biases in computer-mediated knowledge communication – and how they may be overcome*. Dordrecht, Netherlands: Kluwer Academic Publisher.

Fischer, K., & Granoo, N. (1995). Beyond one-dimensional change: Parallel, concurrent, socially distributed processes in learning and development. *Human Development*, 1995(38), 302–314.

Garfinkel, H. (1967). *Studies in ethnomethodology*. Englewood Cliffs, NJ: Prentice-Hall.

Goffman, E. (1974). *Frame analysis: An essay on the organization of experience*. New York: Harper & Row.

Goldman, K. J. (2004). An interactive environment for beginning Java programmers. *Science of Computer Programming*, 53(1), 3–24.

Gruber, S., Peyton, J. K., & Bruce, B. C. (1995). Collaborative writing in multiple discourse contexts. *Computer-Supported Cooperative Work*, 3, 247–269.

Guzdial, M., Hmelo, C., Hubscher, R., Newstetter, W., Puntambekar, S., Shabo, A., ... Kolodner, J. (1997). Integrating and guiding collaboration: Lessons learned in computer-supported collaboration learning research at Georgia Tech. Paper presented at the international conference on Computer-Supported Collaborative Learning (CSCL '97), Toronto, Canada.

Hanks, W. F. (1996). *Language and communicative practices*. Boulder, CO: Westview Press.

Have, P. T. (1999). *Doing conversation analysis: A practical guide*. Thousand Oaks, CA: Sage.

Heritage, J. (1984). *Garfinkel and ethnomethodology*. Cambridge: Polity Press.

Hicks, D. (Ed.) (1996). *Discourse, learning, and schooling*. New York: Cambridge University Press.

Horwitz, E., & Weinberger, K. (2005, May). How to wake up your dormant trade marks. *Managing Intellectual Property*.

Johnson, R. B., & Onwuegbuzie, A. J. (2004). Mixed methods research: A research paradigm whose time has come. *Educational Researcher*, 33(7), 14–26.

Kienle, A., & Wessner, M. (2005). Our Way to Taipei: An analysis of the first ten years of the CSCL community. Paper presented at the international conference of Computer-Supported Collaborative Learning (CSCL 2005), Taipei, Taiwan.

Koedinger, K. R., & Corbett, A. T. (2006). Cognitive tutors: Technology bringing learning sciences to the classroom. In R. K. Sawyer (Ed.), *Cambridge handbook of the learning sciences* (pp. 61–77). New York: Cambridge.

Koschmann, T. (Ed.) (1996a). *CSCL: Theory and practice of an emerging paradigm*. Hillsdale, NJ: Lawrence Erlbaum Associates.

Koschmann, T. (1996b). Paradigm shifts and instructional technology. In T. Koschmann (Ed.), *CSCL: Theory and practice of an emerging paradigm* (pp. 1–23). Mahwah, NJ: Lawrence Erlbaum Associates.

Koschmann, T. (2002a). Dewey's contribution to the foundations of CSCL research. In G. Stahl (Ed.), *Computer support for collaborative learning: Foundations for a CSCL community: Proceedings of CSCL 2002* (pp. 17–22). Boulder, CO: Lawrence Erlbaum Associates.

Koschmann, T. (2002b). Dewey's critique of Thorndike's behaviorism. Paper presented at the AERA 2002, New Orleans, LA.

Koschmann, T., Hall, R., & Miyake, N. (Eds.). (2002). *CSCL2: Carrying forward the conversation*. Mahwah, NJ: Lawrence Erlbaum Associates.

Koschmann, T., Stahl, G., & Zemel, A. (2005). The video analyst's manifesto (or The implications of Garfinkel's policies for the development of a program of video analytic research within the learning sciences). In R. Goldman, R. Pea, B. Barron, & S. Derry (Eds.), *Video research in the learning sciences.*

Koschmann, T., Zemel, A., Conlee-Stevens, M., Young, N., Robbs, J., & Barnhart, A. (2003). Problematizing the problem: A single case analysis in a dPBL meeting. In B. Wasson, S. Ludvigsen, & U. Hoppe (Eds.), *Designing for change in networked learning environments: Proceedings of the International Conference on Computer Support for Collaborative Learning (CSCL '03)* (pp. 37–46). Bergen, Norway: Kluwer Publishers.

Lave, J., & Wenger, E. (1991). *Situated learning: Legitimate peripheral participation.* New York: Cambridge University Press.

LeBaron, C. (2002). Technology does not exist independent of its use. In T. Koschmann, R. Hall, & N. Miyake (Eds.), *CSCL 2: Carrying forward the conversation* (pp. 433–439). Mahwah, NJ: Lawrence Erlbaum Associates.

Levinson, S. C. (2000). *Presumptive meanings: The theory of generalized conversational implicature*. Cambridge, MA: MIT Press.

Lingnau, A., Hoppe, H. U., & Mannhaupt, G. (2003). Computer supported collaborative writing in an early learning classroom. *Journal of Computer Assisted Learning, 19*(2), 186–194.

Lipponen, L., Hakkarainen, K., & Paavola, S. (2004). Practices and orientations of CSCL. In J.-W. Strijbos, P. Kirschner, & R. Martens (Eds.), *What we know about CSCL: And implementing it in higher education* (pp. 31–50). Dordrecht, Netherlands: Kluwer Academic Publishers.

Newman, D., Griffin, P., & Cole, M. (1989). *The construction zone: Working for cognitive change in schools*. Cambridge: Cambridge University Press.

Nicolopoulou, A., & Cole, M. (1993). Generation and transmission of shared knowledge in the culture of collaborative learning: The fifth dimension, its playworld and its institutional contexts. In E. Forman, N. Minnick, & C. A. Stone (Eds.), *Contexts for learning: Sociocultural dynamics in children's development*. New York: Oxford University Press.

Nussbaum, B. (1993, June 7). Hot products: Smart design is the common thread. *Business Week*, 40–43.

O'Malley, C. (1995). *Computer supported collaborative learning*. Berlin: Springer Verlag.

Rommetveit, R. (1974). *On message structure: A framework for the study of language and communication*. New York: Wiley & Sons.

Rorty, R. (1974). *Philosophy and the mirror of nature*. Princeton, NJ: Princeton University Press.

Roschelle, J. (1992). Learning by collaborating: Convergent conceptual change. *Journal of the Learning Sciences, 2*, 235–276.

Rummel, N., & Spada, H. (2005). Learning to collaborate: An instructional approach to promoting collaborative problem solving in computer-mediated settings. *Journal of the Learning Sciences, 14*(2), 201–241.

Sacks, H. (1992). *Lectures on conversation, Volume 1*. Cambridge: Blackwell.

Scardamalia, M., & Bereiter, C. (1991). Higher levels of agency in knowledge building: A challenge for the design of new knowledge media. *Journal of the Learning Sciences, 1*, 37–68.

Scardamalia, M., & Bereiter, C. (1996). Computer support for knowledge-building communities. In T. Koschmann (Ed.), *CSCL: Theory and practice of an emerging paradigm* (pp. 249–268). Mahwah, NJ: Lawrence Erlbaum Associates.

Sfard, A. (1998). On two metaphors for learning and the dangers of choosing just one. *Educational Researcher*, 27(2), 4–13.

Sperber, D., & Wilson, D. (1986). *Relevance: Communication and cognition.* Cambridge, MA: Harvard University Press.

Stahl, G. (2006). *Group cognition: Computer support for building collaborative knowledge.* Cambridge, MA: MIT Press.

Suthers, D. D., & Hundhausen, C. D. (2002, April). Influence of representations on students' elaborations during collaborative learning. Paper presented at the American Educational Research Association, New Orleans, LA.

Thorndike, E. L. (1912). *Education: A first book.* New York: Macmillan.

Van der Pol, J., Admiraal, W., & Simons, R.-J. (2003). Grounding in electronic discussions: Standard (threaded) versus anchored discussion. Paper presented at the international conference of Computer-Supported Collaborative Learning (CSCL 2003), Bergen, Norway.

Vygotsky, L. (1930/1978). *Mind in society.* Cambridge, MA: Harvard University Press.

Whitworth, B., Gallupe, B., & McQueen, R. (2000). A cognitive three-process model of computer-mediated group interaction. *Group Decision and Negotiation*, 9, 431–456.

Zemel, A., Xhafa, F., & Stahl, G. (2005). Analyzing the organization of collaborative math problem-solving in online chats using statistics and conversation analysis. Paper presented at the CRIWG International Workshop on Groupware, Racife, Brazil.

25 Mobile Learning

Mike Sharples and Roy Pea

Since the dawn of humanity, people have learned outdoors while on the move. Now, mobile phones and tablet computers are enhancing this personal form of learning by connecting across time and space. In many developing countries, including most of sub-Saharan Africa, there is no fixed line communication infrastructure, so a wireless mobile device provides the first opportunity to access the Internet or even to hold a telephone conversation. In every country, children and adults increasingly have mobile access to Web resources.

The modern era of mobile learning devices may be traced back to the 1970s and a team led by Alan Kay at the Xerox Palo Alto Research Center. The team members proposed a low-cost wireless handheld device named the Dynabook. Inspired by educational theories from Jerome Bruner and Seymour Papert, the Dynabook would support active involvement and interaction with dynamic simulations of physical systems, and allow learners to share their creative ideas. Figure 25.1 shows an illustration from Kay's 1972 paper "A Personal Computer for Children of All Ages" of two children engaged in a shared simulation game on wirelessly linked Dynabooks, where winning involves understanding and controlling the thrust and motion of rockets in a planet's gravitational field (Kay, 1972).

In the 1970s, technology was not sufficiently advanced to construct a working Dynabook. But four decades later, technology has caught up, through the widespread availability of low-cost tablet computers and sophisticated mobile phones, all connected to the Internet. When well-designed educational software is installed, these networked handheld devices can provide interactive access to learning resources and support learning dialogues across widely differing settings and cultures.

The earliest major mobile learning project was Mobilearn, involving 24 partners from academia and industry across 10 countries (Bo, 2005). Its broad ambition was to develop, implement, and evaluate a learning system for work and leisure, based on theories of effective teaching and learning in mobile environments. The focus of the project was to develop and support learning outside classrooms, including learning in museums, studying for a work-related MBA, and learning to manage medical workplace emergencies. Mobilearn developed a general-purpose software platform for mobile learning incorporating location tracking indoors and outdoors and delivery

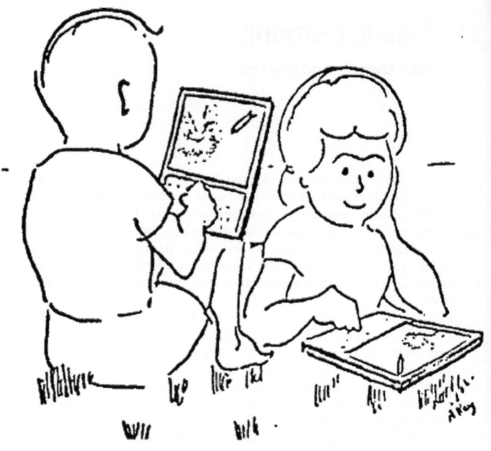

Figure 25.1. *Illustration by Alan Kay of children learning outdoors on wirelessly connected tablet computers through shared simulation games (Kay, 1972).*

of multimedia content to a variety of mobiles. Trials were conducted on university campuses and in Florence's Uffizi Gallery.

In a final meeting of Mobilearn, researchers reflected on what they had learned as project partners. They concluded mobile learning should be reconceived around *learner mobility* rather than technology – that learning interleaves with other everyday activities, complementing yet at times also conflicting with formal education. The project identified a need to provide structure and support for mobilised learners, the challenges involved in evaluating learning occurring outdoors, and ethical issues including people's rights to not have their learning activities continually monitored.

Mobile learning is now moving beyond research and pilot projects towards large-scale applications. One recent initiative is English in Action (EIA): a nine-year project, since May 2008, to help 25 million people in Bangladesh improve their communicative English language skills. A partnership between the Bangladesh government and the United Kingdom's Department for International development (DFID), it also involves The Open University and the British Broadcasting Corporation (BBC). The project is providing audio and visual learning materials on micro-SD cards for mobile phones, with portable rechargeable speakers, to support the professional development of teachers of English. Each video sequence on the mobile phones starts with a narrator explaining the teaching activity, followed by an example of its use in the classroom. After a pilot phase with 690 teachers, EIA conducted two large-scale quantitative studies. One lesson from each of the 350 primary teachers and 141 of the secondary teachers in the project was observed and the results were compared to those found in a baseline study. The study found that teachers' competence in English improved, they used English most of the time for classroom conversation, and they preferred the new communicative classroom activities to traditional English teaching through grammar lessons (Walsh et al., 2012). The pilot study is being scaled up to 12,500 teachers.

Another part of English in Action, BBC Janala, provides daily three-minute audio lessons on mobile phones to adults wishing to improve their English language skills. Anyone can learn and practice English by calling a mobile short code, for the cost of 50 paisa (half a penny) a minute. In the first two years of the project nearly 24 million people (a quarter of the adult population in Bangladesh) accessed English in Action media (English in Action, 2013).

Seamless Learning

As children and adults come to possess networked mobile devices, networked learning extends beyond classrooms and homes to become part of everyday life (Sharples, 2000), blurring the boundaries between formal and informal learning (Crowley, Pierroux, & Knutson, Chapter 23, this volume).

School classrooms offer a limited range of sensory experiences and learning contexts. The world beyond classrooms is much richer and more diverse, but is not designed to foster maximum learning. Mobile devices provide us with opportunities to combine the distinct strengths of formal and informal learning environments (Bransford et al., 2006) – the direct instruction and space for reflection in classrooms and the authentic, contextualized learning that can occur in the world outside schools, in homes, communities, and nature.

Advocates of *seamless learning* (Chan et al., 2006; Kuh, 1996) propose that previously distinct experiences of learning (in-class and out-of-class; academic and nonacademic; curricular and cocurricular; on-campus and off-campus) should be bound together to seem continuous. Such learning may be intentional, when a learning activity starts in a classroom and continues through discussion with colleagues or online at home. It can be accidental, when an interesting piece of information from a newspaper or TV programme sets off a learning journey leading to exploration, discussion, or formal learning. Wong and Looi (2011; MSL5 as revised by Wong, 2012) proposed 10 characteristics of "mobile-assisted seamless learning" (MSL):

(MSL1) Encompassing formal and informal learning;

(MSL2) Encompassing personalised and social learning;

(MSL3) Across time;

(MSL4) Across locations;

(MSL5) Ubiquitous access to learning resources (online data and information, teacher-created materials, student artefacts, student online interactions, etc.);

(MSL6) Encompassing physical and digital worlds;

(MSL7) Combined use of multiple device types (including "stable" technologies such as desktop computers, interactive whiteboards);

(MSL8) Seamless switching between multiple learning tasks (such as data collection, analysis, and communication);

(MSL9) Knowledge synthesis (a combination of prior and new knowledge, multiple levels of thinking skills, and multidisciplinary learning);

(MSL10) Encompassing multiple pedagogical or learning activity models.

So we can see how mobile learning merges into a fluid activity of learning pathways within and across locations, institutions, and social situations. The teacher has a central role, but as a learning orchestrator rather than an authority delivering information to learners. Within classrooms, wireless mobile devices can facilitate access to information while assisting teachers in managing transitions between individual, group, and whole-class activity (e.g., Goldman, Pea, Maldonado, Martin, & White, 2004; Stroup, Ares, & Hurford, 2005; White & Pea, 2011). Outside classrooms, mobile devices can continue to orchestrate and guide learning, offering toolkits to probe the natural environment, storing information for retrieval and annotation, and supporting learning conversations.

Seamless mobile learning provides a powerful vision. There are at least four reasons to suggest such learning would be more effective than traditional classroom instruction. First, seamless learning is interwoven with other everyday activities, such as chatting, reading, shopping, or watching TV, and these activities become resources for learning. As Dewey (1897, 1938) proposed, learning emerges when a person strives to overcome a problem or breakdown in everyday activity, or recognises part of the continual flow of activity and conversation as worth remembering. Second, in seamless learning, the control and management of learning is distributed. In a classroom, the locus of control over learning traditionally remains firmly with the teacher, but for mobile learning it may diffuse across learners, guides, teachers, technologies, and resources such as books, buildings, plants, and animals. Third, seamless learning takes advantage of the fact that we are always *in a context*, situated in a location at a point in time surrounded by objects, persons, and resources, and at the same time we *create context* through interactions with our surroundings, by holding conversations, making notes, and modifying nearby objects. Fourth, with well-designed mobile applications, everyday natural interactions between people and their surroundings can be transformed into learning opportunities by providing tools to interpret objects in the world, collect data, converse with people in other locations, and reflect on experience. For example, augmented reality overlays computer-generated graphics, video, or audio onto a person's experience of the surrounding world.

Mobile Learning in Practice

Two primary motivations drive the increasing interest in mobile learning. The first is a desire to equip each student with a powerful individual device, as this could provide a customised and personalized learning experience, and we know that students learn more effectively when they build on their own current understanding and make learning choices (Gureckis & Markant, 2012; Schwartz & Arena, 2013). The second is an increasing recognition that in the 21st century, people must continue to learn throughout their lifetimes, as knowledge advances and technologies rapidly change (NRC, 2012).

Mobile Devices and the 1-to-1 Classroom

Colella (2000) reported a classroom project run by the MIT Media Lab to design and evaluate small wearable devices ("Tags") for children to engage in a computer simulation of a physical system, not by watching it unfold on a computer screen, but by acting out the simulation themselves. Each Tag had a two-digit number display and five bicolour LED lights. The Tags could communicate automatically as children wearing them moved within range of one another. In one successful game, children acted as virus transmitters. At the start of the game, one child unknowingly carried a simulated virus. The children moved around the classroom as they wished and the virus started to spread, shown by LED lights flashing red when the Tag was "sick." Most of the Tags become infected, but not all of them, because some Tags were "immune." The simulation is governed by five preprogrammed rules – the children's task is to infer these rules of infection by repeatedly running the simulation. The rules (from Colella, 2000) are:

- The virus is latent (invisible) for approximately three minutes.
- Any person with a Tag with the virus, even if it is not visible, can infect another person's Tag.
- The probability for infection when meeting an infected Tag is 100 per cent.

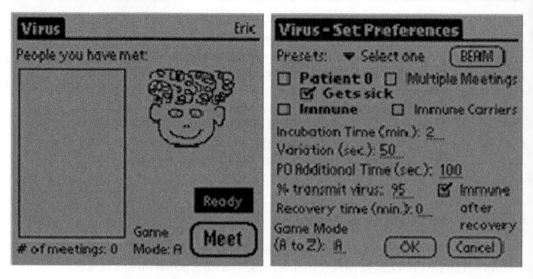

Figure 25.2. *User and settings screens for the handheld version of the* Virus Game.

- People with Tags numbered 1 or 2 in the ones position (1, 2, 11, 12, 21, etc.) (as shown on the number display) are immune to the virus.
- Immune Tags are not carriers of the disease.

A study of children playing the *Virus Game* in class revealed not only that it was highly engaging, but that children collectively enacted an inquiry learning process to uncover the game's rules. The teacher oversaw the activity, but did not guide students towards a correct answer. In one class Colella studied, children started by moving around the classroom without prior planning, reacting to events. They willingly adopted the role allocated by their personal Tags and "died" when the lights flashed red. Then they restarted the simulation and in a series of repeated trials, over five sessions, they began to predict who might be the initial disease carrier ("Patient Zero") and why some children never died. In subsequent sessions they modified their behavior – for example, deliberately not moving – to try and uncover the rules of the virus infection. The children Colella interviewed were able to explain part of the virus transmission rules, and some made analogies to the AIDS virus, exclaiming that they had "caught HIV." A later version of the game was implemented on handheld devices (Figure 25.2).

This early study provides a microcosm of mobile learning, demonstrating many of its opportunities and issues. Class time was devoted to the *Virus Game* for five days over a three-week period, so children repeatedly engaged in a game, reflected on and discussed outcomes, planned to vary the activity, and reran the game. Communication and collaboration were essential *Virus Game* elements, in the embodied interactions between children moving around the room passing on the infection, and in their reflective discussions and agreement on how to run the next game iteration. The potential for learning came from allowing each learner to experience an indeterminate situation and then to inquire into its underlying structure (Colella, 2000).

Personalized learning with mobile devices presents challenges for a teacher to convene and orchestrate the activity. When learning is based on active inquiry, as in the *Virus Game*, then the teacher must guide the learners as they build shared understandings. If all the activity takes place within class – as in the previous example – then the teacher may observe and guide its flow, but if children engage in learning activities with mobile devices at home or outdoors, then the teacher needs to conduct a semi-improvised lesson that integrates their findings into a productive outcome. Managing this process requires teacher professional development to refine these new pedagogical strategies.

Finally, there is the issue of what is actually learned and whether the technology assists or hinders that learning. Children had experiences of playing an active part of a virus simulation, but there is no evidence that the children gained a deep understanding of epidemiology or of scientific inquiry. Subsequent school-based mobile learning projects have explored these same themes: embodied engagement, personalisation and collaboration, orchestration, and teacher development. Roschelle and Pea (2002) identified opportunities for Wireless Internet Learning Devices (or WILDs) to support a new learning dynamic, where a teacher-provided question is shown on each child's device and each child's response is shown on a classroom whiteboard display. For example, the teacher could send a concept map of a topic to all devices, asking each child to indicate the concept or link that is most difficult to understand. All the responses are overlaid on the classroom screen, provoking a class discussion.

Nussbaum and colleagues (Nussbaum et al., 2009) in MCSCL and Roschelle and colleagues with the GroupScribbles environment (Roschelle et al., 2011) established a joint investigation into handheld devices for classroom collaborative learning, building on the WILD design principles. In MCSCL, children work in groups of three to four and attempt to solve problems. The same problem is presented to all the students on their personal devices, requiring a closed response (for example, selecting the answer to a multiple choice question) or an open response (for example, writing a text paragraph or a graph). Each learner attempts to answer the question individually. Then when all are ready, they compare answers within their group. If all answers are correct (or for open responses, if they all agree), then they must all select a consensus answer to send to the teacher. If the answer is shown as wrong or they disagree, then they must talk together till they reach a correct or agreed answer. The teacher then uses responses sent by each group as a focus for classroom discussion.

Zurita and Nussbaum (2004) compared MCSCL learning gains with an equivalent collaborative learning (CL) condition where students are given the same problems, in math and language, and asked to follow the same process, but with pen and paper rather than handheld devices. They found significant gains for MCSCL. One aspect of MCSCL's success appears to result from handhelds performing the dual role of providing external representations and coordinating different types of conversation. Each learner has the opportunity to solve a problem, then to re-represent and discuss it within their group, and then to present it immediately for a teacher-managed discussion.

Mobile Learning outside the Classroom

A parallel stream of mobile learning projects outside the classroom has explored the value of "being in the wild": having a personal experience of a phenomenon or environment, such as a multimedia simulation, museum, or field trip environment. Typically, such environments are engaging, rich, and complex, raising the issue of how to get learners to attend to relevant aspects of the unfolding situation and uncover its essential features or implicit rules (Klopfer & Squire, 2008). In mobile learning during museum visits or field trips, the processes of reflection need to be managed, by designing technologies that encourage children to pause and think (Lonsdale, 2011), or by setting up a classroom-like environment associated with field locations (Facer et al., 2004), or by enabling children to collect appropriately detailed, contextualized information for analysis back in the classroom (Vavoula, Sharples, Rudman, Meek, & Lonsdale, 2009).

The tension between allowing each child to experience the phenomenon and providing opportunities for collaborative sense making and planning is explored in mobile learning projects including WILD (Roschelle, Patton, & Tatar, 2007; Roschelle & Pea, 2002), Collpad (Nussbaum et al., 2009), and Personal Inquiry (Anastopoulou et al., 2012).

Mobile learning projects outside classrooms draw on a long educational tradition of informal, experiential, and inquiry learning (e.g., Dewey, 1916; Freire, 1996; Illich, 1971; Knowles, 1984; Kolb & Fry, 1975; Livingstone, 1999). What principally distinguishes mobile learning from this previous work is that the technology is a means not only of providing learning materials when and where they are needed, but also tools for scaffolding, orchestrating, and connecting the learning across contexts.

The Personal Inquiry project helps young people aged 11–14 understand themselves and their world through scientific processes of active inquiry across formal and informal settings. The project developed an approach of "scripted inquiry," where scripts are like dynamic lesson plans implemented on children's personal devices for orchestrating learning. The nQuire Software runs on personal "netbook" computers and smartphones, using their built-in sensors to provide a mobile scientific toolkit. The project developed a

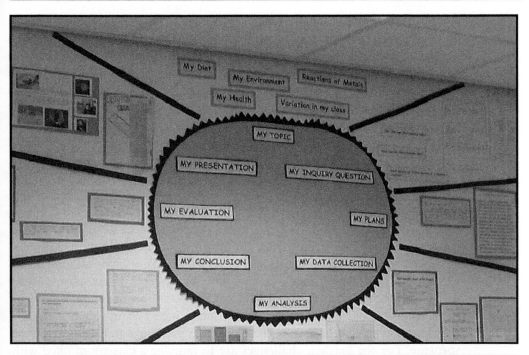

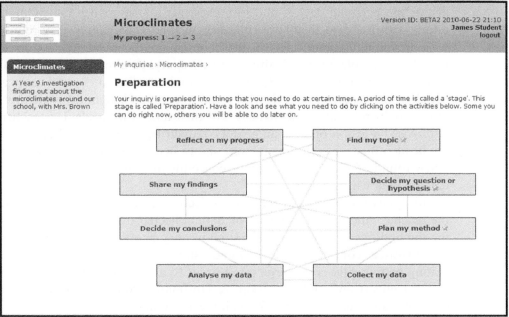

Figure 25.3. *Representation of the personal inquiry process on the classroom wall (top) and on the nQuire screen (bottom).*

depiction of the personal inquiry learning process (Figure 25.3) as both a shared representation in class and an interactive guide on the nQuire screen.

Children typically start a teacher-managed science investigation in class, then continue it at home or outside, supported by nQuire; they then share, discuss, and present findings in class. The Personal Inquiry project conducted trials in two schools with topics engaging and relevant to young people's lives – "healthy eating," "food decay and waste," "micro-climates in school playground," and "the effect of noise pollution on bird feeding." Six school-based trials were conducted to evaluate this combination of technology and pedagogy. Results indicated positive effects on learning outcomes for the personal inquiry children compared with a control class. They also maintained enjoyment of science lessons. Participant interviews across trials revealed how children and their teachers increased understanding of inquiry learning (Anastopoulou et al., 2012).

Personal Inquiry and similar projects, including LETS GO (Pea et al., 2012) and SCY (de Jong et al., 2010), have shown it is possible to connect learning in and out of classrooms using mobile devices to orchestrate the learning, deliver contextually relevant resources, and exploit mobile devices as inquiry toolkits. These efforts also raise deep challenges for extending this type of learning more widely within education systems. Each learner needs to be equipped with a personal Internet device usable at home, outdoors, or in school. Children need to be supported in inquiry and collaboration as they move from instruction by the teacher to guidance and support by the software. For the teacher, challenges are to manage a classroom filled with distracting personal devices and to orchestrate a lesson when the children return with the data they have collected outside. The children may return with broken equipment, inconsistent or missing data, or unexpected findings. For example, in the Healthy Eating inquiry, children took photos of their meals each day, using nQuire to log each meal's content and show a bar chart of its nutrition. In the classroom integration lesson, many children were initially reluctant to share images of their unhealthy meals. The teacher improvised a lesson on data anonymity, reassuring the children they would not be identified when the images were shown in class. They then carried out a new round of photo diary activity, collecting and sharing more complete data on their eating habits.

This type of lesson can be seen as a collective sense-making activity, with the teacher guiding the exposure of data collected outside and interpreting the findings in relation to the initial inquiry question. Sense making is "a motivated, continuous effort to understand connections (which can be among people, places, and events) in order to anticipate their trajectories and act effectively" (Klein, Moon, & Hoffman, 2006). It is an essential cognitive and social process for gaining awareness of a complex situation (De Jaegher & Di Paulo, 2007; also see NRC, 2009), understanding one's place in society, and interpreting scientific findings. Mobile learning provides opportunities to connect sense making outdoors and at home into classroom activities, relating emerging data to a shared inquiry question or hypothesis, and revising the question in the light of the emerging evidence.

A Theory of Mobile Learning

Several decades of learning sciences research have documented how conversation between learners contributes to learning (Miyake & Kirschner, Chapter 21, this volume; Andriessen & Baker, Chapter 22, this volume; Stahl, Koschmann, & Suthers, Chapter 24, this volume). A learning conversation may be with teachers, experts, or peers. One way that conversation contributes to learning is by enabling and requiring learners to externalise their developing understandings (Eisenberg & Pares, Chapter 17, this volume), and this contributes to metacognitive awareness (Winne & Azevedo, Chapter 4, this volume). To engage in a productive learning conversation, all parties need access to a shared external representation of the subject matter.

Even before the advent of computers, technologies were developed to externalise classroom understanding: slate tablets, student notebooks, blackboards, and interactive whiteboards allowed teachers to explain difficult concepts and students to express their thoughts. Shortly after computers were brought into schools, learning scientists began to develop software to structure learning conversations, typically called computer-supported collaborative learning (CSCL – Stahl et al., Chapter 24, this volume). Many learning scientists have developed computer applications that support learners in externalising knowledge, even in abstract and complex subject matter such as complex systems (Wilensky & Jacobson, Chapter 16, this volume).

To optimise learning, teachers must manage these conversations so that they remain aligned with the curriculum and progress towards desired learning outcomes. Learning scientists use the concept of "orchestration" to describe a teacher's management of a classroom in which each child has access to a computational device (Dillenbourg, Järvelä, & Fischer, 2009; Dillenbourg & Jermann, 2010; Roschelle & Pea, 2002). In orchestration, the teacher creates a "script" (like a dynamic lesson plan) that runs on every learner's device and assists the teacher in allocating resources, assigning learners to groups, presenting materials, setting constraints, monitoring progress, enabling communication and shared activity, and integrating outcomes (Collins, Mulholland, & Gaved, 2011). In the ManyScripts software (Dillenbourg & Jermann, 2010), teachers can choose and edit scripts so that they guide lesson flow. One such script is ArgueGraph, where a teacher designs a multiple choice question, with each student selecting an answer. The spread of answers is displayed for all to see and the teacher uses the range of answers to guide a classroom discussion.

With mobile learning, these conversations can be taken outside the classroom. They may be conducted outdoors, or at a distance between people on the move. The common ground is continually shifting as people move in and out of communication and change technologies and contexts.

Context and Learning

Sociocultural and situated perspectives have been influential in the learning sciences (see Greeno & Engeström, Chapter 7, this volume). In the sociocultural perspective, all learning is thought to be unavoidably embedded in a physical and social context, and sociocultural research attempts to identify how different contexts can both enrich and constrain learning. The sociocultural perspective is particularly important as we study mobile learning, because with these wireless handheld devices, learning can occur anywhere, in or out of class and with or without a teacher. Consider a group of friends visiting an art gallery and standing in front of a painting. Each person has arrived at a current understanding of the painting from the path they have made through the gallery – taking in the ambience, stopping at other paintings, reading the guidebook – and also from each person's lifetime of creating and interpreting works of art, starting with childhood drawings. Standing together by the painting, they construct a learning "micro-site" by sharing and discussing their knowledge of art while viewing the painting, resourced by guide books and descriptive labels. To understand mobile learning, we need to examine how people adaptively engage with their surroundings to create impromptu micro-sites of learning – and how they carry that learning from one setting to another (Pea, 1992, 1993, 1994).

Augmentation and Ubiquitous Learning

Today's mobile technologies support ubiquitous learning – learning anywhere, any time. Smartphones and tablet computers are powerful computers capable of guiding learning activities. They are also scientific toolkits, with embedded cameras, voice recorders, increasingly many sensors, and multimedia communications. Further, there are now technologies available that can support mobile learning even when students do not personally carry a mobile device. For example, a building can be augmented with sensors that detect where people are and with communicators that provide occupants with information about energy usage (also see Eisenberg & Pares, Chapter 17, this volume). With the GPS capabilities of today's wireless devices, it is possible to create location-specific messages – for example, "virtual tourist trails" as visitors walk around a city. Thus technology is used to *augment* everyday experience, such that everyday objects and locations become "learning enabled" (Spohrer, 1999).

Mobile devices, combined with augmented environments, potentially allow learners to decide where and when to learn. Rather than sign up for a class and go to a school to learn something, they would instead continue with their everyday activities, retrieving knowledge and learning only when it becomes useful.

The site of a historic battle, the underlying rock formations in a mountain landscape, or the daily energy consumption of a building's rooms cannot be readily seen from visual inspection or data probing. This is why augmenting reality is potentially so powerful for learning. As an example, the fabric of an engineering building at Marquette University in Wisconsin has been instrumented to enable students to gain knowledge about building design and power generation by measuring wind speeds, structural strains, and foundation pressure on the building (Claeys, 2001). Rogers and colleagues (2004) designed forms of digital augmentation and processes by which they could be accessed as part of an outdoor learning experience ("Ambient Wood"), to encourage sixth grade students to conduct contextualized scientific inquiry and reflect on their interactions. Ogata and colleagues (Li, Zheng, Ogata, & Yano, 2005; Ogata, Miyata, & Yano, 2010; Ogata & Yano, 2004) have developed ubiquitous learning environments where support for learning is embedded into sensor-augmented "smart objects," such as furniture and utensils that can speak their names or describe their functions in a foreign language. In their Out There In Here project (Coughlan, Adams, Rogers, & Davies, 2011), students on field trips were connected via voice and video with other students in a base camp room. The two groups of students formed a mutually augmenting learning system, where the students in the base camp room proposed questions and provided reference information, while students in the field collected data to answer the questions and shared the experience of "being there."

Disruptive Activity

Children have always sought to disrupt the routine of the classroom by provoking the teacher or engaging in surreptitious activities. But Internet-connected mobile devices and smartphones make it possible for students to take this to a new level, enabling children to converse with one another and with the outside world by "backchanneling" through social media, breaking the classroom's hermetic seal and challenging the teacher's ability to successfully orchestrate learning (Sharples, 2002).

The early reaction of most schools and teacher organisations has been to forbid the use of mobile devices in class. However, there has been growing recognition of the need to connect formal classroom learning and informal learning (Bevan, Bell, Stevens, & Razfar, 2013), and as we pointed out earlier, mobile devices can do that very effectively. Outside school, children use their mobile devices to create social networks, to constantly converse, and they develop skills in information sharing and online research – and these skills, although developed for personal and social reasons, are valued in the knowledge economy. Although these activities may be severely restricted in school, we believe they should be recognised as complementing rather than conflicting with formal education.

Bringing these themes together, we come to see mobile learning as "processes of coming to know through conversations and explorations across multiple contexts among people and personal interactive technologies" (adapted from Sharples, Taylor, & Vavoula, 2007). This emphasises cognitive and social processes for individuals and groups to gain knowledge and reach shared understanding, by conversing with each other and exploring their surroundings, across locations and over time, enabled by a range of fixed and portable technologies.

Future Trends and Challenges

Over the past decade, the field of mobile learning has expanded from pilot research projects to large-scale deployment of technologies and services. The ubiquity of smartphones and tablets means that Internet access on the move has, for many people, become deeply interwoven into daily life. E-books are already replacing paper books; mobile Internet access is replacing desktop browsing, with a third of all Web traffic now being mobile (ComScore, 2013). A survey of Internet access by the UK Office for National Statistics (Office for National Statistics, 2013) shows that 51 per cent of adults used a mobile phone to access the Internet, rising to 80 per cent for people in the age range 16 to 34. In this age group, more than 60 per cent used their phone or other mobile device for social networking and more than 15 per cent for reading e-books. By contrast, less than 10 per cent of people older than age 55 in the United Kingdom use mobile devices for social networking or reading.

As people go through life constantly connected by mobile devices, their patterns of learning will change. Rather than acting as direct substitutes for books and informational videos, mobile devices are becoming tools for managing a lifetime of education and learning. Social networks provide a peer group of informal learning contacts. Tools such as Evernote, Dropbox, and Google Docs offer support for seamless learning across devices and contexts; emerging Massively Open Online Courses (MOOCs) provide deep dives into the best courses from leading universities (also see Sawyer, Chapter 36, this volume). New technologies for augmented reality and personal information capture will enable annotation of locations and sharing of experience.

Two examples of such innovation are contextual language learning and citizen science. In contextual language learning, people learning a foreign language use an application running on their own mobile phones to find words and phrases relevant to their location (Sweeney, Pemberton, & Sharples, 2011). These vocabulary lists have been provided by other language learners. For example, at a local restaurant a previous language learner may have provided a definition of its specialty "banoffee pie" and taken a photograph of the dessert. Then, when other people visit the restaurant they can see this along with other definitions and photographs, relevant to that specific location, provided by other language learners.

The general approach of "crowd sourced" mobile learning, where many thousands of people contribute and share location-specific information, is also being applied to citizen science. The mobile iSpot application (Woods & Scanlon, 2012) enables people to upload and share location-specific observations of wildlife and nature and to see what observations have been made nearby. The iSpot Web site has more than 18,000 registered users who take photographs and make identifications of plants and animals. Each sighting can be seen by other users who may verify the identification. A system of reputation management promotes those who provide regular and accurate identifications, awarding them virtual badges and also giving more weight to their verifications.

Shared contextual learning activities such as these are increasingly blending into the fabric of daily life. E-books are allowing readers to engage in social reading, sharing margin notes and annotations. Wearable devices, like glasses and badges, will allow location-specific experiences to be captured, shared, and recalled. Buildings and street displays will provide information about their structure, energy use, and history. People will be able to leave "virtual graffiti" at locations to record their impressions and stories.

A long-term Intel labs project has explored context awareness activity recognition. Sensors already used on consumer mobile devices for "hard" sensing (detecting location, relative motion with accelerometers, and ambient light and sound) are combined with "soft" sensing (such as device activity, social networking actions, calendar data) to produce aggregated data streams that can be interpreted to predict what an individual is doing. Intel proposes that such activity recognition may be used to guide, instruct, encourage, inform, and otherwise support a user's activities in a personalized way (Intel, 2013). Intel observes how activity recognition may be combined with elements such as gesture recognition, social proximity, and emotional classifiers (Healey, Nachman, Subramamian, Shahabdeen, & Morris, 2010) to develop a wide range of highly personalized applications.

This emerging future of continual monitoring of ambient activity raises deep ethical issues. Some of these have been identified as part of the information revolution, including problems of information overload, needs to escape from relentless connectivity, and the skills required to filter and discriminate valuable knowledge from background data noise. As information becomes contextualized, these issues will not be confined to online activity. More activity will be taken online, so that all locations become associated with a buzzing profusion of data competing for attention. Each person will face the challenge of using mobile tools to create a coherent life story that connects times, places, and social groupings, to support personally meaningful projects, and filter out unwanted distractions. Formal education may offer a sanctuary, freed from context-specific intrusions, and also an opportunity to plan and reflect on mobilised learning projects. For this to occur, teachers will need to adopt a transformed role: preparing children for a lifetime of contextualised meaning making, helping them tap funds of knowledge and experience gained from learning outside school, and fostering learning with mobile devices.

One ethical problem is that if learning is no longer seen as confined to the classroom or lecture hall, but is embedded into everyday lives, then what rights or responsibilities do schools and colleges have to guide such education across formal and informal environments? Most children are already required to perform homework. Should other online activities outside school be managed, monitored, and assessed? Should children be given inquiry science tasks to record pictures of their daily meals for a healthy eating project, or asked to monitor their heart rate for a project on fitness and exercise? These activities are all technically feasible, but what should be the ethical boundaries?

A related issue concerns the rights of young people to own and control their data and to have online spaces where they can capture and share ideas free from adult monitoring and interference. Parental fear of Internet predators and inappropriate behaviour has resulted in the home online activity of some children being continually monitored. As online activity extends outside, young people may inhabit a world without privacy, where every activity is checked. The converse is true for teachers – their classroom activities may be open to continual scrutiny by children with camera phones. A productive and ethical balance needs to be struck between seamless connectivity and guarded privacy and reflection. A new frontier beckons in mobile learning as it merges with life itself.

Conclusion

From a technology perspective, mobile learning is the provision of educational content and services to people on the move, relevant to their location, across multiple devices including smartphones and tablet computers and even wall-sized displays. To learning scientists, the emphasis and the questions concern context and continuity of learning: How can our learning opportunities be best shaped in relation to location and time?

Mobile learning takes for granted that learners are continually on the move. We learn across space, taking ideas and learning resources gained in one location and applying them in another, with multiple purposes, multiple facets of identity. We learn across time, by revisiting knowledge that was gained earlier in a different context. We move from topic to topic, managing a range of personal learning projects, rather than following a single curriculum. We also move in and out of engagement with technology, for example as we enter and leave phone coverage (Vavoula & Sharples, 2002).

An emphasis on mobility is important for understanding and supporting learning, for many reasons. As parents and teachers, we need to equip our children with skills and strategies not only for learning specific topics, but also for managing learning projects across locations and adapting learning to physical and social contexts. Teachers will need to support children bringing not only mobile devices but also their own personal learning purposes, resources, and networks into classrooms. *Context* is a central and evolving theoretical construct for mobile learning. People learn within multiple contexts; by moving through and comparing contexts; and by creating contexts from interacting with locations, artefacts, resources, and other people.

Because most previous educational research has been conducted in school settings, we know too little about how people learn outside classrooms: how they engage with their surroundings to create micro-sites of learning and carry learning from one setting to another. The science of mobile learning must examine mobility not only of individuals, but groups and societies. We are only beginning to understand how to design cities with buildings, public spaces, and services that enable not only commerce and entertainment, but also technology-enhanced meaning making: for example, enabling immigrants to learn about language and culture through a combination of interactive public displays and personal context-aware applications. How people learn through movement is a central concern, whether in sport and dance, or by moving about a conceptually rich space such as a museum or heritage centre.

New technologies can offer personalized toolsets for mobile learning, combining location-aware sensors with facilities for accessing, communicating, and sharing knowledge on the move. People in a real setting, such as a heritage site, can share situated knowledge with people online moving around a virtual simulation of that location. Citizen scientists may use mobile phones and tablets to perform experiments, to observe and share questions and information about nature. Mobile services allow people to leave "virtual graffiti," hear context-specific stories, and engage in simultaneous shared experiences across multiple locations. These offer new ways of learning, but also raise deep ethical issues of privacy, ownership, and space to reflect in an "always on" society. Learning happens through a cyclical process of engaged flow of experience, interspersed with opportunities for reflective understanding and knowledge sharing. As learning scientists we need to understand how to spark and maintain this learning engine for people, groups, and societies ever on the move.

References

Anastopoulou, A., Sharples, M., Ainsworth, S., Crook, C., O'Malley, C., & Wright, M. (2012). Creating personal meaning through technology-supported science learning across formal and informal settings. *International Journal of Science Education, 34*(2), 251–273.

Bevan, B., Bell, P., Stevens, R., & Razfar, A. (Eds.). (2013). *LOST Opportunities: Learning in out-of-school time.* New York: Springer.

Bo, G. (2005). MOBIlearn: Project Final Report. Available at http://www.mobilearn.org/results/results.htm. Accessed December 1, 2012.

Bransford, J. D., Barron, B., Pea, R., Meltzoff, A., Kuhl, P., Bell, P., Stevens, R., Schwartz, D., Vye, N., Reeves, B., Roschelle, J., & Sabelli, N. (2006). Foundations and opportunities for an interdisciplinary science of learning. In K. Sawyer (Ed.), *The Cambridge handbook of the learning sciences* (pp. 19–34). New York: Cambridge University Press.

Chan, T-W., Milrad, M., and 15 others. (2006). One-to-one technology-enhanced learning: An opportunity for global research collaboration. *Research and Practice in Technology Enhanced Learning Journal*, 1(1), 3–29.

Claeys, M. (2001). Instrumentation of buildings to enhance student learning – A case study at Marquette University's Discovery Learning Complex. Master's Theses (2009–). Paper 86. Available at http://epublications.marquette.edu/theses_open/86.

Colella, V. (2000). Participatory simulations: Building collaborative understanding through immersive dynamic modelling. *Journal of the Learning Sciences*, 9(4), 471–500.

Collins, T., Mulholland, P., & Gaved, M. (2011). Scripting personal inquiry. In K. Littleton, E. Scanlon, & M. Sharples (Eds.), *Orchestrating inquiry learning* (pp. 87–104). Abingdon: Routledge.

ComScore (2013, February). *Mobile future in focus – 2013.* ComScore.

Coughlan, T., Adams, A., Rogers, Y., & Davies, S.-J. (2011). Enabling live dialogic and collaborative learning between field and indoor contexts. In *Proceedings of the 25th BCS Conference on Human Computer Interaction* (pp. 88–98). July 4–8, 2011, Newcastle upon Tyne, UK.

De Jaegher, H., & Di Paolo, E. (2007). Participatory sense-making. *Phenomenology and the Cognitive Sciences*, 6(4), 485–507.

de Jong, T., Van Joolingen, W. R., Giemza, A., Girault, I., Hoppe, U., Kindermann, J., & the SCY Team (2010). Learning by creating and exchanging objects: The SCY experience. *British Journal of Educational Technology*, 41, 909–921.

Dewey, J. (1897). My pedagogic creed. *School Journal*, 54, 77–80.

Dewey, J. (1938). *Experience and education.* New York: Macmillan.

Dillenbourg, P., Järvelä, S., & Fischer, F. (2009). The evolution of research on computer-supported collaborative learning: From design to orchestration. In N. Balacheff, S. Ludvigsen, T. Jong, A. Lazonder, & S. Barnes (Eds.), *Technology-enhanced learning* (pp. 3–19). New York: Springer.

Dillenbourg, P., & Jermann, P. (2010). Technology for classroom orchestration. In M. S. Khine & I. M. Saleh (Eds.), *New science of learning: Cognition, computers and collaboration in education* (pp. 525–552). New York: Springer.

English in Action (2013). English in action, media and adult learning. Accessed March 1, 2013 at http://www.eiabd.com/eia/index.php/en/2012-10-04-07-26-15/adult-learning.

Facer, K., Joiner, R., Stanton, D., Reid, J., Hull, R., & Kirk, D. (2004). Savannah: Mobile gaming and learning? *Journal of Computer Assisted Learning*, 20, 399–409.

Goldman, S., Pea, R., Maldonado, H., Martin, L., & White, T. (2004). Functioning in the wireless classroom. In *Proceedings of the Third IEEE International Workshop on Wireless and Mobile Technologies in Education* (WMTE'04, pp. 75–82). New York: IEEE Press.

Gureckis T. M., & Markant D. B. (2012). Self-directed learning: A cognitive and computational perspective. *Perspectives on Psychological Science*, 7(5), 464–481.

Healey, J., Nachman, L., Subramanian, S., Shahabdeen, J., & Morris, M. (2010). Out of the lab and into the fray: Towards modeling emotion in everyday life. *Pervasive Computing*, 156–173.

Intel. (2013). Context Awareness Activity Recognition: Project. Available at http://goo.gl/PIJy4.

Kay, A. C. (1972, August). A personal computer for children of all ages. *Proceedings of the ACM National Conference*, 1(1), 1–11. Boston, MA.

Kuh, G. D. (1996). Guiding principles for creating seamless learning environments for undergraduates. *Journal of College Student Development*, 37(2), 135–148.

Klein, G., Moon, B., & Hoffman, R. F. (2006). Making sense of sensemaking I: Alternative perspectives. *IEEE Intelligent Systems*, 21(4), 70–73.

Klopfer, E., & Squire, K. (2008). Environmental detectives – the development of an augmented reality platform for environmental simulations. *Educational Technology Research and Development*, 56(2), 203–228.

Li, L., Zheng, Y., Ogata, H., & Yano, Y. (2005). A conceptual framework of computer-supported ubiquitous learning environment. *International Journal of Advanced Technology for Learning*, 2(4), 187–197.

Lonsdale, P. (2011). Design and evaluation of mobile games to support active and reflective learning outdoors. PhD Thesis, University of Nottingham. Available at http://etheses.nottingham.ac.uk/2076/.

National Research Council/NRC. (2009). *Learning science in informal environments: People, places, and pursuits. Committee on Learning Science in Informal Environments*. P. Bell, B. Lewenstein, A. W. Shouse, & M. A. Feder (Eds.). Washington, DC: National Academy Press.

National Research Council/NRC. (2012). *Education for life and work: Developing transferable knowledge and skills in the 21st century*. J. W. Pellegrino & M. L. Hilton (Eds.). Washington DC: National Academy Press.

Nussbaum, M., Alvarez, C., McFarlane, A., Gomez, F., Claro, S., & Radovic, D. (2009). Technology as small group face-to-face collaborative scaffolding. *Computers & Education*, 52(1), 147–153.

Office for National Statistics. (2013). Internet access – Households and individuals, 2012 part 2. Retrieved from http://www.ons.gov.uk/ons/dcp171778_301822.pdf.

Ogata, H., Miyata, M., & Yano, Y. (2010). JAMIOLAS2: Supporting Japanese mimetic words and onomatopoeia learning with wireless sensor networks for overseas students. *International Journal of Mobile Learning and Organisation*, 4(4), 333–345.

Ogata, H., & Yano, Y. (2004). CLUE: Computer supported ubiquitous learning environment for language learning. *IPSJ*, 45(10), 2354–2363.

Pea, R. D. (1992). Augmenting the discourse of learning with computer-based learning environments. In E. de Corte, M. Linn, H. Mandl, & L. Verschaffel

(Eds.), *Computer-based learning environments and problem-solving (NATO Series, subseries F: Computer and System Sciences)* (pp. 313–343). New York: Springer-Verlag.

Pea, R. D. (1993). Learning scientific concepts through material and social activities: Conversational analysis meets conceptual change. *Educational Psychologist*, 28, 265–277.

Pea, R. D. (1994). Seeing what we build together: Distributed multimedia learning environments for transformative communications. *Journal of the Learning Sciences*, 3(3), 285–299.

Pea, R., Milrad, M., Maldonado, H., Vogel, B., Kurti, A., & Spikol, D. (2012). Learning and technological designs for mobile science inquiry collaboratories. In K. Littleton, E. Scanlon, & M. Sharples (Eds.), *Orchestrating inquiry learning* (pp. 105–127). Abingdon: Routledge.

Rogers, Y., Price, S., Fitzpatrick, G., Fleck, R., Harris, E., Smith, H., & Weal, M. (2004). Ambient wood: Designing new forms of digital augmentation for learning outdoors. In *Proceedings of the 2004 conference on Interaction design and children: building a community* (pp. 3–10). New York: Association for Computing Machinery (ACM).

Roschelle, J., Patton, C., Schank, P., Penuel, W., Looi, C-K, Chen, W., Chan, A., Prieto, P, Villagra, S., & Dimitriadis, Y. (2011). CSCL and innovation: In classrooms, with teachers, among school leaders, in schools of education. In *Proceedings of Computer-Supported Collaborative Learning Conference, Volume III – Community Events, pp. 1073–1080*. International Society of the Learning Sciences.

Roschelle, J., Patton, C., & Tatar, D. (2007). Designing networked handheld devices to enhance school learning. *Advances in Computers*, 70, 1–60.

Roschelle, J., & Pea, R. D. (2002). A walk on the WILD side: How wireless handhelds may change computer-supported collaborative learning (CSCL*). The International Journal of Cognition and Technology*, 1(1), 145–168.

Schwartz, D. L., & Arena, D. (2013). *Measuring what matters most: Choice-based assessment in the digital age*. The John D. and Catherine T. MacArthur Foundation Reports on Digital Media and Learning. Cambridge, MA: MIT Press.

Sharples, M. (2000). The design of personal mobile technologies for lifelong learning. *Computers & Education*, 34, 177–193.

Sharples, M. (2002). Disruptive devices: Mobile technology for conversational learning. *International Journal of Continuing Engineering Education and Lifelong Learning*, 12(5/6), 504–520.

Sharples, M., Taylor, J., & Vavoula, G. (2007). A theory of learning for the mobile age. In R. Andrews & C. Haythornthwaite (Eds.), *The Sage handbook of e-learning research* (pp. 221–247). London: Sage.

Spohrer, J. C. (1999). Information in places. *IBM Systems Journal*, 38(4), 602–628.

Stroup, W. M., Ares, N. M., & Hurford, A. C. (2005). A dialectical analysis of generativity: Issues of network-supported design in mathematics and sciences. *Mathematical Thinking and Learning*, 7(3), 181–206.

Sweeney, T., Pemberton, R., & Sharples, M. (2011) Toponimo: A geosocial pervasive game for English second language learning. Proceedings of the 10th World

Conference on Mobile and Contextual Learning (mLearn 2011), October 18–21, 2011, Beijing, China, pp. 436–440.

Vavoula, G. N., & Sharples, M. (2002). KLeOS: A personal, mobile, knowledge and learning organisation system. In M. Milrad, U. Hoppe, & Kinshuk (Eds.), *Proceedings of the IEEE International Workshop on Mobile and Wireless Technologies in Education (WMTE2002)*, August 29–30, Vaxjo, Sweden, pp. 152–156.

Vavoula, G., Sharples, M., Rudman, P., Meek, J., & Lonsdale, P. (2009) Myartspace: Design and evaluation of support for learning with multimedia phones between classrooms and museums. *Computers & Education*, 53(2), 286–299.

Walsh, C. S., Shaheen, R., Power, T., Hedges, C., Katoon, M., & Mondol, S. (2012). Low cost mobile phones for large scale teacher professional development in Bangladesh. In 11th World Conference on Mobile and Contextual Learning (mLearn 2012), 1518 October, Helsinki, Finland.

White, T., & Pea, R. (2011). Distributed by design: On the promises and pitfalls of collaborative learning with multiple representations. *Journal of the Learning Sciences*, 20(3), 1–59.

Wong, L.-H. (2012). A learner-centric view of mobile seamless learning. *British Journal of Educational Technology*, 43(1), E19–E23.

Wong, L.-H., & Looi, C.-K. (2011). What seams do we remove in mobile-assisted seamless learning? A critical review of the literature. *Computers & Education*, 57(4), 2364–2381.

Woods, W., & Scanlon, E. (2012). iSpot Mobile – A natural history participatory science application. In Proceedings of Mlearn 2012, Helsinki, Finland, October 15–16.

Zurita, G., & Nussbaum, M. (2004). Computer supported collaborative learning using wirelessly interconnected handheld computers. *Computers & Education*, 42(3), 289–314.

26 Learning in Virtual Worlds

Yasmin B. Kafai and Chris Dede

Virtual worlds are among the fastest growing online communities, often with millions of participants. Some of the most popular virtual worlds, such as *Minecraft, Second Life*, and *World of Warcraft* (for adults) and *Club Penguin, Habbo Hotel, Neopets*, and *Webkinz* (for children; Kafai & Fields, 2013), have become household names. Virtual worlds can be defined as "synchronous, persistent networks of people, represented as avatars, facilitated by networked computers" (Bell, 2008, p. 2) and are characterized by the psychological feeling of immersion: the subjective sense of having a comprehensive, realistic experience in a place that one is not physically located (Dede, 2012a). The most commercially successful virtual worlds are either multiplayer videogames (e.g., *World of Warcraft*), or they are designed to help sell physical products and to increase brand loyalty among consumers. For example, *Club Penguin* is owned by the Walt Disney Company and *WebKinz* and *NeoPets* are designed to drive sales of stuffed animal toys.

In recent years, several learning scientists have conducted design-based research on the educational potential of virtual worlds technology; some of the best-known examples include *EcoMUVE, Quest Atlantis*, and *River City* (Dawley & Dede, 2014; Messinger, Stroulia, & Lyons, 2008). There are four reasons that learning scientists believe that virtual worlds offer unique potential to contribute to learning. First, virtual worlds enable participants to simulate social and economic phenomena (Bainbridge, 2007; Castronova, 2005), as well as to run experiments and manipulate microworlds, for example to explore health issues and address environmental problems (Kafai & Fefferman, 2011; Metcalf, Kamarainen, Tutwiler, Grotzer, & Dede, 2011). These features of simulation and visualization can potentially support a form of experiential learning regarding complex phenomena (see Wilensky & Jacobson, Chapter 16, this volume) that would not be possible without virtual worlds.

Second, the immersive nature of virtual worlds supports social interaction and identity exploration – and learning scientists have demonstrated that interaction and identity are critical components of learning, as predicted by sociocultural theories that frame learning as a form of legitimate participation in communities (Lave & Wenger, 1991). Participants are represented onscreen in the virtual world as an *avatar*, an image of themselves that they have designed or that they have selected from a menu of existing avatar images. Players can become members of social groups – for example, by organizing themselves in *guilds* for coordinated play – but they can also interact with artifacts, architectures, and automated agents in the virtual world without interacting with another human being. In contrast to single-player videogames, virtual worlds are *persistent*, meaning the interaction space does not cease to exist when the player leaves; rather, it continues to exist and other members of the community may continue to act in it. While virtual worlds contain many spaces to explore and encourage a sense of citizenship, participants within these communities often develop social practices that identify people as insiders and outsiders and thus can constrain membership (Boellstorff, 2008).

Third, virtual worlds tend to be highly engaging and motivating, and a large body of learning sciences research demonstrates the importance of engagement and motivation in learning (see Järvelä & Renninger, Chapter 33, this volume; also see Dawley & Dede, 2014). Many virtual worlds allow the user to decide how to explore the environment, which avatars to interact with, and which purchases to make with their virtual currency. Providing such choices enhances autonomy, and therefore motivation, yet within autonomy guidance can be provided to foster particular learning outcomes (Nelson, 2007). In addition, participation in virtual worlds that simulate scientific phenomena has been found to increase self-efficacy and improve science inquiry skills, in particular among underperforming student groups (Ketelhut, 2007). Likewise, virtual worlds designed to replicate the physical and organizational constraints of real settings, such as *simSchool* (Gibson, 2012), provide opportunities for participants to experiment with new strategies for communication and collaboration, master strategies, and then transfer them to life in the real-world classroom.

Fourth, virtual worlds provide educators with a new way to assess learning in authentic, automated, and embedded ways and then provide feedback to teachers, students, and parents (Dede, 2012b; see Pellegrino, Chapter 12, this volume). In virtual worlds, all user activity (e.g., chats, e-mails, comments, or artifacts created by users; Grimes & Fields, 2012) potentially provides data about learning, and can be used to understand levels of student engagement and patterns of inquiry. The collection and analyses of such different data points can be helpful to document and trace student learning beyond the school day over extended periods of time.

Virtual worlds can be designed for use in schools, for use out of schools, or for hybrid use in both; in the next section, we review various virtual worlds as learning environments inside and outside of schools. We provide examples of various virtual worlds, and then examine the outcomes of various research studies that have evaluated a range of learning outcomes. In the subsequent section, we examine the kinds of assessments that can be embedded in virtual worlds. Although there are many available assessment methods, we highlight two: learning analytics and connective ethnographies that showcase how the design of virtual worlds affords particular opportunities to collect and work with massive datasets. In the final section, we discuss three issues we believe are important for future research on virtual worlds: scaling them up to large number of participants, integrating expert advice with animated pedagogical agents, and creating hybrid learning environments that contain elements of both virtual worlds and the real-world classroom.

Designs for Learning in Virtual Worlds

Any virtual world, by design, can be used anywhere – including both inside and outside of classrooms. But designers frame activities differently when they are designing specifically for a classroom application. When a child participates in a virtual world at home, or in any other out of school setting, the child is free to engage in activities of their own choosing – much like a visitor to a science center or other informal learning environment (see Crowley, Pierroux, & Knutson, Chapter 23, this volume). In contrast, classrooms typically assign a specific time when students engage in virtual worlds and also assign what activities they do in that world, and classroom teachers and curricula can provide degrees of support for learning that are rarely present at home. The strengths and limits of classrooms and homes as sites for virtual worlds are often interwoven, and strategies for use involve managing various trade-offs.

Inside Schools

In recent years, learning scientists have developed several virtual worlds designed for use in science classrooms, and these have been demonstrated to have superior learning outcomes when compared to conventional instruction. Most of these applications involve the development of a virtual world, in combination with off-line curricular elements, including conventional instruction and assessment. One of the most successful examples is *Quest Atlantis* (http://www.questatlantis.org/) (Barab, Sadler, Heiselt, Hickey, & Zuiker, 2007). For example, in the case of the Taiga Virtual Park in *Quest Atlantis*, teachers can support an 11-year-old in taking on the role of a scientist who uses disciplinary understanding of water quality to solve an authentic problem and observe the consequences of his or her choices, thereby providing an element of experiential consequentiality not usually possible in the classroom (Barab et al., 2007). Comparison studies (Barab et al., 2009) show learning and motivation gains over traditional science curricula.

As a second example of a curriculum centered on a virtual world and developed for use in classrooms, *River City* (http://muve.gse.harvard.edu/rivercityproject/) is designed to teach students how to form hypotheses and design experiments, as well as content related to national standards and

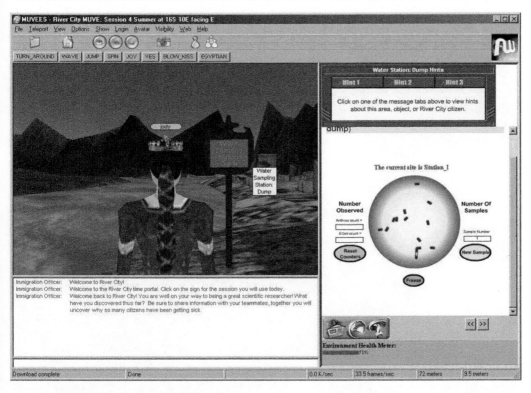

Figure 26.1. *Experimentation in* River City.

assessments in biology and epidemiology (Dede, 2009a). Students learn to behave as scientists as they collaboratively identify problems through observation and inference, form and test hypotheses, and deduce evidence-based conclusions about underlying causes. Learners immerse themselves in a simulated, historically accurate 19th-century city (Figure 26.1). Collaborating in teams of three or four participants, they try to figure out why people are getting sick. They talk to various residents in this simulated setting – such as children and adults who have fallen ill, hospital employees, merchants, and university scientists. Evaluations of *River City* classroom implementations showed that a broader range of students gained substantial knowledge and skills in scientific inquiry than through conventional instruction or equivalent learning experiences delivered via a board game (Clarke & Dede, 2009).

Furthermore, students were deeply engaged by this curriculum, and they developed sophisticated problem-finding skills (in a complex setting with many phenomena, problems must be identified and formulated before they can be solved). Compared with a similar, paper-based curriculum that included laboratory experiences, students overall (regardless of factors such as gender, ethnicity, or English language proficiency) were more engaged in the immersive interface and learned as much or more (Ketelhut, Nelson, Clarke, & Dede, 2010).

Figure 26.2. *Data collection at the* EcoMUVE *pond.*

As a third example, the *EcoMUVE* curriculum (http://ecomuve.gse. harvard.edu) focuses on the potential of immersive authentic simulations to teach ecosystems science concepts, scientific inquiry (collaborative and individual), and complex causality in middle schools (Metcalf, Kamarainen, Grotzer, & Dede, 2012). In *EcoMUVE*, two virtual worlds simulate pond and forest virtual ecosystems, and each represents an ecological scenario involving complex causality (Figure 26.2). Students investigate research questions by exploring the virtual ecosystems and collecting data from a variety of sources over time, taking on roles as ecosystems scientists. *EcoMUVE* uses a jigsaw pedagogy (Dede, 2013: students work in teams of four and are assigned roles based on areas of expertise (e.g., botanist, microscopic specialist) and use interactive learning quests to learn more about the content specific to their module (e.g., what is pH?). Each student then performs data collection specific to his or her assigned role, sharing these data with teammates within the immersive interface via tables and graphs. Each team works collaboratively to analyze the combined data and understand the ecosystem interrelationships. The module culminates in each team creating an evidence-based concept map representing its understanding of the causal relationships in the ecosystem and presenting this to the class. Early findings (Grotzer, Kamarainen, Tutwiler, Metcalf, & Dede, 2012; Kamarainen, Metcalf, Grotzer, & Dede, 2012; Metcalf et al., 2012) document gains in student engagement and learning in ecosystems science and complex causality.

Classroom settings offer the opportunity to design and implement the virtual world with the teacher as a resource. However, there is also the risk that the teacher might not implement the curriculum in the manner its designers intended, inadvertently undercutting student learning (Dede, 2005). As with all educational innovations, teacher professional development is essential (see Fishman, Davis, & Chan, Chapter 35, this volume). For example, over the last two years of the *River City* project, 94 percent of participating teachers rated as useful a four-hour online pre-implementation training program. In-field *River City* trainers reported fewer problems with teachers undercutting intended pedagogy among those educators who invested time in either the face-to-face or the online professional development (Dede, 2009b).

Schools often have inadequate technology infrastructures for the one-to-one student-computer ratios required to make virtual world learning successful. For example, in the *River City* curriculum a chronic implementation problem in classroom settings was teachers' access to an adequate, reliable technology infrastructure. In schools where teachers had to take their class down the hall to a technology lab to use *River City*, other teachers who also wanted to use the technology lab were resentful. When schools instead created just-in-time classroom infrastructures using laptops on carts that could be rolled into different classrooms as necessary, precious time was lost each session in activating the network among machines and the server.

Further, for reasons of security, student safety, and privacy, districts often have idiosyncratic ways of enabling network access to outside resources, some as extreme as simply blocking all external Web sites (see Schofield, 2006). For implementations of the *River City* curriculum in hundreds of schools during the 2008–2009 academic year, the project team included a quarter-time technology specialist to handle, sometimes school by school, these idiosyncratic network configurations (Dede, 2009b). For example, districts sometimes interpret the Child Internet Protection Act (CIPA) to imply that they must disable by default many of the Internet capabilities that are essential to the operation of a virtual world, a situation that is technically, logistically, and organizationally difficult to change. In these contexts, "virtual" environments must be completely closed (e.g., no external URLs). To support these school districts, a closed version of the *EcoMUVE* curriculum has been developed.

After using a virtual world in the classroom, students often are so highly engaged that they want to continue using the environment at home. This can increase immersion, enhance engagement, and more closely align science instruction with students' informal learning strategies. However, allowing students to use the same virtual world in school and at home presents several challenges. Students who have good computers and high-bandwidth Internet at home have an advantage over those who do not. Further, if the virtual world is multiuser, then students might engage in inappropriate behavior when they are unsupervised (e.g., cyberbullying, swearing). Although informal communities like *Whyville* (discussed later) rely on peer pressure to enforce positive social norms, to guarantee a safe setting the developers restricted use of the *River City* curriculum to in-school settings (class, lunch period, before or after school) in which an adult was present as monitor. They also built an automated "swear checker" that would respond to the use of bad words in student chat, reminding them to watch their language. They provided teachers each morning with chat logs of their students from the previous day, so that they could closely monitor student activities to encourage appropriate, on-task behaviors (Clarke & Dede, 2009). Students quickly realized they were being closely monitored in the virtual world.

Outside Schools

When virtual worlds are used outside of schools, players are more self-directed in their activities, and also there are significantly more participants. Many virtual worlds incorporate short casual games, and players can often accrue virtual "currency" by playing these games successfully. Virtual worlds designed by learning scientists likewise often contain educational videogames and currency. For instance, in *Whyville*, playing various science games allows members to accrue virtual resources that can be used to accessorize their avatars and socialize with others (Kafai, 2010). As an illustration, the single-player game "Hot Air Balloon Race" has Whyvillians navigate a hot air balloon, drop a bean bag over a target on the ground, and safely land the balloon. They accomplish this by manipulating the amount of fuel burned and hot air released, thus using the relationship between temperature and density of gas, speed, and wind direction to alter the balloon's position on a coordinate graph. *Whyville* also contains collaborative science games where members sign up in teams to work together on solving a problem. One example is the Solstice Safari, in which a group of players works together to collect data about the sunrise and sunset at different locations around the world. This encourages collaboration and social interactions among Whyvillians and teaches them about the earth's position in relation to the sun, as well as conceptions of time, seasons, temperature, and geography (see Figure 26.3).

In *Whyville*, players can also participate in immersive science simulations, such as a virtual epidemic. For instance, the annual outbreak of Whypox infects players' avatars with red blotches on their faces and interrupts their chat text with sneezing "achoos" (Kafai, Feldon, Fields, Giang, & Quintero, 2008), thus having effects that everyone can see. Players experience not only on a personal level, but also on a community level, the ramifications of an infectious disease as it spreads through the virtual world over the course of

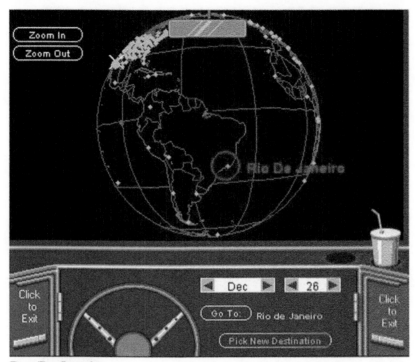

Reo De Janeiro

Figure 26.3. *Solstice Safari in* Whyville *(image provided by Yasmin B. Kafai).*

several weeks. A virtual center for disease control provides information in the form of a graph that tallies the daily status of infections in the online community. Discussion forums provide contexts to evaluate different disease vectors, while the online newspaper gives Whyvillians the space to elaborate in short articles about various impact aspects of the disease. In addition, epidemic simulators allow players to set up and run their own outbreaks and make predictions about the spread and impact of the infection (see Figure 26.4).

Research results from the impact of Whypox showed that online players participated in a range of science inquiry-related activities (Kafai, Quintero, & Feldon, 2010). On a community-wide level, players' science talk during the outbreak increased, as chat records indicated. When we studied after school club members who visited *Whyville* during the Whypox outbreak, we found many conversations not only focused on getting infected, but also putting forward hypotheses about responsible disease vectors and the length of incubation (Kafai & Wong, 2008). The use of epidemic simulators, where players could make and test their predictions about the impact and length of an infectious outbreak by running small-scale versions of epidemics, increased significantly when compared to times before or after the outbreak. Players would not only venture more often into the virtual center for disease control to inspect the status of community infection graphs, but also would test

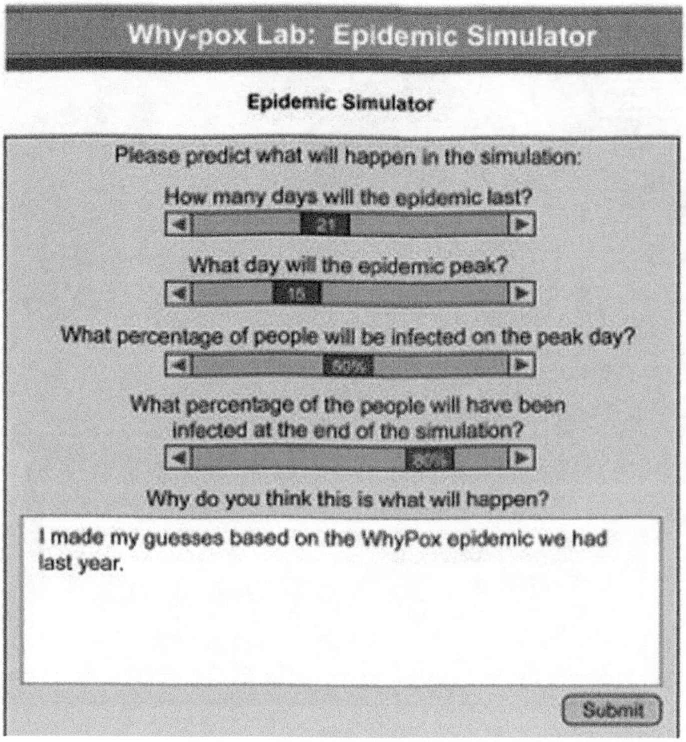

Figure 26.4. *Epidemic simulator in* Whyville *(image provided by Yasmin B. Kafai).*

epidemic designs with the simulators. One important finding was that predictions in successive uses of the epidemic simulators improved, indicating that players were not random in setting up their parameters. Finally, an analysis of more than 100 articles written by youth for the online newspaper indicated that the community at large took notice of the virtual epidemic and discussed issues related to preventive measures, social interactions, and general reactions.

A second example illustrates a very different type of learning opportunity, namely cheat sites players develop to inform others about answers and shortcuts in games, as well as provide information about the cultural norms and practices in virtual worlds (Fields & Kafai, 2010a). Hundreds of such cheat sites can be found for any virtual world on the Web. Some of them just list answers and solutions to games, while others provide detailed explanations about concepts – often supplemented with diagrams – aiming to help players understand the ideas and principles embedded in the educational games. These cheat sites, a common part of gaming communities, illustrate how unpacking the design of educational games can become a rich learning opportunity – at least, when detailed explanations are provided. In addition, cheat sites make a strong case for educational game design that requires players to provide more than just a right answer that can be easily copied; rather, educational games should engage players in inquiry by solving problems and generating explanations.

A third example of an informal virtual world, *Minecraft*, allows players to create objects and buildings using textured 3-D blocks, thus designing their own immersive environments. *Minecraft* provides a rough template with different bio-zones; it runs through a night and day cycle; and it is populated with non-player characters. Different modes of game play are possible, including *explorations* in which players can travel to different parts of the world, *crafting* in which players can build and share objects, and *combat* in which players are required to maintain health and shelter to survive attacks from hostile players and creatures. The crafting modes of *Minecraft* have received considerable attention from learning scientists for their potential learning benefits. For instance, *Minecraft's physics engine* has been used to build simple systems ranging from mechanical devices to electric circuits and more complex systems such as CPUs.

These informal spaces offer massive number of players various ways to engage with content and inquiry. *Habbo Hotel*, the leader among virtual worlds for teens, has more than 268 million registered members, with more than 9 million unique users every month. *Minecraft* has more than 28 million users. *Whyville* has 6.5 million players age 8–14 years. Unlike school settings, where students are required to participate during designated time periods in virtual worlds, participation outside of school is voluntary. This results in an uneven distribution of player participation, ranging from a relatively small proportion of players (7%) being heavily engaged in virtual worlds, to a larger proportion (34%) of involved players that visit the site occasionally, and an even larger proportion (59%) of casual players who only peripherally participate in activities (Kafai & Field, 2013). While the actual numbers of registered players in many commercial and informal virtual worlds is often in the millions, only a small percentage of them actually participate in educational activities and generate the majority of the online traffic and contributions.

Perhaps the biggest challenge facing out-of-school virtual worlds is that the most popular of them are not explicitly designed to foster socially desired learning outcomes. The success of *Whyville* and its community games such as the virtual epidemic Whypox is an exception. This type of community game leverages the massive number of participants to its advantage by providing players with an immersive experience of living through an epidemic outbreak. Such immersive experiences also leverage the virtual world's social dimension by making it part of game play and inviting players to pursue further investigation. While some virtual worlds (e.g., *Minecraft* and *Whyville*) offer opportunities for creative participation by letting players design and contribute content in the form of avatar parts, building blocks, and written articles, most of them limit the players' creative freedom by providing preset menus of options. The learning potential and benefits in virtual worlds outside of school lies in engaging players, not just in participation, but also in contribution in forms of creative design and writings, judging by the tremendous growth of virtual world building communities and by the popularity of youth design online communities around programming constructions and fan fictions.

Assessments of Learning in Virtual Worlds

Virtual worlds collect and store information about players and their actions. This information can be used for generating formative, diagnostic feedback for teachers and students, providing summative assessments of understandings and performances, and ethnographically examining patterns of participation. These data are challenging to analyze because virtual worlds are relatively open-ended learning experiences, and large volumes of data are generated, only some of which is relevant to learning (Dede, 2012b). Furthermore, many of the most beneficial learning outcomes of virtual worlds are complex, higher-level abilities (e.g., learning how to identify a good problem in an unstructured situation) and difficult to analyze in an algorithmic, automated fashion. Consequently, assessment is more complex than in tightly structured computer-based learning environments (e.g., tutoring systems, simple simulations, and games) in which the phenomenon to be studied is clearly defined, with no extraneous or unrelated information clouding the situation, and in which, at each decision point, the range of possible actions is limited to a few alternatives, all directly related to the phenomenon (rather than possibly off-task). Still, because the data collected in virtual worlds is particularly rich in its detail, there is great potential for virtual worlds to provide highly valid assessments of understandings and performances.

Virtual worlds offer unique potential for both formative and summative assessment because of three Es: engagement, evocation, and evidence. Because well-designed virtual worlds are very *engaging*, students try hard to succeed; this means that, unlike many types of testing, all students are putting forth their best efforts. Further, as discussed earlier, virtual worlds can *evoke* a wide spectrum of performances. As *EcoMUVE* illustrates, within the structure of a narrative about problems in an ecosystem, one can simulate almost any performance that students might demonstrate within an internship in a real research group. This means that a very broad palette of learning experiences – and assessment situations by which a mentor would assess progress toward mastery – can create opportunities for students to reveal their degrees of engagement, self-efficacy, understandings, and performances.

The third "e," *evidence*, is complex. Drawing on a broad spectrum of performances is important in determining the true extent of what a student knows and does not know. In a detailed analysis of *River City* students' ongoing activities and interactions, investigators found evidence of learning that was not captured by pre/post-tests or by a scientific conference presentation student teams gave at the end of the unit (Ketelhut, Dede, Clarke, Nelson, & Bowman, 2007). The evidentiary trail of learning trajectories provided by interwoven diagnostic assessments was more detailed and often more valid than a snapshot summative measure, even a rich artifact like a synthesis presentation.

Finally, virtual worlds can collect an impressive array of evidence about what a learner knows (and does not know), what he or she can do (and cannot do), and whether he or she knows when and how to apply disciplinary frames and prior knowledge to a novel problem. Virtual worlds – because of their situated nature and because they generate log files – make it easy to design for eliciting performances, to collect continuous data, and to interpret structures of evidence. The server automatically documents and timestamps actions by each student: movements, interactions, utterances, saved data, and so on (Dede, 2012b).

Displaying Learning Pathways

The path that a student takes in exploring a virtual world – for example, to determine the contextual situation, identify anomalies, and collect data related to a hypothesis for the causes of an anomaly – is an important predictor of the student's understanding of scientific inquiry. In *River City*, we used log file data to generate event paths for both individual students and their three-person teams. Students and teachers found this to be a useful source of diagnostic feedback on the relative exploratory skills and degree of collaboration of these teams. Dukas (2009) extended this research by developing an avatar log visualizer (ALV), which generates a series of slides depicting the relative frequency of events in subpopulations of students, displayed by the pattern of their movements over time. For example, an ALV visualization might contrast the search strategies of the high-performing and low-performing students in a class, displaying the top 10 scores on the content post-test (in green) and the lowest 10 scores (in pink). The high-performing students' preferred locations and their search strategies can be used in diagnostic feedback, and also can be demonstrated to students in subsequent classes. The low-performing students' locations and search strategies may offer insights into what types of understanding they lack.

Analyzing a user's path through the virtual world is a potentially powerful form of embedded assessment. However, choosing the best way to display student paths through a learning environment is a complex type of visualization that is not well understood at present. The utility of this diagnostic approach also depends on the degree to which the exploration path through the virtual world plays a key role in learning. In *EcoMUVE*, for example, while the forest module involves substantial exploration, only one role out of four team roles in the pond module involves searching the region.

However, students can rotate this role from session to session so that all get this experience and benefit from diagnostic feedback.

Understanding Individualized Guidance Use

As another example of the rich analytic power possible through the use of log files, Nelson (2007) developed a version of *River City* that contained an interwoven individualized guidance system (IGS). The guidance system utilized personalized interaction histories collected from each student's activities to generate real-time, customized advice to each student. The IGS offered reflective prompts about each student's learning in the world, with the content of the messages based on in-world events and basic event histories of that individual. As an example, if a student were to click on the admissions chart in the *River City* hospital, a predefined rule stated that if the student had previously visited the tenement district and talked to a resident there, then a customized guidance message would be shown reminding the student that he or she had previously visited the tenement district and asking the student how many patients listed on the chart came from that part of town. Findings from a multilevel multiple regression analysis showed that use of this guidance system in the *River City* curriculum had a statistically significant, positive impact ($p < .05$) on student learning (Nelson, 2007). In addition to using the log files to personalize the guidance provided to each student, the investigators conducted analyses of guidance use to determine when and if students first chose to use the guidance system, which messages they viewed, where they were in the virtual world when they viewed them, and what actions they took subsequent to viewing a given guidance message. Thus the log files provide diagnostic information that could be used to personalize instruction even further.

Tracking Online and Off-line Participation

Making sense of players' navigation and interactions across the hundreds of public and private places that constitute virtual worlds is a complex enterprise. One tool to help make sense of how players interact with virtual worlds is to conduct an ethnography of a classroom, after school club, or any other setting where multiple players are simultaneously participating in the virtual world while in the same physical space (Boellstorff, Nardi, Pearce, & Taylor, 2012). For example, one can longitudinally follow one person or one practice over several months, and this can provide an in-depth account of how learning unfolds in virtual worlds (Kafai & Fields, 2013). These ethnographic data can then be combined with quantitative logfile data (Williams, 2005) to create richer case studies of how players or practices change over time. For instance, case studies of virtual world players can be generated by going click by click through the logfile data, creating minute-by-minute summaries of online activities, and condensing these into short daily narratives that identify patterns and innovations in participation. These accounts can then be complemented with video, field notes, and interview data from observations at other settings. The ethnographic data can identify centers and shifts of participation not visible from the logfile data alone. Likewise, this approach can be adopted to document how players learn a particular practice from other players, such as a secret command. The online tracking data reveals not only when, but also where players first used the secret command, whether they sought any online help, and how the practice spread through the club over a two-week time period. Such analyses capture the multimodal processes at play of how players learn to navigate virtual worlds and how they draw on personal resources online and off-line. These methodological approaches, while time consuming and fine-grained, can also be used to investigate more complex social practices (Fields & Kafai, 2010b).

Further Developments

These examples provide compelling visions about how virtual worlds can enhance learning and enable innovative methods of assessment. Virtual worlds allow learners to experience various academic identities, such as engaging in inquiry practices of scientists, and we know that this sort of identity work contributes to learning (see Nasir, Rosebery, Warren, & Lee, Chapter 34, this volume). Virtual worlds enable new types of formative and summative assessments to guide learning. Virtual worlds offer unique, powerful mechanisms for formative and summative assessment. The opportunity to provide customized, just-in-time formative assessment can help learners surmount challenges and contribute to more effective learning (also see Pellegrino, Chapter 12, this volume).

Future research on virtual worlds and learning should focus on how to design virtual worlds to maximize learning. As we know from learning sciences research more generally, enhancing learning requires scaffolds of various kinds (Reiser & Tabak, Chapter 3, this volume), and these scaffolds are likely to differ in classroom and informal settings. The degree of constraint and guidance to provide toward desired learning outcomes, while not taking away too much of the free-choice element, is one of the key challenges in designing for learning in virtual worlds. We close by identifying three aspects of virtual worlds that warrant additional research – scaling up, integrating expert advice, and developing hybrid models.

Designing Virtual Worlds for Scale

To have a substantial educational impact, designers must be able to develop and implement virtual worlds at scale. We know from commercial counterparts, whose participation numbers can feature millions of players, that virtual worlds can support very large numbers of users. Research has documented that in education, unlike other sectors of society, the scaling of successful instructional programs from a few settings to widespread use across a range of contexts is very difficult, even for innovations that are economically and logistically practical (Dede, 2006; Dede, Honan, & Peters, 2005; see Penuel & Spillane, Chapter 32, this volume). Research typically finds that context-specific variables have a substantial influence in shaping the desirability, practicality, and effectiveness of educational interventions (e.g., the teacher's content preparation, students' self-efficacy, prior academic achievement; Schneider & McDonald, 2007). Therefore, achieving scale in education requires designs that can flexibly adapt to effective use in a wide variety of contexts across a spectrum of learners and teachers.

Based in part on work by Coburn (2003), Clarke and Dede (2009) document the application of a five-dimensional framework for scaling up to the implementation of the *River City* virtual world curriculum for middle school science:

- *Depth* concerns the quality or effectiveness of the innovation. Design-based research studies of virtual worlds seek to enhance their depth.
- *Sustainability* concerns the extent to which the innovation is maintained in ongoing use. Virtual worlds are designed to include many factors for engagement so as to attract and keep a wide variety of participants.
- *Spread* is the extent to which large numbers of people or organizations adopt an innovation. Virtual worlds achieve spread by forming communities whose participants recruit others to join the experience.
- *Shift* is a decentralization of ownership over the creation of an innovation. In virtual worlds that allow participants considerable autonomy in their choices, they come to think of the virtual world as theirs rather than belonging to the designers.
- *Evolution* concerns learning from users by the original creators of an innovation. Using the types of formative evaluation described earlier to improve the design of a virtual world fosters evolution.

River City and *EcoMUVE* demonstrate that, with design for scale, virtual worlds can be implemented across a wide range of classroom settings, teachers, and students.

Integrating "Expert" Advice

Animated pedagogical agents (APAs) are "lifelike autonomous characters [that] co-habit learning environments with students to create rich, face-to-face learning interactions" (Johnson, Rickel, & Lester, 2000, p. 47). Several research studies have shown that APAs can provide virtual mentorship, acting as an expert, motivator, collaborator, and learning companion (Baylor & Kim, 2005; Bowman, 2011; Chou, Chan, & Lin, 2003). Learning would be enhanced if we could design a wide range of APAs to meet various student needs and embed these in virtual worlds (Dede, 2012). APAs have two further advantages: First, the questions students ask of an APA are themselves diagnostic – typically learners will ask for information they do not know, but see as having value. Sometimes a single question asked by a student of an APA may reveal as much about what that learner does and does not know than a series of answers the student provides to a teacher's diagnostic questions. Curricula such as *EcoMUVE* could embed APAs of various types to elicit a trajectory of questions over time that reveal aspects of students' understanding and motivation, while the APA is aiding learning and engagement with its responses. Second, APAs scattered through a virtual world can draw out student performances in various ways. In *EcoMUVE*, for example, a student could meet an APA who requests the student's name and role. Even a simple pattern recognition system could determine if the student made a response indicating self-efficacy and motivation ("ecosystems scientist" or some variant) versus a response indicating lack of confidence or engagement ("sixth grader" or some other out-of-character reply). As another example, an APA could request a student to summarize what the student has learned so far, and some form of latent semantic analysis could scan the response for key phrases indicating understanding of terminology and relevant concepts. The important design considerations of this method for evoking performances are that (a) the interaction is consistent with the overall narrative, (b) the measurement is relatively unobtrusive, and (c) the interactions themselves deepen immersion.

Developing Models of Hybrid Learning Environments

One powerful feature of virtual worlds is that they can be used in a hybrid fashion, incorporating both in-school and out-of-school engagement, thus bridging learning across different settings. While some educational virtual worlds are closed environments only accessible to students in particular classes, the most powerful virtual worlds (like *Whyville*) can be used both inside and outside of schools. For instance, in the case of the virtual epidemic, middle school students participated in Whypox as part of their infectious disease curriculum unit by visiting *Whyville* during class time, by keeping track of infected status of local class members, and by having class discussions with their teacher about possible causes and interventions. Students were also invited to visit *Whyville* outside of classroom time, thus extending exposure and opportunity to observe and experience the outbreak. Results from pre/post surveys that examined students' understanding of infectious disease revealed significant improvements from the hybrid model (Neulight et al., 2007). This case study shows that it is possible to create hybrid models where learning in virtual worlds exists both inside and outside schools, and thus extends classroom time into informal time in meaningful ways. Such approaches, however, have not been widely implemented because of the administrative and legal issues discussed earlier.

In summary, virtual worlds provide both macro and micro lenses for studying learning. They serve as a telescope because huge numbers of people can be involved in individual and collaborative learning in immersive, simulated contexts, providing learning scientists with very large amounts of data about how people differ from each other in their learning strengths and preferences. Virtual worlds also serve as a microscope because, for any individual participant, log files and other data sources can provide very rich knowledge about what and how they have learned. Learning scientists have provided substantial evidence that virtual worlds provide unique and powerful learning benefits. In the future, we anticipate that schools and other education providers will make increasing use of virtual worlds to foster learning.

Acknowledgments

The writing of this chapter was supported by a grant of the National Science Foundation to the first author and by several grants of the National Science Foundation and the Institute for Education Sciences, U.S. Department of Education to the second author. The views expressed are those of the authors and do not necessarily represent the views of the funders, the University of Pennsylvania, or Harvard University.

References

Bainbridge, W. S. (2007). The research potential of virtual worlds. *Science*, 317, 472–476.

Barab, S. A., & Luehrmann, A. L. (2003. Building sustainable science curriculum: Acknowledging and accommodating local adaptation. *Science Education*, 87, 454–467.

Barab, S. A., Sadler, T., Heiselt, C., Hickey, D., & Zuiker, S. (2007). Relating narrative, inquiry, and inscriptions: A framework for socio-scientific inquiry. *Journal of Science Education and Technology*, 16(1), 59–82.

Barab, S. A., Scott, B., Siyahhan, S. Goldstone, R., Ingram- Goble, A., Zuiker, S., & Warren, S. (2009). Conceptual play as a curricular scaffold: Using videogames to support science education. *Journal of Science Education and Technology*, 18(1), 305–320.

Barab, S. A., Zuiker, S., Warren, S., Hickey, D., Ingram-Goble, A., Kwon, E.-J., Kouper, I., & Herring, S. C. (2007). Situationally embodied curriculum: Relating formalisms to contexts. *Science Education*, 91(5), 750–782.

Baylor, A. L., & Kim, Y. (2005). Simulating instructional roles through pedagogical agents. *International Journal of Artificial Intelligence in Education*, 15, 95–115.

Bell, M. (2008). Toward a definition of "virtual worlds." *Journal of Virtual Worlds Research*, 1(1), 1–5.

Boellstorff, T. (2008). *Coming of age in Second Life: An anthropologist explores the virtually human*. Princeton, NJ: Princeton University Press.

Boellstorff, T., Bardi, B., Pearce, C., & Taylor, T. L. (2012). *Ethnography and virtual worlds: A handbook of method*. Princeton, NJ: Princeton University Press.

Bowman, C. D. D. (2011). Student use of animated pedagogical agents in a middle school science inquiry program. *British Journal of Educational Technology*, 43(3). Retrieved from http://onlinelibrary.wiley.com/doi/10.1111/j.1467-8535.2011.01198.x/pdf.

Castronova, E. (2005). *Synthetic worlds: The business and pleasure of gaming*. Chicago: Chicago University Press.

Chou, C., Chan, T., & Lin, C. (2003). Redefining the learning companion: The past, present, and future of educational agents. *Computers and Education*, 40, 255–269.

Clarke, J., & Dede, C. (2009). Robust designs for scalability. In L. Moller, J. B. Huett, & D. M. Harvey (Eds.), *Learning and instructional technologies for the 21st century: Visions of the future* (pp. 27–48). New York: Springer.

Coburn, C. E. (2003). Rethinking scale: Moving beyond numbers to deep and lasting change. *Educational Researcher*, 32, 3–12.

Dawley, L., & Dede, C. (2014). Situated learning in virtual worlds and immersive simulations. In J. M. Spector, M. D. Merrill, J. Elen, & M. J. Bishop (Eds.), *The handbook of research for educational communications and technology*. Fourth Edition. New York: Springer Verlag.

Dede, C. (2005). Why design-based research is both important and difficult. *Educational Technology*, 45(1), 5–8.

Dede, C. (2006). Scaling up: Evolving innovations beyond ideal settings to challenging contexts of practice. In R. K. Sawyer (Ed.), *Cambridge handbook of the learning sciences* (pp. 551–566). Cambridge: Cambridge University Press.

Dede, C. (2009a). Immersive interfaces for engagement and learning. *Science*, 323(5910), 66–69.

Dede, C. (2009b). *Learning context: Gaming, simulation, and science learning in the classroom*. Commissioned Paper for the National Research Council Workshop on Games and Simulations in Science Education. Washington, DC: NRC, September.

Dede, C. (2012a). Customization in immersive learning environments: Implications for digital teaching platforms. In C. Dede & J. Richards (Eds.), *Digital teaching platforms: Customizing classroom learning for each student* (pp. 119–133). New York: Teacher's College Press.

Dede, C. (2012b). Interweaving assessments into immersive authentic simulations: Design strategies for diagnostic and instructional insights (Commissioned White Paper for the ETS Invitational Research Symposium on Technology Enhanced Assessments). Princeton, NJ: Educational Testing Service. http://www.k12center.org/rsc/pdf/session4-dede-paper-tea2012.pdf.

Dede, C. (2013). Opportunities and challenges in embedding diagnostic assessments into immersive interfaces. *Educational Designer, 2*(6).

Dede, C., Honan, J., & Peters. L. (Eds.) (2005). *Scaling up success: Lessons learned from technology-based educational improvement*. New York: Jossey-Bass.

Dukas, G. (2009). Characterizing student navigation in educational multiuser virtual environments: A case study using data from the River City project (Unpublished doctoral dissertation). Harvard Graduate School of Education, Cambridge, MA.

Fields, D. A., & Kafai, Y. B. (2009). A connective ethnography of peer knowledge sharing and diffusion in a tween virtual world. *International Journal of Computer Supported Collaborative Learning*, 4(1), 47–68.

Fields, D. A., & Kafai, Y. B. (2010a). Knowing and throwing mudballs, hearts, pies, and flowers: A connective ethnography of gaming practices. *Games and Culture* (Special Issue), 5(1), 88–115.

Fields, D. A., & Kafai, Y. B. (2010b). Stealing from Grandma or generating knowledge? Contestations and effects of cheating in Whyville. *Games and Culture* (Special Issue), 5(1), 64–87.

Fields, D. A., & Kafai, Y. B. (2012). Navigating life as an avatar: The shifting identities-in-practice of a girl player in a tween virtual world. In C. C. Ching & B. Foley (Eds.), *Constructing identity in a digital world*, Cambridge: Cambridge University Press, 222–250.

Gibson, D. (2012). Living virtually: Researching new worlds. *Journal of Gaming and Computer-Mediated Simulations*, 2(1), 59–61.

Grimes, S. M., & Fields, D. A. (2012). *Kids online: A new research agenda for understanding social networking forums.* New York: Joan Ganz Cooney Center.

Grotzer, T. A., Kamarainen, A., Tutwiler, M. S., Metcalf, S. J., & Dede, C. (2012, April). Learning for focus on processes and steady states in ecosystems dynamics using a virtual environment. Paper presented at the annual meeting of the American Educational Research Association, Vancouver, Canada.

Jenkins, H. (1998). Complete freedom of movement: Videogames as gendered play-spaces. In J. Cassell & H. Jenkins (Eds.), *From Barbie to Mortal Kombat: Perspectives on gender and computer games* (pp. 323–356). Cambridge, MA: MIT Press.

Johnson, W. L., Rickel, J. W., & Lester, J. C. (2000). Animated pedagogical agents: Face-to-face interaction in interactive learning environments. *International Journal of Artificial Intelligence in Education*, 11, 47–78.

Kafai, Y. B. (Ed.) (2010). The world of Whyville: Living, playing, and learning in a tween virtual world. Special issue of *Games & Culture*, 5(1), January 2010.

Kafai, Y. B., & Fefferman, N. (2011). Virtual epidemics as learning laboratories in virtual worlds. *Virtual Worlds Research*, 3(2). Retrieved from http://jvwresearch.org/index.php/past-issues/32-virtual-worlds-for-kids.

Kafai, Y., Feldon, D., Fields, D. A., Giang, M., & Quintero, M. (2007). Life in the time of Whypox: A virtual epidemic as a community event. In C. Steinfeld, B. Pentland, M. Ackerman, & N. Contractor (Eds.), *Communities and technologies* (pp. 171–190). Berlin: Spring-Verlag.

Kafai, Y. B., & Fields, D. A. (2013). *Connected play: Tweens in a virtual world.* Cambridge, MA: MIT Press.

Kafai, Y. B., & Giang, M. (2007). Virtual playgrounds. In T. Willoughby & E. Wood (Eds.), *Children's learning in a digital world* (pp. 196–217). Oxford: Blackwell Publishing.

Kafai, Y., Quintero, M., & Feldon, D. (2010). Investigating the 'Why" in Whypox: Explorations of a virtual epidemic. *Games and Culture* (Special Issue), 5(1), 116–135.

Kafai Y., & Wong, J. (2008). Real arguments about a virtual epidemic: Conversations and contestations in a tween gaming club. In V. Jonker, A. Lazonder, & C. Hoadley (Eds.), *Proceedings of the 8th International Conference of the Learning Sciences* (Vol. 1, pp. 414–421). Utrecht, Netherlands.

Kamarainen, A., Metcalf, S., Tutwiler, S., Grotzer, T., & Dede, C. (2012, April). EcoMUVE: Shifts in affective beliefs and values about science through learning experiences in immersive virtual environments. Paper presented at the annual meeting of the American Educational Research Association, Vancouver, Canada.

Ketelhut, D. J. (2007). The impact of student self-efficacy on scientific inquiry skills: An exploratory investigation in River City, a multi-user virtual environment. *Journal of Science Education and Technology*, 16(1), 99–111.

Ketelhut, D., Dede, C., Clarke, J., Nelson, B., & Bowman, C. (2007). Studying situated learning in a multi-user virtual environment. In E. Baker, J. Dickieson, W. Wulfeck, & H. O'Neil (Eds.), *Assessment of problem solving using simulations* (pp. 37–58). Mahwah, NJ: Lawrence Erlbaum Associates.

Ketelhut, D. J., Nelson, B. C., Clarke, J. E., & Dede, C. (2010). A multi-user virtual environment for building and assessing higher order inquiry skills in science. *British Journal of Educational Technology*, 41(1), 56–68.

Lave, J., & Wenger, E. (1991). *Situated learning: Legitimate peripheral participation.* New York: Cambridge University Press.

Messinger, P., Stroulia, E., & Lyons, K. (2008). A typology of virtual worlds: Historical overview and future directions. *Journal of Virtual Worlds Research*, 1(1), 1–18.

Metcalf, S., Kamarainen, A., Grotzer, T., & Dede, C. (2012, April). Teacher perceptions of the practicality and effectiveness of immersive ecological simulations as classroom curricula. Paper presented at the annual meeting of the American Educational Research Association, Vancouver, Canada.

Metcalf, S., Kamarainen, A., Tutwiler, M. S., Grotzer, T., & Dede, C. (2011). Ecosystem science learning via multi-user virtual environments. *International Journal of Gaming and Computer-Mediated Simulations*, 3(1) (January–March), 86–90.

Nelson, B. (2007). Exploring the use of individualized, reflective guidance in an educational multi-user virtual environment. *Journal of Science Education and Technology*, 16(1), 83–97.

Neulight, N., Kafai, Y. B., Kao, L., Foley, B., & Galas, C. (2007). Children's learning about infectious disease through participation in a virtual epidemic. *Journal of Science Education and Technology*, 16(1), 47–58.

Schneider, B., & McDonald, S.-K. (Eds.) (2007). *Scale-up in education: Ideas in principle* (Volume I) and *Scale-up in Education: Issues in practice* (Volume 2). New York: Rowman & Littlefield.

Schofield, J. W. (2006). Internet use in schools: Promise and problems. In R. K. Sawyer (Ed.), *Cambridge handbook of the learning sciences* (pp. 521–534). New York: Cambridge University Press.

Thomas, M. K., Barab, S. A., & Tuzun, H. (2009). Developing critical implementations of technology-rich innovations: A cross-case study of the implementation of Quest Atlantis. *Journal of Educational Computing Research*, 41(2), 125–153.

Williams, D. (2005). Bridging the methodological divide in game research. *Simulation & Gaming*, 36(4), 1–17.

PART V

Learning Disciplinary Knowledge

27 Research in Mathematics Education: What Can It Teach Us about Human Learning?

Anna Sfard and Paul Cobb

Among the diverse domains of human knowing, mathematics stands out as a hothouse for insights about teaching and learning in general. This chapter summarizes the ways that research on mathematics learning contributes to our understanding of how people learn. We begin with a brief historical overview, which explains what it is about mathematics that has made it the content area of choice for the study of human learning. We then focus our attention on two distinct approaches in education research, the *acquisitionist* and the *participationist* approaches, which have influenced our understanding of learning and the practices of teaching in all content areas. Mathematics education research is particularly important to the learning sciences, because it challenges the first approach (which is still dominant in much education research) and it has helped to introduce and develop the second approach.

Mathematics Education Research – A Historical Overview

Mathematics education is an applied discipline aiming at improving the practice of learning and teaching mathematics. It became established as a full-fledged academic discipline about 50 years ago. However, various scholars began studying mathematical learning at the end of the 19th century, when the currently popular idea of evidence-based pedagogy first came to the fore. The first half of the 20th century saw numerous experimental and quasi-experimental studies (see Campbell & Stanley, 1963, for a review) in which researchers endeavored to compare and evaluate the effectiveness of different teaching approaches. That research, conducted mainly by mathematics educators, attracted the attention of professional mathematicians, whose concern for the teaching of mathematics was accompanied by puzzlement over the question: "How does it happen that there are people who do not understand mathematics?" (Poincaré, 1929/1952, p. 47). These early studies by mathematics educators proved unable to answer the mathematicians' query, in large part because they focused on an "input-output" model that examined causal relations between teaching methods (inputs) and student achievement (outputs) and gave little attention to the intervening *processes* of learning in the context of instruction (on processes, see Chinn & Sherin, Chapter 9, this volume).

A small number of psychologists studied processes of mathematics learning that mathematics educators had ignored during the first part of the 20th century. They hoped that this particular case of learning, in spite of its disciplinary specificity, would bring insights into human learning in general. The psychologists' efforts, initiated by American educational psychologist Edward Thorndike at the turn of the 20th century, and fueled along the way by Jean Piaget's ambition to build "a sort of embryology of intelligence" (Piaget, 1976, p. 10), aimed at identifying and describing the development of those aspects of cognition that were common to all humans, regardless of their sociocultural backgrounds and personal histories. With this goal in mind, psychologists focused their empirical studies on human skills and understandings that they assumed would be more or less the same in every place and every culture. Mathematics, hailed as "the only true universal language" (Rees, 2009), seemed to be ideally suited.

By the 1960s, a reasonable merger was achieved between three academic communities interested in mathematics teaching and learning: psychologists, mathematicians, and mathematics educators. This was the origin of the modern discipline of mathematics education research. Since the 1960s, most studies tended to focus either on teaching or on learning, and not until quite recently did researchers come to view these two processes as too tightly interrelated to be studied separately. Currently, investigators attend to learning even if teaching is their primary focus, and attend to teaching even when learning is the main interest.

The basic questions mathematics educators study have remained the same: How do people learn mathematics? How can our understanding of human cognition inform the way we teach math? What learning environments and curricula are more effective in producing desired learning outcomes? These questions have been studied from within two very different conceptual frameworks that reflect contrasting interpretations of what mathematics is, and consequently, what it means to learn mathematics. The first framework comprises approaches that portray mathematics as pre-given structures and procedures, and view learning mathematics as the *acquisition* of these structures and procedures. The acquired entities may be called *knowledge*, *schemes*, or *conceptions*, and the process of acquisition can be either passive, happening through mere "transmission," or active, achieved by the learner's own constructive efforts. We call this framework *acquisitionism*. The second framework portrays mathematics as a form of human activity rather than as something to be "acquired," and thus views learning mathematics as the process of *becoming a participant* in this distinct type of activity. We call this framework *participationism*. Acquisitionism holds that mathematics is an external body of knowledge that was discovered or constructed by mathematicians and is acquired or reconstructed by the learner. In contrast, participationism holds that mathematics is one of many human ways of doing things, and that it has evolved historically and continues to undergo change (Sfard, 1998). Each of these two frameworks has very different consequences for both research and pedagogy.

Acquisitionist and participationist approaches are both prominent in current research on mathematics learning and teaching. The acquisitionist approach generates research in which learning is conceptualized as a change in *conceptions* (see diSessa, Chapter 5, this volume). The participationist view of learning has given rise to two overlapping lines of study. The first line of study conducts investigations in classrooms, where mathematics learning can be seen as part and parcel of the process of changing *learning-teaching practices*. The second focuses on ways of communicating (or *discourses*) as the primary objects of change in the learning of mathematics. In the reminder of this chapter, we review these three centrally important lines of research in mathematics education: the acquisitionist focus on conceptual change, and the participationist focus on changes in practices and on changes in discourses.

Acquisitionist Research in Mathematics Education: Learning Mathematics as a Change in Conceptions

Many researchers in science as well as mathematics education considered Piaget's theory of learning, which was well developed by the middle of the 20th century, to be the perfect framework for conducting studies that aimed to "look inside the human head" in a rigorous manner. *Constructivism*, as an elaborated version of this approach became known (Kafai, 2006; Von Glasersfeld, 1989), was the predominant framework until the end of the 1980s. The central assumption of constructivism is that learners build their understanding of the world primarily through direct interaction with their environment. In constructivist pedagogy, the teacher is portrayed as a provider of opportunities for learning rather than as someone who delivers information to a passive learner. This characterization of learning in instructional situations pushed the individual learner to center stage and seemed to suggest that there was little need to study instruction per se.

Two complementary lines of constructivist research have made systematic contributions to mathematics education. The first has investigated the often idiosyncratic student *conceptions* that are the products of mathematics learning. The second has modeled the *processes* of conceptual change with the help of empirical data from clinical studies, the most insightful of which are known as *teaching experiments*.

Studying Learners' Conceptions

This line of research started in science education with studies of student *misconceptions* (see diSessa, Chapter 5, this volume), a notion derived from

Piaget's contention that inadequate understandings of reality can be found consistently across situations and people (Piaget, 1962). The term *misconception* referred to students' "*own meanings* – meanings that are not appropriate at all" (Davis, 1988, p. 9). Science educators began to question the assumption that learners' meanings were inappropriate, and the term *misconception* itself, in the 1970s (Driver & Easley, 1978). Resilient student conceptions that were deemed to violate the scientific canon were later described more charitably as *alternative* or *naïve* conceptions, and were characterized as possibly inevitable early version of formal concepts. In mathematics education, researchers spoke in terms of *tacit models* (Fischbein, 1989) or of students' *images of concepts*, which were contrasted with verbal definitions of concepts (Tall & Vinner, 1981). There is hardly a mathematical concept learned in school that was not studied using this framework.

Researchers who engaged in this kind of study found surprising consistencies in alternative conceptions across classrooms, schools, and even nations. This was taken as evidence that idiosyncrasies in how students deal with mathematical concepts were not just a matter of faulty teaching. For instance, research on student conceptions has repeatedly shown that many high school students identify as functions only those mappings that can be represented by simple formulas. This is often the case even for learners who can recite the formal definition of function and know that it does not, in fact, require formulas (Malik, 1980; Vinner & Dreyfus, 1989). Similarly, young children were found to resist the idea that multiplication can yield a value lower than a multiplied number (think, for instance, about one-half times six) or that division can do the opposite (as is the case with three divided by one-half; Fischbein, 1989; Harel, Behr, Post, & Lesh, 1989).

Misconceptions research has been widely disseminated in teacher education programs and has been quite influential, in part because of its methodological simplicity. Initially, research on misconceptions used surveys composed of open-ended or, better still, multi-choice questions that could be administered to large groups of people and processed statistically. Later, structured and semi-structured interviews complemented or replaced surveys. The pedagogical implications of these studies were also enticingly simple: to repair a misconception, the teacher was advised to elicit a *cognitive conflict*, a situation in which students' current conceptions clash with empirical evidence or with a mathematical definition. It was believed that when faced with such conflicts, students would come to realize that their current conception was not accurate, and they would thus be led to a correct conception.

Investigations of students' conceptions have been central in science education for some time. In mathematics education, misconceptions research began relatively late, peaked in the 1980s, and started to decline in the early 1990s. It was at this point that mathematics education research began parting company with research in science education. Science education researchers were aware of various foundational weaknesses of misconceptions studies, including discrepancies with constructivist principles and the lack of a sound theoretical basis (Smith, diSessa, & Rochelle, 1993). However, they opted for repair rather than replacement, and the study of learners' scientific misconceptions evolved into theoretically grounded research on *conceptual change* (see diSessa, Chapter 5, this volume). In contrast, mathematics educators gradually began to reject the misconceptions approach, possibly as a result of insights they gained through investigating processes of concept formation that we review next.

Studying Processes of Constructing Conceptions

In mathematics education, research on students' conceptions has been accompanied almost from the beginning by studies of the cognitive processes that take place as the conceptions develop. The pioneers of this research in mathematics education translated Piagetian theory of human development into discipline-specific research frameworks (see, e.g., Skemp, 1971). Their followers proposed a number of homegrown theories of mathematical thinking and its development, among them the theory of conceptual fields (Vergnaud, 1990), theories of process-object duality of mathematical conceptions (Dubinsky, 1991; Gray & Tall, 1993; Sfard, 1991), and a theory of the growth of mathematical understanding (Pirie & Kieran, 1994). The ultimate purpose of the resulting studies was to produce models of students' evolving conceptions (Steffe, Thompson, & Von Glasersfeld, 2000). The assumption underlying this work was that particular types of interactions with a teacher and other students could give rise to internal cognitive perturbations for students. However, these interactions were viewed as having only limited influence on how students attempt to eliminate perturbations by reorganizing their current conceptions. Students' progress through a sequence of developmental levels was therefore characterized as a process of individual construction that can be precipitated by interactions with others.

This line of inquiry has made two lasting contributions. First, it has produced a number of models of mathematical learning that have informed researchers' thinking about how students learn a range of different mathematical topics. Second, it produced methodological innovations that, although used less frequently in their original form today, were stepping stones to current research methods, with design experiment probably the most notable among them (see the next section and Barab, Chapter 8, this volume).

Models that describe how learners gradually construct different mathematical conceptions differ widely in their scope. Probably the best known model, proposed by Dutch researchers Dina and Pierre van Hiele, was meant to account for students' development of geometric thinking (Van Hiele, 2004/1959). In the spirit of Piaget's theory of development, this model is predicated on the assumption that the way students think about geometric concepts undergoes several transformations that can be characterized as transitions between qualitatively different levels of understanding. However, the Van Hieles departed from Piaget's theory in one important respect. They argued that although progress from one level to the next is as inevitable as the transitions between Piagetian stages, these changes result from teaching rather than from independent construction on the part of the learner. According to the Van Hieles, it is under proper instruction that the student proceeds from the level of *visualization*, where she can recognize a shape as a whole; to that of *analysis*, where she can also name its parts; to that of *abstraction*, where she recognizes the role of a formal definition in establishing the name of a shape; and to that of *deduction*, where she can also derive and justify her claims with the help of the rules of logic. Eventually, the learner may reach the level of *rigor*, where the whole edifice of geometry becomes a formal theory, derivable from a small set of axioms. The Van Hieles's model spurred a flurry of research that indicated that very few secondary school graduates reach the level of deduction, and the great majority end up at the level of analysis or abstraction (Battista, 2007).

The Van Hiele model of mathematical concept construction is particularly robust, and today it remains as influential as ever. This is remarkable, given that the Piagetian approach that inspired this model has declined in influence. The key to this resiliency may be the Van Hieles's emphasis on the critical role of teaching in cognitive change, and their focus on language as the main object of change as students make the transition from one level to another. As a consequence, the Van Hiele model can be reconciled with current sociocultural approaches in general, and with approaches that focus on ways of communicating in particular (see the section on learning as a change in discourse).

The study of learners' development of arithmetical and algebraic conceptions, inspired by Piaget's pioneering work on numerical thinking, has been a particularly active area of research. Researchers have zoomed in on specific, clearly delineated forms of mathematical activity such as counting (Gelman & Gallistel, 1978), using fractions (Kieren, 1992), and solving problems with unknowns (Filloy & Rojano, 1989). This research typically provides meticulous descriptions of how the relevant conceptions and skills evolve (for comprehensive reviews, see Kilpatrick, Swafford, & Findell, 2001 and Kieran, 2007).

Finally, the method of the *teaching experiment* was introduced in the 1980s by researchers who were trying to map trajectories in the development of students' mathematical conceptions. This technique is premised on the assumption that only through teaching can researchers come into contact with those critical moments when students reorganize their thinking (Steffe et al., 2000). And if so, researchers must engage in a long-term process of teaching individual students one on one in order to study the process of concept construction. Consistent with the constructivist principles that inspired this work, teaching involved posing carefully chosen tasks and pressing students to reflect on their problem-solving activity. Video-recorded interactions were analyzed after each teaching session to inform the selection of tasks for subsequent sessions (also see Chinn & Sherin, Chapter 9, this volume, on microgenetic methods). Retrospective analyses of video recordings and transcriptions were conducted once the experiment was completed to model the participating students' learning "in terms of coordinated schemes of actions and operations" (Cobb & Steffe, 1983/2010, p. 24). In spite of the experiment's focus on a small number of individual learners, the models were intended to be "both general and specific" (Cobb & Steffe, 1983/2010, p. 27). The impact of the teaching experiment methodology has extended beyond mathematics education and marked the beginning of the intensive study of learning processes in instructional situations.

To summarize, research on learners' mathematical conceptions and on their development has extended our knowledge of mathematical learning in two important ways. First, it resulted in thorough records of the most common idiosyncrasies of learners' mathematical thinking, and second, it yielded important insights about mechanisms of learning mathematics. In addition to producing detailed models that depict the evolution of specific mathematical ideas, this research has shown that learning is not a linear process, and that some phenomena, even those that seem like "accidents" on the road toward mathematical competency, may be essential even though they are later discarded, as with the larval stage in the development of some insects.

In addition to making these contributions, this research gave rise to several quandaries, with the surprising resilience of "misconceptions" perhaps the most puzzling. Research findings indicated that students' nonstandard ideas are often impervious to both preventive and remedial efforts of the teacher. The vision of learning as "acquisition of conceptions" seemed ill suited for dealing with this phenomenon. Indeed, when conceptions are understood as discrete entities "transmitted" to or "reconstructed" by learners, it is difficult to explain the nonlinear nature of learning, the fact that it often cannot proceed by a simple expansion of what the student already knows. In the next section, we present additional reasons for the emergence of the alternative participationist approach in mathematics education and beyond.

From Learning as Acquisition of Concepts to Learning as Evolving Participation in Activities

By the early 1990s, some researchers concluded that it would not be possible to answer certain core questions about mathematics learning without a thorough revision of the tacit assumptions that ground their work. Many of the mathematics-related critiques of the acquisitionist approach came from cross-cultural and cross-situational research conducted by developmental psychologists who were attempting to further and refine Piaget's theory by conducting ethnographies of mathematical practice in a variety of non-Western societies. Contrary to their intentions, these studies indicated the untenability of Piagetian claims about cross-cultural invariants in human intellectual development and about the primacy of development over learning. Piagetians reserved the term *development* for changes that happen spontaneously and are common to all people. Numerical thinking, considered a universal human capability, was the obvious candidate for cross-cultural and cross-situational examination. However, numerical thinking soon proved anything but culturally invariant. In fact, the very idea of cross-cultural comparisons proved problematic. Investigations of numerical thinking often led to one conclusion if the participants were presented with school-like numerical tasks, and to quite a different one if they were asked to solve mathematically equivalent everyday problems (Cole, 1996, p. 74).

Evidence about the diversity rather than universality of numerical thinking, and thus about its cultural rather than developmental sources, came from numerous investigations, including studies of the counting practices of Oksapmin people in Papua New Guinea (Saxe, 1982), the money transactions and paper-and-pencil arithmetic of unschooled Brazilian street vendors (e.g., Nunes, Schliemann, & Carraher, 1993), and the use of numbers and measurement in a range of work (e.g., Scribner, 1997) and everyday tasks (e.g., Lave, 1988). These studies suggested that mathematics learning is deeply embedded in situated social practices and results in students becoming able to tackle particular types of tasks with the support of particular features of the situated social practices in which the learning takes place (see Greeno & Engeström, Chapter 7, this volume; also Brown, Collins, & Duguid, 1989). Contextual changes that appeared mathematically irrelevant often resulted in previously successful students becoming helpless. These findings revealed a much greater diversity of learning and its outcomes than Piaget and his followers anticipated, and were seen by many researchers as a challenge to the idea that human intellectual growth was primarily a process of development rather than learning.

Mathematics education researchers, who kept teachers and teaching in mind even while focusing on learning, voiced their own doubts about some of the tenets of constructivism. Their findings called for revision of the limited role attributed to instruction. In one of these studies (Erlwanger, 1973), the researcher followed a sixth grader learning on his own as he worked through a "teacher-proof" series of mathematics booklets. The findings shocked mathematics educators by showing that the child produced correct answers by inventing ingenuous, locally effective but mathematically faulty solution procedures. Such findings led many scholars to conclude that mathematics education research had to acknowledge the central role of the teacher in learning.

Growing dissatisfaction could also be felt among researchers who had never underestimated the importance of instruction and who consequently favored the teaching experiment methodology over other investigative techniques. The main cause for their uneasiness was that the restricted role of the teacher in one-on-one teaching experiments was at odds with research on teaching that highlighted the importance of teachers proactively supporting students' learning. In addition, it was becoming increasingly apparent that interactions in one-on-one teaching experiments might be qualitatively different from what occurs in the classroom as the teacher and multiple students interact (Cobb, 2012).

Those constructivist-inspired researchers who argued for the development-over-learning vision of intellectual growth could not account for either the cross-cultural and cross-situational diversity of individual learning, or for learning that occurs at the level of society. This latter type of learning is apparent from historical changes in mathematical practices, and more generally, in the increasing complexity of human ways of thinking and acting across successive generations. A solution to both these problems, inspired mainly by the work of Lev Vygotsky and his associates, was to reconceptualize learning as a process of becoming capable of acting in uniquely human ways (see Nathan & Sawyer, Chapter 2, this volume). An important aspect of human activities is that they are *mediated by artifacts*, that is, performed with the help of material tools, such as hammers or computers on the one hand, and of symbolic systems, such as language, counting systems, and writing, on the other. The artifacts, and thus the activities themselves, are constantly refined and passed from one generation to the next. The activities are historically constituted rather than predetermined, and they can differ from one culture to another. For Vygotsky, therefore, to learn meant to become a competent participant in activities that characterize the times and the culture into which people are born. From this theoretical perspective, learning mathematics is reconceptualized as becoming a competent participant in mathematical activity.

To sum up, the contemporary approaches that we call *participationist* emphasize joint participation in shared cultural activities. In contrast to the acquisitionist approaches reviewed in the previous section, participationist researchers focus on social, predominantly linguistic interaction (see Enyedy & Stevens, Chapter 10, this volume), and they often study the learning that occurs in everyday out-of-school practices as well as learning in classroom encounters (see Greeno & Engeström, Chapter 7, this volume). In the next sections, we give an overview of two prominent interrelated trends in current participationist research in mathematics education. One of these trends foregrounds school learning, whereas the other foregrounds communication and, in its strongest version, leads to the conclusion that learning mathematics is equivalent to changes in patterns of participation in discourse.

Participationist Research in Mathematics Education

Classroom Learning as a Change in Practice

The participationist approach views personal growth as originating on "the social plane" (Vygotsky, 1987, p. 11) rather than in the direct interaction between a person and the world. It therefore emphasizes that children's interactions with more knowledgeable others, such as parents and teachers, play an essential role in their learning. The participationist approach shifts the focus of mathematics education research to students' mathematical learning as it takes place in social contexts – whether classrooms, families, or elsewhere. This development has been supported by technological advances that have made it possible to document classroom occurrences in all their complexity and analyze them at any level of detail (see, for example, the video research methods described in Goldman, Zahn, & Derry, Chapter 11, in this volume).

When researchers began focusing on mathematics as practiced in the school, they soon discovered that more than one type of learning is taking place in the classroom. In addition to individual *student* learning, there is the type of learning that can be called *collective* because it involves overall changes in what is considered in the classroom as acceptable ways of doing things; and there is *teacher* learning, which had previously garnered only marginal attention. Of course, what is being learned is not necessarily the same for all participants in classroom interactions. Still, there are close ties between these three types of learning, and none of them can be adequately understood without considering the other two (note the parallels with the distinction between elemental and systemic approaches described in Nathan & Sawyer, Chapter 2, this volume).

Two innovations, one of them conceptual and the other methodological, have emerged as unifying themes in contemporary participationist studies of mathematics classrooms. First, collective learning is often conceptualized as a *change in practice*, and individual students' and the teacher's learning as a *change in ways of participating in collective practices* (cf. Rogoff, 1990). Cobb and his colleagues introduced the notion of *classroom norms* that characterize the recurrent ways of acting in a classroom. They distinguished among three types of norms. The *social* and *sociomathematical* norms differ in the degree of generality: social norms are those interactional regularities that could be found in any classroom irrespective of subject matter area, whereas sociomathematical norms are unique to the learning of mathematics (Yackel & Cobb, 1996). The third type of norms, those collectively labeled *mathematical practices of the classroom*, pertain to mathematical ways of doing things and encompass the purpose for engaging in mathematical activity, standards of mathematical argumentation, and ways of reasoning with tools and symbols (Cobb, Stephen, McClain, & Gravemeijer, 2001). Thus understood, classroom mathematical practices have been shown to evolve in the course of classroom interactions (Cobb et al., 2001). The notion of norm has proved useful in describing collective learning and in explaining individual participants' actions and interactions. In fact, all types of classroom learning may be thought of as resulting from the mutual shaping of collective norms and the teacher's and students' individual actions.

In order to investigate the interdependence of collective and individual learning and to modify instruction in response to evolving classroom mathematical practices, participationist researchers developed a research technique called the *design experiment* (see Barab, Chapter 8, this volume). This method involves both instructional design and research, with researchers assuming the responsibility for a class and its mathematical learning for an extended period of time (Cobb et al., 2001; see also Barab, Chapter 8, this volume). Rather than planning the entire course of instruction in advance, the researchers satisfy themselves with specifying learning goals, anticipating a possible collective learning trajectory, and identifying possible types of learning tasks and tools. Decisions about the exact shape of instructional tasks and tools are then made "on the run" and are grounded in ongoing analyses of what has happened in the classroom so far.

Student Learning

One of the overall goals of a design experiment is to investigate students' development of important mathematical capabilities such as justifying solutions, evaluating the reasonableness of solutions, generalizing from solutions, and making connections between multiple representations of a mathematical idea (Common Core State Standards Initiative, 2010; Kilpatrick, Swafford, & Findell, 2001). The design experiment methodology makes it possible for the researchers to both support and observe successive patterns in the development of these mathematical capabilities, and to tie the patterns observed to the specific means used to support the students' learning. The analyses of the data collected in an experiment therefore emphasize that both the process of students' mathematical learning and the mathematical capabilities they develop are situated with respect to the classroom learning environment, and are highly dependent on the students' interactions with the teacher (Brown, Collins, & Duguid, 1989).

Participationist research has supported the emergence of a broad consensus about how mathematics lessons should be organized to support students' development of key mathematical capabilities (Hiebert & Grouws, 2007). The findings of a number of studies indicate the value of the teacher introducing mathematical tasks that are challenging for students, then students working to solve the tasks individually or in small groups, and finally the teacher orchestrating a whole class discussion of the students' solutions. Looking beyond this broad recommendation, participationist research in mathematics education has also made a significant contribution by analyzing the major aspects of productive classroom learning environments, including instructional tasks, classroom norms for each phase of lessons, the nature of classroom discourse, and students' use of notations and other types of tools (Lehrer & Lesh, 2003). It is apparent from this work that the various aspects of the classroom learning environment are interdependent. For example, instructional tasks as they are actually implemented in the classroom and experienced by students depend on the tools that are available to students and on whether the teacher simply grades students' solutions or leads a whole-class discussion in which students are pressed to explain and justify their reasoning. In this regard, participationist research focuses on both the nature of instructional tasks and on the classroom activities within which the tasks come to have meaning and significance for students. Although this work is content specific, the conceptualization of the classroom learning environment as composed of interdependent aspects can be adapted to inform research on learning in other content areas.

As stated, participationist research acknowledges the crucial role of the teacher as the more knowledgeable other who proactively supports students' learning. Research on mathematics teaching has emerged during the past 10 years or so as a vibrant area of investigation that draws on research on student learning. Substantial progress has been made in delineating key classroom instructional routines that are likely to give rise to significant learning opportunities for students. As an illustration, let us consider a whole-class discussion, the aim of which is to present, compare, and consolidate students' solutions. Orchestrating such discussion is challenging because it involves drawing on students' contributions while ensuring that classroom discourse focuses on central mathematics ideas. Stein, Engle, Smith, and Hughes (2008) found that accomplished teachers could anticipate the most common types of student solutions and that they purposefully sequenced the order in which solutions were discussed so that particular mathematical issues came to the fore. In addition, they treated student contributions differentially based on whether it would advance their instructional agenda to press students to explain and justify their reasoning, evaluate a peer's solutions, or make connections between different solutions. As this illustration indicates, analyses that identify specific instructional routines make a significant contribution by specifying potential goals for teachers' learning and thus for teacher professional development. This is an important advance over broad instructional recommendations that are relatively abstract and removed from the contingencies of the classroom.

In addition to identifying specific instructional routines, research on mathematics teaching has also begun to clarify some of the types of knowing inherent in the enactment of these routines. The most influential finding in this regard concerns what Hill and her colleagues have labeled as *mathematical knowledge for teaching* and described as knowledge of mathematics specific to the work of teaching (Hill, Sleep, Lewis, & Ball, 2007). Such knowledge involves much more than just solving the problems students are expected to solve. Whereas prior research on teacher knowledge focused on this latter capability, researchers who study mathematical knowledge for teaching also ask whether teachers "understand mathematics in the particular ways needed for teaching, whether they know what their students are likely to make of the content, and whether they can craft instruction that takes into account both students and the mathematics" (Hill et al., 2007, p. 125). The prior studies failed to find a relation between teacher knowledge and the quality of instruction, in large part because the capabilities on which they focused were not specific to the work of teaching. In contrast, Hill and colleagues' finding that there is significant connection between teachers' mathematical knowledge for teaching, the quality of instruction, and student achievement indicates the value of viewing teachers' ways of knowing as situated with respect to the types of decisions and judgments that they make in the course of their work.

Teacher Learning

Participationist research has shown in a consistent manner that teachers, and not just students, may be learning through classroom interactions (see, e.g., Leikin & Zazkis, 2010). It is not surprising that this learning involves changes in instructional routines. However, it is less obvious that the teacher's mathematical ways of doing things can also be evolving in the context of practice.

A number of recent studies have employed the design experiment methodology to investigate the process of mathematics teachers' learning and the means of supporting that learning. These studies have focused on teachers' development of *high-leverage instructional routines*, that is, on routines that teachers enact frequently and that are likely to give rise to significant learning opportunities for students (e.g., Kazemi, Franke, & Lampert, 2009). Examples include eliciting and responding to student contributions, managing small group work on challenging tasks, and leading whole-class discussions of students' solutions to challenging tasks.

The findings of this research call into question the common assumption that teachers' knowledge and beliefs develop prior to practice and that they then remain unchanged as they drive teachers' instructional moves in the classroom. The evidence suggests, instead, that relevant knowledge and beliefs are integral aspects of practice and that they are refined in the context of practice. It appears essential that teachers participate in activities that approximate the targeted classroom routines with the support of professional development leaders who are more accomplished others (Franke, Kazemi, & Battey, 2007). In professional development of this type, teachers do not apply what they learn in one situation to a second situation. Instead, classroom practice is the primary context in which they make sense of their engagement in professional development activities, in the course of which they rework their classroom routines.

The findings of participationist research on teacher learning have broad implications for our understanding of learning more generally. They indicate both that learning is fundamentally situated and that people's learning in one situation (e.g., teacher professional development) can influence what they do in another situation (e.g., the classroom). The situated view (Greeno & Engeström, Chapter 7, this volume) suggests that the transfer of learning across situations is a significant achievement that requires both that the situations be aligned for learners and that learners' participation is supported by more accomplished others. In addition, the findings indicate the value of taking the practices in which people participate (e.g., teaching) as the primary point of reference when attempting to identify and assess potentially relevant types of knowledge (e.g., mathematical knowledge for teaching).

Learning as a Change in Discourse

During the second half of the 20th century, a number of European and American philosophers, with Michel Foucault and Richard Rorty the most prominent among them, suggested almost simultaneously that human knowledge should be viewed as "a kind of discourse" (Lyotard, 1993, p. 3), that is, a special form of multimodal (not just verbal) communication. In making this proposal, they challenged the characterizations of knowledge as static sets of decontextualized propositions produced by "the abstract, denotative, or logical and cognitive procedures usually associated with science" (Jameson, 1993, p. xi). Although this new proposal was made with reference to any kind of human knowledge – scientific, mathematical, or historical – a number of mathematics education researchers have taken its implications particularly seriously (Kieran, Forman, & Sfard, 2003; Lerman, 2001). Whether directly influenced by the philosophers or inspired by the Zeitgeist, these researchers began to view mathematics learners' talk as an object of study in its own right and not just a "window" to something else – conceptions, mental schemes, and so forth (see Enyedy & Stevens, Chapter 10, this volume, for additional discussion of these different perspectives on discourse). Some of these researchers declared explicitly that they view *discourse*, broadly understood as rule-governed multimodal communicational activity, as the thing that changes in the process of learning – in opposition to the acquisitionist view that what changes is the internal mental state of an individual learner (Sfard, 2008). Changes in discourse constitute learning, whether the learning occurs in the classroom or in the course of daily activities, and whether it is observed on the individual or the societal level. From this perspective, studying mathematics learning is synonymous with investigating processes of discourse development. This change of perspective has conceptual, methodological, and practical ramifications, some of them quite far reaching.

Recognition of the discursive nature of mathematics and its learning necessarily affects the very foundations of research on learning. It directly challenges the strict ontological divide between what is going on "inside" the human mind and what is happening "outside."[1] This ontological unification has at least two weighty implications. First, it completes the Vygotskian solution to the puzzle of the human ability to constantly build on previous achievements: human communication, most of which happens in language, serves as the main repository of complexity and the principal carrier of invention. Second, the statement that learning means changes in discourse creates an opportunity to operationalize research vocabulary and to refine methodology. Hypothesized mental constructs such as "mental scheme" or "conception" are then either dispensed with or redefined as aspects of discourse, and discourse is considered to be the same type of activity whether it occurs publicly or is practiced silently by a lone learner.

Equipped with definitions that specify publicly accessible criteria for when and how to apply the different theoretical terms, researchers become accountable for the claims they make. Their claims are generated by means of well-defined, rigorous procedures of data collecting and analysis. In participationist research that focuses on discourse, the basic type of data is the carefully transcribed communicational event. Many of the methods of analysis are adaptations of techniques developed by applied linguists or by discursively oriented social scientists (again, see Enyedy & Stevens, Chapter 10, this volume, for more detail on these methodologies and their historical origins). There is also a rapidly expanding assortment of analytic tools that are tailor made to fit the particular needs of mathematics education research (Moschkovich, 2010). Even so, most of these techniques can be easily transferred to the study of other subjects.

Discursive methods are demanding and time consuming. However, at their best, they allow the analyst to see what inevitably escapes attention when one is engaged in a real-time conversation. The resulting high-resolution picture of learning makes it possible to delineate differences in things or situations that previously appeared identical. The analyst is often able to perceive as rational those discursive actions that in real-time exchange appear as nonsensical. Some of the new insights are achieved through careful documentation of learners' communicational actions and through analyzes carried out at an unprecedented level of detail. Other insights are achieved by adopting

---

[1] It is important to stress that recognition of the discursive nature of mathematics does not entail complete rejection of processes that happen inside human heads. It only means that discourse becomes the superordinate category and that mental phenomena are no longer considered to have a separate ontological status. Admittedly, not all discursively oriented researchers embrace this uncompromising non-dualism, and one can thus speak about weaker and stronger discursive approaches.

a macro perspective and looking for communicational routines characteristic of the learning-teaching interactions. What has been learned thus far suggests tentative answers to some long-standing dilemmas, while also casting doubt on several common beliefs about learning and teaching mathematics (see, e.g., Sfard 2008). For instance, some discursive developments – such as when the transition is made from unsigned to signed numbers – do not just expand discourse, but also change its rules. In these cases, the support of the teacher or the "more knowledgeable other" cannot be limited to encouraging learners' own invention. Instead, it is imperative that students be exposed to, and actively supported to engage in, the discourse of the expert participant, and that they are encouraged to persist even though this discourse is new and seemingly incompatible with their own.

Concluding Remarks

Today, we know a great deal about what is likely to happen as students make their way into the world of mathematics and about how a particular teacher's instructional routines may support or hinder their learning. Moreover, mathematics education researchers now seem more capable than ever of dealing with the complexities of human learning without compromising the standards of scientific quality that such work is expected to meet. In recent years, an increasing number of studies have been successful in satisfying two requirements that previously seemed inherently irreconcilable: the requirement of insightfulness and usefulness on the one hand, and that of trustworthiness and rigor, on the other.

All this said, much work still lies ahead, and there is the constant need for innovations that can make a significant difference both in research and in the practice of teaching and learning. New opportunities seem to be opening, thanks to recent advances in brain-imaging technology. The detailed picture of the processes of learning mathematics emerging from the research reviewed in this chapter may one day be complemented by a corresponding portrayal of mathematics learning as the process of transforming specialized synaptic structures. Whatever the future developments are going to be, one thing seems certain: research in mathematics education will continue to make contributions, the importance and applicability of which go beyond its own boundaries, to the sciences of learning in general.

References

Battista, M. T. (2007). The development of geometric and spatial thinking. In F. Lester (Ed.), *Second handbook of research on mathematics teaching and learning* (vol. 2, pp. 843–908). Charlotte, NC: National Council of Teachers of Mathematics & Information Age Publishing.

Brown, J. S., Collins, A., & Duguid, P. (1989). Situated cognition and the culture of learning. *Educational Researcher*, 18(1), 32–42.

Campbell, D., & Stanley, J. (1963). *Experimental and quasi-experimental designs for research*. Chicago, IL: Rand-McNally.

Clements, D. H., & Barrista, M. T. (1992). Geometry and spatial reasoning. In D. A. Grouws (Ed.), *Handbook of research on mathematics teaching and learning* (pp. 420–424). New York: Macmillan.

Cobb, P. (2012). *Research in mathematics education: Supporting improvements in the quality of mathematics teaching on a large scale*. Paper presented at a meeting of the National Science Board Committee on Education and Human Resources, Washington, DC.

Cobb, P., Confrey, J., diSessa, A. A., Lehrer, R., & Schauble, L. (2003). Design experiments in education research. *Educational Researcher*, 32(1), 9–13.

Cobb, P., & Steffe, L. P. (1983). The constructivist researcher as teacher and model builder. *Journal for Research in Mathematics Education*, 14, 83–94.

Cobb, P., Stephen, M., McClain, K., & Gravemeijer, K. (2001). Participating in classroom mathematical practices. *The Journal of the Learning Sciences*, 10(1&2), 113–163.

Cole, M. (1996). *Cultural psychology: A once and future discipline*. Cambridge, MA: The Belknap Press of Harvard University Press.

Common Core State Standards Initiative. (2010). *Common Core State Standards for Mathematics*.

Davis, R. (1988). The interplay of algebra, geometry, and logic. *Journal of Mathematical Behavior*, 7, 9–28.

Driver, R., & Easley, J. (1978). Pupils and paradigms: A review of literature related to concept development in adolescent science students. *Studies in Science Education*, 5, 61–84.

Dubinsky, E. (1991). Reflective abstraction in advanced mathematical thinking. In D. Tall (Ed.), *Advanced mathematical thinking* (pp. 95–125). Dordrecht, The Netherlands: Kluwer Academic Publishers.

Erlwanger, S. H. (1973). Benny's conception of rules and answers in IPI mathematics. *Journal of Children's Mathematical Behavior*, 1(2), 7–26.

Filloy, E., & Rojano, T. (1989). Solving equations: The transition from arithmetic to algebra. *For the Learning of Mathematics*, 9(2), 19–25.

Fischbein, E. (1989). Tactic models and mathematical reasoning. *For the Learning of Mathematics*, 9(2), 9–14.

Franke, M. L., Kazemi, E., & Battey, D. (2007). Mathematics teaching and classroom practice. In F. Lester (Ed.), *Second handbook of research on mathematics teaching and learning* (pp. 225–256). Greenwich, CT: Information Age Publishing.

Gelman, R., & Gallistel, C. R. (1978). *The child's understanding of number*. Cambridge, MA: Harvard University Press.

Gray, E. M., & Tall, D. O. (1993). Duality, ambiguity, and flexibility: A "proceptual" view of simple arithmetic. *Journal for Research in Mathematics Education*, 25(2), 116–140.

Grossman, P., Compton, C., Igra, D., Ronfeldt, M., Shahan, E., & Williamson, P. W. (2009). Teaching practice: A cross-professional perspective. *Teachers College Record*, 111, 2055–2100.

Harel, G., Behr, M., Post, T., & Lesh, R. (1989). Fishbein's theory: A further consideration. In G. Vergnaud, J. Rogalski, & M. Artigue (Eds.), *Proceedings of the Thirteenth Annual Conference of the Psychology of Mathematics Education* (pp. 52–59). Paris: University of Paris.

Hiebert, J., & Grouws, D. A. (2007). The effects of classroom mathematics teaching on students' learning. In F. K. Lester (Ed.), *Second handbook of research on mathematics teaching and learning* (vol. 1, pp. 371–405). Greenwich, CT: Information Age Publishing.

Hill, H. C., Sleep, L., Lewis, J. M., & Ball, D. L. (2007). Assessing teachers' mathematical knowledge: What knowledge matters and what evidence counts? In F. K. Lester (Ed.), *Second handbook of research on mathematics teaching and learning* (vol. 1, pp. 111–156). Charlotte, NC: Information Age Publishing.

Jameson, F. (1993). Foreword. In J.-F. Lyotard (Ed.), *The postmodern condition: A report on knowledge*. Minneapolis: University of Minnesota Press.

Kafai, Y. B. (2006). Constructionism. In R. K. Sawyer (Ed.), *The Cambridge handbook of the learning sciences* (pp. 35–46). New York: Cambridge University Press.

Kazemi, E., Franke, M., & Lampert, M. (2009). Developing pedagogies in teacher education to support novice teachers' ability to enact ambitious instruction. Paper presented at the Annual Meeting of the Mathematics Education Research Group of Australasia, Wellington, New Zealand.

Kieran, C. (2007). Learning and teaching algebra at the middle school through college levels: Building meaning for symbols and their manipulation. In J. F. K. Lester (Ed.), *Second handbook of research on mathematics teaching and learning* (pp. 707–762). Greenwich, CT: Information Age Publishing.

Kieran, C., Forman, E. A., & Sfard, A. (Eds.) (2003). *Learning discourse: Discursive approaches to research in mathematics education*. Dordrecht, The Netherlands: Kluwer Academic Press. [Also published as a special issue of *Educational Studies in Mathematics*, 46(1–3).]

Kieren, T. E. (1992). Rational numbers and fractional numbers as mathematical and personal knowledge: Implications for curriculum and instruction. In G. Leinhardt & R. T. Putnam (Eds.), *Analysis of arithmetic for mathematics teaching* (pp. 323–371). Hillsdale, NJ: Lawrence Erlbaum Associates.

Kilpatrick, J., Swafford, J., & Findell, B. (Eds.) (2001). *Adding it up: Helping children learn mathematics*. Washington, DC: National Academy Press.

Lave, J. (1988). *Cognition in practice: Mind, mathematics, and culture in everyday life*. New York: Cambridge University Press.

Lehrer, R., & Lesh, R. (2003). Mathematical learning. In W. Reynolds & G. Miller (Eds.), *Comprehensive handbook of psychology* (vol. 7, pp. 357–391). New York: John Wiley.

Leikin, R., & Zazkis, R. (Eds.) (2010). *Learning through teaching mathematics: Development of teachers' knowledge and expertise in practice*. New York: Springer.

Lerman, S. (2001). Cultural, discursive psychology: A sociocultural approach to studying the teaching and learning of mathematics. *Educational Studies in Mathematics*, 46, 87–113.

Lyotard, J.-F. (1993). *The postmodern condition: A report on knowledge.* Minneapolis: University of Minnesota Press.

Malik, M. A. (1980). Historical and pedagogical aspects of definition of function. *International Journal of Math Science and Technology*, 1(4), 489–492.

Moschkovich, J. N. (Ed.) (2010). *Language and mathematics education: Multiple perspectives and directions for research.* Charlotte, NC: Information Age Publishing.

Nunes, T., Schliemann, A., & Carraher, D. (1993). *Street mathematics and school mathematics.* New York: Cambridge University Press.

Piaget, J. (1962). *Comments on Vygotsky's critical remarks concerning the language and thought of the child, and judgment and reasoning in the child.* Boston, MA: MIT Press.

Piaget, J. (1976). Autobiographie. Les sciences sociales avec et ýaprès Jean Piaget. *Cahiers Vilfredo Pareto. Revue européenne des sciences sociales*, XIV(38–39), 1–43.

Pirie, S., & Kieren, T. (1994). Growth in mathematical understanding: How can we characterize it and how can we represent it? *Educational Studies in Mathematics*, 26, 165–190.

Poincaré, H. (1929/1952). *Science and method.* New York: Dover Publications.

Rees, M. (2009). Mathematics: The only true universal language. *New Scientist*, 2695. http://www.newscientist.com/article/mg20126951.800-mathematics-the-only-true-universal-language.html. Retrieved August 15, 2012.

Rogoff, B. (1990). *Apprenticeship in thinking: Cognitive development in social context.* Oxford: Oxford University Press.

Saxe, G. B. (1982). Developing forms of arithmetic operations among the Oksapmin of Papua New Guinea. *Developmental Psychology*, 18(4), 583–594.

Scribner, S. (1997). *Mind and social practice: Selected writings of Sylvia Scribner.* New York: Cambridge University Press.

Sfard, A. (1991). On the dual nature of mathematical conceptions: Reflections on processes and objects as different sides of the same coin. *Educational Studies in Mathematics*, 22, 1–36.

Sfard, A. (1998). Two metaphors for learning and the dangers of choosing just one. *Educational Researcher*, 27(2), 4–13.

Sfard, A. (2008). *Thinking as communicating: Human development, the growth of discourses, and mathematizing.* Cambridge: Cambridge University Press.

Skemp, R. R. (1971). *The psychology of learning mathematics.* Harmondsworth, England: Penguin.

Skemp, R. R. (1976). Relational understanding and instrumental understanding. *Mathematics Teaching*, 77, 44–49.

Smith, J. P., diSessa, A. A., & Rochelle, J. (1993). Misconceptions reconceived: A constructivist analysis of knowledge in transition. *The Journal of the Learning Sciences*, 3(2), 115–163.

Steffe, L. P., Thompson, P. W., & Von Glasersfeld, E. (2000). Teaching experiment methodology: Underlying principles and essential elements. In E. A. Kelly & R. A. Lesh (Eds.), *Handbook of research design in mathematics and science education* (pp. 267–306). Mahwah, NJ: Lawrence Erlbaum Associates.

Stein, M. K., Engle, R., Smith, M., & Hughes, E. (2008). Orchestrating powerful mathematical discussions: Five practices for helping teachers move beyond show and tell. *Mathematical Thinking and Learning*, 10(313–340).

Tall, D., & Vinner, S. (1981). Concept image and concept definition in mathematics with particular reference to limits and continuity. *Educational Studies in Mathematics*, 12, 151–169.

Van Hiele, P. M. (2004/1959). A child's thought and geometry. In T. P. Carpenter, J. A. Dossey, & J. L. Koelher (Eds.), *Classics in mathematics education research* (pp. 60–67). Reston, VA: National Council of Teachers of Mathematics.

Vergnaud, G., Booker, G., Confrey, J., Lerman, S., Lockhead, J., Sfard, A., & Sierpinska, A. (1990). Epistemology and psychology of mathematics education. In P. Nesher & J. Kilpatrick (Eds.), *Mathematics and cognition: A research study of the International Group of the Psychology of Mathematics Education* (pp. 14–30). Cambridge: Cambridge University Press.

Vinner, S., & Dreyfus, T. (1989). Images and definitions for the concept of function. *Journal for Research in Mathematics Education*, 20(4), 356–366.

Von Glasersfeld, E. (1989). Constructivism in education. In T. Husen & T. N. Postlethwaite (Eds.), *The international encyclopedia of education, supplement vol. 1.* (pp. 162–163). Oxford/New York: Pergamon Press.

Vygotsky, L. S. (1978). *Mind in society: The development of higher psychological processes.* Cambridge, MA: Harvard University Press.

Vygotsky, L. S. (1987). Thinking and speech. In R. W. Rieber & A. C. Carton (Eds.), *The collected works of L. S. Vygotsky* (pp. 39–285). New York: Plenum Press.

Yackel, E., & Cobb, P. (1996). Sociomathematical norms, argumentation, and autonomy in mathematics. *Journal for Research in Mathematics Education*, 27(4), 58–477.

28 Science Education and the Learning Sciences as Coevolving Species

Nancy Butler Songer and Yael Kali

Science education has been a popular disciplinary context for research studies within the learning sciences, particularly in classroom-based research studies. In the 2006 handbook, chapters as diverse as conceptual change research (chapter 16), project-based research (chapter 19), authentic practices (chapter 20), design of inquiry-focused curricular units (chapter 21), and model-based reasoning (chapter 22) grounded their discussions in science-based contexts and examples. There are several explanations for this synergy between the learning sciences and science education – including a compelling international recognition of the importance of scientific thinking and problem solving across contexts with a reach far beyond the traditional scientific domains including economics, psychology, medicine, agriculture, and political science (e.g., NRC, 2007).

In biology, scientists use the idea of *coevolution* to describe the process of synchronistic changes in two different species over time, resulting in a strong and often mutually beneficial relationship between the two species. Over historical time, many species of insects and flowering plants have coevolved relative to each other and supported the mutually beneficial existence of the two organisms over thousands of years. Species such as the acacia tree and acacia ants are a good example of coevolution. The acacia tree makes a substance on its leaves that is food for the ants; in return, when predators threaten the tree, the ants release a chemical (pheromone) and organize into a large group to overcome the predator and defend the tree from being eaten.

In this chapter, we argue that the learning sciences and science education have coevolved over the past several years. In particular, our chapter is organized around four areas of educational scholarship in which the learning sciences and science education have worked in mutually beneficial ways over recent time to shape each other's scholarship, resulting in advantageous outcomes for both fields. This chapter presents each of the four areas of scholarship, followed by a brief overview of recent research in the learning sciences and science education. In each area of scholarship, some of the key ideas are represented through one context-rich example to illustrate particular aspects of the learning sciences/science education coevolution. We conclude each of the areas of scholarship with a few suggested research questions that warrant additional study. In selecting our four areas of educational scholarship, we selected themes that illustrate large-scale changes influenced by both learning sciences and science education research, as well as themes that have emerged across multiple countries and continents, particularly since the publication date of the last edition of this handbook (2006). We conclude by describing the relationship and role of technology in the science education/learning sciences coevolution, and suggest four principles for designing technology-enhanced learning that cut across contexts and disciplines.

What Is Science Knowledge? What Science Knowledge should Be Emphasized?

For many years, national policy and standards documents from a variety of nations and government organizations provided descriptions of the nature and amount of science knowledge that should be the focus of teaching and learning for preuniversity students (e.g., NRC, 2012, in the United States; OECD, 2012). Across many countries, there is strong agreement that science knowledge has never been more important. As a major policy document for Israeli science education states:

> For Israel to flourish economically ... boys and girls must receive a scientific education whose scope and quality is equal to the demands of the twenty-first century. The country must apply the latest scientific and technological innovations in teaching all subjects and at all age levels in the education system. Unfortunately, the system has proved incapable of adjusting to the age of science and technology. Here and there, we can point to impressive achievements in certain fields, but there is a pressing need for significant changes, both qualitative and quantitative, in all fields of scientific education. (Israeli Ministry of Education, 1994, p. 9)

Before a country can attain such goals, educators and policy makers must agree on the desired learning outcomes. What types of science knowledge should be fostered in formal and informal educational environments? Fortunately, across many countries and documents, there is strong agreement about the types of science knowledge formal and informal educational environments should foster to best prepare citizens for their futures. For example, a recent policy document from Ontario, Canada emphasizes two different types of scientific knowledge:

> Science refers to certain processes used by humans for obtaining knowledge about nature, and to an organized body of knowledge about nature obtained by these processes. (Science Teachers' Association of Ontario, Canada/APSO, 2006, p. 1)

The first type of science knowledge is called *scientific processes* (NRC, 1996), *ways of knowing*, or *science and engineering practices* (NRC, 2012). These terms refer to the knowledge and skills obtained and practiced by scientists when they do scientific work, including constructing scientific arguments, conducting experiments, analyzing data, and using models to make predictions (NRC, 2012). The second type of science knowledge is called *content knowledge, disciplinary core ideas* (NRC, 2012), or *the body of scientific knowledge*. This type of knowledge refers to scientific information that comprises the large amount of facts, definitions, and formulas such as "matter is made of minute particles called atoms, and atoms are composed of even smaller components" (NRC, 1996, p. 178).

Interestingly, while both types of science knowledge are often declared important in policy documents, research studies across country and age group reveal that the science knowledge emphasized in a majority of science classrooms and science resource materials, such as textbooks, is of the second type: fact-based disciplinary knowledge. There is much less emphasis on the first type of knowledge: science as a way of knowing (e.g., NRC, 2007, OECD, 2012). This emphasis on the disciplinary knowledge is also now deeply embedded in schools as a result of many years of a pedagogy and assessment cycle that places a great deal of emphasis on memorizing facts and definitions that are assessed with paper-and-pencil tests (Shepard, 2000).

During the past decade, however, particularly as a result of research studies that emphasize both the learning sciences and science education foundations, this "instructionist" focus (see Sawyer, Chapter 1, this volume) has been increasingly criticized as out of sync with today's knowledge and innovation age. Recent research suggests that the knowledge emphasized in science education should shift from an emphasis on stand-alone, compartmentalized, discipline knowledge to an emphasis on scientific knowledge that is a fused or blended combination of the two types of science knowledge. Through a recognition that neither disciplinary knowledge nor ways of knowing represent a deep, conceptual understanding of science as stand-alone pieces, policy documents and research studies are increasingly emphasizing a fused or blended knowledge product that not only strengthens and deepens the disciplinary understanding, but that supports critical thinking and problem solving within scientific knowledge domains (e.g., NRC, 2012; Songer, Kelcey, & Gotwals, 2009). As a result, many countries now emphasize the importance of developing 21st-century learning skills, such as critical thinking and problem solving (Partnership for 21st Century Skills, 2011), within science and other disciplines.

In many places in the world this shift from disciplinary facts to blended knowledge emphasizing conceptual understanding and critical thinking is becoming more commonplace in policy documents. For instance, in the United States, new national science standards specifically call for a new emphasis on scientific knowledge that systematically pairs one idea from the body of knowledge (called *disciplinary core ideas* in this document) with one

Table 28.1. *Contrasting standards on ecosystems and arguments from two versions of U.S. national science standards in 1996 and 2013*

	The U.S. National Science Education Standards (1996) (Separate presentation of standards focused on the body of knowledge and the ways of knowing)	The U.S. Next Generation Science Standards (2013) (One standard that blends disciplinary knowledge and ways of knowing)
Body of Knowledge	"Content Standard 5–8: The number of organisms an ecosystem can support depends on the resources available and abiotic factors, such as quantity of light and water, range of temperatures, and soil composition…Lack of resources and other factors, such as predation and climate, limit the growth of populations in specific niches in the ecosystem."	"Middle School, Life Science 2–1: Construct an argument supported by empirical evidence that changes to physical or biological components of an ecosystem affect populations."
Ways of Knowing	"Inquiry Standard: "Develop descriptions, explanations, predictions and models using evidence."	

or more ways of knowing (called *science and engineering practices* in this document). Drawing from foundational theories of learning and a conceptual framework document developed by learning scientists, scientists, and science educators (NRC, 2012), the new national standards are comprised of *performance expectations*, knowledge statements that combine a body of knowledge with ways of knowing into one blended science knowledge statement.

Table 28.1 presents comparative science standards from the United States that illustrate this shift in what type of science knowledge should be emphasized in K-12 science classrooms. The left column presents a life science standard from the U.S. science standards of the 1990s (NRC, 1996). The right column presents a similar life science standard from the U.S. science standards of 2013 (Achieve, 2013). Notice that while both standards include both body of knowledge and ways of knowing, the 2013 standards emphasize these two types of knowledge as blended or fused into one science knowledge goal. In other words, the new standards are crafted so that learners must engage in 21st-century problem-solving and argumentation activities as their means to gain a deep understanding of factual biology knowledge, rather than learning process skills separate from factual knowledge.

This shift in what knowledge is emphasized in science classrooms from isolated facts to the construction of arguments about a topic shifts the instruction activities toward an emphasis on using arguments, data analysis, and models about the topic to foster deep, conceptual understandings of the disciplinary ideas. So although introducing blended standards that combine these two types of knowledge may seem like a minor change, as a result, we have now motivated a shift toward pedagogical activities that discourage memorization of inert, disciplinary science facts, and instead encourage deep conceptual development of science content through engagement with both disciplinary knowledge and ways of knowing. There is already tentative evidence that this pedagogical change has resulted in better learning outcomes: quasi-experimental research has demonstrated that students who engage in curricular programs that emphasize learning disciplinary knowledge while engaging in ways of knowing demonstrated enhanced learning outcomes when compared to students engaged in a curricular program that emphasized facts only (e.g., Songer et al., 2009).

Promising Research Questions in This Area

Blending disciplinary knowledge with ways of knowing provides opportunities for new research studies, such as the following:

- Building from foundational work that characterized students' alternative ideas of disciplinary science knowledge (e.g., Driver, Guesne, & Tiberghien, 1985), what prior knowledge and alternative conceptions do students hold of blended science knowledge prior to instructional interventions focused on fostering blended knowledge development?
- What alternative conceptions and partially correct ideas do students hold of blended knowledge as they engage with instructional interventions focused on fostering blended knowledge development?
- How can individual students' progress in learning content through the practices be monitored and evaluated? What does assessment of blended science knowledge look like?

How Is Blended Science Knowledge Fostered?

Related to this shift from teaching facts and skills as distinct to teaching facts and skills in a blended fashion, a second shift is in the pedagogical practices that support learning. This section explores the shifts that have occurred in teacher moves and instructional materials that support the learning of blended science knowledge and complex reasoning in science.

Previously, many of the instructional models for science classrooms emphasized some combination of science lectures and highly specified "cookbook" laboratories (classroom lab experiments are referred to pejoratively as "cookbook" when students are told exactly what actions to take and in exactly what sequence, as if they are following directions from a cookbook to prepare a recipe). Each of these pedagogical approaches supported a view that to learn science was to listen to lectures, memorize lecture or textbook-based science facts, or repeat steps of a science experiment exactly the same way as others had before. A shift from science knowledge as declarative facts toward science knowledge as blended disciplinary knowledge learned through ways of knowing requires new teacher behaviors, new instructional models, and new instructional supports. We characterize this second shift as a shift from lecture and cookbook labs to guided instruction, including pedagogies that build on prior knowledge, emphasize scaffolds and fading (see Reiser & Tabak, Chapter 3, this volume), and emphasize metacognitive reflection (see Winne & Azevedo, Chapter 4, this volume).

As with the shift in what knowledge is emphasized, the shift in pedagogies to support blended science knowledge has deep roots in learning sciences and science education research. Research studies and learning theories from the learning sciences remind us that the learning of science and other topics is anchored in constructivism (e.g., Inhelder & Piaget, 1958), and this learning takes into account an organized developmental progression of activities that includes higher-order thinking even at younger ages (e.g., Metz, 2000). Research studies by important learning scientists like Ann Brown (e.g., Brown, Ellery, & Campione, 1998) provided evidence in the 1980s and 1990s that the development of deep conceptual understandings of science takes time, guidance such as catalysts and mediation, and repeated exposures (Brown et al., 1998; NRC, 2007). Learners develop deep understandings of disciplinary content as a result of organized "recyclings," for example structured sequences of activities that embrace rich conceptual ideas through repeated interactions at increasingly abstract levels (e.g., Karplus spiral curriculum, 1977; Songer, 2006). A central component of repeated interaction is the idea of organized, learner-focused guidance, often in the form of cognitive scaffolds (Reiser & Tabak, Chapter 3, this volume; Lee & Songer, 2003; Palinscar, 1998; Quintana et al., 2004).

More recently, many research studies have advanced our thinking in teacher moves and instructional resources to foster the new emphasis on critical thinking and blended science knowledge. Recognizing the need to build productively on individuals' prior knowledge, new research studies have provided us with much more effective tools and pedagogical moves to capture and work with students' prior ideas (McNeill & Krajcik, 2009; also see diSessa, Chapter 5, this volume; Reiser & Tabak, Chapter 3, this volume; Scardamalia & Bereiter, Chapter 20, this volume; Andriessen & Baker, Chapter 22, this volume). One emerging approach, learning progressions, points to the importance of not just being cognizant of one's prior knowledge and experiences, but organizing a systematic progression of instructional activities that build on one another toward deep conceptual understandings (e.g., Corcoran, Mosher, & Rogat, 2009). Many researchers have also utilized emerging technologies to build sophisticated scaffolds that are interactive and/or guide and fade on demand (e.g., Peters, Dewey, Kwok, Hammond, & Songer, 2012).

Figures 28.1 and 28.2 illustrate one example of a pedagogical approach that supports critical thinking and blended science knowledge. In the example, middle school students experience eight weeks of activities focused on understanding the concepts of climate change and one particular set of activities focused around the impact of climate change on an animal, the red squirrel, that lives in their region of the world – the state of Michigan, in the north central part of the United States. The science ideas emphasized in the activities blend each of these science practices: (a) data collection, (b) data analysis, and (c) using models to construct explanations with a disciplinary core idea as follows:

a. Collect data on organisms, their interactions, and where they are found to build a definition of habitat.
b. Analyze data to describe where the red squirrel lives.
c. Use a model to construct an explanation about whether there is evidence that climate change will impact where my focal species, the red squirrel, can live.

Figure 28.1 presents an illustration of one of the online curricular activities that students work with toward the end of the eight-week unit to help them develop a deep understanding of the knowledge represented earlier: students use a model to construct an explanation about whether there is evidence that climate change will impact where the red squirrel can live. All curricular units are online and are used in face-to-face classroom settings to provide flexible scaffolds and dynamic visualization resources, such as the U.S. map showing current and future information for where the red squirrel can live (Figure 28.1). Figure 28.2 presents the online curricular activities containing interactive scaffolds for guiding students in the explanation construction portion of their activity. Note that these scaffolds were designed to build productively on students' prior knowledge in the development of blended scientific knowledge, including prior disciplinary content ideas and practices addressed in earlier activities of this unit (e.g., What is a species? What are the parts of an explanation?) In this way the example illustrates the importance of (a) scaffold-rich, (b) guided learning activities along a particular learning progression that can result in (c) deeper conceptual understandings of the disciplinary knowledge through a (d) reduction in cognition load that nevertheless retains a level of "desirable difficulty" for productive engagement and learning (Bjork & Linn, 2006).

Focal Species Current and Future Distributions

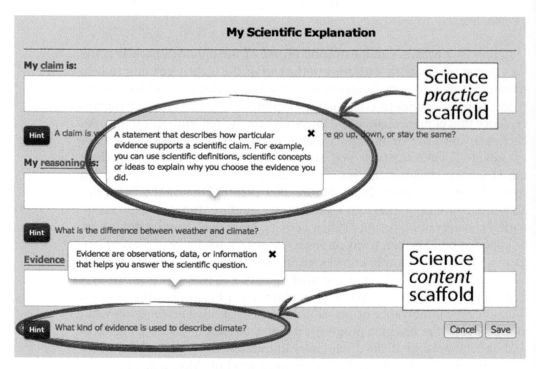

Figure 28.1. *Visualization illustrating where red squirrels can live at the present time (light shading) and in 2100 as predicted by the Intergovernmental Panel on Climate Change (IPCC).*

My Scientific Explanation

My claim is:

Science practice scaffold

Hint   A claim is y...   A statement that describes how particular   ✖   ...re go up, down, or stay the same?
                             evidence supports a scientific claim. For example,
My reasoning is: you can use scientific definitions, scientific concepts
                             or ideas to explain why you choose the evidence you
                             did.

Hint   What is the difference between weather and climate?

Evidence   Evidence are observations, data, or information   ✖   *Science content scaffold*
               that helps you answer the scientific question.

Hint   What kind of evidence is used to describe climate?   Cancel   Save

Figure 28.2. *Online scaffolds for guiding fused content and practices knowledge development.*

Promising Research Questions in this Area

The shift from lectures and cookbook labs to interactive, guided instructional activities and pedagogies that build on prior instruction presents rich new research questions for fruitful study. These include the following:

- How can technological advances such as big data, rapid feedback, or dynamic scaffolds and support be harnessed to foster blended science knowledge for a wide range of learners and stakeholders?
- How can video tutorials, big data, and webinars support a wide range of teachers' pedagogical moves to foster blended science knowledge learning?

Who should Learn Science?

One of the major advances in science education over the past 50 years has been the shift from targeting students who will become "the future scientists" to the notion that science is important for all students and that this knowledge is necessary to be a literate member of the society. This shift can be understood in light of the various reforms that have been made in science education. Pea and Collins (2008) describe four waves of such reforms. The first, which occurred in the United States from the 1950s to the 1960s, and which was followed by similar reforms in other countries, was driven by a sense that schools were not providing the appropriate education that would maintain America's leadership in science and technology. To a large extent this concern stemmed from the Soviet Union's launch of the first man-made space satellite – *Sputnik*. This wave of reform was characterized by the development of new science curricula that introduced scientific advances and emphasized the scientific method. However, these were targeted toward elite students who were most likely to become scientists.

The next three waves of reform, according to Pea and Collins, were the cognitive science reform wave (1970s–1980s), the standards reform wave (1980s–1990s), and the systematic approach reform wave (2000s to date). Focusing on the diversity aspect in these reforms, a gradual increase is evident in terms of addressing the needs of *all* learners. In the cognitive science reform, the study of learners' reasoning enabled science curriculum developers to better diagnose students' developmental level and to design supports for coping with various misconceptions, using strategies such as bridging analogies. In the standards reform, learning assessments were revised to better align with standards that defined, as mentioned previously, not only what all students *should know*, but also what they *should be able to do* at particular grade levels. Finally, in the current wave of reform, systematic means are developed so that all students would be able to reach these standards. Pea and Collins describe these means as follows: "planful coordination of curriculum design, activities, and tools to support (a) different teaching methods that will foster students' expertise in linking and connecting disparate ideas concerning science, (b) embedded learning assessments to guide instructional practices, and (c) teacher professional development to foster continued learning about how to improve teaching practice" (Pea & Collins, 2008, p. 4). They claim that current curricular efforts, such as those we describe here, represent this systematic approach (see also the book *Designing Coherent Science Education* by Kali, Linn, & Roseman, 2008, where Pea and Collins's chapter is introduced).

To illustrate how current science education addresses the issue of diversity, we first present a distinction Tate, Clark, Gallagher, and McLaughlin (2008) made between "general" and "targeted" design strategies to promote deep understanding of science among diverse groups of learners. In the general approach, diversity is attributed to differences stemming from prior knowledge, academic achievement, learning disabilities, or personal interest. In contrast, in the targeted approach, diversity is attributed to racial, linguistic, cultural, and gendered identities and experiences that students bring to the classroom. Tate and colleagues (2008) do not consider general and targeted design approaches to be in competition; they believe that curriculum materials designed to engage and support students who have been underserved have the potential to benefit *all* learners.

An example of a learning environment designed with a targeted strategy is the Technology Enhanced Learning in Science (TELS) module named "Improving your community's asthma problem" (Tate et al., 2008). This module, aimed at high school students from underserved communities, was designed to minimize the gap between their home life and school science. Students investigated how asthma affects the human body and how it is affected by environmental factors such as pollution. Their exploration was situated within their own neighborhoods, which enabled investigating sociopolitical factors that contribute to disparity in disease management (Figure 28.3). In addition to small group Web-based inquiry activities that took place in the classroom to foster deep understanding of physiological and environmental aspects of asthma, students were also involved in off-line evidence collection in their communities and in whole-class debates regarding possible solutions. Findings from eight classroom implementations (Tate, 2008) indicated that students significantly improved their ability to explain complex scientific ideas such as physiological aspects of asthma as an allergic immune response. They were also able to thoughtfully consider trade-offs in making decisions regarding alternative programs (prevention of the disease for everyone before symptoms appear versus treatment of the disease focused only on those who manifest symptoms) to deal with the problem. Improvements in learning were found regardless of whether students came from underserved communities, strengthening Tate and colleagues' (2008) assertion that "targeted" design strategies can result in curriculum materials that are beneficial to all learners.

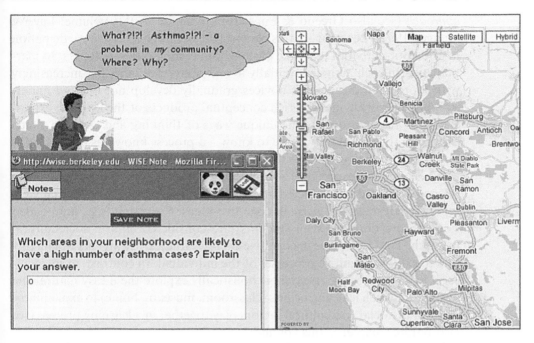

Figure 28.3. *Web page from the "Asthma" module, a community-based curriculum designed to connect school science with students' everyday lives (from Tate et al., 2008).*

Promising Research Questions in this Area

The shift from science education for a select few, to science education as a core component of science literacy and critical thinking for learners of all ages and dispositions, presents rich new research questions for fruitful study. These include the following:

- Are there unique targeted supports that are appropriate for specific audiences and that might hinder other audiences? Do such supports have an added value compared to more generalized supports?
- If so, how can diversity within the classroom be addressed?
- How can curricula be designed so that the cultural differences inherent to school contexts become assets rather than impediments?

Science Knowledge Is Situated and Learned Socially

One of the most important advancements in the learning sciences, which has greatly resonated in science education research, has been the shift away from viewing learning as an individual cognitive process to the idea that knowledge and knowing are situated in social and cultural contexts. This new perspective is referred to as the *sociocultural approach* or the *situated approach* (see also Greeno & Engeström, Chapter 7, this volume; Lave & Wenger, 1991). Learning, in this perspective, is viewed as active participation in authentic activities that take place within communities' practices. By participating in such activities, initially in a peripheral manner but increasingly with more centralized roles, novices gradually develop not only an understanding of the big ideas or rich conceptual products of the learning experience, but also appropriate the unique ways of thinking and doing in which experts in the community come to know – a process known as *enculturation* into the community (see also Collins & Kapur, Chapter 6, this volume).

When science knowledge is considered to be situated, research on how science is learned is conducted in very different ways. Occurrences that were typically referred to as *noise* in cognitive-focused research (e.g., unintended side conversations between students) are considered *data* in sociocultural research. That is because in cognitive-focused studies, researchers isolate factors to explain cognitive processes of the individual. In contrast, in sociocultural research studies, researchers holistically explore the messy naturalistic settings in which learning occurs (classroom, museum, home) to explain how all sorts of social and cultural factors play together in a learning process (see also Barab, Chapter 8, this volume).

In designing science learning environments, the situated perspective has led to the development of rich, contextual learning experiences that, in some cases, are very different from a traditional lecture-delivered approach. For example, Sagy and colleagues (2011) transformed a traditional undergraduate lecture-based course in biology, typically taught in large classes of about 350 students. Their design included knowledge-building teams of five students who worked collaboratively for a few weeks on their own, using a Wiki-based environment, to explore and prepare a presentation regarding a specific aspect (e.g., a specific organelle) of one of the ten course topics (e.g., organelles). Each team's exploration was guided by specific questions (e.g. "What is the connection between the chloroplasts in cells and the changes in concentration of oxygen in a river?"), for which they were provided resources to seed their collaborative knowledge-building process. This unit culminated with a special "mini-conference" meeting, facilitated by the instructor, in which a group of 35 students who chose to focus on one course topic discussed the various team presentations (see Figure 28.4). Sagy and colleagues (2011) demonstrated that this intervention significantly affected students' appropriation of what they called a more "internal-value based culture of learning." In other words, when this intervention was fully implemented, students sought deeper understanding of the contents and took more ownership of their learning process, compared to students who took the course when the intervention was only partially implemented. Furthermore, Tsaushu and colleagues (2012) show that, by participating in one knowledge-building team and mini-conference meeting, students developed deeper understanding of biological ideas that cut across the topics of the course.

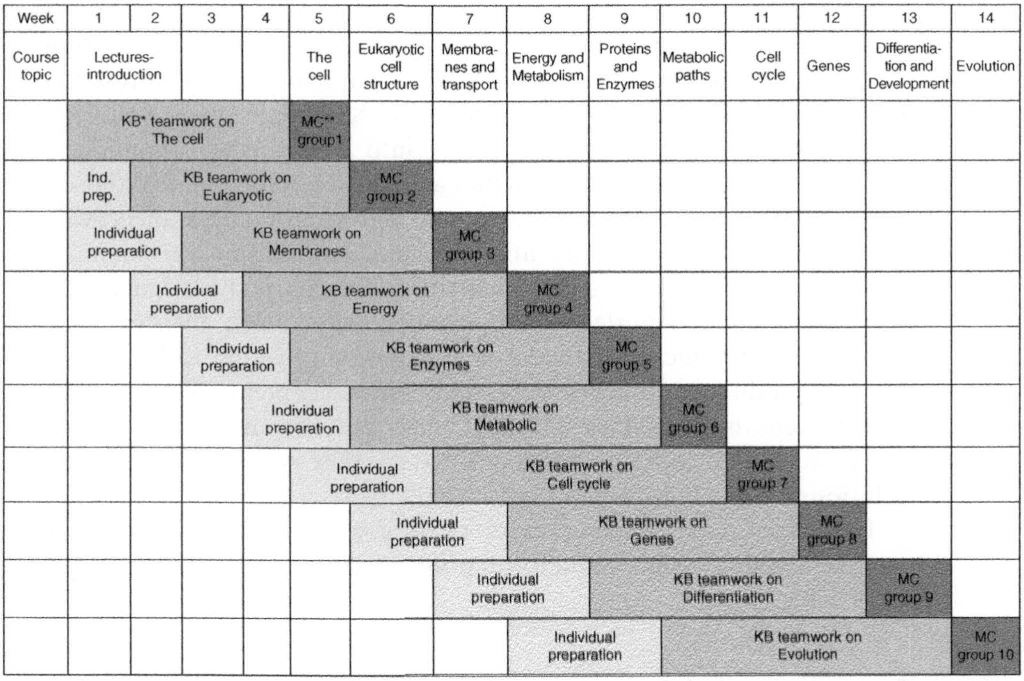

Week	1	2	3	4	5	6	7	8	9	10	11	12	13	14
Course topic	Lectures-introduction				The cell	Eukaryotic cell structure	Membranes and transport	Energy and Metabolism	Proteins and Enzymes	Metabolic paths	Cell cycle	Genes	Differentia-tion and Development	Evolution
	KB* teamwork on The cell				MC** group1									
	Ind. prep.	KB teamwork on Eukaryotic				MC group 2								
	Individual preparation		KB teamwork on Membranes				MC group 3							
		Individual preparation		KB teamwork on Energy				MC group 4						
			Individual preparation		KB teamwork on Enzymes				MC group 5					
				Individual preparation		KB teamwork on Metabolic				MC group 6				
					Individual preparation		KB teamwork on Cell cycle				MC group 7			
						Individual preparation		KB teamwork on Genes				MC group 8		
							Individual preparation		KB teamwork on Differentiation				MC group 9	
								Individual preparation		KB teamwork on Evolution				MC group 10

* KB = Knowledge-building   ** MC = Mini-conference

Figure 28.4. *Course structure in the advanced level of the intervention, showing individual, team, and group work in each of the course topics (adapted from Sagy et al., 2011).*

Increasingly, the theoretical notion of "situatedness" has served as a rationale for designing innovative learning environments and educational interventions in various disciplinary areas, as in the example described earlier. These interventions, in turn, enable further exploration of the ways people learn. Specifically, we would like to highlight two major trends in science education that were motivated by the situated approach. The first has to do with the context for learning, suggesting socio-scientific issues (SSIs) as a productive arena for situated learning of science (Sadler, 2009). The second has to do with innovative technologies that have afforded new ways of participation in communities of learning in science.

SSIs as Contexts for Situated Science Education

In his comprehensive review, Sadler (2009) illustrates how social issues such as genetically modified food (Walker & Zeidler, 2007) or global warming (Khishfe & Lederman, 2006), which are heavily informed by scientific knowledge, can serve as ideal contexts for science education as framed by situated learning theory.

By engaging students in the exploration of ill-structured problems that involve complex undetermined solutions (Kuhn, 2010; Zohar & Nemet, 2002), require negotiation of scientific ideas, and tend to be controversial in nature (Bricker & Bell, 2008), teaching with SSIs, according to Sadler, can transform the culture of school science into a culture of communities of practice. In other words, the activities afforded by SSIs resemble those that active citizens carry out in a modern world, and thus provide students with an opportunity to engage in authentic problem-solving within a community.

Sadler's review shows that such activities, when properly designed (e.g., by supporting students in developing scientific skills during their exploration of the SSI), can increase student interest and motivation to learn science, serve as productive contexts for learning science content, develop students' higher-order thinking skills, and most important, encourage them to become "involved in their communities in new ways as they explore and contribute to solutions for local problems" (Sadler, 2009, p. 33).

This line of research is an example of the coevolution of science education and the learning sciences, and it will probably continue to inspire research in both fields.

Technologies that Support New Ways of Participation in Communities of Learning in Science

The second trend in which the situated approach to learning has played a crucial role in science education has to do with the growing use of educational technologies. Since the 1980s, technological tools have played an increasing role in supporting school learning. When learning is viewed as active participation within a community, technologies that enable new forms of participation have a unique added value in supporting such learning. Increasingly, teachers are using tools such as Wikis, blogs, and other collaborative editing and social networking tools to provide students with creative ways to participate in communities of learning (e.g., Ben-Zvi, 2007). Designated collaborative learning environments such as Knowledge Forum (Scardamalia & Bereiter, Chapter 20, this volume), have also been developed to support knowledge-building processes within communities. More recently, technological tools have been designed to enable students to engage in collaborative learning endeavors using their avatars in Multi-User Virtual Environments (MUVEs) (see Kafai & Dede, Chapter 26, this volume).

Technologies that support participation in learning communities have been developed and explored in a wide variety of disciplinary areas, such as art, history, literature, math, and science. However, in science education, unique participatory technologies have been developed to address specific challenges involved in science learning. Participatory (or immersive) simulations are an example. This type of technology is often designed to assist students in developing understandings of complex scientific phenomena (see also Wilensky & Jacobson, Chapter 16, this volume).

For instance, Colella (2000) explored students' learning about how epidemic diseases are spread. To assist them in understanding this complex phenomenon, she designed a life-sized simulation in which students, wearing small, communicating computers called Thinking Tags, transformed into players in a large-scale microworld. When students met with each other, their tags, if carrying the "virus," infected each other. But, simulating a real epidemic disease, the virus was initially latent (invisible), making it impossible for students to know if they were "sick," while infecting more and more students. By playing the simulation several times, and trying to figure out what the underlying rules of the simulation are, students were deeply engaged in collaborative exploration of the phenomenon – in fact, they spontaneously designed experiments to decipher what was happening.

This particular use of technology, which was initially designed to address challenges in science education, has made an important contribution to our current state of knowledge in the learning sciences regarding the ways learners develop understandings of complex systems, thus contributing to the coevolutionary development of both fields. We further discuss this development in the next section regarding design principles that cut across disciplines and contexts.

Promising Research Questions in this Area

The shift away from viewing science learning as an individual cognitive process to the idea that knowledge and knowing in science are situated in social and cultural contexts presents rich new research questions for fruitful study. These include the following:

- What are the implications of blurring the boundaries between "school culture" with more situated "science culture" in terms of traditional teacher-student hierarchies?
- How should teacher training and professional programs support teachers in developing the skills required to teach situated science?

Design Principles that Stem from the Dual-Domain Coevolutionary Process

Our examples were selected to illustrate recent shifts in the knowledge, pedagogical moves, target audience, and context of emerging learning environments in science. Note that each of these examples utilizes technology to support teaching and learning science. This section will discuss the role of technology in the learning sciences/science education coevolutionary work, and what we know about the design of technological tools that support complex thinking in science.

Productive design of technology-enhanced learning in science combines bottom-up and top-down processes. In top-down processes, designers build learning environments that exploit the unique strengths of technology, based on theories of learning. As Laurillard expressed, designers should "use what we know about what it takes to learn, and build this into a pedagogical framework with which to challenge digital technologies to deliver a genuinely enhanced learning experience" (Laurillard, 2009, p. 5). In contrast, bottom-up processes reflect the fact that design is an iterative process in which theories of learning are developed and refined in repetitive cycles of designing a learning environment, implementing the design in real-world contexts, and analyzing the learning that occurs as a consequence of students' interaction within the designed environment. This iterative, bottom-up process has been developed in the past decade into a methodological approach named design-based research (DBR) (see Barab, Chapter 8, this volume).

In recent years, researchers have come to use notions such as design principles (Kali, 2006, 2008, Kali & Linn, 2007; Merrill, 2002) and design patterns (Goodyear & Retalis, 2010; Linn & Eylon, 2006) to guide the design of learning environments. In the following sections we utilize design principles to illustrate common ideas that are not only relevant to the design of science learning environments, but that can also be used to guide the design of learning environments in disciplines other than science. The fact that these principles cut across disciplines and contexts and employ ideas from both science education and the learning sciences illustrates how research-based knowledge regarding how to support learning has propagated in this dual-domain coevolutionary process.

We use the design knowledge presented in the Design Principles Database (DPD) to illustrate this. The DPD is an archive of design knowledge, which includes a set of interconnected descriptions of features and principles that were contributed by various educational technology design researchers in a collaborative knowledge-building endeavor between 2001 to 2008 (Kali, 2006). Following is a description of how the examples presented in this chapter demonstrate more generalized principles.

Providing Students with Templates to Help Reasoning in the "Distribution of the Red Squirrel" Example

The scaffolds presented in Figure 28.2 in the "distribution of red squirrel" example were designed to blend students' learning of science content with their development of scientific process skills. These scaffolds exemplify a more general design principle described in the DPD as: "provide students with templates to help reasoning," which Janet Kolodner articulated as follows: To support students in articulating complex scientific ideas, designers have created what might be called templates. Templates scaffold students in representing their ideas and revising them as they complete complex activities"

(Kolodner et al., 2004). The template helps students to create a solution to a problem by de-structuring the problem into its components, and by supplying analytical and visual tools to deal with each segment. Apart from the inherent analysis, the template as a whole, allows students to integrate between segments of the solution (The Design Principles Database, 2007, prkey 308).

Providing students with templates to help reasoning can be used in non-science disciplines. For instance, templates are one of the features in the Knowledge Forum environment that help students develop their literacy in a wide range of contexts (Scardamalia & Bereiter, Chapter 20, this volume).

Connecting to Personally Relevant Contexts in the "Asthma in My Community" Example

The "asthma in my community" module (Figure 28.3) was designed to connect school science with students' everyday lives. Connecting to personally relevant contexts is described in the DPD as follows:

> Too often students find academic science lacking personal relevance. This sense of irrelevance leads to lack of personal interest and low engagement levels. Personally-relevant problems drawn from students' everyday lives, such as determining how to keep a drink cold or how to minimize the potential radiation danger associated with cellular phone use can make science accessible and authentic. Such problems can elicit intuitive ideas to fuel inquiry because students have had prior experiences related to the problem scenarios. (The Design Principles Database, 2007, prkey 171)

But connecting to personally relevant contexts can be used as a design principle in other disciplines too. For instance, in the Paidaia curriculum focused on teaching classics such as ancient Greek texts, teachers are instructed to draw analogies between social roles and conflicts in classic novels and those that students face in their neighborhoods and in contemporary society (Wortham, 1994).

Employing Multiple Social Activity Structures in the "Mini-Conference Sequence in Biology Course" Example

In the mini-conference sequence in the biology course, Sagy and colleagues (2011) designed activities that transitioned between individual learning (of informational contents using the online tutorial), small team knowledge building (of a specific aspect), and group meetings (in the mini-conference format). These transitions provided students an opportunity, despite the large class of 350 students, to get a sense of the way scientists share knowledge in conferences. But this design principle can definitely be used in other disciplines such as mathematics (see Sfard & Cobb, Chapter 27, this volume). Working in small teams is, at times, more efficient than working in big groups. In the Computer as Learning Partner research, students were most successful when they collaborated with one peer on a complex project (Linn & Hsi, 2000). This stemmed from the comfort individuals felt in one-on-one discussions as well as from the logistic difficulties of working with large groups. However, larger groups also offer students opportunities. In larger groups students need to justify their opinions more coherently to get them heard and to negotiate tasks more carefully than they do when working with one partner. Multiple social formats also increase the likelihood that all the participants will find an effective format for their learning (The Design Principles Database, 2007, prkey 238).

Engaging Learners in Complex Projects in the Epidemic Disease Participatory Simulation Example

In her discussion, Colella (2000) describes several specific principles for designing participatory simulations. But other, more generalized design principles can also be deduced from the epidemic disease participatory simulation, which can be used for designing learning environments for various disciplines. For instance, one pragmatic design principle in the DPD calls to "engage learners in complex projects." This design principle is described as follows:

> Too often inquiry-based learning environments introduce curricular topics in an isolated and over-simplified manner. In many cases topics are presented as disconnected from one another, which leads to the constructing of superficial knowledge that lacks integration. When students are introduced to real world problems they have the opportunity to struggle with the complexity of the topics and to engage in thoughtful debates. In this manner students can make connections between various ideas of central topics, develop integrated understanding, and be prepared for future learning (The Design Principles Database, 2007, prkey 248).

In fact, in recent years Levy and Wilensky extended the use of participatory simulations, which were earlier studied mostly in scientific contexts, to design "everyday complexity" participatory simulations. Using these simulations, sixth grade students explored ordinary social events, which can be explained in terms of complexity theory as "emergent phenomena" (also see Wilensky & Jacobson, Chapter 16, this volume). For instance, students reasoned about the following situation:

> a sixth-grade classroom goes out on a break to the playground. One can see boys and girls congregating in same-sex groupings. Explaining such a pattern does not require a centralized planned organization. It is enough to think of a small set of simple rules: each individual prefers to be with other individuals of the same gender. If you are by a group of mostly the opposite gender, you move away. If you are by a group of primarily the same gender as yours, you stick around. The emergent pattern is a

gender-segregated community of sixth-graders. However, no one has instructed them to separate in this way! (Levy & Wilensky, 2008, p. 10)

Adopting complexity lenses to explore young students' reasoning about everyday emergent phenomena enabled Levy and Wilensky to describe and characterize a construct they call *mid-level strategy*, which they define as students' expressed understanding of complex systems principles. This is another example of ways science education research has influenced the learning sciences.

Conclusion

The fields of the learning sciences and science education are deeply intertwined. While the exact mechanism and directionality of change is not always easy to articulate, we suggest that there have been shifts and movement in both disciplines that have benefited both fields. In particular, we see evidence of mutual shaping, such as examples where ideas from the learning sciences, such as situated cognition, have been influential in science education. We also see evidence that ideas from science education, such as emphasis on knowledge that blends disciplinary core ideas with practices, is being incorporated into other disciplines within the learning sciences more broadly. And we expect that this coevolution will continue to result in important new developments in our understanding of learning.

References

Achieve. (2013). Next generation science standards. Downloaded from www.nextgenscience.org on May 28, 2013.

Ben-Zvi, D. (2007). Using wiki to promote collaborative learning in statistics education. *Technology Innovations in Statistics Education*, 1(1), 1–18.

Bjork, R. A., & Linn, M. C. (2006). The science of learning and the learning of science: Introducing desirable difficulties. *APS Observer*, 19(3).

Bricker, L. A., & Bell, P. (2008). Conceptualizations of argumentation from science studies and the learning sciences and their implications for the practices of science education. *Science Education*, 92(3), 473–498.

Brown, A., Ellery, S., & Campione, J. C. (1998). Creating zones of proximal development electronically. In J. G. Greeno & S. Goldman (Eds.), *Thinking practices: A symposium in mathematics and science education*. Hillsdale, NJ: Lawrence Erlbaum Associates.

Colella, V. (2000). Participatory simulations: Building collaborative understanding through immersive dynamic modeling. *The Journal of the Learning Sciences*, 9(4), 471–500.

Corcoran, T., Mosher, F. A., & Rogat, A. (2009) Learning progressions in science: An evidence-based approach to reform. Consortium for Policy Research in Education Research Report RR 63.

The Design Principles Database (DPD). (2007). Multiple entries retrieved from http://www.edu-design-principles.org/dp/viewPrincipleDetail.php?prKey=308 (replace prkey number to access different entries cited).

Driver, R., Guesne, E., & Tiberghien, A. (1985) *Children's ideas in science.* Buckingham, UK: Open University Press.

Goodyear, P., & Retalis, S. (2010). *Technology-enhanced learning: Design patterns and pattern languages.* Rotterdam: Sense Publishers.

Inhelder, B., & Piaget, J. (1958). *The growth of logical thinking from childhood to adolescence.* New York: Basic Books.

Israeli Ministry of Education. (1994). Tomorrow 98: Report of the Superior Committee on Science, Mathematics and Technology Education in Israel.

Kali, Y. (2006). Collaborative knowledge building using the Design Principles Database. *International Journal of Computer Support for Collaborative Learning,* 1(2), 187–201.

Kali, Y. (2008). The Design Principles Database as means for promoting design-based research. In A. E. Kelly, R. A. Lesh, & J. Y. Baek (Eds.), *Handbook of design research methods in education* (pp. 423–438). New York: Routledge.

Kali, Y., & Linn, M. C. (2007). Technology-enhanced support strategies for inquiry learning. In J. M. Spector, M. D. Merrill, J. J. G. van Merriënboer, & M. P. Driscoll (Eds.), *Handbook of research on educational communications and technology.* Third Edition (pp. 445–461). Mahwah, NJ: Lawrence Erlbaum Associates.

Kali, Y., Linn, M. C., & Roseman, J. E. (2008). *Designing coherent science education: Implications for curriculum, instruction, and policy.* New York: Teachers College Press.

Karplus, R. (1977). Science teaching and the development of reasoning. *Journal of Research in Science Education,* 14(2), 169–175.

Khishfe, R., & Lederman, N. (2006). Teaching nature of science within a controversial topic: Integrated versus nonintegrated. *Journal of Research in Science Teaching,* 43(4), 395–418.

Kolodner, J. L., Owensby, J. N., & Guzdial, M. (2004). Case-based learning aids. In D.H. Jonassen (Ed.), *Handbook of research for education communications and technology, 2nd Ed.* Mahwah, NJ: Lawrence Erlbaum Associates.

Kuhn, D. (2010). What is scientific thinking and how does it develop? In U. Goswami (Ed.), *Handbook of childhood cognitive development.* Second Edition. Blackwell.

Laurillard, D. (2009). The pedagogical challenges to collaborative technologies. *International Journal of Computer-Supported Collaborative Learning,* 4(1), 5–20.

Lave, J., & Wenger, E. (1991). Situated learning: Legitimate peripheral participation. In R. Pea & J. S. Brown (Eds.), *Learning in doing: Social, cognitive, and computational perspectives* (pp. 29–129). Cambridge: Cambridge University Press.

Lee, H. S., & Songer. N. B. (2003). Making authentic science accessible to students. *International Journal of Science Education,* 25(1), 1–26.

Levy, Sharona T., & Wilensky, U. (2008). Inventing a "mid level" to make ends meet: Reasoning between the levels of complexity. *Cognition and Instruction*, 26(1), 1–47.

Linn, M. C., & Eylon, B. (2006). Science education: Integrating views of learning and instruction. In P. A. Alexander & P. H. Winne (Eds.), *Handbook of educational psychology, second edition* (pp. 511–544). Mahwah, NJ: Lawrence Erlbaum Associates.

Linn, M. C., & Hsi, S. (2000). *Computers, teachers, peers: Science learning partners*. Mahwah, NJ: Lawrence Erlbaum Associates.

McNeill, K., & Krajcik. J. (2009) Synergy between teacher practices and curricular scaffolds to support students in using domain specific and domain general knowledge in writing arguments to explain phenomena. *The Journal of the Learning Sciences*, 18(3), 416–460.

Merrill, M. D. (2002). First principles of instruction. *Educational Technology Research and Development*, 50(3), 43–59.

Metz, K. (2000). Young children's inquiry in biology: Building the knowledge bases to empower independent inquiry. In J. Minstrell & E. van Zee (Eds.), *Inquiring into inquiry learning and teaching in science* (pp. 371–404). Washington, DC: AAAS.

National Academy of Science. (2007). *Rising above the gathering storm: Energizing and employing America for a brighter economic future*. Washington, DC: National Academies Press.

National Research Council (NRC). (1996). *National science education standards*. Washington, DC: National Academies Press.

National Research Council (NRC). (2007). *Taking science to school: Learning and teaching science in grades K-8*. Washington, DC: National Academies Press.

National Research Council (NRC). (2012). *A framework for K-12 science education: Practices, crosscutting concepts and core ideas*. Washington, DC: National Academies Press.

OECD. (2012). OECD Science, Technology and Industry Outlook 2012. http://www.oecd.org/sti/oecdsciencetechnologyandindustryoutlook.htm.

Palincsar, A. S. (1998). Social constructivist perspectives on teaching and learning. *Annual Review of Psychology*, 49, 345–375.

Partnership for 21st Century Skills. (2011). Framework for 21st Century Learning. Downloaded from http://www.p21.org/tools-and-resources/policy-maker#defining on May 29, 2013.

Pea, R., & Collins, A. (2008). Learning how to do science education: Four waves of reform. In Y. Kali, M. C. Linn, & J. E. Roseman (Eds.), *Designing coherent science education: Implications for curriculum, instruction, and policy* (pp. 3–12). New York: Teachers College Press.

Peters, V., Dewey, T., Kwok, A., Hammond, G., & Songer, N. B. (2012). Predicting the impact of climate change on ecosystems: A high school curricular module. *The Earth Scientist*, (28)3, 33–37.

Quintana, C., Reiser, B., Davis, E., Krajcik, J., Fretz, E., Duncan, R., Kyza, E., Edison, E., & Soloway, E. (2004). A scaffolding design framework for software to support science inquiry. *The Journal of the Learning Sciences*, 13(3), 337–386.

Sadler, T. D. (2009). Situated learning in science education: Socio-scientific issues as contexts for practice. *Studies in Science Education*, 45(1), 1–42.

Sagy, O., Kali, Y., Tsaushu, M., Tal, T., Zilberstein, D., & Gepstein, S. (2011). Promoting a culture of learning that is based on internal values in an introductory undergraduate level biology course. Paper presented at the 14th biennial European Association for Research on Learning and Instruction (EARLI) conference, Exeter, United Kingdom.

Scardamalia, M. (2003). Crossing the digital divide: Literacy as by-product of knowledge building. *Journal of Distance Education*, 17 (Suppl. 3, Learning Technology Innovation in Canada), 78–81.

Shepard, L. (2000). The role of assessment in a learning culture. *Educational Researcher*, (20)7, 4–14.

Songer, N. B. (2006). BioKIDS: An animated conversation on the development of curricular activity structures for inquiry science. In R. Keith Sawyer (Ed.), *Cambridge handbook of the learning sciences* (pp. 355–369). New York: Cambridge University Press.

Songer, N. B., Kelcey, B., & Gotwals, A. (2009). How and when does complex reasoning occur? Empirically driven development of a learning progression focused on complex reasoning about biodiversity. *Journal of Research in Science Teaching*, (46)6, 610–631.

STAO/APSO. (2006). Position Paper: The nature of science. downloaded from http://stao.ca/resources/position-statements/Nature_of_Science.pdf.

Tate, E. D. (2008). The impact of an asthma curriculum on students' integrated understanding of biology. Paper presented at the American Educational Research Association, Washington, DC.

Tate, E. D., Clark, D., Gallagher, J., & McLaughlin, D. (2008). Designing science instruction for diverse learners. In Y. Kali, M. C. Linn, & J. E. Roseman (Eds.), *Designing coherent science education: Implications for curriculum, instruction, and policy* (pp. 65–93). New York: Teachers College Press.

Tsaushu, M., Tal, T., Sagy, O., Kali, Y., Gepstein, S., & Zilberstein, D. (2012). Peer learning and support of technology in an undergraduate biology course to enhance deep learning. *CBE life sciences education*, 11(4), 402–412.

Walker, K. A., & Zeidler, D. L. (2007). Promoting discourse about socioscientific issues through scaffolded inquiry. *International Journal of Science Education*, (29)11, 1387–1410.

Wortham, S. E. F. (1994). *Acting out participant examples in the classroom*. Philadelphia, PA: John Benjamins Publishing Company.

Zohar, A., & Nemet, F. (2002). Fostering students' knowledge and argumentation skills through dilemmas in human genetics. *Journal of Research in Science Teaching*, 39(1), 35–62.

29 Learning Historical Concepts

Mario Carretero and Peter Lee

History is about what people have done and what has happened to them, but it can also be about the shape of society or institutions at particular times in the past. History seems to be about everyday, commonsense things – decisions that people make, actions that people take. We all make decisions and take actions every day, so many people believe that history can be understood simply by applying commonsense understandings. In history we learn about *presidents, entrepreneurs, constitutions*, and *trade*, and although most of us have never met a president, we can easily think of the president's actions and decisions as variants of actions and decisions that we ourselves engage in. And although sometimes we read about things that are never encountered in modern life (like *pharaoh, serf, puritan*, or *musket*), we can easily conceive of these as quaint versions of what we know already. The task of learning history, then, is often portrayed as being less about mastering strange and esoteric conceptual tools than about acquiring information about ordinary life, as it was and as it unfolded. In short, history seems to be commonsense and cumulative.

In this chapter, we argue that this simplistic view of history learning is a mistake. Four decades of research suggests that thinking historically is counterintuitive (Lee, 2005). History requires understanding concepts that differ from everyday conceptions and explanations. Some everyday ideas are completely incompatible with history; many students, for example, believe that we can only really know anything by directly experiencing it. Many more students believe that because there was only one past series of events that actually occurred, there can only be one true description of the past. It is likely that children often learn how to "tell the truth" by appeal to a fixed past against which we can measure truth claims. Such an idea is useful in day-to-day affairs where conventions of relevance may be shared, but in history it fails completely. There may be differing views about what questions to ask, and contested conventions of relevance. Moreover, what is asserted may not be something that could have been witnessed by anyone; changes in values, birth rates, or the environment could not be directly witnessed like births or battles: they must be inferred, not observed.

We know from misconceptions research in science education (see diSessa, Chapter 5, this volume) that science learners have to abandon commonsense concepts (like *weight* or *speed*) and struggle with very different tools for handling the world (like *mass* or *velocity*) or even ideas that appear – sometimes despite their labels – to have no analog in common sense (like *entanglement* or *neutron*). We argue that successful learning in history involves similar challenges to learning physics – they both require learners to overcome misconceptions.

If we examine, for example, how the French Revolution is presented to students in many regions, we see that the students are presented with abstract concepts and arguments – such as the structure of French society at that time or the emergence of free-thinking ideas and their connection with economic and sociopolitical factors. This example demonstrates that history shares many of the complexities of the social sciences. For example, numerous investigations indicate that an answer to a question like "Why has poverty existed and why does it still exist in the world?" involves political, economic, social, cultural, and other causes, forming a multicausal structure whose understanding requires complex and abstract thinking. In contrast, many affluent and middle-class students are likely to believe that this question has a simple answer: poverty continues to exist only because certain individuals do not have the will to overcome it (see Barton, 2008, for extended review).

The example of poverty hints at the complexities of substantive history, but does not touch on a more fundamental problem that students face: How can we know anything about the past? Given the fact that no one alive today was present to witness most of the human past, the stories and explanations that history purports to offer seem to many students to be at best a matter of opinion. For students who think like this, history does not seem to be common sense, but rather, it seems to be subjective opinion – which is odd for a field that purports to be scholarly.

The content of historians' stories and explanations are populated with first-order elements, for example *peasants*, *generals*, *laws*, and *priests*, but always behind (or above) any account of these first-order elements are implicit second-order concepts of, for example *historical evidence*, *change*, *significance*, and *accounts*. Professional historians make assumptions about the nature of historical evidence, explanations, and accounts, and these lie behind any substantive claims about the past (Lee, 2005). In this chapter, we consider "learning history" in two sections: how students learn the substantive knowledge of the past – the first-order content, and how they learn the second-order understanding that helps organize and underpin that substantive knowledge.

Understanding Substantive Historical Concepts

Research indicates that students' understanding of events and processes can vary greatly in complexity throughout adolescence and adulthood (Barrett & Barrow, 2005; Furnham, 1994). For example, some students understand revolutions as simple confrontations between groups of people rather than as structural changes affecting all aspects of society. These students also understand monarchy only in terms of the actions of an individual king; they may have difficulty understanding that a modern nation-state is not simply a territory and its inhabitants, but a complex social system that could only have emerged relatively recently in human history because of economic, intellectual, and technological developments (Carretero, Castorina, & Levinas, 2013).

Understanding the conceptual framework that is involved in the processes of societal change – examples include the Neolithic revolution and the transition from feudalism to capitalism – requires a mastery of concepts that have no direct manifestation in empirical reality; rather, they are theoretical elaborations by social scientists and historians. These historical concepts and theories have an intrinsically changing nature. As history teachers know, any historical concept, for example *democracy*, did not mean the same thing in classical Greece as it means now. This is a very well-known teaching issue, and it is also a central and unresolved issue among professional historians.

Historical concepts possess many diverse meanings. Concepts can be used in different ways, not only because of the passing of time, but also in the same historical moment, by different groups and interests. This is extremely important not only from a theoretical point of view, but also when it comes to teaching history, where complex concepts – such as *independence, emancipation, liberty, people, nation, state, patriotism, citizenship*, and so forth – need to be introduced. Such concepts change their meaning through time and have different connotations for individuals and groups. History teaching must therefore take into account how students use such historical concepts and how the student (and the class) could represent different features of the same concept, generating different meanings according to their prior knowledge and cultural experience. Failure to do so means teachers may not be addressing the ideas they intend, leaving students to assimilate what is being taught to existing preconceptions.

According to recent research, the ability to understand historical concepts progresses along with the development of conceptual thinking more generally (Barton, 2008; Limón, 2002). *Conceptual development* refers to both the type of characteristics or attributes with which concepts are defined and the connections that are established between them. Conceptual development takes two forms. First, a student progresses from understanding concepts through their more concrete dimensions to assigning more abstract qualities to the concepts (see Figure 29.1). This development is reflected in (for example) a typical student's conception of social institutions. Younger pupils have a more concrete understanding of institutions and social realities: they are embodied by the people who represent them or by specific events. For example, the French Revolution is associated with Napoleon, or the Industrial Revolution is associated with the invention of the steam

Change	Concepts		
		Initial understanding	Final understanding
From concrete to abstract	Facts	Reduction to superficial aspects (directly perceptible)	Definition by deep features (dependent theoretical elements)
	Institutions	Personalization	Institutionalization
From static to dynamic	Simultaneous realities	The different fields of social and historical reality (e.g., political, economic) appear separate	Integration of the various fields of social and historical reality
	Successive realities	Conception of social reality as immutable (naturalization of social and historical beliefs)	Understanding of social change and consideration of social and historical objects and phenomena as processes and in a distanced manner

Figure 29.1. *Development of the understanding of substantive historical concepts.*

engine. In this naïve understanding, history is composed of a succession of people and events, such as Napoleon or the invention of the steam engine. With increasing understanding, a student begins to understand social and historical concepts better, but in a static and isolated manner. Finally, the student comes to understand history as an increasingly complex conceptual network in which different elements are interconnected and in which every social and historical reality is dynamically defined by its relationship with other aspects of reality.

In their comprehension of the social world at any given time in history, adolescents generally believe that the various elements of the social world are disconnected, seldom establishing any connections between the different aspects of a social reality (e.g., political, economic, social, cultural, military). For example, they think that cultural progress is caused by purely cultural factors, and that it has no connection with any political or economic factors. Voss and Carretero (2000) asked a group of college students to explain the dissolution of the Soviet Union in 1991. Some students provided more complex explanations than others, but any mention of interactions between the factors (e.g., economic problems, nationalism, international context) was rare.

In their comprehension of changes across time, teenagers generally tend to think that things continue as they are, with little change possible (see Figure 29.1). Representations of historical and social phenomena in children and even some adolescents and adults have proven rather static. Students tend to think that different social situations are immutable. And as a result, social change is difficult for them to understand, and a proper learning of history is quite difficult.

We argue that school history should do more than simply teach "first-order" facts and concepts; it should also teach students to "think historically," what we have called "second-order" understanding – the ability to use evidence, to give and assess explanations, and to construct and evaluate narratives of the past. Curriculum and teaching that is designed to develop historical thinking must move beyond asking students to copy, sort, and drill for memory of facts. The most influential and large-scale example of such an approach was the Schools Council History Project in the United Kingdom in the 1980s, and perhaps the most significant current example is the Historical Thinking Project in Canada (Seixas, 2010; Shemilt, 1980).

To develop these new approaches in this educational area, one must know how students of different ages conceive of history. Do students believe that history is an exact reflection of past reality? Or do they understand that history emerges from a reasoning process and therefore from human interpretation? These questions were addressed by Shemilt (1983), who demonstrated that the comprehension of students between 13 and 16 years of age evolves from a realistic conception of historical inquiry – in which they believe that historians simply find written historical data – to a more negotiated conception through which they understand the significant difference between hypotheses and supporting evidence. In a study primarily involving students from 10 to 11 years of age, Brophy, VanSledright, and Bredin (1992) also found that students of this age believed history to be an exact science consisting of unambiguous facts, and that a historian resembles the popular stereotype of the archaeologist who objectively examines remnants of the past. When students move past this misconception to a more negotiated conception, they begin to understand the function of primary sources and the importance of understanding the historical and social context in which those sources were generated.

There is considerable agreement that thinking historically requires at least the following:

a) Being able to use evidence to confirm or disconfirm singular factual statements about the past.
b) Understanding that historical accounts are constructions in answer to questions, and are neither copies of the past nor simply aggregations of singular factual statements.
c) Imagining situations that one cannot experience, and entertaining values and beliefs about the world that one does not share (sometimes employing concepts that are strange and even repugnant, and which no longer have equivalents nowadays).

d)   Defining abstract concepts with precision and demonstrating how the meanings of these concepts, as they are used and defined by others, have changed over time.

e)   Developing hypotheses regarding the causes and effects of past events by considering that a cause can be remote both in time and in the analysis of its effects. This type of thinking implies the added complexity of the need to account for different levels of analysis (for example, some political effects of an event may originate from religious causes), which are sometimes combined with a temporal dimension.

f)   Examining the extent to which the developed hypotheses conform to the facts, while understanding that reality is complex and that one can always find and consider counterarguments.

g)   Analyzing change (and continuity) over time, as indicated by (c), (d), and (e). This also involves understanding ideas related to time, like duration, sequence, and temporal conventions.

The following review focuses on (a) through (e), but the research mentioned often has implications for (f) and (g).

A. Evidence

Historians select and evaluate *evidence* from the past, which often entails using written documents to construct accounts and explanations of past events. Wineburg (1991a, 1991b) demonstrated that historians use three heuristics or strategies known as *corroboration, sourcing,* and *contextualization* that are not used by college students lacking specific knowledge of history. According to the first of these heuristics, a historian always looks to find important details from different sources before accepting them as probable or plausible. The sourcing heuristic means that through the evaluation of evidence, historians pay attention to their original source. Finally, the contextualization heuristic refers to the general tendency of historians to place events in historical space and time within a chronological sequence.

An empirical study on the expulsion of the Moors from Spain during the 17th century confirmed that participants with a high level of expertise (university professors who are specialists in modern history) use the contextualization heuristic (Limón & Carretero, 1999, 2000; see also VanSledright & Limón, 2006 for a review). Their interpretations differed significantly from those of fifth-year university students majoring in history (the other group participating in the study), particularly in two aspects:

i)   The professors accounted for and interrelated various levels of analysis (economic, political, social, and ideological): a difficult task for children and teenagers (Carretero, López-Manjón, & Jacott, 1997).

Figure 29.2. *Christopher Columbus receives presents from the Cacique Quacanagari on Hispaniola (what is now modern Haiti). Theodore de, Bry (1528–1598). Engraving.*

ii) The professors considered the "time" dimension by distinguishing between the analysis and assessment of the problem in the short, medium, and long term, whereas fifth-year history majors do not make such a distinction. This also sheds light on (g), analyzing change over time.

To think historically, students have to abandon the assumption that we rely on *reports* for our knowledge of the past, and develop a genuine concept of *evidence*. Evidence ceases to be a special category of objects: anything can be evidence for appropriate questions, and in this sense evidence is created by questions.

Historians often use images as a method of solving historical problems. In several inquiries, research participants of different ages were shown a historical picture, Figure 29.2, that commonly appears in textbooks, and asked to provide a historical narrative for the picture. Figure 29.2 is an engraving by T. De Bry and it was the focus of our inquiry in a comparative study of textbooks (Carretero, Jacott, & López-Manjon, 2002). Results for adolescents and adults from three different countries (Argentina, Chile, and

Spain) indicate that 12- and 14-year-old students range from considering the image in a "realistic" manner (i.e., almost as a copy of the reality that supposedly occurred) to considering the picture itself as a historiographic product that does not copy the past reality but is a product of history and thus requires distanced and theoretical interpretation and analysis. In some adults and 16-year-old subjects, we found only the last conception. After comparing students from different countries and finding the same developmental sequence, the study concluded that the evolution of this heuristic in the interpretation of historical images does not appear to depend on cultural influences but rather responds to a pattern that is determined by cognitive development. This pattern of change in the representation of historical images demonstrates the transition from a concrete and realistic to an abstract and complex way of considering historical "objects," as shown in the research of the development and change of historical and social concepts.

B. Historical Accounts

Students undergo a developmental trajectory in their understanding of historical *accounts*. These understandings tend to progress from less to more powerful, as shown in Figure 29.3. This model seems to accurately represent student development in several different cultures (Lee & Ashby, 2000). Later in this chapter, we further explore a particularly common form of historical account, the *narrative*.

C and D. Empathy

Empathy has been defined as the ability to understand others' actions in the past and to recognize that other people and other societies had beliefs, values, and goals that differed from our own. Students tend to assume that people in the past had the same beliefs and values as they do (Ashby & Lee, 1987; Shemilt, 1984). Wineburg (2001) described this as a "default" position. Indeed, there is considerable evidence to suggest that many students assume that because people in the past acted in ways we would not, and accepted institutions that would be unacceptable today, they were defective in both intelligence and ethical judgment, compared with us (Lee & Ashby, 2001). In contrast, professional historians understand that beliefs and values are different in different historical periods and different societies; an important element of historical thinking is the ability to imagine oneself in a very different time with a different worldview. Again, it is possible to produce a progression model of ideas likely to be held by students in connection with empathy (see Figure 29.4), allowing teachers to anticipate possible prior conceptions to be addressed in the classroom (Lee & Shemilt, 2011).

1. Accounts are just (given) stories

Accounts are stories that are just 'there'. Competing stories are just different ways of saying the same thing, rather like the school task of telling the same story 'in our own words'.

2. Accounts fail to be copies of a past we cannot witness

Accounts cannot be 'accurate' because we were not there to see the past and therefore cannot know it; they differ because they are just 'opinion', that is, a substitute for knowledge we can never have.

3. Accounts are accurate copies of the past, except for mistakes or gaps

If we know the facts, there is a one-to-one correspondence between the past and accounts. (This is the positive correlate of the previous position.) 'Opinion' is a result of gaps in information and mistakes.

4. Accounts may be distorted for ulterior motives

Accounts are distorted copies of the past. Differing accounts derive not simply from lack of knowledge, but from authors who necessarily distort the past. 'Opinion' is bias, exaggeration and lies stemming from partisan positions. Ideally a story should be written from no position.

5. Accounts are organized from a personal viewpoint

Accounts are arrangements of significant parts of the past chosen by historians. Students who think like this have made a major break with previous ideas by abandoning the idea that accounts should be copies of the past. 'Opinion' re-appears as personal choice in the selection historians make, but this does not make it partisan. A viewpoint and selection are legitimate features of accounts. Historians may be interested in answering different questions.

6. Accounts must answer questions and fit criteria

Differences in accounts are not just a matter of authors' choices; accounts are necessarily selective, and constructed for particular themes and timescales. There can be no complete account. It is in the nature of accounts to differ — legitimately — from one another: they (re-) construct the past in answer to questions. Accounts are assessed against criteria in order to determine their admissibility and relative worth. Rival accounts of the same topics may be accepted because they address equally worthwhile questions about that topic. Disciplinary criteria exclude many possible accounts of the past, but do not prescribe a fixed number of admissible accounts.

Figure 29.3. *A provisional progression model of students' ideas about historical accounts.*

1. A Deficit Past

Past action is unintelligible because people in the past were stupid, not as clever as we are, inept, morally defective, or "didn't know any better".

2. Generalized Stereotypes

Past action explained in terms of conventional stereotypes of roles, institutions etc. Ascription of very generalized dispositions. "They would do that, wouldn't they."

3. Everyday Empathy

Past action explained in terms of the specific situation in which agents found themselves, but this is seen in modern terms. No consistent distinction between what the agent could know and what we now know, or between past beliefs and values and ours.

4. Restricted Historical Empathy

Recognition that the agent's knowledge, beliefs and values may have differed from ours, and that intentions and purposes may be complex, qualified and ramified.

5. Contextual Historical Empathy

Action set in a wider context of beliefs and values, and a recognition that it may require to be understood as having implicit goals related to matters outside its overt concerns.

Figure 29.4. *A highly simplified progression model of students' ideas about historical empathy.*

E. Cause

Another central area of study involves examining the evolution in the understanding of historical *causality* during the school years and the type of explanations participants provide when required to give an account of a specific historical and social event. In one study, students were asked to link boxes to explain an event (Lee, Dickinson, & Ashby, 2001). This study identified three strategies for the formulation of causal explanations: the *additive strategy*, according to which causes are established in a linear and isolated manner; the *narrative strategy*, in which linear chains of cause united by "and then" or "therefore" are formed; and the *analytical strategy*, in which connection nodes are set between causes. Shemilt (1983) analyzed students' ideas to produce a developmental model of causal explanation. In this model, learners gradually transition from the idea that causes are immanent in past events, to the idea that "cause" is a property of persons (a causal power), and finally to a notion of causal chains or networks. As students become more sophisticated in their understanding of historical causality, they begin to realize the possibilities opened up or constrained by prevailing social, economic, and political conditions. At the most advanced level, conditions are understood to be contingent on the contexts in which they operate, and causal explanations are understood to be more like theories than things to be found in the world.

A key component of causal understanding is the understanding of *necessary* and *sufficient conditions*. In one study, university students were asked to explain the collapse of the former Soviet Union. This study found that the students had "a reasonable intuitive sense of the concepts of sufficiency and necessity" (Voss, Ciarrocchi, & Carretero, 2000). Participants with an interest in history and current events tended to have more confidence in their judgments, and receiving training in the meaning of the concepts of sufficiency and necessity increased this confidence.

Another key component of causal understanding is students' ideas about how to test causal explanations. Scholars have conducted very little research on this, but one study indicated considerable differences (probably age-related) in the assumptions and conceptual tools available to 10- and 14-year-olds for deciding whether one explanation is better than another (Lee, 2001).

Carretero and colleagues (1997) conducted a study in which they asked high school students and university students in their fifth year of the history and psychology programs to grade a series of "causes" related to the so-called discovery of America. The primary goal of this work was to study the characteristics and types of explanations offered by participants with little domain-specific knowledge. The results indicate that students with a higher level of domain-specific knowledge (fifth-year history students) attached significantly more importance to "causes" that enabled the contextualization of the event in a broader sociopolitical context, whereas the remaining students (adolescents from 12 to 16 years old and even adult psychology students) gave significantly more prominence to intentional agents who participated in the event (recall the findings that children have more "concrete" understandings of historical change, associating changes with specific individuals rather than with macrosocial forces). Other authors, such as Halldén (2000), have also emphasized the importance of personal agents in the historical explanations of students.

Younger children appear less likely than adolescents to make any distinction between causal and descriptive statements, and are less likely to distinguish between the reasons leading to an action and the conditions and causal antecedents explaining the result of the action. (Actions can lead to unintended outcomes, so explaining why someone did something is not automatically explaining why the outcome event occurred.) There is also evidence that the reasons students give for an *action* and their ideas about giving causal explanations of *events* are decoupled: development in these two aspects of explanation does not necessarily go hand in hand (Lee et al., 2001).

Construction of Historical Narratives

Humans interpret their own actions and behaviors, and those of others, through narrative. Narrative thought is a widespread, and possibly innate, way of understanding social and historical reality; this makes it of particular importance in learning history (Rüsen, 2005; Straub, 2005). Several authors in the philosophy of history (e.g., Ricoeur, 1990; White, 1987) have emphasized that narratives are a powerful cultural tool for understanding history, even though the explicative and logical structure of history does not always conform to psychologically conventional narrative structure.

Narratives are not a sequence of random events; rather, they are used in an attempt to shed light on how one event causes another and the factors that affect these relationships. Nevertheless, the intuitive psychological structure of narrative tends to be more simple than reality; it does not include all of the causes that contribute to an outcome or all of the actors that participated in an event. When it comes to history, many students treat historical narratives as if they were complete and accurate copies of a fixed past. And yet professional historians think of history in very different ways; first, because the past may be described in an indefinite number of ways, and second, because our understanding of the past is dynamic, changing with subsequent events. It could not be said in 1920 that "the 1919 Treaty of Versailles sowed the seeds for Nazi rule in Germany," whereas in 1940 this description was a possible one. If they are to learn history, students must therefore understand that narratives simplify history, they tell some stories and omit others, and they mention some central characters while neglecting others who are lesser known and more anonymous (occasionally entire social groups). In short, narratives are tools for understanding history, but are not history itself (see Figure 29.3).

Historical narratives acquire special importance in the educational context where they are often falsely equated with history itself (Halldén, 1998, 2000). Two types of concrete narratives frequently appear in the realm of education: individual narratives and national narratives (Barton & Levstik, 2004; VanSledright, 2008). Alridge (2006), in an exhaustive analysis of American textbooks, revealed that narratives regarding the great men and events that guided America toward an ideal of progress and civilization continue to be the prototypical way many historians and textbooks disseminate knowledge.

Individual narratives center on the personal lives of relevant historic figures, in comparison with narratives that focus on more abstract entities and events such as nations, economic systems, social change, civilizations, and other impersonal concepts. Examples of individual narratives are easily recalled from our own experiences in school: stories of Columbus, Julius Caesar, and Napoleon are classic examples. The classroom use of individual narrative is justified, in part, on the ground that more abstract accounts are more difficult to understand and less motivating for students. As several authors have indicated (Alridge, 2006; Barton, 2008; Lopez & Carretero, 2012), individual narratives have the power to humanize history. Students may identify with the central characters, they may imagine the thoughts and feelings that guided them, and even try to imagine how they (the student) might have acted in those situations. Through these narratives, students also learn to value the role that one individual can play in a society and contemplate the possible impact of a particular individual, but these representations do not necessarily imply historical disciplinary understanding. In some cases they could be rather simplistic and even unhistorical.

Nevertheless, although individual narratives can be highly motivating and more easily understood by students, they can also produce a series of characteristic biases that complicate the development of historical thinking. For example, they may lack causal explanations of a structural nature based on social, political, or economic factors. The impact produced by collective action is ignored. They almost unavoidably propagate the misconception that long-term processes of change can be identified with deliberate acts carried out by individuals (Barton, 1996). Often, standard histories associate a historic event with a specific historic figure (who is then seen as the cause and the principal actor of the event), thus emphasizing that individuals are causes of historical events (Rivière et al., 1998). Prominent examples in U.S. history include the association of the "discovery of America" with Christopher Columbus or the association of Abraham Lincoln with the end of slavery in the United States.

Another type of narrative found in both education and daily life is the *national narrative* (Carretero, Asensio, & Rodriguez-Moneo, 2012; Symcox & Wilschut, 2009). These narratives are found in history classrooms in practically all countries (Barton & McCully, 2005; Carretero, 2011). This is because history education, beginning at the end of the 19th century, was intended to serve the function of consolidating national identity and building nation-states (Grever & Stuurman, 2008). This type of narrative substantially influences the way students understand and analyze information about the past. National narratives, for example, make it difficult to consider another nation's point of view, or the perspective of nondominant groups. And this interferes with the development of historical thinking, because a fundamental component of historical literacy is the ability to take into account different versions of history. Classes in national history rarely explain conflicts between interpretations; most reproduce the official version of history almost without nuance. Thus, in national history classes, students are likely to encounter an approach to history as closed, unique, and true (VanSledright, 2008).

These national narratives may become socially shared *schematic templates*. For example, in the case of the United States, two have been identified: the concept of progress and the idea of liberty (Barton & Levstik, 2004). When one possesses these schematic templates, the resistance of Native Americans to the encroaching settlements of European colonists is seen as an obstacle to achieving progress; the Vietnam War is explained as a righteous attempt to bring liberty and freedom to that country. Students are typically presented in class with a very conventional version of these national narratives; they rarely are presented with the most controversial aspects of history, and this complicates the development of more advanced historical thinking (Alridge, 2006; Grever & Stuurman, 2008).

Carretero and Bermudez (2012) have presented a theoretical analysis of the interactive processes of production-consumption of school historical narratives. Usually production processes are related to the way cultural artifacts, in this case history textbooks, include specific historical narratives (Foster & Crawford, 2006). Consumption processes have to do with the way students and people in general make sense of and appropriate those produced contents (Bermudez, 2012). Produced and consumed historical narratives do not necessarily share exactly the same features and elements, but some kind of significant interaction is expected. We identify six common features of school historical narratives, present in both the production and consumption process.

a) The establishment of the historical subject through a logical operation of exclusion-inclusion. This is to say, historical narratives are always presented in terms of a national positive "we" as opposed to a negative "they." This logical operation is critical because it determines both the main voice and the logical actions for that national subject.

b) Identification processes as a cognitive but also an affective anchor. It is likely that the national distinction "we-they" is already mastered by children between six and eight years of age. It is very probable that this emotional feature will facilitate the formation of the nation as a concept, through a strong identification process at a very early age.

c) Frequent presence of mythical and heroic characters and motives. Myths and mythical figures, as expressed through narratives, are usually beyond time restrictions. When time and its constraints are introduced, history, as a discipline, is making its appearance. Often in the school context students cannot properly understand historical narratives because they tend to consider historical figures as almost mythical ones.

d) Search for freedom or territory as a main and common narrative theme. Students consider the process by which their own nation gained independence as a historical master narrative, emplotted as the search for freedom, independently of the multiple and complex causes that produced such a process of independence.

e) Historical school narratives contain basic moral orientations. Historical master narratives always present the nation as a moral and justified actor, providing legitimization for the nation's main acts.

f) A romantic and essentialist concept of both the nation and its nationals. This feature implies the view of the nation and its nationals as preexisting political entities, having a kind of eternal and "ontological" nature.

Teaching Implications

Caution is required here: talk of "implications of research for teaching" may be misleading, because changes in teaching and research both stemmed from the same context of changing conceptions of what is involved in "learning history." Nevertheless, the research we review in this chapter has important consequences for teaching, and the three principles set out by the U.S. *How People Learn* (HPL) project – summarizing the robust findings of cognitive research over the previous three decades – indicate why. HPL pointed first to the necessity of addressing students' prior conceptions (to avoid assimilation of what is taught to existing ideas). Second, it emphasized that cognitive competence in any area depends on a deep foundation of factual knowledge, understood and organized in a conceptual framework specific to the relevant discipline, facilitating retrieval and application. Third, it insisted on a metacognitive approach to allow students to take control of their own learning.

As we have seen, research into students' second-order ideas about the nature and status of historical knowledge suggests that learning history is not a matter of extending commonsense factual knowledge to include more past facts, or even stories and explanations. It warns teachers that history is not so simple, and gives them some guidance as to what to expect as students come to grips with specific second-order concepts, and how these concepts are likely to develop. It also offers the beginnings of a picture of how second-order concepts can provide a metacognitive apparatus for students, so that they can ask themselves if a statement they want to make is justified by the evidence, how far their attempted explanation accounts for the facts, or whether the narrative they have constructed answers the question they have posed as well as competing stories do.

If learning history is as complex as research suggests, there is little doubt that teaching history in many schools across the world must continue to change. But this is not something that empirical studies of learning and understanding can determine on their own. Wider conceptions of the place and aims of history in society are also at stake. The research we review in this chapter has increased the tensions between policy makers, politicians, and many citizens – who see history education as a matter of strengthening the social cement – and those who, in developing more sophisticated understanding of "thinking historically," see learning history as acquiring a centrally important way of seeing the world.

If history is indeed an "unnatural act," then how students learn it and how it is taught is a serious matter, and perhaps one where only formal education can be expected to make a difference.

Acknowledgments

This chapter was written with the support of projects EDU-2010 17725 (DGICYT, Spain) and PICT 2008–1217 (ANPCYT, Argentina), both coordinated by the first author, who would like to acknowledge that support.

References

Alridge, D. P. (2006). The limits of master narratives in history textbooks: An analysis of representations of Martin Luther King, Jr. *Teachers College Record*, 108.

Ashby, R., & Lee, P. J. (1987). Children's concepts of empathy and understanding in history. In C. Portal (Ed.), *The history curriculum for teachers* (pp. 62–88). Lewes: Falmer Press.

Barrett, M., & Buchanan-Barrow, E. (Eds.) (2005). *Children's understanding of society*. London: Taylor & Francis.

Barton, K. C. (1996). Narrative simplifications in elementary students' historical thinking. In J. Brophy (Ed.), *Advances in research on teaching: Teaching and learning history* (pp. 51–83). Greenwich, CT: JAI Press.

Barton, K. C. (2008). Research on students' ideas about history. In L. Levstik & C. A. Thyson (Eds.), *Handbook of research on social studies education*. New York. Taylor and Francis.

Barton, K. C., & Levstik, L. S. (2004). *Teaching history for the common good*. Mahwah, NJ: Lawrence Erlbaum Associates.

Barton, K. C., & McCully, A. W. (2005). History, identity, and the school curriculum in Northern Ireland: An empirical study of secondary students' ideas and perspectives. *Journal of Curriculum Studies*, 37, 85–116.

Bermudez, A. (2012). The discursive negotiation of narratives and identities in learning history. In M. Carretero, M. Asensio, & M. Rodriguez-Moneo (Eds.), *History education and the construction of national identities* (pp. 203–220). Charlotte, NC: Information Age Publishing.

Brophy, J., VanSledright, B. A., & Bredin, N. (1992). Fifth graders' ideas about history expressed before and after their introduction to the subject. *Theory & Research in Social Education*, 20(4), 440–489.

Carretero, M. (2011). *Constructing patriotism: Teaching history and memories in global worlds*. Charlotte, NC: Information Age Publishing.

Carretero, M., Asensio, M., & Rodriguez-Moneo, M. (Eds.) (2012). *History education and the construction of national identities*. Charlotte, NC: Information Age Publishing.

Carretero, M., & Bermúdez, A. (2012). Constructing histories. In J. Valsiner (Ed.), *Oxford handbook of culture and psychology* (pp. 625–646). Oxford: Oxford University Press.

Carretero, M., Castorina, J. A., & Levinas, M. L. (2013). Conceptual change and historical narratives about the nation: A theoretical and empirical approach. In S. Vosniadou (Ed.), *International handbook of research on conceptual change* (pp. 269–287). New York: Routledge.

Carretero, M., Jacott, L., & López-Manjon, A. (2002). Learning history through textbooks: Are Mexican and Spanish children taught the same story? *Learning and Instruction*, 12, 651–665.

Carretero, M., López-Manjón, A., & Jacott, L. (1997). Explaining historical events. *International Journal of Educational Research*, 27(3), 245–253.

Foster, S. J., & Crawford, K. A. (Eds.) (2006). *What shall we tell the children? International perspectives on school history textbooks*. Greenwich, CT: Information Age Publishing.

Furnham, A. (1994). Young people's understanding of politics and economics. In M. Carretero & J. F. Voss (Eds.), *Cognitive and instructional processes in history and the social sciences* (pp. 19, 25, 26). Hillsdale, NJ: Lawrence Erlbaum Associates.

Grever, M., & Stuurman, S. (2008). *Beyond the canon: History for the 21st century*. Basingstoke: Macmillan.

Halldén, O. (1994). Constructing the learning task in history. In M. Carretero & J. F. Voss (Eds.), *Learning and reasoning in history* (pp. 187–200). Hillsdale, NJ: Lawrence Erlbaum Associates.

Halldén, O. (1998). Personalization in historical descriptions and explanations. *Learning and Instruction*, 8(2), 131–139.

Halldén, O. (2000). *On reasoning in history*. In J. F. Voss & M. Carretero (Eds.), *Learning and reasoning in history* (pp. 272–278). London: Routledge.

Lee, P. J. (2001). History in an information culture: Project CHATA. *International Journal of Historical Learning, Teaching and Research*, 1(2), 75–98.

Lee, P. J. (2005). Putting principles into practice: Understanding history. In M. S. Donovan & J. D. Bransford (Eds.), *How students learn history in the classroom* (pp. 29–78). Washington, DC: National Academy Press.

Lee, P. J., & Ashby, R. (2000). Progression in historical understanding among students ages 7–14. In P. Seixas, P. Stearns, & S. Wineburg (Eds.), *Teaching, learning and knowing history* (pp. 199–222). New York: New York University Press.

Lee, P. J., & Ashby, R. (2001). Empathy, perspective taking and rational understanding. In O. L. Davis Jr., S. Foster, & E. Yaeger (Eds.), *Historical empathy and perspective taking in the social studies* (pp. 21–50). Boulder, CO: Rowman & Littlefield.

Lee, P. J., Dickinson, A. K., & Ashby, R. (2001). Children's ideas about historical explanation. In A. K. Dickinson, P. Gordon, & P. J. Lee (Eds.), *Raising standards in history education: International Review of History Education, Volume 3* (pp. 97–115). London: Woburn Press.

Lee, P. J., & Shemilt, D. (2011). The concept that dares not speak its name: Should empathy come out of the closet? *Teaching History*, 143.

Limón, M. (2002). Conceptual change in history. In M. Limón & L. Mason (Eds.), *Reconsidering conceptual change: Issues in theory and practice* (pp. 259–289). New York: Kluwers.

Limón, M., & Carretero, M. (1999). Conflicting data and conceptual change in history experts. In W. Schnotz, S. Vosniadou, & M. Carretero (Eds.), *New perspectives on conceptual change* (pp. 137–160). Amsterdam: Pergamon/Elsevier.

Limón, M., & Carretero, M. (2000). Evidence evaluation and reasoning abilities in the domain of history: An empirical study. In J. F. Voss & M. Carretero (Eds.), *Learning and reasoning in history: International review of history education* (vol. 2) (pp. 252–271). London: Routledge.

Ricoeur, P. (1990). *Time and narration*. Chicago: University of Chicago Press.

Rivière, A., Nuñez, M., Barquero, B., & Fontela, F. (1998). Influence of intentional and personal factors in recalling historical text. In J. F. Voss & M. Carretero (Eds.), *Learning and reasoning in history: International Review of History Education, Volume Two* (pp. 214–226). London: Woburn Press.

Rüsen, J. (2005). *History*. New York: Berghahn Books.

Seixas, P. (2010). A modest proposal for change in Canadian history education. In *Contemporary public debates over history education: International Review of History Education, Volume Six* (pp. 11–26). Charlotte, NC: Information Age Publishing.

Shemilt, D. (1980). *History 13–16 Evaluation Study*. Edinburgh: Holmes McDougall.

Shemilt, D. (1983). The Devil's Locomotive. *History and Theory*, XXII(4), 1–18.

Shemilt, D. (1984). Beauty and the philosopher: Empathy in history and the classroom. In A. K. Dickinson, P. J. Lee, & P. J. Rogers (Eds.), *Learning history* (pp. 39–84). London: Heinemann.

Straub, J. (Ed.) (2005). *Narration identity and historical consciousness*. New York: Berghahn.

Symcox, L., & Wilschut, A. (Eds.) (2009). *National history standards. The problem of the canon and the future of teaching history: International Review of History Education, Volume Five*. Charlotte, NC: Information Age Publishing.

VanSledright, B. (2008). Narratives of nation-state, historical knowledge and school history education. *Review of Research in Education*, 32(1), 109–146.

VanSledright, B., & Limón, M. (2006). Learning and teaching in social studies: Cognitive research on history and geography. In P. Alexander & P. Winne (Eds.), *Handbook of educational psychology* (2nd ed.) (pp. 545–570). Mahwah, NJ: Lawrence Erlbaum Associates.

Voss, J. F., & Carretero, M. (Eds.) (2000). *Learning and reasoning in history: International Review of History Education, Volume Two*. New York: Routledge.

Voss, J., Ciarrocchi, J., & Carretero, M. (2000) Causality in history: On the "intuitive" understanding of the concepts of sufficiency and necessity. In J. Voss & M. Carretero (Eds.), *Learning and reasoning in history: International Review of History Education* (pp. 199–213). New York: Routledge.

White, H. (1987). *The content of the form: Narrative discourse and historical representation*. Baltimore, MD: Johns Hopkins University Press.

Wineburg, S. (1991a). Historical problem solving: A study of the cognitive processes used in the evaluation of documentary and pictorial evidence. *Journal of Educational Psychology*, 83(1), 73–87.

Wineburg, S. (1991b). The reading of historical texts: Notes on the breach between school and academy. *American Educational Research Journal*, 28, 495–519.

Wineburg, S. (2001). *Historical thinking and other unnatural acts*. Philadelphia, PA: Temple University Press.

30 Learning to Be Literate

Peter Smagorinsky and Richard E. Mayer

Among the defining features of an advanced modern society is widespread literacy in a print medium. And yet human beings invented writing systems only about 5,500 years ago, well after the human mind had fully evolved, suggesting that the human cognitive architecture could not have evolved specifically to enable reading and writing. Instead, the ability to read and write is based on general cognitive abilities that evolved to satisfy other purposes. For this reason, studies of literacy learning have general implications for all studies of cognition and learning. In this chapter, we review the large body of learning sciences research that examines the fundamental cognitive and social processes whereby people learn to read and write. We conclude by identifying several general implications for learning scientists.

The word *literacy* evolved from the Latin term *litteratus*, which means "being marked with letters." Thus a "literate person" is a person who can read and write text using letters. More recently, a broader and more expansive notion of a *literate performance* has been applied to fields and areas traditionally not focused solely on printed verbal texts: information literacy, media literacy (or mediacy), multimedia literacy, technological literacy, functional literacy, critical literacy, rhetorical literacy, arts literacy, ecological literacy, health literacy, statistical literacy, emotional literacy, computer literacy (or cyberacy), science literacy, mathematical literacy (or numeracy), visual literacy, digital literacy, infomedia literacy, moral literacy, dance literacy, ancient literacy, and countless other notions that refer to one's capabilities within a specific area (Tuominen, Savolainen, & Talja, 2005). This more expansive conception of literacy further posits the need for *intermediality*, the synthesis of various literacies needed to navigate the complex 21st-century world (Elleström, 2010).

In this chapter, we confine our attention to what follows from literacy's etymological origins, considering what is involved in learning how to read and write alphabetic texts. Most cognitive psychological and learning sciences research on literacy has focused on this traditional conception of literacy. Still, we hope that scholars who have extended the scope of reference to these other forms of literacy may find this research useful as well.

Writing can be defined as a one-to-one correspondence between text and speech (Woods, 2010a). This distinction is particularly helpful in drawing a distinction between writing and new definitions of literacy that describe nonverbal representational forms (cf. Mayer, 2008a). Kress (2003) and others have attempted to identify the features of visual representations that are generated with the intention of representing particular authorial intent, but the ambiguity of images does not allow for the same direct correspondence between image and speech as does written text, and generating such images would not be considered "writing" under our definition. A written script's use of characters and grammar represents the boundary between prehistory and history (Woods, 2010a); after the development of orthographic writing systems, people were able to document the present and past and thus provide a record of the evolution of their society.

Societal expectations of literacy have increased over time. Before the effort to promote universal literacy through formal education got under way, adults were deemed literate when they could indicate their signature with an "X" (Reay, 1991). In the 21st century, the U. S. Common Core Standards require that kindergarten children (age five to six) "use a combination of drawing, dictating, and writing to compose opinion pieces in which they tell a reader the topic or the name of the book they are writing about and state an opinion or preference about the topic or book (e.g., *My favorite book is …)*" (National Governors Association, 2012). This ratcheting up of literacy expectations demonstrates that definitions of literacy change across time, as do the standards that should apply to students at different ages of development and schooling.

Three Types of Literate Knowledge

Geary (2005) distinguishes between biologically primary cognitive abilities (those that evolved through natural selection) and biologically secondary cognitive abilities (those that are developed through cultural practice). The primary abilities are part of everyone's genetic architecture; the secondary abilities are learned through engagement with the physical world and with others (cf. Vygotsky's [1934/1987] notion of lower and higher mental functions), and these capacities vary across cultures and groups. Literacy is a secondary cognitive ability. Most cultures teach literacy through formal educational institutions (Gardner, 1991), and literacy is a prerequisite to teaching most school subjects. (There are a few exceptions to this general pattern: Scribner and Cole (1981) have documented that in some cultures, people learn scripts outside the formal confines of school that embody particular forms of cultural knowledge, with these scripts serving more local than abstract social purposes.)

Smagorinsky and Smith (1992) argue that researchers have focused, broadly speaking, on three types of knowledge. First, knowledge can be *general*, such as the ability to decode words or engage in drafting and revision. One could conceivably engage in these practices regardless of what is being read or written. Second, knowledge can be *task specific*: learning to read a novel and learning to read a recipe require different declarative and procedural knowledge, the first relying on the ability to recognize a narrative perspective and determine its reliability, and the second requiring a reader to follow or adapt specific instructions. Third, knowledge can be *community specific*, in which people who are members of a community bring specialized forms of knowledge to bear on their literate actions. In this case, people from different communities might approach a given text using different cognitive and interpretive frameworks. For example, a fundamentalist Christian might first learn to read the Bible as a text embodying an indisputable truth and then adapt that stance to other readings, even when a more interpretive approach is cued by the textual codes and the context of reading (Heath, 1983).

Literacy researchers have studied all three types of literacy knowledge. Each research approach produces different insights, and together they provide a comprehensive picture of what literacy learning involves.

General Knowledge in Learning to Read and Write

Learning scientists have studied how people learn to read a printed word, comprehend a prose passage, write an essay, and engage in other literacy practices. These studies are examples of how researchers have applied the general science of learning to specific educational issues (Mayer, 2008b, 2011), particularly to learning of subject matter (Mayer, 2004). The psychology of subject matter – which investigates how people learn and think in subject matter areas – represents an important advance in the learning sciences away from general theories of learning that dominated in the first half of the 20th century (Mayer, 2004, 2008b; also see the other chapters in Part 5 of this handbook). In this section, we summarize exemplary research on the cognitive science of general knowledge in literacy learning in reading fluency, reading comprehension, and writing, as summarized in Table 30.1.

Reading Fluency

Consider the cognitive processes involved in reading a printed word, such as CAT. Helping students develop this seemingly simple ability to read printed words is perhaps the single most important task of schooling in the primary grades, and understanding how students learn to read fluently falls squarely within the domain of the learning sciences. Huey articulated an important challenge for the learning sciences: "[T]o completely analyze what we do when we read would almost be the acme of a psychologist's achievements, for it would be to describe very many of the most intricate workings of the human mind, as well as to unravel the tangled story of the most remarkable

Table 30.1. *Three content areas in the cognitive science of literacy learning*

Name	Target task
Reading fluency	Pronouncing a printed word
Reading comprehension	Comprehending a printed passage
Writing	Producing a written essay

Table 30.2. *Four cognitive processes in reading fluency*

Name	Example task
Recognizing phonemes	Substitution of first phoneme: You hear the word "ball" and are asked to change the /b/ sound into a /t/ sound.
Decoding words	Word identification: Pronounce the printed word, CAT. Word attack: Pronounce the printed word, BLUD.
Decoding words fluently	Read a paragraph aloud fast and without error.
Accessing word meaning	Give a definition for a word and use it in a sentence.

specific performance that civilization has learned in all its history" (Huey, 1908, p. 6). Since Huey's challenge, researchers have made remarkable progress in understanding the cognitive processes that unfold when a person is reading (Rayner, Pollatsek, Ashby, & Clifton, 2011). As shown in Table 30.2, Mayer (2008b) has analyzed the process of word reading in alphabetic orthographies into four component cognitive skills: recognizing phonemes, decoding words, decoding words fluently, and accessing word meaning.

Recognizing phonemes. Phonemes are the smallest sound units of a language. In English there are approximately 42 phonemes, such as /c/ and /a/ and /t/, that are combined to form the word CAT. Phonological awareness is the ability to recognize and produce each of the sound units of one's language. Reading researchers have produced strong evidence that phonological awareness is a readiness skill for learning to read. Being able to segment a spoken word into phonemes and being able to combine phonemes into a spoken word represent the first step in learning to read in alphabetic languages, even though it does not involve printed words at all. English language readers must form cognitive categories for each of the 42 sounds of English.

What is the evidence for the role of phonological awareness in learning to read? Bradley and Bryant (1985) tested children on phonological awareness at age four or five (e.g., being able to say "call" when asked to change the first sound in the spoken word "ball" to a hard /c/ sound) and then tested them on reading comprehension three years later (e.g., being able to answer questions about a passage they read). The correlation was $r = 0.5$, which indicates a strong positive relation between phonological awareness upon entering school and success in learning to read after three years of instruction. Juel,

Griffin, and Gough (1986) found similar effects in which phonological awareness at the start of the first grade correlated strongly with children's ability to pronounce a printed word ($r = 0.5$) or write a spoken word ($r = 0.6$) at the end of the second grade. Longitudinal studies provide promising correlational evidence for the role of phonological awareness in reading (Wagner & Torgesen, 1987) by showing that students who enter school with weak skills in phonological awareness are less successful in learning to read than those who enter school with strong skill in phonological awareness. However, it is not possible to draw causal conclusions based on correlational findings. For example, it might be the case that general intellectual ability is responsible for both phonological awareness and reading skill.

Experimental studies, where learners are randomly assigned to different instructional conditions, offer a way of testing causal claims about the role of phonological awareness. For example, Bradley and Bryant (1983) provided 40 10-minute sessions of direct instruction in phonological awareness to five- and six-year-olds (such as selecting which of four pictures started with a different sound than the others). On subsequent tests performed two years later, the students who had this training outscored control students on standardized reading tests. In a related study, Fuchs and colleagues (2001) found that providing 15 hours of whole-class activities aimed at improving phonological awareness created large improvements on later tests of phonological awareness and reading comprehension as compared to providing no special instruction in phonological awareness. Overall, reviews of training studies such as these provide strong and consistent support for the claim that phonological awareness is a first step in causing improvements in learning to read (Bus & Van Ijzendoorn, 1999; Ehri et al., 2001a; Goswami & Bryant, 1990; Spector, 1995).

Decoding words. The cognitive skill of decoding refers to the process of pronouncing a printed word. Decoding skill can be assessed through *word identification tasks* (i.e., pronouncing words), such as saying "cat" when reading the printed word CAT; and *word attack tasks* (i.e., pronouncing nonwords), such as saying "blood" when reading the printed pseudo word BLUD. A major issue concerns whether people acquire decoding skill mainly by learning to translate whole words into sounds (called the *whole-word approach*) or by learning to translate individual letters into phonemes that are blended together to form a word (called the *phonics approach*). Of course, in idiographic languages, learning to read involves the whole-word approach, because each idiograph corresponds to one word. In cultures with alphabetic writing systems, the whole-word approach has been criticized on the grounds that it is more efficient to learn the pairings between letters (or letter groups) and 42 individual phonemes than to learn thousands of words.

However, the phonics approach can be criticized on the grounds that phonics rules are somewhat inconsistent, at least in English (Clymer, 1963), so some words are best learned by the whole-word approach, such as "the" (and of course, this approach is necessary with idiographic orthographies). But with alphabetic orthographies, the preponderance of evidence shows that phonics instruction is indispensable in learning to read, and yields better decoding performance than all forms of conventional instruction including whole-word on word identification tasks and word attack tasks, according to a review by Ehri, Nunes, Stahl, and Willows (2001b). For example, Blachman and colleagues (2004) found that providing 100 sessions of systematic phonics training to at-risk students resulted in greater improvement than conventional instruction on word identification tasks and word attack tasks as well as on tests of reading comprehension, even when the tests were given a year later. Overall, there is a strong research base showing that phonics instruction greatly improves students' decoding skill.

Decoding words fluently. Decoding through a phonics approach can initially be a cognitively demanding task in which phonemes must be sounded out and blended together to form a word, so an important step in becoming literate is to automatize the process of decoding words. Automaticity of skills is a central topic in the learning sciences, and automaticity in decoding refers to being able to read words without using conscious mental effort. When readers automatize their decoding process, limited cognitive resources in working memory are freed up to be used for reading comprehension (Perfetti & Hogaboam, 1975).

Automaticity of decoding can be assessed by *decoding fluency*, which refers to being able to read words quickly and without error. Classic research by Bryan and Harter (1897) on the development of decoding fluency in telegraphic operators shows that decoding becomes faster over 36 weeks of practice as operators move from decoding one letter at a time, to one syllable at a time, to one word at a time, to entire clauses at a time. More recently, researchers have shown that reading fluency can be increased through the method of repeated readings in which students read aloud a short passage over and over until they reach a high reading rate and low error rate, and then move on to another passage (Dowhower, 1994; Kuhn & Stahl, 2003; Samuels, 1979). Overall, there is strong evidence that decoding automaticity can be achieved through systematic practice in repeated reading.

Accessing word meaning. Readers must not only be able to decode words, they must also determine the meaning of words, an ability that can be ascertained when a reader is asked to give a definition or use a word in a sentence. To access a word's meaning, a reader has to search for the meaning of the printed word in his or her long-term memory, so an important aspect of becoming literate is to develop a large and accessible vocabulary. Students are expected to acquire at least 1,000 to 2,000 words per year, but direct instruction in vocabulary words is woefully inadequate to reach this goal (Joshi, 2005; Nagy & Scott, 2000). Therefore, the majority of one's vocabulary is learned from context, that is, from being exposed to a literate environment in which students listen to spoken language, read printed language, speak, and

Table 30.3. *Four cognitive processes in reading comprehension*

Name	Example task
Using prior knowledge	Reorganizing the material to fit with an existing schema
Using prose structure	Determining what information is important in a passage
Making inferences	Attributing a motive to justify a character's action
Using metacognitive knowledge	Finding a contradiction in a passage

write. For example, Brabham and Lynch-Brown (2002) found that elementary school students learned more new vocabulary words when their teacher read books aloud and engaged them in discussion before, during, and after the reading than when the teacher simply read the book without class discussion. Research is needed to better pinpoint the mechanism by which exposure to spoken and printed language influences vocabulary growth.

Reading Comprehension

Once a learner has acquired the cognitive skills needed for reading, which can be called *learning to read*, the learner is ready to engage in reading comprehension, which can be called *reading to learn*. This transition to reading comprehension can occur in the third and fourth grades, and is epitomized by being able to make sense of a short text passage (e.g., to be able to answer comprehension questions). Reading comprehension has long been recognized as a creative act of structure building (Bartlett, 1932; Gernsbacher, 1990) in which the reader selects relevant information, mentally organizes it into a coherent structure, and integrates it with relevant prior knowledge activated from long-term memory (Mayer, 2011). As shown in Table 30.3, some of the cognitive processes involved in reading comprehension are: using prior knowledge, using prose structure, making inferences, and using metacognitive knowledge.

Using prior knowledge. Skilled readers use their prior knowledge to guide how they select, organize, and integrate incoming information. Bartlett (1932) proposed that prose comprehension is a constructive activity in which learners assimilate incoming information to an existing schema. Modern research supports the role of prior knowledge in prose comprehension by showing that learners perform better on reading comprehension tests when they have relevant prior knowledge than when they do not (Bransford & Johnson, 1972; Pearson, Hansen, & Gordon, 1979) and they better remember material that fits with their existing knowledge (Lipson, 1983; Pichert & Anderson, 1977). Beck, McKeown, Sinatra, and Loxterman (1991) have shown that students perform much better on comprehension tests when a history text is rewritten to explicitly prime relevant schemas. For example, if the text is about the causes of a war over territory, students comprehend that text better when it is rewritten to evoke a common childhood schema, two children both wanting the same object and fighting over who gets to play with it.

Using prose structure. Skilled readers are able to mentally outline a passage and use the outline to help them determine what is most important. For example, Brown and Smiley (1977) asked students to rate each idea unit in a passage on a scale from 1 (least important) to 4 (most important). They observed a developmental trend: third graders gave the same average rating to important and unimportant idea units, whereas college students gave much higher ratings to important than unimportant idea units. Many studies have confirmed this finding that more skilled readers are better at identifying important information. For example, more skilled readers are more likely to recall important material from a lesson than unimportant material, whereas less skilled readers tend to recall important and unimportant material at similar rates (Taylor, 1980). When learners practice summarizing passages, which requires recognizing important material, they score better on comprehension test performance after reading text passages (Bean & Steenwyk, 1984; Taylor & Beach, 1984).

Making inferences. Skilled readers make inferences as they read to help make sense of the passage. For example, Paris and Lindauer (1976) read a list of sentences (such as "Our neighbor unlocked the door.") to students and then gave them a cued recall test with *explicit cues* – words that had appeared in the text (e.g., "door") or *implicit cues* – words that had not appeared in the text but that were implied (e.g., "key"). Kindergarteners performed much better with explicit cues, indicating they did not infer that a key was used to unlock the door, whereas fourth graders performed just as well with implicit cues as with explicit cues, indicating they did make inferences while listening to the sentences. Inspired by this finding, Hansen and Pearson (1983) examined whether inference-making training could enhance comprehension. When they administered the training to fourth graders, it improved comprehension test performance for poor readers but not good readers. One possible explanation for this finding is that the good readers already knew how to make inferences while reading.

Using metacognitive knowledge. Skilled readers monitor how well they understand what they are reading, that is, they engage in *comprehension monitoring* (also see Winne & Azevedo, Chapter 4, this volume, on metacognition). For example, Markman (1979) found that children in grades 3 through 6 generally were not able to recognize implicit inconsistencies in a passage (e.g., seeing a mismatch between saying there is absolutely no light at the bottom of the ocean and saying fish can see the color of plants at the bottom of the ocean) and recognized explicit inconsistencies (e.g., seeing a mismatch between saying fish can't see anything at the bottom of the ocean and saying fish can see the color of plants at the bottom of the ocean) only about

Table 30.4. *Three cognitive processes in writing*

Name	Example task
Planning	Creating an outline before writing
Translating	Using a word processing program to compose an essay
Reviewing	Detecting and correcting problems in an essay

50 percent to 60 percent of the time. Even in adult readers, those who have larger working memory capacity were more likely to engage in comprehension monitoring than those with low working memory capacity (Linderholm & Van den Broek, 2002). Rubman and Waters (2000) were able to improve third and sixth grade students' recognition of inconsistencies in a passage by asking them to place cutouts on a magnetic board to visually represent the passage. Explicit instruction in how to recognize inconsistencies, along with examples, also improved comprehension-monitoring skill in 8- and 10-year olds (Markman & Gorin, 1981).

Writing

Finally, consider the cognitive processes involved in writing an essay. In an analysis of think aloud protocols of student writers, Hayes and Flower (1980; Hayes, 1996) identified three cognitive processes in writing: *planning*, *translating*, and *reviewing*. These three processes, summarized in Table 30.4, occur iteratively throughout the process of writing an essay rather than in precise linear order.

Planning. Planning includes generating (i.e., retrieving relevant information from long-term memory), organizing (i.e., selecting the most important information and structuring it into a writing plan), and goal setting (i.e., establishing criteria concerning how to communicate with the audience). Gould (1980) found that writers tended to engage in abundant local planning (e.g., pausing after each clause or sentence to plan the next) but not to engage in much global planning (indicated by not pausing before starting to write). When students are instructed to create an outline before they write an essay, the quality of the essay is better than when they are not asked to generate an outline (Kellogg, 1994).

Translating. Translating involves putting words on the page, such as through typing or handwriting. Nystrand (1982) noted that the process of translating is subject to low-level constraints such as graphic constraints (e.g., the words must be legible) and syntactic constraints (e.g., the sentences must be grammatically correct and the words must be spelled correctly), as well as high-level constraints such as semantic constraints (e.g., the sentences must convey the intended meaning) and contextual constraints (e.g., the tone must be appropriate for the audience). Working memory capacity is limited, so if writers focus too much on low-level constraints, their essays may fail to satisfy high-level constraints, and vice versa.

For example, when students receive training in handwriting, their handwriting becomes more legible. But somewhat surprisingly, the handwriting training also results in an increase in the quality of their essays. This finding has been interpreted as evidence that once they have automated their handwriting skill, they can use their working memory mainly for addressing the high-level semantic and contextual constraints that are essential to well-composed essays (Jones & Christianson, 1999). In a related study, Glynn, Britton, Muth, and Dogan (1982) asked students to write an essay by first producing a rough draft that did not need correct sentence structure and spelling, or by first producing a polished draft that had proper grammar and spelling. The rough draft group wound up producing higher-quality final drafts. This finding is best explained using the working memory interpretation: the rough draft group could devote more working memory capacity to addressing higher-level constraints as they wrote the first draft.

Reviewing. Reviewing refers to detecting and correcting problems in the written text, including both syntactic problems and semantic problems. Gould (1980) found that adult writers seldom engage in reviewing of short letters, and Bartlett (1982) found that young writers tend to miss most errors in their own writing and are able to correct fewer than half the errors they find. (Note that these studies were conducted before computer software began providing cues, like automatic spell checking, so might require 21st-century modification.) Explicit training in specific strategies for detecting and correcting errors can be successful in improving essay quality (De La Paz, Swanson, & Graham, 1998; Saddler & Graham, 2005).

Overall, understanding how people learn to read and write contributes to the science of learning by extending the learning sciences to authentic learning tasks. In contrast to classic learning theories that focused on general principles of learning, learning in subject areas such as reading and writing requires domain-specific knowledge and skills and is shaped by working memory limitations. This phenomenon is central to the task-specific and community-specific orientations that most mature readers and writers take. These factors are addressed in the next two sections.

Task-Specific Knowledge in Reading and Writing

Knowledge about how to read and write particular genres of texts involves specific as well as general knowledge. For instance, in the previous section, we summarized research on writing the "essay" genre, which found that composing a well-written essay involves the processes of *planning*, *translating*, and *reviewing*. But one cannot necessarily conclude that all writing involves these processes. It depends on whether one accepts essay writing as embodying the processes and qualities that go into any successful writing effort, and the degree to which one believes that additional knowledge would be critical for one to write effectively in other genres or tasks (Hillocks, 1995; Smagorinsky, Johannessen, Kahn, & McCann, 2010; Smagorinsky & Smith, 1992).

A number of researchers have adopted the position that general knowledge is necessary but not sufficient as people's writing skills mature and they begin to differentiate genres of written expression and begin to read an increasing variety of texts. These researchers have found that when people engage with various types of reading tasks, they use different declarative and procedural knowledge. This perspective has ancient roots; the ancient Greeks identified four classical forms of discourse: exposition, argumentation, description, and narration. Instruction in these forms presumes that each has a distinct set of traits that can be learned.

Hillocks (1982, 1986) and his students and colleagues (e.g., Hillocks, Kahn, & Johannessen, 1983; McCann, 1989; Smagorinsky, 1991; Smith, 1989) have been among the strongest proponents of the idea that writing and reading knowledge become differentiated by genre or task. Hillocks and colleagues, for instance, describe certain "enabling strategies" (Hillocks et al., 1983, p. 276) for compositions involving the definition of abstract concepts: "1) to circumscribe the problem generally, 2) to compare examples in order to generate criteria that discriminate between the target concept and related but essentially different concepts, and 3) to generate examples which clarify the distinctions" (Hillocks et al., 1983, p. 276). These strategies are unique to the task of defining abstract concepts; one would not employ them in writing a personal narrative, although, quite remarkably, Hillocks (2002) has found that in some high stakes writing tests, the same rubric is used for very different writing tasks. For example, both narrative essays and persuasive essays are graded on a rubric that says they must have an introductory paragraph, three body paragraphs, and a concluding paragraph. These assessment criteria suggest that the test developers implicitly subscribe to the general knowledge position. In contrast, scholars like Hillocks have argued that because narrative essays and persuasive essays enlist very different cognitive skills and abilities, the two genres call for very different production and evaluative criteria.

In addition to the debate about rubrics and assessment, the task-specific knowledge position has implications for school instruction. Specifically, instruction in text composition should focus on the particular demands of individual tasks. This position is opposed to the general knowledge position that a writer can approach a poem and a memo in the same way and with the same procedures (e.g., Murray, 1980). The task-specific position suggests further that even different types of poems – a sonnet, a free verse poem, a limerick, or virtually any other poetic type – would require unique knowledge, with each variation (e.g., different types of sonnets) requiring yet more specialized knowledge. The implication is that designing an effective learning environment for these different writing tasks requires a task analysis of the particular knowledge required for each type of composition, and explicit instruction in the appropriate set of procedures identified by the task analysis.

In parallel with research on cognitive variation in writing tasks, researchers have also documented that unique skills are required to read particular types of texts. Rabinowitz, for instance, argued that reading literature "is not even a logical consequence of knowledge of the linguistic system and its written signs. It is, rather, a separately learned, conventional activity" (Rabinowitz, 1987, p. 27). Smith (1989) found that giving students direct instruction in the interpretive strategies that readers use to understand irony (Booth, 1974) significantly improved students' ability to understand ironic poetry, as measured by performance on an objective test and by responses to interview questions. Booth (1974) argued that authors alert readers to the presence of irony through five types of clues, and that, once cued, readers employ particular strategies to reconstruct ironic meanings.

In Smith's 1989 study, students were taught the clues and strategies through the use of songs, short poems, and excerpts of poems before applying them independently to longer and more difficult poems. In addition to increasing students' understanding of ironic poetry, Hillocks (1989) found that such an approach resulted in substantially higher levels of engagement in classroom discussions than did a more traditional approach to teaching poetry. Smith (1989) argued that giving students direct instruction in the conventions of irony may help them become more active interpreters of meaning when irony is employed.

Community-Specific Knowledge in Reading and Writing

In addition to general knowledge used in literate activities and task-specific knowledge used in particular genres, different communities of practice (Lave & Wenger, 1991) require further specificity in the kinds of knowledge they employ when their members read and write, because of the demands and customs of the particular social and discourse communities in which they participate. The shift toward conceiving literacy practices as differentiated by community comprises the "social turn" taken by many writing researchers since the 1990s (Smagorinsky, 2006).

Researchers working from this position find that the process of argumentation, to give one of many possible examples, is not practiced the same by all cultural groups. All cultural groups are likely to employ features of the general outline of argumentative practices identified by Toulmin (1958) (see Andriessen & Baker, Chapter 22, this volume), but in different degrees and with additional requirements to suit their cultural practices. Although Toulmin acknowledged that different situations bring out nuances in the particular argumentative strategy, his widely accepted model stipulates that arguments include the following elements:

1. *Claim*: the points or generalizations emphasized in the argument.
2. *Grounds*: reasons or supporting examples used to support the claim.
3. *Warrant*: the principle, provision, or chain of reasoning that serves to substantiate the grounds as evidence in service of the claim.
4. *Backing*: support, justification, reasons to verify the warrant.
5. *Rebuttal/Reservation*: the identification of counterarguments and response in terms of the argument's driving logic.
6. *Qualification*: acknowledgment of the limits to the claims, grounds, warrants, and backing and conditionality thereof.

These elements, however, do not appear in the same degree in all discourse communities, and various cultural groups often have additional elements and requirements. Kochman (1981), for instance, found that in U.S. public settings, black and white participants foregrounded different aspects of argumentation in their exchanges and distrusted the argumentative practices employed by the other cultural group. White participants in public discussions of neighborhood issues in Chicago tended to rely on logical arguments founded in appropriately grounded claims, yet did so with muted affect, relying instead on the weight of their logic. Black participants meanwhile relied on passionate expression of needs and ideas. To white participants, the black contributors lacked analytic grounding for their opinions, and thus were suspect. To the black participants, the white contributors lacked passion and thus commitment to their ideas, and thus were suspect.

With less volatile consequences, others have found that professional and disciplinary communities of practice foreground different aspects of argumentation. Fahnestock and Secor argue that literary criticism is a unique form of argumentative discourse, one that a Toulminesque purist might find deficient in terms of its implementation of argumentative structure. A literary critic's effectiveness "depends not just on what is said but on the vehicle of its saying" (Fahnestock & Secor, 1991, p. 91), with *metaphor* serving as "the very vehicle by which the argument is framed in language" (Fahnestock & Secor, 1991, p. 92). Literary argument also relies on special conventions, such as the use of paradox, which "may both serve the intellectual content of the argument and be an aesthetic end in itself, demonstrating the cleverness of the critic" (Fahnestock & Secor, 1991, p. 88). Literary criticism, then, must itself include literary elements in order to persuade the literati of its merit.

If argumentation were task-specific only, without being adapted to discourse communities' specialized values, literary criticism would not have such particular requirements and expectations. However, when read independent of its intended context, literary criticism might come across as insufficient as argumentation, because "literary arguments often do not make explicit certain structurally predictable elements – the definitions, causal linkages, comparisons which derive from the stases and common topoi of classical rhetoric" (Fahnestock & Secor, 1991, p. 84). Yet the special conventions of literary critics "invoke the shared assumptions of the community of literary scholars, and at the same time create that community" (Fahnestock & Secor, 1991, p. 84).

Stratman, in contrast, analyzed legal brief writing and found that "legal writing is a distinct, unique kind of writing skill [that] can be taught" (Stratman, 1990, p. 196). Stratman's findings contradict the widely held view of law schools that general practice in critical reasoning will result in good legal writing. Stratman contests this approach, arguing that "What differentiates legal reasoning and argument from ordinary reasoning and argument are the unique rhetorical demands that structure the appellant-appellee (petitioner-respondent) relationships and the way courts may reconstitute opposing arguments in the context of this relationship" (Stratman, 1990, p. 185). Appellate brief writers need to be able to make inferences about certain enduring dispositions common to both judges and their opposing lawyers, and should be able to anticipate the ways judges and opponents frame and interpret their contentions. In the setting of the courtroom, the metaphorical expression of the literary critic would undoubtedly come across as distracting and confusing. The expectations of a knowledgeable audience suggest which aspects of argumentation are most salient.

Implications for Learning Sciences

Our review of the research on how people learn to be literate suggests the following implications for the learning sciences in general:

1. Learning a complex cognitive skill, such as reading and writing, requires a multifaceted array of cognitive components, from decoding letters as a fundamental skill to composing and interpreting texts in a variety of genres in accordance with the expectations of particular communities of practice. This complexity is likely to be found in other complex cognitive skills, including those that are presumed by many to lack such demands. Rose (2005), for instance, has documented how waitresses must develop strategies to aid memory of a routinely changing set of customers in a chaotic environment, requiring the recall of the basic sequences and etiquette (greeting the customer, asking for drink orders, bringing the salad before the main course, and so on as performance schema) as well as more task-specific knowledge, such as the different conventions for serving wine and serving water, and more community-specific knowledge, such as the expectations for serving wine in a roadside diner and

serving wine in a five-star restaurant. The general, task-specific, and community-specific knowledge categories appear to structure performances in diverse areas of endeavor.

2. It is not possible to learn the higher-level cognitive skill (understanding a genre like argumentation) without first mastering the lower-level cognitive skills of letter and word decoding; and the automatization of lower-level skills is necessary before higher-level skills can be learned because of limitations in working memory. Just as a reader or writer could not undertake an argument without knowing how to form words from letters, a soccer player could not attack different types of defenses without first knowing how to kick, pass, and receive a soccer ball at the most basic level.

3. Communities of practice play a substantial role in defining expert cognitive performance in literate domains. As learners mature within fields of endeavor and belief systems that differentiate schools of thought within fields, they must learn the conventions for acceptable communication and action so that they can adapt to local expectations. In diverse areas of cognition and performance, metacognitive awareness helps to enable the adaptation of one's knowledge to new situations in which local conventions require recognition and adjustment for optimal communication and action.

Conclusion

In this chapter we have confined our discussion of literacy practices to those concerned with learning to read and write print-based texts using alphabetic orthographies. In doing so we do not dismiss the abundant field of multimodal textuality that has become of great scholarly and practical interest following the recent proliferation of digital devices that enable combinations of sign systems for communication. These new forms of textuality are increasingly driving research that extends the findings presented in this chapter in new ways.

The body of research reviewed here will continue to form an important base for all forms of multimodal textuality, because in many of them, printed text is a core element used to convey meaning. Even when they do not contain printed text, they typically involve composing and interpreting complex sequences and configurations of symbols, and as such are likely to be based in the same underlying cognitive abilities that we have reviewed here.

Our outline of general, task-specific, and community-specific knowledge provides a useful organizing framework for a large body of research. Roughly speaking, these three types of knowledge follow a developmental curricular path, with general knowledge of how to read and write being the province of younger children and their education, task-specific knowledge available when curricula begin to differentiate in middle and high school into subject areas and their preferred genres, and community-specific knowledge primarily of importance when one enters more intensive concentration on a profession or discipline such that adhering to local conventions is necessary to communicate and succeed within genres.

This chronological approach does include exceptions, such as McCarthey and Raphael's (1992) finding that even young readers are oriented to the expectations and codification of disciplinary texts, and thus to the demands of particular discourse communities; and Hayes and Flower's (1980) reliance on populations of college students in an engineering school engaged in problem-solving tasks to produce general models of composing knowledge. At the same time, this curricular progression maps well onto the finding from the learning sciences that knowledge proceeds from general understandings to those requiring more specific forms of knowledge. The learning sequence governing reading and writing development, then, appears to share fundamental processes involved in learning across the cognitive spectrum.

References

Bartlett, E. J. (1982). Learning to revise: Some component processes. In M. Nystrand (Ed.), *What writers know: The language, process, and the structure of written discourse* (pp. 345–363). New York: Academic Press.

Bartlett, F. C. (1932). *Remembering*. New York: Cambridge University Press.

Bean, T. W., & Stenwyck, F. L. (1984). The effect of three forms of summarization instruction on sixth graders' summary writing and comprehension. *Journal of Reading Behavior*, 16, 297–306.

Beck, I. L., McKeown, M., Sinatra, G. M., & Loxterman, J. A. (1991). Revising social studies text from a text-processing perspective: Evidence of improved comprehensibility. *Reading Research Quarterly*, 26, 251–276.

Blachman, B. A., Schatschneider, C., Fletcher, J. M., Francis, D. J., Clonan, S. M., Shaywitz, B. A., & Shaywitz, S. E. (2004). Effects of intensive reading remediation for second and third graders and a 1 year follow-up. *Journal of Educational Psychology*, 96, 444–461.

Booth, W. (1974). *A rhetoric of irony*. Chicago: University of Chicago Press.

Brabham, E. G., & Lynch-Brown, C. (2002). Effects of teachers' reading aloud styles on vocabulary acquisition and comprehension of students in the early elementary grades. *Journal of Educational Psychology*, 94, 465–473.

Bradley, L., & Bryant, P. (1983). Categorizing sounds and learning to read – a causal connection. *Nature*, 301, 419–421.

Bradley, L., & Bryant, P. (1985). *Rhyme and reason in reading and spelling*. Ann Arbor: University of Michigan Press.

Bransford, J. D., & Johnson, M. K. (1972). Contextual requisites for understanding: Some investigations of comprehension and recall. *Journal of Verbal Learning and Verbal Behavior*, 11, 717–726.

Brown, A. L., & Smiley, S. S. (1977). Rating the importance of structural units of prose passages: A problem of metacognitive development. *Child Development*, 48, 1–8.

Bryan, W. L., & Harter, N. (1897). Studies in the physiology and psychology of telegraphic language. *Psychological Review*, 4, 27–53.

Bus, A. G., & Van Ijzendoorn, M. H. (1999). Phonological awareness and early reading: A meta-analysis of experimental studies. *Journal of Educational Psychology*, 91, 403–414.

Clymer, T. (1963). The utility of phonic generalizations in the primary grades. *The Reading Teacher*, 16, 252–258.

De La Paz, S., Swanson, N., & Graham, S. (1998). The contribution of executive control to the revising by students with writing and learning difficulties. *Journal of Educational Psychology*, 90, 448–460.

Dowhower, S. L. (1994). Repeated reading revisited: Research into practice. *Reading & Writing Quarterly*, 19, 343–358.

Ehri, L. C., Nunes, S. R., Simone, R., Willows, D. M., Schuster, B. V., Yaghoub-Zadeh, Z., & Shanahan, T. (2001a). Phonemic awareness instruction helps children learn to read: Evidence from the National Reading Panel's meta-analysis. *Reading Research Quarterly*, 36, 250–287.

Ehri, L. C., Nunes, S. R., Stahl, S. A., & Willows, D. M. (2001b). Systematic phonics instruction helps students learn to read: Evidence from the National Reading Panel's meta-analysis. *Review of Educational Research*, 71, 393–447.

Elleström, L. (Ed.) (2010). *Media borders, multimodality and intermediality*. New York: Palgrave Macmillan.

Fahnestock, J., & Secor, M. (1991). The rhetoric of literary criticism. In C. Bazerman & J. Paradis (Eds.), *Textual dynamics of the professions: Historical and contemporary studies of writing in professional communities* (pp. 74–96). Madison: University of Wisconsin Press.

Fuchs, D., Fuchs, L. S., Thompson, A., Al Otaiba, S., Yen, L., Yang, N. J., Braun, M., & O'Connor, R. E. (2001). Is reading important in reading-readiness programs? A randomized field trial with teachers as program implementers. *Journal of Educational Psychology*, 93, 251–267.

Gardner, H. (1991). *The unschooled mind: How children think and how schools should teach*. New York: Basic Books.

Geary, D. C. (2005). *The origin of mind: Evolution of brain, cognition, and general intelligence*. Washington, DC: American Psychological Association.

Gernsbacher, M. A. (1990). *Language comprehension as structure building*. Mahwah, NJ: Lawrence Erlbaum Associates.

Glynn, S. M., Britton, B. K., Muth, D., & Dogan, N. (1982). Writing and revising persuasive documents: Cognitive demands. *Journal of Educational Psychology*, 74, 557–567.

Goswami, U., & Bryant, P. (1990). *Phonological skills and learning to read*. Mahwah, NJ: Lawrence Erlbaum Associates.

Gould, J. D. (1980). Experiments on composing letters: Some facts, some myths, and some observations. In L. W. Gregg & E. R. Steinberg (Eds.), *Cognitive processes in writing* (pp. 97–128). Mahwah, NJ: Lawrence Erlbaum Associates.

Hansen, J., & Pearson, P. D. (1983). An instructional study: Improving the inferential comprehension of good and poor fourth-grade readers. *Journal of Educational Psychology*, 75, 821–829.

Hayes, J. R. (1996). A new framework for understanding cognition and affect in writing. In C. M. Levy & S. Ransdell (Eds.), *The science of writing* (pp. 1–28). Mahwah, NJ: Lawrence Erlbaum Associates.

Hayes, J. R., & Flower, L. S. (1980). Identifying the organization of writing processes. In L. W. Gregg & E. R. Steinberg (Eds.), *Cognitive processes in writing* (pp. 3–30), Mahwah, NJ: Lawrence Erlbaum Associates.

Heath, S. B. (1983). *Ways with words: Language life, and work in communities and classrooms.* New York: Cambridge University Press.

Hillocks, G. (1982). The interaction of instruction, teacher comment, and revision in teaching the composing process. *Research in the Teaching of English*, 16, 261–278.

Hillocks, G. (1986). *Research on written composition: New directions for teaching.* Urbana, IL: ERIC, National Conference on Research in English.

Hillocks, G. (1989). Literary texts in classrooms. In P. W. Jackson & S. Haroutunian-Gordon (Eds.), *From Socrates to software: The teacher as text and the text as teacher.* 88th yearbook of the National Society for the Study of Education (pp. 135–158). Chicago: University of Chicago Press.

Hillocks, G. (1995). *Teaching writing as reflective practice.* New York: Teachers College Press.

Hillocks, G. (2002). *The testing trap: How state writing assessments control learning.* New York: Teachers College Press.

Hillocks, G., Kahn, E., & Johannessen, L. (1983). Teaching defining strategies as a mode on inquiry: Some effects on student writing. *Research in the Teaching of English*, 17, 275–284.

Huey, E. B. (1908/1968). *The psychology and pedagogy of reading.* Cambridge, MA: MIT Press.

Jones, D., & Christensen, C. A. (1999). Relationship between automaticity in handwriting and students' ability to generate written text. *Journal of Educational Psychology*, 91, 44–49.

Joshi, R. M. (2005). Vocabulary: A critical component of comprehension. *Reading & Writing Quarterly*, 21, 209–219.

Juel, C., Griffin, P. L., & Gough, P. B. (1986). Acquisition of literacy: A longitudinal study of children in first and second grade. *Journal of Educational Psychology*, 78, 243–255.

Kellogg, R. T. (1994). *The psychology of writing.* New York: Oxford University Press.

Kochman, T. (1981). *Black and white styles in conflict.* Chicago: University of Chicago Press.

Kress, G. (2003, May). Reading images: Multimodality, representation and new media. Paper presented at the International Institute for Information Design Conference, Expert Forum for Knowledge Presentation: Preparing for the Future of Knowledge Presentation, Chicago. Retrieved February 26, 2011 from http://www.knowledgepresentation.org/BuildingTheFuture/Kress2/Kress2.html.

Kuhn, M. R., & Stahl, S. A. (2003). Fluency: A review of developmental and remedial practices. *Journal of Educational Psychology*, 95, 3–21.

Lave, J., & Wenger, E. (1991). *Situated learning: Legitimate peripheral participation.* New York: Cambridge University Press.

Linderholm, T., & Van den Broek, P. (2002). The effect of reading prose and working memory capacity on the processing of expository text. *Journal of Educational Psychology*, 94, 778–784.

Lipson, M. Y. (1983). The influence of religious affiliation on children's memory for text information. *Reading Research Quarterly*, 18, 448–457.

Markman, E. (1979). Realizing that you don't understand: Elementary school children's awareness of inconsistencies. *Child Development*, 50, 643–655.

Markman, E. M., & Gorin, L. (1981). Children's ability to adjust their standards for evaluating comprehension. *Journal of Educational Psychology*, 73, 320–325.

Mayer, R. E. (2004). Teaching of subject matter. In S. T. Fiske, D. L. Shallert, & C. Zahn-Waxler (Eds.), *Annual review of psychology* (vol. 55, pp. 715–744). Palo Alto, CA: Annual Reviews.

Mayer, R. E. (2008a). Multimedia literacy. In J. Coiro, M. Knobel, C. Lankshear, & D. J. Leu (Eds.), *Handbook of research on new literacies* (pp. 359–378). Mahwah, NJ: Lawrence Erlbaum Associates.

Mayer, R. E. (2008b). *Learning and instruction*. Second Edition. Upper Saddle River, NJ: Pearson.

Mayer, R. E. (2011). *Applying the science of learning*. Upper Saddle River, NJ: Pearson.

McCann, T. M. (1989). Student argumentative writing: Knowledge and ability at three grade levels. *Research in the Teaching of English*, 23, 62–76.

McCarthey, S. J., & Raphael, T. E. (1992). Alternative perspectives of reading/writing connections. In J. W. Irwin & M. Doyle (Eds.), *Reading/writing connections: Learning from research* (pp. 2–30). Newark, DE: International Reading Association.

Murray, D. (1980). Writing as process. In T. R. Donovan & V. W. McClelland (Eds.), *Eight approaches to teaching composition* (pp. 3–20). Urbana, IL: National Council of Teachers of English.

Nagy, W. E., & Scott, J. A. (2000). Vocabulary processes. In M. L. Kamil, P. B. Mosenthal, P. D. Pearson, & R. Barr (Eds.), *Handbook of reading research* (vol. 3, pp. 269–284). Mahwah, NJ: Lawrence Erlbaum Associates.

National Governors Association. (2012). *Common Core State Standards Initiative: Preparing America's students for college & career, Kindergarten-Grade 12*. Washington, DC: Author. Available at http://www.corestandards.org/ELA-Literacy/W/K.

Nystrand, M. (1982). An analysis of errors in written communication. In M. Nystrand (Ed.), *What writers know: The language, process, and structure of written discourse* (pp. 57–74). New York: Academic Press.

Paris, S. G., & Lindauer, B. K. (1976). The role of inference in children's comprehension and memory for sentences. *Cognitive Psychology*, 8, 217–227.

Pearson, P. D., Hansen, J., & Gordon, C. (1979). The effect of background knowledge on young children's comprehension of explicit and implicit information. *Journal of Reading Behavior*, 11, 201–209.

Perfetti, C. A., & Hogaboam, T. (1975). The relationship between single word decoding and reading comprehension skill. *Journal of Educational Psychology*, 67, 461–469.

Pichert, J., & Anderson, R. C. (1977). Taking different perspectives on a story. *Journal of Educational Psychology*, 69, 309–315.

Rabinowitz, P. J. (1987). *Before reading: Narrative conventions and the politics of interpretation*. Ithaca, NY: Cornell University Press.

Rayner, K., Pollatsek, A., Ashby, J., & Clifton, C. (2011). *Psychology of reading.* Second Edition. New York: Psychology Press.

Reay, B. (1991). The context and meaning of popular literacy: Some evidence from nineteenth-century rural England. *Past and Present*, 131(1), 89–129.

Rose, M. (2005). *The mind at work: Valuing the intelligence of the American worker.* New York: Penguin.

Rubman, C. N., & Waters, H. S. (2000). A, B seeing: The role of constructive processes in children's comprehension monitoring. *Journal of Educational Psychology*, 92, 503–514.

Saddler, B., & Graham, S. (2005). The effects of peer-assisted sentence-combining instruction on the writing performance of more or less skilled young writers. *Journal of Educational Psychology*, 97, 43–54.

Samuels, S. J. (1979). The method of repeated readings. *The Reading Teacher*, 32, 403–408.

Saxe, G. B. (2012). *Cultural development of mathematical ideas: Papua New Guinea studies.* New York: Cambridge University Press.

Scribner, S., & Cole, M. (1981). *The psychology of literacy.* Cambridge, MA: Harvard University Press.

Smagorinsky, P. (1991). The writer's knowledge and the writing process: A protocol analysis. *Research in the Teaching of English*, 25, 339–364.

Smagorinsky, P. (Ed.) (2006). *Research on composition: Multiple perspectives on two decades of change.* New York: Teachers College Press and the National Conference on Research in Language and Literacy.

Smagorinsky, P., Johannessen, L. R., Kahn, E., & McCann, T. (2010). *The dynamics of writing instruction: A structured process approach for middle and high school.* Portsmouth, NH: Heinemann.

Smagorinsky, P., & Smith, M. W. (1992). The nature of knowledge in composition and literary understanding: The question of specificity. *Review of Educational Research*, 62, 279–305.

Smith, M. W. (1989). Teaching the interpretation of irony in poetry. *Research in the Teaching of English*, 23, 254–272.

Spector, J. E. (1995). Phonemic awareness training: Application of principles of direct instruction. *Reading & Writing Quarterly*, 11, 37–51.

Stratman, J. (1990). The emergence of legal composition as a field of inquiry: Evaluating the prospects. *Review of Educational Research*, 60, 153–235.

Taylor, B. (1980). Children's memory for expository text after reading. *Reading Research Quarterly*, 15, 399–411.

Taylor, B., & Beach, R. W. (1984). The effects of text structure instruction on middle-grade students' comprehension and production of expository text. *Reading Research Quarterly*, 19, 134–146.

Toulmin, S. (1958). *The uses of argument.* New York: Cambridge University Press.

Tuominen, K., Savolainen, R., & Talja, S. (2005). Information literacy as sociotechnical practice. *Library Journal*, 75, 329–345.

Vygotsky, L. S. (1934/1987). Thinking and speech. In L. S. Vygotsky, *Collected works* (vol. 1, pp. 39–285) (R. Rieber & A. Carton, Eds; N. Minick, Trans.). New York: Plenum.

Wagner, R. K., & Torgesen, J. K. (1987). The nature of phonological processing and its causal role in the acquisition of reading skills. *Psychological Bulletin*, 101, 192–212.

Witte, S. (1992). Context, text, intertext: Toward a constructivist semiotic of writing. *Written Communication, 9,* 237–308.

Woods, C. (Ed.) (2010a). *Visible language: Inventions of writing in the ancient Middle East and beyond.* Chicago: The Oriental Institute of the University of Chicago. Retrieved February 11, 2011 from http://oi.uchicago.edu/pdf/oimp32.pdf.

Woods, C. (2010b). Introduction: Visible language: The earliest writing systems. In C. Wood (Ed.), *Visible language: Inventions of writing in the ancient Middle East and beyond* (pp. 15–27). Chicago: The Oriental Institute of the University of Chicago. Retrieved February 11, 2011 from http://oi.uchicago.edu/pdf/oimp32.pdf.

31 Arts Education and the Learning Sciences

Erica Rosenfeld Halverson and Kimberly M. Sheridan

In this chapter, we review research on how people learn disciplinary knowledge and practice in the arts. Learning in the arts is distinct from the other subjects discussed in this handbook (math, science, history, and literacy) for three core reasons. First, the arts are centrally a representational domain and learning in the arts involves becoming increasingly aware of how representational choices communicate meaning to different audiences (Halverson, 2013). Second, form and meaning are deeply integrated in the arts; artistic representations are saturated with meaning, and subtle variations in aspects such as line quality, tone, inflection, and tempo are considered consequential to that meaning. Third, work in the arts often involves explicitly exploring and examining identity and culture, because artistic cognition is intertwined with both. We argue that these three distinctive features of arts learning have potential implications for our understanding of learning more generally.

There is a long history of research in arts education (for reviews, see Deasy, 2002; Fiske, 2000; Gadsden, 2008). However, this chapter is the first review of what we know about learning in the arts from a learning sciences perspective. We consider four complementary questions:

- What do we know about the arts within educational contexts?
- What do we know about learning in and through the arts?
- What are the features of designed learning environments for the arts?
- How can an arts-based perspective contribute to the learning sciences?

To address these questions, we look at arts in K–12 art education and other environments identified as "arts-based" and the types of learning studied therein. Arts education is often associated with four primary disciplines: drama and narrative arts, music, dance/movement, and visual arts (Fleming, 2010; Gadsden, 2008). More recently, digital media arts have entered the conversation as both a component of contemporary practice in all the other art forms and as a fifth arts-based discipline in education (Peppler, 2010).

The desired learning outcomes of arts education across these five disciplines are for learners to be able to produce and critically respond to artworks. Learners develop the ability to represent ideas through techniques for manipulating diverse materials, and the ability to analyze and interpret the forms other artists have created throughout history and across cultures. In the visual arts, tools include two- and three-dimensional visual media from paint to sculpture, physical and digital. Theater includes any art form designed to communicate a story: staged theater, creative writing, performance art, and (more recently) digital video/audio narratives. Dance involves moving in purposeful and rhythmical ways and learning to choreograph the movements of others. Music involves learning to use, compose, and perform with tools such as instruments and voice and to appreciate the performances of others. The digital media arts typically refer to creating using digital technologically enabled modes for representation including video, audio, graphic design, multimedia, virtual design, videogames, and digital stories.

Learning in and through the arts often involves multiple art forms simultaneously – particularly in digital media arts. Hip-Hop, for example, stretches across the visual arts (tagging and clothing design), music (producing beats and rhymes), theater (live performance of storied music), and the digital media arts (recording and producing albums) (Hill & Petchauer, 2013). While traditional arts education has separated artistic media into domain-specific boxes, it is clear that contemporary learning in the arts is often a multidisciplinary act that requires understanding how the tools of a given medium afford representation and communicate meaning.

In the next section, we discuss how the arts have been studied within educational contexts, beginning with a brief history of the study of cognition and learning in the arts. We review studies of learning in each of the five art forms, and then identify and discuss four broad themes: creating representations, engagement in identity processes, language development, and creativity and design thinking. We then describe the key design features of studio arts learning environments: the role of audiences, critique, authentic assessment, and opportunities for role taking. Last, we discuss how these key design features can yield new insights and directions for the learning sciences more broadly.

Defining the Arts within Educational Contexts

A Brief History of the Arts and Learning

Psychologists have been studying arts since the founding of experimental psychology itself, with early experiments on aesthetic perception conducted by William James and Gustav Fechner. At the dawn of the emergence of cognitive psychology, Goodman (1976) argued that cognition in the arts involved mental processing of symbolic representations. This influential work led cognitive psychologists to study how children develop the ability to read and speak those languages of art (Goodman, 1976). Across artistic domains, these researchers have shown how children create intuitive schemas and notational systems to bootstrap themselves to build more complex representations before using more formal or conventional musical notational systems, story structures, and visual schemas (e.g., Bamberger, 1991; Hanna, 2008; Karmiloff-Smith, 1992; Winner, 1982). For instance, Karmiloff-Smith demonstrated how young children learning to draw a figure or play a tune first develop behavioral mastery, but with implicit representations. Then, through a gradual systematic process she terms *representational redescription*, the representations become increasingly explicit and accessible to learners as they manipulate the representational forms with greater flexibility, such as deciding to play a portion of a tune at a faster tempo for a particular effect, or changing the position of the arms on a previously rote drawing of a figure (Karmiloff-Smith, 1992). Many academic competences – such as literacy and numeracy – generally show linear progress with age and experience. In contrast, artistic development is more ambiguous. For instance, Gardner and Winner (1976) argued for steady development in expressiveness and inventiveness in metaphoric language, pretend play, visual arts, and musical composition until about age five, and then a downward trend through middle childhood as children become more literal and conventional, resulting in a plateau through adulthood without further training in an art form (Gardner, 1982; Gardner & Winner, 1976). These assertions about artistic development are not without controversy. For instance, looking at the same middle childhood drawings, expert judges in China who value a traditionalist approach to visual art see a growth, whereas judges in the United States and Europe are more likely to see a loss in expressiveness and originality (see Sheridan & Gardner, 2012).

One way to ground discussions of artistic development has been to look at the "end state" of expert-level ability in various art forms. Experts approach their art form in qualitatively different ways from novices – in particular, they think about the whole piece in relationship to its components with greater fluidity and flexibility (e.g., Ericsson, 1996). With advances in neuroimaging, researchers have identified neurological substrates for arts expertise. For instance, Solso (2001) described evidence from neuroimaging data (EEG and fMRI) that suggests that novices tend to approach drawing as a motoric task whereas experts' brains process it as a higher-order task.

A key line of arts learning research has been to examine how learning in a particular art form transfers to non-arts skills, competences, or outcomes (Deasy, 2002). In meta-analytic reviews of these transfer studies, Hetland and Winner (2000, 2001) found support for some instances of transfer, but primarily asserted that claims for transfer to non-arts skills widely exceed the findings.

This foundational cognitive psychological work has provided insight into the kinds of cognition involved in the arts, the development of artistic thinking, and the nature of expertise in different artistic domains, but less on arts learning processes, noncognitive learning outcomes, and how sociocultural environments shape arts learning. Contemporary arts research in the learning sciences is exploring how to weave these dimensions together.

Disciplinary Research on Learning in the Arts

Much of this research explored the cognitive structures and processes shared across the arts. In addition to this type of research, there is a substantial body of research on arts learning that is focused on each of the five distinct art forms. In visual arts, researchers have described how visual arts develop and integrate habits of mind such as observing, envisioning, expressing, and reflecting (e.g., Eisner, 2002; Hetland, Winner, Veenema, & Sheridan, 2013) and have studied giftedness in children and extraordinary artistic achievements to understand high-level performance and creativity (e.g., Gardner, 1993; Simonton, 1994). Arts education research has evolved to align with changes in conceptions of visual art, the art world, and practices that are prevalent in arts education. For instance, early accounts of visual arts development focused on representational accuracy (e.g., Lowenfeld, 1957), but soon after visual arts learning became conceptualized as facility with a symbolic and communicating language (e.g., Goodman, 1976) rather than a mimetic ability, developmental outcomes such as how flexibly children learned to use media and techniques to represent and communicate were increasingly studied (e.g., Golomb, 2002; Kindler, 2004; Sheridan & Gardner, 2012).

Research in the narrative arts has focused primarily on how young people learn to create and share original narrative art. Dyson's (1997) work with elementary schoolchildren has demonstrated that kids use dramatic play and their knowledge of popular culture as key tools for meaning making through creative writing. Research focused on older learners and creative writing explores niche communities – such as fan fiction Web sites – and describes how writers iterate through composition (Magnifico, 2012), use the composition process for language learning (Black, 2008), and engage in 21st-century creative production activities (Jenkins, Purushotma, Clinton, Weigler, & Robison, 2007). Beyond creative writing as a narrative art form, research explores the dramaturgical process: the telling, adapting, and performing of narratives of personal experiences (Halverson, 2009, 2012; Wiley & Feiner, 2001). This work focuses on how young people extend their narrative production from the written word to multimodal forms of communication including live performance and digital production.

Research on drama in learning is often differentiated by the degree of spontaneity present in the composition process. The most informal, creative drama is defined as "an improvisational, non-exhibitional, process-centered form of drama" (Davis & Evans, 1987, p. 262) enacted in learning environments by field pioneers Dorothy Heathcote and Viola Spolin (Heathcote & Johnson, 1991; McCaslin, 1995). Research on process-oriented drama has demonstrated that drama leads to learning gains on reading and writing assessments (DuPont, 1992; Moore & Caldwell, 1993; Podlozny, 2000).

Cognitive scientists have studied music extensively. One stream of research has explored how children acquire skills to sing, play, notate, appreciate, and interpret the cultural forms of music to which they are exposed and taught (e.g., Bamberger, 1991; Stalinski & Schellenberg, 2012). Researchers have also characterized the effects of musical training, such as how music instruction impacts neurological and cognitive outcomes (e.g., Schlaug et al., 2005) and how receiving musical training earlier rather than later in life improves cognitive and neurological processing and integration of musical components such as pitch, rhythm, and synchronization (see Penhune, 2011, for a review). McPherson, Davidson, and Faulkner (2012) followed more than 150 children through their musical learning, showing how music education extends beyond developing instrumental skill to deeper, more conceptual aspects of musical understanding. They document shifts in motivation, emotional expression, and identity development as young music students weave together the different aspects of their musical lives. Given the centrality of music in the lives of adolescents outside formal education, research also documents more informal music learning, such as how playing music-based videogames such as *Guitar Hero* helps to develop music performance skills without formal musical training (Miller, 2009).

Hanna defined dance as "human behavior composed of purposeful, intentionally rhythmical, and culturally influenced sequences of nonverbal body movements and stillness in time and space with effort" (Hanna, 2008, p. 492). Neuroscientific evidence indicates that *moving* develops learners' capacity for conceptualization, creativity, and memory in the same way as engagement with verbal poetry and prose (Grafton & Cross, 2008). Hanna (2008) outlined the differences in knowledge and skills required for *performing* (learning/imitating someone else's dance) and *choreographing* (making up your own dance), and argued that these two tasks are substantively different teaching and learning enterprises. From a learning sciences perspective, dance provides an opportunity to engage with embodied forms of thinking and learning and to use the body as a conduit for the development of symbolization (Hanna, 1987; see Abrahamson & Lindgren, Chapter 18, this volume).

Learning in digital media arts is a natural topic for learning scientists, because the learning sciences is centrally concerned with how technologies are used in distributed cognitive systems. In fact, the digital media arts have reinvigorated an interest in the role of art making more generally as a path for productive learning. For example, Ito and her colleagues' extended ethnographic studies of kids' technological lives identified "creative production" as a core form of participation in the digital world (Lange & Ito, 2010). There is now substantial research on specific forms of digital art making including videogame design (e.g., Salen & Zimmerman, 2004), radio production (e.g., Chávez & Soep, 2005), video production (e.g., Halverson, 2013), and computational textiles (e.g., Buechley, Eisenberg, Catchen, & Crockett, 2008).

How do People Learn in and through the Arts?

In the following, we identify four broad themes that apply across all arts disciplines: creating representations, engagement in identity processes, language development, and creativity and critical thinking.

Creating Representations

Constructionism, a theoretical framework central to the learning sciences (see Nathan & Sawyer, Chapter 2, this volume), posits that learners create their own knowledge by building physical artifacts and that this gradually leads to the construction of conceptual representations. The sociocognitive approach extends Piaget's original claim by proposing a distributed approach to conceptualizing learning, where teachers and learners work together to design and create an external, public artifact (Kafai, 2006; Papert & Harel, 1991). The externality of physical artifacts – whether sculptures, models of the solar system, or videogames – makes visible the understandings, discoveries, and misconceptions inherent in learners' evolving designs, opening up the possibility for critique by knowledgeable others (Kafai, 2006). Just as representation is an integral process to art making, the design and critique of external artifacts is central in arts learning. Whether the artifacts are paintings, poems, lyrics, dramatic performances, or interactive games, art education primarily involves perceiving, creating, and reflecting on artifacts and the processes involved in making them.

Goodman (1976) argued that art making is a fundamentally representational domain. Producing art is a communicative act that requires learners to master the representational tools of the artistic medium. In learning sciences research, the capacity to construct an external representation of a complex idea is a marker of mastery in many disciplines (Enyedy, 2005; see also Eisenberg & Pares, Chapter 17, this volume). Tools for representation vary with the forms of language described earlier; dance requires bodies, digital media requires multimodal tools, and the visual arts require everything from paintbrushes to clay. To use tools effectively, artists must have an understanding of the design grammar within which they are working and have a sense of how the tools support communication within a specific context (Halverson, 2012). It is not enough to know how to use an audio editing tool like Garage Band; art makers must understand what forms of audio editing are expected and acceptable if they are aiming to produce a piece of documentary radio.

Halverson (2013) proposed that digital art-making processes can be understood as "representational trajectories" that culminate in the creation of digital artifacts. To successfully create a digital artifact, a learner must understand the relationship between the idea to be communicated and how the tools of the digital art medium can be used to communicate that idea. This process mirrors the progressive formalization of representations valued in math and science education (Azevedo, 2000; Enyedy, 2005), which results in metarepresentational competence (MRC) that marks deep engagement with complex content (diSessa, 2004).

Learning in the digital media arts has a close connection with learning in technology, because digital media arts production requires a fairly sophisticated ability to use computer technology, in some cases even computer programming (Clark & Sheridan, 2010; Peppler, 2010). Learning environments in STEM disciplines have begun to incorporate rich representational forms, for instance by incorporating digital video production into science inquiry as a method for measuring competence with scientific constructs and science identity (Calabrese-Barton & Tan, 2010). In learning to produce digital media arts, young people engage with technological tools that support the representation of complex ideas over time, and this is a goal of many reform-oriented learning sciences curricular efforts (see Songer & Kali, Chapter 28, this volume).

Engagement in Identity Processes

Studies of the role of the arts in learning have described the psychosocial benefits of arts participation in broad identity terms, such as how participation in arts organizations supports positive developmental trajectories for young people, especially those who do not affiliate with mainstream academic settings (Ball & Heath, 1993; Heath, 2000). Specifically, participating in arts-based activities supports identity exploration by "placing oneself in the center of a work as observer and actor" (Gadsden, 2008, p. 35). While there is evidence that this form of identity exploration is relevant for learners starting in early childhood, the primary focus of identity exploration work is in adolescence. For example, at Teen Talk, a theater program run through a Boys and Girls Club, McLaughlin and colleagues described the journey of one actress over the course of a given performance:

> During the next half hour Rosa is, in turn, a pregnant mother, the bereaved friend of a drunk-driving victim, and the child of abusive parents. When not portraying one of these characters she takes her turn as both backdrop and stagehand while other players act out scenes (McLaughlin et al., 1994, pp. 76–77).

Drama provides Rosa with the opportunity to experiment with potential selves: What would it be like to be a pregnant teen? Rosa is able to step into those shoes without actually having to go through a pregnancy. In addition, learners are free to take on roles that they would not likely be given the opportunity to take on in "real life." In their community-based theater work with youth, Wiley and Feiner described how one youth with multiple sclerosis had the opportunity to try on a different kind of physical self: "She relished the opportunity to shed her reputation as a klutz, and the rest of the group supported her in taking on the challenge of adapting a role with few lines of dialogue but tremendous physical presence" (Wiley & Feiner, 2001, p. 128).

Identity explorations through the arts have proven especially productive for populations who feel marginalized from mainstream institutions. Ball and Heath (1993) demonstrated that, through dance, young people embraced and expressed their ethnic selves. Halverson (2005) demonstrated that queer youth explore possible selves as they perform the narratives of their peers, literally trying on identities that they had never before imagined for themselves. Artistic production also supports youth as they engage in *detypification*, a mechanism for affiliating with a traditionally stigmatized identity in a positive way (Halverson, 2010a). Fleetwood's (2005) work with adolescents participating in digital media production demonstrates that art making encourages discussions about the construction of stereotypes, their function in art, and how these stereotypes reflect individuals' experiences.

Finally, participating in art-making processes can support both individualistic and collectivistic conceptions of identity (Halverson, Lowenhaupt, Gibbons, & Bass, 2009). Researchers who study identity development tend to conceive of "identity" as a property of an individual (e.g., Fleetwood, 2005; Wiley & Feiner, 2001; Worthman, 2002). However, in some communities, the collective group itself has a prominent role in both the process and the products of students' art (Bing-Canar & Zerkel, 1998; Mayer, 2000). In more collectivist-oriented communities, groups (as opposed to individuals) often determine the topics of youth art and co-compose the products, taking over from one another based on availability, expertise, and interest. Halverson and colleagues provided evidence that adolescents use artistic production to explore collective identity development, specifically in rural communities that orient their young people toward community-oriented visions of identity. In their study, one artistic director describes youth film as "not only ... the story of the individual artist, but it also has this indigenous sense in that it is a collective story of the community and of the people, and of the timelessness of a lot of the stories that are within there" (Halverson et al., 2009, p. 32).

Language Development

While engaging in arts practice, arts learners work with the tools of the medium to communicate to an imagined audience. Across narrative artistic forms, language is a core tool for communication, and participation in arts practice provides unique opportunities for language development (Heath, 2004; Soep, 1996; Worthman, 2002). Heath (2004) pointed out the wide variety of oral and written language activities that learners participate in while engaged in arts practice, including group composition, journal writing, and editing. Members of arts organizations learn to be flexible in their use of language, as the different roles they take on in performance and within the organization require a variety of language resources.

The narrative arts are most directly linked to the development of language. In theater programs where students create their own pieces for performance, they use language as a meditational tool for sense making and empowerment (Worthman, 2002) to construct a representation of self and/or community that can be shared with a public audience. As a result, the majority of their work focuses on linguistic decisions: Should a new character be included to represent a certain aspect of the narrative? Should an individual's narrative be sacrificed for a broader cultural point through the combination of multiple languages or through changing one of the characters' core features, like gender? (Halverson, 2010a). These questions make clear that there is a reciprocal relationship between the development of language and the development of self, as learners negotiate how to represent themselves through language.

The New London Group (1996) first argued that our conceptions of literacy should be expanded to include multiple forms of communication. The digital media arts include not only language, but many other modalities of communication: still and moving images, sound, and music. This shift in thinking has been accelerated by the increasing accessibility of simple digital media tools. There is ample evidence that learners build language skills through their participation in digital media arts learning, including digital storytelling (Hull & Nelson, 2005), filmmaking (Fleetwood, 2005; Halverson, 2010b; Mayer, 2000), radio production (Chávez & Soep, 2005), and appropriation – sampling and remixing media content (Jenkins et al., 2007).

Creativity and Design Thinking

Creativity is not unique to the arts; many national and international standards documents for STEM education describe creativity as a desired characteristic of learners across all disciplines (Sawyer, 2012). Here, we focus on dimensions that are central to inquiries at the intersection of the arts and learning sciences – the qualities of both individual and group creativity processes and experiences and insights into how creativity can be evaluated in designed learning settings.

Historically, creativity has been thought of as an individual trait (Sternberg, 1999; 2006). Csikszentmihalyi's (1990) influential work on *flow* shifted the focus from creativity as belonging to an individual, to identifying the qualities of subjective experience that have ties to creativity. Flow refers to the phenomenological experience of being deeply immersed in an activity, including a sense of intense focus, agency, lack of self-awareness, and a distortion of the experience of time (Csikszentmihalyi, 1990). Flow is intrinsically rewarding, and flow encourages the deeper and more sustained engagements that support creative endeavors.

While flow was initially conceptualized as an individual experience, artistic endeavors often involve groups and creativity often emerges from collaboration (Sawyer, 2003). For instance, Sawyer and DeZutter (2009) provided evidence that creative arts processes are distributed cognitive endeavors by tracing the development of group theatrical performance.

Creativity and design thinking share many characteristics. Research in creativity has focused more on original, novel outcomes and the kinds of thinking that cause or are associated with those outcomes, while acknowledging also that some artistic areas, such as traditional Indian dance, demand "vertical creativity": small innovations on a common artistic form (Keinänen, Sheridan, & Gardner, 2006). Research on design thinking has focused on the iterative process involved in planning, creating, testing, and revising ideas and products for a variety of ends such as coherence, functionality, craft, suitability for audience, along with originality. One of the key contributions of the learning sciences has been to clarify the different components of the creative process involved in design.

While the specifics vary across creative domains such as architecture (e.g., Schön, 1988), digital and video narratives (e.g., Halverson, 2012), engineering (e.g., Campbell, Cagan, & Kotovsky, 2003), and game design (Salen & Zimmerman, 2004), researchers have identified common aspects of an iterative process that moves from an initial phase of exploration and ideation – which often involves finding or describing a problem – to the construction of drafts, sketches, and prototypes that pose potential designs or solutions, to reflection on these through some process such as critique. This creative process is iterative, with a move toward a refinement of the design, often ending with some form of sharing the product either through use, exhibition, sale, or performance (Cross, 2011). Likewise, there are commonalties across design problems and domains in the kinds of thinking encouraged at different stages in the creative process. For instance, in the ideation phase, educators and researchers have highlighted the importance of thorough exploration. In their classic study in the visual arts, Getzels and Csikszentmihalyi (1976) found exploratory behavior before completing an artwork to be strongly associated with work that was judged to be more creative, and furthermore with more general judgments of creativity and artistic success in later years. Hetland and colleagues (2013) identified "Stretch & Explore" as one of the habits of mind repeatedly encouraged by visual art teachers through strategies such as generating multiple drafts, working from multiple exemplars, explicitly trying out different techniques, shifting points of view, and mid-process critiques of multiple versions. Likewise, studies of more structured design problems describe the need for educators to support learners past an "early commitment pitfall" by allowing ample exploration time with tools and materials before posing explicit design problems (e.g., Kafai & Resnick, 1996; Puntambekar & Kolodner, 2005). In engineering design, researchers identify an analogous problem of "design fixation" where designers fixate on a less than optimal design decision and fail to envision meaningful alternatives (Jansson & Smith, 1991; Purcell & Gero, 1996). To overcome design fixation and early commitment, learning environments should provide diverse exemplars and scaffolding tools that encourage multiple design generation (e.g., Puntambekar & Kolodner, 2005; Purcell & Gero, 1996).

The Design of Arts-Based Learning Environments

Hetland and colleagues' (2013) intensive study of high school visual arts studio classrooms described three flexible studio structures that were characteristic of visual arts instruction: *Demonstration-lectures*, where problems are posed and tools and techniques are shown; *Students-at-Work*, where students work on the posed problem while the teacher circles around offering individualized direction and feedback; and *Critique*, where students and teachers pause to reflect on and discuss students' work-in-progress or completed works. These structures were used fluidly in varying sequences, with the bulk of time spent in students-at-work. A fourth overarching structure, *Exhibition*, where works are created and curated to be shown to outside audiences, exists outside the classroom but informs work within it. Additional insights into design features of arts classrooms have come from the United Kingdom, where media studies have made their way into the formal curriculum; these studies describe attention to audience, the role of representation, and use of media language as core components of the designed space (Sefton-Green & Sinker, 2000).

In addition to these studies of school-based arts classes, there has been substantial study of arts learning in informal environments such as youth organizations, community centers, after school programs, and museums (e.g., Chávez & Soep, 2005; Halverson, 2012; Heath, 2000; Sheridan, 2011; Sheridan, Clark, & Williams, 2013) and in self-directed arts learning communities on the Internet (Jenkins et al., 2007; Lange & Ito, 2010; Magnifico, 2012; Sheridan, 2008). In both formal classrooms and in these informal arts learning environments, there are four features associated with effective learning that we discuss in the following sections: attention to an authentic audience, a focus on critique, authentic assessment embedded into both the process and the product, and opportunities for role taking.

The Role of Audiences

Meaning is co-created by artists and their audiences. When people are learning to produce art, they often talk about how external audiences will receive the product (Halverson, 2012; Halverson et al., 2009; Heath, 2004; Wiley & Feiner, 2001; Worthman, 2002). How will the product be perceived and understood? What emotions, feelings, and ideas may the work evoke? In the arts, consideration of the audience is embedded throughout the creative process. First, how art is conceptualized is in part based on who the art is presumed to be for. Fleetwood (2005), for example, described her work with African American youth who employ visual tropes as "racialized" stereotyped images that make their social identities easily identifiable to an external audience. These visual tropes, while potentially offensive to community insiders, serve a function for unfamiliar outsiders. Learners choose whether to include these potentially offensive images in their artwork as they consider who the final audience for their work will be. The decision is made early on, while engaged in compositional decisions. Second, arts learning involves frequent peer and expert critique (e.g., Hetland et al., 2013), where at each stage of the work, the learner must explain and defend the evolving work to this immediate audience. Finally, the sharing of completed work with an audience often serves as an assessment or an evaluation of the work itself (Buckingham, Fraser, & Sefton-Green, 2000; Halverson et al., 2012).

Critique

Studio art teachers dedicate large portions of instructional time to engaging learners in discussions of works-in-progress, specifically asking about the artist's intent, talking about the apparent intent as represented in the unfolding work (which is often quite different from the artist's intent), and providing suggestions for improvement (Hetland et al., 2013). Through critique, learners develop what Hetland and colleagues (2013) refer to as "Studio Habits of Mind," which include engagement and persistence, envisioning possibilities, observation, and reflection. Soep (1996; Chávez & Soep, 2005) has worked across media – from the visual arts to digital video and radio – and has shown that when learners participate collectively in arts practice, they work together to learn the language of critique, developing a discourse similar to that of professional artists. These same conversations are apparent in communities of youth game designers as they evaluate the games created by other young learners (Peppler, Warschauer, & Diazgranados, 2010). Halverson and Gibbons (2010) found that arts organizations offer "key moments" in the artistic production process where learners must stop and talk about the idea they intend to represent and how they plan to use the medium to represent that idea. The use of critique as a form of authentic assessment has the potential to transform the way we understand learning in many non-arts disciplines that involve the production of artifacts.

Authentic Assessment

A long-standing criticism of arts education is that there is no way to objectively evaluate what and how people learn. Some have argued that schools only value what can be objectively assessed, and this inability to objectively assess arts production has destined the arts to remain peripheral in schools (Eisner, 2002). However, in all arts disciplines, evaluation is central to the creative process. Sefton-Green and Sinker's (2000) collection of essays offers examples of how creativity is evaluated across artistic disciplines including music, drama, and the digital media arts.

Arts-based learning environments design opportunities for feedback throughout art making, and to have learners' finished works received by an external audience that is motivated to engage with the work. Each artistic discipline struggles with the question of how to evaluate arts learning and the relative emphasis to put on artistic process and products.

Process assessments include the critiques described earlier, "key moments" in art-making processes that afford reflection and articulation of progress (Halverson & Gibbons, 2010), and the documentation of work over time that can be used to create a post hoc construction of the art-making process. All of these methods point to the creation of a trajectory of participation that values progress, failure, iteration, and reflection as learning outcomes. Treating process as a legitimate component of the assessment of learning is a major contribution of arts-based learning environments to the broader learning sciences discussion of innovative forms of assessment (see Pellegrino, Chapter 12, this volume).

Coupled with a focus on the assessment of process must also be a focus on what is produced. When creative products have been evaluated in research, Amabile's (1982) consensual assessment technique (CAT) – where two or more experts each rate the quality and creativity of diverse artistic products, and assessed for blind inter-rater reliability – has been an important and consistently effective tool (Baer, Kaufman, & Gentile, 2004). Expert judgment is also used in standardized arts assessments such as the Advanced Placement and the International Baccalaureate.

One of the challenges of assessing artistic products is that criteria and/or standards of quality in the arts are culturally situated and therefore often changing (Ito et al., 2008; Sheridan & Gardner, 2012). This cannot be avoided, because developing, understanding, and applying culturally situated evaluative criteria is often a marker of artistic expertise (Halverson et al., 2012). Sefton-Green (2000) argued that assessment begins when a piece of art meets an audience. Empirical studies of film audiences have demonstrated that audiences use consistent criteria to evaluate the quality of films, whether the films are produced by professionals (Sheridan, 2008) or by students (Halverson et al., 2012). These criteria focus on locating the artwork within a genre, evaluating how successful the work is in embracing the standards of the genre, and whether the filmmaker innovates at all within the genre. Simply put, one powerful method for evaluating artistic products is to share final works with external, interested audiences.

Opportunities for Role Taking

Earlier in this chapter, we described the important role that the arts can play in learners' engagement with identity processes. One of the key psychosocial mechanisms for identity is role playing, both within the context of the performance arts and in the organizational work of many arts-based learning environments. Particularly during out-of-school time, learners take on varying roles within the environment, often assuming leadership and mentoring positions (Chávez & Soep, 2005; Heath, 2000, 2004; Jenkins et al., 2007; Sheridan et al., 2013). Many of these learning environments are communities of practice (see Greeno & Engeström, Chapter 7, this volume) where participants move from legitimate peripheral participants to central leadership figures over time (Wenger, 1998). Heath (2000, 2004) described the necessity of role taking for arts organizations that depend on artistic performance or showcase for sources of revenue that keep organizational practices alive. Without youth leadership across a variety of tasks, from ticket sales to marketing, the organizations would not continue to survive. Most arts-based production work encourages (and sometimes requires) learners to generate their own production ideas, developing reciprocal relationships with adult mentors who can offer professional expertise around idea development and use of tools for representation (Halverson, 2012). This form of role taking emerges frequently in arts-based learning environments, and requires negotiation as young people seek to balance participation in these settings with their prior experiences that separate adult-controlled and youth-controlled spaces (Ball & Heath, 1993; Chávez & Soep, 2005; Sheridan et al., in press).

Contributions to the Learning Sciences

We began this chapter with a focus on three concepts central to arts: the centrality and richness of representation in arts, the integration of form and meaning, and the examination and exploration of identity and culture in arts learning. Each of these concepts has both a cognitive and a sociocultural component, made seamless in arts practices, and the elucidation of each lends important insights to the learning sciences. Likewise, we have argued that the learning sciences perspective has added to arts learning research by integrating sociocultural theory, noncognitive learning processes and outcomes, and explicit accounts of the design of learning environments into our growing understanding of learning and the arts.

In terms of representation, we see across the arts a consistent focus on how the tools of each medium influence the representations that are created, and how the generation of successive representations demonstrates a growing understanding of what is being represented. It is through this process that artists develop metarepresentational competence (diSessa, 2004) and through which they develop a sense of the social and cultural context for their work through critique and the presence of audiences. Learners' representational trajectories chart their paths from initial conception to final piece, highlighting how successive representations are both opportunities to assess progress and themselves and evidence of a growing understanding of the importance of representations for "getting smart" in the arts (Halverson, 2013).

Representations in art are *relatively replete* (Goodman, 1976) with form and meaning inseparable. In addition, art representations regularly shift with changes in arts practices, tools, and media. These features suggest a need for learning environments that are likely to be different than those associated with STEM disciplines. Key practices in arts learning environments – such as analyzing professional works of art in relation to the problems youth are working on, ongoing individualized and iterative support from teachers during the work process, and mid-process critiques – support youths' understanding and development of artistic habits of mind (Chávez & Soep, 2005; Hetland et al., 2013). As new media design tools – for video, interactive game design, or music – have become increasingly accessible, they are often used as tools for learning across the academic disciplines. Insights from traditional studio arts environments on how to support the design process in diverse media are critical, but often underused (Peppler, 2010; Sheridan, 2011; Clark & Sheridan, 2010).

Finally, identity plays an important though often neglected role in learning (see Nasir, Rosebery, Warren, & Lee, Chapter 34, this volume). We have argued that the arts add depth to our understanding of how learners engage with identity. Through artistic production, young artists explore possible selves and engage in detypification. Art making can potentially accommodate both individualistic and collectivistic conceptions of identity (Halverson, 2009). Exploring possible selves is one form of role taking; another is the role taking that occurs as artists move from legitimate peripheral participants to central participants, and eventually become mentors (Sheridan et al., 2013). Arts environments provide opportunities to understand how identity is explored and constructed through participation in learning environments.

Learning scientist Seymour Papert said that watching an art class was the original inspiration for his influential writings on constructionism; he envisioned how other academic areas could attain the same level of engagement with an external, public, and evolving representation of learners' thinking that he saw as children carved soap sculptures (Papert & Harel, 1991). We see this chapter as building on Papert's initial inspiration, identifying further potential for the learning sciences and education from studying arts learning, and identifying ways a learning sciences perspective can broaden and enrich our understanding of arts education.

References

Amabile, T. M. (1982). The social psychology of creativity: A consensual assessment technique. *Journal of Personality and Social Psychology*, 43, 997–1013.

Azevedo, F. (2000). Designing representations of terrain: A study in meta-representational competence. *Journal of Mathematical Behavior*, 19, 443–480.

Baer, J., Kaufman, J. C., & Gentile, C. A. (2004). Extension of the consensual assessment technique to nonparallel creative products. *Creativity Research Journal*, 16(1), 113–117.

Ball, A., & Heath, S. B. (1993). Dances of identity: Finding an ethnic self in the arts. In S. B. Heath & M. McLaughlin (Eds.), *Identity and inner city youth: Beyond ethnicity and gender* (pp. 69–93). New York: Teachers College Press.

Bamberger, J. (1991). *The mind behind the ear: How children develop musical intelligence*. Cambridge, MA: Harvard University Press.

Bing-Canar, J., & Zerkel, M. (1998) Reading the Media and Myself: Experiences in critical media literacy with young Arab-American women. *Signs*, 23(3), 735–743.

Black, R. (2008). *Adolescents and online fan fiction*. New York: Peter Lang.

Buckingham, D., Fraser, P., & Sefton-Green, J. (2000). Making the grade: Evaluating student production in media studies. In J. Sefton-Green & R. Sinker (Eds.), *Evaluating creativity: Making and learning by young people* (pp. 129–153). London: Routledge.

Buechley, L., Eisenberg, M., Catchen, J., & Crockett, A. (2008). The LilyPad Arduino: Using computational textiles to investigate engagement, aesthetics, and diversity in computer science education. In *Proceedings of the SIGCHI conference on human factors in computing systems (CHI)* (pp. 423–432). Florence, Italy, April.

Calabrese Barton, A., & Tan, E. (2010). *We be burnin!* Agency, identity, and science learning. *The Journal of the Learning Sciences*, 19, 187–229.

Campbell, M. I., Cagan, J., & Kotovsky, K. (2003). The A-design approach to managing automated design synthesis. *Research in Engineering Design*, 14(1), 12–24.

Chávez, V., & Soep, E. (2005). Youth radio and the pedagogy of collegiality. *Harvard Educational Review*, 75(4), 409–434.

Clark, K., & Sheridan, K. (2010). Game design through mentoring and collaboration. *Journal of Educational Multimedia and Hypermedia*, 19(2), 125–145.

Cross, N. (1993). Science and design methodology: A review. *Research in Engineering Design*, 5(2), 63–69.

Cross, N. (2011). *Design thinking: Understanding how designers think and work*. Oxford: Berg Publishers.

Csikszentmihalyi, M. (1988). Society, culture, and person: A systems view of creativity. In R. J. Sternberg (Ed.), *The nature of creativity: Contemporary psychological perspectives* (pp. 325–339). Cambridge: Cambridge University Press.

Csikszentmihalyi, M. (1990). *Flow: The psychology of optimal experience.* New York: HarperCollins.

Davis, J. H., & Evans, M. J. (1987). *Theatre, children, and youth.* New Orleans, LA: Anchorage Press.

Deasy, R. J. (Ed.) (2002). *Critical links: Learning in the arts and student academic and social development.* Washington, DC: Council of Chief State School Officers.

diSessa, A. (2004). Metarepresentational competence: Native competence and targets for instruction. *Cognition and Instruction, 22*(3), 293–331.

DuPont, S. (1992). The effectiveness of creative drama as an instructional strategy to enhance reading comprehension skills of fifth-grade remedial readers. *Reading Research and Instruction, 31*(3), 41–52.

Dyson, A. H. (1997). *Writing superheroes.* New York: Teachers College Press.

Eisner, E. (2002). *The arts and the creation of mind.* New Haven, CT: Yale University Press.

Eisner, E. W., & Day, M. D. (2004). *Handbook of research and policy in art education: A project of the National Art Education Association.* Mahwah, NJ: Lawrence Erlbaum Associates.

Enyedy, N. (2005). Inventing mapping: Creating cultural forms to solve collective problems. *Cognition and Instruction, 23*(4), 427–466.

Ericsson, K. A. (Ed.) (1996). *The road to excellence: The acquisition of expert performance in the arts and sciences, sports and games.* Mahwah, NJ: Lawrence Erlbaum Associates.

Fleetwood, N. (2005). Authenticating practices: Producing realness, performing youth. In S. Maira & E. Soep (Eds.), *Youthscapes: The popular, the national, the global* (pp. 155–172). Philadelphia: University of Pennsylvania Press.

Fleming, M. (2010). *Arts in education and creativity: A literature review.* New Castle Upon Tyne, UK: Arts Council England.

Fiske, E. B. (2000). *Champions of change: The impact of the arts on learning.* Washington, DC: The Arts Education Partnership.

Freeman, N. H. (2004). Aesthetic judgment and reasoning. In E. W. Eisner & M. D. Day (Eds.), *Handbook of research and policy in art education* (pp. 359–377). Mahwah, NJ: Lawrence Erlbaum Associates.

Gadsden, V. (2008). The arts and education: Knowledge generation, pedagogy, and the discourse of learning. *Review of Research in Education, 32,* 29–61.

Gardner, H. (1982). *Art, mind, and brain: A cognitive approach to creativity.* New York: Basic Books.

Gardner, H. (1993). *Creating minds: An anatomy of creativity seen through the lives of Freud, Einstein, Picasso, Stravinsky, Eliot, Graham, and Ghandi.* New York: Basic Books.

Gazzaniga, M. (2008). Arts and cognition: Findings hint at relationships. In M. deLong & T. Wichmann (Eds.), *Learning, arts, and the brain. The Dana Consortium Arts and Cognition report* (pp. 7–11). New York: Dana Press.

Getzels, J. W., & Csikszentmihalyi, M. (1976). *The creative vision: A longitudinal study of problem finding in art.* New York: Wiley.

Golomb, C. (2002). *Child art in context: A cultural and comparative perspective.* Washington, DC: American Psychological Association Press.

Goodman, N. (1976). *Languages of art: An approach to a theory of symbols.* Cambridge, MA: Hackett Publishing Company.

Grafton, S., & Cross, M. (2008). Dance and the brain. In C. Asbury & B. Rich (Eds.), *Learning, the arts, and the brain: The Dana Consortium Arts and Cognition report* (pp. 61–70). New York: Dana Foundation.

Halverson, E. R. (2005). InsideOut: Facilitating gay youth identity development through a performance-based youth organization. *Identity: An International Journal of Theory & Research*, 5(1), 67–90.

Halverson, E. R. (2009). Artistic production processes as venues for positive youth development. *Revista Interuniversitaria de Formacion del Profesorado (Interuniversity Journal of Teacher Education)*, 23(3), 181–202.

Halverson, E. R. (2010a). Detypification as identity development: The dramaturgical process and LGBTQ youth. *Journal of Adolescent Research*, 25(5), 635–668.

Halverson, E. R. (2010b). Film as identity exploration: A multimodal analysis of youth-produced films. *Teachers College Record*, 112(9), 2352–2378.

Halverson, E. R. (2012). Participatory media spaces: A design perspective on learning with media and technology in the 21st century. In C. Steinkuehler, K. Squire, & S. Barab (Eds.), *Games learning & society: Learning and meaning in a digital age* (pp. 244–270). New York: Cambridge University Press.

Halverson, E. R. (2013). Digital art-making as a representational process. *The Journal of the Learning Sciences*, 23(1), 121–162.

Halverson, E. R., & Gibbons, D. (2010). "Key moments" as pedagogical windows into the digital video production process. *Journal of Computing in Teacher Education*, 26(2), 69–74.

Halverson, E. R., Gibbons, D., Copeland, S., Andrews, A., Hernando Llorens, B., & Bass, M. (2012). What makes a youth-produced film good? The youth audience perspective. *Learning, Media, & Technology, 1–18.*

Halverson, E. R., Lowenhaupt, R., Gibbons, D., & Bass, M. (2009). Conceptualizing identity in youth media arts organizations: A comparative case study. *E-Learning*, 6(1), 23–42.

Hanna, J. L. (1987). *To dance is human: A theory of nonverbal communication.* Chicago: University of Chicago Press.

Hanna, J. L. (2008). A nonverbal language for imagining and learning: Dance education in a K-12 curriculum. *Educational Researcher*, 37(8), 491–506.

Heath, S. B. (2000). Making learning work. *After School Matters*, 1, 33–43.

Heath, S. B. (2004). Risks, rules, and roles: Youth perspectives on the work of learning for community development. In A. Perret-Clermont, C. Pontecorvo, L. Resnick, T. Zittoun, & B. Burge, (Eds.), *Joining society: Social interaction and learning in adolescence and youth* (pp. 41–70). New York: Cambridge University Press.

Heathcote, D., & Johnson, L. (1991). Ed. C. O'Neill. *Collected writings on education and drama.* Evanston, IL: Northwestern University Press.

Hetland, L., Winner, E., Veenema, S., & Sheridan, K. M. (2013). *Studio thinking: The real benefits of visual arts education.* New York: Teachers College Press.

Hill, M. L., & Petchauer, E. (2013). *Schooling Hip-Hop: Expanding Hip-Hop education across the curriculum.* New York: Teachers College Press.

Hull, G. A., & Nelson, M. E. (2005). Locating the semiotic power of multimodality. *Written Communication*, 22(2), 224–261.

Ito, M., Horst, H., Bittani, M., boyd, d., Herr-Stephenson, B., Lange, P. G., Pascoe, C. J., & Robinson, L. (2008). *Living and learning with new media: Summary of findings from the digital youth project.* Chicago, IL: MacArthur Foundation.

Jenkins, H., Purushotma, R., Clinton, K., Weigler, M., & Robison, A. (2007). *Confronting the challenges of participatory culture: Media education for the 21st century. Building the field of digital media and learning.* Chicago, IL: MacArthur Foundation.

Jansson, D. G., & Smith, S. M. (1991). Design fixation. *Design Studies*, 12(1), 3–11.

Kafai, Y. B. (2006). Constructionism. In K. Sawyer (Ed.), *Cambridge handbook of the learning sciences.* Cambridge, MA: Cambridge University Press.

Kafai, Y., & Resnick, M. (1996). *Constructionism in practice: Designing, thinking and learning in a digital world.* Mahwah, NJ: Lawrence Erlbaum Associates.

Karmiloff-Smith, A. (1992). *Beyond modularity: A developmental perspective on cognitive science.* Cambridge, MA: MIT Press.

Keinänen, M., Sheridan, K., & Gardner, H. (2006). Opening up creativity: The lenses of axis and focus. In J. C. Kaufman & J. Baer (Eds.), *Creativity and reason in cognitive development* (pp. 202–218). Cambridge: Cambridge University Press.

Kindler, A. M. (2004). Introduction: Development and learning in art. In E. Eisner & M. Day (Eds.), *Handbook of research and policy in arts education* (pp. 227–232). Mahwah, NJ: Lawrence Erlbaum Associates.

Lange, P. G., & Ito, M. (2010). Creative production. In M. Ito et al. (Eds.), *Hanging out, messing around, and geeking out: Kids living and learning with new media* (pp. 243–293). Cambridge, MA: MIT Press.

Lowenfeld, V. (1957). *Creative and mental growth.* Third Edition. New York: MacMillan.

Magnifico, A. M. (2012). The game of Neopian writing. In E. R. Hayes & S. C. Duncan (Eds.), *Learning in videogame affinity spaces* (pp. 212–234). New York: Peter Lang.

Mayer, V. (2000). Capturing cultural identity/creating community. *International Journal of Cultural Studies*, 3(1), 57–78.

McCaslin, N. (1995). *Creative drama in the classroom and beyond.* Addison-Wesley.

McPherson, G. E., Davidson, J. W., & Faulkner, R. (2012). *Music in our lives: Rethinking musical ability, development, and identity.* Oxford: Oxford University Press.

Miller, K. (2009). Schizophonic performance: Guitar Hero, Rock Band, and Virtual Virtuosity. *Journal of the Society for American Music*, 3(4), 395–429.

Moore, B. H., & Caldwell, H. (1993). Drama and drawing for narrative writing in primary grades. *Journal of Educational Research*, 87(2), 100–110.

New London Group. (1996). A pedagogy of multiliteracies: Designing social futures. *Harvard Educational Review*, 66(1).

Papert, S., & Harel, I. (1991). Situating constructionism. In I. Harel & S. Papert (Eds.), *Constructionism* (pp. 1–11). Norwood, NJ: Ablex Publishing Corporation.

Penhune, V. B. (2011). Sensitive periods in human development: Evidence from musical training. *Cortex*, 47(9), 1126–1137.

Peppler, K. A. (2010). Media arts: Arts education for a digital age. *Teachers College Record*, 112(8), 2118–2153.

Peppler, K., Warschauer, M., & Diazgranados, A. (2010). Game critics: Exploring the role of critique in game-design literacies. *E-Learning*, 7(1), 35–48.

Perani, D., Saccuman, M. C., Scifo, P., Spada, D., Andreolli, G., Rovelli, R., Baldoli, C., & Koelsch, S. (2010). Functional specializations for music processing in the human newborn brain. *Proceedings of the National Academy of Sciences of the United States of America*, 107(10), 4758–4763.

Podlozny, A. (2000). Strengthening verbal skills through the use of classroom drama: A clear link. *Journal of Aesthetic Education*, 34(3–4), 239–276.

Puntambekar, S., & Kolodner, J. L. (2005). Toward implementing distributed scaffolding: Helping students learn science from design. *Journal of Research in Science Teaching*, 42(2), 185–217.

Purcell, A. T., & Gero, J. S. (1996). Design and other types of fixation. *Design Studies*, 17(4), 363–383.

Salen, K., & Zimmerman, E. (Eds.) (2004). *Rules of play: Game design fundamentals*. Cambridge, MA: MIT Press.

Sawyer, R. K. (2003). *Group creativity: Music, theater, collaboration*. Mahwah, NJ: Lawrence Erlbaum Associates.

Sawyer, R. K. (2012). *Explaining creativity*. New York: Oxford University Press.

Sawyer, R. K., & DeZutter, S. (2009). Distributed creativity: How collective creations emerge from collaboration. *Journal of Aesthetics, Creativity, and the Arts*.

Schlaug, G., Norton, A., Overy, K., & Winner, E. (2005). Effects of music training on the child's brain and cognitive development. *Annals of the New York Academy of Sciences, 1060*, 219–230.

Schön, D. A. (1988). Designing: Rules, types and words. *Design studies*, 9(3), 181–190.

Sefton-Green, J. (2000). From creativity to cultural production: Shared perspectives. In J. Sefton-Green & R. Sinker (Eds.), *Evaluating creativity: Making and learning by young people* (pp. 216–231). London: Routledge.

Sefton-Green, J., & Sinker, R. (Eds.) (2000). *Evaluating creativity: Making and learning by young people*. London: Routledge.

Sheridan, K. M. (2008). Reading, writing and watching: The informal education of film fans. In J. Flood, D. Lapp, & S. B. Heath (Eds.), *Handbook on teaching literacy through the communicative, visual and performing arts*. Second Edition (pp. 259–269). Mahwah, NJ: Lawrence Erlbaum Associates.

Sheridan, K. M. (2011). Envision and observe: Using the studio thinking framework for learning and teaching in digital arts. *Mind, Brain, and Education*, 5(1), 19–26.

Sheridan, K. M., Clark, K., & Williams, A. (2013). Designing games, designing roles: A study of youth agency in an informal education program. *Urban Education*, 48(3), 734–758.

Sheridan, K. M., & Gardner, H. (2012). Artistic development: Three essential spheres. In A. Shimamura & S. Palmer (Eds.), *Aesthetic science: connecting minds, brains, and experience* (pp. 276–296). Oxford: Oxford University Press.

Shimamura, A. P., & Palmer, S. E. (2012). *Aesthetic science: Connecting minds, brains, and experience.* Oxford: Oxford University Press.

Simonton, D. K. (1994). *Greatness: Who makes history and why.* New York: Guilford.

Simonton, D. K. (1996). Creative expertise: A life-span developmental perspective. In K. A. Ericsson (Ed.), *The road to excellence: The acquisition of expert performance in the arts and sciences, sports and games* (pp. 227–253). Mahwah, NJ: Lawrence Erlbaum Associates.

Soep, E. (1996). An art in itself: Youth development through critique. In *New Designs for Youth Development*, 12(4), 42–46.

Solso, R. L. (2001). Brain activities in a skilled versus a novice artist: An fMRI study. *Leonardo*, 34(1), 31–34.

Stalinski, S. M., & Schellenberg, E. G. (2012). Music cognition: A developmental perspective. *Topics in Cognitive Science*, 4(4), 485–497.

Sternberg, R. (Ed.) (1999). *Handbook of creativity.* Cambridge: Cambridge University Press.

Sternberg, R. (2006). Creating a vision of creativity: The first 25 years. *Psychology of Aesthetics, Creativity, and the Arts*, 8(1), 1–12.

Wenger, E. (1998). *Communities of practice: Learning, meaning, and identity.* Cambridge: Cambridge University Press.

Wiley L., & Feiner, D. (2001). Making a scene: Representational authority and a community-centered process of script development. In S. C. Haedicke & T. Nellahus (Eds.), *Performing democracy: International perspectives on urban community-based performance* (pp.121–142). Ann Arbor, MI: University of Michigan Press.

Winner, E. (1982). *Invented worlds: The psychology of the arts.* Cambridge, MA: Harvard University Press.

Winner, E., & Hetland, L. (2000). The arts in education: Evaluating the evidence for a causal link. *Journal of Aesthetic Education*, 34(3/4), 3–10.

Winner, E., & Hetland, L. (Eds.) (2001). *Proceedings from beyond the soundbite: What the research actually shows about arts education and academic outcomes.* Los Angeles, CA: J. Paul Getty Trust.

Worthman, C. (2002). *"Just playing the part": Engaging adolescents in drama and literacy.* New York: Teachers College Press.

Moving Learning Sciences Research into the Classroom

32 Learning Sciences and Policy Design and Implementation: Key Concepts and Tools for Collaborative Engagement

William R. Penuel and James P. Spillane

To many learning scientists, the world of policy is a distant concern. Their primary goals are to engineer new forms of learning in a small number of classrooms as a means to develop theories of how children learn. For them, the policies that affect what goes on in these classrooms are at best "mild annoyances" (Donovan, Snow, & Daro, 2013) that interfere minimally with their research efforts. At worst, policies appear to block the very possibility of innovation and change.

Some learning scientists, however, are engaged in the complex work of designing policies and supporting implementation. Their goals are to collaborate with local policy makers in districts and schools, teachers, community members, and researchers in other disciplines in initiatives to transform teaching and learning at scale. For these learning scientists, policies can be instruments for enabling change in systems because they signal what is important to teach and learn and focus attention and resources on particular problems of practice. Instead of seeking to avoid the world of policy, these researchers bring their expertise in disciplinary learning and design research methods to help develop local policies and the means of supporting their implementation (Cobb & Jackson, 2012; Penuel, Fishman, Cheng, & Sabelli, 2011).

In this chapter, we describe how learning scientists can contribute to the work of policy design and implementation. We focus on three strategies teams can employ to do so:

1. Engage in policy design initiatives that aim to redesign system and organizational infrastructures.
2. Use concepts and tools from implementation research to inform design.
3. Partner with a broad group of stakeholders to achieve broad impact and equity.

We draw on examples from both inside and outside the learning sciences that provide concrete models of productive engagement among researchers, policy makers, practitioners, and other educational stakeholders. In so doing, we hope to provide learning scientists with a means to expand their repertoire of strategies for organizing research and development activities.

Engage in Policy Design Initiatives that Aim to Redesign System and Organizational Infrastructures

Policies are attempts by one group (policy makers) to influence or coordinate members of other groups (Coburn & Stein, 2006). People who make educational policies include legislators at the national, state, and local levels, governmental agencies, and leaders of educational organizations. Their policy designs target what they see as key problems of education, such as low achievement or the need for more highly skilled teachers. To address these problems, policy makers seek to influence those charged with implementing policies through a mixture of mandates, incentives, and sanctions, as well as by allocating resources to build capacity and change systems (McDonnell & Elmore, 1987).

The design of policies is a continuous, interactive process that involves a wide range of government and nongovernmental actors that seek to influence the goals and instruments of policy (Feldman & Khademian, 2008). Policy design takes place in a wide variety of *arenas*, or sites of decision making where people initiate, negotiate, and implement policies (Mazzoni, 1991). Some of those arenas are sites where individuals and advocacy groups can openly deliberate about policy goals and strategies, but some of them are at least partly closed or invisible to the public. In these partly closed arenas, small groups of policy entrepreneurs – groups that often include researchers – work to influence policies, typically as a force for innovation and change (Kingdon, 2010; Mazzoni, 1991).

In recent years in the United States, some learning scientists have been effective policy entrepreneurs at the national level. A good example is the new *Framework for K-12 Science Education* (NRC, 2012), which drew on learning sciences research to provide advice for how to teach students core ideas in science. Learning sciences research has also provided advice to policy makers and educational leaders in the areas of assessment (NRC, 2001, 2006), curriculum (NRC, 2004), subject matter teaching in the disciplines (NRC, 2005), and technology (U.S. Department of Education, 2010).

Despite their influence at the national level, learning scientists' policy entrepreneurship has had a limited impact on practice. In assessment, large-scale assessments in core subject areas in most states (and on international tests of student achievement) rarely take into account models of cognition in item design, as learning sciences research would suggest. In curriculum, with just a few exceptions (e.g., the *Carnegie Learning Curricula and Cognitive Tutor®* *Software, Investigations in Number, Data, and Space*), curricula developed by learning scientists are not widely available to students. Instead, school boards adopt trade textbooks in mathematics and science that reflect state standards based on traditional "scope and sequence" models. In teacher education, policies and programs to improve teaching – in English-speaking countries at least – remain incoherent and allocate too few resources to support significant teacher learning.

One reason policy entrepreneurship at the national level rarely translates into changes to practice is that people who implement policies at the local level are always charged with implementing multiple policies at the same time (Hatch, 2002). These policies do not all adhere to the same logic, and they make competing demands on implementers. For policies to contribute to positive changes in practice, local leaders of educational organizations (e.g., principals, managers in community-based organizations that provide educational services) need to strategically manage how to respond to competing policy demands (Honig & Hatch, 2004). Sometimes, the result is instructional coherence, but often it produces incoherence and wide variation in the level and quality of implementation of any single policy.

Researchers can assist local leaders with the task of organizing coherent opportunities for students to learn from competing policy demands in ways that support local leaders' improvement efforts. For example, preparing principals and other school leaders to conduct walkthroughs or "instructional rounds" can be a mechanism for promoting coherence in instructional practices (City, Elmore, Fiarman, & Teitel, 2009; Goldman et al., 2004). In addition, researchers can collect evidence and provide feedback related to the instructional coherence that can support school and district leaders' improving the success of particular programs (e.g., Elmore & Forman, 2010).

Local educational systems are important settings where learning scientists can support policy making and adaptation in ways that can impact practice. Intermediary organizations and groups that include learning scientists can help educational leaders "craft coherence" by guiding the process of design and by providing evidence of student learning relevant for redesign of policies and implementation supports (Donovan et al., 2013). Learning scientists bring a "learning perspective" to the design of policies. This perspective is potentially valuable to local educational leaders, because all new policies demand departures from practice and thus create new learning demands on actors throughout the educational system (Cohen & Barnes, 1993).

Design activities that are likely to have the largest impact on practice are those aimed at redesigning system and organizational *infrastructures*. Infrastructure includes standards, systems of classification for people and processes, networks, buildings, and so forth – all the things that are necessary for any system to function. Most infrastructures are largely invisible; it takes deep investigation to recover and make visible the work infrastructures do, let alone redesign them (Bowker & Star, 1999; Star & Ruhleder, 1996). But redesigning infrastructures is a core task of changing systems, and many innovations require new infrastructures to be used – electricity requires materials and a means to produce it and a power grid to distribute it across a geographic area. Similarly, educational systems require materials and means to prepare educators, acquire materials and technology used in teaching, processes for attracting and enrolling learners, and the like. Redesign of educational infrastructures requires great effort – such as when schools redefine attendance patterns or states adopt new standards and assessment systems – but the consequences are typically far reaching, implicating other components of the educational infrastructure either directly or indirectly.

Redesigning infrastructure in educational systems can encompass various activities. Many redesign efforts in recent decades at the state and national levels in the United States have sought to bring greater coherence and reduce fragmentation of the system of standards, curriculum, assessments, and professional development (Cohen, Moffitt, & Goldin, 2007). At the local level, redesign can involve establishing new networks or linkages across different types of activities and organizations, such as making connections between schools and informal settings for learning (de Kanter, Adair, Chung, & Stonehill, 2003). Redesign can also entail the creation of new organizational routines and tools intended to support coordination within organizations (Spillane & Coldren, 2010). Redesign can also comprise efforts to reorganize district offices to better support instructional improvement in schools or to institute new leadership roles such as instructional coaches who are expected to support content area teachers in schools (Coburn & Woulfin, 2012; Honig, 2013). Similarly, comprehensive school reform models offer new infrastructures for supporting instruction inside schools (Peurach, 2011).

Illustration: The MIST Project

An example of a project in which learning scientists are engaged in an effort focused on changing system and organizational infrastructures is the Middle School Mathematics and the Institutional Setting of Teaching (MIST) project (Cobb & Jackson, 2011, 2012; Cobb & Smith, 2008). In MIST, learning scientists and policy researchers have partnered with four districts to help these districts bring about improvements to mathematics instruction at scale. The object of design in MIST is not a curricular or instructional innovation; in fact, the districts have already adopted the *Connected Mathematics Project (II)* curriculum. Instead, the team is focused on designs for professional development of teachers and building leaders, developing models for effective instructional coaching that aim at improving teaching with the adopted curriculum, and on coordinating these types of supports at the district level. If successful, these tools for supporting the learning of teachers, leaders, and coaches will facilitate the development of a practical theory of action that can guide improvements to instruction at scale and that is informed by and advances theories of both learning and organizing (Cobb & Jackson, 2011).

A perspective that guides the MIST team is a focus on educational policies as "designs for supporting learning" (Cobb & Jackson, 2012, p. 488). At a minimum, such designs specify the "what" of the desired changes to behavior or practice. Cobb and Jackson (2012) also posit that policies should explicitly identify the *how* and *why* of policies, that is, learning supports that will be put into place to help people learn how to implement the policy and why those learning supports might be expected to support policy implementation. Thus, a key focus of the MIST project researchers' and district leaders' analysis has been the nature, efficacy, and coordination of supports available to teachers and leaders at different levels of the district to support their learning the how and why of policies (Jackson & Cobb, 2013).

To support the effort to redesign a coordinated system of supports for changing instructional practice, MIST researchers have collaborated closely with district leaders. They elicited district leaders' own "theories of action," that is, leaders' hypotheses about how particular strategies they had in place or put into place would lead to instructional improvement at scale. The researchers brought to bear frameworks for interpreting those theories in light of research on leadership, teacher learning, curriculum, and learning.

Researchers' role early in the project was primarily as a support to district leaders' own efforts to redesign organizational infrastructures. On an annual basis, researchers collected interview, observation, and assessment data to document the enactment of the districts' strategies for improvement, such as district plans for professional development for instructional coaches in mathematics. Then, on the basis of their analyses of the data, the researchers prepared a report and presentation to the districts about what they found that incorporated specific, actionable recommendations for the district. In these feedback sessions, the researchers and district leaders deliberated about the significance of the findings, and the researchers refined their theory of action on the basis of both the evidence from their research and district leaders' interpretations of them. Over time in one of the MIST districts, the team began to engage in helping the district to devise new strategies for redesigning professional development for instructional leaders on the basis of what had been learned in the research.

The MIST team's work involved at least two broad kinds of infrastructure design. The first target of redesign was the district's infrastructure for instructional improvement. The team aimed to support district and school leaders' goal of developing a shared vision of high-quality mathematics instruction, as well as their goal of helping teachers make effective use of the district's adopted curriculum materials. But an equally important infrastructural redesign involved a change to how MIST researchers organized their own work (Cobb, Jackson, Smith, Sorum, & Henrick, 2013). For example, the team created new processes and artifacts – such as feedback reports and debriefing meetings – that could not be published in journals but that proved useful to districts in supporting iterative refinements to their own reform strategies. The report was a new genre for the researchers, and the debriefing meetings were a new activity structure for researchers and district leaders alike.

Challenges to Redesigning Infrastructures

Crafting a coherent system of supports for learning within the MIST districts is still challenging for district leaders to do, even with the MIST team's help. Infrastructures are layered, and redesign of infrastructures can create new sources of conflict and incoherence in systems (Bowker & Star, 1999). School districts, moreover, are open systems, meaning people and processes from outside strongly influence dynamics and outcomes within them. Advocacy groups, the work of educational service providers in the communities, curriculum developers, parents, and policy makers at the state and national levels can all influence system dynamics and outcomes of schooling.

For learning scientists who engage in or support redesign of infrastructures, there are additional challenges. On the one hand, the MIST team's learning perspective on the design of policies is familiar to most learning scientists. That is, they have appropriated a goal common to many design experiments, engineering and learning about the necessary means of support for learning in a particular context. But, on the other hand, the learners and context are not students in classrooms as is typical in learning sciences research, but rather teachers, coaches, and leaders in districts and schools, and the targets of design are professional development activities and planned and informal interactions to support the learning of instructional leaders. To analyze learning in these contexts, teams need to draw on the additional expertise of policy researchers and on theories from policy and organizational change in order to find relevant concepts and tools to guide their inquiry and support to district change efforts. We turn next to consider some concepts and tools from research on policy implementation that may be useful for projects like MIST that share a focus on redesigning infrastructures.

Use Tools and Theories from Implementation Research to Inform Design

Implementation research focuses on how practice shapes the effects of policies (Berman & McLaughlin, 1975; Cohen et al., 2007; Majone & Wildavsky, 1977; Werner, 2004). In the 1960s, implementation research focused principally on whether policies were implemented as intended. But beginning in the 1970s, implementation researchers began to document the things that practitioners know that policy makers cannot and how practitioners use that knowledge to change policy in practice.

For decades, policy researchers have observed that strategies for producing alignment and coordination from the top down rarely work as intended (e.g., Cohen et al., 2007; Elmore, 1980). Berman and McLaughlin (1975) observed that teachers' adaptations of programs at the classroom level, not policy makers' plans, largely determine programs' effectiveness. Implementation problems multiply, moreover, as programs go to scale, as a consequence of both the adaptations teachers make and changes in the environment (McLaughlin, 1987). Successful efforts to effect change at scale, most policy researchers agree, depends on local actors – district administrators, school leaders, and teachers – making continual, coherent adjustments to programs as they work their way through educational systems (Weinbaum & Supovitz, 2010). Critically – and relevant to learning scientists – tools and processes to support system actors' learning are important conditions for making adaptations that support policy goals (Cohen & Hill, 2001).

Today, implementation research in education develops more than just accounts of the failure of reforms to take hold. It includes empirical analyses on the conditions under which policies support or undermine intended changes to practice. It also includes analyses of the micro-processes through which practitioners reshape policies through their efforts to make sense of what policies ask them to do. Theories of organization, institutional change, and leadership inform these empirical analyses and also provide potentially useful conceptual tools for diagnosing problems of practice and designing for change (Honig, 2006).

Certain perspectives articulated in policy implementation research focus especially on the redesign of system and organizational infrastructures. A *distributed perspective* on practice in general and leadership practice in particular is one example (Spillane, 2006). This perspective draws on theoretical work in distributed cognition, activity theory, and microsociology. It focuses on practice – including but not limited to the practice of leading and managing schools – and the ways that practice in one setting is both enabled and constrained by organizational and system infrastructures.

A distributed perspective on leadership practice in schools involves two key aspects. The first aspect entails moving beyond an exclusive focus on the school principal and documenting how other formal and informal leaders take responsibility for leadership and management work. A second, equally important (though often ignored) pillar of the distributed perspective involves anchoring research in the *practice* of leading and managing. A distributed perspective defines practice not in terms of the actions of individual leaders, but rather in terms of the interactions among school staff and aspects of their *situation* (Spillane, 2006). Framed in this way, practice is stretched over the work of two or more school staff members as mediated by aspects of their situation such as organizational routines. Aspects of our situations, often taken for granted, define practice by enabling and constraining interactions among people. Situational aspects do not simply "affect" what school leaders do or moderate the impact of what they do, but rather are core defining elements of practice (Gronn, 2002; Spillane & Diamond, 2007).

Illustration: The Design and Deployment of New Organizational Routines

The practice of leadership in schools involves the use and redesign of *organizational routines*. Routines are a staple in any organization and often a taken-for-granted aspect of organizational life; routines of various kinds structure daily practice in organizations (March & Simon, 1958). Organizational routines are "repetitive, recognizable pattern[s] of interdependent actions" (Feldman & Pentland, 2003, p. 96). They involve social interactions among two or more organizational members who act interdependently to carry out the routine. Some organizational routines are designed locally to meet specific needs, some are handed down from external governing bodies (e.g., school districts, states, whole-school reform models), and some are appropriated from one situation by organizational members and adapted to serve some new purpose in another situation (Spillane, 2006).

Much of the work of schools is done in and through organizational routines such as weekly faculty meetings, annual school improvement planning, teacher hiring, student assemblies, and teacher evaluations. Routines – whether they are at the classroom, school, or system level – can be thought about as (temporary) agreements about how to do organizational work as well as means of storing organizational experiences and thereby enabling more or less efficient coordinated action, even in the face of substantial change (Argote, 1999; Levitt & March, 1988; March, 1991). Of course, organizational routines also can contribute to inertia, worker deskilling and demotivation, and inappropriate responses (Ashforth & Fried, 1988; Gersick & Hackman, 1990).

The design and deployment of organizational routines or redesign of existing routines can be a means of leveraging change in practice at the classroom, school, district, or state level (Spillane, Parise, & Sherer, 2011). Policy makers attempt to leverage change directly and indirectly using organizational routines. Some states and/or school districts, for example, mandate that schools perform particular organizational routines such as school improvement planning, monitoring instruction, and walkthroughs (brief, structured observations of teaching). Federal, state, and school district policy makers also work indirectly to change organizational routines in schools through supporting the development of extra system providers (e.g., comprehensive school reform models) and either mandating or providing inducements for schools to adopt these models. Each of these models includes, among other things, a set of routines that more or less specify how the routine should be implemented with varying degrees of support in the form of coaching and monitoring (Rowan, Correnti, Miller, & Camburn, 2009).

Both planned and unplanned changes are implicated in organizational routines. Routines may be designed with the intent of supporting planned change, but individuals' enactments of routines may either wittingly or unwittingly deviate from the plan in ways that produce unintended consequences. In addition, the design and redesign of organizational routines figures prominently in school leaders' efforts to respond to external policies and to work at improving instruction (Sherer & Spillane, 2011; Spillane et al., 2011).

Challenges to Planned Change through Organizational Routines

To be sure, efforts at planned change through organizational routines face a number of challenges. Organizational routines involve multiple actors, meaning that their implementation involves distributed expertise, making them difficult to observe, analyze, and transfer from one situation to the next (Cohen & Bacdayan, 1996). The knowledge of different parts of an organizational routine has a tacit dimension, so policy makers and school reformers can at best provide broad scripts for organizational routines that must be elaborated and worked out in local practice. Further, organizational routines extend beyond the individual organization (e.g., school or district office) to connect different organizations within education systems and indeed beyond the education sector to other institutional sectors (Petty & Heimer, 2011). Thus, organizational routines focus our attention on both intra- and inter-organizational practice as well as intra-and inter-institutional practice.

Intentional efforts to reshape organizational routines are a part of what might be called the "designed" as opposed to "lived" organization. As with designs for classroom learning, people adapt organizational routines in ways that transform and sometimes undercut the possibilities for organizational change and improvement. As routines of practice are enacted, they always are adapted and change, even when people do not intend to adapt them (de Certeau, 2002). The analytic concept of designed versus lived organization posits that there is and always will be a gap between how organizations are experienced and what leaders and others intend for an organization's functioning (including the roles, processes, and artifacts that people create to improve it). This gap, though, provides rich opportunities for analysis. For example, researchers can analyze alignments between the formal and informal networks of schools (e.g., Penuel, Riel, Joshi, & Frank, 2009) and analyze the demands for collegial interaction likely to be associated with the introduction of new curriculum materials (e.g., Stein & Kim, 2009).

While some see the gap between the designed and lived organization as something to be lamented – and at times it is when routines are lethally mutated in adaptation – this is also a productive way to think about analysis and diagnosis. For example, a school that deploys an organizational routine to foster greater collaboration on instructional matters among teachers may produce new patterns of help among teachers that align closely with organizational goals. But just as likely, the new routines and patterns of interaction will coexist with informal interactions that are based on past shared history, friendship, and the like. Sometimes, these patterns are congruent, but other times they conflict with one another in ways that can lead schools to have a splintered vision for instructional improvement.

Analyses of congruence can inform iteration in design of organizational routines. Learning scientists can model the degree of congruence as a means to evaluate the success of the new routine in developing a common aim for improvement in a school. Learning scientists can then use these analyses of the gap between the designed and the lived organization or system to iterate on the designs of organizational routines and gain new insights for future designs. Key is avoiding an "implementation mind-set" (Spillane & Healey, 2010) that focuses only on fidelity to a static design; rather, as in other forms of design research, a more useful perspective is to consider the work of diagnosis and design as an ongoing practice.

Partnering with a Broad Group of Stakeholders to Achieve Broad Impact and Equity

To ensure that teachers or informal educators can implement their innovations in real settings, many learning scientists have engaged educators as partners in design. Educators may be involved in all aspects of design, from formulating goals to developing and testing prototypes. Learning scientists have used *codesign* successfully with educators as a strategy for developing curriculum materials in school science and mathematics, assessment materials, and professional development activities for teachers (see Penuel, Roschelle, & Shechtman, 2007, for examples). In most instances, learning scientists work with teacher volunteers in schools as their primary partners in design.

In formal educational settings, sustaining and broadening the reach of innovations beyond teachers involved in the design requires the active support and engagement of multiple school and district leaders. School and district officials make policies and at the same time make sense and give sense of state and national policies in ways that shape their implementation. School and district leaders, for example, allocate resources to purchase programs, to encourage or require their adoption, to hire teachers and other specialists, and to provide for teacher professional development (Spillane, Diamond, Walker, Halverson, & Jita, 2001). Learning scientists that have been successful in bringing codesigned innovations to scale have typically secured the support and involvement of multiple leaders at different levels of systems (Coburn, Penuel, & Geil, 2013). This is necessary both because there are often multiple people responsible in schools and districts for selecting programs and curriculum materials and because turnover and change in leadership in many districts is high.

Increasingly, policies target transformation of systems that comprise multiple stakeholders, including nonsystem actors such as parents and community members. This more expansive purview of policy is significant, because of the sheer number and diversity of different institutions that shape schools. It also reflects a growing recognition that to impact school outcomes requires addressing the ways that children's learning and their futures takes place across multiple, linked settings and practices over time (Banks et al., 2007; Bell, Tzou, Bricker, & Baines, 2012). Policies that target nonsystem actors like community-based organizations that provide programming to youth are thus critical to transforming systems of practice. The design and implementation of such requires correspondingly broad coalitions of stakeholders that represent different interests in communities.

Illustration: Community-Based Design Research with Two Indigenous Communities

An example of a multi-partner change initiative centered in the community is a cooperative effort of reservation-based tribal institutions, an urban tribal institution, and a major research university described by Bang and colleagues (Bang, Curley, Kessel, Marin, & Suzokovich, 2012; Bang & Medin, 2010; Bang, Medin, Washinawatok, & Chapman, 2010). One of the goals of this work was to increase science achievement of Native Americans and their representation in science-related professions. To that end, a team engaged in the design of an innovative community-based program focused on ecology, conservation, and restoration of harmonious relations between the people and the natural environment.

Accomplishing these goals required the team to engage in an inclusive design process to adopt goals for design appropriate to the particular history of the community groups involved. There is a long history of conducting anthropological and educational research in Indigenous communities without consideration for these communities' interest and without their active involvement in participation. In this project, learning scientists adapted a form of participatory action research (Hermes, 1999) to work in their particular Indigenous communities. The approach included input from local elders, gaining support from tribal institutions, use of traditional language and respect for cultural values, and broad community participation in the research agenda, staff selection, and budget.

The goals of the project themselves reflected sensitivity to the history of the different communities engaged, particularly the need to develop among youth an appreciation for Indigenous knowledge. Though the project focused on science, the goal of the design was not to replace students' everyday ways of knowing with scientific ways of knowing. Instead, it was to mobilize students' cultural epistemologies, to help students develop an understanding of their relation to scientific cultural epistemologies and to navigate across these different epistemologies as they move across different settings. In addition, a key aim was to allow community members to reclaim classroom-level authority for teaching and learning of Indigenous children.

To accomplish this last aim, the partners made sure that Indigenous people shared authority for helping to design and implement activities with children and youth. Each of the project principals, including researchers, had close ties with the communities involved. Both of the Indigenous communities engaged in the effort – the Menominee people of rural Wisconsin and the more urban American Indian Center of Chicago – had elders and community experts help design and lead activities. In addition, activities were customized to place, and they reflected the different ecologies and valued relationships to the land for the two communities.

A key component of Bang and colleagues' analysis of the effectiveness of their partnership was a sociohistorical one. She and her colleagues looked for evidence that participants could locate the project as a meaningful event within their community's history. She also documented whether and how participants saw the project's effort to help communities develop a productive relationship to science as interwoven with community concerns. This analysis shows the work the partnership performed toward the goal of changing systems of practice, that is, the collective efforts to reorganize relations among partners and to give appropriate authority to Indigenous community members and educators within the work.

Challenges to Expanding the Scope of Who Participates in Design

Expanding who is involved in design can create new challenges for teams. Adding more people to design teams adds more perspectives and diversity to teams, making it difficult to synthesize input in any straightforward way (see Coburn et al., 2013, for more details about this partnership). Conflict and power struggles may undercut efforts as well, especially when conflicts reinforce traditional dynamics of authority and voice (Engeström, Engeström, & Karkkainen, 1995). Thus, if learning scientists expand participation in design, development of additional strategies for organizing design to make productive use of diverse perspectives is necessary.

Using research to support the work of a coalition of community partners demands skill in facilitation, negotiation, and building and maintaining trust (O'Connor, Hanny, & Lewis, 2011). To succeed in their efforts, researchers must work collaboratively with partners to identify design challenges that are both of interest to community members and of potential interest to their colleagues in research. They must be sensitive to the history of particular communities and design strategies that have the potential to address concerns that participants might have about being part of a design process.

Conclusion and Future Directions

In this chapter we have presented three strategies to support learning scientists' productive engagement with policy design and implementation. Learning scientists need to support the work of redesigning system and organizational infrastructures – not just develop, test, and scale up innovative learning environments. Policy and organizational studies can provide learning scientists with conceptual and practical tools for engaging in systemic change efforts that complement theories and methods from learning sciences. Working at the level of systems benefits from broad stakeholder involvement, because multiple institutional actors with conflicting goals influence those systems. In addition, broad stakeholder involvement can help address problems that are not visible to actors within any one societal sector and has the potential to redress inequities in educational systems.

In our view, productive engagement with the world of policy does not require learning scientists to choose between theories and methods of the learning sciences and those of policy and organizational research. Rather, theories and methods from both fields are necessary (Resnick & Spillane, 2006). Making effective use of both requires diverse teams with broad expertise in designing and testing strategies for changing systems of practice. In addition, to successfully engage with the problems that concern policy makers, educational leaders, teachers, community members, and parents, learning sciences research projects must include a broad range of stakeholders who are not typically part of design research projects. We are also likely to need new research designs.

We argue that to impact school practice and reform, learning scientists will have to expand the repertoires they use to organize their research and development. Many other prominent educational organizations are making similar arguments. A decade ago, a National Research Council (2003) report called for a new infrastructure to support long-term partnerships between researchers and school districts. Subsequently, the Strategic Education Research Partnership (SERP) Institute formed to implement those recommendations. Since its formation, SERP has developed partnerships with two different districts and supported their efforts to improve teaching and learning at scale. More recently, Bryk and Gomez (2008) have called for a new research and development infrastructure that would draw on methods of improvement from health care. Their efforts, along with those of colleagues at the Carnegie Foundation for the Advancement of Teaching, have sought to put these ideas to the test in both K-12 and community college settings (Dolle, Gomez, Russell, & Bryk, 2013). Fishman, Penuel, and colleagues (Fishman, Penuel, Allen, & Cheng, 2013; Penuel et al., 2011) have also called for a new approach to organizing research at the intersection of learning sciences and policy that targets persistent problems of practice and employs participatory approaches to design and research. Advancing these new, interdisciplinary approaches to research that employ the strategies we have described in this chapter will require new infrastructures for collaboration and new models of funding (Sabelli & Dede, 2013) that build from lessons learned from investments in systemic improvement and partnerships to improve mathematics and science supported by both the National Science Foundation and U.S. Department of Education.

Examples from within the learning sciences show that it is possible for learning scientists to draw on perspectives and methods familiar to them when working to change systems of practice in school districts. However, the strategies we have highlighted imply the need for expertise that few learning scientists develop as part of their training. This includes expertise in systems dynamics, knowledge of the structures of educational organizations and systems, and familiarity with the concepts and tools of policy and organizational research. It also includes the capacity to match techniques of participatory design to different kinds of contexts and in situations where divergence of stakeholder perspectives is likely. One way to develop this expertise would be apprenticeship opportunities that provide opportunities to engage with policy issues within educational systems.

We are not arguing for a simplistic one-way "translation" of learning sciences research into practice. Rather, our position is that a more useful stance for learning scientists to take is to see ourselves as agents embedded in social practices pertaining to policy design and implementation alongside community members, policy makers, school leaders, educators, and other researchers. In that respect, it is neither useful nor productive to think of ourselves as either arbiters of policy or as people who stand outside politics and policy. A more productive view positions learning scientists as *contributors* to the design of new infrastructures for supporting changes to practice. As contributors, learning scientists may bring specialized expertise in subject matter learning, as do others whose expertise lies in other areas that are essential for changing practice. At the same time, other stakeholders bring goals, values, perspectives, and experiences that are all relevant to policy design and necessary to engage for effective policy implementation. Learning scientists have much to learn, and also much to contribute, by engaging more directly in policy design and implementation.

Acknowledgments

The authors thank Barry Fishman and Lorrie Shepard for their comments on an earlier version of this chapter.

References

Argote, L. (1999). *Organizational learning: Creating, retaining and transferring knowledge*. New York: Kluwer.

Ashforth, B. E., & Fried, Y. (1988). The mindlessness of organizational behaviors. *Human Relations*, 41, 305–329.

Bang, M., Curley, L., Kessel, A., Marin, A., & Suzokovich, E. (2012, April). Muskrat theories, tobacco in the streets, and living Chicago as indigenous land. Paper presented at the Annual Meeting of the American Educational Research Association, Vancouver, British Columbia.

Bang, M., & Medin, D. (2010). Cultural processes in science education: Supporting the navigation of multiple epistemologies. *Science Education*, 94(6), 1008–1026.

Bang, M., Medin, D., Washinawatok, K., & Chapman, S. (2010). Innovations in culturally based science education through partnerships and community. In M. S. Khine & M. I. Saleh (Eds.), *New science of learning: Cognition, computers, and collaboration in education* (pp. 569–592). New York: Springer.

Banks, J. A., Au, K. H., Ball, A. F., Bell, P., Gordon, E. W., Gutierrez, K. D., ... Zhou, M. (2007). Learning in and out of school in diverse environments: Life-long, life-wide, life-deep. Seattle, Washington: The LIFE Center (The Learning in Informal and Formal Environments Center), University of Washington, Stanford University, and SRI International and Center for Multicultural Education, University of Washington.

Bell, P., Tzou, C., Bricker, L. A., & Baines, A. D. (2012). Learning in diversities of structures of social practice: Accounting for how, why, and where people learn science. *Human Development*, 55, 269–284.

Berman, P., & McLaughlin, M. W. (1975). *Federal programs supporting educational change*, Volume 4: The findings in review. Santa Monica, CA: RAND.

Bowker, G., & Star, S. L. (1999). *Sorting things out: Classification and its consequences*. Cambridge, MA: MIT Press.

Bryk, A. S., & Gomez, L. M. (2008). Reinventing a research and development capacity. In F. M. Hess (Ed.), *The future of educational entrepreneurship: Possibilities for school reform* (pp. 181–187). Cambridge, MA: Harvard Educational Press.

City, E. A., Elmore, R. F., Fiarman, S. E., & Teitel, L. (2009). *Instructional rounds in education: A network approach to improving teaching and learning*. Cambridge, MA: Harvard Education Press.

Cobb, P. A., & Jackson, K. (2011). Toward an empirically grounded theory of action for improving the quality of mathematics at scale. *Mathematics Teacher Education and Development*, 13(1), 6–33.

Cobb, P. A., & Jackson, K. (2012). Analyzing educational policies: A learning design perspective. *Journal of the Learning Sciences*, 21, 487–521.

Cobb, P. A., Jackson, K., Smith, T., Sorum, M., & Henrick, E. C. (2013). Design research with educational systems: Investigating and supporting improvements in the quality of mathematics teaching at scale. In B. J. Fishman, W. R. Penuel, A.-R. Allen, & B. H. Cheng (Eds.), *Design-based implementation research: Theories, methods, and exemplars. National Society for the Study of Education Yearbook*. New York: Teachers College Record.

Cobb, P. A., & Smith, T. (2008). District development as a means of improving mathematics teaching and learning at scale. In K. Krainer & T. Wood (Eds.), *International handbook of mathematics teacher education: Volume 3. Participants in mathematics teacher education: Individuals, teams, communities and networks* (pp. 231–254). Rotterdam, The Netherlands: Sense Publishers.

Coburn, C. E., Penuel, W. R., & Geil, K. (2013). *Research-practice partnerships at the district level: A new strategy for leveraging research for educational improvement.* Berkeley, CA and Boulder, CO: University of California and University of Colorado.

Coburn, C. E., & Stein, M. K. (2006). Communities of practice theory and the role of teacher professional community in policy implementation. In M. I. Honig (Ed.), *New directions in education policy implementation: Confronting complexity* (pp. 25–46). Albany: State University of New York Press.

Coburn, C. E., & Woulfin, S. L. (2012). Reading coaches and the relationship between policy and practice. *Reading Research Quarterly*, 47(1), 5–30.

Cohen, D. K., & Barnes, C. A. (1993). Pedagogy and policy. In D. K. Cohen, M. W. McLaughlin, & J. E. Talbert (Eds.), *Teaching for understanding: Challenges for policy and practice* (pp. 207–239). San Francisco, CA: Jossey-Bass.

Cohen, D. K., & Hill, H. C. (2001). *Learning policy: When state education reform works.* New Haven, CT: Yale University Press.

Cohen, D. K., Moffitt, S. L., & Goldin, S. (2007). Policy and practice: The dilemma. *American Journal of Education*, 113(4), 515–548.

Cohen, M. D., & Bacdayan, P. (1996). Organizational routines are stored as procedural memory: Evidence from a laboratory study. In M. D. Cohen & L. Sproull (Eds.), *Organizational learning* (pp. 403–429). Thousand Oaks, CA: Sage.

de Certeau, M. (2002). *The practice of everyday life.* Berkeley: University of California Press.

de Kanter, A., Adair, J. K., Chung, A.-M., & Stonehill, R. M. (2003). Ensuring quality and sustainability in after-school programs: How partnerships play a key role. *Yearbook of the National Society for the Study of Education*, 102(2), 201–220.

Dolle, J. R., Gomez, L. M., Russell, J. L., & Bryk, A. S. (2013). More than a network: Building professional communities for educational improvement. In B. J. Fishman, W. R. Penuel, A.-R. Allen, & B. H. Cheng (Eds.), *Design-based implementation research: Theories, methods, and exemplars. National Society for the Study of Education Yearbook.* New York: Teachers College Record.

Donovan, M. S., Snow, C. E., & Daro, P. (2013). The SERP approach to problem-solving research, development, and implementation. In B. J. Fishman, W. R. Penuel, A.-R. Allen, & B. H. Cheng (Eds), *Design-based implementation research. National Society for the Study of Education Yearbook*, 112(1).

Elmore, R. F. (1980). Backward mapping: Implementation research and policy decisions. *Political Science Quarterly*, 94(4), 601–616.

Elmore, R. F., & Forman, M. (2010, May). Internal coherence: Building organizational capacity for instructional improvement. Paper presented at the Annual Meeting of the American Educational Research Association, Denver, Colorado.

Engeström, Y., Engeström, R., & Karkkainen, M. (1995). Polycontextuality and boundary crossing in expert cognition: Learning and problem solving in complex work activities. *Learning and Instruction*, 5(4), 319–336.

Feldman, M. S., & Khademian, A. M. (2008). The continuous process of policy formation. In K. Ahmed & E. Sanchez-Triana (Eds.), *Strategic environment assessment for policies: An instrument for good governance* (pp. 37–59). Washington, DC: World Bank.

Feldman, M. S., & Pentland, B. T. (2003). Reconceptualizing organizational routines as a source of flexibility and change. *Administrative Science Quarterly*, 48(1), 94–118.

Fishman, B. J., Penuel, W. R., Allen, A.-R., & Cheng, B. H. (Eds.) (2013). *Design-based implementation research: Theories, methods, and exemplars. National Society for the Study of Education Yearbook*. New York: Teachers College Press.

Gersick, C. J., & Hackman, J. R. (1990). Habitual routines in task-performing groups. *Organizational Behavior and Human Decision Processes*, 47, 65–97.

Goldman, P., Resnick, L. B., Bill, V., Johnston, J., Micheaux, D., & Seitz, A. (2004). *Learning Walk Sourcebook*. Pittsburgh, PA: Institute for Learning, Learning Research & Development Center, University of Pittsburgh.

Hatch, T. C. (2002). When improvement programs collide. *Phi Delta Kappan*, 83(8), 626–639.

Hermes, M. (1999). Research methods as a situated response: Toward a First Nations' methodology. In L. Parker, D. Deyle, & S. Villenas (Eds.), *Race is … race isn't: Critical race theory and qualitative studies in education* (vol. 4, pp. 83–100). Boulder, CO: Westview.

Honig, M. I. (2006). Complexity and policy implementation: Challenges and opportunities for the field. In M. I. Honig (Ed.), *New directions in education policy implementation: Confronting complexity* (pp. 1–23). Albany: State University of New York Press.

Honig, M. I. (2013). Beyond the policy memo: Designing to strengthen the practice of district central office leadership for instructional improvement at scale. In B. J. Fishman, W. R. Penuel, A.-R. Allen, & B. H. Cheng (Eds.), *Design-based implementation research. National Society for the Study of Education Yearbook*, 112(1).

Honig, M. I., & Hatch, T. C. (2004). Crafting coherence: How schools strategically manage multiple, external demands. *Educational Researcher*, 33(8), 16–30.

Jackson, K., & Cobb, P. (2013). Coordinating professional development across contexts and role group. In M. Evans (Ed.), *Teacher education and pedagogy: Theory, policy and practice*. New York: Cambridge University Press.

Kingdon, J. W. (2010). *Agendas, alternatives, and public policies*. Second Edition. Harlow, UK: Longman.

Levitt, B., & March, J. G. (1988). Organizational learning. *Annual Review of Sociology*, 14, 319–338.

Majone, G., & Wildavsky, A. (1977). Implementation as evolution. *Policy Studies Review*, 2, 103–117.

March, J. G. (1991). Exploration and exploitation in organizational learning. *Organization Science*, 2, 71–87.

March, J. G., & Simon, H. A. (1958). *Organizations*. Oxford: Wiley.

Mazzoni, T. L. (1991). Analyzing state school policymaking: An arena model. *Educational Evaluation and Policy Analysis*, 13(2), 115–138.

McDonnell, L. M., & Elmore, R. F. (1987). Getting the job done: Alternative policy instruments. *Educational Evaluation and Policy Analysis*, 9(2), 133–152.

McLaughlin, M. W. (1987). Learning from experience: Lessons from policy implementation. *Educational Evaluation and Policy Analysis*, 9, 171–178.

National Research Council (NRC). (2001). *Knowing what students know.* Washington, DC: National Academies Press.

National Research Council (NRC). (2003). *Strategic education research partnership.* Washington, DC: National Research Council.

National Research Council (NRC). (2004). *On evaluating curricular effectiveness: Judging the quality of K-12 mathematics evaluations.* Washington, DC: National Academies Press.

National Research Council (NRC). (2005). *How students learn: History, mathematics, and science in the classroom.* Washington, DC: National Academies Press.

National Research Council (NRC). (2006). *Systems for state science assessment.* Washington, DC: National Academies Press.

National Research Council (NRC). (2012). *A framework for K-12 science education: Practices, crosscutting concepts, and core ideas.* Washington, DC: National Research Council.

O'Connor, K., Hanny, C., & Lewis, C. (2011). Doing "business as usual": Dynamics of voice in community organizing talk. *Anthropology and Education Quarterly*, 42(2), 154–171.

Penuel, W. R., Fishman, B. J., Cheng, B., & Sabelli, N. (2011). Organizing research and development at the intersection of learning, implementation, and design. *Educational Researcher*, 40(7), 331–337.

Penuel, W. R., Riel, M., Joshi, A., & Frank, K. A. (2009, April). The alignment of the informal and formal organizational supports for reform: Implications for improving teaching in schools. Paper presented at the Social Network Analysis Workshop for Math-Science Partnerships, Rockville, MD.

Penuel, W. R., Roschelle, J., & Shechtman, N. (2007). The WHIRL co-design process: Participant experiences. *Research and Practice in Technology Enhanced Learning*, 2(1), 51–74.

Petty, J., & Heimer, C. A. (2011). Extending the rails: How research reshapes clinics. *Social Studies of Science*, 41(3), 337–360.

Resnick, L. B., & Spillane, J. P. (2006). From individual learning to organizational designs for learning. In L. Verschaffel, F. Dochy, M. Boekaerts, & S. Vosinadou (Eds.), *Instructional psychology: Past, present and future trends. Sixteen essays in honor of Erik de Corte.* (pp. 257–274). Oxford: Pergamon.

Rowan, B., Correnti, R., Miller, R. J., & Camburn, E. (2009). *School improvement by design: Lessons from a study of comprehensive school reform programs.* Ann Arbor, MI: Consortium for Policy Research in Education.

Sabelli, N., & Dede, C. (2013). Empowering design-based implementation research: The need for infrastructure. In B. J. Fishman, W. R. Penuel, A.-R. Allen, & B. H. Cheng (Eds.), *Design-based implementation research. National Society for the Study of Education Yearbook*, 112(1).

Sherer, J. Z., & Spillane, J. P. (2011). Constancy and change in work practice in schools: The role of organizational routines. *Teachers College Record*, 113(3), 611–657.

Spillane, J. P. (2006). *Distributed leadership.* San Francisco, CA: Jossey-Bass.

Spillane, J. P., & Coldren, A. F. (2010). *Diagnosis and design for school improvement: Using a distributed perspective to lead and manage change*. New York: Teachers College Press.

Spillane, J. P., & Diamond, J. B. (2007). *Distributed leadership in practice*. New York: Teachers College Press.

Spillane, J. P., Diamond, J. B., Walker, L. J., Halverson, R., & Jita, L. (2001). Urban school leadership for elementary science instruction: Identifying and activating resources in an undervalued school subject. *Journal of Research in Science Teaching*, 38(8), 918–940.

Spillane, J. P., & Healey, K. (2010). Conceptualizing school leadership and management from a distributed perspective. *The Elementary School Journal*, 111(2), 253–281.

Spillane, J. P., Parise, L. M., & Sherer, J. Z. (2011). Organizational routines as coupling mechanisms: Policy, school administration, and the technical core. *American Educational Research Journal*, 48(3), 586–619.

Star, S. L., & Ruhleder, K. (1996). Steps toward an ecology of infrastructure: Design and access for large information spaces. *Information Systems Research*, 7(1), 111–134.

Stein, M. K., & Kim, G. (2009). The role of mathematics curriculum in large-scale urban reform: An analysis of demands and opportunities for teacher learning In J. T. Remillard, B. A. Herbel-Eisenmann, & G. M. Lloyd (Eds.), *Mathematics teachers at work: Connecting curriculum materials and classroom instruction* (pp. 37–55). New York: Routledge.

U.S. Department of Education. (2010). *National Educational Technology Plan*. Washington, DC: Office of Educational Technology, U.S. Department of Education.

Weinbaum, E. H., & Supovitz, J. A. (2010). Planning ahead: Make program implementation more predictable. *Phi Delta Kappan*, 91(7), 68–71.

Werner, A. (2004). *A guide to implementation research*. Washington, DC: Urban Institute Press.

33 Designing for Learning: Interest, Motivation, and Engagement

Sanna Järvelä and K. Ann Renninger

In order to be productive at home, school, or work, and in their free time, learners are constantly involved in communicating, collaborating, problem solving, and thinking critically. They need to master these skills to participate fully and effectively in society (McLaughlin, 2008). International organizations (e.g., OECD, EU, UNESCO), public-private partnerships (P21, ACTS), educational organizations (e.g., ISTE, NAEP), and researchers have formulated frameworks describing the skills necessary to contribute to the 21st century, and how to design learning environments to foster these skills (e.g., Trilling & Fadel, 2009). However, the roles of interest, motivation, and engagement that enable the development of these skills has not been carefully examined.

In general, learners elect to engage in tasks and activities in which they feel competent and confident, and avoid those in which they do not (e.g., Bandura, 1997). Challenging tasks can lead some learners to feel they are not able to learn; for others, challenge is a reason to persevere. However, only those who believe that their actions will result in the consequences they desire have the incentive to engage (Schunk, 1995). Decades of research have shown that learners with a strong sense of their own competence approach difficult tasks and situations as challenges to be mastered, rather than as threats to be avoided (Zimmermann & Schunk, 2011). Past experience solving problems and individual interest impacts their ability to work with challenge or failure (Tulis & Ainley, 2011). Research on group learning, for example, has shown that learners' interpretations can be positive and lead to increased motivation and engagement for group activities; and, alternatively, that learners' perceptions can be negative and lead to de-motivation and withdrawal (Van den Bossche, Gijselaers, Segers, & Kirchner, 2006).

When we think of engaged learners, we typically think of learners who have more developed interest and are motivated to learn. They are involved behaviorally, intellectually, and emotionally in learning tasks (Fredricks, Blumenfeld, & Paris, 2004). Learners who are not engaged, by contrast, lack interest and are unmotivated. Understanding how to support both groups of learners is critical. Learners with developed interest are ready to engage deeply with content and to master higher-level skills, but at the same time, those with less interest need to be supported (see Renninger, 2010). As such, there are two core questions for the learning sciences regarding the roles of interest, motivation, and engagement in designing for learning:

1. How do we enable those who are not yet engaged to develop their will and skill for learning? How can we help unmotivated learners become motivated to learn?
2. How do we design in order to continue to support those who are already engaged, such that they continue to deepen their interest and, as a result, their motivation to learn particular disciplinary content?

In this chapter, we survey the current state of research to address these questions. We begin by defining interest, motivation, and engagement as distinct and complementary influences on learning. Following this, we identify a set of key themes that emerge from the research, and we review a sample of studies that address interest, motivation, and engagement and focus on differing participant groups across a variety of learning environments. We conclude by proposing potential design principles that emerge from this review.

On Conceptualizing Interest, Motivation, and Engagement

To design learning environments that foster deep learning (Mathan & Koedinger, 2005), it is important to distinguish among three constructs that in everyday use are often assumed to be identical: interest, motivation, and engagement.

Interest

While colloquial usage might suggest that interest is a simple matter of liking one or another type of activity or subject matter, research on interest more precisely defines interest as a psychological state, as well as a predisposition to reengage particular disciplinary content over time (see Hidi & Renninger, 2006; Renninger & Hidi, 2011). Interest is a cognitive and affective motivational variable that develops through four phases, beginning with a triggering of interest that may or may not be sustained (e.g., the opportunity to look through a telescope at cloud formations), and extending to a more well-developed individual interest (e.g., a relatively enduring predisposition to begin looking for a telescope with a larger aperture because of the possibility to track cloud belts). As such, a learner may find weather fascinating and be excited to learn about lightning or different types of clouds, but his or her phase of interest could really vary.

In their Four-Phase Model of Interest Development, Hidi and Renninger (2006) indicate that a learner's phase of interest may be in one of four phases. An interest in weather could be:

- a *triggered situational interest*, meaning that the learner's attention is piqued by information acquired about weather; he or she may, but also may never, return to or make use of this information again;
- a *maintained situational interest*, meaning that other persons or the task to learn about cloud formations itself may help to sustain interest, but the learner may not yet be electing to reengage this content voluntarily. If, for example, the experience of classroom learning is primarily a social experience for the learner, he or she might only work with information about weather when in the classroom with other learners;
- an *emerging individual interest*, meaning that the learner has his or her own questions about weather and, to the extent that the classroom discussion maps onto these, the learner is ready to be a constructive participant in the discussion. Because learners in this phase of interest have some basic knowledge about weather and value this, the classroom could trigger them to ask another question, for example, a question about whether there can be lightning without clouds. This question is an example of a curiosity question, a type of question that characterizes the focus of learners' attention, is novel in terms of learners' own understanding, and may or may not be verbal (Renninger, 2000). Such questioning, in turn, often leads the learner to seek his or her own answers by excitedly asking questions or voluntarily doing research outside of the classroom context to address them. It is also possible that the connection that he or she has made is the only aspect of the classroom discussion that is of interest to him or her, however. Thus, learners with an emerging individual interest have curiosity questions but the scope of these is constrained.
- a *well-developed individual interest*, meaning that the learner has his or her own curiosity questions, is involved in addressing these, and can also think about alternate approaches to them or even varied additional information. Thus, in the class context, others' questions and perspectives on the relation between lightning and clouds and experiments would be enthusiastically and seriously engaged – possibly looking like excitement, and of course interest, but excitement that is qualitatively different than that of the learner who in an earlier phase of interest development.

Learners in each of the phases of interest may look excited; however, their excitement is not an indicator of the phase of their interest nor is it sufficient as an indicator of interest given developments in neuroscience (e.g., Berridge, Robinson, & Aldridge, 2009; Hidi, 2013). Instead, a learner's feelings, value, and knowledge are indicators that together can predict the likelihood of voluntary reengagement with particular content over time (see discussion in

Renninger & Su, 2012). Interest can be triggered for learners of all ages and in all phases of interest – even for learners with little initial interest. Interest can be triggered by the collative variables: novelty, challenge, surprise, complexity, and/or uncertainty (Berlyne, 1960; see related findings in Durik & Harackiewicz, 2007; Hidi & Baird, 1988; Mitchell, 1993; Palmer, 2009).

The phase of a learner's interest is predictive of both motivation and engagement. When learners have a more developed interest, they are motivated to learn, able to self-regulate and set goals for themselves, and to achieve (see Harackiewicz, Durik, Barron, Linnenbrink, & Tauer, 2008; Hidi & Ainley, 2008). They also are likely to begin to identify with the disciplinary content of interest and related occupations (Krapp, 2007).

In later phases of interest, when learners begin to make meaningful connections to the discipline and to ask curiosity questions (e.g., What is the relation between lightening and clouds?), they begin identifying connections between what is known and what still needs to be figured out. They also begin seeking their own answers to their questions and assuming responsibility for what is learned.

Interest is supported to develop through interactions with others (peers, educators) and the tasks (e.g., software, exhibits, worksheets) of the learning environment. In this sense, interest is malleable. Interest can be triggered and supported to develop at any age; however, triggers for interest are needed. Regardless of phase of interest, a learner's interest is sustained and continues to develop in relation to the novelty, challenge, surprise, complexity, and/or uncertainty – the collative variables that lead to the asking of curiosity questions. Without such triggers, or support for learner interest (e.g., if a teacher or parent assumes that the learner is interested in science and there are no opportunities to continue to grow knowledge), interest may fall off, go dormant, or disappear altogether (Bergin, 1999; Hidi & Renninger, 2006).

Motivation

Motivation is a broader construct than interest and is not specifically linked to learning of particular disciplinary content. Motivation comes from the Latin word *motivare*, meaning *to move*. Like interest, motivation involves a complex blend of the environment, cognition, and affect (Volet & Järvelä, 2001); however, while interest is always motivating, what is motivating is not always of interest (Renninger, 2000).

Note that while the literature on motivation has been parsed and studied in terms of intrinsic motivators (personal desires) and extrinsic motivators (such as grades), neuroscience has shown intrinsic and extrinsic motivation to be complementary aspects of motivation that do not exist in isolation (see discussion in Hidi & Harackiewicz, 2000). Here we discuss motivation in relation to achievement, or the will or movement needed to succeed: the initiation, guides for, and maintenance of goal-oriented behavior (e.g., Wigfield,

Eccles, Schiefele, Roeser, & Davis-Kean, 2006). According to Eccles's (2009) *expectancy-value theory*, a learner chooses to take on a challenging task if he or she both expects success and values the task; in other words, if the cost of involvement will yield a benefit. As such, being motivated to succeed is likely to be accompanied by feelings of self-efficacy, appreciation of possibilities or expectancy regarding the utility of engagement, and/or consideration of cost (Wigfield et al., 2006).

Support for changing the motivation of learners is likely to need to start with the triggering of interest, whether this is the trigger provided by a developing understanding of discipline or task utility (e.g., Harackiewicz, Rozek, Hulleman, & Hyde, 2012) or the piquing of attention that occurs, for example, when someone runs into the room and yells, "sex" (Schank, 1979). However, motivation is not a developmental construct in the same sense that interest is, meaning that while interest can be supported to develop through the triggering process and meaningful connections and curiosity questions can be promoted, a learner is typically described as having more or less motivation based on their personal characteristics: their self-efficacy, ability to self-regulate, and/or their expectancy-value. As such, motivation is typically assessed relative to others and learners are described as being more or less motivated, meaning that they may or may not self-regulate to accomplish goals and/or understand the utility of engagement. A learner's present designation as less motivated than others does not preclude the possibility that his or her interest could be triggered for a particular discipline (e.g., science) and be supported by others and/or purposeful design to develop (Renninger, 2010). The quality of the support provided to the learner has implications for changing learner motivation (see Eccles & Midgley, 1989).

When learners are able to persevere on a task independently, they self-regulate their behaviors, whether this involves figuring out how to do an assigned problem set, developing the ability to explain equations in everyday English, or practicing use of a micrometer (e.g., Järvelä, Järvenoja, & Malmberg, 2012). Self-regulated learning involves strategically adopting and adapting tools and strategies to optimize task performance and learning; monitoring progress and intervening if results deviate from plans; and persisting and adapting in the face of challenges (Hadwin & Winne, 2012).

When learners are able to self-regulate effectively, they are also considered to be motivated learners. Being self-regulated does not necessarily suggest that a person has a developed interest for the content to be learned. Having a developed interest for content can mean that a learner is likely to self-regulate without supports to do so, even at very young ages, because he or she wants to master, figure out, or persevere to address curiosity questions (Renninger, 2009). However, older learners who have little interest can and do self-regulate their behaviors effectively (Sansone & Thoman, 2005; Sansone, Weir, Harpster, & Morgan, 1992).

Zimmerman's (1989, 2001) social cognitive model of self-regulation points to promoting the development of self-regulation through: modeling, scaffolding, and other regulation such as support provided by peers, teachers, and parents. Models facilitate self-regulation by providing learners with information about possible actions, processes, and consequences (e.g., Zimmerman & Kitsantas, 2002). Scaffolding refers to supports provided by peers, teachers, and/or parents that promote conceptual understanding by promoting metacognition, strategy use, and study procedures such as how to use resources or perform tasks (see Järvelä & Hadwin, 2013).

This line of research has also addressed features, factors, and characteristics of contexts that support the development of self-regulated learning (e.g., Malmberg, Järvelä, & Kirschner, 2013; Perry, VandeKamp, Mercer, & Nordby, 2002). For example, Perry (1998) reported that second- and third-grade writing instruction could be categorized as high or low in support for self-regulation or based on inclusion of the following: choice about types of tasks and the challenge they provide, self-evaluation, and opportunities to receive support from both teachers and peers. Her study demonstrated that students in classrooms with high levels of support were more likely than those in classrooms with low levels of support to have the skills and attitudes of self-regulated learners.

Engagement

The concept of *engagement* has informed study of whether and the ways in which learners respond to learning environments less as a psychological construct and more as a description of learners' connections to the learning environment. First undertaken as a focus for study in relation to concerns about school disengagement and time on task, studies of engagement have now been undertaken at different levels of granularity ranging from schooling generally to engagement with one or another task type (see Christenson, Reschly, & Wylie, 2012; Tytler & Osborne, 2012).

Skinner and Belmont (1993; see also Skinner & Pitzer, 2012), for example, study engagement in terms of learner initiation of action, effort and persistence in academic tasks, as well as the learners' emotional states during activities. Fredricks, Blumenfeld, and Paris (2004) describe engagement as a multifaceted construct that includes behavior, affect, and cognition. Ainley (1993, 2012) describes engagement as the extent to which a learner is actively involved with content, where "active involvement" suggests that the person acts to maintain or extend their contact in order to increase their knowledge of it.

For the purposes of this chapter, engagement is understood to include socioemotional and cognitive aspects of the learning environment; it is not a psychological variable, per se. Conceptualizing learner engagement in this way acknowledges its multiple facets: the frame of the experience (Engle,

2006), the design and expectations that are facilitated and communicated (Gresalfi & Barab, 2011), as well as the roles of psychological variables such as interest and motivation as contributing to whether engagement is productive (the learners' willingness and/or ability to persevere when a task is challenging and to self-regulate his or her behaviors in order to complete assignments or attain goals). It also describes the learner's lack of response when he or she does not yet recognize expectations as set out by the environment and needs support to do so.

The Learning Environment and the Individual

Interest, motivation, and engagement are products of learners' interactions with the environment. Interactions can occur with the classroom, museum exhibits, videogames, books, or integrative projects, for example, as well as with other people, such as educators, parents, and peers. As a result, interactions have an idiosyncratic quality that both constitute and shape the experiences of the learner. Some environments promote exploration that encourages innovation and the development of problem-solving skills; in others, exploration is constrained by time, the design of the task and/or its facilitation (see related discussions in Azevedo, 2006; Flum & Kaplan, 2006).

Interactions that are responsive to variations in the strengths and needs of learners enhance the possibility for learning (see Eccles & Midgley, 1989; Volet & Järvelä, 2001). Some learners are able to prioritize, to persevere when tasks are difficult, and to plan their work and lives strategically. These learners also tend to be those who have learned to self-regulate, to focus and adapt their actions to fit the demands of the situation (Hadwin, Järvelä, & Miller, 2011). These same learners could be described as engaged or as having made connections to the materials and tasks with which they are to work. Their interest has been triggered and maintained, and they have begun to ask questions that lead them to seek answers (Renninger, 2000). They are likely to regulate their activity so that they can find those answers (Renninger, 2010). In this sense, motivated behavior emerges from the triggering of interest that is then maintained, and from the learners' ability to self-regulate because they want answers to the questions they have generated.

Research suggests that learners may need different types of scaffolding to engage tasks that are set out for them depending on their interest, motivation, and engagement. Research on scaffolding further indicates that beginning learners need more support than more knowledgeable learners (see Reiser & Tabak, Chapter 3, this volume). For those with little interest or understanding about particular content to be learned, scaffolds can promote the making of connections to the content that, in turn, will lead to learners asking curiosity questions about the content and self-regulating so that they can find answers (Renninger & List, 2012). Content can be scaffolded by inserting topics into passages and problems (Renninger, Ewen, & Lasher, 2002; Walkerdine, Petrosino, & Sherman, 2013). Content can also be scaffolded by promoting utility value. For example, Hulleman and Harackiewicz (2009) found that encouraging ninth grade learners with little interest in biology to identify the utility of learning biology enabled them to successfully engage their biology class, whereas learners in the same class with more interest for biology have not benefited by the utility intervention, presumably because they already recognize the utility of learning the content and are ready to work with and be challenged by biology as a discipline.

Although the design of the learning environments is adaptable, the open question is how to design so that the necessary supports are in place to (a) promote the development of interest for those in earlier phases of interest so that they are motivated and engaged, and (b) continue to challenge those in later phases of interest development so that they continue to develop and deepen their interest, maintaining their level of motivation and engagement.

Studies of Interest, Motivation, and Engagement

In this section, we overview methods and findings from five studies as exemplars of those addressing interest, motivation, and/or engagement in the learning sciences. The studies were parsimoniously selected to represent a range of participant groups and learning environments. Although the studies address different research questions and use varied methodologies, they provide convergent evidence for suggesting both that designing for learning requires (1) attending to the possibility that interest, motivation, and/or engagement will vary across learners and (2) supporting learners through content-informed interactions and, in particular, scaffolding that focuses on disciplinary content.

Falk and Needham (2011): Science Center Visits, Interviews, and Sampling Participants and the Broader Community

Visitors to museums make their own choices about which exhibits to visit and how long to stay at one exhibit before moving along to the next (see Crowley, Pierroux, & Knutson, Chapter 23, this volume). Like other out-of-school contexts, the museum environment is considered "free choice" because there are no requirements for participation and, as such, is also assumed to be of interest, motivating, and engaging. To understand visitor attendance and the impact of a science center on its community, Falk and Needham (2011) interviewed visitors and the broader community. They collected data using two semi-structured in-depth telephone interviews of a random sample of Science Center visitors (n= 832, n= 1008) approximately nine years apart. The second interview followed the renovation of the Science Center.

The results show that Science Center visits increased visitors' interest and motivation to learn about science. People who participated in leisure free-choice learning activities (e.g., read books about science or went to a science club) were significantly more likely to visit the science center. Those who had visited believed that the Science Center strongly influenced their science and technology understanding, attitudes, and behaviors. For example, adults reported that a visit to the Science Center resulted in their children engaging in science-related activities following their visit. Adults themselves reported a range of positive outcomes of their visits to the Science Center, such as increased positive attitude toward science or learning one or more things they did not know before the visit.

Falk and Needham used an "outside-in" approach to survey the broader community. Self-reported impacts were slightly higher for cognitive outcomes (e.g., increased understanding and thinking about science) than for affective outcomes (e.g., increased interest and attitudes), which may, as Falk and Needham explain, be because people who choose to visit a science center are likely to already possess higher interest in science. Their findings suggest that visits to a science center help make authentic connections to the disciplinary understanding of science and thus strengthen existing interests. They report that museum visits increased interest among those who had been less engaged in science and that living in a community that had a new science center meant that learning from others' visits to the science museum also had an impact on those who had not yet visited. These findings also point to the connections that visitors and members of the community make to the disciplinary content of the exhibit, providing content-informed interactions and scaffolding for the development of interest and motivation, and, as a result, for engagement.

Ainley and Ainley (2011): PISA, Large-Scale Assessment of Specific Science Topics

International studies comparing learning gains provide the basis for evaluating educational systems and their practice. In the Programme for International Learner Assessment survey (OECD, 2006), the achievement of 15-year-old learners across OECD and partner countries was assessed in multiple disciplinary contents. In their 2011 article, Ainley and Ainley report on analyses of student responses to science problems that emphasize understanding and application of knowledge in real-life situations using data from samples of more than 4,000 learners from Colombia, the United States, Estonia, and Sweden each (total N = 19,044). The assessment contained items that allowed them to examine how overall enjoyment of science contributes to learners' interest in finding out more about specific topics. These items chronicled learners' reactions to the specifics of the topic on which the learners were working.

Ainley and Ainley found correlations between the students' reported enjoyment and their PISA science scores; they also found correlations between their interest for science and their PISA science scores. When learners finished working on the science problems (interest assessments were embedded to the science problems assessment), they were asked to complete a questionnaire assessing measures, such as personal value of science and enjoyment of science. The findings confirmed the expected association between enjoyment of science and interest in learning science and predicted learner interest in learning about specific topics. Path analyses further indicate that the relation between personal value and interest in science is partially mediated through enjoyment of science, and also that the relation between enjoyment and embedded interest is mediated through a strong positive relation between interest in learning science and embedded interest.

These findings are interpreted as suggesting both that learners need to have (a) connections to the content on which they are working in order to experience enjoyment and engagement, and (b) interactions with, and possibly scaffolding from, others such as educators or peers, or from the embedded context of tasks. Such interactions enable learners to identify meaning and relevance in the content of science, possibly leading to reevaluation of their perceptions of science learning.

Patrick, Ryan, and Kaplan (2007): The Role of the Social in Fifth-Grade Mathematics Classrooms, Survey and Achievement Data

The impact of the social context of classroom learning is typically assumed to be beneficial, but its impact on learning is not well understood. Patrick, Ryan, and Kaplan (2007) studied fifth-grade learners' (N=602) perceptions of classroom social environment, their motivational beliefs, and their engagement in a mathematics class. Using survey data and learner achievement data (math grades from learner records), three questions were asked: (a) How do learners' perceptions of various aspects of the classroom social environment (teacher and learner support, promotion of mutual respect, and task-related interaction) relate to their engagement in math? (b) Do measures of engagement (use of self-regulation strategies and task-related interactions with peers) correlate with math achievement? (c) Do learners' motivational beliefs (whether their goals were mastery oriented, and their feelings of academia and social efficacy) mediate the associations hypothesized in questions (a) and (b)?

Briefly, findings from this study help to detail the role of the classroom social environment in learner engagement. They indicate that classroom interactions with teachers about mathematics are related to learners' mathematics achievement beyond what might have been expected based on prior achievement. They also suggest that social interaction can enhance learners' focus on mastery and feelings of efficacy, and in this way, facilitate engagement.

Finally, they underscore the relation among the social environment, the content to be learned, and learner motivation and engagement and suggest that interactions focused on disciplinary content contribute to learning of that content.

Järvelä, Veermans, and Leinonen (2008): CSCL, Case Analysis Using Observations, Interviews, Artifact Analysis, and Experience Sampling

Motivational profiles of learners during classroom computer-supported collaborative learning (CSCL) were the focus of Järvelä, Veermans, and Leinonen's (2008) study of two 14-year-old Finnish girls' work with a science fiction project on Knowledge Forum (see Scardamalia & Bereiter, Chapter 20, this volume). The two learners were selected for study based on differences in their motivational profiles during classroom work that did not involve CSCL. Mixed methods including observations, interviews, content analysis of computer notes, and an experience-sampling questionnaire were employed.

Findings reveal that even though the two learners had different motivational tendencies in a more traditional classroom – one was high and the other low – each benefited and continued to develop as learners in the CSCL context. It appears that both girls were able to succeed because CSCL involves interacting with the content to be learned, and scaffolding that supports the construction of goals consistent with capacities, in turn structuring activity and enabling self-regulation and engagement. The findings further suggest that when learning tasks are authentic and meaningful, learners are likely to work to resolve difficulties that surface because they have made connections to them: they have identified something for which they want an answer, a curiosity question, and are working to address it. Moreover, the process of identifying a research problem related to personal experience served to trigger and sustain the interest of learners identified as having differing levels of motivation.

Renninger, Cai, Lewis, Adams, and Ernst (2011): Motivation and Learning in an Online Unmoderated Workshop, Descriptive Surveys, Artifact Analysis, Logfile Analysis, and Interviews

The role of mathematics teachers' motivation and learning during their work with unmoderated modules developed by the Math Forum (mathforum.org) for online professional development was undertaken by Renninger, Cai, Lewis, Adams, and Ernst (2011). Three questions guided their study: (a) What characterized the mathematics teachers who are working online in the workshop and what are their goals? (b) What is the nature of teacher participation in terms of motivation and learning in an online mathematics workshop? (c) Can participation in an online workshop for teachers be predicted?

Methods to assess motivation and learning in the online workshop context were developed through 13 previous iterations of workshop data. Analysis focused on one workshop that included a total of 164 teachers. Data sources included pre- and post-test descriptive surveys, logfile analysis, workshop artifacts, and interviews including general and contextualized information about teachers' motivation.

Findings from the study indicate that the participants' entering level of interest, self-efficacy, and prior course work in mathematics predicted the quality of their work with nonroutine technology-enhanced challenge problems and journal assignments that prompted exploration and reflection. Three distinct clusters of teachers were identified: (a) teachers with low interest, high self-efficacy, and more background in math course work, (b) teachers with low interest, low self-efficacy, and less math background, and (c) teachers with high interest, high self-efficacy, and more math background. Differences in participation led to three general recommendations for the design of online workshops: (a) recognition that learners do not all enter the learning environment with the same motivational profile, despite their role, in this case as "teacher"; (b) initial tasks that enable all learners to enter and build community with others whose profiles and previous experience differ from their own; (c) a range of activities that allow participants to select from among them. These findings provide strong support for the possibilities and the benefits of tailoring the design of the environment, the unmoderated online course in this case, to learners' motivational profiles.

Potential Design Principles and Some Conclusions

These studies provide us with some answers to questions about the roles of interest, motivation, and/or engagement in designing for learning. There is strong evidence that learners bring different preparations and interest to their activity that results in variation in:

- their motivation and engagement,
- sense that they can be successful, and
- the types of supports needed for learning.

The literature suggests that learning environments can and should ideally enable learners with varying preparation and interest and motivation to work with disciplinary content and also that learning environments can be designed to provide learners with this type of support. Moreover, it appears that learners' levels of interest, motivation, and engagement are often proportional, meaning that with developed interest, there is increased motivation and more effective engagement. In other words, design teams could anticipate differences in the levels of learners' interest, motivation, and engagement and include project or problem features in their designs that are likely to be effective for each, increasing the likelihood that one or another of these features will feel possible to the learner, triggering interest, enabling motivation, supporting productive engagement and learning.

Some learners may of course need more support than others because they do not yet recognize what others regard as learning opportunities. For those with little interest or understanding about particular content, the design of the learning environment can be adapted to enhance the quality and possibility of learner participation. Those who have a more developed interest, however, can, through adjusted supports, continue to be challenged to develop and deepen their interest and understanding.

In summary, it appears that design principles for learning need to account for differences of interest, motivation, and engagement and do so by: (1) supporting content-informed interactions and (2) providing scaffolding for learners to think and work with content.

Supporting Content-Informed Interactions

Learners may be low on interest, motivation, or engagement because they are early in their work with the field or because they have not yet been able to make effective connections to it. If so, design needs to make clear the utility of the content to be learned, its relevance, and/or by triggering their interest for the content through novelty, challenge, surprise, complexity, or uncertainty; design needs to make connections between the real world and the content to be learned or between one and another topic in the domain.

Learners with more developed interest, motivation, or engagement can be expected to already appreciate the utility of the content to be learned and to recognize its relevance. Although their interest is also triggered by novelty, challenge, surprise, complexity, and/or uncertainty, what counts as novelty and so forth differs for those with less interest, motivation, or engagement. For them, design needs to support learners to continue to deepen their thinking about domain-specific content.

Designing activities and tasks that allow multiple ways of accessing content to be learned, and as such varied ways to think and work with content, can increase the likelihood of engagement. This type of design can occur in the museum, the out-of-school workshop, the classroom, and online. Computer-based tools, CSCL, online modules, and social media embedded in learning environments have shown particular promise for enabling the differentiation of learning and instruction because they can provide tailored support for self-regulated and active task interactions such as elaboration and articulation or managing and aggregating information (Dabbagh & Kitsansas, 2012; Gresalfi & Barab, 2011; Laru, Näykki, & Järvelä, 2012). Computer-based tools and online modules have proven particularly effective for supporting active task interactions when learners are expected to function independently with limited interaction with teachers or peers (e.g., Mathan & Koedinger, 2005; Renninger et al., 2011).

Scaffolding Interactions with Disciplinary Content

It is critical that learners in earlier or less developed phases of interest, motivation, and engagement find utility or relevance in the disciplinary content to be learned, or be positioned to have their interest triggered for the content. Like Patrick and colleagues (2007), Hijzen, Boekaerts, and Vedder (2007) reported that student opportunities for collaboration, belongingness, and social support were related to student engagement and the quality of learning. Kempler-Rogat and Linnenbrink-Garcia's (2011) qualitative analyses of group observations across six collaborative groups of upper elementary students further suggest that characteristics of positive interactions are active listening, respectful interactions, and group cohesion.

For learners with more developed interest, motivation, and engagement, scaffolding that directly engages them in the content on which they are working and supports them to stretch their understanding is essential. They need to continue to develop and deepen their thinking and be supported to identify and find answers to their curiosity questions. Scaffolding interactions that promote work with disciplinary content provide learners with a foundation for independently reengaging content – not because they have to but because they want to.

We have provided evidence that learning environments are enhanced by:

- the inclusion of content-informed interaction, and
- the scaffolding of learners' interactions with disciplinary content.

Learning environments with these design features are likely to trigger, sustain, and support the development of learners' interest. As a result, they also can be expected to positively impact learners' motivation and their engagement.

References

Ainley, M. (1993). Styles of engagement with learning: Multidimensional assessment of their relationship with strategy use and school achievement. *Journal of Educational Psychology*, 85, 395–405.

Ainley, M. (2012). Students' interest and engagement in classroom activities. In S. L. Christenson, A. L. Reschly, & C. Wylie (Eds.), *Handbook of research on student engagement* (pp. 283–302). New York: Springer International.

Ainley, M., & Ainley, J. (2011). Learner engagement with science in early adolescence: The contribution of enjoyment to learners' continuing interest in learning about science. *Contemporary Educational Psychology*, 36(1), 4–12.

Azevedo, F. S. (2006). Personal excursions: Investigating the dynamics of student engagement. *International Journal of Computers for Mathematical Learning*, 11, 57–98.

Bandura, A. (1997). *Self-efficacy: The exercise of control*. New York: W. H. Freeman & Company.

Bergin, D. (1999). Influences of classroom interest. *Educational Psychologist*, 34(2), 87–98.

Berlyne, D. (1960). *Conflict, arousal, and curiosity*. New York: McGraw-Hill.

Berridge, K. C., Robinson, T. E., & Aldridge, I. W. (2009). Dissecting components of reward: "Liking," "wanting," and learning. *Current Opinion in Pharmacology*, 9, 65–73.

Christenson, S. L., Reschly, A. L., & Wylie, C. (Eds.) (2012). *Handbook of research on student engagement*. New York: Springer International.

Dabbagh, N., & Kitsantas, A. (2012). Personal learning environments, social media, and self-regulated learning: A natural formula for connecting formal and informal learning. *The Internet and Higher Education*, 15(1), 3–8.

Durik, A. M., & Harackiewicz, J. M. (2007). Different strokes for different folks: Individual interest as a moderator of the effects of situational factors on task interest. *Journal of Educational Psychology*, 99(3), 597–610.

Eccles, J. S. (2009). Who am I and what am I going to do with my life? Personal and collective identities as motivators of action. *Educational Psychologist*, 44(2), 78–89.

Eccles, J. S., & Midgley, C. (1989). Stage/environment fit: Developmentally appropriate classrooms for early adolescents. In R. E. Ames & C. Ames (Eds.), *Research on motivation in education* (vol. 3, pp. 139–181). New York: Guildford Press.

Engle, R. A. (2006). Framing interactions to foster generative learning: A situative explanation of transfer in a community of learners classroom. *Journal of the Learning Sciences*, 15(4), 451–498.

Falk, J. H., & Needham, M. D. (2011). Measuring the impact of a science center on its community. *Journal of Research in Science Teaching*, 48(1), 1–12.

Flum, H., & Kaplan, A. (2006). Exploratory orientation as an educational goal. *Educational Psychologist*, 41, 99–110.

Fredricks, J. A., Blumenfeld, P. C., & Paris, A. H. (2004). School engagement: Potential of the concept, state of the evidence. *Review of Educational Research*, 74, 59–109.

Gresalfi, M., & Barab, S. (2011). Learning for a reason: Supporting forms of engagement by designing tasks and orchestrating environments. *Theory into Practice*, 50(4), 300–310.

Hadwin, A., Järvelä, S., & Miller, M. (2011). Self-regulated, co-regulated, and socially shared regulation of learning. In B. Zimmerman & D. Schunk (Eds.), *Handbook of self-regulation of learning and performance* (pp. 65–84). New York: Routledge.

Hadwin, A. F., & Winne, P. H. (2012). Promoting learning skills in undergraduate learners. In M. J. Lawson & J. R. Kirby (Eds.), *The quality of learning: Dispositions, instruction, and mental structures* (pp. 201–229). New York: Cambridge University Press.

Harackiewicz, J. M., Durik, A. M., Barron, K. E., Linnenbrink, L., & Tauer, J. M. (2008). The role of achievement goals in the development of interest: Reciprocal relations between achievement goals, interest, and performance. *Journal of Educational Psychology*, 100(1), 105–122.

Harackiewicz, J. M., Rozek, C. R., Hulleman, C. S., & Hyde, J. S. (2012). Helping parents motivate their teens in mathematics and science: An experimental test. *Psychological Science*, 23(8), 899–906.

Hidi, S. (2013). Revisiting the role of rewards in motivation and learning: Implications of neuroscientific research. Under review.

Hidi, S., & Ainley, M. (2008). Interest and self-regulation: Relationships between two variables that influence learning. In D. H. Schunk & B. J. Zimmerman (Eds.), *Motivation and self-regulated learning: Theory, research, and applications* (pp. 77–109). Mahwah, NJ: Lawrence Erlbaum Associates.

Hidi, S., & Baird, W. (1988). Strategies for increasing text-based interest and students' recall of expository texts. *Reading Research Quarterly*, 23, 465–483.

Hidi, S., & Harackiewicz, J. (2000). Motivating the academically unmotivated: A critical issue for the 21st century. *Review of Educational Research*, 70, 151–179.

Hidi, S., & Renniger, A. (2006). The Four-Phase Model of Interest Development. *Educational Psychologist*, 41(2), 111–127.

Hijzen, D., Boekaerts, M., & Vedder, P. (2007). Exploring the links between learners' engagement in cooperative learning, their goal preferences, and appraisals of instructional conditions in the classroom. *Learning and Instruction*, 17(6), 673–687.

Hulleman, C. S., & Harackiewicz, J. M. (2009). Promoting interest and performance in high school science classes. *Science*, 326, 1410–1412.

Järvelä, S., & Hadwin, A. (2013). New frontiers: Regulating learning in CSCL. *Educational Psychologist*, 48(1), 1–15.

Järvelä, S., Järvenoja, H., & Malmberg, J. (2012). How elementary school students' regulation of motivation is connected to self-regulation. *Educational Research and Evaluation*, 18(1), 65–84.

Järvelä, S., Veermans, M., & Leinonen, P. (2008). Investigating learners' engagement in a computer-supported inquiry – a process-oriented analysis. *Social Psychology in Education*, 11, 299–322.

Kempler Rogat, T. M., & Linnenbrink-Garcia, L. (2011). Socially shared regulation in collaborative groups: An analysis of the interplay between quality of social regulation and group processes. *Cognition and Instruction*, 29(4), 375–415.

Krapp, A. (2007). An educational-psychological conceptualisation of interest. *International Journal of Educational and Vocational Guidance*, 7(1), 5–21.

Laru, J., Näykki, P., & Järvelä, S. (2012). Supporting small-group learning with use of multiple Web 2.0 tools in blended learning setting: A case study with learning sciences students. *The Internet and Higher Education*, 15, 29–38.

Malmberg, J., Järvelä, S., & Kirschner, P. (2013, accepted). Elementary school students' strategic activity and quality of strategy use: Does task-type matter? *Metacognition and Learning*.

Mathan, S. A., & Koedinger, K. R. (2005). Fostering the intelligent novice: Learning from errors with metacognitive tutoring. *Educational Psychologist*, 40(4), 257–265.

McLaughlin, C. (2008). Emotional well-being and its relationship to schools and classrooms: A critical reflection. *British Journal of Guidance & Counselling*, 36(4), 353–366.

Mitchell, M. (1993). Situational interest: Its multifaceted structure in the secondary school mathematics classroom. *Journal of Educational Psychology*, 85, 424–436.

OECD. (2006). *PISA 2006 science competencies for tomorrow's world*. Paris: OECD.

Palmer, D. H. (2009). Student interest generated during an inquiry skills lesson. *Journal of Research in Science Teaching*, 46(2), 147–165.

Patrick, H., Ryan, A., & Kaplan, A. (2007). Early adolescents' perceptions of the classroom social environment, motivational beliefs, and engagement. *Journal of Educational Psychology*, 99, 83–98.

Perry, N. E. (1998). Young children's self-regulated learning and contexts that support it. *Journal of Educational Psychology*, 90, 715–729.

Perry, N. E., VandeKamp, K. O., Mercer, L. K., & Nordby, C. J. (2002). Investigating teacher-student interactions that foster self-regulated learning. *Educational Psychologist*, 37(1), 5–15.

Renninger, K. A. (2000). Individual interest and its implications for understanding intrinsic motivation. In C. Sansone & J. M. Harackiewicz (Eds.), *Intrinsic motivation: Controversies and new directions* (pp. 373–404). San Diego, CA: Academic Press.

Renninger, K. A. (2009). Interest and identity development in instruction: An inductive model. *Educational Psychologist*, 44(2), 105–118.

Renninger, K. A. (2010). Working with and cultivating interest, self-efficacy, and self-regulation. In D. Preiss & R. Sternberg (Eds.), *Innovations in educational psychology: Perspectives on learning, teaching and human development* (pp. 158–195). New York: Springer.

Renninger, K. A., Cai, M., Lewis, M. C., Adams, M. M., & Ernst, K. L. (2011). Motivation and learning in an online, unmoderated, mathematics workshop for teachers. *Educational Technology Research and Development*, 59(2), 229–247.

Renninger, K. A., Ewen, E., & Lasher, A. K. (2002). Individual interest as context in expository text and mathematical word problems. *Learning and Instruction*, 12, 467–491.

Renninger, K. A., & Hidi, S. (2011). Revisiting the conceptualization, measurement, and generation of interest. *Educational Psychologist*, 46(3), 168–184.

Renninger, K. A., & List, A. (2012). Scaffolding for learning. In N. Seel (Ed.), *Encyclopedia of the sciences of learning* (pp. 989–992). New York: Springer.

Renninger, K. A., & Su, S. (2012). Interest and its development. In R. Ryan (Ed.), *Oxford handbook of motivation* (pp. 167–187). New York: Oxford University Press.

Sansone, C., & Thoman, D. B. (2005). Interest as the missing motivator in self-regulation. *European Psychologist*, 10(3), 175–186.

Sansone. C., Weir, C., Harpster, L., & Morgan, C. (1992). Once a boring task always a boring task? Interest as a self-regulatory mechanism. *Journal of Personality and Social Psychology*, 63, 379–390.

Schank, R. C. (1979). Interestingness: Controlling inferences. *Artificial Intelligence*, 12, 273–297.

Schunk, D. H. (1995). Self-efficacy, motivation, and performance. *Journal of Applied Sport Psychology*, 7(2), 112–137.

Schunk, D. H., & Zimmerman, B. J. (Eds.) (1994). *Self-regulation of learning and performance: Issues and educational applications*. Hillsdale, NJ: Lawrence Erlbaum Associates.

Skinner, E. A., & Belmont, M. J. (1993). Motivation in the classroom: Reciprocal effects of teacher behavior and student engagement across the school year. *Journal of Educational Psychology*, 85, 571–581.

Skinner, E. A., & Pitzer, J. R. (2012). Developmental dynamics of student engagement, coping, and everyday resilience. In S. L. Christenson, A. L. Reschly, & C. Wylie (Eds.), *Handbook of research on student engagement* (pp. 21–44). New York: Springer International.

Trilling, B., & Fadel, C. (2009). *21st century skills: Learning for life in our times*. San Francisco, CA: Jossey-Bass.

Tulis, M., & Ainley, M. (2011). Interest, enjoyment and pride after failure experiences? Predictors of learners' state-emotions after success and failure during learning in mathematics. *An International Journal of Experimental Educational Psychology*, 31(7), 779–807.

Tytler, R., & Osborne, J. (2012). Student attitudes and aspirations towards science. In B. J. Fraser, K. Tobin, & C. J. McRobbie (Eds.), *Second international handbook of science education* (pp. 597–625). New York: Springer International.

Van den Bossche, P., Gijselars, W., Seger, M., & Kirschner, P. A. (2006). Social and cognitive factors driving teamwork in collaborative learning environments. Team learning beliefs and behaviors. *Small Group Research*, 37(5), 490–521.

Volet, S., & Järvelä, S. (Eds.) (2001). *Motivation in learning contexts: Theoretical advances and methodological implications*. London: Pergamon/Elsevier.

Walkington, C., Petrosino, A., & Sherman, M. (2013). Supporting algebraic reasoning through personalized story scenarios: How situational understanding mediates performance. *Mathematical Thinking and Learning*, 15(2), 89–120.

Wigfield, A., Eccles, J., Schiefele, U., Roeser, R., & Davis-Kean, P. (2006). Development of achievement motivation. In R. Lerner & W. Damon (Series Eds.) and N. Eisenberg (Vol. Ed.), *Handbook of child psychology: Vol. 3. Social, emotional, and personality development*. Sixth Edition (pp. 933–1002). New York: Wiley.

Zimmerman, B. (1989). A social cognitive view of self-regulated academic learning. *Journal of Educational Psychology*, 81, 329–339.

Zimmerman, B. (2001). Theories of self-regulated learning and academic achievement: An overview and analysis. In B. J. Zimmerman & D. H. Schunk (Eds.), *Self-regulated learning and academic achievement: Theoretical perspectives*. Second Edition (pp.1–37). Mahwah, NJ: Lawrence Erlbaum Associates.

Zimmerman, B., & Kitsantas, A. (2002). Acquiring writing revision and self-regulatory skill through observation and emulation. *Journal of Educational Psychology*, 94(4), 660–668.

Zimmerman, B., & Schunk, D. (2011). Self-regulated learning and performance: An introduction and an overview. In B. Zimmerman & D. Schunk (Eds.), *Handbook of self-regulation of learning and performance*. New York: Routledge.

34 Learning as a Cultural Process: Achieving Equity through Diversity

Na'ilah Suad Nasir, Ann S. Rosebery, Beth Warren, and Carol D. Lee

In this chapter, we argue that learning and teaching are fundamentally cultural processes (Cole, 1996; Lee, 2008; Lee, Spencer, & Harpalani, 2003; Nasir & Bang, 2012; Rogoff, 2003). The learning sciences have not yet adequately addressed the ways that culture is integral to learning. By *culture*, we mean the constellations of practices communities have historically developed and dynamically shaped in order to accomplish the purposes they value, including tools they use, social networks with which they are connected, ways they organize joint activity, and their ways of conceptualizing and engaging with the world. In this view, learning and development can be seen as the acquisition throughout the life course of diverse repertoires of overlapping, complementary, or even conflicting cultural practices.

Diversity along multiple dimensions is a mainstay of human communities. National boundaries evolve and change, bringing together people from different groups that have different ethnicities, languages, worldviews, and cultural practices. Migration and transmigration are not new phenomena. However, technological advances have accelerated cross-national movement. In 2010, international migrants constituted 3.1 percent of the world population. The greatest concentrations of international migrants relative to the national populations are in the United States, Saudi Arabia, Canada, across Europe, and Oceania (largely New Zealand and Australia).

Levels of both historic and contemporary ethnic diversity within nations are often overlooked. For example, China has 56 officially recognized ethnic groups, including ethnic concentrations in the five autonomous regions. First-generation immigrants represent 10–15 percent of the populations in Belgium, France, the Netherlands, Sweden, and the United Kingdom; 24 percent in New Zealand, Canada, and Switzerland. Thus, diversity in the political, social, and economic organization of nation-states is an ongoing phenomenon with complex implications for education.

Different countries have organized schooling to address diversity in a variety of ways, and we now have increasing evidence of which policies are most effective. While not universally the case, it is not uncommon that ethnic minorities and recent immigrants are more likely to be of lower income and lower socioeconomic status (SES) across nations. However, neither poverty nor immigrant status necessarily equates with low academic performance. The OECD defines resiliency in terms of students who are from the bottom SES quartile of their nation but score in the top quartile on the Program for International Student Assessment (PISA) among students from similar SES backgrounds across countries (Organization for Economic Cooperation and Development, 2010). Using 2009 PISA data, the overall top scoring countries with high percentages of resilient students are: Turkey, Canada, Portugal, Finland, Japan, and Singapore (39%–48%); Korea (50%); Macao-China (56%); Hong Kong (72%); and Shanghai-China (76%). These high resiliency scores cannot be attributed to homogeneity; none of these countries is ethnically homogeneous, and all are linguistically diverse. These societies provide societal safety nets for families; a number of them have school-based policies that explicitly address linguistic and other forms of diversity within their school systems. Additionally, many nations have national policies that directly address the role of cultural diversity in learning, including:

- The official use of Catalan in the Catalan region of Spain and progressive efforts to address the educational needs of recent immigrants from Morocco and other parts of North Africa as well as their historic Roma population;
- Language and other preferential policies in autonomous regions in China such as the Xianjiang Uygur Autonomous Region;
- National policies to include African diaspora history and culture in the curriculum in Brazil and Venezuela; and
- Cross-national attention to the role of indigenous knowledge systems among indigenous populations in North and South America, Australia, New Zealand, and the Pacific Islands.

While these policies and practices are incomplete and often controversial, they help us to understand how an awareness of cultural diversity can enhance the quality of learning when the student population is heterogeneous. The examples we discuss in this chapter are largely based in the United States; however, the underlying principles that we identify are basic to human learning in all its variations, within and across national boundaries.

Across the world, through participation in varied communities of practice, individuals appropriate, over time, varied repertoires of *cultural practices* – ways of being and acting that are socially situated and culturally valued. In children's daily environments – from home to school, mathematics to literature class, basketball team to workplace – they encounter, engage, and negotiate various situated repertoires of these cultural practices. Each repertoire represents a particular point of view on the world, characterized by its own objects, meanings, purposes, symbols, and values (Bakhtin, 1981; Gee, 1990). Navigation among these repertoires can be problematic at any time in any place for any human being. However, for youth from nondominant groups, for students who speak national or language varieties other than an official national language, and for students from low-income communities, this navigation is exacerbated by asymmetrical relationships of power that inevitably come into play around matters of culture, ethnicity, class, gender, and language. Thus these youth must learn to manage multiple developmental tasks: both the ordinary tasks of life course development, as well as tasks that involve managing sources of stress rooted in particular forms of institutional stigmatization due to assumptions regarding race, poverty, language variation, gender, and disability (Burton, Allison, & Obeidallah, 1995; Spencer, 1999). Such stigmatization limits access to opportunities in school and work.

Historically, studies of culture have often viewed nondominant students and communities as different or deficient and assumed a singular pathway of development based on dominant cultural norms. From this viewpoint, the proper way to address diversity is to help nondominant groups become more like dominant groups. In this chapter, we reject this historically dated view and argue for a more sophisticated understanding of diversity and learning – one that shows schools they can use diversity to enhance learning, rather than simply viewing it as a problem to overcome.

In this chapter, we draw on empirical research on the cultural nature of learning, including studies of (a) learning in and out of school settings; (b) relationships between everyday and academic knowledge and discourse, especially for youth from nondominant groups; and (c) classroom-based design research that explores linkages among the varied repertoires of practice of youth and those of academic disciplines. These studies address multiple dimensions of learning including cognition, discourse, affect, motivation, and identity. Our cultural view of learning is closely related to work on *adaptive expertise* (Hatano & Inagaki, 1986), that is, the development of flexible knowledge and dispositions that facilitate effective navigation across varied settings and tasks. Adaptive expertise is crucial for youth from nondominant groups who typically face and must be able to address extreme societal challenges.

Our chapter addresses three critical, related questions:

1. How do children learn when engaged in their own cultures' everyday repertoires of practice?
2. How can we connect these everyday repertoires of practice with academic disciplinary practices, as found in formal school settings?
3. Can we use our increased understanding of these repertoires of practice to help children learn better?

We illustrate each with examples from research on science, literacy, and mathematics learning and teaching.

Question 1: How Do Children Learn When Engaged in Their Own Cultures' Everyday Repertoires of Practice?

Many children who seem to have trouble learning in schools nonetheless learn successfully in everyday, out-of-school cultural practices. In this section, we review research on the out-of-school learning of children from nondominant groups with the purpose of illuminating what such learning looks like and how it happens. Consider the following vignette from a study of learning in the game of dominoes:

> Four 10-year-old African American boys are playing a game of dominoes. In their version, the goal is to score points by creating a sum of the end pieces that is a multiple of five. A novice player puts a play on the board, then uses his finger to count the number of points on the board, but does not know if it is a score. An expert player notices his confusion and says, "It's not nothing!" Later, at the end of this hand of play, the expert player suggests pieces that the novice could have played to create a score. (Nasir & Stone, 2003)

In this vignette, the expert player was an important resource for supporting the sense making of the novice, both through the feedback he offered directly and as an example of what more advanced play looks like. Through interactions like these, domino players come to learn both more competent play and concepts of multiples and serial addition.

Learning happens in a wide range of activities outside of school, including dairy factory work (Scribner, 1985), plumbing (Rose, 2004), hairdressing (Majors, 2003), candy selling (Saxe, 1991), basketball (Nasir, 2000), gardening (Civil, 2005), weaving (Rogoff, 2003), and everyday language use (Ball, 1992, 1995; Heath, 1983; Lee, 1993). Several studies have pointed to the context specificity of the skills and knowledge learned in informal settings (Cole, Gay, Glick, & Sharp, 1971; Lave, 1988). Often, people can competently perform complex cognitive tasks outside of school, but may not display these skills on school-type tasks. This finding indicates the importance of understanding the nature of learning in out-of-school settings and of building on this learning to support learning in school.

As we discuss selected studies of successful out-of-school learning environments, we argue that scaffolding (see Reiser & Tabak, Chapter 3, this volume) plays a critical role in the development of adaptive expertise. Scaffolding involves (1) organizing participation in activities in ways that address basic human needs for a sense of safety and belonging; (2) making the structure of the domain visible and socializing participants for dispositions and habits of mind necessary for expert-like practice; (3) helping novices understand possible trajectories for competence and the relevance of the domain; and (4) providing timely and flexible feedback.

Participation that Addresses Basic Needs

A key part of scaffolding in out-of-school learning involves organizing participation in ways that address basic human needs for safety, belonging and identification, self-esteem and respect (Maslow, 1962). The need for physical and psychological safety is central to the creation of effective learning environments. Psychological safety can be defined as a sense of comfort, willingness to take risks and be oneself, and a feeling of acceptance. Steele's (1997) work documenting stereotype threat demonstrates the profound influence that a *lack* of psychological safety has on learning. This work demonstrated that when the climate was psychologically unsafe (i.e., African American students were made to think that their performance on a test was diagnostic, triggering fears of fitting into a stereotype about their race), performance suffered. However, when testing conditions did not trigger the threat of being stereotyped, performance increased. In other learning settings with more psychological safety, including community-based programs for youth (Heath & McLaughlin, 1993), adult organizers recognized the importance of creating safe spaces for activity and supported youth in attaining high levels of engagement and competence.

Successful learning contexts also attend to students' need for a sense of belonging and identification (Hirsch, 2005). This occurs through both the organization of the practice and the social interaction within these contexts. For instance, in a study of a U.S. high school track and field team (Nasir & Cooks, 2009), coaches explicitly attended to this sense of belonging as an important outcome. These athletes discussed this feeling of belonging and identification as a key reason they persisted in the sport and continued to work to improve their performance, even through difficult races.

Making Visible the Structure of the Domain

Effective out-of-school settings also make visible a deep structural knowledge of the domain. For example, in dominoes, a game played in many African American and South American communities (Nasir, 2002), more expert players not only make their thinking about game strategies (involving multiplication and probability) available to novices, but they do this in a developmental fashion. That is, as players become more skillful, they receive feedback that pushes them to the next level of understanding the game. Language practices are critical to this scaffolding in giving novices access to the structure of the domain.

Language practices also play an important role in the Investigators Club (I-Club), a U.S. after school science program for middle school students who are not experiencing academic success in school (Sohmer & Michaels, 2005). In I-Club, dynamic metaphors that bridge actual situations in the world and scientific concepts scaffold student investigators toward scientific discourses. Participants also talk explicitly about how scientific and everyday talk differ. Thus, I-Club is making visible to participants how specific scientific discourses work.

A number of studies have documented the literacy practices that are embedded in a variety of American out-of-school contexts, including church (Baquedano-Lopez, 1997), blue collar work settings (Rose, 2004), sports (Mahiri, 1998), and the arts (Ball, 1995). Fisher (2003) documented how a number of nontraditional community-based organizations create multigenerational spaces where African American and Latino/a adolescents gather to create "spoken word" poetry. In spoken word communities, public discussions of criteria for quality writing or play are routine.

Trajectories for Competence

Providing novices with a clear view of developing expertise is another form of scaffolding. This allows newcomers to see how experts participate and provides them with a sense of possible learning trajectories. This form of scaffolding has been observed widely, and research has documented how novices work in apprentice roles as they perform tasks in conjunction with experts (see Collins & Kapur, Chapter 6, this volume). Rogoff (2003) has described such learning as "intent participation," highlighting the ways participants learn by observing the flow of an activity. Within after school environments such as the Computer Clubhouse at the Museum of Science in Boston, youth have access to each others' experience and practice. At the Computer Clubhouse, youth work closely with one another and with support and inspiration from adult mentors to learn to use leading-edge software to create their own artwork, animations, virtual worlds, musical creations, Web sites, and robotic constructions (Resnick & Rusk, 1996).

Timely and Flexible Feedback

Timely and flexible feedback takes many forms in out-of-school practices and often involves evaluation and on-the-spot correction. In candy selling among Brazilian children, evaluation and correction occur when sellers are pricing candy or as they are counting their profits. Saxe (1991) described sellers who correct the pricing conventions of others during selling activity. In dominoes (Nasir, 2000, 2005), not only does correction occur in the midst of game play (usually with more competent players advising and correcting less sophisticated players), but evaluation is a part of the regular game structure through postgame analysis, where players discuss the strengths and weaknesses of plays in the previous round. This focus on evaluation and correction is a formative and routine part of the practice, rather than an assessment to judge competence.

It is important to note that these four features are often coordinated. This coordination can be very powerful for learning. These are evident in 5th

Dimension after school clubs (Cole & The Distributed Literacy Consortium, 2006) throughout the United States, where youth have access to a variety of resources to support their developing expertise with computer games, including college-aged tutors, peers, information cards, and the now famous virtual wizard to whom youth and adults can write for advice. In addition, Gutiérrez, Baquedano-López, and Tejada (2000) asserted that the participation structure of play invites engagement, and in conjunction with multiple layers of support facilitates persistence and identification of personal goals. While we have focused on out-of-school settings, the forms of scaffolding that we have highlighted may also be enacted in school learning settings.

Question 2: How Can We Connect these Everyday Repertoires of Practice with Academic Disciplinary Practices?

In this section, we examine research that explores intersections between everyday practices and important disciplinary knowledge. We believe that educators can use the varied and productive resources youth develop in their out-of-school lives to help them understand disciplinary ideas.

Intersections with Science

The following vignette illustrates differences in students' sense-making practices in elementary school science.

> While discussing the question, "Do plants grow everyday?", third grade children in a two-way Spanish-English bilingual program in the U.S. debated the pattern of growth and whether you can *see* it. One girl, Serena, the child of highly educated parents who was considered an excellent student, approached these matters from a stance outside the phenomenon, through the logic of measurement. She argued that growth can be seen through the evidence of measurement on a chart of a plant's daily growth. Another girl, Elena, approached the question differently. The child of immigrant, working class parents, Elena was repeating third grade. She took up the question of how one can *see* a plant's growth by imagining her own growth through "the crinkly feeling" she has when her feet are starting to outgrow her socks. (Ballenger, 2003)

This vignette illustrates two important scientific practices, one commonly recognized, one not. Serena's approach is valued in school; it conforms to widely held conceptions of scientific reasoning. While undoubtedly important, it represents one tool in what ought to be a wide-ranging repertoire of sense-making practices in science. In contrast, Elena's approach is undervalued, sometimes even dismissed as confused (Warren & Rosebery, 2011). In fact, Elena's move to imagine her own growth and, through this, the growth of a plant, reflects scientific practice. Scientists regularly use visual and narrative resources to place themselves inside physical events and processes in order to explore how these may behave (Keller, 1983; Ochs, Jacoby, & Gonzales, 1996; Wolpert & Richards, 1997).

Studies of scientific practice have described the fundamental heterogeneity of science-in-action as an intricate intertwining of conceptual, imaginative, material, discursive, symbolic, emotional, and experiential resources (Biagioli, 1999; Galison, 1997). These analyses of the everyday work of scientists challenge a stereotype of science as largely hypothetico-deductive in nature, discontinuous with everyday experience of the physical world, and represented in thinking practices distinct from those used to make sense of everyday life. Dominant understandings like these have shaped traditional science education to privilege certain ways of displaying understanding (e.g., Serena's) over others (e.g., Elena's).

Classroom-based studies have documented intersections between the sense-making practices of scientists and those of youth from nondominant groups. One result is an expanded view of what counts as scientific thinking and activity, including use of embodied imagining, argumentation, and metaphor to theorize and construct knowledge (Bang, Warren, Rosebery, & Medin, 2012). Let us take argumentation as one example (also see Andriessen & Baker, Chapter 22, this volume).

In *Laboratory Life*, Latour and Woolgar (1986) argued that scientists transform their observations into findings through argumentation and persuasion, rather than through measurement and discovery. They portray the activity of laboratory scientists as a constant struggle for the generation and acceptance of fact-like statements. Similarly, researchers working in bilingual classroom settings in Boston found that Haitian American youth used a common Haitian discourse practice, *bay odyans*, to argue claims and evidence in biology and physics (Hudicourt-Barnes, 2003; Warren & Rosebery, 1996). *Bay odyans* is a form of entertainment comprised of highly spirited and focused debate of ideas. Participants express, defend, and dispute divergent points of view with evidence or logic, often forcing one another to narrow their claims, in a manner similar to disagreement sequences that Lynch (1985) documented in studies of professional scientific activity. *Bay odyans* has been shown to support learning in science by helping students specify meanings for crucial terms, explore potential explanatory models, and develop norms of scientific accountability (Rosebery & Warren, 2008; Warren & Rosebery, 1996). Other studies have documented how youth from nondominant groups use practices of narrative sequencing and metaphor to express arguments and explanations in science (Gee & Clinton, 2000; Sohmer & Michaels, 2005; Warren, Ogonowski, & Pothier, 2005). Although these discourse practices have some different features from those valued in school, they connect deeply with discourse practices used in scientific communities.

Intersections with Literacy

Historically in many countries, the language of speakers of nonstandard dialects (such as African American English (AAE) or Appalachian English in the United States) and of recent immigrants who have not yet fully mastered the national language has been positioned as inadequate when compared to the academic language of formal school settings. However, much research indicates that non-mainstream dialects are complex in their own right with features relevant to learning academic reading and writing (also see Smagorinsky & Mayer, Chapter 30, this volume). For example, Gee (1989) documented complex literary features of what Michaels (1981) called an AAE topic associative narrative style. Ball (1995) illustrated preferred expository patterns among African American adolescents that reflect rhetorically powerful patterns used by great African American orators, but are not typically taught in U.S. high schools. Lee and colleagues (2003) scaffolded everyday knowledge of narrative conventions among young speakers of AAE to produce high-quality written narratives. These everyday conventions include what Smitherman (1977) called the African-American Rhetorical Tradition as well as event scripts from African American cultural life. Smitherman (2000) conducted post hoc analyses of African American writing samples from the 1984 and 1988/1989 National Assessment of Educational Progress (NAEP) writing assessments. She found that these African American rhetorical features were highly correlated with high quality of writing as determined by NAEP examiners.

Other studies document how bilingual speakers use competencies in their first language in reading, writing, and speaking in a second language at the level of vocabulary, syntax, and discourse (Garcia, 2000; Jimenez, Garcia, & Pearson, 1996; Langer, Bartolome, Vasquez, & Lucas, 1990; Moll & Gonzalez, 2004). Literacy in the first language can scaffold reading and writing in the second, particularly in content area learning, making technical distinctions in science (Warren, Ballenger, Ogonowski, Rosebery, & Hudicourt-Barnes, 2001), and reasoning in mathematics (Moschkovich, 1999). Others (Orellana, Reynolds, Dorner, & Meza, 2003; Valdes, 2002) have documented the metalinguistic competencies of bilingual youth who translate for their monolingual parents in consequential settings, that is, adapting speech registers to the setting, comprehending complex technical texts, and managing power relations.

Intersections with Mathematics

Studies in mathematics have shown how sophisticated mathematical thinking occurs across multiple repertoires of practice for nondominant students. For instance, African American high school basketball players learned concepts of average and percent as a part of calculating their own and others' game statistics (Nasir, 2000); with their families, Latino students worked with principles of spacing and geometric design in the context of sewing and gardening (Civil, 2005; Gonzalez & Moll, 2004), budgeting practices, and standard algorithms to find batting averages (Goldman, 2001). Research on younger children has documented Brazilian and African American students' participation in buying (Taylor, 2009) and selling (Saxe, 1991) activities.

This work is striking because the participants rarely viewed what they were doing as mathematics and often claimed to be poor at math. This poses a challenge for teachers and researchers: How do researchers, teachers, and participants learn to "see" the math in what they are doing? On one hand, recognizing mathematics is simple, if we view math as calculation. However, this becomes more difficult with more sophisticated mathematics, such as geometry or probabilistic thinking. Furthermore, even when the mathematics involves simple calculations, in practices outside of school these problems are often solved by estimating. Estimating strategies can result in a deeper understanding of mathematical relationships even as they fail to yield precise mathematical answers of the sort valued in school.

Our point here is that in order to see robust, authentic connections between the everyday knowledge and practices of youth from nondominant groups and those of the academic disciplines, we must look beyond the typical connections made in school curricula and identify important continuities of practice. By identifying and then using practices such as embodied imagining, *bay odyans*, or AAE discursive forms, we not only create spaces in which students can participate in academic disciplinary practices, we also put ourselves in a position to better understand the role such practices play in learning (Lee, 1993, 2007; Rosebery, Ogonowski, DiSchino, & Warren, 2010; Warren et al., 2001).

Question 3: Can We Use Our Increased Understanding of these Repertoires of Practice to Help Children Learn Better?

If culturally embedded learning in repertoires of practice is indeed intellectually related to learning in academic disciplines, there are two implications: first, that we should expand conventional views of knowledge in these disciplines, and second, that we should value and make use of the potential of these discursive and reasoning practices to help youth from nondominant groups learn better. To do this, teachers and researchers must work continually to make sense of youths' varied ideas and experiences (Ballenger & Rosebery, 2003; Lee, 2001; Warren et al., 2001), moving beyond the limiting assumptions of academic discourses, learning and teaching, and language, culture, and race (Ball, 2000; Foster, 1997; Ladson-Billings, 2001; Lee, 2005; Warren & Rosebery, 2011).

To use these repertoires of practice to design better learning environments, we must reorganize school practices in ways that make explicit the linkages between everyday and school-based knowledge and discourse. To do this effectively, we need design principles for:

1. making the structure of the discipline visible;
2. engaging youth in actively populating academic discourses with meaning and intention through participation structures that create roles and relationships through which youth can identify with the practices of the discipline;
3. structuring occasions for meta-level analysis (e.g., talk about thinking and language) that helps youth see relationships between usually tacit everyday knowledge and discourse and academic knowledge and discourse.

Such design work also requires that researchers, curriculum designers, and teachers recognize that learning in academic disciplines includes more than mastery of a body of conceptual knowledge. Crucially, it also involves critical engagement with epistemological assumptions, points of view, values, and dispositions (Bang et al., 2012; Collins & Ferguson, 1993; Lee, 2007; Perkins, 1992; Warren et al., 2005; also see Songer & Kali, Chapter 28, this volume). It brings to the forefront issues of affect and emotion that attend academic risk taking, especially for youth who have not experienced academic success in school (Heath, 2004).

A number of school-based interventions have taken up these design challenges. In the United States, these include the Algebra Project (Moses & Cobb, 2001), Chèche Konnen (Rosebery et al., 2010; Warren et al., 2001, 2005), the Cultural Modeling Project (Lee, 1993, 1995, 2007), the Funds of Knowledge Project (Amanti, González, & Moll, 2008), the Kamehameha Early Education Project (Au, 1980; Tharp & Gallimore, 1988), the Migrant Student Summer Program at UCLA (Gutiérrez, 2005), and the Talent Development Project at Howard University (Boykin, 2000; Boykin & Bailey, 2000). We discuss three of these to illustrate attempts to design classrooms that support deep learning of important disciplinary ideas and practices for nondominant students. Other examples include Learning Communities in Spain (Diez, Gatt, & Racionero, 2011) supported by the European Union and Redesigning Pedagogies in the North (Hattam, Brennan, Zipin, & Comber, 2009) in Australia.

Cultural Modeling (Lee, 1993, 1995, 2001, 2007) is a framework for the design of learning environments that leverages knowledge constructed out of everyday experience to support subject matter learning. Studies in Cultural Modeling have focused on literature and narrative writing with African American youth (Lee et al., 2004). In this work, a detailed analysis of the structure of these domains determined the cultural practices and forms of everyday knowledge that would provide the most leverage. Types of generative problems, strategies, and general heuristics for identifying and tackling such problems and necessary intellective dispositions were identified. This called for a different orientation to the idea of genre in literature and its functionality for helping novice readers make sense of texts. Interpretive problems such as symbolism, irony, satire, and use of unreliable narration were identified as crucial for literary readings across national and other traditions. All of these interpretive tasks require an ability to deal with problems of figuration and often require analogical reasoning. For example, Lee found that AAE speakers' knowledge of *signifying* (Smitherman, 1977) – a form of ritual insult requiring analogical reasoning, appreciation of language play, and comprehension of figurative language – could be leveraged effectively to teach literary reasoning.

The following vignette illustrates such design principles at work:

> Beginning a literature unit on symbolism, a class of African American high school students critique the Hip Hop lyrics "The Mask" by The Fugees. Jonetha offers this explication of the second stanza: "I'm saying I think he had a mask on when he was fighting, when he beat him up, because in order for him to have the mask on – he was spying on that person. He was spying on somebody. I don't know who he was spying on. But in order for him to realize that the man was spying on him, he had to take off his mask. In order to realize that the man was saying ... I don't know – shoot. (laughter from class). I'm saying that the man, in order for him to realize that the other man was spying on him, that he had to take off his mask." (Lee, 2007)

In this example, design principles involved using rap lyrics (see also Mahiri, 2000/01; Morrell, 2002) – or what Lee called "cultural data sets" – where students make public how they understand that the mask is not literal, but symbolic. Jonetha's explication demonstrated analogical reasoning, appreciation of language play, close textual analysis without direct instruction from the teacher, as well as intellectual risk taking. The students went on to apply these interpretive strategies to the analysis of the canonical text *Beloved* by Toni Morrison.

By drawing on models of competence students already have (for example, knowing the features that distinguish good rap from bad), the talk that surrounds these "cultural data sets" privileges reflection about the structure of particular problems in the domain, strategies for tackling such problems, criteria for evaluating the goodness of fit of explanations – in short, for making the practices of the domain public and the trajectories for competence within it visible. The examination of cultural data sets provides models of generative domain problems rooted in everyday experience that facilitate analogical reasoning, a powerful problem-solving strategy used by novices and historically by scientists at the edge of new discoveries. The design challenge is to locate analogies sufficiently rooted in students' everyday experiences such that they bring both relevant knowledge and interest to the task and connect to crucial features of the target learning. Second, teacher-student relationships are fundamentally restructured when instruction begins with texts about which students typically have greater knowledge – of one sort – than teachers. This reorganization of relationships between experts and novices – in this case both students and teachers are functioning simultaneously as expert and novice – facilitates a sense of identification with the practice, and as a consequence a greater sense of belonging to a community of learners.

Chèche Konnen Center teachers and researchers have developed a practice they call *Science Workshop* (Warren & Rosebery, 2004) designed to engage students in exploring possible meanings and functions of their own and others' diverse "ways with words" in science. It explicitly features language as an object of inquiry by focusing students' attention on a repertoire of discursive practices broader than that typically featured in school science and more representative of the practices that children from nondominant groups bring to the classroom. In Science Workshop, the potential meanings and functions of varied ways with words, whether those of a student, a scientist, or a text, are explored.

For example, while discussing possible titles for a student-made mural depicting the life cycle of a pumpkin plant, a second grade African American boy felt a need to enlarge the scope of the discussion. Drawing on metaphoric practices known to be prevalent within African American discourse communities, he likened the life cycle of pumpkin seeds to a spider, "because when the mom dies it lays eggs before it dies." Later as the class probed his analogy, they made visible various relationships implied in it (e.g., the pumpkin forms seeds before it rots just as a spider lays eggs before it dies).

The expansive inquiry fostered in Science Workshop into possible meaning of diverse ways of conceptualizing, representing, and evaluating scientific phenomena has several effects. First, it takes children deeper into the scientific territory (e.g., how are eggs and seeds alike and different). Second, it engages them with varied ways with words, which they explore as tools for their own thinking. Third, by positioning learners as analysts of language, it engages them in thinking through both the affordances and limits of explanations and analogies, which helps make explicit how such practices function as meaning-making tools in science. Finally, talk in Science Workshop is hybrid – combining serious analytic work and playful engagement with language and other symbol systems (e.g., models, tables, graphs). Respect for and explicit attention to the heterogeneity of students' thinking and discourse and that of scientific disciplines, construction of a community of learners, and scaffolding by teachers are fundamental aspects of helping students build a sense of the structure and ways of knowing in academic science.

The Algebra Project (AP) is another intervention that takes up the design challenges we have identified. Operating in 28 cities and serving 10,000 children annually, AP includes curriculum, professional development, and an out-of-school organization, the Young People's Project, in which youth actively assume the banner of mathematics as a 21st-century civil right. Dr. Robert Moses, founder of AP, identified the conceptual shift from arithmetic to algebraic thinking as a major stumbling block to higher mathematics. He asked what in the everyday practices of urban adolescents, particularly African American youth, embodied mathematical problems such as displacement and equivalence. He came up with travel on an urban transit system as an anchor for examining such problems. AP has since developed units on ratio and proportion – one of which uses African drumming traditions.

In linking mathematics learning and social justice (Gutiérrez, 2002; Gutstein, 2003; Tate, 1995), AP explicitly engages important developmental relationships between youth and adults within and outside the school community. It also takes seriously the challenges of translating from everyday language to the symbolic inscriptions of mathematical discourse. Similar to Cultural Modeling and Chèche Konnen, AP supports an understanding of mathematics that is rooted in the students' everyday cultural practices. Thus, students are positioned as competent members of both their home communities and the academic community of "doers of mathematics."

Concluding Remarks

There is great variation in how nation-states address cultural diversity within their borders, both historically and currently. In most countries, the historical emergence of mass, mandatory, and free schools was intended to foster a unitary national culture – typically, a culture associated with the politically dominant group – and to homogenize the population. And yet diversity is a mainstay of the human condition (Bang et al., 2012), and in spite of more than a century of such homogenizing efforts, the world's countries are becoming more diverse than ever. We argue that researchers cannot fully understand learning without viewing learning to be a culturally heterogeneous process of engagement in repertoires of practices (Gutiérrez & Rogoff, 2003; Rogoff, 2003). From this perspective, diversity is not a problem to be solved; it becomes a pedagogical asset (Gutiérrez et al., 2000; Rosebery et al., 2010; Warren et al., 2001). Our perspective is much deeper and more transformational than the simple idea that schools should treat everyone equally and should value everyone's culture. We contend that particular configurations of race, ethnicity, and class require that youth wrestle with pervasive challenges (Spencer, 1999) and that designing learning environments must address multiple (and often neglected) elements of learning, including identity and affect.

This argument has important implications both for the design of learning environments and for the development of learning theory. With regard to design, we are arguing for a radical restructuring of the ways learning is organized in school and of the assumptions that are made about learners and relevant knowledge. Thus, restructuring involves, on one hand, changing our collective understanding of the routine language use and social practices of daily life and their relation to the practices of academic disciplines, and on the other hand, designing classrooms that support the myriad pathways along which learning can proceed. Learning scientists can draw on multiple repertoires of practice in schools to better support learning of core academic disciplines and learners' basic needs for belonging and identification.

The research we have reviewed in this chapter suggests that equity is not only about offering the same resources to all students. True equity will only come if we create learning environments that connect in deep ways to the life experiences of all students.

A note about authorship
All authors have made equal contributions to this chapter.

References

Amanti, C., González, N., & Moll, L. (2008). Case study: Using students' cultural resources in teaching. In A. S. Rosebery & B. Warren (Eds.), *Teaching science to English language learners.* (pp 99–102). Washington, DC: National Science Foundation.

Au, K. (1980). Participation structures in a reading lesson with Hawaiian children: Analysis of a culturally appropriate instructional event. *Anthropology Education Quarterly,* 11(2), 91–115.

Bakhtin, M. M. (1981). *The dialogic imagination: Four essays.* Austin: University of Texas Press.

Ball, A. F. (1992). Cultural preferences and the expository writing of African-American adolescents. *Written Communication,* 9(4), 501–532.

Ball, A. F. (1995). Community based learning in an urban setting as a model for educational reform. *Applied Behavioral Science Review,* 3, 127–146.

Ball, A. (2000). Teachers developing philosophies in literacy and their use in urban schools. In C. D. Lee & P. Smagorinsky (Eds.), *Vygotskian perspectives on literacy research: Constructing meaning through collaborative inquiry.* New York: Cambridge University Press.

Ballenger, C. (2003). The puzzling child: Challenging assumptions about participation and meaning in talking science. *Language Arts,* 81(4), 303–311.

Ballenger, C., & Rosebery, A. (2003). What counts as teacher research? Continuing the conversation. *Teachers College Record,* 105(2), 297–314.

Bang, M., Warren, B., Rosebery, A. S., & Medin, D. (2012). Desettling expectations in science education. *Human Development,* 55(5–6), 302–318.

Baquedano-Lopez, P. (1997). Creating social identities through Doctrina narratives. *Issues in Applied Linguistics,* 8(1), 27–45.

Biagioli, M. (Ed.) (1999). *The science studies reader.* London: Routledge.

Boykin, A. W. (2000). The talent development model of schooling: Placing students at promise for academic success. *Journal of Education for Students Placed At Risk*, 5, 3–25.

Boykin, A. W., & Bailey, C. (2000). *Experimental research on the role of cultural factors in school relevant cognitive functioning: Synthesis of findings on cultural contexts, cultural operations and individual differences.* (Center for Research on the Education of Students Placed At Risk (CRESPAR) Technical Report #42 ed.). Washington, DC and Baltimore, MD: Howard University and John Hopkins University.

Burton, L., Allison, K., & Obeidallah, D. (1995). Social context and adolescents: Perspectives on development among inner-city African-American teens. In L. Crockett & A. Crouter (Eds.), *Pathways through adolescence: Individual development in social contexts* (pp. 119–138). Mahwah, NJ: Lawrence Erlbaum Associates.

Civil, M. (2007). Building on community knowledge: An avenue to equity in mathematics education. In N. Nasir & P. Cobb (Eds.), *Improving access to mathematics: Diversity and equity in the classroom* (pp. 105–117). New York: Teachers College Press.

Cole, M. (1996). *Cultural psychology: A once and future discipline.* Cambridge, MA: Belknap Press of Harvard University Press.

Cole, M., & The Distributed Literacy Consortium (2006). *The Fifth Dimension: An after-school program built on diversity.* New York: Russell Sage Foundation.

Cole, M., Gay, J., Glick, J., & Sharp, D. (1971). *The cultural context of learning and thinking.* New York: Basic Books.

Collins, A., & Ferguson, W. (1993). Epistemic forms and epistemic games: Structures and strategies to guide inquiry. *Educational Psychologist*, 28(1), 25–42.

Díez, D., Gatt, S., & Racionero, S. (2011). Placing immigrant and minority family and community members at the school's centre: The role of community participation. *European Journal of Education*, 46(2), 184–196.

Erickson, F. (2002). Culture and human development. *Human Development*, 45(4), 299–306.

Fisher, M. T. (2003). Open mics and open minds: Spoken word poetry in African diaspora participatory literacy communities. *Harvard Education Review*, 73(3), 362–389.

Foster, M. (1997). *Black teachers on teaching.* New York: The New Press.

Galison, P. (1997). *Image and logic: A material culture of microphysics.* Chicago: University of Chicago Press.

Garcia, G. E. (2000). Bilingual children's reading. In M. Kamil, P. Mosenthal, P. D. Pearson, & R. Barr (Eds.), *Handbook of reading research* (vol. 3, pp. 813–834). Mahwah, NJ: Lawrence Erlbaum Associates.

Gee, J. P. (1989). The narrativization of experience in the oral style. *Journal of Education*, 171(1), 75–96.

Gee, J. P. (1990). *Social linguistics and literacies: Ideology in discourses.* London: Falmer.

Gee, J. P. (1996). Vygotsky and current debates in education: Some dilemmas as afterthoughts to discourse, learning, and schooling. In D. Hicks (Ed.), *Discourse, learning, and schooling* (pp. 269–282). Cambridge: Cambridge University Press.

Gee, J. P., & Clinton, K. (2000). An African-American child's "science talk": Co-construction of meaning from the perspective of multiple discourses. In M. Gallego & S. Hollingsworth (Eds.), *What counts as literacy: Challenging the school standard* (pp. 118–135). New York: Teachers College Press.

Gentner, D. (1989). The mechanisms of analogical learning. In S. Vosniadou & A. Ortony (Eds.), *Similarity and analogical reasoning.* New York: Cambridge University Press.

Goldman, S. (2001). "Factoring families into math success." Unpublished manuscript.

González, N. (2004) Disciplining the discipline: Anthropology and the pursuit of quality education. *Educational Researcher,* 33(5), 17–25.

Goswami, U. (1992). *Analogical reasoning in children.* Hillsdale, NJ: Lawrence Erlbaum Associates.

Gutiérrez, K. (2005). *Intersubjectivity and grammar in the third space.* Talk presented at the annual meeting of the American Educational Research Association, April.

Gutiérrez, K. D., Baquedano-López, P., & Tejada, C. (2000). Rethinking diversity: Hybridity and hybrid language practices in the third space. *Mind, Culture, and Activity,* 6, 286–303.

Gutiérrez, K., & Rogoff, B. (2003). Cultural ways of learning: Individual traits or repertoires of practice. *Educational Researcher,* 32(5), 19–25.

Gutiérrez, R. (2002). Enabling the practice of mathematics teachers in context: Towards a new equity research agenda. *Mathematical Thinking and Learning,* 4(2 & 3), 145–187.

Gutstein, E. (2003). Teaching and learning mathematic for social justice in an urban, Latino school. *Journal for Research in Mathematics Education,* 34(1), 37–73.

Hattam, R., Brennan, M., Zipin, L., & Comber, B. (2009). Researching for social justice: contextual, conceptual and methodological challenges. *Discourse,* 30(3), 303–316.

Hatano, G., & Inagaki, K. (1986). Two courses of expertise. In H. W. Stevenson, H. Azuma, & K. Hakuta (Eds.), *Child development and education in Japan* (pp. 262–272). New York: Freeman.

Heath, S. B. (1983). *Ways with words: Language, life, and work in communities and classrooms..* Cambridge: Cambridge University Press.

Heath, S. B. (2004). Risks, rules, and roles: Youth perspectives on the work of learning for community development. In A. N. Perret-Clemont, C. Pontecorvo, L. B. Resnick, T. Zittoun, & B. Burge (Eds.), *Joining society: Social interaction and learning in adolescence and youth* (pp. 41–70). New York: Cambridge University Press.

Heath, S. B., & McLaughlin, M. (1993). *Identity and inner-city youth.* New York: Teachers' College.

Hirsch, B. (2005). *A place to call home: After-school programs for urban youth.* New York: Teachers College Press.

Hudicourt-Barnes, J. (2003). The use of argumentation in Haitian Creole science classrooms. *Harvard Educational Review,* 73(1), 73–93.

Jimenez, R. T., Garcia, G. E., & Pearson, P. D. (1996). The reading strategies of Latina/o students who are successful English readers: Opportunities and obstacles. *Reading Research Quarterly,* 31(1), 90–112.

Keller, E. F. (1983). *A feeling for the organism: The life and work of Barbara McClintock.* New York: W. H. Freeman.

Ladson-Billings, G. (2001). *Crossing over to Canaan: The journey of new teachers in diverse classrooms.* San Francisco, CA: Jossey-Bass.

Langer, J., Bartolome, L., Vasquez, O., & Lucas, T. (1990). Meaning construction in school literacy tasks: A study of bilingual students. *American Educational Research Journal,* 27(3), 427–471.

Latour, B., & Woolgar, S. (1986). *Laboratory life: The social construction of scientific facts* (2nd edition). Princeton, NJ: Princeton University Press.

Lave, J. (1988). *Cognition in practice.* New York: Cambridge.

Lee, C. D. (1993). *Signifying as a scaffold for literary interpretation: The pedagogical implications of an African American discourse genre.* Urbana, IL: National Council of Teachers of English.

Lee, C. D. (1995). A culturally based cognitive apprenticeship: Teaching African American high school students' skills in literary interpretation. *Reading Research Quarterly,* 30(4), 608–631.

Lee, C. D. (2000). Signifying in the zone of proximal development. In C. D. Lee & P. Smagorinsky (Eds.), *Vygotskian perspectives on literacy research: Constructing meaning through collaborative inquiry* (pp. 191–225). New York: Cambridge University Press.

Lee, C. D. (2001). Is October Brown Chinese: A cultural modeling activity system for underachieving students. *American Educational Research Journal,* 38(1), 97–142.

Lee, C. D. (2005). The state of knowledge about the education of African Americans. In J. King (Ed.), *Black education: A transformative research and action agenda for the new century.* Mahwah, NJ: Lawrence Erlbaum Associates (joint publication with the American Educational Research Association).

Lee, C. D. (2006). "Every good-bye ain't gone": Analyzing the cultural underpinnings of classroom talk. *International Journal of Qualitative Studies in Education,* 19(3), 305–327.

Lee, C. D. (2007). *Culture, literacy and learning: Taking blooming in the midst of the whirlwind.* New York: Teachers College Press.

Lee, C. D. (2008). The centrality of culture to the scientific study of learning and development: How an ecological framework in educational research facilitates civic responsibility. *Educational Researcher,* 37(5), 267–279.

Lee, C. D., Rosenfeld, E., Mendenhall, R., Rivers, A., & Tynes, B. (2004). Cultural modeling as a frame for narrative analysis. In C. L. Dauite & C. Lightfoot (Eds.), *Narrative analysis: Studying the development of individuals in society* (pp. 39–62). Thousand Oaks, CA: Sage Publications.

Lee, C. D., Spencer, M. B., & Harpalani, V. (2003). Every shut eye ain't sleep: Studying how people live culturally. *Educational Researcher,* 32(5), 6–13.

Lynch, M. (1985). *Art and artifact in laboratory science: A study of shop work and shop talk in a research laboratory.* Boston, MA: Routledge and Kegan Paul.

Mahiri, J. (1998). *Shooting for excellence: African American and youth culture in new century schools.* New York: Teachers College Press and National Council of Teachers of English.

Mahiri, J. (2000/2001). Pop culture pedagogy and the end(s) of school. *Journal of Adolescent & Adult Literacy,* 44(4), 382–386.

Majors, Y. (2003). Shoptalk: Teaching and learning in an African American hair salon. *Mind, Culture and Activity*, 10(4), 289–310.

Masingila, J. (1994). Mathematics practice in carpet laying. *Anthropology & Education Quarterly*, 25(4), 430–462.

Maslow, A. (1962). *Toward a psychology of being*. Princeton, NJ: Von Nostrand.

Michaels, S. (1981). "Sharing time," Children's narrative styles and differential access to literacy. *Language in Society*, 10, 423–442.

Moll, L. (2000). Inspired by Vygotsky: Ethnographic experiments in education. In C. D. Lee & P. Smagorinsky (Eds.), *Vygotskian perspectives on literacy research: Constructing meaning through collaborative inquiry* (pp. 256–268). Cambridge: Cambridge University Press.

Moll, L., & González, N. (2004). Engaging life: A funds of knowledge approach to multicultural education. In J. Banks & C. McGee Banks (Eds.), *Handbook of research on multicultural education* (2nd edition) (pp. 699–715). New York: Jossey-Bass.

Morrell, E. (2002). Toward a critical pedagogy of popular culture: Literacy development among urban youth. *Journal of Adolescent & Adult Literacy*, 46(1), 72–78.

Moschkovich, J. N. (1999). Supporting the participation of English language learners in mathematical discussions. *For the Learning of Mathematics*, 19(1), 11–19.

Moses, R.P., & Cobb, C. E. (2001). *Radical equations: Math literacy and civil rights*. Boston, MA: Beacon Press.

Moss, B. (1994). Creating a community: Literacy events in African-American churches. In B. Moss (Ed.), *Literacy across communities* (pp. 147–178). Cresskill, NJ: Hampton Press, Inc.

Nasir, N. (2000). "Points Ain't Everything": Emergent goals and average and percent understandings in the play of basketball among African-American students. *Anthropology and Education Quarterly*, 31(3), 283–305.

Nasir, N. (2002). Identity, goals, and learning: Mathematics in cultural practice. In N. Nasir & P. Cobb (Eds.), *Mathematical Thinking and Learning*, Special issue on Diversity, Equity, and Mathematics Learning, 4(2 & 3), 211–247.

Nasir, N. (2005). Individual cognitive structuring and the sociocultural context: Strategy shifts in the game of dominoes. *Journal of the Learning Sciences*, 14(1), 5–34.

Nasir, N., & Bang, M. (Eds.) (2012). *Conceptualizing culture and racialized processes in learning*. Special issue of *Human Development*, 55(5–6), January 2013.

Nasir, N., & Cooks, J. (2009). Becoming a hurdler: How learning settings afford identities. *Anthropology & Education Quarterly*, 40(1), 41–61.

Nasir, N., & Stone, L. (2003). "'Mo' money, no problem': Learning to talk and play dominoes." Unpublished manuscript, Stanford University.

Ochs, E., Gonzales, P., & Jacoby, S. (1996). "When I come down I'm in the domain state": Grammar and graphic representation in the interpretive activity of physicists. In E. Ochs, E. A. Schegloff, & S. A. Thompson (Eds.), *Interaction and grammar* (pp. 328–369). Cambridge, England: Cambridge University Press.

Organization for Economic Cooperation and Development (2010). *PISA 2009 Results: Overcoming Social Background. Equity in Learning Opportunities and Outcomes*. Paris: OECD Publishing.

Orellana, M., Reynolds, J., Dorner, L., & Meza, M. (2003). In other words: Translating or "para-phrasing" as a family literacy practice in immigrant households. *Reading Research Quarterly*, 38(1), 12–34.

Perkins, D. (1992). *Smart schools: Better thinking and learning for every child.* New York: The Free Press.

Polya, G. (1945). *How to solve it: A new aspect of mathematical method.* Princeton, NJ: Princeton University Press.

Resnick, M., & Rusk, N. (1996, July–August). Access is not enough: Computer clubhouses in the inner city. *American Prospect*, 27, 60–68.

Rogoff, B. (2003). *The cultural nature of human development.* New York: Oxford University Press.

Rogoff, B., & Angelillo, C. (2002). Investigating the coordinated functioning of multifaceted cultural practices in human development. *Human Development*, 45(4), 211–225.

Root-Bernstein, R. S. (1989). *Discovering: Inventing and solving problems at the frontier of scientific knowledge.* Cambridge, MA: Harvard University Press.

Rose, M. (2004). *The mind at work.* New York: Viking.

Rosebery, A. (2005). "What are we going to do next?" A case study of lesson planning. In R. Nemirovsky, A. Rosebery, B. Warren, & J. Solomon (Eds.), *Everyday matters in mathematics and science: Studies of complex classroom events* (pp. 299–328). Mahwah, NJ: Lawrence Erlbaum Associates.

Rosebery, A., & Warren, B. (Eds.) (2008). *Teaching science to English language learners.* Washington, DC: The National Science Foundation.

Rosebery, A., Ogonowski, M., DiSchino, M., & Warren, B. (2010). "The coat traps all your body heat": Heterogeneity as fundamental to learning. *Journal of the Learning Sciences*, 19(3), 322–357.

Saxe, G. B. (1991). *Culture & cognitive development: Studies in mathematical understanding.* Mahwah, NJ: Lawrence Erlbaum Associates.

Scribner, S. (1985). Knowledge at work. *Anthropology and Education Quarterly*, 16(3), 199–206.

Smitherman, G. (1977). *Talkin and testifyin: The language of Black America.* Boston, MA: Houghton Mifflin.

Smitherman, G. (2000). African American student writers in the NAEP, 1969–1988/89 and "The Blacker the berry, the sweeter the juice". In G. Smitherman (Ed.), *Talkin that talk: Language, culture and education in African America* (pp. 163–194). New York: Routledge.

Sohmer, R., & Michaels, S. (2005). The "two puppies" story: The role of narrative in teaching and learning science. In U. Quasthoff & T. Becker, (Eds.), *Narrative interaction* (pp. 57–91). Philadelphia, PA: John Benjamins Publishing Company.

Spencer, M. B. (1999). Social and cultural influences on school adjustment: The application of an identity-focused cultural ecological perspective. *Educational Psychologist*, 34(1), 43–57.

Steele, C. M. (1997). A threat in the air: How stereotypes shape intellectual identity and performance. *American Psychologist*, 52, 613–629.

Tate, W. F. (1995). Returning to the root: A culturally relevant approach to mathematics pedagogy. *Theory into Practice*, 34, 166–173.

Taylor, E. (2009). The purchasing practice of low-income students: The relationship to mathematical development. *Journal of the Learning Sciences*, 18(3), 370–415.

Tharp, R., & Gallimore, R. (1988). *Rousing minds to life: Teaching, learning, and schooling in social context.* New York: Cambridge University Press.

Valdes, G. (2002). *Expanding the definitions of giftedness: The case of young interpreters from immigrant countries.* Mahwah, NJ: Lawrence Erlbaum Associates.

Warren, B., Ballenger, C., Ogonowski, M., Rosebery, A., & Hudicourt-Barnes, J. (2001). Rethinking diversity in learning science: The logic of everyday sensemaking. *Journal of Research in Science Teaching*, 38, 529–552.

Warren, B., Ogonowski, M., & Pothier, S. (2005). "Everyday" and "scientific": Re-thinking dichotomies in modes of thinking in science learning. In R. Nemirovsky, A. Rosebery, J. Solomon, & B. Warren (Eds.), *Everyday matters in mathematics and science: Studies of complex classroom events* (pp. 119–148). Mahwah, NJ: Lawrence Erlbaum Associates.

Warren, B., & Rosebery, A. (2004, February). *"What do you think Hassan means?" Exploring possible meanings of explicitness in the science classroom.* Invited talk at the Center for the Scholarship of Teaching, Michigan State University.

Warren, B., & Rosebery, A. (1996). "This question is just too, too easy!": Perspectives from the classroom on accountability in science. In L. Schauble & R. Glaser (Eds.), *Innovations in learning: New environments for education* (pp. 97–125). Hillsdale, NJ: Lawrence Erlbaum Associates.

Warren, B., & Rosebery, A. (2011). Navigating interculturality: African American male students and the science classroom. *Journal of African American Males in Education*, 2(1), 98–115.

Wolpert, L., & Richards, A. (1997). *Passionate minds: The inner world of scientists.* Oxford: Oxford University Press.

35 A Learning Sciences Perspective on Teacher Learning Research

Barry J. Fishman, Elizabeth A. Davis, and Carol K. K. Chan

Learning scientists conduct basic research into how people learn, and draw on this basic research to design new routines, tools, and curricula to improve learning. When these designs take the form of classroom-level interventions in schools, the teacher is a key participant, determining how any intervention is realized and sustained in practice. For this reason, when our goal is to improve student learning in classrooms, it is important to understand how teachers learn and how to support teachers' development. In this chapter, we examine learning sciences' contributions to research on teacher learning, with particular consideration of how the cognitive, sociocognitive, sociocultural, and systems-oriented perspectives that are prevalent in the field extend research on teacher learning in new and significant directions. The need for a focus on how teachers learn has become even more crucial since the first edition of this handbook (Fishman & Davis, 2006), because in the intervening years accountability-based reforms have led to an increasing focus on teacher quality and performance (e.g., Chetty, Friedman, & Rockoff, 2012) in many of the world's education systems. International policy documents emphasize teacher learning as key to educational improvement (e.g., Directorate-General for Education and Culture, 2005; Singapore Ministry of Education, 2010; U.S. Department of Education, 2010).

Teacher learning research in the learning sciences focuses on the development of teachers' knowledge, beliefs, identity, and practice in context. Since the learning sciences emerged from the cognitive sciences in the 1980s, learning scientists have analyzed disciplinary knowledge and practice in content domains such as math, science, and history, and the focus on teacher expertise is consistent with this broader endeavor. Shulman (1986) conceptualized three primary domains of teacher knowledge. The first two, *content knowledge* and *pedagogical knowledge*, were foci of much traditional teacher learning research. Shulman argued that teachers also need a third domain of knowledge, *pedagogical content knowledge* (PCK), and researchers have found this concept extremely useful in understanding what forms of teacher knowledge lead to effective learning (e.g., Magnusson, Krajcik, & Borko, 1999; Van Driel & Berry, 2010; Van Driel, Verloop, & de Vos, 1998). More recently, Ball, Thames, and Phelps (2008) expanded on Shulman's work and identified six domains of teacher knowledge, including horizon content knowledge (i.e., understanding of how topics are connected over the span of the curriculum across years), common content knowledge, and specialized content knowledge, as well as knowledge of content and students, knowledge of content and teaching, and knowledge of content and curriculum. This expanded taxonomy of teacher knowledge suggests an array of areas for investigation and support.

In addition to a focus on teacher knowledge, learning scientists study how teachers' knowledge, identities, and beliefs shape and are shaped by their work contexts (e.g., Enyedy, Goldberg, & Welsh, 2006). Learning scientists have always considered learning to be unavoidably linked to context (e.g., Brown, Collins, & Duguid, 1989), and thus examine teacher learning as situated within practice (Ball & Forzani, 2009; Putnam & Borko, 2000). The relation of knowledge to context is of critical importance, because growth in teacher knowledge that is not translated into practice cannot influence student learning (Desimone, 2009; Fishman, Marx, Best, & Tal, 2003).

Teacher learning occurs in roughly three major career phases: preservice education (university coursework before becoming a teacher), induction into teaching (the first few years in the profession), and ongoing mastery, or continuing development throughout one's career (Feiman-Nemser, 2001). Learning scientists study teacher learning in all three of these phases. The term *teacher education* is most often used to refer to preservice education in schools of education or alternative certification programs, and teacher education programs vary greatly; for example, programs might focus on teaching diverse learners, incorporating constructivist approaches to teaching, or promoting reflection. Research on preservice teacher education and induction is beginning to focus heavily on teacher practice, exploring how novices learn to do the work of teaching (Ball & Forzani, 2009).

The term *professional development* (PD) refers to teacher learning after teachers are working full-time – often referred to as "in-service" education, to contrast it with "preservice" teacher education. PD may encompass mentoring, supportive curriculum materials, workshops, conferences, and online communities. Research indicates that the most effective PD has the following features:

- It is of extended duration (rather than a single seminar or "one-shot" workshop).
- It emphasizes content knowledge (in addition to domain-general pedagogical strategies) with a focus on student understanding.
- It is coherent with respect to standards, expectations, or other initiatives teachers are experiencing (Borko, Jacobs, & Koellner, 2010; Garet, Porter, Desimone, Birman, & Yoon, 2001; Fishman, Penuel, Hegedus, & Roschelle, 2011).
- It requires that teachers examine and reflect on their own practice (Putnam & Borko, 2000; Richardson & Anders, 1994).
- It provides opportunities for teacher collaboration and social supports (Borko et al., 2010; Putnam & Borko, 2000).

- It is closely coupled to the anticipated or desired classroom practice (Cohen & Hill, 1998; Fishman et al., 2003), so that teachers do not have to do a great deal of interpretation to translate the messages from the PD to their own classrooms.

Much research on teacher learning in the learning sciences is set in the context of classroom practice supported by teacher collaboration, cognitive tools, and use of curriculum materials. The goal is to take advantage of the in-class, on-the-job setting to make teacher learning more effective.

Understanding teacher learning requires an emphasis on situated learning and practice, and toward this end the learning sciences offers an advantage over traditional cognitive or psychological studies of teacher expertise: Learning sciences research is often conducted in interdisciplinary teams that incorporate content-area experts and disciplinary perspectives (see, e.g., Hill, Rowan, & Ball, 2005). As a result, learning sciences research is well positioned to help us understand the nature of and changes in teachers' knowledge and practice, in content-specific and context-specific ways.

The Center for Learning Technologies in Urban Schools (LeTUS) project provides an example of the potential benefits of a learning sciences approach to the study of teacher learning. LeTUS worked to help students and teachers master science inquiry skills by developing new curriculum materials and supportive technologies. The work was conducted by a collaborative team of scholars and practitioners in science education, psychology, computer science, learning technologies, and literacy. LeTUS did not begin with a focus on teacher learning, but initial research quickly revealed that teacher learning was essential if the student learning goals were to be met, and the teacher learning research agenda quickly become central to the overall goals of the collaboration. Consequently, LeTUS focused on design-based work linking teacher learning to student learning (Fishman et al., 2003), on how the curriculum materials promoted teacher learning (Schneider & Krajcik, 2002), and on the development of online PD environments designed to create a community of practice (Wenger, 1998) around the curriculum materials (Fishman, 2003).

A widely accepted, simplified model of how teacher learning improves student learning is: teacher education or PD leads to changes in teachers' beliefs and knowledge; changes in teacher beliefs lead to changes in what teachers do in the classroom; and these changed behaviors contribute to improved student learning (Desimone, 2009). However, it is challenging to simultaneously study all of the steps in this linear chain and thus to document exactly how teacher education helps improve student learning (Fishman et al., 2003). Furthermore, feedback loops and bidirectional relationships complicate research. Design-based research (DBR; Barab, Chapter 8, this volume) is particularly well suited to the study of teacher learning across the elements of the logic model. DBR is rooted in "real-world" contexts of practice, with the dual goals of improving both classroom designs and learning theories that inform design (Collins, Joseph, & Bielaczyc, 2004). In DBR, teachers typically work collaboratively with researchers as codesigners (Oshima et al., 2003; Penuel & Gallagher, 2009), and as a result the team is able to develop materials and supports that are rooted in classroom practice. Because researchers work closely with teachers, the observed teacher practice and change present an ideal opportunity for researchers to study teacher learning in context (Bielaczyc, 2013).

Examples of Learning Sciences Research on Teacher Learning

Learning sciences research on teacher learning falls into two broad categories:

- scholarship that foregrounds social supports for teacher learning and the distributed nature of knowledge, and
- scholarship that foregrounds the situated nature of teacher learning within practice.

Foregrounding Social Supports and Distributed Expertise

Decades of learning sciences research have demonstrated that learning is social and distributed (e.g., see the chapters in Part 4 of this handbook), and this is also the case for teacher learning. The research we review demonstrates that effective social supports for teacher learning aid teachers in constructing, distributing, and sharing expertise.

Building Communities of Practice

Teacher learning is enhanced when teachers can learn productively from each other (Grossman, Wineburg, & Woolworth, 2001; Kubitskey, 2006; Putnam & Borko, 2000). Learning sciences research on teacher communities encompasses both off-line and online work across different scales in schools, universities, districts, and cross-national networks. In a review of teacher learning research, Borko, Jacobs, and Koellner (2010) concluded that the most effective PD provides opportunities for teachers to work collaboratively in professional learning communities. Unfortunately, teachers are typically isolated from one another in everyday work. Many learning sciences-based innovations seek to provide teachers with online communication technologies such as blogs, chat rooms, and discussion forums to allow teachers to construct and project professional identity and to provide opportunities for modeling and support to other teachers (Luehmann, 2008). The goal is to create a teacher *community of practice* (CoP), a supportive group of professionals who share common goals and interests (Wenger, 1998). Effective designs for teacher CoPs support teachers in the sharing of diverse expertise, support them as they collaboratively construct professional knowledge bases, and support newcomers as they are "apprenticed" into increasingly expert practice (Collins & Kapur, Chapter 6, this volume).

The Guided Inquiry supporting Multiple Literacies project (GIsML; Palincsar, Magnusson, Marano, & Brown, 1998) was guided by three design principles for a teacher CoP: (a) the community should have a focus on developing specific teaching orientations (for example, inquiry-based learning needs to be connected to content as opposed to vague notions of student activities); (b) the community should include teachers from heterogeneous teaching contexts to enrich shared intellectual resources; and (c) the community should provide extended opportunities to teachers for planning, enactment, and reflection on practice. This project demonstrated how design supports increased teacher reflection and collaboration. Of course, CoPs can naturally emerge in any human social organization, but a major goal of GIsML was to guide the emergence and interaction of the CoP to maximally enhance teacher learning.

Grossman, Wineburg, and Woolworth (2001) used a "book club" model for supporting teacher learning around disciplinary ideas and practices in English and history, in which teachers from the two departments in the same high school came together once a month to read literary and historical works with the goal of creating an interdisciplinary curriculum and to support the teachers in developing improved perspectives on the nature of each discipline as well as greater appreciation for the work of the other discipline. The researchers saw their role primarily as project organizers and co-participants, not facilitators or group leaders (to the initial frustration of the participating teachers). Grossman and colleagues' study of this evolving group (from pseudo-community to a community of practice) highlighted the ways researchers and teachers can work together to develop professional community learning opportunities and structures.

Networks and other communications technologies have the potential to expand teacher access to PD opportunities, and also to enhance collaboration by providing appropriate scaffolding. Three early efforts included LabNet (Ruopp, Gal, Drayton, & Pfister, 1993), the Math Forum (Renninger & Shumar, 2004), and Tapped In (Schlager, Fusco, & Schank 2002):

- LabNet used e-mail and bulletin boards to create a community of practice among secondary science teachers adopting project-based methods. The researchers attributed its success as a well-functioning online community to the development of peer leaders within its membership, a core component of a community of practice and a theme that has carried through to more recent learning sciences research (e.g., Chan, 2011; Fogleman, Fishman, & Krajcik, 2006).

- The Math Forum has evolved into an ongoing active community in which teachers discuss ideas and ask questions. One of its key innovations is a service known as "Ask Dr. Math," through which volunteers provide peer guidance.
- Tapped In used a "virtual place" metaphor, such that each school and each teacher could create their own "room" and they could visit each other's "rooms." Tapped In could be employed by others to extend their own PD programs. For example, the Math Forum has used Tapped In as a place where visitors can meet with "Dr. Math."

In each of these cases, the technology has been used not merely as a mechanism for accessing information or resources, but also as a tool for supporting the construction of knowledge for the generation and maintenance of communities of practice among teachers. These projects, and the ones we describe later, are good examples of the evolution of a learning sciences perspective on the study of online teacher learning, a growing area in the PD literature (Dede, Ketelhut, Whitehouse, & McCloskey, 2009).

Creating Knowledge-Building Communities

Knowledge-building communities are similar to communities of practice in that both work to enhance teacher understanding with social and technological supports, but in contrast to CoPs, they emphasize teachers as knowledge creators and designers. Teachers who participate in knowledge-building communities are not merely sharing existing community practices, but are continually improving those practices and developing new ones; knowledge-building communities focus on collective progress and the development of teachers' capacity for innovation (Scardamalia & Bereiter, Chapter 20, this volume). Teachers work collectively guided by *principles* that highlight the main ideas of the innovation rather than following *fixed activities* (also see improvisation, Sawyer, 2011) to create new knowledge and practice for the community.

Knowledge-building communities often include researchers and teachers with different experiences working in different contexts, including classrooms, university courses, and research settings supported by technology (e.g., Chan & Van Aalst, 2006). Laferrière, Ericksen, and Breuleux (2007) examined university-school partnership for preservice and in-service education students in several universities in Canada. Participating in a networked community with in-service teachers and university-based teacher educators, preservice teachers learned how to integrate digital resources into their classroom practices. Both preservice teachers and in-service teachers used knowledge-building principles to inquire into their classroom practice, supported by the Knowledge Forum suite of tools, and together they created virtual tours to illustrate the collective knowledge advances of the community.

The Knowledge-Building Teacher Network in Hong Kong (KBTN; Chan, 2011) is designed to support teacher PD for educational innovation through participation in knowledge building. The three design themes of the KBTN are: principle-based understanding, coaching and mentoring, and technology-enhanced assessment. KBTN encourages teachers to work with principles and to take ownership of pedagogical innovations by participating in the creation and development of these innovations. KBTN supported teachers as they worked together to create and to transform practices from Western classrooms into practices more appropriate to Asian culture.

Knowledge-building communities often consist of participants from different sectors and different countries, and this provides new dimensions to teacher PD. For example, the Knowledge Society Network (KSN; Hong, Scardamalia, & Zhang, 2010) spans 20 countries and brings together teachers, teacher educators, researchers, engineers, scientists, and policy makers in developing pedagogical innovations. As a cross-sector and cross-culture network of networks, the KSN provides a context to help teachers create knowledge as they work with other professionals across different parts of the world.

The situated and sociocultural perspectives emerging from learning sciences research help to explain how teacher communities can be designed to support teacher learning. In these communities, teachers are provided with ongoing opportunities to construct knowledge, to develop shared practice, and to solve real-world problems in authentic context. These online communities also provide large volumes of data that learning scientists can use to examine the dynamics of teacher collaboration, thus potentially contributing to our understanding of collaboration and learning more generally. For example, computer-supported collaborative learning researchers (CSCL; see Stahl, Koschmann, & Suthers, Chapter 24, this volume) examined online and off-line discourse of how expert and novice teachers collaborate (Cesareni, Martini, & Mancini, 2011). Studying how teachers with diverse expertise collaborate and how they create knowledge in teacher communities enriches our understanding of how people learn from collaboration and communication (see Enyedy & Stevens, Chapter 10, this volume).

Coaching and Mentoring

Collins and Kapur (Chapter 6, this volume) observe that coaching is an important component of cognitive apprenticeship. Coaching – regular, sustained, and personalized interactions around practice – can be productive for both novice and experienced teachers (Lampert & Graziani, 2009). Providing access to coaches (sometimes also called "mentors") is one way of providing social supports and distributing expertise at a smaller, more personalized scale. More experienced and expert teachers can scaffold newer or less expert teachers in developing new knowledge, beliefs, and practices.

The Web-based Inquiry Science Environment (WISE) is a technology-mediated learning environment for students (Linn, Clark, & Slotta, 2003) with face-to-face and online supports for teachers learning to use the environment in their classrooms (Varma, Husic, & Linn, 2008; Slotta, 2004). The WISE model of mentored PD connects teachers to a personal mentor who interacts with them mostly face to face. The mentored PD is complemented by online supports such as discussion spaces for teachers, assessment and feedback tools teachers can use with students, and an authoring environment for adapting existing curriculum units or creating new ones. Research on the WISE-mentored PD model indicates that, in whole-school implementations, the PD approach successfully supports even teachers with very different teaching styles (Slotta, 2004). More recent work from this group also demonstrates the value of teachers providing one another support using an online community together with face-to-face meetings (Madeira & Slotta, 2011).

Practice-based teacher education and PD (Ball & Forzani, 2009) rely heavily on coaching from teacher educators. In practice-based teacher education, teachers' learning is structured around materials and activities that they employ directly in their own classroom practice or, as novices, that they rehearse with colleagues before employing with students. Coaching is an important element of such rehearsal, supporting novices learning to engage in more sophisticated teaching practices. Teacher educators serve as coaches, providing highly targeted feedback to preservice teachers as they engage in *rehearsals* (Grossman et al., 2009). In a rehearsal, a novice takes on a small slice of teaching practice to enact, typically with peers and one or more teacher educators. The peers and teacher educators may interrupt the enactment, providing an opportunity to pause or to "rewind" to try a move again. The teacher educator can also provide highly targeted feedback on the enactment. For example, Lampert, Beasley, Ghousseini, Kazemi, and Franke (2010) have explored how teacher educators across three institutions engaged novices in rehearsals of mathematical tasks, with the goal of promoting the preservice teachers' ability to do this with children. Similarly, Horn (2010) explored how rehearsals with coaching supported experienced teachers' learning, focusing on the ways rehearsals with colleagues supported teachers in "revisioning" their fine-grained instructional work. This vein of scholarship is still very new, but shows a great deal of promise.

These studies, as with the studies of teacher communities described earlier, demonstrate the critical role social supports play for teachers. These communities provide a mechanism for distributing teacher expertise, giving teachers access to a wide range of ideas. Another interesting side effect of these systems or online communities is that they provide data that can be used to measure teacher learning, by (for example) evaluating the artifacts that teachers produce or through carefully documenting teachers' interactions with a mentor when they begin to use new practices or materials with their students.

Foregrounding Situativity by Focusing on Practice

Situativity is a core concept in learning sciences research; the central idea is that learning is more effective when situated in authentic contexts (see Greeno & Engeström, Chapter 7, this volume). The following examples demonstrate how situating learning can promote teacher learning.

Using Video and other Representations of Practice as a Vehicle for Teachers' Learning

Teachers frequently ask to see other teachers' classrooms in action, as they feel this is a powerful way for them to understand how ideas related to teaching translate into practice (Fishman & Duffy, 1992). But in most schools, all teachers are teaching during the same time periods, making it impossible to leave one's own classroom and enter another's. The most widespread solution is to collect videos of teachers in practice. Several researchers have explored, for example, the use of video clubs or study groups as a way to foster in-service teachers' ongoing learning (Frederiksen, Sipusic, Sherin, & Wolfe, 1998; Sherin, 2004). One face-to-face video club involved videotaping the classroom practice of two of the participating middle school mathematics teachers and then discussing the videotapes once a month (Sherin & Van Es, 2009; Van Es, 2009). This experience, spread over an entire school year, helped these teachers develop *professional vision* – "the ability to see and interpret critical features of classroom events" (Sherin, 2004, p. 179). Teachers – even those whose practice was not the focus of discussion – became more likely to consider student ideas and the relationships between student thinking and pedagogical decisions. Increasingly, video has become a key component of teacher education, allowing preservice teachers both to "see" into multiple classrooms, and to select and present *video cases* of their own teaching for critique and feedback. The design of video cases that represent practice and promote productive critique is an active area of research (Zembal-Saul, 2008). Learning how to look at teaching, to be productively critical, and to develop a mindset for sharing one's practice through video are skills that are now being taught in many preservice curricula (e.g., McDonald, 2010; Star & Strickland, 2008).

Learning sciences researchers at the University of Wisconsin and Rutgers University have collaborated on the Elementary and Secondary Teacher Education Program (eSTEP), which has developed tools to enable the creation of online courses and activities for preservice teachers that systematically integrate collaborative instructional planning with text and video study (Derry & Hmelo-Silver, 2002). eSTEP courses taught at both universities include a hypermedia library of learning sciences concepts applied to teaching, linked to a video database of classroom-based video cases. This project encountered several challenges, including that of striking a balance between teacher expectations and the goals of the learning environment (Derry, Seymour, Steinkuehler, Lee, & Siegel, 2004).

Some projects even use computer-generated videos with animated avatars and computer-generated graphics to help teachers examine and reflect on practice. For instance, the Thought Experiments in Mathematics Teaching project (ThEMaT; Chazan & Herbst, 2012; Chieu, Herbst, & Weiss, 2011) used animated characters that are devoid of markers that would typically identify a character as being of a particular gender or race, allowing teachers to focus on what is said and on how the teacher interacts with the students rather than on the personality, ethnicity, or clothing of particular teachers or students. The ThEMaT team has experimented both with predesigned scenarios and with easy-to-use authoring tools that allow teachers to create their own animated scenarios. The use of these materials in preservice teacher education supports novices in understanding the subtleties of student-teacher and student-student interactions in classrooms (Chen, 2011).

These projects promote teachers' learning by situating their learning in representations of real-world practice, in contrast to more generalized teacher education or PD that might focus on broad concepts, such as "constructivist teaching," "inquiry," or "collaborative learning," but leaves it up to teachers to translate the ideas to their own classrooms. This idea is echoed in research that emphasizes the importance of "coherence" and "utility" in PD design; teachers find PD experiences more valuable when they perceive the connection to their local context and needs (Fishman et al., 2011; Penuel, Fishman, Yamaguchi, & Gallagher, 2007).

Using Educative Curriculum Materials to Support Teacher Learning

Because curriculum materials are a primary source of guidance for what teachers teach, Ball and Cohen (1996) suggested that teacher learning opportunities should be embedded directly into their curriculum materials. These *educative curriculum materials* are powerful because they situate teacher learning within daily practice, and studies have shown their value in supporting teacher learning (e.g., McNeill, 2009). Davis and Krajcik (2005) described how educative curriculum materials can promote particular teacher learning processes, such as adding new ideas about teaching, connecting principles of practice to specific instructional moves, and envisioning new, more ambitious practices. For example, in addition to representing effective approaches to teaching, they provide ongoing supports for specific aspects of teachers' learning. This is a radical change, because most curriculum materials are not designed to help teachers learn (Beyer, Delgado, Davis, & Krajcik, 2009). Educative curriculum materials, in contrast, can support teachers' *pedagogical design capacity*, or their ability to use personal and material resources to design powerful learning experiences for students (Brown, 2009; Remillard, 2005).

The Curriculum Access System for Elementary Science (CASES) environment aimed to support preservice and new elementary science teachers, with a goal of addressing typical challenges novice elementary science teachers face (Davis, Petish, & Smithey, 2006). CASES research explored different forms of support in educative curriculum materials, such as narratives that contextualize pedagogical concepts in stories of teachers' practice, and expository supports that explicated principles behind the concepts (e.g., Beyer & Davis, 2009; Davis, Beyer, Forbes, & Stevens, 2011). Other work explores more experienced teachers' use of educative curriculum materials (e.g., Schultz, Arias, Davis, & Palincsar, 2012). Classroom systems are inherently complex (e.g., Linn, Davis, & Bell, 2004), and work on curriculum materials must acknowledge and account for that complexity.

Knowledge Networks On the Web (KNOW; Fishman, 2003) was an online PD environment developed specifically as an extension to the inquiry-oriented middle school curriculum materials developed in LeTUS. KNOW designers opted to provide two primary types of videos: "images of practice" videos that provide windows onto classroom practice, and "how to" videos that give step-by-step visual instruction about how to set up and use scientific apparatuses. KNOW worked best in conjunction with other PD activities, including face-to-face workshops. This integrated PD approach has been demonstrated to enhance classroom practice and student learning (Fishman et al., 2003; Kubitskey, Fishman, & Marx, 2004).

Using Cognitive and Digital Tools to Support Teacher Learning

The notion that cognition is distributed across people and tools is a core element of the sociocognitive theories of learning (Greeno & Engeström, Chapter 7, this volume; Vygotsky, 1978) that underlie much learning sciences research. Shifting our view of teaching from a solo activity to one where the teacher coordinates with, orchestrates, and manages a network of tools and connections shifts our conception of how people teach and how to best support teaching. This is what the 2010 U.S. National Educational Technology Plan (NETP; U.S. Department of Education, 2010) intended when it employed the metaphor of "connected teaching" to depict the future (and present) of teaching practice. In one sense, any tool that offloads or shares part of the task of teaching fits into this category. We focus on two examples here: cognitive tutors and ASSISTments for individualizing student instruction, and tools to support teacher use of curriculum materials.

Cognitive tutors use artificial intelligence methods to create tools that can provide guidance, feedback, and hints to learners with nearly the same effectiveness as human tutors (Koedinger & Corbett, 2006; VanLehn, 2011). By using cognitive tutors to provide individualized support for student learning, teachers are able to spend more time with students who are confused or need extra support, and classroom time is divided between student time with the tutor software and small-group or whole-class instruction (Corbett, Koedinger, & Hadley, 2001). ASSISTments are a variant on cognitive tutor technology that is "a blend of assess*ment* and instructional *assist*ance" (Heffernan, Heffernan, Bennett Decoteau, & Militello, 2012,

p. 89). ASSISTments collect data on student progress, making it possible for teachers to monitor progress at a detailed level. At times the technology will provide support directly to the learner, but at other times teachers may elect to intervene. One key issue in these systems is the design of information displays for teachers; another is the range of challenges for classroom management entailed by individualizing instruction (Connor et al., 2011).

Teachers often reinterpret materials for their local contexts in ways that contradict their designed intent (Barab & Luehmann, 2003; Davis, 2006). This is the essence of what Brown and Campione (1994) referred to as a "lethal mutation." Recent learning sciences work strives to provide embedded support to help teachers make "congruent adaptations" (Blumenfeld et al., 2006), which allow for variation to meet the demands of teachers' local contexts without violating the core principles of an innovation. One example is the Planning Enactment and Reflection Tool (PERT; Lin & Fishman, 2006), a prototype developed in conjunction with the educative curriculum materials of the LeTUS Project (Blumenfeld, Fishman, Krajcik, Marx, & Soloway, 2000). PERT prompted teachers to indicate their intended curriculum modifications. For instance, a teacher might elect to skip a technology-based lesson because of difficulty accessing computers, or to omit a final presentation because of time constraints. PERT then presents teachers with a dashboard that uses meters and other interface elements to indicate how the teachers' planned enactment aligns with the curriculum designers' intent in terms of pedagogical and content learning goals. The teachers may then make further adjustments.

These environments are increasingly referred to as *digital teaching platforms* (DTP; Dede & Richards, 2012). DTPs are technology-supported environments for teaching that combine models of the learner, rich data analytics, and displays that are designed to support teacher planning and reflection. DTPs represent an area that is likely to see increasing research and development in the near future. DTPs provide a context for integrating many other strands of learning sciences research on teaching and learning.

Whether grounded in teachers' own practice or in the practice of others, the examples reviewed in this section illustrate the power of situativity in designing supports for teacher learning. Teachers, like students, benefit from learning in authentic contexts.

Looking Forward

Learning sciences theories and methodologies have been especially useful for uncovering and understanding the importance of context in teachers' learning, ensuring that practice remains central in our investigations. As the field moves forward, we can extend our work with a focus on creating scalable and sustainable innovations for teaching and learning. One such approach, called *design-based implementation research* (DBIR; see Penuel & Spillane, Chapter 32, this volume), blends design-based and sociocognitive approaches with theory and methods from policy research to better understand how interventions function both within classrooms and also within larger systems (also see Fishman, Penuel, Allen, & Cheng, 2013; Penuel, Fishman, Cheng, & Sabelli, 2011).

Shifting populations, communication infrastructures, and technological development will continue to present new opportunities and contexts for teacher learning. The learning sciences is well positioned to influence the way both policy makers and practitioners think about these new opportunities, as it already has in the 2010 U.S. National Educational Technology Plan (U.S. Department of Education, 2010) and also in many international policy documents. We anticipate increasing growth in the range of learning sciences research that both learns from teachers and contributes to the learning of teachers. Progress in this work is crucial not only to the learning sciences, but to the broader educational research and reform agenda.

Acknowledgments

The contribution of the third author was supported by a General Research Funds grant from the University Grants Council of Hong Kong (Grant HKU 740809H).

References

Ball, D. L., & Cohen, D. K. (1996). Reform by the book: What is – or might be – the role of curriculum materials in teacher learning and instructional reform? *Educational Researcher*, 25(9), 6–8.

Ball, D., & Forzani, F. (2009). The work of teaching and the challenge for teacher education. *Journal of Teacher Education*, 60(5), 497–511.

Ball, D., Thames, M., & Phelps, G. (2008). Content knowledge for teaching: What makes it special? *Journal of Teacher Education*, 29(5), 389–407.

Barab, S. A., & Luehmann, A. L. (2003). Building sustainable science curriculum: Acknowledging and accommodating local adaptation. *Science Education*, 87(4), 454–467.

Beyer, C., & Davis, E. A. (2009). Using educative curriculum materials to support preservice elementary teachers' curricular planning: A comparison between two different forms of support. *Curriculum Inquiry*, 39(5), 679–703.

Beyer, C. J., Delgado, C., Davis, E. A., & Krajcik, J. (2009). Investigating teacher learning supports in high school biology curricular programs to inform the design of educative curriculum materials. *Journal of Research in Science Teaching*, 46(9), 977–998.

Bielaczyc, K. (2013). Informing design research: Learning from teachers' designs of social infrastructure. *Journal of the Learning Sciences,* 22(2), 258–311.

Blumenfeld, P., Fishman, B., Krajcik, J., Marx, R., & Soloway, E. (2000). Creating usable innovations in systemic reform: Scaling up technology-embedded project-based science in urban schools. *Educational Psychologist*, 35(3), 149–164.

Blumenfeld, P., Krajcik, J., Kempler, T., Kam, R., Gallagher, S., & Geier, B. (2006). *Opportunities to learn: Teacher instructional practices that account for variation in achievement in project-based science.* Annual Meeting of the American Educational Research Association. San Francisco, CA.

Borko, H., Jacobs, J., & Koellner, K. (2010). Contemporary approaches to teacher professional development. In P. L. Peterson, E. Baker, & B. McGaw (Eds.), *International encyclopedia of education* (pp. 548–556). New York: Elsevier.

Brown, A. L., & Campione, J. C. (1994). Guided discovery in a community of learners. In K. McGilly (Ed.), *Classroom lessons: Integrating cognitive theory and classroom practice.* (pp. 229–270). Cambridge, MA: MIT Press/Bradford Books.

Brown, J. S., Collins, A., & Duguid, P. (1989). Situated cognition and the culture of learning. *Educational Researcher*, 18(1), 32–42.

Brown, M. (2009). The teacher-tool relationship: Theorizing the design and use of curriculum materials. In J. T. Remillard, B. Herbel-Eisenman, & G. Lloyd (Eds.), *Mathematics teachers at work: Connecting curriculum materials and classroom instruction* (pp. 17–36). New York: Routledge.

Cesareni, D., Martini, F., & Mancini, I. (2011). Building a community among teachers, researchers and university students: A blended approach to training. *International Journal of Computer-Supported Collaborative Learning*, 6, 625–646.

Chan, C. K. K. (2011). Bridging research and practice: Implementing and sustaining knowledge building in Hong Kong classrooms. *International Journal of Computer-Supported Collaborative Learning*, 6(2), 147–186.

Chan, C. K. K., & Van Aalst, J. (2006). Teacher development through computer-supported knowledge building: Experience from Hong Kong and Canadian teachers. *Teaching Education*, 17, 7–26.

Chazan, D., & Herbst, P. (2012). Animations of classroom interaction: Expanding the boundaries of video records of practice. *Teachers' College Record*, 114(3), 1–34.

Chen, C. L. (2011). Planning ahead in learning to teach: Attending to mathematical interactions with students. Unpublished doctoral dissertation, University of Michigan, Ann Arbor.

Chetty, R., Friedman, J. N., & Rockoff, J. E. (2012). The long-term impacts of teachers: Teacher value-added and student outcomes in adulthood. Retrieved May 9, 2012, 2012, from http://obs.rc.fas.harvard.edu/chetty/value_added.html.

Chieu, V., Herbst, P., & Weiss, M. (2011). Effects of an animated classroom story embedded in online discussion on helping Mathematics teachers to notice. *The Journal of the Learning Sciences*, 20(4), 589–624.

Cohen, D. K., & Hill, H. C. (1998). *State policy and classroom performance: Mathematics reform in California (CPRE Policy Brief No. RB-23).* Philadelphia, PA: Consortium for Policy Research in Education.

Collins, A. (2006). Cognitive apprenticeship. In R. K. Sawyer (Ed.)., *The Cambridge handbook of the learning sciences* (pp.47–60). New York: Cambridge University Press.

Collins, A., Joseph, D., & Bielaczyc, K. (2004). Design research: Theoretical and methodological issues. *The Journal of the Learning Sciences*, 13(1), 15–42.

Connor, C. M., Morrison, F. J., Schatschneider, C., Toste, J. R., Lundblom, E., Crowe, E. C., & Fishman, B. (2011). Effective classroom instruction: Implications of child characteristics by reading instruction interactions on first graders' word reading achievement. *Journal of Research on Educational Effectiveness*, 4(3), 173–207.

Corbett, A. T., Koedinger, K. R., & Hadley, W. (2001). Cognitive tutors: From the research classroom to all classrooms. In P. Goodman (Ed.), *Technology enhanced learning: Opportunities for change* (pp. 235–263). Mahwah, NJ: Lawrence Erlbaum Associates.

Davis, E. A. (2006). Preservice elementary teachers' critique of instructional materials for science. *Science Education*, 90(2), 348–375.

Davis, E. A., Beyer, C., Forbes, C., & Stevens, S. (2011). Understanding pedagogical design capacity through teachers' narratives. *Teaching and Teacher Education*, 27(4), 797–810.

Davis, E. A., & Krajcik, J. S. (2005). Designing educative curriculum materials to promote teacher learning. *Educational Researcher*, 34(3), 2–14.

Davis, E. A., Petish, D., & Smithey, J. (2006). Challenges new science teachers face. *Review of Educational Research*, 76(4), 607–651.

Dede, C., Ketelhut, D. J., Whitehouse, P., & McCloskey, E. (2009). A research agenda for online teacher professional development. *Journal of Teacher Education*, 60(1), 8–19.

Dede, C., & Richards, J. (2012). *Digital teaching platforms: Customizing classroom learning for each student*. New York: Teachers College Press.

Derry, S. J., & Hmelo-Silver, C. (2002). Addressing teacher education as a complex science: Theory-based studies within the STEP project. In P. Bell, R. Stevens, & T. Satwicz (Eds.), *International Conference of the Learning Sciences (ICLS)* (pp. 611–615). Mahwah, NJ: Lawrence Erlbaum Associates.

Derry, S. J., Seymour, J., Steinkuehler, C., Lee, J., & Siegel, M. A. (2004). From ambitious vision to partially satisfying reality: An evolving socio-technical design supporting community and collaborative learning in teacher education. In S. A. Barab, R. Kling, & J. H. Gray (Eds.), *Designing for virtual communities in the service of learning* (pp. 256–295). Cambridge: Cambridge University Press.

Desimone, L. (2009). Improving impact studies of teachers' professional development: Toward better conceptualizations and measures. *Educational Researcher*, 38(3), 181–199.

Directorate-General for Education and Culture. (2005). CPD for teachers and trainers. European Commission. Retrieved 12/2/2012 from http://ec.europa.eu/education/lifelong-learning-policy/doc/clusters/reportpeer1_En.pdf.

Enyedy, N., Goldberg, J., & Welsh, K. M. (2006). Complex dilemmas of identity and practice. *Science Education*, 90(1), 68–93.

Feiman-Nemser, S. (2001). From preparation to practice: Designing a continuum to strengthen and sustain teaching. *Teachers College Record*, 103(6), 1013–1055.

Fishman, B. (2003). Linking on-line video and curriculum to leverage community knowledge. In J. Brophy (Ed.), *Advances in research on teaching: Using video in teacher education* (vol. 10, pp. 201–234). New York: Elsevier.

Fishman, B., & Davis, E. A. (2006). Teacher learning research and the learning sciences. In R. K. Sawyer (Ed.), *The Cambridge handbook of the learning sciences* (pp. 535–550). New York: Cambridge University Press.

Fishman, B., & Duffy, T. M. (1992). Classroom restructuring: What do teachers really need? *Educational Technology Research and Development*, 40(3), 95–111.

Fishman, B., Marx, R., Best, S., & Tal, R. (2003). Linking teacher and student learning to improve professional development in systemic reform. *Teaching and Teacher Education*, 19(6), 643–658.

Fishman, B., Penuel, W. R., Allen, A., & Cheng, B. H. (2013). Design-based implementation research: Theories, methods, and exemplars. *National Society for the Study of Education Yearbook* (112)2. Teachers College Press.

Fishman, B., Penuel, W. R., Hegedus, S., & Roschelle, J. M. (2011). What happens when the research ends? Factors related to the sustainability of a technology-infused mathematics curriculum. *Journal of Computers in Mathematics and Science Teaching*, 30(4), 329–353.

Fogleman, J., Fishman, B., & Krajcik, J. S. (2006). Sustaining innovations through lead teacher learning: A learning sciences perspective on supporting professional development. *Teaching Education*, 17(2), 181–194.

Frederiksen, J. R., Sipusic, M., Sherin, M., & Wolfe, E. (1998). Video portfolio assessment: Creating a framework for viewing the functions of teaching. *Educational Assessment*, 5(4), 225–297.

Garet, M. S., Porter, A. C., Desimone, L., Birman, B. F., & Yoon, K. S. (2001). What makes professional development effective? Results from a national sample of teachers. *American Educational Research Journal*, 38(4), 915–945.

Greeno, J. G. (2006). Learning in activity. In R. K. Sawyer (Ed.), *The Cambridge handbook of the learning sciences* (pp. 79–96). New York: Cambridge University Press.

Grossman, P., Compton, C., Igra, D., Ronfeldt, M., Shahan, E., & Williamson, P. (2009). Teaching practice: A cross-professional perspective. *Teachers College Record*, 111(9), 2055–2100.

Grossman, P., Wineburg, S., & Woolworth, S. (2001). Toward a theory of teacher community. *Teachers College Record*, 103(6), 942–1012.

Heffernan, N. T., Heffernan, C. L., Bennett Decoteau, M., & Militello, M. (2012). Effective and meaningful use of educational technology: Three cases from the classroom. In C. Dede & J. Richards (Eds.), *Digital teaching platforms: Customizing classroom learning for each student* (pp. 88–102). New York: Teachers College Press.

Hill, H. C., Rowan, B., & Ball, D. L. (2005). Effects of teachers' mathematical knowledge for teaching on student achievement. *American Educational Research Journal*, 42(2), 371–406.

Hong, H. Y., Scardamalia, M., & Zhang, J. (2010). Knowledge Society Network: Toward a dynamic, sustained network for building knowledge. *Canadian Journal of Learning and Technology*, 36(1).

Horn, I. (2010). Teaching replays, teaching rehearsals, and re-visions of practice: Learning from colleagues in a mathematics teacher community. *Teachers College Record*, 112(1), 225–259.

Koedinger, K., & Corbett, A., (2006). Cognitive tutors: Technology bringing learning sciences to the classroom. In R. K. Sawyer (Ed.), *The Cambridge handbook of the learning sciences* (pp. 61–77). New York: Cambridge University Press.

Kubitskey, B. (2006). Extended professional development for systemic curriculum reform. Unpublished doctoral dissertation. University of Michigan, Ann Arbor.

Kubitskey, B., Fishman, B., & Marx, R. (2004). *Teacher learning from reform-based professional development and its impact on student learning: A case study. Annual Meeting of the National Association of Research on Science Teaching.* Vancouver, Canada.

Laferrière T., Erickson, G., & Breuleux, A. (2007). Innovative models of web-supported university-school partnerships. *Canadian Journal of Education*, 30(1), 211–238.

Lampert, M., Beasley, H., Ghousseini, H., Kazemi, E., & Franke, M. (2010). Using designed instructional activities to enable novices to manage ambitious mathematics teaching. In M. K. Stein & L. Kucan (Eds.), *Instructional explanations in the discipline* (pp. 129–141). New York: Springer.

Lampert, M., & Graziani, F. (2009). Instructional activities as a tool for teachers' and teacher educators' learning. *Elementary School Journal*, 109(5), 491–509.

Lin, H. T., & Fishman, B. (2006). *Exploring the relationship between teachers' curriculum enactment experience and their understanding of underlying unit structures. 7th International Conference of the Learning Sciences* (vol. 1, pp. 432–438). Mahwah, NJ: Lawrence Erlbaum Associates.

Linn, M. C., Clark, D., & Slotta, J. (2003). WISE design for knowledge integration. *Science Education*, 87(4), 517–538.

Linn, M. C., Davis, E. A., & Bell, P. (2004). *Internet environments for science education.* Mahwah, NJ: Lawrence Erlbaum Associates.

Luehmann, A. L. (2008). Using blogging in support of teacher professional identity development: A case study. *Journal of the Learning Sciences*, 17(3), 287–337.

Madeira, C. A., & Slotta, J. D. (2011). Technology-mediated reflection and peer exchange: Supports for teacher professional development communities. In H. Spada, G. Stahl, N. Miyake, & N. Law (Eds.), *Connecting computer-supported collaborative learning to policy and practice: CSCL 2011 Conference Proceedings.* Volume I – Long Papers (pp. 558–565). International Society of the Learning Sciences.

Magnusson, S., Krajcik, J., & Borko, H. (1999). Nature, sources, and development of pedagogical content knowledge for science teaching. In J. Gess-Newsome & N. Lederman (Eds.), *Examining pedagogical content knowledge: The construct and its implications for science education* (pp. 95–132). Dordrecht, The Netherlands: Kluwer Academic Publishers.

McDonald, S. P. (2010) Building a conversation: Preservice teachers' use of video as data for making evidence-based arguments about practice. *Educational Technology*, 50(1), 28–31.

McNeill, K. (2009). Teachers' use of curriculum to support students in writing scientific arguments to explain phenomena. *Science Education*, 93(2), 233–268.

Oshima, J., Oshima, R., Inagaki, S., Takenaka, M., Nakayama, H., Yamaguchi, E., & Murayama, I. (2003). Teachers and researchers as a design team: Changes in their relationship through a design experiment using computer support for collaborative learning (CSCL) technology. *Education, Communication & Information*, 3(1), 105–127.

Palincsar, A., Magnusson, S., Marano, N., Ford, D., & Brown, N. (1998). Designing a community of practice: Principles and practices of the GIsML community. *Teaching and Teacher Education*, 14(1), 5–19.

Pea, R. D. (1993). Practices of distributed intelligence and designs for education. In G. Salomon (Ed.), *Distributed cognitions: Psychological and educational considerations* (pp. 47–87). New York: Cambridge University Press.

Penuel, W. R., Fishman, B., Cheng, B. H., & Sabelli, N. (2011). Organizing research and development at the intersection of learning, implementation, and design. *Educational Researcher*, 40(7), 331–337.

Penuel, W. R., Fishman, B., Yamaguchi, R., & Gallagher, L. (2007). What makes professional development effective? Strategies that foster curriculum implementation. *American Educational Research Journal*, 44(4), 921–958.

Penuel, W. R., & Gallagher, L. P. (2009). Preparing teachers to design instruction for deep understanding in middle school earth science. *Journal of the Learning Sciences*, 18(4), 461–508.

Putnam, R., & Borko, H. (2000). What do new views of knowledge and thinking have to say about research on teacher learning? *Educational Researcher*, 29(1), 4–15.

Remillard, J. (2005). Examining key concepts in research on teachers' use of mathematics curricula. *Review of Educational Research*, 75(2), 211–246.

Renninger, K. A., & Shumar, W. (2004). The centrality of culture and community to participant learning at and with The Math Forum. In S. A. Barab, R. Kling, & J. H. Gray (Eds.), *Designing for virtual communities in the service of learning* (pp. 181–209). Cambridge: Cambridge University Press.

Richardson, V., & Anders, P. L. (1994). The study of teacher change. In V. Richardson (Ed.), *Teacher change and the staff development process: A case in reading instruction* (pp. 159–180). New York: Teachers College Press.

Ruopp, R. R., Gal, S., Drayton, B., & Pfister, M. (1993). *LabNet: Toward a community of practice*. Hillsdale, NJ: Lawrence Erlbaum Associates.

Sawyer, R. K. (2011). What makes good teachers great? The artful balance of structure and improvisation. In R. K. Sawyer (Ed.), *Structure and improvisation in creative teaching*. New York: Cambridge University Press.

Schlager, M. S., Fusco, J., & Schank, P. (2002). Evolution of an online education community of practice. In K. A. Renninger & W. Shumar (Eds.), *Building virtual communities: Learning and change in cyberspace* (pp. 129–158). Cambridge: Cambridge University Press.

Schneider, R. M., & Krajcik, J. S. (2002). Supporting science teacher learning: The role of educative curriculum materials. *Journal of Science Teacher Education*, 13(3), 221–245.

Schultz, A., Arias, A., Davis, E. A., & Palincsar, A. S. (2012). Connecting curriculum materials and teachers: Elementary science teachers' enactment of a reform-based curricular unit. Paper presented at the annual meeting of the National Association for Research in Science Teaching.

Sherin, M. G. (2004). Teacher learning in the context of a video club. *Teaching and Teacher Education*, 20(2), 163–183.

Sherin, M. G., & Van Es, E. (2009). Effects of video club participation on teachers' professional vision. *Journal of Teacher Education*, 60(1), 20–37.

Shulman, L. S. (1986). Those who understand: Knowledge growth in teaching. *Educational Researcher*, 15(2), 4–14.

Singapore Ministry of Education (2010, July). Building a national education system for the 21st century: The Singapore experience. Retrieved from http://www.edu.gov.on.ca/bb4e/materials.html.

Slotta, J. (2004). The Web-based Inquiry Science Environment (WISE): Scaffolding knowledge integration in the science classroom. In M. C. Linn, E. A. Davis & P. Bell (Eds.), *Internet environments for science education* (pp. 203–231). Mahwah, NJ: Lawrence Erlbaum Associates.

Star, J., & Strickland, S. (2008). Learning to observe: Using video to improve preservice teachers' ability to notice. *Journal of Mathematics Teacher Education*, 11(2), 107–125.

U.S. Department of Education. (2010). *Transforming American education: Learning powered by technology*. Washington, DC: U.S. Department of Education.

Van Driel, J. H., & Berry, A. (2010). The teacher education knowledge base: Pedagogical content knowledge. In P. L. Peterson, E. Baker, & B. McGaw (Eds.), *Third international encyclopedia of education* (vol. 7, pp. 656–661). Amsterdam: Elsevier.

Van Driel, J., Verloop, N., & de Vos, W. (1998). Developing science teachers' pedagogical content knowledge. *Journal of Research in Science Teaching*, 35(6), 673–695.

Van Es, E. (2009). Participants' roles in the context of a video club. *Journal of the Learning Sciences*, 18(1), 100–137.

VanLehn, K. (2011). The relative effectiveness of human tutoring, intelligent tutoring systems, and other tutoring systems. *Educational Psychologist*, 46(4), 197–221.

Varma, K., Husic, F., & Linn, M. (2008). Targeted support for using technology-enhanced science inquiry modules. *Journal of Science Education and Technology*, 17(4), 341–356.

Vygotsky, L. S. (1978). *Mind in society: The development of the higher psychological processes*. Cambridge, MA: Harvard University Press.

Wenger, E. (1998). *Communities of practice: Learning, meaning, and identity*. Cambridge: Cambridge University Press.

Zembal-Saul, C. (2008). What were you thinking?! Designing video cases to provide novices access to experienced elementary teachers' reasoned decision-making during science teaching. In K. McFerrin et al. (Eds.), *Proceedings of Society for Information Technology & Teacher Education International Conference 2008* (pp. 4834–4838). Chesapeake, VA: AACE.

36 Conclusion

The Future of Learning: Grounding Educational Innovation in the Learning Sciences

R. Keith Sawyer

The education landscape has changed dramatically since 2006, when the first edition of this handbook was published. In 2006, the following innovations did not yet exist; today, each of them is poised to have a significant impact on education:

- *Tablet computers*, like Apple's iPad and Microsoft's Surface. In 2012, Apple released iBooks Author, a free textbook authoring app for instructors to develop their own customized textbooks.
- Although *smartphones* were well established among businesspeople in 2006 (then-popular devices included the BlackBerry and Palm Treo), their market penetration has grown dramatically since the 2007 release of the iPhone, especially among school-aged children.
- *The App store* – Owners of smartphones including Apple's iPhone, and phones running Google's Android and Microsoft's Windows Phone, can easily download free or very cheap applications, choosing from hundreds of thousands available.
- *Inexpensive e-readers*, like the Kindle and the Nook, have sold well, and are connected to online stores that allow books to be downloaded easily and quickly.

Furthermore, since 2006, the following Internet-based educational innovations have been widely disseminated, widely used, and widely discussed:

- *Massive open online courses* (MOOCs). MOOCs are college courses, delivered on the Internet, that are open to anyone and are designed to support tens of thousands of students. The products used for such courses include Udacity, Coursera, edX, and FutureLearn (the United Kingdom's Open University). MOOCs have gained legitimacy because America's top research universities are involved. Coursera delivers courses offered by Brown, Caltech, Princeton, Stanford, and many other schools; edX delivers courses offered by MIT, Harvard, and others. In 2014, Google and edX released MOOC.org, an open-source platform that any university can use.
- *Learning Management Systems* (LMS). LMS are now used by most colleges to support their on-campus courses with full-time students. LMS

provide online discussion forums, electronic delivery of readings and assignments, and electronic return of graded assignments. The market leader is Blackboard; others include Moodle and Sakai. Newcomers like Piazza and Classroom Salon are increasingly integrating social networking features long associated with sites like Facebook (Kaufer, Gunewardena, Tan, & Cheek, 2011).

- *The flipped classroom.* The Khan Academy, which began as a series of YouTube instructional videos, popularized the notion of the "flipped classroom," where students watch videotaped lectures at home and then use class time for peer collaboration and hands-on, interactive learning. iTunes U offers full courses from MIT and Stanford (www.mit.edu/itunesu). Instructors can create courses for the iPad using iTunes U Course Manager.
- *Online college degrees.* The University of North Carolina at Chapel Hill began offering an online MBA degree in 2011, MBA@UNC; this has been extremely successful. In May 2013, Georgia Tech announced the first online master's degree in computer science, at one-fourth the cost of its traditional on-campus degree.

These innovations contrast sharply with the schools of today, which were largely designed during the 19th and 20th centuries to provide workers for the industrial economy. And the potential is that these innovations might be more effective than traditional schools, which are based in a pedagogical approach sometimes called *instructionism* – with teachers delivering information to passive, attentive students. As I argued in the introduction to this handbook, instructionism is largely ineffective at helping learners acquire the skills and knowledge needed in the 21st century. The world has changed dramatically since modern schools took shape around 100 years ago; in the 1970s, economists and other social scientists began to realize that the world's economies were shifting from an industrial economy to a knowledge economy (Bell, 1973; Drucker, 1993; Toffler, 1980). By the 1990s, educators had begun to realize that if the economy was no longer the 1920s-era factory economy, then traditional schools – instructionist, standardized, focused on memorization and rote learning – were designed for a vanishing world (Bereiter, 2002; Hargreaves, 2003; Sawyer, 2006). In the first decade of the 21st century, it became increasingly clear that the world had entered an *innovation age*. Today, it is widely accepted that companies and countries alike now have to continually innovate, to create *new* knowledge – not simply to master existing knowledge.

Leading thinkers in business, politics, and education are now in consensus that schools, and other learning environments, have to be redesigned to educate for innovation. In May 2013, in language typical of such reports, education consultants Michael Barber, Katelyn Donnelly, and Saad Rivzi wrote, "Our belief is that deep, radical and urgent transformation is required in higher education much as it is in school systems" (Barber, Donnelly, & Rivzi, 2013, p. 3). These arguments have expanded beyond consulting firms and policy circles to reach the general public; for example, a *New York Times Magazine* cover dated September 15, 2013, had this headline: "The All-Out, All-Ages Overhaul of School Is Happening Now" (*The New York Times,* 2013).

Everyone seems to agree that education in the 21st century is in need of transformational innovation. But what sort of innovation? And what will the innovation process look like – how do we get there from here? Most policy makers and media stories tend to focus on two drivers of educational innovation:

1. *The application of market models to the education sector.* Advocates of market models argue that introducing competition and increasing customer choice will drive innovation. Advocates of market competition argue that today's public schools have a monopoly on the delivery of education, and in general, monopolies reduce effectiveness and innovation. Because public schools have a guaranteed revenue stream in government taxes, they are not forced to compete on quality and cost.

2. *The increasing involvement of the private sector in education.* Many influential business leaders have given high-profile public talks arguing that schools are failing to graduate workers for the 21st-century economy. The list of CEOs, companies, and business organizations calling for change is long – Bill Gates, cofounder and former CEO of Microsoft; Louis V. Gerstner, the former CEO of IBM (Gerstner, 2008); Lockheed and Intel (Chaker, 2008); the U.S. Chamber of Commerce and the National Association of Manufacturers (Hagerty, 2011). Two of the most influential recent education reforms in the United States had strong private sector involvement: the Common Core standards, adopted by 45 of the 50 states (with early involvement by CEOs and senior executives at Intel, Prudential Financial, Battelle, and IBM), and the 21st-century skills movement (long sponsored by the Partnership for 21st Century Skills, with its founding organizations including AOL Time Warner, Apple, Cisco, Dell, and Microsoft). Many of these successful business leaders have also funded the push toward market reforms in schools, including the Bill and Melinda Gates Foundation, the Walton Family Foundation, the Eli and Edythe Broad Foundation, and the Michael and Susan Dell Foundation (Ravitch, 2010).

But to date, these potential drivers of educational innovation have not resulted in schools that are more solidly grounded in the learning sciences – the participatory, project-based, constructivist, and collaborative pedagogies suggested by the chapters in this handbook. In many cases, just the opposite has occurred: introducing competition and private sector models into schools has resulted in even more old-fashioned, traditional forms of teaching and learning – instructionism on steroids. To take one example: successful market competition requires a quantified measure of quality and success; consequently, the United States has invested in outcome measures of learning – the famous "high-stakes testing" associated with the No Child Left Behind (NCLB) legislation. (Most other countries already have high-stakes national examinations.) And yet the relatively recent U.S. focus on these high-stakes assessments has, for the most part, resulted in a reversion to instructionist pedagogy. (This is consistent with international experience; in many countries with high-stakes national examinations, instructionism is deeply rooted.) To take another example, the pedagogy used by MOOCs "is a transmission model, relying on video lectures, recommended readings and staged assessment" (Sharples et al., 2013, p. 3) – exactly the opposite of what learning sciences research would advise.

After several years of attempting to "fix" schools with technology, a growing number of techno-skeptics have emerged (see Collins & Halverson, 2009). For example, in 2010 computer pioneer and visionary Alan Kay said that 30 years of technology in schools had failed (Cult of Mac, 2010). In 2012, Peter J. Stokes said, "The whole MOOC thing is mass psychosis, people just throwing spaghetti against the wall to see what sticks"; he was then executive director for postsecondary innovation at Northeastern University's College of Professional Studies (Carlson & Blumenstyk, 2012, pp. A4–A5). A U.S. government review of 10 major software products for teaching algebra, reading, and math found that nine of them did not have statistically significant effects on test scores (Gabriel & Richtel, 2011).

If we are to succeed in creating the schools of the future, educational innovation and technology must be grounded in the learning sciences. The learning sciences are showing us how to design the learning environments of the future – learning environments that teach the deep knowledge and adaptive expertise required in an innovation age. Major governmental and international bodies have commissioned reports summarizing learning sciences research; these reports began with the influential U.S. National Research Council's *How People Learn* (Bransford, Brown, & Cocking, 2000). Since the 2006 publication of the first edition of this handbook, the OECD has published many excellent reviews of this research, including *Innovative Learning Environments* (2013), *The Nature of Learning: Using Research to Inspire Practice* (2010), and *Innovating to Learn, Learning to Innovate* (2008).

Those societies that can effectively restructure their schools on the learning sciences will be the leaders in the 21st century (OECD, 2000, 2004, 2008, 2010, 2013). The issues addressed by the learning sciences have been recognized as critical in all 28 of the countries studied by the ISTE (Kozma, 2003). The leaders of these countries agree that the world economy has changed to an innovation- and knowledge-based economy, and that education must change as well for a society to make this transition successfully. This handbook continues the important work recommended by these reports; the chapters collected here describe how to design the learning environments of the future. If you closely read all of these chapters, various visions of the schools of the future begin to take shape – but the outlines remain fuzzy. The key issue facing the learning sciences in the next 10 to 20 years will be to outline an increasingly specific vision for the future of learning. In this conclusion, I begin by presenting possible visions of the schools of the future. I then discuss unresolved issues that will face the learning sciences as its findings begin to be used to build the learning environments of the future.

Schools and Beyond

The learning sciences has enormous potential to transform schools so that students learn better and more deeply, are more prepared to function in the knowledge economy, and are able to participate actively in an open, democratic society. These chapters provide a wealth of research-based evidence for how learning environments should be designed. Note that these chapters generally talk about "learning environments" rather than "schools" or "classrooms"; this is because learning environments include schools and classrooms but also the many informal learning situations that have existed through history and continue to exist alongside formal schooling, and also include the new computer- and Internet-based alternatives to classrooms. A true science of learning has to bring together understandings of all learning environments, drawing on their best features to build the schools of the future. Instead of studying small incremental changes to today's schools, learning scientists ask a more profound question: Are today's schools really the right schools for the knowledge society?

Most learning sciences researchers are committed to improving schools, and they believe that school reform should involve working together with teachers, engaging in professional development, and integrating new software into classrooms. A new research methodology developed by learning scientists – the design experiment – is conducted in classrooms, and requires that researchers work closely with teachers as they participate in curriculum development, teacher professional development, and assessment (Barab, Chapter 8, this volume).

But learning sciences research might also lead to more radical alternatives that would make schools as we know them obsolete, leaving today's big high schools as empty as the shuttered steel factories of the faded industrial economy. Two of the most influential founders of the learning sciences, Roger Schank (1999) and Seymour Papert (1980), argued that computer technology is so radically transformative that schools as we know them will have to fade away before the full benefits can be realized. The recent technological developments I described earlier seem to finally make this possible. Everything is subject to change: schools may not be physical locations where everyone goes, students may not be grouped by age or grade, students could learn anywhere at any time. I made this same statement in my conclusion to the 2006 edition, when it may have seemed shocking; now, in 2014, such visions have become the conventional wisdom. I already mentioned the September 2013 *New York Times Magazine* cover "The All-Out, All-Ages Overhaul of School is Happening Now"; the cover photograph behind this text shows a shuttered and abandoned red brick school building. In May 2013, Andy Kessler proposed a de-schooled future for Chicago Public Schools in *The Wall Street Journal*, in response to a study showing that under 8 percent of school graduates were ready for college:

> Why not forget the [Chicago] teachers and issue all 404,151 [Chicago students] an iPad or an Android tablet? At the cost of $161 million, that's less than 10% of the expense of paying teachers' salaries. Add online software, tutors and a $2,000 graduation bonus, and you still don't come close to the cost of teachers. You can't possibly do worse than a 7.9% college readiness level. (Kessler, 2013)

As of 2013, 27 states had established online virtual schools; 31 states and Washington, DC have statewide full-time online schools. These schools generally receive per-student funding from the state just like any other district (although typically at a lower amount than an in-school student). In the 2009–2010 school year, an estimated 1,816,400 U.S. students were enrolled in distance learning courses, and 200,000 full-time students were enrolled in full-time online schools (International Association for K-12 Online Learning, 2013). In 2012, Florida became the first U.S. state to offer full-time and part-time online options to all students in grades K-12.

Imagine a nation of online home-based activities organized around small neighborhood learning clubs, all connected through high-bandwidth Internet software. There would be no textbooks, few lectures, and no curriculum as we know it today. "Teachers" would operate as independent consultants who work from home most of the time, and occasionally meet with ad hoc groups of students at a learning club. Each meeting would be radically different in nature, depending on the project-based and self-directed learning that those students were engaged in. In fact, each type of learning session might involve a different learning specialist. The teaching profession could become multitiered, with master teachers developing curriculum in collaboration with software developers and acting as consultants to schools, and learning centers staffed by a variety of independent contractors whose job no longer involves lesson preparation or grading, but instead involves mostly assisting students as they work at the computer or gather data in the field (Stallard & Cocker, 2001).

Educational software gives us the opportunity to provide a customized learning experience to each student to a degree not possible when one teacher is responsible for six classrooms of 25 students each. Well-designed software could sense each learner's unique learning style and developmental level, and tailor the presentation of material appropriately – by using learning analytics (see Baker & Siemens, Chapter 13, this volume). As of 2013, Knewton's adaptive learning offerings were in both K-12 schools and in universities (Selingo, 2013, pp. 73–78; Webley, 2013). Some students could take longer to master a subject, while others would be faster, because the computer can provide information to each student at his or her own pace. And each student could learn each subject at different rates; for example, learning what we think of today as "fifth grade" reading and "third grade" math at the same time. In age-graded classrooms this would be impossible, but in the schools of the future there may be no educational need to age-grade classrooms, no need to hold back the more advanced children or to leave behind those who need more help, and no reason for a child to learn all subjects at the same rate. Of course, age-graded classrooms also serve to socialize children, providing opportunities to make friends, to form peer groups, and to participate in team sports. If learning and schooling were no longer age-graded, other institutions would have to emerge to provide these opportunities.

Conservative critics of public schools see the future emerging through an open market system of competition, in which parents can use local property tax dollars to choose from a wide range of learning environments. To take just one hypothetical possibility, for-profit tutoring centers (such as Kumon Learning Centers) might begin to offer a three-hour intensive workday, structured around tutors and individualized educational software, with each student taking home his or her laptop to complete the remainder of the day at home. Because each tutor could schedule two three-hour shifts in one day, class size could be halved with no increase in cost. Because curriculum and software would be designed centrally, and the software does the grading automatically, these future tutors could actually leave their work at the office – unlike today's teachers, who stay up late every night and spend their weekends preparing lesson plans and grading. For those parents who need an all-day option for their children because of their work schedule, for-profit charter schools could proliferate, each based on a slightly different curriculum or a slightly different software package. Particularly skilled teachers could develop reputations that would allow them to create their own "start-up schools," taking 10 or 20 students into their home for some or all of the school day – the best of them providing serious competition for today's elite private schools, and earning as much as other knowledge workers such as lawyers, doctors, and executives. In 2010, one of Korea's best-known English language teachers earned $4 million (Ripley, 2013, pp. 167–174).

Museums and public libraries might play a larger role in education. They could receive increased funding to support their evolution into learning resource centers, perhaps even receiving a portion of the government's tax-funded education budget. They could contribute to student learning in several ways: for example, by developing curriculum and lesson plans and making these available to students anywhere over the Internet, and by providing physical learning environments as they redesign their buildings to support schooling. Science centers have already taken the lead in this area, developing inquiry-based curricula and conducting teacher professional development, and art and history museums may soon follow suit.

The boundary between formal schooling and continuing education will increasingly blur. The milestone of a high school diploma could gradually decrease in importance, as the nature of learning in school begins to look more and more like on-the-job apprenticeship and adult distance education. Inexpensive tablets and phones allow learning to take place anywhere, anytime; 16-year-olds could work their part-time jobs during the day and take their classes at night, just as many adult students do now. Many types of knowledge are better learned in workplace environments; this kind of learning will be radically transformed by the availability of anywhere, anytime learning, as new employees take their tablets or smartphones on the job with them, with software specially designed to provide apprenticeship support in the workplace. Professional schools could be radically affected; new forms of portable just-in-time learning could increasingly put their campus-based educational models at risk.

These scenarios are all hypothetical; it isn't yet clear how schools will change in response to the new research emerging from the learning sciences, and to the computer technology that makes these new learning environments possible. But if schools do not redesign themselves on a foundation in the learning sciences, alternative learning environments that do so could gradually draw more students – particularly if charter schools, vouchers, and online learning become widespread. Learning scientists Allan Collins and Richard Halverson have predicted that schools will fail to change and that alternative learning environments will emerge and gradually begin to dominate (Collins & Halverson, 2009). And even if schools do not face competition from charters and vouchers, learning will increasingly take place both inside and outside the school walls – in libraries, museums, after school clubs, online virtual schools, Internet-based courses, modules, and certifications, and at home.

What Constitutes Evidence of Learning?

Most of today's schools are organized around a "credit hour" model (the so-called Carnegie unit) and a nine-month calendar. For example, at the university level, a "course" is defined as three hours a week, in a room with a professor, for one term (in the United States, the nine-month year has either two terms of approximately 15 weeks each – called *semesters* – or three terms of approximately 10 weeks each, called *quarters*). A student receives three credit hours with a passing grade at the end of the course. A student's transcript – the document providing evidence of successful learning – is likewise organized by term and credit hour. Primary and secondary schools follow similar frameworks.

Many educational innovations challenge this model – particularly online distance learning. Why, their advocates ask, should the fundamental unit of teaching and learning be so tightly connected to a physical campus and to face-to-face interaction? After all, they argue, the credit hour is a rather poor measure of what learning has occurred. Instead, they propose, why not measure learning outcomes directly, with a culminating examination?

One of the most prominent alternatives to the credit hour model is the proposal to use *badges* as the fundamental unit of learning. Terms like *competency based* or *proficiency based* are used to refer to the practice of granting degrees and certificates based on performance on a final assessment rather than time in the classroom (Selingo, 2013, pp. 112–116). By some measures, 34 states are moving toward competency education (Carnegie Foundation, 2013). The online Western Governor University does not use grades and credit hours, but instead is solely assessment driven (Kamenetz, 2010, p. 101).

A second prominent alternative is the idea of instituting an "exit exam" for universities as a replacement for the school transcript and the grade point average (GPA). One prominent example is the Collegiate Learning Assessment (CLA), released in the United States in 2013. Already in many of the world's countries – including almost all of Asia and Europe – the most important evidence of successful learning at the secondary level is a single high-stakes exit exam. A student's grades in courses are far less important. In the United States, one's high school grades remain important, but in addition all college-bound students take one of the privately developed and privately administered college entrance exams, the ACT or the SAT.

The challenge will be to design badges and other assessments to be grounded in the latest science of how people learn, and to accurately reflect 21st-century skills – creativity, collaboration, and deeper conceptual understanding. Assessment design is an active area of research (see Pellegrino, Chapter 12, this volume), and is poised for dramatic developments in the near future.

Computers and the Schools of the Future

Learning scientists build learning environments that are based on scientific principles. As we've seen throughout this handbook, carefully designed computer software can play a critical role in these learning environments. However, learning scientists know that for 50 years, reformers have been claiming that computers will change schools – and these predictions have never come to pass. Perhaps the first such high-profile prediction was in the 1950s, when legendary behaviorist B. F. Skinner claimed that his "teaching machines" made the teacher "out of date" (Skinner, 1954/1968, p. 22). Criticisms of computer-based learning had already appeared in 1951, with Isaac Asimov's classic science fiction short story, "The Fun They Had," which takes place in a future where children are educated at home by a robot (the "fun" refers to an imagined past when children actually went to school). Decades later, starting from the dramatically different theoretical framework of constructivism, Seymour Papert's 1980 book *Mindstorms* argued that giving every child a computer would allow students to actively construct their own learning, leaving teachers with an uncertain role: "schools as we know them today will have no place in the future" (Papert, 1980, p. 9). Behaviorists and constructivists don't agree about much, but in this case they agreed on the power of computers to transform schools. But both Skinner's and Papert's predictions have been wrong. In 2001, Larry Cuban famously documented the failure of computers and the Internet to improve U.S. schools in his book *Oversold and Underused*. This disappointing history provides a sobering counter-narrative to technological visionaries who today argue that the Internet will transform schooling. How is the software being developed by learning scientists any different?

The fundamental differences are that learning scientists begin by first developing a foundation in the basic sciences of learning, and their computer software is designed with the participation of practicing teachers and is grounded in how people learn. Learning scientists work closely with schools and also with informal learning environments like science centers; part of the reason that the design research methodology (Barab, Chapter 8, this volume) is so central to research practice is that this methodology allows computers and programs to be embedded in a complex and integrated curriculum. Learning scientists realize that computers will never realize their full potential if they are merely add-ons to the existing instructionist classroom; that's why they are engaged in the hard work of designing entire learning environments – not just stand-alone computer applications, as previous generations of educational software designers did.

Curriculum

What should be taught in second grade math, or in sixth grade social studies? Learning scientists have discovered that what seems more simple to an adult professional is not necessarily more simple to a learner. The most effective sequencing of activities is not always a sequence from what experts consider to be more simple to more complex. Children arrive at school with naïve theories and misconceptions; and during the school years, children pass through a series of cognitive developmental stages. Instructionist textbooks and curricula were designed before learning scientists began to map out the educational relevance of cognitive development.

In the next 10 to 20 years, new curricula for K-12 education will emerge that are based in the learning sciences. Major funding should be directed at identifying the specific sequences of activities and concepts that are most effective in each subject – sometimes referred to as "learning trajectories" or "learning progressions" (e.g., Daro, Mosher, & Corcoran, 2011). Developing these new curricula will require an army of researchers, distributed across all grades and all subjects, to identify the most appropriate sequences of material, and the most effective learning activities, based on research into children's developing cognitive competencies and how children construct their own deep knowledge while engaged in situated practices.

Related to the issue of curriculum is the sensitive topic of coverage – how much material, and how many topics, should students learn about at each age? In instructionism, the debate about curriculum is almost exclusively a debate about topic coverage – what should be included at each grade, and how much. But this focus on breadth is misguided. According to the Trends in International Mathematics and Science Study (TIMSS), which compares student achievement in math and science in 50 or more countries every four years, U.S. science and math curricula contain much more content than other countries as a result of their survey approaches to material – but rather than strengthening students' abilities, this survey approach weakens U.S. achievement relative to other countries (Schmidt & McKnight, 1997; Stigler & Hiebert, 2009). Compared to other countries, U.S. science curricula are "a mile wide and an inch deep" (Vogel, 1996, p. 335). Each topic is taught as its own distinct unit – and the new knowledge is often forgotten as soon as the students turn to the next topic. Studies of the TIMSS data show that children in nations that pursue a more focused, coherent, and deep strategy do substantially better on the mathematics assessment than do U.S. children (Schmidt & McKnight, 1997). This is consistent with the learning sciences finding that students learn better when they learn deep knowledge that allows them to think and to solve problems with the content that they are learning.

A near-term task facing the learning sciences is to identify the content of the curriculum for each subject and each grade, and then to design an integrated, coherent, unified curriculum to replace existing textbooks. Learning sciences research could be directed toward identifying which deep knowledge should be the outcome of each grade. These curricula are likely to contain fewer units and fewer overall line items, with more time spent on each item. This will be a political challenge, because some will view it as removing material from the curriculum, "dumbing down" or reducing expectations of students. In the United States, politicians and school boards have frequently responded to concerns about education by adding content requirements to the curriculum – contributing to the "mile wide, inch deep" phenomenon. It will take a paradigm change to shift the terms of this policy debate, and learning scientists could make valuable contributions.

The Teachers of the Future

The learning sciences focuses on learning and learners. Many education researchers are instead focused on teachers and teaching, and these readers may observe that the classroom activities described in these chapters seem very challenging for teachers. How are we going to find enough qualified professionals to staff the schools of the future? The teachers of the future will be knowledge workers, with equivalent skills to other knowledge workers such as lawyers, doctors, engineers, managers, and consultants. They will deeply understand the theoretical principles and the latest knowledge about how children learn. They will be deeply familiar with the authentic practices of professional scientists, historians, mathematics, or literary critics. They will have to receive salaries comparable to other knowledge workers, or else the profession will have difficulty attracting new teachers with the potential to teach for deep knowledge. The classrooms of the future will require more autonomy, more creativity, and more content knowledge (see Sawyer, 2011).

Over a wide variety of international schools, a set of best practices surrounding educational technology is emerging (Kozma, 2003; Schofield & Davidson, 2002). Instead of instructionism – with the teacher lecturing in a transmission-and-acquisition style – these classrooms engage in authentic and situated problem-based activities. If you looked into such a classroom, you'd see the teacher advising students, creating structures to scaffold student activities, and monitoring student progress. You'd see the students actively engaged in projects, managing and guiding their own activities, collaborating with other students, and occasionally asking the teacher for help.

The teachers of the future will be highly trained professionals, comfortable with technology, with a deep pedagogical understanding of the subject matter, able to respond improvisationally to the uniquely emerging flow of each classroom (Sawyer, 2004, 2011). They will lead teams of students, much like a manager of a business or the master in a workshop, preparing students to fully participate in the knowledge society.

Speed Bumps in the Road to the Future

It is too early to predict exactly what the learning environments of the future will look like. Three things now seem certain: first, that learning environments will eventually have to change to meet the needs of the modern knowledge society; second, that schools are complex institutions that have proven quite resistant to change; and third, that alternative learning environments, many enabled by new technologies, are rapidly emerging to challenge schools. The road from instructionism to the schools of the future will be long and unpredictable, but some of the speed bumps can be predicted.

Incompatibilities between Schools and the Learning Sciences

In an influential book, learning scientists Allan Collins and Richard Halverson (2009) identified several entrenched features of today's public schools that might make them resist the necessary changes emerging from the learning sciences:

Uniform learning versus customization. Schools are based on the assumption that everyone learns the same thing at the same time. Courses are structured so that everyone reads the same pages of the text at the same time, and everyone takes the same test on the same day. But in the schools of the future, each learner will receive a customized learning experience.

Teacher as expert versus diverse knowledge sources. In the constructivist and project-based learning advocated by the learning sciences, students gain expertise from a variety of sources – from the Internet, at the library, or through e-mail exchange with a working professional – and the teacher will no longer be the only source of expertise in the classroom. But today's schools are based on the notion that teachers are all-knowing experts, and their job is to transmit their expertise to the students.

Standardized assessment versus individualized assessment. Today's assessments require that every student learn the same thing at the same time. The standards movement and the resulting high-stakes testing are increasing standardization, at the same time that learning sciences and technology are making it possible for individual students to have customized learning experiences. Customization combined with diverse knowledge sources enable students to learn different things. Schools will still need to measure learning for accountability purposes, but we don't yet know how to reconcile accountability with customized learning.

Knowledge in the head versus distributed knowledge. In the real world, people act intelligently by making frequent use of books, papers, and technology. And in most professions, knowledge work occurs in teams and organizations, so that several times every hour, a person is interacting with others. But in today's schools, there is a belief that a student only knows something when that student can do it on his or her own, without any use of outside resources. There is a mismatch between today's school culture and the situated knowledge required in the knowledge society.

Connecting Elemental and Systemic Approaches

In Chapter 2, Mitch Nathan and I grouped learning sciences research into *elemental* and *systemic* approaches. Elemental approaches focus on individual learning, and systemic approaches focus on groups and classrooms. Many learning scientists emphasize the importance of learning in groups, in part because most knowledge work takes place in complexly organized teams.

These group processes are generally analyzed using systemic approaches. In contrast, many psychologists focus on individual learning and assume that all knowledge is individual knowledge. These individual cognitive processes are analyzed using elemental approaches. For these researchers, the basic science of learning must be the science of how individuals learn, and social context is only of secondary importance – as a potential influence on these basically mental processes. Many learning scientists reject this individualist view, and argue that all knowledge is in some sense group knowledge, because it is always used in social and cultural contexts (e.g., Rogoff, 1998).

A challenge facing learning sciences is how to integrate the scientific findings emerging from the elemental and systemic approaches, to develop a "unified grand theory" of teaching and learning. The learning sciences combines a diverse range of positions on how to accomplish this, from cognitive psychologists who focus on the mental structures that underlie knowledge, to socioculturalists who believe that it may be impossible to identify the mental structures corresponding to situated social practice. Most learning scientists reside in the center of this debate, believing that a full understanding of learning requires a combination of elemental and systemic approaches. But there is disagreement among learning scientists about where the emphasis should be placed, and how important it is to focus on individual learning.

Individual learning is always going to be an important goal of schooling. Individuals learn some knowledge better in social and collaborative settings than they do in isolation, but schools will continue to be judged on how well individual graduates perform on some form of individualized assessment. The learning sciences strongly suggests that today's assessments are misguided in design, in part because they isolate individuals from meaningful contexts. New assessments could include components that evaluate the individual's ability to work in a group, to manage diversity of backgrounds, or to communicate in complex, rapidly changing environments. But although new forms of assessment may place individuals in groups, we will still need to tease out the individual learning of each group participant.

Assessment and Accountability

The ultimate goal of learning sciences research is to contribute to the design of learning environments that lead to better student outcomes. Success must be measured using assessments of student learning. However, the learning sciences suggests that many of today's standardized tests are flawed because they focus on the surface knowledge emphasized by instructionism and do not assess the deep knowledge the knowledge society requires. Standardized tests, almost by their very nature, evaluate decontextualized and compartmentalized knowledge. For example, science tests do not assess whether preexisting misconceptions have indeed been left behind (diSessa, Chapter 5, this volume) nor do they assess problem-solving or inquiry skills (Krajcik & Shin, Chapter 14, this volume). As long as schools are evaluated on how well their students do on such tests, it will be difficult for them to leave instructionist methods behind.

One of the key issues facing the learning sciences is how to design new kinds of assessment that correspond to the deep knowledge required in today's knowledge society (Pellegrino, Chapter 12, this volume). Several learning sciences researchers are developing new assessments that focus on deeper conceptual understanding. For example, Lehrer and Schauble (2006) developed a test of model-based reasoning – a form of deeper understanding that is emphasized in their curriculum, but that does not appear on traditional standardized mathematics tests. The Views of the Nature of Science (VNOS) questionnaire assesses deeper understanding of scientific practice rather than content knowledge (Lederman, Adb-El-Khalick, Bell, & Schwartz, 2002).

In classrooms that make day-to-day use of computer software, installed on each student's own personal computer, there is an interesting new opportunity for assessment – the assessment could be built into the software itself (see Baker & Siemens, Chapter 13, this volume; Pellegrino, Chapter 12, this volume). After all, the learning sciences has found that effective educational software has to closely track the student's developing knowledge structures to be effective; because that tracking is being done anyway, it would be a rather straightforward extension to make summary versions of it available to teachers. New learning sciences software is exploring how to track deep learning during the learning process, in some cases inferring student learning from such subtle cues as where the learner moves and clicks the mouse – providing an opportunity for assessment during the learning itself, not in a separate multiple-choice quiz (e.g., Gobert, Buckley, & Dede, 2005).

These new forms of assessment represent the cutting edge of learning sciences research. A critical issue for the future is to continue this work, both in the research setting but also in the policy arena – working with developers of standardized tests and working with state boards of education to develop broad-scale standardized tests. Test construction is complex, involving field tests of reliability and validity for example, and will require learning scientists to work with psychometricians and policy experts.

New Methodologies

Experimental studies that randomly assign students to either a new educational intervention or a traditional classroom remain the gold standard for evaluating what works best to improve learning. This method is known as the randomized controlled trial (RCT) and is commonly used in medicine to evaluate new drugs and treatments. Many educators and politicians have recently applied this medical model of research to education (Shavelson &

Towne, 2002). But medical research does not consist only of RCTs. Medical research proceeds in roughly five phases:

> Preclinical: basic scientific research. A wide range of methodologies are used.
> Phase 1: Feasibility. How to administer the treatment; how much is appropriate. Again, a wide range of methodologies are used.
> Phase 2: Initial efficacy. How well does it work? Quasi-experimental methodologies are typically used.
> Phase 3: Randomized controlled trial (RCT). The gold standard, the controlled experiment is necessary to prove efficacy of the treatment.
> Phase 4: Continuing evaluation and follow-on research.

The learning sciences are still in the Preclinical and Phase 1 stages of research, with a few of the more well-established efforts entering Phase 2. Experimental studies are not sufficient to create the schools of the future, for several reasons (cf. Raudenbush, 2005):

1. Learning sciences researchers are still in a preclinical phase of identifying the goals of schools: the cognitive and social outcomes that we expect our students to attain. Experimental methodologies alone cannot help us to rigorously and clearly identify the knowledge that we want students to learn.

2. Experimental methodologies are premature at the preclinical and first phases, when learning scientists are still developing the learning environments of the future. At these early phases, hybrid methodologies and design experiments are more appropriate. Conducting experimental research is expensive, and it wouldn't be practical to do an experiment at every iterative stage of a design experiment. Once well-conceived and solidly researched new curricula are in place, then experimental methodologies can appropriately be used to compare them.

3. Experimental methodologies identify causal relations between inputs and outcomes, but they cannot explain the causal mechanisms that result in those relations – the step-by-step processes of learning – and as a result, these methodologies are not able to provide specific and detailed suggestions for how to improve curricula and student performance.

A typical learning sciences research project involves at least a year in the classroom; sometimes a year or more in advance to design new software and learner-centered interfaces; and a year or more afterward to analyze the huge volumes of videotape data, interviews, and assessments gathered from the classroom. Many learning scientists have developed new technological tools to help with analyzing large masses of complex data (Baker & Siemens, Chapter 13, this volume), and new tools for digital video ethnography are being developed (Goldman, Zahn, & Derry, Chapter 11, this volume).

The studies reported in this handbook typically took at least three years to complete – and the research behind each chapter has resulted in many books, scientific articles, and research reports. This is complex, difficult, and expensive work. It's almost impossible for any one scholar to do alone; most learning sciences research is conducted by collaborative teams of researchers – software developers, teacher educators, research assistants to hold the video cameras and transcribe the recordings, and scholars to sift through the data, each using different methodologies, to try to understand the learning processes that occurred and how the learning environment could be improved for the next iteration. Because learning sciences research requires such a massive human effort, it has tended to occur at a small number of universities where there is a critical mass of faculty and graduate students, and has tended to cluster around collaborative projects supported by large NSF grants at a small number of universities. The U.S. National Science Foundation recognized this in 2003 and 2005 by creating a few large Science of Learning Centers.

To create the learning environments of the future, we will need more research sites, and governments will have to increase their funding dramatically. Fortunately, a necessary first step is occurring: training the next generation of scholars in doctoral programs to prepare them to take faculty positions and start their own research projects. The number of graduate programs in the learning sciences has increased substantially since the 2006 edition; the ISLS now coordinates the NAPLES consortium of graduate learning sciences programs, with 23 members (as of September 2013). These master's and doctoral students are being trained in interdisciplinary learning sciences programs; they are learning to draw on a wide range of theoretical frameworks and research methodologies, and learning to combine the basic sciences of learning with hands-on issues like classroom organization, curriculum and software design, teacher education, and assessment.

Building the Community

The learning sciences approach is relatively new – the name was coined in 1989, and the research tradition extends only back to the 1970s. There are several groups of scholars engaged in learning sciences research who do not necessarily use that term for their research:

- The large community of *educational technologists* and *instructional system designers* who develop computer software for instructional purposes. This community includes university researchers but also for-profit software companies developing a range of educational technologies for corporations and schools.
- The large community of *cognitive psychologists* and *cognitive neuroscientists* who are studying basic brain functions that are related to learning.

- The large community of *educational psychologists* that are studying a wide range of psychological functions related to learning. A subset of this group that will be particularly important to bring into the learning sciences will be assessment researchers, both in universities and at institutions like the Educational Testing Service (the developer of many widely used tests in the United States, including the SAT, AP, and GRE).

The task facing society today is to design the schools of the future, and that is a massive undertaking that will involve many different communities of practice.

The Path to Educational Innovation

In the next 10 to 20 years, the task facing all knowledge societies will be to translate learning sciences research into educational practice. Perhaps the most solid finding to emerge from the learning sciences is that significant change can't be done by fiddling around at the edges of a system that remains instructionist at the core. Instead, the entire instructionist system will have to be replaced with new learning environments that are based on the learning sciences. Many tasks have to be accomplished:

- Parents, politicians, and school boards must be convinced that change is necessary. The shift will require an initial investment in computers, software, and network infrastructure – perhaps even new buildings with as-yet-undetermined architectural designs – but once the shift is in place the annual costs will not necessarily be any more than current expenditures on textbooks and curricular materials.
- Textbooks must be rewritten (or perhaps reconceived as laptop- or tablet-based software packages), to present knowledge in the developmentally appropriate sequence suggested by the learning sciences, and to present knowledge as a coherent, integrated whole, rather than as a disconnected series of decontextualized facts.
- The shift to customized, just-in-time learning will result in a radical restructuring of the school day, and may make many features of today's schools obsolete: schools years might no longer be grouped by age, school days might no longer be organized into class periods, standardized tests might no longer be administered en masse to an auditorium of students, perhaps not everyone will graduate high school or start college at the same age. Many of the socially entrenched aspects of schools that are not directly related to education would have to change as a result: organized sports, extracurricular activities, class parties that function as rites of passage.
- The relationship between the institution of school and the rest of society may need to change, as network technologies allow learners to interact with adult professionals outside the school walls, and as classroom activities become increasingly authentic and embedded in real-world practice.

- Standardized tests must be rewritten to assess deep knowledge as well as surface knowledge, and to take into account the fact that because of customization, different learners might learn different subject matter.
- Teacher education programs must prepare teachers for the schools of the future – teachers who are experts in disciplinary content, knowledgeable about the latest research on how people learn, and able to respond creatively to support each student's optimal learning.

We are at an exciting time in the study of learning. This handbook was created by a dedicated group of scholars committed to uncovering the mysteries of learning. These researchers have been working since the 1970s, developing the basic sciences of learning – beginning in psychology, cognitive science, sociology, and other disciplinary traditions, and in the 1980s and 1990s, increasingly working closely with educators and in schools. Since the 1990s, the brain research of cognitive neuroscience has made rapid progress that may soon allow it to join with the learning sciences. As these scholars continue to work together in a spirit of interdisciplinary collaboration, the end result will be an increasingly detailed understanding of how people learn. And once that understanding is available, the final step to transform schools must be taken by our whole society: parents and teachers, innovators and entrepreneurs, and the administrators and politicians who we entrust with our schools.

References

Barber, M., Donnelly, K., & Rivzi, S. (2013). *An avalanche is coming: Higher education and the revolution ahead.* London: Institute for Public Policy Research.

Bell, D. (1973). *The coming of the post-industrial society: A venture in social forecasting.* New York: Basic Books.

Bereiter, C. (2002). *Education and mind in the knowledge age.* Mahwah, NJ: Lawrence Erlbaum Associates.

Bransford, J. D., Brown, A. L., & Cocking, R. R. (Eds.) (2000). *How people learn: Brain, mind, experience, and school.* Washington, DC: National Academy Press.

Carlson, S., & Blumenstyk, G. (2012, December 21). The false promise of the education revolution. *The Chronicle of Higher Education,* A1, A4.

Carnegie Foundation. (2013). *50-State Scan of Course Credit Policies.* Stanford, CA: Carnegie Foundation for the Advancement of Teaching.

Chaker, A. M. (2008, March 6). High schools add classes scripted by corporations, *The Wall Street Journal,* pp. A1, A13.

Collins, A., & Halverson, R. (2009). *Rethinking education in the age of technology: The digital revolution and schooling in America.* New York: Teachers College Press.

Cuban, L. (2001). *Oversold and underused: Computers in the classroom*. Cambridge, MA: Harvard University Press.

Cult of Mac. (2010). Computers in schools are a failure, says computer pioneer Alan Kay. Retrieved September 17, 2013, from http://www.cultofmac.com/68757/computers-in-schools-are-a-failure-apple-fellow-alan-kay/.

Daro, P., Mosher, F. A., & Corcoran, T. (2011). *Learning trajectories in mathematics: A foundation for standards, curriculum, assessment, and instruction*. Philadelphia, PA: Consortium for Policy Research in Education.

Drucker, P. F. (1993). *Post-capitalist society*. New York: HarperBusiness.

Gabriel, T., & Richtel, M. (2011, October 9). Inflating the software report card: School-technology companies ignore some results, *The New York Times*, pp. A1, A22.

Gerstner, L. V. (2008, December 1). Lessons from 40 years of education "reform," *The Wall Street Journal*, p. A23.

Gobert, J., Buckley, B. C., & Dede, C. J. (2005). Logging students' learning with hypermodels in BioLogica and Dynamica. Paper presented at the American Educational Research Association, Montreal, Canada.

Hagerty, J. R. (2011, June 6). Industry puts heat on schools to teach skills employers need. *The Wall Street Journal*.

Hargreaves, A. (2003). *Teaching in the knowledge society: Education in the age of insecurity*. New York: Teachers College Press.

International Association for K-12 Online Learning. (2013). *Fast facts about online learning*. Vienna, VA: International Association for K-12 Online Learning.

Kamenetz, A. (2010). *DIY U: Edupunks, edupreneurs, and the coming transformation of higher education*. White River Junction, VT: Chelsea Green.

Kaufer, D., Gunawardena, A., Tan, A., & Cheek, A. (2011). Bringing social media to the writing classroom: Classroom Salon. *Journal of Business and Technical Communication*, 25(3), 299–321.

Kessler, A. (2013, June 3). Professors are about to get an online education, *Wall Street Journal*.

Kozma, R. B. (Ed.) (2003). *Technology, innovation, and educational change: A global perspective*. Eugene, OR: International Society for Technology in Education.

Lederman, N. G., Adb-El-Khalick, F., Bell, R. L., & Schwartz, R. S. (2002). Views of Nature of Science Questionnaire (VNOS): Toward valid and meaningful assessment of learners' conceptions of nature of science. *Journal of Research in Science Teaching*, 39(6), 497–521.

Lehrer, R., & Schauble, L. (2006). Cultivating model-based reasoning in science education. In R. K. Sawyer (Ed.), *Cambridge handbook of the learning sciences* (pp. 371–387). New York: Cambridge University Press.

The New York Times. (2013). *The education issue: The all-out, all-ages overhaul of school is happening now*. New York: The New York Times.

OECD. (2000). *Knowledge management in the learning society*. Paris: OECD Publications.

OECD. (2004). *Innovation in the knowledge economy: Implications for education and learning*. Paris: OECD Publications.

OECD. (2008). *Innovating to learn, learning to innovate*. Paris: OECD Publications.

OECD. (2010). *The nature of learning: Using research to inspire practice*. Paris: OECD Publications.

OECD. (2013). *Innovative learning environments*. Paris: OECD Publications.

Papert, S. (1980). *Mindstorms: Children, computers, and powerful ideas*. New York: Basic Books.

Ravitch, D. (2010). *The death and life of the great American school system: How testing and choice are undermining education*. New York: Basic Books.

Raudenbush, S. W. (2005). Learning from attempts to improve schooling: The contribution of methodological diversity. *Educational Researcher*, 34(5), 25–31.

Ripley, A. (2013). *The smartest kids in the world and how they got that way*. New York: Simon & Schuster.

Rogoff, B. (1998). Cognition as a collaborative process. In D. Kuhn & R. S. Siegler (Eds.), *Handbook of child psychology, 5th edition, Volume 2: Cognition, perception, and language* (pp. 679–744). New York: Wiley.

Sawyer, R. K. (2004). Creative teaching: Collaborative discussion as disciplined improvisation. *Educational Researcher*, 33(2), 12–20.

Sawyer, R. K. (2006). Educating for innovation. *The International Journal of Thinking Skills and Creativity*, 1(1), 41–48.

Sawyer, R. K. (Ed.) (2011). *Structure and improvisation in creative teaching*. Cambridge: Cambridge University Press.

Schank, R. C. (1999). The disrespected student, or, the need for the virtual university: A talk with Roger Schank (interview with John Brockman, 8/16/1999), http://www.edge.org/3rd_culture/schank/schank_index.html, accessed August 1, 2005.

Schmidt, W. A., & McKnight, C. C. (1997). *A splintered vision: An investigation of U.S. science and mathematics education*. Dordrecht, The Netherlands: Kluwer Academic.

Schofield, J. W., & Davidson, A. L. (2002). *Bringing the Internet to school: Lessons from an urban district*. San Francisco, CA: Jossey-Bass.

Selingo, J. J. (2013). *College (un)bound: The future of higher education and what it means for students*. New York: Houghton Mifflin Harcourt.

Sharples, M., McAndrew, P., Weller, M., Ferguson, R., Fitzgerald, E., Hirst, T., & Gaved, M. (2013). *Innovating pedagogy 2013: Open University innovation report 2*. Milton Keynes, UK: The Open University.

Shavelson, R. J., & Towne, L. (2002). *Scientific research in education*. Washington, DC: National Academy Press.

Skinner, B. F. (1954/1968). The science of learning and the art of teaching. In B. F. Skinner (Ed.), *The technology of teaching* (pp. 9–28). New York: Appleton-Century-Crofts. (Original work published in 1954 in the *Harvard Educational Review*, **24**, (2), 86–97).

Stallard, C. K., & Cocker, J. S. (2001). *The promise of technology in schools: The next 20 years*. Lanham, MD: Scarecrow Press.

Stigler, J. W., & Hiebert, J. (2009). *The teaching gap: Best ideas from the world's teachers for improving education in the classroom*. New York: Free Press.

Toffler, A. (1980). *The third wave*. New York: Morrow.

Vogel, G. (1996). Global review faults U.S. curricula. *Science*, 274(5286), 335.

Webley, K. (2013, June 17). A is for Adaptive. *TIME Magazine*, 40–45.

Index

Abrahamson, D., 325, 330–331, 363
absolute accuracy, 71
absolutist epistemology, 444
abstract concepts, 360–361
abstract formalisms, 32
abstraction
  in geometric thinking, 550
  as simulated action, 360–362
abstract knowledge, 11, 25
abstract vs. embodied understanding, 353–354
academically productive talk, 129–130
Academic Talk, 449
accessible fabrication, 341
accountability, 739–740
accountable talk, 129–130, 196, 197
accuracy, in calibration research, 71
achievement
  assessment of, 234
  levels of, 238–239
  motivation and, 671–672
  prediction of, 71
  of student performance, 243
acquisitionism framework, 546–547
acquisition metaphor, 495–496
activation-elaboration hypothesis, 302
activity structures, 51, 403
activity systems
  classroom examples, 137
  cognitive trail in, 142
  communities of practice in, 128–129, 130
  conceptual domain, 141
  contextualizing in, 133
  defined, 128
  development of, 130–131
  distributed cognition in, 138–139
  expansive framing, 133, 138
  expansivity notion in, 131–132
  forms of, 136
  functional/formal concept distinction,
    140–141
  general model of, 131
  for individual learners, 136–138
  learning object in, 133–135
  mechanisms of phenomena, 139
  modes of movement, 142–143

  norms of interaction and, 137
  practice concepts in, 128–129
  properties hypothesis, 139–140
  role of subject in, 132–133
  situated perspective, 143–144
  student participation in, 137–139
  task analysis example, 131
ACT-R Theory, 256
Adams, M. M., 678–679
adaptive expertise, 688
adaptive learning offerings, 731–732
addition strategy, 174–175, 187
additive strategy, in history learning, 596
administrators, 4
adult literacy, 606
"The Adventures of Jasper Woodbury," 21–22,
  34–35, 218
AERA/APA/NCME Standards, 240–241
African American Rhetorical Tradition, 694
Agamanolis, S., 349
age-graded classrooms, 731–732
agent-based modeling (ABM), 324, 330–331
agent-environment dynamics, 361
Ainley, J., 676–677
Ainley, M., 673, 676–677
Algebra Project (AP), 698–699
Alibali, M. W., 28, 36, 178
alignment, 101
Allen, S., 464
Alridge, D. P., 598
alternate reality games (ARGs), 388.
  See also videogames
Alvarez, H., 692
Amabile, T. M., 638
American pragmatism, 26–27
Amershi, S., 258–259
analysis
  in geometric thinking, 550
  levels of, 28–29
analytical strategy, in history learning, 596
analytics. *See* educational data mining (EDM);
  learning analytics (LA)
anchoring upward, 133
anchors, 141
Anderson, N. C., 129–130

747